HAYES AND WILLIAMS' FAMILY LAW

Third Edition

STEPHEN GILMORE

*LL.B (Hons) Leics, LL.M (Family Law and Policy) UEA, M.St Oxon
of Lincoln's Inn, Barrister,
Senior Lecturer in Law, King's College London*

AND

LISA GLENNON

LL.B, Ph.D

OXFORD
UNIVERSITY PRESS

OXFORD
UNIVERSITY PRESS

Great Clarendon Street, Oxford, OX2 6DP,
United Kingdom

Oxford University Press is a department of the University of Oxford.
It furthers the University's objective of excellence in research, scholarship,
and education by publishing worldwide. Oxford is a registered trade mark of
Oxford University Press in the UK and in certain other countries

© Oxford University Press 2012

The moral rights of the authors have been asserted

First Edition Published 1995
Second Edition Published 1999
Impression: 2

Public sector information reproduced under Open Government Licence v1.0
(http://www.nationalarchives.gov.uk/doc/open-government-licence/open-government-licence.htm)

Crown Copyright material reproduced with the permission of the
Controller, HMSO (under the terms of the Click Use licence)

British Library Cataloguing in Publication Data
Data available

Library of Congress Cataloging in Publication Data
Library of Congress Control Number: 2012939872

ISBN 978-0-19-928236-4

Printed in Great Britain by
Ashford Colour Press Ltd, Gosport, Hampshire

ACKNOWLEDGEMENTS

The authors would like to express their gratitude to a number of people whose work, encouragement, and support made a significant contribution to the production of this edition of the book. First, we would like to thank Mary Hayes and Catherine Williams, who co-authored the original Hayes and Williams *Family Law: Principles, Policy and Practice*, for inviting us to take over the book and update its content. It has been a great privilege and pleasure producing this edition and we hope that we have lived up to the high standards of previous editions.

What began as an update, however, transformed into a more extensive task when the book was taken over by Oxford University Press, with a decision to re-structure the book and add new chapters. We are extremely grateful to the team at OUP for their patience and support throughout the project. In particular we would like to record our thanks to Melanie Jackson, Alex Clabburn, Anna Winstanley (our original editors at OUP), and Ben Pettitt who worked tirelessly to see us through the production of the final manuscript. Thanks are also due to Jacqueline Senior, Heather Smyth, and Abbey Nelms at OUP. A special debt of gratitude is owed to our copy-editor, Joy Ruskin-Tompkins, whose efficiency and attention to detail was outstanding, and to Gillian Wright who proofread the manuscript and patiently managed our last minute amendments.

We would also like to acknowledge the contributions of Kate Standley and Jane Sendall in the production of the manuscript. The writing of the book coincided with the birth of Lisa's beautiful son, Daniel. At that time, Kate Standley kindly stepped in to produce outline chapters on formation and dissolution of relationships, which were later developed. Jane Sendall later read the manuscript and advised on pedagogical features.

We must also thank our many friends and colleagues in family law who have helped in various ways. We owe a debt of gratitude to Marilyn Freeman, Robert George, Martin Parry, and Nick Wikeley, who read and commented on parts of the manuscript in their respective areas of expertise. Others helped in ways perhaps unknown to them, in particular Jonathan Herring, Rebecca Probert, and Jens Scherpe.

Lisa would like to dedicate her chapters to her husband Brian and their son Daniel. She would like to thank them for their constant supply of love and laughter! Lisa would also like to express her sincere thanks to her co-author Stephen for his knowledge, dedication, friendship, and patience, in particular, during her period of maternity leave!

Similarly, Stephen would like to thank his co-author Lisa for all her effort and support: it is one thing producing a textbook; quite another to produce a child at the same time! Finally, Stephen would like to dedicate his work to his wife, Penny (a constant source of love and support, without whom the book could not have been completed), and to their children, Libby and Tom, who for too long during the writing suffered their dad's lack of attention.

Lisa was responsible for the adult family law section of the book, and Stephen wrote the introduction and the child law section, although we prefer to think of it all as a joint effort! We have attempted to state the law as at February 2012.

Stephen Gilmore
Lisa Glennon
April 2012

NEW TO THIS EDITION

The third edition of this book is the first to be published by Oxford University Press and to be co-authored by a new team, Stephen Gilmore and Lisa Glennon. The book has been re-named *Hayes and Williams' Family Law* to recognise the important foundations of the text, which was originally co-authored by Mary Hayes and Catherine Williams.

Comparing the content of this edition with the second edition in 1999 shows just how much family law has been transformed in a little over a decade. The last edition appeared prior to the implementation, in October 2000, of the Human Rights Act 1998; and in the years shortly after the second edition there was a flurry of legislative activity on family law matters. Major changes to the regulation of adult relationships came with the enactment of the Civil Partnership Act 2004 and the Gender Recognition Act 2004. In addition, the Domestic Violence, Crime and Victims Act 2004 made significant changes to the criminal justice response to domestic violence. The law on parenthood and parental responsibility also saw significant developments: the Adoption and Children Act 2002 amended the law on parental responsibility and recast the law on adoption; the Human Fertilisation and Embryology Act 2008 extended the law on parenthood in cases of assisted conception. The law on facilitation and enforcement of child/parent contact was strengthened by the Children and Adoption Act 2006. The public law relating to children has also not escaped legislative attention, with enactment of the Children Act 2004, the Childcare Act 2006, and the Children and Young Persons Act 2008. There have also been significant changes in the law on child support as the legislature has struggled to put in place an effective mechanism for assessment and collection of child support maintenance: the Child Support, Pensions and Social Security Act 2000, the Child Maintenance and Other Payments Act 2008, and the Welfare Reform Act 2012. There are no signs of any let-up in this relentless supply of legislation, with the recent announcement of a Children and Families Bill 2013 (see 'Recent Policy Developments' at p viii).

The courts have also been hard at work since the last edition, and case law developments are so extensive that it is only possible to highlight a few major areas of change. Perhaps the most significant development has been in ancillary relief, now called 'financial orders', which was recast by the decisions in *White v White* [2000] UKHL 54, *Miller/McFarlane* [2006] UKHL 24, and *Granatino (formerly Radmacher) v Radmacher* [2010] UKSC 42. There have also been key decisions at the highest level on the welfare principle in section 1(1) of the Children Act 1989 (*Re G (Children)* [2006] UKHL 43, *Re B* [2009] UKSC 5) and its application in various private law areas (eg *Holmes-Moorhouse v London Borough of Richmond Upon Thames* [2009] UKHL 7, on shared residence). The Court of Appeal in *Re P (Child: Financial Provision)* [2003] EWCA Civ 837 has provided guidance on Schedule 1 to the Children Act 1989. There have also been significant developments in the case law on care orders (*Lancashire County Council v A* [2000] 2 AC 147, *Re O and N; Re B* [2003] UKHL 18, *Re B (Children)* [2008] UKHL 35, *Re S-B* [2009] UKSC 17), and several important decisions interpreting the new law on adoption.

In order to accommodate these changes to the law we have adopted a new structure for the book, with the addition of new chapters. The book is now divided into two parts. The first part (Chapters 1 to 5 inclusive) deals principally with the legal regulation of adult family relationships, as follows: (1) the formation of adult relationships; (2) the dissolution of adult relationships; (3) protection from domestic violence and occupation of the family home; (4) money and property distribution on marriage breakdown; and (5) property disputes of unmarried cohabitants on relationship breakdown. The second part (Chapters 6 to 11) focuses on the law relating to children: (6) financial support for children; (7) a child's parents: parentage, parenthood, and parental responsibility; (8) children's rights; (9) private law disputes and issues in children cases; (10) children needing services, care and protection; and (11) adoption and special guardianship. What was originally Chapter 9 of the book is now therefore dealt with in two separate chapters, Chapter 5 on property disputes of unmarried cohabitants, and Chapter 6 on financial support for children. Discussion of orders in section 8 of the Children Act 1989, which was originally split between two chapters (dealing with procedural matters and approaches to welfare respectively) has now been brought together in Chapter 9 on private law disputes and issues in children's cases. There are also entirely new chapters on children's rights and on adoption and special guardianship.

There have been so many changes that the book is rather different from earlier editions. As the coverage of substantive law has expanded, it has not proved possible to maintain coverage of some practice issues (such as the law relating to children's evidence, or representation). The law on international child abduction is also no longer covered, as several reviewers for this edition told us that it was not taught in their undergraduate family law course, and the law in that area can be found in specialist texts. Apologies to those who still do teach it.

However, we have sought to maintain the clear, logical, and straightforward account of the law for which earlier editions of this book were known, and where possible to maintain any existing commentary. In response to reviewers' comments we have tried to include more academic commentary and policy debate, in order to encourage students to engage critically with the law and debates about it. However, we also firmly believe that students must be able to situate their criticisms within a good, detailed understanding of the law. In the spirit of earlier editions we have therefore sought, where possible, to provide quite full (student-friendly) accounts of case law. Our reasons are explained more fully in the Introduction. We have tried to ensure that students are able to identify the wood, whilst also maintaining awareness of the trees.

Stephen Gilmore
Lisa Glennon
June 2012

RECENT POLICY DEVELOPMENTS

On 1 May 2012 the Legal Aid, Sentencing and Punishment of Offenders Act 2012 was passed, drastically curtailing legal aid for legal advice and representation in private family law matters;[1] and a week later the Queen's Speech announced a Children and Families Bill which is expected to be introduced early in 2013.[2] Family justice is encountering a period of major changes. Much of the expected content of the Bill represents the culmination of the Family Justice Review (FJR). This major review of the family justice system, conducted by a panel of civil servants and independent members from across the family justice service, and chaired by David Norgrove, began work in March 2010.[3] A year later, having taken evidence from over 700 individuals and organisations, an interim report was published for consultation.[4] With the benefit of 668 responses to the consultation, and of the Justice Select Committee's report on the operation of the family courts,[5] a final report was presented in November 2011.[6] The Government's response to the final report was published in February 2012[7] as this book was going into production, and came too late for detailed inclusion at relevant points in the text. Similarly too late, the Department for Education published its *Adoption Action Plan: Tackling Delay* in March 2012. This section therefore supplements the main text with an overview of recent policy developments.

THE FAMILY JUSTICE REVIEW RECOMMENDATIONS

Concerns About How Family Justice Operates

The FJR found the family law legal framework robust, but had deep concern about how family justice operates,[8] concluding that it does not operate as a coherent, managed system. In particular, concern was expressed about cost-effectiveness and how long cases

---

[1] The main exceptions are cases involving domestic violence or unlawful removal from the UK. See Sch 1 to the 2012 Act. A case for exceptional funding can be made under s 9. For the human rights implications, see J. Miles, 'Legal Aid, Article 6 and "Exceptional Funding" under the Legal Aid Etc Bill 2011' [2011] Fam Law 1003 and 'Legal Aid and "Exceptional" Funding: A Postscript' [2011] Fam Law 1268. See also M. Maclean and J. Eekelaar, 'Legal Representation in Family Matters and the Reform of Legal Aid: A Research Note on Current Practice' [2012] Child and Family Law Quarterly 223.

[2] See Department for Education, 'Children and Families Bill to give families support when they need it most', Press Notice, 9 May 2012.

[3] The terms of reference were not entirely neutral: mediation was to be preferred over court intervention and the court's role should be 'focused on protecting the vulnerable...and should avoid intervening except where there is clear benefit to children or vulnerable adults in doing so'. As John Eekelaar observes, this is 'a startlingly limited view of the role of a court, and hence of the law which courts apply': J. Eekelaar, '"Not of the Highest Importance": Family Justice Under Threat' (2011) 33(4) Journal of Social Welfare and Family Law 311.

[4] www.justice.gov.uk/downloads/publications/policy/moj/family-justice-reviewinterim-rep.pdf.

[5] *Operation of the Family Courts* Sixth Report of Session 2010–12, Vol 1 (2011) House of Commons Justice Committee (July 2011).

[6] www.justice.gov.uk/publications/policy/moj/family-justice-review-final.htm.

[7] Ministry of Justice and Department for Education, *The Government Response to the Family Justice Review: A System with Children and Families at its Heart* (Cm 8273, February 2012).

[8] For comparative perspectives, see M. Maclean, R. Hunter, F. Wasoff, L. Ferguson, B. Bastard, and E. Ryrstedt, 'Family Justice in Hard Times: Can We Learn from Other Jurisdictions?' (2011) 33(4) Journal of Social Welfare and Family Law 319.

take. The FJR identified complicated, overlapping organisational structures, inadequate information and information technology, and that those using the family justice system are often confused as to what is happening to them.

With a view to addressing these difficulties, the FJR had four main strands of recommendations. The first was the establishment of a new Family Justice Service, with responsibility for court social work services, provision of mediation and out of court resolution services, and monitoring the use of expert witnesses. The FJR recommended that initially an Interim Board should be established to plan towards this change. A second strand of recommendations was directed to judicial leadership and culture, suggesting: judges with leadership responsibilities should have clearer management responsibilities; judicial continuity should be the aim in all family law cases; judges and magistrates should be encouraged to specialise in family matters; and the judiciary should review and plan how to deliver consistently effective case management in the courts. Thirdly, the FJR recommended that, without prejudice to the special position of the Family Division of the High Court,[9] there should be a single family court, with family friendly facilities, in which all levels of the family judiciary (including magistrates) should sit. (Currently family law cases can be heard in the Family Proceedings Court, the county court, or the High Court, depending on the nature of the case.) Fourthly, the FJR recommended a workforce strategy to improve interdisciplinary understanding, including interdisciplinary inductions and training.

Delay in Public Law Children Proceedings

Delay within the 'system' was seen as particularly worrying in the case of public law applications to take a child into the care or supervision of the local authority[10] (discussed in chapter 10 of this work). The FJR cited statistics to show that such cases take an average of 61 weeks in care centres and 48 weeks in Family Proceedings Courts, and that 20,000 children were waiting for a decision in public law cases.[11] It concluded that a firm approach was needed to address this difficulty, and recommended that the Government should legislate to set a time limit on care proceedings of six months, with extensions only by exception. The FJR also recommended that the current time-consuming requirement to renew interim care or supervision orders after eight weeks and thereafter every four weeks should be amended. It saw the growth in the use of experts as a major contributor to unacceptable delay and recommended that primary legislation should assert that expert testimony be commissioned only where necessary to resolve the case, and that the legislation should reinforce that in commissioning an expert's report regard must be had to the impact of delay on the welfare of the child. The FJR also noted that courts had progressively extended their scrutiny of local authority care plans for children and recommended that courts should avoid over-scrutiny and focus on core issues.

Private Law Children Cases

In relation to private law disputes when parents separate (see chapter 9), the FJR concluded that too many cases end up in court, in processes which are hard to navigate, and that there was limited awareness of alternatives to court. One hotly debated issue in recent years is the courts' approach to the allocation of parenting time on the breakdown of parents' relationships. Currently the court can make either a residence order settling the arrangements as to the person(s) with whom the child shall live, and/or a contact order

---

[9] With its inherent jurisdiction, and jurisdiction over international family law matters.
[10] Under Children Act 1989, s 31.   [11] See Final Report, at para 3.2.

providing contact between a child and a non-resident parent,[12] in each case applying
the guiding principle of the paramountcy of the child's welfare.[13] Concerns have been
voiced[14] that the courts' tendency to award residence to one parent (usually the child's
mother) and contact to the other does not adequately value the potential input of both
parents on separation. It has been suggested that there should instead be a presumption
of shared residence (or even a presumption of equal division of the child's time), and a
presumption of contact with a non-resident parent. The FJR was inevitably drawn into
these debates. In its Interim Report the FJR canvassed the possibility of legislation which
might state the importance to the child of a meaningful relationship with both parents
after their separation where this is safe. However, having taken account of further evidence that this language might be misinterpreted (drawing on the Australian experience
of legislating in this area[15]), the FJR concluded in its Final Report that 'no legislation
should be introduced that creates or risks creating the perception that there is a parental
right to substantially shared or equal time for both parents'[16] and which might therefore
compromise the guiding principle of the paramountcy of the child's welfare in such proceedings. The FJR therefore eventually rejected the canvassed change to the legislation
as potentially doing more harm than good. However, the FJR recommended a new 'child
arrangements order' (setting out arrangements for the upbringing of the child in cases of
dispute), which would represent a move away from what it saw as the loaded terms 'residence' and 'contact' that had become a source of contention, and allow greater focus on
practical issues of the day-to-day care of the child.

    As for the process of separation, the FJR recommended that parents should have ready
access to a wide range of information and support via an online information hub and help-
line to help them resolve issues following separation and divorce. Where parents required
support to resolve a dispute they should be expected to attend a session with a mediator
to provide information and assess appropriate intervention (a Mediation and Assessment
Meeting) and a Separated Parents Information Programme before being permitted to
apply to a court.[17] The FJR recommended that children and young people should be given
the opportunity to have their voices heard in cases about them where they wish it.

Disputes on Financial Matters and the Law Commission

With regard to disputes on financial matters, the FJR recommended that the Government
should establish a separate review of financial orders to include examination of the law.
In February 2012 the Law Commission announced that its ongoing project on marital
property agreements[18] would be extended to include a targeted review of two aspects of
the law on financial orders: the extent to which one party to a marriage or civil partnership should be required to meet the other's needs after the relationship has ended, and the
meaning of 'non-matrimonial property'.[19] A final report is expected in 2013.

---

[12] Children Act 1989, ss 8 and 10.   [13] Ibid, s 1(1).

[14] Particularly by fathers' rights organisations: see R. Collier and S. Sheldon (eds), *Fathers' Rights Activism and Law Reform in Comparative Perspective* (Oxford: Hart, 2006).

[15] See Final Report, Annex G—Helen Rhoades' evidence in relation to shared parenting.

[16] Family Justice Review Final Report (November 2011), Executive Summary, para 109.

[17] For discussion of the impact of these suggestions on contact disputes, see J. Hunt, 'Through a Glass Darkly: The Uncertain Future of Private Law Child Contact Litigation' (2011) 33(4) Journal of Social Welfare and Family Law 379.

[18] The Law Commission Consultation Paper No 198, *Marital Property Agreements* (2011).

[19] See E. Cooke, 'Pre-Nups and Beyond: What is the Law Commission Up to Now?' [2012] Fam Law 323.

The Government Response to the Family Justice Review

The Government's response to the FJR largely agreed with the FJR's recommendations, indicating that it would establish an Interim Family Justice Board to plan reform of the system. It agreed to adopt measures to improve management of public law cases and tackle delay, including legislation regulating the use of expert opinion evidence,[20] making clearer the court's role in scrutinising care plans,[21] and providing for a time limit of six months for the completion of care and supervision cases.[22] The Government also agreed in general with the FJR's process for resolution of private law disputes, explaining that it would legislate to make attendance at a Mediation and Assessment Meeting a requirement before a court could be approached,[23] and that the court process would be simplified by the establishment of a single family court as recommended.[24] The Government agreed that the terminology 'contact' and 'residence' has become unhelpfully associated with the idea of losing and winning, and accepted the FJR's recommendation to replace contact and residence orders with a new 'child's arrangement order'.[25] However, controversially, the Government rejected the FJR's conclusion that there should be no change to the substantive approach to deciding post-separation parenting issues, commenting that 'many people continue to have concerns about the proper recognition of the role of both parents by the courts'.[26] The Government concluded:

> there should be a legislative statement of the importance of children having an ongoing relationship with both their parents after family separation, where that is safe, and in the child's best interests...
>
> ...The Government is mindful of the lessons which must be learnt from the Australian experience of legislating in this area, which were highlighted by the Review and led them to urge caution. We will therefore consider very carefully how legislation can be framed to avoid the pitfalls of the Australian experience, in particular that a meaningful relationship is not about equal division of time, but the quality of parenting received by the child.[27]

The Government is currently consulting on how the legislation should be framed.[28]

The Proposed Children and Families Bill 2013 and the Crime and Courts Bill

It is proposed that the FJR's recommendation for a single family court for England and Wales will be enacted in a new Crime and Courts Bill and the legislative changes suggested in the Government's response to the FJR will be brought before Parliament in a Children and Families Bill 2013.[29] The Bill will also contain proposals relating to adoption set out in the Adoption Action Plan published in March 2012, as part of wider reforms to speed up the process of adoption and matching children with prospective adoptive parents. There are also plans to strengthen and widen the remit of the Office of the Children's

---

[20] Note 7 above, at paras 40–44.   [21] Ibid, para 50.

[22] Ibid, paras 54 and 55. The changes will work in tandem with child protection practice reforms: see Department for Education, *The Munro Review of Child Protection: Final Report—A Child-Centred System* (Cm 8062), July 2011.   [23] Note 7 above, at para 69.

[24] Ibid, para 75.

[25] Ibid, at para 77. It is not clear whether 'child's arrangement order' is new terminology or a mistaken reference to the FJR's 'child arrangements order'.   [26] Ibid, at para 60.

[27] Ibid, at paras 61 and 62.

[28] Department for Education and Ministry of Justice consultation paper, *Co-operative Parenting Following Family Separation: Proposed Legislation on the Involvement of Both Parents in a Child's Life* (launch date 13 June 2012). Responses are required by 5 September 2012.

[29] See www.education.gov.uk/inthenews/inthenews/a00208753/childrens-bill-family-support.

Commissioner with a view to promoting and protecting children's rights as set out in the United Nations Convention of the Rights of the Child.[30]

EQUAL CIVIL MARRIAGE CONSULTATION

In a Consultation Paper published by the Government Equalities Office in March 2012, the Government indicated that it no longer considers the ban on same-sex marriage to be acceptable. While same-sex couples can currently enter into a civil partnership and thus acquire marital-like rights and duties, same-sex marriage is not legally permissible. Recognising the views of many that 'having two separate provisions for same-sex and opposite-sex couples perpetuates misconceptions and discrimination',[31] the Government sought views on how to remove the ban on same-sex couples from entering into a civil marriage. Recognising that the commitment involved between same-sex couples in a civil partnership is as significant as the commitment between a man and a woman in a civil marriage, the Government indicated that 'it is only right' that all couples have the 'same opportunity to recognise that commitment in the valued institution of marriage'.[32] However, the Consultation Paper made it clear that no change was planned to how religious organisations define and solemnise religious marriage, noting that no religious organisation will be forced to conduct same-sex religious marriage. In addition, while the Government indicated its intention to retain civil partnerships for same-sex couples, the Consultation Paper did not consider the possibility of introducing opposite-sex civil partnerships.

The Consultation Paper also proposed to amend the current law to allow transsexual people to change their legal gender without having to legally end their existing marriage or civil partnership. Currently, a person can legally change their gender by obtaining a full Gender Recognition Certificate. However, a full certificate cannot currently be given to someone who is already in a marriage or civil partnership. In order to obtain a full Gender Recognition Certificate, the couple have to end their existing marriage or civil partnership.[33] Recognising the distress that this can cause, the Government's proposals allow transsexuals to change their gender legally without having to take these steps. The consultation exercise closed on 14 June 2012.

---

[30] Following a review, see J. Dunford, *Review of the Office of the Children's Commissioner* (England) (Cm 7981), December 2010.

[31] Government Equalities Office, *Equal Civil Marriage: A Consultation*, 15 March 2012, Ministerial Foreword.   [32] Ibid, para 1.9.

[33] Ibid, para 2.27.

OUTLINE CONTENTS

Table of Cases   xxiii

Table of Statutes   xliii

Table of Statutory Instruments   liv

INTRODUCTION: THE CHANGING FAMILY AND
DEVELOPING FAMILY LAW   1

PART 1 ADULT FAMILY LAW

1 THE FORMATION OF ADULT RELATIONSHIPS   11

2 THE DISSOLUTION OF ADULT RELATIONSHIPS   59

3 PROTECTION FROM DOMESTIC VIOLENCE AND
   OCCUPATION OF THE FAMILY HOME   91

4 MONEY AND PROPERTY DISTRIBUTION ON
   MARRIAGE BREAKDOWN   160

5 PROPERTY DISPUTES OF UNMARRIED COHABITANTS
   ON RELATIONSHIP BREAKDOWN   246

PART 2 CHILD FAMILY LAW

6   FINANCIAL SUPPORT FOR CHILDREN   313

7   A CHILD'S PARENTS: PARENTAGE, PARENTHOOD,
    AND PARENTAL RESPONSIBILITY   340

8   CHILDREN'S RIGHTS   413

9   PRIVATE LAW DISPUTES AND ISSUES IN CHILDREN CASES   447

10 CHILDREN NEEDING SERVICES, CARE, AND PROTECTION   566

11 ADOPTION AND SPECIAL GUARDIANSHIP   669

Bibliography   713

Index   747

DETAILED CONTENTS

Table of Cases   xxiii

Table of Statutes   xliii

Table of Statutory Instruments   liv

INTRODUCTION: THE CHANGING FAMILY AND
DEVELOPING FAMILY LAW   1

What is Family Law?   2

Families Today: The Statistical Picture and Trends   3

The Legally Recognised 'Family': Shifting Over Time   3

The Impact of the Human Rights Act 1998 and
International Conventions   5

Some Features of Family Law   6
    Discretion   6
    Interaction with Other Disciplines   7

The Arrangement of the Text   7

PART 1 ADULT FAMILY LAW

1   THE FORMATION OF ADULT RELATIONSHIPS   11

  1 Marriage   11
    1.1 Marriage Today   11
    1.2 The Right to Marry   12
    1.3 The Creation of a Valid Marriage   13
    1.4 Capacity to Marry   13
    1.5 The Law of Nullity   14

  2 Void Marriages   15
    2.1 Marriage within the Prohibited Degrees of Relationship   16
    2.2 Marriage Under the Age of 16   17
    2.3 Failure to Comply with the Required Formalities for Marriage   17
    2.4 A Party Must Not Already Be Married   21
    2.5 The Parties Must Be Respectively Male and Female   21

  3 Voidable Marriages   25
    3.1 Non-Consummation   26
    3.2 Lack of Consent to the Marriage   27
    3.3 Mental Disorder Rendering a Person Unfitted for Marriage   29
    3.4 Venereal Disease   29
    3.5 Pregnancy by Another Man   29
    3.6 Gender Recognition as a Ground for Nullity   29
    3.7 Bars to Relief   30
    3.8 Should the Concept of the Voidable Marriage be Abolished?   30

  4 Sham Marriages   33

5	Forced Marriages	33
	5.1 Annulment	35
	5.2 Inherent Jurisdiction or Wardship	35
	5.3 Forced Marriage Protection Orders	36
6	Recognition of an Overseas Marriage	37
7	Same-Sex Marriage	38
8	The Legal Consequences of Marriage	41
9	Civil Partnership	42
	9.1 The Legal Formation of a Civil Partnership	44
	9.2 Recognition of Overseas Civil Partnerships, Annulments, and Separations	45
	9.3 The Legal Consequences of Civil Partnership	45
10	Non-Formal Adult Relationships	46
	10.1 Cohabitation	46
	10.2 Home-Sharers	55
	Discussion Questions	57
	Further Reading	57

2	**THE DISSOLUTION OF ADULT RELATIONSHIPS**	59
1	The Law of Divorce	59
	1.1 A Brief History of Divorce	59
	1.2 Developments in Divorce Procedure	61
	1.3 Trends in Divorce	62
2	Obtaining a Divorce	62
	2.1 Jurisdiction to Hear a Divorce	62
	2.2 Staying Divorce Proceedings in England and Wales	64
	2.3 Divorce under the Matrimonial Causes Act 1973	64
	2.4 The Legal Effects of Divorce	75
	2.5 Recognition of an Overseas Divorce	76
3	Criticisms of Divorce under the Matrimonial Causes Act 1973 and an Attempt at Reform	78
	3.1 Introduction	78
	3.2 Divorce under the Family Law Act 1996	81
4	The Future of Divorce Law	84
5	Other Decrees under the Matrimonial Causes Act 1973	87
	5.1 Decree of Judicial Separation	87
	5.2 Decree of Presumption of Death and Dissolution of the Marriage	88
6	Dissolution of a Civil Partnership	88
7	The Termination of Cohabitation Relationships	89
	Discussion Questions	90
	Further Reading	90

3	**PROTECTION FROM DOMESTIC VIOLENCE AND OCCUPATION OF THE FAMILY HOME**	91
1	What is Domestic Violence?	91
2	How Prevalent is Domestic Violence?	93

3 Explanations for Domestic Violence 96
  3.1 Psychological Explanations 96
  3.2 Social Structural Explanations 96
  3.3 Feminist Explanations—The Patriarchal Social Order 97
  3.4 A Multifaceted Phenomenon 97

4 The Response of the Law to Domestic Violence 98
  4.1 The Role of the Criminal Law 99
  4.2 Criminal Injuries Compensation 102
  4.3 Civil Law Remedies 103

5 Occupation Orders 118
  5.1 Some Preliminary Points about Occupation Orders 118
  5.2 Who Can Apply for an Occupation Order? 119
  5.3 Entitled Applicants 120
  5.4 Non-Entitled Applicants 129
  5.5 Orders Where Neither Party is Entitled to
      Occupy the Dwelling-House 135
  5.6 The Approach of the Courts to Occupation Orders 136
  5.7 Enforcement of an Occupation Order 140
  5.8 Undertakings 142
  5.9 Ex Parte Orders 143
  5.10 Provision for Third Parties to Act on Behalf of
      Victims of Domestic Violence 145

6 Persons Not Protected under the Family Law Act 1996 145

7 Protection from Harassment Act 1997 146
  7.1 Harassment 147
  7.2 Putting People in Fear of Violence 148
  7.3 Restraining Orders 148

8 Domestic Violence and Local Authority Housing 149
  8.1 'Homeless' 149
  8.2 'Priority Need' 151
  8.3 Intentionally Homeless 152

9 Domestic Violence: Human Rights Implications 153
  9.1 The Human Rights Act 1998 154
  9.2 International Human Rights Law 154

10 Domestic Violence and Child Contact 156

Discussion Questions 158

Further Reading 159

4 MONEY AND PROPERTY DISTRIBUTION ON
  MARRIAGE BREAKDOWN 160

1 Background to the Current Law 160

2 The Legislative Framework 161
  2.1 The Courts' Powers 163

3 Undertakings 168

4   Exercise of the Court's Discretion   169
    4.1   Refusal to Exercise Discretion on Policy Grounds   169
    4.2   The Court's General Direction in Section 25(1)   169
    4.3   The Courts' General Guidance   170
    4.4   Clarification in Subsequent Case Law   176
    4.5   The Statutory Factors: Section 25(2)   177
    4.6   The Clean Break   194

5   Pensions   198
    5.1   Duty to Consider the Parties' Pension Entitlements   199
    5.2   Pensions—The Options   199

6   The Matrimonial Home—What Order is the Most Appropriate?   201
    6.1   The Powers of the Court   201

7   Financial and Property Agreements   217
    7.1   Separation Agreements   217
    7.2   Embodying the Agreement in a Consent Order   219
    7.3   Ante-Nuptial Agreements   222
    7.4   Debate Surrounding Ante-Nuptial Agreements   227

8   Appeals and Rehearings   230
    8.1   The Barder Test   230
    8.2   Variation   235

9   Financial Provision Orders During the Marriage   243

Discussion Questions   244

Further Reading   245

5   PROPERTY DISPUTES OF UNMARRIED COHABITANTS ON
     RELATIONSHIP BREAKDOWN   246

1   Ownership of the Family Home: Property Law Principles   247
    1.1   Establishing Legal Ownership   247
    1.2   Establishing Beneficial Ownership   248
    1.3   The Resulting Trust   250
    1.4   The Constructive Trust   251
    1.5   Distinguishing Two Situations   252

2   Joint Names Cases   252
    2.1   Stack v Dowden: The Facts   253
    2.2   Sole Name Cases   266
    2.3   Quantification of the Beneficial Interest   281
    2.4   Proprietary Estoppel   284
    2.5   Orders under the Trusts of Land and Appointment of
           Trustees Act 1996   290
    2.6   Transfer of Tenancies Between Cohabitants   293
    2.7   Schedule 1 to the Children Act 1989   295
    2.8   The Need for Reform   296

Discussion Questions   310

Further Reading   310

PART 2 CHILD FAMILY LAW

6   FINANCIAL SUPPORT FOR CHILDREN   313

    1   The Child Support Act 1991: Background and Recent Reforms   313
        1.1   Birth of the Child Support Act   313
        1.2   Problems   314
        1.3   Responding to Criticism   315
        1.4   Loss of Confidence and a Review of the System   315

    2   The Child Support Act 1991: The Law   317
        2.1   Parents and Children to Whom the Act Applies   317
        2.2   Each Parent's Duty to Maintain a Qualifying Child   317
        2.3   Applications for a Maintenance Calculation and
              Collection/Enforcement   318
        2.4   The Maintenance Calculation   318
        2.5   Enforcement   321

    3   The Courts' Residual Role with Respect to Child Maintenance   321
        3.1   Section 8(3A): Existing Maintenance Orders   322
        3.2   Section 8(5): Existing Maintenance Agreements   322
        3.3   Section 8(6): A Topping Up Order   322
        3.4   Section 8(7): Educational Expenses   322
        3.5   Section 8(8): Expenses Attributable to a Child's Disability   323
        3.6   Section 8(10): Orders Against a Person with Care   323

    4   The Courts' Powers   324
        4.1   Matrimonial Causes Act 1973   324
        4.2   Available Orders   325
        4.3   Exercise of the Court's Discretion   326
        4.4   Maintenance of a Child by a Party Who is Not the Child's Parent 326
        4.5   Duration of Orders   327
        4.6   Provision for Children as Dependants   327
        4.7   Children Act 1989, Section 15 and Schedule 1   329

    Discussion Questions   338

    Further Reading   338

7   A CHILD'S PARENTS: PARENTAGE, PARENTHOOD,
    AND PARENTAL RESPONSIBILITY   340

    1   A Child's Parents   340
        1.1   Different Senses of 'Parent': Biological, Social, and Legal   340
        1.2   Law's Distinctions: Parentage, Parenthood, and Parental Responsibility   341

    2   Parentage   342
        2.1   The Presumption of Paternity in Favour of the Mother's Husband   342
        2.2   Where Parentage is in Issue: Declarations of Parentage   343
        2.3   Directions for Scientific Testing under Section 20 of
              the Family Law Reform Act 1969   344
        2.4   Legal Recognition of Persons' Interests in Knowing Genetic Origins   346
        2.5   Disclosure of Parentage to Children   356

    3   Legal Parenthood   357
        3.1   Motherhood   357

3.2	Fatherhood	358
3.3	The Human Fertilisation and Embryology Act 1990	360
3.4	Section 28: The Legal but Not Biological Father	362
3.5	The Human Fertilisation and Embryology Act 2008	365
3.6	Lesbian Couples, Assisted Conception, and Parenthood	367
3.7	Biology: The Default Position	367
3.8	Persons Not Regarded in Law as a Parent	367
3.9	Transsexual Persons and Parenthood	369
3.10	Surrogacy and Parental Orders	371

4	Making Sense of the Law on Parenthood	374
4.1	Rationales for Attributing Parenthood	374

5	Criticism of the Law	376

6	Allocation of Parental Responsibility	377
6.1	Acquisition of Parental Responsibility by an Unmarried Father	379
6.2	Should Unmarried Fathers be Afforded Equal Treatment?	393
6.3	Acquisition of Parental Responsibility by a Female Parent	400
6.4	Acquisition of Parental Responsibility by a Step-Parent	400
6.5	Further Methods of Acquiring Parental Responsibility	401

7	Duration of Parental Responsibility	403

8	Removal of Parental Responsibility	404
8.1	The Position of Persons Without Parental Responsibility	405

9	The Nature and Scope of Parental Responsibility	406
9.1	The Complexity of Parental Responsibilities	406
9.2	Statutory Guidance on the Nature and Exercise of Parental Responsibility in Section 2 of the Children Act 1989	407
9.3	The Content and Scope of Parental Responsibility	408
9.4	The Link with Chapters that Follow	411

Discussion Questions	411
Further Reading	411

8	CHILDREN'S RIGHTS	413

1	Fundamental Debates Surrounding Children's Rights	413
1.1	Conceptions of a Right: Will Theory v Interest Theory	413
1.2	Should Children Have Rights?	414
1.3	Children and Childhoods	415
1.4	Different Childhoods	417

2	Categorising Children's Rights: The Interests Children Might Plausibly Claim	418
2.1	Eekelaar's Future-Oriented Consent and Freeman's Liberal Paternalism	419

3	Legal Protection of Children's Interests	420
3.1	Recognition of Children's Autonomy Interest?	420
3.2	Interpreting *Gillick*	424
3.3	*Axon*: A Human Rights Challenge to *Gillick*	427

4	Children's Rights in Cases of Refusal of Medical Treatment	428
4.1	*Re R (A Minor) (Wardship: Consent to Treatment)*	429
4.2	*Re W (A Minor) (Medical Treatment: Court's Jurisdiction)*	432

4.3	Authorising the Use of Reasonable Force	434
4.4	Criticism of *Re R* and *Re W*: The Distinction Between Consent and Refusal	436
4.5	The so-called 'Retreat From *Gillick*'	437
4.6	Will a Child Ever be Considered Sufficiently Competent to Refuse Life-Saving Treatment?	438

5   Children and the European Convention on Human Rights   442

6   Conclusion   444

Discussion Questions   445

Further Reading   445

9   PRIVATE LAW DISPUTES AND ISSUES IN CHILDREN CASES   447

1   The Courts' Focus on Child Welfare: Background   447

1.1	Decision-Making Principles in Section 1 of the Children Act 1989	448
1.2	Section 1(2): 'Delay Likely to Prejudice the Child's Welfare'	451
1.3	Section 1(3): The Welfare Checklist	451
1.4	No Order Unless Better for the Child	452

2   The Meaning of 'Paramountcy'   454

3   Is Section 1(1) of the Children Act 1989 Compatible with the Requirements of the Human Rights Act 1998?   462

4   Criticism of the Welfare Principle   463

4.1	'Welfare' as a Decision-Making Criterion	463
4.2	Criticisms of the Paramountcy of the Child's Welfare	465

5   Section 8 Orders   466

5.1	Giving Directions and Imposing Conditions on Section 8 Orders	466
5.2	The Family Assistance Order	467
5.3	The Courts' Powers to Make a Section 8 Order	469
5.4	Who May Apply for a Section 8 Order?	470
5.5	Leave to Apply for a Section 8 Order	472
5.6	Restrictions on Applications for, and the Use of, Section 8 Orders	483
5.7	Residence Orders	484
5.8	Shared Residence	491
5.9	Attaching Conditions to a Residence Order	500
5.10	The Legal Consequences of a Residence Order	502
5.11	Contact Orders	504
5.12	Facilitation and Enforcement of Contact	522
5.13	Prohibited Steps Order	533
5.14	Specific Issue Order	535
5.15	Restricting Applications for Section 8 Orders Under Section 91(14)	555
5.16	Local Authority Applications for Section 8 Orders	560
5.17	The Inherent Jurisdiction of the High Court	562

Discussion Questions   564

Further Reading   564

10   CHILDREN NEEDING SERVICES, CARE, AND PROTECTION   566

1   Background   568

1.1	The Inadequacies of the Previous Law	568

1.2	Ongoing Practice Concerns: The Climbié Report and the Children Act 2004	570
1.3	The Children Act 2004	570

2　Part III of the Children Act 1989 — 571

2.1	Who Are 'Children in Need'?	573
2.2	Provision of Services: Schedule 2 to the Children Act 1989	574
2.3	Provision of Accommodation for Children	576
2.4	Ways in Which the Child Can Be Accommodated	578
2.5	The Status of a 'Looked After' Child	578
2.6	Representations and Complaints Relating to Part III	582
2.7	The Voluntary Nature of 'Accommodation'	584
2.8	Some Qualifications to the Voluntary Nature of 'Accommodation'	586

3　Significant Harm: The Threshold for Compulsory Intervention — 590

3.1	Health or Development: Comparison with Similar Child	592

4　Investigation — 595

4.1	Investigating Whether a Child is Suffering, or is Likely to Suffer, Significant Harm	595
4.2	Child Assessment Orders	597
4.3	The Power of a Court to Direct a Section 37 Investigation in Family Proceedings	599
4.4	Local Authority Responses to Significant Harm	600

5　Protecting Children in an Emergency — 601

5.1	What is an Emergency Protection Order?	601
5.2	The Grounds for Making an Emergency Protection Order	603
5.3	Including an Exclusion Requirement in an Emergency Protection Order	608
5.4	Executing the Emergency Protection Order: The Assistance of the Police and Health Care Professionals	609
5.5	Applying to Discharge an Emergency Protection Order	609
5.6	Challenging the Making of, or Refusal to Make, an Emergency Protection Order	610

6　Police Protection: Children Act 1989, Section 46 — 611

7　Interim Care and Supervision Orders — 613

7.1	Duration of Interim Orders and Renewal	615
7.2	Interim Care and Supervision Orders: The Threshold	615
7.3	Deciding Whether or Not to Grant the Order	616
7.4	Interim Care Orders and Assessment	619
7.5	The Child's Right to Refuse to be Assessed	624
7.6	Interim Care Orders and Excluding the Alleged Abuser From the Home	625
7.7	The Role of the Children's Guardian	625

8　The Final Hearing in Care Proceedings — 628

8.1	The Threshold Test	628
8.2	'Is Suffering Significant Harm'	628
8.3	'Or is Likely to Suffer Significant Harm'	632
8.4	Proving Actual or Likely Significant Harm	632
8.5	The Burden and Standard of Proof in Care Proceedings	638
8.6	Harm Attributable to Care Not Being What it Would be Reasonable to Expect a Parent to Give	640
8.7	The Harm is Attributable to the Child's Being Beyond Parental Control	648
8.8	The Welfare Question in Care Proceedings	649
8.9	Issues Surrounding Application of the Checklist in Care Proceedings	649

9   The Local Authority's Care Plan and Respective
    Roles of the Local Authority and Court   651
    9.1   Reviewing Implementation of the Care Plan   653

10 The Legal Effect of a Care Order   653

11 Supervision Orders   655

12 Deciding Between a Care Order or Supervision Order   657

13 Discharge of Care Orders   661

14 Contact with a Child in Care   662
    14.1 Regulating Contact with a Child in Care in Cases of Disagreement   663
    14.2 Authorising the Local Authority to Deny Contact   664

Discussion Questions   667

Further Reading   667

11 ADOPTION AND SPECIAL GUARDIANSHIP   669

1   Adoption   669

2   The Adoption Service   673

3   Decision Making in Relation to Adoption   674

4   Adoption Agencies' Role in Assessing Suitable Adoptions   675
    4.1   Can Information about Adoption be Withheld from
          the Child's Father and Other Relatives?   676

5   Rules Relating to Parental Consent in Adoption Cases   680

6   Placement for Adoption   680
    6.1   Meaning of 'Placing a Child for Adoption'   681
    6.2   Placement by Agency with Parental Consent (s 19)   681
    6.3   Placement Orders   682
    6.4   Consequences of a Placement Order   686
    6.5   Placement and Contact   687
    6.6   Effect of Placement or Authorisation to Place   687
    6.7   Duration, and Revocation, of a Placement Order   688

7   Applications to Adopt   692
    7.1   Who May Adopt?   692
    7.2   Who May be Adopted?   695
    7.3   Preliminaries to Adoption   695
    7.4   Conditions for Making an Adoption Order   697
    7.5   Court's Leave Required to Oppose Making of Adoption Order   698
    7.6   Effect of an Adoption Order   699
    7.7   Setting Aside an Adoption Order   700
    7.8   Openness in Adoption and On-Going Contact   702

8   Special Guardianship   707

Discussion Questions   711

Further Reading   711

Bibliography   713
Index   747

TABLE OF CASES

A (A Child) (Contact: Sexual Abuse), Re [2002]
EWCA Civ 1595 . . . 521

A (A Minor) (Care Proceedings), Re [1993]
1 FCR 824 . . . 592

A (A Minor) (Custody), Re [1991] 2 FLR
394 . . . 486

A (A Minor) (Paternity: Refusal of Blood Test),
Re [1994] 2 FLR 463, CA . . . 355, 356

A (A Minor) (Residence Order: Leave to Apply),
Re [1993] 1 FLR 425 . . . 477

A (A Minor), Re [1996] 1 FCR 5, FD . . . 389

A (Abduction: Contempt), Re [2008] EWCA
Civ 1138, [2009] 1 WLR 1482, [2009]
1 FLR 1 . . . 529

A (Adoption: Removal), Re [2009] EWCA
Civ 41, [2010] Fam 9 . . . 696, 697

A (Application for Leave), Re [1998]
1 FLR 1 . . . 560

A (Change of Name), Re [2003] EWCA Civ 56,
[2003] 2 FLR 1 . . . 550, 551

A (Children) (Conjoined Twins: Surgical
Separation), Re [2001] Fam 147 . . . 450

A (Children) (Interim Care Order), Re [2001]
3 FCR 402 . . . 618

A (Contact: Section 91(14)), Re [2009] EWCA
Civ 1548, [2010] 2 FLR 151 . . . 556

A (Father: Knowledge of Child's Birth), Re
[2011] EWCA Civ 273, [2011] 2 FLR
123 . . . 677, 678, 679

A (Joint Residence: Parental Responsibility), Re
[2008] EWCA Civ 867, [2008] 2 FLR 1593,
CA . . . 491, 492, 493

A (Leave to Remove: Cultural and Religious
Considerations), Re [2006] EWHC 421 (Fam),
[2006] 2 FLR 572 . . . 544

A (Residence Order), Re [2007] EWCA Civ
899 . . . 530

A (Residential Assessment), Re [2009] EWHC
865 (Fam), [2009] 2 FLR 443 . . . 624

A (Specific Issue Order: Parental Dispute), Re
[2001] 1 FLR 121 . . . 436

A (Supervision Order: Extension), Re [1995]
1 FLR 335, CA . . . 614, 656

A (Suspended Residence Order), Re [2009] EWHC
1576 (Fam), [2010] 1 FLR 1679 . . . 530

A and B (One Parent Killed by the Other), Re
[2011] 1 FLR 783 . . . 629

A and D (Local Authority: Religious
Upbringing), Re [2010] EWHC 2503 (Fam),
[2011] 1 FLR 615 . . . 653, 654

A and Ors (Minors) (Residence Orders: Leave to
Apply), Re [1992] Fam 182, [1992] 3 All ER
872 . . . 474, 478

A Local Authority v GC and others [2008]
EWHC 2555 (Fam), [2009] 1 FLR
299 . . . 682

A v A (A Minor: Financial Provision) [1994]
1 FLR 657 . . . 295, 333, 335

A v A (Family: Unborn Child) [1974]
Fam 6 . . . 325

A v A (Financial Provision) [1995] 1 FLR
345 . . . 192, 204

A v A (Financial Provision) [1998] 2 FLR
180 . . . 191, 196

A v A (Maintenance Pending Suit: Provision for
Legal Fees) [2001] 1 FLR 377 . . . 163

A v A (Minors) (Shared Residence Order) [1994]
1 FLR 669, CA . . . 495, 497

A v A (Shared Residence) [2004] EWHC 142
(Fam), [2004] 1 FLR 1195 . . . 492, 497

A v B and another (Contact: Alternative
Families) [2012] EWCA Civ 285, [2012]
1 FCR 510 . . . 391

A v C [1985] FLR 445 . . . 510

A v East Sussex County Council and Chief
Constable of Sussex Police [2010] EWCA
Civ 743, [2010] 2 FLR 1596 . . . 612

A v J (Nullity Proceedings) [1989]
1 FLR 110 . . . 27

A v L (Contact) [1998] 1 FLR 361 . . . 510

A v L [2010] EWHC 460 (Fam), [2010]
2 FLR 1418 . . . 77

A v Liverpool City Council [1981] 2 All ER
385 . . . 483, 564

A v Liverpool City Council [1982]
AC 363 . . . 433

A v N (Committal: Refusal of Contact) [1997]
1 FLR 533 . . . 528

A v P (Surrogacy: Parental Order: Death of
Application) [2011] EWHC 1738 (Fam),
[2011] Fam Law 1080 . . . 371

A v UK [1998] 2 FLR 959 . . . 154

A, Re; Coventry County Council v CC
and A . . . 696

AAA v ASH, Registrar General for England
and Wales and the Secretary for Justice
[2009] EWHC 636 (Fam), [2010] 1 FLR
1 . . . 380

Abbott v Abbott [2007] UKPC 53 . . . 251, 266,
269, 274, 275, 276, 278, 281, 282, 283, 284

Adekunle v Ritchie [2007] BPIR 1177 . . . 265

Adoption Application (Payments for Adoption),
Re [1987] Fam 81 . . . 373

Agar-Ellis, Re (1883) 24 ChD 317 . . . 422

Agbaje v Akinnoye-Agbaje [2010] UKSC
13 . . . 76

AJ (Adoption Order or Special Guardianship
    Order), Re [2007] EWCA Civ 55, [2007]
    1 FLR 507 . . . 710, 711
Alfonso-Brown v Milwood [2006] EWHC 642
    (Fam), [2006] 2 FLR 265 . . . 19
Alonso v Alonso (1974) 4 Fam Law 164 . . . 207
A-M v A-M (Divorce: Jurisdiction: Validity of
    Marriage) [2001] 2 FLR 6 . . . 21
AMS v Child Support Officer [1998] 1 FLR
    955 . . . 324
Ansah v Ansah [1977] 2 All ER 638 . . . 141
AR (A Child: Relocation), Re [2010] EWHC 1346
    (Fam), [2010] 2 FLR 1577 . . . 496, 544, 545
Archer v Archer [1999] 1 FLR 327 . . . 74
ASB and KBS v MQS (Secretary of State for
    the Home Department Intervening) [2009]
    EWHC 2491 (Fam) . . . 696
Ash v Ash [1972] 1 All ER 582 . . . 70
Ashley v Blackman [1988] FCR 699 . . . 195
Associated Provincial Picture Houses Ltd
    v Wednesbury Corp [1948] 1 KB 223,
    CA . . . 577
Atkinson v Atkinson (No 2) [1996] 1 FLR
    51 . . . 179, 181, 210, 242
Atkinson v Atkinson [1987] 3 All ER
    849 . . . 210, 242
Atkinson v Atkinson [1988] Fam 93 . . . 164, 180
Attar v Attar [1985] FLR 649 . . . 185
Attorney-General ex rel Tilley v Wandsworth
    London Borough Council [1981] 1 WLR
    854 . . . 577

B (A Child) (Immunisation), Re [2003] EWCA
    Civ 1148, [2003] 2 FLR 1095 . . . 536
B (A Child) (Residence), Re [2009] UKSC
    5 . . . 459
B (A Child: Contact), Re [2001] EWCA Civ
    1968 . . . 504
B (A Minor) (Care Order: Criteria), Re [1993]
    1 FLR 815 . . . 616
B (A Minor) (Care Order: Review), Re [1993]
    1 FLR 421 . . . 651
B (A Minor) (Contact: Stepfather's Opposition),
    Re [1997] 2 FLR 579 . . . 508
B (A Minor) (Natural Parent), Re [2001] UKHL
    70, [2002] 1 FLR 196 . . . 694, 695
B (A Minor) (Wardship: Medical Treatment), Re
    (1982) 3 FLR 717, FD . . . 563
B (A Minor) (Wardship: Sterilisation), Re [1987]
    2 FLR 314 . . . 563
B (A Minor) (Wardship: Sterilisation), Re [1988]
    1 AC 199 . . . 457, 535
B (A Minor), Re, 17 October 1995, CA . . . 383
B (Adoption by One Natural Parent to Exclusion
    of Other), Re [2001] 1 FLR 589 . . . 694
B (Adoption Order: Nationality), Re [1999]
    2 AC 136 . . . 696
B (Adoption: Jurisdiction to Set Aside), Re
    [1995] Fam 239 . . . 700, 701, 702

B (Adoption: Natural Parent), Re [2001] UKHL
    70 . . . 462
B (Care or Supervision Order), Re [1996] 2 FLR
    693 . . . 657
B (Care Proceedings: Interim Care Order),
    Re [2009] EWCA Civ 1254, [2010] 1 FLR
    1211 . . . 616, 617
B (Care Proceedings: Standard of Proof),
    Re [2008] UKHL 35, [2009]
    1 AC 11 . . . 516, 566
B (Care: Interference with Family Life), Re
    [2003] 2 FLR 813 . . . 605
B (Change of Surname), Re [1996] 1 FLR 791,
    CA . . . 551, 553
B (Children) (Care Proceedings: Standard of
    Proof) (Cafcass Intervening), Re [2008]
    UKHL 35, [2009] AC 11 . . . 635, 639
B (Children) (Care: Interference with Family
    Life), Re [2003] EWCA Civ 786, [2004]
    1 FCR 463 . . . 685
B (Children) (Removal from Jurisdiction), Re;
    Re S (A Child) (Removal from Jurisdiction)
    [2003] EWCA Civ 1149, [2003] 2 FLR
    1043 . . . 539
B (Children) (Sexual Abuse: Standard of Proof),
    Re [2008] UKHL 35 . . . 649
B (Contact: Child Support), Re [2006] EWCA
    Civ 1574, [2007] 1 FLR 1949 . . . 320
B (Contact: Stepfather's Opposition), Re [1997]
    [1997] 2 FLR 579, CA . . . 522
B (Fact-Finding Hearing: Evidence), Re [2008]
    EWCA Civ 1547, [2009] 2 FLR 14 . . . 642
B (Interim Care Order: Directions), Re [2002]
    1 FLR 545 . . . 622
B (Interim Care Orders: Renewal), Re [2001]
    2 FLR 1217, FD . . . 615
B (Leave to Remove: Impact of Refusal),
    Re [2004] EWCA Civ 956, [2005] 2 FLR
    239 . . . 538, 540, 542
B (Minors) (Care: Contact: Local Authority's
    Plans), Re [1993] 1 FLR 543 . . . 664
B (Minors: Access), Re [1992] 1 FLR 140,
    CA . . . 517, 518
B (Non-Accidental Injury), Re [2002] EWCA
    Civ 752, [2002] 2 FLR 1133 . . . 637
B (Parentage), Re [1996] 2 FLR 15 . . . 364
B (Placement Order), Re [2008] EWCA Civ 835,
    [2008] 2 FLR 1404 . . . 683
B (Prohibited Steps Order), Re [2007] EWCA
    Civ 1055, [2008] 1 FLR 613, CA . . . 501, 535
B (Psychiatric Therapy for Parents), Re [1999]
    1 FLR 701 . . . 622
B (Residence Order: Status Quo), Re [1998]
    1 FLR 368 . . . 485
B (Role of Biological Father), Re [2007] EWHC
    1952 (Fam), [2008] 1 FLR 1015 . . . 391
B (Section 91(14) Order: Duration), Re [2003]
    EWCA Civ 1966, [2004] 1 FLR 871 . . . 505,
    558, 559

B (Wardship: Abortion), Re [1991] 2 FLR
426 . . . 563

B and L v UK (App no 36536/02) [2006] 1 FLR
35 . . . 16, 17

B v B (A Minor) (Residence Order) [1992] 2 FLR
327 . . . 454

B v B (Adult Student: Liability to Support) [1998]
1 FLR 373 . . . 327

B v B (Ancillary Relief) [2008] 1 FCR
613 . . . 182

B v B (Consent Order: Variation) [1995] 1 FLR
9 . . . 197, 219, 220, 222, 236

B v B (Financial Provision) [1990] 1 FLR
20 . . . 196

B v B (Financial Provision: Leave to Apply)
[1994] 1 FLR 219 . . . 230

B v B (Financial Provision: Welfare of Child and
Conduct) [2002] 1 FLR 555 . . . 170

B v B (Mesher Order) [2002] EWHC 3106
(Fam) . . . 197

B v B (Occupation Order) [1999] 1 FLR
715 . . . 125, 126

B v B (Residence Order: Restricting Applications)
[1997] 1 FLR 139 . . . 487, 555, 557

B v B (Residence: Condition Limiting
Geographic Area) [2004] 2 FLR 979 . . . 502

B v B [1995] 1 FLR 9 . . . 206

B v B [2007] EWHC 2492 (Fam), [2008] 1 FLR
813 . . . 20, 233

B v B [2008] EWCA Civ 483 . . . 176

B v Chief Constable of the Avon and Somerset
Constabulary [2001] 1 WLR 340 . . . 639

B v I [2010] 1 FLR 1721 . . . 36

B v P (Adoption by Unmarried Father) [2000]
2 FLR 717 . . . 694

B v S [2009] EWCA Civ 548 . . . 528

B v United Kingdom [2000] 1 FLR 1 . . . 393, 394

B, Re (Sexual Abuse: Standard of Proof) [2008]
UKHL 35 . . . 126

B, Re; RB v FB [2008] EWHC 1436 (Fam), [2008]
2 FLR 1624 . . . 36

Baker v Baker [1995] 2 FLR 829 . . . 183

Balraj v Balraj (1981) 11 FL 110 . . . 74

Banbury Peerage Case [1803–13] All ER Rep 171,
1 Sim and St 153, 57 ER 62 . . . 342

Banks v Banks [1999] 1 FLR 726 . . . 112

Barca v Mears [2004] EWHC 2170 (Ch) . . . 293

Barder v Caluori [1987] 2 All ER 440 . . . 221,
230, 231, 233, 235

Barnardo v McHugh [1891] AC 388 . . . 378

Barrett v Barrett [1988] 2 FLR 516 . . . 195, 196

Basham (Deceased), Re [1987] 1 All ER
405 . . . 285, 287, 289

Baxter v Baxter [1947] 2 All ER 886 . . . 26

BC (A Minor) (Access), Re [1985] FLR 639,
CA . . . 518

Bellinger v Bellinger [2003] UKHL 21 . . . 11, 23,
24, 38

Belton v Belton [1987] 2 FLR 343 . . . 538

Benham v UK (1996) 22 EHRR 293 . . . 529

Benson v Benson [1996] 1 FLR 692 . . . 231

Berkshire County Council v C and Others [1993]
Fam 203, [1993] 1 FLR 569, [1993] 2 WLR
475, FD . . . 620

Berry v Berry [1986] 1 FLR 618 . . . 182

Bhaiji v Chauhan (Queen's Proctor Intervening)
[2003] 2 FLR 485 . . . 67

Birch v Birch [1992] 1 FLR 564 . . . 70

Birmingham City Council v AG and A [2009]
EWHC 3720 (Fam), [2010] 2 FLR 580 . . . 597

Birmingham City Council v Ali and Ors; Moran
v Manchester City Council [2009] UKHL 36,
HL . . . 151

Birmingham City Council v D; Birmingham City
Council v M [1994] 2 FLR 502 . . . 646

Birmingham City Council v H (A Minor) [1994]
2 AC 212 . . . 450, 451

Birmingham City Council v R [2006] EWCA Civ
1748, [2007] 1 FLR 563 . . . 709, 710

Birmingham City Council v S, R and A [2006]
EWHC 3065 (Fam), [2007] 1 FLR 1223 . . . 677

Blackstock v Blackstock [1991] 2 FLR 308 . . . 124

Boylan v Boylan [1988] 1 FLR 282 . . . 196

Briody v St Helen's and Knowsley Area Health
Authority [2001] EWCA Civ 1010, [2001]
2 FLR 1094 . . . 371

Bremner (A Bankrupt), Re [1999] 1 LR
912 . . . 293

Brixey v Lynas, 1994 SLT 847 . . . 486

Bronda v Italy (App no 22430/93) (2001) 33
EHRR 4 . . . 507

Brooks v Brooks [1995] 2 FLR 13 . . . 198

Brown v Brown (1981) 3 FLR 161 . . . 182

Bryant v Bryant (1976) 120 Sol Jo
165 . . . 192, 204

Buckland v Buckland [1968] P 29 6 . . . 27

Buffery v Buffery [1988] 2 FLR
365 . . . 65, 69, 70

Burden and Burden v UK (App no 13378/05)
[2008] 2 FLR 787 . . . 56

Burgess v Burgess [1996] 2 FLR 981, [2000]
3 FCR 555 . . . 195

Burns v Azadani [1999] 1 FLR 266 . . . 123

Burns v Burns [1984] Ch 317 . . . 52, 271, 273, 299

Burris v Azadani [1995] 4 All ER 802 . . . 146

Burrow v Burrow [1999] 1 FLR 508 . . . 199, 201

C (A Child) (Direct Contact: Suspension), Re
[2011] EWCA Civ 521 . . . 508

C (A Child), Re [2006] EWCA Civ 235 . . . 497

C (A Minor) (Adopted Child: Contact), Re
[1993] 2 FLR 431 . . . 476

C (A Minor) (Adoption Order: Conditions), Re
[1989] 1 AC 1 . . . 706

C (A Minor) (Leave to Seek Section 8 Orders),
Re [1994] 1 FLR 26 . . . 480

C (A Minor) (Wardship: Surrogacy) [1985]
FLR 846 . . . 562

C (Adoption: Disclosure to Father), Re [2005] EWHC 3385 (Fam), [2006] 2 FLR 589 . . . 677, 678, 679

C (Care or Supervision Order), Re [1999] 2 FLR 621 . . . 660

C (Care: Contact), Re [2009] EWCA Civ 959, [2010] 1 FLR 895 . . . 663

C (Care: Discharge of Care Order), Re [2009] EWCA Civ 955, [2010] 1 FLR 774 . . . 661

C (Change of Surname), Re [1998] 2 FLR 656 . . . 549, 554

C (Detention: Medical Treatment), Re . . . 434

C (Domestic Violence: Fact-Finding Hearing), Re [2009] EWCA Civ 994, [2010] 1 FLR 1728 . . . 515, 516

C (Family Assistance Order), Re [1996] 1 FLR 424, FD . . . 468

C (Financial Provision), Re [2007] 2 FLR 13 . . . 337

C (HIV Test), Re [1999] 2 FLR 1004 . . . 536

C (Interim Care Order: Residential Assessment), Re [1997] 1 FLR 1 . . . 620

C (Litigant in Person: Section 91(14) Order), Re [2009] EWCA Civ 674, [2009] 2 FLR 1461 . . . 556

C (Minors) (Parental Rights), Re [1992] 1 FLR 1, CA . . . 385, 393

C (Refusal of Medical Treatment), Re [1994] 1 FLR 31 . . . 430

C (Residence Order), Re [2007] EWCA Civ 866, [2008] 1 FLR 211 . . . 530

C (Residence: Child's Application for Leave), Re [1995] 1 FLR 927, FD . . . 480

C (Welfare of Child: Immunisation), Re [2003] EWHC 1376 (Fam), [2003] 2 FLR 1054 . . . 536

C and B (Children) (Care Order: Future Harm), Re [2000] 2 FCR 614 . . . 684

C and V (Contact and Parental Responsibility), Re [1998] 1 FLR 392, CA . . . 382, 383, 384, 385, 386, 387, 519

C v C (Divorce: Stay of English Proceedings) [2001] 1 FLR 624 . . . 226

C v C (Financial Provision: Personal Damages) [1995] 2 FLR 171 . . . 177

C v C (Financial Relief: Short Marriage) [1997] 2 FLR 26 . . . 196, 329

C v C (Minors: Custody) [1988] 2 FLR 291, CA . . . 487, 488

C v F (Disabled Child: Maintenance Orders) [1998] 2 FLR 1, CA . . . 323, 334

C v Solihull MBC [1993] 1 FLR 290 . . . 451

C v W (A Minor) (Contact: Leave to Apply) [1998] 1 FCR 618 . . . 477

Cackett v Cackett [1950] 1 All ER 677 . . . 26

Camden LBC v Alexandrou (No 2) (1998) 30 HLR 534 . . . 248

Camm v Camm (1983) 4 FLR 577 . . . 218

Carr Glyn v Frearsons (A Firm) [1999] 1 FLR 8 . . . 215

Carroll, Re [1931] 1 KB 317 . . . 455

Carron v Carron [1984] FLR 805, CA . . . 325, 327

Carson v Carson [1983] 1 All ER 478 . . . 206

Carter-Fea v Carter-Fea [1987] Fam Law 131 . . . 69

CB (A Minor) (Parental Responsibility Order), Re [1993] 1 FLR 920, FD . . . 382

CB and JB (Care Proceedings: Guidelines), Re [1998] 2 FLR 211 . . . 644, 645

CF v KM (Financial Provision for Child: Costs of Legal Proceedings) [2010] EWHC 1754 (Fam), [2011] 1 FLR 208 . . . 330

Chadwick v Chadwick [1985] FLR 606, CA . . . 187, 209, 211, 213

Chalmers v Johns [1999] 1 FLR 392 . . . 125, 136

Chamberlain v Chamberlain [1973] 1 WLR 1557 . . . 207, 327, 329

Chamberlain v De La Mare (1982) 4 FLR 434 . . . 538, 539

Charman v Charman [2007] EWCA Civ 503, [2007] 1 FLR 1246 . . . 49, 63, 176, 178, 182, 189, 228

Chaudhuri v Chaudhuri [1992] 2 FLR 73 . . . 203, 204, 207, 233

Chechi v Bashier [1999] 2 FLR 489 . . . 108, 113

Cheshire County Council v M [1993] 1 FLR 463 . . . 474, 664

Chief Adjudication Officer v Bath [2000] 1 FLR 8 . . . 20

Churchard v Churchard [1984] FLR 635 . . . 528

Churchill v Roach [2003] WTLR 779 . . . 210

Citro (A Bankrupt), Re [1991] 1 FLR 71 . . . 293

City of Westminster v IC (By His Litigation Friend the Official Solicitor) and KC and NNC [2008] EWHC 198, [2008] 2 FLR 267 . . . 38

C-J (Section 91(14) Order), Re [2006] EWHC 1491 (Fam), [2006] 2 FLR 1213 . . . 556, 558

CL v East Riding Yorkshire Council, MB and BL (A Child) [2006] EWCA Civ 49, [2006] 2 FLR 24 . . . 641

Clark v Clark [1999] 2 FLR 498, CA . . . 192, 194

Claughton v Charalambous [1999] 1 FLR 740 . . . 293

Cleary v Cleary [1974] 1 All ER 498 . . . 68

Clutton v Clutton [1991] 1 All ER 340 . . . 206, 208, 209, 210

Co v Co [2004] 1 FLR 1095 . . . 186

Coleman v Coleman [1972] 3 All ER 886 . . . 165

Conran v Conran [1997] 2 FLR 615 . . . 171

Coombes v Smith [1986] 1 WLR 808 . . . 288

Corbett v Corbett (Otherwise Ashley) [1971] P 83, [1970] 2 WLR 1306 . . . 21–26, 369

Cordle v Cordle [2002] 1 FCR 97 . . . 170, 183, 184

Cornick v Cornick (No 3) [2001] 2 FLR 1240 . . . 238

Cornick v Cornick [1994] 2 FLR 530 . . . 231, 232

Cossey v UK [1991] 2 FLR 492 . . . 22

Coventry City Council v O (Adoption) [2011] EWCA Civ 729, [2011] 2 FLR 936 . . . 681

Covezzi and Morselli v Italy (2003) 38 EHRR 28 . . . 605

Cowan v Cowan [2001] 2 FLR 192 . . . 188

Crabb v Arun District Council [1976] Ch 179 . . . 289

Crago v Julian [1992] 1 WLR 372 . . . 248

Crossley v Crossley [2007] EWCA Civ 1491 . . . 226, 228, 281

Croydon London Borough Council v A (No 3) [1992] 2 FLR 350 . . . 658

Croydon London Borough Council v A [1992] Fam 169, CA . . . 533

Curley v Parkes [2004] EWCA Civ 1515 . . . 251

Currey v Currey [2006] EWCA Civ 1338 . . . 163

D (A Child) (Care Order: Evidence), Re [2010] EWCA Civ 1000, [2011] 1 FLR 447 . . . 642

D (A Child) (IVF Treatment), Re [2001] 1 FLR 972, CA . . . 381

D (A Child) (Residence: Natural Parent), Re [2000] 1 FCR 97, FD . . . 461

D (A Child), Re [2010] EWCA Civ 470 . . . 559

D (A Minor) (Care or Supervision Order), Re [1993] 2 FLR 423 . . . 659

D (A Minor) (Contact: Mother's Hostility), Re [1993] 2 FLR 1 . . . 519

D (A Minor), Re [1995] 3 FCR 783, FD . . . 387

D (Adoption: Parent's Consent), Re [1977] 1 All ER 145 . . . 684

D (Care Order: Evidence), Re [2010] EWCA Civ 1000, [2011] 1 FLR 447 . . . 636, 642

D (Children), Re [2009] EWCA Civ 1551 . . . 530

D (Contact and Parental Responsibility: Lesbian Mothers and Known Father), Re [2006] 1 FCR 556, FD . . . 388, 391

D (Contact: Reasons for Refusal), Re [1997] 2 FLR 48, CA . . . 519, 520

D (Intractable Contact Dispute: Publicity), Re [2004] EWHC 727 (Fam), [2004] 1 FLR 1226 . . . 512, 522, 529

D (Jurisdiction: Programme of Assessment or Therapy), Re [1999] 2 FLR 632 . . . 622

D (Leave to Remove: Appeal), Re [2010] EWCA Civ 50, [2010] 2 FLR 1605 . . . 539, 545, 546

D (Paternity), Re [2006] EWHC 3545 (Fam), [2007] 2 FLR 26 . . . 344, 345, 353, 356

D (Prohibited Steps Order), Re [1996] 2 FLR 273 . . . 502, 533

D (Residence: Imposition of Conditions), Re [1996] 2 FLR 281 . . . 502

D (Unborn Baby), Re [2009] EWHC 446 (Fam), [2009] 2 FLR 313 . . . 612

D and H (Care: Termination of Contact) [1997] 1 FLR 841 . . . 666

D v D (Child of the Family) (1981) 2 FLR 93, CA . . . 325

D v D (County Court Jurisdiction: Injunctions) [1993] 2 FLR 802 . . . 595

D v D (Lump Sum Order: Adjournment of Application) [2001] 1 FLR 633 . . . 166

D v D (Nature of Recognition of Overseas Divorce) [2005] EWHC 3342 (Fam), [2006] 2 FLR 825 . . . 76

D v D (Nullity: Statutory Bar) [1979] Fam 70 . . . 30

D v D (Shared Residence Order) [2001] 1 FLR 495, CA . . . 495, 496

D v N (Contact Order: Conditions) [1997] 2 FLR 797 . . . 467, 562

Dart v Dart [1996] 2 FLR 286 . . . 161, 169–171, 174

Daubney v Daubney [1976] 2 All ER 453 . . . 177

Davis v Johnson [1978] 1 All ER 1132 . . . 104, 135

De Lasala v de Lasala [1980] AC 546, [1979] 2 All ER 1146, PC . . . 220

De Manneville v De Manneville (1804) 10 Ves 54 . . . 447

DE v AG (1985) 1 Rob Eccl 279 . . . 26

Dean v Stout (Trustee in Bankruptcy) [2005] EWHC 3315 (Ch) . . . 293

Delaney v Delaney [1990] 2 FLR 457 . . . 313

Dellow's Will Trusts, Re [1964] 1 WLR 451 . . . 638

Den Heyer v Newby [2006] 1 FLR 1114 . . . 231

Dennis (Deceased), Re [1981] 2 All ER 140 . . . 329

Dennis v Dennis [1955] P 153 . . . 68

Dennis v Dennis [2000] 2 FLR 231 . . . 66

Devjee v Patel [2006] EWCA Civ 1211 . . . 115, 141

Devon County Council v S [1994] 1 FLR 355 . . . 563

DH (A Minor) (Child Abuse), Re [1994] 1 FLR 679 . . . 454, 651

Dharamshi v Dharamshi [2001] 1 FCR 492 . . . 182

Din v Wandsworth London Borough Council [1983] 1 AC 657 . . . 153

Dixon v Marchant [2008] 1 FLR 655 . . . 231, 233, 235

Dodsworth v Dodsworth (1973) 228 EG 1115 . . . 289

Donohue v Ingram [2006] EWHC 282 . . . 293

Dorney-Kingdom v Dorney-Kingdom [2000] 2 FLR 855 . . . 206

Down Lisburn Health and Social Services Trust v H [2006] UKHL 36, [2007] 1 FLR 121 . . . 705, 706

D-R (Adult: Contact), Re [1999] 1 FLR 1161, CA . . . 508

Drake v Whipp [1996] 1 FLR 826 . . . 281

Duhur-Johnson v Duhur-Johnson (Attorney-General Intervening) [2005] 2 FLR 1042 . . . 77

Duxbury v Duxbury [1987] 1 FLR 7 . . . 166, 210

E (A Minor) (Care Order: Contact), Re [1994]
    1 FLR 146 . . . 665
E (A Minor) (Wardship: Medical Treatment), Re
    [1993] 1 FLR 386 . . . 438, 440, 441
E (A Minor: Access), Re [1987] 1 FLR
    368 . . . 520
E (An Alleged Patient), Re; Sheffield City
    Council v E and S [2004] EWHC 2808 (Fam),
    [2005] 1 FLR 965 . . . 13
E (Family Assistance Order), Re [1999] 2 FLR
    512, FD . . . 468
E (Parental Responsibility: Blood Tests), Re
    [1995] 1 FLR 392 . . . 344, 389
E (Residence: Imposition of Conditions), Re
    [1997] 2 FLR 638, CA . . . 410, 484, 500, 501
E v E (Ouster Order) [1995] 1 FLR 224 . . . 122
EB v France (App no 43546/02) [2008] 1 FLR
    850, ECtHR . . . 676
ECC (The Local Authority) v SM [2010] EWHC
    1694 (Fam), [2011] 1 FLR 234 . . . 696
Edgar v Edgar [1980] 1 WLR 1410 . . . 218, 224, 232
El Fadl v El Fadl [2000] 1 FLR 175 . . . 77
Elliott v Elliott [2001] 1 FCR 477 . . . 205, 206
Elsholz v Germany (App no 25735/94) (2002) 34
    EHRR 58 . . . 507, 508
Elsholz v Germany (App no 25735/94) [2001]
    ECtHR . . . 462
Eroglu v Eroglu [1994] 2 FLR 287 . . . 77
Essex County Council v B [1993] 1 FLR
    866 . . . 626
Essex County Council v F [1993] 1 FLR 847 . . . 610
Estate of Park, Re [1954] P 112 . . . 13
ET (Serious Injuries: Standard of Proof) (Note),
    Re [2003] 2 FLR 1205 . . . 639
Evans v Evans [1989] 1 FLR 351 . . . 191, 193
Evans v UK [2007] 2 FCR 5, ECtHR (Grand
    Chamber) . . . 361
Evelyn, Re [1998] Fam 55, CA . . . 459
Evers Trust, Re; Papps v Evers [1980] 3 All ER
    399 . . . 214, 292
Eves v Eves [1975] 1 WLR 1338 . . . 280, 297

F (A Child) (Contact Order), Re [2001] 1 FCR
    422, CA . . . 515
F (A Minor) (Blood Tests: Parental Rights), Re
    [1993] Fam 314, CA . . . 349, 351, 352
F (A Ward) (Leave to Remove Ward Out of the
    Jurisdiction), Re [1988] 2 FLR 116 . . . 538
F (Care Proceedings: Interim Care Order),
    Re [2010] EWCA Civ 826, [2010] 2 FLR
    1455 . . . 617
F (Child: Surname), Re [1993] 2 FLR 837 . . . 551
F (Children) (DNA Evidence), Re [2007] EWHC
    3235 (Fam), [2008] 1 FLR 348 . . . 344
F (Children), Re [2003] EWCA Civ 592 . . . 492
F (Contact: Child in Care), Re [1995] 1 FLR 510,
    FD . . . 451, 662
F (Contact: Enforcement), Re [1998] 1 FLR
    691 . . . 528

F (In Utero) (Wardship), Re [1988] Fam 122,
    [1988] 2 FLR 307 . . . 613
F (Infants) (Adoption Order: Validity), Re [1977]
    Fam 165 . . . 700
F (Interim Care Order), Re [2011] EWCA Civ
    258, [2011] 2 FLR 856 . . . 645, 646
F (Mental Patient: Sterilisation), Re [1990]
    2 AC 1, [1989] 2 FLR 376 . . . 613
F (Minors) (Denial of Contact), Re [1993]
    2 FLR 677, CA . . . 517
F (Placement Order), Re [2008] EWCA Civ 439,
    [2008] 2 FLR 550 . . . 673, 689, 690
F (Restrictions on Applications), Re [2005]
    EWCA Civ 499, [2005] 2 FLR 950 . . . 557
F (Shared Residence Order), Re [2003] EWCA
    Civ 592, [2003] 2 FLR 347 . . . 492
F (Specific Issue: Child Interview), Re [1995]
    1 FLR 819 . . . 536
F and H (Children: Relocation), Re [2007]
    EWCA Civ 692, [2008] 2 FLR 1667 . . . 541
F and R (Section 8 Order: Grandparent's
    Application), Re [1995] 1 FLR 524,
    FD . . . 473
F v Cambridgeshire County Council [1995]
    1 FLR 516 . . . 484
F v G (Child: Financial Provision) [2004] EWHC
    1848 (Fam), [2005] 1 FLR 261 . . . 337, 338
F v Leeds City Council [1994] 2 FLR 60 . . . 451,
    592
F v S (Adoption: Ward) [1973] Fam 203, [1973]
    1 All ER 722 . . . 474
F v Wirral Metropolitan Borough Council [1991]
    2 All ER 648 . . . 590
F(R) (An Infant), Re [1970] 1 QB 385 . . . 700
FH (Dispensing with Fact-Finding Hearing), Re
    [2008] EWCA Civ 1249, [2009] 1 FLR 349,
    CA . . . 516
Fitzpatrick v Sterling Housing Association Ltd
    [2001] AC 27, [2000] 1 FLR 271 . . . 40, 43
Flavell v Flavell [1997] 1 FLR 353 . . . 195, 236,
    237
Fleming v Fleming [2003] EWCA Civ
    1841 . . . 176
Fleming v Fleming [2004] 1 FLR 667 . . . 164,
    180, 181, 210
Foley v Foley [1981] 2 All ER 857 . . . 185
Fournier v Fournier [1998] 2 FLR 990 . . . 183
Fowler v Barron [2008] EWCA Civ 377 . . . 259,
    260, 261, 262
Foyle v Turner [2007] BPIR 43 . . . 293
Frary v Frary [1993] 2 FLR 696 . . . 180
Fraser v Children's Court Pretoria North and
    Others (CCT31/96) [1997] ZACC 1, 1996 (8)
    BCLR 1085, 1997 (2) SA 218 . . . 396
Frazer Harris v Scholfield Roberts & Hill (A
    Firm) [1998] 2 FLR 679 . . . 222
Frost v Clarke [2008] EWHC 742 (Ch) . . . 275
FS (Child Abuse: Evidence), Re [1996] 2 FLR
    158 . . . 651

G (A Minor) (Care Order: Threshold Conditions), Re [1995] Fam 16 . . . 644

G (A Minor) (Interim Care Order: Residential Assessment), Re [2006] 1 AC 576 . . . 621

G (A Minor) (Parental Responsibility Order), Re [1994] 1 FLR 504, CA . . . 382, 383

G (Care: Challenge To Local Authority's Decision), Re [2003] EWHC 551 (Fam), [2003] 2 FLR 42 . . . 642, 655

G (Child Case: Parental Involvement), Re [1996] 1 FLR 857, CA . . . 560

G (Children Act 1989, Schedule 1), Re [1996] 2 FLR 171 . . . 331

G (Children) (Care Order: Evidence), Re [2001] EWCA Civ 968, [2001] 2 FCR 757 . . . 631

G (Children) (Residence: Same-Sex Partner), Re [2006] UKHL 43, [2006] 4 All ER 241 . . . 340, 358, 451, 458, 459, 460, 461, 462

G (Children), Re [2005] EWCA Civ 1283, [2006] 1 FLR 771 . . . 454

G (Children: Contact), Re [2002] EWCA Civ 761, [2002] 3 FCR 377 . . . 706

G (Contempt: Committal), Re [2003] EWCA Civ 489, [2003] 1 WLR 2051, [2003] 2 FLR 58 . . . 529

G (Interim Care Order: Residential Assessment), Re [2006] 1 AC 576 . . . 616

G (Leave to Remove), Re [2007] EWCA Civ 1497, [2008] 1 FLR 1587 . . . 537, 545

G (Minors) (Interim Care Order), Re [1993] 2 FLR 839, CA . . . 615, 616

G (Parentage: Blood Sample), Re [1997] 1 FLR 360, CA . . . 355

G (Parental Responsibility Order), Re [2006] 2 FLR 1092, CA . . . 388

G (Parental Responsibility: Education), Re [1994] 2 FLR 964 . . . 408

G (Residence: Restriction on Further Applications), Re [2008] EWCA Civ 1468, [2009] 1 FLR 894, CA . . . 466, 558

G (Residence: Same-Sex Partner), Re [2006] UKHL 43, [2006] 2 FLR 629, HL . . . 497

G (Special Guardianship Order), Re [2010] EWCA Civ 300, [2010] 2 FLR 696 . . . 709

G (Surrogacy: Foreign Domicile), Re [2007] EWHC 2814 (Fam), [2008] 1 FLR 1047 . . . 362, 372

G and A (Care Order: Freeing Order: Parents with a Learning Disability), Re [2006] NI Fam 8 . . . 642

G and R (Child Sexual Abuse: Standard of Proof), Re [1995] 2 FLR 867 . . . 634

G v F (Shared Residence: Parental Responsibility) [1998] 2 FLR 799 . . . 476, 489

G v G (Financial Provision: Separation Agreement) [2004] 1 FLR 1011, CA . . . 226

G v G (Maintenance Pending Suit: Costs) [2002] EWHC 306 (Fam) . . . 163

G v G (Occupation Order: Conduct) [2000] 2 FLR 36 . . . 137

G v G (Ouster: Ex Parte Application) [1990] 1 FLR 395 . . . 144

G v G (Periodical Payments: Jurisdiction) [1997] 1 All ER 272 . . . 236

G v Kirklees Metropolitan Borough Council [1993] 1 FLR 805 . . . 472

G v Netherlands (App no 16944/90) (1993) 16 EHRR CD 38 . . . 680

G, Re (Financial Provision: Liberty to Restore Application for Lump Sum) [2004] EWHC 88 (Fam), [2004] 1 FLR 997 . . . 166, 187

Gandolfo v Gandolfo [1980] 1 All ER 833 . . . 168

Garcia v Garcia [1992] 1 FLR 256 . . . 74

Gardner v Gardner (1877) 2 App Cas 723 . . . 342

Gaskin v UK (App no 10454/83) (1989) 12 EHRR 36 . . . 348

Gay v Sheeran [1999] 3 All ER 795 . . . 294

George v George [1986] 2 FLR 347 . . . 104

Gereis v Yagoub [1997] 1 FLR 854 . . . 20

Ghaidan v Godin-Mendoza [2004] UKHL 30, [2004] 2 FLR 600 . . . 40, 43

Ghandi v Patel [2002] 1 FLR 603 . . . 19

Gibson v Revenue and Customs Prosecution Office [2008] EWCA 645 . . . 250

Gillet v Holt [2001] Ch 210 . . . 285, 286

Gillick v West Norfolk and Wisbech AHA [1986] AC 112 . . . 353, 395, 409, 420–431, 435, 436, 437, 438, 440, 442, 445, 553

Gissing v Gissing [1970] 2 All ER 780 . . . 187, 249, 273

Glaser v UK [2001] 1 FLR 153 . . . 526

Glass v UK (App no 61827/00) [2004] 1 FLR 1019 . . . 411

Gloucestershire County Council v P [1999] 2 FLR 61 . . . 469

Gogay v Hertfordshire County Council [2001] 1 FLR 280, CA . . . 596

Golubovich v Golubovich [2010] EWCA Civ 810 . . . 63

Goodman v Gallant [1986] 1 FLR 513 . . . 248

Goodrich v Goodrich [1971] 2 All ER 1340 . . . 68

Goodwin v UK (2002) 35 EHRR 18, [2002] 2 FLR 487 . . . 22, 23, 24, 39

GR (Care Order), Re [2010] EWCA Civ 871, [2011] 1 FLR 669 . . . 615, 617

Granatino v Radmacher (formerly Granatino) [2010] UKSC 42, [2011] 1 AC 534 . . . 222, 223, 227

Grant v Edwards [1986] 2 All ER 426 . . . 268, 280

Greasley v Cooke [1980] 3 All ER 710 . . . 287, 289

Greenham v Greenham [1989] 1 FLR 105 . . . 184, 212

Griffiths v Dawson & Co [1993] 2 FLR 315 . . . 75

Griffiths v Griffiths [1984] Fam 70 . . . 328

Grubb v Grubb [2009] EWCA Civ 976 . . . 138

GW v RW (Financial Provision: Departure from Equality) [2003] 2 FLR 108 . . . 174, 185, 186

H (A Child) (Interim Order), Re [2002] EWCA
    Civ 1932, [2003] 1 FCR 350 . . . 616
H (A Child), Re [2002] EWCA Civ 2005 . . . 491
H (A Child: Parental Responsibility), Re [2002]
    EWCA Civ 542 . . . 382, 519
H (A Child: Residence), Re [2002] 3 FCR
    277 . . . 461
H (A Minor) (Blood Tests: Parental Rights), Re
    [1997] Fam 89, CA . . . 351, 352, 356
H (A Minor) (Care Proceedings: Child's Wishes),
    Re [1993] 1 FLR 440 . . . 627
H (A Minor) (Contact), Re [1994] 2 FLR 776,
    CA . . . 508, 520
H (A Minor) (Custody: Interim Care and
    Control), Re [1991] 2 FLR 109, CA . . . 458
H (A Minor) (Section 37 Direction), Re [1993]
    2 FLR 541 . . . 599, 632
H (A Minor) (Shared Residence), Re [1994]
    1 FLR 717 . . . 495
H (A Minor: Custody), Re [1990] 1 FLR 51 . . . 461
H (Children), Re [2003] EWCA Civ 369, [2003]
    All ER (D) 290 . . . 475, 477
H (Children), Re [2009] EWCA Civ 902 . . . 492
H (Children: Residence Order: Condition),
    Re [2001] EWCA Civ 1338, [2001] 2 FLR
    1277 . . . 501
H (Contact Order) (No 2), Re [2002] 1 FLR 22,
    FD . . . 509, 521
H (Contact: Domestic Violence), Re [2005]
    EWCA Civ 1404, [2006] 1 FLR 943 . . . 515
H (Leave to Apply for Residence Order), Re
    [2008] 2 FLR 848 . . . 475, 476, 515
H (Leave to Remove), Re [2010] EWCA Civ 915,
    [2010] 2 FLR 1875 . . . 545, 546
H (Minors) (Access), Re [1992] 1 FLR 148,
    CA . . . 509
H (Minors) (Local Authority: Parental Rights),
    Re (No 3) [1991] Fam 151; sub nom H
    (Illegitimate Children: Father: Parental
    Rights), Re (No 2) [1991] 1 FLR 214 . . . 385
H (Minors), Re, CA (3 December 1999) . . . 517
H (Parental Responsibility), Re [1998] 1 FLR 855,
    CA . . . 382, 384, 392, 408
H (Prohibited Steps Order), Re [1995] 1 FLR
    638 . . . 534
H (Shared Residence: Parental Responsibility),
    Re [1995] 2 FLR 883 . . . 484, 493, 503
H (Supervision Order), Re [1994] 2 FLR
    979 . . . 657
H and A, Re [2002] EWCA Civ 383, [2002]
    2 FCR 469 . . . 343, 352
H and G (Adoption: Consultation of Unmarried
    Fathers), Re [2001] 1 FLR 745 . . . 677, 678
H and Others (Minors) Sexual Abuse: Standard
    of Proof), Re [1996] AC 563 . . . 632, 633, 635,
    638
H v C [2009] 2 FLR 1540 . . . 322
H v H (Child Abuse: Access) [1989] 1 FLR 212,
    CA . . . 512

H v H (Family Provision: Remarriage) [1975]
    Fam 19 . . . 234
H v H (Financial Provision) [2009] 2 FLR
    795 . . . 182
H v H (Financial Provision: Conduct) [1994]
    2 FLR 801 . . . 192, 193
H v H (Financial Provision: Remarriage) [1975]
    1 All ER 367 . . . 203
H v H (Financial Provision: Short Marriage)
    (1981) 2 FLR 392 . . . 185, 186
H v H (Financial Relief: Attempted Murder as
    Conduct) [2005] EWHC 2911 (Fam), [2006]
    1 FLR 990 . . . 192
H v H (Financial Relief: Conduct) [1998] 1 FLR
    971 . . . 193, 202
H v H (Financial Relief: Costs) [1997] 2 FLR
    57 . . . 201
H v H (Talaq Divorce) [2007] EWHC 2945,
    [2008] 2 FLR 857 . . . 77
H v H (The Queen's Proctor Intervening)
    (Validity of Japanese Divorce) [2006] EWHC
    2989 (Fam), [2007] 1 FLR 1318 . . . 77
H v O (Contempt of Court: Sentencing) [2004]
    EWCA Civ 1691 . . . 115, 116, 141
H v Trafford Borough Council [1997] 3 FCR
    113 . . . 641
H, Barhanu and B v Wandsworth Hackney and
    Islington LBC [2007] EWHC 1082 (Admin),
    [2007] 2 FLR 822 . . . 582
H, Re (Threshold Criteria: Standard of Proof)
    [1996] 1 All ER 1 . . . 126
H, Re [1996] AC 563 . . . 650
Haase v Germany [2004] 2 FLR 39, [2005] 3 FCR
    666 . . . 605, 685
Hadjimilitis (Tsavliris) v Tsavliris (Divorce:
    Irretrievable Breakdown) [2003] 1 FLR
    81 . . . 67
Haines v Hill [2007] EWCA Civ 1284 . . . 221
Hale v Tanner [2000] 2 FLR 879, [2000] 3 FCR
    62 . . . 114, 115, 116, 141
Hammerton v Hammerton [2007] EWCA Civ
    248, [2007] 2 FLR 1133 . . . 529
Hammond v Mitchell [1991] 1 WLR 1127 . . . 52,
    267, 268
Hampshire County Council v S [1993] 1 FLR
    559 . . . 616
Hanlon v Hanlon [1978] 2 All ER 889 . . . 203,
    204, 206, 207
Hanlon v Law Society [1981] AC 124 . . . 201
Hardy v Hardy (1981) 2 FLR 321 . . . 179
Harnett v Harnett [1973] Fam 156 . . . 328
Haroutunian v Jennings (1980) 1 FLR 62 . . . 333,
    334
Harris v Goddard [1983] 3 All ER 242 . . . 215
Harris v Harris [2001] 1 FCR 68 . . . 236
Harris v Harris; Attorney-General v Harris
    [2001] 2 FLR 895, FD . . . 556
Harris v Manahan [1997] 1 FLR 205 . . . 216,
    220, 219, 222

Harwood v Harwood [1991] 2 FLR 274 . . . 166, 253

Heard v Heard [1995] 1 FLR 970 . . . 230, 232

Hedges v Hedges [1991] 1 FLR 196 . . . 185

Hepburn v Hepburn [1989] 1 FLR 373 . . . 195

Hewer v Bryant [1970] 1 QB 357 . . . 422

Hewitson v Hewitson [1995] 1 FLR 241 . . . 186

HG (Specific Issue Order: Sterilisation), Re [1993] 1 FLR 587, FD . . . 535

Hill v Hill [1998] 1 FLR 198 . . . 186

Hillard v Hillard (1982) 12 Fam Law 176 . . . 192

Hipgrave and Hipgrave v Jones [2004] EWHC 2901 (QB) . . . 148

Hirani v Hirani (1983) 4 FLR 232 . . . 27, 28

Hodak v Newman (1993) 16 Fam LR 1 . . . 459

Hoffmann v Austria (App no 12875/87) [1993] ECHR 25, (1994) 17 EHRR 293, [1994] 1 FCR 193, ECtHR . . . 489

Hollens v Hollens (1971) 115 SJ 327 . . . 73

Holman v Howes [2007] EWCA Civ 877 . . . 281, 282, 283, 286, 290

Holmes-Moorhouse v Richmond-Upon-Thames LBC [2009] UKHL 7, [2009] 1 FLR 904 . . . 494, 496

Hopes v Hopes [1949] P 227 . . . 71

Hornal v Neuberger Products Ltd [1957] 1 QB 247 . . . 638

Horner v Horner [1982] 2 All ER 495 . . . 104

Horton v Horton [1947] 2 All ER 871 . . . 26

Hounslow LBC v A [1993] 1 FLR 702 . . . 451

Hudson v Leigh [2009] EWHC 1306 (Fam) . . . 19, 20, 38

Humberside County Council v B [1993] 1 FLR 257 . . . 126, 591

Hunter v Canary Wharf Ltd [1997] 2 All ER 426 . . . 146

Huntingford v Hobbs [1993] 1 FLR 736 . . . 251, 253, 281

Hyde v Hyde [1866] LR 1 P & D 130 . . . 11, 21, 27

Hyett v Stanley [2003] EWCA Civ 942 . . . 283

Hyman v Hyman [1929] AC 601 . . . 218, 222

I v UK [2002] 2 FLR 518 . . . 22, 23, 24

Ignaccolo-Zenide v Romania (App no 31679/96) (2001) 31 EHRR 7 . . . 508

IJ (A Child) (Overseas Surrogacy: Parental Order), Re [2011] EWHC 921 (Fam), [2011] 2 FLR 646 . . . 372

Inwards v Baker [1965] 2 QB 29 . . . 289

Islington London Borough Council v EV [2010] EWHC 3240 (Fam), [2011] 1 FLR 1681 . . . 616

Ismailova v Russia [2008] 1 FLR 533 . . . 489

J (A Child) (Restriction on Applications), Re [2007] EWCA Civ 906, [2008] 1 FLR 369 . . . 558, 559

J (A Minor) (Contact), Re [1994] 1 FLR 729, CA . . . 509, 518, 520

J (A Minor), Re, The Times, 14 May 1992 . . . 433

J (Care Proceedings: Injuries), Re [2009] 2 FLR 99, FD . . . 641

J (Care: Care Plan), Re [1994] 1 FLR 253 . . . 651, 652

J (Child Returned Abroad: Convention Rights), Re [2005] UKHL 40, [2005] 2 FLR 802 . . . 544

J (Children), Re [2012] EWCA Civ 380 . . . 646

J (Costs of Fact-Finding Hearing), Re [2009] EWCA Civ 1350, [2010] 1 FLR 1893 . . . 516

J (Leave to Issue Application for Residence Order), Re [2003] 1 FLR 114, CA . . . 474, 475

J (Leave to Remove: Urgent Case), Re [2006] EWCA Civ 1897, [2007] 1 FLR 2033 . . . 540

J (Minors), Re, 2 October 1997, CA . . . 517

J (Residential Assessment: Rights of Audience), Re [2009] EWCA Civ 1210, [2010] 1 FLR 1290 . . . 623

J (Specific Issue Order: Leave to Apply), Re [1995] 1 FLR 669 . . . 536

J (Specific Issue Orders: Child's Religious Upbringing and Circumcision), Re [2000] 1 FLR 571 . . . 408

J and Another v C and Ors [1970] AC 668 . . . 454, 455, 456, 458, 461

J v C (Child: Financial Provision) [1999] 1 FLR 152 . . . 334, 335, 337

J v C [1969] 1 All ER 788, [1970] AC 668 . . . 684

J v C [2006] EWHC 2837 (Fam), [2007] 1 FCR 365 . . . 357

J v C and Another [2006] EWCA Civ 551, [2007] Fam 1 . . . 359, 362, 370

J v J (A Minor: Property Transfer) [1993] 2 FLR 56 . . . 331

J v J and C's Tutor, 1948 SC 636 . . . 701

J v S (Leave to Remove) [2010] EWHC 2098 (Fam) . . . 543

J v V (Disclosure: Offshore Corporations) [2004] 1 FLR 1042 . . . 226

Jackson v Bell [2001] EWCA Civ 387 . . . 293

Jackson v Jackson [1993] 2 FLR 848 . . . 75

Jäggi v Switzerland (App no 58757/00), ECtHR . . . 349

James v Thomas [2007] EWCA Civ 1212 . . . 268, 275, 277, 278, 279, 286, 289, 297, 299, 300

Jennings v Rice [2002] EWCA Civ 159 . . . 285, 290

JKN v JCN [2010] EWHC 843 (Fam) . . . 64

Jodla v Jodla [1960] 1 WLR 236 . . . 27

Johansen v Norway (App no 17383/90) (1997) 23 EHRR 33 . . . 462, 463, 507, 508

Johnson v UK (1999) 27 EHRR 296 . . . 679

Johnston v Republic of Ireland (1986) 9 EHRR 203 . . . 394

Jones v Challenger [1960] 1 All ER 785 . . . 292

Jones v Jones [1975] 2 All ER 12 . . . 192, 193, 204

Jones v Jones [1976] Fam 8, CA . . . 191

Jones v Jones [2000] 2 FCR 201 . . . 237

Jones v Jones [2011] EWCA Civ 41, [2012]
Fam 1 . . . 177, 179

Jones v Kernott [2011] UKSC 53 . . . 251, 258,
262, 263, 274, 281

J-PC v J-AF [1955] P 215 . . . 183

K (A Minor) (Custody), Re [1990] 2 FLR 64,
CA . . . 458

K (A Minor) (Wardship: Adoption), Re [1991]
1 FLR 57 . . . 461

K (Care Order), Re [2007] EWCA Civ 697,
[2007] 2 FLR 1066 . . . 623

K (Care Proceedings: Care Plan), Re [2007]
EWHC 393 (Fam) . . . 651, 652

K (Care: Threshold Criteria), Re [2005] EWCA
Civ 1226, [2006] 2 FLR 868 . . . 638

K (Contact), Re [2008] 2 FLR 581 . . . 666

K (Contact: Committal Order), Re [2002]
EWCA Civ 1559, [2003] 1 FLR
277 . . . 529

K (Contact: Mother's Anxiety), Re [1999] 2 FLR
703 . . . 520

K (Minors: Foreign Surrogacy), Re [2010]
EWHC 1180 . . . 372

K (Shared Residence Order), Re [2008] 2 FLR
380, CA . . . 492, 497

K (Specific Issue Order), Re [1999] 2 FLR
280 . . . 536

K and H, Re [2006] EWCA Civ 1898, [2007]
1 FLR 2043 . . . 616, 617

K and S (Children) (Contact: Domestic
Violence), Re [2005] EWCA Civ 1660,
[2006] 1 FCR 316 . . . 515

K and T v Finland (2000) 31 EHRR 484, [2000]
2 FLR 79, [2001] 2 FLR 707 . . . 605, 636

K v H (Child Maintenance) [1993] 2 FLR
61 . . . 453

K v K (A Minor) (Removal from Jurisdiction)
[1992] 2 FLR 98 . . . 542

K v K (Ancillary Relief: Pre-Nuptial Agreement)
[2003] 1 FLR 120 . . . 226

K v K (Conduct) [1990] 2 FLR 225 . . . 177

K v K (Financial Provision: Conduct) [1990]
2 FLR 225 . . . 193

K v K (Minors: Property Transfer) [1992] 2 All
ER 727 . . . 333

K v K (Periodical Payment: Cohabitation) [2005]
EWHC 2886 (Fam) . . . 164, 181, 210

K v K (Relocation: Shared Care Arrangement)
[2011] EWCA Civ 793, [2011] 2 FLR . . . 541,
546

K, Re (Contact: Mother's Anxiety) [1999] 2 FLR
703 . . . 157

K, Re; A Local Authority v N and Others [2005]
EWHC 2956 (Fam), [2007] 1 FLR 399 . . . 34,
594

K, W and H (Minors) (Medical Treatment), Re
[1993] 1 FLR 854 . . . 435

Karner v Austria (App no 40016/98) (2004) 38
EHRR 24 . . . 43

Katz v Katz [1972] 1 WLR 955 . . . 68, 71

Kaur v Singh [1972] 1 WLR 10 . . . 27

KD (A Minor) (Access: Principles), Re [1988]
2 FLR 139 . . . 409

KD (A Minor) (Ward: Termination of Access),
Re [1988] AC 806 . . . 456–458, 462, 510,
594

Kehoe v UK [2008] ECHR 528, [2008] 2 FLR
1014 . . . 321

Kelly v BBC [2001] 1 All ER 323 . . . 449

Kendrick v Kendrick [1990] 2 FLR 107 . . . 141

Kensington Housing Trust v Oliver (1997)
30 HLR 608 . . . 168

Kent County Council v C [1993] 1 FLR
308 . . . 651, 666

Kevin: Validity of Marriage of Transexual, Re
[2001] Fam CA 1074 . . . 23

Khoransandjian v Bush [1993] 3 All ER
669 . . . 146

Kiely v Kiely [1988] 1 FLR 248, CA . . . 328

Kinch v Bullard [1999] 1 FLR 66 . . . 215

Kokosinski v Kokosinski [1980] 1 All ER
1106 . . . 185

Kosmopoulou v Greece (App no 60457/00)
[2004] 1 FLR 800 . . . 507

Kotke v Saffarini [2005] EWCA Civ 221 . . . 210

Kutzner v Germany (2002) 35 EHRR
653 . . . 636, 642

Kyte v Kyte [1988] Fam 145 . . . 191

L (A Child) (Contact: Domestic Violence), Re; V
(A Child), Re; M (A Child), Re; H (Children),
Re [2001] Fam 260, CA . . . 157, 510, 512, 514,
515, 522

L (A Child) (Parental Order: Foreign Surrogacy),
Re [2010] EWHC 3146, [2011] Fam
106 . . . 373

L (A Child), Re [2009] EWCA Civ 1239, [2010]
2 FLR 188 . . . 354

L (Adoption: Contacting Natural Father), Re
[2007] EWHC 1771 (Fam), [2008] 1 FLR
1079 . . . 676, 678

L (Care Proceedings: Human Rights Claims),
Re [2003] EWHC 665 (Fam), [2003] 2 FLR
160 . . . 652

L (Care Proceedings: Removal of Child), Re
[2008] 1 FLR 575 . . . 617

L (Care: Assessment: Fair Trial), Re [2002]
EWHC 1379 (Fam), [2002] 2 FLR
730 . . . 655

L (Care: Threshold Criteria), Re [2007] 1 FLR
2050 . . . 591, 594, 630

L (Children) (Care Proceedings: Significant
Harm), Re [2006] EWCA Civ 1282, [2007]
1 FLR 1068 . . . 630, 631, 637, 642

L (Contact: Genuine Fear), Re [2002] 1 FLR 621,
FD . . . 393, 520

L (Contact: Transsexual Applicant), Re [1995] 2 FLR 438 (Fam) . . . 517

L (Interim Care Order: Power of Court), Re [1996] 2 FLR 742 . . . 619

L (Medical Treatment: Gillick Competence), Re [1998] 2 FLR 810 . . . 440, 441

L (Minors) (Care Proceedings: Contact), Re [1998] 3 FCR 339 . . . 662

L (Minors), Re, CA (10 June 1998) . . . 517

L (Sexual Abuse: Standard of Proof), Re [1996] 1 FLR 116 . . . 652, 666

L (Shared Residence Order), Re [2009] EWCA Civ 20, [2009] 1 FLR 1157 . . . 502

L (Special Guardianship: Surname), Re [2007] EWCA Civ 196, [2007] 2 FLR 50 . . . 549, 709

L and H (Residential Assessment), Re [2007] EWCA Civ 213, [2007] 1 FLR 1370 . . . 623

L v Human Fertilisation and Embryology Authority and Secretary of State [2008] EWHC 2149 (Fam) . . . 360

L v L (Child Abuse: Access) [1989] 2 FLR 16, CA . . . 512

L v L [2002] 1 FLR 642 . . . 188

L v L [2006] EWHC 956 (Fam) . . . 222

L v L [2008] 1 FLR 26 . . . 168, 235

L v L [2011] EWHC 2207 (Fam) . . . 195

L v London Borough of Bromley [1998] 1 FLR 709 . . . 663, 664, 665

LA (Care: Chronic Neglect), Re [2009] EWCA Civ 822, [2010] 1 FLR 80 . . . 616, 617

Lambert v Lambert [2003] 1 FLR 139 . . . 188, 191

Lambeth London Borough v S, C, V and J (By His Guardian) [2006] EWHC 326 (Fam), [2007] 1 FLR 152 . . . 349, 352

Lancashire County Council v B [2002] 2 AC 147 . . . 641, 642, 643, 644, 645, 646, 649

Lancashire County Council v D and E [2008] EWHC 832 (Fam) . . . 636

Lancashire County Council v R [2008] EWHC 2959 (Fam), [2010] 1 FLR 387 . . . 637

Lang v Lang [1955] AC 402 . . . 72

Langley v Liverpool City Council [2005] EWCA Civ 1173, [2006] 1 FLR 342 . . . 611, 612

Laskar v Laskar [2008] EWCA Civ 347 . . . 250, 265

Lau v Director of Public Prosecutions [2000] 1 FLR 799 . . . 147

Lauder v Lauder [2007] 2 FLR 802 . . . 240, 241

Lawrence v Gallagher [2012] EWCA Civ 394 . . . 160

LBH (A Local Authority) v KJ and IH [2007] EWHC 2798 . . . 643

Le Foe v Le Foe [2001] 2 FLR 970 . . . 273, 274

Le Marchant v Le Marchant [1977] 3 All ER 610 . . . 168

Leadbeater v Leadbeater [1985] FLR 789 . . . 191, 196

Lee v Lee (1984) FLR 243 . . . 128

Leeds City Council v C [1993] 1 FLR 269 . . . 651

Leeds City Council v YX and ZX (Assessment of Sexual Abuse) [2008] EWHC 802 (Fam) . . . 636

Leeds Teaching Hospital NHS Trust v A and others [2003] 1 FCR 599, [2003] EWHC 259 (QB) . . . 363, 367

Leicestershire County Council v G [1994] 2 FLR 329 . . . 651, 658

Lewis v Lewis [1978] 1 All ER 729 . . . 140

Lissimore v Downing [2003] 2 FLR 308 . . . 286

Livesey v Jenkins [1985] 1 All ER 106 . . . 168, 220

Livingstone-Stallard v Livingstone-Stallard [1974] Fam 47 . . . 69, 70

Lloyds Bank v Rosset [1990] 1 All ER 1111 . . . 187, 246, 247, 248, 266, 268, 269, 270

Lomas v Parle [2004] 1 FLR 812 . . . 114, 115, 116, 141, 142, 149

London Borough of Southwark v D; sub nom R (On the Application of D) v A Local Authority [2007] EWCA Civ 182, [2007] 1 FLR 2181, [2007] Fam Law 701 . . . 582

Lonslow v Hennig [1986] 2 FLR 378 . . . 538

Lord Lilford v Glyn [1979] 1 All ER 441 . . . 193, 328

LW (Children) (Enforcement and Committal: Contact), Re; CPL v CH-W and others [2010] EWCA Civ 1253, [2011] 1 FLR 1095, [2011] 1 FCR 78 . . . 505, 506, 528, 529, 530, 532, 533

M (A Child) (Prohibited Steps Order: Appeal), Re [2002] All ER (D) 401 (Nov) . . . 534

M (A Minor) (Care Order: Threshold Conditions), Re [1994] 2 AC 424 . . . 647

M (A Minor) (Care Order: Threshold Conditions), Re [1994] 3 All ER 298 . . . 629, 631

M (A Minor) (Contact: Conditions), Re [1994] 1 FLR 272 . . . 505, 506

M (A Minor) (No 2) (Appeal), Re [1994] 1 FLR 59 . . . 657

M (A Minor) (Secure Accommodation Order), Re [1995] Fam 108 . . . 449, 450

M (Adoption: Leave to Oppose), Re [2010] 1 FLR 238 . . . 698

M (Care Order: Parental Responsibility), Re [1996] 2 FLR 84 . . . 648

M (Care Proceedings: Judicial Review), Re [2003] EWHC 850 (Admin), [2003] 2 FLR 171 . . . 605

M (Care: Challenging Decisions by Local Authority), Re [2001] 2 FLR 1300, FD . . . 655

M (Care: Contact: Grandmother's Application for Leave), Re [1995] 2 FLR 86, CA . . . 474, 475, 477, 664

M (Care: Leave to Interview Child), Re [1995] 1 FLR 825 . . . 564

M (Child's Upbringing), Re [1996] 2 FCR 473 . . . 461

M (Children) (Residence Order), Re [2004] EWCA Civ 1413 . . . 497

M (Contact) (Parental Responsibility), Re [2001]
2 FLR 342 . . . 389, 390
M (Contact: Family Assistance: McKenzie
Friend), Re [1999] 1 FLR 75, CA . . . 387, 520
M (Contact: Long-Term Best Interests), Re
[2006] 1 FLR 627, CA . . . 527
M (Contact: Violent Parent), Re [1999] 2 FLR
321 . . . 514
M (Contact: Welfare Test), Re [1995] 1 FLR 274,
CA . . . 509
M (Education: Section 91(14) Order), Re [2007]
EWCA Civ 1550, [2008] 2 FLR 404 . . . 555
M (Fact-Finding Hearing: Burden of Proof),
Re [2008] EWCA Civ 1261, [2009] 1 FLR
1177 . . . 636
M (Interim Care Order: Removal), Re [2005]
EWCA Civ 1594, [2006] 1 FLR 1043 . . . 618
M (Intractable Contact Dispute: Interim Care
Order), Re [2003] EWHC 1024 (Fam), [2003]
2 FLR 636 . . . 518, 529, 531
M (Judge's Discretion), Re [2001] EWCA Civ
1428, [2002] 1 FLR 730 . . . 467
M (Medical Treatment: Consent), Re [1999]
2 FLR 1097 . . . 441
M (Minors) (Adoption), Re [1991] 1 FLR
458 . . . 701, 702
M (Minors) (Care Proceedings: Child's Wishes),
Re [1994] 1 FLR 749 . . . 627
M (Minors), Re (unreported), 11 October 1995,
CA . . . 404
M (Minors), Re, CA (26 January 2000) . . . 518
M (Prohibited Steps Order: Application for
Leave), Re [1993] 1 FLR 275 . . . 479
M (Residential Assessment Directions), Re
[1998] 2 FLR 371 . . . 620, 622
M and R (Child Abuse: Evidence), Re [1996]
2 FLR 195 . . . 650
M v A (Contact: Domestic Violence) [2002]
2 FLR 921 . . . 516
M v A (Wardship: Removal from Jurisdiction)
[1993] 2 FLR 715 . . . 5442
M v B (Ancillary Proceedings: Lump Sum)
[1998] 1 FLR 53 . . . 183, 201
M v B, A and S (By the Official Solicitor) [2005]
EWHC 1681 (Fam), [2006] 1 FLR
117 . . . 13
M v Birmingham City Council [1994] 2 FLR
141 . . . 648
M v H (Education: Welfare) [2008] EWHC 324
(Fam), [2008] 1 FLR 1400 . . . 490
M v M (Child of the Family) (1981) 2 FLR 39,
CA . . . 325
M v M (Child: Access) [1973] 2 All ER 81,
DC . . . 509, 510
M v M (Financial Misconduct; Subpoena
against Third Party) [2006] 2 FCR
555 . . . 180
M v M (Financial Provision) [1987]
2 FLR 1 . . . 196

M v M (Financial Relief: Substantial Earning
Capacity) [2004] EWHC 688 (Fam), [2004]
2 FLR 236 . . . 186
M v M (Minors) (Jurisdiction) [1993] Fam Law
396 . . . 542
M v M (Minors) (Removal from Jurisdiction)
[1992] 2 FLR 303 . . . 544
M v M (Parental Responsibility) [1999] 2 FLR
737 . . . 385
M v M (Prenuptial Agreement) [2002] 1 FLR
654 . . . 226
M v M (Property Adjustment: Impaired Life
Expectancy) [1993] 2 FLR 723 . . . 187
M v M (Removal from Jurisdiction) [1993]
1 FCR 5 . . . 544
M v P (Contempt: Committal); Butler v Butler
[1993] Fam 167, [1993] 1 FLR 773 . . . 529
M v Secretary of State for Work and Pensions
[2006] UKHL 11, [2006] 2 AC 91 . . . 39
M v Warwickshire County Council [2007]
EWCA Civ 1084, [2008] 1 FLR 1093 . . . 690,
691, 710
M v Westminster City Council [1985] FLR
325 . . . 658
M, Re (Minors) (Contact: Violent Parent) [1999]
2 FLR 231 . . . 157
M, T, P, K and B (Care: Change of Name), Re
[2000] 2 FLR 645 . . . 554
MA (Care Threshold), Re [2009] EWCA Civ 853,
[2010] 1 FLR 431 . . . 594
Mabon v Mabon [2005] EWCA Civ 634, [2005]
Fam 366 . . . 428, 442
Macey v Macey (1981) 3 FLR 7 . . . 182
MacLeod v MacLeod [2008] UKPC 64, [2010]
1 AC 298 . . . 223
Majrowski v Guy's and St Thomas' NHS Trust
[2005] EWCA Civ 251 . . . 147
Marckx v Belgium (1979) 2 EHRR 330 . . . 679
Marckx v Belgium (1979–80) 2 EHRR 14 . . . 394
Mark v Mark [2005] UKHL 42, [2005] 2 FLR
1193, HL . . . 62
Martin v Martin [1976] Fam 335, [1976] 3 All ER
625 . . . 167, 192
Martin v Martin [1977] 3 All ER 762 . . . 180,
208
Masefield v Alexander [1995] 1 FLR 100 . . . 220
Maskell v Maskell [2003] 1 FLR 1138 . . . 233
Matter of C (A Child) [2002] EWHC 157
(Fam) . . . 373
McCabe v McCabe [1994] 1 FLR 410 . . . 37, 41
McCartney v McCartney Mills [2008] EWHC
401 (Fam) . . . 182
McDowell v Hirschfield Lipson & Rumney and
Smith [1992] 2 FLR 126 . . . 215
McEwan v McEwan [1972] 2 All ER 708 . . . 179
McFarlane v McFarlane; Parlour v Parlour [2004]
EWCA Civ 872 . . . 174, 176
McGrath v Wallis [1995] 2 FLR 114 . . . 250
McGrath, Re [1893] 1 Ch 143 . . . 447

McHardy and Sons (A Firm) v Warren [1994]
2 FLR 338 . . . 283

McLean v Nugent (1980) 1 FLR 26 . . . 140

McMichael v UK (1995) 20 EHRR 205 . . . 394

Mehta v Mehta [1945] 2 All ER 690 . . . 29

Mesher v Mesher and Hall [1980] 1 All ER
126n . . . 180, 206, 207

Metropolitan Borough Council v DB [1997]
1 FLR 767 . . . 430, 434

Michael v Michael [1986] 2 FLR 389 . . . 177

Midland Bank plc v Cooke [1995] 2 FLR
915 . . . 269, 281, 283

Mikulić v Croatia (App no 53176/99) [2002]
1 FCR 720 . . . 347, 348

Miller v Miller; McFarlane v McFarlane [2006]
UKHL 24, [2006] 1 FLR 1186 . . . 49, 76, 173,
175, 176, 178, 179, 183, 184, 185, 189, 191, 194,
196, 229, 240, 241

Minton v Minton [1979] 1 All ER 79 . . . 194

Mirza v Mirza [2009] EWHC 3 (Ch) . . . 275

Mizzi v Malta (App no 2611/02) [2006] 1 FLR
1048, ECtHR . . . 347

M-J (Adoption Order or Special Guardianship
Order), Re [2007] EWCA Civ 56, [2007]
1 FLR 691 . . . 710, 711

M-K (A Child) (Relocation Outside the
Jurisdiction), Re [2006] EWCA Civ 1013,
[2007] 1 FLR 432 . . . 542

Morgan v Hill [2006] EWCA Civ 1602, [2007]
1 FLR 1480 . . . 333, 338

Morgan v Morgan [1977] 2 All ER 515 . . . 180

Morris v Morris [2008] EWCA Civ 257 . . . 277,
278, 286, 289

Mortgage Corporation v Shaire [2001]
Ch 743 . . . 284, 292

Mortimer v Mortimer-Griffin [1986] 2 FLR
315 . . . 203

Moses-Taiga v Taiga [2005] EWCA Civ
1013 . . . 163

Mouncer v Mouncer [1972] 1 All ER 289 . . . 73

MT v MT (Financial Provision: Lump Sum)
[1992] 1 FLR 362 . . . 166, 177

Munro v Munro [2007] EWHC 3315 (Fam),
[2008] 1 FLR 1613 . . . 62

Murphy v Gooch [2007] EWCA Civ 603 . . . 291

M-W (Care Proceedings: Expert Evidence),
Re [2010] EWCA Civ 12, [2010] 2 FLR
46 . . . 636

Myerson v Myerson [2009] EWCA Civ
282 . . . 235

N (Minors) (Care Orders: Termination
of Parental Contact), Re [1994] 2 FCR
1101 . . . 666

N (Section 91(14) Order), Re [1996] 1 FLR
356 . . . 555, 560

N v D [2008] 1 FLR 1629 . . . 295

N v F [2011] EWHC 586 (Fam), [2012] 1 FCR
139 . . . 179

N v N (1928) 44 LR 324 . . . 161

N v N (Jurisdiction: Pre-Nuptial Agreement)
[1999] 2 FLR 745 . . . 226

NA v MA [2007] 1 FLR 1760 . . . 219

Nash v Nash [1973] 2 All ER 704 . . . 538

Newham London Borough v AG [1993] 1 FLR
281 . . . 628, 633

North v North [2007] EWCA Civ 760, [2007]
2 FCR 601 . . . 184, 238–240

Northamptonshire County Council v S [1993]
Fam 136, [1992] 3 WLR 1010 . . . 647

Nottinghamshire County Council v P [1993]
3 All ER 815, [1993] 2 FLR 134 . . . 479, 533,
534, 560, 599, 600, 653

NS v MI [2006] EWHC 1646 (Fam), [2007]
1 FLR 444 . . . 28, 33, 34, 35

NS-H v Kingston Upon Hull City Council and
MC [2008] EWCA Civ 493, [2008] 2 FLR 918,
CA . . . 691

Nutley v Nutley [1970] 1 WLR 217 . . . 72

Nuutinen v Finland (App no 32842/96) (2002) 34
EHRR 15 . . . 508

Nwogbe v Nwogbe [2000] 2 FLR 744 . . . 124

Nylund v Finland (App no 27110/95)
(unreported) 29 June 1999 . . . 680

O (A Child) (Supervision Order: Future Harm),
Re [2001] EWCA Civ 16, [2001] 1 FCR
289 . . . 685

O (A Minor) (Care Order: Education:
Procedure), Re [1992] 2 FLR 7 . . . 592, 593

O (A Minor) (Medical Treatment), Re [1993]
2 FLR 149 . . . 561

O (Care or Supervision Order), Re [1996] 2 FLR
755 . . . 454, 658, 660

O (Care Order: Discharge of Care Order), Re
[1999] 2 FLR 119 . . . 660

O (Contact: Imposition of Conditions), Re
[1995] 2 FLR 124, CA . . . 467, 505, 506, 507,
509, 510, 518, 530

O (Contact: Withdrawal of Application), Re
[2003] EWHC 3031 (Fam), [2004] 1 FLR
1258 . . . 518, 526

O (Minors) (Medical Examination), Re [1993]
1 FLR 860 . . . 620

O (Supervision Order), Re [2001] EWCA Civ 16,
[2001] 1 FLR 923 . . . 605

O and another (Minors) (Care: Preliminary
Hearing); Re B (A Minor) [2003] UKHL 18,
[2004] 1 AC 523 . . . 646, 649, 650

O'D v O'D [1976] Fam 83 . . . 171

O'Donoghue and Others v UK (App
no 34848/07) [2011] 2 FCR 197 . . . 13

O'Hara, Re [1900] 2 IR 232 . . . 456

O'Neill v O'Neill [1975] 1 WLR 1118 . . . 69, 70

Odièvre v France (App no 42326/98) [2002]
1 FCR 621, ECtHR (Grand Chamber) . . . 348

Olsson v Sweden (No 2) (App no 13441/87)
(1994) 17 EHRR 134 . . . 508

O-M, GM (and KM) v The Local Authority, LO
and EM [2009] EWCA Civ 1405, [2010]
2 FLR 58 . . . 636
Omielan v Omielan [1996] 2 FLR 306 . . . 168,
204, 207, 209, 210, 212, 213
Oxfordshire County Council v L (Care or
Supervision Order) [1998] 1 FLR 70 . . . 454,
605, 651, 658, 659
Oxfordshire County Council v X, Y and J [2010]
EWCA Civ 581, [2011] 1 FLR 272 . . . 707
Oxley v Hiscock [2004] EWCA Civ 546, [2004]
2 FLR 669 . . . 90, 257, 267, 281, 282, 283

P (A Child) (Adoption: Leave Provisions),
Re [2007] EWCA Civ 616, [2007] 2 FLR
1069 . . . 698
P (A Minor) (Care: Evidence), Re [1994] 2 FLR
751 . . . 634
P (A Minor) (Leave to Apply: Foster Parents), Re
[1994] 2 FCR 1093 . . . 482
P (A Minor) (Parental Responsibility Order), Re
[1994] 1 FLR 578 . . . 386
P (A Minor) (Residence Order: Child's Welfare),
Re [2000] Fam 15 . . . 555, 556, 557, 558, 560
P (Adoption: Unmarried Couple) [2008] UKHL
38, Re . . . 669, 670, 672, 676
P (Child: Financial Provision), Re [2003] EWCA
Civ 837, [2003] 2 FLR 865, [2003] 2 FLR
865 . . . 295, 335, 337
P (Contact: Discretion), Re [1998] 2 FLR 696
(Fam) . . . 519
P (Contact: Supervision), Re [1996] 2 FLR
314 . . . 509
P (Contact: Discretion), Re [1998] 2 FLR 696
(Fam) . . . 520
P (Emergency Protection Order), Re [1996]
1 FLR 482 . . . 610
P (Identity of Mother), Re [2011] EWCA Civ
795, [2012] 1 FLR 351 . . . 353
P (Medical Treatment: Best Interests), Re [2003]
EWHC 2327, [2004] 2 FLR 1117 . . . 441
P (Minor) (Parental Responsibility Order), Re
[1994] 1 FLR 578, FD . . . 395
P (Minors) (Contact with Children in Care), Re
1993] 2 FLR 156 . . . 663
P (Parental Responsibility), Re [1997] 2 FLR 722,
CA . . . 554
P (Parental Responsibility), Re [1998] 2 FLR
96 . . . 382, 383, 387, 390
P (Placement Orders: Parental Consent),
Re [2008] EWCA Civ 535, [2008] 2 FLR
625 . . . 683, 684, 706
P (Representation), Re [1996] 1 FLR
486 . . . 627
P (Residence: Appeal), Re [2007] EWCA Civ
1053, [2008] 1 FLR 198 . . . 374
P (Section 91(14) Guidelines) (Residence and
Religious Heritage), Re [1999] 2 FLR 573,
CA . . . 490, 491

P (Sexual Abuse: Standard of Proof), Re [1996]
2 FLR 333, CA . . . 634, 650
P (Shared Residence Order), Re [2005] EWCA
Civ 1639, [2006] 2 FLR 347 . . . 494, 496
P v B [2003] EWHC 327 (Fam) . . . 512, 518
P v P (Contempt of Court: Mental Capacity)
[1999] 2 FLR 897 . . . 112
P v P (Financial Provision) [1989] 2 FLR
241 . . . 167
P v P (Financial Provision: Lump Sum) [1978]
3 All ER 70 . . . 167
P v P (Inherited Property) [2004] EWHC 1364
(Fam), [2005] 1 FLR 576 . . . 182
P v P [2003] EWHC 151 (Fam) . . . 518
P v R (Forced Marriage: Annulment: Procedure)
[2003] 1 FLR 661 . . . 28, 35
P, C and S v UK (App no 56547/00) (2002) 35
EHRR 31, [2002] 2 FLR 631, ECtHR . . . 605,
613
Padfield and Others v Minister of Agriculture,
Fisheries and Food and Others [1968] AC
997 . . . 611
Page v Page (1981) 2 FLR 198 . . . 171
Pardy v Pardy [1939] P 288 . . . 72
Pascoe v Turner [1979] 2 All ER 945 . . . 287,
288, 289
Pasha v Pasha [2001] EWCA Civ 466 . . . 183
Paton v British Pregnancy Advisory Service
Trustees [1979] QB 276 . . . 41
Paulik v Slovakia (App no 10699/05) [2007]
1 FLR 1090, ECtHR . . . 347
Payne v Payne [1968] 1 WLR 390 . . . 183
Payne v Payne [2001] EWCA Civ 166, [2001]
Fam 473 . . . 462, 463, 537–546
Pazpena de Vire v Pazpena de Vire [2001] 1 FLR
460 . . . 21
P-B (Contact: Committal), Re [2009] 2 FLR 66,
CA . . . 663
PC (Change of Surname), Re [1997] 2 FLR
730 . . . 408
Peacock v Peacock [1984] 1 All ER 1069 . . . 163
Pearce v Pearce [1980] 1 FLR 261 . . . 177
Pearce v Pearce [2003] 2 FLR 1144 . . . 237, 238,
241
Pettitt v Pettitt [1969] 2 All ER 385 . . . 248, 249,
250, 271
Phillips v Peace [1996] 2 FLR 230 . . . 324
Pierce v Society of Sisters, 268 US 510
(1925) . . . 566
Piglowska v Piglowski [1999] 3 All ER 632,
[1999] 2 FLR 763, HL . . . 162, 169, 201, 202
Pini v Romania (2005) 40 EHRR 132, [2005]
2 FLR 596 . . . 680
Poel v Poel [1970] 1 WLR 1469 . . . 538, 545
Popat v Popat [1991] 2 FLR 163 . . . 217
Pounds v Pounds [1994] 1 FLR 775 . . . 218, 220
Power v Power [1996] 3 FCR 338, CA . . . 230
Practice Direction (Family Proceedings:
Committal) [2001] 1 WLR 1253 . . . 529

Practice Direction: Residence and Contact Orders: Domestic Violence and Harm [2009] 2 FLR 1400 . . . 516

Practice Direction: Residence and Contact Orders: Domestic Violence and Harm [2008] 2 FLR 103 . . . 516

Practice Direction: To Warn or Not To Warn: Contact Enforcement [2009] Fam Law 530 . . . 525

Practice Note [1990] 2 FLR 530 . . . 563

Prescott v Fellowes [1958] P 260 . . . 167

Preston v Preston [1982] 1 All ER 41 . . . 170, 171, 184

Pulford v Pulford [1923] P 18 . . . 71

Q (A Minor) (Parental Order), Re [1996] 1 FLR 369 . . . 364, 373

Q (Adoption), Re [2011] EWCA Civ 1610 . . . 684

Quoraishi v Quoraishi [1985] FLR 780 . . . 72

R (A Child) (IVF: Paternity), Re [2005] UKHL 33, [2005] 2 AC 621 . . . 366

R (A Child), Re [2009] EWCA Civ 1316 . . . 530

R (A Minor) (Blood Transfusion), Re [1993] 2 FLR 757 . . . 536, 561

R (A Minor) (Child Abuse: Access), Re [1988] 1 FLR 206, CA . . . 512

R (A Minor) (Wardship: Consent to Treatment), Re [1992] Fam 11 . . . 429

R (A Minor), Re, CA (12 March 1998) . . . 517

R (A) v Croydon London Borough Council; R (M) v Lambeth London Borough Council [2008] EWCA Civ 1445, [2009] 1 FLR 1324 . . . 576

R (Adoption: Contact), Re [2005] EWCA Civ 1128, [2006] 1 FLR 373 . . . 475, 476, 477

R (Axon) v Secretary of State for Health [2006] EWHC 37 (Admin) . . . 427, 428, 444

R (Baiai and Others) v Secretary of State for the Home Department [2008] UKHL 53, [2008] 2 FLR 1462 . . . 12, 33

R (Care Order: Threshold Criteria), Re [2009] EWCA Civ 942, [2010] 1 FLR 673 . . . 633

R (Family Proceedings: No Case to Answer), Re [2009] EWCA Civ 1619, [2009] 2 FLR 83 . . . 516

R (G) v Barnet London Borough Council; R (W) v Lambeth London Borough Council; R (A) v Lambeth London Borough Council [2003] UKHL 57, [2004] 2 AC 208, [2003] 3 WLR 1194, [2004] 1 FLR 454 . . . 574, 576, 577, 578

R (G) v Nottingham City Council [2008] EWHC 152 (Admin), [2008] 1 FLR 1660, QBD . . . 405, 589

R (G) v Nottingham City Council and Nottingham University Hospital [2008] EWHC 400, [2008] 1 FLR 1668, QBD . . . 589

R (G) v Southwark London Borough Council [2009] UKHL 26, [2009] 2 FLR 380 . . . 577, 582

R (IVF: Paternity of Child), Re [2003] Fam 129, CA . . . 364

R (L) v Nottinghamshire County Council [2007] EWHC 2364 (Admin), [2007] All ER (D) 158 (Sept) . . . 582

R (McCann) v Crown Court at Manchester [2003] 1 AC 787 . . . 639

R (On the Application of A) v Croydon London Borough Council; R (On the Application of M) v Lambeth London Borough Council [2009] UKSC 8, [2009] 3 FCR 607 . . . 576

R (On the Application of Kehoe) v Secretary of State for Work and Pensions [2005] UKHL 48 . . . 321

R (On the Application of Williamson) v Secretary of State for Education and Employment [2005] UKHL 15, [2005] AC 246 . . . 444

R (Parental Responsibility), Re [2011] EWHC 1535 (Fam), [2011] 2 FLR 1132 . . . 400

R (Plumb) v Secretary of State for Work and Pensions [2002] EWHC 1125 (Admin) . . . 320

R (Residence: Contact: Restricting Applications), Re [1998] 1 FLR 749 . . . 556, 557, 559

R (Residence: Religion), Re [1993] 2 FLR 163 . . . 490

R (S) v Sutton London Borough Council [2007] EWCA Civ 790, (2007) 10 CCLR 625 . . . 582

R (S) v Swindon Borough Council and another [2001] EWHC (Admin) 334, [2001] 3 FCR 702 . . . 596

R (Surname: Using Both Parents'), Re [2001] EWCA Civ 1344, [2001] 2 FLR 1358, CA . . . 551

R (W) v Brent London Borough Council [2010] EWHC 175 (Admin), [2010] 1 FLR 1914 . . . 681

R and G (Minors) (Interim Care or Supervision Orders), Re [1994] 1 FLR 793 . . . 657, 659

R v Avon County Council, ex p M [1994] 2 FLR 1006 . . . 584

R v C [2007] EWCA Crim 3463 . . . 101

R v Cannings [2004] EWCA Crim 1, [2004] 1 All ER 725 . . . 636, 637

R v D [1984] AC 778 . . . 410

R v E and F (Female Parents: Known Father) [2010] EWHC 417 (Fam), [2010] 2 FLR 383 . . . 391

R v Ealing London Borough Council, ex p Sidhu (1982) 80 LGR 534 . . . 151

R v Gyngall [1893] 2 QB 232 . . . 447

R v Hills [2001] 1 FLR 580 . . . 147

R v Howes (1860) 3 E & E 332 . . . 423

R v Human Fertilisation and Embryology Authority, ex p Blood [1997] 2 All ER 687, CA . . . 360, 364

R v Northavon District Council, ex p Smith [1994] 2 AC 402, [1994] 2 FLR 671 . . . 572, 577

R v Oldham MBC, ex p Garlick; R v Bexley LBC, ex p Bentham; R v Tower Hamlets LBC, ex p Begum [1993] AC 509 . . . 152

R v Pontlottyn Juvenile Court, ex p R [1990] FCR 900 . . . 626

R v R (Divorce: Hemain Injunction) [2003] EWHC 2113 (Fam), [2005] 1 FLR 386 . . . 78

R v R (Financial Provision: Reasonable Needs) [1994] 2 FLR 1044 . . . 196

R v R (Otherwise F) [1952] 1 All ER 1194 . . . 26

R v R (Rape: Marital Exemption) [1992] 1 AC 599 . . . 99

R v Rahman (1985) 81 Cr App R 349 . . . 411

R v Registrar General, ex p Smith [1991] 1 FLR 255, CA . . . 703

R v Royal Borough of Kingston upon Thames, ex p T [1994] 1 FLR 798 . . . 574

R v S [1988] 2 FLR 339 . . . 140

R v Secretary of State for Social Security, ex p W [1999] 2 FLR 604, FD . . . 381

R v Tameside Metropolitan Borough Council ex p J [2000] 1 FCR 173 . . . 584, 585

R v UK (Case 6/1986/104/152), The Times, 9 July 1987 . . . 456

R v Westminster City Council, ex p Bishop [1993] 2 FLR 780 . . . 153

R (M) v Hammersmith and Fulham London Borough Council [2008] UKHL 14, [2008] 1 FLR 1384 . . . 578, 579, 581

R, Re [1992] Fam 11 . . . 429, 430, 431, 435, 436, 437, 438, 439, 445

RA (Minors), Re (1974) 4 Fam Law 182 . . . 700

Radovanovic v Austria (App no 42703/98) (2005) 41 EHRR 6, EtCHR . . . 559

Rahnema v Rahbari [2008] 2 P & CR DG5 . . . 291

Rampal v Rampal (No 2) [2001] EWCA Civ 989, [2002] Fam 85 . . . 169

Rees v UK (1986) 9 EHRR 56, [1987] 2 FLR 111 . . . 22

Reid v Reid [2003] EWHC 2878 (Fam) . . . 231

Rice v Miller (1993) 16 Fam LR 970 . . . 459

Richards v Richards [1972] WLR 1073 . . . 65, 71

Richards v Richards [1984] AC 174, [1983] 2 All ER 807, HL . . . 124, 449

Richardson v Richardson [1993] 4 All ER 67 . . . 197, 236

Richardson v Richardson (No 2) [1994] 2 FLR 1051 . . . 206

Riley v Riley [1986] 2 FLR 429 . . . 495

Ritchie v Ritchie [1996] 1 FLR 898 . . . 231

Robinson v Robinson [1982] 2 All ER 699n . . . 221

Rochefaucauld v Boustead [1897] 1 Ch 196 . . . 248

Roddy (A Child) (Identification: Restrictions on Publication), Re [2003] EWHC 2927 (Fam), [2004] 2 FLR 949 . . . 443

Rose v Secretary of State for Health and Human Fertilisation and Embryology Authority [2002] EWHC 1593 (Admin) . . . 347

Rossi v Rossi [2006] 2 FLR 1482 (Fam) . . . 182

Rozanski v Poland (App no 55339/00) [2006] 2 FCR 178 . . . 347, 679

Rukat v Rukat [1975] Fam 63 . . . 74

S (A Child) (Residence Order: Condition) (No 2), Re [2002] EWCA Civ 1795, [2002] 1 FCR 138 . . . 500, 501

S (A Child) (Residence Order: Condition), Re [2001] EWCA Civ 847, [2001] 3 FCR 154 . . . 501

S (A Child), In the matter of [2010] EWCA Civ 705 . . . 504

S (A Minor) (Access Application), Re [1991] 1 FLR 161 . . . 664

S (A Minor) (Adopted Child: Contact), Re [1999] Fam 283 . . . 480

S (A Minor) (Adoption: Blood Transfusion), Re [1995] 2 FCR 177, CA . . . 700

S (A Minor) (Care: Contact Order), Re [1994] 2 FLR 222 . . . 662, 664

S (A Minor) (Change of Surname), Re [1999] 1 FCR 304 . . . 654

S (A Minor) (Consent to Medical Treatment), Re [1994] 2 FLR 1065 . . . 439

S (A Minor) (Custody), Re [1991] 2 FLR 388, CA . . . 486

S (A Minor) (Stay of Proceedings), Re [1993] 2 FLR 912, CA . . . 384

S (Adoption Order or Special Guardianship Order), Re [2007] EWCA Civ 54, [2007] 1 FLR 819 . . . 708–711

S (Care or Supervision Order), Re [1996] 1 FLR 753 . . . 659, 660

S (Care: Parental Contact), Re [2004] EWCA Civ 1397, [2005] 1 FLR 469 . . . 666

S (Care: Parenting Skills: Personality Tests), Re [2004] EWCA Civ 1029, [2005] 2 FLR 658 . . . 637

S (Change of Names: Cultural Factors), Re [2001] Fam 1, CA . . . 554

S (Change of Surname), Re [1999] 1 FLR 672 . . . 549

S (Contact Dispute: Committal), Re [2004] EWCA Civ 1790, [2005] 1 FLR 812 . . . 528

S (Contact: Application by Sibling), Re [1998] 2 FLR 897 . . . 451

S (Contact: Children's Views), Re [2002] EWHC 540 (Fam), [2002] 1 FLR 1156 . . . 517

S (Contact: Promoting Relationship with Absent Parent), Re [2004] EWCA Civ 18, [2004] 1 FLR 1279 . . . 462, 526

S (Discharge of Care Order), Re [1995] 2 FLR 639 . . . 661

S (Infants), Re [1967] 1 All ER 202 . . . 562

S (J) (A Minor) (Care or Supervision Order), Re [1993] 2 FLR 919, FD . . . 658, 659

S (Minors) (Care Order: Implementation of Care Plan), Re; Re W (Minors) (Care Order: Adequacy of Care Plan) [2002] 2 AC 291 . . . 651, 653

S (Minors: Access), Re [1990] 2 FLR 166 . . . 528

S (Parental Order), Re [2009] EWHC 2977, [2010] 1 FLR 1156 . . . 373

S (Parental Responsibility), Re [1995] 2 FLR 648, CA . . . 383, 386, 387

S (Parental Responsibility: Jurisdiction), Re [1998] 2 FLR 921 . . . 381

S (Permission to Seek Relief), Re [2006] EWCA Civ 1190, [2007] 1 FLR 482 . . . 556, 558, 560

S (Placement Order: Revocation), Re [2008] EWCA Civ 1333, [2009] 1 FLR 503 . . . 681, 689

S (Practice: Muslim Women Giving Evidence), Re [2007] 2 FLR 461 . . . 35

S (Relocation: Interests of Siblings), Re [2011] EWCA Civ 454, [2011] 2 FLR 678 . . . 544

S (Unmarried Parents: Financial Provisions), Re [2006] EWCA Civ 479, [2006] 2 FLR 950 . . . 337

S and D (Children: Powers of Court), Re [1995] 2 FLR 456 . . . 653

S and P (Discharge of Care Order), Re [1995] 2 FLR 782 . . . 661

S v F (Occupation Order) [2000] 1 FLR 255 . . . 138

S v Oxfordshire County Council [1993] 1 FLR 452 . . . 651

S v P (Contact Application: Family Assistance Order) [1997] 2 FLR 277, FD . . . 468

S v S (Ancillary Relief: Consent Order) [2002] 1 FLR 922 . . . 231

S v S (Ancillary Relief: Consent Order) [2002] EWHC 223 (Fam) . . . 222

S v S (Child Abuse: Access) [1988] 1 FLR 213, CA . . . 512

S v S (Divorce: Staying Proceedings) [1997] 2 FLR 100 . . . 64

S v S (Hemain) Injunction [2009] EWHC 3224 (Fam), [2010] 2 FLR 502 . . . 78

S v S (Interim Contact) [2009] EWHC 1575 (Fam), [2009] 2 FLR 1586 . . . 515

S v S (Matrimonial Proceedings: Appropriate Forum) [1997] 2 FLR 100 . . . 226

S v S (Otherwise W) (No 2) [1962] 3 All ER 55 . . . 26

S v S [1962] 1 WLR 445 . . . 510

S v S [1977] 1 All ER 56 . . . 173, 184

S v S [1987] 1 FLR 71 . . . 181, 210

S v S; W v Official Solicitor [1972] AC 24 . . . 345, 346, 353, 449

SA (Vulnerable Adult with Capacity: Marriage), Re [2005] EWHC 2942 (Fam), [2006] 1 FLR 867 . . . 36

Sahin v Germany (App no 30943/96) [2003] 2 FLR 671 . . . 508

Salgueiro da Silva Mouta v Portugal (App no 33290/96) [1999] ECHR, [2001] 1 FCR 653, ECtHR . . . 488

Sanchez Cardenas v Norway (App no 12148/03) [2007] ECHR 763 . . . 512

Santos v Santos [1972] Fam 247 . . . 73

Saunders v UK (1996) 23 EHRR 313 . . . 529

Sawden v Sawden [2004] 1 FCR 776 . . . 206, 207

SB v RB [2008] EWHC 938 (Fam), [2008] 2 FLR 1588 . . . 36

SC (A Minor) (Leave to Seek Residence Order), Re [1994] 1 FLR 96 . . . 479, 480

S-C (Contempt), Re [2010] EWCA Civ 21, [2010] 1 FLR 1478 . . . 529

Scallon v Scallon [1990] 1 FLR 194 . . . 195, 202

Schalk and Kopf v Austria (App no 30141/04), 24 June 201 . . . 38, 39

Schuller v Schuller [1990] 2 FLR 193 . . . 177, 203

Scozzari and Giunta v Italy (2000) 35 EHRR 243 . . . 636

Secretary of State for Work and Pensions v Jones [2003] EWHC 2163 (Fam), [2004] 1 FLR 282 . . . 352

SH (Care Order: Orphan), Re [1995] 1 FLR 746 . . . 647

SH v NB [2009] EWHC 3274 (Fam) . . . 30

Shaw v Shaw [2002] 2 FLR 1204 . . . 231

Sheffield and Horsham v UK [1998] 2 FLR 92 . . . 22

Shipp v Shipp [1988] 1 FLR 345 . . . 124

Shofman v Russia (App no 74826/01) [2006] 1 FLR 680, ECtHR . . . 347

Singh v Bhakar [2007] 1 FLR 880 . . . 148

Singh v Singh [1971] 2 WLR 963 . . . 26, 27, 28

Smith v McInerney [1994] 2 FLR 1077 . . . 218

Smith v Smith [1975] 2 All ER 19n . . . 204

Sorrell v Sorrell [2005] EWHC 1717 (Fam) . . . 189

Soulsbury v Soulsbury [2007] EWCA 969 . . . 220, 221

South Glamorgan County Council v W and B [1993] 1 FLR 574 . . . 427, 435, 624, 625

Southwark London Borough Council v B [1999] 1 FCR 550, FD . . . 630

Spencer v Camacho (1984) 4 FLR 662 . . . 104

Springette v Defoe [1992] 2 FLR 388 . . . 251, 281

Squire v Squire [1905] P 4 . . . 242

Stack v Dowden [2007] UKHL 17, [2007] 1 FLR 1858 . . . 49, 90, 248, 249, 250, 251, 252, 253, 254, 256, 257, 258, 259, 260, 261, 262, 263, 264, 265, 266, 269, 273, 274, 275, 276, 277, 278, 279, 281, 282, 283, 284, 291, 297, 298

Standley v Stewkesbury [1998] 2 FLR 610 . . . 218

Stringer v Stringer [2006] EWCA Civ 1617, [2007] 1 FLR 1532 . . . 556

Sulaiman v Juffali [2002] 1 FLR 479 . . . 77

Suter v Suter and Jones [1987] Fam 111 . . . 170, 194

Sutton v Mishcon de Reya and Gawor & Co [2003] EWHC 3166 (Ch), [2004] 1 FLR 837 . . . 51, 228

Szechter v Szechter [1970] 3 All ER 905 . . . 27

T (A Child: Contact), Re [2002] EWCA Civ 1736, [2003] 1 FLR 531 . . . 518

T (A Minor) (Care or Supervision Order), Re [1994] 1 FLR 103 . . . 658, 659

T (A Minor) (Care Order: Conditions), Re [1994] 2 FLR 423 . . . 619, 624, 651, 652

T (A Minor) (Contact after Adoption) [1995] 2 FCR 537 . . . 706

T (A Minor) (Guardian ad Litem: Case Record), Re [1994] 1 FLR 632 . . . 627

T (A Minor) (Parental Responsibility: Contact), Re [1993] 2 FLR 450, CA . . . 392

T (Accommodation by Local Authority), Re [1995] 1 FLR 15 . . . 587

T (Adopted Children: Contact), Re [1995] 2 FLR 792 . . . 476

T (Adoption: Contact), Re [1995] 2 FLR 251 . . . 453

T (An Adult) (Consent to Medical Treatment), Re [1993] Fam 95 . . . 440

T (Change of Surname), Re [1998] 2 FLR 620 . . . 551

T (Minors) (Custody: Religious Upbringing), Re (1981) 2 FLR 239 . . . 490

T (Paternity: Ordering Blood Tests), Re [2001] 2 FLR 1190, FD . . . 351, 352

T (Placement Order), Re [2008] EWCA Civ 248, [2008] 1 FLR 1721 . . . 686

T (Termination of Contact: Discharge of Order), Re [1997] 1 FLR 517 . . . 666

T and E (Proceedings: Conflicting Interests), Re [1995] 1 FLR 581, FD . . . 451

T and M (Adoption), Re [2010] EWHC 964 (Fam), [2011] 1 FLR 1487 . . . 692

T v B (Parental Responsibility: Financial Provision) [2010] EWHC 1444 (Fam), [2010] 2 FLR 1966 . . . 331

T v S (Financial Provision for Children) [1994] 2 FLR 883 . . . 295, 334

T v T (Consent Order: Procedure to Set Aside) [1996] 2 FLR 640 . . . 221

T v T (Financial Provision) [1988] 1 FLR 480 . . . 197, 236

T v T (Financial Relief: Pensions) [1998] 1 FLR 1072 . . . 198, 199, 200

T v T (Shared Residence) [2010] EWCA Civ 1366 . . . 494, 497

T v W (Contact: Reasons for Refusing Leave) [1996] 2 FLR 473, FD . . . 472

T, Re [2009] EWCA Civ 388 . . . 484

Tavli v Turkey [2007] 1 FLR 1136, ECtHR . . . 347

Tavoulareas v Tavoulareas [1998] 2 FLR 418 . . . 193, 328, 329

Taylor v Taylor [1987] 1 FLR 142 . . . 212

Teeling v Teeling [1984] FLR 808, CA . . . 325, 326

Thomas v News Group Newspapers [2002] EMLR 78 . . . 147

Thomas v Thomas [1995] 2 FLR 668 . . . 177

Thompson v Thompson [1985] 2 All ER 243 . . . 211, 212, 230, 232

Thorner v Major [2009] UKHL 18 . . . 285, 286

Thurlow v Thurlow [1975] 2 All ER 979 . . . 70

Tibbs v Dick [1998] 2 FLR 1118 . . . 222

TL v ML [2006] 1 FCR 465 . . . 178

Tommey v Tommey [1983] Fam 15 . . . 220

TP and KM v UK (App no 28945/95) [2001] ECtHR . . . 462

Tribe v Tribe [1995] 2 FLR 966 . . . 250

Turner v Avis [2009] 1 FLR 74 . . . 293

Tyler v Tyler [1989] 2 FLR 158 . . . 542

U (A Child) (Department for Education and Skills Intervening) [2005] Fam 134 . . . 639

U (Serious Injury: Standard of Proof), Re; Re B [2004] EWCA Civ 567, [2004] 2 FLR 263 . . . 636, 637

U v W (Attorney General Intervening) [1998] Fam 29 . . . 363

V (A Minor) (Adoption: Dispensing with Agreement), Re [1987] 2 FLR 89 . . . 706

V (Care or Supervision Order), Re [1996] 1 FLR 776, CA . . . 660

V v V (Children) (Contact: Implacable Hostility) [2004] EWHC 1215 (Fam), [2004] 2 FLR 851 . . . 518, 522

Vaughan v Vaughan [1973] 1 WLR 1159 . . . 104

VB v JP [2008] 1 FLR 742 . . . 241

Venema v Netherlands [2003] 1 FLR 552 . . . 605

W (A Child) (Illegitimate Child: Change of Surname), Re; Re A (A Child); Re B (Children) [2001] Fam 1, CA . . . 551, 554

W (A Child) (Parental Contact: Prohibition), Re [2000] Fam 130 . . . 666

W (A Child) (Removal from Jurisdiction), Re [2005] EWCA Civ 1614, [2006] 1 FCR 346 . . . 543

W (A Minor) (Contact), Re [1994] 2 FLR 441 . . . 520

W (A Minor) (Interim Care Order), Re [1994] 2 FLR 892 . . . 616, 658

W (A Minor) (Medical Treatment: Court's Jurisdiction), Re [1993] Fam 64 . . . 429

W (A Minor) (Residence Order), Re [1992] 2 FLR 332, CA . . . 485

W (A Minor) (Residence Order), Re [1993] 2 FCR 589, CA . . . 458

W (A Minor) (Residence Order), Re [1993] 2 FLR 625 . . . 458

W (A Minor) (Medical Treatment), Re [1992] 4 All ER 627 . . . 563

W (A Minor), Re, CA (6 December 1993) . . . 491

W (Adoption Order: Set Aside and Leave to Oppose), Re [2010] EWCA Civ 1535, [2011] 1 FLR 2153 . . . 698

W (Application for Leave: Whether Necessary), Re [1996] 3 FCR 337 . . . 479

W (Assessment of Child), Re [1998] 2 FLR 130 . . . 619, 620

W (Care: Threshold Criteria), Re [2007] EWCA Civ 102, [2007] 2 FLR 98 . . . 641

W (Children) (Residence Order), Re [2003] EWCA Civ 116 . . . 493

W (Contact Application: Procedure), Re [2000] 1 FLR 263 . . . 479

W (Relocation: Removal Outside Jurisdiction), Re [2011] EWCA Civ 345, [2011] 2 FLR 409 . . . 541, 546

W (Residence Order), Re [1999] 1 FLR 869, CA . . . 410

W (RJ) v W (SJ) [1972] Fam 152, [1971] 3 All ER 303 . . . 325, 327, 471

W (Shared Residence Order), Re [2009] EWCA Civ 370, [2009] 2 FLR 436, CA . . . 492, 493, 496, 497

W (Welfare Reports), Re [1995] 2 FLR 142, CA . . . 451

W v Ealing London Borough Council [1993] 2 FLR 788, CA . . . 385, 474

W v J (Child: Variation of Financial Provision) [2003] EWHC 2657 (Fam), [2004] 2 FLR 300 . . . 330

W v W (Ancillary Relief: Non-Disclosure) [2003] 3 FCR 385 . . . 183

W v W (Child of the Family) [1984] FLR 796, CA . . . 325

W v W (Disclosure by Third Party) (1981) 2 FLR 291 . . . 180

W v W (Financial Provision: Lump Sum) [1976] Fam 107 . . . 191

W v W (Physical Inter-Sex) [2001] Fam 111, FD . . . 26

W, Re (A Minor) [1993] Fam 64 . . . 432, 434, 435, 436, 437, 438, 439, 440, 443, 445

Wachtel v Wachtel [1973] Fam 72 . . . 190, 191

Wagstaff v Wagstaff [1992] 1 All ER 275 . . . 177

Walker v Hall [1984] FLR 126 . . . 251, 281

Walsh v Rother District Council [1978] ICR 1216 . . . 641

Waterman v Waterman [1989] 1 FLR 380 . . . 170, 197

Wayling v Jones [1995] 2 FLR 1029 . . . 287

WB (Residence Orders), Re [1995] 2 FLR 1023 . . . 535

Webb [1995] 2 FLR 259 . . . 166

Webster v Norfolk County Council and the Children (By their Children's Guardian) [2009] EWCA Civ 59, [2009] 1 FLR 1378 . . . 700, 701

Weisz v Weisz (1975) The Times, 16 December . . . 192

Wellesley v Duke of Beaufort (1827) 2 Russ Rep 1 . . . 447

Wells v Wells [1992] 2 FLR 66 . . . 204, 233, 234

West v West [1978] Fam 1 . . . 191

West v West [1998] 1 FLR 971 . . . 193

Westbury v Sampson [2001] EWCA Civ 4807 . . . 165

Whiston v Whiston [1995] 2 FLR 268 . . . 169

White v White [1948] 2 All ER 151 . . . 26, 49

White v White [2001] 1 AC 596, [2000] 2 FLR 981 . . . 63, 76, 166, 170, 171, 172, 176, 179, 188, 189, 206, 229, 240

Whiting v Whiting [1988] 2 All ER 275 . . . 195

Wicks v Wicks [1998] 1 All ER 470 . . . 164

Widdowson v Widdowson (1982) 4 FLR 121 . . . 140

Wilcox v Tait [2006] EWCA Civ 1867 . . . 291

Wilkinson v Kitzinger [2006] EWHC 2022 (Fam), [2007] 1 FLR 295 . . . 22, 38, 39, 40

Wilkinson v Kitzinger [2006] EWHC 835 (Fam), [2006] 2 FLR 397 . . . 89

Wilkinson v Wilkinson (1980) 10 Fam Law 48 . . . 182

Williams v Lindley [2005] EWCA Civ 103 . . . 230, 233, 234

Williams v Williams [1974] 3 All ER 377 . . . 179

Wilson v Webster [1998] 1 FLR 1097 . . . 142

Wiseman v Simpson [1988] All ER 245 . . . 124

WM (Adoption: Non-Patrial), Re [1997] 1 FLR 132, FD . . . 693

Wookey v Wookey [1991] 3 All ER 365 . . . 112, 113

Wooton v Wooton (1984) FLR 871 . . . 112

Wright v Wright (1981) 2 FLR 276 . . . 490

Wright v Wright [1970] 1 WLR 1219 . . . 219

Wynne v Wynne and Jeffers [1980] 3 All ER 659 . . . 180

X (A Child) (Injunctions Restraining Publication), Re [2001] 1 FCR 541 . . . 448

X (A Minor) (Adoption Details: Disclosure), Re [1994] 2 FLR 45 . . . 562

X (Children) (Parental Order: Foreign Surrogacy), Re [2008] EWHC 3030 (Fam), [2009] Fam 71 . . . 372, 373

X (Emergency Protection Orders), Re [2006] EWHC 510 (Fam), [2006] 2 FLR 701 . . . 601, 606, 607

X (Minors) (Care Proceedings: Parental Responsibility), Re [2000] Fam 156 . . . 381

X and Y (Children: Foreign Surrogacy), Re [2011] EWHC 3147 (Fam) . . . 373

X and Y v A Local Authority (Adoption: Procedure) [2009] EWHC 47 (Fam) . . . 476

X and Y, Re [2001] 2 FCR 398 . . . 453

X City Council v MB, NB and MAb (By His Litigation Friend The Official Solicitor) [2006] EWHC 168 (Fam), [2006] 2 FLR 968 . . . 14

X Council v B (Emergency Protection Order)
[2004] EWHC 2015 (Fam), [2005] 1 FLR
341 . . . 605, 607, 610

X v X (Y and Z Intervening) [2002] 1 FLR
508 . . . 219, 226

X, Re; Barnet London Borough Council v Y and
X [2006] 2 FLR 998 . . . 652

X, Y and Z v UK [1997] 2 FLR 892 . . . 370

Xydhias v Xydhias [1999] 1 FLR 683 . . . 221

Y (Children) (Occupation Order), Re [2000] 2
FCR 470 . . . 136

Y (Leave to Remove from Jurisdiction), Re
[2004] 2 FLR 330 . . . 540, 541

Yemshaw v Hounslow London Borough Council
[2011] UKSC 3 . . . 92, 150

Yeoman's Row Management Ltd v Cobbe [2008]
UKHL 55, HL . . . 285

Young v Lauretani [2007] EWHC 1244
(Ch) . . . 291

Young v Young [1962] P 27 . . . 167

Young v Young [1998] 2 FLR 1131 . . . 193

Yousef v The Netherlands (Application no
33711/96), 5 November 2002 . . . 462, 463

Z (A Child) (Specific Issue Order: Religious
Education), Re [2002] EWCA Civ
501 . . . 536

Z (A Minor) (Freedom of Publication), Re
[1997] Fam 1 . . . 448, 449

Z (Children), Re [2008] EWCA Civ
1556 . . . 393

Z (In the matter of) (Children) [2008] EWCA
Civ 1556 . . . 382

Z (Unsupervised Contact: Allegations of
Domestic Violence), Re [2009] EWCA Civ
430, [2009] 2 FLR 877 . . . 516

Z and Others v UK [2000] 2 FLR 603 . . . 601

Z County Council v R [2001] 1 FLR 365 . . . 677,
678

Z v Z [2011] EWHC 2878 (Fam) . . . 225

Z, Re (Unsupervised Contact: Allegations
of Domestic Violence) [2009] EWCA Civ
430 . . . 157

TABLE OF STATUTES

Access to Justice Act 1999
  s 10(7) . . . 201
Adoption Act 1926 . . . 669
Adoption Act 1976 . . . 105, 562, 693, 696
  s 15(3) . . . 694
Adoption and Children Act 2002 . . . 40, 43, 105,
  402, 469, 562, 669, 670, 672, 673, 693, 705
  s 1 . . . 371, 674, 684, 685, 690, 697
  s 1(1) . . . 674
  s 1(2) . . . 674, 684, 690
  s 1(3) . . . 674, 684
  s 1(4) . . . 674, 684
  s 1(4)(c) . . . 684
  s 1(4)(f) . . . 684
  s 1(5) . . . 674
  s 1(6) . . . 675
  s 1(7) . . . 674
  s 1(8) . . . 674
  s 2(1) . . . 673
  s 2(2) . . . 673
  s 3(2) . . . 673
  s 4 . . . 673
  s 8 . . . 673
  s 9 . . . 674
  s 10 . . . 674
  s 12 . . . 674, 676
  s 18 . . . 680
  s 18(2) . . . 680
  s 18(4) . . . 692
  s 18(5) . . . 681, 689
  s 19 . . . 680, 682, 687, 688
  s 19(1) . . . 681
  s 20(1) . . . 682
  s 20(4) . . . 682
  s 21 . . . 682
  s 21(1) . . . 682
  s 22(1) . . . 683
  s 22(1)(d) . . . 683
  s 24(2) . . . 689, 690, 696, 710
  s 24(3) . . . 690, 710
  s 24(4) . . . 688
  s 24(5) . . . 688, 689, 690
  s 25 . . . 688
  s 26 . . . 687, 707
  s 26(1) . . . 687
  s 26(2) . . . 687
  s 26(4) . . . 687
  s 26(5) . . . 687, 706
  s 27 . . . 687, 707
  s 27(4) . . . 687
  s 27(5) . . . 687
  ss 28(1)–(4) . . . 688
  ss 29(1)–(3) . . . 686

s 29(4) . . . 686
s 29(5) . . . 686
s 30(1)–(3) . . . 688
ss 31–33 . . . 688
s 42 . . . 695
s 42(2) . . . 696
s 42(3) . . . 696
s 42(4) . . . 696
s 42(5) . . . 696
s 42(6) . . . 696
s 42(7) . . . 697
s 43 . . . 697
s 44(1)–(6) . . . 697
s 44(8) . . . 681
s 45 . . . 676
s 46 . . . 402, 669
s 46(1) . . . 699
s 46(2) . . . 699
s 46(2)(d) . . . 699, 700
s 46(3)(a) . . . 699
s 46(5) . . . 695
s 46(6) . . . 706, 707
s 47 . . . 402, 407, 669, 698
s 47(2) . . . 697
s 47(3) . . . 698
s 47(4) . . . 682, 697
s 47(5) . . . 698, 699
s 47(7) . . . 698
s 47(8) . . . 695
s 47(8A) . . . 695
s 47(9) . . . 695
s 49 . . . 692
s 49(2) . . . 692
s 49(3) . . . 692
s 49(4) . . . 695
s 50 . . . 699
s 50(1) . . . 692
s 50(7) . . . 693
s 51 . . . 693
s 51(1) . . . 693
s 51(2) . . . 693, 699, 700
s 51(3) . . . 694
s 51(3A) . . . 694
s 51(4) . . . 694
s 52 . . . 680, 682
s 52(1) . . . 684
s 52(1)(b) . . . 684, 685
s 52(2) . . . 680
s 52(3) . . . 680
s 52(4) . . . 682
s 52(5) . . . 680
s 52(6) . . . 680
s 52(7) . . . 682

s 52(8) ... 682
s 52(9) ... 680
s 52(10) ... 680
s 52(6) ... 407
s 56 ... 702
s 57 ... 702, 703
s 58 ... 703
s 59 ... 703
s 60 ... 703
s 63 ... 703
s 67 ... 700
s 67(1)–(5) ... 699
s 67(3) ... 700
s 67(6) ... 700
s 68 ... 700
s 74(1)(a) ... 700
s 74(1)(b) ... 700
s 74(2) ... 700
s 80 ... 702
s 84 ... 401, 654
s 84(2) ... 372
s 103 ... 627
s 111 ... 379
s 115 ... 708
s 144(4)(b) ... 692, 693
s 144(5) ... 692
s 144(6) ... 692
s 145(5) ... 692
Attachment of Earnings Act 1971 ... 124

Births and Deaths Registration Act 1953
    s 2A ... 380
    s 2B ... 380
    s 2B(3) ... 380
    s 2B(4) ... 380
    s 2C ... 380
    s 2D ... 380
    s 2E ... 380
    s 10(1)(a)–(c) ... 380
    s 10A(1) ... 380
Borders, Citizenship and Immigration Act 2009
    s 55 ... 571
British Nationality Act 1981 ... 700

Child Abduction Act 1984 ... 537
    s 1 ... 503, 534
    s 1(4) ... 534
Child Care Act 1980 ... 568
    s 3 ... 568
Child Care Act 2006
    s 40 ... 571
Child Maintenance and Other Payments
    Act 2008 ... 316, 318
Child Support Act 1991 ... 50, 204, 244, 313,
    316, 317, 327, 329, 363, 406, 407
    s 1 ... 406
    s 1(1) ... 317, 318
    s 3 ... 317
    s 3(1) ... 317

s 3(2) ... 317
s 3(3) ... 318
s 3(5) ... 317
s 3(6) ... 318
s 4(1) ... 318
s 4(2) ... 318
s 4(2A) ... 318
s 4(10) ... 322
s 4(10)(aa) ... 318
s 5 ... 318
s 6 ... 318
s 7(10) ... 322
s 8 ... 244, 323
s 8(1) ... 321, 323, 324
s 8(3) ... 321, 323, 324
s 8(3A) ... 322
s 8(5) ... 322
s 8(6) ... 322
s 8(6)(a) ... 322
s 8(6)(b) ... 322
s 8(7) ... 322
s 8(9) ... 323
s 8(10) ... 323
s 8(11) ... 322
s 9(2A) ... 316
s 9A ... 316
s 26(2) ... 317
s 27 ... 317
s 27A ... 317
s 28A(1) ... 320
s 28E ... 320
s 28F ... 315, 320
s 28F(1) ... 320
s 28F(2) ... 321
s 32M ... 321
s 35 ... 321
s 39A ... 321
s 39B ... 321
s 44 ... 317
s 44(2A) ... 317
s 54 ... 317
s 55(1) ... 317
s 55(1)(b) ... 407
s 55(2) ... 317
s 55(7) ... 407
s 55(8) ... 407
Sch 1 ... 318
Sch 1 para 2 ... 318
Sch 1 para 2(3) ... 319
Sch 1 para 5A ... 319
Sch 1 para 6 ... 320
Sch 1 para 7(6) ... 320
Sch 1 para 7(7) ... 320
Sch 1 para 8(2) ... 320
Sch 1 para 10(3) ... 319, 322
Sch 1 para 10A(1)(b) ... 322
Sch 4B ... 321
Sch 4B Pt I ... 315, 320
Child Support Act 1995 ... 315

Child Support, Pensions and Social Security
  Act 2000 . . . 315
  Pt I . . . 315
Children Act 1948 . . . 568, 569
Children Act 1975 . . . 670, 707
Children Act 1989 . . . 35, 67, 105, 110, 126, 216,
  329, 374, 377, 396, 403, 427, 513, 562, 567, 568,
  569, 570, 613, 671, 686
  Pt I . . . 88, 469
  Pt II . . . 88, 467, 469
  Pt III . . . 449, 536, 569, 572, 582, 585
  Pt IV . . . 410, 420, 452, 469, 560, 569, 649
  Pt V . . . 410, 420, 560, 569
  s 1 . . . 332, 377, 444, 447, 448, 461, 616, 649,
    674
  s 1(1) . . . 382, 404, 406, 434, 448, 449, 451,
    453, 460, 462, 463, 465, 474, 484, 493, 495,
    510, 515, 540, 549, 557
  s 1(2)–(5) . . . 448
  s 1(2) . . . 451, 627, 665
  s 1(3) . . . 158, 382, 434, 452, 462, 484, 509,
    515, 537, 540, 627, 649, 707
  s 1(3)(d) . . . 490
  s 1(3)(e) . . . 649, 650, 661
  s 1(3)(g) . . . 498, 650
  s 1(4) . . . 382, 452, 649
  s 1(5) . . . 207, 382, 448, 449, 452, 453, 454,
    549, 586, 649
  s 2 . . . 396, 407
  s 2(1) . . . 377, 378
  s 2(1A) . . . 40
  s 2(1A)(a), (b) . . . 46
  s 2(1B) . . . 40
  s 2(2) . . . 378
  s 2(3) . . . 377
  s 2(5) . . . 407
  s 2(6) . . . 407, 653
  s 2(7) . . . 407, 408
  s 2(8) . . . 386, 408, 503
  s 2(9) . . . 408
  s 2(11) . . . 408
  s 3 . . . 385, 405, 406, 407, 535
  s 3(1) . . . 377
  s 3(2) . . . 377
  s 3(3) . . . 377
  s 3(4) . . . 406
  s 3(5) . . . 405, 406, 590
  s 4 . . . 51, 349, 378, 379, 382
  s 4(1)(a) . . . 379, 380
  s 4(1)(b) . . . 379, 380, 400
  s 4(1)(c) . . . 378, 381
  s 4(2A) . . . 404
  s 4(3) . . . 404
  s 4(4) . . . 404
  s 4ZA . . . 46, 400, 401, 493
  s 4ZA(5) . . . 404
  s 4ZA(6) . . . 404
  s 4ZA(7) . . . 404
  s 4A . . . 46, 400, 493, 654, 670

s 4A(1)(a) . . . 400
s 4A(1)(b) . . . 400
s 4A(3) . . . 404
s 5 . . . 402
s 5(1) . . . 402, 482
s 5(2) . . . 402
s 5(5) . . . 402
s 5(6) . . . 402
s 5(7) . . . 503
s 5(7)(a) . . . 403
s 5(7)(b) . . . 403
s 5(9) . . . 402, 403
s 5(10) . . . 402
s 5(13) . . . 402
s 6(1) . . . 403
s 6(2) . . . 403
s 6(3) . . . 403
s 6(3A) . . . 403
s 6(3B) . . . 403
s 7 . . . 67
s 8 . . . 46, 51, 110, 349, 370, 374, 401, 407,
  445, 466–473, 479, 483, 502, 505, 535, 559,
  561, 629, 687, 687, 708, 711
s 8(1) . . . 504, 686
s 8(3) . . . 469
s 8(4) . . . 469, 470
s 9 . . . 440, 561
s 9(1) . . . 483, 504, 560, 561, 564
s 9(2) . . . 482, 483, 484
s 9(3) . . . 481, 482
s 9(3)(a) . . . 482
s 9(3)(c) . . . 482
s 9(5) . . . 466, 534, 653
s 9(5)(a) . . . 534
s 9(7) . . . 587
s 10 . . . 349, 469, 483
s 10(1)(a) . . . 469
s 10(1)(b) . . . 469
s 10(2) . . . 470
s 10(3) . . . 483
s 10(4) . . . 370, 407, 470, 559
s 10(5) . . . 471, 472, 559
s 10(5)(b) . . . 471
s 10(5)(c) . . . 471, 472, 503
s 10(5A) . . . 472, 482
s 10(5B) . . . 472
s 10(6) . . . 479
s 10(7) . . . 535
s 10(8) . . . 479, 481
s 10(9) . . . 472— 475, 480, 481, 483, 559, 664
s 10(9)(d) . . . 478
s 10(10) . . . 471
s 11(4) . . . 491
s 11(7) . . . 466, 467, 500, 501, 502, 506, 533
s 11(7)(b) . . . 524, 532, 533
s 11(8) . . . 533
ss 11A–11P . . . 523
s 11A . . . 523
s 11A(1)–(7) . . . 524

s 11B(2), (4), (5), (7) . . . 524
s 11C(5) . . . 524
s 11D(3) . . . 524
s 11E(2)–(6) . . . 525
s 11F(1) . . . 524
s 11G . . . 525
s 11G(3) . . . 525
s 11H . . . 525
s 11H(3)–(6), (8) . . . 525
s 11I . . . 525
s 11J . . . 526, 531
s 11J(2) . . . 531
s 11J(3) . . . 532
s 11J(4), (6), (7), (9) . . . 532
s 11J(8) . . . 531
s 11J(10) . . . 53
s 11K . . . 531
s 11K(1) . . . 531
s 11K(2) . . . 531
s 11K(4) . . . 531
s 11L . . . 531
s 11L(1)–(4) . . . 532
s 11L(7) . . . 532
s 11M . . . 532
s 11N . . . 532
s 11O(2) . . . 533
s 11O(3)–(4) . . . 533
s 11O(9)–(11) . . . 533
s 11O(14) . . . 533
s 11P . . . 533
s 12(1A) . . . 401
s 12(2) . . . 401, 493, 503, 629
s 12(3) . . . 401
s 12(4) . . . 401
s 13 . . . 408, 503, 534, 537
s 13(1)(b) . . . 537, 539
s 13(2) . . . 537
s 13(3) . . . 537
ss 14A–14F . . . 402, 708
s 14A . . . 708
s 14A(1) . . . 708
s 14A(2) . . . 708
s 14A(4) . . . 708
s 14A(5) . . . 708
s 14A(6) . . . 709
s 14A(7) . . . 709
s 14A(11) . . . 709
s 14B(2) . . . 709
s 14C(2)–(4) . . . 709
s 14D(1), (4), (5) . . . 709
s 15 . . . 50, 329
s 16 . . . 467, 468
s 16(1) . . . 467
s 16(2) . . . 467
s 16(3) . . . 468
s 16(4A) . . . 523
s 16(5) . . . 468
s 16(6) . . . 468
s 16(7) . . . 468

s 17 . . . 536, 572, 574, 576, 578, 579, 582, 585
s 17(1) . . . 574, 585, 654
s 17(3) . . . 576
s 17(4A) . . . 573
s 17(6) . . . 573
s 17(10) . . . 573
s 17(11) . . . 573
s 20 . . . 406, 574, 575, 577, 579, 580, 581, 584,
    588, 589, 646
s 20(1) . . . 576, 578, 582
s 20(1)(a)–(c) . . . 577
s 20(3) . . . 587
s 20(5) . . . 587
s 20(6) . . . 576
s 20(7) . . . 504, 584, 585, 586, 588
s 20(8) . . . 406, 504, 584, 586, 588, 590
s 20(9) . . . 504, 586
s 20(10) . . . 586
s 20(11) . . . 578, 586, 587
ss 22–22G . . . 655
s 22 . . . 578, 579, 646, 658
s 22(1) . . . 579
s 22(2) . . . 579
s 22(3) . . . 478, 654
s 22(3A) . . . 579
s 22(5) . . . 579
s 22A . . . 578
s 22B . . . 579
s 22B(3) . . . 578
s 22C . . . 578
s 22C(4) . . . 578
s 22C(7) . . . 578
s 22C(8) . . . 578
s 22C(9) . . . 578
s 23 . . . 478, 646
s 23A . . . 580, 581, 582
s 23B . . . 579, 580
s 23B(8), (9) . . . 580
s 23C(1) . . . 582
s 23C(2) . . . 580
s 23C(5A) . . . 580
s 23C(6), (7) . . . 580
s 23CA(1) . . . 580
s 23CA(5) . . . 580
s 24B . . . 579
s 24B(1), (2) . . . 580, 582
s 24D . . . 582
s 25 . . . 449, 577, 587
s 26 . . . 583, 653
s 26(3) . . . 582
s 26(3B) . . . 582
s 26(3C) . . . 582
s 26A(1) . . . 582
s 26A(2) . . . 582
s 27 . . . 572
s 27(2) . . . 572
s 31 . . . 35, 126, 469
s 31(2) . . . 563, 614, 616, 628, 631, 632, 633,
    639, 640, 641, 642, 646

s 31(2)(a) . . . 646
s 31(2)(b) . . . 633, 640, 641, 643, 646, 648
s 31(3) . . . 660
s 31(5) . . . 660
s 31(8) . . . 655
s 31(9) . . . 158, 477, 591
s 31(10) . . . 477, 592
s 31A . . . 651
s 33 . . . 401, 653
s 33(3)(b) . . . 381, 631, 654
s 33(5) . . . 654
s 33(6)(a) . . . 653, 654
s 33(6)(b) . . . 654
s 34 . . . 483, 503, 603, 651, 663, 664, 665, 687,
   710
s 34(1) . . . 662, 663, 664, 667
s 34(1)(a)–(d) . . . 664
s 34(2) . . . 450, 662, 663, 667
s 34(3) . . . 450, 474, 662, 664
s 34(4) . . . 450, 664, 665, 666
s 34(5) . . . 662
s 34(6) . . . 664, 665
s 34(8) . . . 663
s 34(9) . . . 666
s 34(10) . . . 662
s 35 . . . 656
s 35(1) . . . 632
s 35(1)(a)–(c) . . . 656
s 37 . . . 530, 531, 599, 600
s 37(1) . . . 531
s 38(1) . . . 614
s 38(1)(b) . . . 531
s 38(2) . . . 615
s 38(3) . . . 614
s 38(4) . . . 615
s 38(5) . . . 615
s 38(6) . . . 427, 608, 619, 620, 621, 622, 623,
   624, 625
s 38(7) . . . 619, 620, 621, 624
s 38(8) . . . 620
s 38(10) . . . 615
s 38A . . . 614, 625
s 38A(2) . . . 625
s 38A(5) . . . 625
s 38A(8) . . . 625
s 38B . . . 625
s 39 . . . 652
s 39(1) . . . 504, 661
s 41 . . . 626
s 41(1) . . . 626
s 41(2) . . . 626
s 41(6)(b) . . . 531
s 42 . . . 627
s 43 . . . 598, 633
s 43(1) . . . 598
s 43(2) . . . 598
s 43(3) . . . 599
s 43(4) . . . 599
s 43(5) . . . 598

s 43(6) . . . 598
s 43(7) . . . 598
s 43(8) . . . 427
s 43(9) . . . 598
s 43(10) . . . 598
s 44 . . . 561, 590, 601, 611
s 44(1) . . . 603, 608
s 44(1)(a) . . . 604
s 44(1)(b) . . . 604
s 44(3) . . . 604
s 44(4)(c) . . . 601
s 44(5) . . . 401
s 44(5)(a) . . . 602, 609
s 44(5)(b) . . . 602
s 44(6)(b) . . . 602
s 44(7) . . . 427, 602
s 44(8) . . . 602
s 44(10) . . . 609
s 44(11) . . . 602
s 44(13) . . . 603
s 44(15) . . . 601
s 44A . . . 625
s 44A(1) . . . 608
s 44A(2) . . . 608
s 44A(3) . . . 608
s 44A(5) . . . 608
s 44A(8) . . . 608
s 44A(10) . . . 608
s 44B . . . 608, 609, 625
s 44B(3)(a) . . . 609
s 45(1) . . . 602
s 45(5) . . . 602, 609
s 45(6) . . . 602
s 45(7) . . . 604
s 45(8) . . . 609
s 45(10) . . . 610
s 45(12) . . . 609
s 46 . . . 577, 611, 612, 633
s 46(1) . . . 611
s 46(6) . . . 611
s 46(7) . . . 611
s 47 . . . 35, 595, 596, 597, 600, 604, 686
s 47(1) . . . 595
s 47(1)(b) . . . 595, 604
s 47(2) . . . 595
s 47(3), (4) . . . 596
s 47(4) . . . 597, 604
s 47(6) . . . 596, 597
s 47(7) . . . 596, 597
s 47(8) . . . 597
s 47(9) . . . 597
s 47(10) . . . 597
s 47(11) . . . 597
s 48(3) . . . 609
s 48(4) . . . 609
s 48(9) . . . 611
s 87 . . . 571
s 91(5A) . . . 710
s 91(12) . . . 652

s 91(14) . . . 555—560
s 93(13) . . . 558
s 100 . . . 429, 440, 562, 563
s 100(2) . . . 563, 610
s 100(2)(b) . . . 653
s 100(2)(d) . . . 563
s 100(3) . . . 561
s 100(4) . . . 563, 610
s 100(5) . . . 563, 625
s 102 . . . 658
s 105 . . . 403, 448, 472
s 105(1) . . . 331, 406, 407, 449, 477, 576
Sch 1 . . . 49, 50, 139, 225, 295, 322, 324, 329,
    331, 335, 337, 338, 453
Sch 1 para 1(1) . . . 330, 331
Sch 1 para 1(2) . . . 330
Sch 1 para 1(2)(a)–(e) . . . 330
Sch 1 para 1(3) . . . 330
Sch 1 para 1(5) . . . 330
Sch 1 para 1(6), (7) . . . 329
Sch 1 para 2 . . . 329, 330, 332, 333
Sch 1 para 2(4) . . . 330
Sch 1 para 2(4) . . . 330
Sch 1 para 3 . . . 331
Sch 1 para 4(1), (2), (3) . . . 332
Sch 1 para 5(2) . . . 331
Sch 1 para 10(3) . . . 338
Sch 1 para 16 . . . 331
Sch A1 . . . 532
Sch 2 . . . 574, 575
Sch 2 Pt I . . . 572
Sch 2 para 4(1) . . . 575
Sch 2 para 5 . . . 575, 614
Sch 2 para 6 . . . 575
Sch 2 para 7 . . . 575
Sch 2 para 8 . . . 575
Sch 2 para 8A . . . 575
Sch 2 para 9 . . . 575
Sch 2 para 10 . . . 575
Sch 2 para 15(1) . . . 662
Sch 2 para 16 . . . 662
Sch 2 para 19 . . . 616
Sch 2 para 19B . . . 579
Sch 2 para 19B(2) . . . 579, 582
Sch 2 para 19B(4), (5) . . . 579
Sch 2 para 19C . . . 579
Sch 3 . . . 656
Sch 3 para 2(1), (3) . . . 656
Sch 3 para 3 . . . 656
Sch 3 para 4(4) . . . 656
Sch 3 para 5(5) . . . 656
Sch 3 para 6(1) . . . 655
Sch 3 para 6(3), (4) . . . 656
Sch 3 para 8(1), (2) . . . 656
Sch 3 para 9(1) . . . 655
Sch 3 para 10 . . . 655
Children Act 2004 . . . 570
    Pt II . . . 570
    s 10 . . . 571
    s 10(3) . . . 571

s 10(4) . . . 571
s 20(5) . . . 571
s 11 . . . 570
s 11(1) . . . 571
ss 13–16 . . . 571
s 13 . . . 571
s 13(2) . . . 571
s 13(4) . . . 571
s 14 . . . 571
s 18 . . . 570
s 35 . . . 626
s 58 . . . 410
Children and Adoption Act 2006 . . . 523
    Pt I . . . 523
    s 6(1) . . . 468, 523
    s 6(3) . . . 523
    s 6(4) . . . 468
Children and Young Persons Act 1933
    s 1(7) . . . 410
Children and Young Persons Act 1969 . . . 568, 569
    s 28 . . . 568, 629
Children and Young Persons Act 2008
    s 22(2) . . . 580
Children (Scotland) Act 1995
    s 1 . . . 408
    s 2 . . . 408
Civil Partnership Act 2004 . . . 38, 40, 42, 44, 56,
    88, 89, 304, 305
    s 1(1) . . . 44
    s 2(1) . . . 44
    s 2(5) . . . 44
    s 3 . . . 44
    s 3(1) . . . 44
    s 8 . . . 44
    s 12 . . . 44
    s 14 . . . 44
    ss 37–64 . . . 89
    s 41 . . . 89
    s 42 . . . 89
    s 44(5) . . . 89
    ss 47–48 . . . 89
    ss 49–54 . . . 45
    s 62(3) . . . 56
    ss 65–72 . . . 45
    s 72 . . . 89
    s 72(4) . . . 45
    s 73 . . . 44, 106
    s 74 . . . 44
    s 74(5) . . . 44
    s 75(2) . . . 400
    ss 18–19 . . . 44
    ss 212–218 . . . 39
    s 215 . . . 39
    s 218 . . . 45
    ss 233–238 . . . 45, 89
    Sch 5 . . . 89, 160, 246, 291, 295, 322, 324, 469
    Sch 5 Pt 9 . . . 244
    Sch 6 . . . 243, 322, 469
    Sch 7 . . . 45, 322
    Sch 9 . . . 106, 217

Contempt of Court Act 1981
  s 14 . . . 114
  s 14(1) . . . 141
Crime and Disorder Act 1998
  s 11 . . . 469
  s 12 . . . 469
Criminal Injuries Compensation Act 1995 . . . 102
Criminal Justice and Court Services
  Act 2000 . . . 571
  s 12 . . . 626

Debtors Act 1869 . . . 124
Divorce (Religious Marriages) Act 2002 . . . 75
Divorce Reform Act 1969 . . . 60, 61, 84, 313
Domestic Proceedings and Magistrates' Courts
  Act 1978 . . . 41, 110, 243, 322, 469
  s 1 . . . 243
  s 2 . . . 243
  s 6 . . . 243
  s 20 . . . 244
Domestic Violence and Matrimonial Proceedings
  Act 1976 . . . 103, 124, 140
Domestic Violence, Crime and Victims Act
  2004 . . . 104, 108, 113, 116, 117, 133, 149
  s 1 . . . 113
  s 2(1) . . . 137
  s 2(2) . . . 137
  s 3 . . . 108
  s 12 . . . 149
  s 58(1) . . . 106
  Sch 10 para 36 . . . 105
Domicile and Matrimonial Proceedings Act
  1973 . . . 62, 64
  s 5(2) . . . 62
  s 5(6) . . . 64
  Sch 1 para 9(1) . . . 61

Education Act 1996
  s 548 . . . 444
Education Act 2002
  s 157 . . . 571
  s 175 . . . 571
Equality Act 2002
  s 202 . . . 43, 44

Family Law Act 1975 . . . 54
Family Law Act 1986
  s 55A . . . 344
  s 55A(1) . . . 343
  s 55A(2)–(4) . . . 343
  s 56 . . . 344
Family Law Act 1996 . . . 61, 76, 78, 81, 83, 84,
  86, 91, 107, 124, 129, 145, 146, 149, 292, 469
  Pts 1–3 . . . 80
  Pt 1 . . . 83
  Pt 2 . . . 76, 78, 83
  Pt 4 . . . 36, 42, 43, 44, 46, 48, 50, 51, 55, 75,
    82, 90, 103, 104, 108, 112, 202, 449, 534,
    557, 560, 614
  Pt 4A . . . 36, 52

Pt 6 . . . 42
s 15 . . . 164
s 30 . . . 46, 50, 75, 121, 246
s 30(1)(a)(i)–(ii) . . . 121
s 30(2) . . . 121
s 30(8) . . . 123
s 32 . . . 121
s 33 . . . 119, 120, 121, 130, 292, 294
s 33(1)(b) . . . 121
s 33(2) . . . 120
s 33(2A) . . . 120
s 33(3) . . . 122, 124, 125
s 33(3)(c) . . . 122
s 33(3)(g) . . . 123
s 33(4) . . . 124
s 33(5) . . . 123, 126, 129, 130
s 33(6) . . . 124, 125, 126, 127, 135, 136, 137,
  138, 292
s 33(6)(c) . . . 128
s 33(6)(d) . . . 128
s 33(7) . . . 124, 125, 135, 292
s 33(10) . . . 123, 129
ss 35–38 . . . 119
s 35 . . . 123, 129
s 35(5) . . . 130
s 35(6) . . . 130
s 35(7) . . . 131
s 35(8) . . . 131
s 35(9) . . . 131
s 35(10) . . . 131
s 36 . . . 123, 129, 131
s 36(3) . . . 132
s 36(4) . . . 132
s 36(5) . . . 133
s 36(6) . . . 132, 134
s 36(6)(e) . . . 133
s 36(8) . . . 134
s 36(10) . . . 123, 134
s 37 . . . 121
s 37(5) . . . 135
s 38 . . . 120, 121
s 38(6) . . . 135
s 39(2) . . . 119
s 39(3) . . . 120
s 40 . . . 123
s 40(1) . . . 123
s 41 . . . 133
s 42 . . . 104
s 42(2)(b) . . . 105
s 42(4) . . . 106
s 42(4ZA) . . . 106
s 42(4A) . . . 105
s 42(5) . . . 110
s 42(6) . . . 104
s 42(7) . . . 105, 113
s 42A . . . 104, 113, 114, 115, 116, 117, 142, 144
s 42A(2) . . . 114, 144
s 42A(4) . . . 114
s 42A(4A) . . . 118
s 42A(5) . . . 114

s 45 . . . 143, 154
s 45(3) . . . 144, 154
s 46 . . . 142
s 46(1) . . . 77
s 46(2) . . . 77, 142
s 46(3) . . . 142
s 46(3A) . . . 142
s 46(4) . . . 142
s 47 . . . 141
s 47(2) . . . 108, 140
s 47(3) . . . 144
s 47(4) . . . 144
s 47(6) . . . 141
s 47(7) . . . 141
s 47(8) . . . 114, 141
s 47(12) . . . 141
s 52 . . . 77, 608, 625
s 53 . . . 217, 293
s 55 . . . 39
s 60 . . . 105, 145
s 62 . . . 150
s 62(1)(a) . . . 131
s 62(2) . . . 105, 106
s 62(2)(b) . . . 105
s 62(2)(c) . . . 106
s 62(3) . . . 106, 120
s 62(3)(ea) . . . 107
s 63 . . . 108
s 63A(1) . . . 36
s 63A(2), (3) . . . 37
s 63A(4) . . . 36
s 63A(6) . . . 36
s 63B(1), (2) . . . 37
s 63C(1) . . . 37
s 63D . . . 37
s 63E . . . 37
s 63F . . . 37
s 63G . . . 37
s 63H . . . 37
s 63Q(1) . . . 36
Sch 2 para 3 . . . 164
Sch 6 para 1 . . . 625
Sch 6 para 3 . . . 608
Sch 7 . . . 217, 293, 295, 333
Sch 7 para 1 . . . 217
Sch 7 para 2 . . . 217, 293
Sch 7 para 3 . . . 294
Sch 7 para 4 . . . 294
Sch 7 para 5 . . . 217, 294
Sch 7 para 10(1) . . . 294
Sch 7 para 10(2), (5) . . . 294
Sch 7 para 11(1), (2) . . . 294
Sch 7 para 13 . . . 217
Sch 7 para 14(1) . . . 294
Sch 8 para 16 . . . 237
Family Law Amendment (De Facto Financial
 Matters and Other Measures) Act 2008 . . . 54
Family Law Reform Act 1969 . . . 433
 Pt III . . . 345

s 8 . . . 421, 431, 432, 433
s 8(1) . . . 432
s 8(3) . . . 432
s 20 . . . 344, 349, 354
s 20(1) . . . 345, 353
s 20(1A) . . . 344
s 20(2A) . . . 344
s 21 . . . 354
s 21(1) . . . 353
s 21(2) . . . 353
s 21(3) . . . 353, 354
s 21(4) . . . 353
s 22 . . . 344
s 23(1) . . . 354, 355
s 23(2) . . . 354
s 25 . . . 353
s 26 . . . 342, 346
Family Law Reform Act 1987 . . . 342, 358
s 1 . . . 377
s 1(3)(b) . . . 377
s 1(3)(c) . . . 378
s 1(3)(d) . . . 378
s 4 . . . 378, 382
s 27 . . . 358, 359, 362, 370
s 27(2) . . . 370
Family Law (Scotland) Act 2006 . . . 308
s 10 . . . 87
Forced Marriage (Civil Protection) Act
 2007 . . . 34, 36

Gender Recognition Act 2004 . . . 24, 26, 29, 30,
 369, 370, 396, 487
s 1(1) . . . 24
s 2(1) . . . 24
s 5 . . . 24
s 9(1) . . . 24
s 9(2) . . . 369, 370
Guardianship of Infants Act 1886 . . . 447
Guardianship of Infants Act 1925 . . . 447
s 1 . . . 447, 455
Guardianship of Minors Act 1971
s 1 . . . 448
s 11B(2)(d) . . . 333

Homelessness Act 2002 . . . 153
Housing Act 1985
s 60(1) . . . 572
s 79 . . . 217, 294
Housing Act 1988
Pt I . . . 217, 294
Housing Act 1996 . . . 91, 149, 151, 494
s 175(1) . . . 149
s 175(2) . . . 150
s 175(3) . . . 150
s 177(1) . . . 91, 150
s 182 . . . 581
s 188 . . . 581
s 188(1) . . . 127
s 189(1) . . . 151, 494

s 190(2) ... 153
s 191 ... 153
s 191(3) ... 153
s 193(2) ... 151, 152
s 195(2) ... 151
Human Fertilisation and Embryology
    Act 1990 ... 358, 359, 360, 372, .373
    s 2(1) ... 363
    s 13(5) ... 360
    s 13(6) ... 360
    ss 27–29 ... 359
    s 27 ... 358
    s 28 ... 365, 694
    s 28(2) ... 359, 362, 363, 364, 365, 367, 370
    s 28(3) ... 359, 362, 363, 364, 365, 367
    s 28(4) ... 365
    s 28(5) ... 362
    s 28(5A)–(5I) ... 369
    s 28(6) ... 374
    s 28(6)(a) ... 368
    s 28(6)(b) ... 368
    s 28(7) ... 362
    s 28(8) ... 362
    s 29(1) ... 365
    s 29(3B) ... 369
    s 30 ... 371, 373
    s 30(7) ... 372
    s 31ZA ... 368
    s 31ZA(2)(a) ... 368
    s 31ZC ... 368
    s 31ZE ... 368
    s 31ZF ... 368
    s 41 ... 374
    s 43 ... 401
    s 49(4) ... 359
    Sch 3 ... 360
    Sch 3 para 3 ... 360
    Sch 3 para 5 ... 360, 368
    Sch 3 para 5(1) ... 360
    Sch 3 para 5(3) ... 360
    Sch 3 para 8 ... 360
    Sch 3ZA Pt I ... 360
Human Fertilisation and Embryology
    Act 2008 ... 358, 360, 376
    ss 35–37 ... 367, 369
    ss 33–48 ... 359
    ss 33–58 ... 365
    s 33 ... 358
    s 33(2) ... 358
    s 33(3) ... 358
    ss 34–47 ... 694
    s 35 ... 370
    s 36 ... 365, 366
    s 37 ... 365, 366
    s 39 ... 369, 694
    s 40 ... 694
    s 41 ... 380
    s 41(1) ... 368
    s 41(2) ... 368

ss 42–44 ... 40, 46, 367, 369
s 42 ... 378
s 43 ... 378, 400
s 46 ... 369, 694
s 49 ... 370
s 54 ... 359, 371, 372, 373, 374
s 54(1) ... 371
s 54(3)–(8) ... 371
s 54(3) ... 372
s 54(5) ... 372
s 54(6) ... 372
s 54(7) ... 372
s 54(8) ... 372, 373
s 54(10) ... 371
s 54(11) ... 372
s 55 ... 371
s 57(1) ... 359
s 57(2) ... 359
Human Rights Act 1998 ... 23, 154, 352, 427,
    442, 444, 460, 462, 463, 475, 537, 584, 655
    s 2(1) ... 23
    s 3 ... 690
    s 3(1) ... 24
    s 4 ... 24
    s 4(2) ... 39
    s 6 ... 154, 442
    s 7 ... 23, 612, 653
    s 45 ... 154
    s 45(3) ... 154

Immigration Act 1971 ... 700
Inheritance (Provision for Family and
    Dependants) Act 1975 ... 42, 46, 49, 50, 51,
    75, 88, 90, 201, 329, 333
Insolvency Act 1986
    s 335A(3) ... 293

Land Registration Act 1925
    s 70(1)(g) ... 270
Land Registration Act 2002 ... 270
Law of Property Act 1925
    s 52(1) ... 247, 287
    s 53(1) ... 248
    s 53(1)(b) ... 248, 249
    s 53(2) ... 249
Law Reform (Husband and Wife) Act 1962
    s 1 ... 41
Law Reform (Married Women and Tortfeasors)
    Act 1935 ... 41
Legitimacy Act 1976
    s 1 ... 377
    s 1(1) ... 377
    s 1(4) ... 377
    s 10 ... 377
Local Authority Social Services Act 1970
    s 7 ... 571

Marriage Act 1949 ... 16, 17, 18, 19
    s 1 ... 17

s 3 . . . 17, 503
s 49 . . . 21
Sch 1 Pts I–III . . . 16
Sch 1 Pt I . . . 17
Marriage (Prohibited Degrees of Relationship)
    Act 1986 . . . 16
Married Women's Property Act 1882 . . . 42, 75
Matrimonial Causes Act 1923 . . . 59
Matrimonial Causes Act 1857 . . . 59
Matrimonial Causes Act 1937 . . . 59
Matrimonial Causes Act 1973 . . . 52, 61, 79, 81,
    89, 161, 330, 331, 333, 469
    Pt I . . . 14, 64, 66, 87
    Pt II . . . 14, 15, 19, 25, 42, 63, 64, 75, 76, 161,
        246, 291, 295, 324
    s 1(1) . . . 64
    s 1(2) . . . 64
    s 1(2)(a) . . . 67, 71
    s 1(2)(b) . . . 31, 70, 71
    s 1(2)(c) . . . 71
    s 1(2)(d) . . . 72
    s 1(2)(e) . . . 72
    s 1(4) . . . 65
    s 2 . . . 60
    s 2(1) . . . 60, 68
    s 2(2) . . . 68
    s 2(3) . . . 71
    s 2(5) . . . 72, 73
    s 2(6) . . . 73
    s 2(7) . . . 72
    s 3 . . . 15
    s 3(1) . . . 66
    s 3(2) . . . 66
    s 4(1) . . . 87
    s 5 . . . 73, 74
    s 6(1) . . . 60, 66
    s 6(2) . . . 60, 66
    s 8 . . . 66
    s 9(2) . . . 66
    s 10 . . . 73, 74
    s 10(1) . . . 72, 74
    s 10(2) . . . 74
    s 10(3) . . . 74
    s 10(4) . . . 74
    s 10A . . . 75
    s 11 . . . 13, 15, 88
    s 11(a)(i) . . . 16
    s 11(a)(ii) . . . 17
    s 11(a)(iii) . . . 20
    s 11(b) . . . 21
    s 11(c) . . . 21, 23, 24, 39, 370
    s 12 . . . 25, 29, 35
    s 12(a) . . . 26
    s 12(b) . . . 26, 68
    s 12(c) . . . 27, 35
    s 12(d) . . . 29, 31
    s 12(e) . . . 29, 31
    s 12(f) . . . 29, 31
    s 12(g) . . . 26, 30

    s 12(h) . . . 26, 30
    s 13 . . . 30
    s 13(1) . . . 30
    s 13(2) . . . 29, 30, 36
    s 13(2A) . . . 30
    s 13(4) . . . 30
    s 16 . . . 14
    s 17 . . . 87
    s 17(2) . . . 87
    s 18(1) . . . 88
    s 18(2) . . . 88
    s 19 . . . 88
    s 19(1) . . . 88
    s 19(2) . . . 88
    ss 21–25D . . . 220
    s 21A(1) . . . 200
    s 22 . . . 163, 164
    s 22A(3) . . . 242
    ss 23–24A . . . 161, 162
    s 23 . . . 164, 325
    s 23(1)(b) . . . 164
    s 23(1)(c) . . . 165, 236
    s 23(1)(d)–(f) . . . 326
    s 23(2) . . . 326
    s 23(3)(c) . . . 165
    s 23(4) . . . 326
    s 23(6) . . . 165
    s 24 . . . 325, 326
    s 24(1)(a) . . . 166, 203
    s 24(1)(b) . . . 167
    s 24A . . . 167, 202, 212, 324, 326
    s 24A(2)(b) . . . 167
    s 24A(4) . . . 167
    s 24A(5) . . . 167
    s 24A(6) . . . 168
    s 24B . . . 236
    s 24B(5) . . . 200
    s 25 . . . 168, 198, 215, 219, 220, 221, 244
    s 25(1) . . . 162, 169, 170, 185, 202, 203, 207,
        216, 325, 329, 332, 449
    s 25(2) . . . 162, 169, 177, 178, 193, 326
    s 25(2)(a)–(h) . . . 162, 193, 199
    s 25(2)(a) . . . 177, 178, 179, 184, 329
    s 25(2)(b) . . . 203, 207
    s 25(2)(c) . . . 184
    s 25(2)(d) . . . 184
    s 25(2)(e) . . . 332
    s 25(2)(f) . . . 185
    s 25(2)(g) . . . 193, 204
    s 25(2)(h) . . . 194
    s 25(3) . . . 326
    s 25(3)(e) . . . 332
    s 25(4) . . . 326
    s 25A . . . 163, 193, 196
    s 25A(1) . . . 194
    s 25A(2) . . . 195, 197
    s 25A(3) . . . 197, 204
    ss 25B–25D . . . 162, 199
    s 25B(1)(a) . . . 199

s 25B(1)(b) . . . 199
s 25B(5) . . . 199
s 25B(7) . . . 200, 201
s 25C(2) . . . 200
s 27 . . . 41, 243, 244
s 28 . . . 199
s 28(1)(a) . . . 164, 180, 209
s 28(1)(b) . . . 164
s 28(1A) . . . 197, 222, 236, 237, 240, 242
s 29(1)–(3) . . . 207
s 29(1) . . . 327
s 29(2)(a) . . . 327
s 29(2)(b) . . . 327
s 29(3) . . . 165, 327
s 31 . . . 163, 195, 236, 237, 238, 239
s 31(1) . . . 165
s 31(2) . . . 235
s 31(7) . . . 197
s 31(7)(a) . . . 237
s 31(7)(b) . . . 237
s 31(7A)–(7G) . . . 237
s 31(7B) . . . 197
s 33(6)(a), (b) . . . 217
s 33A . . . 220
s 33A(3) . . . 220
ss 34–36 . . . 218
s 34(1) . . . 218
s 35 . . . 218, 223
s 41 . . . 49, 469
s 41(1) . . . 67
s 41(2) . . . 67, 469
s 52 . . . 169, 324
Matrimonial and Family Proceedings Act 1984
 Pt III . . . 76, 322, 469
Matrimonial Homes Act 1983 . . . 103
 s 1(3) . . . 124
Matrimonial Proceedings and Property
 Act 1970 . . . 61, 75, 160, 161, 186
 s 37 . . . 279
Matrimonial Proceedings and Property
 Act 1984 . . . 161
Mental Capacity Act 2005 . . . 353, 380
Mental Health Act 1983 . . . 29, 435
 s 2 . . . 429
 s 3 . . . 429

Offences Against the Person Act 1861 . . . 410
 s 57 . . . 21

Pensions Act 1995 . . . 199
Police and Criminal Evidence Act 1984
 s 17(1)(e) . . . 609
 s 24(6) . . . 148
 s 64(1A) . . . 349
Property (Relationships) Act 1976 . . . 55
Protection from Harassment Act 1997 . . . 34, 109,
 115, 116, 142, 146
 s 1(1) . . . 147
 s 1(2) . . . 147

s 2 . . . 147, 148
s 3 . . . 147
s 3(1) . . . 148
s 3(2) . . . 147, 148
s 3(6) . . . 148
s 3(7) . . . 148
s 3(8) . . . 148
s 4 . . . 148
s 5 . . . 148
s 5(4) . . . 149
s 5A . . . 149
s 7(2) . . . 147

Rent Act 1977 . . . 217, 294
Rent (Agriculture) Act 1976 . . . 217, 294

Sexual Offences Act 1956
 s 5 . . . 421
 s 6 . . . 421
 s 28(1) . . . 421
Sexual Offences Act 2003
 s 64 . . . 700
 s 65 . . . 700
Social Security Contributions and Benefits Act 1992
 Pt IX . . . 319
Surrogacy Arrangements Act 1985 . . . 371
 s 1 . . . 371
 s 1A . . . 371
 s 2 . . . 371
 s 3 . . . 371

Trust of Land and Appointment of Trustees Act
 1996 . . . 54, 206, 290, 291
 s 13 . . . 291
 s 13(2) . . . 292
 s 13(4) . . . 292
 s 14 . . . 290, 292, 293
 s 14(1) . . . 292
 s 15 . . . 291, 292
 s 15(1)(d) . . . 293

Welfare Reform Act 2009
 Sch 6 . . . 380, 400
Welfare Reform Act 2012 . . . 316
 ss 136–142 . . . 316
 s 136 . . . 316
 s 137 . . . 318
 s 138 . . . 316
Welfare Reform and Pensions Act 1999 . . . 199, 200
 s 27(1) . . . 200
 s 29 . . . 200
Wills Act 1837
 s 18A . . . 88

Austria

Federal Act on the Religious Education of Children
 art 2(2) . . . 489

TABLE OF STATUTORY INSTRUMENTS

Adoption Agencies Regulations 2005
(SI 2005/389) . . . 674, 675
reg 3 . . . 675
reg 6 . . . 675
reg 12 . . . 675
reg 13 . . . 675
reg 14 . . . 675
reg 15 . . . 675
reg 16 . . . 675
reg 17 . . . 675
reg 17(3) . . . 675
reg 18 . . . 675
reg 22 . . . 675
reg 23 . . . 675
reg 24 . . . 676
reg 25 . . . 676
reg 26 . . . 676
reg 31 . . . 676
reg 32 . . . 676
reg 33 . . . 676
reg 35 . . . 676, 681, 682
reg 35(2) . . . 681
Sch 1 . . . 676
Sch 1 para 3 . . . 676
Sch 5 para 3 . . . 681
Adoption Agencies (Wales) Regulations 2005
(SI 2005/1313) . . . 683
Adoption Support Services Regulations 2005
(SI 2005/691) . . . 673

Blood Tests (Evidence of Paternity) Regulations
1971 (SI 1971/1861) . . . 344

Care Planning, Placement and Case Review
(England) Regulations 2010
(SI 2010/959) . . . 588, 663
reg 8(4) . . . 663
reg 28 . . . 658
reg 30 . . . 658
reg 40 . . . 579
Child Support (Applications: Prescribed Date)
Regulations 2003 (SI 2003/194)
reg 10(1)(a) . . . 318
Child Support (Maintenance Calculation
Procedure) Regulations 2000
(SI 2001/157) . . . 318
Sch 1 para 5(1) . . . 407
Child Support (Miscellaneous Amendments)
Regulations 1993 (SI 1993/913) . . . 318
Child Support (Miscellaneous Amendments)
(No 2) Regulations 2009 (SI
2009/2909) . . . 317

Children Act 1989 Representations Procedure
(England) Regulations 2006
(SI 2006/1738) . . . 583
reg 9(1) . . . 583
reg 14 . . . 583
reg 14(1) . . . 583
reg 15(2) . . . 583
reg 17 . . . 583
reg 19(3) . . . 583
reg 20 . . . 583
Children (Leaving Care) (England) Regulations
2001 (SI 2001/2874)
reg 4(5) . . . 661
Children (Secure Accommodation) Regulations
1991 (SI 1991/1505)
reg 10(1) . . . 587
Community Care, Services for Carers and
Children's Services (Direct Payments)
(England) Regulations 2009
(SI 2009/1887) . . . 573
Community Care, Services for Carers and
Children's Services (Direct Payments) (Wales)
Regulations 2004
(SI 2004/1748) . . . 573
Community Legal Service (Financial)
(Amendment) Regulations 2005
(SI 2005/589) . . . 201
Contact with Children Regulations 1991
(SI 1991/891)
reg 3 . . . 666

Disclosure of Adoption Information
(Post-Commencement Adoptions)
Regulations 2005 (SI 2005/888)
reg 4 . . . 702
reg 5 . . . 702
reg 6 . . . 702
reg 16 . . . 703
Divorce etc. (Pensions) Regulations 2000;
Pensions on Divorce etc. (Provision of
Information) Regulations 2000 . . . 198

Family Procedure Rules 2010
(SI 2010/2955) . . . 64, 65, 161, 626
Pt 6 . . . 67
r 6.2 . . . 627
r 6.3 . . . 627
r 7.6 . . . 66
r 7.12(12) . . . 72
r 7.12(13) . . . 72
r 7.33 . . . 66
r 12.6 . . . 626

Pt 16 . . . 626
r 16.3 . . . 626
r 16.17 . . . 626
r 16.20(1) . . . 626
r 16.20(2) . . . 626
r 16.20(5) . . . 626
Pt 16A PD . . . 626
Pt 16A PD Pt 3 . . . 627
Pt 16A PD para 6.1 . . . 627
Pt 16A PD para 6.6 . . . 627
Pt 16A PD para 6.8(a) . . . 627
Fostering Services (Wales) Regulations 2003
 (SI 2003/237)
 reg 38(2) . . . 624

Homeless (Priority Need for Accommodation)
 (England) Order 2002 . . . 151
Homeless (Priority Need for Accommodation)
 (Wales) Order 2002 . . . 151
Human Fertilisation and Embryology Authority
 (Disclosure of Donor Information) Regulations
 2004 (SI 2004/1511) . . . 348, 368
 reg 2(2) . . . 368
 reg 2(3) . . . 368
Human Fertilisation and Embryology (Parental
 Orders) Regulations 2010
 (SI 2010/985) . . . 371
 reg 2 . . . 371, 373
 Sch 1 . . . 371, 373

Independent Review of Determinations
 (Adoption and Fostering) Regulations 2009 (SI
 2009/395) . . . 674, 676

Local Safeguarding Children Boards Regulations
 2006 (SI 2006/90) . . . 571
Local Safeguarding Children Boards
 (Amendment) Regulations 2010
 (SI 2010/622) . . . 571

Marriage Act 1949 (Remedial Order) 2007
 (SI 2007/438) . . . 17
Marriage and Civil Partnerships (Approved
 Premises) (Amendment) Regulations 2011
 (SI 2011/2661) . . . 43, 44

Occupational Pension Schemes (Disclosure of
 Information) Regulations 1996
 (SI 1996/1655) . . . 198
Occupational Pension Schemes (Disclosure of
 Information) Amendment Regulations 2002
 (SI 2002/1383) . . . 198

Parental Responsibility Agreement Regulations
 1991 (SI 1991/1478) . . . 381
Parental Responsibility Agreement (Amendment)
 Regulations 2005 (SI 2005/2808) . . . 381
Parental Responsibility Agreement
 (Amendment) Regulations 2009
 (SI 2009/2026) . . . 381
Personal and Occupational Pension Schemes
 (Indexation and Disclosure of Information)
 (Miscellaneous Amendments) Regulations
 2005 (SI 2005/704) . . . 198

Special Guardianship Regulations 2005
 (SI 2005/1109) . . . 708

INTRODUCTION: THE CHANGING FAMILY AND DEVELOPING FAMILY LAW

The subject matter of family law is inherently interesting to many because the issues it addresses are often personal matters to which we can relate in our own lives, whether directly, or indirectly through the experiences of those we know. The courts tend to get involved with families when things go wrong, when relationships break down, and there are disputes, and when emotions are running high. The focus of much of family law is thus on the pathology of family life.[1] Not surprisingly, therefore, the family law reports are strewn with mini-dramas, with striking facts, revealing the messiness and complexity of family life. The issues raised are often controversial. By way of examples, take just the following issues which appear within this book. Should the law permit same-sex marriage? What financial provision should be made on divorce to a wife who has incited others to kill her husband? How should the law respond to the issue of domestic violence? Can a child have two female parents? Can a female-to-male transsexual person be the father of a child? Could that person be the mother of one child and the father of another? Can a child be taken into state care in circumstances where it is unclear whether a parent or a childminder has caused injury to a child? Can a child be adopted without a parent's knowledge? In addition to specific questions like these, family law raises many interesting broader issues, such as how the law can meet the needs of diverse cultures and religions within an increasingly plural society; the extent to which families should be permitted to order their family matters privately without law's interference; the extent to which family members' conduct should be material to decision making.[2] Family law develops at a pace, attracting a large body of case law and much policy debate. Indeed, the family justice system has recently been the subject of an extensive review, and the Government has responded with proposals for change.[3] In short, family law is rarely dull. Indeed, we believe it to be one of the most fascinating legal subjects of study. Of course, as teachers of the subject, we might be expected to hold that view. We hope, however, that once you have read this book you will fully understand what we mean.

In this introductory chapter we briefly set the scene for the chapters that follow by exploring some general features of family law and its study, and providing some background information, including a statistical picture of families in England and Wales. So far we have assumed that the term 'family law' is understood, but our first task must be to seek to explain what is meant by this subject—family law—that you are beginning to study.

---

[1] This is of course only a partial view of family law, see R. Probert (ed), *Family Life and the Law Under one Roof* (Aldershot: Ashgate, 2007), exploring law and the intact family.

[2] See A. Bainham, 'Men and Women Behaving Badly: Is Fault Dead in English Family Law?' (2001) 22(1) Oxford Journal of Legal Studies 219–238.

[3] *Family Justice Review Final Report* (Ministry of Justice, November 2011), and see Ministry of Justice and Department for Education, *The Government Response to the Family Justice Review: A System with Children and Families at its Heart* (Cm 8273, February 2012).

WHAT IS FAMILY LAW?

What is family law? This is a question which is difficult, if not impossible, to answer directly. What one can do is give some reasons why it is difficult to answer. First, understandings of 'family' may be contingent on the particular society concerned, influenced by cultural, economic, ideological, or other circumstances and, as illustrated in some of the case law discussed later, such understandings can shift over time. Furthermore, as illustrations given by Lords Nicholls and Slynn in *Fitzpatrick v Sterling Housing Association*[4] show, the word 'family' itself has different connotations depending on how it is used: 'we are thinking of having a family', 'accommodation suitable for families' (adults and children); 'family tree' or 'we're having a family gathering' (wider family/friends); the Christian family (religious community). As these examples show, the meaning may depend on the context, and the purpose for which a definition of family is required. For example, we might give different answers if we are asked to define family in terms of those who should be responsible to each other for economic support, or inheritance, compared with those who should be regarded as family for the purpose of protection from domestic violence.[5] A further difficulty is that a great variety of areas of law impact on the family, so deciding what 'family law' is, as distinct from other areas of law, is essentially a matter of line-drawing. There is a traditional core of study in family law which examines the formation and dissolution of legally recognised relationships, their legal consequences, and protection of individuals in the family. Some areas of law which have important impacts on family life (like taxation or social security law) are not usually included within standard accounts of family law, perhaps because these are also regarded as detailed areas of law in their own right. Alison Diduck has observed, however, that while family law displays this incoherence, there is a glimmer of a thread of normative consistency in family law's role as shaper of responsibility for responsibility.[6] In other words, family law decides who has responsibility for caring for others (the state or individuals), and who within the family is so responsible. The fact that family law is merely a collection of different areas of law collected around the family has led others to suggest that family law might be replaced, for example by a 'personal law'[7] or by a law of domestic relations.[8]

The core areas of study tend to reflect the major functions of family law: defining legally recognised relationships, protection, adjustment, and support,[9] and this is one way of ordering, reflecting on, and assessing family law. If anything, the trend has been towards increased focus on the functions carried out within relationships.[10] Another way of interrogating family law is to look at its impact. In this respect the work of feminist writers has been particularly influential, drawing attention to the gender dimension of many family laws.[11] A recent striking example of this perspective at work in the courts is Baroness

---

[4] [1999] 3 WLR 1113, HL.

[5] Compare those who have a claim under s 1 of the Inheritance (Provision for Family and Dependants) Act 1975, with the definition of associated persons for the purpose of protection from domestic violence in the Family Law Act 1996, s 63(2).

[6] A. Diduck, 'Family Law and Family Responsibility' in J. Bridgeman, H. Keating, and C. Lind (eds), *Responsibility, Law and the Family* (Aldershot: Ashgate, 2008).

[7] J. Eekelaar, *Family Law and Personal Life* (Oxford: Oxford University Press, 2006).

[8] R. Probert, 'Family Law—A Modern Concept?' [2004] Family Law 901.

[9] See eg J. Eekelaar, *Family Law and Social Policy* (London: Weidenfeld & Nicholson, 1984).

[10] For discussion, see L. Glennon, 'Obligations Between Adult Partners: Moving From Form to Function' (2008) 22 International Journal of Law, Policy and the Family 22.

[11] See A. Diduck and K. O'Donovan (eds), *Feminist Perspectives on Family Law* (Abingdon: Routledge-Cavendish, 2006); J. Bridgeman and D. Monk, *Feminist Perspectives on Child Law* (London: Cavendish, 2000); K. O'Donovan, *Family Law Matters* (London: Pluto Press, 1993); R. Hunter, C. McGlynn, and E.

Hale's judgment in *Granatino v Radmacher (formerly Granatino)*[12] in which she pointedly remarked that the legal recognition of ante-nuptial agreements has a gender dimension 'which some may think ill-suited to decision by a court consisting of eight men and one woman'.[13]

FAMILIES TODAY: THE STATISTICAL PICTURE AND TRENDS[14]

There were 26.3 million households in the UK in 2011. The trend is towards smaller household sizes. Twenty-nine per cent of households in 2011 consisted of only one person and only about 20 per cent consisted of four or more people. In 2011, 7.7 million people in UK households lived alone.

In 2011 there were 17.9 million families in the UK, of which 12 million consisted of a married couple with or without children. So married couple families are still the most common family type in the UK. The most common family type is a married or civil partner couple family without dependent children (7.6 million in 2011), then such families with dependent children (4.5 million in 2011).

However, the trend is that the marriage rate is dropping and people are marrying at an older age than in the past. The percentage of marriages ending in divorce increased for those marrying between the 1970s and the early 1990s, 22 per cent of marriages in 1970 ending in divorce by the 15th wedding anniversary compared with 33 per cent of marriages in 1995. However, between 2003 and 2009 there was a consistent downward trend in divorces in England and Wales.

Cohabitation outside marriage, however, is on the increase. The number of opposite-sex cohabiting couple families increased from 2.1 million in 2001 to 2.9 million in 2011. Thirty-eight per cent of cohabiting couples had dependent children.

Lone parenthood is also on the increase. There were 2 million lone parents with dependent children in the UK in 2011 (92 per cent of them women), a figure which has grown significantly from 1.7 million in 2001.

The birth rate is in decline. In 2009 there were 706,200 live births registered in England and Wales, compared with 783,200 in 1971 and 708,700 in 2008. The age distribution for childbirth has changed considerably; women are having children older than they used to.[15]

THE LEGALLY RECOGNISED 'FAMILY': SHIFTING OVER TIME

Many of the cases providing some indication of law's view of what constitutes a family, have arisen in the context of the question whether a person could succeed to a tenancy by reason of being a member of the deceased's family,[16] where unusually the word 'family'

Rackley (eds), *Feminist Judgments From Theory to Practice* (Oxford: Hart, 2010); A. Diduck and F. Kaganas, *Family Law, Gender and the State: Text, Cases and Materials* (Oxford: Hart, 2012).

   [12] [2010] UKSC 42, [2011] 1 AC 534.

   [13] Ibid, para 137.

   [14] The information in this section is taken from ONS national statistics, and from Social Trends, No 41, 2011 edn.

   [15] Social Trends, No 41, 2011 edn.

   [16] In statutes going back to the 1920s, amended several times over the years.

appears in the relevant statutes. The courts initially adopted the test of the ordinary man's view in determining whether someone was a member of another's family. The cases illustrate how notions of the legally recognised 'family' have shifted over time. It was soon established that family was not confined to *de jure* relationships, but also included some *de facto* equivalents. So by 1949, in *Brock v Wollams*,[17] a child who had been adopted as a matter of fact but not law was regarded as a member of her adoptive family. Around the same time, however, application of the same test resulted in the view that to say that unmarried cohabitants of 20 years were members of each other's family would be 'an abuse of the English language'.[18] Where, however, an unmarried couple had children, their family life together was recognised.[19] Yet, by the mid-1970s, in *Dyson Holdings v Fox*[20] the popular view of family had shifted to include unmarried cohabitants without children, although the Court of Appeal cautioned that relationships 'of a casual or intermittent character and those bearing indications of impermanence would not come within the popular concept of a family unit.'[21] In *Joram Developments Ltd v Sharratt*,[22] however, the House of Lords, approving a dictum of the Court of Appeal in *Ross v Collins*,[23] made clear that

> two strangers cannot…ever establish artificially…a familial nexus by acting as brothers or as sisters, even if they call each other such and consider their relationship to be tantamount to that. Nor…can an adult man and woman who establish a platonic relationship establish a familial nexus by acting as a devoted brother and sister or father and daughter would act, even if they address each other as such and even if they refer to each other as such and regard their association as tantamount to such.

Thus a 24-year-old man and 75-year-old woman who had platonic aunt/nephew-type relationship were not members of each other's family.[24]

The 'ordinary person test' was rejected, however, and the *Joram Developments* case distinguished, by a majority of the House of Lords[25] in *Fitzpatrick v Sterling Housing Association*.[26] Mr Thompson was the tenant of a flat. The appellant, Mr Fitzpatrick, lived with Mr Thompson from 1976 until Mr Thompson's death in 1994. They had been 'partners in a longstanding, close, loving and faithful, monogamous, homosexual relationship'. Mr Fitzpatrick had nursed Mr Thompson 24 hours a day for the final eight years of his life, after Mr Thompson had suffered an accident resulting in a blood clot on his brain. Mr Fitzpatrick claimed protection of the Rent Act 1977 either as a statutory tenant because he and Mr Thompson had been living as husband and wife, or as an assured tenant by reason of being a member of Thompson's family.[27] The House held unanimously that the words 'husband and wife' are gender specific, so could not apply, but by a majority found that Mr Fitzpatrick was a member of Mr Thompson's family. Lord Slynn emphasised that 'family' is not a term of art, and needs to be understood in context. The relevant questions were: what were the characteristics of a family as understood by the legislation and could

---

[17] *Brock v Wollams* [1949] 2 KB 388.   [18] *Gammans v Ekins* [1950] 2 All ER 140 at 142.
[19] *Hawes v Evenden* [1953] 2 All ER 737.   [20] [1976] QB 503.   [21] Ibid, per James LJ.
[22] [1979] 1 WLR 928, HL.
[23] [1964] 1 WLR 425 at 432 (woman who began living in an elderly man's property when she was in her 30s, and who subsequently acted as his housekeeper and nurse, not a member of the man's family).
[24] See also *Sefton Holdings v Cairns* [1988] 2 FLR 109, CA (no family relationship in case of *de facto* adoption of an adult 'child', distinguishing member of family and member of household).
[25] Lords Slynn, Nicholls, and Clyde; Lords Hutton and Hobhouse dissenting on the basis that the *Joram Developments* case was binding on the House and any change was a matter for Parliament.
[26] [1999] 3 WLR 1113, HL. For a detailed comment, see L. Glennon, '*Fitzpatrick v Sterling Housing Association*: A Perfectly Pitched Stall' in S. Gilmore, J. Herring, and R. Probert, *Landmark Cases in Family Law* (Oxford: Hart, 2011).   [27] Rent Act 1977, Sch 1, paras 2 and 3.

two same-sex partners satisfy those characteristics? His Lordship saw the hallmarks of the relationship as 'essentially that there should be a degree of mutual inter-dependence, of the sharing of lives, of caring and love, of commitment and support.' Lord Nicholls, although disapproving the 'ordinary person test', approved the *Dyson Holdings* case and concluded that 'there can be no rational or other basis on which the like conclusion can be withheld from a similarly stable and permanent sexual relationship between two men or between two women.' Lord Clyde explained that each case 'will require to depend eventually upon its own facts'. He saw the bond as 'one of love and affection, not of a casual or transitory nature, but in a relationship which is permanent or at least intended to be so' and commented that it would be difficult to establish 'without an active sexual relationship between them or at least the potentiality of such a relationship' and unless the couple were living together in the same house.

In *Ghaidan v Godin-Mendoza*[28] the question was whether the ruling in *Fitzpatrick* on the applicability of the term 'living together as husband and wife' to homosexual relationships could survive in the light of implementation of the Human Rights Act (HRA) 1998. Unanimously the House ruled that the exclusion of homosexual relationships would not pursue a legitimate aim and constituted a breach of Articles 14 and 8 of the European Convention on Human Rights (ECHR).[29] A majority of the House[30] was prepared to reinterpret those words pursuant to section 3 of the HRA 1998 to mean 'living together *as if they were* husband and wife'. Since that decision the Civil Partnership Act 2004 has been enacted giving same-sex couples who have registered their partnership effectively the same legal incidents as those attaching to marriage, so a similar result could now be reached simply by recognition of the *de facto* equivalent of the *de jure* status of civil partnership.

As can be seen, therefore, the law adopts a mixture of form and function to determine the existence of family relationships. Formally legally recognised relationships, such as marriage or civil partnership, are included. Such relationships will usually be loving, caring ones, but need not necessarily be so to qualify. The *de facto* equivalents of such relationships are included provided there is the necessary stability, caring, and mutual interdependence. Usually it will be necessary for the parties to be living under the same roof, and for there to be at least the potential for a sexual relationship. There can be no overarching meaning of 'family'; the meaning attributed may depend upon the context, and each case depends upon its facts.

THE IMPACT OF THE HUMAN RIGHTS ACT 1998 AND INTERNATIONAL CONVENTIONS

As *Ghaidan v Godin-Mendoza* illustrates, English law must now take account of the ECHR as implemented by the HRA 1998. Several Articles of the Convention, particularly Articles 3 (protection from inhuman and degrading treatment), 6 (right to a fair trial), 8 (private and family life), 12 (right to marry and found a family), and 14

---

[28] [2004] UKHL 30.

[29] As Baroness Hale observed, the legitimate aim

> cannot be the protection of the traditional family. The traditional family is not protected by granting it a benefit that is denied to people who cannot, or will not, become a traditional family... it is difficult to see how heterosexuals will be encouraged to form and maintain... marriage-like relationships by the knowledge that the equivalent benefit is being denied to homosexuals.

Ibid, para [143].

[30] Lords Nicholls, Steyn, Rodger, and Baroness Hale; Lord Millett dissenting.

(non-discrimination in application of Convention rights), will often be encountered in family law and their implications are discussed at various points in this book. Article 8 of the ECHR is particularly pertinent since it protects the right to respect for private and family life. The European Court of Human Rights has defined family life widely to include *de facto* family relationships and, in recent case law,[31] has indicated that family life embraces same-sex relationships.

There is an increasing internationalisation of family law, and no comprehensive account of family law can legitimately ignore the impact of international conventions,[32] even where not directly part of English law (such as the United Nations Convention on the Rights of the Child). Mention is made of such provisions at various points in the text where relevant to matters under discussion. However, it is important for us to make clear at the outset that our focus in this book is upon domestic family law (as opposed to international aspects of family law). We have eschewed an encyclopaedic treatment in favour of a clear, detailed examination of domestic case law and statutes and critical commentary thereon. Our focus is on the needs of undergraduate law students commencing their family law studies, by way of providing a foundation for further study. We believe that overload at this stage can easily undermine those foundations.

SOME FEATURES OF FAMILY LAW

DISCRETION

There is another reason why our focus is heavily on the domestic law, and particularly the case law. Family law is different from many other law subjects in that much of family law decision making is discretionary in nature. Appellate courts cannot interfere with a judge's discretion unless he or she has taken into account an irrelevant matter, has omitted a relevant matter, or the judge's balancing of factors in a case is plainly wrong.[33] Frequently, therefore, knowledge of family law involves understanding how judges exercise their wide discretion, which is often guided by statutory frameworks.[34] Unlike in subjects like tort or contract, where students are concerned to learn the *ratio decidendi* or particular legal principle represented by each case, in family law the cases are often not setting precedents in the same sense. Appellate judgments will often merely set guidelines for judges in the exercise of their discretion.[35] In order to understand family law it is necessary therefore to get a feel for how judges are likely to exercise their discretion. This comes with experience and with reading a large number of judgments. That is why we have tried, wherever possible, to deal with the cases in some detail and give as many examples as space permitted.

That is not to say that all of family law relies merely on discretion. Some areas are more rule-based, for example the calculation of child support maintenance.[36] The choice between the use of rules and discretion in family law has provoked debate as to the respective advantages and disadvantages of those approaches, and whether there is any coherence to such choices or whether the responses of family law are nothing more than

---

[31] *Schalk and Kopf v Austria* (App no 30141/04), ECtHR.
[32] Eg the Hague Convention on Civil Aspects of International Child Abduction.
[33] *G v G (Minors) (Custody Appeal)* [1985] FLR 894.
[34] See eg the Children Act 1989 s 1 or the Matrimonial Causes Act 1973, s 25.
[35] For further discussion, see S. Gilmore, 'The *Payne* Saga: Precedent and Family Law Cases' [2011] Family Law 970, esp at 973 et seq.   [36] Child Support Act 1991, Sch 1.

chaotic.[37] Where the court's exercise of discretion is dictated by welfare considerations, as for example in matters with respect to children's upbringing,[38] there is also a tension between utility and rights.[39]

INTERACTION WITH OTHER DISCIPLINES

Another feature of family law is the role that other disciplines play, particularly in children cases. In child protection cases, paediatricians, child psychiatrists, and other specialists may provide valuable expert evidence. Social workers will also be closely professionally involved. Even in private law cases there may be a need for the child's welfare to be safeguarded in the proceedings and for the court to receive professional advice. The Children and Family Court Advisory and Support Service (Cafcass)[40] has statutory duties[41] in family law cases involving children: to safeguard and promote child welfare; to give advice to court; to represent children where necessary; and to provide information and support to families. Officers of the service have various roles: preparing court reports; representing children in public law child protection and adoption cases, and ensuring parents understand what is happening in adoption cases; and, where appropriate,[42] providing separate representation for children in private law cases. The focus in such cases on the welfare of children, and the interaction which law has here with other disciplines, raises issues concerning the use of knowledge from other disciplines in court decision making. To what extent are the courts, and should they be, influenced by social science research evidence on child well-being?[43] At various points in this book we examine the connections between research evidence and the law.

THE ARRANGEMENT OF THE TEXT

The text is arranged as follows. In the first chapter, we begin by examining the law surrounding the formation of the formal relationships of marriage and civil partnership, including the law on nullity. This chapter also explores, by way of contrast, non-formal cohabiting relationships. Chapters 2 and 3 then move on to examine how the law regulates the breakdown of relationships, Chapter 2 exploring the law of divorce and dissolution of civil partnership, before Chapter 3 explores more specifically the problems and legal responses to relationships in which there is domestic violence. Chapters 4 and 5 then consider the financial consequences of relationships (which usually come to the fore on breakdown). Chapter 4 examines the courts' powers to make financial provision and adjust property as between spouses or civil partners ancillary to divorce or dissolution. Chapter 5 explores how the family finances are dealt with in the absence of such a discretionary regime, which particularly affects cohabitants in non-formal relationships. In the case of a former cohabitant who has no entitlement to the former family home, one way of obtaining support may be in his or her role as carer of any child of the relationship. Thus,

---

[37] J. Dewar, 'The Normal Chaos of Family Law' (1998) 61 Modern Law Review 467.

[38] Children Act 1989, s 1(1).

[39] See S. Parker, 'Rights and Utility in Anglo-Australian Family Law' (1992) 55 Modern Law Review 311.

[40] Set up pursuant to the Criminal Justice and Court Services Act 2002, s 11.

[41] Criminal Justice and Court Services Act 2000, s 12.

[42] Usually only in difficult cases.

[43] Indeed, to what extent is law capable of managing knowledge from other disciplines? See for a discussion of autopoietic theory in this context, M. King and C. Piper, *How the Law Thinks About Children*, 2nd edn (Aldershot: Ashgate, 1995).

Chapter 6 follows with a discussion of financial support for children. Having examined parental duties relating to child support, Chapter 7 then examines in more detail the law on parenthood and parental responsibility. Chapters 8, 9, and 10 then examine different areas of law which may result in an interference with parental responsibility. Chapter 8 explores the issue of children's rights, with a particular focus on the child's right to make his or her own decisions as a possible limitation on parental responsibility. Chapter 9 examines how the courts deal with private law issues or disputes relating to children's upbringing, such as post-separation residence or contact disputes, or other specific issues. Chapter 10 examines the relationship between children, parents, and the state, looking at how the law responds to children needing services, care, and protection. The book ends by examining in Chapter 11 the legal mechanisms by which children can be provided with long-term alternative secure family placements: the law on adoption and special guardianship.

It may be helpful to view the arrangement of the text in this book as two halves. The first half (Chapters 1 to 5 inclusive) deals principally with the legal regulation of adult family relationships, and the second (Chapters 6 to 11) focuses on the law relating to children, with the linking point in this arrangement of the book being the chapter on child support. Each half of the book has its own logical arrangement, however, and in this way the book is particularly suitable not only for modules that cover both aspects of family law (or a little of each), but also allows it to be used conveniently in cases where separate family law and child law modules are taught.

PART 1

ADULT FAMILY LAW

1

THE FORMATION OF ADULT RELATIONSHIPS

INTRODUCTION

At one time family law recognised only one sort of status relationship, namely marriage. Today, however, same-sex relationships are similarly recognised in that such couples can register a civil partnership. Over time, the law has also given increasing recognition to couples who cohabit outside marriage or civil partnership, although as we shall see cohabitants have fewer rights and remedies in family law than married couples or civil partners.[1] This chapter looks at the creation of these adult relationships and their legal consequences.

Marriage and civil partnership are regarded as 'formal' in nature, since certain legal formalities must be complied with for their creation (and indeed dissolution). A failure to do so may mean that the legal relationship of marriage or civil partnership will not have been created and the parties will not have the legal rights, obligations, and privileges which attach thereto. By contrast, other relationships, such as cohabitation outside marriage and civil partnership, or home-sharer relationships, are 'informal' in nature. Whether such informal relationships exist depends on the factual nature of the relationship. Proposals for reform of the law to give cohabitants rights on relationship breakdown have struggled with the difficulty of defining cohabitation.[2] Marriage and civil partnership, on the other hand, are proved simply by evidencing the status, for example by production of a marriage certificate.

This chapter deals first with formal relationships of marriage and civil partnership, and then with cohabitation and finally with home-sharer relationships.

1 MARRIAGE

1.1 MARRIAGE TODAY

Although Lord Nicholls stated in *Bellinger v Bellinger (Lord Chancellor Intervening)*[3] that marriage is 'an institution, or a relationship, deeply embedded in the religious and social culture of this country', marriage is no longer as popular as it was, and increasing numbers of couples opt to cohabit rather than marry.[4] Also, the nature of marriage has changed over the years. In 1886, Lord Penzance in the case of *Hyde v Hyde*[5] said: 'I conceive that marriage, as understood in Christendom, may...be defined as the voluntary union for

---

[1] For discussion of the differences and of legal developments and policy, see A. Barlow, S. Duncan, G. James, and A. Park, *Cohabitation, Marriage and the Law: Social Change and Legal Reform in the 21st Century* (Oxford: Hart, 2005).　　　　　　　　　　　　　　　　　　　　　　　　　[2] See Chapter 2.

[3] [2003] UKHL 21.　　　　[4] See Chapter 2.　　　　[5] [1866] LR 1 P & D 130.

life of one man and one woman, to the exclusion of all others.' Today, this definition[6] is no longer accurate. First, the Christian conception of marriage no longer predominates. Many marriages today are civil marriages, and it is possible to marry in a Muslim mosque or a Hindu temple, not just in a Christian church. Marriage is also not necessarily regarded as being for life, as many marriages end in divorce. Also, some polygamous marriages are recognised in this country where the parties have come from an overseas jurisdiction where such marriages are lawful. Furthermore, although only heterosexual marriage is permitted, same-sex partners can now enter into a civil partnership and thereby acquire virtually the same rights as married couples. The only part of Lord Penzance's definition, therefore, which remains material today is that marriage involves a voluntary union, a fact which has been reinforced in recent years by reforms giving greater protection to victims of forced marriage.

Talking point

According to Government statistics[7] the number of marriages has declined significantly over the years, but has remained relatively stable in the last few years. The provisional number of marriages registered in England and Wales rose by 3.7 per cent in 2010 to 241,100 (from 232,443 in 2009).[8] Provisional figures for 2010 also show an increase in both the male and female marriage rate. The provisional male marriage rate rose to 21.8 men marrying per 1,000 unmarried men aged 16 and over (from 21.4 in 2009), and the provisional female marriage rate rose to 19.8 women marrying per 1,000 unmarried women aged 16 and over (from 19.3 in 2009). The average age of marriage has increased over the years although figures for 2010 show a slight decrease in the mean age at marriage for both men and women. The provisional mean age for men marrying in 2010 was 36.2 years, and for women was 33.6 years. Many marriages are second marriages, because of the high incidence of marriage breakdown. In 2010 provisional figures show that 34 per cent of all marriages in England and Wales were remarriages for one or both of the parties. Since 1992, there have been more civil ceremonies in England and Wales than religious ceremonies. In 2010, civil ceremonies accounted for 68 per cent of all ceremonies. Increasing numbers of marriages now take place in approved premises, such as hotels, stately homes, and historic buildings. In 2010, 52 per cent of all marriages took place in such premises.

1.2 THE RIGHT TO MARRY

Key legislation

The right to marry is a human right under Article 12 of the European Convention for the Protection of Human Rights (ECHR),[9] which provides that: 'Men and women of marriageable age have the right to marry and to found a family according to the national laws governing the exercise of this right.'

This is a 'strong' right, as illustrated by the House of Lords decision in *R (Baiai and Others) v Secretary of State for the Home Department*.[10] In that case a legal challenge

---

[6] Or a defence of a particular view of marriage, see R. Probert, '*Hyde v Hyde*: Defining or Defending Marriage?' [2007] Child and Family Law Quarterly 322.

[7] Published by the Office for National Statistics (www.statistics.gov.uk).

[8] Marriage statistics for 2010 are provisional and will be finalised in 2013 when the majority of marriage returns have been received from register offices and the clergy.

[9] On the right to marry, see R. Probert, 'The Right to Marry and the Impact of the Human Rights Act 1998' [2003] International Family Law 29.   [10] [2008] UKHL 53, [2008] 2 FLR 1462.

was made to the immigration rules which required persons subject to immigration control to obtain the written permission of the Home Secretary to marry in the UK, unless they intended to enter into an Anglican marriage. These provisions were held to breach Article 12 and Article 14 (discrimination in respect of a Convention right) of the ECHR. The House of Lords held that, although the right to marry under Article 12 can be regulated by national laws both as to procedure and substance, such laws must not deprive persons of full legal capacity of the right to marry, or substantially interfere with their exercise of that right.[11]

1.3 THE CREATION OF A VALID MARRIAGE

Marriage is an arrangement in which the state has an interest and thus it is not a contract which can be created and terminated at the will of the parties. For this reason there are legal rules governing its formation and dissolution.[12] In order to create a valid marriage in England and Wales, both parties must have the capacity to marry, and the marriage must not fall foul of various grounds in section 11 of the Matrimonial Causes Act (MCA) 1973 upon which a marriage may be regarded as void.

1.4 CAPACITY TO MARRY

As marriage involves a *voluntary* union between a man and a woman, each party must consent to the marriage and thus have the capacity to consent. In *Re E (An Alleged Patient); Sheffield City Council v E and S*[13] a local authority sought to prevent E, a young woman of 21 who was functioning at the level of a 13-year-old, from marrying a 37-year-old man who had a substantial history of sexually violent crimes. The local authority were concerned that the relationship was an abusive one. As a preliminary issue the question arose as to the test for capacity to marry. Munby J, drawing on earlier authority,[14] explained that the test for capacity is whether a person is able to understand the nature of the marriage contract, and whether he or she is mentally capable of understanding the duties and responsibilities that normally attach to marriage.[15] His Lordship went on, however, to indicate that this requires merely an understanding of the essence of the agreement, which is 'to live together, and to love one another as husband and wife, to the exclusion of all others. It creates a relationship of mutual & reciprocal obligations, typically involving the sharing of a common home and a common domestic life and the right to enjoy each other's society, comfort and assistance.' Munby J was concerned not to set the test of capacity to marry too high, 'lest it operate as an unfair, unnecessary and indeed discriminatory bar against the mentally disabled'[16] or become 'too easy to challenge the validity of what appear on the surface to be regular and seemingly valid marriages'.[17]

The High Court's inherent jurisdiction[18] can be invoked to protect vulnerable adults who lack the capacity to marry but who may be at risk of being forced into a marriage. For instance, in *M v B, A and S (By the Official Solicitor)*,[19] the local authority was concerned that the parents of a young woman aged 23 with a severe learning difficulty were

[11] See also *O'Donoghue and Others v UK* (App no 34848/07) [2011] 2 FCR 197.   [12] See Chapter 2.
[13] [2004] EWHC 2808 (Fam), [2005] 1 FLR 965.   [14] *Re Estate of Park* [1954] P 112.
[15] *Re E (An Alleged Patient); Sheffield City Council v E and S* [2004] EWHC 2808 (Fam), [2005] 1 FLR 965. See R. Gaffney-Rhys, '*Sheffield City Council v E & Another*—Capacity to Marry and the Rights and Responsibility of Married Couples' [2006] 18 Child and Family Law Quarterly 139.
[16] Ibid, para [144].   [17] Ibid, para [145].
[18] The High Court's inherent jurisdiction is a parental sort of jurisdiction, of which wardship is also a part, see Chapter 9.   [19] [2005] EWHC 1681 (Fam), [2006] 1 FLR 117.

organising a marriage for her in Pakistan. The High Court, exercising its inherent jurisdiction, granted declarations, on the local authority's application, that she lacked the capacity to marry and that it was not in her best interests to leave the jurisdiction of the UK.[20]

1.5 THE LAW OF NULLITY

Key legislation

The law of nullity of marriage is laid down in Part I of the MCA 1973.[21] The law distinguishes between void and voidable marriages.

A void marriage is one which is not valid because of a fundamental defect. The marriage is void *ab initio*; there never was a valid marriage right from the beginning. Parties to a void marriage are therefore free to marry, and there is no need to apply for a decree to annul the 'marriage'.[22] However the advantage of obtaining a decree of nullity is that it removes any uncertainty as to the status of the parties, and the grant of a decree gives the court jurisdiction under Part II of the MCA 1973 to grant finance and property orders equivalent to those which can be made on divorce.[23] Third parties, not just the parties to the marriage, can apply for a decree of nullity on the ground that the marriage is void and they can do so during the lifetime of the spouses or after their deaths.[24] In rare circumstances, a marriage may be regarded as a 'non-marriage', one which departs so far from the formalities required to contract a valid marriage in England and Wales that it cannot even be regarded as a void marriage.

A voidable marriage, on the other hand, is a valid and subsisting marriage unless and until it is annulled by the court on application of one of the parties during the lifetime of both parties.[25]

Talking point

Nullity petitions are rarely sought and are much less commonly sought than divorce. According to Government statistics, only 290 nullity decrees were filed in the courts in England and Wales in 2009 compared with 132,144 petitions for divorce.[26]

A decree of nullity is granted in two stages: decree nisi followed by a decree absolute. On or after the grant of a decree of nullity the court has jurisdiction to make finance and

---

[20] See also *X City Council v MB, NB and Mab (By His Litigation Friend The Official Solicitor)* [2006] EWHC 168 (Fam), [2006] 2 FLR 968 where an autistic man (aged 25) who lacked capacity to marry was given protection by Munby J under the inherent jurisdiction of the High Court on the application of the local authority, in order to prevent him being taken abroad by his parents to be married in Pakistan.

[21] Which also governs the law of divorce (and judicial separation), see Chapter 4.

[22] The parties to a void first 'marriage' will not commit the crime of bigamy if they enter into a second one without annulling the first.   [23] See Chapter 4.

[24] Eg a third party who wishes to prove there is no valid marriage in order to establish that the children of the relationship have no automatic right to succeed to any property on the death of a party to the 'marriage' who has died intestate.   [25] MCA 1973, s 16.

[26] *Judicial and Court Statistics 2009* (Ministry of Justice, 2010), Ch 2, Table 2.5.

property orders under Part II of the MCA 1973 equivalent to those which can be made on divorce. Nullity differs from divorce, however, in that the grounds for nullity are different, and there is no prohibition on bringing nullity proceedings in the first year of marriage as there is for divorce.[27] Also, the procedure for nullity is very different from that of divorce. Thus, whereas undefended divorces are dealt with by what is essentially an administrative procedure with little judicial involvement and there usually being no need to attend court, nullity proceedings, whether or not defended, are heard in open court with the parties giving oral evidence. This can be distressing and embarrassing for the parties, particularly in forced marriage cases where the petitioner may already be considerably distressed by the experience of being forced into marriage. There has been discussion about whether the law should be changed to remove the need for nullity proceedings to be heard in open court, and a significant majority of persons who responded to a Government consultation were in favour of the court having the power to make nullity orders without hearing oral evidence, but having a discretion to require a hearing where appropriate.[28]

2 VOID MARRIAGES

Key legislation

The grounds on which a marriage may be void are laid down in section 11 of the MCA 1973, which provides that:

A marriage celebrated after 31 July 1971 shall be void on the following grounds only, that is to say—

(a) That it is not a valid marriage under the provisions of the Marriage Acts 1949–1986 (that is to say where—

    (i) the parties are within the prohibited degrees of relationship;

    (ii) either party is under the age of sixteen; or

    (iii) the parties have intermarried in disregard of certain requirements as to the formation of the marriage);

(b) that at the time of the marriage either party was already lawfully married;

(c) that the parties are not respectively male and female;

(d) in the case of a polygamous marriage entered into outside England and Wales, that either party was at the time of the marriage domiciled in England and Wales.

For the purposes of paragraph (d) of this subsection a marriage may be polygamous although at its inception neither party has any spouse additional to the other.

The grounds which render a marriage void are considered in more detail in the following sections.

---

[27] See MCA 1973, s 3.

[28] See the consultation document, *Family Procedure Rules: A New Procedural Code for Family Proceedings*, CP 19/06.

2.1 MARRIAGE WITHIN THE PROHIBITED DEGREES OF RELATIONSHIP

A marriage is void under section 11(a)(i) of the MCA 1973 if the parties are within the prohibited degrees of relationship. The law of England and Wales prohibits marriage between certain relationships of consanguinity (blood relations) and affinity (family relationship created by marriage). The rules governing relationships of consanguinity are more restrictive than those for relationships of affinity.

Under the rules which apply to relationships of consanguinity,[29] a person may not marry his or her parent, grandparent, child, grandchild, sibling, aunt or uncle, niece or nephew. These prohibitions on marriages between persons related closely by blood are founded on biological, moral, and social reasons. The biological reasons are based on genetic factors, as inherited disorders are more liable to arise within the same genetic pool. The moral and social policy reasons which prohibit such marriages relate to what is acceptable to public opinion. People have a strong sense of taboo about sexual relationships taking place between persons who are closely related. Marriage between cousins is permitted, however, despite evidence to show that children of cousin-parents are more likely to suffer from genetic diseases which may cause disability or death. Cousin marriage is particularly common in the Pakistani and Bangladeshi immigrant community, and Baroness Deech has expressed the view that, although human rights and religious and cultural practices are respected by not prohibiting such marriages, those cousins who do marry should be made aware of the possible genetic consequences for their children.[30]

There are also prohibitions on marriages taking place between persons who are related by reason of marriage.[31] These prohibitions are based on social policy considerations designed to discourage sexual relations within the family which cut across taboos of what is generally regarded as acceptable behaviour. However, these prohibitions were made less restrictive by the Marriage (Prohibited Degrees of Relationship) Act 1986, which amended the relevant provisions of the Marriage Act 1949 and permitted certain persons related by marriage to enter into a valid marriage. Thus, it became possible for a step-parent to marry his or her stepchild (the son or daughter of his or her former spouse), provided both parties were over the age of 21 and the step-parent had not treated the stepchild as a child of the family before the stepchild reached the age of 18. It also became possible to marry a former in-law provided both parties to the marriage were over 21 and the parties' former spouses were dead. Thus, for example, a man could marry his mother-in-law, provided his former wife and his former father-in-law were both dead. However, the restrictions on former in-law marriages were removed on 1 March 2007, as they were held by the European Court of Human Rights (ECtHR) in *B and L v UK*[32] to be in breach of the right to marry under Article 12 of the ECHR.

Key case

In *B and L*, a father-in-law (B) and his daughter-in-law (L) wished to marry after each of their marriages had ended in divorce, but the superintendent registrar at the register office refused to give them permission to marry as they were prohibited from doing so on the ground that both their former spouses were alive. B and L took their case to the ECtHR claiming that this bar on 'in-law' marriages was a breach of their fundamental right to marry under Article 12.

---

[29] See the Marriage Act 1949, Sch 1, Pt I.
[30] R. Deech, 'Cousin Marriage' [2010] Family Law 619.
[31] See Marriage Act 1949, Sch 1, Pts II and III.   [32] (App no 36536/02) [2006] 1 FLR 35.

The Court allowed their claim, holding that the relevant sections of the Marriage Act 1949 were incompatible with Article 12 of the ECHR as the prohibition was neither rational nor logical and served no useful purpose of public policy.[33]

After the decision in *B and L v UK*, the UK Government was forced to change the law and remove the restrictions that both former spouses should be dead.[34] Although the UK Government was not obliged to remove the age restriction, as the ECtHR had not considered this matter (as B and L were both over 21), it nonetheless decided to remove the incompatibility with Article 12 'across the board' by removing the age restriction.[35]

2.2 MARRIAGE UNDER THE AGE OF 16

Under section 11(a)(ii) of the MCA 1973, a marriage is void if either party to the marriage is under the age of 16. One of the reasons for making 16 the minimum age for marriage is that it is a criminal offence for a man to have sexual intercourse with a girl aged under 16, and the notion that a man could nonetheless be entitled to have sexual intercourse with a girl under 16 under the cloak of marriage was regarded as offensive to law reformers. The view was taken that it was 'essential that the minimum age of marriage and the age of consent for sexual intercourse should be the same'.[36]

If a party is aged 16 but under 18, the age of majority, the consent of certain persons is required as a preliminary formality. These persons include each parent with parental responsibility (or guardian), a special guardian, anyone with whom the young person lives or is to live under a residence order, and a local authority if the child is in care.[37] The absence of parental consent does not render a marriage void although it does mean that the celebrant can refuse to marry the couple; if the child is a ward of court, the court's consent is required. Consent can be dispensed with, however, if a person whose consent is needed is absent, inaccessible, or suffers from a disability.

2.3 FAILURE TO COMPLY WITH THE REQUIRED FORMALITIES FOR MARRIAGE

As marriage changes the status of the parties and gives them various rights and responsibilities it is important to make sure that a marriage has been contracted. For this reason, various formalities must be complied with. The aim of these formalities is to ensure that the parties have the capacity to marry and consent to doing so, that there are no impediments to the marriage, and that there is proof by registration that a marriage has taken place. These rules are complex and breach of certain formality requirements can attract criminal sanctions.[38]

---

[33] For a discussion of *B and L v UK* and whether the decision has other implications for the law on the prohibited degrees of relationship, see L. Schäfer, 'Marrying an In-Law: The Future of Prohibited Degrees of Affinity and Consanguinity in English Law' [2008] Child and Family Law Quarterly 219.

[34] It did so by passing the Marriage Act 1949 (Remedial Order) 2007, which amended s 1 of and Sch 1 to the Marriage Act 1949, and applied to marriages solemnised on or after 1 March 2007.

[35] The Government was of the view that there would be very few cases involving a party under 21 (because the younger person must have been 16 or over to enter into the first marriage, and could not divorce for at least one year afterwards; and because very few couples marry at so young an age).

[36] *Report of the Committee on the Age of Majority*, Latey Committee (Cmd 3342, 1967), para 177.

[37] See Marriage Act 1949, s 3.

[38] Eg giving a false declaration constitutes the criminal offence of perjury.

The exact nature of the formalities differs depending on whether the marriage is a civil or religious marriage, and whether it takes place in a religious building, a register office, or approved premises. With respect to religious marriages, there are also different rules depending on whether or not the marriage is an Anglican marriage, in other words one celebrated in the Church of England. The different formalities are explained in the following sections.

Preliminary formalities: the parties must satisfy certain preliminary formalities before the marriage can take place. The rules are the same for all marriages, except those which are to be celebrated in the Church of England.

In the case of a non-Anglican marriage, the parties must first obtain a superintendent registrar's certificate giving them approval to marry. Various requirements must be satisfied before the certificate can be granted, and these are laid down in the Marriage Act 1949. Thus, the parties must give notice of the marriage in prescribed form to the superintendent registrar in the district(s) in which each of them has resided for at least the previous seven days, and to the register office where the ceremony is to take place (if this is different). The parties must declare that: there are no lawful impediments to the marriage; the residence requirements have been satisfied; and the required consents have been given. Notice of the marriage is then entered in the marriage notice book and publicly displayed in the register officer for 15 days after which the superintendent registrar issues a certificate (provided there has been no objection to the marriage). The marriage must take place within three months of notice in the marriage notice book. The Registrar-General has the power in exceptional circumstances to reduce the 15-day period; and under the Marriage Act 1983 special provisions permit a person who is housebound due to illness or disability, or who is detained in prison or due to mental ill-health, to marry in the place where he or she is residing or is detained.

A Church of England marriage can only be solemnised after the publication of banns,[39] or after the completion of one of the formalities listed earlier. In the case of other religious marriages a superintendent registrar's certificate must be obtained, but there are additional preliminary formalities for some religions. Thus, under the provisions of the Marriage Act 1949, Quakers must make special declarations when giving notice; and both parties to a Jewish marriage must profess to belong to the Jewish faith.

The marriage ceremony: in England and Wales the ceremony of marriage can take place in a register office, a religious building (such as a church or mosque), or in approved premises.[40]

A marriage ceremony in England and Wales must comply with certain legal formalities which differ depending on whether the marriage is civil or religious. In the case of a civil marriage, once the parties have satisfied the preliminary formalities (see earlier) and obtained the approval of the superintendent registrar (or the Registrar-General) to marry, the marriage can take place in a register office or in 'approved premises', or, in special cases, at the location where a person is housebound or detained. 'Approved premises' are premises which have been approved by the local authority for the purpose of conducting a civil marriage,[41] and include premises such as hotels, stately homes, castles, and other approved places. The civil ceremony, which is public and secular, may be followed

---

[39] An announcement of the intended marriage made by the vicar or rector on three successive Sundays in the parish church of each of the parties.

[40] According to statistics published by the Office for National Statistics, civil ceremonies are more popular than religious ceremonies, and many marriages now take place in approved premises.

[41] Under the provisions of the Marriage Act 1994 and in government regulations.

by a religious ceremony, but it is the civil ceremony which creates the marriage. At the civil ceremony, the parties must declare that there are no lawful impediments to the marriage and they must exchange vows. At least two witnesses must attend.

In the case of a religious marriage, once the preliminary formalities have been complied with, the marriage is celebrated according to the rites of the particular religion and in the presence of at least two witnesses. Quaker and Jewish marriages are celebrated according to their own religious rites, but they need not take place in a registered building or in public or before an authorised person. There are special rules for the registration of Quaker and Jewish marriages. In the case of other religious marriages, the superintendent registrar's certificate will state where the ceremony is to be held, which will usually be a registered building in the district where at least one of the parties resides. Under the Marriage Act 1949, a 'registered building' is one which is registered by the Registrar-General as a place of meeting for religious worship, and includes not only Christian churches but also Sikh and Hindu temples and Muslim mosques. A non-Anglican religious marriage must be attended by a registrar or an 'authorised person' (such as a religious cleric) and must take place in the presence of at least two witnesses and be open to the public. The ceremony can take any form, provided that during the ceremony the required declarations are made.

2.3.1 'Non-marriages'

A failure to comply with the formalities required for contracting a valid marriage will usually mean that the marriage is void, but in some circumstances the court may hold that there was no marriage at all; in other words there was a 'non-marriage'.[42] The distinction between a void marriage and a 'non-marriage' is important because, if there is a 'non-marriage', then a party will not be entitled to a decree of nullity and will therefore be unable to apply for finance and property orders under Part II of the MCA 1973. A 'non-marriage' is one where the formation of the 'marriage' is so flawed that it cannot even be considered a void marriage.

Whether there is a non-marriage depends on the facts of the case, including, for instance, whether the participants, in particular the celebrant, reasonably believed and intended the ceremony to be one which created a lawful marriage. In *Ghandi v Patel*,[43] for instance, a Hindu marriage ceremony conducted by a Brahmin priest in a London restaurant was held to be 'non-marriage'.[44] The court came to the same conclusion in *Alfonso-Brown v Milwood*[45] as the parties had lacked the necessary intent at the time of the ceremony. Neither party had believed that the ceremony, which took place in Ghana, was anything other than an engagement ceremony.

There was also held to be a 'non-marriage' in *Hudson v Leigh*.[46] In that case Miss Hudson was religious and wanted a religious marriage, but Mr Leigh was an atheist. The couple therefore agreed to have a religious ceremony for Miss Hudson's benefit to be followed by a civil ceremony of marriage. The religious ceremony took place but Mr Leigh subsequently refused to go through with the civil ceremony and the question arose as to the status of the religious ceremony. That ceremony was conducted by a minister who was aware of the couple's intentions with respect to the two ceremonies. It was agreed that he would omit the usual words required by law to effect a lawful marriage. So the

---

[42] See R. Probert, 'When Are We Married? Void, Non-Existent and Presumed Marriages' [2000] 22 Legal Studies 398.

[43] [2002] 1 FLR 603. See also *A-M (Divorce: Jurisdiction: Validity of Marriage)* [2001] 2 FLR 6.

[44] The law's classifications are arguably unsatisfactory. A father/daughter marriage is void, yet the ceremony in *Ghandi v Patel* is merely a non-marriage. See R. Probert, 'When Are We Married? Void, Non-Existent and Presumed Marriages' [2000] 22 Legal Studies 398.

[45] [2006] EWHC 642 (Fam), [2006] 2 FLR 265.   [46] [2009] EWHC 1306 (Fam).

minister did not ask if the parties knew of any lawful impediments to the marriage, made no reference to them as 'lawful husband or wife', and did not declare that they were 'lawfully married'. Bodey J found on the facts that the ceremony did not create the status of marriage as between the parties. Neither the parties at the time of the ceremony, nor the celebrant, intended or believed it to be legally binding. While Bodey J emphasised that the test for non-marriage is a flexible one, with questionable ceremonies being addressed on a case-by-case basis, he provided a non-exhaustive list of factors for consideration. First, whether the ceremony or event set out or purported to be a lawful marriage; secondly, whether it bore all or enough of the hallmarks of marriage; thirdly, whether the three key participants (most especially the officiating official) believed, intended, and understood the ceremony as giving rise to the status of lawful marriage; and finally the reasonable perceptions, understandings, and beliefs of those in attendance.[47]

These cases may be contrasted with *Gereis v Yagoub*.[48] In that case a couple went through a marriage ceremony at a Coptic Orthodox Church which was not licensed for marriage. The ceremony was conducted by a priest who was not licensed to conduct marriages, and who told the couple that they would also require a civil ceremony to effect a valid marriage. The court held that the ceremony bore all the hallmarks of an ordinary Christian marriage[49] and that the marriage had been treated as a subsisting marriage by all those who had attended. The court rejected the submission that there was no marriage at all, and granted a decree of nullity under section 11(a)(iii) of the MCA 1973, on the basis that the parties had knowingly and wilfully disregarded the formalities.[50] In light of the criteria set out in *Hudson v Leigh*, however, and especially the focus on the belief of the person officiating, it may be that a case like *Gereis v Yagoub* would now be decided differently.

2.3.2 The presumptions of marriage[51]

In some cases it may be necessary to rely on the common law presumptions of marriage in order to make a finding that there is a valid marriage. There are two presumptions of marriage. There is a presumption of marriage arising from cohabitation after a ceremony of marriage. In such cases everything necessary for the validity of the marriage is presumed in the absence of decisive evidence to the contrary. A second presumption arises merely from long cohabitation, where a couple have cohabited for such length of time and in such circumstances as to acquire the reputation of being married, even though there is no positive evidence of a ceremony. This presumption can be rebutted only by strong and weighty evidence. In *Chief Adjudication Officer v Bath*[52] the respondent, Kirpal Bath had gone through a marriage ceremony with Mr Bath at a Sikh Temple in 1956 when she was 16. The couple believed the marriage ceremony to be legally valid and were ignorant of the requirements of the Marriage Acts. They had two children and lived together for 37 years until Mr Bath's death. Mr Bath had paid National Insurance contributions as a married man. On his death, however, Mrs Bath was declined a state widow's pension on the ground that there was not a valid marriage ceremony, since there was no evidence that the Sikh temple was registered at the material time. However, there was also no positive evidence that it was not registered. In those circumstances the Court of Appeal held

---

[47] For a discussion of this case, see R. Gaffney-Rhys, '*Hudson v Leigh*—The Concept of Non-Marriage' (2010) Child and Family Law Quarterly 351.   [48] [1997] 1 FLR 854.

[49] See R. Probert, 'When Are We Married? Void, Non-Existent and Presumed Marriages' [2000] 22 Legal Studies 398 for criticism of this arguably unjustifiable emphasis on the Christian nature of the ceremony.

[50] See also *B v B* [2007] EWHC 2492 (Fam), [2008] 1 FLR 813.

[51] See A. Borkowsi, 'The Presumption of Marriage' [2002] Child and Family Law Quarterly 251.

[52] [2000] 1 FLR 8.

that the presumption of marriage from long cohabitation was not rebutted and Mrs Bath was entitled to her pension. Evans and Schiemann LJJ also held that since Mr and Mrs Bath had not knowingly and wilfully married in disregard of the formalities contrary to section 49 of the Marriage Act 1949, there was no provision in the Marriage Act which rendered the marriage void.[53]

2.4 A PARTY MUST NOT ALREADY BE MARRIED

Under section 11(b) of the MCA 1973 a marriage is void if at the time of the marriage either party was already lawfully married. As Lord Penzance said in 1866 in *Hyde v Hyde*,[54] marriage is 'the voluntary union for life of one man and one woman to the exclusion of all others'. A person who enters into a subsequent marriage without the previous marriage being terminated by annulment, divorce, or death, may commit the criminal offence of bigamy.[55] If a spouse has disappeared and is thought to be dead, the other spouse should therefore consider applying for a decree of presumption of death and dissolution of marriage which, if granted, prevents the second marriage being void or possibly bigamous even if the first spouse reappears.

2.5 THE PARTIES MUST BE RESPECTIVELY MALE AND FEMALE

The parties to a marriage must be respectively male and female otherwise the marriage is void under section 11(c) of the MCA 1973. Same-sex marriage, which is discussed later, is thus not permitted in English law. The main issues which arise under this subsection are whether a transsexual person can validly marry in his or her acquired gender,[56] and how the law treats intersexual persons.[57]

2.5.1 Transsexual persons and marriage

The starting point for discussion of the law relating to transsexual persons and marriage is the case of *Corbett v Corbett (Otherwise Ashley)*.[58] April Ashley, a male-to-female transsexual person, had gone through a ceremony of marriage with Arthur Corbett, who at the time was fully aware of Ashley's background. Subsequently, however, Corbett sought a decree of nullity on the basis that Ashley was male. Ormrod J heard medical evidence which accepted at least four criteria for determining a person's sex, namely: (i) chromosomal factors; (ii) gonadal factors (ie, presence or absence of testes or ovaries); (iii) genital factors (including internal sex organs); and (iv) psychological factors. The witnesses were clear, however, that 'the biological sexual constitution of an individual is fixed at birth

---

[53] See also *Pazpena de Vire v Pazpena de Vire* [2001] 1 FLR 460 (marriage by proxy in Uruguay with neither party present at the ceremony was held to be valid by applying the presumption of long cohabitation, as the parties had lived in England for 35 years as husband and wife); and *A-M v A-M (Divorce: Jurisdiction: Validity of Marriage)* [2001] 2 FLR 6.   [54] (1866) LR 1 P & D 130.

[55] Offences Against the Person Act 1861, s 57. See C. Barton, 'Bigamy and Marriage—Horse and Carriage?' [2004] Family Law 517.

[56] Transsexualism is a medically recognised gender identity disorder, gender dysphoria, whereby a person who appears to be biologically of a particular sex believes or feels that he or she is psychologically a member of the opposite sex. Some persons with gender dysphoria opt to have a gender reassignment, which involves hormone treatment and in some cases surgery. Gender reassignment is available on the National Health Service.   [57] Persons whose gender is ambiguous at birth.

[58] [1971] P 83, [1970] 2 WLR 1306. For a detailed discussion of this case and its impact, see S. Gilmore, '*Corbett v Corbett*: Once a Man, Always a Man?' in S. Gilmore, J. Herring, and R. Probert, *Landmark Cases in Family Law* (Oxford: Hart, 2011).

(at the latest)'. Having regard to this evidence and the essentially heterosexual nature of marriage, Ormrod J concluded that the law 'should adopt in the first place, the first three of the doctors' criteria, i.e. the chromosomal, gonadal and genital tests, and if all three are congruent, determine the sex for the purpose of marriage accordingly, and ignore any operative intervention.'[59]

Accordingly, even though Ashley had undergone gender reassignment surgery and hormone treatment and lived as a woman, 'she' was male, and 'her' marriage to the petitioner was void.

The biological test propounded in *Corbett* made it impossible for transsexual persons to have their acquired gender legally recognised and to enter into a valid marriage in that gender. In a series of cases, transsexual persons took their cases to the ECtHR arguing that UK laws breached their human rights.[60] It was argued that the UK Government was in breach of Article 8 (the right to respect for family life) and Article 12 (the right to marry) of the ECHR taken in conjunction with Article 14 (the right not be discriminated against in respect of a Convention right). At first the claims failed, the ECtHR affording the UK a wide margin of appreciation on these issues. However, the Court had stressed the need for the law to be kept under review by contracting states and by the European Court itself, having regard to scientific and societal developments. In *Sheffield and Horsham v UK*[61] the Court stressed the importance of the increasing social acceptance of transsexualism and the growing recognition of the problems which post-operative transsexuals encountered.

Key case

Eventually, taking account of these factors, in *Goodwin v UK*[62] (heard with *I v UK*[63]), the ECtHR changed its approach. In *Goodwin*, the applicant, a male-to-female transsexual, claimed that the UK had violated her rights under Articles 8 and 12 of the ECHR because UK law was failing to recognise the legal status of transsexual persons in respect of a wide range of matters, such as employment, social security, the state pension, car insurance, and marriage. The UK's defence was that it enjoyed a margin of appreciation in respect of legislating on such matters. However, the European Court refused to accept this argument and unanimously held that both Articles 8 and 12 had been breached.

With regard to Article 8, the ECtHR held that the unsatisfactory situation whereby post-operative transsexuals lived in an intermediate zone where they were not quite one gender or another was no longer sustainable. The UK could no longer claim it enjoyed a margin of appreciation in such matters. As there were no significant factors of public interest which weighed against the interest of the applicant in obtaining legal recognition of her reassignment, the Court held that the fair balance inherent in the European Convention tilted in her favour. It held that a 'serious interference with private life can arise where domestic law conflicts with an important aspect of personal identity, and that the stress and alienation'[64] suffered by a post-operative transsexual could not be considered as a minor inconvenience arising from a formality. The Court also recognised that

---

[59] [1971] P 83 at 106.

[60] *Rees v UK* (1986) 9 EHRR 56, [1987] 2 FLR 111; *Cossey v UK* [1991] 2 FLR 492; *Sheffield and Horsham v UK* [1998] 2 FLR 928.   [61] [1998] 2 FLR 928.

[62] (2002) 35 EHRR 18, [2002] 2 FLR 487. *Goodwin* was used in argument in *Wilkinson v Kitzinger* [2006] EWHC 2022 (Fam), [2007] 1 FLR 295, see p XXX (Section 8).   [63] [2002] 2 FLR 518.

[64] (2002) 35 EHRR 18, [2002] 2 FLR 487 at [77].

developments in medical science necessitated a change of approach, and that it was not apparent that chromosomal tests alone should necessarily be decisive for the purposes of attributing gender identity.

With regard to Article 12, the ECtHR held that the term 'man and woman' in relation to the right to marry could no longer be assumed to refer to a test of gender based on purely biological criteria, as had been laid down in *Corbett v Corbett*.[65] It held that such a test was no longer appropriate to the current understanding of transsexualism and could no longer be decisive in denying legal recognition to the change of gender of a post-operative transsexual. Another factor which influenced the Court to find in favour of the applicants was that the condition of gender identity disorder was recognised by the medical profession and treatment, including surgery, was available on the National Health Service. It held that, as the applicant had no possibility of marrying a man even though she lived as a woman and was in a relationship with a man and would only wish to marry a man, the very essence of her right to marry had been infringed and there was no justification for barring her from enjoying that right in the circumstances.[66] The reasoning in *Goodwin* was adopted by the ECtHR in *I v UK*,[67] heard with *Goodwin*, where the applicant, a male-to-female transsexual, had not been admitted to a nursing course because she had failed to show her birth certificate which stated she was male. The ECtHR found in her favour.

Key case

Around the same time as the *Goodwin* decision, a case involving a transsexual person and the right to marry was progressing through the domestic courts, reaching the House of Lords in 2003. In *Bellinger v Bellinger (Lord Chancellor Intervening)*,[68] the House of Lords had to consider the legal position of transsexuals in light of its obligations under the Human Rights Act (HRA) 1998. The *Bellinger* case was different from the transsexual cases cited earlier in that it involved an application by a transsexual person, Mrs Bellinger, for a declaration under section 55 of the Family Law Act 1986 that her 1981 marriage was a valid and subsisting marriage, even though she was a male-to-female transsexual and had married a man. The High Court and the Court of Appeal by a majority (Thorpe LJ dissenting) refused to grant the declaration as, applying the biological test of gender laid down in *Corbett*, they had not entered into a valid marriage, as section 11(c) of the MCA 1973 required the parties to be respectively male and female.

Mrs Bellinger appealed to the House of Lords arguing that the Court of Appeal's decision was incompatible with the ECHR and was therefore unlawful under section 7 of the HRA 1998. As section 2(1) of the HRA 1998 requires courts in the UK to take account of the judgments of the ECtHR when determining any question arising in connection with a Convention right, the House of Lords had to take into account the decision in *Goodwin v UK*

---

[65] That a person's biological sex is fixed at birth and could only be established by chromosomal, gonadal, and genital criteria, see earlier.

[66] In *Goodwin*, the European Court was referred to the case of *Re Kevin: Validity of Marriage of Transsexual* [2001] Fam CA 1074 where Chisholm J in the Family Court of Australia had strongly criticised the reasoning in *Corbett* and had upheld the validity of a marriage between a woman and a female-to-male transsexual on the basis that sex was to be determined at the date of marriage having regard not just to biological factors but to all other relevant factors, such as life experiences and self-perception. [67] [2002] 2 FLR 518.

[68] [2003] UKHL 21, [2003] 1 FLR 1043. See S. Gilmore, '*Bellinger v Bellinger*—Not Quite Between the Ears and Between the Legs—Transsexualism and Marriage in the Lords' (2003) 15(3) Child and Family Law Quarterly 295; C. Bessant, 'Transsexuals and Marriage after *Goodwin v United Kingdom*' [2003] Family Law 111; A. Bradney, 'Developing Human Rights? The Lords and Transsexual Marriages' [2003] Family Law 585.

(and *I v UK*), which had been decided after the decision of the Court of Appeal in *Bellinger* but before the case was heard by the House of Lords. As the courts are required by section 3(1) of the HRA 1998 to read and give effect to primary legislation in a way which is compatible with the ECHR, the House of Lords was obliged to consider whether section 11(c) of the MCA 1973, which requires the parties to a marriage to be male and female, was incompatible with the European Convention. However, despite the provisions of the HRA 1998 and the decisions of the European Court in *Goodwin* and *I v UK*, the House of Lords dismissed Mrs Bellinger's appeal on the ground that such an important change in the law was better left to Parliament not the courts, particularly as the UK Government had already said it would introduce legislation to change the law. The House of Lords, however, made a declaration of incompatibility under section 4 of the HRA 1998 that section 11(c) of the MCA 1973 was incompatible with Articles 8 and 12 of the ECHR.

2.5.2 The Gender Recognition Act 2004

After the decisions of the ECtHR in *Goodwin v UK* and *I v UK*,[69] and *Bellinger v Bellinger (Lord Chancellor Intervening)*,[70] the UK was forced to comply with its Convention obligations and change the law to give transsexuals new rights. The UK Government announced that it would introduce new laws which would include not only changes in respect of birth certificates, inheritance provision, and pension rights, but also give transsexuals the right to enter into a valid marriage or civil partnership in their acquired sex. These changes were enacted in the Gender Recognition Act 2004, which came into force on 4 April 2005, and which gives legal recognition to transsexuals who have shown that they have taken decisive steps towards living fully and permanently in their acquired gender.

Under the Gender Recognition Act, a transsexual person aged 18 who has lived in the other gender or who has changed gender under the law or a country or territory outside the UK can apply for a gender recognition certificate from the Gender Recognition Panel,[71] which it must grant if it is satisfied that: the applicant has or has had gender dysphoria; has lived in the acquired gender for two years ending on the date on which the application is made; intends to continue to live in the acquired gender until death; and complies with certain evidential requirements laid down in section 3 of the Act.[72] There is no requirement that the applicant must have had gender reassignment surgery or have been sterilised. The effect of a full gender recognition certificate[73] is that the applicant's gender 'becomes for all purposes the acquired gender'.[74] Thus, the practical effect of a gender recognition certificate is to provide a transsexual person with legal recognition in the acquired gender, so that he or she is entitled to various rights which include a new birth certificate reflecting the acquired gender and the right to enter into a valid marriage or civil partnership in the acquired gender.[75] In the absence of a gender recognition certificate, however, the common law in *Corbett* still applies; indeed it was apparently endorsed by the House of Lords in *Bellinger*.

---

[69] See earlier in this section.   [70] [2003] UKHL 21, [2003] 1 FLR 1043.
[71] Section 1(1). The Panel is comprised of lawyers and medical practitioners.   [72] Section 2(1).
[73] If the applicant is a spouse or civil partner, only an interim gender recognition certificate can be issued (s 4), but, if the marriage or civil partnership is terminated by divorce or dissolution within six months of the issue of the interim certificate, the applicant can seek a full gender recognition certificate (s 5).
[74] Section 9(1).
[75] With regard to parenthood, however, the grant of a gender recognition certificate does not affect the applicant's parental status as a father or mother, so that it is not thereby possible to remove parental rights and responsibilities: see s 12, and S. Gilmore, 'The Gender Recognition Act 2004' [2004] Family Law 741.

2.5.3 Intersexuals and marriage

The law treats transsexual and intersexual persons differently. In the latter case the biological indicia of sex are not congruent at birth and in *W v W (Physical Inter-Sex)*[76] Charles J distinguished *Corbett* on that basis. In *W v W* the respondent to an application for a decree of nullity had been diagnosed with a physical intersex condition. At birth her chromosomal sex was male, but the external genital appearance was ambiguous. She had no internal sex organs or genitalia of a woman and no vaginal opening, although she subsequently had gender reassignment surgery. Her body now looked more female than male, and she chose to live as a woman. Charles J concluded that the decision whether the respondent was male or female was to be ascertained at the time of the marriage, having regard to her development and all of the indicia of sex listed in *Corbett* (ie, the biological factors, psychological factors, hormonal factors, and secondary sexual characteristics, such as distribution of hair, breast development, physique etc).[77] Applying those criteria, the respondent was female and the decree was refused.

3 VOIDABLE MARRIAGES

A voidable marriage is a valid and subsisting marriage unless and until a decree of nullity is granted. Unlike a void marriage, a voidable marriage can only be annulled during the lifetime of both parties and only the parties to the marriage can petition for a decree. However, like a void marriage, on a decree being granted the court has jurisdiction under Part II of the MCA 1973 to make finance and property orders equivalent to those which can be made on divorce.[78]

The grounds upon which a marriage may be declared voidable are laid down in section 12 of the MCA 1973, which provides that:

Key legislation

A marriage celebrated after 31st July 1971 shall be voidable on the following grounds only, that is to say—

(a) that the marriage has not been consummated owing to the incapacity of either party to consummate it;

(b) that the marriage has not been consummated owing to the wilful refusal of the respondent to consummate it;

(c) that either party to the marriage did not validly consent to it, whether in consequence of duress, mistake, unsoundness of mind or otherwise;

(d) that at the time of the marriage either party, though capable of giving a valid consent, was suffering (whether continuously or intermittently) from mental disorder within the meaning of the Mental Health Act 1983 of such a kind or to such an extent as to be unfitted for marriage;

(e) that at the time of the marriage the respondent was suffering from venereal disease in a communicable form;

---

[76] [2001] Fam 111, FD, *per* Charles J. See A. Barlow, '*W v W (Nullity: Gender) and B v B (Validity of Marriage: Transsexual)*—A New Approach to Transsexualism and a Missed Opportunity?' [2001] Child and Family Law Quarterly 225 and also P.-L. Chau and J. Herring, 'Defining, Assigning and Designing Sex' (2002) 16 International Journal of Law, Policy and the Family 327 and J. Herring and P.-L. Chau, 'Assigning Sex and Intersexuals' [2001] Family Law 762.   [77] Ibid, 146.   [78] See Chapter 4.

(f) that at the time of the marriage the respondent was pregnant by some person other than the petitioner;

(g) that an interim gender recognition certificate under the Gender Recognition Act 2004 has, after the time of the marriage, been issued to either party to the marriage;

(h) that the respondent is a person whose gender at the time of the marriage had become the acquired gender under the Gender Recognition Act 2004.[79]

Each of these grounds is now considered in turn.

3.1 NON-CONSUMMATION

A marriage is voidable under section 12(a) of the MCA 1973 if there is non-consummation owing to the incapacity of either party to the marriage; or under section 12(b) if non-consummation is due to wilful refusal on the part of the respondent. Sexual intercourse for the purposes of consummation must be 'ordinary and complete, and not partial and imperfect'.[80] Incapacity to consummate, unlike wilful refusal to consummate, can be brought by either party to the marriage and can therefore be based on either the petitioner's or respondent's incapacity. The incapacity must be permanent and incurable. It is unclear whether a transsexual person can consummate a marriage. In *Corbett v Corbett*[81] Ormrod J stated *obiter* that a male-to-female transsexual person with an artificially constructed vagina was incapable of consummating. However, the courts may not take the same view now that the Gender Recognition Act 2004 permits transsexual marriage. In *W v W (Physical Inter-Sex)*[82] Charles J distinguished *Corbett* in holding that an intersexual person who had had surgery was not necessarily incapable of consummating.

It has been held that incapacity to consummate can include not just physical incapacity, but also 'an invincible repugnance to the respondent due to a psychiatric or sexual aversion'.[83] With wilful refusal to consummate, 'a settled and definite decision not to consummate without just excuse' must be established.[84]

Incapacity to consummate and wilful refusal to consummate are closely linked even though the two grounds are conceptually quite different. A petitioner who wishes to plead that the marriage has not been consummated may be unsure which of the two grounds is the relevant one, and may decide to plead them in the alternative. The question of whether a marriage had not been consummated due to incapacity or wilful refusal sometimes arose in the earlier case law on forced marriage.[85] In some religions it is the practice to have a civil ceremony of marriage followed by a religious ceremony. Only after the religious ceremony are the parties deemed to be married in the eyes of their

---

[79]   Sections 12(g) and 12(h) were inserted by the Gender Recognition Act 2004.

[80]   *DE v AG* (1985) 1 Rob Eccl 279, *per* Dr Lushington. This should be contrasted with the law of rape, and adultery, where sexual intercourse occurs where the penis makes the slightest penetration of the vagina. Case law has established that a marriage is consummated where there is *coitus interruptus* (where the husband withdraws before ejaculation (*White v White* [1948] 2 All ER 151 and *Cackett v Cackett* [1950] 1 All ER 677); or where the husband is not capable of ejaculation (*R v R (Otherwise F)* [1952] 1 All ER 1194). The use of contraceptives does not prevent consummation occurring (*Baxter v Baxter* [1947] 2 All ER 886); and it is the fact of intercourse which is the sole issue, not whether it is qualitatively satisfactory (*S v S (Otherwise W) (No 2)* [1962] 3 All ER 55).   [81]   [1971] P 83.

[82]   [2001] Fam 111, FD, *per* Charles J.

[83]   See *Singh v Singh* [1971] 2 WLR 963 (see further at n 90), but where the Court of Appeal held that the evidence was not sufficient to prove an invincible repugnance.

[84]   *Horton v Horton* [1947] 2 All ER 871, *per* Lord Jowitt LC.   [85]   See further at p 33 (Section 5).

religion whereupon consumption can take place. In some of these cases there was held to be wilful refusal to consummate if a party refused to go through with the religious ceremony,[86] refused to make arrangements for the religious ceremony when it was his duty to do so,[87] or postponed the religious ceremony indefinitely.[88] Such behaviour has been held to be wilful refusal because the defaulting party knew that, by failing to satisfy the religious requirements, he or she was in effect refusing to have sexual intercourse.[89] However, a woman who has been forced into marriage and who refuses to consummate the marriage cannot petition on the basis of her own wilful refusal to consummate, but must instead prove incapacity to consummate, which can include not just a physical incapacity but 'an invincible repugnance to the respondent due to a psychiatric or sexual aversion'.[90]

3.2 LACK OF CONSENT TO THE MARRIAGE

Consent is regarded as an essential component of marriage. As Lord Penzance said in *Hyde v Hyde*[91] marriage involves a '*voluntary* union' between a man and a woman. Under section 12(c) of the MCA 1973 a marriage is voidable if 'either party to the marriage did not validly consent to it, whether in consequence of duress, mistake, unsoundness of mind or otherwise'. Most of the reported case law has concerned duress, mistake, and lack of capacity to marry.

3.2.1 Duress

With regard to duress, the question is what degree of duress suffices to vitiate consent. At one time the test for establishing duress was much more stringent. In *Szechter v Szechter*[92] Simon P said that the test was whether the will of one of the parties had been 'overborne by a genuine and reasonably held fear caused by threat of immediate danger (for which the party is not himself responsible), to life, limb or liberty.'[93] This test was approved and adopted by the Court of Appeal in *Singh v Singh*[94] in refusing the claim of a 17-year-old Sikh woman that she had been forced by her parents into an arranged marriage to a man whom she had never met and who was neither handsome nor intelligent as she had been told. The *Szechter* test made it particularly difficult for victims of forced marriages to obtain a decree on this ground.[95] However, in *Hirani v Hirani*[96] a different and less stringent test for establishing duress was adopted.

---

[86] *Jodla v Jodla* [1960] 1 WLR 236.   [87] *Kaur v Singh* [1972] 1 WLR 105.

[88] *A v J (Nullity Proceedings)* [1989] 1 FLR 110.

[89] In *Kaur v Singh* [1992] 1 WLR 105 the husband's refusal to arrange the Sikh wedding ceremony after the civil ceremony was held to constitute wilful refusal to consummate the marriage and his wife was successful in obtaining a nullity decree.

[90] In *Singh v Singh* [1971] 2 WLR 963 the wife petitioned on the ground of her husband's incapacity to consummate due to her invincible repugnance to him (she had never met him until the civil ceremony and went back to live with her parents and refused to take part in a Sikh religious ceremony). Her petition was dismissed, as her refusal to go through with the religious ceremony was held to be a very long way away from having an invincible repugnance to sexual intercourse. See *D v D* (1982) 12 Fam Law 150.

[91] (1886) LR 1 P & D 130 at 133.

[92] [1970] 3 All ER 905. See also *Buckland v Buckland* [1968] P 296.

[93] Ibid, 915.   [94] [1971] 2 All ER 828.

[95] In *Singh v Kaur* (1981) 11 Fam Law 152 a young man petitioned for a decree on the basis that the pressure put upon him by his parents was so great that his consent had no validity. The Court of Appeal dismissed his case holding that it did not wish to see the *Szechter* test watered down.

[96] (1983) 4 FLR 232.

Key case

In *Hirani v Hirani* the petitioner, a woman aged 19, formed an association with an Indian Muslim. Her parents, who were Hindus, were horrified at this relationship and quickly arranged for her to marry a Hindu man, Mr Hirani, whom she had never met. Reluctantly, and crying throughout, she went through a ceremony of marriage with Mr Hirani. After the marriage, the wife petitioned for nullity on the ground of lack of consent owing to duress. She claimed that she was wholly dependent on her parents and that they had threatened to throw her out of the house if she did not go through with the marriage. The Court of Appeal held that a threat to life, limb, or liberty, as required in *Szechter*, was no longer required. Instead, the crucial question was whether the threats, pressure, or other acts were sufficient 'to destroy the reality of consent and overbear the will of the individual'.[97] This test is a subjective test, considering whether the particular petitioner's will has been overborne, not whether a reasonable person would find there to be lack of consent due to duress. As the Court of Appeal found that the petitioner's will had been clearly overborne by parental pressure, it held that she had not consented to the marriage and was therefore entitled to have the marriage annulled.

In *NS v MI*[98] Munby J drew attention to the different approaches in the cases and preferred the *Hirani* approach, declaring that the *Szechter* approach no longer represents the law, if it ever did. The preferred approach in practice is certainly the subjective approach in *Hirani*.[99] However, the conflict as a matter of doctrine at Court of Appeal level[100] has not been resolved, since the Court of Appeal decision in *Singh v Singh* (which adopted the objective test) was not cited in *Hirani*. In *NS v MI* the petitioner had been taken to Pakistan by her parents when she was 16, supposedly for a two-month holiday. She was stranded in a remote region of Pakistan for over a year, because her mother held her passport, and eventually it emerged that arrangements had been made for her to marry a cousin there. She went through the ceremony under great family pressure to go ahead with the marriage. Upon her return to England she sought a decree of nullity on the ground of lack of consent. Applying a subjective approach Munby J granting the decree, commenting:

> where the influence is that of a parent or other close and dominating relative, and where the arguments and persuasion are based upon personal affection or duty, religious beliefs, powerful social or cultural conventions, or asserted social, familial or domestic obligations, the influence may…be subtle, insidious, pervasive and powerful. In such cases, moreover, very little pressure may suffice to bring about the desired result.[101]

The 'overborne will' test for duress has made it easier for victims of forced marriage to succeed in obtaining a decree of nullity based on lack of consent. Forced marriages are condemned by the courts and by the Government, and various provisions in addition to nullity exist to protect victims.[102]

3.2.2 Mistake

Consent to marriage may be vitiated where there is mistake, and this may entitle either party to the marriage to a decree of nullity. Mistake can relate either to the identity of

---

[97] Ibid, *per* Ormrod LJ at 234.   [98] [2007] 1 FLR 444.
[99] See eg *P v R (Forced Marriage: Annulment: Procedure)* [2003] 1 FLR 661, *per* Coleridge J.
[100] See A. Bradney, 'Duress, Family Law and Coherent Legal System' [1994] Modern Law Review 963.
[101] [2007] 1 FLR 444 at [34].   [102] See Section 2.5.2.

the other person or to the nature of the ceremony. However, with respect to identity, a mistake as to a party's attributes or characteristics does not constitute a mistake and will not invalidate a marriage. Mistake as to the nature of the ceremony could include, for example, a situation where a party mistakenly believes that he or she is taking part in an engagement ceremony, not a marriage ceremony.[103]

3.3 MENTAL DISORDER RENDERING A PERSON UNFITTED FOR MARRIAGE

Under section 12(d) of the MCA 1973 a marriage is voidable on the ground that 'either party, though capable of giving a valid consent, was suffering (whether continuously or intermittently) from mental disorder within the meaning of the Mental Health Act 1983 of such a kind or to such an extent as to be unfitted for marriage.' This ground differs from unsoundness of mind for the purposes of consent discussed earlier, in that a party is capable of giving a valid consent, but the state of his or her mental health is such that it would be appropriate to annul the marriage. A petitioner may rely on his or her own mental disorder for the purpose of petitioning for a decree of nullity on this ground.

3.4 VENEREAL DISEASE

Under section 12(e) a marriage is voidable where the respondent was suffering from venereal disease in a communicable form at the time of the marriage. The basis of this ground clearly ties in with the non-consummation grounds, as it is looked upon as an impediment to sexual intercourse.

3.5 PREGNANCY BY ANOTHER MAN

Section 12(f) provides a husband with a ground for nullity if he can prove that at the time of the marriage his wife was pregnant by some person other than himself. Thus, if at the time of the marriage the wife conceals from her husband the fact that she is pregnant by another man, he can subsequently seek an annulment. The petition must be presented within three years of the marriage,[104] so that if a wife keeps the child's true paternity secret for more than three years, then the marriage cannot be annulled on this ground.

3.6 GENDER RECOGNITION AS A GROUND FOR NULLITY

Two new grounds for establishing a voidable marriage were introduced into section 12 of the MCA 1973 by the Gender Recognition Act 2004 which was passed to give transsexual persons new rights, including the right to enter into a valid marriage in their acquired gender on the issue of a full gender recognition certificate granted by a Gender Recognition Panel.[105] If a person who applies to a Gender Recognition Panel meets the statutory criteria and is unmarried, the Panel will issue a full gender recognition certificate which will entitle this person to a new birth certificate reflecting their acquired gender, thus allowing marriage in this new gender. However, if a married applicant applies to the Gender Recognition Panel for recognition of his or her 'acquired' gender, the Panel,

---

[103] See eg *Mehta v Mehta* [1945] 2 All ER 690 where the wife mistakenly thought that the marriage ceremony was one of conversion to the Hindu religion, and who was granted a decree of nullity on this basis.

[104] MCA 1973, s 13(2).

[105] See Section 2.5.2.

on the satisfaction of the criteria, will only issue an interim gender recognition certificate (due to the existing marriage). This becomes a ground for annulment of the existing marriage as under section 12(g) of the MCA 1973 a marriage is voidable if an interim gender recognition certificate has, after the time of the marriage, been issued to either party to the marriage.[106] Under section 12(h) a marriage is voidable if the respondent is a person whose gender at the time of the marriage had become the acquired gender under the Gender Recognition Act 2004. In other words, a marriage is voidable if at the time of the marriage one party to the marriage did not know that the other was previously of another gender and had obtained a gender recognition certificate.

3.7 BARS TO RELIEF

There are certain statutory prohibitions (bars) to relief in respect of voidable marriages. Thus, under section 13 of the MCA 1973 there are time limits for certain nullity petitions, and for all petitions there is a general bar based on the approbation of the petitioner.

A nullity petition must be instituted within three years of the date of the marriage unless the petitioner is relying on incapacity or wilful refusal to consummate the marriage.[107] Where the ground relied on is venereal disease or pregnancy by another man, the petitioner must be ignorant of those facts at the date of the marriage.[108] Where a decree is sought on the basis of the issue of an interim gender recognition certificate,[109] the proceedings must be instituted within six months of the interim gender recognition certificate being issued.[110]

A general bar based on approbation by the petitioner applies to all nullity petitions brought on the basis that a marriage is voidable.[111] Thus, the court must not grant a decree if the respondent proves that the petitioner knew that it was open to him or her to have the marriage annulled but led the respondent reasonably to believe that he would not seek to do so; *and* that it would be unjust to the respondent to grant the decree. It will be very difficult to satisfy this test, as the facts of *D v D (Nullity: Statutory Bar)*[112] illustrate. The wife had a physical impediment, preventing consummation, which could have been cured by a comparatively common operation but the wife refused and the marriage was never consummated. Although the husband knew he could have the marriage annulled, the couple fostered then adopted two children at the request of the Church of England Children's Society. The husband subsequently sought a decree of nullity. Dunn J found that the first limb of section 13(1) was fulfilled but it could not be shown that there would be any injustice to the wife. She would have access to the same orders for financial provision as on divorce.

3.8 SHOULD THE CONCEPT OF THE VOIDABLE
MARRIAGE BE ABOLISHED?

There are arguments in favour of abolishing the concept of the voidable marriage, something which has been done in Australia.[113] One argument is that there are so few nullity

---

[106] Where a person obtains a decree absolute of nullity on this ground, the court must issue that person with a full gender recognition certificate. In a recent Consultation Paper, the Government has proposed to allow transsexual people to change their gender without having to legally end their existing marriage: Government Equalities Office, *Equal Civil Marriage: A Consultation*, 15 March 2012.

[107] See s 13(2). This is subject to the proviso that the period may be extended where the petitioner has suffered from a mental disorder during the three years, and it is just to do so (s 13(4)). For a case involving the non-availability of a nullity petition after three years (on the ground of lack of consent), see *SH v NB* [2009] EWHC 3274 (Fam).   [108] Section 13(3).

[109] Under s 12(g).   [110] Section 13(2A).   [111] Section 13(1).   [112] [1979] Fam 70.

[113] By the Family Law Act 1975, s 51.

petitions today that it would cause no great hardship if the voidable grounds were abolished. In 2009, only 290 nullity petitions were filed in the courts in England and Wales, with 199 decrees absolute of nullity being granted, whereas 116,576 decrees absolute of divorce were granted in that year.[114] The reasons why there are so few nullity petitions is partly because the facts upon which a nullity petition can be based do not often arise, and partly because of the ease with which it is now possible to obtain a divorce. Also, divorce no longer carries the stigma that it once did.[115]

Another argument is that some of the grounds seem rather archaic and with little or no relevance today. Thus, for instance, should non-consummation be abolished as a ground for nullity on the basis that it is an archaic relic of medieval ecclesiastical law? In the view of the Church, marriage is important for begetting children, and hence there is a need to consummate the marriage. However, some couples may choose to marry for companionship and may not consider consummation to be particularly important, whether or not they are capable of it. Probert[116] has argued that it might be better if non-consummation were abolished in order to 'define marriage in a way that is relevant for the twenty-first century'[117] since it is arguably too intrusive and embarrassing for the law to examine parties' sexual lives in this way. Furthermore, doing away with the grounds based on non-consummation would remove the possibility that transsexual marriages are always voidable for lack of capacity. If non-consummation were abolished as a ground for nullity, a person who wished to terminate the marriage could still do so by petitioning for a divorce on the ground of unreasonable behaviour[118] due to the respondent's failure to consummate the marriage. The only disadvantage of this would be that a petitioner would have to wait for one year after the marriage to do so as there is a statutory prohibition on divorce in the first year of marriage. A decree of judicial separation, on the other hand, is available at any time after the marriage.

Some of the other grounds for rendering a marriage voidable are also open to criticism, and might justifiably be abolished. Thus mental disorder as a ground for nullity under section 12(d) seems somewhat outmoded and offensive, as it stems from the days when mental illness was misunderstood and those suffering from such illness were regarded with fear and suspicion. It is also difficult to understand why mental illness should be singled out as a ground for nullity when an adult who is prone to violence or paedophilia, for example, may also be equally unfit for marriage. The venereal disease ground in section 12(e) is also out of touch with developments in medical science and is also somewhat limited. It is difficult to know what to make of this ground today as, when it was first introduced in 1937, antibiotics were not available. Medical practitioners today no longer talk about 'venereal diseases' but about 'sexually transmitted diseases'.

The pregnancy by another man ground for nullity under section 12(f) is also questionable. The Law Commission's original explanation for this ground was that a husband who marries in these circumstances has given conditional consent only to the marriage. The ground therefore appears to rest on one of two bases. Either the husband has married a woman knowing her to be pregnant and believing that he is the father of the child, in which case he might then argue that, but for the pregnancy, he would not have married her. Alternatively, he might argue that he was marrying a woman who was chaste, but the lack of chastity has self-evidently been demonstrated. Whichever of these two bases

---

[114] *Judicial and Court Statistics 2009* (Ministry of Justice, 2010), Ch 2, Table 2.5.

[115] The Law Commission's claim in its 1970 *Report on Nullity of Marriage* (Law Com No 33), about the stigma associated with divorce, but not with nullity, is no longer true today.

[116] R. Probert, 'How Would *Corbett v Corbett* Be Decided Today?' [2004] Family Law 382.

[117] It should also be noted that consummation has no relevance to the annulment of a civil partnership.

[118] Under the MCA 1973, s 1(2)(b), see Chapter 2.

applies, it is suggested that such thinking has no place in the law today. In 1937, when the ground was first introduced, men might well be forced to marry if they were believed to be responsible for the pregnancy of a woman. This would not normally be the case nowadays; but if it was, the ground of duress might apply. The chastity basis is not relevant or sensible in today's society. There are other forms of behaviour by a spouse which could just as easily be said to strike at the fundamental root of a marriage, in the sense that a spouse is giving conditional consent to the marriage. For example, the woman who marries a man not knowing that he is a convicted rapist, or paedophile, could claim her consent to the marriage should be characterised as conditional. However, her escape route is to use the law of divorce. It is suggested that, similarly, divorce is a more appropriate response in the case of pregnancy by another man.

Nevertheless, the fact that the woman is pregnant by another man undoubtedly strikes at the heart of the marriage. A man is unquestionably entitled to say that he certainly would not have married his wife had he known she was carrying another man's child. But is not a woman equally entitled to state that she would not have married her husband if, at the time of the marriage, she had known that another woman was pregnant by him? It is suggested that the law should treat spouses in an equal manner in this regard.

If voidable marriages were abolished, the parties to a marriage would instead have to seek a divorce. The question which therefore arises is whether divorce can provide an adequate alternative to nullity in the case of voidable marriages. In its 1970 *Report on Nullity of Marriage*[119] the Law Commission referred to the stigma associated with divorce. Today, however, there is little stigma attached to divorce, and it could be argued that greater stigma may attach to the grounds for nullity. Thus, there may be a stigma attached to a finding that a person has wilfully refused to consummate the marriage or a woman has deceived a man into marrying by concealing the true paternity of the baby. For these reasons, the Law Commission's arguments about stigma are no longer so valid. As regards the Law Commission's comments in its Report about the Christian Church's distinction between nullity and divorce, it can be argued that this distinction is no longer so valid now that society is more secular and multicultural. It could be argued that it is inappropriate for the Christian Church to have such a large influence on the law relating to marriage when only a minority of the population attend organised Christian worship and when many people today are either of a religious persuasion which is not Christian, or have no religion at all.

The Law Commission's argument in its *Report on Nullity of Marriage* in favour of retaining the concept of voidable marriage, because there was no advantage to be achieved in abolishing it, is perhaps the strongest argument for retaining the concept. Thus, if the concept of voidable marriage is useful for a few parties to a marriage, then why do away with it? Although the number of nullity decrees compared with decrees of divorce is small, they do show that nullity is still useful for some people. One of the main advantages of nullity is that a petition can be brought straightaway after a marriage whereas with divorce there is an absolute bar on bringing a petition in the first year of marriage. Also, there may be a small number of persons who choose to have their marriage annulled for religious reasons, perhaps because they may wish to marry in the future and be able to marry in a church or other religious building. Some religions will not allow a divorced person to marry in church, but other religions are now less strict about this. Thus, while the Church of England teaches that marriage is for life, it recognises that marriages do break down and since 2002 has permitted divorced persons to marry in church provided the local parish priest agrees to this. Other churches are more lenient about remarriage

---

[119] Law Com No 33, see n 115.

after divorce, but the Catholic Church's views on this matter is much stronger and it does not tolerate divorce. Another important reason in favour of retaining the concept of a voidable marriage is that it allows victims of forced marriages to have their marriage annulled, for instance on the ground that there was no consent as a result of duress. However, if consent is regarded as a fundamental flaw existing at the inception of a marriage, which the formalities for marriage show it to be, then lack of consent should be a ground for rendering a marriage *void*, not voidable. This would give victims of forced marriages the option of nullity, instead of having to rely on divorce. It would also send out a strong message that consent is a requirement going to the root of a marriage in England and Wales and that lack of consent will not be tolerated.

4 SHAM MARRIAGES

A 'sham' marriage, or what is sometimes called a 'marriage of convenience', is a marriage which is entered into for an ulterior motive, such as to gain British citizenship and/or to enter the UK. With respect to immigration, the immigration authorities are keen to ensure that these sorts of marriages do not take place as they allow the parties to circumvent the immigration rules. For this reason the immigration rules attempt to prevent such marriages taking place. However, although this is a legitimate role for immigration law, it was held by the House of Lords in *R (Baiai and Others) v Secretary of State for the Home Department*[120] that the powers of the immigration authorities must not interfere with the right to marry in Article 12 of the ECHR. Thus, the immigration authorities must exercise their powers in a proportionate and non-discriminatory way.

5 FORCED MARRIAGES

A forced marriage is a marriage which is entered into without the true consent of one or both of the parties and where some degree of duress is involved, which may include, for example, physical, psychological, financial, sexual, and emotional pressure, and even violence. A forced marriage is different from an 'arranged marriage', which is one where the families of both parties take a leading role in choosing a marriage partner but where consent to the arrangement remains with the parties themselves. The courts are not opposed to arranged marriages but are strongly opposed to forced marriages. In *NS v MI*[121] Munby J said that while forced marriages were utterly unacceptable, arranged marriages were to be respected and supported. Forced marriages are common in some religious and ethnic groups and are sometimes used for immigration purposes, such as to enable a foreign relative to gain entry into the UK. Forced marriage victims can suffer traumatic and distressing experiences, which may include physical and emotional threats, violence, blackmail, abduction, and imprisonment in the home.

In recent years there has been increasing recognition of the problem of forced marriages and the need to prevent them happening and to protect victims. A special unit, the Forced Marriage Unit (FMU) based in the Foreign & Commonwealth Office,[122] was established in 2005 as a joint initiative with the Home Office. It is responsible for

---

[120] [2008] UKHL 53, [2008] 2 FLR 1462.   [121] [2006] EWHC 1646 (Fam), [2007] 1 FLR 444.

[122] See the Foreign & Commonwealth Office website: www.fco.gov.uk. The Unit, together with relevant government departments and agencies, has published practice guidelines for police officers, health professionals, social workers, and education professionals on how to deal with forced marriage cases.

developing Government policy on forced marriages and for providing support, information, and advice for actual and potential victims and for practitioners working in the field. Most cases of forced marriage in the UK involve South Asian families, particularly families of Pakistani and Bangladeshi origin, which is partly due to the fact that there is a large South Asian population in the UK.[123] Some cases occur within the UK and have no overseas element, but others involve a party coming from overseas or a British citizen being sent abroad. Most cases involve young women, but some cases involve the coercion of men. Many cases go unreported.

Forced marriages are not tolerated in England and Wales, being regarded by the Government and the courts as a gross abuse of human rights and as a form of domestic violence. In *NS v MI*[124] where a nullity decree was granted to the petitioner who had entered into a forced marriage, Munby J said that 'the court must not hesitate to use every weapon in its protective arsenal if faced with what is, or appears to be, a case of forced marriage.' In *Re K; A Local Authority v N and Others*[125] Munby J described forced marriage as an 'appalling practice' and 'a gross abuse of human rights'. He said it was 'a form of domestic violence that dehumanises people by denying them their right to choose how to live their lives'. In addition to remedies for victims under the general law, the Government has taken steps to give greater protection to victims and, as a result, there are now specialised remedies in family law under the Forced Marriage (Civil Protection) Act 2007.[126]

With regard to the criminal law, the police take forced marriages very seriously and have policy guidelines on how to deal with them. There are various criminal offences which can be committed by those perpetrating a forced marriage (such as assault, abduction, kidnapping, and false imprisonment). Although there is no specific criminal offence of forcing someone to marry, there has been discussion about introducing such an offence but, after consulting on the matter,[127] the Government decided not to introduce this new offence as there was little support from the Crown Prosecution Service and the Probation Service for such a move. Although the Government recognised that an offence of forcing someone to marry would have advantages (such as creating a change of culture, having a deterrent effect, and empowering young people), it considered that these advantages were outweighed by the disadvantages. In other words, it was of the view that the introduction of a criminal offence of forcing someone to marry might drive forced marriages underground and isolate victims, and also cause racial problems at a time of heightened racial tension. Instead of introducing a new criminal offence, the Government decided instead to introduce a new civil remedy which would be available in the family courts (see Section 5.3), but it nonetheless recommended that the law should be kept under review. In addition to the criminal law, there are remedies which can be sought under the civil law. Thus, forcing a person to marry can constitute a tort of trespass to the person, false imprisonment, or harassment under the Protection from Harassment Act 1997, and may

---

[123] Figures published by the Forced Marriage Unit (FMU) in 2009 (see its website) showed an increase in the number of persons coming forward to seek protection. The majority of reportings to the FMU involved families of Pakistani (70 per cent) and Bangladeshi (11 per cent) origin, with smaller percentages of those of Indian, Middle Eastern, European, and African origin. Victims in 14 per cent of cases were male; 33 per cent of all assistance cases involved under 18-year-olds and 14 per cent were under 16. In 2009 the FMU gave advice and support to 1,682 cases, 86 per cent of which involved females and 14 per cent males.

[124] [2006] EWHC 1646 (Fam), [2007] 1 FLR 444.

[125] [2005] EWHC 2956 (Fam), [2007] 1 FLR 399.   [126] See further Section 5.3.

[127] See the consultation paper, *Forced Marriage: A Wrong Not a Right*, published by the Home Office and the Foreign & Commonwealth Office in September 2005.

give the victim a right to obtain damages by way of compensation and/or protection by way of injunctive relief.

Family law provides actual and potential victims of forced marriage with the following remedies: annulment of the marriage; protection under the High Court's inherent and wardship jurisdictions; and forced marriage protection orders. A multi-agency approach is taken in forced marriage cases involving a wide range of agencies, such as social workers, the police, and health authorities. If a victim is under 18, the Children Act 1989 will be relevant, as forcing someone to marry may constitute significant harm for the purposes of that Act.[128]

5.1 ANNULMENT

A person who enters into a forced marriage can have the marriage annulled on the ground that the marriage is voidable under section 12 of the MCA 1973. In most cases, victims will petition on the ground of lack of consent to the marriage as a result of duress caused by parental and/or family pressure.[129] Thus, for example, in *P v R (Forced Marriage: Annulment)*[130] a 20-year-old woman who had been forced to enter into a marriage in Pakistan successfully petitioned for a decree of nullity on the ground of lack of consent as a consequence of duress. Her brother had threatened her with violence and she believed that if she failed to go ahead with the marriage she would be unable to return to England. She was told by her parents that she would bring shame and disgrace on the family if she did not go ahead with the marriage. During the ceremony in Pakistan she was forced to nod in agreement to the marriage by her mother pushing her head forward three times, and she signed the marriage certificate out of fear. When she returned to the UK, she successfully petitioned for a decree of nullity. Coleridge J found that she had not validly consented to the marriage as her consent had been vitiated by physical and emotional force.

Although a petitioner for a decree of nullity will have to give oral evidence in open court, the court will do whatever it can to protect the petitioner (eg where the petitioner is reluctant to give evidence because of the presence of family members).[131]

5.2 INHERENT JURISDICTION OR WARDSHIP

The inherent jurisdiction of the High Court can be invoked to protect a person who is being forced into marriage, or the High Court's wardship jurisdiction if the victim is under 18. Because of the flexible and parental nature of these jurisdictions, they can be invoked, in exceptional circumstances, even though the victim is not present or living in

---

[128] Where there is significant harm, or a risk of significant harm, a local authority has a duty to make enquiries (under s 47) to decide whether to take action to safeguard or promote the welfare of a child; and where there is an actual or potential risk of significant harm a local authority can bring care proceedings (under s 31) to protect a child or young person who is being forced into marriage. See Chapter 10.

[129] See MCA 1973, s 12(c). In some of the older reported cases, non-consummation was sometimes used as a ground.

[130] [2003] 1 FLR 661. See also *Re S (Practice: Muslim Women Giving Evidence)* [2007] 2 FLR 461 where a young Muslim woman was granted a decree of nullity because she had entered into a forced marriage after a two-year campaign of family pressure.

[131] *Per* Munby J in *NS v MI* [2006] EWHC 1646 (Fam), [2007] 1 FLR 444.

the UK but is living overseas, for instance in Pakistan[132] or Bangladesh.[133] These 'parental' jurisdictions of the High Court can also be invoked where there is merely a risk that someone will be forced into a marriage, and where a person needs protection even though they may have capacity.[134] Forced marriage protection orders (see Section 5.3) now provide protection for such persons but, where there is an overseas element, the High Court's inherent and wardship jurisdictions may be more appropriate because of their more flexible jurisdictional rules. This may include, for instance, the High Court under its inherent jurisdiction making a declaration that a forced marriage entered into overseas is not capable of being recognised as a valid marriage in England and Wales. The inherent jurisdiction may also prove useful in a case where a victim of a forced marriage is unable to petition for a decree of nullity on the ground of lack of consent because of being statute barred under section 13(2) of the MCA 1973.[135]

5.3 FORCED MARRIAGE PROTECTION ORDERS

Under Part 4A of the Family Law Act 1996, the Family Division of the High Court and county courts have jurisdiction to make a forced marriage protection order, which is an order providing legal protection for an actual or potential victim of a forced marriage or an attempted forced marriage.[136] These provisions were introduced by the Forced Marriage (Civil Protection) Act 2007.[137] The remedies are modelled on those available under Part 4 of the Family Law Act 1996 to protect victims of domestic violence.[138] A multi-agency approach is adopted for dealing with forced marriages, and Government guidance sets out the responsibilities of the various agencies involved in protecting victims.[139] Part 2 of the guidance is issued as statutory guidance under section 63Q(1) of Part 4A of the Family Law Act 1996, and must be taken into account by those exercising a public function.[140]

'Forced marriage' is defined in the Act as a marriage where a person has not given full and free consent;[141] and 'force' is defined to include not just physical coercion but coercion by threats or other psychological means.[142] The court has wide powers to include in the order such prohibitions, restrictions, or requirements or other such terms as are considered appropriate, and the terms of the order can relate to conduct outside and/or

---

[132] See *Re B; RB v FB* [2008] EWHC 1436 (Fam), [2008] 2 FLR 1624, where a girl (aged 15) who was a British national living in Pakistan was made a ward of court as it considered her to be a British national who was in desperate need of help, even though her only connection with the UK was that her late father was British.

[133] See *SB v RB* [2008] EWHC 938 (Fam), [2008] 2 FLR 1588 where a girl (aged 11) was made a ward of court because she had been forced to marry a 20-year-old man in Bangladesh. She was subsequently returned to the UK with the assistance of the FMU in London, and the marriage was subsequently annulled.

[134] See *Re SA (Vulnerable Adult With Capacity: Marriage)* [2005] EWHC 2942 (Fam), [2006] 1 FLR 867 where the inherent jurisdiction of the High Court was successfully invoked by the local authority as it feared that the girl (aged 17, who was profoundly deaf, unable to speak, and had an intellect of a 13- or 14-year-old) might be taken by her family to Pakistan for the purposes of an arranged marriage.

[135] See *B v I* [2010] 1 FLR 1721 where an English woman of Bangladeshi origin who had been forced into a marriage in Bangladesh but who was unable to petition for nullity, as the 'marriage' had taken place in 2005, was granted a declaration under the court's inherent jurisdiction that the ceremony in Bangladesh had not given rise to a marriage capable of recognition in England and Wales.   [136] Section 63A(1).

[137] See G. Vallance-Webb, 'Forced Marriage: A Yielding of the Lips Not the Mind' [2008] Family Law 565.   [138] See Chapter 3.

[139] *The Right to Choose: Multi-Agency Statutory Guidance for Dealing with Forced Marriage* (available at www.fco.gov.uk).

[140] Eg persons performing a child protection function, teachers, police, local authorities, police authorities, youth offending teams, Cafcass, Local Safeguarding Children Board, and NHS Trusts.

[141] Section 63A(4).   [142] Section 63A(6).

within England and Wales.[143] Thus, for example, an order could be made to prohibit a potential victim being taken outside the UK for the purpose of marrying overseas (which could include handing over a passport), or to prevent a family member from molesting or contacting a victim who has escaped from her family and taken refuge elsewhere. An order can be made for a specified period or until varied or discharged.[144]

An application for an order can be made by: a victim, a person on the victim's behalf with permission of the court, or a relevant third party. Local authorities have been specified as relevant third parties. As with certain other family proceedings, the court has the power to make an order of its own motion (in other words, where no application has been made for an order but it is appropriate to make one).[145]

When deciding whether to exercise its powers to make an order and, if so, in what manner, the court must consider all the circumstances of the case including the need to secure the health, safety, and well-being of the victim; and, when ascertaining 'well-being', it must have regard in particular to the victim's wishes and feelings (so far as they are readily ascertainable) as the court considers appropriate in light of the victim's age and understanding.[146]

Orders can be made without the respondent having been given notice of the proceedings, provided it is just and convenient to do so.[147] In appropriate cases the court can, instead of making an order, accept an undertaking from the respondent, but not if the respondent has used or threatened violence.[148] The court can attach a power of arrest to an order (but not to an order without notice) if the respondent has used or threatened violence against the victim or otherwise in connection with the matters being dealt with in the order.[149] If a power of arrest is attached, a police officer can arrest the respondent without warrant if there is reasonable cause for suspecting that person to be in breach of a forced marriage protection order. Breach of a forced marriage protection order is not a criminal offence but a constable may arrest a person whom he has reasonable cause to suspect is in breach or otherwise in contempt of the order. A respondent can be brought back to the original court for it to consider the alleged breach. Failure to comply with an order is contempt of court, which can result in a fine or imprisonment.

6 RECOGNITION OF AN OVERSEAS MARRIAGE

A marriage contracted in a country outside the jurisdiction of the UK is recognised as valid in the UK provided each party had the capacity to marry according to his or her place of domicile and the formalities required by the law of the place where the marriage was celebrated were complied with.[150] Thus, even though the formalities might be invalid under the law of England and Wales, the court can still recognise the marriage as valid, provided it complied with the rules laid down in the place in which it was celebrated. For this reason an overseas marriage celebrated by local custom can be recognised in the UK.[151] These rules, however, are subject to the overriding rule that an overseas marriage will not be recognised in the UK if it is manifestly unjust or contrary to public policy.

---

[143] Section 63B(1) and (2).   [144] Sections 63F and 63G.   [145] Section 63C(1).
[146] Section 63A(2) and (3).   [147] Section 63D.   [148] Section 63E.   [149] Section 63H.
[150] See *Dicey, Morris and Collins on the Conflict of Laws*, 14th edn (London: Sweet & Maxwell, 2010).
[151] As it was, eg, in *McCabe v McCabe* [1994] 1 FLR 410, where a marriage in Ghana between a Ghanaian woman and an Irish man, involving a bottle of gin and a sum of money, was upheld as valid by the English court, even though the parties were not present at the ceremony. The Court of Appeal held that on the evidence of local law, the essential components of a marriage ceremony (ie, the consent of both parties and of their families) was present and so it was a valid marriage ceremony and would be recognised in the UK.

Special legal provisions apply to certain overseas marriages, for instance where persons are serving abroad in HM Forces. If the marriage is recognised in England and Wales, then recognition of the marriage will affect the legitimacy of children and the availability of divorce or other marital claims, as well as nationality, immigration rights, inheritance rights, and tax and welfare benefits.

Key case

Whether the courts in England and Wales will recognise an overseas marriage as a valid marriage in the UK depends on the facts of each case. In *Hudson v Leigh*,[152] for example, Bodey J made a declaration that a 'marriage' conducted in South Africa was not a valid marriage in England and Wales as the formal requirements for a valid marriage had not been satisfied. Furthermore, both the parties and the minister who had conducted the religious ceremony did not at the time of the ceremony intend or believe it to be legally binding. Bodey J held that, while the ceremony had the trappings of a marriage, it had fundamentally failed to effect a valid one. Lack of capacity to marry may invalidate an overseas marriage. Thus, for instance, in *City of Westminster v IC (By His Litigation Friend the Official Solicitor) and KC and NNC*,[153] a Muslim arranged marriage which had taken place over the telephone between an autistic man (aged 26, but with a mental age of 3) in England and a woman in Bangladesh, was held to be invalid even though it was agreed by all the parties that the marriage had validly taken place in Bangladesh under Shariah law. The Court of Appeal refused to recognise the marriage as valid as the man, due to his disability, lacked capacity under the law of England and Wales and was therefore unable to give valid consent.[154]

---

7 SAME-SEX MARRIAGE

Some countries[155] permit same-sex marriages, but they are not permitted in the UK although same-sex partners can enter into a civil partnership under the Civil Partnership Act 2004[156] which gives the partners virtually the same rights, responsibilities, and privileges as married couples. Thus, civil partnerships are regarded as being similar to marriage but not identical.[157] Marriage in England and Wales and the rest of the UK involves a union which is only possible between a man and a woman. As Lord Nicholls said in *Bellinger v Bellinger (Lord Chancellor Intervening)*, marriage is 'deeply embedded [in the religious and social culture of this country] as a relationship between two persons of the opposite sex'.[158]

While the legal obligations between civil partners are based on marriage, same-sex marriage remains unlawful and, in *Wilkinson v Kitzinger*, it was held that this is not in violation of the principles of the ECHR.[159] It was also held that a same-sex marriage

---

[152] [2009] EWHC 1306 (Fam), [2009] 2 FLR 1129.   [153] [2008] EWHC 198, [2008] 2 FLR 267.

[154] See R. Probert, 'Hanging on the Telephone: *City of Westminster v IC*' (2008) Child and Family Law Quarterly 395.

[155] Such as in Holland, Spain, South Africa, Mexico City, and in some provinces of Canada (Ontario, Quebec, and British Columbia).   [156] See Section 9.

[157] See Section 10.   [158] [2003] UKHL 21.

[159] [2006] EWHC 2022 (Fam), [2007] 1 FLR 295. See also *Schalk and Kopf v Austria* (App no 30141/04), 24 June 2010. For commentary on *Wilkinson v Kitzinger*, see N. Bamforth, ' "The Benefits of Marriage in All But Name"? Same-Sex Couples and the Civil Partnership Act 2004' [2007] Child and Family Law Quarterly 133 and R. Auchmuty, 'What's so Special about Marriage? The Impact of *Wilkinson* v *Kitzinger*' [2008] Child and Family Law Quarterly 475.

validly entered into in an overseas jurisdiction is not recognised as a valid marriage in the courts in this country, although it can be recognised as a valid civil partnership.[160]

Key case

In *Wilkinson v Kitzinger* the parties, Ms Kitzinger and Ms Wilkinson, two feminist scholars who lived and worked in England, applied to the English court to have their Canadian marriage, which had been validly entered into in British Columbia, recognised in the UK. They applied for a declaration as to marital status under section 55 of Family Law Act 1986. They argued that the provisions of the Civil Partnership Act 2004,[161] which treated an overseas marriage as a civil partnership, and section 11(c) of the MCA 1973, which requires the parties to a valid marriage in England and Wales to be respectively male and female,[162] violated their human rights under the ECHR. They argued that the provisions breached their rights to respect for private and family life (Article 8), to marry (Article 12), and not to suffer discrimination in respect of those Convention rights (Article 14). In the alternative they contended that the common law definition of marriage in English law as a union between a man and a woman[163] should be developed so as to recognise same-sex marriages. They also sought a declaration under section 4(2) of the HRA 1998 that the statutory provisions were incompatible with Articles 8, 12, and 14 of the ECHR.

Potter P dismissed the petition on the basis that there had been no violation of their human rights. He said that this was a controversial topic which lacked consensus throughout Europe, with the result that the ECtHR had declared itself slow to trespass into this area. Potter P rejected the Article 8 argument on the basis that Strasbourg jurisprudence did not regard relationships between same-sex partners as 'family life'.[164] (It should be noted that this view no longer holds following the ECtHR's ruling in *Schalk and Kopf v Austria*.[165]) Insofar as the claim was based on a 'private life', Potter P referred to *M v Secretary of State for Work and Pensions*[166] in which the majority of the House of Lords had guarded against an expansive interpretation of Article 8. For the same reasons, Potter P found no breach of Article 8 taken together with Article 14.

Potter P also held that there was no breach of Article 12, the right to marry, because Strasbourg jurisprudence referred to marriage in the traditional sense, in other words as a marriage between a man and a woman. The petitioner in *Wilkinson v Kitzinger* relied on *Goodwin v UK*[167] (a case on transsexuals) to argue that it was possible to apply the 'living instrument' doctrine (which requires the Convention to be interpreted in light of present-day conditions) and to interpret and extend the right to marry in Article 12 to recognise the unqualified right of a man or a woman to marry a person of the same, as well as the opposite, sex. Potter P rejected this argument, holding that there were 'clear limitations' to the 'living instrument' doctrine and that it could not be said that this was an area where there was European-wide consensus on the matter. Potter P therefore declined to find a violation of Article 12. He held that the 'living instrument' doctrine could not be applied

---

[160] Provided the parties had the capacity to marry in the overseas jurisdiction and complied with the required overseas formalities, see the Civil Partnership Act 2004, s 215.   [161] Sections 212–218.

[162] See Section 2.5.

[163] The common law definition of marriage, as stated by Lord Penzance in *Hyde v Hyde* (1866) LR 1 P & D 130 at 133, 35 LJP & M 57, is: 'The voluntary union for life of one man and one woman, to the exclusion of all others'.   [164] See paras 70–75.

[165] (App no 30141/04), 24 June 2010.   [166] [2006] UKHL 11, [2006] 2 AC 91.

[167] (2002) 35 EHRR 18, [2002] 2 FLR 487. See further at Section 2.5.1.

to Article 12 to bring it within the scope of Convention issues which were plainly outside its contemplation.

By contrast, Potter P held that Article 12 was engaged for the purpose of Article 14. He concluded, however, that the difference in treatment of same-sex couples pursued a legitimate aim and represented a proportionate response to achieving that aim. Potter P referred to the Civil Partnership Act 2004, which he said Parliament had enacted as a policy choice to create a legal status for same-sex partners while at the same time demonstrating support for marriage. Prefacing his comments with the observation that same-sex relationships are not inferior, he nevertheless adopted a traditional view of marriage to justify his conclusion. He held that marriage is a heterosexual institution, the primary (although not exclusive) aim of which is procreation in a family environment where children are nurtured by both maternal and paternal influences.[168] To allow same-sex couples to marry would, he concluded, 'fail to recognise physical reality'.[169]

Potter P's reasoning in *Wilkinson v Kitzinger* has been criticised as being unconvincing, in particular for its adoption of a 'traditional' view of marriage which, it has been argued, is out of step with other areas of the law and societal trends.[170] The traditional view that marriage can only be a relationship between opposite-sex partners, because one of the main functions of marriage is to beget children, is open to challenge now that same-sex couples can adopt children[171] and a lesbian woman who has a child by artificial reproduction or surrogacy, whether or not she is a civil partner, now has parental responsibility for a child of the partnership.[172] If marriage is the best environment for raising children, why deny it to same-sex couples who have children? Bamforth has criticised Potter P for choosing to ignore a line of authority in English law which found that childless same-sex couples were 'family' in other contexts, for instance in the context of the Rent Acts.[173] He also argues that Potter P's view that the parties were adequately compensated by having their union recognised as a civil partnership is unconvincing. Potter P's insistence that marriage is the relationship that 'best encourages stability in a well regulated society' means that 'anything else must be second-best, or worse', yet the thrust of Wilkinson and Kitzinger's argument was that they were not being treated equally to those who marry because civil partnership was considered to be different from marriage.

Auchmuty[174] has argued that English law will have to accept same-sex marriage one day. She says that *Wilkinson v Kitzinger* 'bears all the hallmarks of law in transition' and that same-sex marriage 'will doubtless come to the UK, one way or another'. She concludes that a declaration of incompatibility seems 'a likely route' as, while Potter P ruled that Article 12 was engaged by Article 14, he nevertheless offered 'a fairly feeble justification for discrimination which should be easy to demolish'.

There are arguments for and against allowing same-sex marriages in England and Wales, and difficult policy issues are involved. Some argue that marriage is for heterosexuals, and same-sex couples should not be 'landed' with the religious 'baggage' and gender dimensions that marriage carries. It can be argued that some same-sex couples have lifestyles different from heterosexual couples and should not be required to conform

---

[168] [2006] EWHC 2022 (Fam), [118] and [120].   [169] Ibid, [120].

[170] By Bamforth and Auchmuty (n 159).

[171] Under the Adoption and Children Act 2002, see Chapter 11.

[172] See the Children Act 1989, ss 2(1A) and 2(1B) and the Human Fertilisation and Embryology Act 2008, ss 42 and 43.

[173] He referred to *Fitzpatrick v Sterling Housing Association Ltd* [2001] AC 27, [2000] 1 FLR 271 where the House of Lords had held that a same-sex couple should be considered 'family' for the purposes of tenancy succession, and to *Ghaidan v Godin-Mendoza* [2004] UKHL 30, [2004] 2 FLR 600 where Lord Nicholls had stated that the existence of children should not be used as a means of differentiating between heterosexual and homosexual couples.   [174] Auchmuty (n 159).

to norms that are designed for heterosexuals.[175] By contrast, however, although civil partnership is effectively same-sex marriage in all but name, there are those who believe that
same-sex partners should be entitled to marry. If a transsexual person whether or not he or
she has had gender assignment surgery, can now marry a person of the same sex as his or
her birth sex, then it may be only fair and logical to extend the right to marry to same-sex
partners. The case for recognising a same-sex marriage validly entered into in an overseas
jurisdiction as a valid marriage in England and Wales seems even stronger, particularly
as increasing numbers of countries are beginning to accept and permit such marriages. It
seems rather strange that Wilkinson and Kitzinger could not have their valid Canadian
marriage recognised in this country whereas in *McCabe v McCabe*,[176] a marriage in Ghana
between a Ghanaian woman and an Irish man involving a bottle of gin and a sum of money,
was recognised as valid by the English court even though the parties were not present at the
ceremony. In a positive development, on 15 March 2012 the Government launched a consultation on how to remove the bar on same-sex couples being able to have a marriage through
a civil ceremony (Government Equalities Office, *Equal Civil Marriage: A Consultation*).

8 THE LEGAL CONSEQUENCES OF MARRIAGE

Married persons, as a result of their marital status, have various legal rights and responsibilities which are prescribed by the state. There is no statutory list of these rights and responsibilities but they are found in a wide range of statutory provisions and cover a wide range
of matters, such as taxation, inheritance, immigration, social security, financial obligations,
and tenancies. On marriage breakdown, married persons also have various rights and
responsibilities, for instance to provide financial provision for the other spouse in certain
circumstances. However, despite their rights and responsibilities, which are outlined in
the following text, husbands and wives have separate legal personalities. This means that
they can own property in their sole name (or jointly) and can bring proceedings in tort and
contract separately against each other or against third parties.[177] They can also enter into
contracts with each other, make unilateral decisions about their own medical treatment,[178]
and make their own decisions on how their property is to be administered on their death.

Married persons have the following rights and responsibilities.

Financial obligations: the parties to a marriage have financial obligations to each other during
their marriage and, depending on the circumstances, on the termination of the marriage by
divorce or annulment. They can seek orders from the court in respect of financial provision
during marriage[179] and on divorce. Married couples, like all parents, have a duty to provide
maintenance for any child of the family during the marriage and on and after marital breakdown. They can enter into agreements about maintenance provision for themselves and also
their children, but they cannot exclude the jurisdiction of the court in respect of the terms of
such agreements; and any provision in an agreement restricting the right of either spouse or
any other relevant person to apply for child support maintenance for a relevant child is void.

---

[175] K. McK. Norrie, 'Marriage is for Heterosexuals—May the Rest of Us be Saved From It' [2000] Child
and Family Law Quarterly 363.   [176] [1994] 1 FLR 410.

[177] Law Reform (Married Women and Tortfeasors) Act 1935; Law Reform (Husband and Wife) Act 1962,
s 1.

[178] This includes the right of a wife to make a unilateral decision to abort a child born of the marriage (see
Paton v British Pregnancy Advisory Service Trustees [1979] QB 276 where the husband's application for an
injunction to prohibit the defendant carrying out an abortion on his wife failed).

[179] In the family proceedings court (under the Domestic Proceedings and Magistrates' Courts Act 1978)
and in the county court or High Court (under the MCA 1973, s 27).

Property rights: each spouse can own property solely or jointly with the other spouse. During the marriage the rules governing property ownership are the same as those which apply to other persons, with the exception of some special statutory provisions which apply only to spouses,[180] of particular importance being the statutory right to occupy the family home ('home rights').[181] Thus, who owns what during marriage depends on which spouse bought the property or to whom the property was given, subject in all cases to a contrary intention. On divorce, however, the position is different, as the divorce court has wide powers to adjust the property rights of spouses, irrespective of who owns what but according to the circumstances of the case.[182] In respect of property on death, each spouse is free to make a will leaving his or her property to whomsoever he or she wishes. On intestacy the surviving spouse will succeed to the estate of the deceased spouse, subject to certain restrictions and financial limits. A surviving spouse can apply to the court for reasonable financial provision from the other spouse's estate under the Inheritance (Provision for Family and Dependants) Act 1975, and is treated more favourably than other applicants.[183]

Children: parents who are married have 'automatic' parental responsibility in law for their children[184] unlike unmarried parents, where only the unmarried mother has automatic parental responsibility. In respect of any stepchild of either party, parental responsibility is not 'automatic' but can be acquired. Married parents, like all parents, have a duty to provide maintenance for any child of the family. They can adopt a child jointly, and in some circumstances solely, and they also have a right to give or refuse consent to the adoption of their child.

Other miscellaneous rights: spouses (and former spouses) can seek remedies under Part IV of the Family Law Act 1996 to protect themselves against domestic violence. Special rules apply to spouses in respect of giving evidence in criminal proceedings. The marriage of a non-British person to a British citizen may provide a way of acquiring British citizenship and/or the right to enter the UK. Married couples enjoy certain tax and pension privileges. For instance, transfers between parties to a marriage are exempt from inheritance tax, and a transfer between spouses does not give rise to a chargeable gain for the purpose of capital gains tax. A married person can also benefit from a deceased spouse's pension rights.

9 CIVIL PARTNERSHIP

Persons in a same-sex relationship have been given increasing recognition in family law and can now enter into a registered civil partnership under the Civil Partnership Act 2004 which came into force in December 2005.[185] Even before the introduction of civil partnership, the law had begun to give same-sex couples various rights, for instance to

---

[180] Such as the Married Women's Property Act 1882.

[181] Under the Family Law Act 1996, Part IV, s 30.   [182] Under the MCA 1973, Pt II, see Chapter 4.

[183] The applicant spouse (or former spouse) can do so without having to prove dependency on the deceased or that he or she was being maintained by the deceased.

[184] On parental rights and responsibilities and children, see Chapter 7.

[185] See R. Deech, 'Civil Partnership' [2010] Family Law 468. On the history of the legal treatment of homosexuality, see S. Cretney, *Same Sex Relationships: From 'Odious Crime' to 'Gay Marriage'* (Oxford: Oxford University Press, 2006). See also the government consultation paper, *Civil Partnership: A Framework for the Legal Recognition of Same-Sex Couples* (Women and Equality Unit of the Department of Trade and Industry, June 2003), which set out the proposals for reform.

seek protection against domestic violence under Part IV of the Family Law Act 1996[186] and to succeed to a tenancy held in the name of their deceased partner.[187] Gay and lesbian partners can now adopt children jointly.[188]

The Government's intention in introducing civil partnership was to create an institution which would be parallel, but not identical, to marriage. It was keen to emphasise that civil partnership would not undermine the institution of marriage or offend religious beliefs.

Talking point

Baroness Scotland, introducing the second reading of the Civil Partnership Bill in the House of Lords, said:

> The Bill offers a secular solution to the disadvantages which same-sex couples face in the way they are treated by our laws.... This Bill does not undermine or weaken the importance of marriage and we do not propose to open civil partnership to opposite-sex couples. Civil partnership is aimed at same-sex couples who cannot marry. However, it is important for us to be clear that we continue to support marriage and recognise that it is the surest foundation for opposite sex couples raising children.[189]

Although the Government has been keen to stress that civil partnership is not 'gay marriage', civil partnership is in fact almost identical to marriage as it creates a status from which virtually the same rights and responsibilities flow. One of the reasons for refusing to equate civil partnership with marriage is that marriage is considered by many to be a religious sacrament, and the law of marriage has ecclesiastical origins. Whether such an approach should continue to be taken today when we live in a multi-ethnic and multi-religious society is perhaps questionable especially as civil partnerships can be celebrated in religious premises.[190] Civil partnership does, however, have the following differences from marriage. Adultery is not a ground for the dissolution of a civil partnership as it is in the case of divorce; and non-consummation and venereal disease are not available as grounds for the voidability of a civil partnership.[191] In essence, there is therefore very little difference between the status relationship of civil partnership and that of marriage.

Talking point

According to Government statistics,[192] in 2009 there were 6,281 civil partnerships registered in the UK (3,227 male and 3,054 female), a fall of 12 per cent compared with 2008. The number of civil partnerships in both England and Wales in 2009 fell by 13 per cent to 5,443 and 244 respectively.

---

[186] See Chapter 3.

[187] See *Fitzpatrick v Sterling Housing Association Ltd* [2001] 1 AC 27, [2001] 1 FLR 271, where the House of Lords held that a same-sex partner was capable of being a member of the other partner's family for the purpose of the Rent Act legislation; and *Ghaidan v Godin-Mendoza* [2004] UKHL 30, [2004] 2 AC 557, [2004] 2 FLR 600, where the House of Lords held that a surviving homosexual partner's right to succeed to a tenancy was a human right under Art 14 in conjunction with Art 8 of the ECHR (applying *Karner v Austria* (App no 40016/98) (2004) 38 EHRR 24). For a discussion of *Fitzpatrick* see L. Glennon, '*Fitzpatrick v Sterling Housing Association*: A Perfectly Pitched Stall' in S. Gilmore, J. Herring, and R. Probert (eds), *Landmark Cases in Family Law* (Oxford: Hart, 2011).   [188] Under the Adoption and Children Act 2002, see Chapter 11.

[189] Hansard, HL 22 April 2004, col 388.

[190] See section 202 of the Equality Act 2010. The Marriage and Civil Partnerships (Approved Premises) (Amendment) Regulations 2011.

[191] See Sections 3.1 and 3.4.   [192] See Office for National Statistics (www.statistics.gov.uk).

In 2009, 11 per cent of men and 21 per cent of women forming a civil partnership in the UK had been in a previous marriage or civil partnership. As in 2008, London had the highest number of civil partnership registrations in the UK with a quarter of all partnerships taking place there.

9.1 THE LEGAL FORMATION OF A CIVIL PARTNERSHIP

A civil partnership is defined in the Civil Partnership Act 2004 as 'a relationship between two people of the same sex...which is formed when they register as civil partners of each other.'[193] To be able to register a civil partnership, the parties must be of the same sex, and each party must not be under 16, not be within the prohibited degrees of relationship, and not be already civil partners or lawfully married.[194]

Local registration services are responsible for registration, which involves a process similar to that for a civil marriage. Like a civil marriage, various preliminary formalities must be satisfied, such as residence and notice requirements. Each party must declare that there is no impediment to the formation of the partnership and that the residence requirements are satisfied.[195] Notice of the proposed registration will be published and, after a 15-day waiting period and in the absence of any objections, the registration authority will issue a 'civil partnership schedule' authorising registration to take place.[196] The 15-day waiting period can be reduced in special cases;[197] and special provision exists for housebound persons, hospital patients, and prisoners.[198] Once these preliminary formalities have been satisfied, registration can take place. The Civil Partnership Act 2004 prohibited civil partnership registrations taking place on religious premises. However, section 202 of the Equality Act 2010 and the Marriages and Civil Partnerships (Approved Premises) (Amendment) Regulations 2011 enable civil partnerships to be registered on approved religious premises where permitted by religious organisations, although there must be no religious service at the registration.[199] Registration is completed when each party has signed the civil registration document at the invitation of, and in the presence of, the civil partnership registrar; and in the presence of each other and two witnesses.[200]

9.1.1 Civil partnership agreements

Civil partners can enter into a civil partnership agreement. This is the equivalent of an engagement to marry and the rules which apply are the same as those which apply to engagements. Thus, a civil partnership agreement does not have contractual effect, and the same rules about rights in property apply on the termination of a civil partnership agreement as apply on the termination of an engagement.[201] A party to a civil partnership agreement can also seek protection against domestic violence under Part IV of the Family Act 1996.[202]

9.1.2 Termination of a civil partnership

Under the Civil Partnership Act 2004 a civil partner can apply to have the partnership annulled (on the ground that it is void or voidable) or have it dissolved. These legal processes and the laws which apply are virtually the same as those for married couples who are applying to have their marriage annulled or terminated by divorce. Civil partners can also apply

---

[193] Section 1(1).   [194] Section 3(1).   [195] Section 3.
[196] Section 8.   [197] Section 14.   [198] Section 12.
[199] Sections 18–19.   [200] Sections 2(1) and 2(5).
[201] See ss 73 and 74. Thus, where a party makes a gift to the other party on the condition (express or implied) that it is to be returned if the civil partnership agreement is terminated, that party is not prevented from recovering the property merely because he or she was responsible for terminating the agreement (s 74(5)).   [202] See Chapter 3.

for a separation order, which is equivalent to a decree of judicial separation in the case of married persons; and an order equivalent to the decree of presumption of death.

9.1.3 Annulment of a civil partnership

Under the Civil Partnership Act 2004 the court has the power to make nullity orders in respect of void and voidable civil partnerships. These provisions are virtually the same as those for nullity of marriage.[203] Unlike nullity of a marriage,[204] however, there are no non-consummation and venereal disease grounds to render a civil partnership voidable.

9.1.4 Dissolution of a civil partnership

Dissolution of a civil partnership is the same as the termination of a marriage by divorce, except that there is no adultery ground.

9.2 RECOGNITION OF OVERSEAS CIVIL PARTNERSHIPS, ANNULMENTS, AND SEPARATIONS

The Civil Partnership Act 2004 makes provision[205] for the recognition of overseas civil partnerships in the UK, and also the recognition of overseas civil partnership dissolutions, annulments, and separations. These are equivalent to the provisions governing the recognition of overseas marriages, divorces, annulments, and separations. This is subject, however, to the provision that an overseas civil partnership will not be recognised if it 'would be manifestly contrary to public policy to recognise the capacity, under the relevant law, of one or both of them to enter into the relationship.'[206] Although, as the case of *Wilkinson v Kitzinger*[207] showed, an overseas same-sex marriage is not recognised in the UK, it can be recognised in the UK as a valid civil partnership. The court has jurisdiction to make finance and property orders after an overseas dissolution, annulment, or legal separation of a civil partnership.[208]

9.3 THE LEGAL CONSEQUENCES OF CIVIL PARTNERSHIP

Civil partners have virtually the same rights, responsibilities, and privileges as married couples both during the partnership and on and after its breakdown. Thus, the effect of registration is to give the partners various rights, responsibilities, and obligations broadly analogous to those of married couples.

During the partnership, civil partners, like spouses, have a mutual duty to maintain each other, and a civil partner can apply against the other partner for financial provision in the family proceedings court.[209] Civil partners have the same pension rights as married couples; and they are treated in the same way as married couples for tax and state benefit purposes.

On the grant of a dissolution order or a decree of annulment, the family courts have jurisdiction to make finance and property orders in favour of civil partners equivalent to those which it can make on divorce.

On the death of a civil partner, the surviving partner is in the same position as a surviving spouse. Thus, if a civil partner dies intestate, then the surviving partner is treated in the same way as a surviving spouse in respect of inheriting the deceased's estate. The survivor is also entitled to inherit a tenancy belonging to the deceased partner in the same

---

[203] See Section 1.5. [204] Sections 49–54. [205] See ss 233–238. [206] Section 218.
[207] [2006] EWHC 2022 (Fam), [2007] 1 FLR 295, and see further at Section 7.
[208] See s 72(4) and Sch 7. [209] Sections 65–72.

way as a surviving spouse, and the surviving partner can also bring a claim for financial provision on the death of a partner under the Inheritance (Provision for Family and Dependants) Act 1975 in the same way as a married person.

In respect of children and parenting, a civil partner who is not the biological parent can obtain parental responsibility for his or her civil partner's child by entering into a parental responsibility agreement with his or her partner or by obtaining a parental responsibility order from the court.[210] Provisions have recently been introduced which give lesbian partners (whether or not they are civil partners) 'automatic' parental responsibility for a child of the partnership conceived as a result of assisted reproduction or surrogacy;[211] and which allow a lesbian partner (whether or not a civil partner) of a child's mother to acquire parental responsibility where the partners have a child by means of assisted reproduction or surrogacy.[212] Civil partners can apply for residence and contact orders and other orders under section 8 of the Children Act 1989.[213] They have a duty to provide maintenance for any child of the family; and they can apply for financial provision for a child in the same way as married couples. Like a married couple, they can apply to adopt a child jointly and, in some circumstances, solely.

Civil partners who are actual or potential victims of domestic violence can apply for non-molestation orders and occupation orders under Part IV of the Family Act 1996 in the same way as married couples, and a non-owning civil partner has 'home rights' (a statutory right of occupation in the home) under section 30 of the 1996 Act.[214]

10 NON-FORMAL ADULT RELATIONSHIPS

The only two formal adult relationships in family law are marriage and civil partnership. These are relationships which can only be created by complying with various statutory formalities. These requirements have been considered earlier. Family law also recognises the non-formal relationship of cohabitation, but not to the same extent as marriage and civil partnership. There is also another type of non-formal adult relationship, that between home-sharers, but although these relationships have been considered by law reformers, such as by the Law Commission, and provision was made for them in the Cohabitation Bill 2008, no recognition has been given to such relationships in family law.

10.1 COHABITATION

Cohabitation[215] is an increasingly popular relationship choice whether between heterosexual or homosexual partners, and social attitudes to cohabitation have changed over

---

[210] See Children Act 1989, s 4A and Chapter 7.

[211] See the Children Act 1989, s 2(1A)(a) and (b) and the Human Fertilisation and Embryology Act 2008, ss 42 and 43. 'Automatic' means that parental responsibility arises 'automatically' in the sense that there is no need to apply for it. On parental responsibility generally, see further Chapter 7.

[212] See Children Act 1989, s 4ZA.   [213] See Chapter 9.   [214] See Chapter 3.

[215] On cohabitation, see A. Barlow, S. Duncan, G. James, and A. Park, *Cohabitation, Marriage and the Law: Social Change and Legal Reform in 21st Century Britain* (Oxford: Hart, 2005); C. Burgoyne and S. Sonnenberg, 'Financial Practices in Cohabiting Heterosexual Couples: A Perspective from Economic Psychology' in J. Miles and R. Probert (eds), *Sharing Lives, Dividing Assets, An Inter-Disciplinary Study* (Oxford: Hart, 2009), pp 89–108; K. Kiernan, 'Unmarried Cohabitation and Parenthood in Britain and Europe' (2004) 26(1) Journal of Law and Policy 33–55; C. Grant Bowman, *Unmarried Couples, Law, and Public Policy* (Oxford: Oxford University Press, 2010); C. Vogler, M. Brockmann, and R. Wiggins, 'Intimate Relationships and Changing Patterns of Money Management at the Beginning of the 21st Century' (2008) 37 British Journal of Sociology 455; G. Douglas, J. Pearce, and H. Woodward, *A Failure of Trust: Resolving Property Disputes on*

the years. Although cohabitation is on the increase, while marriage is on the decline, it is difficult to measure accurately how many people are actually living in cohabiting relationships and also how many relationships break down. This is because there is no proof by public record, as there is with marriage and civil partnership, as to the existence of a cohabitation relationship. Also, there is no proof of the termination of a cohabiting relationship as there is with divorce and dissolution of a civil partnership. The problem of estimating the number of cohabiting relationships and how many break down is particularly difficult to determine because of the difficulty of defining what the terms 'cohabitants' and 'cohabitation' mean.[216]

Talking point

According to Government statistics, in 2011 there were approximately 2.9 million opposite-sex cohabiting couples living in England and Wales and this figure is projected to rise to 3.8 million by 2033.[217] The median duration of cohabiting relationships is two years, after which the parties either marry or separate. Sixty-five per cent of cohabiting relationships terminate; and about half the number of cohabiting parents split up before a child is 5 years old. Thirty-five per cent of cohabitants' children will have both parents up to the age of 16, compared to 70 per cent of children with married parents.[218] The Office for National Statistics has predicted that unmarried adults will soon outnumber married ones; and that by 2014 married couples will form fewer than half of all British families.

10.1.1 Defining cohabitants and cohabitation

One of the difficulties for the law, and for any law reform, is defining what the terms 'cohabitant' and 'cohabitation' mean. Defining these terms is important for determining whether the parties possess, or should possess, various legal rights and responsibilities. But defining them is difficult because cohabitation relationships can take many forms. In fact the parties to a relationship may themselves have divergent views about whether or not they are cohabiting, and whether or not they should be subject to mutually enforceable legal obligations.

Persons cohabit for different reasons. Some couples may cohabit as a preference choice to marriage. Some may cohabit as a precursor to marriage. In some cohabiting relationships the parties may not be in agreement—one of the parties may be committed to the relationship whereas the other party might not be, or not to the same degree. A study by

---

Cohabitation Breakdown (2007), available at www.law.cf.ac.uk/researchpapers/papers/1.pdf; A. Barlow, C. Burgoyne, and J. Smithson, *The Living Together Campaign: An Investigation of its Impact on Legally Aware Cohabitants* (Ministry of Justice, 2007), available at www.justice.gov.uk/publications/docs/living-together-research-report(1).pdf; A. Barlow, 'Legal Rationality and Family Property: What has Love Got to Do With It?' in J. Miles and R. Probert (eds), *Sharing Lives, Dividing Assets: An Interdisciplinary Study* (Oxford: Hart, 2009); A. Dnes, 'Rational Decision-Making and Intimate Cohabitation' in J. Miles and R. Probert (eds), *Sharing Lives, Dividing Assets: An Interdisciplinary Study* (Oxford: Hart, 2009); A. Barlow, C. Burgoyne, E. Clery, and J. Smithson, *Cohabitation and the Law: Myths, Money and the Media, British Social Attitudes 24th Report* (London: Sage, 2008); S. Duncan, A. Barlow, and G. James, 'Why Don't They Marry? Cohabitation, Commitment and DIY Marriage' [2005] Child and Family Law Quarterly 383.

[216] See further Section 10.1.1.

[217] According to figures from the Office for National Statistics (www.statistics.gov.uk).

[218] K. Kiernan, LSE Case Paper 65 (2003) and J. Ermisch, 'The Achievements of the British Household Panel Survey' (2008).

Barlow and Smithson[219] found that cohabitants are of the following four psychological types: 'idealogues' (those who cohabit as they have an ideological objection to marriage); 'romantics' (those where cohabitation is a step towards marriage); 'pragmatists' (those who make decisions about whether to marry or cohabit on legal or financial grounds); and 'uneven couples' (those where one party to the relationship wishes to marry and the other does not, thereby leaving the person who wishes to marry in a vulnerable position). Barlow and Smithson concluded that these different styles of cohabiting relationship underlined the need for any legal reforms to provide a range of legal options for cohabitants.

How the terms 'cohabitation' and 'cohabitants' are defined raises certain policy issues. Some argue that a wide definition giving a wide category of cohabitants new legal rights and remedies similar, or identical, to those of married couples and civil partners would undermine the institution of marriage. Such presumptive-based recognition (ie, where rights and duties arise by virtue of the cohabiting relationship itself and not through the parties opting in to marriage or civil partnership) would, it is argued, also undermine the autonomy of cohabiting couples, some of whom may have made a conscious decision not to marry in order to avoid the rights and obligations which the state imposes on married couples or civil partners. On the other hand, one could argue that such presumptive-based legal recognition is necessary in order to protect economically vulnerable parties in cohabiting relationships.

Current statutory provisions giving cohabitants rights do not adopt a consistent definition of the term 'cohabitants'. Although they define 'cohabitants' as persons living in a quasi-marital or civil partnership relationship, there is not necessarily a minimal duration and residence requirement. Thus, to apply for financial provision from a deceased cohabiting partner's estate under the Inheritance (Provision for Family and Dependants) Act 1975, a cohabitant must have lived in the same household as the deceased for at least two years as if he or she were the spouse or civil partner of the deceased; but for the purposes of obtaining protection against domestic violence under Part IV of the Family Law Act 1996 the term 'cohabitant' is defined less restrictively as there is no minimum duration requirement. The reason for this is to ensure that persons who are living together come under the umbrella of the 1996 Act and are able to gain protection against violence.

Determining the length of a cohabitation relationship for the purpose of reforming the law and giving cohabitants new rights is difficult, and there have been divergent views on this. Lord Lester's Cohabitation Bill 2008 initially recommended two years, but this was increased to five when the Bill was debated in the House of Lords. Deech, however, has suggested that ten years is a better 'gateway', if there is to be one at all, on the basis that 'only 5% of cohabiting unions in this country last for more than 10 years'.[220] There is also the question of whether short periods of separation should be ignored when calculating the duration of a cohabiting relationship and whether the nature of the parties' commitment should be taken into account, although that would be virtually impossible to assess. Difficulties about whether someone is or is not a cohabitant could result in protracted and expensive litigation being brought, which would result in the assets of cohabitants being significantly reduced and be counterproductive in any attempt to give them new rights.

10.1.2 The vulnerability of cohabitants and their children

Cohabitants are given some recognition in family law but not to the same extent as married couples and civil partners. Thus, for instance, they can seek orders from the court to

---

[219] A. Barlow and J. Smithson, 'Legal Assumptions, Cohabitants' Talk and the Rocky Road to Reform' [2010] Child and Family Law Quarterly 328.

[220] R. Deech, 'Cohabitation' [2010] Family Law 39.

protect themselves against domestic violence[221] and make a claim for financial provision from the estate of their deceased partner.[222] In respect of property and financial matters, however, there are no special family law provisions and cohabitants must turn instead to the general principles of the law of property and contract. This makes them particularly vulnerable on relationship breakdown as cohabiting partners have no duty to provide each other with financial provision (maintenance); and any dispute about the family home must be determined by property law principles and in the ordinary courts where the outcome may be uncertain and the cost of litigation prohibitive. This is quite different from marriage and civil partnerships where the family court has a wide discretion to make property and finance orders according to the needs and resources of the parties and by applying principles of fairness and non-discrimination.[223] In a property dispute involving cohabitants, on the other hand, the court will exercise its jurisdiction by looking at the express or inferred intentions of the parties,[224] and not base its decision on what is fair in the circumstances. The only remedy cohabitants have in family law is that, if they have a child, they can apply for a property order for the benefit of the child under Schedule 1 to the Children Act 1989.[225]

There is also the problem that there is a widespread but erroneous belief that there exists something in English law called a 'common law marriage' which gives cohabiting couples after a period of time the same rights and remedies as married couples.[226] This is a myth about which cohabiting couples need to be informed and made aware. Probert[227] argues that the origin of the 'common-law marriage myth' can be traced back to no earlier than the 1970s, basing her hypothesis on the fact that the media used this term during the 1970s when Parliament and the courts began to confer rights on such couples. A two-year study by Barlow, Burgoyne, Clery, and Smithson (2008)[228] found that cohabitation is a popular choice of relationship in Britain but that, despite the Living Together Campaign,[229] few cohabitants had taken steps to safeguard their legal position. Thus, only 15 per cent of those who owned their accommodation had a written agreement about their share of the ownership; and only 19 per cent had sought advice about their legal position.

Children of cohabiting couples are also likely to be in a more vulnerable position than children whose parents are married, not only because cohabiting relationships are more prone to breakdown, but because the court has no power to oversee the residence and contact arrangements for children of cohabiting parents on family breakdown, whereas it has if parents are divorcing.[230] Children may also be vulnerable if one of their cohabiting

---

[221] Under the Family Law Act 1996, Part IV, see Chapter 3.

[222] Under the Inheritance (Provision for Family and Dependants) Act 1975.

[223] See, in particular, *White v White* [2001] 1 AC 596, [2000] 2 FLR 981; *Miller v Miller; McFarlane v McFarlane* [2006] UKHL 24, [2006] 1 FLR 1186; and *Charman v Charman* [2007] EWCA Civ 503, [2007] 1 FLR 1246. See Chapter 4.

[224] See, in particular, Baroness Hale in *Stack v Dowden* [2007] UKHL 17, [2007] 1 FLR 1858 at [61]. See further at Chapter 5.   [225] See Chapter 5.

[226] In fact some 53 per cent of the 2006 British Social Attitudes survey's nationally representative sample believed there was something called a 'common law marriage' (see A. Barlow, C. Burgoyne, E. Clery, and J. Smithson, 'Cohabitation and the Law: Myths, Money and the Media' in A. Park, J. Curtice, K. Thompson, M. Phillips, and E. Clery (eds), *British Social Attitudes—The 24th Report* (London: Sage, 2008), pp 29–51).

[227] See R. Probert, 'Common-Law Marriage: Myths and Misunderstandings' [2008] Child and Family Law Quarterly 1.   [228] See n 228.

[229] Its website provides cohabitants with information about their legal rights and remedies.

[230] A petitioner to a divorce must present a Statement of Arrangements for the Children to the divorce court and the district judge has an obligation under the MCA 1973, s 41, to consider those arrangements. See further Chapter 9.

parents loses a right to remain in the family home on relationship breakdown, and also because there is no maintenance obligation between unmarried partners.

10.1.3 The rights and obligations of cohabitants

Cohabitants have some legal rights and obligations but these are much more limited than those of married couples and civil partners.

Financial obligations: unlike married couples and civil partners, cohabitants have no duty during their relationship or on its breakdown to provide each other with financial support, and therefore have no right to apply for court orders in respect of financial provision during their relationship or on its breakdown. They do, however, have a right to seek financial provision in certain circumstances from the estate of their deceased partner on his or her intestacy.[231] In respect of their children, cohabiting parents, whether or not they have parental responsibility, have a duty to provide financial provision for their children and, if a parent fails to do so, an application can be made to the Child Maintenance and Enforcement Commission[232] and, in certain circumstances, to the court, where they can apply not just for maintenance but also lump sum orders for the benefit of a child.[233]

Property rights: cohabitants, unlike married couples and civil partners, have no special property rights in family law either during the relationship or on relationship breakdown. To establish an interest in property, such as the family home, cohabitants must rely on equitable doctrines, such as trusts and proprietary estoppel.[234] This is quite different from divorce or dissolution of a civil partnership.[235] This may mean that, on relationship breakdown, cohabitants may find themselves without any entitlement to the former family home and with no right to any pension provision from their former cohabiting partner. Also, cohabitants, unlike married couples and civil partners, have no statutory rights of occupation of the family home ('home rights'), which means that they will only have a right to occupy the home if they have a right of ownership in the property, a licence to live there, a right under a tenancy, or they have been granted an occupation order permitting them to reside in the home where there is domestic violence.[236] However, if cohabitants have children they are in a slightly better position as they can seek property orders for the benefit of a child under section 15 of and Schedule 1 to the Children Act 1989, which give the court power to transfer, for instance, the family home to the non-owning cohabitant during a child's dependency which may enable the child and the residential parent to continue living in the home after the age of majority.[237]

Property rights on the death of a cohabiting partner: on the death of a cohabiting partner who dies intestate, the surviving cohabitant is in a vulnerable position compared with a married person or civil partner, as the survivor has no right to inherit from the deceased partner's estate. Instead any property goes to the deceased's children or parents. There has, however, been discussion about whether the rules of intestacy should be reformed to

---

[231] Under the Inheritance (Provision for Dependants) Act 1975.
[232] Under the Child Support Act 1991, as amended, see Chapter 6.
[233] Under the Children Act 1989, s 15 and Sch 1.   [234] See Chapter 5.
[235] See Chapter 4.
[236] Married couples and civil partners have 'home rights' under the Family Law Act 1996, Pt IV, s 30 in certain circumstances, see Chapter 3.
[237] See Chapter 5.

give cohabitants a right to succeed to their deceased partner's estate.[238] In 2007 the Law Commission in its report on cohabitation law reform was not in favour of this, as it considered it would be difficult to reflect appropriately the diverse range of cohabiting relationships.[239] It proposed instead making better provision for cohabitants by amending the Inheritance (Provision for Family and Dependants) Act 1975. However, in 2008 the Law Commission announced that it would carry out a general review of the law of intestacy and the 1975 Act, and in 2009 published a Consultation Paper in which it reviewed the law and discussed options for reform including a proposal that unmarried couples who had lived together for at least two years should be automatically entitled to half their deceased partner's estate on intestacy, which would put them in the same position as surviving spouses and civil partners.[240]

Because of the danger that a surviving cohabitant may be left with nothing on his or her partner's death, it is particularly important for cohabiting partners to make a will even though the surviving cohabitant can apply to the court for financial provision from the deceased partner's estate under the Inheritance (Provision for Family and Dependants) Act 1975. Under this Act, however, cohabitants are not treated as favourably as spouses and civil partners. It is also possible to bring a claim against a deceased partner's estate by applying to the court to establish a beneficial interest in the deceased cohabitant's property under a trust or proprietary estoppel. A surviving partner can succeed to a tenancy belonging to a deceased cohabitant.

Cohabitants and their children: cohabiting parents have virtually the same rights and responsibilities with regard to their children as married couples, but with the important exception that the unmarried father has no 'automatic' parental responsibility in law for his children, although he can acquire it in various ways.[241] Cohabitants have the same maintenance obligations to their children as married couples, and all other parents, irrespective of whether the father has parental responsibility, and cohabiting parents (including fathers without parental responsibility) can apply for residence and contact orders and other orders under section 8 of the Children Act 1989.[242] Eligibility to apply for section 8 orders is based on parenthood, not on whether a parent has parental responsibility. Only the unmarried mother, not the father, has a duty to register the child's birth, but both parties can choose to do so jointly whereupon the father acquires parental responsibility. Under the law of adoption[243] a cohabiting couple can make a joint application to adopt a child, but an unmarried father without parental responsibility has no statutory right to consent to the adoption of his child.

Other rights: cohabitants and former cohabitants, opposite-sex and same-sex, can apply for non-molestation orders and occupation orders under Part IV of the Family Law Act 1996 to protect themselves and their children against domestic violence. Cohabitants

---

[238] See C. Williams, G. Potter, and G. Douglas, 'Cohabitation and Intestacy: Public Opinion and Law Reform' [2008] Child and Family Law Quarterly 499 which considers the position of cohabitants whose partners die, and also the approach of the courts to claims under the Inheritance (Provision for Family and Dependants) Act 1975.

[239] Law Commission, *Cohabitation: The Financial Consequences of Relationship Breakdown* (Law Com No 307, 2007), Part 6.

[240] *Intestacy and Family Provision Claims on Death* (Law Com CP No 191, 2009).

[241] Eg by registering his child's birth with the mother, by entering into parental responsibility agreement with the mother, or obtaining a parental responsibility order from the court (see Children Act 1989, s 4), or by subsequently marrying the child's mother (see further Chapter 7).

[242] Such as for residence and contact, see Chapter 9.   [243] See Chapter 11.

have a right to enter into a contract to regulate their affairs, for example to make arrangements about the allocation of property and other matters should their relationship break down, but in practice few do so.[244]

10.1.4 Reforming the law

For many years there has been discussion about reforming the law to give cohabitants rights in respect of property and finance on relationship breakdown, and on the death of their partner. Proposals for reform have come not only from the Law Commission[245] but from the Law Society[246] and from Resolution, the body of family lawyers.[247] At the end of 2008, Lord Lester of Herne Hill[248] introduced the Cohabitation Bill into the House of Lords,[249] a Bill which was supported by Resolution. The Bill had its second reading in the House of Lords in March 2009, but met with resistance from some members of the House and went no further. Thus, the discussions and proposals for reform have gone no further and there are currently no proposals to reform the law.

There are several arguments for and against reforming the law to give cohabitants new rights on relationship breakdown and on the death of a partner. One of the main arguments given in favour of reform is that under the current law cohabitants and their children are vulnerable and suffer unfairness and injustice particularly on relationship breakdown.[250] Thus, for instance, Lord Lester of Herne Hill, when presenting the Cohabitation Bill to Parliament at the end of 2008, said that legislation was 'urgently needed to tackle the vulnerability not only of unmarried cohabiting couples and their children but also co-dependent carers and siblings who live together.'[251] He said that it is

---

[244] See *Sutton v Mishcon de Reya and Gawor & Co* [2003] EWHC 3166 (Ch), [2004] 1 FLR 837 where a cohabitation agreement was held not to be valid in the circumstances of the case, as it was an agreement about sexual relations not one about the parties' property, and see commentary by R. Probert, 'Sutton v Mishcon de Reya and Gawor & Co: Cohabitation Contracts and Swedish Sex Slaves' [2004] Child and Family Law Quarterly 453.

[245] In 2002 it published *Sharing Homes: A Discussion Paper* (Law Com No 278), in which it discussed reforming the law not just for cohabitants but home-sharers generally. It did so by discussing a 'contribution-based' model for reform, but it found it to be unworkable in practice. In 2006 the Law Commission published a Consultation Paper, *Cohabitation: The Financial Consequences of Relationship Breakdown* (Law Com CP No 179) making proposals for reform of the law relating to the property and financial consequences of cohabitation breakdown. This was followed in 2007 by the publication of its Report, *Cohabitation: The Financial Consequences of Relationship Breakdown* (Law Com No 307).

[246] See *Cohabitation: The Case for Clear Law; Proposals for Reform.*

[247] In 2000 the Solicitors' Family Law Association (now called Resolution) published *Fairness for Families,* in which it recommended reforms similar to those recommended by the Law Society.

[248] A human rights lawyer, and the person who was responsible for driving the reforms giving victims of forced marriages greater protection under the Family Law Act 1996, Pt 4A.

[249] The Bill was drawn up after a consultation paper, *Reforming the Law for People Who Live Together,* had been published in 2008 setting out two main options for reform: one similar to that proposed by the Law Commission in 2007 being based on economic disadvantage; and the other a more discretionary scheme similar to that on divorce under the MCA 1973. It was the latter option which was chosen and incorporated into the Bill. For details of the Bill, see R. Probert, 'The Cohabitation Bill' [2009] Family Law 150.

[250] The 'classic' case of unfairness which is often cited is that of *Burns v Burns* [1984] Ch 317 where the female cohabitant (she had taken her partner's name) failed on relationship breakdown to gain an interest under a trust in the home owned by her male partner, even though they had cohabited for nearly 20 years and she had looked after the house and brought up the children. Cf *Hammond v Mitchell* [1991] 1 WLR 1127 where the female cohabitant obtained an interest in the home under a trust on facts similar to those in *Burns,* except that a conversation she had had with her partner (even though brief and many years earlier) was held to be sufficient evidence of an inferred intention that she was to have a half-share.

[251] The Burden sisters supported the Bill, see p 56 (later in this section).

'a scandal in modern Britain that existing law does almost nothing to prevent such people from losing their home or sliding into poverty if their relationship breaks down or their partner dies.'

Other arguments are posited as reasons for reforming the law. One is that the law should keep up to date with changing social conditions and provide new rights for cohabitants, as cohabitation is increasingly popular and is predicted to increase even further in the future. Another argument is that the law of property, which cohabitants must use to determine property disputes, is unsatisfactory and their property rights should be determined by a family law, not a property law, regime. The drawbacks of the law of property were referred to by the Law Commission in its 2006 Consultation Paper[252] where it stated that in cohabitation cases the rules 'have proved to be relatively rigid and extremely difficult to apply, and their application can lead to what many would regard as unfairness between the parties.' The Law Commission said that any claim based on these rules was time-consuming and expensive and resulted in protracted hearings. It also said that the inherent uncertainty of the underlying principles made effective bargaining difficult to achieve as parties found it difficult to predict the outcome of contested litigation.

There are, however, arguments against reforming the law, such as that cohabitants can, if they wish, enter into a marriage or civil partnership and thereby acquire the rights which attach to that status. One of the major arguments against reform is that it would undermine the autonomy of cohabitants, some of whom may have consciously chosen to cohabit in order to avoid the state imposing on them legal obligations which they do not wish to have. Deech,[253] for instance, is of the view that the autonomy and privacy of those who live together should be respected and that, rather than reforming the law, any disputes should be 'dealt with by the ordinary law of the land, of agreements, wills, property and so on'. She argues that any reform of the law degrades the emancipation of women and that any legal reform 'should build on cohabitants' autonomy rather than take it away'. She is in favour of recognising cohabitation contracts and encouraging cohabitants to make wills leaving their property to each other if that is what they wish.[254] In other words, Deech is in favour of maintaining the autonomy and contractual freedom of cohabitants, but ensuring that they know what their rights and remedies are. Herring, on the other hand, is of the view that individual conceptions of autonomy 'are inconsistent with the realities of family life; are dissonant with how people understand their intimate lives; and work against the interests of women.'[255] Instead, he argues that a vision of autonomy is needed which recognises the interdependency and vulnerability of both children and adults within family relationships.[256] However, despite the arguments against reform based on autonomy, a compromise is possible, as any legal reform giving cohabitants new rights could

---

[252] *Cohabitation: The Financial Consequences of Relationship Breakdown* (Law Com No 179, 2006).

[253] R. Deech, 'Cohabitation' [2010] Family Law 39.

[254] Deech is also not in favour of the proposals providing for automatic inheritance on intestacy for cohabitants (see Law Commission Consultation Paper, *Intestacy and Family Provision* (Law Com CP No 191, 2009), Part 4).

[255] J. Herring, 'Relational Autonomy in Family Law' in J. Wallbank, J. Herring, and S. Choudhry (eds), *Rights, Gender and Family Law* (Abingdon: Routledge, 2009), p 275.

[256] See also L. Glennon, 'The Limitations of Equality Discourses on the Contours of Intimate Obligations' in J. Wallbank, J. Herring, and S. Choudhry (eds), *Rights, Gender and Family Law* (Abingdon: Routledge, 2009), pp. 169–198.

include provisions allowing cohabitants to contract out of any new regime should they wish to do so.[257]

If it is decided that the law must be changed, then one of the most difficult policy issues is defining the terms 'cohabitants' or 'cohabitation' for the purpose of giving those who live together new rights and obligations. Should there be a minimum duration requirement and, if so, how long should the relationship have lasted; and should the fact the couple have children automatically bring them within the definition of cohabitants?[258] A definition of cohabitation which gives a wide category of persons living together new legal rights might undermine the autonomy of cohabitants; and may also be seen to undermine the institution of marriage if those who come within the definition are given quasi-marital rights. How cohabitation is defined for the purposes of eligibility for new legal rights has been, and will be, an important part of any discussions of reform of the law.

Another difficult and important policy issue is whether cohabitants who are eligible should have the same rights and remedies as married couples and civil partners on relationship breakdown. In other words, what should be the scope of any new rights? Should, for instance, cohabitants be entitled to maintenance, property orders, and a share of their partner's pension on relationship breakdown in the same way as spouses and civil partners? The Law Commission in its 2007 Report and the Cohabitation Bill 2008 took different approaches in respect of what entitlements cohabitants should have.

The Law Commission was against cohabitants having the same rights as divorcing couples as it would 'impose an equivalence with marriage which many people would find inappropriate' and which would be 'politically unattainable'.[259] The Law Commission therefore recommended a statutory discretionary regime for adjusting the property of cohabitants, although limited to addressing the need to adjust for any disadvantage or retained benefit arising from the relationship. There would be no power to order periodical payments as cohabitants do not necessarily give each other a commitment of future support.[260]

The Cohabitation Bill 2008, on the other hand, would have given cohabitants rights which were similar, although not identical, to those of married couples on divorce. Reforms in Australia and New Zealand have also given cohabitants virtually the same rights as married couples on relationship breakdown. Thus, in Australia[261] cohabiting couples (those who are able to prove according to various statutory criteria that they living in a 'de facto' relationship) have rights equivalent to those of married couples on relation-

---

[257] Provision was made for this in both the Law Commission's proposals for reform in 2007 and in the Cohabitation Bill 2008.

[258] The Cohabitation Bill 2008 originally defined cohabitants as persons who live together as a couple (opposite-sex or same-sex) for a continuous period of at least two years; or live together as a couple and are the parents of a minor child or have a joint residence order in respect of a child. However, the two-year requirement was later amended to five after debate in the House of Lords.

[259] See the Law Commission Report, paras 4.5–4.10.

[260] S. Bridge, 'Financial Relief for Cohabitants: How the Law Commission's Scheme would Work' [2007] Family Law 998 and S. Bridge, 'Financial Relief for Cohabitants: Eligibility, Opt-Out and Provision on Death' [2007] Family Law 1076. For criticism, see G. Douglas, J. Pearce, and H. Woodward, 'The Law Commission's Cohabitation Proposals: Applying them in Practice' [2008] Family Law 1076.

[261] Under the Family Law Amendment (De Facto Financial Matters and Other Measures) Act 2008, which amends the Family Law Act 1975, and which came into force in March 2008. See H. Baker, 'Family Law Down Under: Can the Old World Learn from the New?' [2009] International Family Law 165 (for an edited version of this article, see [2009] Family Law 1201).

ship breakdown, and which are similar to those which married couples have on divorce in England and Wales.[262] In New Zealand, 'relationship property' (home, chattels, post-relationship acquisitions) are shared equally after three years' cohabitation, subject to the parties contracting out.[263]

There are other important and difficult issues to address. One is whether cohabitants should be entitled to opt out of any new scheme and, if so, how this should be achieved. Any discussion of reform would have to consider whether, when, and in what circumstances the court would have the power to vary or revoke such agreements.[264] Another issue is whether heterosexual cohabiting partners should be given the opportunity to enter into a civil partnership, which is currently only available to same-sex couples.[265] In some countries heterosexual couples can register such a partnership.[266] Any reforms will also have to address the issue of whether those who cohabit should be able to continue to bring claims under the general law, such as for a beneficial interest in the home under a trust.

Despite differing views about whether the law should be reformed to give cohabitants new rights, and the advantages and disadvantages of reforming the law, it is not disputed that cohabitants should have access to easily understandable information about their rights and remedies and about their lack of them compared with married couples, including the fact that there is no such thing as a 'common law marriage'. The Government's Living Together Campaign, launched in 2004, aimed to provide information and guidance for cohabitants,[267] and a survey conducted for the Ministry of Justice by Barlow, Burgoyne, and Smithson[268] found that those who used the Living Together Campaign's website were of the view that they had become better informed about their rights and obligations as cohabitants as a result of visiting the website.

10.2 HOME-SHARERS

Some people live together in informal relationships but are not cohabitants. Thus, some people live together as companions, or as friends, or because they have a family relationship.[269] Such 'home-sharers' may live together for different reasons. Some may live together because this is the only way they can afford to buy a house. Some may do so for companionate reasons, and others may live together to care for another person or a family member. Persons living in informal home-sharing relationships do not have those family law rights which are available to married couples and civil partners except in respect of protection from domestic violence when they can apply for remedies under

---

[262] Under the MCA 1973, Pt II, see Chapter 4.   [263] See the Property (Relationships) Act 1976.

[264] The Law Commission's proposals for reform (see its 2007 Report) and the Cohabitation Bill 2008 made provision for such agreements to be set aside by the court where they would cause manifest unfairness.

[265] See Section 9.

[266] In the Netherlands heterosexual and homosexual cohabitants can enter into a civil partnership, and in France they can enter into a *pacte civile de solidarité* (a state-endorsed contract).

[267] Its website (www.advicenow.org.uk/living-together) provides advice and guidance for cohabitants which explains what rights cohabitants have and how they differ from those of married couples.

[268] See para 5, p 7, in A. Barlow, C. Burgoyne, and J. Smithson, *The Living Together Campaign: An Investigation of its Impact on Legally Aware Cohabitants* (Ministry of Justice, 2007), available at www.justice.gov.uk/publications/docs/living-together-research-report(1).pdf.

[269] See L. Glennon, 'Displacing the "Conjugal" Family in Legal Policy—A Progressive Move?' (2005) Child and Family Law Quarterly 17.

Part IV of the Family Law Act 1996 in certain circumstances.[270] 'Home-sharers' can be vulnerable in the same was as cohabitants can be in respect of ownership of the home when the home-sharing arrangement comes to an end and also when the other home-sharer dies. They can also suffer tax disadvantages as the case of *Burden and Burden v UK*,[271] which follows, has shown. The Law Commission has considered whether the law should be changed to give home-sharers certain property rights, and in 2002 published a discussion paper[272] in which it discussed a 'contribution-based' model of reform, but in which it came to the conclusion that this was unworkable in practice and the discussion was taken no further.

Key case

In the *Burden* case two unmarried sisters (aged 90 and 82) considered that they were discriminated against in respect of inheritance tax under UK law as they did not have the same inheritance rights as same-sex couples even though they had lived together for the whole of their adult lives in the same home which they owned in their joint names. On the death of one of them, the survivor would be forced to sell the house to pay the 40 per cent inheritance tax owed on its value. After their claim failed before the English courts they took their case to the ECtHR, arguing that UK inheritance tax laws discriminated against them under Article 14 of the ECHR taken in conjunction with Article 1 of Protocol 1 to the Convention which provides that 'Every natural or legal person is entitled to the peaceful enjoyment of his possessions'. They also argued that the Civil Partnership Act 2004 breached their human rights under the ECHR as it was discriminatory in that it gave rights to same-sex, but not opposite-sex, couples. Their claim failed. The Grand Chamber of the ECtHR held by 15 votes to 2 that there had been no violation of the Convention, as the UK had not exceeded the wide margin of appreciation afforded to it; and the difference of treatment for the purposes of the grant of inheritance tax exceptions was reasonably and objectively justified for the purpose of Article 14. It was of the view that any workable tax system was bound to create marginal situations and individual cases of apparent hardship or injustice; and it was up to national authorities to decide how to strike the right balance between raising revenue and pursuing social policy objectives.

The outcome of the decision in *Burden* was that the UK was justified in not treating siblings in the same way as married couples and civil partners for the purpose of inheritance tax, even though they had lived together for all their adult lives.[273] The UK was entitled to differentiate between marriage and other relationships in respect of tax. However, some commentators have been critical of the decision. Deech, for instance, considered it 'inequitable' that the Burden sisters, who had lived 'at least as companionably and interdependently as any two same sex partners' were denied any sort of benefits.[274] She referred to other carer situations, such as the child who looks after a parent and does not inherit, or if he or she inherits has to pay inheritance tax. Deech proposes that a 'sensible reform'

---

[270] As associated persons, which includes persons who 'live or have lived in the same household, otherwise than merely by reason of one of them being the other's employee, tenant, lodger or boarder' and persons who are relatives (s 62(3)).   [271] (App no 13378/05), [2008] 2 FLR 787.

[272] *Sharing Homes: A Discussion Paper* (Law Com No 278).

[273] See R. Auchmuty, 'Beyond Couples' (2009) 17 Feminist Legal Studies 205.

[274] See R. Deech. 'Sisters Sisters—And Other Family Members' [2010] Family Law 375.

would be 'to grant deferral of IHT to any two family members who are co-dependent and are within the prohibited degrees so that the option of civil partnership or marriage is not open to them.' Lord Lester's Cohabitation Bill[275] put before Parliament at the end of 2008 made provision for sibling home-sharers but the Bill went nowhere and there are currently no proposals for reform.

DISCUSSION QUESTIONS

1. Is the 'legal' family becoming more fragmented in the face of greater cohabitation between adults?

2. Argue for or against the extension of marriage to same-sex couples in light of the court's decision in *Wilkinson v Kitzinger*.

3. Is nullity a relevant remedy in the twenty-first century?

FURTHER READING

BAMFORTH, N., '"The Benefits of Marriage in All But Name"? Same-Sex Couples and the Civil Partnership Act 2004' [2007] Child and Family Law Quarterly 133

BARLOW, A., BURGOYNE, C., CLERY, E., and SMITHSON, J., *Cohabitation and the Law: Myths, Money and the Media*, British Social Attitudes 24th Report (London: Sage, 2008)

BARLOW, A., DUNCAN, S., JAMES, G., and PARK, A., *Cohabitation, Marriage and the Law: Social Change and Legal Reform in 21st Century Britain* (Oxford: Hart, 2005)

BESSANT, C., 'Transsexuals and Marriage after *Goodwin v United Kingdom*' [2003] Family Law 111

BRADNEY, A., 'Developing Human Rights? The Lords and Transsexual Marriages' [2003] Family Law 585

CRETNEY, S., *Same-Sex Relationships* (Oxford: Oxford University Press, 2006)

DIDUCK, A. and O'DONOVAN, K. (eds), *Feminist Perspectives on Family Law* (London: Routledge, 2007)

DUNCAN, S., BARLOW, A., and JAMES, G., 'Why Don't They Marry? Cohabitation, Commitment and DIY Marriage' [2005] Child and Family Law Quarterly 383

EEKELAAR, J., *Family Life and Personal Life* (Oxford: Oxford University Press, 2006)

EEKELAAR, J., and MACLEAN, M., 'Marriage and the Moral Bases of Personal Relationships' (2004) Journal of Law and Society 244

GILMORE, S., '*Bellinger v Bellinger*—Not Quite Between the Ears and Between the Legs—Transsexualism and Marriage in the Lords' (2003) 15(3) Child and Family Law Quarterly 295

GILMORE, S., 'The Gender Recognition Act 2004' [2004] Family Law 741

---

[275] Lord Lester of Herne Hill introduced a Private Member's Bill in the House of Lords on 11 December 2008. See Chapter 5.

GLENNON, L., 'Displacing the Conjugal Family in Legal Policy—A Progressive Move?' (2005) 17(2) Child and Family Law Quarterly 141

GLENNON, L., 'Strategizing for the Future through the Civil Partnership Act' (2006) 33(2) Journal of Law and Society 244

GLENNON, L., 'The Limitations of Equality Discourses on the Contours of Intimate Obligations' in J. Wallbank, J. Herring, and S. Choudhry (eds), *Rights, Gender and Family Law* (Abingdon: Routledge, 2009), 169

GRANT BOWMAN, C., *Unmarried Couples, Law, and Public Policy* (Oxford: Oxford University Press, 2010)

PROBERT, R., 'When Are We Married? Void, Non-Existent and Presumed Marriages' (2002) Legal Studies 398

2

THE DISSOLUTION OF ADULT RELATIONSHIPS

INTRODUCTION

This chapter deals with the termination of adult relationships, in particular divorce. It also considers the dissolution of civil partnerships, and the termination of cohabitation. The property and financial consequences of termination and arrangements for children on relationship breakdown are dealt with in other chapters in the book.

1 THE LAW OF DIVORCE

1.1 A BRIEF HISTORY OF DIVORCE

Divorce has only been generally available as a means of ending a marriage since the middle of the nineteenth century. Prior to that the Ecclesiastical Courts could grant a decree *a mensa et thoro*, a decree which, like the current decree of judicial separation, relieved the parties of the duty to live together but did not terminate the marriage. For a very few couples it was possible to end a marriage and thereby obtain the right to remarry, but this could only be achieved by means of a private Act of Parliament.[1] It was not until the Matrimonial Causes Act 1857 that a law of divorce applicable to the public at large was introduced.[2] This Act, and subsequent divorce legislation until 1969, was strictly fault-based.[3] Divorce law was built around the notion that one spouse was guilty of a matrimonial offence.[4] Parties were referred to as 'guilty' and 'innocent', and divorce was a remedy for a legal wrong. This conceptual base led to the inclusion in legislation, and the development by case law, of a legal infrastructure of rules and principles which often bore little relationship to the physical, mental, and emotional circumstances of marriage breakdown. The matrimonial offences were difficult to prove whether or not the petition was defended. Divorce was barred where the respondent had connived at the commission of the offence relied on. An attempt at reconciliation was regarded as condonation (evidence that a party approved of the divorce) which could also provide a defence to divorce. Thus, evidence that the parties were in agreement that divorce was the solution

---

[1] For discussion of the first ever divorce, see R. Probert, 'The *Roos* Case' in S. Gilmore, J. Herring, and R. Probert (eds), *Landmark Cases in Family Law* (Oxford: Hart, 2011).

[2] For an account of the history of the law of divorce, see L. Stone, *Road to Divorce* (Oxford: Oxford University Press, 1991).   [3] Matrimonial Causes Act 1923; Matrimonial Causes Act 1937.

[4] Between 1937 and 1969 the grounds for divorce were adultery, cruelty, desertion for a continuous period of three years or more, and incurable insanity on the part of the respondent. This last ground was the only concession to the notion that a marriage could be terminated despite there being no 'fault' by either party.

to their matrimonial difficulties resulted in the decree being denied on the ground of collusion, polarising the position of the parties. It led to spurious cases where the husband provided false evidence of adultery (often allegedly committed in a hotel), and to snooping and gross invasions of privacy in order to obtain evidence of adultery where this was denied. It prevented divorces where marriages had clearly broken down and it prevented spouses from making realistic attempts at reconciliation. In short, the law was out of touch with natural human responses to matrimonial difficulties and positively encouraged acrimony. It allowed the notion that one spouse was guilty and the other innocent to influence arrangements about the children, and it penalised sensible agreements arrived at by consent. Moreover, it made no provision for those persons who had left their spouses and formed a new family unit. It was impossible for such persons to marry for a second time where their first spouse refused to divorce them. By the middle of the twentieth century change was clearly long overdue.

In 1956 a Royal Commission, the Morton Commission,[5] published a report which advocated reform of the law and recommended the introduction of the concept of no-fault divorce. In 1966, a group appointed by the Archbishop of Canterbury published a report, *Putting Asunder*, which advocated that divorce should be based on a single concept, namely the irretrievable breakdown of the marriage. *Putting Asunder* recommended that in every case there should be a judicial enquiry to ensure that breakdown had really occurred and that no abuse of the system had taken place. *Putting Asunder* was followed shortly afterwards by a discussion paper issued by the Law Commission,[6] which similarly advocated proof of marital breakdown as the basis for dissolving a marriage, but recommended that this should be inferred from one or more of five specified facts. The law was amended in 1969 by the Divorce Reform Act 1969, which represented a compromise between the positions taken by the Archbishop of Canterbury's group and the Law Commission.

The underlying purpose of the reformed divorce law was to:

(i) to buttress, rather than to undermine, the stability of marriage;

and

(ii) when, regrettably, a marriage has irretrievably broken down, to enable the empty shell to be destroyed with the minimum fairness, and the minimum bitterness, distress and humiliation.[7]

Provisions were therefore introduced which were designed to assist parties to remain together and resolve their differences. Parties were no longer to be barred from petitioning if they continued to live together after a party committed adultery or after other behaviour which under the old law would have prevented them from obtaining a decree of divorce.[8] Some encouragement was given to parties to consider reconciliation rather than proceeding to a divorce. A solicitor acting for the petitioner would be obliged to file a certificate stating whether or not he or she had discussed reconciliation with the client or had given the client names and addresses of people qualified to help.[9] A court could adjourn the proceedings at any time if it appeared that there was a reasonable prospect of successful reconciliation.[10]

---

[5] *Royal Commission on Marriage and Divorce* (Cmd 9678, 1956).
[6] *Reform of the Grounds of Divorce: the Field of Choice* (Cmd 3123, 1966).   [7] Ibid, para 15.
[8] MCA 1973, s 2, although in relation to adultery s 2(1) creates a bar where the parties live together for longer than six months after the discovery of the adultery.   [9] MCA 1973, s 6(1).
[10] Section 6(2). It was subsequently established that these provisions had limited value, see the Booth Report (*Report of the Matrimonial Causes Procedure Committee*, Matrimonial Causes Procedure Committee,

Parliament properly took the view that it would be wrong to liberalise divorce law without at the same time ensuring that dependent spouses could be protected from suffering some of the more serious economic consequences of divorce.[11] Therefore, legislation was introduced, the Matrimonial Proceedings and Property Act 1970, which gave the courts wide powers to make financial provision and property adjustment orders on the grant of a decree.[12] Implementation of the new law by the Divorce Reform Act 1969 was delayed and the two Acts came into force together. The 1969 Act and the 1970 Act were subsequently consolidated in the Matrimonial Causes Act (MCA) 1973, which remains the law today.

1.2 DEVELOPMENTS IN DIVORCE PROCEDURE

Changes to the procedure for obtaining a divorce have been made over the years. At one time all divorces, undefended and defended, were heard in London and only by senior judges. This was because divorce was considered a serious matter. Divorces were heard in open court with the petitioner giving oral evidence to prove the ground and fact alleged. This was not only distressing for the parties, but also costly and time-consuming. With the huge increase in divorces, particularly after the more liberal grounds for divorce were introduced by the Divorce Reform Act 1969, the courts became overloaded with divorces, even though undefended divorces were taking only a short time to be heard. Owing to these difficulties, a new procedure called the 'special procedure' was introduced in the 1970s with the aim of simplifying the divorce process, making it quicker and less costly. It was initially introduced, in 1973, for childless couples divorcing with consent, but in 1975 was extended to all childless couples, except those petitioning on the basis of unreasonable behaviour. In 1977 it was extended to all undefended divorces. All undefended divorces today are therefore dealt with by what is an essentially administrative procedure, a 'paper exercise' whereby the district judge in the divorce court examines the papers to establish whether the marriage has irretrievably broken down and whether the fact alleged in the divorce petition (eg adultery, behaviour etc) is proved and whether there is any reason for refusing to grant the divorce. A list of those petitioners who have satisfied the district judge that a decree nisi of divorce should be granted is drawn up and read out in open court, after which the district judge pronounces decrees nisi of divorce en bloc. If a divorce is undefended there is usually no need for the parties to attend court. Defended divorces, on the other hand, which are virtually non-existent because of the futility of defending a divorce, are still heard in open court with the parties giving oral evidence.

From time to time there has been discussion about reforming the divorce procedure. For instance in the 1980s the Matrimonial Causes Act Committee, chaired by Hon Mrs Justice Booth (the 'Booth Committee')[13] was requested by the Government to look at the divorce procedure and to make recommendations for reform. The recommendations were not implemented, but the attempt at divorce reform in the Family Law Act 1996 included some of the Booth Committee's recommendations, such as changes of terminology to make divorce law more understandable.

---

chaired by Hon Mrs Justice Booth (HMSO, 1985), paras 4.42–4.43); Law Com No 170, para 3.9; and G. Davis and M. Murch, *Grounds for Divorce* (Oxford: Clarendon Press, 1988), Ch 4.

[11] There was particular concern about the so-called 'Casanova's charter' provision, which enabled an 'innocent' spouse to be divorced against his or her will after the parties had lived apart for at least five years.   [12] See Chapter 4.

[13] See *Report of the Matrimonial Causes Procedure Committee*, Matrimonial Causes Procedure Committee, chaired by Hon Mrs Justice Booth (HMSO, 1985).

1.3 TRENDS IN DIVORCE

Talking point

In respect of the number of divorces, Government statistics show a decline in the numbers of divorce petitions filed annually. Thus, in 2009, 116,576 decrees absolute of divorce were granted in England and Wales, a drop of 5 per cent on 2008 and continuing the steady downward trend.[14] In 2006, for instance, 142,116 decrees absolute were granted.[15] The average age of those who divorce has risen over the years. In 2008 it was 43.9 years for men and 41.4 years for women, figures which partly reflect the rise in the age at which people marry. Many divorces involve persons who have had a previous divorce. Thus, in 2008, 1 in 5 of those divorcing had a previous marriage ending in divorce, a proportion which has almost doubled since 1981. More divorces are brought by and granted to wives (67 per cent of divorces in 2008); and for all divorces the behaviour of the respondent is the most common fact relied on for divorce. Men and women in their late 20s have the highest divorce rate of all age groups.

---

2 OBTAINING A DIVORCE

2.1 JURISDICTION TO HEAR A DIVORCE

Key legislation

The rules governing the jurisdiction of the courts in England and Wales to hear a divorce (and annulment and judicial separation) are laid down in section 5 of the Domicile and Matrimonial Proceedings Act 1973, as amended by Council Regulation (EC) No 2201/2003 Concerning Jurisdiction and the Recognition and Enforcement of Judgments in Matrimonial Matters and in Matters of Parental Responsibility ('Brussels II Revised'). Section 5(2) of the Domicile and Matrimonial Proceedings Act 1973 sets out, with reference to Brussels II, the circumstances when the courts have jurisdiction to entertain proceedings for divorce.

These jurisdictional rules are complex, but in very general terms the courts in England and Wales have jurisdiction in divorce proceedings if either spouse is domiciled in England or Wales when the proceedings are begun, or is habitually resident in England or Wales throughout the period of one year ending with the date on which proceedings are begun.[16] The issue of jurisdiction can be complex and may involve difficult questions, for instance about domicile.[17]

---

[14] See *Judicial and Court Statistics 2009* (Ministry of Justice, 2010), Ch 2, Table 2.5. The Office for National Statistics (www.ons.gov.uk) also provides statistics on divorce and provides the remainder of the information contained in this section.   [15] Ibid.

[16] In *Mark v Mark* [2005] UKHL 42, [2005] 2 FLR 1193 the House of Lords held that, for the purpose of jurisdiction to entertain a divorce petition under s 5(2) of the Domicile and Matrimonial Proceedings Act 1973, residence in England and Wales need not be lawful residence. Thus a person can be habitually resident or domiciled in England and Wales even if his or her presence in the UK is a criminal offence under the Immigration Act 1971.

[17] See eg *Munro v Munro* [2007] EWHC 3315 (Fam), [2008] 1 FLR 1613 where Bennett J had to decide whether the wife should be allowed to petition for divorce in England and Wales even though she and her husband had moved to Spain shortly after marrying in England. On the facts, Bennett J held that the English court had jurisdiction.

Establishing whether England and Wales has jurisdiction to hear a divorce is particularly important for parties in 'big money' cases, because if a decree of divorce is granted by the divorce court in England and Wales then the courts in England and Wales also have jurisdiction to make property and finance orders on divorce under Part II of the MCA 1973.[18] Because the divorce courts in England and Wales have wide discretionary powers to make property and financial orders depending on the circumstances of the case and exercise an approach based on fairness and equality,[19] some parties to a marriage, particularly those where there are substantial property assets to distribute, are keen to divorce in England and Wales. In 'big money' international cases the parties may compete with each other to have their case heard in the country whose court will give them the more favourable award. Thus, even though it is time-consuming and expensive, parties to 'international' marriages will sometimes engage in what is called 'forum shopping' and there will be a race between the parties so that one of them (usually the wife) can win the race and have the divorce dealt with in London or in another part of England and Wales. Such disputes are not about which jurisdiction is the better one for obtaining the actual divorce, but about which jurisdiction will provide a better finance and property award on divorce.

Talking point

The former President of the Family Division, Sir Mark Potter, in a postscript to his decision in *Charman v Charman*[20] drew attention to this:

> Thus, in very big money cases, the effect of the decision in *White* was to raise the aspirations of the claimant hugely. In big money cases the *White* factor has more than doubled the levels of award and it has been said by many that London has become the divorce capital of the world for aspiring wives.

Key case

Attempts by the husband and wife to hear their cases in different jurisdictions were the subject of the litigation, for example, in *Golubovich v Golubovich*,[21] which provides an example of how parties are willing to engage in complex and costly jurisdictional disputes in order to gain a financial advantage on divorce. In this case, the husband (who came from a hugely wealthy Russian family) and his Russian wife had lived in London following their marriage. On marriage breakdown, he invoked the jurisdiction of the Russian courts and she the jurisdiction of the English courts. It was therefore a question of which court had priority to hear their divorce. The husband won the race to the divorce decree but, it appeared, by allegedly

---

[18] See Chapter 4.

[19] See *White v White* [2001] 1 AC 596 where the House of Lords held that fairness and non-discrimination were the principles to be applied by the courts in ancillary relief proceedings on divorce and that the court should apply a 'yardstick of equality' and not just make an award limited to the reasonable needs of the applicant. After *White*, in big money cases, wives in particular were successful in gaining a much bigger share of the matrimonial assets on divorce than had hitherto been the case, as the court was no longer restricted to making an order that merely satisfied their reasonable needs. See Chapter 4 on finance and property on divorce.   [20] [2007] EWCA Civ 503 at [116]. See Chapter 4 on finance and property on divorce.

[21] [2010] EWCA Civ 810.

forging documents. The English court subsequently made a '*Hemain* injunction'[22] precluding him from taking any further steps in the Russian courts to have his divorce decided there. However, despite being aware of the injunction, the Russian court, on his application, granted him a divorce. The wife thereupon sought an order in the English court asking for the Russian divorce decree to be refused recognition in England and Wales. She was successful at first instance but the Court of Appeal allowed the husband's appeal, holding that the Russian court had found itself with jurisdiction to dissolve the marriage and, absent any treaty with the jurisdiction of England and Wales, the Russian court had found itself unfettered by the existence of the *Hemain* injunction.

2.2 STAYING DIVORCE PROCEEDINGS IN ENGLAND AND WALES

In connection with jurisdiction, the divorce courts in England and Wales have jurisdiction to stay proceedings for divorce if they consider the matter would be better dealt with in another jurisdiction. Thus, if divorce proceedings are pending in a country outside England and Wales, then, under the Domicile and Matrimonial Proceedings Act 1973,[23] the divorce courts in England and Wales have a discretionary jurisdiction to stay the English divorce proceedings which it will usually do if it considers the foreign court is the more appropriate forum for hearing the divorce.[24] With regard to EU divorces, even though Brussels II governs the jurisdiction of divorces in England and Wales, a party to a marriage can nevertheless apply for a stay of the English proceedings under the Domicile and Matrimonial Proceedings Act 1973.[25]

2.3 DIVORCE UNDER THE MATRIMONIAL CAUSES ACT 1973

The current law governing the substantive law of divorce is set out in Part I of the MCA 1973, and the rules governing divorce procedure are laid down in the Family Procedure Rules 2010. Part II of the 1973 Act deals with property and financial matters on divorce, which are discussed in detail in Chapter 4. Other statutory provisions apply to disputes about children on divorce, whether it be about residence, contact, or child maintenance.[26]

2.3.1 The ground for divorce

Key legislation

Under section 1(1) of the MCA 1973, irretrievable breakdown of marriage is the sole ground for divorce, but irretrievable breakdown is only established on proof of at least one of the five facts listed in section 1(2) of the Act.[27] Section 1(2) provides as follows:

---

[22] This is an 'anti-suit' injunction requiring a person not to take steps to bring proceedings in another jurisdiction.   [23] See Domicile and Matrimonial Proceedings Act 1973, s 5(6) and Sch 1, para 9(1).
    [24] See eg *S v S (Divorce: Staying Proceedings)* [1997] 2 FLR 100 (and see *JKN v JCN* [2010] EWHC 843 (Fam)).   [25] See *JKN v JCN* [2010] EWHC 843 (Fam).
    [26] See Chapters 9 and 6.
    [27] In discussions leading up to the current law of divorce, it was recognised by the Law Commission and accepted by Parliament that it would be impossible for courts to adjudicate on the individual circumstances of every marriage to establish whether the marriage had irretrievably broken down. Hence the introduction of the five facts.

The court hearing a petition for divorce shall not hold the marriage to have broken down irretrievably unless the petitioner satisfies the court of one or more of the following facts, that is to say—

(a) that the respondent has committed adultery and the petitioner finds it intolerable to live with the respondent;

(b) that the respondent has behaved in such a way that the petitioner cannot reasonably be expected to live with the respondent;

(c) that the respondent has deserted the petitioner for a continuous period of at least two years immediately preceding the presentation of the petition;

(d) that the parties to the marriage have lived apart for a continuous period of at least two years immediately preceding the presentation of the petition…and the respondent consents to a decree being granted;

(e) that the parties to the marriage have lived apart for a continuous period of at least five years immediately preceding the presentation of the petition.

Talking point

These five facts are commonly referred to as the 'grounds' for divorce, when, technically speaking, there is only one ground for divorce, irretrievable breakdown of the marriage. However, both irretrievable breakdown *and* at least one of the five facts must be proved,[28] requirements which have provoked criticism, and have caused some rather strange decisions in the earlier case law.[29]

In Section 2.3.3 we examine in some detail how the five facts have been judicially interpreted. Before doing so, however, it is convenient to outline some procedural matters relating to obtaining a divorce.

2.3.2 Divorce procedure

The divorce petition is the key document in the divorce proceedings, as it informs the respondent and the court of the basis on which the petitioner is seeking the divorce and of any orders that he or she will be seeking as part of the divorce. It must contain specified information,[30] and also a statement that the marriage has broken down and brief particulars of the fact(s) relied on. The petition must conclude with a prayer for dissolution of the marriage, any claim for costs, and a prayer setting out any claims for property and finance orders and any child support maintenance claimed. To begin proceedings, the petition, and other required documents, must be presented to a divorce county court (or the Principal Registry in London).[31]

---

[28] Section 1(4).

[29] See eg *Richards v Richards* [1972] WLR 1073 and *Buffery v Buffery* [1988] 2 FLR 365, where in both cases the Court of Appeal found that the marriage had irretrievably broken down but that the fact alleged ('unreasonable behaviour') had not been satisfied.

[30] See the Family Procedure Rules (FPR) 2010 and the supporting notes to the divorce petition.

[31] The marriage certificate, the Statement of Arrangements for the Children, certified copies of any court orders, and any certificate in respect of public funding.

2.3.2.1 The one-year bar on petitions

A petition for divorce cannot be presented within the first year of marriage.[32] This is an absolute bar. In other words, there is no discretion to waive or reduce the time limit, however extreme a petitioner's case. But, despite the one-year bar, a petition can be based on matters which occurred during the first year of marriage,[33] such as any evidence of adultery or unreasonable behaviour.

2.3.2.2 Encouraging reconciliation

One of the policy objectives of the law of divorce is to encourage the saving of saveable marriages and in order to promote this objective, certain provisions in Part I of the MCA 1973 encourage reconciliation. Thus, the court can adjourn divorce proceedings at any stage if there is a reasonable possibility of a reconciliation being effected between the parties;[34] and certain periods of resumed cohabitation are ignored when establishing whether a fact is proved in order to satisfy the court that the marriage has irretrievably broken down.[35] If a solicitor is acting in the proceedings, then a reconciliation certificate must be filed with the court stating whether or not the solicitor has discussed with the client the possibility of a reconciliation and has given the client details of persons qualified to help effect a reconciliation.[36] The solicitor is not obliged to discuss reconciliation with the client.[37]

Divorce involves a two-stage procedure: a decree nisi followed by a decree absolute.[38] The marriage is not terminated until the grant of decree absolute, which is automatically granted on the application of the petitioner who can apply for it six weeks or later after the grant of decree nisi. If the petitioner fails to apply, the respondent can do so after three months have passed from the earliest day on which the petitioner could apply,[39] but the decree cannot be granted without a hearing by a judge or district judge.[40] If no application has been made after 12 months, the court may require the applicant to provide evidence accounting for the delay. The court then has a discretion whether to make the decree absolute or to rescind it altogether. These rules are strict; a decree absolute obtained in breach of the rules is void.[41] When a divorce is sought on either of the separation grounds, a decree absolute can be refused if the respondent has not been satisfactorily financially provided for by the petitioner.[42]

The period between decree nisi and decree absolute can be used to sort out outstanding issues relating to financial and property matters and children, but there is no requirement that these should be resolved before the divorce is finalised. The purpose of the gap between decree nisi and decree absolute is to enable a respondent to appeal and for the Queen's Proctor and other persons to show just cause why the decree should not be made absolute.[43] Intervention by the Queen's Proctor is rare, but was more common under

---

[32] MCA 1973, s 3(1).

[33] Ibid, s 3(2). In the law prior to the current law there was as a bar on divorce in the first three years of marriage, unless a party could prove exceptional hardship on the part of the petitioner or depravity on the part of the respondent. There is no bar in respect of nullity proceedings; a petition for nullity can be sought at any time after a marriage.   [34] Section 6(2).

[35] See Section 2.3.3.2.3.   [36] See FPR 2010, r 7.6.   [37] MCA 1973, s 6(1).

[38] A decree nisi may be rescinded by the court if both spouses agree to this and are of sound mind (see eg *S v S (Rescission of Decree Nisi: Pension Sharing Provision)* [2002] 1 FLR 457, where the parties wished to do so in order that they could be subject to the new legislation on pensions which had just come into force).

[39] MCA 1973, s 9(2)).   [40] See FPR 2010, r 7.33.

[41] See *Dennis v Dennis* [2000] 2 FLR 231.   [42] See Section 2.3.4.   [43] MCA 1973, s 8.

the 'old' law when a decree could be refused if the parties had colluded in obtaining the divorce, for instance by fabricating adultery.[44]

As one of the policy objectives of divorce law is to protect the interests of children, if there are children under 16, or over 16 but receiving higher education or training, then the divorce cannot be made absolute until the judge[45] is satisfied with the arrangements for the children as set down in the Statement of Arrangements for the Children, a form containing specified information and which must be submitted to the court with the divorce petition.[46] The purpose of the 'Statement' is to enable the court to fulfil its duty under section 41(1) of the MCA 1973 which requires the judge to consider whether, in light of the actual or proposed arrangements made for the children, the court should exercise any of its powers under the Children Act 1989 with respect to the children. If the court is satisfied with the arrangements, the judge will certify to that effect. If not, he or she can direct that further evidence be filed, or order a welfare report under section 7 of the Children Act 1989, or order the parent(s) to attend court. If the child's welfare requires it, and the court is not able to exercise any of its powers under the Children Act 1989 without further consideration of the case, the judge can exceptionally direct that the decree of divorce should not be made absolute.[47] In practice this rarely happens.

In the case of undefended divorces (virtually all divorces because of the futility of defending a divorce), there is usually no need for the parties or their legal representatives to attend court. The judge may request further information or evidence, if needed. The judge, sitting in private in the divorce court, scrutinises the divorce application and, if satisfied that the ground is made out, files a certificate to that effect, and a date, time, and place are fixed for the judge to pronounce decree nisi. Both parties receive a certificate and notice of the date and place for the pronouncement, which takes place in open court, but which neither the parties nor their legal representatives need attend. The process of pronouncement of decree nisi is a mere formality. The decrees are listed together in batches and collectively read out by the clerk of the court (or by the judge), with the judge pronouncing decrees nisi orally or by nodding.

Defended divorces begin in the same way as an undefended divorce, but the respondent will indicate in the Acknowledgement of Service his or her intention to defend the divorce. Once various notice requirements have been satisfied,[48] there is an exchange of pleadings and the hearing takes place in open court with the parties giving oral evidence and with there being cross-examination of the parties.[49]

2.3.3 The five facts in section 1(2)

2.3.3.1 Adultery by the respondent and intolerability

A petition based on adultery must establish that the respondent has committed adultery *and* that the petitioner finds it intolerable to live with the respondent.[50] The requirement

---

[44] See *Bhaiji v Chauhan (Queen's Proctor Intervening)* [2003] 2 FLR 485 where the Queen's Proctor intervened and opposed the grant of decrees absolute in cases where bogus allegations of unreasonable behaviour had been made to obtain divorces in respect of five marriages which had been entered into solely for the purpose of circumventing the immigration rules.

[45] The word 'judge' is used here, but in practice it is usually a district judge who hears divorces.

[46] The Statement of Arrangements for the Children (Form D8A) must include details relating to the child's home, education and training, care, child maintenance, contact, and health. The form is available on the HM Courts Service website. [47] Section 41(2).

[48] See FPR 2010, Pt 6.

[49] For a rare case involving a defended divorce, see *Hadjimilitis (Tsavliris) v Tsavliris (Divorce: Irretrievable Breakdown)* [2003] 1 FLR 81. [50] Section 1(2)(a).

of intolerability was added to buttress the stability of marriage, one of the policy aims of the law, so that adultery on its own would not be sufficient to terminate a marriage. Adultery involves a voluntary act of sexual intercourse between a married person and another person not being married to him or her and who is of the opposite sex, and who may or may not be married.[51]

Adultery may be proved in a number of ways. The Acknowledgment of Service form used in relation to petitions based on adultery asks the question: 'Do you admit the adultery alleged in the petition?' If the respondent answers 'Yes', and signs the form, that is sufficient proof. Where the respondent does not admit the adultery, and fails to file an answer, the petitioner will have to prove the adultery in other ways, such as by providing evidence that the respondent is living with another person.

In addition to adultery, the petitioner must also prove that he or she finds it intolerable to live with the respondent. The intolerability need not follow from the adultery,[52] but it may well be the adultery which makes living with the respondent intolerable. The test to be applied when establishing intolerability is subjective,[53] in other words it depends on the petitioner's view of the matter.

To encourage reconciliation, one of the policy objectives of divorce, if the parties continue living together for a period of up to six months after the discovery of the adultery this period must be disregarded in determining whether the petitioner finds it intolerable to live with the respondent.[54] However, if the parties live together for a period in excess of six months after the discovery of adultery then this operates as a complete bar to the presentation of a petition based on adultery.[55]

2.3.3.2 Behaviour by the respondent

The petitioner must prove, in addition to establishing irretrievable breakdown of the marriage, that 'the respondent has behaved in such a way that the petitioner cannot reasonably be expected to live with the respondent'.[56]

Talking point

This fact is often referred to colloquially as 'unreasonable behaviour', but this is not strictly correct as it is a question of whether the respondent's behaviour is such that it is unreasonable for the *petitioner* to continue living with the respondent, not whether the respondent's behaviour is unreasonable. The Court of Appeal has held that behaviour can take the form of an act or an omission.[57]

The respondent's behaviour is the most commonly alleged ground for divorce.[58] This is regrettable, since the policy of terminating a marriage with the minimum bitterness, distress, and humiliation is undermined when either party sets out to prove the behaviour fact. Petitions often contain a catalogue of incidents in support of the allegation so that they add up cumulatively to sufficient behaviour to satisfy the court. Also, because of its pejorative connotations, a petition based on behaviour may be hotly contested in respect of ancillary matters. Allegations of behaviour may make settlement more difficult

---

[51] *Dennis v Dennis* [1955] P 153.
[52] See *Cleary v Cleary* [1974] 1 All ER 498.   [53] *Goodrich v Goodrich* [1971] 2 All ER 1340.
[54] Section 2(2).   [55] Section 2(1).   [56] Section 1(2)(b).
[57] See *Katz v Katz* [1972] 1 WLR 955.
[58] According to statistics published by the Office for National Statistics.

which is often contrary to the best interests of the parties and any children. As long ago as 1985, the Booth Committee, which was asked by the Government to look at divorce procedure with a view to reform, found that allegations of unreasonable behaviour made it worse for the parties and their children. Those findings still hold good today, perhaps even more so, as since 1985 there has been an even greater emphasis on the parties to divorce settling matters in a civilised and non-hostile way and with solicitors having an obligation to deal with family matters in a conciliatory way.[59] In its Report, the Booth Committee stated:[60]

> We are satisfied that the bitterness and unhappiness of divorcing couples is frequently exacerbated and prolonged by the fault element in divorce and that this is particularly so where the fact relied upon is behaviour, whether or not the suit is defended. Great hostility and resentment may be generated by the recital in the petition of allegations of behaviour, often exaggerated and sometimes stretching back over many years, to the extent that no discussion can take place between the parties or any agreement be reached on any matter relating to their marriage or their children.

'Unreasonable behaviour' can cover a wide range of behaviour and be of varying degrees of severity. In some cases, a single serious incident of behaviour might be sufficient to establish the petitioner's case. However, it is important to appreciate that the focus is not on the gravity of the behaviour per se but on its impact on the petitioner. An accumulation of trivial incidents may suffice.[61] There must, however, be some behaviour from which the court can conclude that the petitioner cannot reasonably be expected to live with the respondent, and more than a mere drifting apart of the parties. In *Buffery v Buffery*,[62] for instance, a decree was denied where the wife alleged that her husband was insensitive and never took her out, and that they had nothing to talk about and nothing in common after their children had grown up and left home.

In some circumstances conduct which is not actually directed at the marriage itself, but which has a serious effect on the petitioner, will be sufficient. Thus, a conviction for a serious criminal offence would undoubtedly give the petitioner the facts on which to base a petition, but minor acts of violence might require more than one incident to satisfy the court. Behaviour such as drunkenness, alcoholism, and drug addiction are frequently relied on by petitioners. Causing financial difficulties can constitute unreasonable behaviour,[63] and so may even a failure to finish 'DIY' jobs over a long period.[64]

---

[59] Members of Resolution (an association of family lawyers) adhere to a Code of Practice which requires them to 'see the advantages of a constructive and non-confrontational approach as a way of resolving differences' (r 2). The principles of the Code have been adopted by the Law Society as rules of good practice for family law solicitors generally (see the *Family Law Protocol*, 2nd edn (2006), Appendix 2).

[60] *Report of the Matrimonial Causes Procedure Committee*, para 2.8, under the chairmanship of Hon Mrs Justice Booth (HMSO, 1985).

[61] As they did in *Livingstone-Stallard* [1974] Fam 47 where Dunn J held that the wife 'was subjected to a constant atmosphere of criticism, disapproval and boorish behaviour on the part of her husband'.

[62] [1988] 2 FLR 365.

[63] See *Carter-Fea v Carter-Fea* [1987] Fam Law 131 where the wife complained that her husband was incapable of managing his own affairs, and she was faced with mounting debt due to his failure to take any action in response to his financial difficulties. She was held to be entitled to a decree of divorce.

[64] As it did in *O'Neill v O'Neill* [1975] 1 WLR 1118 where the husband's DIY behaviour caused the wife so much stress that her health suffered. The final straw was when his renovation work on their bungalow involved mixing cement on the living room floor and leaving the lavatory door off for eight months. He had also written to the wife's solicitors casting doubt on the paternity of the children which the Court of Appeal thought of itself was sufficient to establish the ground alleged.

2.3.3.2.1 The test under section 1(2)(b)

The question to be asked under section 1(2)(b) is: 'Can this particular petitioner be expected to live with this particular respondent?'[65]

Key case

When considering the subsection in *Ash v Ash*[66] Bagnall J stated:

> Can this petitioner, with his or her character and personality, with his or her faults and other attributes, good and bad, and having regard to his or her behaviour during the marriage reasonably be expected to live with the respondent?

In *O'Neill v O'Neill* the Court of Appeal endorsed Dunn J's formulation of the test in *Livingstone-Stallard v Livingstone-Stallard*:[67]

> would any right-thinking person come to the conclusion that the husband has behaved in such a way that this wife cannot reasonably be expected to live with him, taking into account the whole of the circumstances and the characters and personalities of the parties?

These judicial statements show how the test for behaviour combines both an objective and a subjective approach.

It is objective in that the court must decide whether the petitioner can *reasonably* be expected to live with the respondent, but the essence of section 1(2)(b) is subjective in its focus on the parties concerned.

2.3.3.2.2 Behaviour arising through illness

Cases involving illness, particularly mental illness, have posed problems for the courts as they have had to grapple with the difficulty of deciding whether to grant a decree where a respondent is not morally responsible for his or her behaviour. Whilst it is generally accepted that marriage entails taking on certain obligations, including the burden of illness, the court will recognise the strain that illness can impose on the other spouse. The courts have made it clear that granting a decree of divorce does not necessarily involve blameworthiness.

Key case

In *Thurlow v Thurlow*[68] Rees J held that, in cases involving illness, the court must take into account:

> …all the circumstances including the disabilities and temperaments of both parties, the causes of the behaviour and whether the causes were or were not known to the petitioner, the presence or absence of intention, the impact of it on the petitioner and the family unit, its duration, and the prospects of cure or improvement in the future.

---

[65] *Birch v Birch* [1992] 1 FLR 564.   [66] [1972] 1 All ER 582.

[67] [1974] Fam 47. The test in *Livingstone-Stallard* was approved by the Court of Appeal in *O'Neill v O'Neill* (n 64); and endorsed by the Court of Appeal in *Buffery v Buffery* (n 29). See also *Birch v Birch* [1992] 1 FLR 564.   [68] [1975] 2 All ER 979 at 988.

Each case depends on its facts, and a divorce may be granted even though the respondent is not responsible for his or her own behaviour, particularly if the behaviour is serious or harmful. In *Katz v Katz*[69] despite making allowances for the husband's manic depression, the impact on his wife was held to be sufficiently serious to justify granting her a decree. She was so distressed by the situation that she had attempted suicide. But in *Richards v Richards*[70] where the husband was very moody, sat staring into space, and had assaulted the wife on two occasions (one incident was very trivial), the court held that this was not sufficient for granting a decree.

2.3.3.2.3 Living together after the behaviour

Where a petitioner continues to live with the respondent for a period of up to six months after the date of the last incident of behaviour relied on in the petition, this period must be disregarded by the court when determining whether the petitioner can reasonably be expected to live with the respondent.[71] The aim of this provision is to facilitate a reconciliation between the parties. Where the period of living together exceeds six months, the court must take it into account, but this does not provide an automatic bar to the granting of a decree. It depends on the facts of the case.

2.3.3.3 Desertion for two years by the respondent

To establish desertion, the respondent must have deserted the petitioner for a continuous period of at least two years immediately preceding the presentation of the petition.[72] Desertion occurs where one spouse abandons the other spouse and leaves the household[73] with the intention of not returning. In practice, desertion is rarely used as a fact because the petitioner will normally use the two years' separation fact if the respondent consents to the divorce. Therefore a petitioner will only need to use this fact where the deserting spouse refuses to consent to a divorce and has not behaved in such a way as to enable the petitioner to petition under either section 1(2)(a) or (b).

Desertion requires the following to be proved: factual separation; an intention to desert on the part of the respondent; no consent by the petitioner to the desertion; and no just cause to desert. The first element, the parties' physical separation, is most obviously established by one spouse leaving the family home. However, the parties can still be regarded as separated even if they are still living under the one roof if one spouse has deliberately retreated from the common household. In *Pulford v Pulford*[74] desertion was described as 'not the withdrawal from a place, but from a state of things'. Thus desertion can be established where there is a total cessation of cohabitation between the parties, even though they remain living under the same roof. In *Hopes v Hopes*,[75] Denning LJ said that a husband who 'shuts himself up in one or two rooms of his house, and ceases to have anything to do with his wife, is living separately and apart from her as effectively as if they were separated by the outer door of a flat'.[76] To satisfy this test, however, the parties must be living separate lives under one roof and no longer operating as one household but two.

The second element requires the deserting spouse to intend to leave the marriage permanently and not to be absent for any other reason such as work commitments, holiday, or imprisonment. Where the parties are forcibly absent from one another, for example because the respondent is in prison, or on a posting abroad, or where the parties agree to separate, that will not normally amount to desertion, unless evidence can be brought to show that the respondent intended to have nothing more to do with the petitioner.[77] The third element requires it to be shown that the innocent spouse does not consent to the desertion.[78]

---

[69] [1972] 1 WLR 955.   [70] [1972] 3 All ER 695.
[71] Section 2(3).   [72] Section 1(2)(c).   [73] See *Hopes v Hopes* [1949] P 227.   [74] [1923] P 18.
[75] [1949] P 227.   [76] Ibid, 235.
[77] See *Nutley v Nutley* [1970] 1 WLR 217.   [78] *Pardy v Pardy* [1939] P 288.

Finally, there must be no justification for the deserting party's absence from the marriage.[79] In circumstances where the behaviour of the non-deserting spouse (ie, the spouse left behind) can be called into question, 'constructive' desertion may be possible. This occurs when a spouse is physically forced out of the household or feels compelled to leave because of the respondent's actions.[80] In these circumstances it is not the party who leaves the household who is in desertion, but his or her spouse whose actions have resulted in the former's absence. To establish constructive desertion, the petitioner must show that the respondent's behaviour was sufficiently serious to drive him or her out. In *Lang v Lang*, Lord Porter said that the course of conduct leading to one spouse leaving must be 'grave and convincing'.[81]

Desertion can come to an end in various ways, for example by a spouse moving back into the home or by the parties agreeing to separate. In order to encourage reconciliation, a period of up to six months' cohabitation does not terminate the desertion, but the period of failed reconciliation must be added on to the two years required to establish desertion.[82]

2.3.3.4 Two years' separation with consent and five years' separation

A divorce can be granted on the basis of two years' separation with consent to the divorce (s 1(2)(d)) or on the basis of five years' separation (s 1(2)(e)). These are the only no-fault facts, but in practice they are much less relied on by petitioners than the fault facts of adultery and unreasonable behaviour.

A petitioner who relies on two years' separation must show that the parties have been 'living apart' for two years and must also obtain the respondent's consent to the divorce before a decree will be granted. Prior to 1969, when the current law was enacted, divorce by consent was completely forbidden.[83] When two years' separation with consent to the divorce was introduced it was the hope of the law reformers that this simple, non-judgemental state of affairs, with no allegations of any kind against the respondent being required, would become the main fact relied on for divorce purposes, but this has not been the case. The fact that few petitioners rely on these two no-fault separation grounds has provided one of the arguments for reforming the law.

Positive consent is required under section 1(2)(d); mere passive non-objection is not sufficient. Consent must be freely given with an understanding of what it entails,[84] and it can be withdrawn at any time before decree nisi is pronounced whereupon the proceedings must be stayed.[85] At any time before decree absolute is granted, the respondent can apply to have the decree nisi rescinded if he or she has been misled by the petitioner in respect of any matter which the respondent took into account in deciding whether to give consent.[86] The usual way in which notice of consent is given is by the respondent signifying to that effect in the Acknowledgement of Service form.

With five years' separation, all that is required is proof that the parties have lived apart for a period of five years. This was highly controversial when first introduced because it permitted divorce against the respondent's will even though the respondent had done nothing 'wrong', a consideration of particular significance for those who were opposed to divorce on religious grounds. Such a respondent was, and still is, helpless to prevent such a divorce, unless he or she is able to raise a defence under section 5 that he or she will suffer grave financial or other hardship; a defence which is highly unlikely to succeed.[87]

---

[79] See eg *Quoraishi v Quoraishi* [1985] FLR 780 where the husband took a second wife which justified his first wife's desertion of the marriage when she left him.   [80] *Lang v Lang* [1955] AC 402.

[81] Ibid, 418.   [82] See s 2(5).   [83] See Section 1.1.

[84] See s 2(7) and the FPR 2010, r 7.12(12) and (13).   [85] FPR 2010, r 7.12(12) and (13).

[86] Section 10(1).   [87] See Section 2.3.4.

2.3.3.4.1 Living apart

The parties will not be held to be living apart for the purpose of the two or five years separation grounds merely by reason of physical separation (eg where a spouse is abroad on military service or in prison). Living apart also requires a mental element, the belief by one of the parties that the marriage is at an end, although it is not necessary for this belief to be communicated to the other.

For the purpose of establishing physical separation, section 2(6) provides that a husband and wife 'shall be treated as living apart unless they are living with each other in the same household'. This is a question of fact in each case, but 'living with each other in the same household' is not the same as living with each other in the same *house*. For this reason, it is possible for the parties to be separated even if they are living under the same roof. It depends on whether or not they have a communal life together. Thus, where there has been no communal life under the same roof, the parties may succeed in obtaining a decree of divorce on the basis of separation. In *Hollens v Hollens*,[88] for example, the husband and wife continued living in their two-bedroomed council house, but had not spoken or eaten together since a violent quarrel more than two years previously. Neither party had done anything for the other since the quarrel. This degree of separation was sufficient to satisfy the court that all common life between them had ceased and that they were living apart. By contrast, in *Mouncer v Mouncer*[89] it was held that the parties were not living apart as, although they were on very bad terms and slept in separate bedrooms, they continued to eat meals together and in the company of their children. In other words, they enjoyed some communal life together. It is unfortunate that the more civilised the parties, and the more willing they are to behave well, cooperate with each other, and share the care of their children, the less chance there is of them obtaining a divorce under one of the seperation grounds. This is because the court will consider they have a communal life together and are not therefore living separately. This is likely to affect, in particular, those couples who, due to financial constraints, cannot afford to separate and live in separate dwellings. The Law Commission has described it as being 'unjust and discriminatory of the law to provide for a civilised "no fault" ground for divorce which, in practice, is denied to a large section of the population'.[90] Thus, some petitioners are forced to rely on the fault grounds of adultery and unreasonable behaviour, because of the difficulty of separating even though allegations of fault may create hostility and bitterness and may make sorting out the consequences of divorce much more difficult. As previously indicated, physical separation will not be enough by itself to establish that the parties are living apart. This must be accompanied by a belief by one of the parties that the marriage is over.[91]

The period living apart must be continuous. However, to facilitate attempts at reconciliation, the spouses are permitted to resume living together for one or more periods totalling up to six months without the continuity of the period being broken.[92] However, any period spent living together is not counted for the purpose of the period of living apart therefore the time living together must be made up with a further period living apart.

2.3.4 Special protection for respondents in separation divorces

Sections 5 and 10 of the MCA 1973 provide protection for respondents in petitions brought on the separation grounds. These provisions were introduced with the aim of

---

[88] (1971) 115 SJ 327. [89] [1972] 1 All ER 289. [90] See Law Com No 192, para 2.12.
[91] See *Santos v Santos* [1972] Fam 247. It is worth noting that Parliament did not intend there to be any mental element to 'living apart' for the purposes of the two- and five-year separation facts. This requirement was introduced by the Court of Appeal in *Santos v Santos* [1972] Fam 247 where it held that to establish living apart not only must there be a physical separation, but there must also be a mental element of wishing to live apart on the part of at least one of the spouses. [92] See s 2(5).

protecting 'innocent' and vulnerable spouses, in other words those who were respondents to a 'no-fault' divorce and who had therefore committed no matrimonial offence.

Key legislation

Where the only fact relied on for divorce is five years' separation, the petitioner can be refused a decree under section 5 of the MCA 1973 if the respondent establishes that dissolution of the marriage will cause him or her to suffer grave financial or other hardship *and* that it would be wrong in all the circumstances to dissolve the marriage.

This provision, however, is rarely used in practice and, if used, rarely succeeds, but it may be useful for putting pressure on a petitioner to offer the respondent a reasonable financial settlement.[93] In respect of the 'other hardship' part of the 'defence' in section 5, this might include, for example, religious or social hardship that a respondent might suffer due to ostracism in the community as a result of religious or social objections to the divorce.[94]

Key legislation

The court has jurisdiction under section 10 to protect a respondent in a divorce case where a decree nisi has been obtained on the basis of two or five years' separation. Thus, under section 10(1) the court has jurisdiction to rescind the decree nisi where a respondent can prove that the petitioner misled the respondent (intentionally or unintentionally) about any matter which the respondent took into account in deciding to give consent to the decree being granted in a two-year separation case. Under section 10(2) a respondent may apply to the court for his or her financial position after divorce to be considered, in which case the court hearing the application shall by virtue of section 10(3) consider all the circumstances including a list of circumstances in section 10(3); and can refuse to grant a decree absolute unless it is satisfied that 'the petitioner should not be required to make any financial provision for the respondent, or that the financial provision made by the petitioner for the respondent is reasonable and fair or the best that can be made in the circumstances.' However, the court has an overriding discretion (under s 10(4)) to make a decree absolute, notwithstanding the requirements of section 10(3) if there are circumstances making it desirable that the decree should be made absolute without delay and the court has obtained a satisfactory undertaking from the petitioner that he or she will make such financial provision for the respondent as the court may approve.

These provisions therefore afford a respondent valuable protection where a petitioner is, for example, being unreasonable or obdurate over financial arrangements or is in arrears with payments due under an existing order.[95] The effect of section 10 is to delay decree absolute while financial matters are looked into. These provisions were at one time occasionally used to protect respondents who were at risk of losing their entitlement to pension

---

[93] At one time it was sometimes used to put pressure on a petitioner to make pension provision for the respondent (see eg *Archer v Archer* [1999] 1 FLR 327), but now that the court has the power to make pension orders on divorce (see Chapter 4), this is no longer necessary.

[94] See eg *Rukat v Rukat* [1975] Fam 63 and *Balraj v Balraj* (1981) 11 FL 110.

[95] In *Garcia v Garcia* [1992] 1 FLR 256, for instance, the wife successfully invoked s 10(3) to delay the grant of decree nisi because her Spanish husband owed her a substantial sum in unpaid child maintenance.

rights on divorce,[96] but now that the divorce court has wider powers to make orders with respect to pensions, this is no longer necessary.

2.3.5 Religious decrees of divorce and the Matrimonial Causes Act 1973

The MCA 1973 was amended[97] to provide protection to those requiring a religious as well as a civil decree of divorce as there were a number of cases of women being refused a religious divorce by their spouse. Section 10A will apply where a decree of divorce has been granted but not made absolute and the parties to the marriage:

(a) were married in accordance with—

    (i) the usages of the Jews, or

    (ii) any other prescribed religious usages; and

(b) must co-operate if the marriage is to be dissolved.

Either party can apply to the court for an order that the divorce decree is not to be made absolute until a declaration by both parties that they have taken such steps as are required to dissolve the marriage in accordance with those usages is produced to the court. Such an order will be made if the court believes it is just and reasonable to do so considering all the circumstances of the case.

This will prevent the dissolution of the marriage until the court is satisfied that all steps have been taken to secure a religious divorce. This clearly would be a bargaining point for the party wishing to obtain a religious decree of divorce. Currently there are no other prescribed religious usages. In future, other religious marriages, for example under Islamic law, may come within the ambit of this section.

2.4 THE LEGAL EFFECTS OF DIVORCE

The status of being married gives rise to various rights, and responsibilities.[98] Termination of the marriage by decree absolute of divorce therefore has important legal consequences.

On the grant of decree absolute, the marriage is dissolved and each party is free to remarry. The decree has other legal consequences. Thus, any finance and property orders made under Part II of the MCA 1973 in favour of a party to a marriage take effect and orders for the settlement or variation of a settlement can take effect in respect of any child of the family. All other orders for children take effect as soon as they are made. Divorce also has an effect on a will made by either party so that, subject to any contrary intention in a will, any legacies and gifts to a former spouse lapse. However, a former spouse can make a claim for reasonable financial provision from the deceased's estate under the Inheritance (Provision for Family and Dependants) Act 1975.[99] Termination of the marriage also affects social security, pension, and taxation rights. Both parties also lose their rights under legislation governing their 'matrimonial' rights, in particular the statutory right of occupation of the family home,[100] although they still have a right to apply for protection against domestic violence under Part IV of the Family Law Act 1996 in

---

[96] See eg *Griffiths v Dawson & Co* [1993] 2 FLR 315 and *Jackson v Jackson* [1993] 2 FLR 848.

[97] Divorce (Religious Marriages) Act 2002.   [98] See Chapter 1.

[99] A provision can be included in the divorce settlement precluding such an application.

[100] Under the Family Law Act 1996, Pt IV, s 30. They also lose rights under, for instance, the Matrimonial Proceedings and Property Act 1970 and the Married Women's Property Act 1882.

their status as former spouse.[101] With regard to children, divorce does not terminate the parties' parental responsibility, and the obligation to provide financial support for their children continues after divorce.[102]

2.5 RECOGNITION OF AN OVERSEAS DIVORCE

In certain circumstances divorces obtained in an overseas jurisdiction are recognised in the UK. Part II of the Family Law Act 1986 makes provision for the recognition of overseas divorces (and annulments and separations), but special rules apply to the recognition of divorces obtained in other member states of the European Union.[103]

Disputes about the recognition of an overseas divorce usually arise in the context of 'big money' international marriage cases. This is because if an overseas divorce is recognised as valid in England and Wales, then a party to the marriage will not be able to apply for a divorce in the English courts and will therefore have no access to the financial order jurisdiction of the divorce court in England and Wales under Part II of the MCA 1973, which requires a divorce decree to be granted in the divorce court in England and Wales. If the divorce has already been granted overseas then a party to the marriage may attempt to argue before the courts in England and Wales that the overseas divorce should not be recognised. If successful, then the divorce may be able to be heard in the English courts with the 'reward' possibly being a more lucrative finance and property award than the one that would have been awarded in the court of the overseas jurisdiction.

It is usually wives who argue that an overseas divorce should not be recognised in England and Wales, because the English courts adopt a generous approach in financial proceedings and apply principles of fairness and non-discrimination.[104] If, on the other hand, the overseas divorce is recognised by the courts in this country as being valid in England and Wales, then a party will have to apply instead for financial orders under Part III of the Matrimonial and Family Proceedings Act 1984, which gives the English court jurisdiction to grant financial relief after a marriage has been dissolved (or annulled) in a foreign country, but where the award may not be as great as that which might be obtained in the divorce court under Part II of the MCA 1973.[105]

Key legislation

The law governing the recognition in England and Wales of overseas divorces is found in the Family Law Act 1986 (which applies to all overseas divorces other than those obtained in the EU).

The Act makes a distinction between divorces obtained in proceedings (judicial or other proceedings) and those which are not. For divorces obtained in proceedings, recognition is much broader and such a divorce will be recognised as a valid divorce in this country if it is effective under the law of the country where it was obtained and at the commencement of the proceedings either party was habitually resident or domiciled in that country

---

[101] See Chapter 3.   [102] See Chapter 6.

[103] See Council Regulation (EC) No 2201/2003 Concerning Jurisdiction and the Recognition and Enforcement of Judgments in Matrimonial Matters and in Matters of Parental Responsibility (Brussels II Revised); and see eg *D v D (Nature of Recognition of Overseas Divorce)* [2005] EWHC 3342 (Fam), [2006] 2 FLR 825 where a Greek divorce was recognised in England and Wales under Brussels II.

[104] See *White v White* [2001] 1 AC 596, [2000] 2 FLR 981 and *Miller v Miller; McFarlane v McFarlane* [2006] UKHL 24, [2006] 1 FLR 1186. See Chapter 4.

[105] See *Agbaje v Akinnoye-Agbaje* [2010] UKSC 13.

or was a national of that country.[106] An overseas divorce not obtained in proceedings is recognised in this country if it is effective in the country where it was obtained, and on the date it was obtained one or both parties were domiciled in that country, or one party was domiciled there and the other party was domiciled in a country which recognised the divorce, and in any case neither party was habitually resident in the UK for one year immediately preceding the divorce.[107]

Notwithstanding these rules, the court in England and Wales has an overriding discretion to refuse recognition of an overseas divorce where, in the case of a divorce obtained by proceedings, reasonable steps were not taken to give notice of the proceedings to a party to the marriage or to give a party to the marriage an opportunity to take part in those proceedings;[108] and, in all cases, where recognition would be manifestly contrary to public policy.[109] It is often difficult to succeed in arguing that a divorce should not be recognised on grounds of public policy.[110] Cases are decided on their own facts, but the courts are keen to ensure that the principles of international law are upheld, in particular the principle of comity which requires the courts to respect the jurisdiction of courts in countries overseas.

In some cases the courts have had to consider whether a talaq should be recognised in England and Wales. A talaq is an Islamic divorce whereby the husband can divorce his wife by uttering the words 'I divorce you' three times without being in the presence of another person and without his wife giving consent. A talaq made *within* the jurisdiction of England and Wales is not valid, as only divorces obtained in court proceedings are recognised in this country.[111] On the other hand, a talaq validly made *outside* the UK may, at the discretion of the court, be recognised as a valid divorce in the UK, and is likely to be recognised unless the court considers there are public policy reasons for refusing to do so.

Key case

In *H v H (Talaq Divorce)*[112] where a talaq divorce validly announced in Pakistan was upheld by the High Court, Sumner J said it was important that marriages and divorces recognised in one country should be recognised in another unless there were good reasons for not doing so, particularly where many people moved freely between the two countries. However, in *A v L*,[113] where the husband applied to the High Court for his wife's petition for divorce to be adjourned on the ground that the Egyptian court had made an order confirming that he had already divorced his wife by talaq over the telephone, the High Court refused to accept

---

[106] Section 46(1).   [107] Section 46(2).

[108] Section 51(3). See eg *Duhur-Johnson v Duhur-Johnson (Attorney-General Intervening)* [2005] 2 FLR 1042 where a Nigerian divorce was refused recognition as the husband had not taken reasonable steps to give his wife notice of the divorce proceedings.   [109] Section 52.

[110] See Thorpe LJ in *Eroglu v Eroglu* [1994] 2 FLR 287 where the wife's argument that her Turkish divorce should not be recognised on the ground that it had been obtained by fraud was dismissed. See also *H v H (The Queen's Proctor Intervening) (Validity of Japanese Divorce)* [2006] EWHC 2989 (Fam), [2007] 1 FLR 1318 where a Japanese divorce by agreement (a Kyogi rikon) was recognised as a valid divorce, as there was no reason to refuse recognition on public policy grounds.

[111] See eg *Sulaiman v Juffali* [2002] 1 FLR 479 where a talaq pronounced in England, and subsequently registered in Saudi Arabia, was held not to be a valid divorce under the provisions of the Family Law Act 1986 as the court held that it had been obtained in England, not Saudi Arabia.

[112] [2007] EWHC 2945, [2008] 2 FLR 857. See also *El Fadl v El Fadl* [2000] 1 FLR 175 where a talaq divorce registered with the Shariah court in Lebanon was recognised by the High Court in England and Wales, as registration constituted proceedings for the purpose of the Family Law Act 1986.

[113] [2010] EWHC 460 (Fam), [2010] 2 FLR 1418.

his argument. Although a talaq is not normally regarded as a divorce by means of proceedings, in this case it was regarded as being granted in proceedings because the Egyptian court had been involved. As the wife had not been given notice of the proceedings or been able to attend them, recognition was refused.[114]

Where the court in England and Wales considers that a party to a marriage has acted unconscientiously, oppressively, or vexatiously by stealing a forensic advantage by disputing that England is the appropriate forum to hear the divorce proceedings and thereby hold ups the English proceedings while at the same time pursuing his or her own proceedings abroad, then the court in England and Wales can grant a '*Hemain*' injunction to prevent this happening.[115]

3 CRITICISMS OF DIVORCE UNDER THE MATRIMONIAL CAUSES ACT 1973 AND AN ATTEMPT AT REFORM

3.1 INTRODUCTION

The current law of divorce has been criticised by judges, academics, and politicians for many reasons. In 2000 a radical reform of divorce was due to come into force under Part II of the Family Law Act 1996 but it was shelved at the eleventh hour much to the relief of those who had argued against it. This part of the chapter considers the criticisms of the current law of divorce and gives an overview of the radical reform of divorce which was due to come into force under the Family Law Act 1996 but which was never implemented.

In the years following the implementation of the current law there was growing disquiet in some quarters that the aims of the new law were not being achieved in practice. This disquiet, coupled with a significant increase in the divorce rate, provided fertile ground for a fresh examination of the legal framework. Thus, in 1982 a committee chaired by Booth J was established to examine the procedure associated with matrimonial causes. The committee was displeased with what it discovered, particularly with regard to divorces based on the behaviour fact, and in its Report published in 1985[116] recommended that changes be made which would lead to a reduction in acrimony between the parties. The Law Commission, taking the lead from the Booth Report, carried out an examination of the law governing the grounds for divorce, against the background of the divorce law's professed objectives, and found it to be wanting. The Law Commission's findings were published in a discussion paper in 1988.[117] These findings were that the law had failed to satisfy its original objectives. Indeed the criticisms were devastating: the law was found to be confusing and misleading; to be discriminatory and unjust; to exacerbate hostility;

---

[114] See earlier in this section.

[115] See eg *S v S (Hemain) Injunction* [2009] EWHC 3224 (Fam), [2010] 2 FLR 502 where the wife's application for a *Hemain* injunction (an 'anti-suit' injunction) against her husband to order him not to take any further steps to register a talaq divorce in the Sunnite Shariah Court of Beirut was dismissed as she had started the English proceedings with the deliberate aim of frustrating the Lebanese process in which she had previously participated. It was held that to order a *Hemain* injunction against the husband would also offend the principles of comity and the principles and policy underpinning the *Hemain* injunction procedure. See also *R v R (Divorce: Hemain Injunction)* [2003] EWHC 2113 (Fam), [2005] 1 FLR 386.

[116] *Report of the Matrimonial Causes Procedure Committee* (1985).

[117] *Facing the Future: A Discussion Paper on the Ground for Divorce* (Law Com No 170, 1988).

to distort the parties' bargaining positions; to do nothing to save the marriage; and to make matters worse for the children. In its discussion paper the Law Commission invited views on different suggestions for how the law might be altered. In light of the responses, the Law Commission made proposals for the reform of divorce in its report, *Family Law: The Ground for Divorce*.[118]

Talking point

The aims of the law of divorce as expressed in both Law Commission papers were encapsulated in the following four propositions: (i) to support those marriages capable of being saved; (ii) to enable those not so capable of being dissolved to be dissolved with the minimum of avoidable distress, bitterness, and hostility; (iii) so far as possible, to encourage the amicable solution of practical issues relating to the couple's home, finances, and children, and the proper discharge of their responsibilities to one another and their children; and (iv) to minimise the harm the children of the family might suffer, both at the time of the divorce and in the future, and to promote, so far as possible, the continued sharing of parental responsibility for them.

The Law Commission's 1988 discussion paper contained three possible models for reform: a mixed system with both fault and no-fault grounds for divorce, as under the current law in the MCA 1973, but with some modifications; divorce after a fixed minimum period of separation; and divorce after a fixed minimum period of reflection and consideration, in other words a divorce involving a process over time. The last model was chosen as the Law Commission's preferred option and which it recommended in its final report.

The Lord Chancellor's Department[119] took up many of the Law Commission's suggestions and in 1993 published a Consultation Paper, *Looking to the Future: Mediation and the Ground for Divorce*.[120] In the introduction, the Government's objectives in relation to the law and procedure surrounding the dissolution of marriage were expressed rather differently from those put forward by the Law Commission. These objectives were: (i) to support the institution of marriage; (ii) to include practicable steps to prevent the irretrievable breakdown of marriage; (iii) to ensure that the parties understand the practical consequences of divorce before taking any irreversible decision; (iv) where divorce is unavoidable, to minimise the bitterness and hostility between the parties and to reduce the trauma for the children; and (v) to keep to the minimum the cost to the taxpayer.

In the Government's Consultation Paper, the objections to the divorce law in the MCA 1973 and the reasons for wishing for change, were spelled out in some detail.[121] The Government claimed that the law in the 1973 Act, particularly the manner in which it was applied in practice, allowed divorce to be obtained too quickly and too easily without the parties being required to consider the consequences. It claimed that the system did nothing to save a marriage; it could make things worse for the children; it was unjust and exacerbated bitterness and hostility; it was confusing, misleading, and open to abuse; it was discriminatory; and it distorted the parties' bargaining positions. The Consultation Paper listed nine possible options for reform but with the preferred option being the Law Commission's recommended model, namely that the sole ground for divorce should be

---

[118] Law Com No 192.

[119] In 2003 the Lord Chancellor's Department was renamed the Department for Constitutional Affairs, but the responsibilities of the latter were in May 2007 transferred to the newly formed Ministry of Justice.

[120] HMSO, 1993.   [121] *Looking to the Future* (1993), Ch 5.

irretrievable breakdown of the marriage to be established by the passage of time, during which time the parties would be expected to consider and reflect on the divorce and its consequences.

A considerable number of comments were received in response to the Consultation Paper, and in the spring of 1995, the Government published a White Paper, *Looking to the Future: Mediation and the Ground for Divorce*[122] setting out fresh proposals for change.

Talking point

The White Paper stated, *inter alia*, that the proposals would:

- require couples to attend a compulsory information session before starting the divorce process;
- remove the incentive to make allegations of fault in order to divorce quickly;
- require a 12-month period of reflection by the parties on whether the marriage could be saved;
- require couples to think through and face up to the consequences of divorce before it happened;
- ensure that arrangements for children and other matters were settled before a divorce was granted;
- allow divorces to be barred where the dissolution of the marriage would cause grave financial or other grave hardship; and
- introduce comprehensive family mediation as part of the divorce process.

The Government's proposals had a strong marriage-saving rhetoric. The aim of the reforms was not to make divorce easier as key aspects of the Government's proposals concentrated as much on 'marriage saving' as 'marriage ending'. Thus, it was proposed that:[123] saveable marriages would be identified; referrals for marriage guidance, and opportunities to explore reconciliation, would be facilitated; adequate time would be given to test whether the marriage had genuinely broken down; acrimony, hostility, and conflict would be removed or minimised, thereby reducing the worst effects of divorce on children; parents would be encouraged to focus on their joint responsibility to support and care for their children; couples would be encouraged to meet these responsibilities before the marriage was dissolved; and couples would be assisted in this process through family mediation.

The resultant Family Law Bill had a difficult progress through Parliament. A large number of amendments were made in response to pressure from both Houses. However, the Lord Chancellor was determined that the Bill would become law and it received the Royal Assent in July 1996. However, the reforms, which were contained in Parts I–III of the Family Law Act 1996,[124] were never introduced and were eventually repealed.[125] For this reason, only an outline of the reforms is given below.[126]

---

[122] Cm 2799.   [123] See the Preface to the White Paper.

[124] Part IV contains provisions providing protection against domestic violence. Part 4A contains provisions giving protection to victims of forced marriage.

[125] Except for some general principles by which the law should be guided, set out in s 1, which remain in force.

[126] For a detailed account of the divorce provisions of the 1996 Act, see S. M. Cretney and R. Bird, *Divorce: The New Law* (Bristol: Family Law, 1996).

3.2 DIVORCE UNDER THE FAMILY LAW ACT 1996

3.2.1 An outline of the reform

The new divorce law laid down in Parts I–III of the Family Law Act 1996[127] would have radically reformed the law of divorce, in both substance and procedure. It would have swept away the provisions in the MCA 1973. The 1996 Act introduced 'divorce over a process of time', in fact a significant period of time, in which divorcing parties were required to face up to the emotional and practical consequences of divorcing. Under the 1996 Act, divorce law, like the current law, required proof that the marriage had irretrievably broken down, but instead of requiring factual evidence to prove breakdown (such as adultery, behaviour, or separation), the parties were required to follow and complete a complex sequence of procedural steps before being able to obtain a divorce. If the process was complied with, this provided evidence of irretrievable breakdown. The main stages in the process involved: attendance at an information meeting; making a statement of marital breakdown; passing a period of time for reflection and consideration; and finally the granting of a divorce order. Orders were also available to protect vulnerable parties to divorce, similar to those which exist under the current law.

One of the main differences between the current law and the proposed new law was that the parties were required to sort out arrangements ancillary to the divorce (such as arrangements about their children and in respect of property and financial matters) *before* being able to obtain a divorce. Under the current law, on the other hand, a divorce can be obtained relatively quickly (in a matter of weeks) but sorting out the consequences may take several years. The Government took the view in discussions leading to the enactment of the Family Law Act 1996 that, by making the parties settle their arrangements for the future, it would emphasise the responsibilities of marriage and parenthood.[128] The new law also included a much greater use of mediation in divorce and related disputes. There were also changes in the terminology used for divorce law and joint applications for divorce were possible.

Attendance at an information meeting: the spouse (or both spouses) contemplating divorce would first have to attend an information meeting where information about matters relating to divorce would be given, including not only information about the divorce and separation process but on other matters, such as: marriage counselling and marriage support services; the importance of the welfare needs of any children; the nature of the financial issues which might arise; mediation; and legal aid. The actual details about the content and length of these information meetings, however, proved to be complex and unclear, and because of these concerns the Government decided to conduct pilot studies before the new law came into force. The results of the pilot studies found that there were various problems relating to the information meetings, and it was these results which eventually led to the reforms being 'ditched' and the relevant Parts of the Family Law Act 1996 being repealed.

Statement of marital breakdown: three months or more after attendance at an information meeting, one spouse (or both) would be required to make a 'statement of marital breakdown' declaring that the party (or parties) were aware of the purposes of the period

---

[127] Part I laid down a set of general principles governing the divorce legislation. Part II contained provisions relating to divorce and separation. Part III laid down provisions relating to legal aid for mediation.

[128] The Law Commission, by contrast, had recommended that making arrangements should not be a precondition of divorce, as this might rush the parties into making unsuitable arrangements and play into the hands of one of the parties.

of reflection and consideration and wished to make arrangements for the future. A statement of breakdown could not be made in the first year of marriage.

A period for reflection and consideration: once the statement of marital breakdown had been made, a period for reflection and consideration would begin to run. The purpose of this period was to give the parties time to reflect on whether their marriage could be saved, to have an opportunity to effect a reconciliation, and to consider what arrangements should be made for the future. The minimum period for reflection and consideration in all cases was nine months, but this was automatically extended for a further six months (making 15 months in total) where there was a child of the family aged under 16, unless a non-molestation or occupation order[129] had been made to protect a party and/or a child against domestic violence by the other party, or where delay in making a divorce order would be significantly detrimental to the welfare of any child of the family. The period could also be extended by six months if the party who had not applied for the divorce order applied to the court for further reflection.

During the period for reflection and consideration the parties were required to make financial arrangements for the future and arrangements about their children, because, unless they did so to the court's satisfaction by the end of the required period, then a divorce order would not be made. However, in certain circumstances this requirement to make arrangements could be waived (eg where the other party was obstructive or where there was ill health, disability, or domestic violence or where delay would be significantly detrimental to the welfare of a child of the family).

The divorce order: after complying with the above requirements, one or both parties (irrespective of who set the divorce in motion) could then apply for a divorce order which the court could make if: the marriage had irretrievably broken down; the requirements listed earlier had been satisfied; and the application had not been withdrawn. Irretrievable breakdown was proved if the parties had complied with the process for obtaining a divorce. The effect of a divorce order was to dissolve the marriage, although it could not be made if an order preventing divorce was in force.

Orders preventing divorce: the court could make an order preventing divorce if dissolution of the marriage would result in substantial financial or other hardship to the other party or to a child of the family; and it would be wrong in the circumstances for the marriage to be dissolved.

3.2.2 The decision not to implement the reform

The proposed radical reforms of divorce law were due to come into force on 1 January 1999, but implementation was suspended until 2000 until after the Government had received the results of pilot projects to see how the information meetings would work in practice. However, the results of these pilot projects turned out to be disappointing,[130] as it was found that the information meetings failed to achieve their aims, which were to save marriages and promote mediation. The results showed that only a minority of couples were diverted to marriage counselling, that few people attended a meeting with a view to saving their marriage, and that the meetings were not very successful in diverting couples into mediation.

---

[129] Under the Family Law Act 1996, Pt IV, see Chapter 3.

[130] Only 7 per cent of those attending information meetings were diverted into mediation and very few couples attended the meetings together. The information meetings had therefore failed to achieve the Government's stated objectives of saving saveable marriages and encouraging mediation.

Although the aim of the pilot projects was simply to test the format for information delivery, the Government evaluated the results of the pilots by reference to the likelihood of the parties electing to use mediation rather than seeking legal advice. Thus, the Law Commission's original scheme changed its emphasis as it developed in the hands of successive Governments. The use of mediation had not been central to the scheme as was originally proposed by the Law Commission, but it became central to the Government's scheme, particularly when the Conservative Government took over the reform. As marriage-saving and cost-saving had become the new rhetoric, the Government came to the conclusion that the proposed reform had failed to fulfil the policy objectives laid down in Part I of the 1996 Act, namely to save saveable marriages and, where they had broken down, to bring them to an end with the minimum of distress to the parties and any children. For this reason, the reforms were never introduced and Parts I and II of the 1996 Act were eventually repealed.

3.2.3 Reaction to the proposed reform

The proposed reform of divorce law by the Family Law Act 1996 generated fierce debate; and the decision not to implement the new law was greeted with considerable relief by those who had considered the reforms to be inherently flawed and unworkable in practice. Some of the main criticisms were that the new divorce law was unnecessarily complicated and that it would place impossible demands on divorcing couples to sort out arrangement about their property and children, often at a time of emotional turmoil, before they would be able to get a divorce. The Solicitors' Family Law Association (now called Resolution) considered the reforms to be cumbersome and confusing, and said that they would create delay and uncertainty which were contrary to the best interests of divorcing couples and their children.

Some commentators considered the length of the period of reflection and consideration to be much too long. Freeman,[131] for example, was critical of the length of the process because, among other things, it would create more conflict, more tension, more domestic violence, and unnecessary abortions. Cretney[132] considered the Government to be 'curiously naive' about what was likely to happen during the period of reflection. He said that some couples would not spend time considering whether their marriage could be saved or making arrangements for the future, but would instead spend the time conceiving children, or exploiting their emotional or financial advantage, or brooding on their grievances. Eekelaar[133] was critical of the need for information meetings and considered them to be a form of 'social engineering'. His main objection was that the reforms had strong implications for the rule of law, in that the Government was using 'the institutions of law itself to obstruct individuals from access to the rights conferred on them by law'.[134] He said that this could be 'deeply corrupting of the law itself', and that it should not be forgotten that both marriage and divorce were legal rights. In other words, Eekelaar found the requirement that those wishing to divorce should be compulsorily required to attend an information meeting was obstructive of justice.

Thus, despite more than ten years of debate and an attempt to devise and introduce 'divorce over a period of time' (a rather appropriate name for a divorce law which took so

---

[131] M. Freeman, 'Divorce Gospel Style' [1997] Family Law 413 at 414.
[132] S. Cretney, 'The Divorce White Paper—Some Reflections' [1995] Family Law 302 at 304.
[133] J. Eekelaar, 'Family Law—Keeping Us "On Message"' [1999] Child and Family Law Quarterly 387.
[134] Ibid.

long to gestate),[135] divorce law in England and Wales remains the same as it was in 1971 when the Divorce Reform Act 1969 introduced what are now the current grounds for divorce. Furthermore, there are no current proposals to reform the law.

4 THE FUTURE OF DIVORCE LAW

Although there are no current proposals to reform the law,[136] the law of divorce has been criticised by many commentators,[137] and some have argued for the need for it to be reformed. Concerns about divorce law cover a range of issues and there is also the added difficulty of deciding what form any new law should take. As the attempt at divorce reform by the Family Law Act 1996 showed in the previous section, any reform of the law is difficult and raises difficult policy issues.

However, the criticisms which led to the reforms under the 1996 Act still remain true today; and, after the Government's decision not to implement the reforms, some judges, practitioners, academics, and politicians have continued to voice concerns about the current law. For instance, the Rt Hon Elizabeth Butler-Sloss, a former President of the Family Division, described obtaining a divorce on the ground of unreasonable behaviour as a 'hypocritical charade', and she said there was a need to introduce a truly no-fault divorce.[138] In 2001, the Lord Chancellor's Advisory Board on Family Law in its final report[139] said that it regretted the missed opportunity to reform divorce, and it urged that serious consideration be given to replacing the current adversarial system and partly fault-based divorce regime. The Advisory Board stated that serious defects identified by the Law Commission in discussions leading up to reform in the Family Law Act 1996 still remained, in particular that allegations of fault (unreasonable behaviour and adultery) caused unnecessary conflict between the parties, and that their distress and anger impacted on their children. Resolution, a group of family lawyers which adopts a non-confrontational approach to family disputes, is also in favour of reform and has spent many years campaigning for the introduction of no-fault divorce on the basis that the current system does not sit well with the non-confrontational settlement culture which is encouraged and promoted in the rest of the family justice system. Resolution has asked for divorce reform to be put back on the political agenda, and in a more recent statement Resolution proposed that both divorce and civil partnership dissolution should be

---

[135] It was 1988 when the Law Commission first 'set the ball rolling' with it discussion paper, and it was 1999 when the divorce reforms under the Family Law Act 1996 were due to come into force.

[136] In October 2010 there was a debate in Parliament on the reform of divorce, including no-fault divorce (and making pre-nuptial agreements binding). The debate was tabled by Baroness Ruth Deech. However, Lord McNally, responding to the motion on behalf of the Government, said that the Government would await the outcome of the Family Justice Review before making any decisions on comprehensive divorce law reform.

[137] On divorce reform, see eg R. Deech, 'Divorce—A Disaster?' [2009] Family Law 1048; E. Hasson, 'Setting a Standard or Reflecting Reality? The "Role" of Divorce Law, and the Case of the Family Law Act 1996' [2003] International Journal of Law, Policy and the Family 338; R. Kay, 'Whose Divorce is it Anyway? The Human Rights Aspect' [2004] Family Law 892; E. Hasson, 'Wedded to "Fault": The Legal Regulation of Divorce and Relationship Breakdown' (2006) Legal Studies 267; S. Cretney, 'Marriage, Divorce and the Courts' [2002] Family Law 900; M. Freeman (ed), *Divorce: Where Next?* (Aldershot: Dartmouth, 1996).

[138] At her inaugural speech on being appointed President of the Family Division.

[139] See its final report, *Making Contact Work*, in which it made a number of serious criticisms of the family justice system, particularly, but not exclusively, relating to contact proceedings.

reformed in order to end the 'blame game'.[140] Cretney[141] has described the law of divorce as being in 'a state of confusion', because the theory of divorce (that the state has a vital interest in the matter and divorce is only available on proof of irretrievable breakdown) does not match up with the practical reality (which is that divorce is readily and quickly available, whether or not the parties agree, because 'there is no point in denying that the marriage has broken down if one party firmly asserts it has').

One of the main criticisms of divorce relates to the fault element, which is particularly pertinent as most divorces are brought on the fault grounds of adultery and unreasonable behaviour, partly because these grounds, unlike the separation grounds, enable the marriage to be terminated quickly. Allegations of fault increase bitterness and hostility which may make agreement between the parties about the consequences of divorce more difficult. Allegations of fault also run counter to the settlement culture which is adopted in respect of ancillary matters on divorce. Also, fault has little relevance to arrangements for children and to finance and property matters, unless behaviour is of an extreme kind, a fact which some parties find difficult to understand.

Another concern relates to the speed with which a divorce can be granted. A divorce can be obtained in a matter of weeks, but sorting out disputes relating to finance and property and children involves separate court proceedings which can sometimes drag on for years. One of the few advantages of the reforms under the Family Law Act 1996 was that obtaining a divorce and sorting out the consequences were integrated, and the requirement of a 'period of reflection and consideration' meant that couples were not 'steamrollered' into divorce and regretted it later.

Reforming divorce raises difficult questions, and there is no point in reforming the law unless any reform is a significant improvement on the current system. However, reforming the law and getting the balance right is difficult. Thus, if divorce is made too easy it may send out a message that marriage can be treated lightly but, on the other hand, if it is made too difficult then people may decide not to marry and opt instead for cohabitation. In terms of the substantive law, one of the most important policy decisions is whether there should be fault, no fault, or a mixed system of fault and no fault. Allegations of fault may make marriage breakdown and divorce more difficult for the parties and make things worse for the children. However, one possible advantage of fault is that it sends out a message that marriage involves a moral code, although this raises the question of whether it is the function of family law to provide a moral code of behaviour and also whether the law can actually influence human conduct. Also, ascribing and apportioning fault to parties to a marriage is difficult and complex. In many cases, both parties may be to blame, but only one of them can petition for divorce.

Although it seems to be generally agreed that fault divorce is not the preferred option, then it becomes a question of what the alternative is. Should, for instance, divorce be available on the unilateral demand of one of the parties or by mutual consent of the parties? Divorce on unilateral demand is the most liberal form of divorce, but it may give too much freedom to the individual and possibly send out a message that divorce is something which is easy to obtain. However, on the basis that a divorce is relatively easy to obtain today, it could be argued that we already have what is in effect divorce on unilateral demand. Divorce by mutual consent[142] seems to be a 'civilised' way of permitting a

---

[140] See [2007] Family Law 1053; and N. Shepherd, 'Ending the Blame Game: Getting No Fault Divorce Back on the Agenda' [2009] Family Law 122.

[141] S. Cretney, *Family Law in the Twentieth Century* (Oxford: Oxford University Press, 2003), p 391.

[142] The Law Commission, when it was considering reform of divorce in the early 1990s, found substantial support for divorce on the basis of mutual consent, with a survey showing that 90 per cent of those persons

divorce, and would tie in with the settlement culture which pervades the rest of the family justice system. But, there are also problems with mutual consent. Thus, for instance, procedural safeguards would have to be put in place to ensure that consent has been truly and freely given and also to ensure that both parties have the capacity to consent. Divorce by mutual consent might also threaten the balance of power between the parties and act as a bargaining chip whereby one party may agree to succumb to an unfavourable divorce settlement in relation to, say, the family home and the children, in order to 'escape' from the marriage. Grounds other than mutual consent would also be needed to provide a basis for divorce for those persons not able to consent.

Another policy issue is whether divorce law should promote the institution of marriage. However, whether the law can actually do this is questionable, for marriages may break down despite divorce law, not because of it. Some commentators, on the other hand, have argued that the more liberal the divorce law, the more likely it is that the number of divorcing couples will rise. Deech,[143] for example, is against any wholesale reform of the grounds for divorce as those whose marriage has broken down 'can easily obtain divorces under the existing law, so there is no need to "liberalise" it'; and she is of the view that any reform is 'dangerous' as '[e]ach successive attempt in the twentieth century to bring the statute law into line with "reality" has resulted in an increase in the divorce rate'.[144]

Other difficulties relate to the process of divorce. One difficulty is deciding whether there should be a 'cooling off' period before the parties are permitted to divorce and, if so, how long this period should be. Resolution[145] has recommended *inter alia* that there should be a 'waiting period' of six months before one party (or both) is able to file a declaration that the marriage has broken down. Deech[146] recommends that a waiting period should be introduced to delay divorces based on adultery or unreasonable behaviour being processed so quickly, which she says would be achieved by adding to those grounds 'a provision that no decree shall be granted until at least 12 months have elapsed from the service of the petition'.

There are other questions to be addressed, such as whether joint applications for divorce should be permitted[147] and whether there should be a purely administrative form of divorce without judicial and court involvement. Cretney[148] has questioned the need for judicial involvement in the divorce process:

> Should we not accept that the routine processing of marriage breakdown is no longer a judicial function and that it should accordingly be removed altogether from the courts and the judicial system, leaving them with more time to deal with the problems that do require their expertise and procedures? If we believe that respect for the law and the legal system is important, and that the 1996 reforms would have made the law even more complex and difficult to understand, should we not begin to ask whether there is not a simpler and better alternative?

Other issues relate to the role to be played by mediation, and whether it should be compulsory, and the role played by marriage counselling and information provision for those

who responded to a survey thought that divorce should be available on this basis (see Law Com No 183, 1990).

[143] R. Deech, 'Divorce—A Disaster?' [2009] Family Law 1048.

[144] Ibid.

[145] See N. Shepherd, 'Ending the Blame Game: Getting No Fault Divorce Back on the Agenda' [2009] Family Law 122.

[146] R. Deech, 'Divorce—A Disaster?' [2009] Family Law 1048.

[147] Resolution is in favour of joint applications, and joint applications were available under the reforms proposed in the Family Law Act 1996.

[148] S. Cretney, 'Marriage, Divorce and the Courts' [2002] Family Law 900.

persons contemplating divorce. Another issue is whether marriage and divorce education should be made part of the national curriculum.

Currently there are no reforms of divorce on the horizon, but one simple change which could easily be implemented in England and Wales would be for the Government to follow the lead of the Scottish Parliament[149] which has made a simple adjustment to the law of divorce (which is virtually the same as divorce law in England and Wales) so that the period of two years' separation and consent to the divorce has been reduced to one, and the five-year separation ground reduced to three. Scotland has also abolished desertion as a ground for divorce. The aim of these simple reforms is to encourage the use of the separation grounds and thereby lessen the acrimony and conflict which can be associated with fault-based divorces, and to allow parents and children to move on.

5 OTHER DECREES UNDER THE MATRIMONIAL CAUSES ACT 1973

There are two decrees other than divorce (and nullity) which can be made by the court under Part I of the MCA 1973. These are a decree of judicial separation and a decree of presumption of death and dissolution of marriage.

5.1 DECREE OF JUDICIAL SEPARATION

Talking point

Some spouses may have objections to divorce (eg because of their religious beliefs), but if their marriage has come to an end they may wish to separate from the other spouse. A decree of judicial separation, which the court has jurisdiction to make under section 17 of the MCA 1973, provides such spouses with the judicial assistance they need. It may also be useful for persons who cannot divorce because one year of marriage has not elapsed, as the one-year bar which applies to divorce does not apply.

In practice, compared with divorce, the number of petitions for a decree of judicial separation each year are small and the trend over the years has been downwards.[150]

A decree can be obtained in reliance on the same facts as those for divorce (adultery, unreasonable behaviour etc), but there is no need to prove that the marriage has irretrievably broken down.[151] If one of the facts is made out, the court must grant the decree, which comes into effect immediately. There is no two-stage process as there is in divorce. It is also not possible to raise the defence of grave financial or other hardship in section 5; and section 10[152] does not apply because the parties' status as a married couple does not alter. A petitioner who successfully petitions for a decree of judicial separation is entitled to petition for divorce in reliance on the same facts.[153]

---

[149] By the Family Law (Scotland) Act 2006, s 10.

[150] In 2009, 360 petitions were filed, a drop of 14 per cent on the previous year, and continuing the steady downward trend (see *Judicial and Court Statistics 2009* (Ministry of Justice, 2010), Ch 2, Table 2.5).

[151] See s 17(2).

[152] Which makes provision for the rescission or withholding of a decree of divorce when the petitioner has misled the respondent to a petition based on the two- or five-year fact.   [153] MCA 1973, s 4(1).

A decree of judicial separation does not terminate the marriage but merely relieves the parties of the duty to live with each other,[154] although they are not obliged to separate. Once a decree has been obtained, neither party is in desertion for refusing to live with the other party and so desertion cannot be relied upon as a fact for divorce. A spouse may decide to seek a decree of judicial separation in order to take advantage of the court's ancillary powers to make financial provision and property orders[155] and, where appropriate, orders in relation to the upbringing of the children.[156] For succession purposes, the parties are treated as if they have pre-deceased one another. Consequently, they are not entitled to succeed to one another's property on intestacy.[157] However, where one party is a beneficiary under the other party's will the position is different from divorce. On divorce any gift made to a spouse in a will automatically lapses,[158] but this rule does not extend to where the parties are judicially separated.

5.2 DECREE OF PRESUMPTION OF DEATH AND DISSOLUTION OF THE MARRIAGE

A difficult situation arises where a spouse disappears and the other spouse does not know whether the spouse who has disappeared is alive or dead. If the spouse marries again and the other spouse is not dead, the second 'marriage' is void as section 11 of the MCA 1973 provides that the parties must not be already married.[159] Also, to enter into another marriage when a spouse is not dead and where the first marriage has not been annulled or terminated by divorce, may result in a party being convicted of the criminal offence of bigamy.[160] In a case of this kind, a spouse can be assisted by obtaining a decree of presumption of death and dissolution of the marriage under section 19 of the MCA 1973.

Under section 19 the court can make such a decree if the petitioner is able to prove that there are reasonable grounds for supposing that the other party to the marriage is dead.[161] For this purpose, the other party is presumed dead if after a period of seven years or more he or she has been continually absent from the petitioner and the petitioner has no reason to believe that the other party has been alive during that period.[162] The court can grant the decree before the seven years have elapsed, but any shorter period does not raise the presumption that the absent person has died. The decree both presumes death and dissolves the marriage. Thus, if the missing person should reappear after a second marriage has taken place, his or her reappearance has no effect on the validity of the second marriage. Before a decree can be granted, the petitioner must establish that the petitioner has made reasonable enquiries as to the whereabouts of the other spouse.

6 DISSOLUTION OF A CIVIL PARTNERSHIP

A civil partnership can be terminated by a dissolution order made under the Civil Partnership Act 2004 in virtually same way as a divorce. The court also has the power to

---

[154] Section 18(1).   [155] Under the MCA 1973, Pt II, see Chapter 4.
[156] Under the Children Act 1989, Pts I and II.
[157] MCA 1973, s 18(2). However, they can make an application for reasonable financial provision under the Inheritance (Provision for Family and Dependants) Act 1975.   [158] Wills Act 1837, s 18A.
[159] See Chapter 1.   [160] Ibid.   [161] Section 19(1).   [162] Section 19(2).

make separation orders and presumption of death orders in the same way as the court can under the MCA 1973.[163]

Dissolution is a court-based process like that of divorce and, with the exception of adultery, the ground and the fact(s) which must be proved to obtain a dissolution order are the same as those for divorce. Thus, the applicant must prove that the partnership has irretrievably broken down on the basis of:[164] 'unreasonable behaviour'; two years' separation with consent to the dissolution; five years' separation; and desertion for at least two years. Like divorce, an application for a dissolution order cannot be made until one year has passed from the date on which the civil partnership was created[165] and attempts at reconciliation are permitted when calculating the periods of separation and desertion.[166] Provision is also made for the refusal of a dissolution order in five-year separation cases and for the protection of respondents in separation cases, just as there is in separation cases on divorce.[167] Dissolution, like divorce, involves a two-stage procedure: a conditional order followed by a final order.[168] The civil partnership is not terminated until the final order is made.

Like divorce, the court has the power on or after making a dissolution order to make finance and property orders equivalent to those which the court can make on divorce.[169] Thus, the court has a discretionary jurisdiction to make periodical payments and lump sum orders, orders for the sale and transfer of property, and pension orders. The court also has the power to make finance and property orders after the overseas dissolution (annulment and legal separation) of a civil partnership.[170]

Under the Civil Partnership Act 2004,[171] the family courts in England and Wales have the power to recognise overseas civil partnerships and overseas civil partnership dissolutions (and annulments and separations), and these powers are the same as those governing the recognition of overseas marriages and divorces. However, overseas same-sex marriages are not recognised in the UK, as the case of *Wilkinson v Kitzinger*[172] shows, although they may be converted to a civil partnership within this jurisdiction.

The number of civil partnership dissolutions granted in the UK has increased since civil partnership was introduced. Thus, in 2008, 189 dissolutions were granted (compared to 42 in 2007), but in 2009 this increased to 351.[173] This increase reflects the fact that the Civil Partnership Act 2004 came into force in December 2005 and there is a bar on seeking dissolution within the first year of a civil partnership.

7 THE TERMINATION OF COHABITATION RELATIONSHIPS

There are no special legal provisions governing the termination of cohabitation relationships as there are for marriage and civil partnership. Thus, there is nothing equivalent to divorce or the dissolution of a civil partnership. This makes cohabitants particularly vulnerable on relationship breakdown because there is no discretionary jurisdiction,

---

[163] Under the Civil Partnership Act 2004, ss 37–64.   [164] Section 44(5).   [165] Section 41.

[166] Eg a period of up to six months' cohabitation can be disregarded when calculating periods of separation or desertion (see s 42).   [167] Sections 47 and 48.

[168] It should be noted that the terminology for dissolution of a civil partnership is different from that of divorce in order to make the terms less archaic and the law more understandable, eg applicant (not petitioner) and order (not decree).

[169] Under the Civil Partnership Act 2004, s 72 and Sch 5. For more details on these orders and the principles governing the making of them, see Chapter 4 which deals with the courts' power to make finance and property orders in ancillary proceedings on divorce.   [170] See s 72(4) and Sch 7.

[171] See ss 233–238.   [172] [2006] EWHC 835 (Fam), [2006] 2 FLR 397, and see Chapter 1.

[173] Office for National Statistics (www.statistics.gov.uk).

as there is on divorce and civil partnership dissolution, to distribute the parties' financial and property assets according to the present and future needs and resources of the parties. Instead any dispute about property, for instance ownership of the family home, must be dealt with in the civil courts, not the family courts, using the general principles of property and contract law, in particular the law of equity.[174] Ownership of property will depend largely on the intentions of the parties, and proving the existence of intention can involve costly and protracted litigation. Cohabitants are also at a disadvantage, compared with spouses and civil partners, in that they have no statutory right of occupation of the family home,[175] although they can apply under Part IV of the Family Law Act 1996 for non-molestation orders and occupation orders if they are actual or potential victims of domestic violence.

Cohabitants are also vulnerable on the death of their partner, for on their partner's intestacy they have no right to succeed to their deceased partner's property, as is the case for married persons and civil partners, although they can apply for financial provision from their deceased partner's estate under the Inheritance (Provision for Family and Dependants) Act 1975. However, applications by cohabitants under that Act are not treated as favourably as applications by married couples and civil partners.

Although there has been discussion and debate about reforming the law to give cohabitants new family law rights on relationship breakdown and also on a partner's intestacy, there are no current proposals to reform the law, despite the fact that there is some considerable support for changing the law.[176]

DISCUSSION QUESTIONS

1. Given the relative ease with which a divorce can be obtained under the special procedure, is there 'divorce on demand'?

2. The Family Law Act 1996 attempted to reform the law on divorce. Discuss the failure to implement the Act and the reasons for this.

3. Would the provisions contained in the 1996 Act in relation to the divorce procedure have been an improvement on the current law?

FURTHER READING

CRETNEY, S., 'Marriage, Divorce and the Courts' [2002] Family Law 900

DEECH, R., 'Divorce—A Disaster?' [2009] Family Law 1048

FREEMAN, M. (ed), *Divorce: Where Next?* (Aldershot: Dartmouth, 1996)

HASSON, E., 'Setting a Standard or Reflecting Reality? The "Role" of Divorce Law, and the Case of the Family Law Act 1996' [2003] International Journal of Law, Policy and the Family 338

HASSON, E., 'Wedded to "Fault": The Legal Regulation of Divorce and Relationship Breakdown' (2006) 26 Legal Studies 267

KAY, R., 'Whose Divorce is it Anyway? The Human Rights Aspect' [2004] Family Law 892

REECE, H., *Divorcing Responsibly* (Oxford: Hart, 2003)

---

[174] See eg *Oxley v Hiscock* [2004] EWCA Civ 546, [2004] 2 FLR 669; *Stack v Dowden* [2007] UKHL 17, [2007] AC 432, [2007] 1 FLR 1858; and see further Chapter 5.

[175] See the Family Law Act 1996, Pt IV, s 30, and see further Chapter 3.

[176] For details of these reforms, see Chapters 1 and 5.

3

PROTECTION FROM DOMESTIC VIOLENCE AND OCCUPATION OF THE FAMILY HOME

INTRODUCTION

The purpose of this chapter is to consider the civil law remedies which are designed to protect a victim from domestic violence. While domestic violence resulting in a physical assault can be prosecuted as a crime such as common assault or under the Offences Against the Person Act 1861, there may be particular reasons why the victim may not want to have the perpetrator prosecuted and classed as a criminal. The civil law provides a range of remedies which are specifically designed to tackle the problem of family violence and abuse. The two primary protective orders under Part IV of the Family Law Act (FLA) 1996 are the non-molestation order and the occupation order. They can be applied for and obtained in conjunction with each other, or separately. In addition, it is important to be aware that the occupation order can also be used to regulate occupation of the family home in non-violent situations when a dispute arises between family members about who is entitled to occupy the home, and on what basis.

1 WHAT IS DOMESTIC VIOLENCE?

Talking point

The government has adopted the following definition of domestic violence:

Any incident of threatening behaviour, violence or abuse (psychological, physical, sexual, financial or emotional) between adults who are or have been intimate partners or family members, regardless of gender or sexuality.[1]

The Supreme Court has recently held that 'domestic violence' for the purposes of the Housing Act 1996[2] is not limited to violence involving physical contact but also includes threatening or intimidating behaviour and any other form of abuse which, directly or

---

[1] *Domestic Violence: National Plan* (London: Home Office, 2005).
[2] Section 177(1). See below at Section 8.1.

indirectly, may give rise to the risk of harm.[3] Thus, it is clear that domestic violence is not simply understood as physical violence but that it encompasses a broad spectrum of abusive and controlling behaviour from actual violence, and the threat of such, to psychological, sexual, financial, and emotional abuse. As will be seen in this chapter, the legal understanding of domestic violence which entitles a victim to seek a protective civil order is similarly broad.[4]

The words which are used to describe or define the abuse which takes place within the family are important. This terminology has changed over the years. In the nineteenth century, the common term used was 'wife beating'. However, as the phenomenon came to be understood as involving a wide-ranging type of controlling abuse which can occur between different family members and not just between a husband and a wife, other terms such as 'family violence' and 'domestic violence' came to be used.[5] The selection of appropriate terminology is important because it can affect a victim's perception of her own situation and the abuse which she suffering. For example, if the term 'battered wives' is used, then individuals who either are not married to the perpetrator or who are suffering non-physical mental or emotional abuse may not identify with this term and thus may not feel that they are suffering from domestic violence for which help is available.[6] Some argue that the use of the modifier 'domestic' to describe violence between family members should be avoided because it locates this form of abuse within the private sphere of the family, and marks a distinction between violence which occurs between strangers and violence between family members, leading to the perception that the latter is not as serious.[7] It has been suggested that the term 'domestic violence' be replaced by terminology which underpins the serious nature of the abuse. Marcus, for example, argues that domestic violence should be seen as a form of 'terrorism' because of the parallels between terrorism, in its conventional usage, and gender-based violence.[8] Terrorists use three tactics to achieve their goals: unannounced and calculated attacks of violence; psychological as well as physical warfare; and the creation of an atmosphere of intimidation. Marcus argues that perpetrators of violence against women in intimate relationships use similar tactics to maintain domination, control, and superiority within the relationship.

The use of a more general term such as 'family violence' is also problematic because it obscures the fact that the most prevalent and severe form of domestic violence is that perpetrated by men against women in a marriage or a marriage-like relationship.[9] While there is no doubt that domestic violence can, and does, take place between a variety of family members and that the perpetrators are not always men, some definitions of domestic violence are deliberately gendered. For example, the UN Declaration on the Elimination of Violence against Women says that domestic violence is:

---

[3] *Yemshaw v Hounslow London Borough Council* [2011] UKSC 3.

[4] See Section 4.3.1 for a description of the non-molestation order which is available to protect the victim from all forms of abuse including non-physical harassment.

[5] R. Dobash and R. Dobash, 'Violence Against Women in the Family' in S. A. Katz, J. Eekelaar, and M. Maclean, *Cross-Currents: Family Law Policy in the US and England* (Oxford: Oxford University Press, 2000), 495.

[6] A. Mullender, *Rethinking Domestic Violence* (Abingdon: Routledge, 1996), p 26.

[7] I. Marcus, 'Reframing "Domestic Violence": Terrorism in the Home' in M. Fineman and R. Mykitiuk (eds), *The Public Nature of Private Violence: The Discovery of Domestic Abuse* (Abingdon: Routledge, 1994), pp 11–36. [8] Ibid.

[9] R. Dobash and R. Dobash, Violence Against Women in the Family' in S. A. Katz, J. Eekelaar, and M. Maclean, *Cross-Currents: Family Law Policy in the US and England* (Oxford: Oxford University Press, 2000), p 496.

Any act of gender-based violence that results in, or is likely to result in, physical, sexual or psychological harm or suffering to women, including threats of such acts, coercion or arbitrary deprivations of liberty, whether occurring in public or private life.

While this chapter will use the term 'domestic violence' as this is the term which is most commonly used to describe violence within the home, cognisance is taken of the fact that the most recurrent and severe form of domestic violence takes place by men against women.[10]

2 HOW PREVALENT IS DOMESTIC VIOLENCE?

Domestic violence occurs in all types of families and is not confined to any particular social class, racial or religious group, or age group. Commentators agree that it is very difficult to be precise about the prevalence of domestic violence. One of the main problems is victim under-reporting. Another difficulty in collecting precise statistical evidence is that some data only portrays violence between intimate partners and not that which occurs between other family members.[11] In addition, the fact that domestic violence not only refers to physical violence but also to other forms of abuse, such as emotional abuse and financial deprivation, makes it hard to quantify as the incidence of these non-physical forms of abuse are difficult to measure.

Statistical evidence does give us some idea of the prevalence of domestic violence, although certainly not its full extent. Evidence shows that domestic violence accounts for 14 per cent of all violent incidents.[12] It is estimated that 1 in 4 women and 1 in 6 men will experience domestic violence at some point in their lives and around two women each week are killed by their partner or former partner.[13] The Home Affairs Select Committee observed in 2008 that domestic violence is the largest cause of morbidity worldwide in women aged 19–44, greater than deaths caused by war, cancer, or motor accidents.[14] The report also calculated that in one year alone domestic violence cost public services in the UK £25.3 billion.

While there is evidence to show that men are at times the victims of domestic violence at the hands of their female partners, it remains the case that there is *asymmetry* in domestic violence with men more likely to be the perpetrator and women more likely to be the victim.[15] Others take a different view and argue that intimate partner violence is just as likely to involve a female perpetrator and a male victim. In light of this, some argue that the focus should be on 'family violence' as opposed to constructing the problem primarily as one of 'violence against women'.[16] However, studies continue to show that men are more likely than women to perpetrate violence against an intimate partner, and that women's violence to men does not equate in terms of frequency, severity, or in terms of its impact on the victim's sense of safety and well-being.[17] Dobash and Dobash reject evidence which suggests that domestic violence is gender-neutral arguing that it is based

---

[10] See the following section.   [11] Home Affairs Select Committee (2008).

[12] HM Government, National Domestic Violence Delivery Plan, Annual Progress Report 2008–09.

[13] Home Affairs Select Committee (2008).

[14] Home Affairs Select Committee (2008). See also *Domestic Violence: A National Report* (London: Home Office, 2005).

[15] R. Dobash and R. Dobash, 'Violence Against Women in the Family' in S. A. Katz, J. Eekelaar, and M. Maclean, *Cross-Currents: Family Law Policy in the US and England* (Oxford: Oxford University Press, 2000).

[16] R. Dobash and R. Dobash, 'Women's Violence to Men in Intimate Relationships: Working on a Puzzle' (2004) British Journal of Criminology 324.   [17] Ibid.

on narrow research methodologies which rely on the measurement of individual 'acts' of abuse such as a slap or a punch. The problem with this type of approach is that it measures these individual acts out of context and does not consider either the history of violence and abuse which may have preceded the act in question, or the outcome of the specific act. For example, they point to the fact that this approach will equate 'the physical impact/consequences of a "slap" delivered by a slight, 5 ft 4 inch woman with the "slap" of a heavily built man of 6 ft 2 inches.'[18] In addition, this approach simply looks at the fact of an act of violence taking place but does not consider the motives or intentions of the perpetrator such as whether it took place in the context of self-defence.

Statistics from the British Crime Survey also reveal that while less serious violence tends to be gender-neutral, the majority of serious and recurring violence is carried out by men against women.[19] A study in 2004 revealed that while 45 per cent of women and 26 per cent of men had experienced at least one incident of domestic violence in their lifetime, women were much more likely to be the victims of repeat incidents, and more severe attacks. Recent research based on studies of 96 cases reported by the Northumbrian police over a six-year period, found that the majority of perpetrators of domestic violence in cases which were reported to the police were men, and that the majority of repeat incidents were recorded for male rather than for female perpetrators.[20] Men were also more likely to use physical violence, threats, and harassment. The authors noted that:

> Men's violence tended to create a context of fear and related to that, control. This was not similarly the case where women were perpetrators.

Incidents where women were the perpetrators usually involved verbal abuse, some physical violence, and only a small proportion of threats or harassment. Women were, however, more likely to use a weapon although this was, at times, in an attempt to stop further violence from their partners. The study also found that in over half of the cases, children were recorded as having been present when the violence or other abuse took place.

Crime and other statistics only provide a rough estimate of the nature and extent of domestic violence, but it is very clear that those living in households where abuse and violence occur are damaged by this behaviour, both physically and emotionally. It is estimated that at least 750,000 children a year witness domestic violence.[21] There is also evidence to show that witnessing domestic violence has a detrimental impact on a child's health and well-being.[22] Children who have lived in a household where domestic violence occurs are more likely to have behavioural problems and other such difficulties. Mullender observes that:

> children are likely to be affected by the fear, disruption and distress in their lives. Children show distress in their own ways, depending on their age and developmental stage. They may have physical, emotional, learning, behavioural or developmental problems, and

---

[18] Ibid, 329.

[19] S. Walby and J. Allen, *Domestic Violence, Sexual Assault and Stalking: Findings from the British Crime Survey*, Home Office Research Study 276 (London: Home Office, 2004). See also Home Affairs Select Committee (2008).

[20] M. Hester, *Who Does What to Whom? Gender and Domestic Violence Perpetrators* (Bristol: University of Bristol in association with the Northern Rock Foundation, 2009). However, the study found that women were arrested to a 'disproportionate degree' given that they were much less likely to be perpetrators of violence than men. During the six-year period of the study, men were arrested once in every ten incidents, and women were arrested every three incidents. See also M. Hester and N. Westmarland, *Tackling Domestic Violence: Effective Interventions and Approaches*, Home Office Research Study 290 (London: Home Office, 2005).   [21] *Secure Futures for Women: Making a Difference* (London: Department of Health, 2002).

[22] *Domestic Violence: A National Report* (London: Home Office, 2005), para 39.

their educational performance and achievement may also be affected. These symptoms can easily be misdiagnosed or wrongly assessed as illness, permanent learning difficulties or naughtiness.[23]

Given the very damaging consequences of domestic violence, one question which is often asked is: why did the victim not leave the relationship? Victims of such violence and abuse very often do not report the violence or seek help, either through fear of the repercussions or because they may be too embarrassed to tell anyone what is happening to them. One of the most notable characteristics of domestic violence is that it rarely occurs as an isolated incident. It is much more likely to occur as an ongoing process of abuse and intimidation with the attacks escalating in both frequency and severity. Parmar and Sampson note that:

> A particular feature of domestic violence is that it occurs as part of a continuum of violence; sometimes there may be serious physical violence, and at other times there are verbal taunts about the incompetence of the woman and her 'ugliness' ... The forms of abuse can include controlling behaviour, such as limiting a woman's contact with her family and friends, scrutiny of and restriction of her actions, threats to hurt, rape and murder.[24]

Repeat victimisation, particularly against female victims, is very common. Hester describes domestic violence whether physical, psychological, emotional, verbal, or financial as an 'ongoing pattern of fear and coercive control'.[25] She continues:

> Such 'archetypal' domestic violence ... will usually involve one partner being violent, involve frequent abuse, and is likely to escalate and to result in serious injury.[26]

At the start of the abuse, the victim is unlikely to report it as she may believe the abuser's promises that it will not happen again and is likely to be committed to the relationship.[27] However, as the abuse continues and escalates in severity, a victim may become less confident in her ability to leave the situation and regain her independence, and more fearful of the abuser and of the repercussions of leaving. The victim may also blame herself, and many victims do not regard the abuse which they suffer as a crime, or as something with which the law can help. There may also be very practical reasons why a person remains in an abusive relationship, especially if the victim has little independent economic resources and is financially dependent on the abuser. Also, leaving the relationship does not mean that the abuse will come to an end. Studies show that women are at the greatest risk of being killed by their former partner after they leave a violent relationship,[28] and that women find the first six months after they leave their partner to be the most dangerous.[29] It should also be pointed out that querying why the victim did not leave removes the focus

[23] A. Mullender, *Tackling Domestic Violence: Providing Support for Children Who Have Witnessed Domestic Violence* (London: Home Office, 2005).

[24] A. Parmar and A. Sampson, 'Evaluating Domestic Violence Initiatives' (2007) British Journal of Criminology 671 at 674. The authors cite R. Dobash et al, *Research Evaluation Programmes for Violent Men* (Edinburgh: The Scottish Office Central Research Unit, 1996); S. Edwards, 'Police Attitudes and Dispositions in Domestic Disputes: The London Study' (1986) Police Journal, July; J. Hanmer and S. Saunders, *Well-Founded Fear* (London: Hutchinson, 1984); L. Kelly, *Surviving Sexual Violence* (Cambridge: Polity Press, 1987); B. Stanko, *Intimate Intrusions: Women's Experience of Male Violence* (London: Routledge, 1985).

[25] M. Hester, *Who Does What to Whom? Gender and Domestic Violence Perpetrators* (Bristol: University of Bristol in association with the Northern Rock Foundation, 2009), p 4.   [26] Ibid.

[27] A. Mullender, *Rethinking Domestic Violence* (Abingdon: Routledge, 1996).

[28] S. Lees, 'Marital Rape and Marital Murder' in J. Hanmer and C. Itzin (eds), *Home Truths about Domestic Violence: Feminist Influences on Policy and Practice: A Reader* (Abingdon: Routledge, 2002).

[29] C. Humphreys and R. K. Thiara, 'Neither Justice nor Protection: Women's Experiences of Post-Separation Violence' (2003) 25 Journal of Social Welfare and Family Law 195.

of attention from the perpetrator. This places responsibility on the victim for not leaving and, in doing so, implicates her in the allocation of blame for what has taken place.[30]

3 EXPLANATIONS FOR DOMESTIC VIOLENCE

There are several schools of thought around the reasons why domestic violence takes place.[31]

3.1 PSYCHOLOGICAL EXPLANATIONS

Some argue that domestic violence is perpetrated by deviant individuals who, for a variety of reasons connected with their background, character, and psychology, are predisposed to violence.[32] Risk factors such as alcohol or drug abuse may also explain the violence, as might the fact that the perpetrator has also suffered abuse and is repeating the cycle of violence. According to the British Crime Survey, 32 per cent of incidents of domestic violence occurred when the perpetrator was under the influence of alcohol.[33] A study in 2003 of 336 convicted domestic violence offenders identified two main types of perpetrator of domestic violence.[34] First, there were 'borderline/emotionally dependent offenders' who tended to display high levels of anger and jealousy, formed intense relationships with high levels of interpersonal dependency, and tended to suffer from depression and/or anxiety and have low self-esteem. Secondly, the study identified 'antisocial/narcissistic' offenders who had hostile attitudes towards women, had difficulty empathising with others, and who also had the highest rate of alcohol dependence and previous convictions.

3.2 SOCIAL STRUCTURAL EXPLANATIONS

From another perspective, broader social and environmental factors, such as unemployment, poverty, and bad housing, are said to contribute to the occurrence of domestic violence. From this sociological perspective, the more social stress which individuals and families face, the greater the likelihood of conflict occurring within the family.[35] According to Straus and Gelles, the family as a social institution has unique features which make it prone to violence.[36] These characteristics include the sheer amount of time spent with family members engaging in a wide-ranging number of activities; the intensity of this involvement; the age and sex differences of family members and the ascribed roles of individuals within the family; the perception of the family as a private institution; and the stresses and strains associated with family life and the dependency of ageing

---

[30] See E. M. Schneider, *Battered Women and Feminist Lawmaking* (New Haven, CT: Yale University Press, 2000).

[31] For an interesting discussion see J. Miles, 'Domestic Violence' in J. Herring (ed), *Family Law: Issues, Debates, Policy* (Cullompton: Willan Publishing, 2001), pp 78–124.   [32] Ibid, p 80.

[33] C. Mirrlees-Black, *Domestic Violence: Findings from a New British Crime Survey Self-Completion Questionnaire*, Home Office Research Study 191 (Home Office, 1999). See *Alcohol and Intimate Partner Violence* (London: Home Office, 2004).

[34] *Domestic Violence Offenders: Characteristics and Offending Related Needs* (London: Home Office, 2003).

[35] See R. Gelles, 'Through a Sociological Lens: Social Structures and Family Violence' in R. Gelles and D. Loseke (eds), *Current Controversies on Family Violence* (Thousand Oaks, CA: Sage, 1993), pp 31–47.

[36] R. Gelles and M. Straus, 'Determinants of Violence in the Family: Toward a Theoretical Integration' in R. Burr et al (eds), *Contemporary Theories About the Family*, vol. 1 (New York: Free Press, 1979), pp 549–581.

family members. However, this approach can also be criticised because it downplays the gendered nature of violence within families, and suggests that violence only occurs in families facing poverty and other social stresses which we know not to be the case. It also fails to answer the question of why such social and environmental stresses should lead to violence against women.[37]

3.3 FEMINIST EXPLANATIONS—THE PATRIARCHAL SOCIAL ORDER

Another school of thought frames the problem of domestic violence within the patriarchal social order where male violence against women is viewed as a mechanism of control and domination within marriage and marriage-like relationships.[38] On this view, domestic violence is the product of the unequal power relationship between men and women in society and is used to perpetuate female subordination which is central to the patriarchal social order.[39] Many argue that male violence against women is characterised by the desire to control the victim's behaviour.[40] The historical legitimisation of domestic violence and the reluctance of the law to take it seriously give credence to the abuser's belief that he is entitled to use force, either physical or otherwise, in order to exercise power and control within the relationship. Thus while the law has changed and domestic violence is no longer lawful, attitudes about female subordination in society and within intimate relationships persist.

3.4 A MULTIFACETED PHENOMENON

While focusing on pathological explanations is a limited viewpoint because it means that the response to domestic violence will be based upon the need to address the individual deviance of the abuser, one must be careful that the personal responsibility of the perpetrator is not diminished by an approach which blames broader social factors. Thus, the preferred approach may be to view domestic violence as caused by a combination of factors. According to Dobash and Dobash:

> Men's violence towards their partners has been part of a world culture for most of written history and should be understood both as an individual and as a sociocultural phenomenon.[41]

In addition, looking at the social structural explanations for domestic violence recognises that the family, as an institution, can be a dangerous environment. Moreover, the prevalence of male violence against women cannot be ignored and thus domestic violence must also be understood within the context of the patriarchal social order. Viewing domestic violence as a product of the patriarchal social structure 'that is built on male superiority

---

[37] A. Mullender, *Rethinking Domestic Violence* (Abingdon: Routledge, 1996).

[38] See D. Martin, *Battered Wives* (New York: Pocket Books, 1976); R. Dobash and R. Dobash, *Violence Against Wives: A Case Against the Patriarchy* (New York: Free Press, 1979); J. Radford and E. Stanko, 'Violence Against Women and Children: The Contradictions of Crime Control under Patriarchy' in M. Hester, L. Kelly, and J. Radford (eds), *Women, Violence and Male Power* (Buckingham: Open University Press, 1996) pp 65–80.   [39] Ibid.

[40] P. Romito, *A Deafening Silence: Hidden Violence against Women and Children* (Bristol: Policy Press, 2008); R. B. Felson and S. F. Messner, 'The Control Motive in Intimate Partner Violence' (2000) 63 Social Psychology Quarterly 86.

[41] R. Dobash and R. Dobash, *Violence Against Wives: A Case Against the Patriarchy* (New York: Free Press, 1979).

and female inferiority, sex-stereotyped roles and expectations, and economic, social and political predominance of men and dependency of women'[42] means that social and political structures which perpetuate female inequality must be challenged. Not only does this involve strategies to maximise women's economic independence, but also a break from notions which legitimise male domination of women in intimate relationships. Madden Dempsey forcefully argues that domestic violence reflects the intersection between three key elements—violence, domesticity, and structural inequality.[43] She uses a conceptual framework which defines violence in the home by its location within the private sphere of the family, and by the relationship between the parties which is usually characterised by intimacy, familial ties, or a shared household. In addition, the two key concepts which underpin the structural inequalities within relationships which form part of her analytical framework are power and control. Power is defined as the 'ability or entitlement to exercise control over another person'. For Madden Dempsey, domestic violence can manifest itself on a continuum from a 'strong' to a 'weak' representation of the phenomenon. The location of different acts of violence and abuse on this continuum depends on the extent of the intersection between the three key elements of violence, domesticity, and structural inequalities. Domestic violence in its 'strong' sense refers to illegitimate violence which occurs in a domestic context and which sustains or perpetuates the structural inequalities between the parties. The classic example of this is 'wife beating'. On the other end of the spectrum is domestic violence in its 'weak' sense which refers to illegitimate violence in a domestic context which does not sustain or perpetuate structural inequalities. An example of this is the actions of a victim of domestic violence in its 'strong' sense who engages in violent actions against his or her abuser. This work is interesting as it shows how the power differentials within relationships impact on the interpretation of violence between the parties, and confirms the notion that dominance, power, and control are at the heart of domestic violence.

4 THE RESPONSE OF THE LAW TO DOMESTIC VIOLENCE

It is only in recent years that domestic violence has been regarded as a social problem requiring state intervention to protect victims. The fact that it occurred within the private realm of the family meant that in social consciousness and by the law it was regarded as a private matter. Historically a husband was responsible for his wife's behaviour and, as such, he had the right to apply moderate chastisement to her.[44] This did not begin to change until the mid-nineteenth century when legal provisions were introduced to protect women from violence. However, these provisions were largely ineffective and it was not until the late 1960s that the pernicious nature of domestic violence became an issue for policy-makers. The first women's refuge was opened in Chiswick in 1971 by Erin Pizzey who subsequently published a dramatic account of the true nature of domestic violence and the failure of the law to provide safeguards for its victims.[45] In the 1970s, domestic violence came to be recognised as a serious social problem. The growing women's movement in the 1970s led to the creation of the Select Committee on Violence in Marriage

[42] R. Copelon, 'Intimate Terror: Understanding Domestic Violence as Terror' in R. Cook (ed), *Human Rights of Women* (Philadelphia, PA: University of Pennsylvania Press, 1994).

[43] M. Madden-Dempsey, 'What Counts as Domestic Violence: A Conceptual Analysis' [2006] 12 William and Mary Journal of Women and the Law 301.

[44] W. Blackstone, *Commentaries on the Laws of England* (1765).

[45] E. Pizzey, *Scream Quietly or the Neighbours Will Hear* (Harmondsworth: Penguin Books, 1974).

in 1974 which resulted in a legislative framework of civil remedies to meet the needs of victims of domestic violence. Before looking at these civil remedies in detail, we must first look at how the criminal justice system responds to domestic violence.

4.1 THE ROLE OF THE CRIMINAL LAW

While there is no specific offence of 'domestic violence', domestic assaults are criminal offences and the perpetrator can be prosecuted under the criminal justice system for offences such as assault, harassment, and rape. Until relatively recently, a husband could not be charged with the rape of his wife because, on marriage, she was deemed to give irrevocable consent to sexual intercourse throughout the marriage. However, following the decision of the House of Lords in *R v R (Rape: Marital Exemption)*[46] this common law rule was abolished and a man can now be charged with raping his wife.[47] In terms of other forms of assault, there is nothing to prevent a perpetrator of domestic abuse from being dealt with by the criminal justice system, and guidelines issued by the Sentencing Guidelines Council state that domestic violence offences are just as serious as offences committed in a non-domestic context.[48] In addition, the Guidelines make it clear that because the offence took place between family members, there are likely to be aggravating factors to make it more serious when it comes to sentencing. The court will consider, in particular, whether the perpetrator abused his position of trust and power within the relationship or exploited the victim's vulnerability and whether there has been a proven history of violence or threats of violence by the offender in a domestic setting. Offences involving serious violence will result in a prison sentence in the majority of cases.[49]

However, domestic violence has not always been regarded as a serious problem by the criminal justice system. The official attitudes of the police and criminal justice agencies towards domestic violence have changed dramatically in the latter half of the twentieth century. Throughout the 1970s and 1980s, the police were reluctant to intervene in situations of domestic violence which tended to be regarded as a private family matter, or a mere 'domestic'. The fact the victims quite often withdrew complaints led to a perception that they were 'fickle', and that this type of violence was less serious that violence between strangers.[50] By 1990, however, criminal justice agencies were taking domestic violence much more seriously and emphasis was placed on pro-arrest policies and prosecution. A Home Office Circular was issued to all police forces in England and Wales in 1990 directing a more proactive response to incidents of domestic violence.[51] However, subsequent research found that putting these policies into practice had not been that successful.[52] A revised circular was introduced in 2000 which emphasised, once again, the need for proactive policing of domestic violence, with a focus on pro-arrest policies.

Official government policy is also focused on improving the criminal justice response to domestic violence in order to achieve justice for victims and to bring perpetrators to account.[53] This change in emphasis has had some success. Reports show an increase in the number of domestic violence offenders being convicted, and pleading guilty. Figures from the Crown Prosecution Service (CPS) reveal that in 2005, 59 per cent of domestic violence

---

[46] [1992] 1 AC 599.   [47] See Sexual Offences Act 2003, s 1.

[48] Sentencing Guidelines Council, 'Overarching Principles: Domestic Violence' (2006).   [49] Ibid.

[50] See S. Edwards, *Policing 'Domestic' Violence: Women, the Law and the State* (London: Sage Publications, 1989).   [51] Home Office Circular 60/1990.

[52] S. Grace, *Policing Domestic Violence in the 1990s*, Home Office Research Study 139 (London: Home Office, 1995).

[53] *Safety and Justice: the Government's Proposals on Domestic Violence* (Cm 5847, 2003); HM Government, National Domestic Violence Delivery Plan: Annual Progress Report 2008–09.

cases resulted in a conviction, compared to 53 per cent in 2004.[54] Further, 52 per cent of defendants pleaded guilty, compared to 45 per cent in the previous year.[55] Central to the more proactive government policy on domestic violence is the introduction of a network of Specialist Domestic Violence Courts (SDVCs) which have developed a specialist way of dealing with domestic violence cases.[56] These specialist courts offer a combined approach to tackling domestic violence by bringing together the police, the Crown prosecutors, magistrates, courts, and specialist support services for victims. This integrated system aims to enhance the effectiveness of court and support services for victims, to improve victim participation and satisfaction, and to increase public confidence in the criminal justice system.[57]

4.1.1 Failure to report the abuse

However, despite these improvements there are still problems with the criminal justice response to domestic violence. Domestic violence remains an under-reported crime.[58] In the 2004 British Crime Survey, the police were only aware of 1 in 4 of the worst cases of domestic violence.[59] When asked why victims did not report the domestic violence to the police:

- 41 per cent of women and 68 per cent of men thought that it was too trivial;

- 38 per cent of women and 39 per cent of men thought that it was a private family matter;

- 7 per cent of women and 5 per cent of men said that they did not want to suffer any more humiliation; and

- 13 per cent of women (and no discernible percentage of men) feared more violence or that the situation would deteriorate if the police were involved.

There are a range of reasons why a victim may be reluctant to report the abuse.[60] Some may have low expectations of the police and criminal justice system, others may feel fear and shame, or regard the abuse to be their own fault. A person may also be deterred by the fact that, once an attack is reported to the police, the matter is no longer under her control. It will be up to the police to decide whether and how they wish to investigate the complaint, and it will be the decision of the CPS whether or not to go ahead and press charges. This loss of control acts as a disincentive to women to report incidents of violence as they may fear the consequences of their actions if the police and the CPS fail to respond in an appropriate fashion. Other factors which may deter a victim from becoming involved in the criminal process include the fear of further, and perhaps more vicious, assaults in retaliation for reporting the abuse; anxiety about the financial hardship which the family may suffer if the perpetrator were to lose his job; and a more general reluctance to be instrumental in the perpetrator obtaining a criminal record, and perhaps being sent to prison.

4.1.2 High levels of 'attrition'

In relation to incidents that are reported to the police, very few make it through the criminal justice system. A Home Office report on domestic violence noted that while there are

[54] CPS, 'Domestic Violence Monitoring Snapshot' (2005) available on CPS website www.cps.gov.uk.

[55] Ibid.

[56] *Domestic Violence: A National Report* (London: Home Office, 2005), para 51.

[57] Ibid, para 53. See D. Cook et al, *Evaluation of Specialist Domestic Violence Courts/Fast Track Systems* (London: CPS/Department of Constitutional Affairs, 2004); A. Robinson and D. Cook, 'Understanding Victim Retraction in Cases of Domestic Violence: Specialist Courts, Government Policy, and Victim-Centred Justice' (2006) 9 Contemporary Justice Review 189.

[58] See Home Affairs Select Committee (2008).

[59] S. Walby and J. Allen, *Domestic Violence, Sexual Assault and Stalking: Findings from the British Crime Survey*, Home Office Research Study 276 (London: Home Office, 2004).

[60] See A. Mullender, *Rethinking Domestic Violence* (Abingdon: Routledge, 1996), p 33.

estimated to be some 500,000 domestic violence-related calls to the police, only around 7,000 incidents result in prosecution.[61] The occurrence where cases fall out of the criminal justice system is known as 'attrition'. There are a variety of reasons why cases do not progress through the system from arrest to conviction. Not only might the police fail to obtain the necessary evidence, but victims may withdraw from the system.[62] Some victims may have concerns about giving evidence in court against a partner or a former partner. For example, a victim could be concerned that even if her partner is convicted, a non-custodial sentence may be imposed which could place her in immediate danger for giving evidence.[63] A study in 2003 examined the attrition rate in domestic violence cases entering the criminal justice system in Northumbria.[64] Of the 869 domestic violence incidents recorded by the police during the sample period, only 3.6 per cent resulted in conviction for criminal offences and there were only four custodial sentences. The researchers found that the victims were considered by the police as key to attrition. If the victim was unable or unwilling to provide a statement, there was little chance of a successful prosecution. However, it is possible for a prosecution to proceed even without the victim's testimony and the policy of the CPS is to consider other evidence which may be available either to support the victim's evidence or as an alternative to the victim's evidence.[65] If the victim does not wish to give evidence, the CPS will decide whether to proceed with the case on public interest grounds, taking into account a number of factors such as whether the defendant used a weapon, the seriousness of the attack, the nature of the victim's injuries, and the effect of the violence on any children living in the household. Given this, the police are encouraged to gather all evidence, such as photographic evidence and witness statements, which may make prosecution possible even if the victim does not wish to provide evidence. This is called 'enhanced evidence gathering'. However, in the Northumbrian study it was found that enhanced evidence was only rarely collected, and the extent to which the police gathered other evidence (such as CCTV footage and interviews with neighbours) depended on what was requested by the CPS.[66]

Despite the changes in the criminal justice system concerning pro-arrest policies and the need to take domestic violence seriously, improvements are still required to translate this rhetoric into practice. However, some argue that regardless of the criminal sanction imposed on a violent partner, women can benefit from simply engaging with the criminal justice system.[67] Lewis says that:

> the process of 'going public' can make women feel that their attempts to challenge their partner's violence are acknowledged and validated. It can offer women immediate and longer-term support, represent a challenge to their partner's tactic of isolation, and/or facilitate a shift in the balance of power in the relationship as men reduce their violence and abuse under the threat of further intervention.[68]

---

[61] *Domestic Violence: A National Report* (London: Home Office, 2005).

[62] See M. Hester, 'Making It Through the Criminal Justice System: Attrition and Domestic Violence' (2005) 5(1) Social Policy and Society 79.

[63] See B. James, 'In Practice: Prosecuting Domestic Violence' [2008] Family Law 456. See also *R v C* [2007] EWCA Crim 3463.

[64] M. Hester et al, *Domestic Violence: Making it Through the Criminal Justice System* (University of Sunderland, Northern Rock Foundation and the International Centre for the Study of Violence and Abuse, 2003); M. Hester, 'Making it Through the Criminal Justice System: Attrition and Domestic Violence' (2005) 5(1) Social Policy and Society 79.

[65] M. Burton, *Legal Responses to Domestic Violence* (Abingdon: Routledge-Cavendish, 2008), p 98.

[66] M. Hester, 'Making it Through the Criminal Justice System: Attrition and Domestic Violence' (2005) 5(1) Social Policy and Society 79 at 86.

[67] R. Lewis, 'Making Justice Work: Effective Legal Interventions for Domestic Violence' (2004) British Journal of Criminology 204.   [68] Ibid.

However, from another perspective, some point out that there are negative aspects of pro-arrest and prosecution policies. For example, some argue that such policies may result in the arrest of women who have used violence in retaliation and defence which may contribute to the emergence of statistics which show than women are also the perpetrators of domestic violence.[69] Others point out that engaging with the criminal justice system means that the victim loses control of how the case is managed which could 'further disempower and endanger the victim' if prosecution is not what she wants.[70] Evidence has shown that court outcomes of domestic violence cases did not stop chronic offenders from continuing their course of violence and harassment.[71]

4.2 CRIMINAL INJURIES COMPENSATION

A victim of domestic violence may be able to claim compensation from the state for the injuries sustained (both physical and mental) as a result of domestic violence. An application can be made to the Criminal Injuries Compensation Scheme which is established under the Criminal Injuries Compensation Act 1995. Compensation may be paid to an individual who has sustained personal injury as a direct result of an act of violence (including arson, fire-raising, or an act of poisoning).[72] A claim should be made as soon as possible, and not usually more than two years after the incident giving rise to the injury.[73] It is not necessary for the assailant to have been convicted of a criminal offence in connection with the injury.[74] However, a claims officer may withhold or reduce an award if the applicant failed to take, without delay, all reasonable steps to inform the police of the circumstances giving rise to the injury;[75] or if the applicant failed to cooperate with the police in attempting to bring the assailant to justice or other disqualifying criteria.[76] In addition, an award will only be made where there is no likelihood that an assailant would benefit from the award.[77] If, at the time the injury was sustained, the victim and the assailant were living in the same household as members of the same family, an application for compensation will be rejected unless:

    (a) the assailant has been prosecuted in connection with the offence, or a claims officer considers that there are practical, technical, or other good reasons why a prosecution has not been brought; and

    (b) in the case of violence between adults in the family, a claims officer is satisfied that the applicant and the assailant stopped living in the same household before the application was made and are unlikely to share the same household again.[78]

For the purposes of the scheme, a man and woman living together as husband and wife (whether or not they are married) or same-sex partners living together (whether or not they are civil partners) will be treated as member of the same family.[79] Where the applicant is entitled to compensation for a series of assaults, she will qualify for an award as the victim of a pattern of abuse, rather than for a separate award for each incident.[80]

---

[69] M. Chesney-Lind, 'Patriarchy, Crime and Justice: Feminist Criminology in an Era of Backlash' (2006) 1 Feminist Criminology 6. See also S. Walklate, 'What is to be Done About Violence Against Women? Gender, Violence, Cosmopolitanism and the Law' (2008) British Journal of Criminology 39.

[70] M. Burton, 'Civil Law Remedies for Domestic Violence: Why are Applications for Non-Molestation Orders Declining?' (2009) 31(2) Journal of Social Welfare and Family Law 109.

[71] M. Hester, 'Making it Through the Criminal Justice System: Attrition and Domestic Violence' (2005) 5(1) Social Policy and Society 79.   [72] Criminal Injuries Compensation Scheme (2008), para 8.

[73] Ibid, para 18.   [74] Ibid, para 10.   [75] Ibid, para 13(1)(a).   [76] Ibid, para 13(1)(b).

[77] Ibid, para 16(a).

[78] Ibid, para 17.   [79] Ibid, para 17(2).   [80] Ibid, p 33.

4.3 CIVIL LAW REMEDIES

The criminal law and civil law have very different objectives. The criminal law is concerned with identifying and punishing criminals, whereas the civil law is designed to respond to the needs of the victim. This is an important distinction, particularly in this area where the victim has an emotional attachment to the abuser which may affect how she wishes the matter to be dealt with. It is often the case that a victim of domestic violence does not wish to bring the relationship to an end permanently, but wants the violence to stop and to receive protection from further assaults. The civil law is designed to take account of the victims' differing needs, and civil law orders are prospective in nature. In other words, they are designed to protect the victim from future violence, as opposed to punishing the abuser for past behaviour.[81]

> ### Key legislation
>
> The civil law remedies for domestic violence are found in Part IV of the FLA 1996. Before the enactment of this legislation, the relevant civil law orders were contained in two pieces of legislation: the Domestic Violence and Matrimonial Proceedings Act 1976 and the Domestic Proceedings and Magistrates' Court Act 1978. Another piece of legislation, the Matrimonial Homes Act 1983, gave the courts the power to regulate occupation of the family home, and to enforce and restrict the respective rights of spouses to occupy the family home.

The Law Commission reviewed the law in 1992 and concluded that the civil remedies were complex, confusing, and lacked integration.[82] Different remedies were available to different applicants in different courts. The legislation also failed to give protection to a number of family members (such as siblings and former cohabitants) who fell outside of the categories of person who were eligible to apply for relief under the various pieces of legislation. The Law Commission made recommendations to deal with two 'distinct but inseparable problems'. First, it sought to provide protection for one member of the family against molestation or violence by another. Secondly, it sought to design provisions to regulate occupation of the family home when a relationship had broken down whether temporarily or permanently. The Law Commission recommended that a new legislative code be enacted to provide a single and consistent set of remedies which are available in all courts to deal with these two situations. The result was the Family Homes and Domestic Violence Bill 1995. However, this draft legislation was withdrawn due to political pressure after a high-profile campaign led by Conservative backbench Members of Parliament and the tabloid press complained that its provisions gave unmarried cohabitants the same property rights as married parties.[83] The draft legislation was amended and the final version was enacted as Part IV of the FLA 1996.

The two main orders under Part IV of the FLA 1996 are the non-molestation order and the occupation order. Not only was the law streamlined under the 1996 Act to ensure that these orders are available in all courts, but enforcement mechanisms were strengthened to provide that powers of arrest should be attached to orders if the victim or a child had been subjected to violence or threats of violence unless the court was satisfied that this was not necessary. In addition, the legislation introduced a new category of 'associated

---

[81] See B. James, 'In Practice: Prosecuting Domestic Violence' [2008] Family Law 456.

[82] Law Com No 207 (1992).

[83] This incorrect assessment of the legislation led to a campaign against its enactment which was instigated by the *Daily Mail*, 23 October 1995.

persons' who are entitled to apply for an order under the legislation although, as we shall see, there are differences between the list of persons who can apply for the two orders.

The law has been amended again in recent years. The enactment of the Domestic Violence, Crime and Victims Act 2004 sought to enhance the criminal justice response to domestic violence. One of the primary changes brought about by this Act was in making a breach of a non-molestation order made under Part IV of the FLA 1996 a criminal offence.[84]

4.3.1 Non-molestation orders

Section 42 of the FLA 1996 allows the court to make a non-molestation order which is an order which prohibits the respondent from molesting an 'associated person' or a 'relevant child'. The non-molestation order is aimed at providing a speedy remedy for a victim of domestic violence, and the Domestic Violence, Crime and Victims Act 2004 makes breach of this civil order a criminal offence.[85] 'Molestation' is not defined in the FLA 1996 as it was feared that this would be over-restrictive and lead to borderline results.[86] Thus, molestation is an 'umbrella term which covers a wide range of behaviour'.[87] It covers the most obvious type of case where the victim is subject to a physical assault or battery which could also give rise to criminal proceedings. However, it is much wider than this as the courts have accepted that while:

> violence is a form of molestation … molestation may take place without the threat or use of violence and still be serious and inimical to mental and physical health.[88]

Molestation can take a variety of forms such as writing abusive letters and shouting obscenities[89] or following the applicant around and making a 'perfect nuisance' of oneself.[90] In *Horner v Horner*[91] the molestation by the husband took the form of handing the wife upsetting notes, and intercepting her on her way to work. Ormrod LJ said that molestation did not 'imply necessarily either violence or threats of violence. It applies to any conduct which can properly be regarded as such a degree of harassment as to call for the intervention of the court.' In *Spencer v Camacho*[92] after a series of other activities for which the woman had obtained non-molestation orders, riffling through her handbag was held to be sufficient conduct to amount to molestation.

Where a non-molestation order is made, the actual wording of the order can be tailored to meet the needs of the particular case and can prohibit the respondent from carrying out very specific acts of molestation such as sending emails or letters.[93] However, a more generally phrased prohibition can be used and a usual form of wording is that the respondent is restrained from 'assaulting, molesting, annoying or otherwise interfering with the applicant or any relevant child living with the applicant'. Some have argued that the term 'non-molestation order' should have been replaced with clearer words which accurately portray the harm at which the order is aimed.[94] At the time the legislation was enacted, the police had concerns about the term 'non-molestation' because they had information to suggest that either the people seeking protection, or those to whom they

---

[84] See the following sections.   [85] Section 42A.

[86] Following the recommendation of the Law Commission (Law Com No 207), para 3.1.   [87] Ibid.

[88] *Davis v Johnson* [1978] 1 All ER 1132, *per* Viscount Dilhorne at 1144.

[89] *George v George* [1986] 2 FLR 347.   [90] *Vaughan v Vaughan* [1973] 1 WLR 1159.

[91] [1982] 2 All ER 495.   [92] (1984) 4 FLR 662.

[93] Section 42(6).

[94] Eg see the written evidence of M. L. Parry to the Special Committee on the Family Homes and Domestic Violence Bill (1994–95) HL Paper 55, p 66. He suggested that terms like 'no harm', 'non-abuse', or 'protection' orders would be more appropriate.

turned for assistance, did not fully understand what the term means. They took the view that some kind of definition, designed to be inclusive not exclusive, could usefully have been provided containing such words as 'pester', 'threaten', or 'harass'.[95] There is a risk that the phrase may be narrowly interpreted by victims and those working within the legal system because of a lack of a clear indication of how wide the term's meaning is meant to be. Unfortunately, recent evidence confirms this. It seems that some solicitors are informing their clients that the non-molestation order only covers physical violence which leads to physical injury, and not non-physical forms of abuse such as emotional abuse.[96] In taking this narrow interpretation, some clients who are suffering from non-physical abuse are being incorrectly advised that they cannot apply for a non-molestation order. One of the problems which may cause such misapprehensions is the lack of specialisation of family law solicitors and the 'large number of untrained lawyers and judges operating in domestic violence cases'.[97]

4.3.2 Some preliminary points about non-molestation orders

A non-molestation order can be made in the magistrates' family proceedings court, county court, and the High Court. The order can be made by the court on application by an eligible person. However, even if no such application has been made, the court has the power to make an order of its own motion in any family proceedings to which the respondent is a party where it considers that the non-molestation order should be made for the benefit of any other party to the proceedings or any relevant child.[98] In addition, the court can make the order when it is considering whether to make an occupation order.[99] The Law Commission had recommended that, on occasion, certain third parties (such as the police) should be able to bring proceedings on behalf of a victim of domestic violence.[100] While section 60 of the FLA allows prescribed persons to bring such proceedings on behalf of another, this provision has not yet been enacted.[101] The non-molestation order can be made for a specified period or until further order.[102]

The order can prohibit the respondent from molesting an 'associated person' or any 'relevant child'. The Law Commission considered that the court should have the discretion to make orders in relation to as wide a range of children as possible.[103] Thus, a 'relevant child' is given a very broad definition and does not just relate to the biological child of the applicant or the respondent but to any child whose interests the court considers relevant. Children who are living, or expected to live, with either the applicant or the respondent will be considered by the court,[104] as will children whose welfare is already before the court (under the Adoption Act 1976, the Adoption and Children Act 2002, or the Children Act 1989).[105] In addition, Parliament was so concerned to ensure that all relevant children fell within the scope of the protection afforded by non-molestation

---

[95] Ibid, oral evidence, p 41.

[96] M. Burton, 'Civil Law Remedies for Domestic Violence: Why are Applications for Non-Molestation Orders Declining?' (2009) 31(2) Journal of Social Welfare and Family Law 109 at 115.

[97] Home Affairs Committee, 'Domestic Violence, Forced Marriage and "Honour"-Based Violence', Sixth Report of Session 2007–08, vol I, HC 263-I.

[98] Section 42(2)(b). Such an order which is made under the court's own motion powers ceases to have effect if the family proceedings in which it is made are withdrawn or dismissed (s 42(8)).

[99] Section 42(4A), inserted by the Domestic Violence, Crime and Victims Act 2004, Sch 10, para 36.

[100] Law Com No 207 (1992), paras 5.18–5.23.

[101] For an assessment of the views of service providers on third party applications, see M. Burton, 'Third Party Applications for Protection Orders in England and Wales: Service Provider's Views on Implementing Section 60 of the Family Law Act 1996' (2003) 25(2) Journal of Social Welfare and Family Law 137–150.

[102] Section 42(7).

[103] Law Com No 207 (1992), para 3.27. [104] Section 62(2). [105] Section 62(2)(b).

injunctions that it included a catch-all provision which gives the court the discretion to make orders to protect 'any other child whose interests the court considers relevant'.[106] The gate-keeping role in relation to this provision is vested in the court which will decide whether the interests of any other child are relevant to the application.

4.3.3 Who can apply for a non-molestation order?

A non-molestation order can be made in respect of any relevant child (s 62(2)), or any person associated with the respondent. Under section 62(3), persons will be 'associated' with one another if:

(a) they are spouses and civil partners, former spouses, and former civil partners;

(b) they are cohabitants or former cohabitants: the definition of cohabitants was amended by the Civil Partnership Act 2004 and the Domestic Violence, Crime and Victims Act 2004 to include same-sex cohabitants. Under section 62(1) cohabitants are now defined as 'two persons who are neither married to each other nor civil partners of each other but are living together as husband and wife or as if they were civil partners';

(c) they live or have lived in the same household, otherwise than merely by reason of one of them being the other's employee, tenant, lodger, or boarder;

(d) they are relatives: the term relatives is defined in section 63 as:

(i) the father, mother, stepfather, stepmother, son, daughter, stepson, stepdaughter, grandmother, grandfather, grandson, or granddaughter of that person or of that person's spouse or former spouse, or

(ii) the brother, sister, uncle, aunt, niece, nephew, or first cousin[107] (whether of the full blood or of the half blood or by affinity) of that person or of that person's spouse or former spouse, and includes, in relation to a person who is cohabiting or has cohabited with another person, and any person who would fall within paragraph (i) or (ii) if the parties were married to each other;

(e) they are engaged or formerly engaged couples: to come within this definition the parties must produce evidence that there was actually an agreement to marry or enter into a civil partnership. First, the parties can produce written evidence of the agreement to marry or enter into a civil partnership.[108] Secondly, the agreement can be proven by the gift of an engagement ring by one party to the other in contemplation of their marriage. In the case of an agreement to enter into a civil partnership, this can be proven by a gift by one party to the other as a token of the agreement.[109] Thirdly, a ceremony entered into by the parties in the presence of one or more other persons assembled for the purpose of witnessing the ceremony can evidence such an agreement. The application must be made within three years of the agreement to marry or enter into a civil partnership being terminated;[110]

(f) they have or have had an intimate personal relationship with each other which is or was of significant duration: this category was inserted by the Domestic Violence, Crime and Victims Act 2004[111] and it plugs a gap in the law whereby dating couples who had neither lived together nor been engaged were not classed as 'associated persons'. No

---

[106] Section 62(2)(c).
[107] First cousins were included within the definition of relative by the Domestic Violence, Crime and Victims Act 2004, s 58(1).
[108] For the definition of a civil partnership agreement see the Civil Partnership Act 2004, s 73.
[109] Civil Partnership Act 2004, Sch 9.   [110] Sections 42(4) and 42(4ZA).
[111] Section 4.

statutory guidance is given on what constitutes an 'intimate personal relationship' or what length of time will suffice to constitute 'significant duration'. Case law will determine the scope of these terms. However, the explanatory notes accompanying the legislation make it clear that this category covers 'a long-standing relationship which may, or may not, be a sexual relationship, but which is an intimate and personal one. It does not include long-term platonic friends or "one-night stands" ';[112]

(g) in relation to any child, persons who are either a parent of the child or have parental responsibility for the child: if a child has been adopted, two persons are also associated with each other if one is a natural parent of the child or a parent of such a natural parent; and the other is the child or any person who has become a parent of the child by virtue of an adoption order or has applied for an adoption order; or with whom the child has at any time been placed for adoption;

(h) parties to the same family proceedings other than proceedings under Part IV of the FLA 1996. Family proceedings are defined under section 63 of the FLA 1996 and include proceedings under the Matrimonial Causes Act 1973, the Adoption Act 1976, and the Children Act 1989.

4.3.4 The approach of the courts to defining 'associated persons'

In *G v F (Non-Molestation Order: Jurisdiction)*[113] the court emphasised that a purposive construction should be taken when deciding whether an applicant was associated with the respondent for the purposes of the legislation. In this case the applicant did not live with the respondent but they stayed with each other two or three nights of the week and for a time had a joint back account. Wall J held that the parties were cohabitants within the meaning of the FLA 1996. The characteristics of their relationship met three of the six 'signposts' which had been set out in *Crake v Supplementary Benefits Commission*[114] to assist in determining what amounts to cohabitation. The signposts were (i) whether they are members of the same household; (ii) whether the relationship is stable; (iii) whether there is financial support; (iv) whether there is a sexual relationship; (v) whether they have children; and (vi) whether there is public acknowledgement of the relationship. In the present case, the parties were in a sexual relationship, they lived in the same household part of the time, and operated a joint bank account. As such, the court held that there was sufficient evidence to demonstrate that they had been cohabitants and therefore 'associated persons' for the purpose of section 42. The general approach of the court in this case is important because it illustrates that in borderline cases where there is some uncertainty about whether an applicant falls into one of the categories of 'associated person', a purposive interpretation will be taken. Wall J said that:

> where domestic violence is concerned [judges] should give the statute a purposive construction and not decline jurisdiction, unless the facts of the case before them are plainly incapable of being brought within the statute.

The legislation is designed to provide 'swift and accessible protective remedies' to victims of domestic violence which mandates against a narrow interpretation of associated persons. In light of recent amendments, this approach may be important when the courts are called upon to decide whether a potential applicant was in an 'intimate relationship' with the respondent which is, or was, of 'significant duration'.[115]

---

[112] www.opsi.gov.uk/acts/acts2004/en/ukpgaen_20040028_en.pdf.
[113] [2000] Fam 186.   [114] [1982] 1 All ER 498.
[115] FLA 1996, s 62(3)(ea).

Case law also illustrates that an applicant who is associated with the respondent can apply for a non-molestation order even where the disharmony is not borne from the family relationship between the parties but from a civil dispute. In *Chechi v Bashier*[116] a bitter family dispute over land in Pakistan led to the applicant's claim for a non-molestation order against his brother and nephews, all of whom were resident in the UK. Even though this was a dispute over land, the court held that it had been intensified by the family relationship between the parties. As such, it was genuinely within the ambit of the FLA 1996 and the applicant was eligible to apply for a non-molestation order against his brother and nephews because he was 'associated' with them under the wide definition of relative in the legislation.[117] However, even though he was entitled to apply for this order, the court rejected his application. Under section 47(2), the court is mandated to attach a power of arrest to a non-molestation order if the respondent has used or threatened violence against the applicant or relevant child unless it is satisfied in all the circumstances that the applicant or child will be adequately protected without such a power of arrest. In the circumstances, the court felt compelled to attach a power of arrest to the order in line with this provision but it feared that in doing so the applicant would have unacceptable power over the respondents. The application for a non-molestation order was rejected on that basis. Some are critical of this decision. Burton, for example, points out that section 47(2) which was designed to strengthen the enforcement of non-molestation orders operated to deny the applicant an order in the first place.[118] She says that in the alternative:

> the court could have granted the order but exercised the discretion afforded by the legislation to not attach a power [of arrest] in circumstances where the applicant is adequately protected without it. If they did not think that the applicant would have been adequately protected without a power of arrest then the case for a non-molestation order was compelling and the courts were arguably wrong to refuse one.

As we shall see later in this chapter, amendments made by the Domestic Violence, Crime and Victims Act 2004 ensures that breach of a non-molestation order is now a criminal offence which means that the police have, in all cases, the power of arrest.[119]

4.3.5 The arguments for and against the wide definition of 'associated persons'

One of the most significant changes brought about by Part IV of the FLA 1996 was the creation of the new category of 'associated persons' where the aim was to ensure that a much wider range of person was eligible to apply for the civil remedies under the legislation.[120] As we have seen, this statutory list has been extended even further by the Domestic Violence, Crime and Victims Act 2004 to include 'those who have or have had an intimate personal relationship with each other which is or was of significant duration',[121] and to include same-sex couples within the definition of cohabitant.[122] The reason for such a wide category of eligible applicants was the recognition that domestic violence can occur in many types of family relationship, and not just between spouses or cohabitants, and that those who fell outside the legislation were

---

[116] [1999] 2 FLR 489.   [117] FLA 1996, s 63.
[118] M. Burton, *Legal Responses to Domestic Violence* (Abingdon: Routledge-Cavendish, 2008), p 27.
[119] See Section 4.3.9.
[120] See A. Bainham, 'Changing Families and Changing Concepts—Reforming the Language of Family Law' (1998) 10 Child and Family Law Quarterly 1.
[121] Domestic Violence, Crime and Victims Act 2004, s 3.   [122] Ibid, s 3.

not receiving the protection which they may need.[123] The Law Commission originally mooted the idea of removing all eligibility requirements to ensure that any person who required protection from abuse was able to obtain it. In effect, this would have created a new tort of harassment or molestation where the protective orders could be used to resolve disputes between neighbours or harassment in the workplace where 'there is no domestic or family relationship to justify special remedies or procedures'.[124] However, this approach was rejected on the grounds that the special nature of family relationships, the strength of the emotions involved in these relationships, and the stresses and strains of family life meant that violence and molestation within the family has to be considered as a special case. Thus, the Law Commission adopted a 'middle path' and widened the range of applicants to include anyone who is associated with the respondent by virtue of a family relationship or something closely akin to such a relationship.[125] No longer are the protective remedies only available to spouses and cohabitants, but also to those within family relationships of sufficient proximity to require the flexibility of a specialist family law regime.

However, this approach can be criticised and some have argued that the protective orders should be available to whoever needs them, regardless of the relationship between the parties. As the Law Commission recognised, restricting the law's remedies to pre-determined categories of persons associated through a family relationship can give rise to strange results. It gave the example of four friends sharing a flat. If they are all joint tenants then any one of them would be able to apply for a non-molestation order as they all live in the same household. However, if one party took the tenancy and then sub-let to his friends, the order would not be available in relation to him because the category of co-residents in a household excludes those who share a household on a commercial basis (such as tenant, lodger, or boarder).[126] It seems unfortunate to legislate knowing in advance the difficult problems that are liable to arise, particularly if those difficulties can be avoided. Limiting the scope of the Act's provisions to associated persons may prevent the court from dealing in an even-handed manner with potential litigants where one is being molested but, in failing to come within the definition of associated person, is unable to avail herself of the court's injunctive powers. Where the behaviour is such that the law should provide a remedy, and given that the legislation focuses on the effect of the conduct in question on the victim rather than on its intrinsic nature, one could question the efficacy of limiting the remedies to certain classes of applicant.[127] Some argue that a simple, accessible remedy available to all who are subject to molestation, not just those in a familial relationship, should have been provided. Of course, it is worth pointing out that another option for such persons is to seek a remedy under the Protection from Harassment Act 1997 where there are no limitations on who can apply for an order.[128]

Others take the opposite view and argue that the definition of 'associated person' is too widely drawn in the legislation. Reece, for example, argues that the category of 'associated

---

[123] Law Com No 207 (1992), para 2.28.

[124] Ibid, para 3.19.   [125] Ibid, para 3.19.

[126] Ibid, para 3.22.

[127] Eg if a university student becomes the object of the obsessive attentions of an unbalanced lecturer (or vice versa) why should not he or she be able to obtain a non-molestation order? See M. Hayes and C. Williams, 'Domestic Violence and Occupation of the Family Home: Proposals for Reform' [1992] Family Law 497 at 498; M. Hayes, 'Non-Molestation Protection—Only Associated Persons Need Apply' [1996] Family Law 134.   [128] See Section 7.

person' upon whom enhanced civil protection for domestic violence is conferred, is mis-guided. Not only is there little evidence to suggest that the breadth of 'family members' identified as associated persons are vulnerable to domestic violence, but their inclusion within the legislation gives rise to the perception that domestic violence occurs in every type of family relationship. This, Reece argues, obscures the 'true character of the phe-nomenon' and the fact that domestic violence is typically perpetuated by men against women in partnering relationships. Pointing to statistics which show that domestic vio-lence is usually carried out by men against their present or former female partners, Reece argues that the range of associated persons do not share the features of wives and female heterosexual cohabitants which make them particularly vulnerable to domestic violence. These features include:

- the victim's isolation;
- the victim's unequal power relations with her spouse or partner;
- the presence of barriers to leaving the relationship (such as one's identity being fixed on the relationship to the extent that it becomes impossible to consider leaving);
- the victim's financial dependence on her spouse or partner.

While some associated persons may face similar issues, for example an elderly person who is being abused in the family home, Reece concludes that for the most part those included within the statutory list do not have these characteristics. In short, she argues that the wide category of associated persons 'endangers the specificity of the category of domestic violence'.

4.3.6 The child as applicant for a non-molestation order

Under section 43, children under the age of 16 can apply for a non-molestation order provided that the child obtains the leave of the court. The court will grant leave only if it is satisfied that the child has sufficient understanding to make the proposed application. No statutory guidance is provided to the court on what criteria should apply to such a leave application. However, it is likely that parallels will be drawn with applications for leave to apply for section 8 orders made by children under the Children Act 1989, where the same restriction applies. Persuading a parent or other adult associated with the respondent to apply for a non-molestation order, particularly where the application is coupled with an application for an occupation order, might sometimes avoid the necessity to institute care proceedings on behalf of a child who is suffering, or likely to suffer, significant harm as a result of domestic violence. It also avoids the child becoming embroiled in taking legal proceedings against his or her own parent.

4.3.7 Criteria for granting non-molestation orders

Under the pre-1996 domestic violence legislation, protection orders could only be granted by the court where the respondent had used, or threatened to use, violence against the applicant or a child of the family.[129] However, the 1996 legislation heralded a change in emphasis. The Law Commission took the view that the criteria for granting a non-moles-tation order should focus on the *effect* of the respondent's behaviour on the applicant and any relevant child.[130]

---

[129] Under the Domestic Proceedings and Magistrates' Court Act 1978.
[130] Law Com No 207 (1992), para 3.6.

Key legislation

Thus under section 42(5) of the 1996 Act:

In deciding whether to exercise its powers under this section and, if so, in what manner, the court shall have regard to all the circumstances including the need to secure the health, safety and well-being—

(a) of the applicant or in a case [where the court proposes to make an order of its own motion], the person for whose benefit the order would be made; and

(b) of any relevant child.

For the purposes of this provision, 'health' includes both physical and mental health. This victim-focused provision mandates the court to consider the *effect* of the respondent's behaviour on the applicant or any relevant child rather than on the nature of the conduct itself. It is clear that the purpose of the legislation is to provide protection from harm rather than to assign punishment or blame. The court has a wide discretion when deciding whether to grant a non-molestation order. No specific evidence of violence or threats of violence is required before the court will make an order. The standard of proof required to obtain a non-molestation order is the civil standard (the balance of probabilities) even though breach of this order is a criminal offence.[131]

A very wide definition of molestation, and a victim-focused approach to the criteria to be applied to the exercise of judicial discretion, is to be welcomed. Any conduct which has the effect of harassing or pestering the applicant or any relevant child will come under the scope of a non-molestation order if sufficiently serious. However, as previously indicated, while a non-molestation order can be made to protect the victim from non-physical abuse, research has called into question the extent to which orders are made to protect against this sort of behaviour.[132] While, technically, a non-molestation order is available to protect against non-physical forms of abuse, there may be practical reasons why a victim of such abuse may find it hard to obtain a legal remedy. In particular, the victim might face obstacles in securing legal aid funding to support their case.[133] Research has shown through interviews with representatives from the Legal Services Commission that victims of non-physical violence would not be considered as a priority for public funding and that those suffering from mental abuse would have to produce medical documentation to verify the effect that this had on their health.[134]

4.3.8 Can an order be made to protect the applicant against unintentional conduct?

One question which has arisen is whether it is a requirement that the conduct complained of is intentional on the part of the respondent. In *Johnson v Walton*,[135] a case which was decided under the pre-1996 legislation, the court took the view that molestation involving harassment includes an intent to cause distress or harm. However, earlier case law

---

[131] The Government said that 'in criminalising the breach of the non-molestation order it is not the Government's intention to affect the law in respect of the making of such orders, in particular the standard of proof required for the courts to grant orders', House of Commons Standing Committee E, Hansard, 22 June 2004, col 27, see S. Gore, 'In Practice: The Domestic Violence, Crime and Victims Act 2004 and Family Law Act 1996 Injunctions' [2007] Family Law 739.   [132] See Section 4.3.1.

[133] M. Burton, 'Civil Law Remedies for Domestic Violence: Why are Applications for Non-Molestation Orders Declining?' (2009) 31(2) Journal of Social Welfare and Family Law 109.

[134] M. Burton, *Legal Responses to Domestic Violence* (Abingdon: Routledge-Cavendish, 2008), p 40.

[135] [1990] 1 FLR 350.

confirmed that where the respondent is physically violent towards the applicant an order can be granted regardless of intention. In *Wooton v Wooton*[136] the respondent only became violent during epileptic episodes. The Court of Appeal held that the court had jurisdiction to grant an injunction because it was the actual violence and the consequences suffered by the applicant which were the important factors to be considered by the court.

However, what is the position under Part IV of the FLA 1996: must the respondent have the 'intent' to molest for a victim to obtain a non-molestation order? The answer to this question appears to be that an order can be made regardless of the respondent's actual intent. This, it is suggested, is the correct approach. Given that the criteria for making non-molestation orders are deliberately focused on the *effect* of the conduct on the victim as opposed to the actual nature of the respondent's actions, it would be contradictory for the courts to impose a requirement that the conduct was carried out with the deliberate intention of harassing the applicant. Although the respondent's behaviour in a large number of instances of domestic violence may well satisfy a threshold of intent, making this a pre-requisite to obtaining an order would give the respondent the scope to put forward a defence on the ground that due to a medical condition or drug/alcohol consumption he was unable to control his actions. Given the statistical evidence which shows the clear link between alcohol/drug abuse and domestic violence,[137] such a requirement would limit the scope of the non-molestation order. An abuser who, perhaps due to mental illness, is behaving in such a way that the court would normally intervene, may be causing as much distress as an abuser who is deliberately acting out of spite. As Sedley LJ observed in *P v P (Contempt of Court: Mental Capacity)*:[138] 'The court has an invidious choice to make in a situation like this between the compulsive behaviour of a most unfortunate individual and the safety and well-being of his family.' It is also arguable that this same principle should apply where the abuser was behaving whilst under the influence of drugs or alcohol. Thus it seems that a non-molestation order can be made against someone whose actions are not deliberately wilful, but are unintentional.

However, this gives rise to a related issue. If the respondent is suffering from a mental illness or some other disability which impairs their understanding of the nature of the order and the fact that it prohibits certain conduct, the court may refuse to grant the order on the ground that it could not be effectively enforced. In such circumstances, the order would have no deterrent effect because the respondent would not be capable of complying with it, and any breach could not be subject to effective enforcement proceedings.[139]

Key case

In *Banks v Banks*,[140] which was a decision of the Oxford County Court, the court refused to grant a non-molestation order against a 79-year-old woman who suffered from manic depression and dementia. The woman had been looked after by her husband and other carers for many years in the matrimonial home. When her condition deteriorated, she was admitted to hospital but after responding to treatment, the hospital wished to discharge her and send her home as it was felt to be best for her to be in familiar surroundings rather than in residential care. Her husband, who was aged 75 and both physically and emotionally frail, petitioned for divorce on the ground that he could no longer cope with her illness. She had

---

[136] (1984) FLR 871.

[137] See eg C. Mirrlees-Black, *Domestic Violence: Findings from a New British Crime Survey Self-Completion Questionnaire*, Home Office Research Study 191 (London: Home Office, 1999); K. E. Leonard and B. M. Quigley, 'Drinking and Marital Aggression in Newlyweds: An Event-Based Analysis of Drinking and the Occurrence of Husband Marital Aggression' (1999) 60(4) Journal of Studies on Alcohol 537–545.

[138] [1999] 2 FLR 897.   [139] *Wookey v Wookey* [1991] 3 All ER 365.   [140] [1999] 1 FLR 726.

been both physically and verbally abusive towards him although at no point had he suffered any physical injury. According to the wife's consultant psychiatrist, it was unlikely that she posed a threat to his health and the intention was that she was to be looked after by a team of daily carers. The husband's application for a non-molestation order was refused by the court. Judge Geddes held that her behaviour was a symptom of her condition and thus outside her control. He concluded that an order would serve no practical purpose, even if she were capable of understanding it.[141]

In short, therefore, when dealing with a respondent whose actions are caused by a medical condition, or some other ailment which impairs his judgement, the fact that the abuse may be unintentional will not prevent the court from making the order. However, if the respondent's condition affects his ability to understand the nature of the order, the court may refuse to grant the order on the ground that it would serve no useful purpose. But an order will be made if the respondent understands that an order prohibits him or her from doing certain things and that if this is ignored punishment will follow.

4.3.9 Enforcement of the non-molestation order

The non-molestation order is designed to protect the applicant against violence and other forms of molestation. However, this order may be worthless unless it is backed up by strong enforcement powers which courts are prepared to use, and the police to operate in practice. One of the major changes introduced by the Domestic Violence, Crime and Victims Act 2004 concerns the enforcement of a non-molestation order. Under the old law, breach of this order was dealt with as a civil contempt of court and the exact method of enforcement depended on whether the court had attached a power of arrest to the order. While this was a matter for the court's discretion, section 47(2) of the 1996 Act compelled the court to attach a power of arrest to a non-molestation order if it appeared that the respondent had used or threatened violence against the applicant or relevant child unless it was satisfied in all the circumstances that the applicant or child would be adequately protected without such a power of arrest.[142] A power of arrest allowed the police to arrest the respondent without warrant if there was reasonable cause to suspect that the respondent was in breach of the order to which the power of arrest was attached. If no power of arrest was attached to the order, the victim had to apply to the civil court for an arrest warrant and then enforce the order through the contempt of court procedure.

In line with the general trend to take domestic violence more seriously and to use the criminal justice system to punish domestic violence offenders, the Government sought to strengthen the legal protection afforded to victims of domestic violence.[143] A new provision was introduced by the Domestic Violence, Crime and Victims Act 2004 which criminalised the breach of a non-molestation order.

Key legislation

Under the new section 42A in the 1996 Act:[144]

> a person who without reasonable excuse does anything that he is prohibited from doing by a non-molestation order is guilty of an offence.

---

[141] See *Wookey v Wookey* [1991] 3 All ER 365.   [142] See *Chechi v Bashir* [1999] 2 FLR 489.
[143] *Safety and Justice: The Government's Proposals on Domestic Violence* (Cm 5847, 2003).
[144] Inserted by the Domestic Violence, Crime and Victims Act 2004, s 1.

This means that breach of a non-molestation order is now an arrestable offence.[145] Enforcement of this order no longer depends on whether a power of arrest has been attached, nor does the victim have to apply to the civil court to get an arrest warrant.[146]

4.3.10 Why was the law changed?

There were various reasons put forward to justify the criminalisation of non-molestation orders.[147] First, enforcing a non-molestation order through the criminal courts takes the matter out of the hands of the victim. It is the police and the CPS who will decide whether to proceed with the prosecution and it was thought that this would be helpful to victims who may not want to have the responsibility of instigating proceedings against a husband or partner. The aim was to encourage greater use of the criminal justice system and the application of criminal sanctions for domestic violence. Secondly, it was hoped that this would address the uncertainty which police officers faced around whether they could arrest someone for an alleged breach of a non-molestation order. Previously this depended on whether a power of arrest was attached to the order and it was not always clear to police officers who were called to an incident of domestic violence whether or not this power was in existence. The matter is now much more straightforward. Under section 42A, the police in all cases have the power to arrest a person who is in breach of a non-molestation order. Thirdly, as an action under section 42A will be taken by the police, the cost of enforcing the non-molestation order will not fall to the victim. The victim may be a witness but she will not be enforcing the action personally. In addition, the available sanctions are much more extensive in the criminal courts. While the maximum custodial sentence for breach of a non-molestation order under section 42A is five years,[148] the maximum period of imprisonment for breach of an injunction in civil contempt cases is two years.[149]

4.3.11 Can a victim still enforce the order in the civil courts?

The court no longer has the power to attach a power of arrest to a non-molestation order. However, a victim who wishes to enforce the order in the civil courts can apply for a warrant to arrest the respondent[150] or make an application for committal proceedings.[151] This may be particularly relevant where the police have decided not to arrest the alleged abuser, or where the CPS does not proceed with the prosecution. In such circumstances, the victim retains the option of enforcing the non-molestation order through civil proceedings for contempt of court.

However, the legislation makes it clear that the non-molestation order cannot be enforced as *both* a civil and criminal matter. Section 42A(4) and (5) states that a person cannot be convicted of breach of a non-molestation order under section 42A where the conduct has already been dealt with under contempt of court proceedings. The converse is also true. If a respondent has been convicted for breach of a non-molestation order under section 42A, the victim cannot subsequently bring proceedings for contempt of court in the civil courts.[152] In other words, the order can be enforced in one of two ways, under section 42A or as a contempt of court, but not both.

---

[145] Under the Police and Criminal Evidence Act 1984, s 24(1).

[146] Note: for orders made without notice, an individual will only be guilty of a criminal offence if he is aware of the existence of the order (s 42A(2)). See Section 5.14.

[147] See C. Bessant, 'Enforcing Non-Molestation Orders in the Civil and Criminal Courts' [2005] Family Law 640.   [148] Section 42A(5).

[149] Contempt of Court Act 1981, s 14.   [150] Under s 47(8).

[151] J. Platt, 'The Domestic Violence, Crime and Victims Act 2004 Part 1: Is it Working?' [2008] Family Law 642.   [152] Section 42A(3). See *Hale v Tanner* [2000] 3 FCR 62; *Lomas v Parle* [2004] 1 FLR 812.

This does give rise to some concerns surrounding the extent to which a victim of domestic violence can control the manner in which any breach of a non-molestation order is dealt with. It has already been pointed out that a victim of domestic violence may want to salvage the relationship with the abuser, or may fear the practical consequences of the abuser being labelled a criminal and the impact which this may have on the family (eg if the abuser loses his job). It is these sorts of factors which may have led the victim to apply for a civil order in the first place, as opposed to seeking the protection of the criminal law. However, breach of a non-molestation order is now a criminal offence. Thus, what is to happen if the police decide to pursue the matter through the criminal courts but the victim opposes this and prefers, in the alternative, to enforce the order through the civil courts? While, in theory, the legislation preserves the right of the victim to enforce the order through the civil courts, in practice this option will be denied to the victim if the police and CPS adopt a rigorous policy of prosecuting breaches as a criminal offence under section 42A. Some have criticised this change to the law on the grounds that it undermines the autonomy of the victim and fails to appreciate the very particular nature of domestic violence. Indeed, some point out that the enforcement of non-molestation orders could have been strengthened by simply extending the penalties available in civil proceedings for contempt.[153] It remains to be seen to what extent a victim's reluctance to involve the criminal justice system will impact upon the decision of the police and the CPS whether or not to prosecute under section 42A.[154] Indeed, this may turn out to be little more than a hypothetical problem as the reality may be the exact opposite. In other words, it is possible that the police will fail to treat breach of a non-molestation order as a matter for the criminal courts.[155] Indeed, early evidence on the implementation of section 42A suggests that the police are using cautions to deal with perpetrators who have breached a non-molestation order under section 42A,[156] and that the CPS is not charging perpetrators with a criminal offence.[157]

While a breach of a non-molestation order cannot be dealt with through both civil and criminal enforcement proceedings, there is nothing to prevent a perpetrator whose actions in breaching the order also constitute a substantive criminal offence from being prosecuted under the criminal law for this offence,[158] and also being prosecuted for breach of the non-molestation order under section 42A (or facing contempt of court proceedings).

4.3.12 Sentencing for breach of a non-molestation order in the civil courts

A range of orders may be made in civil contempt cases and every case must be considered on its own facts.[159] In particular, the court will consider the nature of the breach, the presence of children, and whether the order was breached more than once.[160] The sentence imposed by the civil courts has a dual function. It will indicate the court's disapproval

---

[153] M. Burton, 'Criminalising Breaches of Civil Orders for Protection from Domestic Violence' [2003] Crim LR 301.

[154] See C. Bessant, 'Enforcing Non-Molestation Orders in the Civil and Criminal Courts' [2005] Family Law 640.

[155] M. Burton, *Legal Responses to Domestic Violence* (Abingdon: Routledge-Cavendish, 2008), p 54.

[156] J. Platt, 'The Domestic Violence, Crime and Victims Act 2004 Part 1: Is it Working?' [2008] Family Law 642.

[157] Home Affairs Committee, 'Domestic Violence, Forced Marriage and "Honour"-Based Violence', Sixth Report of Session 2007–08, volume I, HC 263-I.

[158] Including under the Protection from Harassment Act 1997.

[159] *Devjee v Patel* [2006] EWCA Civ 1211. For guidance see *Hale v Tanner* [2000] 2 FLR 879; *Lomas v Parle* [2004] 1 FLR 812; *H v O (Contempt of Court: Sentencing)* [2004] EWCA Civ 1691.

[160] *Lomas v Parle* [2004] 1 FLR 812.

of the respondent's breach of the order, and will also attempt to secure the perpetrator's future compliance with the order.[161] A custodial sentence can be imposed, the maximum of which is two years. While there are no precise tariffs set for the appropriate sentence to be handed down when enforcing breach of a non-molestation order as a contempt of court,[162] case law shows that the courts take such breaches very seriously. In *Lomas v Parle*,[163] for example, the court indicated that the sentence imposed for breach of a non-molestation order as a civil contempt matter should not be 'manifestly discrepant' with the sentences imposed for criminal offences for breach of the orders under the Protection from Harassment Act 1997.[164] Where the respondent has used violence in breach of a non-molestation order, the court is likely to order imprisonment.

4.3.13 Sentencing for breach of a non-molestation order in the criminal courts

Under section 42A breach of a non-molestation order is an arrestable offence which can be enforced in the criminal courts. The sentences which can be imposed by the criminal courts are more extensive than those available to the civil courts and include fines, imprisonment, or community sentences and rehabilitation orders. Guidance issued by the Sentencing Guidelines Council on the approach to be taken to breach of a non-molestation order under section 42A makes it clear that the aim of the order is to protect the victim from harm. Thus, the sentence imposed for breach of this order should be primarily concerned with 'ensuring that the order is complied with and that it achieves the protection that it was intended to achieve'.[165]

One question which arises on sentencing is the relevance of the nature and context of the conduct which led to the non-molestation order being made in the first place. The Sentencing Guidelines state that the nature of the original conduct is relevant to the extent that it allows an assessment to be made regarding the severity of the breach. For example, if the non-molestation order was made in relation to very serious behaviour, then even relatively minor conduct which constitutes a breach (emails, telephone calls) could cause significant anxiety for a victim. Notwithstanding this, it must be remembered that the sentence following a breach is for the actual breach and is not designed to punish the offender for the original conduct which led to the order being made.

The nature of the conduct which caused the breach will also be considered and where the order is breached by the use of physical violence, the Guidelines make it clear that the starting point should normally be a custodial sentence. Non-violent behaviour that causes a high degree of harm or harassment can also result in a custodial sentence.

4.3.14 Recent research on the use of non-molestation orders

Burton observes that an increase in the number of non-molestation orders sought may have been expected after the implementation of the Domestic Violence, Crime and Victims Act 2004 given that a greater number of people could apply for this order, and the fact that it had strengthened enforcement mechanisms.[166] However, this has not been

---

[161] *Hale v Tanner* [2000] 2 FLR 879.   [162] Ibid.   [163] [2004] 1 FLR 812.

[164] See also *H v O (Contempt of Court: Sentencing)* [2004] EWCA Civ 1691. Although this approach has been criticised on the basis that there are discrepancies between the range of remedies which are available in the civil and criminal courts respectively, and that the two systems have different objections and functions. While civil orders are designed to mark the court's disapproval at the respondent's breach of the civil order and ensure future compliance, the criminal courts are primarily concerned with punishing the offender. See M. Burton, 'Case Commentary—*Lomas v Parle*—Coherent and Effective Remedies for Victims of Domestic Violence: Time for an Integrated Domestic Violence Court' [2004] Child and Family Law Quarterly 317.

[165] Breach of a Protective Order, Sentencing Guidelines Council (2006), para 3.3.

[166] M. Burton, 'Civil Law Remedies for Domestic Violence: Why are Applications for Non-Molestation Orders Declining?' (2009) 31(2) Journal of Social Welfare and Family Law 109 at 112.

the case. Recent studies have revealed that since the criminalisation of the non-molestation order, there has been a reduction in the number of applications for this order.[167] His Honour Justice Platt notes that across six courts during a six-month period after the changes introduced by the Act, the drop in applications for a non-molestation order varied from 15–30 per cent, with an average drop of around 25 per cent. Judge Platt suggests that there may be several possible explanations for this trend. First, the more severe sanctions for domestic violence may have led to a reduction in the incidence of such abuse, which means that fewer people actually need to apply for protective orders. However, this optimistic view is unlikely. As Platt points out, the new provisions only affect the sanctions for breach and not the criteria for initially making the order. Secondly, it may be that more victims are choosing to initiate criminal proceedings to tackle domestic violence. The fact that there has been an increase in the number of criminal prosecutions adds weight to this argument. However, the most likely explanation for the drop in applications is that the criminalisation of a breach of a non-molestation order has discouraged some victims from applying for the order. Platt regards this as entirely possible saying that:

> there are serious shortcomings in the way the 2004 Act has been implemented and there remains, as the Government acknowledged, serious disagreement as to whether the civil or criminal route is more effective in achieving the common goal which is to get the domestic abuse to stop.[168]

Even though these enhanced measures have been designed to increase the level of protection afforded to victims, the factors which deter victims from seeking the prosecution of the perpetrator may now act as a similar deterrence when deciding whether to initiate civil proceedings. However, it has also been pointed out that there may be other reasons which help to explain the reduction in the number of applications. For example, the perception that seeking an order is an expensive business,[169] the reduction in the availability of legal aid, and that some victims may simply be receiving poor legal advice may all be relevant factors.[170] In addition, it is worth pointing out that even before the enactment of the 2004 Act there had been a steady decrease in the number of applications for non-molestation orders which may mean that the current reductions may be a 'consolidation of the previous downward trend'.[171]

[167] J. Platt, 'The Domestic Violence, Crime and Victims Act 2004 Part 1: Is it Working?' [2008] Family Law 642. Platt also notes, however, that during the same period there was a significant increase in the number of applications for occupations orders under s 33(3)(g) which 'are non-molestation orders in all but name and to which a power of arrest can be attached'. M. Burton, 'Civil Law Remedies for Domestic Violence: Why are Applications for Non-Molestation Orders Declining?' (2009) 31(2) Journal of Social Welfare and Family Law 109.

[168] Platt notes that police training in the aftermath of the new changes was inadequate as police were still using the civil courts when arresting someone for breach of a non-molestation order. Also it is unclear whether a person is charged under the new s 42A, charged with a criminal offence (if their conduct also constitutes an existing criminal offence), or both. There is also evidence that the police are using cautions to deal with those arrested under s 42A. See J. Platt, 'The Domestic Violence, Crime and Victims Act 2004 Part 1: Is it Working?' [2008] Family Law 642.

[169] C. Humphreys and R. K. Thiara, *Routes to Safety: Protection Issues Facing Abused Women and Children and the Role of Outreach Services* (Bristol: Women's Aid Federation England, 2002); M. Burton, 'Civil Law Remedies for Domestic Violence: Why are Applications for Non-Molestation Orders Declining?' (2009) 31(2) Journal of Social Welfare and Family Law 109.   [170] Burton, ibid.

[171] M. Hester, N. Westmarland, J. Pearce, and E. Williamson, *Early Evaluation of the Domestic Violence, Crime and Victims Act 2004*, Ministry of Justice Research Series 14/08 (2008), p 27 cited in Burton, ibid at 112.

5 OCCUPATION ORDERS

The breakdown of a personal relationship often occurs after a long period of time and it may be punctuated by incidents of violence and molestation. Victims of domestic assaults do not necessarily want their relationship with their spouse or partner to end, rather they may want it to continue but for the violence and threatening behaviour to stop. A spouse or partner who is being assaulted, harassed, threatened, or otherwise abused and molested may reach the stage where it is no longer tolerable to live under the same roof as the perpetrator. Indeed, many victims of domestic violence are forced to flee the family home because of the risks to which they, and their children, may be exposed. The question of whether an order can be obtained to force the abuser to leave the home and, where the victim has already been driven from the home, whether an order can be obtained which will entitle this person to return to the property, arises as a matter of real urgency. This is particularly true where the parties have few assets and a relatively low income. In such cases, the parties often cannot agree about who should stay in the home and who should leave, because the person who leaves may have nowhere suitable to go. The occupation order is, therefore, an important protective order. As noted by the Law Commission: 'in cases of domestic violence as where the parties live together, an occupation order ousting the respondent from the home will often be the only way of supporting a non-molestation order and giving the applicant effective protection.'[172] It is worth noting that when the court is considering whether to make an occupation order, it is also under a duty to consider whether to make a non-molestation order.[173]

The issue may be more complicated where children are living in the home. In this situation, a spouse or partner may insist on remaining in the home because they feel that to leave would impact on their relationship with their children, and would prejudice any chance they have of obtaining a residence order in respect of the children.[174] In addition, where allegations of violence have been made against one of the parties, the alleged perpetrator may refuse to leave the home on the basis that this would amount to an admission of guilt. While non-molestation orders can be granted which focus solely on the person of the victim, these may have little value if the perpetrator of an assault (or other form of molestation) is living in the same household as the victim. By giving the court the power to make occupation orders, the law therefore makes provision for the temporary removal of one of the parties from the home. The occupation order can also be used to give one party the right to enter the home and remain in occupation.

5.1 SOME PRELIMINARY POINTS ABOUT OCCUPATION ORDERS

While an occupation order will usually be sought by a victim of domestic violence, it is not limited to these situations. The occupation order can be used to regulate occupation of the family home where a non-violent dispute arises between the parties as to who is entitled to occupy the property. However, due to the temporary nature of the order, it is unlikely that parties will seek an occupation order to resolve the long-term consequences of a relationship breakdown. Case law shows that the courts do not regard an occupation order as being designed to fulfil this function but instead view it as a serious interference with one's occupation rights in the family home.

---

[172] Law Com No 207 (1992), para 4.6.
[173] Section 42(4A).   [174] On residence orders and the status quo principle, see Chapter 9.

Not all those who are entitled to apply for a non-molestation order can apply for an occupation order. Occupation orders interfere with the parties' property rights and the law takes such interference very seriously. Thus, the legislation restricts eligibility to apply for occupation orders to a narrow range of persons. There are two categories of applicant: entitled and non-entitled applicants. Entitled applicants have some existing legal rights in the property, while non-entitled applicants do not.[175]

An occupation order can only be made in relation to a dwelling-house which is, was, or was intended by both of them at any time to be the home of the parties.[176] Under section 39(2), an occupation order may be made on a free-standing application brought under section 33 or sections 35–38 of the FLA 1996. An occupation order can also be made in other family proceedings,[177] but the court does not have the power to make an occupation order by its own motion.[178]

There are two types of occupation orders. First, a 'declaratory occupation order' which declares, confers, or extends occupation rights in the home. This order must be obtained as a preliminary order by non-entitled applicants who have no pre-existing right to occupy the home. Secondly, a 'regulatory occupation order' which controls the exercise of the parties' existing rights of occupation. For example, this order can require one party to leave the home, or require one party to allow the other to enter and/or remain in the home.

5.2 WHO CAN APPLY FOR AN OCCUPATION ORDER?

Entitled applicants are those who have an existing right of occupation in the home arising from a legal or beneficial interest in the property, or spouses/civil partners who have a statutory right of occupation in the home (known as 'home rights'). Entitled applicants can seek an occupation order against anyone with whom they are 'associated'. Non-entitled applicants are persons who do *not* have any existing legal or beneficial interest in the property, nor do they have 'home rights'. The legislation provides that non-entitled applicants can only seek an occupation order against a former spouse/civil partner, cohabitant, or former cohabitant. However, for non-entitled applicants the order is simply a short-term protective measure to give the applicant time to find suitable alternative accommodation or to 'await the outcome of an application for a property law remedy'.[179]

Thus, there are five categories of person who are eligible to apply for an occupation order. They are:

(i) those entitled to occupy the property (s 33);

(ii) a former spouse/civil partner with no existing rights of occupation in the property where the other former spouse/civil partner is so entitled (s 35);

(iii) a cohabitant or former cohabitant with no existing rights of occupation in the property where the other partner/former partner is so entitled (s 36);

(iv) a spouse or civil partner who has no existing right to occupy the property where the other spouse/civil partner also has no entitlement to remain in occupation (s 37);

---

[175] See Section 5.2.

[176] Under the previous law the court had no power to make an order in respect of property which the parties intended to be their home but where they never actually lived together. This was amended by the FLA 1996 and thus an occupation order can be made in relation to property which the parties intended to be their joint home.   [177] Section 39(2).

[178] Section 39(2).   [179] Law Com No 207 (1992), para 4.7.

(v) a cohabitant or former cohabitant who has no existing right to occupy the property where the other cohabitant or former cohabitant also has no entitlement to remain in occupation (s 38).

It is very important to establish which category a person falls under as this will affect the manner of their application, and the nature of any order made. Where an application is made under the wrong section the court may make an order under the correct section.[180] The following sections will detail the situation for each category of applicant.

5.3 ENTITLED APPLICANTS

Entitled applicants have an existing estate or interest in the family home and already have an entitlement to occupy the property.

Key legislation

The provision dealing with entitled applicants is section 33 which provides that:

(1) If—

  (a) a person ("the person entitled)—

    (i) is entitled to occupy a dwelling-house by virtue of a beneficial estate or interest or contract or by virtue of any enactment giving him the right to remain in occupation, or

    (ii) has home rights in relation to a dwelling-house, and

  (b) the dwelling-house—

    (i) is or at any time has been the home of the person entitled and of another person with whom he is associated, or

    (ii) was at any time intended by the person entitled and any such other person to be their home,

  (c) the person entitled may apply to the court for an order containing any of the provisions specified in subsections (3), (4) and (5).

Thus, under section 33 there are two types of entitled applicant. First, those who are already entitled to occupy the home by virtue of a beneficial estate or other interest in the property provided that the respondent is an 'associated person'.[181] This covers someone who is the sole or joint legal owner of the property or has a beneficial interest in the property by virtue of a resulting or constructive trust, or proprietary estoppel.[182] Under this provision, an application for an occupation order can be made between a variety of associated persons, for example siblings, unmarried partners, and engaged couples. This has nothing to do with the nature of the applicant's personal status but instead depends on whether the applicant has an existing estate or interest in the property which he or she shared, or intended to share, as a home with the respondent. Secondly, a spouse or

---

[180] Section 39(3).

[181] The meaning of 'associated person' is found in s 62(3); it is discussed in Section 4.3.3 in relation to non-molestation orders. Persons who have agreed to marry or enter into a civil partnership (whether or not that agreement has been terminated) are associated, but where the agreement has been terminated no application for an occupation order may be made under s 33 by reference to that agreement after three years beginning with the day on which it is terminated (s 33(2) and (2A)).   [182] See Chapter 5.

civil partner is almost always entitled to apply for an occupation order under section 33 because he or she has a personal right to occupy the family home, known as 'home rights'.[183] Under section 30 of the 1996 Act, 'home rights' automatically arise in the following situation. Where one spouse or civil partner ('A') is entitled to occupy the home,[184] but the other spouse or civil partner ('B') is not so entitled, B, by virtue to being married or in a civil partnership with A obtains 'home rights' in the home. 'Home rights' are basically a statutory right of occupation: that is, a right to remain living in the home.[185]

Key legislation

The precise nature of this personal right is described in section 30(2) of the 1996 Act:

(a) if in occupation, a right not to be evicted or excluded from the dwelling-house or any part of it by the other spouse/civil partner except with the leave of the court given by an order under section 33;

(b) if not in occupation, a right with the leave of the court to enter into and occupy the dwelling-house.

This is a crucial provision because it not only gives a non-owning spouse/civil partner the right to live in the family home, it also gives that person certain rights against third party purchasers. Any purchaser from the entitled owning spouse/civil partner will take the property subject to the other spouse/civil partner's 'home rights' (provided that these have been registered in accordance with the Act's provisions).[186]

5.3.1 What order(s) can be made?

In terms of the property to which the order applies, it must be a dwelling-house that either is or at any time has been, or was intended to be, the home of the applicant and of the person with whom she is associated.[187] The court, under section 33(4), can make a preliminary order which simply declares that the applicant falls into one of the earlier mentioned categories of entitled applicant. That is, that the applicant already has an estate or interest in the dwelling-house or has 'home rights' in the property. This may be particularly useful in situations where it may not be clear whether an applicant who is not a spouse or civil partner has a sufficient property interest to be entitled to apply for an order under section 33. This can be clarified by an order under section 33(4) declaring that the applicant is so entitled.

In the case of any entitled applicant the court can make a variety of orders to *regulate* occupation of the family home.

---

[183] Where the spouses or civil partners are bare licensees or squatters they are both non-entitled and will not be able to apply for an occupation order against each other under s 33. Instead, an application may be made under either s 37 or 38.

[184] This entitlement can arise by virtue of a beneficial estate or interest or contract, or any enactment giving that person the right to remain in occupation (s 30(1)(a)(i) and (ii)).

[185] Spouses and civil partners have 'home rights' simply by being married to, or in a civil partnership with, the person who is entitled to occupy the home under s 30. For the purposes of obtaining occupation orders it does not matter whether these rights have been registered. It is only where a third party is claiming rights in the family home that notification of matrimonial home rights becomes a crucial issue.

[186] Sections 31 and 32.   [187] Section 33(1)(b).

Key legislation

Section 33(3) provides that the court may:

(a) enforce the applicant's entitlement to remain in occupation as against the other person ('the respondent');

(b) require the respondent to permit the applicant to enter and remain in the dwelling-house or part of the dwelling-house;

(c) regulate the occupation of the dwelling-house by either or both parties;

(d) if the respondent is entitled as mentioned in subsection (1)(a)(i), prohibit, suspend or restrict the exercise by him of his right to occupy the dwelling-house;

(e) if the respondent has home rights in relation to the dwelling-house and the applicant is the other spouse, restrict or terminate those rights;

(f) require the respondent to leave the dwelling-house or part of the dwelling-house; or

(g) exclude the respondent from a defined area in which the dwelling-house is included.

Together these provisions give the court wide powers to control the occupation of the home. It is important to understand that an occupation order is not simply confined to removing the respondent from the home. That may, indeed, be one manifestation of the order but it is much more flexible than that. For example, under section 33(3)(c) the court can make an order which regulates the occupation of the home by either or both parties. This gives the court considerable flexibility to impose certain arrangements about how the property is to be used by the parties. In some instances the court may order that while the respondent is to remain living in the home, he is only allowed to use certain rooms. Indeed, the court may be more inclined to make such an order to carve up the parties' living arrangements rather than remove the respondent from the home, particularly in view of the general approach of the courts which has been to view the actual removal of one party from the home as being draconian.[188] It may also make sense for the applicant to accept such an arrangement as the difficulties in obtaining an occupation order removing the respondent from the property mean that the parties are frequently left living together. Thus, to have an order restricting occupation may be better than no order at all. While this type of remedy may be considered to be inappropriate in situations of violence because the applicant may remain at risk, there are cases which show that even in these sorts of circumstances the court may refuse to remove the respondent from the property. In *E v E (Ouster Order)*,[189] despite accepting the evidence of the wife that the husband attempted to rape her, the Court of Appeal confirmed the trial judge's decision simply to exclude the husband from one of the two bedrooms in the house. In her evidence-in-chief the wife had said: 'separate rooms would help, yes. I don't necessarily want him to go. I want my safety and peace. I don't want any more aggravation.' The Court of Appeal considered that normally it should be expected that an order removing the respondent from the property would follow where the judge finds allegations of rape or attempted rape. However, the evidence of the wife, coupled with other factors,[190] indicated that it was not possible for them to say that the judge had been plainly wrong in the exercise of his discretion.

---

[188] See Section 5.6.   [189] [1995] 1 FLR 224.

[190] This included a living pattern whereby the parties were not in the house together very often, no children, and the wife's uncertain immigration status, which meant she might be reluctant to bring divorce proceedings. This latter consideration meant that the wife was in a particularly vulnerable position, but still the court was willing to accept at face value her evidence that separate bedrooms would give her adequate protection.

Section 33(3)(g) which permits the court to 'exclude the respondent from a defined area in which the dwelling-house is included' is also useful as it allows the court to throw a ring around the property and order the respondent not to come within its vicinity. For example, if the home was located in a block of flats, the respondent could not only be ordered to keep away from the home, but also the block in which the home is situated. In *Tuck v Nicholls*[191] the order stated that the respondent should not enter 'that area of King's Lynn in which lies the matrimonial home'.[192] This broad exclusionary order confers considerable protection on the applicant as she can take action to have the respondent brought before the court for breach of the order before he comes near enough to attack her. So, for example, if he is hanging around in the road outside the house, or threatening her when she goes out, and an injunction is in force prohibiting him from being in that area, she can have him brought back before the court for breach of the order.[193]

In the case of spouses and civil partners two additional orders are available, and each may have a radical effect on the applicant's position in relation to the property. Section 33(3)(e) allows the court to restrict or terminate the 'home rights' of a respondent spouse or civil partner. In other words, if the respondent simply has 'home rights' in relation to the property, the court can restrict or even terminate those rights. Such an order not only ends the respondent's right to live in the home, but also frees the applicant spouse/civil partner who is the sole owner of the property to dispose of the property as he or she wishes. By contrast, section 33(5) is a protective provision which enables a court to order that the 'home rights' of a spouse or civil partner are not brought to an end by the death of the other spouse/civil partner, or the termination (otherwise than by death) of the marriage or civil partnership.[194]

Section 40 specifies additional orders which may be included where an occupation order is made under section 33.[195] Under this provision either party can be obliged to take responsibility for the repair and maintenance of the dwelling-house, or the discharge of rent, mortgage repayments, or other outgoings.[196] One of the main concerns of a person who is in a financially vulnerable position is to keep a roof over her head and not to fall behind with payments owed to third parties, as default may entitle them to take possession proceedings. Thus, section 40 aims to address this concern by giving the court the power to require either party to take responsibility for the rent or mortgage repayments in relation to the house. For example, if one party has been ousted from the home under an occupation order, that person can be ordered to pay the rent, mortgage, or other outgoings in relation to the property. When deciding whether to make an order under section 40, the court is directed to have regard to all the circumstances of the case including the financial needs and resources of the parties and their present and future financial obligations. Section 40 orders are likely to be less useful to unmarried partners and other persons entitled to apply for orders under sections 35 and 36, as any provision ceases to have effect when the occupation order to which it relates comes to an end.[197] While section 40 orders appear to be very useful, they have a serious defect. Orders made under section 40 lack effective enforcement mechanisms: there is no provision for enforcement under the

---

[191] [1989] 1 FLR 283.

[192] The order was discharged on appeal, but not for excess of powers in this regard.

[193] See also *Burns v Azadani* [1999] 1 FLR 266.

[194] Which is when they would normally terminate (s 30(8)).

[195] Section 40 also applies to orders made under ss 35 and 36.   [196] Section 40(1).

[197] Section 40(3). Orders for entitled applicants under s 33 may be made for a specified period, until the occurrence of a specified event or until further order (s 33(10)). In the first instance orders relating to former spouses under s 35 cannot last for longer than six months, although they may be extended on one or more occasion for a further six months (s 35(10)). However, orders between unmarried partners made under s 36 may be extended by six months on one occasion only (s 36(10)).

FLA 1996 and they cannot be enforced under other enforcement legislation, namely, the Debtors Act 1869 and the Attachment of Earnings Act 1971. The Court of Appeal identified this gap in the law in *Nwogbe v Nwogbe*[198] and recommended that courts do not exercise their powers under section 40 until an effective enforcement procedure is provided by legislation. Despite the fact that this plea for reform was made in 2000, no action has yet been taken and section 40 remains a toothless provision.

5.3.2 Criteria for making an occupation order

Before the introduction of occupation orders under the FLA 1996, the court had the power to make an ouster order under the Domestic Violence and Matrimonial Proceedings Act 1976. The criteria for making such an order were contained in section 1(3) of the Matrimonial Homes Act 1983. This provision directed the court:

> to make such order as it thinks just and reasonable having regard to the conduct of the spouses in relation to each other and otherwise, to their respective needs and financial resources, to the needs of any children and to all the circumstances of the case.

These factors were not listed in any kind of hierarchy[199] and the courts made it very clear that an order ousting someone from their home was a very serious order which required strong justification. Indeed, it was felt by the courts that such an order should only be made where the judge was satisfied that no lesser measure would suffice to protect the welfare of the applicant and any child.[200] This approach was criticised on a number of grounds. First, it was argued that it did not give sufficient priority to the applicant's need for personal protection but instead balanced this against other factors, such as the hardship to the respondent.[201] Secondly, it was felt that the requirement to consider the conduct of the parties encouraged parties to make allegations of fault which conflicts with the general trend in family law to remove recrimination and fault-finding from decision making. Thirdly, it was also thought that the test gave insufficient weight to the welfare of children as each of the factors listed in the legislation were given equal weight. It was pointed out that this was inconsistent with the emerging ethos of family law to give priority to the interests of children.[202] While the statutory criteria for making an occupation order was amended in light of these shortcomings, it could be argued that very similar concerns can be levelled at the current criteria and its interpretation by the courts. The fear by some that the test which was recommended by the Law Commission would lead to 'occupation orders almost on demand' has certainly proved to be far from the case.[203]

The court can make a declaratory occupation order under section 33(4) or a regulatory occupation order under section 33(3). A declaratory order will simply confirm that the applicant either has 'home rights' or has an existing interest in the property. However, to enforce the entitled applicant's existing right of occupation or to restrict the respondent's use of the property a regulatory occupation order must be obtained. There are two tests for the court to consider when deciding whether to grant a regulatory occupation order. The first test,[204] if met in favour of the applicant, confers a mandatory duty on the court to make an order, while the second[205] gives the court the discretion whether to make the

---

[198] [2000] 2 FLR 744.

[199] In *Richards v Richards* [1983] 2 All ER 807 the House of Lords rejected the submission that in cases where children were involved their needs were paramount and held that each of the factors listed in s 1(3) should be given equal weight.

[200] *Wiseman v Simpson* [1988] All ER 245; *Shipp v Shipp* [1988] 1 FLR 345; *Blackstock v Blackstock* [1991] 2 FLR 308.   [201] Law Com No 207 (1992), para 4.23.

[202] Ibid, para 4.23.   [203] Ibid, para 4.23.   [204] Under s 33(7).   [205] Under s 33(6).

order or not. Initially there was some confusion over the relationship between these two sets of criteria with early authority suggesting that they fed into one another. In other words, the general checklist of factors outlined in section 33(6) was used by the court when considering the test under section 33(7).[206] However, it is now clear that these tests are applied separately.[207] In practical terms, when deciding whether to make a regulatory occupation order for an entitled applicant the court will approach the matter in the following way:

(i) it will first consider the 'balance of harm' test under section 33(7) and if this is satisfied in favour of the applicant or any child, then the court will be under a mandatory duty to make the order;

(ii) if the 'balance of harm' test does not apply or is not met in favour of the applicant, the court will consider whether to make an order at its discretion by considering the general checklist of factors under section 33(6).

5.3.3 The 'balance of harm' test

The first set of criteria that the court will consider when deciding whether to make an occupation order in favour of an entitled applicant is the 'balance of harm' test under section 33(7).

Key legislation

Under this provision:

If it appears to the court that the applicant or any relevant child is likely to suffer significant harm attributable to the conduct of the respondent if an order under this section containing one or more of the provisions mentioned in subsection (3) is not made, the court shall make the order unless it appears to it that—

(a) the respondent or any relevant child is likely to suffer significant harm if the order is made; and

(b) the harm likely to be suffered by the respondent or child in that event is as great as, or greater than, the harm attributable to conduct of the respondent which is likely to be suffered by the applicant or child if the order is not made.

This test mandates the court to carry out a balancing exercise which weighs the harm likely to be suffered by the applicant and any relevant child if the order is not made against the harm likely to be suffered by the respondent and any relevant child if the order is made. This test states that the court *must* make an order where it appears that the applicant or any relevant child is likely to suffer significant harm attributable to the conduct of the respondent if the order is not made. The court must make an order in favour of the applicant in these circumstances although section 33(7) leaves open the type of protective action the court should take. The orders under section 33(3) range from simply enforcing the applicant's right to live in the house to excluding the respondent.[208] However, where the harm likely to be suffered by the respondent or child if the order were to be made is as

---

[206] See eg *B v B (Occupation Order)* [1999] 1 FLR 715.   [207] *Chalmers v Johns* [1999] 1 FLR 392.

[208] It could be maintained that it is implicit that a finding of hardship to the applicant under s 33(7) must lead to an order which, at a minimum, regulates the respondent's occupation of the home, because this is what the court must do in a case of an applicant former spouse or civil partner with no existing right to occupy: s 33(5), (8).

great as, or greater than, the harm which is likely to be suffered by the applicant or child if the order is not made, then the court has a choice about what order, if any, to make. Where the likelihood of significant harm to both parties is deemed to be equal, then the court is not obliged to make an order but can do so at its discretion by applying the general checklist under section 33(6).

There are several points which are worth noting about this provision. First, if this test is established in favour of the applicant or any relevant child then the court is under a duty to make the order. However, this test only applies where 'likely significant harm attributable to the conduct of the respondent' is established. 'Harm' in relation to both adults and children is defined as the ill-treatment or the impairment of physical or mental health; but in relation to a child it also includes the impairment of a child's development.[209] The legislation also states that ill-treatment in relation to children includes sexual abuse, although why this is specified in relation to children and not adults is not entirely clear. While the term 'significant' is not defined in the FLA 1996, for the purposes of the Children Act 1989, 'significant' has been taken to mean 'considerable, noteworthy or important'.[210] It is clear from the case law that a similarly high threshold applies to the definition of 'significant harm' in the 1996 Act which means that minor types of harm will not be considered. While the standard of proof required to establish the likelihood of significant harm has not been made clear in the FLA 1996, the term 'likely' in section 31 of the Children Act 1989 has been interpreted to mean 'a real possibility' which is to be established on the balance of probabilities.[211]

Contrary to the prevailing ethos of other family law provisions, the welfare of any children is not the paramount consideration under the 'balance of harm' test. The Law Commission considered this point head on and did not find it easy to strike an acceptable balance between what it termed a 'balance of hardship' test and a test which made the welfare of the children paramount.[212] In the end it recommended a middle-ground approach as it was felt that the paramountcy principle was not appropriate to occupation order cases.

Unfortunately while the Law Commission was careful not to link the test to the respondent's conduct, Parliament thought otherwise and introduced conduct as an element to be considered.[213] Not only must significant harm to the applicant or child be shown before the balance of harm test comes into play, but the test only applies where it is established that the harm is *attributable* to the respondent's conduct. This means that the balancing exercise is immediately weighted in favour of the respondent. It is only where the respondent's conduct is causative of the likely harm that the court is under a duty to make an order. There is no similar requirement to show that the harm to the respondent is caused by the applicant's conduct: any type of harm which the respondent may suffer on making the order can be taken into account. This means that the test does not apply in a morally neutral fashion.

The test's concentration on conduct and causation in addition to proof of significant harm gives ample scope for argument on behalf of the respondent that the order should not be made. It also means that the test will not apply where the significant harm is brought about by the applicant's decision to move out of the home without good cause. Further, if the harm is caused by the poor accommodation in which the applicant finds herself after moving out of the home, the court may not regard this harm as attributable to the conduct

---

[209] Section 63(1).   [210] *Humberside County Council v B* [1993] 1 FLR 257 at 263, *per* Booth J.
[211] *Re H (Threshold Criteria: Standard of Proof)* [1996] 1 All ER 1; *Re B (Sexual Abuse: Standard of Proof)* [2008] UKHL 35.   [212] Law Com No 207 (1992), paras 4.20–4.34.
[213] And under the general criteria in s 33(6).

of the respondent even though it was this conduct that may have caused the applicant to leave the home in the first place.[214]

A useful example which shows how the courts weigh up the competing interests of the parties is *B v B (Occupation Order)*.[215] This case also illustrates how the courts can face some difficult decisions about the needs of different children. In this case the wife had been forced out of council property she shared with her husband due to his serious violence. She left the home with her baby and was temporarily housed by the local authority in bed and breakfast accommodation. The husband remained in the property with his 6-year-old son from a previous relationship. Allowing the husband's appeal against an occupation order made in favour of the wife, the Court of Appeal found that all that the baby needed was to be securely with her mother. Although the baby's present accommodation was unsuitable it was likely to be temporary as the local authority were bound to treat the wife as homeless and in priority need for suitable accommodation.[216] However, the local authority's duty to the husband, at its highest, was simply to provide advice and to secure temporary accommodation for him after which he would have to source accommodation for himself.[217] Applying the balance of harm test, the court found that if the husband were ordered out of the house this would cause his son to suffer significant harm. It would result in the boy changing school for the fifth time in 18 months, and this would be very damaging and disruptive to his mental and emotional well-being. The boy's security depended not only on being with his father, but on his other day-to-day support systems of which his home and school were plainly the most important. Thus, when the respective likelihoods of harm to the two children were weighed, the balance came down on the son suffering the greater harm if the occupation order were made. One should not take from this case that the court tolerated the husband's violence in the home: the Court of Appeal was emphatic that the husband's behaviour had been disgraceful, and it stressed that perpetrators of domestic violence cannot expect to remain in shared accommodation. However, the interests of all the parties had to be weighed against each other and a critical factor in this case was that the son was not the child of both parties, and that there was no question of him being cared for by anyone other than the father.

5.3.4 The general checklist

Key legislation

If the 'balance of harm' test is not met in favour of the applicant, the court can still make an order at its discretion taking into account all of the circumstances of the case including:[218]

(a) the housing needs and housing sources of each of the parties and of any relevant child;

(b) the financial resources of each of the parties;

(c) the likely effect of any order, or of any decision by the court not to exercise its powers…
on the health, safety or well-being of the parties and of any relevant child; and

(d) the conduct of the parties in relation to each other and otherwise.

These factors are given equal weight and, once again, the welfare of the children is not the court's paramount consideration.

---

[214] M. Burton, *Legal Responses to Domestic Violence* (Abingdon: Routledge-Cavendish, 2008), pp 21–22.

[215] [1999] 1 FLR 715.   [216] Housing Act 1996, s 188(1). See Section 8.1 on homelessness.

[217] See Section 8.1 on homelessness.   [218] Section 33(6).

5.3.4.1 Housing and financial needs and resources

The court will consider the parties' respective housing and financial needs and their available resources. One issue will be what alternative accommodation each party has open to them. The court will, therefore, consider the ability of the respondent to rehouse himself. However, even where this is thought to be feasible, it is no guarantee that the court will make an occupation order, despite the fact that the court may accept that it is undesirable for the two parties to continue living together under the same roof.

Where the parties live in accommodation provided by the local authority the court may be influenced by the authority's housing policies in determining whether or not to make an occupation order. Where the court is satisfied that suitable alternative accommodation will be provided for the respondent, the decision to remove him from the home becomes less draconian. However, if the order will effectively render him homeless, then this is an extremely serious matter.[219] In these sorts of situations much will depend on whether the local authority would rehouse the respondent if he were forced to leave the family home. If the local authority is under no obligation to rehouse the respondent, but if the applicant were to leave the family home and would be treated by the local authority as in priority need for housing, then this may persuade the court that no order should be made.

5.3.4.2 The likely effect of the court's decision on the health, safety, or well-being of the parties or a child

Under section 33(6)(c), when exercising its discretion whether to make an order, the court must take into account the effect of its decision to grant, or refuse to grant, an order. Even though the welfare of any child is not the court's paramount consideration, there are some instances where their interests may persuade the court that an order should be made. In *Lee v Lee*,[220] for example, the wife had left the home and was unable to find accommodation for herself and her children to live together as a family. The court held that the needs of the children to be together, and to be with their mother, were sufficient to establish the necessity for an order. However, the prevailing judicial view is that occupation orders are draconian measures because they interfere with the respondent's property rights and, as such, they should only be made in exceptional circumstances. Indeed, in general, the courts have been more concerned about the impact of an occupation order on the respondent than on the impact of a refusal to make an order on the applicant and children. In other words, removing the respondent from his home tends to be viewed as more serious than the applicant fleeing the home to live in unsuitable accommodation.

5.3.4.3 Conduct

Under the old law, the courts tended to focus almost entirely on whether the respondent's conduct was sufficiently grave to justify exclusion from the home. The Law Commission considered that this placed too much emphasis on allegations of the parties' behaviour at the expense of giving priority to the applicant's personal protection and the interests of the children.[221] However, the conduct of the parties is specifically listed as one of the factors to consider under the general checklist.[222] This means that there remains a tension in the law between those cases where, after balancing all the factors, decisive weight is given to whether the respondent's conduct has been sufficiently serious to justify making an order

---

[219] See Section 8.1 on homelessness.   [220] (1984) FLR 243.
[221] Law Com No 207 (1992), para 4.23.   [222] Section 33(6)(d).

removing him from the home, and those cases where the financial and housing needs of the applicant and her children appear to demand an order requiring the respondent to leave. Burton argues that the case law suggests that 'occupation orders will be difficult to obtain in the absence of serious physical violence'.[223] One could say, therefore, that unless the court is satisfied that the respondent has been blameworthy in carrying out physical violence an order may not be made. Arguably this gives greater priority to the conduct element in the criteria than to the other considerations, such as the harm caused to the children in witnessing domestic violence and, if the applicant moves out of the home, the harm caused by living in unsuitable accommodation. It is suggested that the courts should re-focus on the role of the civil law which is to afford protection in cases of domestic violence, in contrast with the role of criminal law which is to apportion blame and to punish. While the Law Commission sought to centralise the welfare of the applicant and children in the decision-making process, one can question whether the provisions under the FLA 1996 (as interpreted by the courts) 'do in fact tip the balance away from conduct and towards the welfare of applicant and child'.[224]

5.3.5 Duration of orders made in favour of entitled applicants

The Law Commission recommended that a distinction be made between entitled and non-entitled applicants in relation to the duration of the order.[225] They took the view that where an applicant is entitled to occupy the home, it is inappropriate to impose statutory time limits on the duration of the order. Thus, section 33(10) provides that 'An order under this section may, in so far as it has continuing effect, be made for a specified period, until the occurrence of a specified event or until further order.' This means that an occupation order can be made in favour of an entitled application for an unlimited duration, or until further order.

5.4 NON-ENTITLED APPLICANTS

An occupation order can also be sought by a limited range of persons who are not entitled to occupy the home. There are two types of non-entitled applicant. First, those who are seeking an order against a respondent who is entitled to occupy the property. Secondly, there are those who are seeking an order against a respondent who is also non-entitled. As the Law Commission noted, in the latter case 'the court is only adjusting occupation rights as between the parties themselves, both of whom may well be subject to almost immediate ejection at the behest of a third party'.

In situations where the respondent is entitled to occupy the property, only a former spouse or civil partner (s 35) or a cohabitant or former cohabitant can apply for an order (s 36).[226]

5.4.1 One former spouse with no existing right to occupy (s 35)

When a marriage or a civil partnership is brought to an end by divorce or dissolution, the non-entitled party's 'home rights' come to an end unless they have been extended under section 33(5). The non-entitled spouse or civil partner can, therefore, be in a vulnerable position if the entitled person asserts his sole right to occupy the former family home

---

[223] M. Burton, *Legal Responses to Domestic Violence* (Abingdon: Routledge-Cavendish, 2008), p 25.

[224] Ibid, p 21.

[225] Law Com No 207 (1992), paras 4.35–4.37.

[226] The legislation makes provision for the situation where neither party is entitled to occupy the home: see Section 5.5.

while any pending financial provision and property adjustment arrangements within the divorce/dissolution proceedings are resolved.[227] The applicant may wish to take steps to obtain the right to remain in the property, and may wish to remove the respondent from the property in situations of domestic violence or to reduce the tension associated with the breakdown of the parties' relationship.

A non-entitled former spouse can make an application for an occupation order under section 35. However, this is a two-stage process as the court must first decide whether to make a declaratory order which will give this person rights of occupation in the property: that is, the right not to be evicted from the home or if she is not currently in occupation of the property, the right to enter the property and remain in occupation. If occupation rights are granted, the court will then decide whether to make a regulatory order.

Key legislation

In deciding whether to make a declaratory order, the court will have regard to all the circumstances of the case including the range of factors listed under section 35(6). These are:

(a) the housing needs and housing resources of each of the parties and of any relevant child;

(b) the financial resources of each of the parties;

(c) the likely effect of any order, or of any decision by the court not to exercise its powers under subsection (3) or (4), on the health, safety or well-being of the parties and of any relevant child;

(d) the conduct of the parties in relation to each other and otherwise;

(e) the length of time that has elapsed since the parties ceased to live together;

(f) the length of time that has elapsed since the marriage was dissolved or annulled; and

(g) the existence of any pending proceedings between the parties—

    (i) for an order under section 23A or 24 of the [1973 c. 18.] Matrimonial Causes Act 1973 (property adjustment orders in connection with divorce proceedings etc.);

    (ii) for an order under paragraph 1(2)(d) or (e) of Schedule 1 to the [1989 c. 41.] Children Act 1989 (orders for financial relief against parents); or

    (iii) relating to the legal or beneficial ownership of the dwelling-house.

Thus the court will take into account the general checklist of factors, paragraphs (a) to (e), before considering certain issues pertinent to the situation of a former spouse: that is, the length of time since the parties ceased to live together; the length of time since the marriage/civil partnership was brought to an end; and the existence of any pending proceedings between the parties. The latter point may be particularly important to the court.

If the court makes a declaratory occupation order giving the non-entitled former spouse the right to live in the home, it will then consider whether to make a regulatory order regulating this right of occupation. The regulatory order in favour of a former spouse/civil partner can do all of the things which can be done for the entitled applicant under section 33. For example, it can remove the respondent from the home or exclude the respondent from a defined area around the home.[228]

---

[227] See Chapter 4.   [228] See s 35(5).

> **Key legislation**
>
> Under section 35(7), the court will decide whether to make a regulatory order by taking into account all the circumstances of the case including:
>
> (a) the housing needs and housing resources of each of the parties and of any relevant child;
>
> (b) the financial resources of each of the parties;
>
> (c) the likely effect of any order, or of any decision by the court not to exercise its powers under subsection (3) or (4), on the health, safety or well-being of the parties and of any relevant child;
>
> (d) the conduct of the parties in relation to each other and otherwise;
>
> (e) the length of time that has elapsed since the parties ceased to live together.
>
> The balance of harm test also applies under section 35(8) which means that the court is under a duty to make an order if the applicant or any relevant child is likely to suffer significant harm attributable to the conduct of the respondent if the order is not made, unless the respondent or relevant child would suffer harm as great or greater.

The occupation order for a non-entitled former spouse/civil partner will only last for six months initially under section 35(10). However, the order may be extended on one or more occasion for a further period of six months although the Law Commission made it clear that an occupation order for a non-entitled applicant is designed to be a short-term measure to give the applicant time to find suitable alternative accommodation or to await the outcome of financial and property proceedings between the parties.[229] Under section 35(9), an order cannot be made after the death of either party and ceases to have effect on the death of either party.

5.4.2 Cohabitant or former cohabitant with no existing right to occupy (s 36)

A cohabitant or former cohabitant with no existing rights in the property can apply as a non-entitled applicant against an entitled respondent under section 36. Under section 62(1)(a) cohabitants are defined as 'two persons who are neither married to each other nor civil partners of each other but are living together as husband and wife or as if they were civil partners'.

The Select Committee on Violence in Marriage,[230] which produced its report in 1975, revealed that there were grounds for serious concern about the lack of protective safeguards for women abused by their violent husbands or partners. The home continues to be a dangerous place, and cohabitants and former cohabitants have an undoubted need for protection from eviction and to be able to evict their abusive partners. However, the thrust of the House of Lords' ruling in *Davis v Johnson*[231] was that the purpose of domestic violence relief is to provide a swift but temporary response to an urgent situation and to give the applicant a secure roof over her head while she looks for alternative accommodation. Consequently, the courts were normally unwilling to interfere with the undoubted right of the respondent to live in his own home except on the most temporary of bases. The FLA 1996 continues to reflect this view.

The application of a non-entitled cohabitant or former cohabitant is similar to the application of a non-entitled former spouse. That is, there is a two-step process. First the

---

[229] Law Com No 207 (1992), para 4.19.
[230] HC 553 (1974–75).   [231] [1978] 1 All ER 1132.

court will decide whether to grant the applicant occupation rights. Secondly, if these are granted, the court will then decide whether to regulate those rights by making a regulatory occupation order.

5.4.2.1 *Granting occupation rights*

Under section 36(3) a non-entitled cohabitant who is in occupation may apply for an order:

(a) giving the applicant the right not to be evicted or excluded from the dwelling-house or any part of it by the respondent for the period specified in the order; and

(b) prohibiting the respondent from evicting or excluding the applicant during that period.

Subsection (4) covers the converse situation, and provides that where the cohabitant is not in occupation, an order must contain provisions:

(a) giving the applicant the right not to be evicted or excluded from the dwelling-house or any part of it by the respondent for the period specified in the order; and

(b) requiring the respondent to permit the exercise of that right.

Key legislation

When the court is determining whether to make an order under either of these subsections and, if so, in what manner, section 36(6) directs it to have regard to all the circumstances including:

(a) the housing needs and housing resources of each of the parties and of any relevant child;

(b) the financial resources of each of the parties;

(c) the likely effect of any order, or of any decision by the court not to exercise its powers under subsection (3) or (4), on the health, safety or well-being of the parties and of any relevant child;

(d) the conduct of the parties in relation to each other and otherwise;

(e) the nature of the parties' relationship and in particular the level of commitment involved in it;

(f) the length of time during which they have lived together as husband and wife;

(g) whether there are or have been any children who are children of both parties or for whom both parties have or have had parental responsibility;

(h) the length of time that has elapsed since the parties ceased to live together; and

(i) the existence of any pending proceedings between the parties—

(i) for an order under paragraph 1(2)(d) or (e) of Schedule 1 to the Children Act 1989 (orders for financial relief against parents); or

(ii) relating to the legal or beneficial ownership of the dwelling-house.

Orders under section 36(3) and (4) give the applicant the right to live in the property but do not otherwise interfere with the owning cohabitant's rights. They are thus the least intrusive on the respondent's sole right of occupation. The criteria governing the exercise of the court's discretion in paragraphs (a) to (d) are identical to those which apply to entitled applicants and non-entitled former spouses/civil partners. The additional criteria in paragraphs (e) to (i) focus on the nature and duration of the personal relationship between the cohabitants, whether they have children, and whether proceedings designed to resolve the financial and property-owning issues stemming from their joint occupation and joint parenthood are pending. These criteria enable the court to take account of matters which reflect the parties' legitimate expectations according to the circumstances of the case.[232] In cases where the cohabitation has lasted for a short period of time, the claim of the non-entitled cohabitant is relatively weak. However, the court is also directed to take account of both the respondent's conduct and the applicant's needs and these considerations may strengthen the applicant's case for immediate relief.

Particular note should be taken of paragraph (e). This requires the court to consider the nature of the parties' relationship and the 'particular level of commitment involved in it'. Originally the court had to take into account the fact that the parties had not given each other the commitment involved in marriage.[233] This provision was included to pacify those opposed to legislation on the ground that it gave increased protection to unmarried cohabitants, thus undermining the institution of marriage. However, its inclusion can be criticised as being unhelpful to courts when deciding upon the civil remedies which may be necessary to protect a victim of domestic violence. It also involves a sweeping judgement of unmarried relationships as lacking the commitment of marriage when research illustrates that the level of commitment involved in relationships does not simply depend on marital status.[234] It is to be welcomed that this provision was repealed by the Domestic Violence, Crime and Victims Act 2004[235] although it added to section 36(6)(e) that when the court is considering the nature of the parties' relationship, it should consider the 'particular level of commitment involved in it'.[236] Quite how the court should assess this level of commitment is unclear, particularly when one considers that the court is, in another subsection, directed to consider the length of the parties' relationship and whether they had children. One could argue that this direction to consider the functional characteristics of the parties' relationship is quite sufficient for the court to draw a conclusion on the nature of the relationship without having to assess the 'level of commitment' under a separate provision.

5.4.2.2 Regulatory orders

Key legislation

Section 36(5) is a more draconian order because it allows the court to interfere directly with the entitled cohabitant's right to occupy the home. A regulatory order may:

(a) regulate the occupation of the dwelling-house by either or both of the parties;

(b) prohibit, suspend or restrict the exercise by the respondent of his right to occupy the dwelling-house;

(c) require the respondent to leave the dwelling-house or part of the dwelling-house; or

(d) exclude the respondent from a defined area in which the dwelling-house is included.

---

[232] Law Com No 207 (1992), para 4.12.

[233] FLA 1996, s 41: repealed by the Domestic Violence, Crime and Victims Act 2004.

[234] See eg M. Maclean and J. Eekelaar, 'The Obligations and Expectations of Couples Within Families' (2004) 26(2) Journal of Social Welfare and Family Law 117.

[235] Section 2(1).   [236] Inserted by the Domestic Violence, Crime and Victims Act 2004, s 2(2).

When deciding whether to grant a regulatory order, the court takes into account the general checklist of factors under section 36(6)(a)–(d)—that is: the housing needs and housing resources of each of the parties and of any relevant child; the financial resources of each of the parties; the effect of the court's decision whether to make an order on the health, safety, or well-being of the parties and of any relevant child; and the conduct of the parties in relation to each other and otherwise. This excludes the matters mentioned in paragraphs (e) to (h) of subsection (6).[237] This is important, because those paragraphs contain considerations which may be unhelpful to the applicant's case. It is plain that once paragraphs (e) to (h) have been overcome, and an order has been made allowing the applicant to enter and remain in the dwelling-house, they should not be revisited when consideration is given to making a harsher order containing a subsection (5) provision.

The court must also consider the balance of harm test, but this applies in a very different way to the other category of applicants. Under section 36(8) the court considers the following questions:

(a) whether the applicant or any relevant child is likely to suffer significant harm attributable to conduct of the respondent if the subsection (5) provision is not included in the order; and

(b) whether the harm likely to be suffered by the respondent or child if the provision is included is as great as or greater than the harm attributable to conduct of the respondent which is likely to be suffered by the applicant or child if the provision is not included.

There is a crucial distinction between the application of the balance of harm test for non-entitled cohabitants and the other applicants (ie, an entitled applicant and a non-entitled former spouse/civil partner). For other applicants, the court is under a duty to make an order where the harm to the applicant or child exceeds the likely harm to the respondent or child. However, in the case of non-entitled cohabitants or former cohabitants, the balance of harm provision in section 36(8) merely provides a set of questions for the court to take into account when exercising its discretion: they do not determine what, if any, order should be made. This means that even if the applicant or child is likely to suffer greater significant harm than the respondent, the court is not under a duty to make an order but instead retains its discretion in this matter. It is argued that this is an unacceptable distinction which elevates the status of the parties' relationship, or former relationship, over the applicant's need for protection. Surely the balance of harm test which seeks to safeguard the welfare of the applicant and children in situations where inaction will result in significant harm should apply in exactly the same way for all applicants, especially in light of the fact that all applicants are 'entitled' applicants by the time the court comes to make a decision on an application for a regulatory occupation order.

5.4.2.3 Duration and nature of an order for a non-entitled cohabitant or former cohabitant

Another significant difference between the position of a spouse and civil partner (who will always been an entitled applicant) and a non-entitled cohabitant is that an order made in favour of the latter will be limited in duration. In the first instance they can last for up to six months, but may be extended on one occasion for a further maximum period of six months.[238] This means that an order for a non-entitled cohabitant can only last for a maximum of one year irrespective of the length of the parties' cohabitation, their relative need for accommodation, or the nature of the conduct which led to the order being made.

---

[237] See the previous section.   [238] Section 36(10).

The court has no residual discretion so, for example, where the couple have lived together for many years and have brought up children who are now no longer dependent, the non-entitled partner must leave at the end of the specified period.[239] The six-month period, with the possibility of its extension, is intended to give the applicant time in which to sort out her financial affairs, to claim a beneficial entitlement to the property where evidence to support this is disputed, or otherwise to make new housing arrangements. It should be remembered that if a cohabitant already has either a legal or beneficial interest in the property, then she will be an entitled applicant under section 33 and will be treated in the same way as a spouse or civil partner. This illustrates the extent to which the legislation both prioritises and seeks to protect the proprietary interests of the parties. There is no distinction made between a spouse/civil partner and a cohabitant where the latter has an interest in the property because both have an equal right to occupy and, in this situation, the Law Commission did not think that it was appropriate to impose a time limit on the regulation of occupation between such entitled parties. However, where a cohabitant does not have an interest in the property then the occupation order is simply designed as a temporary measure and is thus subject to a statutory time limit. The maximum total period for which this order can be made is one year, and the Law Commission considered this sufficient time to enable the applicant to find alternative accommodation. Whatever the circumstances which initially led to the order being granted, the length of the parties' relationship and the applicant's need for protection, the fact that the applicant does not have an interest in the property and the respondent does, means that the interests of the latter take priority.

5.5 ORDERS WHERE NEITHER PARTY IS ENTITLED TO OCCUPY THE DWELLING-HOUSE

In a case where neither party is entitled to occupy the home, the court is not interfering with property rights, it is merely adjusting occupation rights as between the parties. This situation may arise, for example, if the couple is living with relatives or friends. Section 37 governs the situation where the parties are spouses or former spouses, and section 38 where they are cohabitants or former cohabitants. Either party may obtain an order against the other containing the usual regulatory provisions, but this order will have no effect on a third party who may also be occupying the property or who may own it.

In the case of spouses and former spouses the court's discretion is governed by exactly the same criteria which apply to entitled applicants under section 33(6) and (7). That is: the balance of harm test is applied and, if not met in favour of the applicant, the general checklist of factors are taken into account by the court in the exercise of its discretion. The order must initially be limited to six months, but may be extended on one or more occasion for a further specified period of not more than six months.[240]

In the case of cohabitants and former cohabitants, the Act continues to distinguish these applicants from their married counterparts[241] even though, in this instance, there are no property rights involved. The balance of harm test does not result in a mandatory duty to make an order and must merely be considered as a series of questions affecting the exercise of the court's discretion. In addition, the six-month maximum duration of any order applies, and may be extended on one occasion only for a period of not more than six months.[242]

---

[239] Where the children continue to be dependent, she may be able to obtain an order maintaining a roof over the children's (and therefore her own) heads until their dependency ends: see the Children Act 1989, Sch 1, and Chapter 5.   [240] Section 37(5).

[241] And civil partners.   [242] Section 38(6).

5.6 THE APPROACH OF THE COURTS TO OCCUPATION ORDERS

The courts regard occupation orders as an extremely serious invasion of the rights of the respondent, and thus considerations relating to the well-being of the applicant and any children will not, on their own, persuade the court to grant an occupation order; more will be required. Despite the intention of the Law Commission that the criteria for making occupation orders should remove the focus on the parties' conduct and concentrate, more specifically, on the needs of the parties, the courts have confirmed earlier authorities which took the view that such orders were draconian. In *Chalmers v Johns*[243] the Court of Appeal held that the string of authorities which emphasise the harsh nature of the occupation order had not been overtaken by the new provisions in the 1996 Act, and that an order which overrides proprietary interests was only justified in exceptional circumstances. In addition, the courts have been adamant that where divorce is imminent an occupation order should not be made as a short-term measure to give the parties breathing space from the tension surrounding the marital breakdown.

In *Chalmers v Johns*[244] the parties, who were not married, lived together for 25 years and occupied the family home as joint tenants. They had two children, an adult son and a daughter aged 7. The relationship between the parties had always been volatile and the year before they separated, the police had been called to the house on four occasions to investigate complaints of assault, by both the mother and the father, which resulted in minor injuries. The mother subsequently left the home with her daughter and moved into temporary council accommodation which was a mile and a half from the daughter's school. By contrast, the family home was approximately a ten-minute walk from the school. The judge made an interim occupation order in the mother's favour but the father successfully appealed against this decision. The Court of Appeal first considered the balance of harm test and held that neither the mother nor the child would be likely to suffer significant harm attributable to the conduct of the father if the order were not made. There was no risk of the child suffering violence and the inconvenience involved in her longer journey to school could not amount to harm. Thorpe LJ did not regard the facts of this case as coming anywhere near the level of harm required which would place the court under a duty to make the order on the balance of harm test.[245] The court then had to decide whether to make the order at its discretion under section 33(6). In light of the pending family law proceedings between the parties to decide upon the residence of the daughter, the court held that it was not appropriate to make an occupation order as an interim measure given, in particular, its severe consequences. Thus the fact that the final issues regarding the couple's separation and residence of the daughter had yet to be decided was of great relevance when the court was exercising its discretion.

In *Re Y (Children) (Occupation Order)*,[246] the parties had been married for 20 years and had four children. Two of the children, a boy aged 13 and a girl aged 16 who was pregnant, remained with them in the family home. The wife began divorce proceedings which had become protracted and, in the meantime, the husband applied for an occupation order against the wife. The husband had diabetes, had lost his sight in one eye, and was registered disabled. The family was described as dysfunctional with the mother and the daughter allied against the son and the father. In particular, the father and daughter had an appalling relationship. The parties lived in separate camps in the house, with the mother and daughter on one side and the father and son on the other. The Court of Appeal allowed the mother's appeal against the granting of an occupation order saying that this order was a draconian remedy which should only be used as

---

[243] [1999] 1 FLR 392.   [244] Ibid.   [245] Ibid, 396.   [246] [2000] 2 FCR 470.

a last resort. In making the order, the judge at first instance was persuaded by the fact that the local authority would more easily accommodate the mother and her pregnant 16-year-old daughter than the father and son thus concluding that the father and son would suffer greater harm. The Court of Appeal disagreed holding that the balance of harm test was not established. First, the court was not persuaded that the father would suffer significant harm if the order were not made. Secondly, even if this could be established the balance of harm test would fail because the harm to the husband was associated with his disability and thus was not attributable to the wife's conduct—there was no evidence that she had been violent towards the husband. The court also felt that the judge had failed to consider the harm which would be caused to the daughter if she were to be rehoused with the mother, and considered that the father would be in a stronger position to be rehoused by the local authority given his disability. However, the court did not wish to allow this to become the determinative factor when applying the balance of harm test.

It then considered the matter under section 33(6). First, when considering the housing needs and resources of the parties, the court felt that the matrimonial home could be divided to meet the needs of both parties. The family factions had already established their separate camps within the house and given that the issues would be resolved on a permanent basis when the parties divorced, the court held that there was no reason why the current arrangements could not continue until that time. In terms of financial resources, while the wife was working there was nothing to suggest that this income would provide enough for her to rent accommodation privately. The likely effect of the order on the health, safety, and well-being of the parties and of any relevant child may have tipped the balance in favour of the husband in light of his health. However, the court concluded that any potential effect on his health was not due to the wife's misconduct but rather was more to do with his poor relationship with his daughter. In relation to the conduct of each of the parties, the court felt that they were as bad as each other. In light of emphasis placed on the fact that an occupation order is a harsh remedy which should only be used as a 'last resort',[247] the court held that the judge had been wrong to make the order to bring to an end the atmosphere in the house during the protracted divorce proceedings. That was not the purpose of an occupation order. As Sedley LJ noted:

> The purpose of an occupation order ... is not to break matrimonial deadlock by evicting one of the parties ... nor is it to use publicly-funded emergency housing as a solution for domestic strife.[248]

That the occupation should not be used as a 'weapon in domestic warfare'[249] is further illustrated in *G v G (Occupation Order: Conduct)*.[250] In this case the wife had issued divorce proceedings against the husband. They had two children, aged 15 and 12, and the parties continued to live in the family home during the divorce proceedings. This caused considerable tension and the wife sought an occupation order to remove the husband from the property. The judge at first instance refused to make the order on the ground that the husband's conduct was unintentional. However, the Court of Appeal held that this approach was incorrect. The court clarified that when considering under the balance of harm test whether any harm likely to be suffered by the applicant or child was attributable to the conduct of the respondent, the important factor was the effect of the conduct rather than the intention of the respondent. Even if the respondent's conduct had been

---

[247] Ibid, 477.　　[248] Ibid, 478.　　[249] Ibid, 480.　　[250] [2000] 2 FLR 36.

unintentional, while lack of intent may be a relevant consideration this did not mean that any resulting harm could not be attributed to the respondent. Thorpe LJ said:

> the court's consideration must be upon the effect of the conduct rather than the intention of the doer. Whether misconduct is intentional or unintentional is not the question. An applicant under section 33 is entitled to protection from unjustifiable conduct that causes harm to her or the children of the family.[251]

However, on the facts there was no significant harm and so the balance of harm test did not apply. The court considered whether the occupation order should be made at its discretion under section 33(6). The answer was no. The husband had not been violent to the wife and this was not one of those exceptional cases which justified such a draconian order. Of significance was the fact that the wife had made applications for residence of the children and financial relief orders against the husband. As these substantive issues would be determined within a short time, an occupation order was not warranted in the meantime. It is clear that an occupation order will not be made to deal with the 'heightened tensions that any family has to live with whilst the process of divorce and separation is current'.[252] This is especially the case when a substantive hearing will take place within a short time to resolve the parties' affairs in the aftermath of the divorce or separation.

However, in *S v F (Occupation Order)*[253] an occupation order was made in the absence of physical violence. In this case the parties had divorced and the children lived with their mother in the matrimonial home in London. When the mother remarried she wanted to sell the family home and move to the country. One son was opposed to the move and wished to remain living in London so that he could continue with his examinations. The father, who had been living in Kuala Lumpur, applied for an occupation order which would allow him to move back into the matrimonial home in London in order to provide a home for his son.[254] The court made the order allowing the father to return to the property for six months or until the ancillary relief proceedings between the parties were resolved, whichever was the sooner. Even though the court was prepared to make an occupation order in the absence of the respondent's violence, it should be remembered that, on the facts, the order operated in a positive as opposed to a negative way. In other words, it permitted the father to move into the former matrimonial home to provide a home for his son who wished to remain in London to continue his education, as opposed to removing the mother from the home. The mother was already living in another property in the country and so this is not an example of the occupation order at its most draconian. The restriction on the wife's proprietary rights was simply that her wish to sell the property was delayed for a short time and so, given these facts, one cannot take this case as evidence of the court's willingness to make occupation orders removing the respondent from the property in the absence of serious physical violence.

The courts have consistently taken the view that occupation orders are not designed to provide respite for the parties from the usual tensions associated with relationship breakdown. However, a recent decision by the Court of Appeal took a slightly different approach. In *Grubb v Grubb*,[255] the Court of Appeal refused the husband's application for leave to appeal against an occupation order which removed him from the property which

---

[251] Ibid, 40.   [252] Ibid, 41.   [253] [2000] 1 FLR 255.

[254] Note the father, as a former spouse, had to apply for an occupation order as a non-entitled applicant: a former spouse with no existing right to occupy the home under s 35. This was because the property was in the mother's name and as a former spouse he no longer had 'home rights' in the property and there was insufficient evidence to satisfy the court that he was entitled to occupy the property by virtue of having a beneficial interest in it.

[255] [2009] EWCA Civ 976.

was his family's ancestral home. They parties were married for over 25 years and had five children, the youngest of whom was 13. The children were to remain living with the mother which meant that she required accommodation with at least five bedrooms. The matrimonial home was a large six-bedroom property in an estate which had been in the husband's family for over a century. The husband, who had substantial wealth, also had other properties on the estate. The wife sought an occupation order under section 33(6), the general checklist, and did not argue that the either she or the children were likely to suffer significant harm if the order were not made. While the wife accepted that the husband was never physically violent towards her, she alleged that he was verbally abusive and was domineering and controlling.

The judge at first instance accepted that the wife was under stress: she was diagnosed with a moderately severe depressive disorder and was on medication. It was agreed that the current living arrangements were intolerable and that a separation was required. Thus, the judge made an occupation order removing the husband from the family home. The Court of Appeal refused leave to appeal against this decision despite accepting existing authority that an occupation order is 'always serious, and no doubt can sometimes be particularly serious when it relates to a spouse's removal from what one might almost call his ancestral home'.[256] However, the court indicated that the seriousness of the order was compounded when the evicted party did not have alternative accommodation readily available. In this case, the husband had another property at his disposal which was big enough for his needs but too small for the wife and children. In addition, he also had sufficient resources to fund comfortable accommodation elsewhere. The court noted, and was most likely persuaded by the fact that, the husband's removal from the home was simply a short-term interim measure, the duration of which was within his control as the wife was willing to move out when suitable accommodation had been found for the family. The husband was ordered to leave the property within 28 days and the order was to last until financial order proceedings between the parties were finalised.

A couple of points are worth noting. First, the fact that a case was not mounted under section 33(7) and that no 'significant harm' was alleged, but that the applicant was successful under section 33(6) confirms that significant harm is not a necessary threshold for making the order at the court's discretion.[257] Secondly, that the respondent was not guilty of any physical violence, and yet he was still removed from the home, could be taken to suggest a liberalisation of the criteria. Thirdly, this case suggests that an occupation order can be used to resolve the tensions associated with relationship breakdown. It has been observed that:

> This decision may have the consequent effect of making it easier to persuade a judge to grant an occupation order under s 33(6), where conduct is not really the main issue, but a solution is needed to difficult living arrangements. Essentially, it would appear that if the applicant can demonstrate the existence of credible alternative accommodation for the other party, or rely upon that party's greater financial resources, then he or she need not cite very much by way of conduct to justify the order. Where the line is drawn, as to what may constitute credible alternative accommodation or adequate financial resources, remains to be seen.

However, it is important not to overemphasise the significance of this case. There were very particular facts which persuaded the court that an order should be made. Most notably, the husband owned another property which was readily available to

[256] Ibid, [26].
[257] B. James, 'Occupation Orders after *Grubb*', available at www.familylawweek.co.uk.

him and which met his needs. In addition, the court noted the fact that the wife was willing to move out of the property but the husband had not made the necessary arrangements for her accommodation at another property on the estate which was large enough for the family. Despite the outcome of this case, it remains unlikely that the court will make an occupation order either in the absence of physical violence or to deal with the normal tensions of divorce where the respondent has no alternative accommodation.[258]

5.7 ENFORCEMENT OF AN OCCUPATION ORDER

Where the court has issued an occupation order requiring the respondent to permit the applicant to enter and remain in the home, excluding the respondent from the home, or forbidding him from a specified area in which the home is included, such orders will only be effective if steps can be readily taken to enforce them should the respondent choose to ignore them. Unlike the situation with the non-molestation order, breach of an occupation order is not a criminal offence. Instead breach of the order will be enforced as a contempt of court.

Historically there were problems with the enforcement of civil orders as the correct procedures had to be followed before the respondent was brought before the court for contempt. Normally the respondent must be served personally with notice of an application to commit him for breach and then must be arrested by officers of the court, all of which took time when the applicant required protection. The lack of speedy enforcement mechanisms was recognised by the Select Committee on Violence in Marriage, and it recommended that the police should become involved in the enforcement of the civil orders made to protect against domestic violence. This recommendation was accepted, and since 1976[259] courts have been able to attach a power of arrest to these civil orders. However, although the introduction of the power of arrest assisted victims of domestic violence, the Law Commission found that powers of arrest were being attached to a relatively small proportion of orders.[260]

Reluctance to make use of the power of arrest stemmed from the Court of Appeal's decision in *Lewis v Lewis*[261] where the court ruled that attaching a power of arrest to an injunction should not be a routine remedy and that the use of this power was quite plainly intended for the exceptional situation 'where men or women persistently disobey injunctions and make nuisances of themselves to the other party and to others concerned.'[262] This set the pattern for the approach in subsequent cases, and the courts consistently stated that the power of arrest should only be attached in exceptional circumstances.[263]

This gate-keeping attitude failed to recognise the very real dangers associated with domestic violence and suggested that speedy enforcement was only essential in the most extreme cases. Such an approach failed to recognise that a power of arrest is a 'simple, immediate and inexpensive means of enforcement which underlines the seriousness of the breach to the offending party'.[264] The FLA 1996 creates a presumption in favour of attaching a power of arrest in certain cases. Under section 47(2), the court shall attach a power of arrest to an occupation order if it appears that the respondent has used or threatened violence against the applicant or relevant child unless it is satisfied that the applicant will

---

[258] Ibid.   [259] Domestic Violence and Matrimonial Proceedings Act 1976.

[260] In 1989, the latest year for which figures were available to the Law Commission, powers of arrest were attached to only 29 per cent of orders made under the 1976 Act: Law Com No 207 (1992), para 5.11.

[261] [1978] 1 All ER 729. Similarly in *Widdowson v Widdowson* (1982) 4 FLR 121, it was held that magistrates should only attach a power of arrest where it was really necessary, and that they should specifically state their reasons for doing so.   [262] [1978] 1 All ER 729 at 731.

[263] See *R v S* [1988] 2 FLR 339; *McLean v Nugent* (1980) 1 FLR 26.

[264] Law Com No 207 (1992), para 5.13.

be adequately protected without this measure.[265] 'Violence' is undefined in relation to this provision. Under the previous legislation, 'actual bodily harm' to the applicant or child had to be established although this was held to encompass both physical and psychological violence.[266] However, the 1996 Act has extended the occasions when a power of arrest shall be attached by including threatened as well as actual violence. This is an important change because it recognises that the applicant or child should not have to be physically assaulted before a power of arrest can be attached to the order. Statistics show that the majority of occupation orders have a power of arrest attached.[267] Given that the power of arrest will only be attached where violence or threats of violence have been used, this illustrates the extent to which the occupation order is made to deal with this type of situation.

If a power of arrest is attached, a constable can arrest a person without warrant where there is reasonable cause to suspect that he or she is in breach of the order.[268] The respondent must be brought before the relevant judicial authority within 24 hours from the time of the arrest, and where the matter is not disposed of forthwith he may be remanded either in custody or on bail (to which conditions may be attached).[269] If the court has not attached a power of arrest to the order, then the applicant will have to apply to the court for a warrant for arrest if she considers that the respondent has breached the order.[270] The court will not issue a warrant unless the application is substantiated by a statement under oath and there are reasonable grounds to suspect that the respondent has been in breach.

If the respondent is arrested under section 47 for breaching an occupation order, he will be punished for contempt of court. The sanctions that can be imposed for contempt are a fine or imprisonment although the maximum sentence which can be imposed is two years.[271] The court does not have the power in contempt proceedings to impose other sanctions such as enforced enrolment on anger management or rehabilitation programmes. A range of orders may be made in civil contempt cases and every case must be considered on its own facts.[272] In particular, the court will consider the nature of the breach, the presence of children, and whether the order was breached more than once.[273] A custodial sentence can be imposed, the maximum of which is two years. There have been some cases where the courts have appeared reluctant to impose a custodial sentence. In *Ansah v Ansah*,[274] for example, the court thought that committal orders are remedies of last resort, particularly in family cases because they could damage the applicant as much as the respondent. However, the position today is that the court will impose a sanction which reflects the gravity of the breach. While there are no precise tariffs set for the appropriate sentence to be handed down when enforcing breach of a civil order,[275] case law shows that the courts take such breaches very seriously. In *Lomas v Parle*,[276] for example, the court indicated that the sentence imposed for breach of a non-molestation order as a civil contempt matter should not be 'manifestly discrepant' with the sentences imposed for criminal offences for breach of the orders under the Protection from Harassment

---

[265] Section 47(2). The legislation originally provided that the court should attach a power of arrest to a non-molestation order where there was violence or threats of violence. This is no longer the case because breach of a non-molestation order is now a criminal offence.

[266] *Kendrick v Kendrick* [1990] 2 FLR 107.

[267] In 2004, 90 per cent of occupation orders had a power of arrest attached; in 2005 and 2006 it was 91 per cent; in 2007 it was 81 per cent and in 2008 it was 66 per cent.   [268] Section 47(6).

[269] Section 47(7) and (12). No account is taken of Christmas Day, Good Friday, or any Sunday in reckoning this period of time.   [270] Section 47(8).

[271] Contempt of Court Act 1981, s 14(1).

[272] *Devjee v Patel* [2006] EWCA Civ 1211. For guidance see *Hale v Tanner* [2000] 2 FLR 879; *Lomas v Parle* [2004] 1 FLR 812; *H v O (Contempt of Court: Sentencing)* [2004] EWCA Civ 1691.

[273] *Lomas v Parle* [2004] 1 FLR 812.   [274] [1977] 2 All ER 638.

[275] See *Hale v Tanner* [2000] 2 FLR 879.   [276] [2004] 1 FLR 812.

Act 1997.[277] Where the respondent has used violence when breaching an order, the court is likely to order imprisonment.[278]

It may be the case that breach of the civil order also gives rise to criminal proceedings. In these circumstances the civil and criminal proceedings may run concurrently, although it is likely that the civil proceedings will be dealt with more swiftly. One issue is whether the respondent is punished twice for the same offence. In *Lomas v Parle*,[279] the Court of Appeal laid down some guidelines for sentencing in concurrent proceedings. First the Court of Appeal said that it is 'essential that the second court should be fully informed of the factors and circumstances reflected in the first sentence' in order to ensure that the defendant is not punished twice.[280] The first court, which is most likely to be dealing with the civil proceedings, is not to try to second-guess the likely outcome of the subsequent proceedings or alter its sentence to take account of these proceedings, but must explain its reasoning fully for the benefit of the second court. The civil contempt proceedings must be dealt with swiftly and decisively in order to ensure that this information is available to the court dealing with the criminal proceedings.

5.8 UNDERTAKINGS

An undertaking is a promise given by the respondent to the court which is enforceable like a court order. Prior to the FLA 1996, when an application was made for a non-molestation order it was frequently the case that pressure was put on the applicant to withdraw her application in return for the respondent giving an undertaking to the court not to molest her. Similarly, when faced with an application for an occupation order, the respondent often agreed to leave the home, thus obviating the need for the court to make an order. In theory, the protection afforded by such an undertaking to the court is just as effective as a court order, and breach of an undertaking can give rise to proceedings for contempt.[281] It was often to the respondent's advantage to give an undertaking because the court did not then make any findings of fact about his alleged behaviour.

The FLA 1996 makes provision for the practice of accepting undertakings in non-molestation and occupation order cases to continue. Under section 46, in any case where the court has the power to make an occupation order or a non-molestation order, it may accept an undertaking from any party to the proceedings.[282] However, while the undertaking is enforced through contempt proceedings,[283] no power of arrest can be attached to the order.[284] As a result, the occasions when the court can accept an undertaking appear to be limited by provisions which prohibit the court's acceptance of an undertaking where a power of arrest would be attached to an occupation order,[285] or where it is necessary to make a non-molestation order which is enforceable as a criminal offence under section 42A.[286] This suggests that an undertaking will not be accepted by the court

---

[277] See also *H v O (Contempt of Court: Sentencing)* [2004] EWCA Civ 1691. Although this approach has been criticised on the basis that there are discrepancies between the range of remedies which are available in the civil and criminal courts respectively, and that the two systems have different objections and functions. While civil orders are designed to mark the court's disapproval at the respondent's breach of the civil order and ensure future compliance, the criminal courts are primarily concerned with punishing the offender. See M. Burton, 'Case Commentary—*Lomas v Parle*—Coherent and Effective Remedies for Victims of Domestic Violence: Time for an Integrated Domestic Violence Court' [2004] Child and Family Law Quarterly 317.

[278] *Wilson v Webster* [1998] 1 FLR 1097.   [279] [2004] 1 FLR 812.   [280] Ibid, [48].

[281] Section 46(4).

[282] Section 46 did not appear in the Law Commission's Draft Bill, or in the original Family Homes and Domestic Violence Bill 1995, but was introduced into the final legislation at the Committee stage of the legislative process.   [283] Section 46(4).

[284] Section 46(2).   [285] Section 46(3).   [286] Section 46(3A).

instead of making a non-molestation or occupation order in cases where the respondent has used or threatened violence against the applicant or relevant child. Thus there is still scope for a court to accept an undertaking from the respondent instead of making an order even though the legislation discourages this in cases of violence or threatened violence. There is evidence to suggest that undertakings are still used and that solicitors remain keen to deal with domestic violence cases by undertakings.[287]

5.9 EX PARTE ORDERS

Normally a respondent to an application for an order in civil proceedings must be given adequate notice of the proceedings in accordance with the rules of court. However, in an emergency, the normal notice procedures can be dispensed with and the court can make an order ex parte (without notice).

Key legislation

Section 45 provides that in any case where the court considers it just and convenient to do so it may grant a non-molestation order or an occupation order in ex parte proceedings. In determining whether to do so the court must have regard to all the circumstances including:

(a) any risk of significant harm to the applicant or a relevant child, attributable to the conduct of the respondent if the order is not made immediately;

(b) whether it is likely that the applicant will be deterred or prevented from pursuing the application if an order is not made immediately; and

(c) whether there is reason to believe that the respondent is aware of the proceedings but is deliberately evading service and the applicant or a relevant child will be seriously prejudiced by the delay involved—

  (i) where the court is a magistrates' court, in effecting service of proceedings; or

  (ii) in any other case, in effecting substituted service.

These criteria stress that ex parte applications should only be granted where there are compelling reasons for doing so. As the Law Commission pointed out:

> The danger of a misconceived or malicious application being granted or the risk of some other injustice being done to the respondent is inevitably greater where the court has only heard the applicant's side of the story and the respondent has had no opportunity to reply.[288]

Other drawbacks in ex parte orders were pointed out such as the fact that 'the judge has no opportunity to try to resolve the parties' differences by agreed undertakings or otherwise to try to reduce the tension of the dispute'; and 'there is no opportunity to bring home the seriousness of the situation to the respondent and to underline the importance of complying with the order or undertaking'.[289] Accordingly, ex parte orders will be rare, although the courts are more likely to be willing to make an ex parte non-molestation order than an occupation order. The former restrains the respondent from carrying out an act(s) which he is prohibited from doing under the general law, while the latter involves a balancing

---

[287] M. Burton, 'Civil Law Remedies for Domestic Violence: Why are Applications for Non-Molestation Orders Declining?' (2009) 31(2) Journal of Social Welfare and Family Law 109 at 115.

[288] Law Com No 207 (1992), para 5.6.   [289] Ibid.

exercise which is difficult to carry out without the respondent having the opportunity to present evidence. Evidence confirms that the courts are reluctant to grant ex parte occupation orders.[290]

The criteria for making an ex parte order concentrate on those situations where it is necessary or desirable. Paragraph (a) focuses on cases where the respondent's conduct is creating a risk of significant harm to the applicant or relevant child unless the order is made immediately. It is more likely that this threshold of 'significant harm' will be met in cases where physical violence has taken place, or there is a threat of imminent violence. In addition, an ex parte order may be particularly appropriate where the applicant is frightened that the respondent will react violently to service of the proceedings. Paragraph (b) is a significant provision as it recognises the real risk that many applicants may be deterred from pursuing an application if an order is not made immediately. It also ties in with paragraph (c) which is aimed at the difficult situation where the respondent is deliberately evading service, sometimes as a device to wear down the applicant's resolve to press ahead with proceedings by causing delay.[291]

Where an ex parte order is granted it should be strictly limited in time and section 45(3) makes it clear that the respondent must be given an opportunity to make representations relating to the order as soon as just and convenient at a full hearing. Provided the court fulfils its obligations to secure a full hearing as soon as just and convenient, Article 6 of the European Convention on Human Rights (ECHR) which provides that everyone is entitled to a fair and public hearing of the determination of his civil rights, will not be breached. If a non-molestation order is made in ex parte proceedings, breach of that order will only constitute a criminal offence under section 42A if the respondent was aware of the existence of the order at the time the conduct was carried out.[292] It has been pointed out that the respondent simply has to be aware of the existence of the order, but not its terms[293] which means that a respondent could be guilty of a criminal offence (for breaching a non-molestation order) without knowing that he was prohibited from carrying out the precise conduct in question in the first place.[294] This has led to the observation that this may constitute an infringement of the respondent's rights under Articles 5,[295] 6,[296] and 8[297] of the ECHR.[298] It is also worth noting that the court's powers to attach a power of arrest to an occupation order are more circumscribed in ex parte proceedings than in a full hearing.[299] A power of arrest may be attached if it appears that the respondent has used or threatened violence against the applicant or a relevant child, and that there is a risk of significant harm to them attributable to the conduct of the respondent if a power of arrest is not attached to the order immediately.[300] In these circumstances, the court may order that the power of arrest is to last for a shorter period than other provisions in the order.[301]

---

[290] J. Barron, 'Five Years On: A Review of Legal Protection from Domestic Violence' (Bristol: Women's Aid, 2002); M. Burton, Legal Responses to Domestic Violence (Abingdon: Routledge-Cavendish, 2008), pp 38 and 41. See eg G v G (Ouster: Ex Parte Application) [1990] 1 FLR 395.

[291] The Law Commission was informed by a number of respondents that this evasion gives rise to considerable problems and expense, Law Com No 207 (1992), para 5.9.

[292] Section 42A(2).

[293] B. Soni, 'Domestic Violence and Family Law: A New Era', available at www.familylawweek.co.uk.

[294] Ibid.   [295] Right to respect for liberty and security of person.

[296] Right to a fair and public hearing.   [297] Right to respect for one's private and family life.

[298] B. Soni, 'Domestic Violence and Family Law: A New Era', available at www.familylawweek.co.uk.

[299] Section 47(3).   [300] Section 47(3).   [301] Section 47(4).

5.10 PROVISION FOR THIRD PARTIES TO ACT ON
BEHALF OF VICTIMS OF DOMESTIC VIOLENCE

Section 60 of the FLA 1996, which has not been implemented, states that rules of court may provide for prescribed persons to apply for a non-molestation order or an occupation order on behalf of another. This provision stems from the Law Commission's recommendation that where the police have been involved in an incident of domestic violence or its aftermath, they should have the power to apply for civil remedies on behalf of the victim.[302] The Commission modelled its recommendation on similar provisions which apply in several Australian states where it has been found to serve a useful and valuable function.[303] The purpose behind involving the police is to remove the burden of taking action from the victim, to reduce the scope for further intimidation by the perpetrator, and to lead to fewer cases being withdrawn: 'The fact that the police are initiating the proceedings also has the beneficial effect of bringing home to the respondent the seriousness of the matter and giving civil proceedings the "weight" they can lack in the eyes of some of the less law abiding members of society.'[304]

The Commission found the question of whether the victim's consent should be necessary before the police can bring civil proceedings a difficult one to resolve.[305] It concluded that the best solution was to require the police to consult the victim and take account of her views, but not to make her consent or approval the decisive factor in determining whether or not civil proceedings are issued. Research carried out by the Lord Chancellor's Department which investigated the views of service providers on whether section 60 should be enacted revealed clear support for this provision.[306] It was felt that third party applicants would remove the burden on the victim to seek protective remedies which would be useful in cases where the victim was discouraged from taking such action for fear of reprisals. However, despite the anticipated advantages of this provision, it has not yet been enacted.

6 PERSONS NOT PROTECTED UNDER THE
FAMILY LAW ACT 1996

As we have seen, the FLA 1996 sought to achieve a balance between widening the scope of the protective remedies to a wider class of family member whilst maintaining the requirement that a familial link exist between the parties. One could argue, however, that if the objective of the legislation is to provide protection to those suffering violence or molestation, it is counterproductive to restrict the availability of the protective remedies. Whilst recognising this, the Law Commission did not wish to create a new tort of harassment or molestation and thus took the view that it was inappropriate to remove all restrictions on applicants and open the legislation to all in need of protection, as has been done in some Australian states.[307] Consequently, the protective remedies in the FLA 1996 are

---

[302] Law Com No 207 (1992), paras 5.18–5.23.

[303] The Australian Law Reform Commission, Domestic Violence, Report No 30 (1986); D. Chappell and H. Strang, 'Domestic Violence—Findings and Recommendations of the National Committee on Violence' [1990] Australian Journal of Family Law 211.   [304] Law Com No 207 (1992), para 5.18.

[305] Ibid, para 5.22.

[306] M. Burton, 'Third Party Applications for Protections Orders in England and Wales: Service Provider's Views on Implementing Section 60 of the Family Law Act 1996' (2003) 25(2) Journal of Social Welfare and Family Law 137–150. Two-thirds of the respondents supported the implementation of s 60.

[307] Eg in New South Wales it has been possible since 1989 for anyone to apply for an 'apprehended violence order' regardless of their connection with the applicant.

limited to certain categories of applicant who are connected by family ties on the grounds that 'violence and molestation within family relationships need to be treated as a special case'.[308] This means that neighbours, work colleagues, tenants, doctors, teachers, and others who may be vulnerable to threats of violence, sexual harassment, and other forms of molestation are excluded from the Act's provisions. Unless the behaviour was criminal or tortious, such as where there had been violence, those falling outside the scope of the 1996 Act were not protected under the general criminal or civil law either. This left a gap in the law because as there was no distinct tort of harassment, a person who was harassed in a non-physical way by someone with whom they were not 'associated' (such as neighbours) may not be able to obtain the protection afforded by the general law.

Attempts were made to create a tort of harassment. In *Khoransandjian v Bush*[309] the Court of Appeal moved away from limiting an action in nuisance to those who had an interest in land, and opened up the possibility of future developments. In this case the plaintiff was a young woman whose relationship with the defendant had come to an end. Despite this, the defendant persecuted the plaintiff with telephone calls to her mother's house. The defendant conceded that the mother could complain about the persistent telephone calls made to the parental home if she had a freehold or leasehold interest in the property as such conduct would fall within the tort of private nuisance. However, he claimed that as the plaintiff was a mere licensee in her mother's property, with no proprietary interest, she did not fall within the scope of the law. This argument was rejected by the Court of Appeal. Dillon LJ commented:

> to my mind, it is ridiculous if in this present age the law is that the making of deliberately harassing and pestering telephone calls to a person is only actionable in the civil courts if the recipient of the calls happens to have the freehold or a leasehold proprietary interest in the premises in which he or she has received the calls.[310]

He went on to approve the wording of the injunction granted by the judge which prohibited the defendant from 'using violence to, harassing, pestering or communicating with' the plaintiff. However, the potential of this development in the common law was short-lived because the decision was overruled by the House of Lords in *Hunter v Canary Wharf Ltd*.[311] Their Lordships held that a person who has no right in the land affected by the nuisance, such as a licensee or occupier, cannot bring an action in nuisance. Moreover, it was wrong to treat actions in respect of discomfort, interference with personal enjoyment, or personal injury by the plaintiff as actions in nuisance.

7 PROTECTION FROM HARASSMENT ACT 1997

Fortunately many of the limitations of both the 1996 Act and the common law have been addressed by the Protection from Harassment Act 1997. The 1997 Act came into force after public concern about stalking.[312] Although it can cover situations where there is no relationship or connection between the parties, the Act can also be used in domestic disputes and, notably, breach of the orders under the legislation attracts both civil and criminal remedies. The Act creates two new criminal offences and a statutory tort of harassment.

---

[308] Law Com No 207 (1992), para 3.16.
[309] [1993] 3 All ER 669. See also *Burris v Azadani* [1995] 4 All ER 802.
[310] [1993] 3 All ER 669 at 675.   [311] [1997] 2 All ER 426.
[312] *Stalking—The Solutions: A Consultation Paper* (London: Home Office, 1996).

7.1 HARASSMENT

Section 1(1) creates an arrestable offence of harassment and gives victims of harassment both criminal[313] and civil remedies,[314] including the right to claim damages.[315] A victim does not have to pursue both civil and criminal sanctions. Civil enforcement may be particularly useful where there is insufficient evidence to satisfy the standard of proof required for a criminal prosecution (beyond reasonable doubt) but where there is sufficient evidence to meet the civil standard (on the balance of probabilities). The defendant can try to defend the allegations of harassment by showing that it was pursued for the purpose of preventing or detecting crime, it was pursued under an enactment or rule of law, or in the particular circumstances the conduct was reasonable.

Section 1 states that a person must not pursue a course of conduct which amounts to harassment of another, and which he knows or ought to know amounts to harassment of the other.[316] Such a person will be taken to know that his behaviour amounts to harassment 'if a reasonable person in possession of the same information would think the course of conduct amounted to harassment of the other'.[317] This provision focuses on the defendant's behaviour as well as its impact on the victim. The concept of harassment has no statutory definition but it appears to be very broad as it includes 'alarming the person or causing the person distress'.[318] This was considered by the Court of Appeal in *Majrowski v Guy's and St Thomas' NHS Trust*[319] where May LJ said that:

> The conduct … has to be calculated, in an objective sense, to cause distress and has to be oppressive and unreasonable. It has to be conduct which the perpetrator knows or ought to know amounts to harassment, and conduct which a reasonable person would think amounted to harassment.[320]

In addition, a 'course of conduct' must involve conduct on at least two occasions and 'conduct' includes speech. It seems that harassment also encompasses the same types of behaviours as those which amount to molestation for the purposes of the 1996 Act, although unlike for the non-molestation order, a one-off act will not suffice. In addition, while the focus for the court when deciding whether to make a non-molestation order is on the effect of the behaviour on the victim, the court when deciding whether conduct amounts to harassment under the 1997 legislation, must consider the fact that this is a criminal offence which means that 'a series of very minor annoyances may not meet the criteria'.[321] To constitute a 'course of conduct' it seems that there must be some connection between the incidents complained of. In *R v Hills*,[322] the incidents of alleged harassment were six months apart and in this intervening period the parties had cohabited and had sexual relations. The Court of Appeal held that this prevented the assaults from constituting a course of conduct as they did not possess the 'necessary cogent linkage'.[323] It could be argued, therefore, that the 'fewer the number of incidents and the wider the time

---

[313] Section 2.

[314] Section 3.   [315] Section 3(2).   [316] Section 1(1).   [317] Section 1(2).

[318] Section 7(2). See *Thomas v News Group Newspapers* [2002] EMLR 78.

[319] [2005] EWCA Civ 251.

[320] See R. Noon, 'Compensation for Domestic Abuse after *Singh v Bhaker*', available at www.familylawweek.co.uk.

[321] *Majrowski v Guy's and St Thomas' NHS Trust* [2005] EWCA Civ 251; R. Noon, 'Compensation for Domestic Abuse after *Singh v Bhaker*', available at www.familylawweek.co.uk.   [322] [2001] 1 FLR 580.

[323] R. Noon, 'Compensation for Domestic Abuse after *Singh v Bhaker*', available at www.familylawweek. co.uk. See also *Lau v Director of Public Prosecutions* [2000] 1 FLR 799 where the fact that the incidents were four months apart prevented the court from viewing them as a 'course of conduct'.

lapse between them, the less likely that they give rise to a "course of conduct".[324] A person who pursues a course of conduct which amounts to harassment is guilty of an offence, the penalty for which is imprisonment for up to six months, or a fine, or both. The court can also make a restraining order when someone is convicted of harassment, and breach of the order will be a further offence.[325]

A civil action for damages may also be brought by the victim of an actual or apprehended offence of harassment.[326] Various responses are open to the civil court. Damages may be awarded for (among other things) any anxiety or financial loss caused by, or resulting from, the harassment.[327] In *Singh v Bhakar*[328] the claimant was a Sikh woman who married a Hindu and subsequently moved in with her mother-in-law who disliked her and caused her 'four months of hell'. As a result of this abuse the claimant was diagnosed with a moderate depressive episode and sought damages from her mother-in-law under the 1997 legislation. Given the nature of the harassment and the fact that the claimant was the deliberate target of this conduct, the judge awarded her £35,000. This led some to point out that lawyers acting on behalf of victims of domestic violence should no longer be reticent about seeking damages from their client under the 1997 legislation either as a free-standing application or in conjunction with an injunction application.[329] Injunctions may also be granted to restrain the defendant from pursing the course of conduct, any breach of which may be enforced by the issue of an arrest warrant in proceedings brought by the victim. Breach of an injunction prohibiting harassment under section 3 amounts to an offence as well as contempt of court, but where the defendant is convicted he may not also be punished for contempt, and vice versa.[330] Even though the breach of this civil injunction is a criminal offence, the standard of proof required for making the injunction remains the civil standard (on the balance of probabilities).[331]

7.2 PUTTING PEOPLE IN FEAR OF VIOLENCE

Section 4 of the Act makes it an offence for a person to carry out a course of conduct on at least two occasions which causes another person to fear that violence will be used against him, if the perpetrator knows or ought to know that he will cause such a fear on each occasion. No warrant is needed where there is a breach because the offence falls within the normal arrest powers given to the police.[332] It is a defence to show that the conduct was pursued for the purpose of preventing or detecting crime, was pursued under a statutory provision, or was reasonable for the protection of himself or someone else or for the protection of property.

7.3 RESTRAINING ORDERS

A court sentencing a person convicted of an offence under section 2 (harassment) or section 4 (putting people in fear of violence) may also make a restraining order, and breach of it will be further offence.[333] The restraining order can be used to prohibit the

---

[324] R. N. Hill, 'Protection from Harassment' [2005] Family Law 364. Hill points out that in such circumstances, and where appropriate, a charge of assault may be the preferred course of action. Domestic Violence, Crime and Victims Act 2004, s 10 makes common assault an arrestable offence.   [325] Section 5.

[326] Section 3(1).   [327] Section 3(2).   [328] [2007] 1 FLR 880.

[329] J. Rosley, 'In Practice: Mother-in-law Harassment: *Singh v Bhakar*' [2006] Family Law 968.

[330] Section 3(6), (7), and (8). Breach of an injunction under s 3 is an arrestable offence which means that an arrest can be made without a warrant.

[331] *Hipgrave and Hipgrave v Jones* [2004] EWHC 2901 (QB).

[332] Police and Criminal Evidence Act 1994, s 24(6).   [333] Section 5.

offender from engaging in conduct which amounts to harassment or will cause a fear of violence. It is an arrestable offence for the offender to breach this order without reasonable excuse.[334] The Domestic Violence, Crime and Victims Act 2004 inserted a new provision (s 5A) into the 1997 legislation giving the court the power to issue a restraining order in a wider range of circumstances.[335] If a defendant is acquitted in criminal proceedings of an offence, the court now has the power to make a restraining order where it considers it necessary to do so to protect a person from harassment from the defendant.[336] While the victim could, of course, apply for a non-molestation order and/or an injunction under the 1997 legislation, the court's power to make a restraining order 'would not only avoid delay and increased costs to the legal aid budget, but also provide a more seamless protection for the victim'.[337]

The 1997 Act clearly has widespread civil and criminal law implications, and where the victim wishes to pursue an action in damages it may be advantageous to apply under this Act even though she is entitled to apply for orders under the FLA 1996. Further, there is nothing to prevent a victim of domestic violence from making applications under both pieces of legislation.[338] In such a situation, the application should be issued in the same court and tried by a judge with jurisdiction in both sets of proceedings.[339] Despite the benefits of making an application under the 1997 legislation which offers the potential of being awarded damages which are not available under the FLA 1996, research shows that the remedies under the 1997 Act are not pursued on many occasions.[340]

8 DOMESTIC VIOLENCE AND LOCAL AUTHORITY HOUSING

Victims of domestic violence who have been forced to leave, or otherwise been driven, from the family home, may turn to their local housing authority for assistance. Statistics show that domestic violence is one of the primary causes of homelessness: in 2002, 40 per cent of homeless women indicated that domestic violence was a factor which led to their homelessness.[341] Under the Housing Act 1996, as amended by the Homelessness Act 2002, a local authority is obliged to provide accommodation for certain categories of person who are deemed to be 'unintentionally homeless'.[342]

8.1 'HOMELESS'

A person is homeless if they have no accommodation which is available for their occupation in the UK or elsewhere,[343] or if they have such accommodation but cannot secure entry to

---

[334] Section 5(4).

[335] Home Office Circular 017/2009.

[336] Protection from Harassment Act 1997, s 5A, inserted by the Domestic Violence, Crime and Victims Act 2004, s 12. This provision came into force on 30 September 2009.

[337] Home Office Circular 017/2009.

[338] *Lomas v Parle* [2004] 1 FLR 812 at [44]. For a comparison of the two pieces of legislation see R. N. Hill, 'Protection from Harassment' [2005] Family Law 364.   [339] *Lomas v Parle*, ibid.

[340] M. Burton, 'Civil Law Remedies for Domestic Violence: Why are Applications for Non-Molestation Orders Declining?' (2009) 31(2) Journal of Social Welfare and Family Law 109.

[341] Shelter Scotland, *Repeat Homelessness and Domestic Abuse* (2002) cited in T. Rubens, 'Domestic Violence and Priority Need' (2008) Journal of Housing Law 28.

[342] Although research suggests that local authorities are failing to provide persons leaving a situation of domestic violence with the help which they need: Crisis, *Homeless Women: Still Being Failed Yet Striving to Survive* (London: Crisis, 2006).   [343] Housing Act 1996, s 175(1).

it.[344] If accommodation is available and accessible but it is not reasonable for the applicant to continue to occupy this property, they will also be deemed to be homeless.[345]

Key legislation

Whether it is reasonable to continue to occupy accommodation is defined in section 177(1) which states:

It is not reasonable for a person to continue to occupy accommodation if it is probable that this will lead to domestic violence against him, or against—

(a) a person who normally resides with him as a member of his family, or

(b) any other person who might reasonably be expected to reside with him.

For this purpose 'domestic violence', in relation to a person, means violence from a person with whom he is associated, or threats of violence from such a person which are likely to be carried out.

This means that if a person is forced to flee the family home due to violence, or threats of violence from an associated person, they will be deemed to be homeless and thus entitled to the help of the local authority. 'Associated person' is defined in section 178, the definition being almost identical to that contained in section 62 of the FLA 1996.[346] It is worth noting that the legislation does not actually require the perpetrator of the domestic violence to be living in the same property as the victim, merely that the parties are within an associated relationship. The Code of Guidance accompanying the legislation makes it clear that domestic violence does not just refer to incidents which take place within the home, but also covers violence outside the home.[347] The legislation follows the ethos of the FLA 1996 by giving 'domestic violence' a wide meaning. It includes:

> threatening behaviour, violence or abuse (psychological, physical, sexual, financial or emotional) between persons who are, or have been, intimate partners, family members or members of the same household, regardless of gender or sexuality.[348]

The definition of domestic violence in section 177(1) of the Housing Act 1996 has now been considered by the Supreme Court in *Yemshaw v Hounslow London Borough Council*.[349] In this case the court unanimously ruled that 'domestic violence' includes physical violence, threatening or intimidating behaviour, and any other form of abuse which, directly or indirectly, may give rise to the risk of harm. In this case the appellant left the matrimonial home in which she lived with her husband, taking her two young children with her. She sought assistance from the local housing authority, saying that her husband would shout at her in front of the children and that she was scared that if she confronted him he might hit her. The housing authority in this case felt that there was a low risk of domestic violence against her as her husband had never actually hit her or threatened to do so, and therefore that it was reasonable for her to continue to live in the matrimonial home. This meant that she had, in the housing authority's eyes, made herself intentionally homeless

---

[344] Section 175(2)(a). [345] Section 175(3).

[346] See Section 4.3.3. The only significant difference is that where the parties live or have lived in the same household, then employees, tenants, lodgers, and boarders are not excluded.

[347] Department for Communities and Local Government, *Homelessness Code of Guidance for Local Authorities* (2006), para 8.19. [348] Ibid, para 8.21.

[349] [2011] UKSC 3.

and, as such, it had no duty to provide her with alternative accommodation. The Supreme Court held unanimously that the Housing Act's definition of domestic violence should include not just physical violence, but also threatening or intimidating behaviour and other abuse that may give rise to the risk of harm. As such, the court held that the appellant had not made herself intentionally homeless and ruled that the case should be remitted to the local housing authority to make a fresh decision.

The Code of Guidance accompanying the legislation also makes it very clear that the safety of the applicant is the primary consideration, and thus the threat of violence is not based on whether there has been violence in the past.[350] Nor should any value judgement be made about the conduct of the applicant or the extent to which action could have been taken to mitigate the threat of violence.[351] While the applicant may be able to seek a non-molestation order to prevent future molestation, or an occupation order to remove the abuser from the home, there is no obligation on them to do this. The Code of Guidance recognises that victims may not have the confidence in these measures to prevent future abuse and thus their potential availability does not detract from the duty on the Local Authority to provide assistance to the victim as a homeless person.[352] In short, the Act makes provision both for a person who has been locked out of the home, and for a person who is too frightened either to stay in the home[353] or to return there, to seek accommodation from the local authority as a homeless person. A person who takes shelter in a refuge is still regarded as homeless.[354]

8.2 'PRIORITY NEED'

The local authority will owe 'stronger' duties to homeless people who are deemed to have a priority need for accommodation. This includes the duty to secure accommodation for the homeless person[355] and to take reasonable steps to prevent the loss of accommodation.[356] Those in priority need of accommodation include:[357]

(i) a pregnant woman or a person with whom she resides or might reasonably be expected to reside;

(ii) a person with whom dependent children reside or might reasonably be expected to reside;

(iii) a person who is vulnerable as a result of old age, mental illness, or handicap or physical disability or other special reason, or with whom such a person resides or might reasonably be expected to reside;

(iv) a person who is vulnerable as a result of ceasing to occupy accommodation because of violence from another person or threats of violence from another person which are likely to be carried out;

(v) a person who is vulnerable for any other special reason, or with whom such a person resides or might reasonably be expected to reside.

---

[350] Department for Communities and Local Government, *Homelessness Code of Guidance for Local Authorities* (2006), paras 8.22 and 8.24.   [351] Ibid, para 8.22.

[352] Ibid, para 8.23.   [353] *R v Broxbourne Borough Council, ex p Willmoth* (1989) 22 HLR 118.

[354] *R v Ealing London Borough Council, ex p Sidhu* (1982) 80 LGR 534; *Birmingham City Council v Ali and Others; Moran v Manchester City Council* [2009] UKHL 36. The House of Lords accepted that while a 'refuge is a safe haven in which to find peace and support … it is not a place to live' [2009] UKHL 36 at [43].

[355] Section 193(2).   [356] Section 195(2).

[357] Section 189(1) as amended by the Homeless (Priority Need for Accommodation) (England) Order 2002 and the Homeless (Priority Need for Accommodation) (Wales) Order 2002.

Dependent children do not qualify as being in priority need in their own right, neither will they qualify as being vulnerable either because of their youth or because of some sort of disability.[358] However, applicants who have dependent children who live with them, or who might reasonably be expected to live with them, have a priority need. The Code of Guidance states that while the child need not be wholly and exclusively resident with the applicant, there must be actual residence (or a reasonable expectation of residence) with some degree of permanence or regularity as opposed to just a temporary arrangement.[359] The legislation does not define 'dependent child' but the Code of Guidance suggests that it should cover children under 16, and those aged 16–18 who are still in full-time education or training, or who are unable to support themselves and live at home.[360]

A person who has been forced out of accommodation because of violence, or threats of violence, from another will be classed as 'vulnerable' and in priority need for accommodation. The Code of Guidance specifies that when considering if a victim of actual or threatened domestic violence is 'vulnerable', the housing authority may wish to consider:

(i) the nature of the violence or threats of violence;

(ii) the impact of the violence/threats of violence on the applicant's current and future well-being;

(iii) whether the applicant has any existing support networks, particularly by way of family and friends.[361]

Thus, a person who leaves the family home due to violence may not be considered to be 'vulnerable' by the housing authority if they have a network of family and friends to support them. Of course, if they have dependent children residing with them, or expected to reside with them, they will already be in priority need of housing without having to show vulnerability. It may also be possible for a person to establish that they are in priority need under the category of vulnerability where they have a child living with them, but that child is now over the age of 18, if the child himself is vulnerable. Where the child is severely handicapped he may not be able to make an application for housing on his own behalf, as he may be considered to lack the capacity to do so.[362] However, section 189(1)(c) also encompasses the carer of a vulnerable person. Provided that the applicant's homelessness is not intentional, she will qualify for an offer of accommodation which will enable her to continue to look after her vulnerable child.

8.3 INTENTIONALLY HOMELESS

If the applicant is found to be homeless and in priority need, a local authority must then assess whether or not they are intentionally homeless. Where their homelessness is unintentional, the authority are under a duty to secure accommodation that becomes available for her occupation.[363] If, however, the local authority decides that they are intentionally

---

[358] *R v Oldham MBC, ex p Garlick; R v Bexley LBC, ex p Bentham; R v Tower Hamlets LBC, ex p Begum* [1993] AC 509.

[359] Department for Communities and Local Government, *Homelessness Code of Guidance for Local Authorities* (2006), para 10.6.

[360] Ibid, para 10.7. The Guidance also stresses that dependency can be non-financial and thus a child who is over 16 and financially dependent may still lack the maturity to live independently from their parents (para 10.7).   [361] Ibid, para 10.29.

[362] *R v Oldham MBC, ex p Garlick; R v Bexley LBC, ex p Bentham; R v Tower Hamlets LBC, ex p Begum* [1993] AC 509.   [363] Section 193(2).

homeless[364] their duty is limited to providing only temporary accommodation simply in order to enable her to have a reasonable opportunity of securing her own accommodation, and to furnishing her with advice and assistance.[365] The relevant date for determining whether or not homelessness is intentional is the date the person leaves the accommodation, and the cause of homelessness must be assessed as at that date.[366] Under section 191(3), a person becomes homeless intentionally if he deliberately does or fails to do anything as a result of which he ceases to occupy accommodation which is available for his occupation and which it would be reasonable for him to continue to occupy.[367]

Local authorities are anxious to preserve scarce resources for those who cannot make housing provision for themselves. For victims of domestic violence, there is evidence to suggest that some authorities will not assist a person if they have not taken steps to attempt to secure an exclusive right to occupy their present accommodation through seeking an occupation order.[368] However, the Code of Guidance suggests that a different view is taken. It states that:

> In cases where there is a probability of violence against an applicant if they continue, or had continued, to occupy their accommodation, and the applicant was aware of measures that could have been taken to prevent or mitigate the risk of violence but decided not to take them, their decision cannot be taken as having caused the probability of violence, and thus, indirectly, having caused the homelessness. Authorities must not assume that measures which could have been taken to prevent actual or threatened violence would necessarily have been effective.[369]

The safety of the applicant is deemed to be the paramount consideration and the Guidance continues that 'in assessing whether it is likely that threats of violence are likely to be carried out, a housing authority should only take into account the probability of violence, and not actions which the applicant could take (such as injunctions against the perpetrators).'[370] In light of this it would be counter-intuitive to then suggest that an applicant who does not attempt to remain in their current accommodation by seeking an occupation order is intentionally homeless and thus only entitled to temporary accommodation and the advice of the local authority.[371]

9 DOMESTIC VIOLENCE: HUMAN RIGHTS IMPLICATIONS

As we have seen, domestic violence is a significant social problem which has not always been taken seriously by the police or the courts. One question which arises is whether domestic violence can be seen as a human rights issue. While theorising such violence under a human rights framework may help the victim, it should be remembered that it may also help the perpetrator of the violence who could argue, for example, that legal sanctions (such as an occupation order) violate his or her property rights. Once a human rights

---

[364] Housing Act 1992, s 191, as amended by the Homelessnes Act 2002.   [365] Section 190(2).
[366] *Din v Wandsworth London Borough Council* [1983] 1 AC 657.   [367] See also ss 191(3) and 196.
[368] See *R v Westminster City Council, ex p Bishop* [1993] 2 FLR 780.
[369] Department for Communities and Local Government, *Homelessness Code of Guidance for Local Authorities* (2006), para 11.13.   [370] Ibid, para 10.29.
[371] See *R v Westminster City Council, ex p Bishop* [1993] 2 FLR 780.

framework is initiated, the rights of the victim must be balanced against the competing rights of the alleged perpetrator.[372]

Domestic violence has several implications under international human rights law, as well as under the Human Rights Act 1998, which incorporates the principles of the ECHR into domestic law.

9.1 THE HUMAN RIGHTS ACT 1998

Several provisions of the ECHR are relevant to domestic violence. Article 2 requires everyone's right to life to be protected by the law and Article 3 protects individuals from torture or inhuman or degrading treatment or punishment. Section 6 of the Human Rights Act 1998 requires courts and other public authorities to act compatibly with parties' rights under the ECHR. This means that if the police or the courts fail to take reasonable steps to protect family members from violence or abuse which falls within the ambit of Article 2 or 3, they may be violating the victim's rights under the ECHR. This is the case even though it is another private individual, and not an agent of the state, who is carrying out the abuse. Indeed, the European Court of Human Rights made it very clear in *A v UK*[373] that the state is under a positive obligation to take measures to ensure that no one is subjected to inhuman or degrading treatment or punishment at the hands of another private individual.

Article 8 requires protection for an individual's right to respect for their private and family life and it could be argued that failing to protect a person from violence in the home, breaches their rights under Article 8. Balanced against this, however, is the alleged perpetrator's rights under the same Article which could be infringed by an occupation order which interferes their property rights in the home and thus with their enjoyment of their private and family life. Indeed, unlike Articles 2 and 3 of the ECHR (which are absolute rights), a person's rights under Article 8 are qualified. Interference with one's right to a private and family life may be justified under Article 8(2) if it is in accordance with the law and is deemed to be necessary on the grounds of public safety; prevention of disorder or crime; protection of health or morals; or for the protection of the rights and freedoms of others. This means that the court must conduct a balancing exercise considering both the rights of the victim and the rights of the perpetrator under Article 8.

The human rights implications of an ex parte order have already been mentioned earlier in the chapter. Under Article 6 of the ECHR, a respondent has a right to a fair and public hearing of the determination of his civil rights. This has implications for ex parte orders which are made in emergency situations where the normal notice procedures are dispensed with.[374] However, section 45(3) of the Family Law Act 1996 makes it clear that where an ex parte order is granted, the respondent must be given an opportunity to make representations relating to the order as soon as just and convenient at a full hearing. Provided the court fulfils its obligations to secure a full hearing as soon as just and convenient, Article 6 of the ECHR is unlikely to be breached.

9.2 INTERNATIONAL HUMAN RIGHTS LAW

The Human Rights Act (and the ECHR) is not the only human rights law relevant to domestic violence. The subject is also dealt with in several UN treaties, notably the Convention

---

[372] See J. Herring and S. Choudhry, 'Domestic Violence and the Human Rights Act 1998: A New Means of Legal Intervention' (2006) Public Law 752.   [373] [1998] 2 FLR 959.
[374] Family Law Act 1996, s 45.

on the Elimination of All Forms of Discrimination Against Women (CEDAW). The Convention, and several later declarations and statements, set out detailed guidelines as to what steps states should take to tackle domestic violence, among other problems. While such international human rights treaties do not give individuals direct rights in domestic courts, their provisions (if ratified) are binding on the UK Government. The UN monitors compliance with the provisions of the various treaties by requiring the production of periodic national reports to a committee, which then issues a report stating its concerns about the state of compliance in that country. This means that while the UN cannot force a state to change its policies or laws on a particular issue, the monitoring procedure can be used to try to persuade states to comply with their international obligations.[375]

International human rights law has not always been concerned with domestic violence. Thomas and Beasley suggest that there are various reasons why domestic violence has, in the past, been excluded from international human rights practice.[376] One of the main reasons is that international human rights law was historically designed to protect individuals from abuses carried out by the state as opposed to other private individuals. Domestic violence, by contrast, occurs in private and, as such, was regarded as being outside the scope of international human rights law. However, thinking began to change as it became accepted that abuse which takes place in the private sphere between private citizens is also a human rights violation for which the state is accountable.[377] As Thomas and Beasley note:

> the concept of state accountability has expanded to include not only actions directly committed by states, but also states' systemic failure to prosecute acts committed by ... private actors.[378]

The extension of state accountability to cover abuse which takes place in the private sphere, coupled with the growth in information about the gender-specific nature of domestic violence and typical low rates of prosecution, have made it possible to consider domestic violence under international human rights law.[379] Indeed, many commentators argue that gender-based violence *must* be seen as a human rights issue as this shifts conceptions of such violence from being seen as an individual problem or simply part of 'family dynamics' to a more intense focus on the actions of the perpetrator and the 'traditional complicity of law and custom in giving license to violent "impulses" against women'.[380]

As already mentioned, one of the most important UN treaties to deal with domestic violence is CEDAW. CEDAW (also known as the Women's Convention) was adopted by the UN General Assembly in 1979 and is the only international human rights treaty to focus exclusively on the rights of women. The UK ratified CEDAW in 1986. However, the provisions of CEDAW do not deal directly with the issue of domestic violence. The Committee on the Elimination of Discrimination against Women (which monitors state compliance with CEDAW) recognised that the failure explicitly to address the issue of domestic violence within the Convention was a serious omission. Thus, in 1992 the

---

[375] R. McQuigg, 'The Responses of States to the Comments of the CEDAW Committee on Domestic Violence' (2007) 11(4) International Journal of Human Rights 461.

[376] D. Thomas and M. Beasley, 'Domestic Violence as a Human Rights Issue' (1993) 15 Human Rights Quarterly 36–62.

[377] See A. S. Fraser, 'Becoming Human: The Origin and Development of Women's Human Rights Law' (1999) 21 Human Rights Quarterly 853–906.

[378] D. Thomas and M. Beasley, 'Domestic Violence as a Human Rights Issue' (1993) 15 Human Rights Quarterly 36–62 at 41. [379] Ibid.

[380] R. Copelon, 'Intimate Terror: Understanding Domestic Violence as Torture' in R. Cook (ed), *Human Rights of Women: National and International Perspectives* (Philadelphia, PA: University of Pennsylvania Press, 1994).

Committee issued General Recommendation No 19 which makes it clear that violence against women is a form of discrimination which falls within the remit of CEDAW:

> The definition of discrimination includes gender-based violence, that is, violence that is directed against a woman because she is a woman or that affects women disproportionately. It includes acts that inflict physical, mental or sexual harm or suffering, threats of such acts, coercion and other deprivations of liberty. Gender-based violence may breach specific provisions of the Convention, regardless of whether those provisions expressly mention violence.[381]

This means that the Committee, when monitoring state compliance with CEDAW, will seek information on how the problem of domestic violence is being addressed at state level. It also means that states must include in their reports to the Committee details on the prevalence of such violence and on the measures which have been taken to deal with it. This is significant for a number of reasons. First, it is symbolically important in conceptualising domestic violence as a gendered issue and a form of discrimination against women. Secondly, the monitoring procedures may encourage governments to take domestic violence seriously in order to avoid the wrath of the Committee. Thirdly, it gives activists and lobbyists working within the area the leverage to apply pressure on governments to develop strategies to tackle domestic violence in order to ensure compliance with CEDAW.[382] However, as enforcement is limited to these reporting procedures, much depends on the will of the state to comply with the provisions of the UN treaties. If a state does not comply then there is little that can be done as the UN has no real way of forcing states to alter their policies or change their laws.[383]

10 DOMESTIC VIOLENCE AND CHILD CONTACT

The fact that a parent has perpetrated domestic violence does not constitute a bar to contact with his/her children.[384] Moreover, many agree that the extent to which children are harmed by domestic violence has not always received the attention which it deserves. Certainly, until recent years allegations or findings of domestic violence had little impact at all on the issue of child contact in the aftermath of parental separation.[385] Courts tended to view violence against a parent and contact with children as separate issues and there was insufficient recognition of the effects of the violence on either the parent or the child. A presumption in favour of contact, the assumed benefits of continued contact between

---

[381] The Committee on the Elimination of Discrimination against Women, General Recommendation No 19, para 6: www.un.org/womenwatch/daw/cedaw/recommendations/recomm.htm.

[382] When Governments submit their reports to the Committee, NGOs and other lobbyists are also encouraged to submit their own 'shadow' reports outlining their own views on the compliance of the state with the provisions of CEDAW.

[383] R. McQuigg, 'The Responses of States to the Comments of the CEDAW Committee on Domestic Violence' (2007) 11(4) International Journal of Human Rights 461. It is worth noting that CEDAW has been augmented by an Optional Protocol, introduced in 1999, which provides for an individual complaints and inquiry procedure. Under the complaints procedure, the Committee can receive claims of state violations of CEDAW by individuals or groups. However, before hearing a complaint the Committee must be satisfied that all domestic remedies in relation to the issue have been exhausted. In addition, an inquiry procedure allows the Committee to initiate inquiries into situations of 'grave or systematic' violations of women's rights under CEDAW.

[384] The issue of child contact is considered more fully in Chapter 9.

[385] J. Barron, *Not Worth the Paper...? The Effectiveness of Legal Protection for Women and Children Experiencing Domestic Violence* (Bristol: Women's Aid Federation England, 1990).

a child and the non-residential parent, and the suspicion that allegations of violence were being made or encouraged by a hostile parent who opposed contact out of spite or revenge operated to minimise the impact of domestic violence on child contact arrangements.[386]

However, in recent years increased attention has been paid to the issue of contact between parents who are perpetrators of domestic violence and their children following separation. The Department of Health recognised in 2003 that:

> At least 750,000 children a year witness domestic violence. Nearly three quarters of children on the 'at risk' register live in households where domestic violence occurs.[387]

Studies have also highlighted the dangers of allowing perpetrators of domestic violence to have contact with their children. Indeed, domestic violence does not end when a relationship breaks down as victims can be exposed to even greater risk from an ex-partner. Research has established that post-separation contact between children and a violent parent, particularly during handovers, can be particularly dangerous.[388] In addition, there has been a growing awareness of the harmful effects of domestic violence on children. Not only have researchers established a clear connection between domestic violence and child abuse,[389] but it is clear that children who witness such violence (either through seeing or hearing it) also suffer significant harm. An influential report by child psychiatrists Drs Sturge and Glaser highlighted the dangers to children of witnessing domestic violence and the potential harm caused by allowing contact between a child and a violent parent.[390] They found that domestic violence was a 'very serious and significant failure in parenting' which meets any definition of child abuse.

Despite these recommendations, there is still no presumption against contact in situations of domestic violence, and allegations or findings of such violence will not constitute a bar to contact.[391] However, judicial attitudes have changed in recent years as the courts now recognise the harmful effects of domestic violence on children and their primary carers.[392] In one of the most important cases on the relevance of allegations of domestic violence on child contact disputes, the Court of Appeal laid down guidelines which direct a court to consider, amongst other things, whether the allegations are well founded and, if so, the impact of the violence on the child.[393] These guidelines reflect the need to take

---

[386] R. Bailey-Harris, J. Barron, and J. Pearce, 'From Utility to Rights? The Presumption of Contact in Practice' (1999) 13 International Journal of Law, Policy and the Family 111–131.

[387] *Into the Mainstream—Strategic Development of Mental Health Care for Women* (London: Department of Health, 2003).

[388] L. Richards, *Domestic Violence Murder Review Analysis of Findings* (London: Metropolitan Police Service, 2003).

[389] M. Hester, C. Pearson, and N. Harwin, *Making an Impact: Children and Domestic Violence—A Reader* (London: Jessica Kingsley, 2007).

[390] C. Sturge and D. Glaser, 'Contact and Domestic Violence—The Experts' Report' (2000) 30 Family Law 615.

[391] *Re L, V, M, H (Children) (Contact: Domestic Violence)* [2001] Family Law 260. See F. Kaganas, 'Re L (Contact: Domestic Violence) ... Contact and Domestic Violence' (1999) 12 Child and Family Law Quarterly 311.

[392] *Re K (Contact: Mother's Anxiety)* [1999] 2 FLR 703; *Re M (Minors) (Contact: Violent Parent)* [1999] 2 FLR 231.

[393] *Re L, V, M, H (Children) (Contact: Domestic Violence)* [2001] Fam 260. See also Practice Direction: Residence and Contact Orders: Domestic Violence and Harm [2009] All ER(D) 122 (Jan). The Court of Appeal made it clear in *Re Z (Unsupervised Contact: Allegations of Domestic Violence)* [2009] EWCA Civ 430 that while the Practice Direction was not designed to tell judges what to decide in an application for contact or residence, its purpose was to inform them of how to go about deciding such issues where there were allegations of domestic violence. For a fuller discussion of the approach of the courts when determining child contact and residence disputes, see Chapter 9.

allegations of domestic violence more seriously and to recognise that children who are exposed to violence indirectly (through seeing or hearing incidents of abuse) as opposed to being directly involved in it also suffer harm.[394] The danger associated with indirect exposure to domestic violence is also recognised in legislation. The definition of 'harm' in the Children Act 1989 for the purposes of the welfare checklist[395] and for making a care or supervision order[396] has been amended to include the 'impairment suffered from seeing or hearing the ill-treatment of another'. This means that, when making decisions regarding a child's welfare, there is a statutory obligation to consider the harm a child will suffer through witnessing domestic violence. However, it has been argued that this does not go far enough to challenge the entrenched view that contact is almost always in the best interests of the child.[397]

Despite changes in both judicial attitudes and official thinking about the seriousness of domestic violence and its impact on children, many argue that little has changed in practice and that contact between a child and a violent partner is still too readily ordered. Indeed, less than 1 per cent of applications for child contact are rejected.[398] In a study for Women's Aid, Hilary Saunders compiled a list of 29 children in 13 families who were killed by their fathers during contact arrangements between 1994 and 2004.[399] It was established that domestic violence was involved in at least 11 out of the 13 families. In addition, in five of the cases contact had been ordered by the court, and in three of these cases the court granted orders for unsupervised contact or residence to very violent fathers against professional advice. It was also found that in five cases the father killed the children in order to take revenge on his ex-partner for leaving him. As such, there have been calls for the introduction of a rebuttable statutory presumption, as in New Zealand, that contact should not be granted to a perpetrator of domestic violence unless the court is satisfied that it will be safe for the child and the other parent[400] although the government remains resistant to such a change.

DISCUSSION QUESTIONS

1. Domestic violence has historical, patriarchal, and multifaceted explanations for its prevalence. Describe the theories which attempt to explain domestic violence.

2. Do the civil law remedies available in the Family Law Act 1996 adequately protect victims of domestic violence?

---

[394] Although evidence suggests that the implementation of these guidelines has been 'patchy', DCA, DfES, and DTI, 'Parental Separation: Children's Needs and Parents' Responsibilities (Cm 6273, London: HMSO, 2004), para 48.   [395] Children Act 1989, s 1(3), see Chapter 10.

[396] Children Act 1989, s 31(9), see Chapter 10.

[397] H. Saunders, 'Twenty-Nine Child Homicides: Lessons Still to be Learnt on Domestic Violence and Child Protection' (Bristol: Women's Aid, 2004).

[398] DCA, DfES and DTI, 'Parental Separation: Children's Needs and Parents' Responsibilities, Cm 6273 (London: HMSO, 2004), para 25.

[399] H. Saunders, Twenty-Nine Child Homicides: Lessons Still to be Learnt on Domestic Violence and Child Protection (Bristol: Women's Aid, 2004).

[400] See eg Refuge, Response to Domestic Violence, Crimes and Victims Bill (July 2004); L. Radford, S. Sayers, and Aid for Mothers Involved in Contact Action (AMICA), Unreasonable Fears? Child Contact in the Context of Domestic Violence: A Survey of Mothers' Perception of Harm (Bristol: Women's Aid Federation England, 1999).

3. Occupation orders differentiate between applicants according to their legal right to occupy a property. Discuss whether this is satisfactory and what issues arise from this situation.

4. Critically evaluate the courts' approach to granting occupation orders.

FURTHER READING

BURTON, M., 'Criminalising Breaches of Civil Orders for Protection from Domestic Violence' [2003] Crim LR 301

BURTON, M., *Legal Responses to Domestic Violence* (Abingdon: Routledge-Cavendish, 2008)

CHOUDRY, S. and HERRING, J., 'Righting Domestic Violence' (2006) 20 International Journal of Law, Policy and the Family 95

HERRING, J. and CHOUDHRY, S., 'Domestic Violence and the Human Rights Act 1998: A New Means of Legal Intervention' (2006) Public Law 752

HESTER, M., *Who Does What to Whom? Gender and Domestic Violence Perpetrators* (Bristol: University of Bristol in association with the Northern Rock Foundation, 2009)

HOME OFFICE, *Domestic Violence: A National Report* (London: Home Office, 2005)

HUMPHREYS, C. and THIARA, R. K., 'Neither Justice nor Protection: Women's Experiences of Post-Separation Violence' (2003) 25 Journal of Social Welfare and Family Law 195

MADDEN-DEMPSEY, M., 'What Counts as Domestic Violence: A Conceptual Analysis' [2006] 12 William and Mary Journal of Women and the Law 301

MULLENDER, A., *Rethinking Domestic Violence* (Abingdon: Routledge, 1996)

REECE, H., 'The End of Domestic Violence' (2006) Modern Law Review 770

WALBY, S. and ALLEN, J., *Domestic Violence, Sexual Assault and Stalking: Findings from the British Crime Survey*, Home Office Research Study 276 (London: Home Office, 2004)

4

MONEY AND PROPERTY DISTRIBUTION ON MARRIAGE BREAKDOWN

INTRODUCTION

When relationships break down, questions invariably arise about whether, and if so how, the parties' property will be divided. A further issue is whether one party should be required to provide ongoing financial support to the other. The answers depend on how legal and social policy views the now-ended relationship. For spouses and civil partners there are statutory regimes which allow the courts to respond flexibly to their specific circumstances by way of orders for financial provision and property adjustment. No similar scheme applies to cohabitants who are not in a marriage or civil partnership[1] and, as we shall see in the next chapter, disputes between such cohabitants on relationship breakdown are governed by strict property law principles. This chapter will examine the legal framework which determines how money and property are distributed between spouses or civil partners when the relationship ends. The focus will be on spouses since it is in that context that the guideline case law has emerged, and the relevant statutory provisions are similar for civil partners.[2] As in many areas of family law, the legal and social policy preference is for parties to reach agreement on these issues. However, in the absence of such agreement, the courts have very wide powers to resolve disputes, and of course agreements are reached in the shadow of knowledge of how the courts are likely to exercise discretion.

1 BACKGROUND TO THE CURRENT LAW

Legislation was introduced in the early 1970s which gave the courts much greater powers to distribute the parties' assets ancillary to divorce, nullity, or judicial separation. The impetus for change was the introduction of no-fault divorce in the Divorce Reform Act 1969. The removal of 'fault' as the conceptual basis for divorce necessitated a new way of thinking about post-divorce economic obligations. It was feared that the new legislation would prove a 'Casanova's Charter', with innocent wives being divorced against their will and left in poverty. The Matrimonial Proceedings and Property Act 1970 thus

---

[1] Although there have been proposals for a scheme: see Law Commission's proposals (Law Commission, *Cohabitation: The Financial Consequences of Relationship Breakdown* (Law Com No 307, 2007). See Chapter 5.

[2] Civil Partnership Act 2004, Sch 5. The Court of Appeal has recently heard the first financial provision case involving the dissolution of a civil partnership. In *Lawrence v Gallagher* [2012] EWCA Civ 394, the Court of Appeal confirmed that the principles of financial provision following the dissolution of a civil partnership are to be applied in the same way as financial provision on divorce.

introduced wide-ranging powers to adjust property as well as to make orders for financial provision ancillary to decrees of divorce, nullity, or judicial separation. The power to adjust property was one of the main innovations of the new legislation.[3] The provisions of the 1970 Act were consolidated with the substantive law of divorce in the Matrimonial Causes Act (MCA) 1973, and are now contained in Part II of that Act.[4] They have been amended on several occasions, most notably by the Matrimonial and Family Proceedings Act 1984.

When the legislation was first enacted in 1970, it stated that the court's powers should, as far as possible, be exercised in such a way as to place the parties in the financial position in which they would have been in had the marriage not broken down and had each properly discharged his or her financial obligations and responsibilities towards the other.[5] This was known as the 'minimal loss principle'. However, it was criticised as being inconsistent with the modern notions of the dissoluble marriage and proved unworkable in practice.[6] There was a growing dissatisfaction with the law among a powerful lobby of former husbands who resented having to support their former wives for life (so-called 'alimony drones'),[7] and the Law Commission examined the law again in the early 1980s. The Law Commission reported that the consensus was for a change of emphasis rather than a radical restructuring of the law. Its recommendations which were enacted by the Matrimonial and Family Proceedings Act 1984 were that: (i) emphasis should be on giving priority to the needs of children; (ii) greater weight should be attached to the wife's earning capacity and to the desirability of both parties becoming self-sufficient (the idea of seeking to effect a clean break); and (iii) that the principle of minimal loss should be repealed to allow more emphasis to be given to the individual facts of cases. The removal of the principle of minimal loss, however, signalled the advent of an even more unpredictable discretionary system as it was not replaced by an alternative overriding objective. Instead, the statute instructed the courts to give first consideration to the welfare of any minor children and to consider the appropriateness of a 'clean break', two objectives which can pull in different directions. In the absence of an overriding objective, it has been left to the judiciary to interpret the statutory criteria. This means that we must pay close attention to case law in this area.

In 2010, the Family Procedure Rules 2010 introduced new terminology and the system is now described as 'proceedings for financial orders'.

2 THE LEGISLATIVE FRAMEWORK

The court's powers are contained principally in sections 23 to 24A of the MCA 1973. Section 23 contains what are known as 'financial provision orders': powers to make orders for periodical payments, secured periodical payments, and lump sums. Section 24

---

[3] Introducing the remedy of 'equitable distribution' of matrimonial property reflecting 'social change and compelling social need': see *Dart v Dart* [1996] 2 FLR 286 at 294.

[4] As Glendon observed, this 'sounded the death knell for the old marital property system of separation of assets, so far as divorce was concerned': see M. A. Glendon, *The Transformation of Family Law; State, Law, and Family in the United States and Western Europe* (Chicago, IL: University of Chicago Press, 1989), p 199.

[5] Matrimonial Proceedings and Property Act 1970, s 5(1). There was little discussion of this but it seems the approach taken was from the common law: see *N v N* (1928) 44 LR 324 at 328, quoted in Law Commission, *Family Law: The Financial Consequences of Divorce: The Basic Policy: A Discussion Paper* (Law Com No 103, 1980), para 9.   [6] See Law Com No 103 (1980), para 24.

[7] Cf C. Smart, *The Ties That Bind* (Abingdon: Routledge, 1984), who argues that the alimony drone was a myth.

contains powers to adjust property by way of transfer or settlement of property. Section 24A gives the court power to order the sale of property. In addition, there are powers to deal specifically with a party's pension in sections 25B–25D of the Act. The orders are discussed in detail in later sections of this chapter.

Section 25(1) and (2) gives guidance to the court on the matters to which it must have regard when deciding whether, and if so how, to exercise its powers.

Key legislation

Section 25(1) provides the court with the general direction that:

It shall be the duty of the court in deciding whether to exercise its powers…and, if so, in what manner, to have regard to all the circumstances of the case, first consideration being given to the welfare while a minor of any child of the family who has not attained the age of eighteen.

Section 25(2) then highlights particular matters, providing that:

As regards the exercise of the powers of the court…in relation to a party to the marriage, the court shall in particular have regard to the following matters—

(a) the income, earning capacity, property and other financial resources which each of the parties to the marriage has or is likely to have in the foreseeable future, including in the case of earning capacity any increase in that capacity which it would in the opinion of the court be reasonable to expect a party to the marriage to take steps to acquire;

(b) the financial needs, obligations and responsibilities which each of the parties to the marriage has or is likely to have in the foreseeable future;

(c) the standard of living enjoyed by the family before the breakdown of the marriage;

(d) the age of each party to the marriage and the duration of the marriage;

(e) any physical or mental disability of either of the parties to the marriage;

(f) the contributions which each of the parties has made or is likely in the foreseeable future to make to the welfare of the family, including any contribution by looking after the home or caring for the family;

(g) the conduct of each of the parties, if that conduct is such that it would in the opinion of the court be inequitable to disregard it;

(h) in the case of proceedings for divorce or nullity of marriage, the value to each of the parties of any benefit which by reason of the dissolution or annulment of the marriage, that party will lose the chance of acquiring.

In *Piglowska v Piglowski*[8] the House of Lords made clear that the considerations in section 25(2)(a)–(h) are not ranked in any hierarchy; consequently some factors will assume great importance in some cases, and lesser or no importance in others.

In addition, when a court is exercising its powers to make financial provision between the parties, it must consider whether a clean break or a deferred clean break order would be appropriate. The relevant legislative provisions are laid out below.

---

[8] [1999] 3 All ER 632, [1999] 2 FLR 763, HL.

Key legislation

Section 25A provides:

(1) Where on or after the grant of a decree of divorce or nullity of marriage the court decides to exercises its powers under [the legislation] in favour of a party to a marriage... it shall be the duty of the court to consider whether it would be appropriate so to exercise those powers that the financial obligations of each party towards the other will be terminated as soon after the grant of the decree of nullity as the court considers just and reasonable.

(2) Where the court decides in such a case to make a periodical payments or secured periodical payments order in favour of a party to the marriage, the court shall in particular consider whether it would be appropriate to require those payments to be made or secured only for such term as would in the opinion of the court be sufficient to enable the party in whose favour the order is made to adjust without undue hardship to the termination of his or her financial dependence on the other party.

(3) Where on or after the grant of a decree of divorce or nullity of marriage an application is made by a party to the marriage for a periodical payments or secured periodical payments order in his or her favour, then, if the court considers that no continuing obligation should be imposed on either party to make or secure periodical payments in favour of the other, the court may dismiss the application with a direction that the applicant shall not be entitled to make any further application in relation to that marriage for an order [for periodical payments or secured periodical payments].

2.1 THE COURTS' POWERS

The court can make a variety of income-based orders and property adjustment orders which redistribute the parties' capital assets on divorce, which can be combined if necessary to achieve what it considers to be a fair settlement between the parties.

2.1.1 Maintenance pending suit

Under section 22 of the MCA 1973 the courts can, on a petition for divorce, nullity, or judicial separation, order either spouse to make such periodical payments to the other pending suit as it thinks reasonable. The court will take account of all the circumstances of the case although the applicant's immediate financial needs and those of the children will be particularly relevant.[9] Maintenance has been defined widely in this context so that it is not limited to a spouse's daily living expenditure and could include a component for legal costs in situations where the applicant has no other means to fund the litigation.[10] In *A v A (Maintenance Pending Suit: Provision for Legal Fees)*[11] Holman J stated that meeting the costs of the ancillary relief claim was, outside food and housing, the applicant's most 'urgent and pressing need and expense'.[12] While Thorpe LJ suggested in *Moses-Taiga v Taiga*,[13] that the court will only exercise its jurisdiction to make a costs allowance as part of a section 22 order in exceptional cases, the Court of Appeal made it clear in *Currey v Currey*[14] that the proper test is whether the applicant 'cannot *reasonably*

---

[9] *Peacock v Peacock* [1984] 1 All ER 1069.

[10] Such orders were made in *A v A (Maintenance Pending Suit: Provision for Legal Fees)* [2001] 1 FLR 377 and *G v G (Maintenance Pending Suit: Costs)* [2002] EWHC 306 (Fam).

[11] [2001] 1 FLR 377.   [12] Ibid, 382.   [13] [2005] EWCA Civ 1013.

[14] [2006] EWCA Civ 1338 at [20]. Although this case concerned an application to increase the quantum of periodical payments under the MCA 1973, s 31 in order to meet legal costs, the court confirmed that the

procure legal advice and representation by any other means'. Note, however, that under section 22 the court can only make periodical payments and cannot make an interim lump sum order.[15]

2.1.2 Periodical payments order

Under section 23 of the MCA 1973, the court can make a periodical payments order in favour of a spouse and/or for the benefit of any child. These payments simply amount to ongoing payments of maintenance from the payer to the payee. They can be made for any amount, including a nominal sum which can be increased should the payer's circumstances change. Under section 28(1)(a) of the MCA 1973, the payments will end on the death of either party or the remarriage of the payee.[16] The payments may be paid at any regular interval, including annually and may be for a fixed period or until further order. Any order for periodical payments, however small,[17] is capable of being varied upwards should either of the spouses' circumstances alter in the future. Thus, if at the time of divorce, the parties' resources are limited, the court could make an order for a nominal sum which can be increased should the parties' circumstances change.

2.1.3 Secured periodical payments order

A secured periodical payments order can be made under section 23(1)(b). Under a secured periodical payments order, payments are secured against specific property belonging to the payer. Sometimes the chosen property is income-producing, and sometimes it is property against which the charge can be enforced with the sum due should the payer default on the payments. Usually the payer is required to transfer the property to trustees and to execute a deed of security. Normally the trusts of the deed provide that, as long as the payer makes the payments ordered to the payee, the income from the property on which the payments are secured should be paid to the payer. In this way the payer is allowed to retain some choice and control over how he fulfils the requirements of the order. The security will, of course, revert to the payer on the payee's death or remarriage;[18] or to his estate when these events occur after the payer's death.

The main advantage of a secured order over an unsecured order is that it can last for the payee's lifetime,[19] which means that when the payer dies the payee can still look to the security as a source of income. The other main advantage of a secured order is to be found in the improved opportunities for enforcement. When an unsecured order is in existence, and the payer is determined to be obdurate in refusing to pay, one response might be to make a fresh application for a secured periodical payments order, rather than to attempt

---

legal principles were the same as those which applied to determine an application for a costs allowance under s 22 (maintenance pending suit).

[15] See *Wicks v Wicks* [1998] 1 All ER 470. While such a power was to be given by the Family Law Act 1996, s 15 and Sch 2, para 3, it was never implemented.

[16] Cohabitation of the recipient with another will not automatically extinguish a periodical payments order. However, the court can take the recipient's new living arrangements into account which may result in the payments being varied or brought to an end under the MCA 1973, s 33: see *Atkinson v Atkinson* [1988] Fam 93; *Fleming v Fleming* [2004] 1 FLR 667. In *Fleming* the Court of Appeal rejected the argument that marriage should be equated with cohabitation for the purposes of bringing a periodical payments order to an end. However, in *K v K (Periodical Payment: Cohabitation)* [2005] EWHC 2886 (Fam), Coleridge J observed that the social acceptance of cohabitation had changed dramatically over the last 30 years. As such he questioned why the consequences of cohabitation should not be the same as the consequences of a further marriage on an existing periodical payments order. See also P. Moor, 'Key Developments in Ancillary Relief' [2008] Family Law 44 at 46.   [17] Even 1p a year.

[18] MCA 1973, s 28(1)(b).

[19] By contrast, an unsecured order can last only for the spouses' joint lives.

to enforce the original order. In the case of a secured order, should the payer default on the payments, the trustees of the security must make payments directly to the payee from the income produced by the security. Should that income prove to be insufficient, the trustees have power to resort to the capital. In cases where the order is secured on property which does not produce income, the amount of the arrears will be charged on the property, and the payee can realise her charge by forcing a sale. Either process could be invaluable to the payee when the payer is refusing to pay, has disappeared, has emigrated, or has defaulted for some other reason. Sometimes it might be appropriate for the order to be secured on the payer's interest in the former matrimonial home. It is relatively commonplace for the sale of the former matrimonial home to be postponed to some future date when the proceeds will then be divided between the spouses in predetermined amounts, and for one spouse to be given a right to live in it in the meantime. In a case of this kind, the periodical payments order could be secured on the payer's postponed share and, in the event of his default, his eventual share in the proceeds of sale would be reduced by the arrears outstanding. While this arrangement would not directly assist the payee to obtain a regular income, it would ensure that the payer ultimately pays for his or her default, and would give the payee a growing share in the proceeds of sale of the matrimonial home, which might be needed where income has been reduced.

Despite the advantages of the secured periodical payments order, they are now rarely made. If there is sufficient capital to provide security for periodical payments, the preferred option is to use the capital to make a clean break transfer between the parties. This can be achieved by either a lump sum or property adjustment order.

2.1.4 Lump sum

A lump sum order is 'an order that either party to the marriage shall pay to the other such lump sum or sums as may be so specified'.[20] Although the legislation refers to sums in the plural, only one lump sum order can be made.[21] The plural allows for it to be paid in instalments[22] in which case the payments can be secured[23] and interest can be ordered on the amount deferred.[24] The lump sum order is designed to represent a final order and, as such, it will not usually be varied. However, as confirmed by the Court of Appeal in *Westbury v Sampson*,[25] the court has the power under section 31(1) to re-timetable and adjust the amounts of individual instalments under a lump sum order payable by instalments and can also vary, suspend, or discharge the principal lump sum itself under such an order. However, the latter power should only be used sparingly.[26]

A lump sum may be made on the grant of a decree or at any time thereafter, but it must be remembered that the right to apply for lump sum and property adjustment orders is lost in the event of the applicant's remarriage.[27] However, provided that the application has been made before the remarriage, the court has jurisdiction even though the application is not heard until after the remarriage has taken place. One consequence of the rule that an application for financial provision and property adjustment orders cannot be made after remarriage is that it is normal practice to make an application for all types of relief at the time of the divorce. Generally speaking, this practice is sensible and desirable, and it deals with the danger of a swift remarriage depriving a spouse of his or her claim to a share in the property. However, it is clearly inadvisable to apply for an order when it is obvious that the respondent is in no position to make a lump sum payment. This is

---

[20] MCA 1973, s 23(1)(c).   [21] *Coleman v Coleman* [1972] 3 All ER 886.
[22] MCA 1983, s 23(3)(c).   [23] Section 23(3)(c).   [24] Section 23(6).
[25] [2001] EWCA Civ 4807.   [26] *Westbury v Sampson* [2001] EWCA Civ 4807 at [18].
[27] Section 28(3).

because when an application for a lump sum payment is dismissed, no further application can subsequently be made. The applicant may, therefore, have everything to lose and nothing to gain from making a comprehensive application at the time of the divorce. In a case where the respondent has no capital resources, but is likely to acquire them at a later date, for example when he will inherit under his parents' will or intestacy, it may be wiser not to make an application at the time of the divorce, but to take the chance that leave will be granted by the court at some time in the future. Alternatively, a court may be prepared to adjourn the application for a lump sum where there is a real possibility that the respondent will shortly obtain capital out of which it can be paid.[28]

Where there are sufficient resources, a lump sum order may be used to capitalise an applicant's maintenance requirements in line with the clean break principle. The *Duxbury* formula can be used to calculate the quantum to be paid via a lump sum which will be sufficient to meet the applicant's income needs. Taken from the case of *Duxbury v Duxbury*,[29] this arithmetical formula will take into account factors such as the applicant's life expectancy, the rate of inflation, and interest rates, to generate a lump sum which when invested will provide a sufficient income for the remainder of the recipient's life. However, this formula is only a guide when assessing the quantum of a lump sum order, it is not determinative. The House of Lords in *White v White*[30] referred to the 'Duxbury paradox' which means that reliance on these actuarial calculations could result in unfair outcomes on the basis that 'the longer the marriage and hence the older the wife, the less the capital sum required for a Duxbury type fund'.[31] Thus, while the Duxbury calculation may be a useful tool to capitalise maintenance requirements, it is not determinative of the final award.

2.1.5 Property adjustment orders

Section 24 enables a court to adjust the spouses' interests in the ownership of property, such as the family home, a car, furnishings, and investments,[32] so that it can make provision for the current circumstances of all the family members. It cannot be emphasised too strongly that there is no power subsequently to vary a property adjustment order. Consequently, very close attention must be paid to ensuring that any such order makes fair and just provision for each party, both immediately and in the future.[33] A property adjustment order can take various forms.

2.1.5.1 Property transfer orders

Section 24(1)(a) provides that the court may order that 'a party to the marriage shall transfer to the other party, to any child of the family or to such person as may be specified in the order' any property to which that party is entitled either in possession or reversion. Property transfer orders, like lump sum orders, may be used to bring about a clean break

---

[28] See eg *D v D (Lump Sum Order: Adjournment of Application)* [2001] 1 FLR 633 where Connell J adjourned the wife's application for a lump sum order as the husband's prospective bonus under an incentive scheme was not known at the time of the proceedings. It was emphasised, however, that this should only be done in cases where there was a real possibility of capital from a specific source becoming available in the near future and where justice to the parties could only be achieved if there was an adjournment. See also *MT v MT (Financial Provision: Lump Sum)* [1992] 1 FLR 362 and *Re G (Financial Provision: Liberty to Restore Application for Lump Sum* [2004] EWHC 88 (Fam).   [29] [1987] 1 FLR 7.

[30] [2001] AC 596.   [31] Ibid, 609.

[32] Including property owned with a third party: see eg *Harwood v Harwood* [1991] 2 FLR 274 in which the husband was ordered to assign to the wife the whole of his share of the assets of a dissolved partnership.

[33] The only possibility open to an aggrieved party is to seek leave to appeal out of time, see Section 8.1.

between the parties. This order may be made in respect of any property of the spouses, although it is usually made in respect of the matrimonial home.

2.1.5.2 Settlement orders

Section 24(1)(b) provides that the court can order a spouse to settle property for the benefit of the other party and of the children of the family, or either or any of them. A settlement arises where any property has been purchased in the spouses' joint names, or where they each have a beneficial interest in it. It includes any disposition made in favour of the spouses as spouses which makes continuing provision for them.[34] A settlement creates successive interests in land, and can be invaluable where the spouses' resources are insufficient to make adequate provision for them both, and where one spouse needs the immediate use of property more urgently than the other. It may, for example, be appropriate to direct that the matrimonial home be jointly owned, that one spouse should have exclusive use of the property for a period of time, and that the other should become entitled to his or her share in the proceeds of sale of the property when the settlement period comes to an end. In this way a settlement enables a court to make provision for one of the party's needs without entirely taking away the other party's rights in the property concerned.

2.1.6 Power of sale

Section 24A provides that:

> Where the court makes...a secured periodical payments order, an order for the payment of a lump sum or a property adjustment order, then, on making that order or at any time thereafter, the court may make a further order for the sale of such property as may be specified in the order, being property in which or in the proceeds of sale of which either or both of the parties to the marriage has or have a beneficial interest, either in possession or reversion.

This provision is an essential adjunct to those other orders, and used imaginatively it can extend and complement the court's other powers. For example, it may only be possible to order a lump sum payment if property is sold to raise the necessary cash. Sometimes one spouse is obdurate about complying with an existing lump sum order. In these circumstances, provisions in section 24A may come to the assistance of the other spouse. Thus, the court can order sale but direct that the sale shall not take effect until a specified event occurs or until after a specified period of time has expired.[35] This power could be used to coerce the obdurate spouse into compliance. Clearly there are some situations in which sale of property may be unwise: for example if ordering the sale of the former matrimonial home will result in both spouses and their children being homeless or if liquidating assets which are income-producing will destroy the owning spouse's means of earning his livelihood.[36]

Where a sale order is made, it can contain a provision requiring the proceeds to be invested in a fund designed to secure an order for periodical payments for one of the parties, but such an order will cease to have effect on the death or remarriage of that party.[37] The court can require specified property to be offered for sale to a specified person.[38]

---

[34] *Young v Young* [1962] P 27. However, an outright transfer is not a settlement, see *Prescott v Fellowes* [1958] P 260. [35] Section 24A(4).

[36] *Martin v Martin* [1976] 3 All ER 625; *P v P (Financial Provision: Lump Sum)* [1978] 3 All ER 70; *P v P (Financial Provision)* [1989] 2 FLR 241.

[37] Section 24A(5).   [38] Section 24A(2)(b).

In effect, this means that the court can give one spouse the first option to buy out the other spouse's share in the matrimonial home (or other specified property). This is a valuable provision where one spouse is hostile to the other acquiring a particular family asset, and where he or she plans to dispose of it to someone else. Where someone other than the spouses has a beneficial interest in the property in question, this does not prevent an order for sale being made. However, the court must give that person the opportunity to make representations in relation to the order which are then taken into account alongside the other matters it is required to consider under section 25.[39]

3 UNDERTAKINGS

Undertakings given to the court enable spouses to promise the court to do certain things which the court cannot order them to do because they fall outside the scope of the statutory framework.[40] As put by Butler-Sloss LJ (as she then was) in *Kensington Housing Trust v Oliver*:[41]

> Undertakings are convenient since a party can promise to do or abstain from that which a court would be unable to order. In that way an undertaking may cover a situation not capable of being the subject of a court order.

For example, it is commonplace for a husband to undertake to make the mortgage repayments on the former matrimonial home, to use his best endeavours to secure the release of the wife from her own obligations to the mortgagee, and to indemnify her should she be pursued for payments owing. Or he might undertake to take out insurance on his life in order to compensate his wife for her loss of expectation of a widow's pension,[42] to pay the children's school fees,[43] or to be solely responsible for specified debts. The advantage of arrangements agreed in this manner is that they can be more flexible, and more imaginative, than the range of orders available to courts. For example, Munby J held in *L v L*[44] that while the court was prohibited from awarding a spouse periodical payments beyond their remarriage, neither the legislation nor public policy prevented a former spouse from voluntarily assuming to pay maintenance beyond the payee's remarriage. Such a promise could be embodied in a formal undertaking.[45] Importantly, such undertakings are enforceable just as effectively as direct orders,[46] but of course a court cannot require a party who is not willing to do so to give undertakings. Undertakings, particularly when combined with consent orders, allow for consideration of a wide range of proposals about how best to untangle spouses' financial affairs, and how best to make financial and property provision for their future.

---

[39] Section 24A(6).

[40] For a general review on undertakings, see D. Burrows, 'Undertakings and Consent Orders' [1998] Fam Law 158.   [41] (1997) 30 HLR 608 at 611.

[42] *Le Marchant v Le Marchant* [1977] 3 All ER 610.

[43] *Gandolfo v Gandolfo* [1980] 1 All ER 833. See too *Omielan v Omielan* [1996] 2 FLR 306 where the husband gave up his share altogether in the house, and the wife's share was reduced from 50 per cent to 25 per cent, the children to gain the remaining 75 per cent. Such an arrangement was one which could not properly have been ordered by the court.   [44] [2008] 1 FLR 26.

[45] [2008] 1 FLR 26 at [101].   [46] *Livesey v Jenkins* [1985] 1 All ER 106.

4 EXERCISE OF THE COURT'S DISCRETION

4.1 REFUSAL TO EXERCISE DISCRETION ON POLICY GROUNDS

On rare occasions the court may refuse to exercise its discretion for reasons of public policy. In *Whiston v Whiston*[47] the 'wife' was a bigamist and applied for financial orders ancillary to nullity proceedings. The Court of Appeal refused to exercise its discretion in her favour, holding that as a matter of public policy the 'wife' should not benefit from her crime. The court held that the fact that conduct is one of the factors in section 25(2) of the MCA 1973 should not prevent the application of this doctrine. There is, however, no universal rule precluding the exercise of the court's discretion in favour of a bigamist, for example where both spouses are knowing parties to a bigamous marriage.[48]

4.2 THE COURT'S GENERAL DIRECTION IN SECTION 25(1)

4.2.1 All the circumstances

Section 25(1) enjoins the court to have regard to all the circumstances of the case. The courts are thus given a very wide discretion to make financial orders which suit the needs of individual cases, albeit guided by the various factors in the statutory framework.[49] The legislation 'provides the jurisdiction for all applications for financial relief from the poverty-stricken to the multimillionaire'[50] and so the application of the statutory criteria will depend very much on the facts and circumstances of each individual case. Thus the value of precedent is limited. The Court of Appeal can only interfere with the judge's exercise of discretion if he or she has taken into account an irrelevant matter or failed to take into account a relevant matter, or the judge's weighing of factors is plainly wrong. As Lord Hoffmann observed in *Piglowska v Piglowski*[51] appellate courts must permit pluralism in these matters. Thus there is no easy and straightforward answer to the question: 'How will the parties' property and income be divided and distributed between the spouses when their marriage is terminated by divorce?' Moreover, in many cases there will be a range of possible solutions which could either be negotiated between the spouses or ordered by a court. So the law in this area can be unpredictable, with obvious impact on the length of time sometimes needed to reach a negotiated settlement, if at all.

4.2.2 First consideration to welfare of children of the family

Section 25(1) provides that 'first' consideration must be given to the welfare whilst a minor of any child of the family who has not attained the age of 18. A child of the family is defined in section 52 of the MCA 1973 as a child of both of the parties; and any other child, not being a child who is placed with those parties as foster parents by a local authority or voluntary organisation, who has been treated by both of those parties as a child of

---

[47] [1995] 2 FLR 268.   [48] See *Rampal v Rampal* (No 2) [2001] EWCA Civ 989, [2002] Fam 85.

[49] See *Dart v Dart* [1996] 2 FLR 286 at 294 where Thorpe LJ commented: 'Parliament might have opted for a community of property system or some fraction approach. It opted instead for a wide judicial discretion that would produce a bespoke solution to fit the infinite variety of individual cases.'

[50] *Dart v Dart* [1996] 2 FLR 286 at 303, *per* Butler-Sloss LJ.   [51] [1999] 2 FLR 763, HL.

their family. Whether a child has been so treated is a matter of fact, determined according to how the parties have behaved towards the child.[52]

In *Suter v Suter and Jones*[53] the Court of Appeal explained that the words 'first consideration' mean that the child's welfare is to be 'regarded as of first importance to be borne in mind throughout consideration of all the circumstances'.[54] The section requires 'the court to consider all the circumstances…always bearing in mind the important consideration of the welfare of the children, and then try to attain a financial result which is just as between husband and wife'.[55] In that case the judge had erred by treating the child's welfare as the paramount (overriding) consideration.

The focus on the welfare of the children required by section 25(1) means that 'in the ordinary case the court's first concern will be to provide a home for the primary carer and the children' and 'in many cases the satisfaction of that need may absorb all that is immediately available'.[56] Although financial support for children themselves is dealt with in law as a separate issue, the welfare of the children will be integrally bound with the appropriate level of financial provision for the spouse who is continuing to provide the primary care for the children.[57] This will usually mean that the spouse who is looking after the children will need an appropriate home, if possible by way of retention of the use of the former matrimonial home.[58]

In cases where the parties have few assets, these financial circumstances will largely dictate the outcome as the assessment of the parties' needs will 'lean heavily in favour of the children and the parent with whom they live'.[59] However, in cases where the parties have assets which go beyond their financial needs, 'policy' questions become much more visible and 'it becomes necessary to consider the ultimate limits of the court's discretionary powers'.[60] In such situations difficult questions have to be answered about the underlying rationale for distribution of these assets.[61] The House of Lords has provided some general guidance on how the statutory framework should be applied.

4.3 THE COURTS' GENERAL GUIDANCE

Key case

White v White

In *White v White*[62] the husband and wife had been married for over 30 years. Both came from farming families and during their marriage they ran a dairy farm business in partnership.

---

[52] See further discussion in Chapter 6 on child support.   [53] [1987] Fam 111.   [54] Ibid, 123.
[55] Ibid.
[56] *Cordle v Cordle* [2002] 1 FCR 97 at [33], *per* Thorpe LJ; and see E. Jackson, F. Wasoff, M. Maclean, and R. Dobash, 'Financial Support on Divorce: The Right Mixture of Rules and Discretion?' (1993) 7 International Journal of Law and the Family 230.   [57] See eg *Waterman v Waterman* [1989] 1 FLR 380.
[58] See *B v B (Financial Provision: Welfare of Child and Conduct)* [2002] 1 FLR 555. See also the recognition in *Miller; McFarlane* [2006] UKHL 24 at [142], that the law has been extremely 'successful in retaining a home for the children'.
[59] *Dart v Dart* [1996] 2 FLR 286 at 303, *per* Butler-Sloss LJ. See J. Eekelaar, 'Some Principles of Financial and Property Adjustment on Divorce' (1979) Law Quarterly Review 253; E. Jackson, F. Wasoff, M. Maclean, and R. Dobash, 'Financial Support on Divorce: The Right Mixture of Rules and Discretion?' (1993) 7 International Journal of Law and the Family 230.
[60] *Preston v Preston* [1982] 1 All ER 41 at 47, *per* Ormrod LJ.
[61] See J. Eekelaar, 'Uncovering Social Obligations: Family Law and the Responsible Citizen' in M. Maclean (ed), *Making Law for Families* (Oxford: Hart, 2000), p 19 on the difficulty the courts found with identifying underlying rationales for provision.   [62] [2001] 1 AC 596.

One farm belonged to the couple jointly, having been purchased with the assistance of a mortgage and a loan from Mr White's father; and the other, which had been inherited from the husband's father, was in the husband's sole name. The couple's net assets were worth £4.6 million, £1.5 million of which belonged to the wife. When the marriage broke down, the trial judge awarded Mrs White £980,000, to meet what were seen as her 'reasonable requirements' by way of provision of a home and a lump sum to provide her with an income for life.[63] Thus, under the order the wife was to receive slightly over one-fifth of the parties' total assets. In adopting this approach, the judge was following Court of Appeal authority[64] which had established that even in big money cases a spouse's award would be limited to reasonable requirements assessed in light of the available wealth and the marital standard of living. On the wife's appeal to the Court of Appeal, the amount of the husband's payment was increased to £1.5 million which meant that, after deducting the parties' costs, her share was increased to about two-fifths. The husband appealed to the House of Lords seeking the restoration of the trial judge's order, and the wife cross-appealed seeking an order giving her an equal share in all the assets. The key issue for the House of Lords was the principles that should determine applications for financial relief in so-called 'big money' cases where the assets exceed the parties' financial needs in terms of housing and income. The facts of the case starkly called into question the 'reasonable requirements' approach, since Mrs White received less than her share of jointly owned property, and she would have fared better under partnership law than she did in the ancillary relief jurisdiction.

The House of Lords could find no justification for departing from the outcome reached by the Court of Appeal. Lord Nicholls of Birkenhead delivered an opinion with which all their Lordships agreed.[65] He indicated that 'the objective must be to achieve a fair outcome'[66] and the courts' 'powers must always be exercised with this objective in view, giving first consideration to the welfare of the children'.[67] His Lordship recognised, however, that 'fairness, like beauty, lies in the eye of the beholder'.[68] He therefore stressed the desirability of identifying guiding principles as clearly as possible in order to 'promote consistency in court decisions and in order to assist parties and their advisers and mediators in resolving disputes by agreement as quickly and inexpensively as possible'.[69]

By way of guidance, the House of Lords introduced a non-discrimination principle, indicating that in 'seeking to achieve a fair outcome, there is no place for discrimination between husband and wife and their respective roles'.[70] As Lord Nicholls explained:

> whatever the division of labour chosen by [the parties]…if, in their different spheres, each contributed equally to the family, then in principle it did not matter which of them earned the money and built up the assets. There should be no bias in favour of the money-earner and against the home-maker and the child-carer.[71]

He then went on to advise that:

> a judge would always be well advised to check his tentative views against the yardstick of equality of division. As a general guide, equality should be departed from only if, and to the extent that, there is good reason for doing so. The need to consider and articulate

---

[63] A Duxbury fund: see *Duxbury v Duxbury (Note)* [1992] Fam 62.

[64] See *O'D v O'D* [1976] Fam 83; *Page v Page* (1981) 2 FLR 198 at 201; *Preston v Preston* [1982] Fam 17 at 25; *Dart v Dart* [1996] 2 FLR 286; and cf *Conran v Conran* [1997] 2 FLR 615. As Baroness Hale has described the practice, 'the wife was entitled to her "reasonable requirements" (preferably capitalised) and the husband got the rest': *Miller; McFarlane* [2006] UKHL 24 at [135].

[65] Lord Cooke of Thorndon added a short judgment by way of supplement and emphasis.

[66] [2001] 1 AC 596 at 604.   [67] Ibid, 605.   [68] Ibid, 599.   [69] Ibid, 600.

[70] Ibid, 605.   [71] Ibid.

reasons for departing from equality would help the parties and the court to focus on the need to ensure the absence of discrimination.[72]

Lord Nicholls was clear that this was 'not to introduce a presumption of equal division under another guise'[73] since 'a presumption of equal division would go beyond the permissible bounds of interpretation of section 25'.[74] Neither is there a starting point of equality since 'a starting point principle of general application would carry a risk that in practice it would be treated as a legal presumption'.[75]

The House of Lords rejected the 'reasonable requirements' ceiling as expressed in the earlier Court of Appeal authorities. Lord Nicholls commented that the statutory provisions 'lend no support to the idea that a claimant's financial needs, even interpreted generously and called reasonable requirements, are to be regarded as determinative' and that there was 'much to be said for returning to the language of the statute'.[76]

The final issue addressed related to inherited property or property brought into a marriage by one spouse. Lord Nicholls explained the view that such property comes from a source external to the marriage and that in fairness the owning spouse should be permitted to keep it. He pointed out that in English law, when present, this factor is one of the circumstances of the case and the judge should assess its importance, and other relevant matters including the 'nature and value of the property, and the time when and circumstances in which the property was acquired'.[77] However, 'in the ordinary course, this factor can be expected to carry little weight, if any, in a case where the claimant's financial needs cannot be met without recourse to this property'.[78] Applying this approach to the facts of the case, Lord Nicholls concluded that the 'initial cash contribution made by Mr White's father in the early days cannot carry much weight 33 years later'.[79]

Talking point

The decision in *White* got a mixed reception amongst commentators. One leading commentator, Stephen Cretney,[80] wondered whether it might have been a trifle rash for the House of Lords to overrule, in an untypical case like *White*, the well-settled practice of the courts. He was led to the view that legislation was now required. He commented that it does not follow that a spouse should be entitled to the division of assets which might have been made had Parliament in 1970 not specifically rejected the incorporation of community of property in marriage. He argued that it may be rather simplistic to equate home-making contributions with commercially motivated money-making activity. Other commentators were more welcoming of the decision, but pointing out, as Professor Cooke did, that *White* raised a whole host of further issues (eg whether and how it would apply to shorter marriages, to the not-so-diligent spouse, or in cases of scarce resources).[81] Professor Bailey-Harris welcomed the case as a step towards marriage as an equal partnership but questioned the extent to which it provides workable guidance.[82] Did it, she asked, elevate contributions in the same way as the reasonable requirements approach had elevated needs? She predicted (correctly as we shall see) that there would be scope in future for argument

---

[72] Ibid.   [73] Ibid.   [74] Ibid, 606.

[75] Ibid. Lord Cooke doubted 'whether the labels "yardstick" or "check" will produce any result different from "guidelines" or "starting point"' ([2001] 1 AC 596 at 615).   [76] Ibid, 608.

[77] Ibid, 610.   [78] Ibid.   [79] Ibid, 611.   [80] [2001] Fam Law 3.

[81] See E. Cooke, 'White v White—A New Yardstick for the Marriage Partnership' [2001] Child and Family Law Quarterly 81.

[82] R. Bailey-Harris, 'Dividing the Assets on Family Breakdown: The Content of Fairness' [2001] Current Legal Problems 533.

over whether there had been equality of contribution. Bailey-Harris pointed out that the House's analysis of equality was simple formal equality, and that substantive equality may require more than equal division. She questioned the ability of the statute to provide justice or equality given the lack of any clear objective. While inappropriate, at the very least the reasonable requirements approach provided some certainty in predicting and assessing the likely outcome of cases.[83]

Key case

Miller v Miller; McFarlane v McFarlane

An opportunity for the House of Lords to clarify the law further arose in two cases heard together, *Miller v Miller; McFarlane v McFarlane*.[84] In *Miller*, the spouses were married for two years and nine months and had no children. The marriage broke down because of the husband's relationship with another woman. The husband was a very wealthy accountant and unit trust fund manager. In 2000 he had earned a cash payment of £13 million and subsequently acquired shares worth £12–18 million. The wealth creation in relation to the shares took place during the period of the marriage. The wife, who had a good career before giving it up during the marriage to concentrate on renovation projects, had net assets in the region of £100,000. At first instance Singer J awarded the wife £5 million (£2.3 million for a home and a £2.7 million lump sum). He said that Mr Miller had given his wife a legitimate expectation that she would be living on a higher financial plain in the future, and took into account that it was the husband's marital misconduct which had brought the marriage to an end. The husband's appeal was dismissed by the Court of Appeal which similarly held that the judge had been entitled to take into account that the husband was responsible for the breakdown of the marriage as a 'defence' to the shortness of the marriage. The husband further appealed to the House of Lords.

In *McFarlane v McFarlane* the parties were married for 16 years and had three children. Both were professionally qualified, the wife as a solicitor and the husband as an accountant. After the second child was born, the wife gave up her job. The husband proceeded in his career to a partnership in an accountant's firm, earning £753,000 net per annum. The parties assets were valued at £3 million and they agreed an equal share, the wife retaining the matrimonial home worth £1.5 million. The only dispute was as to the level of the wife's periodical payments. The husband's income represented a significant surplus after the parties' needs had been satisfied and the key question was the basis upon which this should be distributed, if at all. In the first instance, the district judge ordered £250,000 per annum (which was approximately 33 per cent of husband's current net income). Bennett J reduced this to £180,000 per annum and, on appeal, the Court of Appeal restored the original order, albeit for a five-year extendable term to enable the wife to accumulate a capital reserve.[85]

---

[83] See per Ormrod LJ in *S v S* [1977] 1 All ER 56.

[84] [2006] UKHL 24, [2006] 2 AC 618. For comment see E. Cooke, 'Miller/McFarlane: Law in Search of Discrimination' [2007] Child and Family Law Quarterly 98; District Judge Glen Brasse, 'It's Payback Time! Miller, McFarlane and the Compensation Culture' [2006] Family Law 647; L. Glennon, 'Obligations between Adult Partners: Moving from Form to Function?' (2008) 22(1) International Journal of Law, Policy and the Family 22.

[85] For commentary on the Court of Appeal decision in *McFarlane*, see K. O'Donovan, 'Flirting with Academic Categorizations—*McFarlane v McFarlane and Parlour v Parlour*' [2005] Child and Family Law Quarterly 418.

MORE GENERAL GUIDANCE

Two main opinions were delivered, by Lord Nicholls and Baroness Hale respectively.

Lord Nicholls made clear that the principles in *White* are applicable to all marriages. He acknowledged, however, that the removal of the needs-based approach had 'accentuated the need for some further judicial enunciation of general principle'.[86] He pointed out that an important aspect of fairness is that 'like cases are decided alike' and therefore the court must articulate, if only in the broadest fashion, what the applicable principles are.[87] Lord Nicholls then set out three underlying rationales for a seeking to achieve fairness:

(i) *The needs of the parties*, reflecting their interdependence. Most cases will end here.[88]

(ii) *Compensation* aimed at addressing any significant prospective economic disparity due to the manner in which the marriage was conducted.[89] Lord Nicholls acknowledged that there is potential overlap between needs and compensation and indicated that there is no invariable rule on how they are to be approached.

(iii) *Sharing*: the idea of marriage as a partnership of equals right from the outset, with spouses sharing the financial fruits of the marital partnership.[90] Lord Nicholls made clear that this applies equally to a short marriage as a long one[91] and the House disapproved of the idea that a non-earning spouse would accrue a share in the marital assets over time.[92]

Lord Nicholls said that the court must have regard to all property but need not treat all property the same. Here Lord Nicholls distinguished, as he had done in *White*, between marital and non-marital property (eg gifts, inheritances, or other property brought into the marriage), but he was of the opinion that the courts should be slow to introduce a distinction between 'family assets' and 'business assets'. Lord Nicholls indicated that the position in relation to non-marital assets was summarised in *White*. He added:

24 In the case of a short marriage fairness may well require that the claimant should not be entitled to a share of the other's non-matrimonial property. The source of the asset may be a good reason for departing from equality. This reflects the instinctive feeling that parties will generally have less call upon each other on the breakdown of a short marriage.

25 With longer marriages the position is not so straightforward. Non-matrimonial property represents a contribution made to the marriage by one of the parties. Sometimes, as the years pass, the weight fairly to be attributed to this contribution will diminish, sometimes it will not. After many years of marriage the continuing weight to be attributed to modest savings introduced by one party at the outset of the marriage may well be different from the weight attributable to a valuable heirloom intended to be retained in specie.

He added another relevant matter, the way the parties organised their financial affairs, and that the court can distinguish property with the necessary degree of particularity or generality as the circumstances dictate.

---

[86] Ibid, [8].   [87] Ibid, [6]. See also per Baroness Hale at [122].

[88] Ibid, [11]; [138]–[139] *per* Lord Nicholls and Baroness Hale.

[89] Ibid, [13]; [140] *per* Lord Nicholls and Baroness Hale.

[90] Ibid, [16]–[17]; [141]–[143] *per* Lord Nicholls and Baroness Hale.   [91] Ibid, [17].

[92] Ibid, [19]. This approach had been suggested in *GW v RW (Financial Provision: Departure from Equality)* [2003] 2 FLR 108 at 121–122, and see J. Eekelaar, 'Asset Distribution on Divorce—The Durational Element' (2001) 117 LQR 552. Cf R. Bailey-Harris, 'Comment on *GW v RW (Financial Provision: Departure from Equality)*' [2003] Family Law 388.

Addressing some of the general issues raised by the *McFarlane* case, Lord Nicholls held that periodical payments are not confined to maintenance and can be made for the purpose of affording compensation. The desirability of the clean break should be a sufficient reason for depriving the claimant of compensation.

Baroness Hale delivered an opinion which, in the main, reflected what Lord Nicholls had said. However, Baroness Hale indicated that arguments about the provenance of some business assets could not be ignored. Unlike Lord Nicholls she made a distinction between family assets and non-family business assets. Family assets are the home and its contents, other assets obviously acquired for the benefit of the family, for example holiday homes, furniture, caravans, family savings, including family businesses/joint ventures. By contrast, business or investment assets generated solely or mainly by the efforts of one party, that is, 'non-business partnership non-family assets' are not to be treated as family assets.[93] The distinction is founded on the basis that there is no obvious causal connection between the home-making contributions of the primary carer and the creation of these assets. The balance of opinion amongst the Lords appeared to favour the approach of Baroness Hale.[94]

THE SPECIFIC ISSUES RAISED BY THE FACTS OF *MILLER* AND *MCFARLANE*

Having set out the general principles, the House then addressed the specific issues raised in the cases. In *Miller* the marriage was less than three years in duration. Prior to this case the courts' approach in such cases tended to try to restore the parties to their position had the marriage not existed. The House made clear that, in light of the principles discussed earlier, that approach is no longer valid. The House also held that Singer J had been wrong to talk of the legitimate expectation of wealth that the husband had given the wife, since this would be tantamount to re-introducing the principle of minimal loss. In addition, the judge and the Court of Appeal had been wrong to take account of the husband's matrimonial conduct (in having an affair). The statute draws the line at conduct which it would in the opinion of the court be inequitable to disregard. As we shall see later in this chapter, by this is meant conduct which is material to the fairness of the proceedings, sometimes characterised as 'obvious and gross' conduct. It does not include 'run-of-the-mill' marital misconduct leading to a divorce. The House of Lords agreed with the judge's overall assessment. Having regard to the marital standard of living and the accretion of wealth during the marriage, the House considered the award of £5 million, amounting to less than one-sixth of the value of the husband's total worth,[95] was not inappropriate.

However, basing the decision on the career sacrifices made by Mrs McFarlane, the House of Lords restored the joint lives order on the grounds that, over and above her financial needs, she was entitled to compensation for her economic disadvantage arising as a result of the division of labour within the marriage. This, according to Lord Nicholls, resulted in the double-loss of a 'diminution in her earning capacity and the loss of a share in husband's enhanced income'.[96] Thus, it seems that a compensatory award can mitigate both opportunity costs and expectation losses.[97] The House concluded that the five-year limitation on the

---

[93] [2006] UKHL 24, [2006] 2 AC 618 at [150].

[94] Lord Hoffmann agreed with Lady Hale, as did Lord Mance who noted that in relation to 'non-business partnership, non-family assets' the yardstick of equal sharing 'may not apply with the same force especially in the case of short marriages' (p 168). Lord Hope agreed with both Lord Nicholls *and* Lady Hale.

[95] Ibid, [73] *per* Lord Nicholls.   [96] Ibid, [13] *per* Lord Nicholls.

[97] At [13]. However, the interaction between the two is unclear. Can these elements operate independently of one another? Eg a wife who did not ostensibly sacrifice a lucrative career will still, on divorce, lose the opportunity to share in her husband's enhanced income. Will this only be compensable for a wife whose commitment at home, which allowed the husband to concentrate on his career unfettered by daily caring responsibilities, resulted in a tangible (non-speculative) loss in her own earning capacity? For a wife who

periodical payments order should be removed. The Lords considered that the responsibility of applying for any variation to the term should rest with the husband, especially in light of the high threshold which is set for justifying an extension of the term.[98]

Reading the two leading decisions together, the ethos of the two guiding principles in *White* (the non-discrimination principle and the yardstick of equal division) have now been incorporated within three bases of wealth distribution. Financial need, once the ceiling in big money cases, is now just one part of a more complex financial award. The net result is a more complex, layered approach to the redistribution of assets which has required, and continues to require, further clarification by the courts.

4.4 CLARIFICATION IN SUBSEQUENT CASE LAW

One question which arose following *Miller; McFarlane* was whether the equal sharing principle was still to be treated as an end-of-assessment yardstick, as stated in *White*, or whether it was now perhaps to be viewed as a starting point for the redistribution exercise. In *Charman v Charman*,[99] the Court of Appeal held that following *Miller; McFarlane* the question of equality need no longer be postponed to the end of the statutory exercise. The yardstick of equality propounded in earlier cases is now a principle of financial provision law[100] and any departure is not from the principle but takes place within the principle. The starting point of every inquiry in an application for financial orders is the financial position of the parties. The inquiry is always in two stages, namely computation and distribution; the court must decide what assets are available to the parties and then decide how they should be distributed. The Court of Appeal confirmed in *Charman* that once the parties' assets have been established, the equal sharing principle is now a starting point for the distributive exercise rather than an end-of-assessment yardstick. Unhelpfully, however, in *B v B*[101] the Court of Appeal appeared to suggest that the principle should be applied as a yardstick[102] although emphasised that the decision depended on the unusual facts of the case and thus should not be regarded as establishing any new point of principle.[103] The Court of Appeal also confirmed in *Charman* that the sharing principle applies to all property, but there are likely to be better reasons to depart from equality with non-matrimonial property.

A further issue which arose was whether the *White* principles apply to the division of income. In *McFarlane v McFarlane; Parlour v Parlour*[104] Thorpe LJ posed the following question:

> If the decision in [*White*] introduces the yardstick of equality for measuring a fair division of capital, why should the same yardstick not be applied as the measure for the division of income?[105]

While the Court of Appeal did not provide a clear answer, it seemed to draw a distinction between the distribution of capital and income on the basis that while the division of

---

did not make such a clear sacrifice, will the expectation loss associated with the divorce simply evidence her financial needs as she loses the opportunity to enjoy the resource of her husband's income?

[98] See *Fleming v Fleming* [2003] EWCA Civ 1841.

[99] [2007] EWCA Civ 503. For commentary, see J. Miles, '*Charman v Charman (No 4)*—Making Sense of Need, Compensation and Equal Sharing after *Miller/McFarlane*' [2008] Child and Family Law Quarterly 378.

[100] Ibid, [65]. For criticism, see S. Davis, 'Equal Sharing: A Judicial Gloss Too Far?' [2008] Family Law 428 (arguing that the working wife suffers a detriment relative to the non-working wife, in that if she works she will not be compensated for loss of a career, ie, the non-working wife is rewarded for not working).

[101] [2008] EWCA Civ 543.   [102] Ibid, [50]–[60].   [103] Ibid, [57], [60].
[104] [2004] EWCA Civ 872.   [105] Ibid, [4].

capital can be seen as the division of the 'accumulated fruits of past-shared endeavours' the same could not be said of future income.[106]

4.5 THE STATUTORY FACTORS: SECTION 25(2)

Section 25(2) provides a list of factors to which the court must have regard when deciding upon an ancillary relief application.

4.5.1 Financial resources of each spouse

Key legislation

Specifically, section 25(2)(a) provides that the court must have regard to:

the income, earning capacity, property and other financial resources which each of the parties to the marriage has or is likely to have in the foreseeable future, including in the case of earning capacity any increase in that capacity which it would in the opinion of the court be reasonable to expect a party to the marriage to take steps to acquire.

Section 25(2)(a) concentrates attention on the spouses' resources. In *Pearce v Pearce*[107] Ormrod LJ commented that:

The word 'resources' in s. 25 is entirely unqualified, there are no words of limitation upon it, and so the court should approach the matter realistically, taking into account all the available resources and doing justice in all the circumstances of the case between the spouses in a realistic fashion, dealing with real figures and not with artificially produced figures.[108]

Thus, for example, the court has taken account of inherited wealth acquired after the parties separated, and which in no way formed part of the original matrimonial assets.[109] Expectations of inheritance give rise to difficulty because there is no knowing when the testator will die and whether his or her will may be altered. These expectations have therefore sometimes been deemed too uncertain to be included.[110] In some cases, however, the court may adjourn the proceedings pending receipt of the inheritance.[111] However, the courts have been prepared, in principle, to take account of all present and future resources and they have been prepared to widen the purse to the maximum extent. Personal injury damages awarded under all heads of damage, including for pain and suffering and loss of amenity, can be taken into account.[112] The manner of the distribution of such damages is, of course, still a matter within the court's discretion, and likely to be influenced by paragraph (e), which looks to any mental or physical disability of either party. Moreover, where the injured party has very considerable needs there may be no readily available capital which is transferable to the other party.[113]

A difficulty occurs where a spouse enjoys access to wealth but is not entitled to it, or where he or she has substantial means but has an immediate liquidity problem. In *Thomas v Thomas*[114]

---

[106] J. Eekelaar, 'Shared Income After Divorce: A Step too Far' (2005) LQR 1. See *Jones v Jones* [2011] EWCA Civ 41.

[107] [1980] 1 FLR 261.   [108] Ibid, 267.   [109] *Schuller v Schuller* [1990] 2 FLR 193.

[110] *Michael v Michael* [1986] 2 FLR 389; *K v K (Conduct)* [1990] 2 FLR 225.

[111] See eg *MT v MT (Financial Provision: Lump Sum)* [1992] 1 FLR 366 where the husband was entitled to a substantial inheritance from his elderly father under German law. Bracewell J adjourned the proceedings until the inheritance vested, although it seems that this power will only be exercised in unusual cases.

[112] *Daubney v Daubney* [1976] 2 All ER 453; *Wagstaff v Wagstaff* [1992] 1 All ER 275.

[113] *C v C (Financial Provision: Personal Damages)* [1995] 2 FLR 171.   [114] [1995] 2 FLR 668.

the husband was a prosperous businessman and the court would normally have made a substantial financial order for the benefit of the wife and children. However, he had a large loan secured on the family home and he claimed that he was unable to offer any alternative security which would be acceptable to the bank. He also stated that his immediate income was modest. However, this was because it was derived from a family business of which he was joint managing director, and the company had a policy of ploughing back profits and paying relatively modest salaries to the directors, while at the same time making very generous provision for them by way of pension provision. The Court of Appeal adopted a robust approach. Waite LJ made it plain that 'the court is not obliged to limit its orders exclusively to resources of capital or income which are shown actually to exist. The availability of unidentified resources may, for example, be inferred from a spouse's expenditure or style of living, or from his inability or unwillingness to allow complexity of his affairs to be penetrated with the precision necessary to ascertain his actual wealth or the degree of liquidity of his assets.' Moreover 'there will be occasions when it becomes permissible for a judge deliberately to frame his orders in a form which affords judicious encouragement to third parties to provide the maintaining spouse with the means to comply with the court's view of the justice of the case'.[115] However, this must be viewed alongside the general rule that, when assessing resources, the court cannot take account of the assets of a third party. As such, the willingness of the court to make an award which can only be met through the provision of funds from a third party is limited. In *TL v ML*[116] the claimant wife argued that the court should take into account the husband's parents' resources under section 25(2)(a) and that the court should 'judicially encourage' his parents to make funds available to meet her award. The court rejected this claim on the basis that the husband had no beneficial interest in these assets and, as such, it would be wrong in principle to make an award which ranged outside resources which were the husband's as of right.[117] In *TL v ML* the court commented:

> if the court is satisfied on the balance of probabilities that an outsider will provide money to meet an award that a party cannot meet from his absolute property then the court can, if it is fair to do so, make an award on that footing. But if it is clear that the outsider, being a person who has only historically supplied bounty, will not, reasonably or unreasonably, come to the aid of the payer then there is precious little the court can do about it.[118]

4.5.1.1 Income and earning capacity

The court must have regard to any income and earning capacity, and the reference to increase in earning capacity in section 25(2)(a) reinforces the clean break provisions in section 25A, and the thinking that, where appropriate, the aim should be to enable the spouses to become financially independent of one another. This is discussed further in Section 4.6 on the clean break.

One issue which the courts have had to grapple with is whether earning capacity should be viewed as a capital asset of the marriage. The Court of Appeal in *Charman v Charman*[119] accepted that certain dicta of Baroness Hale in *Miller; McFarlane*[120] could be relied upon to construct an argument that a spouse's earning capacity might be

---

[115] Ibid, 670. The husband was appealing against a lump sum order of £150,000 plus £8,000 for a car and periodical payments of £1,500 per month on the ground that he had neither the capital nor income to pay because his resources were all absorbed by the family business. His appeal was dismissed.

[116] [2006] 1 FCR 465.

[117] The court noted that, by contrast, in *Thomas v Thomas* [1996] 2 FLR 668 'no part of the ancillary relief award ranged over assets or income that were not Mr Thomas' as of right', at [82].

[118] [2006] 1 FCR 465 at [101].   [119] [2007] EWHC Civ 503.

[120] See *Miller; McFarlane* at [149].

considered as a capital asset. However, the court concluded that this was an issue of 'complexity and potential confusion' which did not fall to be determined in the context of the case. In *Jones v Jones*[121] the Court of Appeal clarified that a spouse's earning capacity is not to be capitalised or otherwise brought into account for the purpose of the sharing principle.

If a spouse deliberately reduces his working hours, gives up a job, or is paid less than the normal rate for the work he is doing, the court can base its order on what he or she could earn.[122] A court may deem a person to be deliberately unemployed and make an order on the assumption that they could obtain work if they tried.[123] However, there is a risk that a court will make the assumption that a spouse could obtain work if he or she makes the effort, without there being any real evidence to substantiate this approach. The danger to the spouse who is wrongly labelled as 'work shy' by a court, and being ordered to make periodical payments on the basis of what the court believes him to be capable of earning, was graphically spelled out by Finer J in *Williams v Williams*,[124] when he reminded courts that the ultimate sanction for non-payment of periodical payments is imprisonment. He also stated that it is wrong for courts to make decisions on the footing of impressions about demeanour or generalised local knowledge, important as these factors may be, unchecked by all the hard information that may be available about a man's earning capacity and his chances of employment.[125] These were salutary words, which should be borne in mind particularly at times of high unemployment. There is a real risk that orders may be based on hunch and prejudice, especially if the political climate is one in which those persons who cannot obtain work are labelled as lacking the requisite initiative and drive to seek the employment which is allegedly available.

4.5.1.2 Resources provided by a new spouse or partner

One of the most difficult issues of principle and policy which a court may have to grapple with is to what extent, if at all, it should take account of a new partner's resources when considering the spouses' resources. This difficulty is exacerbated when the new relationship is an unmarried relationship.[126] The simple answer to the question whether property belonging to a new spouse or partner can be treated as a resource under section 25(2)(a) is 'yes'. However, the extent to which a new spouse or partner's resources will influence the way the parties' own assets are distributed is a question for the discretion of the judge, 'not to be circumscribed by declarations of principle which run the risk of fettering the future exercise of what was meant to be a very flexible discretion indeed'.[127]

If, after *White v White*,[128] the focus is on the parties' entitlement to the assets, rather than simply being limited to satisfying the economically vulnerable party's financial needs, then remarriage, or cohabitation, or their prospect, is likely to assume little significance on that issue. However, there will be cases where there are barely enough assets to meet the basic financial needs of both parties. Where the resources available for distribution are being stretched, then the actual, or anticipated, contribution by a

---

[121] [2011] EWCA Civ 41, [2012] Fam 1.
[122] *Hardy v Hardy* (1981) 2 FLR 321.   [123] *McEwan v McEwan* [1972] 2 All ER 708.
[124] [1974] 3 All ER 377.
[125] See *N v F* [2011] EWHC 586 (Fam), [2012] 1 FCR 139 (evidence required, not anecdotal scraps).
[126] Given that unmarried couples, in legal terms, do not owe each other mutual obligations of financial support, it would be inconsistent then to *assume* that the cohabiting couple will share their resources and provide for each other.   [127] *Atkinson v Atkinson (No 2)* [1996] 1 FLR 51 at 54.
[128] [2001] AC 596.

new spouse or partner will assume greater significance and may need to be taken fully into consideration by the court when it decides what orders to make. It will normally not be possible for a court accurately to quantify the extent of a new spouse's, or partner's, assets, because he or she cannot usually be compelled to give precise evidence of means to the court.[129] However, as the court pointed out in *Frary v Frary*,[130] where the husband cannot persuade his partner to give such evidence, he takes the risk that the court will base its order on general assertions and assumptions about the extent of the new partner's means.[131]

For example, the fact that one spouse has accommodation provided by a new spouse may lead to the postponement of the realisation of his or her interest in the property, and to the quantification of his or her share in the value of the property being reduced. In *Martin v Martin*[132] the husband was living with a woman, whom he intended to marry, in her council house. He gave evidence that the tenancy could be transferred into their joint names. The court took account of the husband's occupation of the council house and treated it as part of his resources affecting his needs. Consequently, it gave the wife a life interest in the former matrimonial home, followed by an equal division of the proceeds of sale.[133] Provision made for the husband by a second partner was taken into account in *Mesher v Mesher and Hall*.[134] Here the woman whom the husband intended to marry had provided a deposit for their new home. Her injection of these resources meant that the husband's housing needs were being met, whereas the wife needed to live in the former matrimonial home. The wife's greater needs led to the husband's entitlement to receive his share in the proceeds of sale of the former matrimonial home being postponed until the spouses' youngest child reached 17.

4.5.1.3 Periodical payments where a spouse is living with a new partner

Under section 28(1)(a) of the MCA 1973, an order for periodical payments automatically comes to an end when the recipient spouse remarries. This rule does not apply to a party's mere cohabitation with another. However, the court can take the recipient's new living arrangements into consideration which may result in the payments being varied or brought to an end under section 33.[135] In *Atkinson v Atkinson*[136] it was argued that a wife who cohabits permanently with another man should not be in a better position than a wife who remarries, especially if the motive for cohabitation rather than remarriage is financial. In *Atkinson* the wife was receiving £6,000 per annum in periodical payments which she would automatically lose if she remarried. The man with whom she was living had only a very modest income, and she was therefore heavily reliant on the money she was receiving from her ex-husband. The Court of Appeal held that the fact of cohabitation is a matter to be taken into account by the court, and is conduct which it would be

---

[129] *Wynne v Wynne and Jeffers* [1980] 3 All ER 659; *Frary v Frary* [1993] 2 FLR 696; *Morgan v Morgan* [1977] 2 All ER 515. The court held in *M v M (Financial Misconduct; Subpoena Against Third Party)* [2006] 2 FCR 555, Art 8 of the European Convention on Human Rights (right to respect for private and family life, home and correspondence) reinforces the 'principle that an order for disclosure is an intrusion into an individual's privacy that is oppressive and unwarranted unless it can be shown to be both necessary and proportionate to the issues in the case', at [115].   [130] [1993] 2 FLR 696.

[131] See also *W v W (Disclosure by Third Party)* (1981) 2 FLR 291.   [132] [1977] 3 All ER 762.

[133] This case was heavily influenced by the policy target under s 25 as originally drafted. However, the principle is clear, namely that housing provided by a new partner is a relevant consideration.

[134] [1980] 1 All ER 126n.

[135] *Atkinson v Atkinson* [1988] Fam 93; *Fleming v Fleming* [2004] 1 FLR 667.

[136] [1987] 3 All ER 849.

inequitable to disregard under paragraph (g). Thus, according to the court, the financial consequences of cohabitation may be such that it would be inappropriate for maintenance to continue because the cohabitant can be expected to contribute to the running costs of the household. However, the court stated that, in general, there is no statutory requirement to give decisive weight to the fact of cohabitation and that it should *not* be equated with remarriage without legislative sanction.[137]

Another attempt to persuade the Court of Appeal that it was manifestly unjust for a cohabiting wife of a wealthy ex-husband to receive anything other than nominal periodical payments was made in *Atkinson v Atkinson (No 2)*.[138] The court rejected this submission, stating that it was 'too crude a view', and held that Thorpe J had been entitled to take into account 'the length of the marriage, the contribution made during the marriage by the wife to the care of the home, the upbringing of the children...and the opportunity she provided to the husband to pursue his very successful business activities'.[139] On the broader policy issue of the proper principles to be adopted in cases where a spouse is living in a new and permanent relationship, the Court of Appeal responded that Parliament had intended that this should be a matter for the discretion of the judge, and that the discretion should not be circumscribed by declarations of principle which ran the risk of fettering the exercise of what was meant to be a very flexible discretion indeed.[140] In *Fleming v Fleming*,[141] the Court of Appeal similarly rejected the argument that marriage should be equated with cohabitation for the purposes of bringing a periodical payments order to an end. However, in *K v K (Periodical Payment: Cohabitation)*[142] Coleridge J observed that the social acceptance of cohabitation had changed dramatically over the last 30 years, commenting:

> The concept of cohabitation is now as normal, commonplace and acceptable as marriage. At every level of society and amongst all adult age groups people cohabit without a second thought. It carries no social stigma whatever. Nor for that matter does the birth of children outside marriage.[143]

Given this 'social revolution',[144] he questioned why the consequences of cohabitation should not be the same as the consequences of a remarriage on an existing periodical payments order.[145] As Moor notes, 'for the first time in any reported judgment' the court considered that 'as a matter of principle, cohabitation was a relevant factor on an application to vary/terminate a spousal maintenance order'.[146] The court also considered that there was nothing in the legislation to prevent a court from making an order with would terminate on cohabitation after a certain period.

A different question arises when the respondent to an application for periodical payments, usually the husband, has remarried or is living with another woman who has an income of her own. To what extent can the new partner's income be taken into

---

[137] On the facts of the case, the wife's payments were reduced to £4,500.   [138] [1996] 1 FLR 51.

[139] Ibid, 54.

[140] See too *S v S* [1987] 1 FLR 71 where Waite J held that the weight given to a new partner's income will turn on such factors as the permanency of the relationship, the amount of support the wife is obtaining, and how much she needs.   [141] [2004] 1 FLR 667.

[142] [2005] EWHC 2886 (Fam).   [143] Ibid, [2].   [144] Ibid.

[145] In this case, the husband and wife had been divorced for seven years. On divorce the wife had been awarded periodical payments of £16,000 per annum index linked (currently worth £18,955 per annum) and the husband now sought a downward variation of the payments to take account not only of his changed financial circumstances but of his former wife's settled cohabitation for three years. In taking account of the wife's cohabitation, the court reduced the periodical payments to £12,000 per annum, capitalising the payment at the sum of £100,000.

[146] P. Moor, 'Key Developments in Ancillary Relief' [2008] Family Law 44 at 46.

account when assessing how much the husband ought to pay for the support of his first family? It has been held that a court cannot require a second wife directly to contribute to the periodical payments paid by a husband for the support of his former wife and children. Consequently, if the husband has no income at all of his own, and his second wife is the breadwinner in the family, no order for periodical payments can be made against the husband.[147] In *Macey v Macey*[148] it was held that a magistrates' court had erred in law when taking into account the second woman's income as part of the available funds from which an order for periodical payments could be paid. However, the position is a subtle one. The court held that where the husband derives benefits from his new partner's income, which means that a greater part of his own income is available to pay maintenance to his first wife and children, an order can be made on the basis that the husband may need less money to support his new family.[149] While the new partner's income cannot be brought directly into account, it can be taken into consideration as a cushion for the spouse's expenses. This has the practical consequence that a husband can be ordered to pay more by way of periodical payments to his first family when his new partner has her own income, than he would be required to do where she has not.

4.5.1.4 *Classifying property: matrimonial/non-matrimonial property*

As we have seen, while no assets will be ring-fenced or quarantined to make them unavailable for distribution, their source may be a relevant factor for the court when making its assessment and may justify a departure from equal division, in the sense that 'there is likely to be better reason for departure from equality' in relation to non-matrimonial property.[150] Thus the court will need to consider more carefully than perhaps in the past, the nature of property and particularly whether it is matrimonial or non-matrimonial property.[151] This may raise some difficult questions as to which side of the line resources lie, for example where a spouse receives a bonus shortly after the marriage breakdown. In *Rossi v Rossi*,[152] a limit of one year from the date of the break-up was suggested as a cut-off point and thereafter any bonus should not be regarded as matrimonial in nature. However, in *H v H (Financial Provision)* the idea of such a fixed cut-off point was disapproved.[153] The nature of the property and the use put to it will need to be assessed in all the circumstances.

If one party has substantial assets which were earned prior to the marriage,[154] or the property held by the couple at the time of divorce has been largely generated by one person's inheritance, for example by starting a business using inherited capital,[155] the courts may use this as a reason to depart from equality. In *B v B (Ancillary Relief)*,[156] the husband built a business based on the wife's inheritance and the court justified a departure from equality on this basis. The nature of the property also may be important. For example, in *P v P (Inherited Property)*[157] farming land had been in the husband's family for generations and had been brought into the marriage with the expectation that it would remain in specie for future generations. For these reasons, and since an order for sale of the farm would

---

[147]   *Brown v Brown* (1981) 3 FLR 161; *Berry v Berry* [1986] 1 FLR 618.   [148]   (1981) 3 FLR 7.

[149]   See also *Wilkinson v Wilkinson* (1980) 10 Fam Law 48.

[150]   See discussion of *Charman v Charman* [2007] EWHC Civ 503 in Section 4.4.

[151]   In *Rossi v Rossi* [2006] EWHC 1482 (Fam) Mostyn QC (sitting as deputy High Court judge) held that in all cases it is now a 'primary function' of the court to identify the matrimonial and non-matrimonial property.   [152]   [2006] 2 FLR 1482 (Fam).

[153]   [2009] 2 FLR 795.   [154]   Eg *McCartney v McCartney Mills* [2008] EWHC 401 (Fam).

[155]   *Dharamshi v Dharamshi* [2001] 1 FCR 492.   [156]   [2008] 1 FCR 613.

[157]   [2004] EWHC 1364 (Fam), [2005] 1 FLR 576.

be little short of devastating to the husband, Munby J held that fairness required an order which merely addressed the wife's reasonable requirements which could be achieved without recourse to the farm assets.

4.5.1.5 Full and frank disclosure of resources is required

Each party is under a duty to make full and frank disclosure of all material facts to the other party and to the court. What can a judge do where he or she forms the opinion that one party has deliberately failed or refused to make full and frank disclosure and has concealed his true financial position from the other party? Courts have been encouraged to adopt a robust response to deliberate non-disclosure, to draw adverse inferences against the recalcitrant party,[158] and to make findings about their actual financial circumstances applying a simple balance of probabilities test. Where this results in the non-disclosing party being assumed to have more assets than is the true position, they have only themselves to blame.[159] A costs penalty can also be imposed on the dishonest party. The courts are conscious that the integrity of the legal process would be severely undermined if a party were able deliberately to evade the duty to disclose.[160]

4.5.2 Financial needs, obligations, and responsibilities

Section 25(2)(b) requires the court to take account of:

> the financial needs, obligations and responsibilities which each of the parties to the marriage has or is likely to have in the foreseeable future.

The court's first consideration will be the parties' housing needs.[161] Where there is sufficient to go beyond housing provision for children and a primary caretaker, 'the court's concern will be to provide the means for the absent parent to rehouse'.[162] As Thorpe LJ has commented:

> in any case where there is, by stretch and a degree of risk-taking, the possibility of a division to enable both to rehouse themselves, that is an exceptionally important consideration and one which will almost invariably have a decisive impact on outcome.[163]

It is usually only the financial needs which have been generated by the marriage which become the responsibility of a former spouse on divorce.[164] Moreover, it is only financial obligations which have been reasonably assumed which will be taken into account, although the courts have accepted that the words 'obligations and responsibilities' embrace obligations not only to the ex-spouse and children, but also other family obligations, such as to elderly parents or other relatives. The inclusion of these words allows the claims of any new dependants to be brought into the weighing-up process. Thus, if by the time the court makes its order one of the parties has remarried and undertaken financial responsibility for a new spouse and her children, or if he is cohabiting and has taken on

---

[158] *Pasha v Pasha* [2001] EWCA Civ 466.

[159] *Baker v Baker* [1995] 2 FLR 829; *Payne v Payne* [1968] 1 WLR 390; *J-PC v J-AF* [1955] P 215; *Fournier v Fournier* [1998] 2 FLR 990, where the husband's deliberate concealment of his assets and his failure to pay an order for periodical payments led to the capitalisation of the wife's periodical payments.

[160] In *W v W (Ancillary Relief: Non-Disclosure)* [2003] 3 FCR 385 the court said that 'where it is found that a party has deliberately...misrepresented facts then he must expect judicial censure and penalties in costs', at [3].   [161] *Cordle v Cordle* [2002] 1 FCR 97 at [33], *per* Thorpe LJ.

[162] Ibid, [33].   [163] *M v B (Ancillary Proceedings: Lump Sum)* [1998] 2 FLR 53 at 60.

[164] *Miller; McFarlane* [2006] UKHL 24 at [11], *per* Lord Nicholls. (Baroness Hale said the three strands of fairness which underpin resource distribution on divorce are 'linked to the parties' relationship, either causally or temporally, and not to extrinsic, unrelated factors, such as a disability arising after the marriage has ended', at [137].)

similar obligations, this will be taken into account. However, the court will not allow one party to live a lavish or extravagant lifestyle and claim this as a source of needs.[165]

The importance of the parties' financial needs to the determination of the final outcome depends on the level of available assets. Where resources are limited, the parties' needs will take priority.[166]

4.5.3 The standard of living before the breakdown of the marriage

Paragraph (c) of section 25(2) requires the court to take account of:

the standard of living enjoyed by the family before the breakdown of the marriage.

In the case of families of limited or average means, it is inevitable that the standard of living of each spouse will fall because resources which are adequate to keep one family at a standard of living which allows for small luxuries, when divided between two households will often barely keep each household in necessities. In the case of a wealthy spouse, there will be greater scope for the standard of living enjoyed during the marriage to impact on the outcome. In *Preston v Preston*,[167] Ormrod LJ said 'the wife of a millionaire and 23 years married is entitled to expect a very high standard of living which would include a home in a house or flat at the top end of the market, and probably a second home in the country or abroad, together with a very high spending power'.[168] Thus, where resources permit such an assessment, the marital standard of living is important when determining the level of award to which the claimant is entitled. However, the marital standard of living is a consideration but, as noted earlier in the discussion of *Miller; McFarlane*, there is no legitimate expectation that a particular standard of living will be maintained.

4.5.4 The age of each party and the duration of the marriage

Section 25(2)(d) directs the court's attention to:

the age of each party to the marriage and the duration of the marriage.

A person's age is likely to impact on their financial prospects and, in particular, their 'earning capacity' to which the court has specific regard under section 25(2)(a). Thus, in light of these provisions, a court is likely to want to be given information about the following matters: the impact of an unemployed wife's age on whether she can be expected to obtain work; how old she will be when the children cease to be dependent; where the husband is unemployed, whether at his age he can expect to gain further employment; and where both parties are in middle age, what their financial positions will be on retirement. The age of the husband was an important consideration in *Greenham v Greenham*.[169] The trial judge had ordered that the former matrimonial home, in which the husband was living, should be sold when the husband attained the age of 70. The Court of Appeal held, however, that the judge had been wrong to include this provision. Even though the husband would probably be in a secure financial position at that age, and would be able to afford to pay the wife her share in the property, it was unreasonable to force him to move house at the age of 70.[170]

---

[165] *North v North* [2007] 2 FCR 601.

[166] See eg *Smith v Smith* [1975] 2 All ER 19n; *Suter v Suter and Jones* [1987] 2 All ER 336; *Wells v Wells* [1992] 2 FLR 66. In *Cordle v Cordle* [2002] 1 FCR 97 the court said that in low-income cases, the needs of the parent with care will determine the outcome. This may absorb all of the assets but any surplus will be used to house the absent parent.   [167] [1982] 1 All ER 41.

[168] Ibid, 48.   [169] [1989] 1 FLR 105.

[170] See also *S v S* [1977] 1 All ER 56, where the parties married over the age of 50 and the wife had pressing housing needs.

As we have seen, the idea of marriage as a partnership of equals applies to all marriages, and thus awards in short marriage cases are no longer limited to the pre-*White* position of simply getting the wife back on her feet, or to compensate her for any financial disadvantage arising as a result of the marriage.[171]

As we have seen, the duration of the marriage has assumed importance on the question how property is to be dealt with, in the sense that it may be less likely that the assets will be divided equally in short marriages, especially in relation to property that can be considered as belonging solely to one spouse (perhaps because they have inherited it, or because they generated it solely by their own business efforts with no help from the other party).

4.5.4.1 Can pre-marital cohabitation be taken into account?

It is becoming increasingly commonplace for couples to cohabit before they marry, and consequently various cases have had to consider whether pre-marital cohabitation can be taken into account, either as part of the circumstances of the case or, more interestingly, as part of the duration of the marriage.

In *Foley v Foley*[172] the Court of Appeal made clear that the statute refers to the 'duration of the marriage' and that periods of cohabitation and marriage are not the same. In that case, the parties had lived together for seven years and had three children. They subsequently married but the marriage broke down and they divorced eight years later. The court treated the period when they were living together as 'one of the circumstances' to which the court was required to have regard, the weight to be attached to it being a matter for the court's discretion. The court held that it was entitled to give less weight to the period of cohabitation than to events occurring during the marriage, although the court also said that, where the parties cannot marry, the court could regard their cohabitation as a very weighty factor. This was the case in *Kokosinski v Kokosinski*,[173] where the husband had a wife in his native Poland from whom he was unable to obtain a divorce. The parties lived together for 25 years and had a son. They subsequently married but then only lived together for about four months. Wood J held that the 'welfare of the family' in section 25(2)(f) referred only to events which had occurred after the marriage took place. However, that did not mean that, on these exceptional facts, the 25 years' cohabitation was to be disregarded. Wood J pointed out that the court must also have regard to conduct,[174] and to all the circumstances of the case, and under both of these he could take account of behaviour which had occurred outside the span of marriage, at least in a case where the conduct had affected the finances of the other spouse.[175]

In *GW v RW*,[176] however, the court counted a period of 18 months pre-marital cohabitation as part of the duration of the marriage. Nicholas Mostyn QC said that:

> where a relationship moves seamlessly from cohabitation to marriage without any major alteration in the way the couple live, it is unreal and artificial to treat the periods differently.[177]

---

[171] As in the earlier case law such as *H v H (Financial Provision: Short Marriage)* (1981) 2 FLR 392, *Attar v Attar* [1985] FLR 649, and *Hedges v Hedges* [1991] 1 FLR 196. Of course, cases of limited financial resources will still have to focus primarily on meeting the parties' needs: *Miller; McFarlane* [2006] UKHL 24 at [55], *per* Lord Nicholls.   [172] [1981] 2 All ER 857.

[173] [1980] 1 All ER 1106.   [174] Now under para (g), then under the final target in s 25(1).

[175] But it should be noted that the wife did not obtain the type of order she would have obtained had the marriage lasted for 25 years. She obtained a lump sum which was less than the amount she was seeking, and might have expected to obtain, and no periodical payments.   [176] [2003] 2 FLR 108.

[177] Ibid, [33].

This approach has been criticised,[178] and in *Co v Co*[179] Coleridge J, whilst agreeing with the sentiment of Mostyn QC in *GW v RW*, preferred a different route.[180] Instead of treating the eight years' pre-marital cohabitation as part of the duration of the marriage, he viewed it as an important factor which could be considered as part of 'all the circumstances of the case', or if necessary under a 'specific section 25 pigeonhole', either as a species of contribution or conduct.[181] Similarly in *M v M (Financial Relief: Substantial Earning Capacity)*[182] Baron J regarded a 12-year marriage preceded by four years' cohabitation as a 16-year relationship, commenting:

> I take fully into account the precise wording of the Statute but I am clear that in modern society it is a couple's commitment to each other by co-habiting that is the relevant start date for consideration in most cases. Indeed, I consider that it is the norm for most couples to live together for a period before marriage…I am well aware of the decision in *Foley -v- Foley* [1981] 3 WLR 284 and the dicta of Eveleigh LJ at page 290. There are many other old cases dealing with the importance of the married years per se but I consider that society has moved on and it would be old-fashioned (indeed, senseless) to ignore the manner in which people now choose to order their lives. I prefer the modern view and draw a measure of comfort from *GW -v- RW* [2003] 2 FLR 108 …[183]

Thus the courts have more routinely regarded seamless preceding cohabitation as akin to the duration of the marriage.[184]

Cases of post-divorce cohabitation between former spouses can also give rise to the question whether such cohabitation should be taken into account. If at the time of the divorce a clean break order was made between the spouses, then property and financial disputes which arise from any subsequent cohabitation between them are likely to be dealt with under the normal rules governing cohabitation.[185] However, where there has been no final settlement the applicant can ask for leave to apply for financial relief under the MCA 1973. In *Hill v Hill*[186] the parties had cohabited for 25 years after they divorced. Commenting on the relevance of this, Ward LJ said that since pre-marital cohabitation could be taken into account when the court was doing justice between the parties on ancillary relief, 'then I do not see how the court can deny that cohabitation after the divorce is not a similar circumstance to take into account'. Thus the court concluded that the wife should be granted leave to apply for a property adjustment order, where the husband and wife had divorced in 1969, prior to the availability of the remedy of property adjustment.[187] According to the court, this claim was based not on the parties' cohabitation but

---

[178] S. Gilmore, 'Duration of Marriage *and* Seamless Preceding Cohabitation?' [2004] Family Law 205.

[179] [2004] 1 FLR 1095.

[180] Ibid, [47], commenting that the exact method was perhaps little more than 'a distinction without a difference'. See contra, S. Gilmore, 'Duration of Marriage *and* Seamless Preceding Cohabitation?' [2004] Family Law 205.   [181] [2004] 1 FLR 1095 at [45].

[182] [2004] EWHC 688 (Fam), [2004] 2 FLR 236.   [183] Ibid, [55].

[184] See J. Edwards, 'Duration of Marriage: From "I Do", "I Promise" or "I May"?' [2004] Family Law 726.

[185] See Chapter 5. See *obiter* comments of Butler-Sloss LJ in *Hewitson v Hewitson* [1995] 1 FLR 241 at 245 that:

> there has to be finality and an end to litigation. In my view the umbrella of the dissolved marriage which covers the post-divorce period cannot remain open forever. Upon the making and implementing of a 'clean break' order between spouses with no children, that umbrella has to be closed. Thereafter the relationship which may develop between former spouses is to be dealt with under civil law.

Balcombe J said that 'cohabitation subsequent to an English divorce is not the basis for the English court to grant matrimonial financial relief' (at 246).

[186] [1998] 1 FLR 198.

[187] Which was introduced on 1 January 1971 by the Matrimonial Proceedings and Property Act 1970, the Act having retrospective effect.

on the decree of divorce, the wife's claims from which were 'put in abeyance during the subsequent cohabitation'.

4.5.5 Any physical or mental disability of either of the parties to the marriage

Paragraph (e) requires the court to take account of:

any physical or mental disability of either of the parties to the marriage.

The courts have yet to determine to what extent the needs of a disabled party should impose an obligation on the other spouse to provide financial support which exceeds the norm.[188] For example, should there be a life-long obligation to provide periodical payments for a disabled spouse where the marriage has been relatively short-lived, and where an immediate or deferred clean break order would normally be considered appropriate? This raises the broader question of when the private obligations of ex-spouses to one another should end, and when those of the welfare state should take over. This is an issue of principle which has not yet received a settled answer. In line with the clean break ideal, it seems that the courts will strive to achieve a full and final settlement at the time of the divorce in order to avoid burdening the respondent with a continuing obligation. However, sometimes this will not be possible. For example in *M v M (Property Adjustment: Impaired Life Expectancy)*,[189] the wife suffered a brain tumour which reduced her life expectancy. When the parties divorced, after a 13-year marriage, the court held that the wife's ill-health and its effect on her income-earning capacity, meant that a clean break was not appropriate. She was always going to require periodical payments from her former husband. She was also awarded 75 per cent of the proceeds of sale of the matrimonial home, although this sum was charged back to the husband in the event of the wife's death. A spouse's illness may also impact upon the nature or quantum of an award. In *Re G (Financial Provision: Liberty to Restore Application for Lump Sum)*,[190] the wife, who suffered from multiple sclerosis, had run up debts to pay for her children's education and had had to move into rented accommodation. The husband inherited £2.1 million, and the court awarded the wife a lump sum of £460,000, noting that one of the wife's health needs was to avoid stress.

4.5.6 Contributions made to the welfare of the family

Under section 25(2)(f), the court has regard to:

the contributions which each of the parties has made or is likely in the foreseeable future to make to the welfare of the family, including any contribution by looking after the home or caring for the family.

Prior to the enactment of the current ancillary relief regime, ordinary property law principles governed disputes concerning the family home on divorce.[191] Under these principles, non-financial contributions to the welfare of the family were of little, or no, relevance when determining who owned the parties' property on divorce.[192] The new

---

[188] In *Chadwick v Chadwick* [1985] FLR 606 the Court of Appeal declined to take account of the wife's disability when determining what order to make in respect of the matrimonial home: see Section 6.1.6.2.

[189] [1993] 2 FLR 723.   [190] [2004] 1 FLR 997.

[191] These principles still apply to resolve the property disputes between spouses outside divorce, and all property disputes between cohabitants. See Chapter 5.

[192] *Gissing v Gissing* [1970] 2 All ER 780; *Lloyds Bank v Rosset* [1990] 1 All ER 1111. As Lord Simon of Glaisdale commented on the position: 'The cock bird can feather his nest precisely because he is not required to spend most of his time sitting on it': 'With All My Worldly Goods', Holdsworth Club (1964).

ancillary relief legislation[193] meant that for the first time the court was unfettered by the restrictions inherent in trust law and could take into account the full range of contributions which a spouse makes to the welfare of the family. However, the courts' initial 'reasonable requirements' approach meant that 'those contributions became subservient to a subjective assessment of "desert", rather than a free-standing assessment of the value they may have added to the family's wealth'.[194]

This all changed with the decision of the House of Lords in *White v White*. By articulating the non-discrimination principle, the Lords replaced 'needs' as the central principle with the parties' respective 'contributions to the welfare of the family'. However, this shift of approach left room to argue over what contributions might justify a departure from equality.

4.5.6.1 *The 'special contribution' argument*

In the immediate aftermath of *White*, claims were therefore made, usually by wealthy husbands, that their wealth creation was exceptional and, as such, they should be regarded as having made a 'special contribution' which justified them being awarded more of the assets on divorce. In *Cowan v Cowan*,[195] for example, the Court of Appeal said that the husband should receive a greater share of the capital assets on divorce because his contribution to the welfare of the family in building up a very successful business was 'exceptional'. However, this approach was criticised by the Court of Appeal in *Lambert v Lambert*.[196] The parties' marriage had lasted 23 years and at the time of the divorce the wife was 49 and the husband was 57. There were two children of the marriage, aged 19 and 20 respectively. Both were at university and were very wealthy as a result of a trust created for them by their parents. Prior to the marriage, the husband had started a business which became very successful and which generated the family's substantial wealth. In 1999, shares in the husband's company were sold for £75 million. Of this, the husband received £19.7 million, the wife received £500,000, and the trust in favour of the children received £6 million. At the date of the ancillary relief hearing, the total assets amounted to £20.2 million. The wife sought 50 per cent of the assets on the basis that her contribution to the family had been equal to that of the husband. Throughout the marriage the wife had been the primary homemaker and parent although she also claimed that she had played an important role in the success of the husband's business. By contrast, the husband argued that the family's assets had been generated as a result of his labour, that his wife's involvement in the business had been more or less ornamental, and that this should be reflected in the settlement. The first instance judgment of Connell J gave the wife 37.5 per cent of the family's assets which included the marital home; the departure from equal division being justified on the basis of the husband's special contributions.[197] Relying on the Court of Appeal decision in *Cowan v Cowan*, Connell J concluded that the husband's contribution, although not the product of genius, was a 'special achievement, via special business skills, acumen and effort'. Against this, the wife's contributions could not be described as 'really special' and despite Connell J's admission that there was nothing more that she could have done to justify equal division, this did not mean that an award of less than 50 per cent was unfair. This approach was strongly criticised by the Court of Appeal where Thorpe LJ emphasised that it was unacceptable to place greater value on the

---

[193] Addressing concerns identified by the Law Commission in its *Report on Financial Provision in Matrimonial Proceedings* (Law Com No 25, 1969), para 69.

[194] J. Eekelaar, 'Back to Basics and Forward into the Unknown' [2001] Family Law 30.

[195] [2001] 2 FLR 192.   [196] [2003] 1 FLR 139.   [197] *L v L* [2002] 1 FLR 642.

contribution of the breadwinner than that of the homemaker as justification for unequal division of assets.[198] He said:

> there must be an end to the sterile assertion that the breadwinner's contribution weighs heavier than the homemaker's.[199]

In addition, the court did not accept that its duty to assess the statutory criteria in an ancillary relief application requires a detailed critical appraisal of the performance of each of the parties during the marriage. Indeed, the court foresaw that it was only a matter of time before this 'forensic analysis' approach led to arguments about a spouse's substandard contributions thus resulting in the re-emergence of conduct which, under the legislation, can only be considered if it is 'inequitable to disregard'. To avoid this, the court preferred to *assume* that the parties' contributions to this 23-year marriage had been equal.[200] This is not to suggest that finding that one party has made a special contribution will never be possible.[201] However, refusing to engage in a discussion as to the circumstances which would justify such a finding, Thorpe LJ preferred to leave the issue open-ended stating that it would only be successful in exceptional circumstances to be explored in future case law.

The House of Lords considered the 'special contributions' argument in *Miller; McFarlane* and, in doing so, approved *Lambert* and emphasised that the ethos of *White* must be followed. That is, domestic and financial contributions should be treated equally.[202] This meant that the while it still remains possible for one spouse to argue that they have made a 'special contribution', this will only be successful in exceptional cases. Lord Nicholls said that:

> Parties should not seek to promote a case of 'special contribution' unless the contribution is so marked that to disregard it would be inequitable. A good reason for departing from equality is not to be found in the minutiae of married life.[203]

This approach was followed by the Court of Appeal in *Charman v Charman*.[204] The husband in this case, through his work in the insurance industry, had built up assets of approximately £130 million and he argued, amongst other things, that he had therefore made a 'special contribution' to the family. On this point, the Court of Appeal confirmed that a special contribution to the welfare of the family could be non-financial as well as financial although the court pointed out that, in practice, the claim of 'special contribution' has only been made by someone who has generated great wealth during the marriage. When assessing such claims the court said that:

> the court will no doubt have regard to the amount of the wealth; and in some cases, perhaps including the present, its amount will be so extraordinary as to make it easy for the party who generated it to claim an exceptional and individual quality which deserves special treatment. Often, however, he or she will need independently to establish such a quality, whether by genius in business or in some other field. Sometimes, by contrast, it will immediately be obvious that substantial wealth generated during the marriage is a

---

[198] [2003] 1 FLR 139.   [199] Ibid, [38].

[200] Note, however, that equality of contributions does not mean equal division: 'a distinction must be drawn between an assessment of equality of contribution and an order for equality of division. A finding of equality of contribution may be followed by an order for unequal division because of the influence of one or more of the other statutory criteria as well as the over-arching search for fairness.' Ibid, [38].

[201] Eg in *Sorrell v Sorrell* [2005] EWHC 1717 (Fam) the wife was awarded 40 per cent of the assets on the ground that her husband has made an exceptional contribution in building up a business worth £546 million.   [202] [2006] UKHL 24 at [146].

[203] Ibid, [67].   [204] [2007] EWCA Civ 503.

windfall—the proceeds, for example, of an unanticipated sale of land for development or of an embattled takeover of a party's ailing company—which is not the product of a special contribution.[205]

While the Court of Appeal did not set a threshold of wealth which would evidence a special contribution, it did offer some guidance on how the finding of a special contribution on behalf of one party would affect the award. According to the court, in such circumstances, as a guideline the departure from equal division should be somewhere between 66.6/33.3 per cent and 55/45 per cent. In the case of *Charman* itself, the husband's contribution in generating the massive wealth was regarded as special and, as such, he was awarded 63.5 per cent of the assets.

4.5.7 Conduct

Under section 25(2)(g), the court shall have regard to:

> the conduct of the parties, if that conduct is such that it would in the opinion of the court be inequitable to disregard it.

At one time, the provision of maintenance on divorce was linked to the attribution of blame for the marital breakdown and a wife who was guilty of a matrimonial offence lost her right to maintenance. However, the introduction of no-fault divorce in the 1970s reduced the significance of fault in both the availability of divorce and financial provision in its aftermath. However, the extent to which the conduct of the parties should be taken into account when making financial provision and property adjustment orders has been a controversial issue. When, in 1980, the Law Commission issued a discussion paper which included the question of what policy ought to be adopted on the impact of conduct,[206] it received a large amount of conflicting comment in response. Many individuals felt a considerable sense of injustice because the court had not been prepared to take account of the other spouse's behaviour on divorce.[207] Despite this, the Law Commission expressed the view that courts cannot reasonably be expected to apportion responsibility for marriage breakdown, save in exceptional circumstances. It relied in particular on the words of Ormrod J in *Wachtel v Wachtel*[208] when he said:

> The forensic process is reasonably well adapted to determining in broad terms the share of responsibility of each party for an accident on the road or at work because the issues are relatively confined in scope, but it is much too clumsy a tool for dissecting the complex inter-actions which go on all the time in a family. Shares in responsibility for breakdown cannot be properly assessed without a meticulous examination and understanding of the characters and personalities of the spouses concerned, and the more thorough the investigation the more the shares will, in most cases, approach equality.

The Law Commission also gave more pragmatic reasons for rejecting an inquiry into the parties' mutual recriminations in other than exceptional cases. These included that it would be expensive of court time and legal aid; that resurrecting past matters, sometimes stretching back over many years, for forensic investigation would not assist the parties to come to terms with their deep feelings about the breakdown of their marriage; and

---

[205] Ibid, [80].   [206] Law Com No 103 (1980).   [207] Law Com No 112 (1980), para 36.

[208] [1973] 1 All ER 113 at 119. For detailed discussion, see G. Douglas, 'Bringing an End to the Matrimonial Post Mortem: *Wachtel v Wachtel* and its Enduring Significance for Ancillary Relief' in S. Gilmore, J. Herring, and R. Probert, *Landmark Cases in Family Law* (Oxford: Hart, 2011).

that such feelings are better dealt with during conciliation.[209] As Thorpe LJ explained in *Lambert v Lambert*,[210] considering the parties' conduct during the marriage requires a 'detailed retrospective at the end of a broken marriage just at a time when the parties should be looking forward not back'.[211] Not only does this involve a determination of fact, but it calls for 'a value judgement of the worth of each side's behaviour and translation of that worth into actual money'.[212] Thus, despite recognising the 'widespread feeling' that 'when making orders for financial ancillary relief the judge should know who was to blame for the breakdown of the marriage' and take it into account,[213] the courts will not 'seek to unravel mutual recriminations about happenings within the marriage'.[214] As such, conduct will only be relevant to the ancillary relief assessment in a minority of cases where the conduct is such that it would be inequitable to disregard it. Consequently, judges have refused to penalise a spouse who has committed adultery,[215] or otherwise behaved in a manner which has caused offence or distress to the other party, taking the view that the conduct is not of sufficient seriousness and that this would be to 'impose a fine for supposed misbehaviour in the course of an unhappy married life'.[216] If conduct is not of a serious enough nature to be considered 'inequitable to disregard', then it will not be taken into account.

4.5.7.1 What type of conduct is 'inequitable to disregard'?

As Baroness Hale explained in *Miller; McFarlane*, conduct will only be material where 'one party is much more to blame than the other' through misconduct which is both 'obvious and gross'.[217] In *Leadbeater v Leadbeater*[218] Balcombe J found that the spouses had both behaved as badly as each other and left conduct out of account.

Relevant conduct is not confined to conduct during the marriage and can relate to behaviour after the marriage has broken down.[219] The conduct need not be morally blameworthy. In *West v West*,[220] for example, account was taken of a wife's refusal to cohabit after the marriage in the house purchased by the husband, preferring instead to remain living at her parents' home. In several of the cases, however, conduct which has been seen as material has been seriously morally wrong.

Some examples may help to illustrate the type of conduct which has been seen as 'inequitable to disregard'. In *Kyte v Kyte*[221] the wife, knowing that her husband had attempted suicide on previous occasions, complied with his request to help him to commit suicide by taking a bottle of whisky and some drugs to his office and did not try to dissuade him. She stood to gain from the husband's death and wanted him out of the way so that she could set up home with her new partner. The Court of Appeal reduced the wife's award of £14,000 by £5,000, holding that this was conduct which was inequitable to disregard. In *Evans v Evans*[222] the husband had conscientiously paid maintenance for his ex-wife for many years. She was then convicted of inciting others to kill him. Balcombe LJ commented that if 'the courts were in these circumstances not to discharge the order, the public might think that we had taken leave of our senses'.

---

[209] Law Com No 112 (1980), para 37.   [210] [2003] 1 FLR 139.   [211] Ibid, [20].

[212] Ibid, [20].   [213] *Miller; McFarlane* [2006] UKHL 24 at [60].   [214] Ibid, [61].

[215] *Miller; McFarlane* [2006] UKHL 24.

[216] *Wachtel v Wachtel* [1973] 1 All ER 829; *A v A (Financial Provision)* [1998] 2 FLR 180.

[217] Ibid, [146], *per* Baroness Hale borrowing the words of Ormrod J in *Wachtel v Wachtel* [1973] Fam 72 at 80. As Sir George Baker P put it: conduct 'of the kind that would cause the ordinary mortal to throw up his hands and say, "surely that woman is not going to be given any money" or "is not going to get a full award"': *W v W (Financial Provision: Lump Sum)* [1976] Fam 107 at 114.   [218] [1985] FLR 789.

[219] *Jones v Jones* [1976] Fam 8, CA (discussed in later in this section).   [220] [1978] Fam 1.

[221] [1988] Fam 145.   [222] [1989] 1 FLR 351.

Similarly, in *H v H (Financial Relief: Attempted Murder as Conduct)*[223] the husband attacked the wife with knives in front of the children inflicting serious wounds to her neck, face, and hands. He was convicted of attempted murder and sentenced to 12 years' imprisonment. The court held that the husband's conduct should be taken into account when assessing the financial outcome on divorce. In relation to the effect of the conduct on the final award, the court held that it 'should not be punitive or confiscatory for its own sake'.[224] According to Coleridge J:

> the proper way to have regard to conduct is as a potentially magnifying factor when considering the wife's position under the other subsections and criteria. It is the glass through which the other factors are considered. It places her needs, as I judge them, at a much higher priority to those of the husband because the situation the wife now finds herself in is, in a very real way, his fault. It is not just that she is in a precarious position, which she might be for a variety of medical reasons, but that he has created this position by his reprehensible conduct. So she must, in my judgment and in fairness, be given a greater priority in the share-out.[225]

Sometimes a spouse's behaviour (as well as being morally wrong) may have a direct financial impact, as in *Jones v Jones*,[226] where, after the marriage had ended, the husband maliciously attacked his wife with a knife, injuring her wrist so severely that he impaired her earning capacity as a nurse. The Court of Appeal found that it would be repugnant to justice not to take the husband's conduct into account when securing the position of the wife in the future. In *H v H (Financial Provision: Conduct)*,[227] where the husband violently assaulted his wife as a result of which he was sent to prison for wounding and attempted rape, the husband was no longer able to support his wife and children to the standard which had preceded the attack. Furthermore, the wife had been left in a psychologically vulnerable position. The husband's conduct was one of the factors which influenced Thorpe J to transfer the husband's half share in the matrimonial home to the wife. There was a causative link between the conduct of one of the spouses and the parties' current financial circumstances which it was inequitable for a court to disregard.[228]

The fact that a spouse has behaved very badly will not necessarily mean that he or she will lose all provision. A striking example is provided by *Clark v Clark*,[229] in which Thorpe LJ commented that it 'would be hard to conceive graver marital misconduct', and that the history was 'as baleful as any to be found in the family law reports'. As the judge found, the wife had married a wealthy man 36 years her senior for his money, and spent considerable sums on luxury items such as a boat, a Bentley car, and an expensive home. The marriage had never been consummated and at one stage the wife required the husband to live in a caravan in her garden. She had made him a virtual prisoner in their home and he was eventually rescued by his niece and nephew. The Court of Appeal reduced the judge's award of just over £500,000 to reflect the marital misconduct, but nevertheless the wife still received a lump sum of £125,000.

In *A v A (Financial Provision)*[230] the husband's violent conduct was partly attributable to his uncontrollable psychological state. Allowing the husband's appeal against an

---

[223] [2005] EWHC 2911 (Fam), [2006] 1 FLR 990.   [224] Ibid, [44].

[225] Ibid. Douglas notes that the husband's conduct in this case was exceptionally grave and that the question for the future is 'how far less serious forms of criminal misconduct should "colour" the court's assessment' of the statutory factors: [2006] Fam Law 265.   [226] [1975] 2 All ER 12.

[227] [1994] 2 FLR 801.

[228] See for other examples: *Martin v Martin* [1976] Fam 335; *Bryant v Bryant* (1976) 120 Sol Jo 165; *Weisz v Weisz* (1975) Times, 16 December; *Hillard v Hillard* (1982) 12 Fam Law 176.

[229] [1999] 2 FLR 498, CA.

[230] [1995] 1 FLR 345.

order which reduced his share in the parties' jointly owned property to 10 per cent, and increasing it to one-third, Thorpe J held that although an incident of serious violence could not be disregarded, particularly where it had long-standing effects on the psychological well-being of the injured spouse, conduct was only one of the factors to be considered, and it should not drive the court to conclude that a violent husband should be deprived of his entire capital.[231]

In *H v H (Financial Relief: Conduct)*[232] the husband in the last three years of an 18-year marriage had deceitfully used capital provided by his father-in-law (who was very wealthy) for his own purposes, including placing some of it in a Swiss bank account and financing an adulterous relationship. However, the court found that his breach of trust was out of character, and that the children had a good relationship with him. Singer J held that it was in the children's interests that their father should be securely and adequately housed even if this meant selling the former matrimonial home in which the children lived with their mother. Accordingly he ordered that £375,000 should be settled on the husband for the purchase of a house to be held on trust. However, because it was inequitable to disregard the husband's conduct, Singer J ordered that the property should revert to the children on the husband's death, and not pass to his estate.[233]

Section 25(2)(g) may be criticised as possibly inviting further animosity between the parties. An argument can certainly be made that it may be more beneficial for issues of conduct to be subsumed within the other paragraphs in section 25(2). For example, where one spouse refuses to cohabit as in *West v West*,[234] those allegations could have been considered under paragraph (d) or (f), which focuses on the duration of the marriage, and each spouse's contributions to the welfare of the family. Even extreme cases like *Jones v Jones*,[235] in which the husband attacked the wife with a knife, or *H v H (Financial Provision: Conduct)*,[236] where the husband's attack on his wife had led to his imprisonment, and to her being psychologically harmed, could probably have been adequately considered under paragraphs (a), (b), and (e) which focus respectively on each spouse's earning capacity, resources, needs, and any physical or mental disabilities. Where a spouse has squandered resources, this could be considered as a matter relating to the spouses' resources. While some situations would not easily fall within the other paragraphs in the section,[237] abolishing conduct as a separate category may be more in keeping with the desire to keep the parties from making allegations and counter-allegations of fault. The counter-argument to this is that there ought to be the opportunity for the types of reprehensible conduct examined earlier to be positively condemned in proceedings ancillary to the divorce itself.

It should be noted that section 25(2)(g) relates to the parties' 'marital' misconduct which, as we have seen, can affect the quantum of the award. Conduct connected to the financial proceedings (known as 'litigation' misconduct) is a separate issue which will not usually affect the final award but can lead to one party being penalised in costs.[238]

[231] See eg *K v K (Financial Provision: Conduct)* [1990] 2 FLR 225.   [232] [1998] 1 FLR 971.
[233] The husband also received a lump sum of £100,000, principally to cover his debts. The exceptional nature of the capital order for the benefit of the children was emphasised. Cf *Lord Lilford v Glyn* [1979] 1 All ER 441.   [234] [1977] 2 All ER 705.
[235] [1975] 2 All ER 12.   [236] [1994] 2 FLR 801.
[237] It is hard to see where *Evans v Evans* [1989] 1 FLR 351 would fall, but it might have been considered under the clean break provisions in s 25A.
[238] The distinction between marital misconduct and litigation misconduct was made by the Court of Appeal, per curiam, in *Tavoulareas v Tavoulareas* [1998] 2 FLR 418. Thorpe LJ suggested that para (g) is aimed at marital conduct. However, if one party's misconduct is limited to misconduct within the ancillary relief proceedings, whilst this might affect the award of costs, it was doubtful whether it should diminish the quantum of the financial award. This approach was followed in *Young v Young* [1998] 2 FLR 1131 where

4.5.8 Loss of pension

Section 25(2)(h) directs the court to have regard to:

> the value to each of the parties to the marriage of any benefit which, by reason of the dis-
> solution or annulment of the marriage, that party will lose the chance of acquiring.

A spouse's expectation under a pension scheme is often considered under this provision and the court has specific powers to re-allocate prospective pension entitlements on
divorce. This is discussed further in Section 5.

4.6 THE CLEAN BREAK

The introduction of the clean break provisions in the legislation marked a shift in thinking away from the desirability of requiring a husband to provide continuing maintenance
for his wife for the rest of her life, which had previously been a commonplace feature
of court orders, towards an approach which, in appropriate cases, leads to each spouse
becoming financially independent of the other. This shift had already started to permeate
the reasoning of the courts before it received legislative approval. The motive was succinctly expressed by Lord Scarman in *Minton v Minton*[239] when he said:

> The law now encourages spouses to avoid bitterness after family breakdown and to settle
> their money and property problems. An object of the modern law is to encourage the par-
> ties to put the past behind them and to begin a new life which is not over-shadowed by the
> relationship which has broken down.[240]

As Baroness Hale made clear in *Miller; McFarlane*, the 'ultimate objective is to give each
party an equal start on the road to independent living'.[241] The following salient features
should be noted about the clean break provisions.

4.6.1 Section 25A(1)

Section 25A(1) imposes a duty on a court to consider, in all cases, whether the parties'
obligations towards each other should be terminated as soon after the decree as the court
considers just and reasonable.[242] This is a strong directive, but it is ameliorated by the
language in which the court's discretion is couched. The court must ask itself whether it
is *appropriate* so to exercise its powers; and whether the outcome will be *just and reasonable*. It can be seen that neither spouse is given preferential treatment. Rather the requirement is framed in terms which allow the court to consider the circumstances of both
parties. Baroness Hale described the approach under section 25A(1) as follows:

> It assumes that the court has decided that some award is appropriate... The court is then
> required to consider whether it could achieve an appropriate result by bringing their
> mutual obligations to an end. This is a clear steer in the direction of lump sum and prop-
> erty adjustment orders with no continuing periodical payments. But it does not tell us
> much about what an appropriate result would be.[243]

There is no presumption for a clean break but there may be some circumstances when
a clean break may be appropriate and the courts strive for 'independent finances and

---

the Court of Appeal ruled that the husband's financial misconduct had already been taken into account in a
reduced lump sum order, and that it should not have been brought into account a second time to increase his
liability for costs. See also *Clark v Clark* [1999] 2 FLR 498, CA.

[239] [1979] 1 All ER 79.   [240] Ibid, 87.   [241] [2006] UKHL 24 at [144].
[242] See *Suter v Suter and Jones* [1987] 2 All ER 336.
[243] *Miller; McFarlane* [2006] UKHL 24 at [130].

self-sufficiency'.[244] In some cases, a continuing set of orders may not offer any benefit to the spouse, for example where periodical payments in a small sum are accompanied by a similar reduction in welfare benefits.[245] In such cases the policy of the clean break is in tension with the policy that spouses should make financial provision for each other and not the state. Where, however, the latter policy would be to tie the spouses together long term with little advantage, the policy of the clean break may prevail. If the marriage is very short and childless, or the parties are in established careers, the court may be persuaded that the parties can reach a state of financial independence.[246] If the parties are very wealthy; the courts may be able to find sufficient capital to produce a clean break.

4.6.1.1 Nominal orders

The clean break provisions do not prevent the court, in an appropriate case, from making a nominal sum periodical payments order (of say, 1p annually), to keep in place the possibility of variation upwards should the parties circumstances change.[247] For example, in *Whiting v Whiting*[248] the Court of Appeal held that the trial judge had been entitled to take the view that periodical payments should be kept alive by a nominal sum order in case unforeseen contingencies, such as illness or redundancy, should prevent the wife from making adequate provision for her own needs, and made it necessary for her to look again to her ex-husband for support. Hence the making of a nominal sum order may have profound implications for both parties.

4.6.2 Section 25A(2)

The court's duty under subsection (2) arises in a case when the court has found it appropriate to make an order for periodical payments. The court is then required to consider whether it would be appropriate to limit the term of these payments only to such term as would be sufficient to enable the recipient to adjust *without undue hardship* to the termination of his or her financial dependence on the other. In *Barrett v Barrett*[249] the Court of Appeal made clear that this provision does not say that there must be termination unless there are good reasons for there not to be. Rather the court must be satisfied on the evidence of the spouse's ability to adjust without undue hardship within any proposed term to be set. As the Court of Appeal commented in *Flavell v Flavell*,[250] there is:

> often a tendency for these orders to be made more in hope than in serious expectation. Especially in judging the case of ladies in their middle years, the judicial-looking into a crystal ball very rarely finds enough of substance to justify a finding that adjustment can be made without undue hardship. All too often these orders are made without evidence to support them.

To what extent then are non-working claimants expected to obtain employment and become economically self-sufficient on divorce? The answer to this question depends on the circumstances of the case, in particular the reasons for lack of employment, their age, and length of time which they have been out of the labour market. A spouse who is not hampered by childcare responsibilities is not entitled simply to lapse into apathy with regard to obtaining employment; he or she is expected to make real efforts to obtain work. However, if the claimant is middle-aged and has been absent from the labour market for some time, the courts will not usually expect her to be able to secure full-time employment

---

[244] Ibid, [39]. [245] *Ashley v Blackman* [1988] FCR 699.
[246] *Burgess v Burgess* [1996] 2 FLR 981, [2000] 3 FCR 555. [247] See s 31 for variation.
[248] [1988] 2 All ER 275; see also *Scallon v Scallon* [1990] 1 FLR 194; *Hepburn v Hepburn* [1989] 1 FLR 373. [249] [1988] 2 FLR 516.
[250] [1997] 1 FLR 353. See *L v L* [2011] EWHC 2207 (Fam).

on divorce.[251] Thus the courts recognise the difficulties middle-age spouses face in obtaining employment. As Heilbron J said of the wife in *M v M (Financial Provision)*:[252]

> The wife (and she will not mind my saying so) is no longer a young woman and she is beginning to enter the world of work from a base of 46 or 47 years of age. She is embarking on a difficult and unpredictable life in an increasingly difficult world of work—things do not get easier—and the older she gets, in all probability, the more difficult will it be for her, in my opinion, to work and make her way in that world of employment.

In *Boylan v Boylan*[253] it was held that it would be wrong to construe the words 'undue hardship' as referring solely to the bare needs of a former wife when assessing her ability to adjust to the termination of periodical payments. Rather, her reasonable requirements should be judged by the standard that she was the former wife of a man of substantial wealth.[254] As these cases show, one spouse's *past* contributions as primary caretaker may justifiably limit their economic self-sufficiency as their age and lack of recent training or qualifications may hinder their opportunities to re-enter the labour market.

The same may apply where the spouse currently has childcare responsibilities. In *Miller; McFarlane*[255] Baroness Hale indicated that prioritising the children's welfare 'should also involve ensuring that their primary carer is properly provided for, because it is well known that the security and stability of children depends in large part upon the security and stability of their primary carers'.[256] Thus, although the clean break provisions in section 25A encourage the court to promote each party's self-sufficiency on divorce, the children's welfare will impact on the court's assessment of the financial needs of the residential parent. Indeed, it is unlikely that a court would expect a parent who is caring for young children to seek employment on divorce.[257] Much will depend on the facts of each individual case, but if the residential parent is caring for young children at the time of the divorce, then there may well be uncertainty about her capacity to achieve economic independence. As such, the court may not be able to predict when it would be appropriate to bring the maintenance obligation to an end and, in these circumstances, the court is likely to impose no time limit on the periodical payments order and to leave the payer to seek a variation of the order.[258] Even after a short marriage, the court may reach the same conclusion. In *C v C (Financial Relief: Short Marriage)*,[259] the wife's marriage to a very wealthy man had only lasted for a little over nine months, but the parties had a child who had health problems. The wife, too, had a 'fragile personality', and 'at the age of 40 [was] in that uncertain period in which it may be said she is not young and so her position in the labour market is obviously less favourable than when she was 30'.[260] The Court of Appeal, while acknowledging that the judge's award was at the very top end of the bracket, refused to interfere with the trial judge's decision to award her a lump sum

---

[251] *M v M (Financial Provision)* [1987] 2 FLR 1; *Leadbeater v Leadbeater* [1985] FLR 789; *Barrett v Barrett* [1988] 2 FLR 516; *A v A (Financial Provision)* [1998] 2 FLR 180.   [252] [1987] 2 FLR 1.

[253] [1988] 1 FLR 282.

[254] It was therefore held that the only way in which the wife's right to periodical payments could be terminated, in such a way as not to cause her undue hardship, would be by the payment to her of a lump sum sufficient to provide her with an income comparable to the amount she was receiving in periodical payments; see too *B v B (Financial Provision)* [1990] 1 FLR 20; *R v R (Financial Provision: Reasonable Needs)* [1994] 2 FLR 1044.   [255] [2006] UKHL 24.

[256] Ibid, [128]. Baroness Hale cited the work of Lewis in support of this argument. See J. Lewis, 'Debates and Issues Regarding Marriage and Cohabitation in the British and American Literature' (2001) 15(1) International Journal of Law, Policy and the Family 159.

[257] *Leadbetter v Leadbetter* [1985] 1 FLR 789.   [258] Ibid.   [259] [1997] 2 FLR 26.

[260] Ibid, 32.

of £195,000, and secured periodical payments of £19,500 per annum for herself, without limit of time.[261]

4.6.2.1 Extension of the term

An order will come to an end when its term expires. However, the initial decision to set a time limit on the periodical payments is not necessarily final, for there is a possibility of the order being varied in the future under section 31, and this could include the extension of the term during which payments are to be made, provided the application for extension is made during the currency of the term.[262] If a spouse applies for an extension of the periodical payments order, the court is again under a duty to consider bringing the payments to an end as soon as possible,[263] and it can order a lump sum, property adjustment order, or pension sharing order instead in order to achieve a clean break.[264]

4.6.2.2 A section 28(1A) direction

Clearly, the knowledge that such an application might be made could undermine the purpose of a clean break order which is intended to bring finality to the financial dependence of the payee, albeit postponed for the duration of the order.[265] Section 25A(2) should therefore be considered alongside section 28(1A). This provides:

> Where a periodical payments or secured periodical payments order in favour of a party to a marriage is made on or after the grant of a decree of divorce or nullity of marriage, the court may direct that that party shall not be entitled to apply under section 31 below for the extension of the term specified in the order.

Where such a direction is made it prevents the party in receipt of periodical payments from applying in variation proceedings for an extension of the order. In this way a postponed or deferred clean break can truly be achieved. In *Waterman v Waterman*[266] a judge set a term of five years in the case of a 38-year-old former secretary who had recently undertaken a computer course to obtain employment, and who had a 5-year-old child. The judge also attached a section 28(1A) direction. The Court of Appeal held that, while the five-year term was not of itself wrong, the section 28(1A) direction was inappropriate in such a case given a 'child of tender years' and uncertainty regarding the mother's future employment.

4.6.3 Section 25A(3)

Subsection (3) of section 25A contains the most draconian provision from the point of view of an applicant for a periodical payments order. It entitles a court to dismiss an application for periodical payments, and to direct that the applicant shall not be entitled

---

[261] The husband was determined to pay his wife very little. He had met her when she was working as a 'high-class call-girl'. The husband deliberately concealed the extent of his assets and income. This led the judge to assume that he had capital assets of £1 million and an income of £100,000. Ward LJ commented more than once that he would not necessarily have made the same high level of provision as the trial judge. He emphasised the point which applies to all appeals, namely that it does not matter what the appeal court would have done, the question is whether the trial judge was plainly wrong. See also *B v B (Mesher Order)* [2002] EWHC 3106 (Fam).

[262] *T v T (Financial Provision)* [1988] 1 FLR 480; *Richardson v Richardson* [1993] 4 All ER 673. See also *B v B (Consent Order: Variation)* [1995] 1 FLR 9 where Thorpe J held that a limited order should not have been agreed in a consent order, as the wife could not possibly adjust to termination without suffering undue hardship.   [263] MCA 1973, s 31(7).

[264] Section 31(7B).

[265] For discussion, see E. Cooke, 'Making the Clean Break Squeaky Clean' [1994] Family Law 268.

[266] [1989] 1 FLR 380.

to make any further application for an order for either secured or unsecured periodical payments. There are no words of guidance in subsection (3) on how a court should determine whether or not a continuing obligation should be imposed on one party to make, or secure, periodical payments in favour of the other, which seems to be a weakness in the drafting of this provision. The court will, of course, follow the statutory guidelines provided in section 25 in the exercise of its powers in general, but they are not specifically focused on periodical payments orders. It seems paradoxical that a court must consider the issue of the payee's adjustment without undue hardship to an order being terminated when limiting the duration of a periodical payments order, but not when refusing to make one altogether.

5 PENSIONS

For many people who are divorcing the two most valuable assets they possess are the matrimonial home and any expectation they may have under a pension scheme.[267] Divorce has serious implications in relation to the parties' pension rights, particularly in cases where one spouse has substantial pension provision and the other has not. For example, a divorced wife will lose the opportunity to share in her husband's pension once it becomes payable and further, because a divorced wife is no longer her husband's widow for the purposes of his pension scheme, if he should predecease her, she will not obtain a widow's pension. Similarly, if the wife has a pension scheme which pays benefits to a widower, the husband will not be able to benefit from it if the parties divorce. The loss of pension entitlements therefore usually represents a real financial deprivation to a spouse, particularly one divorced in middle age who may not have a pension scheme of their own. Where spouses divorce fairly late in life their opportunity to make adequate substitute pension arrangements is likely to be limited. Indeed, it may often be sensible to discuss the alternative of obtaining a separation order with a middle-aged or elderly person whose marriage has broken down and who wishes to rearrange his or her financial and property affairs. Orders for financial provision and property adjustment are available in the same way as they are to divorcing spouses, but a separation order does not lead to the automatic loss of pension entitlements.

There are many types of benefit which can accrue under pension schemes. These include lump sum benefits, a regular income entitlement, a widow/widower's pension, death in service benefits, and life cover. The valuation of a person's interest in his pension scheme is by no means problem free even though the process of gathering information is assisted by regulations.[268] For example, future interest, inflation, and taxation rates can only be predicted. This can therefore give rise to differing valuations, depending on the expectations and assumptions of the actuary doing the calculation.[269] This necessarily makes it difficult for any adviser to reach a conclusion as to the worth of a pension.

---

[267] See the comments of Lords Nicholls in *Brooks v Brooks* [1995] 2 FLR 13 at 15.

[268] See Occupational Pension Schemes (Disclosure of Information) Regulations 1996; Occupational Pension Schemes (Disclosure of Information) Amendment Regulations 2002; Personal and Occupational Pension Schemes (Indexation and Disclosure of Information) (Miscellaneous Amendments) Regulations 2005; Divorce etc. (Pensions) Regulations 2000; Pensions on Divorce etc. (Provision of Information) Regulations 2000.

[269] For a helpful analysis of how to assess the value of a pension, see *T v T (Financial Relief: Pensions)* [1998] 1 FLR 1072.

5.1 DUTY TO CONSIDER THE PARTIES' PENSION ENTITLEMENTS

The court when making financial and property arrangements on divorce is mandated to have regard to 'any benefits under a pension scheme which a party to the marriage has or is likely to have' when considering the spouses' resources under paragraph (a) of section 25(2);[270] and when considering paragraph (h) the court must have regard to 'any benefits under a pension scheme which, by reason of the dissolution or annulment of the marriage, a party to the marriage will lose the chance of acquiring.'[271] However, while the parties' respective pension entitlements and any loss of pension rights have to be considered, the court is not bound to make an order distributing the value of the pension between the parties.[272] Rather, redistributing the parties' pension rights on divorce is just one tool at the court's disposal to do justice between the parties in the exercise of its overall discretion. However, should the court wish to compensate one party for loss of pension rights or distribute the capital value of the pension fund between the parties as part of the financial settlement, there are a number of options available to it. These are detailed in Section 5.2. The law relating to pensions after divorce was amended by the Pensions Act 1995 which inserted sections 25B–25D into the MCA 1973 and introduced the 'earmarking order', and by the Welfare Reform and Pensions Act 1999 which established pension splitting, which is the most effective means of redistributing the value of a pension on divorce.

5.2 PENSIONS—THE OPTIONS

5.2.1 Compensation to off-set the loss of pension entitlements

The simplest means by which a court can take account of the potential loss of pension rights is to compensate the loser when adjusting the division of the parties' present financial and property assets. For example, where the husband can anticipate a lump sum payment and a regular income under his pension scheme, this might persuade a court to transfer the entire beneficial interest in the former matrimonial home to the wife, and/or to order that her periodical payments should last for the parties' joint lives, and/or to make a lump sum order. In appropriate cases, it could defer payment of the lump sum until the pension lump sum becomes payable. In many cases, however, it is not possible to make present provision for lost pension rights which adequately takes account of the pensioner's future entitlement and so this is only an option where resources permit such a compensatory award to be made.

5.2.2 Earmarking order

Sections 25B–25D give the court the power to earmark part of the pensioner's entitlement for the benefit of the other spouse and to order that the trustees or managers of the pension make payments to that person from the pension fund once it becomes payable. Thus under section 25B(4) the court 'may require the person responsible for the pension arrangement in question, if at any time any payment in respect of any benefits under the arrangement becomes due to the party with pension rights, to make a payment for the benefit of the other party.'[273] Thus, once the pensioner begins to draw benefits, a proportion of the pension can immediately become payable to his ex-spouse.[274] Similarly,

---

[270] Section 25B(1)(a).   [271] Section 25B(1)(b).   [272] See *Burrow v Burrow* [1999] 1 FLR 508.

[273] Under s 25B(5), an earmarking order must be expressed in percentage terms.

[274] Pension payments are periodical payments and therefore they do not survive the death or remarriage of the payee (s 28). Applications to vary the order can be made under s 31. See also *T v T (Financial Relief: Pensions)* [1998] 1 FLR 1072 at 1085.

the court may require the trustees or managers to pay the whole or part of a lump sum, when it becomes due, to the other party.[275] A disadvantage of earmarking arrangements is that it ties the parties together financially although their marriage has ended, and the receiving spouse is vulnerable should the pensioner spouse die prematurely as this brings any earmarking arrangements to an end. There may also be vulnerability where the pensioner delays taking his pension entitlement or stops paying into the scheme prematurely. Given these difficulties, greater powers were given to the court by the Welfare Reform and Pensions Act 1999 which provides for full pension splitting at the time of the divorce proceedings.

5.2.3 Pension splitting

Pension splitting allows the court to split the pension between the parties at the time of the divorce. In other words, the pension is split into two sections (in equal or unequal proportions) to be allocated to each party who thereafter will be responsible for making their own pension arrangements from their provision. As it splits the pension at the time of the divorce it ties in with the principle that it is normally desirable to achieve a clean break between the parties at the time of the divorce. Pension splitting is available 'in relation to a person's shareable rights under any pension arrangement other than an excepted public service pension scheme'.[276] Under the order, a percentage of one party's rights under a pension scheme is transferred to the other party to enable her to establish her own pension provision either within or outside the current scheme.[277] While the transferee is credited with the percentage value of the pension ordered by the court, the transferor's fund is reduced accordingly.[278] It should be noted that pension splitting, while a more effective remedy, does not replace the earmarking order which can still be made. However, a pension splitting order cannot be made where an earmarking order is already in force in relation to the pension.[279] Also, an earmarking order cannot be made where a pension splitting order is already in force.[280]

In short, under section 25B the court *must* consider the current and/or likely pension entitlements of the parties on divorce and, in particular, any pension benefits which a spouse will lose on divorce. However, that is not to say that the court must make an order which either compensates the spouse for this loss or splits the value of the pension fund between the parties. In *T v T (Financial Relief: Pensions)*[281] it was argued on behalf of a wife that the earmarking provisions of section 25B–25D did not merely enable the court to compensate her for loss of pension benefits, they *required* the court to compensate her. Singer J rejected this argument.[282] He stated that giving consideration to pension

---

[275] Section 25C(2). In common with ordinary lump sums, lump sum payments from a pension are treated as capital payments and are therefore unaffected by the remarriage of the recipient spouse.

[276] Welfare Reform and Pensions Act 1999, s 27(1). Thus pension splitting can be applied to private and occupational pension schemes, as well as State Earnings Related Pension Scheme (SERPS) contributions, but not the basic state pension.   [277] MCA 1973, s 21A(1).

[278] See the Welfare Reform and Pensions Act 1999, s 29.   [279] MCA 1973, s 24B(5).

[280] Section 25B(7B).   [281] [1998] 1 FLR 1072.

[282] In this case the wife had applied for an order directing the trustees of the husband's pension fund to pay her a proportion of his pension. Singer J declined to earmark part of the husband's pension in this fashion as he foresaw that such a direction could give rise to a number of potential 'pitfalls, disadvantages, complications and distractions'. These included the fact that it was impossible to predict the appropriate quantum of periodical payments so far ahead; the husband might delay the date when he took his pension rights; an application to vary the order could be made even before it came into effect; the court would be in a far better position to determine the amount of an order at the time when the husband took his pension rights; and there was no reason for supposing that the husband would not meet an appropriate periodical payments order from his pension receipts after retirement. For similar reasons, the court declined to require

provision was simply included as part of the conventional discretionary balancing exercise the court was required to perform.[283] Thus whether the court makes an order in relation to the pension is simply part of the court's discretionary powers under section 25 which will be exercised to achieve a fair result between the parties.

6 THE MATRIMONIAL HOME—WHAT ORDER IS THE MOST APPROPRIATE?

Often the parties' only major asset is the matrimonial home and it may require some ingenuity to make adequate provision for each spouse from one main resource, particularly where they have dependent children. The dilemma faced by those assisting the parties to reach an agreement in such circumstances, and the court when determining what order to make, is how can arrangements be made which give proper recognition to the rights of both spouses in the property, protect a financially dependent spouse and any children of the family, create a clean break where appropriate, bring finality, and allow for an adjustment of the position if the circumstances of the parties should significantly alter. Clearly, these very different objectives nearly always conflict. Moreover, there is a real risk that any property they own will be worth much less than it was originally by the time the parties have finished negotiating over what should happen to it, because of escalating legal costs. Indeed, how the costs will be paid is often a factor which influences the final order.[284] Where a spouse is legally aided, if any property is recovered or preserved for the assisted person,[285] the costs payable are a first charge on the property, with interest accumulating the longer the charge remains unredeemed.[286] As we have already seen, the court will endeavour to ensure that the children are adequately housed with the residential parent and that sufficient resources are left to house the non-residential parent.[287] However, in cases where resources are limited, this may not always be possible and thus it is not the case that both spouses 'invariably have a right to purchase accommodation'.[288]

6.1 THE POWERS OF THE COURT

The options in relation to distribution of the family home are not limited to simply transferring the property into the sole name of one spouse or ordering immediate sale and a distribution of the proceeds between the parties. Rather, the courts have a variety of

the husband to commute part of his pension benefits (s 25B(7)) so that a deferred lump sum could be paid to the wife. However, the pension trustees were ordered to pay a lump sum equal to ten times her annual maintenance payable from any death in service benefits, as these benefits might not fall into the husband's estate and would therefore not be available to the wife as a dependant in an application made under the Inheritance (Provision for Family and Dependants) Act 1975.

[283] See also *Burrow v Burrow* [1999] 1 FLR 508.

[284] See eg *H v H (Financial Relief: Costs)* [1997] 2 FLR 57.

[285] Property has been 'recovered or preserved' if it has been in issue between the parties in the proceedings and has either been recovered by the claimant if it has been the subject of a successful claim or preserved to the respondent if the claim fails. Whether the property in question was at issue in the proceedings is one of fact, see *Hanlon v Law Society* [1981] AC 124.

[286] Access to Justice Act 1999, s 10(7). Until recently the first £3,000 of a lump sum or the value of any property 'recovered or preserved' was exempt from payment. However, this exemption has been abolished in respect of applications for funding made on or after 1 April 2005 (Community Legal Service (Financial) (Amendment) Regulations 2005). Periodical payments remain exempt from the statutory charge.

[287] See *M v B (Ancillary Proceedings: Lump Sum)* [1998] 1 FLR 53.

[288] *Piglowska v Piglowski* [1999] 3 All ER 632 at 642–643.

options to achieve the immediate housing of the children and residential parent, whilst preserving the rights of the non-residential parent in the property. The following sections will discuss the main methods of disposition of the matrimonial home on divorce in situations where the property is owned by the parties (it may, of course, be subject to a mortgage). The court's power to order the transfer of tenancies under Part IV of the Family Law Act 1996 will also be highlighted.

6.1.2 The property to be sold and the proceeds of sale divided (s 24A)

The attractive feature of an agreement, or order, under which the matrimonial home is sold and the proceeds of sale divided between the parties is that each spouse is able to realise his or her investment in the property. The court can order that the proceeds of sale be divided in whatever proportions it sees fit in the exercise of its overall discretion to achieve fairness between the parties. This solution is particularly appropriate where there are no children and where each spouse can be adequately housed in alternative accommodation from his or her share of the proceeds. It is also appropriate where the spouses are young. They can go their separate ways, using their shares in the money realised as a down payment on fresh property should they so wish. Sale promotes a clean break and finality.

In *Scallon v Scallon*[289] the spouses were beneficial co-owners. The Court of Appeal took the view that it was fairer to divide the proceeds of sale of the matrimonial home between the spouses than to transfer the property to the wife only and make no order for periodical payments. It approved an order that the house be sold, and that the net proceeds be divided three-fifths to the wife and two-fifths to the husband. The court found that this division would enable both spouses to be housed in alternative accommodation which, the court said, was the correct objective. In addition, it ruled that the wife should have the additional protection of a nominal periodical payments order in case she should need maintenance in the future.[290] With a sale order, the spouse with care of the children (the residential parent) can receive a larger percentage of the proceeds than the other spouse (the non-residential parent), reflecting the requirement that the children's interests must be put first.[291] In some cases, the size of the non-residential parent's share of the sale proceeds may be sufficient for him to set himself up in a home which is of adequate size to provide a setting where his children can enjoy staying in contact with him. The objective of securing homes where the children can stay with either parent may override other considerations in the statutory guidelines, as in *H v H (Financial Relief: Conduct)*[292] where the matrimonial home was sold in order to release a sufficient sum with which the husband could purchase a property. In this case it was held to be in the children's interests that their father was securely housed. However, much depends on the circumstances of the case and as noted previously there is no rule that both spouses 'invariably have a right to purchase accommodation'.[293]

---

[289] [1990] 1 FLR 194.

[290] *Scallon v Scallon* was also concerned with the vexed issue of legal aid, and whether the loan from the Legal Aid Fund must be repaid when the property is sold. If any property is 'recovered or preserved' for a person who has been assisted by legal aid, the Legal Aid Fund has first charge on any such property in order to recoup its expenditure on legal fees. However, since 1989 the Legal Aid Board has had the power to postpone the enforcement of its charge where the money, or property, is to be used for the purchase of a home for the assisted person. In *Scallon v Scallon* the wife asserted that the court had failed to take account of the impact of the charge on her means, and that once she had paid her legal aid contribution she would have insufficient money with which to buy a new home. However, the Court of Appeal, while recognising that postponement of the realisation of the charge is a discretionary power, said that it was right to assume that the Board would not seek to frustrate the order of the court by refusing to exercise its discretion, and by realising its charge immediately.   [291] Section 25(1).

[292] [1998] 1 FLR 971.   [293] *Piglowska v Piglowski* [1999] 2 FLR 763.

The disadvantage of sale is that where there are children they lose their home at a time when they are likely to be suffering distress at the termination of their parents' marriage, and experiencing the loss of the day-to-day presence of one parent. When moving to a new house will involve losing the companionship and support of friends in the neighbourhood, or going to a new school, this may be to deprive the children of much needed emotional security. It may also make more difficult the position of the caring parent who is in, or who is seeking, employment because she may have built up a network of persons on whom she can rely to assist her with care of the children while she is at work.[294]

6.1.3 The property to be transferred into the sole name of one of the spouses (s 24(1)(a))

Transferring the matrimonial home into the sole name of one spouse, like sale, has the advantage that it helps to achieve a clean break. It also has the beneficial outcome that the owning spouse is not in the position of being fearful that he or she will have to sell the property at some date in the future in order that the other spouse can have his share.[295] Courts have been willing to order that the matrimonial home should belong solely to one of the parties where, on the circumstances of the case, the other party has alternative accommodation or sufficient resources to secure accommodation. Thus where one spouse enjoyed secure accommodation as part of his employment, as in *Hanlon v Hanlon*,[296] or had acquired an interest in property through marriage to another, as in *H v H (Financial Provision: Remarriage)*,[297] or had additional wealth as a result of inheritance, as in *Schuller v Schuller*,[298] the property was vested in the name of the other spouse alone. Essentially, in these cases the court took account of all available resources under section 25(2)(a), and used the matrimonial home to house one of the parties secure in the knowledge that the other spouse was provided for. Although one spouse was obtaining a disproportionate share in the matrimonial home, this could be justified by reference to each spouse's needs under section 25(2)(b) and, where there were children, by the requirement under section 25(1) to give first consideration to their interests.

When transferring the matrimonial home to one spouse on divorce, the court can order that the other spouse be compensated for his or her loss by a lump sum payment, raised perhaps through the property being mortgaged or remortgaged. An order requiring the spouse to whom the property is transferred to pay the other spouse a lump sum is similar in effect to one in which sale of the home is ordered, because in each case both acquire a share in the value of the property.[299] However, a transfer of property has the advantage that the original property is retained thus preserving familiarity of surroundings and continuity for any children of the family.

Another way of compensating a spouse for giving up his or her claim to a share in the matrimonial property, particularly where there is insufficient capital to make a compensatory payment, is to make no order for periodical payments. In *Hanlon v Hanlon*[300] the husband, who was living rent free in a police flat, was ordered to transfer his entire interest in the matrimonial home to his wife who was looking after their four children, and in return he was no longer required to make periodical payments for the two children who

---

[294] See *Chaudhuri v Chaudhuri* [1992] 2 FLR 73, in which it had been a central part of the wife's case that she needed to stay in the matrimonial home in order to provide a secure home for the children in a neighbourhood where she would have the support of friends.

[295] See *Hanlon v Hanlon* [1978] 2 All ER 889; *Mortimer v Mortimer-Griffin* [1986] 2 FLR 315.

[296] [1978] 2 All ER 889. The husband lived rent-free in a police flat.   [297] [1975] 1 All ER 367.

[298] [1990] 2 FLR 193.

[299] In many instances, however, the owner spouse will not have sufficient resources to make any, or any substantial, payment.   [300] [1978] 2 All ER 889.

were still dependent.[301] However, *Hanlon v Hanlon* preceded the Child Support Act 1991. Nowadays a husband could sensibly agree that in return for him transferring his share in the home to his wife, she will not seek an order for periodical payments for herself either at that time or in the future.[302] But a husband would be extremely unwise to accept such an arrangement in relation to his financial responsibility for his children. He would be vulnerable to an application for child support being made under the Child Support Act 1991 at any time by his former wife[303] which would not take account of the property transfer.

The conduct of one of the parties, provided that it is grave enough to be considered inequitable to disregard,[304] may lead the court to make an order which secures the matrimonial home solely for the other with no compensatory arrangement, as in *Jones v Jones*,[305] discussed earlier. In *Jones v Jones* the conduct of the husband had a direct bearing on the wife's financial circumstances. Similarly, where the husband had dissipated the family assets or previously failed to make periodical payments, courts have chosen to make an order transferring the home to the wife.[306]

In *A v A (Financial Provision)*[307] the matrimonial home, which the parties jointly owned, had a net value of £50,000 and as the wife had overall responsibility for the care and upbringing of the parties' three children, she needed all the capital until they achieved independence. Consequently, the husband's realisation of his share had to be postponed until the children reached adulthood. The most difficult decision for the court was how to balance the wife's need for the immediate use of all the capital against the husband's claim to receive his adjusted portion at the end of that term.[308] Normally, the court would have made an order for a deferred charge. However, there was a history of violence by the husband, and he continued to have obsessional feelings about his wife. Thorpe J therefore took the view that it would be unwise to perpetuate a financial relationship between the parties for many years to come, and instead he ordered the wife to make a lump sum payment of £15,000 to the husband. There were various methods by which the wife might raise the lump sum, but because of her responsibilities and the uncertainties of her resources he held that it would be wrong at that stage to specify a date for payment.[309]

The disadvantage of an order which transfers the parties' only substantial asset into the name of only one spouse is that, unless it is made with compensating provisions, it may give unfair weight to one spouse's needs at the expense of the other spouse's rights. This position is exacerbated when the order has been based on the parties' respective needs, and if the needy spouse's circumstances change for the better after the order in her favour has been finalised, for example if she remarries,[310] comes into an inheritance, or obtains gainful employment. At this stage there is no way of reopening the matter and correcting the imbalance of the original distribution of the property.[311] In the interests of fairness,

---

[301] In *Smith v Smith* [1975] 2 All ER 19n the husband was ordered to transfer his half interest in the matrimonial home to his wife despite the fact that he had no other secure accommodation. His wife had a pressing need for the home because their child had a serious kidney complaint. In return, no periodical payments were ordered for the wife, and only a modest sum for the child.

[302] The transferor should ensure that an order is made under s 25A(3) directing that the transferee shall not be entitled to make any further application for periodical payments.

[303] The position would, of course, be identical if the parties' roles were reversed.

[304] Under the MCA 1973, s 25(2)(g).   [305] [1975] 2 All ER 12.

[306] *Bryant v Bryant* (1976) 120 Sol Jo 165.   [307] [1995] 1 FLR 345.

[308] The husband's share was reduced from a half to a third.

[309] Each party was given liberty to apply as to the date of payment, but Thorpe J expressed the hope that the lump sum would be paid without either party having to exercise their liberty to apply.

[310] *Wells v Wells* [1992] 2 FLR 66.

[311] *Chaudhuri v Chaudhuri* [1992] 2 FLR 73; *Omielan v Omielan* [1996] 2 FLR 306.

the court may find it preferable to shape the order to allow both spouses to retain an interest in the former matrimonial home. There are particular legal devices which can be used to facilitate this.

6.1.4 Retaining an interest for each spouse in the matrimonial home

Satisfying the immediate needs of one spouse at the time of divorce should not necessarily outweigh the legitimate expectation of the other spouse to have some share in the property, the purchase of which he or she has paid towards. If both spouses have contributed towards the purchase of the house, either financially or in kind by looking after the home and caring for the family, then, applying paragraphs (c) and (f) (looking to the parties' standard of living and contribution to the welfare of the family) it may seem inequitable to deprive one spouse of any share in the parties' only substantial asset. Indeed, the principles of equality and non-discrimination inherent in *White v White* strengthen the argument that the fairest solution is that each spouse should retain, or be awarded, a proprietary interest in the former matrimonial home.[312]

There are two main ways of achieving this outcome. Where the parties are joint owners of the property at the time of the divorce a court can order that their co-ownership should continue, but that the right of occupation should be given solely to the spouse who remains in occupation. Alternatively, one sole or co-owner can be ordered to transfer his or her interest in the property to the other. In return, the (now) sole owner spouse can be required to execute a charge over the property in favour of the other spouse. In either case a court can order that realisation of the non-occupying or non-owning spouse's interest in the property should be postponed until the earliest date at which one or more of various contingencies should occur.

One of the most difficult questions to be determined in cases where the property is held in co-ownership, or where a former spouse has the benefit of a charge over the property, is 'when should the spouse kept out of his share in the former matrimonial home be entitled to realise his share?' When that share is substantial, its realisation will often mean that the house must be sold, so the chosen time has very serious implications for the spouse who has remained living in the property. Equally, the party kept out of his share in the property has a very real interest in the choice of eventualities which will lead to him being able to realise that share. Various eventualities present themselves as an appropriate date. These include:

(i) the youngest child of the family reaching a specified age, or completing full-time education;

(ii) the death of the wife;

(iii) the remarriage of the wife;

(iv) the wife's cohabitation with another;

(v) the sale of the property.

6.1.5 Postponing realisation of one party's share until the children reach adulthood (a *Mesher* order)

An order that the property remain in co-ownership, with the sale postponed, or the charge not to be redeemable, until the youngest child reaches a specified age, is often

---

[312] See S. Gerlis, '*White*—The Unlearned Lesson' [2002] 32 Family Law 628; L. Fisher, 'The Unexpected Impact of *White*—Taking "Equality" Too Far' [2002] Family Law 108 at 111–112. See also *Elliott v Elliott* [2001] 1 FCR 477.

referred to as a *Mesher* order.[313] The original *Mesher* order involved a settlement of the property on the spouses on trust for sale in equal shares, sale postponed until the youngest child reached 17.[314] But the term a '*Mesher* order' has been used by lawyers and judges to describe any order under which one of the spouses is kept out of his or her share in the former matrimonial home until a specified event relating to the children occurs.[315] When *Mesher* orders were first introduced the chosen age was typically 18, coinciding with the child reaching majority, and the statutory obligation to give first consideration to the welfare of minor children coming to an end.[316] However, in recent years there has been a tendency to select the date when the youngest child reaches 17 or completes full-time education, including further and higher education whichever is the later.[317] An even more generous approach was taken by the Court of Appeal in *Sawden v Sawden*[318] where the sale of the property was postponed until the adult children had left the family home and had settled in homes of their own.

It was suggested that *Mesher* orders would become more popular in the aftermath of *White v White* where the need to ensure fairness between the parties could be achieved by meeting the immediate housing needs of the wife and children by giving them occupancy of the property, but allowing the husband to retain an interest in its capital.[319] However, *Mesher* orders are not popular with the judiciary. They have dropped out of favour, not only because they contradict the ideal of producing finality between the parties at the time of divorce but also because they are said to store up problems for the future.[320] *Obiter* dicta in *Clutton v Clutton*[321] suggest that a *Mesher* order may be appropriate where the spouses' assets are amply sufficient to house both parties if the home is sold immediately, but where it is in the interests of the children that they remain in the same home for the time being.[322] In such a case, said Lloyd LJ, it may be sensible and just to postpone sale until the children have left home, since the wife's share in the proceeds of sale when that time arrives will be sufficient to enable her to rehouse herself. However, he continued, 'where there is doubt as to the wife's ability to rehouse herself, on the charge taking effect, then a *Mesher* order should not be made.'[323] This statement highlights the reservations which the courts have expressed about *Mesher* orders in recent years. When the children reach the specified age the parent who has been looking after them in the former matrimonial home, usually the wife, may not have enough remaining money after sale of the property, or redemption of the charge, to buy a new property.[324] Hence the anxiety that *Mesher* orders store up trouble for the future. The application of the principles of *White v White* could be said to encourage the use of *Mesher* orders so that the husband can retain an interest in the former matrimonial home. However, the same principles could also discourage the use of such orders in situations where the wife has insufficient capital either to buy-out her former husband's share in the property or to secure alternative accommodation when this share is realised.

[313] *Mesher v Mesher and Hall* [1980] 1 All ER 126n.

[314] The concept of a trust for sale has since been overtaken by the concept of a trust in land, see the Trusts of Land and Appointment of Trustees Act 1996. However, the principles applying to postponement of sale of jointly owned property after divorce remain the same.

[315] See eg *Carson v Carson* [1983] 1 All ER 478, in which the property was ordered to be held on trust for sale for the spouses jointly until the youngest child attained 18, or completed full-time education.

[316] Section 25(1).   [317] *Richardson v Richardson (No 2)* [1994] 2 FLR 1051; *B v B* [1995] 1 FLR 9.

[318] [2004] 1 FCR 776.

[319] See eg *Elliott v Elliott* [2001] 1 FCR 477. See S. Gerlis, '*White*—The Unlearned Lesson' [2002] 32 Family Law 628; L. Fisher, 'The Unexpected Impact of *White*—Taking "Equality" Too Far' [2002] Family Law 108 at 111–112.   [320] *Carson v Carson* [1983] 1 All ER 478.

[321] [1991] 1 All ER 340.   [322] See also *Dorney-Kingdom v Dorney-Kingdom* [2000] 2 FLR 855.

[323] [1991] 1 All ER 340 at 343.   [324] *Hanlon v Hanlon* [1978] 2 All ER 889.

Another disadvantage of a *Mesher* order is that children do not stop needing a family home merely because they leave school, complete further education, or start work. It is noticeable that in those cases where the children were not expected to go into higher or further education the courts have sometimes chosen 17 as the date for sale.[325] Yet orders which lead to the family home being sold when children are on the threshold of adulthood, or have attained their majority, are based on inappropriate expectations of independence at such a young age, and they fail to recognise that the crucial date may arise at a time when a child is taking important examinations.[326] It is suggested that 21 is a more suitable age,[327] or the completion of the youngest child's education, whichever is the later.[328] The age of 21 is, of course, a higher age than the ages of 17 or 18 which bring to an end the obligation of parents to make periodical payments for their children (unless the child is receiving further education or training).[329] Also, once the children of the family reach majority, they are no longer the court's first consideration under section 25(1). However 'adult children' can still be characterised as an obligation and responsibility under section 25(2)(b). Moreover, it is suggested that the higher age is justifiable because there is a difference between an obligation to maintain a child through the provision of income, and an obligation to continue to provide him with a home. Whilst it may be realistic to expect a child to be able to earn a living once he attains his majority, it is usually not realistic to expect him to earn sufficient income to rent or buy adequate accommodation. There are sound social policy reasons for enabling young adults to remain in the family home for some period of time after reaching 18. These include that they will continue to benefit from the influence and guidance of their parents. They are more likely to delay marrying, or cohabiting, and having children of their own before they have sufficient resources to make proper provision for their own family. And, in the case of students in higher education, they need a home to return to in vacations.[330] It is interesting that in *Sawden v Sawden*, the Court of Appeal added to the list of trigger events which would realise the husband's charge on the property when the children (aged 28 and 21) had left home and settled independently in homes of their own.[331]

A significant disadvantage of a *Mesher* order is that it makes the assumption that the children will continue to make their permanent home with the parent who is living in the property throughout their minority. But this may sometimes come into conflict with reality, and with the philosophy of the Children Act 1989. The Act is founded on the premise that after divorce both parents continue to have parental responsibility for their children. It also builds on the notion that parents should be encouraged to make their own arrangements about their children, and that court orders should not be made which settle the arrangements as to the person with whom the children are to live unless making such an order is better for the children.[332] In the case of an order where the non-owning spouse's interest in the former matrimonial home is preserved by a charge over the property, there is no power to re-transfer the home should either the children wish, or a court order, that they move from one parent to the other.[333] A co-ownership order which simply

---

[325] As in *Mesher v Mesher and Hall* [1980] 1 All ER 126n itself.

[326] Relying, probably, on the fact that a parent will normally not try to force a sale at an inappropriate stage in his child's life. But should the date of sale, which relates so directly to the welfare of the child, be left to the goodwill of the non-residential parent?　　　[327] As in *Alonso v Alonso* (1974) 4 Fam Law 164.

[328] It would usually be appropriate to state that education includes undergraduate, but not post-graduate, education.　　　[329] Section 29(1)–(3).

[330] Contrast the approaches to the continuing need of the children for the family home taken in *Hanlon v Hanlon* [1978] 2 All ER 889 and *Chamberlain v Chamberlain* [1974] 1 All ER 33.

[331] See [2005] Fam Law 116.　　　[332] Children Act 1989, s 1(5). See further Chapter 9.

[333] See eg *Omielan v Omielan* [1996] 2 FLR 306; *Chaudhuri v Chaudhuri* [1992] 2 FLR 73.

contains a provision that one spouse is entitled to remain in the matrimonial home until the children reach a specified age similarly does not provide for this eventuality. This is because, once made, a property adjustment order (giving the non-owning spouse a charge over the property, or occupancy rights) cannot usually be varied. Thus, in both scenarios the spouses are locked into a fixed property arrangement which cannot be departed from unless both agree.

6.1.6 Remarriage or cohabitation precipitating sale or realisation of the charge (a *Martin* order)

One spouse, usually the wife, may have a particularly pressing need to be accommodated in the former matrimonial home. Sometimes this need is likely to continue for the rest of her life. Because one of the main concerns of the court is to make sure that, wherever possible, each spouse is securely housed, it has sometimes been thought appropriate to order that while the matrimonial home remains jointly owned, the wife should be allowed to live in the property for the rest of her life. This means that the husband will never himself obtain his share in the property if he predeceases her. He must draw what comfort he can from the knowledge that his share will at some time enure to the benefit of his estate. However, usually such an order contains the contingencies that the property should be sold, or the charge be realisable, 'if the wife should remarry or cohabit with another man'. This is often described as a *Martin*[334] order.

In *Clutton v Clutton*[335] the Court of Appeal ruled that the trial judge had been wrong to order the transfer of the matrimonial home to the wife free of any charge in favour of the husband. It emphasised that the clean break approach did not mean that the court should disregard other considerations, and deprive one spouse for all time of any share in the matrimonial home. In *Clutton v Clutton* both spouses were aged 48 and were divorcing after a 20-year marriage. Their only asset of substance was the matrimonial home, the equity in which was about £50,000. The husband was earning about £20,000 per annum but had substantial debts. The wife had an income of £66 per week working part time as a typist. She was in a stable sexual relationship with a man, but she said that she did not intend either to marry him or to cohabit with him. The Court of Appeal considered whether remarriage, or cohabitation, should affect the wife's future position, and found that it should. The essence of the court's judgment was that it would be unfair to the husband if he lost his entire interest in the property through the wife obtaining an outright transfer order, if she was later joined in the house by a new husband, the latter having contributed nothing towards its acquisition. In relation to cohabitation, Lloyd LJ said that if the reason underlying the clean break principle is the avoidance of bitterness, 'then the bitterness felt by the husband when he sees the former matrimonial home occupied by the wife's cohabitee must surely be greater than the bitterness felt by the wife being subject, as she fears, to perpetual supervision'.[336] The court therefore ordered that the sale of the house should be postponed until the wife died, remarried, or cohabited with another man, and that the proceeds should then be divided on the basis of two-thirds to the wife and one-third to the husband.

6.1.6.1 Remarriage as a triggering event

Consider the effect of such an order, namely that the charge should be enforceable by the husband or that the property should be sold in the event of the wife's remarriage, and measure it against the principle that it is normally fair that each spouse is entitled to a share in the value of the former matrimonial home. Look at it first from the point of view

---

[334] After *Martin v Martin* [1977] 3 All ER 762.   [335] [1991] 1 All ER 340.   [336] Ibid, 345.

of the husband. His position was succinctly expressed by Ormrod LJ in *Leate v Leate*[337] when he recognised that it is 'very galling' for a husband if the family assets are handed over to the wife who then remarries. It could strongly be asserted on behalf of the husband that remarriage is a new relationship which should not be subsidised in any way by an ex-husband. He could argue that a wife who has remarried has all the protection of the legal code which surrounds that new marriage, and that her ex-husband's obligation to provide her with housing should now be brought to an end. Indeed, on behalf of the husband it could be asserted that if remarriage is not a contingency which should precipitate him acquiring his share in the property, it is hard to think of what other change of circumstance should bring this about.

But now consider such a clause from the point of view of the wife. It could be asserted that it may act as a serious restraint on her remarrying, or on her being able to do so only at the cost of losing her home and, where there are children, the children's home too.[338] Such a clause is based on the assumption that her new husband will either be able to provide her with accommodation or that he will be able to buy out the husband's share in the former matrimonial home. But this may prove to be incorrect. It could also be pointed out that where the wife is in receipt of periodical payments, her entitlement to these comes to an end on remarriage.[339] Thus remarriage, for her, will mean that not only will she lose her source of income, she may also lose the roof over her head and, when there are children, over their heads too. Yet, the wife is not at risk of losing her home (and may continue to receive periodical payments) provided that she does not remarry. It could be maintained on behalf of the wife that the insertion of the contingency of remarriage is liable to perpetuate the wife's tie to her ex-husband, it is liable to dissuade her from making a fresh start, and that it is a restraint on marriage which is arguably contrary to public policy.

6.1.6.2 Cohabitation as a triggering event

In *Clutton v Clutton* the Court of Appeal not only made remarriage a reason for the property being sold, it also said that the wife's 'cohabitation with another man' should have the same effect. In *Chadwick v Chadwick*[340] the Court of Appeal specifically endorsed the inclusion of such a cohabitation clause. In this case, after divorce, the trial court had ordered that the former matrimonial home be held in joint names with the parties as trustees, with the wife to have sole occupation of the property unless she decided to move, remarry, or cohabit with another man. On the occurrence of any of these events the house was to be sold and the proceeds divided equally between her and her former husband. The wife, who was severely disabled, appealed on two grounds: (i) that she might wish to move in order to live nearer the hospital where she had regular medical appointments; and (ii) that any new spouse or partner might not have enough resources to be able to assist her with the purchase of the specially adapted accommodation which she needed. She argued that, in either situation, her share in the proceeds of sale might not be sufficient to enable her to buy a new home, and therefore that the order put her at risk of being rendered homeless. The husband's position was that he had no other major resources, and he was purchasing a new property with the assistance of a 100 per cent mortgage.

Approving and upholding the trial judge's order, Cumming Bruce LJ stated that in order to do justice to the husband it was necessary to impose some 'real inconvenience'

---

[337] (1982) 12 Fam Law 121.   [338] See *Omielan v Omielan* [1996] 2 FLR 306.
[339] Section 28(1)(a).
[340] [1985] FLR 606; see too *Simpson v Simpson* [1984] CA Transcript 119; *Hendrix v Hendrix* [1984] CA Transcript 57.

on the former wife, which here meant that if she remarried or cohabited the house must be sold. He continued:

> That imposes on her the necessity, if she decides either to marry another gentleman or to cohabit with another gentleman, to select as her consort a gentleman who is in a position to provide her with accommodation suitable to her needs. [If] she does decide to marry or to cohabit with a gentleman who cannot provide her with such accommodation, that must be regarded as a grave misfortune which she will bring upon herself. Although material considerations are sometimes not the main considerations that lead spouses to the altar, they are not irrelevant.[341]

The practice of equating cohabitation with remarriage may give rise to problems of definition. First, it will not always be clear whether or not the wife is cohabiting. For example, is a woman cohabiting when a long-distance lorry driver spends part of the week at his parents' home and the other part at the wife's home?[342] It may also not be clear for how long the cohabiting relationship must last before it can precipitate sale of the property. Sometimes a time provision is included in the order such as 'the property to be sold if the wife should cohabit with another man for a period exceeding six months'. But even this may be uncertain in its application. For example, what would be the position if the cohabitation continued for more than six months, but then came to an end? Would the husband nonetheless be entitled to demand that the property now be sold in accordance with the court's order? It appears after *Omielan v Omielan*[343] that the answer to this question is 'yes'. An order to that effect had been made in *Omielan* and the wife had cohabited for more than six months. The Court of Appeal ruled that she was bound by the terms of the order. This places the wife, and any children living with her, in a very vulnerable position, for now she can turn to neither man for a roof over her head or other forms of financial assistance.

It appears both anomalous, and contradictory, that the courts have equated cohabitation with remarriage for the purposes of precipitating sale of the matrimonial home, but not for the purposes of terminating periodical payments in an application brought in variation proceedings. In *Atkinson v Atkinson*[344] the Court of Appeal was emphatic that it is for Parliament, not the courts, to determine whether the fact of cohabitation should *automatically* bring to an end the right of a wife to receive periodical payments, and it refused either to extinguish, or even substantially to reduce, the cohabiting wife's order despite evidence that the wife had deliberately refrained from marrying because remarriage would lead to the termination of her periodical payments. This view has since been reiterated on several occasions,[345] although in *K v K (Periodical Payment: Cohabitation)*[346] Coleridge J questioned why the consequences of cohabitation should not be the same as the consequences of remarriage on a periodical payments order. Courts also appear to have lost sight of the principle expounded in *Duxbury v Duxbury*[347] that, after divorce, a wife should be free to live as she chooses and to spend money on, or provide a home for, whomsoever she wishes. In *Clutton v Clutton*[348] the wife argued that a cohabitation clause would encourage constant surveillance of her private life by her husband. This fear was

---

[341] [1985] FLR 606 at 608.

[342] Case law demonstrates a diverse range of domestic living arrangements. See eg *Kotke v Saffarini* [2005] EWCA Civ 221; *Churchill v Roach* [2003] WTLR 779.   [343] [1996] 2 FLR 306.

[344] [1987] 3 All ER 849.

[345] See eg *S v S* [1987] 1 FLR 71; *Atkinson v Atkinson (No 2)* [1996] 1 FLR 51; *Fleming v Fleming* [2004] 1 FLR 667. While cohabitation with a new partner will not automatically bring one's periodical payments from a former spouse to an end, the court can take the new living arrangements into account which may result in the payments being varied or terminated under s 33.   [346] [2005] EWHC 2886 (Fam).

[347] [1987] 1 FLR 7.   [348] [1991] 1 All ER 340.

dismissed by the court, but it seems likely that steps to obtain evidence to confirm his suspicions will sometimes be taken by a husband who suspects that his wife is cohabiting when this is denied. This type of 'snooping' is at best distasteful and, at worst, may amount to an invasion of the wife's privacy.

It is suggested that it is most unfortunate that courts have advocated the making of orders in which cohabitation is a factor which automatically precipitates sale of the home, or the right to realise the charge. Cohabitation does not give a wife the same financial security as remarriage. She has no automatic right to live in any new property purchased solely by her cohabitant. If her cohabiting relationship comes to an end, she has no claims against her new partner for financial provision and property adjustment orders.[349] Should her cohabitant die, she has no automatic succession rights and no pension rights. Thus there are no safeguards, let alone guarantees, that a cohabiting relationship will make provision for a wife's future needs, which was the fear of the wife in *Chadwick v Chadwick*.[350] It would be more acceptable, and less gender-biased,[351] if orders were made in such a manner as to allow the courts to respond in the most appropriate manner to the eventualities of the wife's remarriage, or cohabitation, if and when they occur. This could be achieved by giving the husband 'liberty to apply' to the court for an order that jointly-owned property should now be sold, or that he should be entitled to realise his charge if the wife should remarry or cohabit with another man. This allows the court to deal with the issue, on its merits, at the time when it happens. In some cases it will be appropriate to order immediate sale. In others the needs of the wife compared to those of the husband may be such as to persuade the court that to order sale, or the realisation of the charge, would cause her too much hardship. It should be recalled that unless the wife remarries, or cohabits, the husband will, in any event, be deprived of his share of the property. Making these eventualities automatic factors precipitating sale is arguably to put a strong and unacceptable restraint on an ex-wife forming an intimate relationship with a new partner.[352]

6.1.7 *Mesher and Martin* orders are final orders

Property adjustment orders are final, and cannot be varied. Questions have arisen, however, over whether the specified date for sale of the former matrimonial home, or the realisation of a charge over it, can be altered. In *Thompson v Thompson*[353] spouses remained co-owners of the matrimonial home, and sale of the property was postponed until the children reached 17 or until further order. The wife wanted to move and therefore wished to sell the property while the children were still young. The husband refused to agree to the sale because he feared losing contact with his children. The wife therefore applied to the court for a further order compelling the husband to consent to the sale of the property. It was held by the Court of Appeal that provided the order included a 'liberty to apply'

---

[349] Recommendations proposed by the Law Commission to introduce such a scheme to apply to cohabitants have been put on the back burner. See Chapter 5.

[350] [1985] FLR 606. See further M. Hayes, 'Cohabitation Clauses in Financial Provision and Property Adjustment Orders: Law, Policy and Justice' (1994) 110 LQR 124.

[351] It is suggested that it is most unlikely that a court would order that a husband who remains in occupation of the matrimonial home under a *Martin* or *Mesher* order should be forced to sell the home if he should remarry, or cohabit, with another woman. The assumption is more likely to be made that such a union will add to the husband's responsibilities, rather than provide him with additional resources.

[352] Indeed, it could be asked whether such orders are a modern version of the much discredited *dum sola et casta* (while unmarried and chaste) clauses.

[353] [1985] 2 All ER 243.

provision, the court had jurisdiction to order a sale under section 24A.[354] But it also held that a sale order must be seen as a *working out* of the original order and not a *variation* of it. It held that an early sale at the instance of the party (here the wife) for whose protection the order had been made would give effect to the original order rather than vary it.

Thompson v Thompson should, however, be contrasted with *Taylor v Taylor*,[355] in which the Court of Appeal held that there was jurisdiction to hear an application for an earlier sale under section 24A, whether or not the original order gave liberty to apply for an earlier sale. However, it was held that the trial judge had been wrong to order an earlier sale under section 24A without hearing evidence, or exercising his discretion, on the merits of the case. More significantly, it was held that the discretion to order an earlier sale would not be exercised if the consequence would be to displace rights which had already vested under the earlier order.

This line of reasoning was followed by the Court of Appeal in *Omielan v Omielan*.[356] The court made it plain that section 24A is purely procedural and that it was inserted into the Act to clarify or expand the court's powers of implementation and enforcement. It further made it plain that it is not possible to amend a property adjustment order by making an order under section 24A. In *Omielan* the parties made a consent order whereby the wife was entitled to occupy the former matrimonial home with their four children but the property was to be sold on the occurrence of one of four events. These included the wife's cohabitation with another man for a period of not less than six months.[357] Subsequently, two of the children went to live with the husband, and the wife gave birth to a child by a man with whom she had been cohabiting for more than six months. The husband applied for an order that the matrimonial home be sold, which the wife resisted. She applied for an order varying the original order and postponing sale until the youngest child reached 18. Ordering that the property be sold and dismissing the wife's application, the Court of Appeal held that there was no jurisdiction to vary the original order. The effect of the wife's cohabitation for more than six months was to bring to an end her beneficial interest in possession and to bring into possession the vested beneficial interests in reversion.

6.1.8 Overcoming the 'moving house' problem

In cases of co-ownership, the courts seem invariably to have ordered that the parties' respective interests in the fund tied up in the matrimonial home must be shared between them on sale of the property. When making charge orders, almost invariably the courts have provided that the charge will be realisable when the property is sold. However, the contingency that sale of the property leads to distribution of the proceeds of sale may cause particular hardship to the owning or occupying spouse who wishes to move house. Whether there has been a limited term order, as in the case of a *Mesher* order, or a *Martin* order giving the wife a right to live in the house for life, the security afforded by that order disappears if the property is sold at an earlier date, and the proceeds of sale are divided.

---

[354] Section 24A:

> Where the court makes…a secured periodical payments order, an order for the payment of a lump sum or a property adjustment order, then, on making that order or at any time thereafter, the court may make a further order for the sale of such property as may be specified in the order, being property in which or in the proceeds of sale of which either or both of the parties to the marriage has or have a beneficial interest, either in possession or reversion.

[355] [1987] 1 FLR 142.   [356] [1996] 2 FLR 306.

[357] The other three were the wife's remarriage, her death, or her ceasing to reside at the property on a full-time basis. Unusually, the husband divested himself of any beneficial interest, and the wife's was reduced to 25 per cent. The children had a vested 75 per cent beneficial interest in reversion, subject to the wife's prior right of occupation. The husband and wife were joint owners of the legal estate and trustees of the proceeds of sale.

The wife may wish to move for various reasons such as to take up an offer of employment, to be closer to the children's schools, to care for elderly parents, or to be near to a hospital.[358] Yet the effect of the order may prevent her from moving.

How might the moving house problem be overcome? In co-ownership cases the property is already vested in trustees (usually the husband and wife). It is suggested that any order or agreement should impose a specific duty on the husband and wife to reinvest the proceeds of sale in a new property, where the wife makes such a request.[359] But in order to be fair to the husband, the order or agreement could include a provision allowing him liberty to apply for the proceeds to be divided when the sale occurs. This would enable the court to consider the respective merits of the spouses' positions at that time. In cases where there is a charge, provision could be made that the charge should not be realisable on sale of the property, provided that the proceeds of sale are reinvested in new property which is similarly intended to provide a home for the wife, and any dependent children who are living with her, the charge to be attached to the new property. Again, in order to be fair to the husband, liberty to apply for realisation of the charge when the property is sold could be given.

Does it seem likely that courts would be willing to accept such a flexible approach? There is no reason in principle why they should not. The answer probably would depend on how they perceive the way in which it would affect the balance of interests between the husband and wife.[360] On the one hand, if the main focus of the original order was to make provision for the wife's needs, then an order which would ensure that those needs will continue to be provided for, should she wish to move house, might well be considered desirable. It could usefully be pointed out that one reason for the wife's desire to move might be because she has employment opportunities elsewhere and that, were she to obtain employment, this could bring about a clean break from any periodical payments requirements imposed on the husband. Thus both parties would gain from such an arrangement. On the other hand, if the court's focus has been on the preservation of the absent spouse's share in that particular piece of property, then it would be likely to be reluctant to allow for such a scheme. In *Chadwick v Chadwick*,[361] which appears to be the only reported case which directly deals with this matter, the Court of Appeal was entirely unsympathetic to the wife's position.

6.1.9 More open-ended *Mesher* and *Martin* orders

It has been seen that the insertion in orders of specific contingencies which give rise to the enforcement of sale of the property, or the entitlement to demand that the charge over the property should now be realisable, have the potential to cause hardship for the occupying or owning spouse. This potential may dissuade a court from making an order containing a specific contingency, as in the case of *Mesher* orders, which have fallen out of favour for this reason. Yet a refusal to contemplate a *Mesher* order may cause equal hardship for the non-occupying spouse if the other option is a *Martin* order. Such an order often means that the husband never realises his share in the property during his lifetime.

---

[358] Cf *Chadwick v Chadwick* [1985] FLR 606.

[359] See eg *Omielan v Omielan* [1996] 2 FLR 306. The order, which included the provision that the property be sold if the 'wife ceased to reside in the property on a full-time basis', contained a paragraph which enabled the wife to substitute for the former matrimonial home an alternative property.

[360] For an unusual example see *Greenham v Greenham* [1989] 1 FLR 105, in which the Court of Appeal deleted a provision requiring a husband who was occupying the former matrimonial home to pay his wife 20 per cent of its value when he reached his 70th birthday. The court said that although he would have sufficient capital and income to do so, it would still involve him in having to move house at an age when he might not wish to do so.   [361] [1985] FLR 606.

An alternative approach is for courts to make more open-ended orders. Sometimes they have done this by inserting a contingency in an order, but also including a clause which gives either spouse 'liberty to apply to the court for an earlier sale of the property, or earlier realisation of the charge'. An even more open-ended order is one in which sale is postponed until 'the parties consent to the sale or until further order of the court, with liberty to apply'.[362]

The disadvantage of a more open-ended type of order is that it is vague and leaves the parties in a state of uncertainty. It is difficult for either of them to make plans if they do not know what events might precipitate sale. Also, when they cannot agree that the appropriate time for sale has now been reached, they may then become embroiled in further litigation, which is costly. However, an open-ended order has the advantage that the merits of ordering a sale can be reviewed at the time of the application. Thus where, for example, the youngest child has not yet reached 18, but where the husband has a particularly pressing need to realise his share in the property, this would allow the husband to take the matter back to court. Where the wife is in fact in the position to be able to accommodate herself from her share in the property, or able to buy the husband out, the court could take account of this when reaching its decision. Equally, if the youngest child has reached 18, but where both the wife and the 'child' have pressing needs to remain in the property, and where the husband is adequately accommodated elsewhere, this too could be borne in mind by the court when determining whether sale should be ordered. It has been argued that an order which states that the property must be sold where the wife cohabits with another man may be unduly restrictive. But a more open-ended order, which would give the husband liberty to apply in the event of his wife's cohabitation would be fair to him, but would also allow the wife to form a relationship with a man of limited means, without the fear of automatically losing the roof over her head.

Normally, the proportion each spouse will receive in the proceeds of sale of the property is fixed at the time when the order is made. However this is not imperative, and in *Sakkas v Sakkas*[363] Wood J ordered that the property be held on trust for sale, sale to be postponed until the younger child attained the age of 20. He further ordered that before the house was sold the matter should be brought back before the court for directions to be given as to the proportions in which the proceeds were to be divided. Again there is uncertainty, and the potential for further litigation is actually built into the court's order; however such an order has the advantage of flexibility and gives the opportunity to achieve fairness when the date for sale arrives.

6.1.10 Choosing between co-ownership or a charge over the property

It has been seen that there is a choice to be made where each spouse retains an interest in the former matrimonial home. Should they be co-owners, or should the property be transferred into the sole name of one party and the interest of the other be protected by giving him a charge over the property?

6.1.10.1 Co-ownership

There are various considerations which might usefully be borne in mind when making this choice. In many cases co-ownership will be the starting position because it has become increasingly common for the matrimonial home to be conveyed into the spouses' joint names, usually as beneficial joint tenants. When determining what should happen

---

[362] See *Re Evers Trust, Papps v Evers* [1980] 3 All ER 399, in the context of postponing the enforcement of a trust for sale (now a trust in land): see Chapter 5.

[363] [1987] Fam Law 414.

to the matrimonial home it may be the easiest solution simply to maintain the joint tenancy. This has two significant consequences: first, on the death of one joint tenant the whole beneficial interest enures to the benefit of the survivor; and, secondly, each spouse's share in the proceeds of sale is fixed at 50 per cent. Therefore, when a marriage breaks down and the parties are joint tenants of the matrimonial home, one of the first matters to consider is whether the joint tenancy should be severed. Succession rights through operation of the doctrine of survivorship may represent what the parties wish, especially where the home is being used for the children, or where each spouse agrees that, in the event of death, the surviving parent should own the house. However, where there is no such joint intention, a spouse who fails to sever the joint tenancy and then dies is likely to have his or her testamentary wishes defeated by operation of the right of survivorship.[364]

It is suggested that a conscious decision should always be made about whether to sever the joint tenancy at an early stage in divorce proceedings. If the divorce proceedings are concluded before the death, presumably questions of severance will be dealt with by the court under section 24. The danger lies if either party dies before the conclusion of the divorce proceedings. Here, in the absence of severance, the survivor takes all. For example, in *McDowell v Hirschfield Lipson & Rumney and Smith*[365] the husband and wife were joint tenants of the matrimonial home. The husband had petitioned for divorce after living apart from his wife for more than five years. He had been living with another woman, the plaintiff, and she had borne him two children. The husband had died while the divorce proceedings were pending and there had been no express severance of the joint tenancy. The court held that, for severance to be implied, a course of dealing must be shown in which both parties clearly evince an intention that the property should henceforth be held in common and not jointly, and this the plaintiff had failed to establish. The husband's interest therefore passed to the wife. The other danger in simply allowing a joint tenancy to continue is that such an arrangement is dependent on trust and cooperation between ex-spouses in circumstances which cannot be foreseen. There is always the risk that one of the spouses might sever the joint tenancy at some future date, and devise his or her share to a third party, without the other spouse being aware of the implications of severance for succession purposes.

Another problem associated with preserving the joint tenancy is that if the property is sold during the lifetime of the spouses the proceeds of sale must be equally distributed between them. This may mean that one of the parties has insufficient resources with which to purchase a new property. It may therefore be more appropriate to retain co-ownership, but for the parties, or the court, to convert the joint tenancy into a tenancy in common and to alter the proportionate share of each spouse's beneficial interest in the property, after taking account of the different factors in section 25.

Where it is agreed that the spouses are already co-owners in equity, but where the legal title is in the name of one spouse alone, say the husband, it is important to ensure that the name of the wife is added to the legal title so that she is equally in control of the property for the future. Otherwise the wife's position as against a purchaser could be put at risk. There is some danger that her beneficial interest could be defeated by sale of the property without her knowledge, or she might find that the property has been used as security for a loan without her consent.[366] Of course, where each spouse's name is on the legal title, then

---

[364] Failure by a lawyer to ensure the severance of a joint tenancy could lead to an action in negligence, see *Carr Glyn v Frearsons (A Firm)* [1999] 1 FLR 8. See *Kinch v Bullard* [1999] 1 FLR 66 for discussion of when notice to sever a joint tenancy becomes effective.

[365] [1992] 2 FLR 126; see too *Harris v Goddard* [1983] 3 All ER 242.

[366] The wife's position would turn on the application of the doctrine of notice.

each must be involved in any future transactions concerning the property. The advantages and disadvantages of such an arrangement need to be considered when deciding whether co-ownership or a charge is the better way of maintaining an interest in the property for both spouses. Where the spouses are hostile to one another, or where there is likely to be disagreement over sale or other transactions concerning the property, then any arrangement which depends on the parties' future cooperation is to be avoided. However, such lack of cooperation may be able to be overcome where the obduracy of one co-owner threatens to defeat the court's original order. In *Harvey v Harvey*[367] the husband flatly refused to join with the wife in applying for a second mortgage and improvement grant to effect repairs to the property. The court ordered the appointment of a receiver of the husband's interest in the property, who would be invited to act on the husband's behalf on the applications which the wife wished to make.

The advantage of co-ownership over a charge order is that it allows for more flexibility, because it is possible to create the settlement in such a way that it can be responsive to changes in circumstances. This could be particularly valuable where there are dependent children of the family, and when any order must reflect the needs of the parent caring for the children to provide them with a home. The Children Act 1989 places considerable emphasis on the continuing parental responsibility of each parent after divorce, and where both parents maintain involvement with their children there may be a real possibility that the children may wish to move from one parent to the other during the course of their upbringing. It would be unfortunate, and not in the interests of the children which section 25(1) requires should be given first consideration, if such a move was impossible because of inflexible arrangements about the use of the matrimonial home during their minority. Where it seems likely that the parties will agree, or a court may wish to order, a change of residence for a child, then continuing co-ownership of the property may best provide for this eventuality. It would be possible (although apparently unprecedented) to settle the property so that the right of occupation is vested in whichever parent is providing a home for the children, with liberty to apply for the transfer of the right of occupation if that situation should alter. This would allow for the situation where the children move from one parent to the other after the financial and property arrangements have been completed.

6.1.10.2 A charge over the property

In most cases the preferred method of preserving the absent spouse's interest in the former matrimonial home is by means of a charge. The legal estate and entire beneficial interest in the property is vested in the sole name of one spouse, but she is required to execute a charge over it in favour of the other spouse to secure to him the payment of a sum of money. It is particularly popular where the property is mortgaged. Many mortgagees, that is the banks and building societies, will release a husband from his personal covenants under the mortgage on the wife giving an undertaking to take full responsibility for these, provided that she is in the financial position to do so. If the husband should then wish to obtain a fresh mortgage to purchase a new home, he will be in a better position to do so because he has no liabilities. Indeed, he may even be able to claim that he is particularly creditworthy because he has a charge on property which he will be able to enforce at some time in the future. Thus a charge order is usually advantageous for the husband.

The advantage of a charge order from the wife's point of view is that she now has full control over the property, and can deal with it without consulting the husband. This is in contrast to her position where there is co-ownership. She is also entitled to redeem the

---

[367] [1987] 1 FLR 67.

charge at any time, thereby ending the husband's claim over the property.[368] However, the wife could well find herself in the position of owning property subject to two, and possibly three, charges, namely the original mortgage, the husband's charge, and, in cases when she has been legally aided, the charge in favour of the Legal Aid Fund. Consequently she would be unlikely to be able to raise any further loan for such things as improvements and repairs using the home as security.

6.1.11 Transfer of tenancies

A court has power under section 53 of the Family Law Act 1996 to make an order transferring a relevant tenancy from one spouse/civil partner to the other at any time where it has the power to make a property adjustment order.[369] Consequently, the order may not take effect before a divorce/dissolution or separation order is made, or a decree of nullity is made absolute, unless the circumstances are exceptional.[370] A relevant tenancy means a protected or statutory tenancy within the meaning of the Rent Act 1977, a statutory tenancy within the meaning of the Rent (Agriculture) Act 1976, a secure tenancy within the meaning of section 79 of the Housing Act 1985, or an assured tenancy or assured agricultural occupancy within the meaning of Part I of the Housing Act 1988.[371] The provisions in Schedule 7 to the Family Law Act 1996 only apply if one spouse/civil partner is entitled, either in his own right or jointly with the other spouse/civil partner, to occupy a dwelling-house by virtue of a relevant tenancy.[372] As with any other property adjustment order, an application for a tenancy transfer cannot be made if the applicant has remarried or entered into another civil partnership.[373] The court is given guidelines on the matters to which it must have regard when determining whether to make a tenancy transfer order.[374] These are not the same as those detailed in the MCA 1973. Rather, the court's attention is directed towards the circumstances in which the tenancy was granted, the criteria for making occupation orders specified in section 33(6)(a), (b), and (c),[375] and the suitability of the parties as tenants[376] but, interestingly, conduct is not a relevant consideration.

7 FINANCIAL AND PROPERTY AGREEMENTS

7.1 SEPARATION AGREEMENTS

Instead of using the courts to resolve their post-divorce financial and property arrangements, it is possible for the parties to enter into a separation agreement to govern those matters. Indeed spouses are encouraged to settle their financial and property affairs without recourse to litigation, and most arrangements are arrived at through negotiation, mediation, and agreement, such bargaining taking place in the shadow of what a court would be likely to do.[377] Privately negotiated agreements are preferable for a

---

[368] *Popat v Popat* [1991] 2 FLR 163.

[369] See the Family Law Act 1996, Sch 7, as amended by the Civil Partnership Act 2004, Sch 9. Thus, a civil partner is treated in exactly the same way as a spouse and all references to spouse in this section should be taken to include civil partners.   [370] MCA 1973, s 23B(1); Family Law Act 1996, Sch 7, para 12.

[371] Family Law Act 1996, Sch 7, para 1.   [372] Ibid, para 2.   [373] Ibid, para 13.

[374] Ibid, para 5.   [375] See Chapter 3.

[376] The Family Law Act 1996 extends the court's property adjustment jurisdiction to cohabitants where they are tenants of property, and the details of the provisions in Sch 7 are more fully discussed in Chapter 3.

[377] See the research on the pressure on parties to reach agreements in G. Davis, S. M. Cretney, and J. Collins, *Simple Quarrels* (Oxford: Clarendon Press, 1994).

variety of reasons. Not only can they reduce legal costs, but parties may have a greater sense of ownership over a negotiated agreement and may thus be more likely to abide by its terms.

Subject to general principles of contract law, a separation agreement is enforceable.[378] However, in *Hyman v Hyman*[379] the House of Lords held that no agreement can oust the jurisdiction of the court since the court's powers are designed not only to protect a spouse's interest but also the public interest.[380] Section 34(1) of the MCA 1973 clarifies that any provision within such an agreement which purports to do so is void.[381] Such a term will not, however, render the rest of the agreement void. Sections 34–36 of the MCA 1973 regulate agreements between spouses, and either party can apply to the court under section 35 to vary the terms of the agreement. A privately negotiated agreement cannot prevent an application to the court to vary the agreement or an application for a financial order. Even an express agreement by one spouse not to apply for financial and property provision after divorce does not preclude that spouse from seeking such relief in the courts. Thus the parties are in the paradoxical position that the court may refuse to give effect to an agreement but the parties themselves are not able to resile from the agreement except where normal contractual principles would allow this, such as fraud, misrepresentation, or undue influence.[382]

This is not to say, however, that the court will ignore the terms of the parties' agreement. On the contrary, the agreement reached may be highly relevant to the court's deliberations. *Edgar v Edgar*[383] is the leading case on the weight to be given to a separation agreement. The husband and wife executed a deed of separation under which the wife agreed not to apply for a lump sum or property transfer order on divorce. The husband was very wealthy and the wife's solicitors advised her that she could obtain a far better settlement in divorce proceedings. The wife, however, was eager to separate from the husband and therefore was insistent upon concluding matters between the parties. Nearly three years later the parties divorced and the wife sought a lump sum payment. The trial judge declined to give effect to the agreement and ordered the husband to pay the wife £670,000. The Court of Appeal allowed the husband's appeal. With regard to the weight to be given to a separation, Ormrod LJ said:

> To decide what weight should be given, in order to reach a just result, to a prior agreement not to claim a lump sum, regard must be had to the conduct of both parties, leading up to the prior agreement, and to their subsequent conduct, in consequence of it. It is not necessary in this connection to think in formal legal terms, such as misrepresentation or estoppel; all the circumstances as they affect each of two human beings must be considered in the complex relationship of marriage. So, the circumstances surrounding the making of the agreement are relevant. Undue pressure by one side, exploitation of a dominant position to secure an unreasonable advantage, inadequate knowledge, possibly bad legal advice, an important change of circumstances, unforeseen or overlooked at the time of making the agreement, are all relevant to the question of justice between

---

[378] Such arrangements are normally embodied in a deed, which resolves any difficulties over whether there was a final binding agreement, cf *Standley v Stewkesbury* [1998] 2 FLR 610, or whether the agreement was supported by consideration.   [379] [1929] AC 601.

[380] Ibid, 644. The state has an interest in ensuring that divorce settlements are just and reasonable, and that arrangements are not made which improperly impose the burden of providing housing and income for a spouse and children onto income support or other state funds.   [381] MCA 1973, s 34(1).

[382] The unsatisfactory nature of the law in this area is neatly analysed by Hoffmann LJ in *Pounds v Pounds* [1994] 1 FLR 775 at 791.

[383] [1980] 1 WLR 1410. See also *Camm v Camm* (1983) 4 FLR 577; *Smith v McInerney* [1994] 2 FLR 1077.

the parties.[384] Important too is the general proposition that formal agreements, properly and fairly arrived at with competent legal advice, should not be displaced unless there are good and substantial grounds for concluding that an injustice will be done by holding the parties to the terms of their agreement. There may well be other considerations which affect the justice of this case; the above list is not intended to be an exclusive catalogue.

His Lordship went on to comment that, where there is an agreement, prima facie evidence of material facts which show that justice requires that the spouse should be relieved from the effects of the agreement will be required.[385]

Oliver LJ concluded that:

the court must…start from the position that a solemn and freely negotiated bargain by which a party defines her own requirements ought to be adhered to unless some clear and compelling reason, such as, for instances, a drastic change of circumstances, is shown to the contrary.[386]

Since there was no evidence of pressure by the husband to force the wife to accept the terms of the deed, and since the wife had received advice from her lawyers which she had refused to take, it had not been shown that justice required the court to relieve her of her agreement.

Thus where a separation agreement has been arrived at with the benefit of legal advice and with none of the vitiating factors outlined by the Court of Appeal,[387] a court will normally make a financial provision and property adjustment order in identical terms.[388] However, where a party to an agreement is not wilfully or capriciously seeking to depart from a formal agreement freely negotiated, and where the circumstances are totally different from the circumstances contemplated by the contracting parties, the court may not adhere rigidly to the agreement as this would be to depart from the criteria in section 25.[389] Further, if there is evidence of unfair or improper pressure applied to one party to sign the agreement, then it is unlikely to be upheld by the court. In *NA v MA*,[390] for example, the court found that improper pressure had been exerted on the wife by the husband to sign a post-nuptial agreement. After the husband had discovered that the wife had committed adultery, he gave her an ultimatum that she either sign the agreement (the terms of which had not been properly negotiated between the parties) or the marriage was over. The court held that the wife's free will was overborne and that the terms of the agreement were unfair. Accordingly, it was not factored into the exercise of the court's discretion under section 25.

7.2 EMBODYING THE AGREEMENT IN A CONSENT ORDER

In order to make the terms of any agreement 'watertight' and not subject to a further claim for court provision, it is necessary to embody the agreement in an order of the court,

---

[384] See *B v B (Consent Order: Variation)* [1995] 1 FLR 9, where a consent order was set aside because the wife was in a depressed and confused state when agreeing to it. She was also given bad legal advice, but cf *Harris v Manahan* [1997] 1 FLR 205. The difficulty with allowing a spouse to repudiate an agreement where she has received bad legal advice is that the other spouse has not been responsible for the wrongful advice being given, yet it is he who will be affected by the agreement being overturned.

[385] Agreeing with Sir Gordon Willmer in *Wright v Wright* [1970] 1 WLR 1219 at 1224.

[386] [1980] 1 WLR 1410 at 1424.

[387] Such as non-disclosure, change of circumstances, duress, or lack of legal advice.

[388] The fact that one party would have achieved a better outcome by going to court is not usually a ground for allowing them to resile upon the terms of the agreement, *per* Munby J in *X v X (Y and Z Intervening)* [2002] 1 FLR 508 at [103].   [389] *Beach v Beach* [1995] 2 FLR 160.

[390] [2007] 1 FLR 1760.

known as a 'consent order' (an order made with the consent of the parties). When this is done, the agreed terms derive their authority not from the contract but from the order of the court,[391] and can be enforced in the same way as a non-consensual order. A consent order cannot increase the range of possible disposals of the parties' assets.[392] The order may only contain terms which fall within the court's powers to make financial provision and property adjustment orders under the MCA 1973.[393] Where parties agree to the provisions of a consent order, and the court subsequently gives effect to their agreement by approving the provisions and embodying them in an order of the court, it is important to appreciate that the legal effect of those provisions is derived from the court order itself. It no longer depends on the agreement between the parties.[394] Consequently, consent orders do not have a contractual basis, they are court orders just like any other court orders. [395] Therefore they must be treated in the same way as non-consensual orders.[396]

On an application for a consent order, the court retains the power to examine the agreement and to consider the factors in section 25. Parties are wrong, however, to rely on judges being assiduous in examining the terms of a consent order. Section 33A provides:

(1) ... [O]n an application for a consent order for financial relief[397] the court may, unless it has reason to think that there are other circumstances into which it ought to inquire, make an order in the terms agreed on the basis only of the prescribed information[398] furnished with the application.

Thus, although a judge is no 'mere rubber stamp', he is under no obligation to make inquiries or require evidence. The effect of section 33A is to confine the function of the court to a broad appraisal of the parties' financial circumstances, and only to probe more deeply where that survey puts the court on inquiry.[399] Thus, '[t]he fact that [the judge] was not told facts which, had he known them, might have affected his decision to make a consent order, cannot of itself be a ground for impeaching the order'.[400] The judge's position was neatly summed up by Ward LJ in *Harris v Manahan*:[401] 'Whilst the court is no rubber stamp, nor is it some kind of forensic ferret.'[402]

---

[391] *De Lasala v de Lasala* [1980] AC 546, PC, and see also *Soulsbury v Soulsbury* [2007] EWCA 969 at [35].   [392] *Livesey v Jenkins* [1985] 1 All ER 106.
[393] MCA 1973, ss 21–25D.   [394] *De Lasala v de Lasala* [1979] 2 All ER 1146.
[395] *Thwaite v Thwaite* [1982] Fam 1. Although, as the court has not adjudicated on the evidence, a consent order cannot be challenged on the ground that the court has reached a wrong conclusion on the evidence before it.
[396] So eg in *Masefield v Alexander* [1995] 1 FLR 100 an application to extend the agreed period under which a lump sum payment should be made was granted by the court. As Butler-Sloss LJ explained, if the order had been imposed by a court and not made by consent there would have been no doubt that the time could be extended. See also *B v B (Consent Order: Variation)* [1995] 1 FLR 9 where a periodical payments order was extended contrary to the terms of the original agreement.
[397] This means any financial provision order, any property adjustment order, any order for sale of property, or any interim order for maintenance: s 33A(3).
[398] That is prescribed by rules of court. The information which must be given includes the duration of the marriage; the parties' ages and the ages of their dependent children; an estimate of the value of their property and their respective net incomes; their intended accommodation arrangements; and whether either party has remarried or intends to remarry.   [399] *Pounds v Pounds* [1994] 1 FLR 775.
[400] *Tommey v Tommey* [1983] Fam 15 at 21. This statement was approved by the House of Lords in *Livesey v Jenkins* [1985] 1 All ER 106 (although the implication that there was no duty to make full and frank disclosure was disapproved).   [401] [1997] 1 FLR 205 at 213.
[402] As Ward LJ explained, 'officious inquiry may uncover an injustice but it is more likely to disturb a delicate negotiation and produce the very costly litigation and the recrimination which conciliation is designed to avoid'. Ibid.

Very often the parties will negotiate their position with a view to the court incorporating it in a consent order, and in *Xydhias v Xydhias*[403] Thorpe LJ opined that an agreement reached in such negotiations to compromise an ancillary relief application is not intended to give effect to an enforceable agreement and does not do so.[404] Of course, where there are no pending proceedings for ancillary relief before the court, a valid agreement will be binding.[405]

With the growing pressure on parties to reach a consensual settlement of their property and financial affairs, it is all the more important that the strictures of the House of Lords in *Livesey v Jenkins*[406] concerning full and frank disclosure are properly observed. Parties are under a duty in both contested proceedings and where a consent order is being negotiated to make proper disclosure of all the material facts. Material facts include those matters in section 25 to which the court must have regard when exercising its discretion, for unless the court has such information it is not in the position properly to exercise that discretion. In *Livesey v Jenkins*, the parties reached a final agreement about the form and the terms of a consent order under which the husband agreed to transfer his half share of the matrimonial home to the wife for the express purpose of providing her and their two children with a home. A week later the wife became engaged to be married, but she failed to disclose this fact either to her solicitor or the husband or his solicitor. Shortly afterwards the agreement was embodied in a consent order, the wife remarried, and within two months she advertised the matrimonial home for sale. Setting aside the consent order, the House of Lords held that the wife's engagement was a material circumstance which was directly relevant to the parties' agreement. She had therefore been under a duty to disclose her engagement and her failure to do so invalidated the consent order which would accordingly be set aside.[407] However, Lord Brandon concluded his speech with 'an emphatic word of warning':

> It is not every failure of frank and full disclosure which would justify a court setting aside an order of the kind concerned in this appeal. On the contrary, it will only be in cases when the absence of full and frank disclosure has led to the court making, either in contested proceedings or by consent, an order which is substantially different from the order which it would have made if such disclosure had taken place that a case for setting aside can possibly be made good.[408]

It is clear that a consent order will be set aside where there has been fraud[409] or mistake, as well as where there has been non-disclosure, as in *Livesey v Jenkins*. In *Middleton v Middleton*[410] the entire basis upon which the order had been made, namely that the family home was also a business asset with considerable goodwill, had been undermined by the husband secretly separating the business from the house, resulting in the house plummeting in value. The Court of Appeal set the order aside and made fresh provision

---

[403] [1999] 1 FLR 683.   [404] Ibid, 691.

[405] See eg *Soulsbury v Soulsbury* [2007] EWCA 969 in which *Xydhias* was distinguished. There a contract was upheld where there was agreement that if the wife did not make a claim for periodical payments during the husband's lifetime she would receive £100,000 on his death. See also *Haines v Hill* [2007] EWCA Civ 1284 at [31]: while 'the jurisdiction of the court ... cannot be ousted by the agreement of the spouses ... [e]qually such an agreement is not devoid of any legal effect'.   [406] [1985] 1 All ER 106.

[407] See also *Robinson v Robinson* [1982] 2 All ER 699n.   [408] [1985] 1 All ER 106 at 119.

[409] See eg *T v T (Consent Order: Procedure to Set Aside)* [1996] 2 FLR 640, where the husband, by his deliberate concealment that he was engaged in active negotiations to acquire shares in a private company at the time when the consent order was being negotiated, was held to have acted fraudulently. Where there is fraudulent non-disclosure, the court is deprived of the opportunity properly to exercise its powers under s 25. Thus the situation is different from where there is a supervening event after the original order was made, as in *Barder v Caluori* [1987] 2 All ER 440.   [410] [1998] 2 FLR 821.

for the wife. Outside these rather extreme circumstances, however, there is a deep reluctance to interfere with such orders. Consequently in *Harris v Manahan*,[411] despite having real sympathy for the wronged wife, the Court of Appeal reiterated that only in the most 'exceptional case of the cruellest injustice' would the public interest in the finality of litigation be overridden, and that the bad legal advice which the wife had clearly been given was no reason for setting the consent order aside.[412]

Where a provision in a consent order includes an order for periodical payments of limited duration, then unless a direction is included in the consent order under section 28(1A), an application to extend the term is not debarred, despite the original agreement.[413]

7.3 ANTE-NUPTIAL AGREEMENTS

Another form of private ordering is where the parties agree *before* the marriage how their property and assets should be split in the event of their marriage breaking down (an ante-nuptial agreement). Historically, such agreements, being in anticipation of, and thereby possibly encouraging, separation and divorce, were considered void as contrary to public policy.[414]

Key case

Following the Supreme Court decision in *Granatino v Radmacher (formerly Granatino)*,[415] however, the status of ante-nuptial agreements is a little more complex to discern. In that case, the appellant Mr Granatino, a French national, and Ms Radmacher, a German national, signed an ante-nuptial agreement in Germany in August 1998. Mr Granatino did not take advantage of the wish of the German notary who had drafted the agreement, to postpone execution of the agreement until after Mr Granatino had taken advice, and neither did Mr Granatino take any advice after signing but prior to the marriage. The couple married in November 1998. The couple lived together in London and had two children, before separating after eight years of marriage. The ante-nuptial agreement was instigated by the wife who came from a very rich family and whose father had insisted upon it as the wife was to receive a portion of the family wealth in due course. It provided that the effects of the marriage were to be subject to German law.[416] The effect of the agreement was that 'neither party was to derive an interest in or benefit from the property of the other during the marriage or on its termination'.[417] The agreement made no mention of children. At the time of the agreement Mr Granatino earned about £120,000 per annum in the banking industry, and in subsequent years achieved higher earnings, until 2002 when he gave up his career to embark on a DPhil degree at Oxford University. Despite the terms of the agreement, the husband sought periodical payments and a lump sum against the wife ancillary to the divorce. Baron J

---

[411] [1997] 1 FLR 205.

[412] See also *Tibbs v Dick* [1998] 2 FLR 1118, where the Court of Appeal held that bad or negligent legal advice per se could never be a ground for setting aside a consent order. This was applied in *S v S (Ancillary Relief: Consent Order)* [2002] EWHC 223 (Fam) and *L v L* [2006] EWHC 956 (Fam). However, a party may have a remedy in negligence, *Frazer Harris v Scholfield Roberts & Hill (A Firm)* [1998] 2 FLR 679.

[413] *B v B (Consent Order: Variation)* [1995] 1 FLR 9. For discussion of clean break orders, s 28(1A) and time-limit traps, see Section 8.2.1.   [414] *Hyman v Hyman* [1929] AC 601.

[415] [2010] UKSC 42, [2011] 1 AC 534. For comment, see J. M. Scherpe, 'Fairness, Freedom and Foreign Elements—Marital Agreements in England and Wales After *Radmacher v Granatino*' [2011] Child and Family Law Quarterly 513.

[416] Although, as the Supreme Court found, the issues in the case were governed exclusively by English law: see [2010] UKSC 42, [2011] 1 AC 534 at [108].   [417] Ibid, [12].

concluded that, having regard to the circumstances surrounding the conclusion of the agreement, reduced weight should be given to it, and she awarded the husband approximately £5.5 million to provide a home and income. On the wife's appeal, the Court of Appeal[418] held that Baron J's approach to the circumstances of the agreement was wrong and she should have given the agreement decisive weight, in that there should be provision for Mr Granatino in his role as the children's father but not otherwise in his own right.

Mr Granatino appealed to the Supreme Court, where the issue was what weight should be given to the ante-nuptial agreement. However, the case provided the court with an opportunity to consider more widely the issue of nuptial agreements, particularly in light of the then recent decision of the Privy Council in *MacLeod v MacLeod*,[419] and nine Justices heard the case.

Before explaining the reasoning in *Granatino v Radmacher (formerly Granatino)*, it is convenient first briefly to outline what was said in the *MacLeod* case. In that case the Privy Council heard an appeal from the High Court of Justice of the Isle of Man, where the law on ancillary relief is similar to that in England and Wales. The husband and wife married after signing an ante-nuptial agreement. Substantial variations to that agreement were made by a deed executed during the marriage (a post-nuptial agreement). Baroness Hale, who delivered the Board's advice, referred to the position of ante-nuptial agreements, commenting: 'The Board takes the view that it is not open to them to reverse the long standing rule that ante-nuptial agreements are contrary to public policy and thus not valid or binding in the contractual sense.'[420] However, the Board drew a distinction between ante-nuptial and post-nuptial agreements. It noted that there is no statutory power to vary an ante-nuptial agreement, and it would be unfair to render them enforceable if they could not be varied. By contrast, the Board interpreted the relevant statutory provision (the equivalent of the MCA 1973, s 35) to include power to vary a post-nuptial agreement. The Board also noted that the reasoning which led to the rule that agreements during marriage which anticipated breakdown of the relationship were void relied on an enforceable duty of husband and wife to live together, which had since been abolished. Consequently, since the reasoning had disappeared, it was time for the rule itself also to disappear.[421] It held that in the case of a post-nuptial agreement, the agreement is no longer the price which one party may extract for willingness to marry.[422]

In *Granatino v Radmacher (formerly Granatino)*[423] the Supreme Court delivered its view by way of a majority judgment of seven members of the court, together with a concurring separate judgment by Lord Mance. Baroness Hale was the sole dissentient. The majority endorsed the view that the reasons given in *MacLeod* for declaring post-nuptial agreements void were obsolete, but could see no reason for maintaining a distinction in this regard between a post-nuptial and an ante-nuptial agreement.[424] The court did not accept that the protection of 'section 35 must be a precondition to holding that a nuptial agreement takes effect as a contract',[425] nor that there was any material distinction between the two types of agreement (eg one made the day before the wedding and one the day after). The court pointed out that, in any event, the issue did not arise for decision in *MacLeod*, any more than it arose in *Granatino*. Furthermore, it was a red herring; regardless of whether these types of nuptial agreement are enforceable, the court in ancillary relief proceedings should apply the same principles to ante-nuptial agreements as it

---

[418] [2009] 2 FLR 1181. [419] [2008] UKPC 64, [2010] 1 AC 298. [420] Ibid, [31].
[421] Ibid, [38] and [39]. [422] Ibid, [36]. [423] [2010] UKSC 42, [2011] 1 AC 534.
[424] Ibid, [52]. See also [51]. [425] Ibid, [56].

applies to post-nuptial agreements.[426] The court indicated that the approach in *Edgar v Edgar* with regard to a separation agreement will not necessarily be appropriate for all post-nuptial agreements.[427]

As to disclosure of information, the Supreme Court held that the Court of Appeal had been 'correct in principle to ask whether there was any *material* lack of disclosure'.[428] What is important is that each party should have all the information material to the decision and intend the agreement to govern the end of the relationship.[429] As to factors detracting from the weight given to an agreement, the court commented:

> The first question will be whether any of the standard vitiating factors: duress, fraud or misrepresentation, is present. Even if the agreement does not have contractual force, those factors will negate any effect the agreement might otherwise have. But unconscionable conduct such as undue pressure (falling short of duress) will also be likely to eliminate the weight to be attached to the agreement, and other unworthy conduct, such as exploitation of a dominant position to secure an unfair advantage, would reduce or eliminate it.
>
> The court may take into account a party's emotional state, and what pressures he or she was under to agree. But that again cannot be considered in isolation from what would have happened had he or she not been under those pressures. The circumstances of the parties at the time of the agreement will be relevant. Those will include such matters as their age and maturity, whether either or both had been married or been in long-term relationships before. For such couples their experience of previous relationships may explain the terms of the agreement, and may also show what they foresaw when they entered into the agreement. What may not be easily foreseeable for less mature couples may well be in contemplation of more mature couples. Another important factor may be whether the marriage would have gone ahead without an agreement, or without the terms which had been agreed. This may cut either way.

As to factors enhancing the weight to be given to the agreement, the court commented that the 'fact of the agreement is capable of altering what is fair. It is an important factor to be weighed in the balance'.[430] The court suggested the following proposition:

> The court should give effect to a nuptial agreement that is freely entered into by each party with a full appreciation of its implications unless in the circumstances prevailing it would not be fair to hold the parties to their agreement.

The court explained that the circumstances in which it will not be fair to hold the parties to their agreement will depend on the particular facts of the case.[431] However, the court gave the following guidance:[432]

(i) A nuptial agreement cannot be allowed to prejudice the reasonable requirements of any children of the family.

(ii) The court should accord respect to the parties' autonomy, and should not override the agreement simply on the basis that the court knows best.

(iii) There is nothing inherently unfair in an agreement which seeks to preserve non-matrimonial property for one party.

(iv) There is scope for what happens to the parties over time to make it unfair to hold them to an agreement. It is unlikely that the parties will have intended that one party should be left in a predicament of real need.

---

[426] Ibid, [63].   [427] Ibid, [65].   [428] Ibid, [69].   [429] Ibid.   [430] Ibid, [75].
[431] Ibid, [76].   [432] Ibid, [77]–[83].

(v) It is in relation to the sharing of assets beyond those addressing need that the court will be most likely to make an order in the terms of the nuptial agreement.

The Supreme Court concluded that it was fair in this case for Mr Granatino to be held to the agreement and unfair to depart from it. It could detect no error of principle on the part of the Court of Appeal.[433]

Baroness Hale delivered a dissenting judgment, in which she observed that the law was in a mess and ripe for systematic review and reform.[434] She observed that a court can all too easily lose sight of the fact that the object of an ante-nuptial agreement is to deny the economically weaker spouse provision to which he (and usually she) would otherwise be entitled, and that 'there is a gender dimension to the issue which some may think ill-suited to decision by a court consisting of eight men and one woman'.[435] She disagreed with the view that ante-nuptial agreements are legally enforceable, and that there are no relevant differences between post-nuptial and ante-nuptial agreements. She also saw the majority's formulation of the test to be applied for considering the effect of an ante-nuptial agreement (at para 75 of the judgment) as placing an impermissible gloss on the statute. Instead, she would ask: 'Did each party freely enter into an agreement, intending it to have legal effect and with a full appreciation of its implications? If so, in the circumstances as they now are, would it be fair to hold them to their agreement?'[436] In Baroness Hale's view the Court of Appeal also erred in principle when it treated Mr Granatino in the same way as a parent who was not married to the other parent,[437] namely by making similar provision to that which he could have obtained in such circumstances under Schedule 1 to the Children Act 1989.[438] As she commented: 'Marriage still counts for something in the law of this country and long may it continue to do so.'[439]

Lord Mance delivered a separate judgment, concurring in the conclusion of the majority. However, like Baroness Hale, he expressed no view on the binding or other nature of an ante-nuptial agreement.[440] Lord Mance agreed with the majority view, expressed at paragraph 75 of the judgment, as to the onus or starting point for considering the effect of an ante-nuptial agreement, but did not 'think the difference in wording likely to be important in practice'.[441] He commented that 'the ultimate question remains on any view what is fair, and the starting point or onus is…unlikely to matter once all the facts are before the court'.[442]

Subsequent case law has now had the opportunity to consider and apply the principles of *Radmacher*. In *Z v Z*,[443] which was the first contested case in the High Court to consider *Radmacher*, Moor J observed that the Supreme Court had 'changed the position fundamentally'[444] regarding pre-nuptial agreements. In this case the parties, a French couple, were married for 14 years and had three children. Before marrying, they entered into a standard pre-nuptial agreement in France (known as a *separation de biens*). The couple relocated to England during their marriage and when the marriage broke down, the weight to be given to the pre-nuptial agreement had to be decided according to the principles of English law. The parties' assets totalled £15 million and the wife argued that it would be unjust to hold the parties to the French agreement and that everything should be shared equally. There was no dispute that the agreement was entered into by the parties freely and with a full understanding of its implications. The husband argued, following the *Radmacher* decision, that the agreement, which excluded the equal sharing principle, should be upheld. He accepted, however, that the agreement did not exclude maintenance claims and that the wife's claim should be determined on the basis of a pre-*White*

---

[433] Ibid, [123].   [434] Ibid, [133].   [435] Ibid, [137].   [436] Ibid, [169].   [437] Ibid, [193].
[438] For detailed discussion, see Chapter 6.   [439] At [195].   [440] Ibid, [128].
[441] Ibid, [129].   [442] Ibid.   [443] [2011] EWHC 2878 (Fam).   [444] Ibid, [34].

assessment of her needs (which, he argued, should result in an award to her of approximately 35 per cent of the assets). Moor J held that this would have been an appropriate case for equal division of the assets in the absence of the French agreement. However, he upheld the agreement insofar as it excluded the equal sharing principle and awarded the wife 40 per cent of the assets which was held to be a suitable departure from equality to reflect the agreement. The fact that the agreement excluded the sharing principle but still allowed the wife to make a claim based upon her reasonable needs was relevant as the Supreme Court had taken the view in *Radmacher* that it would be easiest to show that such agreements, which still allowed maintenance claims to be made, were not unfair.

By way of illustrating the role that ante-nuptial agreements can play in a particular case, we will explore a few examples.[445] In *M v M (Prenuptial Agreement)*,[446] at the husband's behest, the parties entered into a prenuptial agreement shortly before they were married. The terms of the agreement were that in the event of marriage breakdown, the wife was to receive a lump sum payment of £275,000. When the marriage broke down five years later, the wife sought £1.3 million from the husband's assets which had a net worth of £7.5 million. On the facts of the case, the agreement was relevant in guiding the court to a more modest award for the wife than may otherwise have been the case and thus she received a lump sum of £875,000 plus child maintenance and school fees. Connell J held that it would have been as unjust to the husband to ignore the existence of the agreement, as it would have been to the wife to hold her strictly to it.

In *K v K (Ancillary Relief: Pre-Nuptial Agreement)*[447] the husband, who was very wealthy, married his pregnant girlfriend after coming under pressure from her family to marry before the birth of the child. The day before they married they signed a prenuptial agreement which specified the capital award the wife would receive if the marriage broke down within five years. The marriage broke down after 14 months. The wife sought a lump sum of £1.6 million while the husband contended that she should receive, in line with the terms of the prenuptial agreement, a lump sum of £120,000. The court upheld the capital award as specified in the agreement on the basis that the wife had signed the agreement knowing what it meant and in the absence of pressure from the husband. It was one of the circumstances of the case and, in light of the short duration of the marriage, there would be no injustice to the parties to hold them to this part of the agreement. However, the court did not uphold the maintenance aspects of the agreement on the ground that the wife was making an 'enormous contribution' to the upbringing of the couple's child. Thus the court substituted its own view of what was fair in terms of maintenance to enable her and the child to live to a reasonable standard commensurate with the wealth of the husband/father.

In *S v S (Matrimonial Proceedings: Appropriate Forum)*[448] Wilson J predicted that 'there will come a case … where the circumstances surrounding the pre-marital agreement and the provision therein contained might, when viewed in the context of the other circumstances of the case prove influential or even crucial.'[449] Such an opportunity came in the Court of Appeal decision in *Crossley v Crossley*[450] where, on the facts of the case, the parties' prenuptial agreement was determinative as to the outcome of the wife's ancillary

---

[445] Other cases include: *N v N (Jurisdiction: Pre-Nuptial Agreement)* [1999] 2 FLR 745 at 752 *per* Wall J; *C v C (Divorce: Stay of English Proceedings)* [2001] 1 FLR 624 *per* Johnson J (French ante-nuptial agreement was a significant factor in staying English proceedings); and *G v G (Financial Provision: Separation Agreement)* [2004] 1 FLR 1011, CA (parties had been married before); *J v V (Disclosure: Offshore Corporations)* [2004] 1 FLR 1042, *per* Coleridge J (agreement on the eve of marriage without advice or disclosure and without allowance for arrival of children); *X v X (Y and Z intervening)* [2002] 1 FLR 508 at [78]–[103], *per* Munby J.
[446] [2002] 1 FLR 654.   [447] [2003] 1 FLR 120.   [448] [1997] 2 FLR 100.   [449] Ibid, 103.
[450] [2007] EWCA Civ 1491.

relief claim on divorce. In this case, the facts of which were regarded as exceptional, the wife, aged 50, and the husband, aged 62, separated after a 14-month marriage. Both had been married several times before and both were independently wealthy prior to the marriage. The husband had assets of £45 million and the wife had her own assets of £18 million. Prior to the marriage, the parties entered into a prenuptial agreement which specified that both of them would walk away from the marriage with whatever they brought into it; that any joint property would be divided equally; and that neither party would apply to the court for financial provision based on their marriage. When the marriage broke down and the wife applied for ancillary relief, the husband argued that the wife be ordered to 'show cause' why her claim should not be resolved in accordance with the prenuptial agreement. He also argued that the usual court procedure should be circumvented, and that the judge should resolve the preliminary question of the enforceability of the prenuptial agreement. Bennett J at first instance agreed with this approach. The wife appealed on the basis that the judge had erred in departing from the normal court procedure and allowing the husband's summons to be heard as a preliminary issue. This, she argued, effectively ousted the jurisdiction of the court to carry out its own investigations under section 25 and precluded her from alleging the husband's non-disclosure of assets at the time the agreement was signed. The Court of Appeal dismissed her appeal. The court did not accept the argument that the case management approach adopted by Bennett J ousted the obligation of the court to apply section 25. The prenuptial agreement remained just one aspect of the case although, on the particular facts, it was of 'magnetic importance'.[451] This was a short, childless marriage between mature adults, both of whom had previously been married and divorced and both of whom were independently wealthy. Thus, taking these facts into account, the court agreed that there was a very strong case that a possible result of the section 25 exercise would be that the wife receive nothing.[452] Thorpe LJ said that while all cases are fact-dependent:

> this is a quite exceptional case on its facts, but if ever there is to be a paradigm case in which the court will look to the prenuptial agreement as not simply one of the peripheral factors in the case but as a factor of magnetic importance, it seems to me that this is such a case.[453]

7.4 DEBATE SURROUNDING ANTE-NUPTIAL AGREEMENTS

The majority decision in *Granatino* goes some way to addressing the calls by many commentators for ante-nuptial agreements to be given greater weight in the regulation of the financial affairs of married couples.[454] It should be recalled, however, that the statements in *Granatino* as to the enforceable nature of an ante-nuptial agreement are merely *obiter*, and there is no suggestion that an ante-nuptial agreement is binding in the sense of determinative of the parties' financial affairs. Nevertheless the approach of the majority in *Granatino* will be welcomed by some. Prior to *Granatino*, Stephen Cretney pointed to the 'remarkable anomaly' created by the fact that while marriage can be described as a

---

[451] Ibid, [15].   [452] Ibid, [14].   [453] Ibid.

[454] See eg S. Cretney, 'The Family and the Law—Status or Contract?' [2003] Child and Family Law Quarterly 403; B. Clark, 'Should Greater Prominence be given to Pre-Nuptial Contracts in the Law of Ancillary Relief' [2004] Child and Family Law Quarterly 399; J. Morley, 'Enforceable Pre-Nuptial Agreements: Their Time Has Come' [2006] Family Law 772; see also Resolution, 'A More Certain Future—Recognition of Pre-Marital Agreements in England and Wales' (2004), arguing for binding prenuptials except in cases of significant injustice. It was accepted that defining 'significant injustice' may result in litigation, but that this was a small price to pay for the certainty of legally binding prenuptial agreements, para 7.7.

partnership, English law did not 'allow husband and wife by contract (whether pre- or post-nuptial) to exercise the right, which it accords virtually all other partners, to make their own agreement as to the terms'.[455] Yet, a couple who are not married could enter into a binding cohabitation contract to regulate their financial and property affairs.[456] While it is sometimes said that prenuptial agreements undermine marriage, there is also an argument that attaching greater weight to prenuptial agreements, may encourage people to marry, or more correctly, counter any disincentive to marry caused by the potential of court-imposed solutions particularly in big money cases. It is also the case that such agreements direct parties away from litigation, thus reducing legal costs and court time.

Prenuptial agreements are recognised in many other European countries and throughout the world.[457] Thus greater recognition of ante-nuptial agreements may bring the position in England and Wales more in line with international experience. It may reduce 'forum shopping' in relation to international divorces. This is where one spouse who does not want to be bound by a prenuptial agreement entered into in another jurisdiction where it is binding, would seek to initiate divorce proceedings in the UK.[458] Indeed in *Crossley v Crossley*[459] Thorpe LJ observed that a strong argument for the codification of the law on prenuptials was to address the difficulties caused by the different approaches taken to divorce and financial matters across Europe. He said:

> there is an obvious divide between the provisions of the civil law jurisdictions and the absence of any marital property tradition in the common law systems. Undoubtedly there would be some narrowing between this European divide if greater opportunity were given within our justice system for parties to contract in advance of marriage to make provision for the possibility of dissolution. The approach that Bennet J took in this case seems to me to accord with a developing view that prenuptial contracts are gaining in importance in a particularly fraught area that confronts so many parties separating and divorcing.[460]

The Court of Appeal had previously voiced its support for prenuptial agreements in *Charman v Charman*:[461]

> If, unlike the rest of Europe, the property consequences of divorce are to be regulated by the principles of needs, compensation and sharing, should not the parties to the marriage, or the projected marriage, have at the least the opportunity to order their own affairs otherwise by a nuptial contract?[462]

However, George, Harris, and Herring[463] have observed that arguments:

> should not blind us to the possibility that, in practice, giving pre-nuptial agreements greater recognition might not only fail to increase the certainty and simplicity of the law, reduce conflict and litigation, and lower costs, but, on the contrary, might cause greater legal uncertainty and complexity, and/or increase opportunities and incentives to litigate.

---

[455] S. Cretney, 'The Family and the Law—Status or Contract?' [2003] Child and Family Law Quarterly 403.   [456] *Sutton v Mischon De Reya and Gawor and Co* [2004] 1 FLR 837.

[457] For a detailed treatment, see J. Scherpe (ed), *Marital Agreements and Private Autonomy in Comparative Perspective* (Oxford: Hart, 2012) and K. Boele-Woelki, J. Miles and J. M. Scherpe (eds), *The Future of Family Property in Europe* (Antwerp: Intersentia, 2011).

[458] J. Morley, 'Enforceable Pre-Nuptial Agreements: Their Time Has Come' [2006] Family Law 772 at 775.   [459] [2007] EWCA Civ 1491.

[460] Ibid.   [461] [2007] EWCA Civ 503.   [462] At [124].

[463] R. H. George, P. G. Harris, and J. Herring, 'Pre-Nuptial Agreements: For Better or For Worse?' [2009] Family Law 934.

It would also constrain the court's ability to impose, and the parties' incentives to agree, fair settlements.[464]

Making the parties' agreement binding inevitably leads to the question of how to build in safeguards to protect the economically vulnerable in relationships, or to prevent the enforcement of a contract in situations where circumstances have changed to make its terms unfair to one party.[465] Statutory force could be given to agreements alongside carefully drafted protective mechanisms to filter out agreements which are problematic due to some procedural or substantive unfairness. In 1998, the Home Office consultation document, *Supporting Families*, recommended that written prenuptial agreements should be binding subject to certain safeguards.[466] There was a mixed response to the consultation document and no further action taken. The Law Commission is currently looking at this issue, and a report and draft Bill are expected in 2012.

While a systematic examination of this issue should be welcomed, the use of ante-nuptial agreements should arguably not be relied upon as the sole or primary policy initiative to improve the law on ancillary relief. Given the width of judicial discretion and the lack of certainty in relation to application of the principles laid down in *White* and *Miller; McFarlane*, serious policy consideration needs to be given to the statutory framework. This should be done in conjunction with looking at the law on prenuptial agreements. Reform in this area of the law is not solely about producing fair outcomes in individual cases, whether imposed by the court or reached between the parties themselves. Indeed, as Herring points out, the bases of financial provision on divorce have implications beyond constructing a fair settlement between the parties. Amongst a range of wider social and political interests, Herrings cites the 'symbolic value of childcare', noting that the message sent by the courts through the construction of financial orders on divorce will to some extent 'influence the perception of childcare (and the caring of dependants generally) in the wider society'.[467] Due to their symbolic importance, the rules which govern the law on ancillary relief should be clear and principled because they send important social messages about the obligations created by being in a formalised relationship of a marriage or civil partnership. That means that it is not enough to attempt to improve the operation of the law by giving statutory force to prenuptial contracts thus allowing parties to achieve certainty and predictability by making their own agreements. Instead, the law on financial orders following divorce needs to be looked at by policy-makers to establish clear reasons for financial and property distribution on divorce and dissolution of civil partnerships.

---

[464] Ibid, 938.

[465] However, problems should not be overstated: Morley points out that

> None of the many common law jurisdictions that enforce prenuptial agreements have given the parties the freedom to create unconscionable or seriously unjust agreements... in every case the courts have retained full power to scrutinise prenuptial agreements to prevent injustice.

J. Morley, 'Enforceable Pre-Nuptial Agreements: Their Time Has Come' [2006] Family Law 772 at 773.

[466] If one or more of the following applied, then the agreement would not be binding: where there was a child of the family, whether or not the child was alive or a child of the family at the time the agreement was made; where under the general law of contract the agreement is unenforceable including if the contract attempted to lay an obligation on a third party who had not agreed in advance; where one or both of the couple did not receive independent legal advice before entering the agreement; where the agreement would cause significant injustice to one or both of the parties or a child of the marriage; where there was not full disclosure of assets before the agreement was made; and where the agreement was entered into less than 21 days before the marriage: *Supporting Families: A Consultation Document* (London: Home Office, 1998), para 4.23.

[467] J. Herring, 'Why Financial Orders on Divorce Should be Unfair' (2005) 19(2) International Journal of Law, Policy and the Family 218.

8 APPEALS AND REHEARINGS

8.1 THE BARDER TEST

A rigorous approach is taken to appeals against a court order or applications for a rehearing. An appeal must be lodged within days of the order being made and not the date from when the order is to be implemented, as must an application for a rehearing.[468] Appeals or a rehearing are occasionally allowed out of time, but only if the stringent conditions laid down by the House of Lords in *Barder v Caluori*[469] are satisfied. These are that:

(i) new events have occurred since the order was made;

(ii) these events invalidate the basis on which the order was made so that an appeal would be certain, or very likely, to succeed;

(iii) the new events have occurred within a relatively short time of the order being made;

(iv) the application for leave to appeal out of time has been made reasonably promptly; and

(v) the granting of leave does not prejudice third parties who have acquired interests in good faith and for value in the property which is the subject of the order.

Point (ii) is the most problematic aspect of the *Barder* criteria as it can be difficult to determine the assumption upon which an order has been made and assess whether this has been invalidated or falsified by subsequent events. The approach to be taken was neatly summed up by Smith LJ in *Williams v Lindley*:[470]

> the task of the judge considering the application for leave is, first, to identify the supervening event. He must then consider whether that event has invalidated the basis upon which the original order was made, so that an appeal would almost certainly succeed. The words 'so that', linking the invalidation of the basis of the original order with the prospects of success of an appeal, mean that the two must be causally related to each other. In my view, the judge should consider whether the supervening event is such that, if it had been foreseen at the time of the order, the order made would have been significantly different. If so, an appeal from the order would be almost certain to succeed.[471]

Lord Brandon in *Barder v Caluori* explained that this is a difficult question because it involves a conflict between two important principles: the principle that it is in the public interest that there should be finality to litigation, and the principle that justice required cases to be decided on the true facts and not on assumptions or estimates which were conclusively shown by later events to have been erroneous.[472] In *Thompson v Thompson*,[473] Mustill LJ, when applying the *Barder* principles, emphasised the severity of the requirements laid down by Lord Brandon. He said that the reviewing court should look in broad terms at the balance of the financial relationship created by the order under review, and ask itself how this balance had been affected by the new state of affairs. Broadly speaking, it should make no difference whether something had happened to alter the original evaluation of the parties' assets or liabilities, or whether an entirely new factor had come

---

[468] *B v B (Financial Provision: Leave to Apply)* [1994] 1 FLR 219.

[469] [1987] 2 All ER 440. In *Power v Power* [1996] 3 FCR 338 the Court of Appeal stated that the same test should be adopted where there is an application for a rehearing; see too *B v B (Financial Provision: Leave to Apply)* [1994] 1 FLR 219. For a clear example of the application of the test see *Heard v Heard* [1995] 1 FLR 970.   [470] [2005] EWCA Civ 103.

[471] Ibid, [46].   [472] [1987] 2 All ER 440 at 451.   [473] [1991] 2 FR 530.

into play, such as the receipt of an unexpected legacy. The cause of the change should not have been foreseen[474] and taken into account when the order was made. However, Mustill LJ also expressed the view that the change should not have been brought about by the *conscious* fault of the person who sought to take advantage of it. He explained that 'merely to say that the applicant must not have brought the change on himself is not enough, for this would disqualify an applicant who had been ruined by an honest error of business judgment.'[475] Despite this concession, the judgment laid emphasis on the exceptional nature of the circumstances which had to be established before leave out of time would be granted, 'otherwise the whole basis of this essentially practical jurisdiction will be put out of joint'.[476] This means that it is only in an 'exceptionally small' number of cases that a court order will be revised.[477] In *Shaw v Shaw*[478] Thorpe LJ said that '[a]n appeal, albeit perhaps necessary to correct error or to redress an unfair result, is nevertheless a misfortune for the family in that it increases costs and extends the duration of conflict... The public interest in finality of litigation in this field must always be emphasised.'[479] Thus, as noted by Lawrence Collins LJ in *Dixon v Marchant*[480] 'the reported cases, with very few exceptions, apply the [*Barder* principle] strictly, and with good reason'.[481]

It was the death of one of the parties which led to the application to appeal out of time being allowed in *Barder v Caluori*. In this case a consent order was made, under which the husband was ordered to transfer the matrimonial home and its contents to the wife. The order had been agreed on the tacit assumption that the wife and the two children would require a home for many years. Tragically, before the order had been executed the wife killed the two children of the family and committed suicide. The wife had devised her estate to her mother. Clearly, the assumption on which the order had been made had been totally invalidated. The husband's appeal against the order was therefore allowed despite the fact that it was out of time. Similarly in *Reid v Reid*[482] the wife, who was aged 74, died two months after the consent order was made. The husband's application to appeal out of time against the order was granted on the ground that the wife's death was a new event which was not reasonably foreseeable. Once it was accepted that the wife's death was a new event within the meaning of the *Barder* principles, the question then arose of what would have been the appropriate order at the time, had it been known that the wife had only two months to live. The court held that the severe contraction of the length of the wife's future needs would have led to a significantly different result and thus permission to appeal was given and a new order was substituted.

[474] See *Cornick v Cornick* [1994] 2 FLR 530; *S v S (Ancillary Relief: Consent Order)* [2002] 1 FLR 922.

[475] [1991] 2 FLR 530 at 538.

[476] The other key factor influencing the court was that the trial judge had found that the wife's appeal would be certain to succeed. Cf *Ritchie v Ritchie* [1996] 1 FLR 898 where the Court of Appeal held that the new events which had occurred, namely for the husband to accept redundancy and fail to pay the mortgage, could not invalidate the fundamental assumption upon which the order had been made and therefore the proposed appeal was neither certain nor very likely to succeed.

[477] *Shaw v Shaw* [2002] 2 FLR 1204 at [44].   [478] [2002] 2 FLR 1204.   [479] Ibid.

[480] [2008] 1 FLR 655 at [100].

[481] However, in cases where one party has been guilty of bad conduct such as fraud, misrepresentation, or non-disclosure, the courts are more willing to invoke the *Barder* principles: S. Hughes, 'Over the *Barder*line' [2008] Family Law 670 at 672. Moreover, in situations such as one party's non-disclosure of assets, that party cannot subsequently complain about the other party's delay in bringing an application to appeal out of time. The other party would have to make an application within a reasonable time from the non-disclosure coming to light and not from the date of the original order. See *Den Heyer v Newby* [2006] 1 FLR 1114 where Thorpe LJ said that 'the duty of promptitude on the applicant has to be measured in the context of the obligation that clearly rests on the respondent to furnish, if not detailed information, then at least the core information to enable the enquiry to be professionally evaluated', at [28].

[482] [2003] EWHC 2878 (Fam).

However, the premature death of one of the parties will not lead to an appeal out of time in all cases. In *Benson v Benson*[483] six months after a consent order was made the wife died from cancer. A compromise agreement was reached between the husband and those acting on behalf of the wife's estate under which part of the consent order would not be enforced. Meanwhile, the husband was also having business difficulties which worsened his financial position and he sought leave to appeal against the consent order, although he did not make this application until a year after his wife's death. Bracewell J was satisfied that the first three requirements in *Barder* were satisfied with respect to the wife's premature death. However, she rejected the husband's contention that his deteriorating financial circumstances amounted to a new event, as the potential seeds for disaster had been sown and were plain to the husband prior to him entering into the consent order. She further found that the delay in mounting the appeal had been lengthy and lacked the promptness which cases of this kind require, and that the reason was that the compromise arrangement was originally acceptable to the husband, and that it only became unpalatable at a later date. Bracewell J dismissed the husband's application on two grounds. Applying the principle in *Edgar v Edgar*[484] that an agreement which had been freely entered into should not be displaced unless there are compelling grounds, she held that the husband had reached an agreement after receiving both legal and financial advice, and therefore the principle applied. Moreover, by delaying so long he failed to satisfy the fourth test in *Barder* that an application for leave to appeal should be made reasonably promptly.

Appeals have occurred where orders have been made on the basis that property or business assets have a particular value, and where the actual value has proved to be considerably higher, as in *Thompson v Thompson*;[485] or considerably lower, as in *Heard v Heard*.[486] In *Cornick v Cornick*[487] Hale J (as she then was) distinguished between cases where an asset which was correctly valued at the date of the hearing changes value within a short time due to 'natural processes of price fluctuation', and those cases where either the asset was incorrectly valued at the date of the hearing or where, subsequent to the hearing, something unforeseen happened to alter the value of the asset. While the latter circumstances could possibly come within the *Barder* principles (provided the other conditions were satisfied) the 'natural processes of price fluctuation' would not. Thus, in this case, the wife was awarded periodical payments and a lump sum payment which amounted to 51 per cent of the husband's capital assets. Shortly after the hearing the value of the husband's shares rose to such an extent that the lump sum payment now only represented 20 per cent of the capital assets. The wife sought leave to appeal out of time on the basis that the increase in the value of the shares was a new event which meant that the issue could be reopened. The court dismissed the application. The assets were correctly valued at the date of the hearing and there was nothing on the facts to require the court to disregard the principle that the natural processes of price fluctuation did not entitle the wife to the relief sought. Hale J (as she then was) said '[o]nce the couple are divorced and their capital

---

[483] [1996] 1 FLR 692.   [484] [1980] 3 All ER 887, discussed in Section 7.1.

[485] [1991] 2 FLR 530. In this case the husband's business had been valued at £20,000 but was sold for £45,000 just five days after the time limit for appealing an order had expired. The Court of Appeal granted the wife leave to appeal out of time.

[486] [1995] 1 FLR 970. The main family asset, the matrimonial home, could only be sold at about half its estimated value, and since the intention had been that the husband would be able to rehouse himself out of the proceeds of sale this amounted to a new event invalidating the basis of the original order. The husband's delay in appealing could be explained and his appeal was therefore allowed and the case remitted.

[487] [1994] 2 FLR 530.

divided, they cannot normally expect to profit from, anymore than they expect to lose by, later changes in the other's fortune.'[488]

To come within the *Barder* principles, it is clear that the new event or change in circumstances must have been unforeseeable at the time the order was made.[489] In *B v B*[490] the wife appealed out of time against a consent order on the basis that the matrimonial home which was valued at £1.25 million at the date of the hearing was subsequently sold by the husband for £1.6 million. The application was dismissed. The property rose in value due to the rising property market and as a result of the husband's refurbishment of the property which cost over £60,000. The court held that even if the renovations and the rise in the property market had not been foreseen at the time the order was made, they were foreseeable. The rising property market was a matter of common knowledge and there was no reason to suppose that the husband, who was a property developer, would not have made clear his intention to refurbish the property if inquiry had been made of him.[491] The circumstances which caused the increase in the value of the property were foreseeable and, as such, the increase was not a new and supervening event within the *Barder* principles. Similarly in *Maskell v Maskell*[492] the Court of Appeal held that the husband's redundancy just two months after the order was made was not a supervening event. Rather, loss of employment was a foreseeable challenge that happened to hundreds of thousands of breadwinners.[493]

Another situation where the *Barder* principle has been successfully applied is the remarriage of the recipient spouse shortly after an order has been made. In *Wells v Wells*[494] six months after the husband was ordered to transfer his entire interest in the matrimonial home to his wife, the wife remarried and went to live with the children in the second husband's house. The husband was granted leave to appeal out of time on the ground that the wife's situation had fundamentally changed, and the whole basis of the order had been vitiated.[495] Similarly in *Williams v Lindley*[496] the parties separated and the wife and one of the parties' two children went to live in the home of her employer. The wife denied that she was in a relationship with her employer and she sought a transfer of the husband's share in the matrimonial home to enable her to return there to live with the children. A consent order was made which provided for a 70:30 split in the equity in the home in her favour. Shortly afterwards the wife married her employer and the husband applied to set aside the consent order. The Court of Appeal held that this was a 'plain case' for the grant of leave to appeal out of time.[497] The main foundation for the original order was the wife's urgent need to rehouse herself and her children. This foundation was destroyed within one month by her engagement and subsequent remarriage. However, this case was distinguished by the Court of Appeal in *Dixon v Marchant*.[498] In this case the parties divorced in 1993 and the husband was ordered to pay a lump sum plus periodical payments during the parties' joint lives or until the wife's remarriage or further order. In 2005 the husband sought a variation of the original order and a consent order was made in 2006 which capitalised the periodical payments into a lump sum payment of £125,000. During this time the husband believed that the wife was cohabiting with her long-term partner. However, as part of the negotiations leading to this agreement, the wife indicated that she was not cohabiting and had no intention of either doing so or remarrying. Seven months after the consent order was made, the wife married the man with whom her husband had believed

---

[488] Ibid.   [489] Ibid.   [490] [2007] EWHC 2472 (Fam).   [491] Ibid, [40].
[492] [2003] 1 FLR 1138.   [493] Ibid, [4].   [494] [1992] 2 FLR 66.
[495] The husband in *Chaudhuri v Chaudhuri* [1992] 2 FLR 73 failed when relying on similar facts because, crucially, the order appealed against contemplated the possibility of the wife remarrying.
[496] [2005] 2 FLR 710.   [497] Ibid, [24].   [498] [2008] EWCA Civ 11.

her to be cohabiting. The husband applied to have the consent order set aside. The main issue was whether the wife's remarriage was a new event which invalidated the basis and fundamental assumption upon which the consent order had been made. The Court of Appeal was divided on this question. The majority rejected the husband's application holding that the basis of the consent order was a straightforward capitalisation of the wife's periodical payments in order to achieve a clean break between the parties. As this was the core purpose of the order, the wife's remarriage was not a special factor on the facts of the case. While the husband had made inquiry about the wife's relationship with her future husband, this was to quell his suspicion that she was cohabiting with him. He was not, according to the court, protesting about nor seeking to protect himself from the risk of her remarriage.[499] Further, the wife's indication of her present situation during the negotiations leading to the consent order carried no implication of her future intention and thus the risk of remarriage was a risk that the husband had to bear.[500] Ward LJ pointed out that the capitalisation of the wife's periodical payments in the consent order carried risks for both parties. For the husband, there was the risk that the wife would remarry and in that event he would have been better off continuing to make maintenance payments as these would have ceased on her remarriage. For the wife, the risk was that the lump sum would be exhausted during her lifetime and thus she would have been better off preserving her rights to maintenance.[501] To succeed in his application, the husband had to show that there was a mutual assumption between the parties, and shared by the court, that for an indefinite period to be measured in years rather than months or weeks the wife would not remarry.[502] However, according to Ward LJ there was nothing in the agreement to suggest that the husband was given any right to claw back any part of the lump sum if the wife should remarry soon after the payment had been made.[503] Both *Wells v Wells*[504] and *Williams v Lindley*[505] were distinguished on the basis that the respective orders had been made to provide a roof over the heads of the wife and children and, in both cases, the wife's remarriage removed this need. In the present case, however, the reason for making the consent order was to capitalise the wife's periodical payments and thus her subsequent remarriage did not invalidate the basis upon which this order was made. Lawrence Collins LJ also dismissed the application noting that the facts of the case 'fall far below the necessary standard' to meet the *Barder* principle.[506] However, he based his judgment on the importance of achieving finality and emphasised that the application of the *Barder* principle is reserved for exceptional cases. Indeed, those cases where the principle was successfully invoked were cases in which 'justice cried out for a remedy'.[507] This, however, was not one of those cases. Wall LJ provided the dissenting judgment. In his view, the fundamental assumption behind the agreement was that the wife would not remarry. Relying upon *Williams v Lindley*,[508] he took the view that the fact of the wife's remarriage made 'the order not merely unsustainable, but—on its face—unjust'.[509]

This case confirms that in the public interest of finality in litigation, it is only in exceptional cases that new events will allow the court to revise a clean break order. The fact of the recipient's remarriage will not, by and of itself, constitute a *Barder* event where periodical payments have been capitalised. Indeed, Ward LJ noted that there is no reported case 'where remarriage as such is the one and only decisive event'.[510] In other cases (such as *Williams v Lindley*) where remarriage was relied upon, the purpose of the original

[499] Ibid, [23].

[500] On this point the court relied upon *Smith v Smith* [1976] Fam 18 and *H v H (Family Provision: Remarriage)* [1975] Fam 19.   [501] [2008] EWCA Civ 11 at [24].

[502] Ibid, [25].   [503] Ibid, [26].   [504] [1992] 2 FLR 66.   [505] [2005] 2 FLR 710.

[506] [2008] EWCA Civ 11 at [100].   [507] Ibid, [95].   [508] Ibid, [70].   [509] Ibid, [34].

[510] Ibid, [20].

order was obviated by the changing circumstances created by the remarriage and not by the remarriage itself. This case also reveals the uncertainty surrounding the application of the *Barder* criteria. The court was divided on whether the consent order was based on the assumption that the wife would not remarry. Zuckerman points out that 'the difference between situations in which justice cries out and those where no such cry is heard is largely a matter of degree and evaluation and liable to be influenced by the judge's moral views about the rights and wrongs of the couple'.[511] He suggests that a preferable solution to appealing out of time in these sorts of case is to use a provisional order subject to a change of circumstances:

> rather than try to work out after the event what was and what was not a fundamental assumption, the court making the order should set out the circumstances that would justify an application for variation … this approach … would do no more than spell out the assumptions that the court already makes and it would have the added advantage that parties would have to work out more carefully what they want to achieve.[512]

Indeed, in *Dixon v Marchant*, the agreement to capitalise the husband's maintenance payments could have provided for the eventuality of the wife's remarriage within a specified time frame of the order being made thus allowing him to recoup some of his money on the occurrence of this event. Douglas notes that Ward LJ appears to have based his reasoning on the fact that the husband could have required such a clause within the agreement[513] which would have allowed him to claw back part of the lump sum and thus he would not have had to appeal out of time against the original order. Of course, an obvious problem with this approach which requires eventualities to be written into capitalised maintenance agreements is in securing the other party's agreement to it.

In *Myerson v Myerson*[514] the husband received a bundle of high-risk assets upon the order of the court but shortly after the making of the order the economy declined and the assets reduced to 14 per cent of their previous value. Thorpe LJ held that this was not a *Barder* event; the husband had agreed to the order and had known that his assets were subject to the natural process of price fluctuation.

8.2 VARIATION

Section 31 governs the variation of financial provision orders. Under section 31, the court has the power to vary or discharge an order or suspend or revive any provision contained within an order. However, this only applies to the following ancillary relief orders:[515]

(i) maintenance pending suit or interim maintenance;

(ii) periodical payments order (secured or unsecured);

---

[511] A. Zuckerman, 'Finality of Litigation—Setting Aside a Final Judgment' (2008) 27(2) Civil Justice Quarterly 151 at 157.   [512] Ibid.

[513] A. Douglas, 'Comment on *Dixon v Marchant*' [2008] Family Law 306. Douglas cites *L v L* [2008] 1 FLR 26 as an example of where a particular eventuality was built into a consent order. In this case a consent order included a clause that the husband would pay the wife an annual income of £75,000 should her earning fall below that sum. Shortly afterwards when the wife gave up work and sought payment, the husband applied to have the consent order set aside on the ground, *inter alia*, that her lack of income was a *Barder* event. This argument was rejected by the court as the order had made specific provision for this eventuality even though it had happened sooner than expected. As noted by Douglas:

> the possibility of the wife's income reducing was expressly covered in the consent order. It was held, inter alia, that the husband could not therefore claim that her giving up work sooner than expected was a Barder 'event' – far from invalidating the basis of the order, it was the occurrence of an event for which the order itself made specific provision.

[514] [2009] EWCA Civ 282.   [515] MCA 1973, s 31(2).

(iii) an order for the payment of a lump sum by instalments;

(iv) any deferred order made by virtue of s 23(1)(c) (lump sums) which includes provision in respect of pension rights;

 (v) an order for the sale of property;

(vi) a pension sharing order under s 24B which is made before the decree absolute.

Property adjustment orders and lump sum orders cannot be varied.[516] Once made, they are final orders and the only way in which they can be altered is for one party to appeal against the order or to seek to have it set aside. Periodical payment orders can, however, be varied upwards, downwards, or they can be terminated altogether. The court can also vary the period for which payments are to be made. The only exception to this is if the court has made an order under section 28(1A) which prevents the recipient of fixed-term periodical payments from applying under section 31 for an extension of the term specified in the order.

8.2.1 Timing of the application to vary

The court's variation powers under section 31 are unfettered[517] and apply with equal force to consent orders.[518] The applicant is not required to establish exceptional circumstances or a material change in circumstances before a variation order can be made, but the exercise of the discretion may, of course, be affected by that consideration.[519] One very important issue, however, relates to the timing of the application to vary. It is essential to ensure that an application to vary a limited term order is made before the order expires, for otherwise there will be no order in existence which is capable of being varied. In *T v T (Financial Provision)*[520] a periodical payments order had been made in favour of a wife which was expressed to take effect 'until such date as the wife shall remarry or until the husband retires or further order'. After the husband retired the wife applied to vary the order. It was conceded that the court would have had jurisdiction to extend the order to beyond the husband's retirement date had the wife made her application before the husband retired.[521] However, the court ruled that its jurisdiction had come to an end once the retirement took place. The addition of the words 'or further order' did not come to the wife's assistance because the Court of Appeal held that these words meant 'a further order in the meantime'. Thus, it is very important that an application to vary is made within good time of the original order coming to an end. Leaving it too late will mean the failure of the variation application because it falls into a time-limit trap.

This was illustrated by *G v G (Periodical Payments: Jurisdiction)*.[522] A consent order was made which contained the following terms: 'The respondent to pay or cause to be paid to the petitioner…periodical payments at the rate of £14,000 per annum…until the petitioner shall remarry, cohabit with another man for a period of 6 months…or until the child of the family, C, shall attain the age of 18 years whichever shall be sooner or until further order.' There was no direction given under section 28(1A) that the wife could not apply for an extension of the term specified in the order, so provided she made her application in time she could have obtained a variation of the order under section 31. However, the wife made her application to vary the original order one month after C reached her

---

[516] The instalments by which a lump sum order by instalments is to be paid can be varied.
[517] See Thorpe LJ in *Harris v Harris* [2001] 1 FCR 68.
[518] *B v B (Consent Order: Variation)* [1995] 1 FLR 9.   [519] *Flavell v Flavell* [1997] 1 FLR 353.
[520] [1988] 1 FLR 480.
[521] This concession was confirmed in *Richardson v Richardson* [1993] 4 All ER 673.
[522] [1997] 1 All ER 272.

eighteenth birthday, one of the cut-off points specified in the consent order. Accordingly, the Court of Appeal ruled that the court had no jurisdiction to vary the original order because it had already expired. Interestingly, however, Ward LJ expressed the *obiter* view that 'it is essential not only that application be made but that an order be made before the expiration of the term.'[523] In other words, suggesting a more stringent test that not only had the application to vary to be made before the time limit in a periodical payment order expired, but that the actual variation order had to be made before this date. However, the Court of Appeal did not follow this dictum in *Jones v Jones*.[524] In this case under the terms of a consent order the parties agreed that the husband would make periodical payments to the wife until 12 January 1998. No direction was made under section 28(1A) which prevented the wife from seeking to extend that term. On 8 January 1998, the wife applied for an extension and the application was granted in June 1998. On appeal the question that fell to be determined was whether after the original termination date of 12 January, the judge had jurisdiction to hear the wife's application. The Court of Appeal held that the judge did have jurisdiction to extend the order even though the application was determined after the period referred to in the consent order had expired. The crucial point was that the wife's application was made *before* the order expired. Thus, the court can vary or extend an order under section 31 provided that the application is made during the life of the order and it does not matter if the application is not determined after the specified term has expired.

8.2.2 Which factors must the court consider?

When exercising its powers under section 31 the court has regard to all the circumstances of the case, first consideration being given to the welfare of any child of the family under the age of 18.[525] The court also considers any change of circumstances in any of the matters to which the court had regard when the original order was made, although in *Flavell v Flavell*[526] the Court of Appeal held that the power of the court to vary orders was not dependent on exceptional circumstances or material change. While these are issues that can affect the exercise of the court's discretion, they are not a requirement of a successful application. The court must, however, consider the possibility of a clean break on a variation application. Under section 31(7)(a), the court must consider whether to vary a periodical payments order so that payments shall only be made for a period of time which will be sufficient, in the opinion of the court, to enable the recipient to adjust without undue hardship to the termination of the payments. So where a clean break has not been possible at the time of the original order, subsequent developments such as one party's increased capital, may make it possible at a later date.[527]

To achieve a clean break, the court has the power to capitalise a periodical payments order. This simply means that the court can substitute a periodical payments order with a capital order, such as a lump sum. This power is given by section 31(7A)–(7G) which were inserted into the MCA 1973 by the Family Law Act 1996.[528] Under these provisions when discharging a periodical payments order or varying that order so that payments are to be made for a limited time only, the court has the power to make one or more of the following orders: a lump sum order; a property adjustment order; and a pension-sharing order. Further, the court can also direct that the payee is not entitled to make any further application for a periodical payments order

---

[523] Ibid, 284.   [524] [2000] 2 FCR 201.   [525] MCA 1973, s 31(7).   [526] [1997] 1 FLR 353.
[527] *Pearce v Pearce* [2003] 2 FLR 1144 at [39]. In a case where the payer has died, the court shall also consider the changed circumstances resulting from his/her death, s 31(7)(b).
[528] Family Law Act 1996, Sch 8, para 16. This followed the recommendation of the Law Commission in its Report, *Family Law: The Ground for Divorce* (Law Com No 192, 1990), para 6.10.

or an extension of the order.[529] When the court is capitalising a periodical payments order, one important question is in determining the quantum of the capital order. Is the court limited to a strict mathematical calculation of the capital equivalent of the ongoing periodical payments or can the court conduct a broader assessment which reopens how the couple's assets should be distributed? The Court of Appeal provided a very clear answer to this question in *Pearce v Pearce*.[530] When terminating one party's entitlement to future periodical payments, the function of the court is not to reopen capital claims but to substitute for the ongoing payments a capital order which compensates the payee and achieves the clean break.[531] The court said that:

> There is simply no power or discretion to embark on further adjustment of capital to reflect the outcome of unwise or unfortunate investment on one side or prudent or lucky investment on the other.[532]

Thorpe LJ laid down the following approach to be taken by a judge faced with capitalising periodical payments: the judge should first determine what, if any, variation should be made in the order for periodical payments; second, fix the date when the new order will commence, and finally substitute a capital order, calculated in accordance with the Duxbury tables, for the periodical payments which are being terminated.[533] According to Thorpe LJ such an approach was necessary 'as a safeguard against the temptation to further adjust the capital division between the parties to reflect the factors which were not foreseen or which did not pertain at the date of the original division'.[534]

Section 31 confers on the court a 'broad discretion' to determine variation applications.[535] The question of when the court will vary a periodical payments order, either upwards or downwards or perhaps terminate it altogether, is an interesting one because it raises issues surrounding the legal obligation one has to a former spouse.

Key case

This was the central issue in *North v North*[536] where the wife applied for an upwards variation of a nominal periodical payments order which had been in place for many years. The parties divorced after 14 years of marriage. They had two children who remained with the husband after the divorce. The financial order, which was made in 1981, made provision for a house for the wife and for the transfer of ground rents to her which provided her with an annual income. The order also contained provision for a nominal order of periodical payments to the wife at a rate of 5p per annum for the parties' joint lives, until the wife remarried or until further order. The wife did not attempt to find employment after the divorce and the husband had, on several occasions, helped her out financially. In 2000 the wife realised all her assets, worth some £328,000, and moved to Australia. She rented an apartment in one of the most expensive areas in Sydney Harbour and placed her money in various investments which incurred substantial losses. She returned to the UK and sought an upwards variation of the nominal periodical payments order made in 1981. Her assets at the time amounted to around £155,000 (after legal costs) which generated an income of £5,000. The husband's

---

[529] Section 31(7B)(c).   [530] [2003] 2 FLR 1144.

[531] Ibid, [45]. In reaching the conclusion, the dicta of Charles J in *Cornick v Cornick (No 3)* [2001] 2 FLR 1240 at 1262–1264, was disapproved.   [532] [2003] 2 FLR 1144 at [36].

[533] Ibid, [37]. Thorpe LJ also said that when determining what substitute order should be made first consideration should be given to the option of carving out of the payer's pension funds a pension for the payee equivalent to the discharged periodical payments order.

[534] [2003] 2 FLR 1144 at [39].

[535] *North v North* [2007] EWCA Civ 760 at [31], *per* Thorpe LJ.   [536] [2007] EWCA Civ 760.

financial position meanwhile had improved significantly since the original order was made. His net assets were worth almost £5 million and he had an income of £60,000. In relation to the wife's application to vary the periodical payments upwards, the district judge found that her diminished financial circumstances were of her own making. However, he awarded her periodical payments of £16,500 per annum, capitalised into a lump sum of £202,000. The husband's appeal against the order was upheld by the Court of Appeal. This is an interesting case because it raised the thorny issue of whether the husband should bear any responsibility for his former wife's current financial position, over 25 years after the parties divorced. Given the findings of the district judge that the wife's financial circumstances were of her own making, in particular due to her lifestyle choices of opting not to work, moving to Australia, and making investments, and that the husband had acted generously and honourably, one could speculate that the court, rather than increasing the periodical payments, would have terminated them. However, the Court of Appeal distinguished between circumstances where assets were dissipated through financial mismanagement, extravagance, or irresponsibility, for which a former spouse would bear no responsibility, and where losses were incurred as a result of misfortune. In relation to the latter, the court did not rule out the possibility that, if so able, the payer be ordered to provide financial assistance in such circumstances. When determining an application under section 31, the court has unfettered discretion. Thorpe LJ made it clear, however, that the overarching objective is to achieve a fair result, which has two elements: 'the order must be fair to the applicant in need, and to the respondent who must pay'.[537] He continued:

> In any application under Section 31 the applicant's needs are likely to be the dominant or magnetic factor. But it does not follow that the respondent is inevitably responsible financially for any established needs. He is not an insurer against all hazards nor, when fairness is the measure, is he necessarily liable for needs created by the applicant's financial mismanagement, extravagance or irresponsibility. The prodigal former wife cannot hope to turn to a former husband in pursuit of a legal remedy, whatever may be her hope that he might out of charity come to her rescue.[538]

This meant that the wife's financial needs which were created by her lifestyle choices (such as her failure to utilise her earning potential and her choice of a more hazardous future in Australia) were of her own making, for which the husband could not be held responsible.[539] However, Thorpe LJ held that the losses incurred by her investments were in a different category. They were 'more the outcome of hazard and therefore to be characterised as misfortune rather than mismanagement'.[540] Thus the court held that the wife had an entitlement to a modest award, quantified at £3,000 per annum to be capitalised.[541]

So it seems that while a former spouse will not be obliged to meet the financial needs of the applicant which have been caused by his or her 'financial mismanagement, extravagance or irresponsibility', an award could be made to compensate for financial needs which were not self-created. As Merrigan points out, while the payee has a responsibility to 'manage the money she has as best she can', poor conduct which has a significant financial impact 'is a factor to reduce but not necessarily defeat the wife's claim for upward variation of maintenance'.[542] Thus much depends on the facts and circumstances of each

---

[537] Ibid, [32].   [538] Ibid.   [539] Ibid, [33].   [540] Ibid, [34].

[541] Indeed, it is clear that if an upwards variation is ordered, the court will strive to capitalise the order, should resources allow, and dismiss the periodical payments order.

[542] D. Merrigan, 'Variation of Nominal Periodical Payment Orders' [2007] Family Law 1009 at 1011.

individual case. However, will it always be clear whether financial losses are incurred by 'misfortune' rather than 'mismanagement'? It is unfortunate that the court did not take the opportunity to articulate clearly why the husband should bear some responsibility for his former wife's investment losses incurred by misfortune. Was this simply on the basis that she found herself in an unfortunate financial position, not all of her own making, and that as the husband had sufficient money to provide assistance he should, in the interests of fairness, be ordered to do so?[543] However, there has to be some rational ground upon which to base a legal obligation and appealing to one's sense of subjective fairness is simply not enough. One should remember that the wife's losses were incurred as a result of decisions made many years after the divorce. While these may have been unfortunate and not the fault of the wife, neither were they the fault of the husband whose obligations to the wife could have been regarded as extinguished after payment of the capital sum on the original order and his financial assistance over the years. Indeed, this was not a situation where a nominal order was made because one's obligation to a spouse could not be fulfilled on divorce and thus the nominal order allowed the court to revisit the issue should the payer's financial circumstances improve. In such situations, an upwards variation of the nominal order (capitalised if resources permit) may be entirely appropriate. But this will have been done to fulfil outstanding obligations created by the marriage. In *North*, however, this was not the case. By contrast, the husband was ordered to bear some responsibility for investment losses incurred by the wife which had nothing to do with the marriage, or by the wife's contributions to the family. This type of thinking is in contrast to other jurisprudence in the area of ancillary relief where, for example, property acquired or bonuses awarded after the parties' separation is generally unavailable in the financial settlement.[544] In other words, assets which are generated after separation or divorce are usually regarded as belonging to those to whom they have accrued. Similarly then, why are financial losses, which are incurred after the parties' separation or divorce, not regarded as being the sole responsibility of the one who incurs them. This, it is suggested, is a particularly strong argument on the facts of *North* where the losses were incurred many years after the parties had divorced.

In another unusual variation application, *Lauder v Lauder*,[545] the court had to decide whether to vary the parties' pre-*White* settlement which was made in 1988 to take account of the fact that the wife's earning capacity had been restricted by her contributions to the family in line with the 'compensation' strand in *Miller; McFarlane*. Given that the parties' settlement had been made long before this decision, the question was whether the wife could increase her award in line with the more generous interpretation of recent jurisprudence. The parties had been married for 24 years and had three children who were aged 20, 18, and 14 at the time of the divorce. The wife, who was aged 50 at the time of the divorce, was awarded periodical payments of £8,000 per annum which equated to 35 per cent of the husband's net income. The order also envisaged that the wife would receive two-thirds of the value of the matrimonial home. However, the couple agreed not to implement the order so that the wife and children could live in the matrimonial home. During this time, the husband paid for the upkeep of the home and supplemented the wife's income. The wife secured employment earning £23,500 by the date of her retirement at the age of 62. In 2003, the matrimonial home was sold. In line with the original order the wife received £414,000 from the proceeds of sale, and the husband received some £314,000. By now the husband was worth in the region of £4.5 million and had a net

---

[543] Of course, this will only be possible where a variation application is permitted and so is not an option where, eg, the court has made an order under s 28(1A).

[544] See Section 4.5.1.4.   [545] [2007] 2 FLR 802.

income of £200,000. By contrast, the wife's income was £9,000. The wife applied for an upwards variation of the periodical payments order. At first instance, the district judge awarded her £40,000 per annum, capitalised at £500,000. On appeal, Baron J opined that the core issue was whether this figure was fair, noting that the decision was handed down before *Miller; McFarlane* and so it had to be considered how that decision impacted on this case.[546]

Baron J held that the proper approach was to apply the terms of the Act in light of the facts and to give proper consideration to the guidance given by the House of Lords in *Miller; McFarlane*.[547] Thus, on the variation application, the court had to interpret the wife's needs generously and consider whether compensation was required. In terms of her needs, Baron J held that the wife's needs had not been 'generously interpreted'. Drawing attention to the fact that the marriage had lasted 24 years, producing three children, and that the wife had continued to spend many years caring for the youngest child after the divorce, Baron J awarded the wife capitalised periodical payments of £725,000. This award included an element of compensation for the wife's relationship-generated economic disadvantage.[548] Even though the wife had attempted to become self-sufficient after the divorce, she had a modest earning capacity which was a 'direct result of the marriage and the parties' decision that she should be a wife and mother'.[549] The court held that 'this requires proper compensation'.[550] The husband argued that the strength of this compensation claim was diminished because so many years had passed since the divorce in 1985. Baron J rejected this assertion:

> This wife, who suffered ill health during the course of the marriage, could never, after 24 years of marriage at the age of 50 years, be expected to earn substantial sums of money which would enable her to save sufficient to look to her own resources in old age. Her salary, at its zenith, was just over £23,000 per annum gross, that was about one tenth of the husband's net income. Her caring role within the family inevitably affected her ability to generate income or assets as she grew older. When this marriage came to an end she was past the age of being able to start a career anew.[551]

In addition, the fact that they did not implement the original order, an unusual decision which placed them in economic limbo, resulted in greater economic disadvantage to the wife. However, it is of note that the court held that the 'sharing' principle in *Miller; McFarlane* was not relevant. As made clear in *Pearce v Pearce*,[552] the court cannot reopen capital claims on a variation application even if the law had progressed to make the original order appear 'discriminatory and unfair'.[553] One is 'not entitled to a second bite of the capital cherry'[554] and thus in *Lauder* the court held that 'this application cannot be used as a basis to distribute capital by the back door' and thus no element of sharing was provided.[555]

The significance of this case lies in the fact that the guidance of the House of Lords in *Miller; McFarlane* on needs and compensation (but not equal sharing) applies not only to an original application for ancillary relief but also on an application for variation of an original order. This was confirmed by the President of the Family Division in *VB v JP*.[556] In this case the wife applied for an increase in the amount of periodical payments awarded in 2002 on the basis that she was entitled to compensation for her lost earning potential.

---

[546] Ibid, [42].   [547] Ibid, [57].

[548] It is of note that Baron J did not quantify the wife's compensation as a separate element of the award but within an assessment of the wife's needs as 'generously interpreted'. See earlier Section 5.2.1 on compensation.   [549] [2007] 2 FLR 802 at [65].

[550] Ibid, [65].   [551] Ibid, [67].   [552] [2003] 2 FLR 1144.   [553] [2007] 2 FLR 802 at [21].

[554] Ibid.   [555] Ibid, [70].   [556] [2008] 1 FLR 742.

The court rejected the husband's assertion that compensation could not be considered on a claim for variation saying that the language of the House of Lords in *Miller; McFarlane* is 'of general application and extends where appropriate to consideration by the court of the overall fairness of an order made upon an application to vary a joint lives periodical payments order.'[557] The court held, therefore, that it was right to have regard to the wife's 'undoubted relationship generated disadvantage'[558] and found that there was a mutual decision between the parties that the wife would sacrifice her career for the 'role of mother and carer for a husband who was busy, worked long hours, and, despite his wish, could devote only a very minor part of his time to his "family life", given the demands of his job and his ability to pursue it successfully to the full as a result'.[559] By contrast to the wife's diminished earning capacity, the husband's career had progressed and his income had increased significantly since the original order was made. Although the wife had clearly suffered lost earning potential and was thus entitled to compensation, this was difficult to quantify. However, because a clean break was not possible on the facts and the parties agreed that there was an indefinite continuing need for periodic maintenance, it was not necessary to quantify the element of compensation separately. Instead, it was considered as part of the assessment of the wife's needs generously assessed against the standard of living during the marriage and husband's increased income.

A contingency which is sometimes included in consent orders for periodical payments is that the order will cease if the wife should cohabit with another man for longer than a specified period.[560] The risk to the wife of an order containing such a clause is that her new partner may not be in the position to maintain her himself. Although courts have clearly stated that cohabitation should not be equated with remarriage when a periodical payments order is made,[561] or when an application has been made in variation proceedings to discharge the order,[562] there seems to be nothing to prevent the inclusion of a clause of this type in a periodical payments order. The wife can apply for a variation of this (or any other) term before the cut-off date has been reached, provided that no direction to the contrary has been made under section 28(1A). But once the specified period of cohabitation has been fulfilled it seems that the order for periodical payments terminates automatically. Moreover, the order cannot be revived even if the cohabitation subsequently ceases, and there is a general rule against repeat applications being made for orders.[563]

It is suggested that orders containing a clause that periodical payments should cease automatically if a former wife should cohabit with another man should be avoided. Such provisions are the modern equivalent of the old *dum casta* orders, which at one time used to stipulate that the wife must remain 'chaste' if she wished her periodical payments to continue.[564] They are objectionable in that they may lead to snooping and may restrain the wife from forming an intimate relationship out of fear that she will lose her source of income from her ex-husband. Whereas cohabitation may provide good cause to apply for variation or termination of an order for periodical payments, for an order to terminate automatically in the event of the wife cohabiting, irrespective of her partner's income, could cause such a wife a great deal of financial hardship.[565]

---

[557] Ibid, [64].   [558] Ibid, [66].   [559] Ibid, [38].

[560] See eg *G v G (Periodical Payments: Jurisdiction)* at Section 8.2.1.

[561] *Atkinson v Atkinson (No 2)* [1996] 1 FLR 51.   [562] *Atkinson v Atkinson* [1987] 3 All ER 849.

[563] Section 22A(3).   [564] Cf *Squire v Squire* [1905] P 4.

[565] See further on this issue, M. Hayes 'Cohabitation Clauses in Financial Provision and Property Adjustment Orders: Law, Policy and Justice' (1994) 110 LQR 124.

9 FINANCIAL PROVISION ORDERS DURING THE MARRIAGE

Before spouses even get to the stage of petitioning for divorce, their relationship may be breaking down in circumstances in which one spouse is failing to make reasonable financial provision for the other. In such cases it is possible for an application to be made to the court for reasonable financial provision during the marriage, although such applications are not that common.[566]

Two pieces of legislation give courts the powers to address these circumstances. An application can be made to the magistrates' court under the Domestic Proceedings and Magistrates' Courts Act 1978 for an order to be made for periodical payments and/or a lump sum not exceeding £1,000.[567] Alternatively, the applicant can apply to a county court, or to the High Court, under section 27 of the MCA 1973, for an order for secured or unsecured periodical payments, and a lump sum, unlimited in amount. In either case orders are limited to periodical payments or lump sums and no property adjustment order can be made. In either case the applicant must establish that the respondent spouse has failed to provide him or her with reasonable maintenance.

Key legislation

Section 1 of the Domestic Proceedings and Magistrates' Courts Act 1978[568] provides:

Either party to a marriage may apply to a magistrates' court for an order under section 2 of this Act on the ground that the other party to the marriage—

(a) has failed to provide reasonable maintenance for the applicant; or

(b) has failed to provide, or to make a proper contribution towards, reasonable maintenance for any child of the family; or

(c) has behaved in such a way that the applicant cannot reasonably be expected to live with the respondent; or

(d) has deserted the applicant.

In practice it is unlikely that the respondent will litigate over whether he or she has wilfully neglected to maintain the applicant. Instead this ground is likely to be conceded and any contest will be over whether an order should be made in light of the parties' respective financial circumstances and, if so, how it should be quantified. In relation to failure to provide reasonable maintenance for the applicant, this is relatively easy to establish in a case where the applicant has no independent income, or only a limited income. Even where a respondent has no source of income from which he or she can pay their spouse maintenance, the ground of failure to provide reasonable maintenance can nonetheless be established. In such cases, the magistrates' courts can make nominal orders, for

---

[566] J. Eekelaar, 'Post-Divorce Financial Obligations' in S. Katz, J. Eekelaar, and M. Maclean (eds), *Cross-Currents: Family Law and Policy in the United States and England* (Oxford: Oxford University Press, 2000), p 407.

[567] The order would be made under s 2. However, where the parties agree that a financial provision order should be made, the application should be brought under s 6.

[568] The equivalent provisions for civil partners are contained in the Civil Partnership Act 2004, Sch 6.

example for 10p per annum, in favour of an applicant.[569] The advantage of such a nominal order is that it recognises that spouses have a legal duty to maintain each other and it is an order which can be varied upwards should the respondent's circumstances subsequently improve.[570] Paragraph (b) has been rendered virtually obsolete because the Child Support Act 1991[571] in general prevents a court making orders for periodical payments in favour of a child.[572]

Where the grounds for making an order are established or conceded, the court, in deciding whether to exercise its powers and, if so, in what manner, must have regard to all the circumstances of the case, must give first consideration to the welfare while a minor of any child of the family, and have regard to the several matters which are listed in section 3. These are virtually the same matters as those to which a court must have regard in the exercise of financial provision and property adjustment powers on the grant of a decree of divorce, nullity, or judicial separation.[573] The differences are that, because the parties are still married, the clean break principle does not apply, since the spouses' mutual obligation to maintain one another continues, and of course there is no need to consider benefits which might be lost by reason of the marriage being terminated.

Proceedings may also be brought in the county court or the High Court for periodical payments and/or a lump sum on the grounds of failure to provide reasonable maintenance for a spouse, or a child of the family, under section 27 of the MCA 1973.[574] Under section 27, the court can make a secured periodical payments order and there is no limit on the amount which can be awarded as a lump sum.[575]

DISCUSSION QUESTIONS

1. The decisions of the House of Lords in *White v White* and *Miller; McFarlane* completely transformed the guiding principles which apply when courts are considering financial orders following divorce. In pursuit of gender-based equality between the parties, the courts have introduced the default rule of equal sharing on divorce. To what extent do you agree with this statement? What issues do you think require further clarification?

2. As indicated, the courts have developed the principle of equality when considering financial orders following divorce. Is this principle sustainable in cases involving families of modest or very limited means?

3. 'The court should give effect to a nuptial agreement that is freely entered into by each party with a full appreciation of its implications unless in the circumstances prevailing it would not be fair to hold the parties to the agreement' (*Radmacher v Granatino*). Critically analyse this statement.

---

[569] See eg *Chase v Chase* (1983) 13 Fam Law 21.

[570] The court can vary or revoke a periodical payments order under the Domestic Proceedings and Magistrates' Courts Act 1978, s 20.

[571] As amended by the Child Support, Pensions and Social Security Act 2000. See Chapter 6.

[572] Child Support Act 1991, s 8. On the Act, and financial and property provision for children generally, see Chapter 6.

[573] MCA 1973, s 25.

[574] The equivalent provisions for civil partners are contained in the Civil Partnership Act 2004, Sch 5, Pt 9.

[575] Although, just like the magistrates' court, the court cannot make a property adjustment order. In relation to children, the court's powers are similarly negated by the Child Support Act 1991, s 8.

FURTHER READING

COOKE, E., '*Miller/McFarlane*: Law in Search of a Definition' [2007] Child and Family Law Quarterly 98

CRETNEY, S., 'The Family and the Law—Status or Contract?' [2003] Child and Family Law Quarterly 403

EEKELAAR, J. 'Post-Divorce Financial Obligations' in S. Katz, J. Eekelaar, and M. Maclean (eds), *Cross-Currents: Family Law and Policy in the United States and England* (Oxford: Oxford University Press, 2000)

EEKELAAR, J., 'Property and Financial Settlement on Divorce—Sharing and Compensating' [2006] 36 Family Law 754

FREEMAN, J., FRANCIS, V., CUNNIFF, P., and COVENEY, H., 'Guarding the Triple Crown: Pre-Nuptial Agreements in Three Jurisdictions' [2008] Family Law 239

GLENNON, L., 'Obligations between Adult Partners: Moving from Form to Function?' (2008) 22(1) International Journal of Law, Policy and the Family 22

GLENNON, L., 'The Limitations of Equality Discourses on the Contours of Intimate Obligations' in J. Wallbank, S. Choudhry, and J. Herring (eds), *Rights, Gender and Family Law* (Abingdon: Routledge, 2010)

JACKSON, E., WASOFF, F., MACLEAN, M., and DOBASH, R., 'Financial Support on Divorce: The Right Mixture of Rules and Discretion?' (1993) 7 International Journal of Law and the Family 230

KELLY, A., 'Rehabilitating Partnership Marriage as a Theory of Wealth Distribution at Divorce: In Recognition of a Shared Life' (2004) 19 Wisconsin Women's Law Journal 141

MILES, J., '*Charman v Charman* (No 4)—Making Sense of Need, Compensation and Equal Sharing after *Miller/McFarlane*' [2008] Child and Family Law Quarterly 378

O'DONOVAN, K., 'Flirting with Academic Categorisations' [2005] 17 Child and Family Law Quarterly 415

SCHERPE, J. M., 'Fairness, Freedom and Foreign Elements—Marital Agreements in England and Wales After *Radmacher v Granatino*' [2011] Child and Family Law Quarterly 513

5

PROPERTY DISPUTES OF UNMARRIED COHABITANTS ON RELATIONSHIP BREAKDOWN

INTRODUCTION

Unmarried and unregistered cohabitants face a host of practical issues on relationship breakdown which are identical to those confronting spouses on divorce. Namely, how is one home to be shared between two persons who each have rights and needs? How is provision to be made for housing the children? Should one party continue to provide financial support to the other? However, at this point the similarity between married and unmarried couples ends. Although their problems are the same, the legal solutions are different. Spouses have the benefit of a statutory regime which takes regard of their married status and which allows courts to respond flexibly to their specific circumstances. A spouse who has no right to occupy the matrimonial home flowing from a proprietary interest, has a statutory right of occupation in the matrimonial home while married;[1] and where the marriage is ended by divorce, a separation order, or a nullity decree, the court has power to distribute the parties' full range of assets (including the family home, pensions, and income provision) to achieve a fair outcome.[2] It is therefore comparatively unusual nowadays for disputes between spouses relating to their rights in the home to be determined by the application of principles which are not specific to their marital status.[3]

There is no such statutory right of occupation or property adjustment regime available to unmarried or unregistered couples.[4] As we have seen, a cohabitant can apply under Part IV of the Family Law Act 1996 for an occupation order in relation to the family home but, if successful, this will only confer short-term occupancy rights.[5] Upon relationship breakdown, courts have no power to make an order about the house, or any other property, on

---

[1] Family Law Act 1996, s 30. See Chapter 3.

[2] Matrimonial Causes Act 1973, Part II; Civil Partnership Act 2004, Sch 5.

[3] Where a third party has a claim on the property then the spouses' respective rights in the property take on a different significance, as in *Lloyds Bank plc v Rosset* [1991] 1 AC 107, which is discussed on pp. 248 (Section 1.2.1). A detailed account of third party claims on the property of spouses and cohabitants is beyond the scope of this book.

[4] Unmarried cohabitants are recognised in some legislative contexts where cohabitation for a period of time will confer certain rights and duties. For a discussion of the legal status of cohabitants, see A. Barlow and G. James, 'Regulating Marriage and Cohabitation in 21st Century Britain' (2004) 67(2) Modern Law Review 143. Unregistered same-sex cohabitants are in the same position as unmarried opposite-sex cohabitants. For ease of reference, however, this chapter will refer to unmarried cohabitants and this should be taken to include unregistered cohabitants.   [5] See Chapter 3.

the basis that an adjustment of the parties' respective rights would be fair and reasonable between them.[6] Instead the entitlement of unmarried partners to ownership of the family home is governed by the ordinary principles of law and equity. These are principles of general application which have not been designed specifically to deal with the financial consequences of relationship breakdown between cohabitants. As such they are generally regarded as inadequate to resolve family property disputes, producing unfair outcomes in certain situations. That there are no specially designed family law principles to govern these situations has attracted considerable criticism from scholars and practitioners and while the Law Commission has made recommendations for reform,[7] there is still no sign of legislation to remedy the inadequacies of the current law. It remains the case that when the court is called upon to resolve a property dispute between unmarried cohabitants on relationship breakdown, the 'focus is on determining who *owns* what as a strict matter of property law, rather than to whom it *should* in fairness be given'.[8]

Before discussing these property law principles, it is worth highlighting the situations to which they apply. As already stated, the main 'domestic' situation which falls prey to the inadequacies of trust law is when unmarried couples separate and there is a dispute concerning ownership of the former family home. However, on some occasions, a spouse must also have recourse to these general principles. While disputes between spouses on divorce are resolved by the flexible and discretionary-based financial regime, if a spouse wishes to establish their interest in the family home *during* the marriage, the financial regime has no jurisdiction. Instead, ordinary property law principles will determine the matter. This is likely to arise when a dispute concerns the family home and a third party.[9] For example, if a third party creditor, such as a mortgagee, seeks possession of the home, another family member whether it be a spouse, civil partner, or cohabitant may seek an ownership interest in the home under ordinary trust principles in an attempt to defeat the third party's claim to possession. The question that we must now ask is: what are the ordinary property law principles which apply in these situations?

1 OWNERSHIP OF THE FAMILY HOME: PROPERTY LAW PRINCIPLES

1.1 ESTABLISHING LEGAL OWNERSHIP

The starting point for determining the parties' respective rights in the family home is to look at the conveyance or other document of title which will establish who has *legal title* to the property. It may be alleged that the person with the legal title has made a gift of land to his or her partner. However, a basic rule of property law is that:

all conveyances of land or of any interest therein are void for the purpose of conveying or creating a legal estate unless made by deed.[10]

---

[6] The courts have limited powers to make property-based orders for the benefit of any children under the Children Act 1989, Sch 1. See Section 2.7.

[7] Law Commission, *Cohabitation: The Financial Consequences of Relationship Breakdown* (Law Com No 307, 2007).

[8] Law Commission, *Cohabitation: The Financial Consequences of Relationship Breakdown, A Consultation Paper* (Law Com No 179, 2006), para 3.3 (emphasis added).

[9] Such a dispute arose in *Lloyds Bank v Rosset* [1991] 1 AC 107.

[10] Law of Property Act 1925, s 52(1).

Thus with regard to the legal estate there is certainty, and any informal written transaction designed to dispose of the legal estate is void.[11]

1.2 ESTABLISHING BENEFICIAL OWNERSHIP

However, establishing the identity of the legal owner is not the end of the matter because the whereabouts of the beneficial ownership in the property must also be considered. The person who has the legal title may hold the property on trust for another person who will have a beneficial interest in the property. It is here that the law becomes more complex because a trust may be created expressly (express trusts), or by implication (implied trusts).

1.2.1 Express trusts

Key legislation

Under section 53(1)(b) of the Law of Property Act 1925 an express trust of land must be in writing. The provision states that:

> a declaration of trust respecting land or any interest therein must be manifested and proved by some writing signed by some person who is able to declare such a trust or by his will.

Without such writing, any purported declaration of trust of land is unenforceable.[12] As such, an oral agreement that the legal owner is to hold the property on trust for his or her partner will not be sufficient to create an express trust. This is well illustrated in *Lloyds Bank v Rosset*.[13] The wife claimed a beneficial entitlement to share in the matrimonial home which had been conveyed into the sole name of her husband on the basis that this had been agreed between the parties. Responding to her claim, Lord Bridge said:

> Even if there had been the clearest oral agreement between Mr. and Mrs. Rosset that Mr. Rosset was to hold the property in trust for them both as tenants in common, this would, of course, have been ineffective since a valid declaration of trust by way of gift of a beneficial interest in land is required by section 53(1) of the Law of Property Act 1925 to be in writing.[14]

Sometimes there is an express declaration of beneficial entitlement in the conveyance which will specify how the beneficial interest in the property is to be split between the parties. Such an express declaration will, in the absence of fraud or mistake at the time of the transaction, conclusively determine the question of title between the parties.[15]

---

[11] See *Crago v Julian* [1992] 1 WLR 372 in which it was held that a deed is necessary even to assign an informal weekly tenancy. See also *Camden LBC v Alexandrou (No 2)* (1998) 30 HLR 534.

[12] The requirement of writing may not be enforced in a case of fraud, *Rochefaucauld v Boustead* [1897] 1 Ch 196.   [13] [1991] 1 AC 107.

[14] Ibid, 129.

[15] *Pettitt v Pettitt* [1969] 2 All ER 385 at 407 *per* Lord Upjohn. See also *Goodman v Gallant* [1986] 1 FLR 513 at 517 and 523. Baroness Hale suggested in *Stack v Dowden* [2007] UKHL 17 at [49] that an express declaration of trust can also be varied by subsequent agreement or affected by proprietary estoppel. While a subsequent declaration of trust which is in writing can vary an earlier express trust, it is doubtful that an oral agreement could vary an express trust. It has also been pointed out that while it is conceivable that an express trust could be varied by a subsequent proprietary estoppel, there is no direct authority for this proposition, A. Chandler, 'Express Declarations of Trust, Rectification and Rescissions: *Goodman v Gallant* Revisited' [2008] Family Law 1210.

This means that if the property is conveyed into the parties' joint names with an express declaration that it is to be held by them as beneficial joint tenants, each is entitled to a half share in the proceeds of sale of the property.[16]

1.2.2 Implied trusts

Problems surface, however, when there is no written declaration of trust. This is likely to arise in circumstances where the property was not jointly purchased by the parties. Say, for example, one person moves into their partner's house and they live together for many years in the property and raise a family together.[17] If the relationship breaks down the non-owner (ie, the person who simply moved in) may claim that it would be unconscionable to allow the other to retain the entire beneficial interest in the property. However, because there is no written declaration of trust falling within section 53(1)(b), the only way the non-owner will be able to establish an interest in the home is through the law of implied trusts which may arise, by implication, from the circumstances of the case.[18]

Talking point

The law of implied trusts enables equity to require the legal owner of land to hold the property on trust for another where it would be inequitable to allow him or her to deny the other a beneficial interest in the land. The broad determining principle is that equity will step in and impose a trust where not to do so would allow the legal owner to become unjustly enriched at the expense of the other.

However, while section 53(2) allows the creation of an implied trust in the absence of a formal declaration of trust, it does not specify how the courts should decide whether such a trust has, in fact, arisen. It is the courts themselves which have created the principles to determine whether an implied trust has been created. It is important to remember that these principles are not confined to family law cases. They are property law principles of universal application and are not specifically designed to resolve disputes relating to ownership of the family home.[19] The general nature of these principles has created tensions. Courts have struggled over the years to remain true to the doctrinal principles underpinning implied trusts while, at the same time, applying them in a way which takes account of the somewhat vague and haphazard way in which couples often deal with their financial and property affairs when they are living together in harmony. Thus there remains a considerable amount of uncertainty about the application of these general principles to family law cases. Recent case law has emphasised that judges must apply the technical requirements of ordinary property law principles and not impose their own idea of fairness between the parties.[20] However, as will be seen in this chapter, dicta from the same

---

[16] Of course, the express declaration of trust may specify that the parties are to share the beneficial interest in some other proportion.

[17] Research in 2001 showed that about one-quarter of cohabitants taking part in a large survey reported that they had moved into their partner's property at the start of the relationship, J. Haskey, 'Cohabiting Couples in Great Britain: Accommodation Sharing, Tenure and Property Ownership' (2001) 103 Population Trends 26. See G. Douglas, J. Pearce, and H. Woodward, Cardiff Law School Research Paper No 1, 'A Failure of Trust: Resolving Property Disputes on Cohabitation Breakdown' (2007), para 2.22.

[18] Under the Law of Property Act 1925, s 53(2), the lack of a written declaration of trust does not prevent the creation or operation of resulting, implied, or constructive trusts.

[19] *Pettitt v Pettitt* [1970] AC 777; *Gissing v Gissing* [1971] 1 AC 886.

[20] *Stack v Dowden* [2007] UKHL 17 at [61].

cases also suggest that the principles do apply in a slightly different way when being used to resolve disputes in the 'domestic' context, that is, concerning the family home.[21]

Implied trusts fall into two main categories: resulting trusts and constructive trusts. The following sections will highlight the core elements of each. It should be understood at the outset, however, that the resulting trust has much less significance in the resolution of domestic property disputes than in the past. The constructive trust is now the primary legal mechanism which will determine the whereabouts of the beneficial interest in the property in the absence of an express declaration of trust.

1.3 THE RESULTING TRUST

Talking point

A resulting trust will arise where the person whose name is not on the legal title to the property makes a direct financial contribution to its purchase price.

These direct payments to the acquisition of the property will entitle the contributor to a share in the property proportionate to the amount of their contribution. For example, if one person pays 20 per cent of the purchase price of a house, the law will presume that this was not a gift and, as such, they will acquire a 20 per cent share in the value of the property. This presumption can be rebutted by evidence that the contribution was made as a gift or a loan. Further, the presumption of resulting trust will not apply where a husband makes a transfer of money or property to his wife or a father makes such a transfer to his child. In these circumstances it will be presumed that a gift was intended and the recipient wife or child will hold the property absolutely. This is known as the presumption of *advancement* and it is based on the historic duties imposed on husbands and fathers to maintain their wives and children. However, this presumption can be rebutted by evidence to the contrary which indicates that a gift was not intended. Given the changing contours of familial obligations where husbands and fathers no longer have a unilateral duty to support their wives and children financially, the presumption of advancement is now much less relevant in modern family law.[22] Indeed, the strength of the presumption of advancement has considerably diminished and is readily rebutted by comparatively slight evidence.[23]

---

[21] Ibid, [3], [14], [33], [42], [56], [60].

[22] The Family Law (Property and Maintenance) Bill 2005 sought, amongst other things, to abolish the presumption of advancement. However, this Bill has not been enacted. See G. Andrews, 'The Presumption of Advancement: Equity, Equality and Human Rights' (2007) Conveyancer and Property Lawyer 340.

[23] See *Pettitt v Pettitt* [1970] AC 777 at 814. See also *Stack v Dowden* [2007] UKHL 17 at [16] *per* Lord Walker and [101] *per* Lord Neuberger. In *McGrath v Wallis* [1995] 2 FLR 114 the Court of Appeal said that the presumption of advancement should only be used as a last resort where there is no evidence of the parties' intentions. In this case the court confirmed that slight evidence can rebut the presumption of advancement between parent and child, and in *Tribe v Tribe* [1995] 2 FLR 966 the Court of Appeal allowed a father to rebut the presumption of advancement to his son. In *Laskar v Laskar* [2008] EWCA Civ 347, Lord Neuberger observed that the presumption of advancement between a parent and child, already a weak presumption, is even weaker where the child was over 18 and managed her own affairs, at [20]. In *Gibson v Revenue and Customs Prosecution Office* [2008] EWCA 645, Arden LJ said that if property is transferred into the parties' joint names, the presumption of advancement does not arise. Instead, in light of the decision of the House of Lords in *Stack v Dowden* [2007] UKHL 17, the 'function of the presumption of advancement is now performed by the presumption of equal beneficial ownership of property held in joint names', at [27]. For a discussion of *Stack v Dowden*, see Section 2.1.

The resulting trust doctrine has several limitations when applied in the domestic context to determine the parties' respective beneficial interests in the family home. First, only direct financial contributions to the acquisition of the property will give rise to a resulting trust and it is doubtful whether more indirect contributions such as the payment of household bills and domestic labour (housework and childcare) will suffice. Secondly, it seems that only initial contributions to the purchase price will generate a resulting trust, and not contributions made after the purchase.[24] Thirdly, the contributor's share in the property under the resulting trust analysis will only be proportionate to the amount of their contributions. However, following the House of Lords' decision in *Stack v Dowden*[25] it would appear that the resulting trust framework is now much less relevant in determining the whereabouts of the beneficial interest in the family home. The majority of the House of Lords stated that the resulting trust will no longer operate as a legal presumption in domestic cases[26] and in *Abbott v Abbott*[27] Baroness Hale confirmed that, in such cases, 'the constructive trust is generally the more appropriate tool of analysis'.[28]

1.4 THE CONSTRUCTIVE TRUST

Talking point

A constructive trust will arise where there was a common intention (either express or implied) between the parties to share the beneficial ownership of the property, and the person claiming such a share has relied on this intention to his or her detriment.

This is known as the common intention constructive trust. While it is a more flexible legal tool than the resulting trust, particularly in the context of relationships where the parties may make a range of important financial and non-financial contributions to the family, it does have its problems. In particular, it is based on finding evidence (express or implied) of the parties' *common intention* to share ownership of the property. However, the problem is that parties to a romantic relationship may not discuss or even think about their expectations or intentions regarding ownership of the family home until the relationship breaks down and then, of course, the demise of the relationship will give the parties a very different perspective about what they intended regarding the property. Retrospectively seeking to ascertain the parties' respective intentions about property ownership at the time of acquisition or any time thereafter is a somewhat fictitious exercise with clear evidential difficulties, but it is at the heart of the common intention constructive trust. In addition, there is a considerable amount of uncertainty about the type of conduct from which the court will infer that the parties had a common intention to share ownership of the property, and of the acts of reliance which will suffice to give rise to the constructive trust. Thus while the constructive trust gives the courts more leeway to consider a broader range of familial contributions when determining ownership of the family home, they still must adhere to its doctrinal requirements. Courts will not be able to impose a constructive trust just because it appears to be the correct thing to do on the facts or because justice requires it.

---

[24] *Curley v Parkes* [2004] EWCA Civ 1515. [25] [2007] UKHL 17.
[26] *Stack v Dowden* [2007] UKHL 17 at [31] *per* Lord Hope, at [60] *per* Baroness Hale. Lord Neuberger dissented and considered that unequal contributions to the acquisition of the property gives rise to the presumption of a resulting trust, at [123]. He pointed out, of course, that this is just a presumption which can be rebutted by other evidence and thus replaced by a constructive trust. [27] [2007] UKPC 53.
[28] Ibid, [4]. See also *Jones v Kernott* [2011] UKSC 53.

1.5 DISTINGUISHING TWO SITUATIONS

The law of implied trusts will have to step in to determine the whereabouts of the beneficial interests in the property in two main situations where the conveyance does not contain an express declaration of trust:

Situation 1: where the legal title to the property is in the *joint names* of the parties but the conveyance does not indicate how the beneficial interest is to be shared between them. We will call these 'joint names cases'. In this situation the crucial question is whether joint beneficial ownership is to be presumed. And, if so, can this be displaced by evidence that unequal beneficial ownership was intended?

Situation 2: where the property is conveyed into the *sole name* of one party, and there is no declaration of beneficial entitlement. We will call these 'sole name cases'. In this situation, equity will presume that the owner of the legal estate has the sole beneficial entitlement. In order to rebut this presumption and acquire a beneficial interest, the non-legal owner must establish that the legal owner holds the property as trustee for both parties in equal or unequal shares. The question which the courts have tried to answer is: how can this be done?

In both situations, the law of implied trusts (in particular, the common intention constructive trust) will resolve these issues and determine the respective entitlement of each party to the property. The following sections will take each situation in turn and discuss the legal principles to determine the whereabouts of the beneficial interests.

2 JOINT NAMES CASES

To re-cap, in this situation the parties are joint legal owners of the property but there is no express declaration of the parties' beneficial entitlement. Which legal principles will determine how the beneficial interest is to be shared? That there are difficult issues regarding the quantification of the beneficial interest in such cases may seem to be surprising. One might assume that if property is held legally in the parties' joint names, then the beneficial interests will automatically, as a matter of logic, be shared equally between them. However, prior to the House of Lords' decision in *Stack v Dowden*, this was not the case. The whereabouts of the beneficial interest was determined by the application of ordinary trust principles and case law suggested that if one party had made a greater financial contribution to the purchase price of the property, they would, under the presumption of a resulting trust, receive a share of the beneficial interest which was proportionate to their contribution.[29] For example, if one person contributed 75 per cent of the purchase price of the property, this greater financial contribution would give them a 75 per cent share of the beneficial interest despite the fact that the property was held in the parties' joint names. However, this all changed when the House of Lords in *Stack v Dowden*,[30] which was the first case concerning a property dispute between unmarried cohabitants to reach the House of Lords, set out a new set of principles to determine the quantification of the beneficial interests in joint names cases. The judgment in *Jones v Kernott*[31] has also considered the position of joint names in trust law.

---

[29] See *Walker v Hall* [1984] FLR 126; *Springette v Defoe* [1992] 2 FLR 388; *Huntingford v Hobbs* [1993] 1 FLR 736.

[30] [2007] UKHL 17.   [31] [2011] UKSC 53.

2.1 *STACK V DOWDEN*: THE FACTS

Key case

The parties (an unmarried couple with four children) purchased a home in joint names. The purchase of the property was financed primarily by Ms Dowden who earned more than her partner, Mr Stack. In particular, it was funded by the sale of another property which had been in Ms Dowden's sole name, plus savings in her sole name as well as a mortgage held in joint names. At the time of the purchase the parties had already been living together for around ten years and had four children. Nine years later the relationship broke down and Mr Stack applied to the court for an order for sale of the property and an equal division of the proceeds. While the property was registered in joint names, there was no declaration of trust specifying how the beneficial interest was to be shared. The transfer deed simply included a clause which contained a declaration that the survivor of the parties could give a valid receipt for capital money arising from the sale of the property. In the Court of Appeal, Mr Stack was awarded just 35 per cent of the value of the property and he appealed to the House of Lords. The House of Lords upheld the decision of the Court of Appeal. All their Lordships reached the same outcome although Lord Neuberger dissented on the reasoning.

2.1.1 Was there an express trust?

The first issue that had to be decided was whether there was any evidence of an express trust. In particular, did the declaration in the transfer deed that the survivor of the parties could give a valid receipt for capital money received on the sale of the property amount to an express declaration of a beneficial joint tenancy? The House of Lords, confirming earlier case law,[32] held that it did not. Even though this 'valid receipt clause' could be consistent with the declaration of a beneficial joint tenancy (where, on the death of one party, the other automatically takes his or her share under the doctrine of survivorship), the court held that it could also be consistent with another form of property ownership.[33] As a result, there was *no express declaration of trust* and the whereabouts of the beneficial interest in the property had to be determined by ordinary trust principles.[34]

2.1.2 The starting point presumption

Talking point

The Lords confirmed that in all cases where there is no express declaration of the beneficial interests in the family home, the starting presumption is that *equity follows the law* and the beneficial

---

[32] *Harwood v Harwood* [1991 2 FLR 274; *Huntington v Hobbs* [1993] 1 FLR 736.

[33] [2007] UKHL 17 at [51] *per* Baroness Hale.

[34] It should be noted that a new form was introduced in 1998 for conveyances of registered land into joint names. Form TR1 contains a section for the transferees to declare whether they are to hold the property on trust for themselves as joint tenants, as tenants in common in equal shares, or in any other way (see J. Wilson, 'Tripping up on the TR1' [2006] Family Law 305). Completion of this part of the form will ensure that there is an express declaration of the beneficial interests which will be conclusive in the absence of fraud or mistake, *Goodman v Gallant* [1986] 1 FLR 513. However, as Baroness Hale made it clear in *Stack v Dowden*, completing this section of the form is not compulsory and non-completion does not affect the validity of the transfer, at [52] (see Editorial, 'Anything to Declare? Express declaration of trust on Land Registry form TR1: The Doubts Raised in *Stack v Dowden*' (2007) 71 Conveyance and Property Lawyer 364). As such, there will still be cases where registered land is transferred into joint names but there is no express declaration of the beneficial interests. Further problems lie in the fact that the language used in the form is not comprehensible to the lay person and so legal advice is usually required to ensure that the parties understand how to complete it. G. Douglas, J. Pearce, and H. Woodward, 'Cohabitants, Property and the Law: A Study of Injustice' (2009) 72(1) Modern Law Review 24 at 40–41.

interests will reflect the legal interests in the property.[35] This means that where there is joint legal ownership, the starting point is joint beneficial ownership.[36] As Baroness Hale made clear:

> at least in the domestic consumer context, a conveyance into joint names indicates both legal and beneficial joint tenancy, unless and until the contrary is proved.[37]

If one party wants a greater share, then the onus is on them to show that there was a common intention that the beneficial ownership was to be different from the legal ownership. Baroness Hale made it clear, however, that this is a very heavy burden to discharge in the domestic context and so 'is not a task to be lightly embarked upon'.[38] Applying this to the facts of the case: the property was in joint names and so the starting presumption was that the parties were to share the beneficial interests equally. If Ms Dowden wanted a greater share, then she had the onus of establishing that the property should be held in unequal beneficial shares. The obvious question is: in what circumstances will the court be persuaded that this is the case?

2.1.3 How to establish that the property is to be held in unequal shares?

There were two approaches open to the court. First, in line with previous case law, the Lords could have confirmed that the presumption of the resulting trust means that the parties' shares in the property mirror their respective financial contributions to its acquisition.[39] Alternatively, the court had the option of taking a broader approach by looking at all the relevant circumstances (and not just financial contributions) to ascertain the parties' common intention regarding the ownership of the property.[40] The majority of the court took the latter approach, making a distinction between the operation of trust principles in commercial situations and when applied to cases concerning the family home. Baroness Hale said that 'these days, the importance to be attached to who paid for what in a domestic context may be very different from its importance in other contexts or long ago'.[41] While the resulting trust operates as a legal presumption in commercial cases where the parties are dealing with each other at arm's length, the majority considered that this is not appropriate in the 'domestic consumer context' where the dispute concerns the family home.[42] In the words of Lord Hope:

> cohabiting couples are in a different kind of relationship. The place where they live together is their home. Living together is an exercise in give and take, mutual co-operation and compromise. Who pays for what in regard to the home has to be seen in the wider context of their overall relationship. A more practical, down-to-earth, fact-based approach is called for in their case.[43]

This is a significant point because it indicates the emergence of a different jurisprudence for domestic cases where the resulting trust will no longer operate as a legal presumption. It means that the presumption of joint beneficial ownership will not be rebutted by the mere fact that the parties have made unequal financial contributions to the acquisition of the property. However, if the resulting trust does not apply, how

---

[35] *Stack v Dowden* [2007] UKHL 17 at [33] *per* Lord Walker, at [54] *per* Baroness Hale.

[36] Ibid, [56] *per* Baroness Hale. The starting point when there is sole legal ownership is sole beneficial ownership.   [37] Ibid, [58].

[38] Ibid, [68].   [39] Unless, of course, a contrary intention could be shown.

[40] *Stack v Dowden* [2007] UKHL 17 at [59] *per* Baroness Hale.   [41] Ibid, [60].

[42] Lord Neuberger dissented on this reasoning and did not agree that different principles should apply in the domestic and commercial context, at [101]–[107].   [43] Ibid, [3].

are the parties' respective beneficial shares to be quantified when the home is in the parties' joint names? In other words, how is the presumption of joint and equal beneficial interests to be rebutted, if at all?

Talking point

The House of Lords made it clear in *Stack* that the presumption will only be rebutted if there is evidence that the parties had a shared intention to hold the property in unequal shares. If there is no evidence of an express agreement between the parties, the task of the court is to undertake a survey of the parties' whole course of dealing taking account of their conduct insofar as it throws light on the question of what they must 'be taken to have intended'.[44] Each case will be decided on its own facts and 'many more factors than financial contributions may be relevant to divining the parties' true intentions'.[45] According to Baroness Hale, these include:[46]

- any advice or discussions at the time of the transfer;
- the reasons why the home was acquired in the parties' joint names;
- the reasons why (if this is the case) the survivor was authorised to give a valid receipt for the capital moneys;
- the purpose for which the home was acquired;
- the nature of the parties' relationship;
- whether they have children for whom they had a responsibility to provide a home;
- how the purchase was financed, both initially and subsequently;
- how the parties arranged their finances;
- how the parties discharged the outgoings on the property and their other household expenses.

In addition, Baroness Hale considered that the parties' individual characteristics and personalities may also be relevant when ascertaining their intentions in relation to the property.[47] The majority took the view that cases where joint legal owners will be found to have intended that their beneficial interests should be different from their legal interests will be 'very unusual'.[48] As it turned out, however, *Stack v Dowden* was regarded as being one of these 'unusual' cases and the House of Lords held that Ms Dowden was able to rebut the presumption of joint beneficial ownership. Indeed, Baroness Hale said that there were 'many factors to which Ms Dowden can point to indicate that these parties did have a different common intention'.[49]

The first factor was that Ms Dowden contributed far more financially to the acquisition of the property than Mr Stack. There was evidence that Mr Stack had made some improvements to the parties' earlier property but it was not possible to quantify their value to the eventual sale price which was then put towards the purchase of the new property. Secondly, the parties did not pool their separate resources, even notionally, for the common good.[50] All of their finances and property, except for the house in question and an associated endowment policy, were kept strictly separate. Thirdly, both parties undertook separate responsibility for that part of the expenditure which they had agreed to pay and, significantly, the court found that it was Ms Dowden who undertook primary

---

[44] Ibid, [61] *per* Baroness Hale.   [45] Ibid, [69] *per* Baroness Hale.   [46] Ibid.
[47] Although it is very unclear how such subjective considerations would be applied.   [48] Ibid, [69].
[49] Ibid, [87].   [50] Ibid, [90].

financial responsibility for the property. By contrast, it was implied that Mr Stack did not contribute as much as he could have done to the family's expenditure. Indeed, Probert concludes that Baroness Hale strongly implied that Mr Stack simply did not pull his weight in contributing to the parties' finances, contributing only to the interest and premiums on the property while all other regular commitments were undertaken by Ms Dowden.[51] Taken together these factors, according to the court, made this a 'very unusual case'.[52] Baroness Hale said:

> there cannot be many unmarried couples who have lived together for as long as this, who have had four children together, and whose affairs have been kept as rigidly separate as this couple's affair were kept. This is all strongly indicative that they did not intend their shares, even in the property which was put into both their names, to be equal.[53]

As a result, the court held that Mr Stack was only entitled to a 35 per cent share in the beneficial interest. Lord Neuberger concurred in the result but dissented on the reasoning. His Lordship disagreed with the view that different principles should apply in domestic cases[54] and, as such, he applied ordinary resulting trust principles.[55] Under Lord Neuberger's analysis, Mr Stack was only entitled to a 35 per cent share of the beneficial interest in light of his financial contribution to the acquisition of the property.

This is a very important decision which has altered the way in which the beneficial interests in the family home will be determined in joint names cases. While it has provided some welcome clarification, particularly in laying down the starting presumption that equity follows the law, it has also come under criticism for leaving several questions unanswered. The important elements of the decision and some points of confusion arising from it are detailed in the following section. But at the outset it is worth nothing that Lord Neuberger, speaking extra-judicially, has expressed concern at the majority's reasoning.[56] His Lordship outlined four main concerns. First, he questioned the assumption that unmarried couples intended to share the property as joint tenants in equity, speculating that one reason such couples do not marry is to keep their assets separate. Secondly, the application of a different set of rules to the domestic consumer context gives rise to the issue of to which familial relationships this exactly refers. Thirdly, under what circumstances will it be appropriate to depart from the presumption of joint beneficial ownership? Fourthly, he considered that the approach of the majority in *Stack*, in particular the search for what the parties must be taken to have intended, will encourage lengthy and costly legal disputes.

2.1.4 Ascertaining the parties' common intention

Talking point

The core issue in *Stack* was the test adopted by the House of Lords for quantifying the parties' shares in joint names cases. The majority concluded that if there is no evidence of an express agreement between the parties, then the task of the court is to ascertain the parties' shared

---

[51] R. Probert, 'Equality in the Family Home' (2007) Feminist Legal Studies 341 at 347. *Stack v Dowden* [2007] UKHL 17 at [91] *per* Baroness Hale.

[52] *Stack v Dowden* [2007] UKHL 17 at [91] *per* Baroness Hale.   [53] Ibid, [92].   [54] Ibid, [107].

[55] Ibid, [110]–[116].

[56] Lord Neuberger, 'The Conspirators, the Tax Man, the Bill of Rights and a Bit About the Lovers', Chancery Bar Association Annual Lecture, 10 March 2008, available at www.chba.org.uk/library/seminar_notes/news4.

intention from their whole course of conduct. By contrast, in the earlier sole name case of *Oxley v Hiscock*,[57] Chadwick LJ considered that the court's task was to search for a fair outcome, noting that each party 'is entitled to that share which the court considers fair having regard to the whole course of dealing between them in relation to the property'.[58] In *Stack v Dowden*, Baroness Hale rejected this approach. She preferred the 'holistic' approach to quantification advocated by the Law Commission in its 2002 Discussion Paper, *Sharing Homes*, where they said that:

> there is much to be said for adopting what has been called a 'holistic approach' to quantifi-cation, undertaking a survey of the whole course of dealing between the parties and taking account of all conduct which throws light on the question what shares were intended.[59]

Baroness Hale preferred this approach for two reasons.[60] First, it emphasises that the court's search is for the result which the parties must have intended. Secondly, this search cannot be abandoned in favour of the result which the court itself considers fair. Thus, Baroness Hale 're-asserted strongly' the need to find the parties' common intention in relation to the property.[61] One could say that, in terms of finding the correct approach, Baroness Hale tried to steer a middle course. On the one hand, her Ladyship expressed disapproval at an approach which gives the court the power to impose its own sense of fairness but, on the other hand, she did not wish to adhere to strict resulting trust prin-ciples which would decide the issue solely on the basis of the parties' direct financial contributions to the acquisition of the property. Instead, she sought a middle ground which took a holistic approach to quantification but under the auspices of searching for the parties' true intentions in relation to be property.

Talking point

However, *Stack* did not make clear whether the court can *impute* an intention to the parties which they did not in fact hold. The majority suggested that the parties' intention could be inferred, or even imputed, from their conduct in relation to the property.[62] There is a subtle but important distinction between *inferring* and *imputing* an intention. Lord Neuberger described the distinction as follows:

> An inferred intention is one which is objectively deduced to be the subjective actual inten-tion of the parties, in the light of their actions and statements. An imputed intention is one which is attributed to the parties, even though no such actual intention can be deduced from their actions and statements, and even though they had no such intention. Imputation involves concluding what the parties would have intended, whereas inference involves con-cluding what they did intend.[63]

---

[57] [2004] EWCA Civ 546.   [58] Ibid, [69].

[59] Law Commission, *Sharing Homes: A Discussion Paper* (Law Com No 278, 2002), para 4.27.

[60] *Stack v Dowden* [2007] UKHL 17 at [60]–[61].

[61] G. Battersby, 'Ownership of the Family Home: *Stack v Dowden* in the House of Lords' [2008] Child and Family Law Quarterly 255.

[62] Baroness Hale said that the 'search is to ascertain the parties' intentions, actual, inferred or imputed, with respect to the property in light of their whole course of conduct in relation to it', *Stack v Dowden* [2007] UKHL 17 at [60].

[63] Ibid, [126]. His Lordship accepted that the parties' intention may be inferred from their conduct but rejected the idea that a court can impute an intention to the parties. He said that the process of impu-tation would be a 'difficult, subjective and uncertain' exercise which is contrary to established principle, at [125]–[127].

Piska observes that an imputed intention is not regarded as representing the parties' actual intentions at all. Rather, it is 'the court's estimation of what is fair'.[64] However, there is a contradiction here. Even though Baroness Hale said that the search was to ascertain the parties' shared intentions, actual, inferred, or *imputed*,[65] her Ladyship was clear that the court should not impose its own sense of fairness. However, if the court is permitted to impute an intention to the parties which they may never have had (which the majority appeared to suggest was permissible) then this, by implication, could import subjective notions of fairness as the court assigns an 'intention' to the parties based on its view of their mutual interaction. Does this mean, then, that the court can covertly impose its own sense of fairness by adopting the guise of searching for the parties' intentions, or more precisely, searching for what the parties must 'be taken to have intended'?[66] The Supreme Court has now had the opportunity to re-visit this issue in *Jones v Kernott*.[67]

2.1.5 Why were the facts of *Stack v Dowden* regarded as unusual?

The actual outcome of the case has attracted considerable criticism. In particular, commentators have posed the question of why the facts were regarded as being so unusual as to allow Ms Dowden to discharge the 'considerable burden' of rebutting the presumption of joint beneficial ownership.[68]

Despite the majority's rejection of the resulting trust framework under which the parties' financial contributions determine their respective beneficial entitlement in a strict arithmetical fashion, it was these contributions which emerged as the most important factor under the constructive trust analysis.[69] Baroness Hale said that the fact that Ms Dowden contributed far more to the acquisition of the property in relation to the initial purchase price and subsequent capital repayments of the mortgage, were factors to 'support an inference of an intention to share otherwise than equally'.[70] It is also worth pointing out that the same outcome was reached from the analyses of the majority, whose reasoning was based on the common intention constructive trust, and the dissenting speech of Lord Neuberger who applied the resulting trust. Thus, despite the sentiment of the majority who urged consideration of a range of factors from which to ascertain the parties' intentions, it is hard not to reach the conclusion that, at the end of the day, it was Ms Dowden's greater financial contribution which was the determining factor. Lord Neuberger (the dissenting voice in *Stack*) speaking extra-judicially has criticised this reasoning saying:

> If the presumption of equality is to be rebutted because the contributions are significantly different, it is a pretty useless presumption: the only time you need it, it isn't there.[71]

---

[64] N. Piska, 'Intention, Fairness and the Presumption of Resulting Trust after *Stack v Dowden*' (2008) 71(1) Modern Law Review 114 at 127.   [65] *Stack v Dowden* [2007] UKHL 17 at [60] (emphasis added).
[66] N. Piska, 'Intention, Fairness and the Presumption of Resulting Trust after *Stack v Dowden*' (2008) 71(1) Modern Law Review 114 at 128.   [67] [2011] UKSC 53, see Section 2.1.7.
[68] See eg M. Dixon, 'The Never-Ending Story—Co-ownership after *Stack v Dowden*' (2007) Conveyancer and Property Lawyer 456 at 460; W. Swadling, 'The Common Intention Constructive Trust in the House of Lords: An Opportunity Missed' (2007) Law Quarterly Review 511 at 515.
[69] As noted by Lord Walker, the facts which traditionally gave rise to a resulting trust (direct contributions to the purchase price) will be relevant when considering the full range of the parties' contributions, both direct and indirect, in the constructive trust analysis and the search for the parties' common intention, [2007] UKHL 17 at [31].   [70] Ibid, [89].
[71] Lord Neuberger, 'The Conspirators, the Tax Man, the Bill of Rights and a Bit About the Lovers', Chancery Bar Association Annual Lecture, 10 March 2008, para 15, available at www.chba.org.uk/library/seminar_notes/news4.

In addition, the court seemed to regard the couple's independent financial arrangements as unusual. However, empirical evidence suggests that independent money-management arrangements are not that uncommon among cohabiting couples and it has been observed that this 'would hardly mark *Stack* as an exceptional case'.[72]

Thus, the 'whole course of conduct' approach to quantification advocated by the majority was undermined in practice by the actual outcome of the case which placed considerable emphasis on the parties' financial contributions and money-management practices. Further, while Baroness Hale provided a non-exhaustive list of factors to be considered when ascertaining the parties' intentions, no further guidance was given on how they should be applied. Even though one factor in this list was the 'nature of the parties' relationship, it is clear from the court's reasoning that general familial characteristics had little relevance when determining the parties' intentions in relation to the property. Indeed, Mr Stack was left with only 35 per cent of the property notwithstanding the fact that this was a very lengthy relationship which had produced four children. However, Baroness Hale ruled that the trial judge had erred in looking at the:

> parties' relationship rather than the matters which were particularly relevant to their intentions about this property. He found his conclusion on the length and nature of their relationship, which he repeatedly referred to as a partnership.[73]

According to Baroness Hale, these factors could not provide an adequate answer to the question of property ownership amounting to 'little more than saying that these people were in a relationship for 27 years and had four children together'.[74] Thus, it is clear that the only conduct from which inferences can be drawn in relation to the parties' intentions is conduct *relating to the property*. While the majority permitted, and indeed advocated, a consideration of the whole course of dealing between the parties, the wider contributions of the parties (beyond their financial contributions) and other relationship-based factors (such as the length of the relationship, whether the parties have children) had little bearing on the actual outcome of the case.

There was a great deal of uncertainty about the implications of *Stack v Dowden*. Several questions arose. In particular, what factual circumstances will lead a court to displace the presumption that the beneficial interest is to be shared equally in joint names cases? Would future courts follow the reasoning implicit in the actual outcome of *Stack*, that is, by attaching greater weight to the parties' respective financial contributions? Or, would courts follow the rhetoric of the speeches of the majority by looking at the whole course of dealing between the parties in relation to the property?[75] In short, how easy or difficult will it be to displace the starting presumption in joint names cases that equity follows the law and the beneficial interest is to be shared equally?

2.1.6 *Fowler v Barron*

The Court of Appeal had the opportunity to apply *Stack* in *Fowler v Barron*.[76] The parties had been in an unmarried relationship for 23 years and had two children. They bought a house in 1998 and made a conscious decision to put the property into joint names but did

---

[72] R. Probert, 'Equality in the Family Home' (2007) Feminist Legal Studies 341 at 347. Probert cites C. Vogler, M. Brockmann, and R. Wiggins, 'Intimate Relationships and Changing Patterns of Money Management at the Beginning of the Twenty-First Century' (2006) 57(3) British Journal of Sociology 455–482. See also G. Douglas, J. Pearce, and H. Woodward, 'Cohabitants, Property and the Law: A Study of Injustice' (2009) 72(1) Modern Law Review 24–47.   [73] [2007] UKHL 17 at [86].
[74] Ibid.   [75] R. Probert, 'Equality in the Family Home' (2007) Feminist Legal Studies 341 at 348.
[76] [2008] EWCA Civ 377.

not receive legal advice about the consequences of doing so. Mr Barron, a retired fireman who was 30 years older than Miss Fowler, paid the deposit on the property and paid the balance of the purchase price out of the proceeds of sale of his flat where the parties had previously been living. The parties took a joint mortgage of £35,000 and Mr Barron paid the instalments. The parties never had a joint bank account and Mr Barron paid all of the direct costs associated with the property, such as the council tax and utilities bills. Miss Fowler worked for most of the duration of the relationship and spent her income on gifts, school expenses, clothing, holidays, and special occasions. The parties also had mutual wills, each leaving his or her interest in the property to the other on their death. While the property was held in the parties' joint legal names, the transfer document did not contain any declaration of trust stating how the beneficial interest was to be shared. In addition, there was no evidence of any discussion between them as to how the property was to be held. When the relationship broke down, the question arose as to the whereabouts of the beneficial interest. Mr Barron argued that in light of his much greater financial contributions to the acquisition of the property, he should receive more than a 50 per cent of the beneficial interest in it.

In light of the outcome in *Stack v Dowden*, one might think this an even more persuasive case for rebutting the presumption of joint beneficial ownership given that (unlike Mr Stack) Miss Fowler had made *no* financial contribution, either direct or indirect, to the purchase price of the property or to the mortgage repayments. However, the Court of Appeal distinguished *Stack v Dowden* and left Miss Fowler with a 50 per cent share in the property. In doing so, it put the rhetoric of the House of Lords into practice by holding that it was incorrect to concentrate on financial contributions instead of looking more broadly at the parties' whole course of conduct in relation to the property. This worked in favour of Miss Fowler.

In distinguishing *Stack v Dowden*, Arden LJ said that the facts of *Fowler v Barron* were 'different in many respects'.[77] First, the couple had executed mutual wills which indicated to the court that they each had a beneficial interest to leave to the other. Secondly, unlike the position in *Stack*, the parties in this case had no substantial assets other than the property. This led Arden LJ to decide that it was not reasonable to infer that the parties intended that Miss Fowler should have no share of the house if the relationship broke down leaving her potentially dependent on state benefits and housing support.[78] In addition, the court inferred from the couple's money-management arrangements that they treated their 'incomes and asset as one pool from which household expenses were paid'.[79] While they maintained separate bank accounts, it was this general pulling of resources for the good of the family that allowed Arden LJ to draw the inference that it made no difference to them who paid for what expense. There was no prior agreement between the parties as to who would pay for what and, taken with the evidence of the mutual wills, the inference was that 'the parties simply did not care about the respective size of each other's contributions'.[80] Thus, according to the Court of Appeal, Mr Barron had not discharged the onus of showing that there was a common intention that the parties would own the property in unequal shares. While Mr Barron gave evidence that when he put the property into the parties' joint names he only ever intended that Miss Fowler have a beneficial interest in the property in the event of his death, the court held that this could not be relied upon. It was only a secret intention on his part and was not a shared intention from which inferences could be drawn. Thus, the presumption of joint beneficial interest was not rebutted, notwithstanding the fact that Miss Fowler had made no financial contribution to the acquisition of the property.

---

[77] Ibid, [46].   [78] Ibid.   [79] Ibid.   [80] Ibid, [41] *per* Arden LJ.

This is a welcome decision which offers some much needed clarification, in particular in determining when the 'default rule'[81] of joint beneficial ownership is rebutted. When ascertaining whether the parties had a shared intention to hold the property in unequal shares, the Court of Appeal said that the task is to:

consider whether the facts as found are inconsistent with the inference of a common intention to share the property in equal shares to an extent sufficient to discharge the civil standard of proof on the person seeking to displace the presumption arising from a transfer into joint names.[82]

In other words, is there anything on the facts which is *inconsistent* with the presumption that the parties are to share the beneficial ownership equally? The parties' respective financial contributions to the acquisition of the property is just one factor for consideration and the mere fact that one party has contributed more than the other will not, by itself, rebut the presumption of equal beneficial shares.[83] In taking this approach, the Court of Appeal has allayed some of the concerns about the implications of *Stack*. It also illustrates just how questionable the actual outcome was in that case. Given the similarities between the two cases, one can ask why *Stack* was deemed to be a very unusual case which justified Mr Stack's share being limited to 35 per cent and yet there was 'nothing at all unusual' about *Fowler v Barron* to rebut the presumption of equal beneficial ownership. Both involved lengthy cohabiting relationships with children. We know that Mr Stack made a much smaller financial contribution to the acquisition of the property than his female partner, although he did pay the mortgage interest and contributed towards paying off the capital. Outside this, the parties kept their finances separate. The facts of *Fowler v Barron* reveal a similar pattern. In fact, Miss Fowler made no direct or indirect financial contribution to the purchase price of the property or to any mortgage repayment. She kept her income separate but used it to contribute to family's general expenditure, and the parties did not have a joint bank account. So, what exactly made *Stack* an unusual case and *Fowler* not?

As indicated, the Court of Appeal put forward various reasons for distinguishing the two cases. However, none are particularly convincing. For example, the evidence of the mutual wills in *Fowler* was deemed to be important in giving rise to the inference that they intended that each should have an interest in the property. However, surely the only proper inference that can be drawn from the mutual wills is that, on death, each intended their interest in the property to pass to the other. It does not necessarily indicate that they intended, should the relationship break down, that the property be split equally between them.[84] Further, the inference that it was unlikely that the parties intended Miss Fowler to have no share of the house if the relationship broke down, leaving her potentially dependent on state benefits, is not fully explained. There is, of course, another contrast between the two cases which may have had some part to play in persuading the majority of the House of Lords that *Stack* was an exceptional case. The only feature of that case which

---

[81] Ibid, [34].   [82] Ibid, [35] *per* Arden LJ.

[83] Arden LJ said that it was not the mere fact that the parties had made unequal contributions to the purchase price which allowed Ms Dowden to rebut the presumption of equal shares in *Stack v Dowden*. What mattered more was the 'inferences to be drawn as to their shared intentions to be gleaned from the evidence overall', ibid, [45]. The fact that they kept their financial affairs 'rigidly separate', did not pool their separate resources for the common good, and that Mr Stack did not contribute as much as he could have done to the family's finances made *Stack* an unusual case, ibid, [20] *per* Arden LJ.

[84] See N. Piska, 'Distinctions without a Difference? Explaining *Stack v Dowden*' (2008) Conveyancer and Property Lawyer 451 at 458–459. Piska points out that they may instead have intended a beneficial tenancy in common in unequal shares.

marks it as unusual was the fact that it was the female partner who was the primary breadwinner and who contributed more financially to purchasing the family home than her male partner.[85] In addition, it was implied that Mr Stack did not contribute as much financially as he could have done.[86] By contrast, there was a much more conventional division of responsibility in *Fowler* where the male partner was the primary economic provider and both parties contributed what they could to the household expenses. One wonders, therefore, whether gender-based assumptions surrounding the conventional division of economic responsibility within families had some intuitive role to play in *Stack*. Indeed, Piska observes that 'with the exception that it was the woman who contributed more financially *Stack* was not an unusual case in the slightest'.[87]

Overall, the decision of the Court of Appeal in *Fowler v Barron* is to be welcomed. It confirms the strength of the 'default rule' in joint names cases that the parties are presumed to hold the beneficial interest in equal shares, with a person who wishes to claim otherwise facing a very difficult task. Indeed, both the reasoning and the outcome of the case clearly confirm that parties can be equal beneficial owners of the property even if their financial contributions to the purchase price had been unequal. The Court of Appeal provided welcome clarification that in determining whether the presumption of joint beneficial ownership is rebutted, the court will consider whether the facts of the case are 'inconsistent with the inference of a common intention to share the property in equal shares'.[88] It seems that if there is 'cogent evidence'[89] that the parties maintain rigidly separate and independent finances and, most importantly, do not pool their resources for the common good then this may be sufficient to rebut the presumption of equal ownership in joint names cases. However, in the absence of such clear evidence, it seems that the presumption that the parties intended their beneficial interests to be equal will prevail.

2.1.7 *Jones v Kernott*

> **Key case**
>
> The Supreme Court has now had the opportunity to revisit the decision in *Stack* in *Jones v Kernott*.[90] The parties, Ms Jones and Mr Kernott, met in 1980 and five years later bought 39 Badger Hall Avenue in joint names for £30,000. The conveyance did not contain a declaration of trust. Ms Jones contributed £6,000 towards the purchase price and the balance was raised by way of a mortgage in their joint names. The parties shared the household expenses until October 1993 when Mr Kernott moved out of the property leaving Ms Jones and their children residing there. Ms Jones paid all the household expenses from that point on and Mr Kernott made no further contribution towards the acquisition of the property.
>
> At some point, the parties cashed in a joint life insurance policy. Mr Kernott used his share of the proceeds as a deposit for a home of his own. In May 1996, he bought 114 Stanley Road. The judge at first instance had found that he was only able to afford this new home because he no longer contributed towards the cost of the Badger Hall property. This arrangement continued until 2006 when Mr Kernott indicated to Ms Jones that he wanted his share of the Badger Hall

---

[85] This can be regarded as unusual because studies show that men continue to earn more than women, see Office for National Statistics, 2010 Annual Survey of Hours and Earnings (2011), available at www.ons. gov.uk/ons/rel/ashe/annual-survey-of-hours-and-earnings/2010-revised-results/index.html; C. Dobbs, 'Patterns of Pay: Results of the Annual Survey of Hours and Earnings 1997 to 2008' (2009) 3(3) Economic & Labour Market Review 24–32.   [86] [2007] UKHL 17 at [91] *per* Baroness Hale.

[87] N. Piska, 'Distinctions without a Difference? Explaining *Stack v Dowden*' (2008) Conveyancer and Property Lawyer 451 at 460.   [88] [2008] EWCA Civ 377 at [35] *per* Arden LJ.

[89] Ibid, [51] *per* Toulson LJ.   [90] [2011] UKSC 53.

property which remained in the parties' joint names. In October 2007, Ms Jones applied for a declaration that she owned the entire beneficial interest in the Badger Hall property. At this time, the Badger Hall property was valued at £245,000. She claimed that since 1993, the parties' actions showed that their intentions with respect to the Badger Hall property had altered from the original intention to hold the beneficial interest jointly into unequal shares.

The judge at first instance accepted this contention, stating that he had to consider what was just and fair between the parties having regard to the whole course of dealing between them. He decided that Ms Jones was entitled to a 90 per cent share in the property. Mr Kernott appealed to the High Court where his appeal was dismissed.[91] An appeal to the Court of Appeal was allowed by a majority with Jacob LJ dissenting. Rix and Wall LJJ held that there was nothing to indicate that the parties' intentions had changed after their separation. Rix LJ held that *Stack v Dowden* was authority for the proposition that the courts could not impute an intention 'where none was expressly uttered or inferentially formed'.[92] Neither Rix nor Wall LJJ considered that there was sufficient evidence to infer a change in the parties' intentions in this case.

In the Supreme Court, their Lordships unanimously restored the judgment made at first instance and Ms Jones recovered 90 per cent of the proceeds of the disputed property.[93] However, the judges reached their decisions by different routes as they failed to agree on whether it was possible, on the facts of the case, to draw inferences as to a change over time in the parties' intentions regarding their shares in the disputed property. In their leading judgment, Lord Walker and Lady Hale (with whom Lord Collins agreed) held that there was no need for the court to impute an intention to the parties as it could be inferred from their conduct that their intention regarding ownership of the home had changed after separation. Post-1993, Ms Jones had paid the mortgage and all of the household expenses. In light of this, the majority ruled that it was logical to infer that the parties intended Mr Kernott's interest in the property to crystallise when he purchased his own house.[94] In reaching this conclusion, the court made it clear that the presumption of joint beneficial ownership in joint names cases can be displaced by showing that the parties had a different common intention as to the quantum of their respective shares in a property, either at the time of acquisition or at a later date. In other words, the parties' intentions as to shares can change over time and can be ambulatory in nature.[95] In terms of finding this common intention, the court confirmed that a broad-brush approach was to be taken with the court looking at the parties' whole course of dealing and not just at their financial contributions. Their Lordships took the view that courts should use their best efforts to infer the parties' actual intentions from their conduct and should not 'shrink from making findings on disputed evidence'.[96] However, even though the majority inferred the parties' intentions from their conduct, they suggested that if this had not been possible, the court must then consider what shares are fair. According to Lord Walker and Lady Hale, where it is not possible to ascertain by direct evidence or by inference what the parties' actual intention was as to the shares in which they would own the property, the court has to consider what shares are fair, having regard to the whole course of dealing between them in relation to the property.[97]

While the majority were able to infer from the parties' conduct that their intentions regarding their shares in the disputed property had changed, Lord Wilson and Lord Kerr felt that such inferences could not be drawn. Instead, Lord Wilson openly imputed an intention to the parties that the house was to be held in unequal proportions as determined by the county court judge, and Lord Kerr held that this was a fair outcome which should stand. This calls into question the

[91] [2009] EWHC 1713 (Ch).   [92] [2010] EWCA Civ 578 at [77].   [93] [2011] UKSC 53.
[94] Ibid, [48].   [95] Ibid, [14].
[96] R. Bailey-Harris and J. Wilson, *'Jones v Kernott*—Another Helping of the Witches Brew?*, available at www.familylawweek.co.uk.   [97] [2011] UKSC 53 at [51], point 4.

legitimacy of openly imputing an intention to the parties which they may never have held to give effect to an outcome which the court considers fair. It is unfortunate that the court did not take the opportunity to clarify this issue, or to thrash out the consequences of the imputation process. Indeed, Lord Collins stated that in his view, in the present context, the differences between inference and imputation are 'largely terminological and conceptual and are likely to make no difference in practice'.[98] While Lord Walker and Lady Hale felt that the conceptual difference between inferring and imputing an intention was clear, they considered that the difference in practice may not be so great.[99] By contrast, Lord Kerr held that the divergence between inference and imputation might well produce a difference in practice.[100] While his Lordship questioned the aptness of imputation, he considered that it may not be practicable to discard it. He concluded that 'the court should anxiously examine the circumstances in order, where possible, to ascertain the parties' intention but it should not be reluctant to recognise, when it is appropriate to do so, that inference of an intention is not possible and that imputation of an intention is the only course to follow'.[101]

That there is a significant difference between inferring and imputing an intention has already been highlighted,[102] and for many commentators the latter is a step too far. For example, Bailey-Harris and Wilson[103] persuasively comment that rebutting the presumption of joint beneficial ownership arising from joint registration by anything other than evidence of actual intention is highly questionable. They lament the fact that Lord Kerr did not develop his scepticism regarding imputation further and take a critical view of the approach of the court saying that:

According to the Supreme Court, imputation is a process of last resort where there is no evidence of the parties' actual intention to hold the property otherwise than as equal owners in equity. But in that situation, surely the presumption should simply hold, since it is not rebutted by evidence? How can a presumption (and a fortiori one which is supposed to be strong) be rebutted not by evidence but by the court filling the black hole in the evidence by its own determination of what is fair? This is surely highly unconventional. What is the point of having a presumption at all, if it can be rebutted not only by evidence of the parties' actual contrary intention but also by the court's own determination of what is fair?[104]

Bailey-Harris and Wilson further speculate that such an approach will encourage litigation as it provides an 'incentive for joint registered owners in cases where there is no express declaration of trust to "have a go" at arguing in court that the interests are other than equal'.[105]

2.1.8 To which 'domestic' situations will the presumption of joint beneficial ownership apply?

Another question arising from *Stack* is the range of domestic relationships to which the presumption of joint beneficial ownership will apply. The presumption of a joint beneficial tenancy will only apply in the domestic context where the property which is in the parties' joint names is their home, and not where it was purchased as an investment (even if the

---

[98] Ibid, [58] and [65].   [99] Ibid, [34].   [100] Ibid, [73]–[75].   [101] Ibid, [72].
[102] See Section 2.1.4.
[103] R. Bailey-Harris and J. Wilson, '*Jones v Kernott*—Another Helping of the Witches Brew?', available at www.familylawweek.co.uk.   [104] Ibid.
[105] Ibid.

owners are also family members). If the presumption does not apply, and if there is no express declaration of the beneficial interest, then the resulting trust will determine the parties' respective beneficial shares in the property.

Key case

This was made clear by the Court of Appeal in the post-*Stack* decision of *Laskar v Laskar*.[106] In this case, the mother purchased a council house at a discount under a right to buy scheme. In order to secure the mortgage, the property was transferred into the joint names of her and her daughter and both became jointly liable under it. The daughter also contributed a small amount of money towards the purchase price. The property was bought as an investment and shortly after the purchase it was rented out. The mother was solely responsible for the property and for the mortgage repayments which were funded from the rental income. When relations between the mother and daughter broke down, the daughter claimed that as the property was in the parties' joint names, there was a presumption at law that the beneficial ownership would be shared equally. The Court of Appeal held that this presumption did not apply because even though the parties were family members, the property was bought as an investment.[107] Instead, the parties' shares in the property were determined by resulting trust principles and thus the daughter received a 33 per cent interest in the property which reflected her contribution to its acquisition. It is worth noting that Lord Neuberger was of the view that even if the presumption of joint beneficial ownership applied, it would have been rebutted by several factors, in particular the fact that the parties maintained separate finances; that the property was purchased as an investment; that the mother had several other children which suggested that it was unlikely that she intended to benefit one over the others; that there was a disparity in the value of the parties' contributions to the purchase price; and that the daughter was a co-purchaser only because the mother could not afford the property on her own.[108]

However, this decision should not be taken to mean that the principles of *Stack v Dowden* only apply to cohabitants in a sexual relationship as opposed to other family members who share a property as a home. In *Adekunle v Ritchie*[109] a mother and her son (who was one of ten children) bought property jointly but there was no declaration of the beneficial interests. The property was purchased as a home for them both where they lived for some years before the mother's death. Judge Behrens held that the presumption of beneficial joint tenancy applied. However, the judge also suggested that it may be easier to rebut the presumption 'when one is not dealing with the situation of a couple living together'.[110] Indeed, although the presumption applied in this case it was rebutted on the facts and the son received only a one-third share in the property. The judge said that this was an unusual case where the evidence indicated that the parties did not intend their shares in the property to be equal.[111] In particular, attention was drawn to the following factors: the property was bought primarily to provide a home for the mother; the parties' finances were separate; the reason the property was put into joint names was because the mother was unable to fund the mortgage without assistance from her son; and the mother had nine other children with whom she was on good terms and there was no reason to think that she would have wanted the whole of her estate to pass to one son

---

[106] [2008] EWCA Civ 347.   [107] Ibid, [17] *per* Lord Neuberger.   [108] Ibid, [19].
[109] [2007] BPIR 1177.   [110] Ibid, [65].   [111] Ibid, [67].

alone.[112] However, the fact that the property was conveyed into joint names, that the son was jointly liable under the mortgage, that he was occupying the property at the time of acquisition, and that he contributed to the mortgage led the judge to conclude that he was to have some beneficial interest in the property. A strict arithmetical calculation based on his financial contribution to the acquisition of the property would have given him no more than a 25 per cent share in the property. However, taking a holistic approach to quantification, the judge awarded him a one-third share.

2.2 SOLE NAME CASES

The second situation that we must consider is the 'sole name case'—where the property is conveyed into the sole name of one party (the legal owner), and the other person claims that they have a beneficial interest in it.

It is clear from *Stack v Dowden* that the starting point in all cases is that equity follows the law. There is thus an immediate difference between sole and joint names cases. In joint names cases, the law will presume that both parties have an equal beneficial interest in the property, although one party can try to rebut this in an attempt to receive a larger share. However, if the property is registered in the sole name of one party, it will be presumed that this person also holds the sole beneficial title.[113] The onus is on the person claiming that the beneficial ownership is different from the legal ownership to show that there was a common intention to hold the property in some other shares. This means that in sole ownership cases, the non-legal owner must establish that he or she has a beneficial interest in the first place, before showing exactly what that interest is.[114]

Talking point

There are thus two separate questions that have to be considered in sole name cases:[115]

- Applying the principles of the common intention constructive trust, can the non-legal owner establish that the legal title is held on trust for both parties?

- If he or she can, the court must then decide the size of this person's beneficial interest (the quantification issue).

2.2.1 Establishing the existence of a beneficial interest

In order to *establish* a beneficial interest under a constructive trust, the non-legal owner must show that the parties had a common intention to share the ownership of the property. On top of this, the non-legal owner must also show that he or she acted to their detriment, or significantly altered their position, in reliance on this common intention.

2.2.1.1 Common intention

The most difficult question is whether or not there was a common intention between the parties to share the property. It is important to be aware that the common intention must relate to sharing the *ownership* of the property and not just its *occupation* as a joint family home. The leading case on establishing the existence of a beneficial interest is *Lloyd's Bank v Rosset*.[116] Lord Bridge stated that common intention can be established

---

[112] Ibid, [66].   [113] *Stack v Dowden* [2007] UKHL 17 at [56] *per* Baroness Hale.
[114] Ibid, [56] and [61].   [115] *Abbott v Abbott* [2007] UKPC 53 at [4] *per* Baroness Hale.
[116] [1991] 1 AC 107 at 133.

in one of two ways. It can be evidenced from the oral statements exchanged between the parties (express common intention), or it can arise from the parties' conduct (inferred common intention).

2.2.1.2 Express common intention

A common intention can be established by evidence of express discussions between the parties (however informal) which show that they had an agreement, arrangement, or understanding to share the beneficial ownership of the property.

Talking point

Indeed, Lord Bridge said that the first question to be resolved is whether:

> there has at any time prior to the acquisition [of the property], or exceptionally at some later date, been any agreement, arrangement or understanding reached between [the parties] that the property is to be shared beneficially. The finding of an agreement or arrangement to share in this sense can only, I think, be based on evidence of express discussions between the partners, however imperfectly remembered and however imprecise their terms may have been.[117]

The emphasis on express discussions between the parties means that:

> the tenderest exchanges of a common law courtship may assume unforeseen significance many years later when they are brought under equity's microscope and subjected to an analysis under which many thousands of pounds of value may be liable to turn on fine questions as to whether the relevant words were spoken in earnest or in dalliance and with or without representational intent.[118]

Case law shows that the common intention which is evidenced by the parties' express discussions can be purely 'notional'.[119] There may be circumstances where one party held no intention to share the ownership of the property with their partner, but through their words and conduct (in particular, excuses made for not putting the property into joint names) led the other to believe that such an intention was held. Two cases where the court found evidence of an express common intention demonstrate this. In *Eves v Eves*[120] an unmarried couple, who had a child, decided to buy a house. The man provided the deposit and paid the mortgage. At the time of the purchase the man told the woman that 'it was to be their house and a home for themselves and their children'. He said that as she was under 21 years of age, the property could not be put into their joint names but had to be in his name alone. He told her that, but for her age, it would have been purchased in joint names. In fact, he was being dishonest and all along he intended that the property should be his alone. However, the woman accepted his explanation. The house itself was in a very dilapidated condition and the woman carried out a great deal of work in the

---

[117] Ibid, 132. The agreement does not have to define the extent or size of each party's share (see *Oxley v Hiscock* [2004] EWCA Civ 546 at [37] and [40]). Quantification is an issue that only follows if a common intention to share is found between the parties.

[118] *Hammond v Mitchell* [1992] 2 All ER 109 at 121 *per* Waite J.

[119] G. Douglas, J. Pearce, and H. Woodward, Cardiff Law School Research Paper No 1, 'A Failure of Trust: Resolving Property Disputes on Cohabitation Breakdown' (2007), para 3.13. See also N. Glover and P. Todd, 'The Myth of Common Intention' (1996) Legal Studies 325.

[120] [1975] 3 All ER 768.

house and garden to make it habitable.[121] Subsequently the man left her and married someone else.[122] The Court of Appeal held that the man clearly led the woman to believe that she would have some undefined interest in the property. This allowed the court to find that there was an express common intention to share the ownership of the property. The woman's performance of manual labour in reliance upon this common intention was sufficient to constitute detrimental reliance, and the court imposed a constructive trust in her favour. She was awarded one-quarter of the equity of the property.

Similarly, in *Grant v Edwards*[123] the house was conveyed into the sole name of the man because the woman was already married to someone else. Here, too, the man falsely led the woman to believe that her name was being excluded from the title deeds for good reason; he told her that if she were to be named as joint legal owner this might prejudice her position in the matrimonial proceedings between her and her husband. Subsequently the women made substantial indirect contributions towards the mortgage by applying her earnings towards the joint household expenses, without which the mortgage instalments could not have been paid by the man. The Court of Appeal held that the man's statement that the woman's name would be on the title deeds but for the matrimonial proceedings was sufficient to show the necessary common intention that the ownership should be shared.[124]

These cases, described by Lord Bridge in *Lloyds Bank v Rosset* as 'outstanding examples' of express common intention,[125] show that such an intention can be found even if one party did not actually hold the intention professed but led the other to believe that he or she did so. However, the Court of Appeal took a tougher line in *James v Thomas*[126] refusing to find that the assurances made by the legal owner to the claimant established a common intention between them. In this case Miss James moved into a property which was registered in the sole name of her partner, Mr Thomas. Both parties carried out work on the property and whenever the parties discussed these improvements, Mr Thomas told her that they would 'benefit us both'. The court rejected the argument that this evidenced a common intention to share the beneficial ownership of the property, holding instead that this was simply intended to mean that the improvements would make their home more comfortable and would improve the quality of their life together. It was neither intended nor understood to be a promise of some proprietary interest either at the time the statement was made or in the future.[127] This was reinforced by Mr Thomas's unwillingness to put the property into joint names when asked to do so by Miss James. He also told her that she would be 'well provided for' in the event of his death. The court said that this was not a representation that she was to have a proprietary interest in the property during his lifetime. It was a representation of what would happen on his death based on the assumption that they would still be living together when that eventuality occurred.[128] This decision has been criticised as inconsistent with earlier case law.[129] Greer says:

---

[121] This included painting and decorating, breaking up concrete in the garden, demolishing and rebuilding a shed, and preparing the garden for turfing.

[122] The women by then had given birth to their second child.   [123] [1986] 2 All ER 426.

[124] At one stage the man paid insurance moneys relating to the house into a savings account in the parties' joint names, which reinforced the evidence of how the parties intended the property to be shared, namely that each should be entitled to a half share. See also *Hammond v Mitchell* [1992] 2 All ER 109 where an express agreement between an unmarried couple was found after the man said to the woman, 'Don't worry about the future because when we are married [the house] will be half yours anyway and I'll always look after you and [our child].'   [125] [1991] 1 AC 107 at 133.

[126] [2007] EWCA Civ 1212.   [127] Ibid, [33].   [128] Ibid, [35].

[129] See eg *Hammond v Mitchell* [1992] 2 All ER 109.

Ms James would have been more successful if Mr Thomas had simply lied to avoid putting the property into joint names, rather than evaded the issue, which seems to make a nonsense of the law.[130]

It seems, then, that if the legal owner makes an excuse for not putting the property into joint names this may be sufficient to allow the court to find an express common intention on the basis that the non-owner reasonably believed that such an intention existed. However, more general references to the couple's mutual well-being and quality of life will not, without more, evidence an express common intention regarding ownership of the property.

In the absence of a representation from one party to the other as in *Eves v Eves*, or a mutually held intention evidenced by express discussions between the parties, no express common intention will be found to exist. More often than not, this will be the case.

Talking point

While it would, of course, be sensible for cohabitants to discuss important financial and property-related matters either at the beginning, or during, their relationship, it is unsurprising that this tends not to happen.[131] Instead, couples will usually deal with each other on the basis of mutual trust and in the expectation that their 'relationship will endure'.[132] As has been pointed out:

> for a couple embarking on a serious relationship, discussion of the terms to apply at parting is almost a contradiction of the shared hopes that have brought them together.[133]

A related problem with finding an express common intention is that when a relationship breaks down, particularly when this is accompanied by feelings of hostility, the parties' respective memories about past discussions regarding the family home are likely to become selective and self-serving.[134] So, in many cases, there will be no clear and reliable evidence of an express agreement or understanding between the parties about how the property was to be shared between them.

2.2.1.3 Inferred common intention

Failure to establish an express agreement or arrangement between the parties regarding ownership of the property is not necessarily fatal to the non-legal owner's claim to a beneficial interest in it. Evidence relating to the parties' conduct may be sufficient to establish a constructive trust where the conduct is such that the court can infer that the parties both intended that the beneficial ownership of the property should be shared.[135] However, from what conduct will the court infer such a common intention? This remains one of the most controversial questions in family law.

---

[130] S. Greer, 'Back to the Bad Old Days?' (2008) 158 New Law Journal 174.

[131] See A. Barlow, C. Burgoyne, and J. Smithson, *The Living Together Campaign—An Investigation of its Impact on Legally Aware Cohabitants* (London: Ministry of Justice, 2007).

[132] *Midland Bank plc v Cooke* [1995] 2 FLR 915 at 927 *per* Waite LJ.

[133] Ibid.

[134] See the observations of Baroness Hale in *Stack v Dowden* [2007] UKHL 17 at [68].

[135] Even if it is clear that the parties neither discussed nor intended any agreement as to how the beneficial interest was to be shared, this does not prevent the court from inferring, on general equitable principles, that such an agreement existed, see *Midland Bank plc v Cooke* [1995] 4 All ER 562 at 574–575; and *Stack v Dowden* [2007] UKHL 17 at [25] where Lord Walker said that the House of Lords in *Lloyds Bank v Rosset* agreed that a '"common intention" trust could be inferred even when there was no evidence of an actual agreement'. See *Abbott v Abbott* [2007] UKPC 53 at [5].

Key case

In *Lloyds Bank v Rosset*,[136] Lord Bridge, speaking *obiter*, gave a very restrictive answer. He said that direct contributions to the purchase price were the *only* conduct from which such a common intention could be inferred:

> direct contributions to the purchase price by the partner who is not the legal owner, whether initially or by payment of mortgage instalments, will readily justify the inference necessary for the creation of a constructive trust. But … it is at least extremely doubtful whether anything less will do.[137]

In *Lloyds Bank v Rosset* the issue to be resolved was whether Mrs Rosset had acquired a beneficial interest in the matrimonial home, a derelict farmhouse, which had been purchased in her husband's sole name and which she had helped to renovate. Mr Rosset had used the property as security for a bank loan without Mrs Rosset's knowledge and when he was unable to repay the loan the bank started proceedings for possession and sale of the property. Mrs Rosset resisted the bank's claim. She alleged that she had made a significant contribution to the acquisition of the property by the work she had personally undertaken in the course of its renovation. This included doing some painting and decorating, designing two rooms, coordinating work with the builders, and engaging in various other tasks connected with the house. She claimed that the parties had a common intention that she should share in the ownership of the property and that therefore she had a beneficial interest under a constructive trust.[138] The trial judge and the Court of Appeal were each satisfied that Mr and Mrs Rosset held the necessary common intention that she should have an interest in the property, that she had acted on the basis of that common intention to her detriment, and that therefore she had acquired a beneficial interest under a constructive trust. However, Lord Bridge, stating the unanimous opinion of the Law Lords, ruled that the two inferior courts had been wrong.

The House of Lords rejected Mrs Rosset's claim of a beneficial interest, holding that she could not establish the requisite common intention that ownership of the property be shared either by proving that the parties had informally agreed to this or by establishing conduct on her own part such that the court should infer an agreement. Lord Bridge emphasised that there must be a common intention to share *ownership* of the property, saying that:

> neither a common intention by spouses that a house is to be renovated as a 'joint venture' nor a common intention that the house is to be shared by the parents and children as the family home throws any light on their intentions with respect to the beneficial ownership of the property.[139]

In relation to Mrs Rosset's efforts in respect of the renovation of the property, from which the trial judge had drawn the inference of a common intention that she should have a beneficial interest, Lord Bridge said:

> By itself this activity, it seems to me, could not possibly justify any such inference. It was common ground that Mrs. Rosset was extremely anxious that the new matrimonial home should be ready for occupation before Christmas if possible. In these

---

[136] [1991] 1 AC 107.   [137] Ibid, 133 *per* Lord Bridge.

[138] She therefore claimed that she had an overriding interest under the Land Registration Act 1925, s 70(1)(g), which would prevail against the bank because she had been in actual occupation of the land on the date when the bank's charge was created. The 1925 Act has been repealed and replaced by the Land Registration Act 2002. The third party aspects of this and other cases are beyond the scope of this book.

[139] [1991] 1 AC 107 at 130.

circumstances it would seem the most natural thing in the world for any wife, in the
absence of her husband abroad, to spend all the time she could spare and to employ
any skills she might have, such as the ability to decorate a room, in doing all she could
to accelerate progress of the work quite irrespective of any expectation she might have
of enjoying a beneficial interest in the property ... On any view the monetary value of
Mrs. Rosset's work expressed as a contribution to a property acquired at a cost exceeding £70,000 must have been so trifling as to be almost de minimis.[140]

Thus Lord Bridge not only took the view that this conduct could not justify the inference that
there had been a common intention that Mrs Rosset should have a beneficial interest in the
matrimonial home, he also characterised her contribution as so trifling that it was doubtful
whether it amounted to sufficient detriment.

This restrictive view means that someone who makes no direct financial contribution
towards the acquisition of the property, nor pays off any part of the mortgage instalments,
but who makes other important financial and non-financial contributions (such as contributing towards the household bills, looking after the house, and taking care of the children)
may not be able to establish a beneficial interest in the family home should the relationship
break down.[141]

The clearest example of courts giving no monetary value to domestic labour is *Burns
v Burns*.[142] In this case a woman lived with her male partner for 19 years in a property
which was conveyed into the man's sole name. They were known as Mr and Mrs Burns
and had two children. There was no express declaration that Mrs Burns should have
a share in the beneficial ownership of the family home, nor had she made any direct
financial contribution to its acquisition. She gave up her job to have the children and
when she returned to work she used her income to contribute to the household expenses
and to purchase clothes for the family. At no time did Mr Burns ask her to contribute
to the household expenses in order to relieve the financial burden on him, and her
purchases did not release his earnings to enable him to pay the mortgage. When the
relationship broke down Mrs Burns sought to establish a common intention that she
should have a beneficial interest in the property on the grounds that she had brought
up the children, carried out domestic tasks, redecorated the interior of the house, used
her earnings to contribute towards the housekeeping expenses, and had bought fix-
tures and fittings and various consumer durables. Her claim was rejected by the Court
of Appeal. There was no evidence of any express common intention that she was to
have a share in the home. Further, as she had made no direct financial contribution to
its acquisition, there was no conduct from which such a common intention could be
inferred. The Court of Appeal held that none of her expenditure was referable to the
acquisition of the property. It held that paying for chattels and decorating the property
did not amount to evidence of a common intention that she should have an interest in
the house.[143] Fox LJ said:

---

[140] Ibid, 131.

[141] Unless, of course, there is evidence of an express common intention to share ownership of the
property.   [142] [1984] Ch 317.

[143] See too *Pettitt v Pettitt* [1969] 2 All ER 385 at 416 where Lord Diplock was dismissive of the notion
that handiwork around the house by a husband should give rise to him acquiring a beneficial interest in the
property owned by the wife.

the mere fact that the parties live together and do the ordinary domestic tasks is, in my view, no indication at all that they thereby intended to alter the existing property rights of either of them.[144]

Thus Mrs Burns was denied any share in the property which had been the family home for 19 years. Mr Burns, on the other hand, was entitled to retain the entire beneficial interest in the property which Mrs Burns had cleaned, decorated, and otherwise looked after and in which she had laboured for his benefit as well as for the benefit of herself and the children. It has been observed that:

> the continuing criticism of this case lies in the failure of the law to call her partner to account for the benefits he had enjoyed during their relationship, simply because these were not valued in financial terms.[145]

While the Court of Appeal felt some sympathy for Mrs Burns' position, it held that it was not for the courts to attempt to remedy any inequity; this was a matter for Parliament. Unfortunately, there has been no such statutory reform and it has been left to the courts to continue to apply these principles to domestic cases. This restrictive approach has been heavily criticised as being too dependent on financial contributions which works against a partner (usually the woman) who has made indirect financial contributions to the general household expenses, or has made wholly domestic contributions through looking after the home and raising children.

2.2.1.4 Are there signs of a more flexible jurisprudence?

The strict requirements laid down by Lord Bridge in *Rosset* certainly make it very difficult to establish a beneficial interest. Unfortunately, there is no evidence that the courts may be persuaded to take a more flexible approach to purely domestic labour. Thus, it remains the case that the economic sacrifices involved with carrying out purely domestic work and other non-financial contributions which benefit the family will not, by themselves, give rise to an interest in the home. For Mrs Burns this meant that she 'had no financial remedy for the loss she sustained as a result of the time and efforts she had devoted to the family'.[146] However, there is some evidence of a more flexible approach being taken by some judges in relation to *indirect financial contributions*. That is, where one person contributes towards the general household expenses which enables their partner to pay the mortgage instalments. There is a very strong argument that such indirect contributions should give rise to a constructive trust. As the Law Commission has pointed out:

> In many cases, a couple will not engage in discussion, but agree to an ordering of the household finances such that one pays off the mortgage while the other pays the household bills.[147]

The Law Commission concluded that the payer of the bills should be given credit for their contribution and therefore such an indirect contribution to the mortgage should give rise to the common intention that the beneficial entitlement to the home be shared.[148] Indeed, others have pointed out that, under trust principles, there is

---

[144] [1984] Ch 317 at 331.
[145] G. Douglas, J. Pearce, and H. Woodward, 'Cohabitants, Property and the Law: A Study of Injustice' (2009) 72(1) Modern Law Review 24 at 31.
[146] Law Commission, *Sharing Homes: A Discussion Paper* (Law Com No 278, 2002), para 5.17.
[147] Ibid, para 4.26.   [148] Ibid, para 4.27.

no reason why indirect financial contributions should not give rise to a constructive trust:

> So long as the claimant has made an indirect contribution that is referable to the acquisition of the house, the requisite inference of an intention to share the property should apply, given that the contribution to joint household expenses has enabled the legal owner more easily to pay the mortgage instalments out of his (or her) own money.[149]

However, in *Rosset*, Lord Bridge appeared to rule out the possibility of a common intention being inferred from such *indirect* financial contributions when he said that 'it is at least extremely doubtful that anything less' than direct financial contributions would suffice. However, Nicholas Mostyn QC, sitting as deputy High Court judge in the first instance decision of *Le Foe v Le Foe*[150] thought otherwise. In this case Mrs Le Foe had not made any direct contributions to the purchase of the family home, although she made substantial financial contributions to the family's day-to-day expenditure. Mostyn QC interpreted the speech of Lord Bridge in *Rosset* in a flexible manner. He suggested that Lord Bridge did not state the proposition that, in the absence of an agreement, *only* direct financial contributions would give rise to a constructive trust, in absolute terms. Rather, in his view, Lord Bridge was simply saying that it is only in exceptional cases that conduct other than direct contributions to the purchase price would give rise to a common intention to share the equity.[151] As a result, Mostyn QC inferred from the wife's indirect contributions to the mortgage, a common intention between the parties to share the property beneficially. In support of this view, he cited dicta from May LJ in *Burns v Burns*[152] and Lord Diplock in *Gissing v Gissing*[153] who said:

> It may be no more than a matter of convenience which spouse pays particular household accounts, particularly when both are earning, and if the wife goes out to work and devotes part of her earnings or uses her private income to meet joint expenses of the household which would otherwise be met by the husband, so as to enable him to pay the mortgage instalments out of his moneys which would be consistent with and might be corroborative of an original common intention that she should share in the beneficial interest in the matrimonial home and that her payments of other household expenses were intended by both spouses to be treated as including a contribution by the wife to the purchase price of the matrimonial home.

The majority of the House of Lords in *Stack v Dowden*[154] also appeared to support a more flexible interpretation of Lord Bridge's *obiter* comments in *Lloyds Bank v Rosset*, although unfortunately no reference was made to *Le Foe v Le Foe*. Lord Walker questioned whether Lord Bridge's narrow view of the contributions which give rise to a constructive trust was in line with earlier authorities, and he noted that this restrictive approach had attracted considerable academic criticism for producing injustice. He continued that 'the law has moved on, and your Lordships should move it a little more in the same direction'.[155] Unfortunately, as *Stack v Dowden* was a joint names case, these comments were merely *obiter*. Indeed, Baroness Hale noted that the question of what is required to *establish* a common intention 'does not concern us now', but she nonetheless accepted the view of the Law Commission that Lord Bridge had 'set the hurdle rather too high' in holding that only direct financial contributions will suffice as conduct from which to infer common intention.[156]

---

[149] M. Pawlowski, 'Beneficial Entitlement—No Longer Doing Justice' (2007) Conveyancer and Property Lawyer 354 at 361.   [150] [2001] 2 FLR 970.
[151] Ibid, [43].   [152] [1984] Ch 317.   [153] [1971 AC 886 at 907–908.   [154] [2007] UKHL 17.
[155] Ibid, [26].   [156] Ibid, [63].

This view was reiterated by Baroness Hale in *Abbott v Abbott*.[157] Following the sentiments of her *obiter* comments in *Stack*, Baroness Hale said that in relation to the view of Lord Bridge that nothing less than direct contributions to the purchase price would give rise to the inference to share the beneficial interest, the 'law has undoubtedly moved on'.[158] However, her Ladyship did not specify in exactly what way and, once again, no reference was made to the decision of Mostyn J in *Le Foe*. Her Ladyship continued by citing from her speech in *Stack* where she said that:

> the law has indeed moved on in response to changing social and economic conditions. The search is to ascertain the parties' shared intentions, actual, inferred or imputed, with respect to the property in light of their whole course of conduct in relation to it.[159]

However, the exact implications of this observation for how 'the law has moved on' in relation to the conduct from which a common intention to share the beneficial interest can be inferred in sole name cases are very unclear. Was Baroness Hale suggesting that where there is no express agreement evidencing the parties' intention, the court will undertake a survey of the whole course of dealing between the parties in relation to the property, taking account of all conduct which throws light on the question of what shares were intended? Is this broad-brush approach, which up to now has only been applied when quantifying an already established beneficial interest, to be taken when ascertaining whether the parties intended to share the beneficial interest in a property that was conveyed into the name of one party only? Does this mean that, in line with *Le Foe v Le Foe*, a common intention to share ownership of the home can be inferred from indirect contributions to the general household expenses?

While comments in both *Stack* and *Abbott* suggest that this is the direction in which the law is moving, it would be premature to say that this is where it has now reached. It should be remembered that comments about the 'law moving on' in relation to *establishing* a beneficial interest were strictly *obiter* in both *Stack* and *Abbott*. *Stack* was a joint names case and in *Abbott* the wife already had a beneficial interest and so the issue for the court was in quantifying the size of her interest. One source of confusion is that there are two separate questions in these cases, and it is unclear to what extent the test for one applies to the other. The first question in sole name cases is whether there is a common intention to share the beneficial interest. The second question, which arises in both sole name and joint names cases, concerns the search for the parties' common intention regarding the quantification of an already established beneficial interest. The 'whole course of conduct test' which Baroness Hale approved in *Stack* was adopted in relation to the second question on quantification. The issue is, to what extent does this test apply to the first question of *establishing* a beneficial interest in sole name cases? Despite the articulation of general sentiments about the law moving on, the speeches of the Lords in *Stack* and *Abbot* do not provide any guidance on how such a test would apply to this first question in sole name cases: that is, how a common intention to share could be inferred from the parties' whole course of conduct.[160] The matter is further complicated when one considers that Baroness Hale also said in *Abbott* that the law has moved on in relation

---

[157] [2007] UKPC 53 at [3]. It was accepted that the claimant had a beneficial interest in the property and so the issue for the Privy Council was the size of each parties' share. For a discussion of the case see Section 2.3.   [158] Ibid, [3] *per* Baroness Hale.

[159] Ibid, [6] citing *Stack v Dowden* [2007] UKHL 17 at [60] *per* Baroness Hale.

[160] The Supreme Court did not offer any further clarification in *Jones v Kernott* [2011] UKSC 53 on the type of conduct from which the court can infer the parties' common intention to share beneficial ownership of the property in sole name cases.

to the question of 'quantifying an acknowledged beneficial interest'.[161] But what of the case where there is no acknowledged beneficial interest and the court is trying to ascertain whether the non-legal owner has *established* a beneficial interest from the parties' conduct? Despite the clear sentiments in both *Stack* and *Abbott* that the speech of Lord Bridge was too restrictive, there remains a considerable amount of uncertainty regarding whether and how the law has moved on in sole name cases when, in the absence of an express agreement between the parties, the court has to look at their conduct from which to infer a common intention to share the property beneficially.

2.2.1.5 An opportunity missed?

Two Court of Appeal cases have now addressed the implications of *Stack* for sole name cases. Unfortunately, in both a very restrictive view has been taken of the type of conduct from which a common intention can be inferred, thus failing to capitalise on the *obiter* remarks made in *Stack* and *Abbot* which suggested that Lord Bridge had set the bar too high.[162] In *James v Thomas*[163] an unmarried couple lived together for almost 15 years in a property which was in the man's sole name. Mr Thomas purchased the property a number of years before the parties had even met. Shortly afterwards, he and Miss James formed a relationship and she moved in with him but she did not financially contribute to the acquisition of the property. She did, however, work with Mr Thomas in his business as a building and drainage contractor without payment. She initially carried out manual labour but, after a number of years, focused on the bookkeeping and paperwork associated with the business on a part-time basis. Their household, living, and personal expenses were paid out of a bank account which was in the sole name of Mr Thomas, and this account also operated as a business account. After some time, the business was carried on as a partnership between the parties and the bank account was put into their joint names. They both carried out extensive renovations to the property which were funded by the income generated by the business. When the relationship broke down, Miss James claimed that she had a beneficial interest in the property by way of a constructive trust or proprietary estoppel. The Court of Appeal rejected her claim.

It is significant that Mr Thomas had purchased the property before the parties met because the main issue was whether a common intention to share it could be formed *after* the property had been acquired. The court confirmed that, in principle, it could. The common intention necessary to give rise to a constructive trust may be formed at any time before, during, or after the acquisition of the property.[164] The court also confirmed that the common intention regarding the beneficial interests in the property may be inferred from evidence of the parties' conduct during the whole course of their dealings in relation to the property.[165] While this seems promising, a sting in the tail was to follow. The Court of Appeal said that:

> in the absence of an express post-acquisition agreement, a court will be slow to infer from conduct alone that parties intended to vary existing beneficial interests at the time of acquisition.[166]

This unfortunately means that it will be very hard for a claimant to establish a common intention to share the beneficial interest from conduct which takes place *after* the property has been acquired. On the facts of the case, there was no express agreement between the parties and so the question was whether a common intention could be inferred from

---

[161] *Abbott v Abbott* [2007] UKPC 53 at [19].
[162] See also *Frost v Clarke* [2008] EWHC 742 (Ch) and *Mirza v Mirza* [2009] EWHC 3 (Ch).
[163] [2007] EWCA Civ 1212.   [164] Ibid, [19].   [165] Ibid.   [166] Ibid, [24] *per* Chadwick LJ.

the parties' whole course of dealings in relation to the property. The real question was whether her contributions to the business, which helped to generate the income to pay off the mortgage, gave rise to the inference of a common intention to share the property. The court said it did not. Given that the couple's only source of income came from the business, the court thought that it was unsurprising that Miss James did all she could to ensure its success. Thus her contributions were 'wholly explicable on other grounds' and did not give rise to the inference that the parties had agreed, or reached a common understanding, that she was to have a share in the property.[167] As such, the Court of Appeal held that Miss James was not entitled to a beneficial interest.

In light of her contributions to the business, and the fact that it was the money generated by the business which paid off the mortgage as well as other household and personal expenses, this seems to be a very unfair outcome. Indeed, it is particularly harsh when one considers that, in his evidence, Mr Thomas conceded that in fairness Miss James was entitled to some interest in the property.[168] However, Chadwick LJ emphasised that this assessment is not about what was fair.[169] He said:

> Her interest in the property (if any) must be determined by applying principles of law and equity which (however inadequate to meet the circumstances in which parties live together in the twenty-first century) must now be taken as well-established. Unless she can bring herself within those principles, her claim … must fail.[170]

Unfortunately the court took a very restrictive view of the post-acquisition conduct from which a common intention could be inferred, flying in the face of the *obiter* views expressed in *Stack* and *Abbott* that the law had moved on. Looking at the reasoning of the court, it is very hard to see how the law has moved on at all. On the type of conduct which would suffice to establish a common intention, Chadwick LJ said:

> although it is possible to envisage circumstances in which the fact that one party began to make contributions to capital repayments due under a mortgage might evidence an agreement that that party was to have a share in the property, the circumstances of this case are not of that nature.[171]

Thus, according to Chadwick LJ, capital repayments to the mortgage may evidence an agreement to share the property. This bears a striking resemblance to the suggestion of Lord Bridge in *Rosset* that direct contributions to the purchase price were required. While Chadwick LJ did not expressly say that nothing else would suffice, the restrictive nature of the language he used (it is *possible* that such contributions *might* evidence an agreement) does not augur well for the argument that more indirect contributions (such as paying household bills) would be enough. The substantial contributions Miss James made to the business were not enough because they were explicable on other grounds. However, it is arguable that this was a strong case from which to infer from Miss James's substantial, unpaid, contributions to the business, a common intention to share the property:

> this was not a case where a live-in-lover claims a share on the ground of paying for a new shag-pile rug, plasma television and a share of the gas, Sky Plus and other essential outgoings … This was a case where all apparent wealth … was the result of joint effort.[172]

[167] Ibid, [27] *per* Chadwick LJ.   [168] Ibid, [37].   [169] Ibid, [38].
[170] Ibid, *per* Chadwick LJ.   [171] Ibid, [27].
[172] A. Ralton, 'Establishing a Beneficial Share: *Rosset* Revisited' [2008] Family Law 424 at 426.

This decision was relied upon in a subsequent Court of Appeal case. In *Morris v Morris*[173] the claimant who was married to Mr Morris, claimed a beneficial interest in the assets of a farming partnership, including the farm, which Mr Morris ran with his mother (who was now deceased). The mother had been the sole legal owner of the farm, and she granted a tenancy of the land year-on-year to the farming partnership. In the early years of the relationship, the claimant provided substantial assistance to the farming business without remuneration. She paid towards the construction of a riding school on the farm which she then ran herself. The riding school became very successful and she eventually incorporated a company and transferred the riding school business to it. When her relationship with Mr Morris broke down, the claimant moved out of the farmhouse and sought a beneficial interest in the farm premises. The trial judge awarded her a 25 per cent share on the basis that her contributions to the farming business and the riding school gave rise to a common intention between the parties (the claimant, her husband, and his mother) that she was to have a beneficial interest in the farm. The claimant had relied upon this to her detriment and thus a constructive trust was established in her favour. The Court of Appeal disagreed and drew a distinction between claiming a share in the business of the farming partnership and claiming a proprietary share in the farm itself. Sir Peter Gibson said:

> It is one thing to say that the claimant believed herself to be an integral part of a business conducted on particular land. It is another to find that the claimant has established an interest in the land itself.[174]

There was no express agreement or discussion between the parties, and neither Mr Morris nor his mother led the claimant to believe that she was to get an interest. The only hope the claimant had of establishing a constructive trust was for the court to infer a common intention from the parties' conduct.

In terms of the correct approach to be taken in these cases, Sir Peter Gibson recited the test from *Stack* that the task of the court is to ascertain the parties' shared intentions in relation to the property in light of their whole course of conduct. However, he then undermined the use of this test when the non-owner is trying to *establish* a beneficial interest in sole name cases. He pointed out that the 'whole course of conduct test' in *Stack* was directed at the second question relating to quantification after a common intention to share had already been established. In terms of the first question he said that:

> the authorities make clear that a common intention constructive trust based only on conduct will only be found in exceptional circumstances.[175]

He confirmed the view of Chadwick LJ in *James v Thomas*[176] that in the absence of an express post-acquisition agreement, a court will be slow to infer from conduct alone that parties intended to vary existing beneficial interests established at the time of acquisition.[177] In terms of the present case, the Court of Appeal concluded that the evidence was 'wholly inadequate' to establish a common intention. The claimant's work on the farm was not of such an exceptional nature as to lead to any inference that she must have acted in the belief that she was acquiring an interest. In addition, the development of the riding school, even though it did add to the capital value of the farm, was for her own financial benefit.[178]

Despite the *obiter* remarks in *Stack* about the law moving on, it remains the case that in the absence of an express agreement or direct financial contributions to the acquisition of

[173] [2008] EWCA Civ 257.   [174] Ibid, [16]. See also [49] *per* Pill LJ.   [175] Ibid, [23].

[176] [2007] EWCA Civ 1212.   [177] [2008] EWCA Civ 257 at [19].   [178] Ibid, [26].

the property, it remains very difficult for a non-legal owner to establish a beneficial interest. In light of the recent decisions of the Court of Appeal, it seems that it is premature to speak of the 'demise of the direct contributions rule' for inferring a common intention to share the property.[179] Of course, it must be pointed out that in both *James v Thomas* and *Morris v Morris*, the property was acquired *before* the parties had even met. Not only did the claimants have to rely on post-acquisition conduct from which to infer a common intention, but they were relying on this conduct to establish a beneficial interest in a property which was not even acquired as the family home. What of a case where the parties are in a relationship and property is acquired in the sole name of one, but it was to be the family home for both of them? Would these circumstances persuade the court to take a more generous view of the conduct of the non-legal owner which would justify the inference of a common intention to share? Would indirect financial contributions be enough then? Some think they might,[180] but dicta from the cases discussed suggest otherwise. The Court of Appeal has made it very clear that courts will be slow to infer from post-acquisition conduct that the parties intended to vary the beneficial interests that existed at the time of acquisition (in our example, in the sole name of one party). Ongoing domestic labour associated with running a household, and indirect financial contributions (such as paying bills), by their very nature, fall into the category of post-acquisition conduct. Given the reluctance to infer from such conduct alone that the parties intended to share the beneficial interest, there is nothing to suggest that the purpose for which the property was acquired would have a significant impact on this reasoning.

Indeed, the reasoning of the Court of Appeal may actually make it more difficult for a common intention to be inferred from indirect financial contributions. Let us recall that in *James v Thomas* the court rejected the claimant's argument that her indirect contributions evidenced an intention to share the property because her conduct was explicable on other grounds. However, this aspect of the court's reasoning is particularly worrying because it appears to set a very high threshold in relation to conduct from which an intention can be inferred. It suggests that one of the questions to be asked in relation to a person's indirect contributions (such as labour in a business without remuneration; paying bills or contributing to the general household expenditure) is whether the contributions can be explained on another basis.[181] This does not bode well for the argument that such contributions give rise to an inference that the parties had agreed or reached a common understanding that the contributor was to receive a share of the property. Instead, it could readily be argued that these contributions were made for the general welfare of the family and to ensure the smooth running of the household and not out of any pecuniary self-interest.[182] The domestic context in which this issue arises works against one who makes indirect contributions because in the cut and thrust of day-to-day family living it will generally be possible to find another reason why such contributions were made.

In this respect, a conundrum may be emerging. The majority in *Stack* thought that property law principles should apply in a slightly different (and more flexible) way when

---

[179] Gardner speculates that, in light of *Stack v Dowden* and *Abbott v Abbott*, this rule (which suggests that common intention can only be inferred from direct contributions to the purchase price) may no longer exist, S. Gardner, 'Family Property Today' (2008) Law Quarterly Review 422 at 424 and 433.

[180] N. Piska, 'A Common Intention or a Rare Bird? Proprietary Interests, Personal Claims and Services Rendered by Lovers Post-Acquisition: *James v Thomas*; *Morris v Morris*' [2009] Child and Family Law Quarterly 104.

[181] That is, there was another reason for the contributor to make these contributions outside an agreement or common understanding between the parties that the contributor was to receive a share of the property.

[182] *James v Thomas* [2007] EWCA Civ 1212 at [36].

dealing with the family home.[183] In particular, the resulting trust no longer operates as a legal presumption because to restrict the size of a party's share in the beneficial interest to an amount proportionate to their direct financial contributions would ignore their whole course of conduct and overall contributions.[184] However, in another way, the domestic context may make some of the evidential hurdles harder to overcome. In particular, after *James v Thomas* it seems that to give rise to the inference of a common intention, the court must be persuaded that the conduct in question was performed by the claimant in the belief that she was getting an interest in the property.[185] If the conduct can be explained on other grounds, this may negate the finding of a common intention. However, in the domestic context, it may be relatively easy for a non-legal owner's contributions to be explained on the ground that her actions were for the benefit of the family rather than a pecuniary interest on her part to acquire a beneficial interest in the property.

2.2.1.6 Improvements to the property

Another type of indirect financial contribution to the property is where one party carries out substantial work on the property which adds value to it.

Key legislation

Under section 37 of the Matrimonial Proceedings and Property Act 1970, if a spouse, civil part-ner, or engaged person makes a substantial contribution in money or money's worth to the improvement of property in which their spouse, civil partner, or fiancé(e) has an interest, the contributions of the former will generate an interest in the property in their favour.

This is subject to any agreement which the parties may reach themselves. This provision does not apply to unmarried cohabitants. However, the majority in *Stack* suggested that improvements, such as manual labour, which add significant value to the property will generate an interest under a constructive trust. Lord Walker pointed out that as most homes are now bought with mortgage finance, 'buying a house does very often continue, in a real sense, throughout the period of its ownership'.[186] He opined that the law should recognise this by taking a wide view of what counts towards a contribution to the acquisi-tion of the property. While he was sceptical about the value of alleged improvements that are really insignificant, there was support for the argument that improvements which added significant value to the property should be taken into account to create an interest in the property.[187]

2.2.1.7 Detrimental reliance

Establishing that there was a common intention (either express or implied) between the parties to share the ownership of the house will not, by itself, create a constructive trust. On top of this the party claiming a beneficial interest must demonstrate that they signifi-cantly altered their position or acted to their detriment on the basis of the common inten-tion. Direct contributions to the purchase price or mortgage instalments will constitute

---

[183] *Stack v Dowden* [2007] UKHL 17 at [3], [14], [33], [42], [56], [60].

[184] Ibid, [31], [33], [60].

[185] This built on the reasoning of *Stack* where the court said that the conduct from which a common intention can be inferred must be conduct relating to the property.

[186] [2007] UKHL 17 at [34].

[187] Ibid, [12] *per* Lord Hope; [36] *per* Lord Walker, and [70] *per* Baroness Hale.

detrimental reliance. This means that if the claimant makes a direct contribution to the purchase price of the property, these contributions will have a dual function. They will give rise to the requisite common intention and will also act as detriment to establish the constructive trust in the claimant's favour.

In the case of express common intention, however, it is unclear exactly what type of contributions will constitute detrimental reliance, and the extent to which there has to be a link between the common intention and the conduct relied upon as a detriment. It seems that what is required is conduct upon which the claimant 'could not reasonably have been expected to embark *unless* she was to have an interest in the house'.[188] In other words, if someone carries out activities which would have ordinarily been expected of them regardless of whether they were to obtain an interest in the house, then this may not be regarded as detrimental reliance. However, if someone's conduct goes beyond that which was expected of them, then a court is more likely to conclude that this constitutes detrimental reliance. For example, in *Eves v Eves*, the woman's manual labour on the property which included breaking up the concrete in the front garden and carrying the pieces to a skip and helping to demolish a shed and construct a new one, was detrimental reliance because the court inferred that she would not have carried out such work if she was not to have an interest in the property. In the words of Brightman J:

> I find it difficult to suppose that she would have been wielding the 14 lb. sledge hammer, breaking up the large area of concrete, filling the skip and doing the other things which were carried out when they moved in, except in pursuance of some expressed or implied arrangement and on the understanding that she was helping to improve a house in which she was to all practical intents and purposes promised that she had an interest.[189]

The court said that this work was 'much more than many wives would do' and had no difficulty in holding that this constituted detrimental reliance. However, it is by no means certain that a court will regard a person's 'ordinary' domestic labour (such as looking after the home, raising children, even paying household bills) as detrimental reliance and may instead view it as work which the claimant would have been doing in any event.[190] As the Law Commission observed:

> if the applicant oversteps the boundary of what might be 'expected' of a partner, particularly in light of the applicant's gender, a finding of detrimental reliance is more likely.[191]

In *James v Thomas*, the question of detrimental reliance did not even arise because the claimant failed at the first hurdle of trying to establish a common intention. However, Chadwick LJ suggested that, in any event, she would not have been able to establish that her contributions amounted to detrimental reliance. He said that she had:

> worked in the business, and contributed her labour to the improvements to the property, because she and Mr Thomas were making their life together as man and wife. The [property] was their home: the business was their livelihood. It is a mistake to think that the motives which lead parties in such a relationship to act as they do are necessarily attributable to pecuniary self-interest.[192]

---

[188] *Grant v Edwards* [1986] Ch 638, *per* Nourse LJ (emphasis added).

[189] *Eves v Eves* [1975] 1 WLR 1338 at 1345.

[190] However, in *Grant v Edwards* [1986] Ch 638, Sir Nicolas Browne-Wilkinson V-C (as he then was) took a more liberal approach suggesting that detriment could be interpreted broadly as 'any act done by [the claimant] … to her detriment relating to the joint lives of the parties', at 657.

[191] Law Commission, *Cohabitation: The Financial Consequences of Relationship Breakdown* (Law Com No 307, 2007), para A.37.   [192] [2007] EWCA Civ 1212 at [36].

So the reasoning which may prevent the court from inferring the existence of a common intention where the performance of the conduct can be explained on other grounds, may also prevent the court from finding detrimental reliance.

2.3 QUANTIFICATION OF THE BENEFICIAL INTEREST

Once it is established that the claimant is to have a beneficial interest in the property, the next question is the size (quantum) of their interest. The first matter the court will look at is whether there was an actual agreement between the parties about the size of their respective shares. The Court of Appeal made it clear in *Crossley v Crossley*[193] that:

> where the parties have reached a consensus on the beneficial interests in the property, the court will give effect to it, unless there is very good reason for not doing so, such as subsequent renegotiation.

If there is no evidence of such an express agreement between the parties, the court will have to quantify their respective shares in the property. As confirmed by the House of Lords in *Stack v Dowden*, and the Supreme Court in *Jones v Kernott*,[194] it will do so by surveying the whole course of dealing between the parties taking account of all conduct which throws light on the question what shares were either intended or fair. This is the test to be used in both joint names and sole name cases.[195]

Stack marked a real turning point for joint names cases. Prior to *Stack*, resulting trust principles determined the size of the parties' shares.[196] However, for some time a more flexible approach to quantification had been taken in sole name cases.[197] In *Midland Bank plc v Cooke*[198] the matrimonial home had been conveyed into the sole name of the husband. The purchase price was provided by a mortgage, some of Mr Cooke's personal savings, and a gift from the husband's parents to the couple. As this was a joint gift, Mrs Cooke's share of it amounted to a 6.47 per cent contribution to the purchase price. She had therefore made a direct contribution to the acquisition of the property which established the necessary common intention. The question for the Court of Appeal was whether her share should be limited to the percentage of the purchase price which she contributed directly (ie, 6.47 per cent). The Court of Appeal answered this question with an unequivocal 'no'. Instead, Waite LJ said that where there is no express evidence of the parties' intentions, it is the duty of the judge to undertake a survey of the whole course of dealing between the parties. That scrutiny should relate to matters relevant to the parties' ownership and occupation of the property and their sharing of its burdens and advantages, and should not confine itself to the limited range of acts of direct contribution of the sort that were needed to found a beneficial interest in the first place. Instead, the court should take into consideration all conduct which threw light on what shares were intended. On the facts, although the wife had made no further financial contribution to the acquisition of the property, there was evidence that, in addition to bringing up the parties' three children, she had worked and paid household bills, and had undertaken liability under a

---

[193] [2005] EWCA Civ 1581 at [32] *per* Sir Peter Gibson. See also *Oxley v Hiscock* [2004] EWCA Civ 546 at [69]. [194] [2011] UKSC 53.

[195] *Abbott v Abbott* [2007] UKPC 53; *Holman v Howes* [2007] EWCA Civ 877. The Supreme Court made it clear in *Jones v Kernott* [2011] UKSC 53 that the approach to quantification is the same in sole name and joint names cases, at [52].

[196] See *Walker v Hall* [1984] FLR 126; *Springette v Defoe* [1992] 2 FLR 388; *Huntingford v Hobbs* [1993] 1 FLR 736.

[197] *Oxley v Hiscock* [2004] EWCA Civ 546; *Midland Bank plc v Cooke* [1995] 4 All ER 562; *Drake v Whipp* [1996] 1 FLR 826. [198] [1995] 2 FLR 915.

second charge on the property for the benefit of the husband's business. This led Waite LJ to conclude that:

> One could hardly have a clearer example of a couple who had agreed to share everything equally; the profits of his business while it prospered, and the risks of indebtedness suffered through its failure; the upbringing of their children; the rewards of her own career as a teacher; and most relevantly, a home into which he put his savings and to which she was to give over the years the benefit of the maintenance and improvement contribution.[199]

He added that when in addition the parties had taken on the commitment of marriage, the conclusion was inescapable that their presumed intention was to share the beneficial interest of the property in equal shares.

In *Oxley v Hiscock*,[200] Chadwick LJ attempted to inject even more flexibility into the quantification exercise when he said that the task of the court was to determine what was a *fair outcome* between the parties in light of their whole course of conduct in relation to the property. However, this approach was rejected by the House of Lords in *Stack v Dowden* and Baroness Hale asserted that the correct approach to quantification was a 'holistic' one where the court surveyed the whole course of dealing between the parties, taking account of all conduct which throws light on the question of what shares were intended. While this was expressed in the context of a joint names case, the same applies to sole name cases. This was confirmed by the Privy Council in *Abbott v Abbott*.[201] This case concerned the divorce of a couple in Antigua. However, the law in Antigua and Barbuda does not have a matrimonial finance regime and thus property disputes have to be resolved by applying ordinary property and trust law principles. The wife claimed that she had a beneficial interest in the former matrimonial home which was held in the husband's sole name. The property was built on a plot of land which had been given to the couple by the husband's mother. The construction of the property was financed partly by a mortgage executed by the husband and by funds provided by the husband's mother. The funds were paid into the couple's joint bank account. The wife worked on and off during the marriage and all the couple's income went into their joint bank account from which the mortgage instalments and insurance premiums were paid. The wife also made herself jointly and severally liable for the mortgage. The husband accepted that the wife had a beneficial interest in the home and thus the real question for the court was in quantifying the size of her share.[202] The Court of Appeal held that the wife was only entitled to around an 8 per cent share of the beneficial interest in the home, a percentage which reflected her direct contributions to the mortgage instalments. The wife successfully appealed to the Privy Council where it was held that she was entitled to a half share in the property.

The Privy Council confirmed that the constructive trust is 'the more appropriate tool of analysis in most matrimonial cases'.[203] As such, the resulting trust did not operate as a legal presumption to limit the wife's share to 8 per cent which reflected her direct financial

---

[199] Ibid, 928. The wife's contribution to the 'maintenance and improvement of the property' was through redecoration, alterations, and improvements and repairs carried out with or without the assistance of contractors, whose bills she paid.   [200] [2004] EWCA Civ 546.

[201] [2007] UKPC 53 at [6]. See also *Holman v Howes* [2007] EWCA Civ 877 where the Court of Appeal made it clear that if it is accepted that both parties have a beneficial interest, then the same approach will be taken to quantification and 'there need not necessarily be any difference according to whether the legal estate is in one or two names', at [28]. The Court of Appeal also made it clear that the only conduct that can be relied upon is conduct which evidences the parties' *shared* intentions. The claimant's conduct in this case could not be relied upon because it was simply *unilateral* conduct which had taken place after the property had been acquired.   [202] [2007] UKPC 53 at [19].

[203] Ibid, [4].

contribution to its acquisition. In this case the home was built on a plot of land given to the couple by the husband's mother and further funds provided by the mother helped to finance the construction of the property. The court recited the accepted principle that if a parent gives financial assistance to a newly married couple to acquire their matrimonial home, the usual inference is that it was intended as a gift to both of them rather than to one alone.[204] This inference of a joint gift was supported by the behaviour of the parties during the marriage. They organised their finances jointly and all of their income went into a joint bank account from which the mortgage was paid and for which they were jointly liable. The couple were married for almost 20 years and had children. The Privy Council confirmed that the task of the court was to survey the whole course of the parties' conduct in order to ascertain their shared intentions in relation to the property. Placing emphasis on the fact that the parties organised their finances jointly and undertook joint liability for the mortgage,[205] the court concluded that the wife was entitled to a half share.

It should be pointed out, however, that although the general approach to quantification is the same in both sole name and joint names cases, Baroness Hale did suggest in *Stack* that there were some differences.[206] First Baroness Hale said that in joint names cases, the 'fact' that the property has been registered in joint names must be taken into account. Her Ladyship continued:

> it will almost always have been a conscious decision to put the house into joint names … Committing oneself to spend large sums of money on a place to live is not normally done by accident or without giving it a moment's thought.[207]

In addition, Baroness Hale considered that:

> when a couple are joint owners of the home and jointly liable for the mortgage, the inferences to be drawn from who pays for what may be very different from the inferences to be drawn when only one is owner of the home. The arithmetical calculation of how much was paid by each is also likely to be less important.[208]

This suggests that who paid for what may be more relevant in sole name cases. However, in both *Midland Bank plc v Cooke* and *Abbott v Abbott*, which were both sole name cases, the court took a broad-brush approach to quantifying the parties' shares, looking at their whole course of conduct in relation to the property. For example, Mrs Cooke was able to establish that she had a beneficial interest after making a small contribution to the purchase price of the property. Once this hurdle was crossed, the court took a broad view of the parties' whole course of dealing and awarded her a half share of the property. It must be remembered, however, that in both of these cases the parties were married. It is entirely possible that a less generous approach would be taken in a sole name case where the parties are not married. There are a number of reasons for this. First, in *Stack*, Baroness Hale said that 'in the cohabitation context, mercenary considerations may be more to the fore than they would be in marriage'.[209] Indeed, in *Midland Bank v Cooke*, Waite LJ stated at the conclusion of his judgment that the fact that the parties were married was important in his determination that Mrs Cooke should receive a half share in the beneficial interest. If the case concerned an unmarried couple it is questionable whether he would have

---

[204] Ibid, [17]. See *McHardy and Sons (A Firm) v Warren* [1994] 2 FLR 338 at 340; *Midland Bank plc v Cooke* [1995] 4 All ER 562 at 570.

[205] The court noted that this has always been regarded as a significant factor. [2007] UKPC 53, [18] *per* Baroness Hale citing *Hyett v Stanley* [2003] EWCA Civ 942.

[206] As Lloyd LJ observed in *Holman v Howes* [2007] EWCA Civ 877 at [28].

[207] *Stack v Dowden* [2007] UKHL 17 at [66].   [208] Ibid, [69].   [209] Ibid.

quantified a cohabitant's share so generously. Indeed, in *Mortgage Corporation v Shaire*[210] Neuberger J (as he then was) said that:

> the extent of the financial contribution is perhaps not as important an aspect as it was once thought to be. It may well carry more weight in a case where the parties are unmarried than where they were married.[211]

It is possible that there are enough hooks within these dicta to persuade the courts to prioritise the parties' financial contributions in sole name cases where the parties are unmarried. In addition, it must be remembered that when ascertaining the parties' intentions, the court is concerned with conduct *relating to the property*. More general relationship factors, such as how long the parties lived together and whether they had children, are less important than factors which reveal the parties' approach to their financial affairs, such as whether they were economically interdependent. In *Abbott* the court placed considerable emphasis on the fact that the parties organised their finances jointly and undertook joint liability for the mortgage. The wife was awarded a half share in the property. However, it is by no means certain that the same outcome would have been reached if there had been no such evidence of financial solidarity but the parties had nevertheless lived a lengthy, emotionally interdependent life together as an *unmarried* couple. Thus, while the same general approach is taken to quantification in sole and joint names cases, it is possible that the courts will apply this in a more restrictive way in sole name cases where the parties are unmarried by paying more attention to the parties' financial contributions.

2.4 PROPRIETARY ESTOPPEL

An alternative to establishing a constructive trust is for the claimant to make out a case of 'proprietary estoppel' in order to acquire a share in the property or to obtain some other remedy in relation to it. There are some overlaps between the theoretical bases of the constructive trust doctrine and proprietary estoppel, to the extent that there has been some debate about whether the doctrines should be assimilated. However, recent jurisprudence has emphasised the significant differences between the two, in particular in the nature of the relief available. Lord Hope said in *Stack v Dowden*[212] that he was:

> now rather less enthusiastic about the notion that proprietary estoppel and 'common interest' constructive trusts can or should be completely assimilated. Proprietary estoppel typically consists of asserting an equitable claim against the conscience of the 'true' owner. The claim is a 'mere equity'. It is to be satisfied by the minimum award necessary to do justice … which may sometimes lead to no more than a monetary award. A 'common intention' constructive trust, by contrast, is identifying the true beneficial owner or owners, and the size of their beneficial interests.

While establishing a constructive trust will give the claimant a beneficial interest in the property, making out a case of proprietary estoppel gives the court the discretion to grant whatever remedy is necessary to satisfy the equity. Thus 'the claimant who establishes a proprietary estoppel may do less well that the claimant who establishes a constructive trust'.[213]

The law relating to proprietary estoppel is complex. The doctrine lacks precise definition and it has been left to the courts to mould it through the development of case law. As noted recently, 'there is no definition of proprietary estoppel that is both comprehensive

---

[210] [2001] Ch 743.   [211] Ibid, 750.   [212] [2007] UKHL 17 at [37] *per* Lord Hope.
[213] *Q v Q* [2008] EWHC 1874 at [113].

and uncontroversial (and many attempts at one have been neither).'[214] Given the complex nature of proprietary estoppel, it is important to look at case law to ascertain the central elements of the doctrine and the circumstances when it can be invoked.

2.4.1 What is proprietary estoppel?

Proprietary estoppel prevents the owner of land from insisting on his or her strict legal rights. It arises where the claimant is deliberately misled into believing, or mistakenly believes, that he or she has a present interest in property owned by another, or that he or she will be given such an interest in the future. The owner of the property must have assured, encouraged, or acquiesced in the claimant's wrongful or mistaken belief and the claimant, in reliance on this belief, must act to his or her detriment. If the owner then seeks to take unconscionable advantage of the claimant by denying him or her the right or benefit which had been expected, a proprietary estoppel may give rise to an equity to which the court will seek to give effect.[215] Recent case law has emphasised that although there are different elements to proprietary estoppel, a broad inquiry must be undertaken to see whether it arises on the facts of a particular case to prevent the unconscionable conduct of the legal owner.[216] In *Gillet v Holt*,[217] Walker LJ said that:

> the doctrine of proprietary estoppel cannot be treated as subdivided into three of four watertight compartments ... the fundamental principle that equity is concerned to prevent unconscionable conduct permeates all the elements of the doctrine. In the end the court must look at the matter in the round.

Thus, while there are several elements to the doctrine (most notably an assurance or representation by the legal owner, and the non-owner's induced detrimental reliance) these elements are 'often intertwined' and will be considered as part of the court's broad inquiry into whether the legal owner's repudiation of the assurance was unconscionable or unfair in all the circumstances.[218]

2.4.2 Was there an assurance or representation by the owner?

To make out a case of proprietary estoppel, there must first be a representation or assurance by the owner that the claimant is to have some interest in the property. What type of assurance will suffice?[219] In *Thorner v Major*,[220] the House of Lords said that the relevant

---

[214] S. Gardner, *An Introduction to Land Law* (2007), p 101: cited by Lord Walker in *Thorner v Major* [2009] UKHL 18. [215] *Re Basham (Deceased)* [1987] 1 All ER 405 at 410.

[216] *Gillet v Holt* [2001] Ch 210; *Jennings v Rice* [2002] EWCA Civ 159.

[217] *Gillet v Holt* [2001] Ch 210 at 225. [218] Ibid.

[219] In *Yeoman's Row Management Ltd v Cobbe* [2008] UKHL 55 the House of Lords cast doubt on the extent to which statements made during commercial negotiations can found a claim of proprietary estoppel should one party subsequently renege on a mere 'gentleman's agreement' that had been reached between the parties. It was held that, in a commercial setting where a formal contract was expected to be formed, the parties cannot rely upon proprietary estoppel to protect their expectations arising from the negotiations. While the decision concerned a commercial case where 'the claimant is typically a business person with access to legal advice and what he or she is expecting to get is a *contract*', at [68] *per* Lord Walker (emphasis in original), one wonders what its impact would be on domestic cases. Indeed, some thought that this restrictive approach sounded the death knell for the doctrine of proprietary estoppel, see B. McFarlane and A. Robertson, 'The Death of Proprietary Estoppel' (2008) Lloyd's Maritime and Commercial Law Quarterly 449. This view, which was described by Lord Walker in *Thorner v Major* [2009] UKHL 18 at [31] as 'apocalyptic', was premature. In *Thorner v Major* [2009] UKHL 18, the House of Lords confirmed that the observations of the court in *Yeoman's Row Management Ltd v Cobbe* were not relevant in the domestic context. See *Yeoman's Row Management Ltd v Cobbe* [2008] UKHL 55 at [68] *per* Lord Walker.

[220] [2009] UKHL 18.

assurance must be 'clear enough'. Whether this is so depends on the facts and circumstances of each individual case. Indeed, the Lords said in *Thorner* that the meaning to be ascribed to one party's words depends on the 'factual context' in which they were made,[221] and it seems that the character of the individuals will also be relevant. This 'factual context' will help to determine how the statements were intended by their maker, how they were understood by the person to whom they were made, and whether such understanding and subsequent reliance were reasonable.[222] The assurance must also relate to some particular asset or property. As Sir Peter Gibson made clear in *Morris v Morris*:[223]

> it is well-established that the representation or assurance must be specific, such as would entitle the person to whom it was made reasonably to rely on it or change his or her position.

While the assurance must relate to an interest in specific property, the actual nature of that interest does not have to be specified.[224] However, more general assurances that the non-owner 'would never want for anything' or 'would be taken care of' will not be enough to found a proprietary estoppel.[225] These are simply general representations regarding the non-owner's well-being and because they do not relate to any specific property, they cannot be relied upon to found an estoppel claim. Indeed, words or conduct which lead the non-owner to harbour a mere expectation that he or she will be allowed to continue to live in the property will not be enough.[226] In *James v Thomas*,[227] the owner (Mr James) assured the non-owner that their joint work improving the property would benefit them both and that she would be provided for on his death. Chadwick LJ, in the Court of Appeal, held that these general statements were not 'intended or understood to be a promise of some proprietary interest, either present or in the future' and so were insufficient to found a claim based on proprietary estoppel.[228] Similarly in *Morris v Morris*,[229] the Court of Appeal found that there was no representation made to the claimant which led her to believe that she had an interest in the property in question. While Sir Peter Gibson considered that her partner had behaved badly after the parties had separated, this was not enough, by itself, to show that there had been unconscionable disadvantage for the purposes of establishing proprietary estoppel.[230]

2.4.3 Detrimental reliance

If an assurance or representation that the non-owner is to have an interest in the property has been made, the non-owner must rely upon this to his or her detriment. Detriment, for the purposes of proprietary estoppel, is not a 'narrow or technical concept' and, although it can, it does not have to consist of the expenditure of money.[231] A range of conduct, such as domestic labour, indirect financial contributions to the family's general expenditure, and foregoing paid employment, may constitute detrimental reliance as long as it is something substantial.[232] In *Gillett v Holt*,[233] the court said:

---

[221] Ibid, [80].   [222] Ibid.

[223] [2008] EWCA Civ 257 at [28]. In *Thorner v Major* [2009] UKHL 18, Lord Walker said that the assurances given to the claimant must relate to identified property owned (or perhaps about to be owned) by the defendant, at [61].   [224] *James v Thomas* [2007] EWCA Civ 1212 at [32].

[225] *Lissimore v Downing* [2003] 2 FLR 308; *James v Thomas* [2007] EWCA Civ 1212 at [31]–[32].

[226] See N. Piska, 'A Common Intention or a Rare Bird? Proprietary Interests, Personal Claims and Services Rendered by Lovers Post-Acquisition: *James v Thomas; Morris v Morris*' [2009] Child and Family Law Quarterly 104.   [227] [2007] EWCA Civ 1212.

[228] Ibid, [33]–[34]. See also *Holman v Howes* [2007] EWCA Civ 877.   [229] [2008] EWCA Civ 257.

[230] Ibid, [29].   [231] *Gillet v Holt* [2001] Ch 210 at 232.   [232] Ibid.   [233] Ibid, 232.

whether the detriment is sufficiently substantial is to be tested by whether it would be unjust or inequitable to allow the assurance to be disregarded.

A good example of proprietary estoppel is *Greasley v Cooke*.[234] Doris Cooke had lived all her adult life with the same family: living as man and wife with one brother, working in the house without payment, looking after a mentally ill member of the household, and remaining there after several members of the family had left or died. She had been encouraged by the family to believe that she could regard the property as her home for the rest of her life and she therefore did not ask for payment for her contributions. At the age of 62 she was told to leave the house by the one surviving brother. The trial judge held that her belief that she could remain in the house for as long as she lived had been induced by assurances given to her by family members, but that she had failed to prove that she had acted to her detriment in reliance on these assurances. The Court of Appeal held that it was to be presumed that she had acted on the faith of these assurances, and that it was up to those who wished to evict her to prove that she had not acted to her detriment or otherwise been prejudiced by remaining in the house, and they failed to do so. The Court of Appeal granted her a declaration that she was entitled to remain rent free in the house for the rest of her life.[235]

The owner's representation regarding the conferral of an interest in the property does not have to be the only reason for the non-owner's conduct, but it does have to be a factor. In *Wayling v Jones*[236] the plaintiff (as they were then called) lived with the deceased and acted as his companion for 16 years. He provided substantial help in running the deceased's business and, in return, received pocket money, living expenses, and an express promise that he would inherit the deceased's property, a hotel. On the deceased's death, the plaintiff argued that he was entitled to the value of the hotel as promised to him but the judge at first instance rejected this claim holding that the plaintiff had failed to prove that the detriment he had suffered (not receiving adequate wages and continuing to serve the deceased until his death) had been in reliance on his belief that he would inherit the deceased's property. Allowing the plaintiff's appeal and giving the judgment of the court, Balcombe LJ held that the following principles applied: first, there must be a sufficient link between the promises relied upon and the conduct which constituted detriment; secondly, the promises relied upon did not have to be the sole inducement for the conduct, it was sufficient if they were an inducement; and, thirdly, once it had been established that promises had been made, and that there had been conduct by the plaintiff of such a nature that an inducement could be inferred, then the burden of proof shifted to the defendant to establish that the plaintiff did not rely on the promises.[237]

Proprietary estoppel may therefore come to the assistance of a person who claims an interest in the home he or she shared with their partner in whose name the property is vested. An example of this is *Pascoe v Turner*.[238] After the breakdown of their relationship, Mr Pascoe told Mrs Turner, with whom he had been living for ten years, that the house and its contents were hers. However, no conveyance of the property was ever drawn up. Therefore, although there was evidence of intention by Mr Pascoe to make a gift of the house to Mrs Turner, it was an imperfect gift.[239] However, Mrs Turner, having been told that the house was hers, set about improving it and spent a substantial sum on the property. Mr Pascoe allowed this to happen and at no time suggested that she was

[234] [1980] 3 All ER 710.

[235] See also *Re Basham (Deceased)* [1987] 1 All ER 405, where the plaintiff also worked without receiving payment.   [236] [1995] 2 FLR 1029.

[237] The plaintiff was awarded the net proceeds of the sale of the hotel.   [238] [1979] 2 All ER 945.

[239] Law of Property Act 1925, s 52(1).

putting her money and her labour into his house. Subsequently he brought proceedings for possession. The Court of Appeal held that Mr Pascoe had encouraged or acquiesced in the manner in which Mrs Turner had changed her position for the worse in the belief that the house was hers, and that she was thus able to establish proprietary estoppel. The court satisfied the equity arising in this case by transferring the house to Mrs Turner.[240] Thus, where a person has been assured that he or she will be able to remain in property owned by their partner, and where the former acts to his or her detriment in reliance on this assurance (eg by spending money on the property) equity may intervene to grant a remedy.

2.4.4 Conduct found insufficient to give rise to proprietary estoppel

In *Coombes v Smith*[241] Mrs Coombes, a married woman, formed a relationship with Mr Smith, a married man, and had his child. Mr Smith bought a house intended for them both, but although Mrs Coombes left her husband and moved in, Mr Smith never did. He refused her requests to put the property in joint names, but reassured her that he would always look after her. He paid the bills and the mortgage and frequently visited her and their child. Mrs Coombes decorated the house on a number of occasions and tidied the garden. When their relationship eventually broke down Mrs Coombes sought an order that Mr Smith transfer the property and its contents to her absolutely, or alternatively sought a declaration that he was bound to allow her to occupy the property and to use its contents for the rest of her life.

Mr Smith conceded that Mrs Coombes had an equity to remain in the property until their daughter reached 17, although he said that she had no entitlement to remain in the property after that time. The court upheld his claim and said that no proprietary estoppel had arisen. It held that Mrs Coombes's belief that Mr Smith would always provide her with a roof over her head was quite different from a belief that she had the legal right to remain in the property against his wishes, and therefore she was unable to establish that she had acted under a mistaken belief that she had security of tenure. It distinguished *Pascoe v Turner*[242] on the grounds that there were no words of gift and there were no improvements made to the property in the mistaken belief that the property was hers.

The most significant feature of the judgment from the point of view of a person who claims that she has an entitlement to remain in her ex-partner's house, was the manner in which the court approached the assurance given by Mr Smith to Mrs Coombes that 'he would never see her without a roof over her head'. The court said that all of the statements relied upon by the plaintiff were made by the owner while the relationship was continuing and thus did not amount to an assurance of what would happen in the event of the relationship breaking down. The court further held that, even if Mrs Coombes had been led to believe that she had a right to remain in the property for the rest of her life, she had not behaved in a way which was detrimental to her or changed her position in reliance on Mr Smith's representation. It held that it would be wholly unreal to find that she had allowed herself to become pregnant in reliance on some mistaken belief as to her legal rights and, in any event, allowing oneself to become pregnant could not amount to detriment in the context of proprietary estoppel. Nor did any prejudice arise from her having

---

[240] In granting this remedy the court was clearly influenced by the fact that the court regarded Mr Pascoe as a man who would pursue his purpose of evicting Mrs Turner from the house by any legal means at his disposal, and that therefore Mrs Turner needed a remedy which would be effective to protect her against any future manifestations of Mr Pascoe's ruthlessness. It rejected the remedy of granting her a licence to live in the house for the rest of her life because she could not protect this right against a purchaser for value without notice.   [241] [1986] 1 WLR 808.
[242] [1979] 2 All ER 945.

redecorated the property, as this was done in the context of her continuing relationship with Mr Smith. Thus even if the court assumed the existence of the requisite mistaken belief about her legal rights, Mrs Coombes failed in her claim because she was unable to establish that she had acted in such a way as to give rise to an equity in her favour.

More recent case law has confirmed this view. Thus, if the owner of the property makes general assurances to his or her partner during the course of the relationship regarding their continued well-being, the court is unlikely to find that this equates to a representation regarding either the ownership or occupation of the family home should the relationship break down.[243] Similarly, as with the constructive trust, the court may be unwilling to find that the claimant has acted to his or her detriment in reliance on the owner's assurance if their conduct was carried out for some reason other than the claimant thought that he or she was acquiring an interest in the property. In *James v Thomas*,[244] for example, the claimant's activities in contributing to her partner's business and working to improve the property were explained by Chadwick LJ on the basis that the couple were making their joint life together as man and wife. He said:

> the Cottage was their home: the business was their livelihood. It is a mistake to think that the motives which lead parties in such a relationship to act as they do are necessarily attributable to pecuniary self-interest.[245]

There is a realism in the court's view that assurances made by the owning party about property rights when an unmarried cohabiting relationship was happy was almost certainly not intended to have binding force when the relationship broke down. However, these cases also show that proprietary estoppel, like the constructive trust, cannot handle the economic fall-out of a relationship breakdown and the disadvantageous situation which one partner may find themselves in if he or she had not paid for, or financially contributed towards, the acquisition of the family home. The law relating to the acquisition of a beneficial interest in the family home, and the law of proprietary estoppel, are not truly part of family law; they are about property law and its amelioration by equity. It is persons who have been living in a family relationship who usually need to rely on equity at its most generous, but it has been seen that this generosity is limited by doctrines which have universal application. Equity has a part to play in assisting the unmarried where there is unfairness, but this part is limited.

2.4.5 Satisfying the equity in a case of proprietary estoppel

If proprietary estoppel is made out, the court has discretion as to what remedy to provide in light of the assurances and the nature of the detrimental reliance.[246] When deciding what remedy to grant, the court will consider what is 'the minimum equity to do justice to the plaintiff'.[247] A wide-ranging number of remedies are available such as granting a licence to the claimant,[248] monetary compensation,[249] or conferring some sort of proprietary interest on the claimant.[250] However, case law has made it clear that there must be

---

[243] *James v Thomas* [2007] EWCA Civ 1212; *Morris v Morris* [2008] EWCA Civ 257.
[244] [2007] EWCA Civ 1212.   [245] Ibid, [36].
[246] Thus in *Re Basham (Deceased)* [1987] 1 All ER 405 the plaintiff had been encouraged to believe that she would inherit a cottage in return for caring for the deceased. Since the plaintiff had subordinated her own interests and wish to move away in reliance on this belief, it was held that she was entitled to inherit the cottage.   [247] *Crabb v Arun District Council* [1976] Ch 179 at 198.
[248] *Inwards v Baker* [1965] 2 QB 29.   [249] *Dodsworth v Dodsworth* (1973) 228 EG 1115.
[250] This could be a life interest (*Greasley v Cooke* [1980] 1 WLR 1306), a fee simple (*Pascoe v Turner* [1979] 1 WLR 431), or an easement (*Crabb v Arun District Council* [1976] Ch 179).

proportionality between the expectation of the claimant and the detriment that he or she has actually suffered:

> the value of [the equity which arises] will depend upon all the circumstances including the expectation and detriment. The task of the court is to do justice. The most essential requirement is that there must be proportionality between the expectation and the detriment.[251]

In *Jennings v Rice*[252] the claimant began working for the deceased as a gardener in 1970. Over time he became her carer and from the late 1980s she stopped paying him for his services telling him instead that he would have the house and furniture on her death. During the last few years of her life, the claimant, at the deceased's request, spent nearly every night on a sofa in a sitting room of her house to provide her with security. However, when she died she did not leave a will and the claimant argued that he was entitled to the value of the house and furniture (worth £435,000) under the doctrine of proprietary estoppel. The Court of Appeal said that when deciding how to satisfy an equity based on proprietary estoppel, it was essential that there was proportionality between the claimant's expectation and the detriment suffered. While the claimant may have expected to receive the full value of the house, the Court of Appeal said that this would not be proportionate to the detriment which he had incurred. The court upheld the decision of the judge at first instance to award him £200,000 as the minimum necessary to satisfy his equity. Thus, the remedy will not necessarily meet the claimant's expectations in relation to what was promised and may simply compensate the claimant for the detriment which was incurred by reliance on the assurance or representation.

2.5 ORDERS UNDER THE TRUSTS OF LAND AND APPOINTMENT OF TRUSTEES ACT 1996

If the family home is co-owned by the parties but, upon relationship breakdown, they cannot reach agreement about whether the property should be sold and how the proceeds divided, or whether one party should continue living in the property (particularly where it is still a home to the parties' children) the provisions of the Trusts of Land and Appointment of Trustees Act 1996 (TOLATA) will apply. Where beneficial entitlement to land is shared, the TOLATA provides that it is held as a trust of land.

Key legislation

Under section 14 of the TOLATA, any person who is a trustee of land, or who has an interest in property which is subject to a trust of land may apply to the court for an order to resolve the disputes concerning the occupation and sale of the property. The court has the power to make an order which relates to the exercise by the trustees of any of their functions, or it will declare the nature or extent of a person's interest in the property subject to the trust, and in either case the court may make any such order as it thinks fit.

This means that the court can order a sale of the property, or order that the sale be postponed. If the court orders that the sale is postponed and one partner is allowed to remain

---

[251] *Jennings v Rice* [2002] EWCA Civ 159 at [36] *per* Aldous LJ; *Holman v Howes* [2007] EWCA Civ 877 at [40]. See A. Robertson, 'The Reliance Basis of Proprietary Estoppel Remedies' (2008) 72 Conveyancer and Property Lawyer 295–321.   [252] [2002] EWCA Civ 159.

in occupation, that person may be ordered to pay compensation (occupation rent) to the excluded party during their period of occupation.[253]

It must be emphasised, however, that the TOLATA is not a property-adjustment regime similar to that available to govern the property disputes of divorcing spouses or civil partners who are dissolving their partnership.[254] Although under section 14 the court is empowered to make 'such order as it thinks fit', it cannot alter the parties' respective beneficial interests. If the property is in the sole name of one party and the non-owner fails to establish that he or she has a beneficial interest in the property under the application of ordinary trust principles, the court does not have the power under the TOLATA to confer any such interest on the non-owner. Thus the TOLATA operates within the strict confines of the parties' existing beneficial interests in the property and while it can determine the sale and occupation of the property, it cannot alter the parties' existing beneficial interests in it.

2.5.1 Criteria for determining applications made under the TOLATA

Key legislation

Section 15 of the TOLATA details the matters to which the court must have regard when determining an application. They include:

   (a) the intentions of the person or persons (if any) who created the trust,

   (b) the purposes for which the property subject to the trust is held,

   (c) the welfare of any minor who occupies or might reasonably be expected to occupy any land subject to the trust as his home, and

   (d) the interests of any secured creditor or beneficiary.

Section 15(2) further provides that where the application concerns the power of the trustees to exclude or restrict the right of a beneficiary to occupy the land,[255] the court must also have regard to the circumstances and wishes of each of the beneficiaries who is entitled to occupy the land.

How do the provisions of the Act affect the real difficulties faced by cohabitants when their relationship breaks down? Can the Act assist them when they are unhappy living together under the same roof? What are the implications for cohabitants who enjoy a shared beneficial entitlement as equitable joint tenants or tenants in common where one wishes to realise his or her beneficial share in the property and the other wishes to remain in occupation? The following sections will consider these questions.

---

[253] TOLATA, s 13. These statutory provisions replace the old powers of equitable accounting where a beneficiary in occupation of the property would be ordered to pay an occupation rent to a beneficiary who was excluded from the property. However, the House of Lords pointed out in *Stack v Dowden* [2007] UKHL 17 that although the governing principles are now found in the TOLATA rather than under the old principles of equity, the results will usually be the same, at [94], *per* Baroness Hale and [150] *per* Lord Neuberger. In *Stack*, Mr Stack applied for occupation rent to compensate him for his exclusion from the property and to cover the cost of his alternative accommodation. His claim was rejected by the majority on the basis that the house was to be sold as soon as possible and thus he 'would not be kept out of his money for long', at [94]. See also *Wilcox v Tait* [2006] EWCA Civ 1867; *Murphy v Gooch* [2007] EWCA Civ 603; *Young v Lauretani* [2007] EWHC 1244 (Ch); *Rahnema v Rahbari* [2008] 2 P & CR DG5. See further E. Cooke, 'Accounting Payments: Please Can We Get the Maths Right?' [2007] Family Law 1024.

[254] This adjustive regime is found under the Matrimonial Causes Act 1973, Pt II; Civil Partnership Act 2004, Sch 5. See Chapter 4.   [255] Section 13.

2.5.2 Disputes over occupation of the property

Consider first a dispute between beneficially entitled cohabitants over occupation of the property. There is an overlap here with the powers of the courts to make occupation orders under the Family Law Act 1996, section 33.[256] It is suggested that a cohabitant would be ill-advised to apply for an order under section 14 of the TOLATA because the courts' powers under the Family Law Act 1996 are more extensive. Furthermore, under the Family Law Act 1996 the criteria guiding the courts' decision making focus on matters such as the parties' respective resources, the likely effect of any order on the health, safety, or well-being of the parties and any relevant child, and, where significant harm is alleged, a balance of harm test is applied.[257] These welfare-orientated criteria are more appropriate to disputes over occupation of the family home than those contained in section 15 of the TOLATA. A cohabitant might well face difficulty in persuading a court to exclude his or her partner's right to occupy the family home under the Family Law Act 1996 because courts regard exclusion orders of this nature as draconian. However, he or she has more of a chance of success under that Act than under the TOLATA. The court's powers under section 14(1) only relate to the exercise by the trustees of any of their functions, and trustees may not unreasonably exclude or restrict entitlement to occupy the land.[258]

2.5.3 Disagreement over sale of the family home

It is where cohabitants cannot agree over whether the property should be retained or sold that the provisions of the TOLATA may come to their assistance. The 1996 Act repeals section 30 of the Law of Property Act 1925 (which governed the execution of the trust for sale), and the criteria in section 15 are aimed at consolidating and rationalising the approach previously adopted by the courts when applying section 30.[259] The framers of the Act did not intend to change the law on how the courts had exercised their powers under section 30. Rather, it was their intention to mirror the position which had been reached through the development of case law. Nevertheless, an important difference between the old law and the TOLATA is that cases prior to the Act which involved a trust for sale were decided against a background of a duty to sell. That duty no longer exists, meaning that courts enjoy greater flexibility when determining whether to postpone sale.[260] Another difference is the introduction of statutory criteria to guide the courts in the exercise of their discretion.[261] When the court is exercising its powers under the TOLATA and deciding whether to order or postpone the sale of the property, one important factor will be the underlying *purpose* of the trust. If the property was bought as a home for the couple but the parties' relationship has broken down, the court is likely to order sale because the purpose for which the property was acquired has come to an end.[262] However, where the purpose was to provide a home for the family and this has not been extinguished because children are still living in the property, then sale may be postponed whilst this purpose still exists.[263]

---

[256] Occupation orders are explained in Chapter 3.   [257] Family Law Act 1996, s 33(6), (7).

[258] TOLATA, s 13(2). The trustees must take account of the intentions of the person(s) who created the trust, the purposes for which the land is held, and the circumstances and wishes of the beneficiaries (s 13(4)).

[259] Following proposals for reform made in *Transfer of Land, Trusts of Land* (Law Com No 181, 1989). Section 30 provided:

> If the trustees for sale refuse to sell or to exercise any of [their] powers …, or any requisite consent cannot be obtained, any person may apply to the court for a vesting or other order for giving effect to the proposed transaction or for an order directing the trustees for sale to give effect thereto, and the court may make such order as it thinks fit.

[260] *Mortgage Corpn v Shaire* [2001] Ch 743 at 758 *per* Neuberger J (as he then was).

[261] Section 15. These criteria are given equal weight.   [262] *Jones v Challenger* [1960] 1 All ER 785.

[263] *Re Evers' Trust* [1980] 3 All ER 399.

In situations where third parties have a financial interest in the proceedings or where one of the parties is bankrupt, the courts have wider concerns. Section 15(1)(d) of the TOLATA directs the court to consider 'the interests of any secured creditor of any beneficiary' when exercising its discretion. A trustee in bankruptcy has the duty to realise the debtor's assets for the benefit of the creditors, and this may involve seeking a sale of the family home under section 14 of the TOLATA. Case law has established that the rights of creditors will usually prevail over the rights of other family members living in the property even if it is still being used as the family home. An order for the sale of the home will be made unless there are exceptional circumstances, and the fact that family members, including children, face eviction which would cause them hardship does not amount to an exceptional circumstance which would either prevent sale or justify its postponement.[264] Nourse LJ said in the leading case of *Re Citro (A Bankrupt)* that while such circumstances engender:

a natural sympathy in all who hear of them, [they] cannot be described as exceptional. They are the melancholy consequences of debt and improvidence with which every civilised society has been familiar.[265]

It seems that only circumstances which are inherently unusual will qualify as exceptional.[266] For example, cases where a sale has been postponed due to the presence of exceptional circumstances have related to a family member's illness.[267] However, even if there are exceptional circumstances, the court can still order sale of the property.[268]

In addition, section 335A(3) of the Insolvency Act 1986 provides that once a year has elapsed since the first vesting of the bankrupt's estate in a trustee, the court must assume, unless the circumstances of the case are exceptional, that the interests of the bankrupt's creditors outweigh all other considerations. In *Barca v Mears*[269] it was questioned whether this narrow construction of 'exceptional circumstances' under which the rights of creditors will usually prevail was compatible with the European Convention on Human Rights and the right to respect for private and family life under Article 8. The court did not reach a firm conclusion on the issue. However, subsequent cases have suggested that human rights considerations do not require any 'significant modification' to the approach currently taken when balancing the interests of the creditors, the bankrupt, and the bankrupt's family.[270] It seems that, until further clarification, the impact of human rights considerations on the law in this area remains a moot point.

2.6 TRANSFER OF TENANCIES BETWEEN COHABITANTS

Section 53 of and Schedule 7 to the Family Law Act 1996 introduced for the first time a form of property transfer order between unmarried cohabitants.[271] The power to transfer

---

[264] *Re Citro (A Bankrupt)* [1991] 1 FLR 71; *Dean v Stout (Trustee in Bankruptcy)* [2005] EWHC 3315 (Ch); *Barca v Mears* [2005] 2 FLR 1; *Donohue v Ingram* [2006] EWHC 282.   [265] [1991] 1 FLR 71 at 82.
[266] *Re Citro (A Bankrupt)* [1991] 1 FLR 71.
[267] *Re Bremner (A Bankrupt)* [1999] 1 LR 912; *Claughton v Charalambous* [1999] 1 FLR 740.
[268] *Dean v Stout* [2005] EWHC 3315 (Ch).
[269] [2004] EWHC 2170 (Ch). See also *Donohue v Ingram* [2006] EWHC 282 (Ch) and *Jackson v Bell* [2001] EWCA Civ 387.   [270] *Foyle v Turner* [2007] BPIR 43; *Turner v Avis* [2009] 1 FLR 74.
[271] A transfer of tenancy order can also be made between spouses on the granting of a decree of divorce, a decree of nullity, or a decree of judicial separation, or between civil partners when the court has the power to make a property adjustment order (Family Law Act 1996, Sch 7, para 2). Remarriage or the formation of a subsequent civil partnership prevents a spouse or civil partner from applying for a transfer of tenancy order. However, the marriage of a cohabitant does not affect his or her right to apply for such an order.

specified tenancies on making divorce or separation orders, or a nullity decree, was re-enacted and extended to cohabitants where they separate. The legislation provides that where a cohabitant is entitled either solely or jointly with the other cohabitant to occupy a dwelling-house by virtue of a relevant tenancy,[272] and where the cohabitants cease to live together as husband and wife, the court may make an order transferring the tenancy from one to the other, provided that the dwelling-house was a home in which they lived together as husband and wife.[273] A relevant tenancy means:

(a) a protected tenancy or statutory tenancy within the meaning of the Rent Act 1977;

(b) a statutory tenancy within the meaning of the Rent (Agriculture) Act 1976;

(c) a secure tenancy within the meaning of section 79 of the Housing Act 1985; or

(d) an assured tenancy or assured agricultural occupancy within the meaning of Part 1 of the Housing Act 1988.

In determining whether to exercise its power to transfer the tenancy, the court must have regard to all the circumstances of the case including when and how the tenancy was granted or otherwise acquired, the housing needs and housing resources of the parties and any relevant child, their financial resources, and the likely effect of an order or the decision not to make an order on the health, safety, or well-being of the parties or any relevant child. Where only one cohabitant is entitled to occupy the dwelling-house by virtue of the tenancy, the court, in addition, must take account of the conduct of the parties in relation to each other and otherwise, the nature of their relationship, the length of time during which they have lived together as husband and wife, whether there are or have been children who are children of both parties or for whom both parties have or have had parental responsibility, and the length of time that has elapsed since the parties ceased to live together.[274] The court must also consider the suitability of the parties as tenants[275] and the landlord must be given an opportunity to be heard.[276]

If a transfer order is made, the transferor can be compensated for his or her loss. The transferee may be directed by the court to make payments to the transferor.[277] The court when deciding whether to make such an order must have regard to the financial loss which would otherwise be suffered by the transferor, the parties' needs, their financial resources, and their financial obligations.[278] Such payments may be deferred or made in instalments but only where immediate payment of the sum by the transferee would cause the transferee greater financial hardship than any financial hardship to the transferor caused by postponement.[279] In addition, the court may direct that both cohabitants are to be jointly and severally liable to discharge or perform the liabilities and obligations in respect of the dwelling-house.[280] It may further direct that one cohabitant is to indemnify the other against payments made, or expenses incurred, in discharging or performing such liabilities and obligations.[281]

Research has shown that cohabiting couples are more likely to rent their home than married couples[282] and so, upon relationship breakdown, it is useful that courts have

---

[272] See *Gay v Sheeran* [1999] 3 All ER 795 which indicates that an order can only be made where the tenancy was held either solely by one cohabitant or jointly between the two cohabitants but not where the tenancy was held by a cohabitant and a third party.   [273] Schedule 7, paras 3 and 4.

[274] Schedule 7, para 5. These criteria are the same as those which the court must take into account when determining whether to make an occupation order under the Family Law Act 1996, ss 33 and 36; see Chapter 3.   [275] Family Law Act 1996, Sch 7, para 5(c).

[276] Ibid, para 14(1).   [277] Ibid, para 10(1).   [278] Ibid, para 10(4).   [279] Ibid, para 10(2), (5).

[280] Ibid, para 11(1).   [281] Ibid, para 11(2).

[282] Office for National Statistics, General Household Survey 2007 (2008), Table 4.10, available at www.ons.gov.uk/ons/rel/ghs/general-household-survey/2007-report/index.html.

the power to transfer a relevant tenancy into the name of one party. Not only do they allow a tenancy in joint names to be transferred into the applicant's sole name, but they also confer power on the court to transfer a tenancy to one partner even where the other partner was the sole tenant. The criteria which guide the court, although different from the criteria which guide courts when making property adjustment orders between spouses and civil partners on divorce/dissolution,[283] nonetheless direct the court to engage in a similar exercise, namely to discover the nature and extent of the parties' resources and to balance their respective needs. However, there is little evidence to indicate how this power is exercised and how often it is used.[284] Further, even though, in comparative terms, cohabitants may rent more often than married couples, overall cohabitants are more likely to be owner-occupiers.[285] However, the property adjustment power under Schedule 7 to the Family Law Act 1996 only relates to certain residential tenancies in the social and private sector and does not apply to disputes concerning an owner-occupied family home. As we have seen, these disputes are resolved according to trust law principles which do not give the courts the discretionary power to consider welfare-based criteria and to resolve disputes in the interests of fairness.

2.7 SCHEDULE 1 TO THE CHILDREN ACT 1989

The only time settlements of property and property transfer orders can be made between cohabitants is under Schedule 1 to the Children Act 1989. However, these orders are of limited use because they can only be made for the benefit of the child where the couple have children and not in order to reach a fair outcome between the cohabitants themselves. Under these provisions, if an unmarried couple with a child separate, the court may order that the child and the primary carer are allowed to remain in the family home or that a property be purchased for their accommodation while the child is dependent. However, once the child has reached the age of majority or has ceased full-time education, the property will revert to its true owner and the court does not have the power to adjust the parties' strict property entitlements in the interests of fairness.[286] This is clearly of only short-term use to a person who has no ownership interest in the property but has been allowed to live there while caring for a child:

> although a carer may be secure for the duration of the child's dependency, she is likely eventually to lose her home and, unless she has been able to establish a [beneficial] share … or has saved hard in the interim (or established a new relationship), be in the position of Mrs Burns with nowhere to go. This makes Schedule 1 a less attractive option than it might otherwise appear.[287]

---

[283] Matrimonial Causes Act 1973, Pt II; Civil Partnership Act 2004, Sch 5. See Chapter 4.

[284] See Law Commission, *Cohabitation: The Financial Consequences of Relationship Breakdown* (Law Com No 307, 2007), para A.66. Recent research suggests that many lawyers have no experience of an application to transfer a tenancy, G. Douglas, J. Pearce, and H. Woodward, Cardiff Law School Research Paper No 1, 'A Failure of Trust: Resolving Property Disputes on Cohabitation Breakdown' (2007), para 8.40.

[285] Office for National Statistics, General Household Survey 2007 (2008), Table 4.10, available at www.ons.gov.uk/ons/rel/ghs/general-household-survey/2007-report/index.html.

[286] See *A v A (A Minor: Financial Provision)* [1994] 1 FLR 657; *T v S (Financial Provision for Children)* [1994] 2 FLR 883; *Re P (Child: Financial Provision)* [2003] EWCA Civ 837; *N v D* [2008] 1 FLR 1629. These provisions and relevant case law are discussed in more detail in Chapter 6.

[287] G. Douglas, J. Pearce, and H. Woodward, Cardiff Law School Research Paper No 1, 'A Failure of Trust: Resolving Property Disputes on Cohabitation Breakdown' (2007), para 3.46. See J. Tod and E. Cooke, 'Schedule 1 and the Need for Reform: *N v D*' [2008] Family Law 751.

Evidence suggests that this provision is not used that much,[288] that there are procedural difficulties surrounding its application,[289] and that it is only suitable where there are enough assets to fund two properties.[290]

2.8 THE NEED FOR REFORM

As we have seen, when unmarried couples separate their property disputes are resolved by the application of ordinary trust law principles. It is generally accepted, however, that these principles, which are not specially designed for application to family law cases, are unsuitable. Under these principles, the courts cannot redistribute the parties' property to achieve a fair outcome between them but must instead search for the parties' shared intentions in relation to ownership (not occupation) of the property. By contrast, when spouses and civil partners end their relationship by divorce or dissolution, a specifically designed set of family law principles determines their post-relationship property and financial arrangements. Under these principles, the courts can re-distribute property ownership unfettered by the restrictions inherent in trust law and can specifically take account of the contributions which each party has made to the welfare of the family. It has been said many times that the lack of a similar legal framework to govern the disputes of unmarried cohabitants on relationship breakdown remains one of the most urgent policy questions in family law. Many have argued that specially designed family law principles which are capable of taking the full range of the parties' contributions into account and assessing their prospective needs should be introduced to resolve these disputes. In 2007, the Law Commission recommended proposals to reform the law in this area but these have been shelved by the Government for the time being.

The following section will outline some deficiencies in the current law, before outlining the recommendations of the Law Commission and other policy-driven initiatives to reform the law which have, as yet, come to nothing.

2.8.1 Arguments in favour of reform

2.8.1.1 The search for the parties' shared intentions

The constructive trust, which is now the primary legal mechanism to determine the parties' respective shares in the family home, is based on ascertaining the parties' shared intentions in relation to ownership of the property. However, more often than not, cohabitants will have given no thought to these issues during the relationship either due a reluctance to contemplate their relationship breaking down or perhaps because they do not appreciate the importance of articulating their intentions in this regard. Indeed, a large number of cohabitants falsely believe that once they have lived together for a period of time they have the same rights as married couples.[291] This failure to communicate gives rise to serious difficulties both in determining whether a trust arises and in quantifying the extent of the claiming party's beneficial interest. Furthermore, even if the parties have

---

[288] See S. Arthur, J. Lewis, M. Maclean, S. Finch, and R. Fitzgerald, 'Settling Up: Making Financial Arrangements after Divorce or Separation' (National Centre for Social Research, 2002); G. Douglas, J. Pearce, and H. Woodward, Cardiff Law School Research Paper No 1, 'A Failure of Trust: Resolving Property Disputes on Cohabitation Breakdown' (2007).

[289] Douglas, Pearce and Woodward, ibid, paras 7.28–7.30.

[290] Ibid, para 8.50.

[291] A. Barlow, C. Burgoyne, E. Clery, and J. Smithson, 'Cohabitation and the Law: Myths, Money and the Media' in A. Park et al (eds), British Social Attitudes: The 24th Report (London: Sage, 2008).

discussed the matter, there may be no clear and reliable evidence of their intentions. The court's task will then be to infer the parties' intention from their conduct.

It has been observed that this judicial search for the parties' common intention is an uncertain and artificial exercise which can give rise to illogical outcomes.[292] For example, as we have seen, a common intention may be found where the legal owner lied about the reasons why the property was not put into joint names thus giving the impression that he or she intended to share ownership of the property when no such intention existed (such as in *Eves v Eves*[293]). By contrast, no common intention will be found by the legal owner's mere promises of future support to his or her partner (as in *James v Thomas*[294]). It also remains very unclear from what conduct the court will infer a common intention.

The core problem is that this doctrinal framework, which is fixated on the parties' intentions, is based on assumptions about the behaviour of cohabiting couples. However, empirical research casts doubt on the reliability of these assumptions. For example, the presumption that equity follows the law, which means that joint legal ownership will lead to the presumption of joint beneficial ownership, may not reflect the parties' actual intentions. As Lord Neuberger (dissenting) recognised in *Stack v Dowden*:[295]

> The property may be bought in joint names for reasons which cast no light on the parties' intentions with regard to beneficial ownership. It may be the solicitor's decision or assumption, the lender's preference for the security of two borrowers, or the happenstance of how the initial contact with the solicitor was made.

This view is confirmed by research which shows that couples who put their home into joint names did not tend to understand the consequences of their actions and did not appreciate that the property would then be owned equally.[296] This study also found that these couples typically showed little interest in the significance of sole or joint ownership. This was due to the fact that they simply did not understand the legal jargon associated with these concepts, and also when they were at the point of moving in together, they were generally unwilling to contemplate the relationship breaking down.[297]

In addition, the case law shows that when ascertaining the parties' shared intentions, the courts pay great attention to the way in which the parties organised their finances, asking questions such as whether the parties were financially interdependent; whether they had a joint bank account; and how responsibility for the household finances was shared. Such evidence will have significant consequences when determining the beneficial interests in the home because it gives the court a basis upon which to draw conclusions about the parties' intentions in relation to property ownership. For example, in *Stack*, the fact that the parties retained their financial independence led the court to conclude that this was an unusual case which meant that the presumption of joint beneficial ownership was rebutted. However, research has shown that the manner in which the parties organised their property and finances is not a reliable indicator of other aspects of their relationship, such as their commitment or their intentions regarding ownership of the family home.[298] For example, if a couple have separate bank accounts this does

---

[292] Law Commission, *Sharing Homes: A Discussion Paper* (Law Com No 278, 2002), para 2.106; Law Commission, *Cohabitation: The Financial Consequences of Relationship Breakdown, A Consultation Paper* (Law Com No 179, 2006), Part 4.   [293] [1975] 3 All ER 768.

[294] [2007] EWCA Civ 1212.   [295] [2007] UKHL 17 at [113].

[296] G. Douglas, J. Pearce, and H. Woodward, 'Cohabitants, Property and the Law: A Study of Injustice' (2009) 72(1) Modern Law Review 24 at 39.   [297] Ibid.

[298] Ibid, 37–38; A. Barlow, C. Burgoyne, and J. Smithson, *The Living Together Campaign—An Investigation of its Impact on Legally Aware Cohabitants* (London: Ministry of Justice, 2007), p 42.

not necessarily indicate separate finances.[299] Once again, Lord Neuberger was cautious about drawing such conclusions in *Stack* and said:

> There is a substantial difference, in law, in commercial terms, in practice, and almost always in terms of value and importance, between the ownership of a home and the ownership of a bank account or, indeed, furniture, furnishings and other chattels.[300]

2.8.1.2 Evidential problems

The search for the parties' shared intentions is made all the more artificial when one considers that the court is attempting, *retrospectively*, to ascertain these intentions. It should be borne in mind that this inquiry arises on relationship breakdown when the parties are in dispute about ownership of the property. This means that the parties' recollections of their past dealings are likely to be tainted by the breakdown and the probable ill-feeling associated with this, and it is unlikely that the parties will offer an unbiased account of their own intentions towards the property. As Baroness Hale pointed out:

> In family disputes, strong feelings are aroused when couples split up. These often lead the parties, honestly but mistakenly, to reinterpret the past in self-exculpatory or vengeful terms.[301]

Thus, it is very hard to obtain reliable evidence about the parties' actual intentions surrounding the property either when it was acquired or during the parties' relationship.

2.8.1.3 The law is unclear and open to interpretation

As the Law Commission has pointed out, the content of the law in this area is wholly dependent on the development of case law. The lack of a statutory framework to govern the financial and property disputes of unmarried cohabitants on relationship breakdown means that any change in the law is dependent on the right case coming along and reaching the Supreme Court,[302] and even then it is open to interpretation. For example, it remains very unclear whether common intention can now be inferred from indirect financial contributions. Thus, the law in this area is extremely complex and research has shown that many solicitors are uncomfortable in dealing with these cases.[303] This creates obvious difficulties when advising clients about the likely outcome of a legal dispute.

2.8.1.4 Property law principles can produce unfair outcomes

It has been pointed out that the current law is unfair, uncertain, and illogical.[304] One of the main problems is that property law principles do not give value to the contributions a partner makes to the welfare of the family, nor do they take any account of the economic sacrifices made by a partner who foregoes or limits a career in order to take care of the house and children.[305] In a sole name case, a common intention to share the property will not be inferred from domestic contributions and thus such contributions, by

---

[299] A. Barlow, C. Burgoyne, E. Clery, and J. Smithson, 'Cohabitation and the Law: Myths, Money and the Media' in A. Park et al (eds), *British Social Attitudes: The 24th Report* (London: Sage, 2008).

[300] *Stack v Dowden* [2007] UKHL 17 at [133]–[134].   [301] Ibid, [67].

[302] Law Commission, *Cohabitation: The Financial Consequences of Relationship Breakdown, A Consultation Paper* (Law Com No 179, 2006), para 5.100.

[303] G. Douglas, J. Pearce, and H. Woodward, 'Cohabitants, Property and the Law: A Study of Injustice' (2009) 72(1) Modern Law Review 24 at 41.

[304] Law Commission, *Cohabitation: The Financial Consequences of Relationship Breakdown, A Consultation Paper* (Law Com No 179, 2006), para 4.1.   [305] Ibid, para 4.5.

themselves, will not be sufficient to establish a constructive trust.[306] In addition, even if there is evidence of express common intention, the non-owner's performance of domestic contributions is unlikely to be sufficient to constitute detrimental reliance because they may be classed as contributions which he or she would have made in any event and not because it was thought that they would generate an interest in the property.[307] This assessment is probably correct in that such familial contributions are unlikely to have been made due to 'pecuniary self-interest'.[308] However, a different outcome would result if these contributions were considered within a remedial family law framework which had the flexibility to recognise their value to the welfare of the family as well as acknowledging the economic sacrifices associated with making these contributions. The doctrinal framework of the property law principles within which they are currently assessed is wholly inadequate because these principles require the contributions in question to evidence an intention to share ownership of the property and to constitute detrimental reliance which insists that their performance is due to a belief that a proprietary interest would result. This led the Law Commission to conclude that:

> the current law can produce unfair outcomes for cohabitants, in particular for the primary carer of children who may experience significant economic disadvantage following separation.[309]

Indeed, empirical research has identified four situations where the current law can result in unfair outcomes.[310] As outlined earlier, the obvious situation is the 'Mrs Burns' scenario where a cohabitant fails to establish a beneficial interest in the family home, even after a lengthy relationship, because she has made no direct financial contribution to its acquisition. In the study, the disadvantaged non-owner was always the female partner who had cared for the children during a lengthy cohabitation.[311] Secondly, the researchers identified a 'newer category of injustice' where a home was owned by one partner before the cohabitation began but was then re-mortgaged and put into the joint names of the original owner and his or her new partner in order to demonstrate a higher joint income to cover an increase in mortgage payments. The subsequent transfer into joint names meant that the property was shared equally 'with no recognition of the partner's prior ownership'. Thirdly, unfairness can arise where one partner provided all or most of the money to purchase a property which was then put into joint names. The research revealed the fact that the property may have been put into joint names for a variety of reasons, such as lack of understanding of the legal position or an unwillingness to consider the possibility of the relationship breaking down. The researchers concluded that these instances of unfairness arise:

> from the mismatch between the result given by adherence to the legal title and the underlying reality of the situation. The ... law as it currently stands may just as unfairly reward

---

[306] *Burns v Burns* [1984] Ch 317. [307] *James v Thomas* [2007] EWCA Civ 1212.

[308] Ibid, [36].

[309] Law Commission, *Cohabitation: The Financial Consequences of Relationship Breakdown* (Law Com No 307, 2007), para 2.13. See R. Tennant, J. Taylor, and J. Lewis, 'Separating from Cohabitation: Making Arrangements for Finances and Parenting', Department for Constitutional Affairs Research Report 7/2006 (London, DCA, 2006); G. Douglas, J. Pearce, and H. Woodward, Cardiff Law School Research Paper No 1, 'A Failure of Trust: Resolving Property Disputes on Cohabitation Breakdown' (2007).

[310] G. Douglas, J. Pearce, and H. Woodward, 'Cohabitants, Property and the Law: A Study of Injustice' (2009) 72(1) Modern Law Review 24 at 34–36.

[311] G. Douglas, J. Pearce, and H. Woodward, Cardiff Law School Research Paper No 1, 'A Failure of Trust: Resolving Property Disputes on Cohabitation Breakdown' (2007); G. Douglas, J. Pearce, and H. Woodward, 'Cohabitants, Property and the Law: A Study of Injustice' (2009) 72(1) Modern Law Review 24.

a party who has done little to deserve their share, as penalise a party who has done much but cannot quantify it in the terms required by the technicalities of the case-law.[312]

Finally, unfairness can arise where one party made a substantial contribution (financial and otherwise) to the relationship and to the home, but this did not result in any or a greater proprietary interest due to lack of evidence regarding the contribution or of the couple's common intention. An example of this is *James v Thomas*.[313]

2.8.1.5 The increase in cohabitation and public support for reform

The rate of unmarried cohabitation has consistently grown since the 1980s. Statistics show that in 2006 around one-quarter (25 per cent) of unmarried men and women between the ages of 16 and 59 were cohabiting.[314] By contrast, in 1986, only 11 per cent of unmarried men and 13 per cent of unmarried women were cohabiting.[315] While the rate of unmarried cohabitation has been on the rise, the number of couples marrying is in decline and figures indicate that in 2007 the marriage rates in England and Wales fell to the lowest level since records began.[316]

Research also shows that public attitudes to unmarried cohabitation are positive and that there is public support for reform. In the 2000 British Social Attitudes Survey, 67 per cent of those surveyed thought that it was acceptable for a couple to live together without intending to get married, and only 27 per cent believed that married couples make better parents than unmarried ones.[317] This has led to the view that, in terms of social attitudes, the 'centrality of the formally married couple has diminished'.[318] Research has also revealed that the majority of people think that the law should treat cohabiting couples the same as married couples when relationships break down, especially where the couple have children.[319]

2.8.2 Arguments against reform

Despite the strength of the case for reform, some arguments have been made against reform:

2.8.2.1 Respecting the choice of cohabitants not to marry or enter into a civil partnership

Some argue that as cohabitants choose not to marry or enter into a civil partnership, this should be respected and thus the law should not impose a regulatory regime to govern their affairs.[320] As Deech argues, 'there ought to be a corner of freedom for such couples to which they can escape and avoid family law'.[321] However, the notion of 'choice' in this context is not as straightforward as it may appear. One party may want

---

[312] G. Douglas, J. Pearce, and H. Woodward, 'Cohabitants, Property and the Law: A Study of Injustice' (2009) 72(1) Modern Law Review 24 at 32.   [313] [2007] EWCA Civ 1212.

[314] National Statistics, Social Trends 2008 (London: Office for National Statistics, 2008), p 21.

[315] Ibid.   [316] See www.guardian.co.uk/news/datablog/2010/feb/11/marriage-rates-uk-data#data.

[317] A. Barlow, S. Duncan, G. James, and A. Park, 'Just a Piece of Paper? Marriage and Cohabitation in Britain' in A. Park, J. Curtice, K. Thomson, L. Jarvis, and C. Bromley (eds), *British Social Attitudes: The 18th Report* (London: Sage, 2001), pp 29–57.

[318] S. Duncan and M. Phillips, 'New Families? Tradition and Change in Modern Relationships' in A. Park et al (eds), *British Social Attitudes: The 24th Report* (London: Sage, 2008), p 25.

[319] A. Barlow, C. Burgoyne, E. Clery, and J. Smithson, 'Cohabitation and the Law: Myths, Money and the Media' in A. Park et al (eds), *British Social Attitudes: The 24th Report* (London: Sage, 2008).

[320] R. Deech, 'The Case against the Legal Recognition of Cohabitation' (1980) 29 International and Comparative Law Quarterly 480.   [321] Ibid, 483.

to formalise the relationship through marriage or civil registration, but the other may not and so it cannot be assumed that the fact that the parties are cohabiting indicates a deliberate mutual choice to avoid relationship regulation. In addition, this argument is complicated by the fact that research has shown that the majority of unmarried cohabitants mistakenly believe that cohabitation for a period of time gives rise, under general law, to the same or similar legal rights as marriage. Known as the 'common law marriage myth',[322] this statistical evidence contradicts the simplistic argument that cohabitants deliberately avoid legal regulation because it shows that a large number of cohabitants falsely believe that such marital-like regulation will, in time, be conferred upon them.

2.8.2.2 Educating cohabitants about their legal position is enough

The government's initial response to the 'common law marriage myth' was to attempt to educate cohabitants regarding their lack of rights and responsibilities and to encourage them to put agreements in place to govern their affairs. A public information campaign called the 'Living Together Campaign' (LTC) was set up to provide advice on the legal rights which cohabitants have. The LTC website also contains downloadable agreements which the parties can use to agree, in advance, the terms of their relationship and outcomes should the relationship break down. However, researchers discovered that by the end of the research project, very few individuals had actually taken these steps. There were a diverse range of reasons for this inaction, including situations when one partner to the relationship would not agree to action being taken or 'optimism bias' where the parties did not feel that they had to consider eventualities such as death or relationship breakdown.[323] Thus, this study shows that even cohabitants who are aware of their legal position do not tend to take immediate action to protect themselves which undermines the argument that merely educating cohabitants about their rights and duties under the current law is a sufficient response to the inadequacies of this law.

2.8.2.3 The lack of commitment in cohabiting relationships

Allied with the argument that cohabitants make a deliberate and mutual decision to avoid legal regulation, those who oppose giving greater legal rights to unmarried couples often point to statistical evidence which shows that cohabiting relationships tend to break down more often than marriage.[324] It is argued that as cohabitants do not display the same level of mutual commitment as spouses, they do not deserve the same level of family law regulation. However, it is too simplistic to make the argument that cohabiting couples lack commitment and consequently should be denied greater legal protection when the relationship breaks down. Indeed, research has shown that different levels of commitment can be found in the broad continuum of cohabiting relationships from the 'mutually committed' where the parties consider their relationship to be akin to marriage, to the more 'contingently committed' where parties do not presume that the

---

[322] In the 2008 British Social Attitudes Report, 53 per cent of unmarried cohabitants falsely believed that common law marriage exists, A. Barlow, C. Burgoyne, E. Clery, and J. Smithson, 'Cohabitation and the Law: Myths, Money and the Media' in A. Park et al (eds), British Social Attitudes: The 24th Report (London: Sage, 2008), pp 40–42.

[323] A. Barlow, C. Burgoyne, and J. Smithson, The Living Together Campaign—An Investigation of its Impact on Legally Aware Cohabitants (London: Ministry of Justice, 2007), pp 33–36.

[324] Law Commission, Cohabitation: The Financial Consequences of Relationship Breakdown, A Consultation Paper (Law Com No 179, 2006), para 2.36, fn 67.

relationship will endure.[325] In a recent research study, the relationships of unmarried cohabitants fell into four categories identified by the researchers:[326]

- *the ideologues*: cohabitants within this category were in long-term and committed relationships, but one or both partners had an ideological objection to marriage;
- *the romantics*: couples within this group saw marriage as a very serious commitment and while they expected to get married eventually, they viewed their cohabitation as a step towards this;
- *the pragmatists*: couples within this group were also mutually committed to the relationship but made decisions about whether to marry on legal or financial grounds;
- *the uneven couples*: couples within this group did not hold mutually compatible views about their relationship. One may have wanted to marry but the other partner did not, or one was more committed to the relationship than the other.

This research shows that cohabitants do not form a homogenous group upon which generalised assumptions can be made about their level of mutual commitment or their views on the desirability of legal regulation.

Furthermore, it is misleading to draw bright-line distinctions between the commitment involved in married and unmarried relationships when research shows that different levels of commitment and interdependencies can also be found in marriage.[327] It is also worth pointing out the irony involved in these arguments which focus on the more durable nature of marriage over unmarried relationships and thus to the different levels of commitment as a justification for privileging marriage. The statutory regime which gives the court the power to re-adjust the parties' property and finances on divorce/dissolution does not apply whilst the parties are still married or in a civil partnership. These redistributive powers are *only* available when the marriage or civil partnership has come to an end and when the parties' commitment has been breached either by mutual consent or the will of one spouse. This somewhat undermines the centralisation of marital commitment when justifying the distinction between married and unmarried relationships.

The relevance of the nature of the parties' commitment to the relationship must also be questioned, alongside consideration of the purpose of the law. If it is accepted that one important function of family law is to protect vulnerable family members, then it would seem that, regardless of the parties' commitment to the relationship, a regulatory regime is required to address the economic fall-out associated with the breakdown of a cohabiting relationship where one partner (and the children) may be left in a weak economic position as a result of the relationship. As Barlow observes:

> Arguably, those who are more likely to separate are in greater need of family law regulation to protect not only the weaker economic partner but more importantly the children of the relationship who are currently impoverished when their parents' relationship breaks down to a far greater extent than children of divorced parents.[328]

---

[325] C. Smart and P. Stevens, *Cohabitation Breakdown* (London: FPSC/Rowntree, 2000). See also G. Douglas, J. Pearce, and H. Woodward, Cardiff Law School Research Paper No 1, 'A Failure of Trust: Resolving Property Disputes on Cohabitation Breakdown' (2007), para 4.4.

[326] A. Barlow and J. Smithson, 'Legal Assumptions, Cohabitants Talk and the Rocky Road to Reform' [2010] Child and Family Law Quarterly 328.

[327] J. Eekelaar and M. Maclean, 'Marriage and the Moral Bases of Personal Relationships' (2004) 31(4) Journal of Law and Society 510; A. Barlow, S. Duncan, G. James, and A. Park, *Cohabitation, Marriage and the Law: Social Change and Legal Reform in the 21st Century* (Oxford: Hart, 2005).

[328] A. Barlow, 'Cohabitation Law Reform—Messages from Research' (2006) 14 Feminist Legal Studies 167 at 172.

2.8.2.4 The fear of undermining marriage

There is a fear that extending the legal protection afforded to unmarried cohabitants would undermine marriage. This fear certainly impacts upon the political will to introduce legislation in this area as politicians are cautious about appearing to undermine this important social institution. However, research has shown that in countries where cohabiting couples have been given greater recognition and protection in law, there has been no negative impact on the marriage rates.[329] Furthermore, one could also ask why it is necessary to maintain the current law for unmarried cohabitants in order to support the institution of marriage. Indeed, the Law Commission has said that:

> the objective of promoting marriage does not require us to deny any remedy to individuals experiencing financial hardship at the end of a cohabiting relationship. The institution of marriage, and individual marriages, can be supported without perpetuating the hardship experience by such individuals.[330]

Further, given the stark contrast between the two regimes in terms of providing financial relief on separation, unmarried cohabitation may be the preferred choice for the wealthier party in a relationship who wishes to protect his or her assets.[331] Maintaining the current law for unmarried cohabitants could therefore 'create a disincentive for one partner to marry'.[332]

2.8.3 Reform initiatives

Whether and how to replace trust law principles with a flexible family law regime to resolve the financial and property disputes between cohabitants on relationship breakdown is not a new question facing policy-makers.

Talking point

In 1995 Charles Harpum, then Law Commissioner for England and Wales, wrote:

> the law which regulates the rights and obligations of those who, in many disparate relationships (whether sexual or otherwise), share a home together but are not married is acknowledged to be thoroughly unsatisfactory by lawyers and non-lawyers alike… Homesharers are not denizens of some black hole of outlawry. Is it better for the law that regulates their affairs to be developed by legislation after an exhaustive consideration of the issues or should it continue to be left to the chances of litigation?[333]

Recommendations for reform have been made a number of times.

[329] K. Kiernan, A. Barlow, and R. Merlo, 'Cohabitation Law Reform and its Impact on Marriage: Evidence from Australia and Europe' (2007) 63 International Family Law 71.

[330] Law Commission, *Cohabitation: The Financial Consequences of Relationship Breakdown, A Consultation Paper* (Law Com No 179, 2006), para 5.34; Law Commission, *Cohabitation: The Financial Consequences of Relationship Breakdown* (Law Com No 307, 2007), paras 2.36–2.45.

[331] Law Commission, *Cohabitation: The Financial Consequences of Relationship Breakdown, A Consultation Paper* (Law Com No 179, 2006), para 5.19, which cited B. Hale, 'Unmarried Couples and Family Law' (2004) 34 Family Law 419 at 422; A. Barlow, S. Duncan, G. James, and A. Park, *Cohabitation, Marriage and the Law: Social Change and Legal Reform in the 21st Century* (Oxford: Hart, 2005), p 109.

[332] Law Commission, *Cohabitation: The Financial Consequences of Relationship Breakdown, A Consultation Paper* (Law Com No 179, 2006), para 5.19.

[333] C. Harpum, 'Cohabitation Consultation' [1995] 25 Family Law 657.

2.8.3.1 The Law Society (2002)

The Law Society reviewed the legal position of cohabitants in 2002 and produced recommendations for reform.[334] It drew attention to the fact that opt-in schemes where couples have to register their relationship formally in order to acquire legal protection do 'not provide for parties in long-term relationships where one party refuses to marry or register the relationship and, as a result, the other party has no financial rights on relationship breakdown'. In light of this, it recommended that cohabitants who had lived together for a continuous period of at least two years or who had a child together would be eligible to apply for financial relief on relationship breakdown.[335] The core objective of the proposals was to protect economically vulnerable cohabitants, especially those who may 'suffer financial disadvantage as a result of having shared their home, income and the upbringing of any children with another person'.[336] While the Society sought to improve the legal position of cohabitants on relationship breakdown, it did not seek to achieve the practical or symbolic assimilation of marriage and cohabitation. In terms of capital provision on separation, the Society recommended a less extensive and operationally distinct system from the financial provision system which applies on divorce.

The Society proposed that the court would have the power to make property adjustment orders and lump sum orders between eligible cohabitants on relationship breakdown. Each claim would be assessed according to the principle that fair account should be taken of any economic advantage derived by either party from contributions by the other, and of any economic disadvantages suffered by either party in the interests of the other or of the family. 'Contributions' included domestic labour such as maintaining or running the home or the family. The Society recommended that cohabitants would only be allowed to apply for maintenance for limited periods and only to provide resources to facilitate the recipient's retraining or to reflect capital payments which could not be made by way of a lump sum. As well as recommending financial relief between separating cohabitants, the proposals also included the conferral of rights for eligible cohabitants in other areas of law such as succession, tax, immigration, transfer of tenancies, and occupation of the home. The Society recommended that the current law relating to property disputes should continue to apply to cohabitants who were not eligible to apply under the scheme (ie, cohabitants who had lived together for less than two years and had no relevant children). These proposals were not acted upon but in the same year that they were published, the Law Commission published a much anticipated Discussion Paper on the property rights of home-sharers.

2.8.3.2 The Law Commission (2002)

The Law Commission embarked on a review of the property rights of home-sharers in 1994 and despite the intention to produce a consultation paper in 1996, it was not until July 2002 that a Discussion Paper was published.[337] This paper examined the property rights of those who shared a home, and included not only unmarried cohabitants but also 'friends, relatives and others who may be living together for reasons of companionship or care and

---

[334] Law Society, *Cohabitation: The Case for Clear Law. Proposals for Reform* (London: Representation and Law Reform Directorate, 2002).

[335] The report also recommended civil registration for same-sex couples which has now been enacted in the Civil Partnership Act 2004.

[336] Law Society, *Cohabitation: the Case for Clear Law. Proposals for Reform* (London: Representation and Law Reform Directorate, 2002), para 12.

[337] Law Commission, *Sharing Homes: A Discussion Paper* (Law Com No 278, 2002).

support'.[338] The paper cited the well-known criticisms of the law in this area including the myth of searching for the parties' common intention and the confusion in case law about the types of contribution from which a common intention will be inferred. The Commission concluded that:

> The current requirements for establishing the existence of an interest under a trust are not ideally suited to the typical informality of those sharing a home. We feel that to demand proof of an intention to share the beneficial interest in the home can be somewhat unrealistic, as people do not tend to think about their home in such legalistic terms. The emphasis on financial input towards the acquisition of the home fails to recognise the realities of most cohabiting relationships. Finally, and importantly, the uncertainties in the present law can cause lengthy and costly litigation, wasting court time, public funding and the parties' own resources.[339]

The Commission then laid out a property-based model for reform under which home-sharers would acquire a proprietary interest in the home, behind a statutory trust, based on a range of contributions (both financial and non-financial) to the shared home. However, in the end the Commission did not recommend this proposal for the determination of shares in the home because it was not convinced that it could 'operate fairly and evenly across the diverse circumstances which are now to be encountered'.[340]

Ultimately the broad remit of the project which looked at the rights of home-sharers in the shared home, as opposed to just unmarried cohabitants, contributed to the defeat of the Commission as the Discussion Paper merely suggested the need for a relationship-based solution to the problem but did not offer any concrete proposals.

2.8.3.3 The Law Commission (2007)

By 2005, however, the legal position of unmarried cohabitants was on the political agenda and the Law Commission was tasked by the Department for Constitutional Affairs to conduct a review of cohabitation law and, in particular, the financial hardship suffered by cohabitants or their children on the termination of their relationship by breakdown or death. The impetus for this policy review came from the enactment of the Civil Partnership Act 2004. During the passage of this legislation through Parliament, concerns were raised about the legal position of unmarried/unregistered relationships and, in particular, the economic hardship suffered by cohabitants 'owing to the current lack of any coherent legal remedies addressing their financial and property disputes' on relationship breakdown.[341] It seems that the refusal to allow unmarried opposite-sex couples to register their relationship under the newly enacted civil partnerships scheme created the impression that same-sex couples were being given preferential treatment.[342] Thus, it became politically important to be seen to take steps to remedy the difficulties faced by unmarried opposite-sex couples on the termination of their relationships.

---

[338] Ibid., Executive Summary, para 1.

[339] Ibid, para 2.11.

[340] Ibid, Executive Summary, para 15.

[341] Law Commission, *Cohabitation: The Financial Consequences of Relationship Breakdown* (Law Com No 307, 2007), para 1.18.

[342] See L. Glennon, 'Obligations Between Adult Partners: Moving from Form to Function?' (2008) 22(1) International Journal of Law, Policy and the Family 22.

The Law Commission published a Consultation Paper in 2006[343] and its final report which contained recommendations for reform was published in 2007.[344] Once again, the Commission was critical of the current law and concluded that:

> The general law … is not equipped to provide a comprehensive solution to problems arising on separation, responding to the economic consequences of the parties' contributions to their relationship. Moreover, since it is limited to addressing the beneficial ownership of individual assets, the general law of property and trusts offers very little remedial flexibility.[345]

Given the inadequacy of the current law which was described as complex, uncertain, expensive to rely on, and not designed for family circumstances,[346] the Law Commission recommended that the courts be given powers to adjust the parties' property rights on relationship breakdown in order to minimise the economic detriment one party may suffer as a result of a cohabiting relationship.

Under the proposals, financial relief upon separation would be available to eligible cohabitants who had not disapplied the statutory scheme[347] and who had made 'qualifying contributions to the relationship giving rise to certain enduring consequences at the point of separation'.[348] To be eligible to apply, cohabitants must have had a child together or have lived together for a specified number of years. The Commission recommended that the requisite period should be set by statute but suggested a period of between two and five years. Under the proposals, being eligible to apply for financial relief would not be enough to obtain an award. In order to obtain a remedy, applicants would have to prove that they had made *qualifying contributions* to the relationship which gave rise to a *retained benefit* in the hands of the respondent, or to their *economic disadvantage*. By contrast to the limited types of contributions which are recognised under the law of trusts, a qualifying contribution, for the purposes of the proposed statutory scheme, was defined as any financial or non-financial contribution which was made to the parties' shared life or to the welfare of members of their families. The scheme did not try to quantify, in financial terms, the value of these contributions to the family, but instead considered the lasting economic impact of these contributions on the parties.

Under the proposals, the court could grant financial relief to reverse any *retained benefit* which the respondent had acquired as a result of the relationship. This could take the form of capital, income, or earning capacity that had been acquired, retained, or enhanced. The court could also grant financial relief to share the *economic disadvantage* suffered by the applicant. An economic disadvantage is a present or future loss and could include a diminution in current savings as a result of expenditure or of earnings lost during the relationship, lost future earnings, or the future cost of paid childcare. Such economic disadvantage could arise, for example, where one party gave up work or worked part time in order to look after the family. However, the economic disadvantage claimed must be 'susceptible to proof of an actual loss on the balance of probabilities' and the applicant would also be under a duty to mitigate this loss.[349] It is important to note that,

---

[343] Law Commission, *Cohabitation: The Financial Consequences of Relationship Breakdown, A Consultation Paper* (Law Com No 179, 2006).

[344] Law Commission, *Cohabitation: The Financial Consequences of Relationship Breakdown* (Law Com No 307, 2007).   [345] Ibid, para 2.16.

[346] Ibid, Executive Summary, para 1.4.   [347] Ibid, para 2.94.

[348] Ibid, Executive Summary, para 1.13.

[349] Ibid, para 4.62. The Law Commission make it clear that an applicant who is claiming on the basis of incurred economic disadvantage is expected to mitigate their loss by making the best of their existing

under the proposals, there must be a causal link between the contributions made by the applicant and the alleged benefit retained by the respondent or disadvantage suffered by the applicant.[350]

In granting financial relief, the court could make lump sums, property transfers, property settlements, orders for sale, and pension sharing orders. Awards under the scheme would be made on a clean break basis and, unlike the position on divorce and dissolution of a civil partnership, periodical payments would not generally be available. The Commission envisaged that the only situation where such payments could be made would be to meet the continuing childcare costs incurred by the applicant to enable him or her to take up employment. In deciding what order to make in order to reverse the retained benefit held by the respondent, or share the economic disadvantage suffered by the applicant, the court would have regard to the following list of 'discretionary factors', first consideration being given to the welfare of any child of both parties who had not attained the age of 18:

- the financial needs and obligations of both parties;
- the extent and nature of the financial resources which each party has or is likely to have in the foreseeable future;
- the welfare of any children who live with, or might reasonably be expected to live with, either party; and
- the conduct of each party (defined restrictively) but to include cases where a qualifying contribution was made despite the express disagreement of the other party.

While there is a discretionary element to this proposed scheme, it is very different to the discretionary-based financial provision system which applies to divorcing spouses or civil partners who are dissolving their partnership. The Commission rejected the extension of this system to cohabitants because:

> cohabitants have not given each other the legal commitment, or accepted the status, of marriage or civil partnership. We therefore believe that it is necessary to find a middle ground between, on the one hand, the law that currently applies to cohabitants and, on the other, the law that applies to spouses and civil partners on their separation.[351]

Thus, the objective of the proposed scheme for cohabitants was not to distribute the fruits of the parties' joint life together nor to meet the financial needs of the applicant (unless they were caused by their contributions to the relationship). Instead, the objective of the scheme was to allow the court to make an order to ensure that the 'pluses and minuses of the relationship' were fairly shared between the couple.[352]

The Commission also attempted to find a balance between ensuring that the contributions and sacrifices made in an intimate relationship are fairly distributed between the parties on separation, whilst taking account of the 'importance of preserving individuals' freedom to conduct their private relationships on their own terms'.[353] Thus, to respect the autonomy of couples who wish to define the terms of their relationships themselves, the Commission recommended that couples should be allowed to opt-out of the statutory scheme leaving them free to make their own arrangements. To be valid, such an agreement would have to be in writing and signed by both parties. While the court would have

---

resources and minimising their disadvantage as far as possible, ibid., para 4.63.

[350] Ibid, para 4.43. [351] Ibid, para 4.2. [352] Ibid, Executive Summary, para 1.19.
[353] Ibid, para 2.93.

the power to set such agreements aside, the Commission said that this should only be done if their enforcement would give rise to manifest unfairness.

However, in March 2008, the Justice Minister announced that 'for the time being' no further action would be taken in relation to the Law Commission's proposals. The decision on their implementation was postponed pending research into the cost and efficacy of provisions in Scotland (under the Family Law (Scotland) Act 2006) which gave rights to cohabitants similar to those proposed by the Law Commission.[354]

2.8.3.4 The Cohabitation Bill (2008)

In response to this impasse, Lord Lester of Herne Hill (backed by Resolution which is an association of family lawyers) introduced a Private Member's Bill in the House of Lords on the rights of unmarried cohabitants. The Cohabitation Bill was introduced to the House of Lords on 11 December 2008 and had its second reading in March 2009. During its second reading, both the Government spokesperson and the Opposition spokesperson indicated that they did not support the Bill.

The Bill sought to establish a legal framework for financial provision on separation for unmarried and unregistered cohabitants.[355] Eligible cohabitants could apply for a financial settlement order on separation. To be eligible, cohabitants must have lived together as a couple for at least two years or have had a child together. The Bill provided that the court could make a financial settlement order on the parties' separation if, having regard to all the circumstances, the court considers that it is just and equitable to do so. The court could make the full range of orders that are available in the context of financial relief—that is: lump sum orders; periodic payments; transfer of property orders; property settlements; sale of property orders; and pension sharing orders. In determining an application, the Bill provided a range of matters to which the court to have regard, including:

- the welfare of any child (this is the first consideration);
- the nature of the commitment between the parties (including the degree of dependency or interdependency) and the duration of the relationship;
- the contributions each party has made to the relationship in financial terms or by caring for the relevant children or looking after the home;
- any economic advantage retained by either party as a result of the relationship;
- any economic disadvantage suffered by either party as a result of the relationship;
- the income, property, and resources of each party;
- the financial needs and obligations of the parties;
- the scope of each partner to obtain paid work, taking into account the cost of any childcare required to facilitate the primary caregiver's employment;
- any written agreement indicating the couple's intentions.

As with the Law Commission's proposals, there are some significant differences between this proposed system and the financial provision system which applies to divorcing spouses and civil partners who are dissolving their partnership. As Probert indicates, under the Cohabitation Bill the 'degree of commitment within the relationship is to be tested rather

---

[354] Hansard, HC 6 March 2008, vol 472, col 123WS.

[355] For a comparison between the recommendations of the Law Commission and the provisions of Lord Lester's Cohabitation Bill see E. Hess, 'The Rights of Cohabitants: When and How Will the Law be Reformed' [2009] Family Law 405.

than assumed'.[356] In addition, the court's discretion under the Cohabitation Bill was limited by several underlying principles. First, there was no presumption that the parties should share equally in the property belonging to either or both of them. Secondly, the Bill provided that both parties should be self-supporting as soon as reasonably practicable. Finally, any award should not exceed the applicant's reasonable needs. While it would be possible for the court to make periodical payments in favour of an applicant, the maximum period for such payments would generally be three years unless a longer period was necessary to avoid the recipient's exceptional hardship caused by the cohabitation or to meet the costs of childcare to enable the primary carer to maintain gainful employment.

While this was a useful attempt to fill the void left by the Government's decision to delay progress on reform, the Bill was not without its problems. In particular, it is unclear exactly what a financial settlement order would be designed to achieve. As Probert points out, while equalising the economic impact of the relationship between the parties was the clear objective of the Law Commission's proposals, the economic advantages and disadvantages which flow from the cohabitation are just factors to be considered within Lord Lester's Cohabitation Bill. Probert wonders how the scheme would apply in different contexts. For example, take the situation where one party contributes to the purchase price of the property which is registered in the sole name of the other. Under property law principles (which currently apply), the contributor would be entitled to a share under a trust. The Law Commission's scheme would also have generated a remedy because this contribution would constitute a retained benefit in the hands of the respondent which the court would have to reverse. But under Lord Lester's Cohabitation Bill this was just one factor to be taken into account. Probert asks: 'given the principle that the award should not exceed the reasonable needs of the applicant, does this mean that contributions made by a self-supporting cohabitant will simply be disregarded?'[357] Given the Bill's lack of focus, it is unclear how its provisions would work in practice.

It is clear, however, that reform is necessary. What is also clear is that the financial provision system which governs financial provision on divorce and dissolution of civil partnerships is not without its problems as the courts continue to grapple with emerging new principles in the application of their broad discretion.[358] One useful approach for reform may be to combine these debates at the level of policy. In a parliamentary debate, Lord Goodhart suggested such an approach when he said:

> as the rights of cohabitees are necessarily linked at least indirectly to those of married couples and civil partners, would it not be a good idea to include in the Law Commission's review the rights arising on the dissolution of a marriage or civil partnership?[359]

Thus, it has been argued that the debates on married and unmarried couples should be considered as integrated policy issues as they raise similar questions concerning obligations within domestic relationships of varying duration and circumstance.[360] However, it is worth noting that all the policy considerations of the legal position of unmarried cohabitants have deliberately sought to distance their proposals from the financial provision system which applies on divorce and dissolution of civl partnerships in order to maintain the practical and ideological superiority of marriage (and now civil partnerships). Indeed, given the political imperative of being seen not to undermine marriage, it is likely that the economic consequences of married and unmarried relationships will continue to be seen as separate policy issues. In the context of cohabitation law, it seems

---

[356] R. Probert, 'The Cohabitation Bill' [2009] Family Law 150.   [357] Ibid.   [358] See Chapter 4.
[359] See Hansard, Lords Debates 6 June 2006, vol 682, col 1136, *per* Lord Goodhart.
[360] L. Glennon, 'Obligations Between Adult Partners: Moving from Form to Function?' (2008) 22(1) International Journal of Law, Policy and the Family 22.

that the objective of any reforming law will be to provide the 'basic protections'[361] or a 'safety net, no more and no less' to avoid unfairness on the termination of long-term cohabiting partnerships, particularly those involving children.[362] At the very least, however, this would be an improvement to the current outcomes generated by the ill-suited law of implied trusts.

DISCUSSION QUESTIONS

1. A cohabitant seeking a share of a beneficial interest in a property where they are not a legal owner is subject to the law of trusts. Explain what such a cohabitant would have to prove to claim a share of the property.

2. The law of trusts is ill-suited to resolving the property disputes of unmarried cohabitants on relationship breakdown. Giving reasons for your answer, discuss the extent to which you agree with this statement.

3. A cohabitant may not wish to marry or enter a civil partnership for a range of different reasons. Should the law of cohabitation be reformed at all?

FURTHER READING

BARLOW, A. and JAMES, G., 'Regulating Marriage and Cohabitation in 21st Century Britain' (2004) 67(2) Modern Law Review 143

BARLOW, A. and SMITHSON, J., 'Legal Assumptions, Cohabitants' Talk and the Rocky Road to Reform' [2010] Child and Family Law Quarterly 328

BARLOW, A., BURGOYNE, C., CLERY, E., and SMITHSON, J., 'Cohabitation and the Law: Myths, Money and the Media' in A. Park et al (eds), *British Social Attitudes: The 24th Report* (London: Sage, 2008)

BATTERSBY, G., 'Ownership of the Family Home: *Stack v Dowden* in the House of Lords' [2008] Child and Family Law Quarterly 255

DOUGLAS, G., PEARCE, J., and WOODWARD, H., Cardiff Law School Research Paper No 1, 'A Failure of Trust: Resolving Property Disputes on Cohabitation Breakdown' (2007)

GARDNER, S., 'Rethinking Family Property' (1993) 109 Law Quarterly Review 263

GARDNER, S. and DAVIDSON, K., 'The Future of *Stack v Dowden*' (2011) 127 Law Quarterly Review 13

GLOVER N. and TODD, P., 'The Myth of Common Intention' (1996) Legal Studies 325

PROBERT, R., 'The Cohabitation Bill' [2009] Family Law 150

---

[361] The Cohabitation Bill 2008, cl 1.
[362] See Hansard, Lords Debates 6 June 2006, vol 682, col 1137, per Baroness Ashton of Upholland (Parliamentary Under-Secretary, Department for Constitutional Affairs).

PART 2
CHILD FAMILY LAW

6

FINANCIAL SUPPORT FOR CHILDREN

INTRODUCTION

When a child's parents are separated, an issue frequently arises as to the appropriate financial support which should be provided for the child by the parent with whom the child is not living (the non-resident parent). This issue is regulated by one or more of several statutes depending on the circumstances: the Child Support Act 1991 (CSA 1991), as amended; Schedule 1 to the Children Act 1989; the Matrimonial Causes Act 1973; and the Civil Partnership Act 2004. The applicability of the CSA 1991 in a particular case can limit to some extent the use of the other statutes mentioned, so it is convenient to begin our explanation of this area of law[1] with an account of the CSA 1991 and its background.

1 THE CHILD SUPPORT ACT 1991: BACKGROUND AND RECENT REFORMS

1.1 BIRTH OF THE CHILD SUPPORT ACT

Prior to 5 April 1993, the date on which the CSA 1991 came into force, parental disputes about child support were dealt with by the courts. While in theory this had the benefit of a judge's careful consideration of the individual circumstances of each case, it had proved problematic in practice: the amounts of court-ordered maintenance tended to be small and poorly enforced.

Talking point

There was a natural tendency for lawyers, acting in the interests of their clients, to try to maximise the availability of welfare benefits on family breakdown.[2] The impact of this on the public purse became more visible with increasing numbers of lone-parent families on welfare benefits, in part as a result of the increase in divorce following the Divorce Reform Act 1969. A change of approach was instigated by Prime Minister Margaret Thatcher, who thought it 'scandalous that only one in three children entitled to receive maintenance actually benefited from regular

---

[1] This chapter provides an overview of the most important features. For detailed scholarly discussion of theory, law, and policy, see N. Wikeley, *Child Support Law and Policy* (Oxford: Hart, 2006).

[2] And see *Delaney v Delaney* [1990] 2 FLR 457.

payments'.[3] Thatcher's intervention led to the passing of the CSA 1991,[4] which sought to address the problems by establishing an administrative process for the assessment, collection, and enforcement of child maintenance. A body called the Child Support Agency was set up to carry out these functions, under the control of a Secretary of State.

In the case of parents who were on certain welfare benefits, the Act placed a duty on parents to authorise the Secretary of State to assess and collect child maintenance.

The Act aligned well with an increasing sensitivity to children's rights[5] and the idea of parental responsibility[6] and, as an initiative which both helped children and saved public money, commanded broad political appeal. Furthermore, the adoption of an administrative scheme could draw support from similar initiatives in other jurisdictions, notably the USA and Australia.[7]

1.2 PROBLEMS

From the outset, however, there was dissatisfaction with some of the detail of the implementation of the new policy.[8] The task of formulating how child support was to be calculated fell, with advice from the Treasury, to the Department of Social Security (DSS). This resulted in a complex, social security-style, mathematical formula for calculating child support maintenance. The formula was quite unlike the model in Australia, where child support was calculated by reference to a simple percentage of a parent's income in the previous year, ascertained from income tax records.[9] It produced in some cases what appeared to be disproportionately high assessments and there was little flexibility to accommodate exceptional circumstances. For example, little thought was given to the Act's impact on clean break financial settlements upon divorce prior to the Act.[10]

---

[3] M. Thatcher, *The Downing Street Years* (London: Harper Collins, 1995), p 630, quoted in S. Cretney, *Family Law in the Twentieth Century: A History* (Oxford: Oxford University Press, 2003), p 475. Thatcher's 'interest drove the project forward at a breath-taking pace': see M. Maclean with J. Kurczewski, *Making Family Law* (Oxford: Hart, 2011), p 45. The recommendations of an Interdepartmental Working Group led straight to a White Paper, DSS, *Children Come First: The Government's Proposals on the Maintenance of Children* (Cm 1263, 1990), omitting the usual public consultation by way of a Green Paper. Cf A. Garnham and E. Knights, *Putting the Treasury First* (London: Child Poverty Action Group, 1994), pp 84–92.

[4] For a look behind the scenes of the making of this legislation, see 'Prime Ministerial Intervention: The Child Support Act 1991' in M. Maclean with J. Kurczewski, *Making Family Law* (Oxford: Hart, 2011). The scheme had many of the hallmarks of Thatcherism: the 'natural' family as a site of social control and as a defence of freedom for the individual: see M. Maclean and J. Eekelaar, 'Child Support: The British Solution' (1993) 7 International Journal of Law and the Family 205.

[5] As illustrated by the *Gillick* case in 1986, see ch 8. See J. Eekelaar, 'Families and Children: From Welfarism to Rights' in J. C. McCrudden and G. Chambers (eds), *Individual Rights and the Law in Britain* (Oxford, Oxford University Press, 1994).   [6] In, eg, the then recently enacted Children Act 1989.

[7] M. Maclean, 'The Making of the Child Support Act: Policy Making at the Intersection of Law and Social Policy' (1994) 21(4) Journal of Law and Society 505.

[8] See R. Collier, 'The Campaign Against the Child Support Act, Errant Fathers and Family Men' [1994] Family Law 384. See also C. Glendinning, K. Clarke, and G. Craig, 'Implementing the Child Support Act'(1996) 18(3) Journal of Social Welfare and Family Law 273–289; G. Gillespie 'Child Support—The Hand that Rocks the Cradle' [1996] Family Law 162.

[9] Such records were then not available in this jurisdiction. For comparison of developments in Australia and the UK since the late 1980s, see B. Fehlberg and M. Maclean 'Child Support Policy in Australia and the United Kingdom: Changing Priorities But A Similar Tough Deal for Children?' (2009) 23(1) International Journal of Law, Policy and the Family 1–24.

[10] Eg a father might transfer his whole interest in the matrimonial home to his former wife in return for not having to make periodical payments to her and their children. See eg *Crozier v Crozier* [1994] 1 FLR 126.

There were also concerns about the Act's emphasis on legal parenthood,[11] and its failure to take sufficient account of the duties of social parenthood which some parents also had within newly constituted families. There was some evidence that the Act was 'failing to improve the financial situation of children', and that it was perceived (at least by some parents) as 'coercive and intrusive', and as providing little incentive to cooperate with the Child Support Agency.[12] Not surprisingly given the dissatisfaction, from its inception the Child Support Agency encountered difficulties enforcing and collecting child support maintenance.[13]

1.3 RESPONDING TO CRITICISM

The Government responded to sustained criticism by enacting the Child Support Act 1995,[14] which introduced greater flexibility, with departures from the formula in prescribed circumstances ('departure directions', now known as 'variations').[15] However, problems with collection and enforcement persisted and further amendments were made. Part I of the Child Support, Pensions and Social Security Act 2000[16] strengthened the powers available to the Secretary of State to enforce payment of child support and introduced a new scheme for calculating child support maintenance. The calculation of child support was simplified so that in most cases the amount payable was a percentage of a non-resident parent's net income, depending on the number of dependent children (15 per cent for one child, 20 per cent for two children, and 25 per cent for three or more). Allowance for the cost of bringing up other 'relevant children' in the parent's household (eg a stepchild) was also introduced. Overall, however, the complexity of the system had increased because there were now two schemes running in parallel.

1.4 LOSS OF CONFIDENCE AND A REVIEW OF THE SYSTEM

Despite all these attempts to improve the system, by 2006 public confidence in the Child Support Agency had reached such a low that the then Prime Minister, Tony Blair, asked Sir David Henshaw to undertake a thoroughgoing review. Henshaw reported[17] that the Child Support Agency was not fit for purpose and that there were such negative

---

[11] For a critical examination of how the CSA 1991 constructed 'family', see A. Diduck, 'The Unmodified Family: The Child Support Act and the Construction of Legal Subjects' (1995) 22(4) Journal of Law and Society 527.

[12] D. Abbott, 'The Child Support Act 1991: The Lives of Parents With Care Living in Liverpool' (1996) 18(1) Journal of Social Welfare and Family Law 21.

[13] G. Davis, N. Wikeley, R. Young et al, *Child Support in Action* (Oxford: Hart, 1998).

[14] Preceded by a White Paper, *Improving Child Support* (Cm 2745, 1995). For criticism, see A. Horton, 'Improving Child Support—A Missed Opportunity' [1995] Child and Family Law Quarterly 26.

[15] CSA 1991 s 28F and Sch 4B, Pt 1. There was also a change of terminology, from 'absent parent' which was perceived by some as offensive, to 'non-resident parent': see J. Wallbank, 'The Campaign for Change of the Child Support Act 1991: Reconstructing the "Absent Father"' (1997) 6 Social and Legal Studies 191.

[16] Preceded by a Green Paper in July 1998, *Children First: A New Approach to Child Support* (Cm 3992, 1998) (see C. Barton 'Third Time Lucky for Child Support?—The 1998 Green Paper' [1998] Family Law 668; N. Mostyn, 'The Green Paper on Child Support' [1999] Family Law 95), and a White Paper, *A New Contract for Welfare: Children's Rights and Parents' Responsibilities* (Cm 4349, 1999), on which see C. Barton, 'Child Support—Tony's Turn' [1999] Family Law 704. See also J. Pirrie, 'The Child Support, Pensions and Social Security Bill' [1999] Family Law 199.

[17] Sir David Henshaw's Report to the Secretary of State for Work and Pensions, *Recovering Child Support: Routes to Responsibility* (Cm 6894, July 2006).

perceptions of it that it should be replaced by a completely new body, now called the Child Maintenance and Enforcement Commission (C-MEC), with increased powers of enforcement. He also recommended further amendments to the CSA 1991, which were adopted by the Government[18] and enacted in the Child Maintenance and Other Payments Act 2008.[19] The 2008 Act has recently been amended by the Welfare Reform Act 2012.[20]

Perhaps the most significant change effected by the 2008 Act is that parents on welfare benefits are no longer compelled to pursue child maintenance through C-MEC. The new policy is to encourage all parents, whether on welfare benefits or not, to make their own arrangements for child support and only to invoke the assistance of C-MEC where agreement cannot be reached. Indeed, this policy has been underlined further by section 136 of the Welfare Reform Act 2012, which inserts a new provision into the CSA 1991,[21] providing that C-MEC 'may take such steps as it considers appropriate to encourage the making and keeping of maintenance agreements' and, before accepting an application to it, may 'invite the applicant to consider with the Commission whether it is possible to make such an agreement'.[22] Thus the new legislation represents an attempt to effect a significant shift towards private ordering of child maintenance. In addition, the 2008 Act introduced another formula for calculating child maintenance, this time based on percentages of historic gross income (as opposed to current net income under the 2000 Act's changes). Thus there are potentially now three possible schemes in place depending on when calculation of maintenance was requested, although the aim is that eventually all cases will be dealt with under the 2008 Act's scheme.

At the time of writing, many of the provisions of the Child Maintenance and Other Payments Act 2008 have yet to be brought into force, and this chapter faces the difficulty of an area of law which is in transition, and of seeking to anticipate when the 2008 Act's scheme will be implemented. The C-MEC indicates that the new gross income scheme will be established some time in 2012, with Child Support Agency clients on both the existing schemes then being actively supported either to apply to the new scheme or to make a family-based arrangement.[23] It is envisaged that by around 2015 a single system of child maintenance will be in place.[24] For those reasons, and to avoid an overcomplex exposition, this chapter discusses the scheme as implemented by the 2008 Act.

---

[18] Department for Work and Pensions, *A New System of Child Maintenance* (Cm 6979, December 2006).

[19] For an account of the principal changes effected by the 2008 Act and the role of the new Commission, see N. Wikeley, 'Child Support: the Brave New World' [2008] Family Law 1024 and 'Child Support: Carrots and Sticks' [2008] Family Law 1102.

[20] See ss 136–142. For policy debate surrounding the proposed reforms of the Welfare Reform Bill that led to the 2012 Act, see DWP, *Strengthening Families, Promoting Parental Responsibility: The Future of Child Maintenance* (Cm 7990, 2011), available at www.dwp.gov.uk/docs/strengthening-families.pdf; DWP, *Government's Response to the Consultation on Strengthening Families, Promoting Parental Responsibility* (Cm 8130, 2011), available at www.dwp.gov.uk/docs/strengthening-families-response.pdf; Work and Pensions Select Committee, *The Government's Proposed Child Maintenance Reforms* (2011), available at www.publications.parliament.uk/pa/cm201012/cmselect/cmworpen/1047/104702.htm.

[21] Section 9(2A).

[22] A new s 9A of the CSA 1991 (to be inserted by the Welfare Reform Act 2012, s 138) allows C-MEC to provide an indicative calculation of maintenance under the CSA 1991, thus providing some basis for privately agreeing an appropriate amount of maintenance.

[23] See www.childmaintenance.org/en/childsupport/timetable.html.   [24] Ibid.

2 THE CHILD SUPPORT ACT 1991: THE LAW

2.1 PARENTS AND CHILDREN TO WHOM THE ACT APPLIES

An important point to grasp right at the outset is that, unlike other statutes in this context, the CSA 1991 is only concerned with imposing liability for child support as between a child and his or her legal parent.[25]

2.1.1 Parents

Parent is defined in section 54 as a 'person who is in law the father or mother of a child'.[26] For the purposes of the 1991 Act a parent must be habitually resident in the UK,[27] unless employed abroad by the civil service, armed forces, a UK company, or prescribed body.[28] Section 26(2) sets out certain cases in which it is assumed that a person is the parent of a child, for example where a child is adopted, where parents are parents pursuant to a parental order or other assisted-conception provisions of the Human Fertilisation and Embryology Acts, or where there has been a declaration of parentage, or the person concerned has been adjudged to be the child's parent in court proceedings. Where section 26(2) does not apply, it is possible for the parent with care to apply for a declaration of parentage, in which a direction for scientific testing can be made.[29]

2.1.2 Child

Section 55(1) provides that, for the purposes of the Act, a person is a child if he has not attained the age of 16, or has not attained the age of 20 and satisfies conditions as may be prescribed. Under the previous legislation the conditions were that the person was receiving full-time education which is not advanced education (ie, below degree level).[30] A person is not a child if he or she is or has been married or in a civil partnership.[31]

2.2 EACH PARENT'S DUTY TO MAINTAIN A QUALIFYING CHILD

Section 1(1) provides that 'each parent of a qualifying child is responsible for maintaining him'. Note that this statutory duty to maintain is not imposed in respect of every child, only those who qualify under the Act. Put simply, the Act only applies to children whose parents do not live with each other. Section 3 of the Act puts this more precisely, defining a 'qualifying child' by reference to the situation of the parents, who may be either a 'non-resident parent' or a 'parent with care'. A child is a qualifying child if one or both of his parents are in relation to him non-resident.[32] A non-resident parent is a parent not living in the same household with the child, where the child is living with 'a person with care'.[33] A person with care is the person with whom the child has his home; who usually

---

[25] To be contrasted with the courts' residual powers to award financial provision for children, which can in certain circumstances be made against step-parents.

[26] See Chapter 7 for a detailed discussion of who in law a child's parent is, and see in this context *Re M (Child Support: Parentage)* [1997] 2 FLR 90.   [27] CSA 1991, s 44.

[28] Ibid, s 44(2A).

[29] See ibid, s 27. Fees for testing can be recovered, see s 27A. See further Chapter 7 for discussion of establishing legal parentage.

[30] See Child Support (Miscellaneous Amendments) (No 2) Regulations 2009 (SI 2009/2909).

[31] Section 55(2). This includes void marriages and civil partnerships.   [32] Section 3(1).

[33] Section 3(2). There may be more than one person with care: see s 3(5).

provides day-to-day care for the child (whether exclusively or in conjunction with any other person); and who does not fall within a prescribed category of person.[34]

2.3 APPLICATIONS FOR A MAINTENANCE CALCULATION AND COLLECTION/ENFORCEMENT

A person with care[35] or a non-resident parent may apply under section 4 for a calculation of maintenance for the child under the provisions of the Act (known as a maintenance calculation).[36] A non-resident parent has a duty to make—and meets his or her responsibility under s 1(1) by making—any periodical payments determined in accordance with a maintenance calculation under the Act.[37] Such payments are called 'child support maintenance'.[38] Where a calculation has been made, C-MEC may arrange for the child support maintenance to be collected or the support obligation to be enforced if the parent applies for those services.[39]

No application can be made where there is in force: a written maintenance agreement made before 5 April 1993 (ie, before the CSA 1991 was first implemented);[40] or a maintenance order made before 3 March 2003;[41] or if a maintenance order made on or after the date 3 March 2003 is in force but has been so for less than the period of one year beginning with the date on which it was made.[42]

2.4 THE MAINTENANCE CALCULATION

The maintenance payable by a non-resident parent is calculated with reference to provisions in Schedule 1 to the Act. Payment of maintenance is calculated according to gross weekly income and is paid at four different rates depending on the non-resident parent's income: a basic, reduced, flat, or nil rate.

2.4.1 The basic rate[43]

Where the non-resident parent's weekly income is £200 or more, the basic rate is applied. The following percentage of the non-resident parent's gross weekly income is applied up to a ceiling of £800 weekly income:

- 12 per cent for one qualifying child;
- 16 per cent for two qualifying children;
- 19 per cent for three or more qualifying children.

---

[34] Section 3(3). See Child Support (Miscellaneous Amendments) Regulations 1993 (SI 1993/913) and the Child Support (Maintenance Calculation Procedure) Regulations 2000 (SI 2001/157).

[35] Where there is more than one person with care, but all do not have parental responsibility for the qualifying child, only those with parental responsibility may apply: see s 5.

[36] Under s 4(1). As mentioned earlier in this chapter, s 6 of the Act, which used to compel use of the Child Support Agency by those who were on prescribed benefits, was repealed from 14 July 2008 by the Child Maintenance and Other Payments Act 2008.   [37] See s 1(2) and (3).

[38] CSA 1991, s 3(6).

[39] Ibid, s 4(2). Section 137 of the Welfare Reform Act 2012 inserts a new s 4(2A) providing that the Commission may only make arrangements under subs (2)(a) if—'(a) the non-resident parent agrees to the arrangements, or (b) the Commission is satisfied that without the arrangements child support maintenance is unlikely to be paid in accordance with the calculation.'   [40] Ibid, s 4(10)(a).

[41] Ibid. See the Child Support (Applications: Prescribed Date) Regulations 2003 (SI 2003/194), reg 10(1)(a).   [42] CSA 1991, s 4(10)(aa).

[43] Ibid, Sch 1, para 2.

For any gross weekly income above £800 up to £3,000,[44] the following percentages apply:

- 9 per cent for one qualifying child;
- 12 per cent for two qualifying children;
- 15 per cent for three or more qualifying children.

If the non-resident parent also has one or more relevant other children, gross weekly income used for these calculations is treated as reduced by the following percentage:

- 12 per cent where the non-resident parent has one relevant other child;
- 16 per cent where the non-resident parent has two relevant other children;
- 19 per cent where the non-resident parent has three or more relevant other children.[45]

Relevant other children are children other than qualifying children in respect of whom the non-resident parent or his or her partner receives child benefit.[46]

2.4.2 Reduced rate

A reduced rate (determined in accordance with regulations) is payable where the non-resident parent's income is less than £200 but more than £100, but the reduced rate may not be less than £7.

2.4.3 Flat rate

Where the non-resident parent's weekly income is £100 or less or he or she, or his or her partner, is receiving prescribed benefits or a pension, a flat rate of £7 is payable.

2.4.4 Nil rate

A nil rate is payable where the non-resident parent is of a prescribed description, or has a gross weekly income below £7.

2.4.5 Where the non-resident parent is maintaining another child under an arrangement

Where the non-resident parent has other non-qualifying children who are nevertheless maintained under a maintenance order or agreement, all of the maintained children are used to identify the appropriate rate within Schedule 1.[47] The amount calculated is divided by the total number of maintained children, and then multiplied by the number of qualifying children. Take the following example. A non-resident parent, living alone,[48] has weekly gross income of £400. He has three children, two of whom are maintained under a maintenance agreement and one of whom is a qualifying child for CSA purposes. The child support maintenance payable is one-third (19 per cent of £400), that is, £25.33. In this way the calculation recognises a higher percentage rate would apply if claims were being made under the Act for all the children, but at the same time recognises that the non-resident parent is already maintaining some of the children under other arrangements. Thus, he or she pays less than if the percentage relating to one qualifying child were simply applied, that is, 12 per cent of £400, which would be £48.

---

[44] Income over £3,000 is ignored for the purposes of Sch 1: Sch 1, para 10(3).
[45] Schedule 1, para 2(3).
[46] Under Pt IX of the Social Security Contributions and Benefits Act 1992: see CSA 1991, Sch 1, para 10C.   [47] Schedule 1, para 5A.
[48] To avoid additional complexity in calculation that would occur if he or she had other 'relevant children'.

2.4.6 Apportionment

Sometimes a non-resident parent may have qualifying children who do not all live together, so that there is more than one person with care. In such cases the amount payable to each person with care is calculated by apportioning the rate between the persons with care. The rate of maintenance liability is divided by the number of qualifying children, and shared among the persons with care according to the number of qualifying children in relation to whom each is a person with care.[49]

2.4.7 Reduction for shared care

If the overnight care of a qualifying child is, or is to be, shared between a non-resident parent and the person with care, in the case of the basic or reduced rates there is a decrease in maintenance payable according to the number of such nights which C-MEC determines there to have been, or expects there to be, or both during a prescribed 12-month period. The amount of that decrease for one child is set out in Table 6.1 (although the amount payable can never fall below £7 per week).[50]

Table 6.1 Reduction for shared care

Number of nights	Fraction to subtract
52–103	One-seventh
104–155	Two-sevenths
156–174	Three-sevenths
175 or more	One-half[51]

The flat rate is reduced to nil if a non-resident parent has care of the child for at least 52 nights in a prescribed 12-month period.[52] It should be emphasised that the reduction applies for *overnight* care. These provisions do not assist a non-resident parent who might incur considerable expenses in providing substantial daytime care of the child but who does not have the child sufficiently overnight to qualify for a reduction.[53] This is arguably unfair and, of course, the current scheme provides an obvious incentive for parents to argue about amounts of staying contact.[54]

2.4.8 Variations from the calculation

It is possible for either parent to apply to obtain a variation from the usual calculation in certain circumstances[55] under section 28F and Part 1 of Schedule 4B. The making of a variation is informed by the general principles that parents should be responsible for maintaining their children whenever they can afford to do so; and where a parent has more than one child, his obligation to maintain any one of them should be no less of an obligation than his obligation to maintain any other of them.[56] C-MEC may agree to a variation if satisfied that the case is one which falls within one or more of the cases set out in Part I of Schedule 4B or in regulations made under that Part; and it is its opinion that, in all the circumstances of the case, it would be just and equitable to agree to a variation.[57] In considering whether it

---

[49] Schedule 1, para 6.   [50] Schedule 1, para 7(7).

[51] If the fraction is one-half, the amount payable is further decreased by £7: see Sch 1, para 7(6).

[52] Schedule 1, para 8(2).

[53] See eg *R (Plumb) v Secretary of State for Work and Pensions* [2002] EWHC 1125 (Admin).

[54] Although see *Re B (Contact: Child Support)* [2006] EWCA Civ 1574, [2007] 1 FLR 1949 (in deciding on contact, the court should not have regard to the impact of its determination upon a parent's liability to pay child support). For criticism, see S. Gilmore, '*Re B (Contact: Child Support)*—Horses and Carts: Contact and Child Support' [2007] Child and Family Law Quarterly 357.   [55] CSA 1991, s 28A(1).

[56] Ibid, s 28E.   [57] Ibid, s 28F(1).

would be just and equitable in any case to agree to a variation, C-MEC must have regard, in particular, to the welfare of any child likely to be affected if it did agree to a variation.[58]

Schedule 4B sets out cases in which a departure direction may be given. First there is the category of prescribed special expenses, which include costs incurred in travelling to work, in maintaining contact with children, costs attributable to a long-term illness or disability of the applicant or of a dependant of the applicant, debts incurred for the family or members of the family before the non-resident parent became a non-resident parent in relation to a child, and costs incurred by a parent in supporting a child who is not his child but who is part of his family. A second category is property or capital transfers made prior to 5 April 1993 (date of implementation of the CSA 1991). There are also some additional cases, such as where a person's lifestyle is inconsistent with the level of his income, or housing or travel costs are unreasonably high.

2.5 ENFORCEMENT

The 1991 Act provides C-MEC with wide powers of collection and enforcement. Section 31 enables it to order a non-resident parent's employers to deduct child support directly from earnings or from accounts. If this proves impossible or ineffective, C-MEC can apply to the magistrates' court for a liability order.[59] This can be enforced by levying distress or sale of the non-resident parent's goods.[60] Where this fails, the applicant can apply for a warrant committing the non-resident parent to prison or disqualifying him or her from holding a driving licence.[61] Where the Commission has failed to recover maintenance by means of enforcement action and maintenance still remains payable and the Commission is of the opinion that there has been wilful refusal or culpable neglect on the part of the person concerned, then it can apply for an order disqualifying the person from holding a driving licence or a UK passport.[62] The court must be satisfied of wilful refusal or culpable neglect.

In *R (On the Application of Kehoe) v Secretary of State for Work and Pensions*[63] the House of Lords held that this was a comprehensive scheme for enforcement of child support under the CSA 1991 by the Secretary of State (now C-MEC) and that the applicant in that case, Mrs Kehoe, did not have an individual right to pursue enforcement of child maintenance before the courts against her former husband. The European Court of Human Rights rejected Mrs Kehoe's claim that the CSA 1991 and the House of Lords' ruling violated her right under Article 6 of the European Convention.[64]

3   THE COURTS' RESIDUAL ROLE WITH RESPECT TO CHILD MAINTENANCE

In order to give effect to the Child Support Act's policy of a general administrative scheme for calculation and collection of child support maintenance, it was necessary to limit the exercise of the courts' powers to make orders for maintenance which still exist in various statutes. Section 8(1) and (3) of the CSA 1991 read together provide that in any case where C-MEC would have jurisdiction to make a maintenance calculation with respect to a qualifying child and a non-resident parent 'no court shall exercise any power which it

---

[58]   Ibid, s 28F(2), together with prescribed matters.   [59]   Ibid, s 32M.   [60]   Ibid, s 35.
[61]   Ibid, s 39A.   [62]   Ibid, s 39B.
[63]   [2005] UKHL 48. For a detailed account and criticism, see N. Wikeley, 'A Duty but Not a Right: Child Support after *R (Kehoe) v Secretary of State for Work and Pensions*' [2006] Child and Family Law Quarterly 287.   [64]   *Kehoe v UK* [2008] ECHR 528, [2008] 2 FLR 1014.

would otherwise have to make, vary or revive any maintenance order[65] in relation to the child and non-resident parent concerned'.[66] In other words, as a general rule the courts' powers to make periodical payments are paralysed when C-MEC has jurisdiction over child support maintenance.

However, there are some exceptions to the general rule which are set out in section 8 of the CSA itself.

3.1 SECTION 8(3A): EXISTING MAINTENANCE ORDERS

Where there is a pre-March 2003 maintenance order and by reason of that order an application for a maintenance calculation is prevented,[67] the courts retain jurisdiction to vary the maintenance order. The courts also retain jurisdiction to vary a maintenance order which was made on or after 3 March 2003 provided no maintenance calculation has actually been made.

3.2 SECTION 8(5): EXISTING MAINTENANCE AGREEMENTS

If there is a written agreement providing that a non-resident parent shall make or secure the making of periodical payments to or for the benefit of the child, a court has power to make a maintenance order which is, in all material respects, in the same terms as the agreement.

3.3 SECTION 8(6): A TOPPING UP ORDER

As discussed earlier, only income up to £3,000 per week is used in the basic rate calculation of child support maintenance in Schedule 1 to the CSA 1991. That figure is likely to exhaust the available income of most non-resident parents. However, in the case of a very wealthy non-resident parent whose gross weekly income exceeds that figure,[68] the courts have jurisdiction to top-up the provision made under the CSA 1991 with court-ordered periodical payments, provided that there is a maintenance calculation in force with respect to the child.[69] The court must be satisfied that the circumstances of the case make it appropriate for the non-resident parent to make or secure the making of periodical payments under a maintenance order in addition to the child support maintenance payable in accordance with the maintenance calculation.[70]

3.4 SECTION 8(7): EDUCATIONAL EXPENSES

Section 8(7) provides that a court may make a maintenance order if:

(a) the child is, will be or (if the order were to be made) would be receiving instruction at an educational establishment or undergoing training for a trade, profession or vocation (whether or not while in gainful employment); and

---

[65] By s 8(11) a 'maintenance order' means an order requiring the making or securing of periodical payments to or for the benefit of the child made under the MCA 1973, Pt II; the Domestic Proceedings and Magistrates' Courts Act 1978; the Matrimonial and Family Proceedings Act 1984, Pt III; the Children Act 1989, Sch 1; the Civil Partnership Act 2004, Sch 5, 6, or 7.

[66] Subsection (4) clarifies that subs (3) does not prevent a court from revoking a maintenance order.

[67] By s 4(10) or 7(10).

[68] Ie, exceeds the figure referred to in para 10(3) of Sch 1 (as it has effect from time to time pursuant to regulations made under para 10A(1)(b)). See s 8(6)(b).

[69] Section 8(6)(a). See S. Mahmood and C. Hallam, 'Schedule 1 and the CSA: Getting into the Top-up Zone' [2011] Family Law 266.   [70] For an example, see *H v C* [2009] 2 FLR 1540, [2009] 2 FLR 1540.

(b) the order is made solely for the purposes of requiring the person making or securing the making of periodical payments fixed by the order to meet some or all of the expenses incurred in connection with the provision of the instruction or training.

3.5 SECTION 8(8): EXPENSES ATTRIBUTABLE TO A CHILD'S DISABILITY

A court may make a maintenance order where a child is disabled[71] and 'the order is made solely for the purpose of requiring the person making or securing the making of periodical payments fixed by the order to meet some or all of any expenses attributable to the child's disability'.

3.6 SECTION 8(10): ORDERS AGAINST A PERSON WITH CARE

Nothing in section 8 prevents a court from exercising any power which it has to make a maintenance order in relation to a child if the order is made against a person with care of the child.

Key case

In *C v F (Disabled Child: Maintenance Orders)*[72] the Court of Appeal held that the courts' powers under these exemptions were limited by the conditions imposed within each exemption. So in the case of a child under a disability, or in further or higher education, the order must be designed simply to meet expenses attributable to these circumstances. Thorpe LJ expressed the view, *obiter*, that the limits imposed by the CSA 1991 would continue to apply until the child reached an age when that Act no longer applied, and thereafter the broader provisions of Schedule 1 to the Children Act 1989 would prevail.[73] The court was clear, however, that the duration of any orders made by a court under the exemption provisions were not limited to the latest date for payments made under the CSA 1991. Such a restriction would undermine the purpose of some of the exemption provisions. For example, there is no reason why a maintenance agreement embodied in a court order should not provide for maintenance beyond the age of 16 even though the child is not receiving full-time education. Moreover, the courts' powers allow orders in respect of children in tertiary education and of children, including adult children, under a disability, and it would be absurd if an order had to come to an end when, for example, a child had just completed his or her first year at university.

There will, of course, be some situations where the restriction in section 8(1) and (3) of the CSA 1991 will simply not apply because the CSA 1991 is not applicable in the first place. An example is the case of a non-resident father who is not habitually resident in the UK within the meaning of the Act. The CSA 1991 does not apply because he is not a parent within the meaning of the Act and there would therefore be no restriction on use of court-ordered periodical payments should an application be made against him.[74]

---

[71] For this purpose a child is disabled if he is blind, deaf, or dumb or is substantially and permanently handicapped by illness, injury, mental disorder, or congenital deformity or such other disability as may be prescribed (s 8(9)).   [72] [1998] 2 FLR 1, CA.

[73] Ibid, 8, a view with which Butler-Sloss and Hutchinson LJJ were inclined to agree but expressed no firm conclusion.

[74] See eg *A v A* , discussed in Section 4.7.5.

Capital provision is unaffected by the CSA 1991, although in a case to which it applies, the power to make a lump sum award should be exercised only 'to meet the need of a child in respect of a particular item of capital expenditure'. Lump sums should not be used 'in such a way as to provide for the regular support of the child, which would ordinarily have been provided by an order for periodic payments',[75] since to do so would circumvent the policy in section 8(1) and (3) of the CSA 1991.

4 THE COURTS' POWERS

Having clarified the relationship between the CSA 1991 and the courts' powers, we now turn to consider the various statutes under which court-based provision might be made. The High Court or county court has powers under the Matrimonial Causes Act 1973 to address financial support for children on or after a decree of divorce or nullity; and the Civil Partnership Act 2004 makes similar provision in the case of dissolution or annulment of a civil partnership.[76] Of these jurisdictions, only the Matrimonial Causes Act (MCA) 1973 will be considered in the following section in order to simplify the exposition, and also because the case law has been developed in relation to those provisions. Reference will be made only to 'marriage', but it should borne in mind throughout that the statutory framework is similar (and is likely to be applied similarly) in respect of the children of civil partners.

Later in this chapter we shall discuss another jurisdiction in Schedule 1 to the Children Act 1989 which is available to provide support for all children irrespective of their parents' marital status.[77] There is thus a choice of jurisdiction in the case of children whose parents are married. Where the parents' circumstances are such that the MCA 1973 would apply, however, there may be advantages in using those provisions. The MCA 1973 contains wider powers than those in Schedule 1 to the Children Act 1989, for example a power to order the sale of property.[78]

4.1 MATRIMONIAL CAUSES ACT 1973

Under Part II of the MCA 1973, on or after the grant of a decree of divorce or nullity the court has power to make various orders for financial provision or property adjustment to or for the benefit of a child of the family.

Key legislation

Section 52 of the 1973 Act provides that child of the family in relation to the parties to a marriage, means:

(a) a child of both of those parties; and

(b) any other child, not being a child who is placed with those parties as foster parents by a local authority or voluntary organisation, who has been treated by both of those parties as a child of their family.

---

[75] *Phillips v Peace* [1996] 2 FLR 230 at 235B–D, *per* Johnson J. For comment, see J. A. Priest, 'Child Support and the Non-Standard Earner—Pass the Heineken, Please! *Phillips v Peace*' [1997] Child and Family Law Quarterly 63. See also on the distinction between a lump sum and a maintenance order as defined in the CSA 1991, s 8(11), and *AMS v Child Support Officer* [1998] 1 FLR 955. See further, J. Priest, 'Capital Settlements and the Child Support Act' [1998] Family Law 115 and 170.   [76] Civil Partnership Act 2004, Sch 5.

[77] Or civil partnership status.

[78] MCA 1973, s 24A. There are also wider powers relating to disclosure and preservation of assets.

The concept of the child of the family recognises that a person who chooses to marry someone who already has children may take on responsibility for the children as well as for his spouse.[79] If the marriage ends, this responsibility may involve making financial and property provision for these children, although as we shall see it is tempered by the liability of anyone else to maintain the child. Before any obligation can be imposed, it must first be established that the non-parent has treated the child as a child of the family. This is a question of fact turning on evidence of how he or she behaved towards the child.[80] It is an objective test:[81] 'The independent outside observer has to look at the situation and say: "Does the evidence show that the child was treated as a member of the family?".'[82]

It is not possible to treat an unborn child as a child of the family, as a foetus is not a child.[83] Thus if a married couple live together during the woman's pregnancy but split up before the child is born, the child will not be a child of the family.[84] This will be so even though the husband may allow it to be thought he is the father of the child when he is not.[85] Where, however, a child lives in the same household with a step-parent for some considerable period of time it is almost inevitable that he or she will be treated as a child of the family.[86] By contrast, if the child has his home with other family members but merely visits his parent and step-parent, this does not make him a child of the family and the step-parent is not financially responsible for him if the marriage breaks down.[87] A child can be treated as a child of the family even where a husband has treated him as such in the mistaken belief that the child is his own child. In *W (RJ) v W(SJ)*[88] a husband was deceived by his wife about the paternity of their two children, and after the marriage broke down blood tests revealed that he was not the father. Park J held that both children had been treated as children of the family and that the husband's lack of knowledge of the facts relating to the children's paternity was immaterial to their status.

As discussed in Chapter 4, the welfare whilst a minor of any child of the family who has not attained the age of 18 will be the court's first consideration when considering financial orders for (former) spouses upon their divorce.[89] Providing support for any such children (eg by provision to the children's primary carer of a secure home) is likely to form an important part (and focus) of many financial relief packages. The power of the court to transfer property to a spouse in his or her own right clearly provides greater flexibility surrounding provision for children. Here, however, we focus specifically on the orders which can be made to or for the benefit of the children.

4.2 AVAILABLE ORDERS

The available orders are set out in sections 23 and 24 of the MCA 1973, which will already be familiar to those conversant with the law relating to financial orders for spouses discussed in

---

[79] However, note that the liability may be to children other than stepchildren, eg an orphaned relative who has lived with the parties and has been treated as a child of their family; or a foster child who was placed privately, who has been treated as a child of the family for some considerable time, and whose parents cannot support him financially.

[80] *M v M (Child of the Family)* (1981) 2 FLR 39, CA; *D v D (Child of the Family)* (1981) 2 FLR 93, CA; *W v W (Child of the Family)* [1984] FLR 796, CA; *Carron v Carron* [1984] FLR 805, CA; *Teeling v Teeling* [1984] FLR 808, CA.

[81] *D v D (Child of the Family)* (1981) 2 FLR 93 at 96.   [82] Ibid, 97.

[83] *A v A (Family: Unborn Child)* [1974] Fam 6 at 15F: 'A man cannot behave towards a child and therefore cannot treat a child as part of the family, unless the child has been born and is living', *per* Bagnall J.

[84] *A v A (Family: Unborn Child)* [1974] Fam 6.

[85] *M v M (Child of the Family)* (1981) 2 FLR 39, CA (couple split up before child's birth).

[86] See *Teeling v Teeling* [1984] FLR 808 (six-month period of cohabitation, discussed in Section 4.4).

[87] *D v D (Child of the Family)* (1981) 2 FLR 93.   [88] [1972] Fam 152.   [89] MCA 1973, s 25(1).

Chapter 4. Paragraphs (d), (e), and (f) of section 23 set out various financial provision orders that can be made to or for the benefit of a child of the family: periodical payments, secured periodical payments, and lump sums respectively. Under section 24 the court can order lump sums, transfers of property, and settlements of property to or for the benefit of such children.

4.3 EXERCISE OF THE COURT'S DISCRETION

The exercise of the court's discretion is guided by section 25(3) and (4).

Key legislation

Section 25(3), which applies in all cases, sets out particular matters to which the court must have regard when making orders to or for the benefit of children. These are:

(a) the financial needs of the child;

(b) the income, earning capacity (if any), property and other financial resources of the child;

(c) any physical or mental disability of the child;

(d) the manner in which he was being and in which the parties to the marriage expected him to be educated or trained;

(e) the considerations mentioned in relation to the parties to the marriage in paragraphs (a), (b), (c) and (e) of subsection (2) above.

The considerations in section 25(2) in relation to the parties to the marriage mentioned in paragraph (e) are discussed in detail in Chapter 4. Put briefly, the court is required to consider the parties' resources, obligations, standard of living before the breakdown, and whether they have any physical or mental disability.

4.4 MAINTENANCE OF A CHILD BY A PARTY WHO IS NOT THE CHILD'S PARENT

As regards the exercise of the courts' powers[90] in favour of a child who is not the child of that party, section 25(4) provides that the court must also have regard:

(a) to whether that party assumed any responsibility for the child's maintenance, and, if so, to the extent to which, and the basis upon which, that party assumed such responsibility and to the length of time for which that party discharged such responsibility;

(b) to whether in assuming and discharging such responsibility that party did so knowing that the child was not his or her own;

(c) to the liability of any other person to maintain the child.

In *Teeling v Teeling*[91] a wife left her husband and had a child by another man. The husband and wife then got back together for only six months before the wife left again. The court found that the baby had been treated as a child of the family, but that the husband's best answer to a claim was to be found in section 25(4), commenting that 'if ever a case was *de minimis* so far as the assumption of any responsibility by this husband for this child

---

[90] Under s 23(1)(d), (e), or (f), (2) or (4), 24, or 24A.　　[91] [1984] FLR 808.

was concerned, it is this case.'[92] The court is specifically required to consider the basis on which such a husband had assumed and discharged his financial responsibility for the child and whether he did so knowing that the child was not his own. Thus lack of knowledge on the part of a deceived husband is material to whether he should be ordered to make provision for a child who is a child of the family but not his own. In *W (RJ) v W(SJ)*,[93] the case of the husband who was deceived about the paternity of two children (mentioned earlier), it was implicit in the judgment that no order for financial provision would be made against the husband. The obligation of a person who has treated a child as a child of the family must also be considered with regard to the liability of any other person to maintain the child.

The court's power to make an order is not precluded by the fact of a legal parent's liability[94] and in an appropriate case the child could receive payments from both adults concerned. However, as we have seen, the CSA 1991 emphasises that the primary responsibility for child support remains with the legal parent regardless of the length of time for which a step-parent has been providing for the child. A step-parent who is pursued for child maintenance in the courts will therefore normally be well advised to insist that the applicant first seeks to obtain support for the child from his or her parent through the intervention of the C-MEC.

4.5 DURATION OF ORDERS

In the first instance, periodical payments are not to extend beyond the child's 17th birthday,[95] unless the court considers that in the circumstances of the case the welfare of the child requires that it should extend to a later date.[96] In any event, the general rule is that periodical payments or secured periodical payments are not to extend beyond a child's 18th birthday.[97] Furthermore, no order for financial provision or for transfer of property is to be made in favour of a child who has attained the age of 18.[98]

The restrictions on making provision for a child over the age of 18 do not apply if it appears to the court that:

(a) the child is, or will be, or if an order were made … would be, receiving instruction at an educational establishment or undergoing training for a trade, profession or vocation, whether or not he is also, or will also be, in gainful employment; or

(b) there are special circumstances which justify the making of an order without complying with either or both of those provisions.[99]

4.6 PROVISION FOR CHILDREN AS DEPENDANTS

The statute enables the courts to make financial provision for children 'as dependants, rather than as persons with an interest or a potential interest in the assets of the family'.[100] This has been said by the Court of Appeal on several occasions. In *Chamberlain v Chamberlain*,[101]

---

[92] Ibid, 810.   [93] [1972] Fam 152.   [94] *Carron v Carron* [1984] FLR 805.

[95] Ie the birthday following attaining the upper limit of compulsory school age: s 29(2)(a).

[96] Section 29(2)(a).   [97] MCA 1973, s 29(2)(b).   [98] Ibid, s 29(1).

[99] Ibid, s 29(3). The fact that the child may be receiving a student award does not preclude the court making further provision: see *B v B (Adult Student: Liability to Support)* [1998] 1 FLR 373. See further T. Costley-White, 'Maintenance Liability for Students' [1999] Family Law 45.

[100] G. Miller, 'Capital Provision for Children' (1997) 1 Private Client Business 51. See also J. Miller, 'Children and Family Capital on Divorce' (1993) 5 Journal of Child Law 113.   [101] [1973] 1 WLR 1557.

for example, the Court of Appeal held that a judge had erred in settling a house 'so that the beneficial interest, at the end of the day, became that of the children in equal shares'. The court observed that there were 'no circumstances to suggest that any of the children had special circumstances which required them to make demands on their parents after the completion of their full-time education'.[102] The court made clear that, provided the parents met their responsibilities to their children as dependants, the house, acquired by the work and resources of the parents, should revert to the parents.[103] In *Lilford (Lord) v Glynn*,[104] the Court of Appeal stated that the wealth of a parent did not amount to special circumstances, and held that the same principle applied even where the child's parent was a millionaire. The court held that it had not been right to order a child's father to settle funds to provide income to a child during the child's whole lifetime, observing:

> A father—even the richest father—ought not to be regarded as having 'financial obliga-
> tions [or] responsibilities' to provide funds for the purposes of such settlements as are
> envisaged in this case on children who are under no disability and whose maintenance
> and education is secure.[105]

However, *Lilford (Lord) v Glynn*[106] was distinguished in *Tavoulareas v Tavoulareas*.[107] In that case neither parent was employed, being supported by their wealthy families. The trial judge ordered the husband to settle on the wife a lump sum of £250,000 to provide for housing for both the wife and their child, which sum would revert to the husband at the end of the child's dependency. The Court of Appeal substituted an order that the sum of £250,000 should be paid to trustees to hold the same for the benefit of the wife during the child's dependency for the purpose of providing them both with accommodation, but that at the conclusion of the child's dependency the reversion would be to the child. Thorpe LJ stated that this was an exceptional case where the reversion to the child was fully justified. Within these wealthy families there was a tradition of making capital provision to children upon attaining adulthood, and the outcome therefore reflected the traditions and convictions of those involved.[108]

The parties' capital had been derived from their respective families, and neither had made any contribution to the sum which would go into the settlement, and neither had a foreseeable need for that sum when the settlement came to an end.

While Thorpe LJ described this as an exceptional case, he also stated that 'in an infinite number of cases since [*Lilford (Lord) v Glynn*] settlements have been ordered during the dependency of a child or children and the court invariably chooses, at the conclusion of the dependency, whether the reversion should be for the settlor, for the parties in some shares, or to the child'.[109] This statement, or the outcome in *Tavoulareas*, is certainly

---

[102] Ibid, 1564 *per* Scarman LJ. See also *Kiely v Kiely* [1988] 1 FLR 248, CA at 252B–C, *per* Booth J: 'the provisions of the 1973 Act make it clear that the statutory scheme is to enable the court to make proper financial
provision for children as children or dependants'; and *Harnett v Harnett* [1973] Fam 156 at 161, *per* Bagnall J:
'In the vast majority of cases the financial position of a child of a subsisting marriage is simply to be afforded
shelter, food and education according to the means of his parents.'

[103] Compare *Griffiths v Griffiths* [1984] Fam 70 where capital provision was appropriate because a parent
had failed to meet responsibilities to a child.   [104] [1979] 1 WLR 78.

[105] Ibid, 85 *per* Orr LJ.

[106] *Lilford (Lord) v Glynn* [1979] 1 WLR 78, (1978) FLR Rep 427, [1979] 1 All ER 441, CA.

[107] [1998] 2 FLR 418.

[108] See at 429 *per* Thorpe LJ. Gilmore criticises the prominence given to the family tradition of passing property between generations and questions whether children from families which do not have such
traditions should be treated any differently: S. Gilmore, 'Re P (Child)(Financial Provision)—Shoeboxes and
Comical Shopping Trips—Child Support From the Affluent to Fabulously Rich' (2004) 16(1) Child and
Family Law Quarterly 103.   [109] *Tavoulareas v Tavoulareas* [1998] 2 FLR 418 at 429.

not easy to reconcile with earlier Court of Appeal authorities, since the judgment in *Tavoulareas* does not explain satisfactorily how the award of the reversion to the child absolutely on reaching adulthood related to needs of the child as a dependant during minority.[110] It also seems to be out of line with the decision of the Court of Appeal in *C v C (Financial Relief: Short Marriage)*.[111] The facts were equally unusual, if not more so. The parties had met when the wife was working as a high-class prostitute. They married, had a child, and separated. The husband, who was very wealthy, wanted any lump sum that he was required to pay to be settled on the wife for the purpose of providing her and the child with a home, and for that sum to revert to the child when the settlement came to an end. The trial judge refused to accede to this request for the reason that the wife should have more than a limited interest in the property. The Court of Appeal dismissed the husband's appeal on two grounds. It found that the trial judge had not been plainly wrong with regard to the needs of the wife; and it held that there was a long line of authorities from *Chamberlain v Chamberlain* to *Lilford (Lord) v Glynn* that the powers to make lump sum and settlement orders were not normally exercised to provide funds directly for the children.

4.7 CHILDREN ACT 1989, SECTION 15 AND SCHEDULE 1

If a child's parents are not married, the jurisdiction which will need to be used to make provision beyond that made under the CSA 1991 is contained in Schedule 1 to the Children Act 1989.[112] The provisions are similar to those under the MCA 1973, although there are some differences which are highlighted in the following sections.[113] The core provisions are in paragraphs 1 to 4: in brief, paragraph 1 sets out the available orders and who (apart from the child himself) can apply for them; paragraph 2 deals with applications by the child himself as an adult; paragraph 3 explains various matters relating to the duration of orders; and paragraph 4 sets out the criteria by which the court exercises its discretion.

4.7.1 Who can apply?

4.7.1.1 Applications on behalf of the child

In most cases the court will be exercising its powers under Schedule 1 in response to an application (although there are some circumstances in which the powers can be exercised even though no application has been made[114]). Those who can apply on behalf of the child are a parent, guardian, or special guardian of a child or any person in whose favour

---

[110] See Gilmore (n 108) who also points out that the assumption of the child's dependency in *Tavoulareas* seems out of line with the policy adopted in claims under the Inheritance (Provision for Family and Dependants) Act 1975 (see eg Browne-Wilkinson J in *Re Dennis (Deceased)* [1981] 2 All ER 140 at 145: 'why should anybody else make provision for you if you are capable maintaining yourself?').

[111] [1997] 2 FLR 26.

[112] See generally, J. Bazley QC et al (One Garden Court Chambers), *Applications under Schedule 1 to the Children Act 1989* (Bristol: Family Law, 2010).

[113] For example, there is in the Children Act 1989 no provision equivalent to the part of s 25(2)(a) of the MCA 1973, requiring the court to have regard to any increase in earning capacity which it would be reasonable for a party to take steps to acquire; unlike s 25(1) of the MCA 1973, the Children Act 1989 does not treat a child's welfare as the 'first consideration'; and under the Children Act 1989, applications can be made by adult children: see Sch 1, para 2.

[114] Where a child is a ward of court or where a court is making, varying, or discharging a residence order or special guardianship order: see Sch 1, paras 1(6) and 1(7).

a residence order is in force with respect to a child.[115] The category of potential applicants is thus wider in some respects than under the MCA 1973. The provision which allows an application by a person in whose favour a residence order is in force is an important one which comes to the assistance of relatives or friends of the child who have undertaken the burden of responsibility for caring for the child but do not have the means to support the child. It seems likely that the power of the courts to make orders in favour of a person with a residence order is not generally known. This is unfortunate because it might persuade relatives and others interested in the child to look after the child where the parents are unable or unwilling to do so. Moreover, those who are already looking after a child on an informal basis in a case where parents are refusing, or failing, to contribute towards the costs of their child's upbringing would sometimes be well advised to apply for a residence order so that they can obtain income, and possibly a capital contribution, towards the child's upkeep.

4.7.1.2 Applications by adult children

It is also possible for an adult child who is a trainee or student, or who can show special circumstances, to apply for his or her own provision pursuant to Schedule 1, paragraph 2. In order for provision to be made it must appear to the court:

(a) that the applicant is, will be or (if an order were made) would be receiving instruction at an educational establishment or undergoing training for a trade, profession or vocation, whether or not while in gainful employment; or

(b) that there are special circumstances which justify the making of an order.

In such cases the court's available powers are limited to making periodical payments or lump sum orders, and the orders can only be made against a parent[116] (not step-parents or others), and only where parents are not living in the same household as each other.[117] In what follows, we shall concentrate on the more usual case of applications on behalf of minor children.

4.7.2 Available orders

Schedule 1, paragraph 1(2) contains a range of powers to make financial provision or property adjustment to or for the benefit of a child.[118] The courts can require either or both of the child's parents to provide financially for the child by way of periodical payments, secured periodical payments,[119] lump sums,[120] or through the settlement[121] or transfer[122] of property.[123] The powers can be exercised at any time[124] although orders for transfer or settlement of property may be exercised only once against the same person in respect of the same child.[125] Whether the full range of orders is available, however,

---

[115] Schedule 1, para 1(1). A person against whom an order is made can apply to vary or discharge an order: see Sch 1, para 1(4).   [116] Schedule 1, para 2(2).

[117] Schedule 1, para 2(4). An application may also not be made under para 2 if, immediately before the applicant reached the age of 16, a periodical payments order was in force with respect to him or her (Sch 1, para 2(3)).

[118] In *CF v KM (Financial Provision for Child: Costs of Legal Proceedings)* [2010] EWHC 1754 (Fam), [2011] 1 FLR 208, Charles J held that an interim lump sum could be awarded for the benefit of the child in respect of the legal fees of Sch 1 proceedings. Charles J said that Bennett J's view in *W v J (Child: Variation of Financial Provision)* [2003] EWHC 2657 (Fam), [2004] 2 FLR 300 at paras [45]–[49] that the words 'for the benefit of the child' in para 1(2)(a) were not wide enough to cover moneys payable by one parent for the other's legal fees had been overtaken by subsequent case law.

[119] Schedule 1, para 1(2)(a) and (b). The orders may be for such term as may be specified in the order.

[120] Schedule 1, para 1(2)(c).   [121] Schedule 1, para 1(2)(d).   [122] Schedule 1, para 1(2)(e).

[123] To which either parent is entitled (either in possession or in reversion).

[124] Schedule 1, para 1(3). Unlike, eg, under the MCA jurisdiction, where the order must be on or after divorce or annulment.   [125] Schedule 1, para 1(5).

depends on which court is hearing the application. Applications under Schedule 1 can be to the High Court, a county court, or a magistrates' court. The High Court or a county court can make any of the available orders. However, the magistrates' court can only make periodical payments and/or lump sums[126] and lump sums in the magistrates' court shall not exceed £1,000.[127]

4.7.3 Against whom can orders be made

Orders can be made against either or both of a child's parents as defined in Schedule 1, paragraph 16.[128] Parent includes any party to a marriage or civil partnership (whether subsisting or not) in relation to whom the child is a child of the family. Child of the family, in relation to parties to a marriage, or to two people who are civil partners of each other, means: (a) a child of both of them, and (b) any other child, other than a child placed with them as foster parents by a local authority or voluntary organisation, who has been treated by both of them as a child of their family.[129] So, in the same way as discussed in relation to the MCA 1973 earlier in this chapter, orders can be made not only against parents, but against step-parents and former step-parents, indeed against any person who is or was a party to a marriage or civil partnership where both parties to that relationship treated the child as part of that family (subject to the exceptions relating to certain foster parents).

In *T v B (Parental Responsibility: Financial Provision)*[130] a child had been raised for several years by a lesbian couple, the child's mother having conceived through anonymous sperm donation at a clinic. The couple's relationship had broken down and a shared residence order had been made conferring parental responsibility on the mother's former partner. The mother then sought orders under Schedule 1 to the Children Act 1989 against the former partner, and the question arose as to the meaning of 'parent' within Schedule 1. Moylan J held that the mother's former partner was a 'social and psychological parent',[131] but that the word 'parent' in Schedule 1 means legal parent.[132] Here the mother's former partner could not be a legal parent because the child had been born prior to enactment of the Human Fertilisation and Embryology Act 2008 which now confers legal parenthood in such a case; and Moylan J was clear that 'the mere obtaining of parental responsibility is clearly not intended to make someone a legal parent when they would not otherwise be such'.[133]

4.7.4 Duration of orders

Similar rules to those in the MCA 1973 apply with respect to the duration of orders.[134]

---

[126] Schedule 1, para 1(1)(b).   [127] Schedule 1, para 5(2).
[128] A court has power to make an order under Sch 1 notwithstanding the bankruptcy of the respondent, *Re G (Children Act 1989, Schedule 1)* [1996] 2 FLR 171. As Singer J said at 177:

> It would be quite wrong…for the mother and, of course in particular the child, to be left with no order simply because a third party had got round to the exercise of their rights to obtain a bankruptcy order against the father.

[129] See Children Act 1989, s 105(1).   [130] [2010] EWHC 1444 (Fam), [2010] 2 FLR 1966.
[131] Ibid, [54].   [132] Ibid, [67]. See also *J v J (A Minor: Property Transfer)* [1993] 2 FLR 56 at 59.
[133] [2010] EWHC 1444 (Fam) at [63].
[134] Schedule 1, para 3. Periodical payments

> (a) shall not in the first instance extend beyond the child's seventeenth birthday unless the court thinks it right in the circumstances of the case to specify a later date; and (b) shall not in any event extend beyond the child's eighteenth birthday.
>
> (2) Paragraph (b) [above] shall not apply in the case of a child if it appears to the court that—
>
> (a) the child is, or will be or (if an order were made without complying with that paragraph) would be receiving instruction at an educational establishment or undergoing training for a trade, profession or vocation, whether or not while in gainful employment; or
>
> (b) there are special circumstances which justify the making of an order without complying with that paragraph.

4.7.5 Exercise of the court's discretion

Key legislation

In deciding whether to exercise its powers under paragraph 1 or 2, and if so in what manner, paragraph 4(1) provides that the court must have regard to all the circumstances including—

(a) the income, earning capacity, property and other financial resources which each person mentioned in sub-paragraph (4) has or is likely to have in the foreseeable future;

(b) the financial needs, obligations and responsibilities which each person mentioned in sub-paragraph (4) has or is likely to have in the foreseeable future;

(c) the financial needs of the child;

(d) the income, earning capacity (if any), property and other financial resources of the child;

(e) any physical or mental disability of the child;

(f) the manner in which the child was being, or was expected to be, educated or trained.

The persons mentioned in sub-paragraph (4) are any parent,[135] the applicant, and any other person in whose favour the court proposes to make the order. Unlike section 25(2)(c) of the MCA 1973 as applied to children's claims, by section 25(3)(e) of the MCA 1973, paragraph 4(1) of the Children Act 1989 does not include any reference to the standard of living enjoyed by the family before the breakdown of the marriage, although standard of living is clearly relevant to 'needs'. The omission no doubt recognises that unmarried parents may never have lived together as a family. In addition, the physical or mental disabilities of the parent are not expressly in issue under the Children Act 1989,[136] an omission which is not easy to understand.

Where the court is deciding whether to make an order against a person who is not the mother or the father of the child, additional considerations in paragraph 4(2) apply:

(a) whether that person has assumed responsibility for the maintenance of the child and, if so, the extent to which and basis on which he assumed that responsibility and the length of the period during which he met that responsibility;

(b) whether he did so knowing that the child was not his child;

(c) the liability of any other person to maintain the child.[137]

The principle of the paramountcy of the child's welfare in section 1 of the Children Act 1989 does not apply to orders for financial and property provision made under Schedule 1 to the Act. This is made plain in section 105 which states that a child's 'upbringing' does not include a child's maintenance. Neither is the child's welfare the first consideration as under section 25(1) of the MCA 1973. There is no reference to the child's welfare at all in Schedule 1, and the only guidance provided by the statute

---

[135] In the case of an application under Sch 1, para 2 by an adult child, 'parent' is confined to the mother and father of the child, although in the case of a child who has a parent by virtue of s 42 or 43 of the Human Fertilisation and Embryology Act 2008, any reference in Sch 1, para 4, to the child's father is a reference to the woman who is a parent of the child by virtue of that section.

[136] Unlike s 25(2)(e) of the MCA 1973, as applied by s 25(3)(e).

[137] If the court makes such an order, it must record in the order that the order is made on the basis that the person against whom the order is made is not the child's father (see para 4(3)).

is the criteria in paragraph 4. In *K v K (Minors: Property Transfer)*[138] the trial judge ordered a father of four children to transfer his interest in a joint tenancy of the council house in which the family were living to the children's mother for the benefit of the children of the family.[139] When arriving at his decision, the judge treated the children's welfare as paramount and omitted to refer to the criteria then governing orders for children. In particular he did not take account of the father's nine years of accrued rights under the right to buy provisions of the Housing Act 1980, his ability to find and pay for other accommodation, and his very low income. The Court of Appeal ordered a retrial,[140] finding that the judge had erred in principle in treating the child's welfare as paramount and failing to conduct this balancing exercise.

In *A v A (A Minor: Financial Provision)*[141] Ward J concluded that, notwithstanding any differences between the Children Act 1989 and the MCA 1973, the claims of children of married and unmarried parents should be dealt with similarly. He noted that the trend against making provision in favour of adult children who have ceased their full-time education is reinforced in the Children Act 1989 jurisdiction by paragraph 2 of Schedule 1, where, in the case of an application by an adult child, there is no power to make a property adjustment order.[142] In that case the father of one child of a family of three children was a multi-millionaire who was resident outside the jurisdiction. The mother applied for periodical payments and for an outright transfer of property either to herself for the benefit of the child, or to the child herself. Ward J awarded £20,000 per annum[143] for the child's maintenance, commenting that insofar as that sum indirectly benefited the child's half-sisters,[144] for whom the father was not financially responsible, it could be justified by reference to the child's welfare which, while not an express consideration under the statute, was one of the circumstances that his Lordship took into account.[145] Ward J included within that sum an allowance for the mother's care of the child, which, it had been established in *Haroutunian v Jennings*,[146] is not wrong in principle. Ward J quantified this allowance by reference to the cost of professional childcare, such as a nanny, or mother's help such as an *au pair*.[147]

Applying the same approach as under the 1973 Act jurisdiction, however, Ward J rejected the application for property transfer and ordered that the house owned by the father, in which the mother and the three children were living, should be settled on the child to terminate six months after she attained the age of 18, or completed full-time tertiary education, whichever was the later.[148] It was a term of the settlement that 'while A is under

---

[138] [1992] 2 All ER 727.

[139] Under the Guardianship of Minors Act 1971, s 11B(2)(d). The power to order one unmarried cohabitant to transfer the tenancy in the family home to the other is found in the Family Law Act 1996, Sch 7.

[140] Although the Court of Appeal ordered a retrial, it nonetheless accepted that such an order was for the benefit of the children and that it therefore fell within the court's powers under Sch 1. However, the willingness of the court to contemplate making a property transfer order for the benefit of children, as distinct from a settlement order with reversion to the settlor, seems to have been unique, and is probably limited to cases involving the transfer of a council or other tenancy.   [141] [1994] 1 FLR 657.

[142] Ibid, 661.

[143] Because the father lived a 'precarious life' and was domiciled abroad, and thus a claim under the Inheritance (Provision for Family and Dependants) Act 1975 was not possible, the periodical payments were to be secured against the father's home in London.

[144] There is no jurisdiction to order sums of direct benefit to such children: see *Morgan v Hill* [2006] EWCA Civ 1602, [2007] 1 FLR 1480 at [38].

[145] Ward J commented ([1994] 1 FLR 657 at 667): 'Somewhat to my surprise and for reasons I cannot understand, welfare plays no express part in the considerations to which I have to have regard.'

[146] (1980) 1 FLR 62.   [147] [1994] 1 FLR 657 at 665H–666B.   [148] Ibid, 663.

the control of her mother and thereafter for so long as A does not object, the mother shall have the right to occupy the property to the exclusion of the father and without paying rent therefor for the purpose of providing a home and care and support for A'. Arguably this was a rather legalistic and insensitive approach to a mother's role in caring for her child. Acceptance of the idea that a child should be entitled to object to her mother continuing to occupy the family home once the child reached the age when she was no longer under the control of her mother is at best surprising. It surely cannot be in the interests of a child that she should have this kind of power over her mother, and the order made had the potential to be extraordinarily damaging to the relationship between the child, her mother, and her siblings.

In *J v C (Child: Financial Provision)*[149] Hale J also held that the child's welfare, 'even if neither the paramount nor the first consideration, must be one of the relevant circumstances to be taken into account when assessing whether and how to order provision'.[150] In that case, after the breakdown of the (unmarried) parents' relationship, the father won £1.4 million on the National Lottery. The child, her mother, and her two half-sisters, lived in three-bedroom rented accommodation, supported by public funds. There was a dispute between the parties as to the nature of their relationship and whether the child was wanted. Hale J did not consider that 'any great weight should be attached' to those disputed circumstances,[151] and held that the child was 'entitled to be brought up in circumstances which bear some sort of relationship with the father's current resources'.[152] It was to the child's benefit to be brought up with, and in similar circumstances to, her half-sisters. This required the purchase[153] of a four-bedroom property, together with reasonable furnishings and a motor car.

In *T v S (Financial Provision for Children)*[154] the parents and their five children had lived in considerable style, with a house in the country and a London flat, until the father was sentenced to two years' imprisonment for possession of cocaine.[155] Upon the mother's application under Schedule 1, the District Judge found the father an unsatisfactory witness who seemed unwilling to give accurate disclosure of his means. By then it seemed that there was only £36,000 left to support the children, which the judge held was to be used to purchase a family home, settled until the children reached 21 or completed their education, then to pass to the children in equal shares. On the father's appeal, Johnson J, following the case law approach in the MCA 1973 jurisdiction, held that the property should revert to the father, not the children. He rejected counsel's argument that the difficulty of establishing the father's resources should be seen as a special circumstance justifying provision for the children's beyond their education. Johnson J held that 'in its reference to special circumstances in relation to the duration of periodical payments, Parliament was intending the court ordinarily to look at special circumstances related to the children—such, for example, as some physical or other handicap'.[156] Johnson J commented: 'The sadness here is that, after a long and seemingly happy relationship, this mother of five

---

[149] [1999] 1 FLR 152.   [150] Ibid, 156G.   [151] Ibid, 154B.

[152] Ibid, 160A–B. See also *Haroutunian v Jennings* (1981) 1 FLR 62 at 65, where Sir George Baker P acknowledged a 'long historical precedent for accepting that a rich man will pay more than a poor man for the maintenance of his child, legitimate or illegitimate'.

[153] Therefore, where resources allow, making provision, as a matter of public policy, to reduce or eliminate the children's need to be supported by public funds.   [154] [1994] 2 FLR 883, *per* Johnson J.

[155] Found, together with £75,000, in a vacuum cleaner, following a police raid on the London flat.

[156] [1994] 2 FLR 883 at 889. See also, agreeing with this passage, Butler-Sloss LJ in *C v F (Disabled Child: Maintenance Orders)* [1998] 2 FLR 1 at 3F.

children, never having been married to their father, has no rights against him of her own. She has no right to be supported by him in the short, still less the long term; no right in herself to have even a roof over her head.'As this case illustrates, an unmarried parent who brings up the children has no continuing claim for support and shelter in her declining years and can literally be turned out into the street once her mothering role has ended.[157]

Key cases

The leading decision on Schedule 1 to the Children Act 1989 is now *Re P (Child: Financial Provision)*[158] in which the Court of Appeal held that the decisions in *A v A (A Minor: Financial Provision)* and *J v C (Child: Financial Provision)* were 'unquestionably sound and should be clearly endorsed',[159] albeit with two qualifications. First, commenting on *A v A (A Minor: Financial Provision)*, Thorpe LJ, delivering the leading judgment, indicated that 'a more generous approach to the calculation of the mother's allowance is not only permissible but also realistic'.[160] The court suggested that quantification of such allowance should not be limited to the cost of a professional nanny, as this may not do full justice to a mother's role in providing 24-hour care for a child. Secondly, the court amplified Hale J's discussion, in *J v C (Child: Financial Provision)*,[161] of the role of welfare by adding that 'welfare must be not just "one of the relevant circumstances" but, in the generality of cases, a constant influence on the discretionary outcome'.[162]

In *Re P* the child had been conceived towards the end of the parents' four-year, intermittent, sexual relationship. The father was a successful international businessman, who described himself as 'fabulously rich' and whose London home was valued at over £10 million. The mother's earnings and home were modest. In her application under Schedule 1, the mother sought a lump sum in the range of £1.2–2.3 million. The judge allowed £450,000 for provision of a home, with £30,000 to furnish the property, and £20,000 for a car, and annual periodical payments of £35,360. In reaching this conclusion the judge attached some importance to the fact that the father had no financial obligations to the child beyond her minority, and he did not therefore wish to create an expectation of luxury from which the child would need to adapt should the father then withdraw his support. The mother appealed, contending that the judge's ruling failed 'to reflect the scale of the father's fortune and expenditure'.[163]

---

[157] For further comment on *T v S* and *A v A*, see E. Cooke, 'Children and Real Property—Trusts, Interests and Considerations' [1998] Family Law 349.

[158] [2003] EWCA Civ 837, [2003] 2 FLR 865. For commentary, see S. Gilmore '*Re P (Child) (Financial Provision)*—Shoeboxes and Comical Shopping Trips—Child Support From the Affluent to Fabulously Rich' (2004) 16(1) Child and Family Law Quarterly 103.   [159] Ibid, [41].

[160] Ibid, [43].   [161] [1999] 1 FLR 152 at 156G.

[162] [2003] EWCA Civ 837, [2003] 2 FLR 865 at para [44]. Thorpe LJ explained that this amplification was justified by reference to the purpose of the statutory exercise, which is: 'to ensure for the child of parents who have never married and who have become alienated and combative, support and also protection against adult irresponsibility and selfishness, at least insofar as money and property can achieve those ends' (ibid, [44]). Expressing it differently, but in an approach that may be indistinguishable in practice, Bodey J suggested that welfare was 'naturally a very relevant consideration as one of "… all the circumstances …" of the case' (ibid, [76]).

[163] [2003] EWCA Civ 837, [2003] 2 FLR 865 at para [20]. The judge's award of £450,000 for a home represented only 5 per cent of the cost of the father's own principal residence.

Allowing the mother's appeal, the Court of Appeal offered a useful method by which a judge should determine a case similar to this. A judge's starting point should be 'to decide, at least generically, the home that the respondent must provide for the child', since it 'introduces some useful boundaries'.[164] The court confirmed that the usual provision would be a settlement with reversion to the settlor. The next step is to assess, in the light of the choice of home, the 'cost of furnishing and equipping the home and the cost of the family car'. The judge should then determine what 'the mother reasonably requires to fund her expenditure in maintaining the home and its contents and in meeting her other expenditure external to the home'.[165] Here Thorpe LJ emphasised that 'what is required is a broad commonsense assessment'.[166] The final step is to consider quantification of an allowance for the mother's care of the child. Here the court drew attention to the tension between the latter and the fact that the mother has no personal entitlement to funds from the father. Bodey J commented that 'it is not possible to reduce to words any formula for seeking to ensure that the above distinction is maintained',[167] and there will 'inevitably be numerous grey areas, where the need asserted is of no direct benefit to the child, but is (or is arguably) of legitimate indirect benefit in helping reasonably to sustain the mother's physical/emotional welfare'.[168] It is 'these fine (and largely insoluble) distinctions of fact and degree within the grey area of indirect benefit to the child' which justify 'a broad budgetary approach by the court in bigger money cases'.[169] Thorpe LJ explained the court's approach, as follows:

the court must recognise the responsibility, and often the sacrifice, of the unmarried parent (generally the mother) who is to be the primary carer for the child, perhaps the exclusive carer if the absent parent disassociates from the child. In order to discharge this responsibility the carer must have control of a budget that reflects her position and the position of the father, both social and financial. On the one hand she should not be burdened with unnecessary financial anxiety or have to resort to parsimony when the other parent chooses to live lavishly. On the other hand whatever is provided is there to be spent at the expiration of the year for which it is provided. There can be no slack to enable the recipient to fund a pension or an endowment policy or otherwise to put money away for a rainy day. In some cases it may be appropriate for the court to expect the mother to keep relatively detailed accounts of her outgoings and expenditure in the first and then in succeeding years of receipt.[170]

Applying this guidance to the facts, the court held that a budget of £1 million was realistic to provide a home for the child, with a further sum of £100,000 to finish, furnish, and equip such a property. The court also awarded annual periodical payments of £70,000, to include the cost of running the home. In reaching its more generous conclusions, it held that the judge had been wrong to allow the speculative risk that the father would withdraw or reduce support at the end of the child's minority to influence the determination of the application.[171]

---

[164] Ibid, [45].

[165] Such as school fees, holidays, routine travel expenses, entertainment, presents, etc, ibid, [47].

[166] Ibid.   [167] Ibid, [80]

[168] Ibid, [81].   [169] Ibid, [82].

[170] Ibid, [48] and [49]. The last point was made once again at para [54] of the judgment:

> Again the father may be entitled to reasonably detailed accounts of expenditure so that he can be satisfied that, taking one year with another, all is spent to meet the needs for which it is provided and none goes to the personal or exclusive benefit of the mother.

[171] Ibid, [68] and [95].

In *Re S (Unmarried Parents: Financial Provisions)*[172] the Court of Appeal made clear that *Re P* should not be interpreted as setting a benchmark for assessment of quantum in future cases. In *Re S* there was a dispute as to quantum of a housing trust fund; the mother was seeking to remain in Kensington, London at a suggested cost of £1.6–2 million, while the father suggested more modest accommodation in Parsons Green/Fulham. In reaching a middle-ground figure of £800,000, Bennett J had regarded the quantum of the housing fund of £1 million in *Re P* as a benchmark and had scaled down that provision to reflect the disparity in wealth between the father in *Re P* and the father in this case. The Court of Appeal held that that was an erroneous fetter on the wide discretionary exercise required by Schedule 1.[173] In addition, Bennett J had been influenced by the mother's egocentricity and the fact that what motivated her to wish to live in Kensington was her own selfish need. The Court of Appeal was concerned that the judge had thereby been distracted from the real focus which should have been an appraisal of the daughter's needs and interests, which were distinct from the mother's and not tainted simply by association with the mother's.[174] The judge should have asked: what would be the consequence for the daughter if she lost the security of her familiar environment in Kensington?[175] The court indicated that this was 'a neat illustration of the advantages of ensuring separate representation for the child in some cases' brought under Schedule 1.[176]

In *Re C (Financial Provision)*[177] District Judge Million, sitting in the Family Division, explained that *Re P* did not establish a rule of law that housing provision must be by way of a settlement; the distinction made in *Re P* was between outright transfer and a settlement. The ruling in *Re P* did not preclude the possibility that provision might, in an appropriate case, be made by financing a rented property.[178] In *Re C* a mother and her 4-year-old boy had recently moved from abroad to London and the mother was seeking a variation to periodical payments in part to cover payment of rent on a flat they were occupying. The father, whose wealth was approximately £100 million, was willing to finance a suitable property through a trust (at a cost of approximately £2 million), because payment of rent would be 'dead money'. The mother preferred to rent because she did not wish to feel that her property was controlled by the father, wanted to retain more flexibility about where she could live in the future, and wished the boy to remain in a place with which he was familiar.[179] The judge held that on the facts the mother's objections did not provide a rational basis for rejecting a trust, as the father was content for the mother to have a choice as to the trustees, the trust document could include the ability to move home, and the child's familiarity with the home was over exaggerated.[180]

The facts in *F v G (Child: Financial Provision)*[181] differed from *Re P* in that the couple had cohabited until the child was 2 years old. Singer J held that statements in *Re P*[182] endorsing the view expressed in *J v C* that the considerations as to the length and nature of the parents' relationship are generally of little if any relevance, had to be viewed in the context of the facts of that case. Singer J held in *F v G* that although 'standard of living' is not one of the specific considerations in paragraph 4(1) of Schedule 1, 'the extent to which the unit of primary carer and child have become accustomed to a particular level of lifestyle can impact legitimately on an evaluation of the child's needs, reasonably to viewed against his or her history'.[183] His Lordship thus sought to mitigate the disparity between the father's spending power and the child's household by adopting a level of

---

[172] [2006] EWCA Civ 479, [2006] 2 FLR 950.
[173] Ibid, [14].   [174] Ibid, [15].   [175] Ibid.   [176] Ibid, [17].   [177] [2007] 2 FLR 13.
[178] Ibid, [45].   [179] See at [46].   [180] See at [47]–[50].
[181] [2004] EWHC 1848 (Fam), [2005] 1 FLR 261 *per* Singer J.
[182] See [2003] EWCA Civ 837, [2003] 2 FLR 865, *per* Bodey J at [76].
[183] [2004] EWHC 1848 (Fam), [2005] 1 FLR 261 at [35]. See also *N v D* [2008] 1 FLR 1629.

award which would enable the mother to provide 'a fabric of home life not too brutally remote from that which the father's hard work enables him to sustain'. In that case the father was worth £4.6 million. The mother had limited capital and a net salary of £37,000 per annum. Singer J awarded a housing fund of £900,000 and periodical payments to include a parent as carer element of £60,000 per annum. Singer J allocated to the mother's salary the cost of a nanny (approximately £24,000) as the mother's contribution to her and the child's lifestyle, and awarded a full parent as carer allowance from the father, thus allowing the mother to make her own decision about employment and whether a nanny were needed or not.[184]

4.7.6 The significance of a prior maintenance agreement

In some cases a child's parents may have concluded a written agreement for financial provision for the child. Such an agreement does not prevent an application under Schedule 1 to the Children Act 1989. Indeed, Schedule 1, paragraph 10(3), provides that provisions of a maintenance agreement can be varied or revoked by the court upon application if the court is satisfied that the agreement does not contain proper financial arrangements with respect to the child. In *Morgan v Hill*[185] the Court of Appeal held that whether an application is made under paragraph 10(3) or under paragraph 1 of Schedule 1, the same approach applies. The pre-existing agreement is seen as the starting point of the court's assessment,[186] which if it is to be departed from must be either demonstrated to be unenforceable given the circumstances surrounding its creation or inadequate in its extent.[187]

DISCUSSION QUESTIONS

1. To what extent do you think that the Child Support Act 1991 has been successful in achieving Mrs Thatcher's goal of ensuring that children are supported by their parents?

2. Is the recent policy effected by the Child Maintenance and Other Payments Act 2008 encouraging parents to make their own agreements relating to child support a welcome improvement to the child support system?

3. When do the courts retain jurisdiction in relation to child support?

4. What principles guide the courts' exercise of discretion when making orders for financial provision for children? Is the courts' approach satisfactory?

FURTHER READING

BAZLEY, J. et al (One Garden Court Chambers), *Applications under Schedule 1 to the Children Act 1989* (Bristol: Family Law, 2010)

COLLIER, R., 'The Campaign Against the Child Support Act, Errant Fathers and Family Men' [1994] Family Law 384

DIDUCK, A., 'The Unmodified Family: The Child Support Act and the Construction of Legal Subjects' (1995) 22(4) Journal of Law and Society 527

---

[184] [2004] EWHC 1848 (Fam), [2005] 1 FLR 261 at [50]–[53].
[185] [2006] EWCA Civ 1602, [2007] 1 FLR 1480.   [186] Ibid, [33], [57], and [61]   [187] Ibid, [33].

FEHLBERG, B. and MACLEAN, M., 'Child Support Policy in Australia and the United Kingdom: Changing Priorities but a Similar Tough Deal for Children?' (2009) 23(1) International Journal of Law, Policy and the Family 1–24

GILMORE, S., '*Re P (Child) (Financial Provision)*—Shoeboxes and Comical Shopping Trips—Child Support from the Affluent to Fabulously Rich' (2004) 16(1) Child and Family Law Quarterly 103

GLENDINNING, C., CLARKE, K., and CRAIG, G., 'Implementing the Child Support Act' (1996) 18(3) Journal of Social Welfare and Family Law 273–289

MACLEAN, M. and EEKELAAR, J., 'Child Support: The British Solution' (1993) 7 International Journal of Law and the Family 205

WIKELEY, N., 'A Duty But Not a Right: Child Support after *R (Kehoe) v Secretary of State for Work and Pensions*' [2006] Child and Family Law Quarterly 287

WIKELEY, N., *Child Support Law and Policy* (Oxford: Hart, 2006)

WIKELEY, N., 'Child Support: The Brave New World' [2008] Family Law 1024

WIKELEY, N., 'Child Support: Carrots and Sticks' [2008] Family Law 1102

7

A CHILD'S PARENTS: PARENTAGE, PARENTHOOD, AND PARENTAL RESPONSIBILITY

INTRODUCTION

This chapter examines how English law answers the question 'Who is a child's parent?'[1] The answer has become increasingly complex as the law has responded to social change and to scientific developments in artificial reproduction techniques.[2] The semen used to fertilise a woman's egg may have been donated by a man who is not her husband or partner, and the donor may be anonymous. Eggs, as well as semen, can be donated and this can result in a woman giving birth to a child which has grown from another woman's egg. The child's mother may be in a same-sex relationship or partnered with a transsexual person. The law has had to address questions such as: who is a child's mother when a woman gives birth to a child conceived as a result of egg donation by another woman? Is the child to have two mothers? Can a female-to-male transsexual person become a child's father? Is a mother's same-sex partner to be recognised as her child's parent too? If so, in what sense? As this last question suggests, the law's response is also complicated by the fact that the notion of 'being a parent' has several different facets.

1 A CHILD'S PARENTS

1.1 DIFFERENT SENSES OF 'PARENT': BIOLOGICAL, SOCIAL, AND LEGAL

Sometimes reference is made to a child's 'natural' parent.[3] This focuses on parenthood in a biological sense, recognising a person's genetic connection as a natural progenitor

---

[1] A. Bainham, S. Day Sclater, and M. Richards (eds), *What is a Parent? A Socio-Legal Analysis* (Oxford: Hart, 1999).

[2] See S. Sheldon, 'Fragmenting Fatherhood: The Regulation of Reproductive Technologies' (2005) 68(4) *Modern Law Review* 523–553 for discussion of the ability of reproductive technologies to disrupt and confuse our understandings of parenthood.

[3] See the discussion by Baroness Hale of Richmond in *Re G (Children) (Residence: Same-Sex Partner)* [2006] UKHL 43, [2006] 4 All ER 241 at [33]–[37].

of the child and/or a person's[4] gestational contribution: bearing and delivering the child. It is also possible to talk of a social and psychological parent. This, as Baroness Hale has explained, describes a relationship developing through the fulfilment of the child's psychological, and day-to-day physical, needs.[5] These two aspects of parenthood are succinctly captured by the ideas of a parent 'by being' and a parent 'by doing'.[6] Frequently, of course, the same person (usually the child's natural mother or father) will combine these aspects of parenthood. A third way in which parenthood can be understood (which is the focus of this chapter) is its legal sense: the person who, *in law*, is regarded as a child's parent. From among the various understandings of parenthood within a society, choices may be made as to who is to be regarded in law as a parent. For example, in English law a biological parent will not always be regarded in law as a parent, and a child's legal parent may sometimes be someone who is not biologically related to the child. Furthermore, a legal parent may not necessarily be the child's social and psychological parent. As this last example shows, the law must address not merely the question of who a child's parent is, but also the rights and responsibilities attending that status, and whether and how legal responsibility for a child's upbringing is to be allocated to those caring for a child.

1.2 LAW'S DISTINCTIONS: PARENTAGE, PARENTHOOD, AND PARENTAL RESPONSIBILITY

Andrew Bainham has usefully observed that the law's engagement with the question 'who is a parent?' involves three 'subtle, elusive, yet important distinctions' in terminology: 'parentage', 'parenthood', and 'parental responsibility'.[7] The term 'parentage' is concerned with the genetic connection between the child and the persons who provided the gametes which led to the child's conception.[8] 'Parentage' is thus a matter of fact, focusing on genetic truth or presumed genetic truth. As Bainham points out, keeping this concept distinct is important, particularly from the child's perspective, because it focuses attention on the child's interest in knowing his or her origins. By contrast, the term 'parenthood' conveys the idea of a status associated with the raising of a child, and the term 'legal parenthood' is concerned with who, *as a matter of law*, is recognised as a parent.

---

[4] The word 'person' rather than 'woman' is chosen here because following enactment of the Gender Recognition Act 2004 it is possible for a man to give birth to a child. In the rest of this chapter, however, 'woman' is used, recognising the usual gender of a person giving birth to a child.

[5] [2006] UKHL 43, [2006] 4 All ER 241 at [35]:

> the relationship which develops through the child demanding and the parent providing for the child's needs, initially at the most basic level of feeding, nurturing, comforting and loving, and later at the more sophisticated level of guiding, socialising, educating and protecting.

[6] J. Masson, 'Parenting by Being; Parenting by Doing—In Search of Principles for Founding Families' in J. R. Spencer and A. Du Bois-Pedain (eds), *Freedom and Responsibility in Reproductive Choice* (Oxford: Oxford University Press, 2006), ch 8.

[7] A. Bainham, 'Parentage, Parenthood and Parental Responsibility: Subtle, Elusive Yet Important Distinctions' in A. Bainham et al, *What is a Parent? A Socio-Legal Analysis* (Oxford: Hart, 1999), ch 2.

[8] Shapiro prefers use of the term 'progenitor' because it does not automatically link that person with the term 'parent': see J. Shapiro, 'Changing Ways, New Technologies and the Devaluation of the Genetic Connection to Children' in M. Maclean (ed), *Family Law and Family Values* (Oxford: Hart, 2005), p 90.

Key legislation

The third term, 'parental responsibility' is defined in section 3 of the Children Act 1989 as 'all the rights, duties, powers, responsibilities and authority which by law a parent of a child has in relation to the child and his property.'

This status is allocated as a matter of law. As we shall see, some legal parents will have parental responsibility while others may not. Parental responsibility can also be conferred on someone who is not a legal parent, thus providing a person with the necessary legal status to carry out his or her social role of looking after a child.

It is helpful to an understanding of the law to keep these three concepts distinct although, as we shall see, the law makes many connections between them. For example, in most cases parentage and legal parenthood coincide because the general rule in English law is that legal parenthood is attributed according to biological connection;[9] and there are also important links between legal parenthood and how parental responsibility is allocated or acquired: for example, all mothers are initially allocated parental responsibility for their children.

2 PARENTAGE

2.1 THE PRESUMPTION OF PATERNITY IN FAVOUR OF THE MOTHER'S HUSBAND

The common law established a presumption of fact that a child born or conceived during the mother's lawful marriage is her husband's child.[10] The presumption relates to children conceived prior to a marriage and born within marriage, and to children who are born within the normal gestation period after a marriage has ended by death or divorce.[11] The presumption was created at a time when society's expectation was that children would not be born outside wedlock, when birth outside marriage could bring significant legal disadvantages to the child, and when great importance was therefore attached to a child's so-called 'legitimate' birth within marriage. The presumption is known therefore as the presumption of legitimacy, and at one time the importance of this status meant that the presumption could only be rebutted to a high standard of proof. Nowadays, however, the legal disadvantages to children born outside marriage have largely been eradicated by the Family Law Reform Act 1987, and section 26 of the Family Law Reform Act 1969 provides that the presumption may be rebutted on the balance of probabilities, that is by evidence which shows that it is more probably true than not that the husband is not the father.

Where applicable account will also need to be taken of the presumption of legitimacy in any case of disputed paternity. However, the importance of this presumption as a factor in deciding such cases, has diminished over time and it is now probably of limited practical

---

[9] Whether actual or presumed. For criticism of automatic deference to biology, see J. G. Dwyer, *The Relationship Rights of Children* (New York: Cambridge University Press, 2006).

[10] *Banbury Peerage Case* [1803–13] All ER Rep 171, 1 Sim and St 153, 57 ER 62.

[11] *Gardner v Gardner* (1877) 2 App Cas 723.

significance. In *Re H and A*[12] Thorpe LJ questioned 'the relevance of the presumption or the justification for its application' in that context, commenting:

> In the nineteenth century, when science had nothing to offer and illegitimacy was a social stigma as well as a depriver of rights, the presumption was a necessary tool, the use of which required no justification...But as science has hastened on and as more and more children are born out of marriage it seems to me that the paternity of any child is to be established by science and not by legal presumption or inference.

2.2 WHERE PARENTAGE IS IN ISSUE: DECLARATIONS OF PARENTAGE

Where there is an issue or dispute as to a child's parentage, it may be necessary ultimately to resolve it in court proceedings.

Key legislation

Section 55A(1) of the Family Law Act 1986 provides that 'any person[13] may apply to a court[14] for a declaration as to whether or not a person named in the application is or was the parent of another person so named.'[15]

The declaration is binding on all persons.[16] Where one of the persons named in the application is a child the court may refuse to hear the application if it considers that the determination of the application would not be in the best interests of the child.[17]

2.2.1 Proving paternity

Nowadays the usual method of proving parentage is by scientific evidence in the form of a DNA profile which can demonstrate to a degree of probability approaching certainty whether a person is the child's genetic parent or not.[18] Prior to the availability of DNA profiling, scientific testing would take the form of blood tests which could exclude the possibility that a man was a child's father or provide some probability that he was, but could not prove the same conclusively. In the past, therefore, there would be much greater emphasis than is the case now on other evidence, in the absence of scientific evidence, or supplementing it. This might consist of witness statements showing the alleged father's inclination and opportunity to have sexual intercourse with

---

[12] [2002] EWCA Civ 383, [2002] 2 FCR 469 at [30].

[13] In certain cases the court must refuse to hear the application unless satisfied that the applicant has a sufficient personal interest in the determination of the application: see s 55A(3) and (4).

[14] High Court, a county court, or a magistrates' court.

[15] Either of the persons named must be domiciled in England and Wales or have been habitually resident in England and Wales for at least one year: see Family Law Act 1986, s 55A(2).

[16] It may be important, therefore, in the child's interests that an application for leave to appeal out of time is granted where a declaration has been made erroneously: see [2003] EWHC 2163 (Fam), [2004] 1 FLR 282 at [17].   [17] Family Law Act 1986, s 55A(5).

[18] For a discussion of DNA testing and kinship, see T. Freeman and M. Richards, 'DNA Testing and Kinship: Paternity, Genealogy and the Search for the "Truth" of our Genetic Origins' in F. Ebtehaj, B. Lindley, and M. Richards (eds), *Kinship Matters* (Oxford: Hart, 2006); for a discussion of the impact in the USA, see M. A. Rothstein, T. H. Murray, G. E. Kaebnick, and M. Anderlik Majunder (eds), *Genetic Ties and the Family. The Impact of Paternity Testing on Parents and Children* (Baltimore, MD: Johns Hopkins University Press, 2005). See also H. Draper and J. Ives, 'Paternity Testing: A Poor Test of Fatherhood' (2009) 31(4) Journal of Social Welfare and Family Law 407–418.

the mother at the relevant time (or indeed the lack of the same, and perhaps evidence of the mother's relationship with a different man). There might also be evidence after the birth, such as the mother entering (or failing to enter) the father's name on the register of births. In *Brierley v Brierley and Williams*[19] a husband petitioned for divorce on the basis of his wife's adultery, the evidence being the birth of a child at a time when the husband, who had been absent on military service in France during the First World War, could not have been the father. To prove the adultery the husband produced a registration of the child's birth, signed by the mother, which had left the father's name blank. McCardie J could see 'no reason to doubt that prima facie evidence may be furnished by the entry in the register or a certified copy.' Such circumstantial evidence is now unlikely to be crucial in most instances, but in cases where forensic testing is unavailable, for example where the alleged father has died and/or cannot be traced, evidence other than scientific evidence may still assume some importance, and indeed the presumption of legitimacy might still command the outcome. Where scientific evidence could assist, however, the court has a power in Part III of the Family Law Reform Act 1969 to direct scientific testing.

2.3 DIRECTIONS FOR SCIENTIFIC TESTING UNDER SECTION 20 OF THE FAMILY LAW REFORM ACT 1969

Key legislation

A court has a discretion to direct scientific testing to ascertain parentage under section 20 of the Family Law Reform Act 1969,[20] which provides:

(1) In any civil proceedings in which the parentage of any person falls to be determined, the court may, either of its own motion or on an application by any party to the proceedings, give a direction—

  (a) for the use of scientific tests to ascertain whether such tests show that a party to the proceedings is or is not the father or mother of that person; and

  (b) for the taking, within a period specified in the direction, of bodily samples from all or any of the following, namely, that person, any party who is alleged to be the father or mother of that person and any other party to the proceedings;[21]

It can be seen that the court cannot make a direction for scientific testing on a free-standing application under section 20.[22] The jurisdiction only arises where there are already civil proceedings before the court in which the parentage of a person falls to be determined. This would be the case, for example, where a formal application for a declaration of parentage has been made pursuant to section 55A of the Family Law Act 1986, although such an application is not essential.[23] The issue of parentage could be raised in other proceedings, as is sometimes the case when a man makes an application for a parental responsibility

---

[19] [1918] P 257.

[20] Any direction for such testing should indicate that it is being made pursuant to s 20 and should specify the body which is to carry out the testing, which should be accredited by the Ministry of Justice: Family Law Reform Act 1969, s 20(1A), and see *Re F (Children) (DNA Evidence)* [2007] EWHC 3235 (Fam), [2008] 1 FLR 348 (Anthony Hayden QC). The manner of giving effect to a direction is regulated by s 22 of the 1969 Act and the Blood Tests (Evidence of Paternity) Regulations 1971 (SI 1971/1861), as amended.

[21] Where the proceedings consist of an application under s 55A or 56 of the Family Law Act 1986, reference to a 'party to the proceedings' includes a reference to any party named in the application: see Family Law Reform Act 1969, s 20(2A).   [22] *Re E (Parental Responsibility: Blood Tests)* [1995] 1 FLR 392.

[23] *Re D (Paternity)* [2006] EWHC 3545 (Fam), [2007] 2 FLR 26, *per* Hedley J at [4].

order or contact order and the child's mother claims that he is not the father and therefore not entitled to apply for the order.

2.3.1 Sufficient evidential basis to justify consideration of the application

The first question, upon any application under section 20, is whether there is sufficient evidential basis to justify serious consideration of the application.[24] This was the approach adopted by Hedley J in *Re D (Paternity)*[25] who concluded (and thus appeared to require) in that case that there were 'reasonable grounds for believing' that the applicant was the child's father, 'sufficient to warrant scientific testing'.[26] If such grounds exist, the court will then go on to consider whether to exercise its discretion.

2.3.2 The discretion to direct scientific testing

General guidance on the discretion to direct scientific testing was given in two cases heard together by the House of Lords in *S v S; W v Official Solicitor*.[27] The point of law to be resolved was whether a blood test could be ordered despite the fact that the child might not benefit from the outcome of the test. The concern was that testing would risk the child's loss of the benefit of the presumption of legitimacy. The Official Solicitor argued that testing should not take place unless it could be shown to be in the child's best interests. Despite the similarity of their facts, the two cases had elicited different responses in the Court of Appeal. In *S v S*, a husband, who was petitioning for divorce on the ground of his wife's adultery, denied paternity of his wife's child. The Official Solicitor, representing the child, objected to testing. The Court of Appeal held that a test should be directed. In *W v Official Solicitor* a wife who had given birth to a child who was strikingly dissimilar to her older children who were conceived with the husband, confessed to adultery with a man who had now disappeared. In contrast to *S v S*, the husband's request for testing to ascertain the child's paternity was refused by the Court of Appeal. The House of Lords unanimously dismissed the first appeal and allowed the second, the outcome in each case being that testing was directed.

The case was decided in relation to the courts' jurisdiction to direct testing prior to implementation of Part III of the Family Law Reform Act 1969, although the principles expounded by the House of Lords are equally applicable to directions under the Act. Indeed, in *obiter* comments Lord Reid observed that it could not have been intended that the then soon to be implemented section 20(1) of the 1969 Act should confer upon the courts an unfettered discretion. That discretion was to be exercised according to principles settled by the superior courts.[28] His Lordship held that 'the court ought to permit a blood test of a young child to be taken unless satisfied that that would be against the child's interests'.[29] The House of Lords made clear, therefore, that the paramountcy of the child's welfare is *not* the governing principle. This is because, as Lord Hodson commented:

> the interests of other persons than the infant are involved in ordinary litigation. The infant needs protection but that is no justification for making his rights superior to those of others.[30]

---

[24] Ibid, [5].   [25] [2006] EWHC 3545 (Fam), [2007] 2 FLR 26.   [26] Ibid, [10].

[27] [1972] AC 24. For a detailed commentary, see A Bainham, 'Welfare, Truth and Justice: The Children of Extra-Marital Liaisons' in S. Gilmore, J. Herring, and R. Probert (eds), *Landmark Cases in Family Law* (Oxford: Hart, 2011), pp 113–134.   [28] [1972] AC 24 at 45.

[29] Ibid, p 45. See also Lord MacDermott at p 51: 'while the court should be alert to exercise its protective jurisdiction on behalf of an infant, it does not need to be satisfied before ordering a blood test that the outcome thereof will be for the benefit of the infant.'

[30] [1972] AC 24 at 58.

Thus the interests of justice, as well as the interests of the child, are raised. Lord Hodson went on to observe that:

> The interests of justice in the abstract are best served by the ascertainment of the truth and there must be few cases where the interests of children can be shown to be best served by the suppression of truth.[31]

The House recognised, however, that there:

> may be a conflict between the interests of the child and the general requirements of justice. Justice requires that available evidence should not be suppressed but it may be against the interests of the child to produce it.[32]

The House held that a court's duty to protect children will not ordinarily provide a ground for refusing to direct forensic testing merely because, in revealing the truth, it might show that the child was not born in lawful wedlock. It explained that following the enactment of section 26 of the 1969 Act, which allows the presumption of legitimacy to be rebutted on the balance of probabilities, 'the presumption of legitimacy now merely determines the onus of proof'[33] and 'public policy no longer requires that special protection should be given by the law to the status of legitimacy'.[34] The House added that while the child must be protected:

> it is not really protecting the child to ban a blood test on some vague and shadowy conjecture that it may turn out to be to its disadvantage: it may equally well turn out to be for its advantage or at least do no harm.[35]

Since this leading decision in *S v S; W v Official Solicitor*, examination of the interests at stake in this context has been refined by increased emphasis on human rights, in particular a person's 'identity rights'. The focus on the child's various interests has been refined by increased emphasis within English law upon children's rights. Before examining various examples of how the court has exercised its discretion under section 20, it is convenient first to explain the human rights context in which decisions must now be taken.

2.4 LEGAL RECOGNITION OF PERSONS' INTERESTS IN KNOWING GENETIC ORIGINS

The law recognises a child's interest in knowing his or her genetic origins. It is specifically protected by Article 7 of the United Nations Convention on the Rights of the Child (UNCRC),[36] which provides that a child has, 'as far as possible, the right to know and be cared for by his or her parents'. In addition, the European Court of Human Rights has said that the right to respect for private life within Article 8(1) of the European Convention on Human Rights (ECHR):

> includes a person's physical and psychological integrity and can sometimes embrace aspects of an individual's physical and social identity. Respect for 'private life' must

---

[31] Ibid, 57. See also Lord Morris' opinion, in which (at 55) he talked of the 'general desirability of arriving at the truth' which 'points to the further desirability of having the best evidence available'. He commented (at 56) that in most cases comparable to *S v S* 'the interests of the child are best served if the truth is ascertained'.   [32] Ibid, 44.

[33] Ibid, 41 *per* Lord Reid.   [34] Ibid, 43 *per* Lord Reid.   [35] Ibid, 45.

[36] New York, 20 November 1989; Treaty Series No 44 of 1992 (Cm 1976).

also comprise to a certain degree the right to establish relationships with other human beings.[37]

Key case

In *Mikulić v Croatia*[38] the Court added that there appears to be 'no reason why the notion of "private life" should be taken to exclude the determination of the legal relationship between a child... and her natural father.'[39] In that case a girl sought to establish in legal proceedings that a particular man was her father. After five years the proceedings were still pending before an appellate court and the child alleged a breach of the right to a fair trial within Article 6(1) in that the proceedings were not concluded in a reasonable time. She further alleged that consequently there had been a breach of Article 8. The Court reiterated that 'particular diligence is required in cases concerning civil status and capacity'[40] and held that in all the circumstances Article 6(1) had been breached. In addition, the Court unanimously held that the Croatian courts' inefficiency had 'left the applicant in a state of prolonged uncertainty as to her personal identity', and failed to secure respect for her private life.[41]

The interest which a parent, or presumed parent, may have in establishing or disputing a child's parentage is also recognised. In a series of decisions,[42] the European Court of Human Rights has also found breaches of the Convention where fathers have not been afforded an opportunity to present DNA evidence to establish paternity, or to deny paternity where the law has presumed it. It has held that 'the situation in which a legal presumption is allowed to prevail over biological and social reality, without regard to both established facts and the wishes of those concerned and without actually benefiting anyone, is not compatible, even having regard to the margin of appreciation left to the State, with the obligation to secure effective "respect" for private and family life.'[43]

The decision in *Mikulić* was applied in domestic law in *Rose v Secretary of State for Health and Human Fertilisation and Embryology Authority*,[44] in which the claimants were both an adult and a child. Both had been born as a result of artificial insemination by anonymous donor sperm. They requested the Secretary of State to make available non-identifying information about sperm donors and to institute a voluntary contact register to facilitate contact between donors and their offspring where they wished to have it. The Secretary of State responded that a consultation paper would be published shortly and ministers would

---

[37] *Mikulić v Croatia* (App no 53176/99) [2002] 1 FCR 720, para 53. See S. Besson, 'Enforcing the Child's Right to Know her Origins: Contrasting Approaches under the Convention on the Rights of the Child and the European Convention on Human Rights' (2007) 21(2) International Journal of Law, Policy and the Family 137.

[38] (App no 53176/99) [2002] 1 FCR 720.   [39] Ibid.   [40] At para 44.   [41] Ibid, para 66.

[42] *Tavli v Turkey* [2007] 1 FLR 1136, ECtHR; *Paulik v Slovakia* (App no 10699/05) [2007] 1 FLR 1090, ECtHR; *Shofman v Russia* (App no 74826/01) [2006] 1 FLR 680, ECtHR (no challenge possible because of expiry of one-year time limit); *Mizzi v Malta* (App no 2611/02) [2006] 1 FLR 1048, ECtHR (no mechanism to disavow parenthood arising from presumption of legitimacy despite scientific tests); *Rozanski v Poland* (App no 55339/00) [2006] 2 FCR 178. See A. Bainham, 'Truth Will Out: Paternity in Europe' [2007] Cambridge Law Journal 278.

[43] See also *Paulik v Slovakia* (App no 10699/05) [2007] 1 FLR 1090, ECtHR (breach of convention where no legal mechanism to disclaim legal paternity of 40-year-old 'daughter' who had no objection to the applicant disclaiming paternity on the basis of DNA tests which showed he was not her father: see esp paras [43], [44], and [47]); and *Tavli v Turkey* (App no 11449/02) [2007] 1 FLR 1136, ECtHR (breach of Art 8 where Turkish law did not permit admission of fresh DNA evidence to annul earlier decision as to applicant's paternity of his wife's child and to permit re-trial): 'domestic courts should interpret the existing legislation in the light of scientific progress and the social repercussions that follow' (at [36]).

[44] [2002] EWHC 1593 (Admin), QB, Scott Baker J.

then consider the matter. The claimants sought judicial review of this response, arguing that their rights under Article 8 of the ECHR were engaged and that the state had positive obligations to comply with their requests. Scott Baker J found that Article 8 was engaged, holding that the concept of personal identity within Article 8 recognised by the European Court of Human Rights 'plainly includes the right to obtain information about a biological parent who will inevitably have contributed to the identity of his child'.[45] Following this decision, the Human Fertilisation and Embryology Authority (Disclosure of Donor Information) Regulations 2004 made provision regulating the disclosure of donor information (see Section 3.8.2).

There is, however, no absolute right to knowledge of origins, as demonstrated by the decision of the Grand Chamber of the European Court of Human Rights in *Odièvre v France*.[46] The case concerned the procedure permitted by French law (known as 'accouchement sous X') which allowed a mother to give birth anonymously, and prohibited subsequent disclosure of information identifying the mother. The policy underlying the French law was to protect the mother's health during pregnancy, to prevent abortions, and to avoid children being abandoned in other, possibly harmful, ways.[47] Ms Odièvre, whose mother had given birth anonymously under this law, claimed that her inability to establish the identity of her mother breached Article 8 of the ECHR. The Court, distinguishing *Mikulić v Croatia*,[48] found by a majority of 10 to 7, no violation of the applicant's rights. The majority observed that Article 8 also applied to the mother, and the mother's interests, for example in remaining anonymous in order to protect her health by giving birth in appropriate medical conditions, were not easily reconciled with the applicant's interests.[49] The Court also recognised that the general interest was at stake, one of the aims of the legislation being respect for life, a higher ranking value guaranteed by the Convention.[50] In these circumstances, the Court found that France had not exceeded its margin of appreciation. There was a strong dissenting opinion, however, which did not accept the Court's distinguishing of earlier authorities. The minority pointed out that the Court's role is to examine whether a fair balance has been struck between the competing interests, and it is not a matter of determining which interest, in a given case, must take absolute precedence over others.[51] They observed that no balancing of interests was possible in this case since French law accepted the mother's decision as an absolute defence to requests for information.[52] Furthermore, there were no reliable data to show that there would be an increased risk of abortion or infanticide if the system of anonymous births were abolished.[53] As to the margin of appreciation afforded to France, the minority observed that 'no other legislative system is so weighted in favour of the protection of maternal anonymity',[54] and that the majority failed to take account of the consensus to be found in international instruments such as in Article 7 of the UNCRC. The minority was 'firmly of the opinion that the *right to an identity*... is within the inner core of the right to respect for one's private life' and accordingly 'the fairest scrutiny was called for when weighing up the competing interests'.[55]

---

[45] Ibid, [48].

[46] (App no 42326/98) [2002] 1 FCR 621, ECtHR (Grand Chamber). See E. Steiner, 'Desperately Seeking Mother—Anonymous Births in the European Court of Human Rights' (2003) 15(4) Child and Family Law Quarterly 425–448. See also the discussion of secret adoptions in Chapter 11.

[47] See N. Lefaucheur, 'The French 'Tradition' of Anonymous Birth: The Lines of Argument' (2004) 18(3) International Journal of Law, Policy and the Family 319.

[48] (App no 53176/99) [2002] 1 FCR 720 and *Gaskin v UK* (App no 10454/83) (1989) 12 EHRR 36 (adult's claim for access to social services records regarding his upbringing in care).

[49] (App no 42326/98) [2002] 1 FCR 621, ECtHR (Grand Chamber), para 44.   [50] Ibid, para 45.

[51] Ibid, Dissenting Opinion, para 6.   [52] Ibid, para 7.   [53] Ibid, para 9.   [54] Ibid, para 13.

[55] Ibid, para 11.

Later decisions have adopted this view that there must be a very careful weighing of the competing interests against a person's interest in establishing his or her identity. In *Jäggi v Switzerland*[56] the Court found a violation of Article 8 where it was unconvinced by the Swiss authorities' reasons for refusing a 67-year-old man's request for DNA testing of the corpse of a man who, in 1939, had been declared his father. The Court observed:

> the right to an identity, which includes the right to know one's parentage, is an integral part of the notion of private life. In such cases, particularly rigorous scrutiny is called for when weighing up the competing interests.

In line with the approach established by the European Court of Human Rights, Ryder J observed in *Lambeth London Borough v S, C, V and J (By His Guardian)*[57] that:

> A person's right to establish their identity is not absolute in the sense that there is no absolute right of access to genetic information. Access to genetic information may be controlled by the state, but if that control is to be lawful ie human rights compliant there has to be a mechanism that provides that any interference is only that which is lawful, necessary in a democratic society for the specified Art 8(2) purposes and proportionate.

In that case a boy, aged 7, was the subject of care proceedings. D, a man assumed to be the boy's father, had been unlawfully killed by the mother's husband. In the course of their investigation, the police obtained from a blood sample a DNA profile. In the care proceedings the local authority's plan was to place the boy with D's mother (his paternal grandmother), which the child's mother resisted on the basis of her allegation that there was no genetic link between the child and D. The local authority sought a direction that the DNA evidence held by the police be released in order to determine conclusively the child's paternity. Ryder J held that there was no power to order disclosure and dismissed the application. He held that the use of the sample was restricted to the purposes specified in section 64(1A) of the Police and Criminal Evidence Act 1984, which regulates the use of retained samples. To remain human rights-compliant that provision had to be construed strictly, and the prohibition on other uses was a proportionate interference having regard to the public policy which underpins the 1984 Act.[58]

The increased focus on individual rights, together with scientific developments, has meant that if any general trend can be identified in the case law on section 20 of the Family Law Reform Act 1969, it has been towards ascertaining the truth by recognising parentage. However, the case law illustrates that the child's interests may occasionally demand that forensic testing does not take place.[59]

In *Re F (A Minor) (Blood Tests: Parental Rights)*[60] a child, E, was conceived at a time when her mother, Mrs F, was having sexual relations with both her husband (Mr F) and the applicant, Mr B. The relationship between Mrs F and Mr B ended before E's birth, and E had been brought up as a child of Mr and Mrs F's family. B had had no contact with E. Believing that he was her natural father, B applied for a parental responsibility order under section 4 of the Children Act 1989, and an order for contact under sections 8 and 10 of that Act. Those applications raised the issue of B's paternity, since the court only has jurisdiction under section 4 to make a parental responsibility order in favour of the child's father, and Mr B could only apply for a contact order (without leave of the court) if he was

---

[56] App No 58757/00, ECtHR.   [57] [2006] EWHC 326 (Fam), [2007] 1 FLR 152.
[58] Ibid, [44]–[46].
[59] For discussion of the role of rights and welfare in this context, see J. Wallbank, 'The Role of Rights and Utility in Instituting a Child's Right to Know her Genetic History' (2004) 13 Social and Legal Studies 245–263.   [60] [1993] Fam 314, CA.

E's father. B applied in the proceedings, therefore, for a direction for testing to determine paternity. Judge Callman dismissed the application on the basis that the father's prospects of success in his applications for contact and parental responsibility were 'remote and unlikely', and it would thus be unfair to expose the child to the risk of losing the presumption of legitimacy.[61] The Court of Appeal upheld this decision. While finding that the judge had perhaps placed rather more emphasis on the presumption of legitimacy than is appropriate in modern circumstances, the court held that this did not detract from the general thrust of the judge's approach, with which it could find no error. The court agreed with the judge, commenting:

> If the probable outcome of [the] proceedings will be the same whoever may be the natural father of E., then there can be no point in exposing E. to the possible disadvantages of a blood test.

The Court of Appeal was unmoved by Mr B's argument that it was in E's interests to know the truth about her parentage, for example to allow her knowledge of her genetic make-up which might be relevant for the possible diagnosis, prevention, mitigation, or cure of some medical disorder. The court saw the chance that this 'might operate so as to harm E's interests' as 'infinitesimal when brought into balance against the harm that might be caused to her if B were able to proceed with his applications'.[62] In addition, Mr B's argument based on Article 7 of the UNCRC,[63] which provides that a child shall have 'as far as possible, the right to know and be cared for by his or her parents' was given short shrift. Balcombe LJ responded that in this case it was 'not in fact possible for E to be cared for by both her parents (if B is such)'.[64] The court commented:

> E's welfare depends for the foreseeable future primarily upon her relationship with her mother...Anything that may disturb that relationship or the stability of the family unit within which E has lived since her birth is likely to be detrimental to E's welfare, and unless that detriment is shown to be counter-balanced by other positive advantages to her which an order for the taking of blood tests could confer, then the judge's refusal to order blood tests was not merely an exercise of his discretion with which we can not interfere, but one with which in the circumstances of this case we agree.[65]

This decision may be criticised for placing 'very little weight on the value to E of knowing the truth about her parentage, as a benefit in its own right, quite detached from the potential value of a parent–child relationship with B'.[66] As Fortin argues, the court 'should have given greater weight to the psychological value to E of knowing the truth about her origins'.[67] She rightly points out that the link between the issue of testing and the outcome of the substantive applications was illogical, since it is 'perfectly possible for a court to decide that though it will not benefit a child ever to meet her natural parent, it is psychologically important for her to know the truth about her origins'.[68] In other words, the law might become more coherent if the issue of biological parentage were detached from the issue of the child's social relationships.[69]

---

[61] Ibid, 319.   [62] Ibid, 320.   [63] Treaty Series No 44 of 1992 (Cm 1976).

[64] [1993] Fam 314 at 321.

[65] Ibid. For another example, see *O v L (Blood Tests)* [1995] 2 FLR 930, CA, explained in the second edition of this book.

[66] J. Fortin, '*Re F*: "The Gooseberry Bush Approach"' (1994) 57 Modern Law Review 296 at 297.

[67] Ibid, 298.   [68] Ibid.

[69] Ibid, 306. See for a similar view, J. Eekelaar, 'Parenthood, Social Engineering and Rights' in D. Morgan and G. Douglas (eds), *Constituting Families: A Study in Governance* (Stuttgart: Steiner, 1994).

Some of the difficulties with the Court of Appeal's approach in *Re F* received acknowledgement in *Re H (A Minor) (Blood Tests: Parental Rights)*,[70] which adopted a different emphasis. There a mother and her husband had two children together. The husband then had a vasectomy and for the following five years the couple continued to have sexual intercourse without conceiving a child. The marriage fell into difficulties and the mother began a sexual relationship with another man, the applicant. She fell pregnant at a time when she was having sexual relations with both her husband and the applicant. She believed, however, that the applicant was the baby's father, and involved him in her antenatal care. The husband moved out of the matrimonial home, and initially there was an understanding that the applicant would move in. In preparation for this, the mother told her eldest child (then aged 13) about her pregnancy and plans, and that the baby's father was not her husband. The plans did not materialise, however, as the mother terminated the affair and was reconciled with her husband, who accepted the baby as his own. The applicant applied for a parental responsibility order and a contact order and, if paternity was denied, a direction for scientific testing. The judge made the direction and on appeal by the mother the Court of Appeal upheld the judge's decision.

In contrast to the court's approach in *Re F*, the Court of Appeal held that the paternity issue is 'entitled to consideration on its own'[71] as distinct from the parental responsibility and contact order proceedings. The 'outcome of the proceedings in which the paternity issue has been raised, in so far as it bears on the welfare of the child, must be taken into account' but whilst those proceedings 'are obviously factors which impinge on the child's welfare', they are 'not determinative' of the question whether there should be testing.[72] Ward LJ observed that there are two separate rights in Article 7 of the UNCRC, 'the one to know, and the other to be cared for by, one's parents', and that Balcombe LJ's judgment in *Re F* had concentrated on the child's right to be cared for.[73] In Ward LJ's view (with which Neill LJ agreed) 'every child has a right to know the truth unless his welfare clearly justifies the cover up'.[74]

Ward LJ, while emphasising that in cases which depend on the exercise of a discretion it is seldom useful to draw factual similarities between cases, addressed counsel's submission that there was similarity between *Re F* and this case, but remained unpersuaded. The applicant here had a substantial claim to be the child's father as evidenced by the mother's belief that he was the father, and by her husband's vasectomy. Thus the claimant would have a good chance of establishing paternity irrespective of whether a direction were given. The judge had been correct, therefore, to make the direction to obtain the best evidence. Moreover, the truth could not be repressed forever as the eldest child was already aware of the paternity issue. As the court put it, better that the child should know the truth rather that 'a time-bomb ticking away'.[75]

In *Re T (Paternity: Ordering Blood Tests)*[76] a husband and wife, who had been unable to have a baby (it having been established that the husband had a low sperm count) agreed that the wife would have sexual intercourse with another man. The wife did so with the applicant and with three other men during a period when she was likely to conceive. The wife became pregnant and gave birth to a child, T, who was brought up by his mother and her husband. When the child was about 1 year old, the applicant had applied for parental responsibility and contact without success and the magistrates had refused

---

[70] [1997] Fam 89, CA. For comment see B. Gilbert, 'Paternity, Truth and the Interests of the Child—Some Problems of *Re H (Paternity: Blood Test)*' [1996] Child and Family Law Quarterly 361; A. Bainham, 'Vasectomies, Lovers and Disputed Offspring: Honesty is the Best Policy (Sometimes)' (1996) 55 Cambridge Law Journal 444–446.   [71] [1997] Fam 89 at 105.

[72] Ibid.

[73] See J. Fortin, '*Re F*: "The Gooseberry Bush Approach"' (1994) 57 Modern Law Review 296 at 305.

[74] [1997] Fam 89 at 106.   [75] Ibid, 108.   [76] [2001] 2 FLR 1190, FD (Bodey J).

to give a direction for DNA testing. At that time the child's paternity was put in the public domain by doubts and suspicions 'going round' a local school and by the applicant's behaviour. He proclaimed himself the father on citizens-band radio, attended the husband's workplace with a placard proclaiming the same, and put leaflets with the same message through local letterboxes. The applicant renewed his applications when T was aged 7, following the passing of the Human Rights Act 1998. Bodey J gave a direction for testing. In his Lordship's view this was not a situation in which tests would create a serious risk of de-stabilising the present family, and any such risk was outweighed by the risk of T learning of the suspicions about his paternity given that they were public knowledge. Bodey J explained that T 'has a right to respect for his private life (in the sense of having knowledge of his identify, which encompasses his true paternity)'. T also had a right to respect for his family life which should not be put at risk except as held to be in T's interests. In addition, the mother and the husband had rights to respect for family life which should not be intruded upon, except as might be necessary to give effect to T's rights, or the applicant's (if he were to be found to have a right to respect for family life within Article 8).[77] Evaluating and balancing those various interests, Bodey J concluded:

> the weightiest emerges clearly as being that of T, namely that he should have the possibility of knowing, perhaps with certainty, his true roots and identity. I find that any such interference as would occur to the right to respect for the family/private life of the mother and her husband, to be proportionate to the legitimate aim of providing T with the possibility of certainty as to his real paternity, a knowledge which would accompany him throughout his life.[78]

In *Re H and A (Children)*[79] the Court of Appeal made clear that the approaches taken in *Re H* and in *Re T* are not necessarily confined to cases with similar facts, namely when there is some doubt surrounding the procreative capacity of the husband concerned. In *Re H and A (Children)* Mrs R had a sexual relationship with Mr B for four years, during which time twins were conceived and born. Her husband, Mr R, remained in ignorance of his wife's adultery and accepted the twins as his own, taking over their primary care when his wife went out to work. Upon the breakdown of the adulterous relationship, Mr B sought contact and parental responsibility in respect of the children. For a year Mrs R managed to conceal the litigation from her husband while she challenged Mr B's paternity. Mr R became aware of the proceedings when he stumbled upon some court papers in his wife's handbag (here lies a lesson for every man!). Mr R subsequently gave evidence in the proceedings, stating that if Mr B were found to be the father he would be unable to continue to care for the children. Mr R stated that he was 99 per cent certain that he was the father. The judge dismissed the application for fear of the 'disastrous disintegrative effects' on the existing family of a finding that Mr B was the father. He distinguished the case from *Re H* and *Re T* on the basis that in this case the husband did not have a low sperm count nor had he had a vasectomy.[80] The Court of Appeal remitted the case for re-trial,[81] holding that the judge had erred in the balancing process. He had given too simplistic an emphasis to the strength of the marriage given the wife's continuing lack

---

[77] Bodey J suggested *obiter* that it was unlikely on the facts that the applicant could make out a successful case for existing 'family life'.

[78] *Re T (Paternity: Ordering Blood Tests)* [2001] 2 FLR 1190 at 1197–1198. See for other human rights analyses in this context, Dame Elizabeth Butler-Sloss P in *Secretary of State for Work and Pensions v Jones* [2003] EWHC 2163 (Fam), [2004] 1 FLR 282 at [18] and Ryder J in *Lambeth London Borough v S, C, V and J (By His Guardian)* [2006] EWHC 326 (Fam), [2007] 1 FLR 152 at [29].

[79] [2002] EWCA Civ 383, [2002] 2 FCR 469.   [80] Ibid, [16].   [81] Ibid, [31].

of candour about her relationship with Mr B.[82] He had also given insufficient weight to the possibility of the matter coming to the children's attention in the future, given the existence of gossip at the mother's workplace and the fact that Mr B had made known his convictions to his family and friends.[83] The Court of Appeal doubted whether the judge gave sufficient weight to the importance of certainty, and held that the factual differences between this case and others did not begin to:

> displace the points of principle to be drawn from the cases, first that the interests of justice are best served by the ascertainment of the truth and second that the court should be furnished with the best available science and not confined to such unsatisfactory alternatives as presumptions and inferences.[84]

2.4.1 Consent and the effect of a direction

Section 20(1) does not empower the court to *order* an adult to be tested;[85] all that it does in that context is permit a direction for the use of tests to ascertain paternity.[86] Section 21(1) of the 1969 Act makes clear that, subject to provisions of that section, a person's consent is required to the taking of a bodily sample[87] in order to give effect to a direction under section 20. Section 21(4) provides, however, that a sample may be taken from a person who lacks capacity[88] to give his consent, if consent is given by the court, or certain persons authorised to consent on that person's behalf.[89] In respect of children, section 21(2), in line with section 8 of the 1969 Act, clarifies that the consent of a child aged 16 or over is as effective as if he or she were of full age. In the case of a child under 16 (not being such a person as is referred to in s 21(4)) a sample can be taken if the person who has care and control of the child consents, or if the court considers that it would be in the child's best interests for the sample to be taken.[90] A notable omission from section 21 is any reference to the ability of the competent child under 16 to consent to testing but presumably a competent child under 16 could provide consent under the common law in *Gillick v West Norfolk and Wisbech AHA*.[91] The section implies, in line with the common law's approach to children's refusal of consent, that the child's refusal to be tested can be overridden by the child's carer,[92] and explicitly states that the sample can be taken if the court considers it would be in the child's best interests.[93] However, in *Re D (Paternity)*[94] Hedley J held that 'best interests' in section 21(3) 'must pay particular regard to the views of the child having regard to his age

---

[82] Ibid, [26] and [27].   [83] Ibid, [20].   [84] Ibid, [29].

[85] See *S v S; W v Official Solicitor* [1972] AC 24 at 43 *per* Lord Reid, at 52 *per* Lord Morris of Borth-y-Gest, and at 57 *per* Lord Hodson.

[86] [1997] Fam 89, CA at 100D (discussion in context of direction for blood tests).

[87] Defined in the Family Law Reform Act 1969, s 25, as a 'sample of bodily fluid or bodily tissue taken for the purpose of scientific tests'.

[88] Within the meaning of the Mental Capacity Act 2005.

[89] Eg the donee of an enduring, or lasting, power of attorney, or a deputy appointed by the Court of Protection: see Family Law Reform Act 1969, s 21(4).   [90] Family Law Reform Act 1969, s 21(3).

[91] [1986] AC 112.

[92] A person who probably will, but may not necessarily, have parental responsibility within the meaning of the Children Act 1989, s 3. The statutory provisions do not sit easily with the comment of Lord Reid in *S v S; W v Official Solicitor* [1972] AC 24 at 45, that 'as soon as a child is able to understand these matters it would generally be unwise to subject it to this operation against its will'.

[93] However, see *Re P (Identity of Mother)* [2011] EWCA Civ 795, [2012] 1 FLR 351, where at [13] the Court of Appeal commented that it was not envisaged that a sample would be taken from the 15-year-old child concerned without her consent; but the court added that that 'does not leave the court powerless, or reliant on findings of fact based on the balance of probabilities. The statute is very clear that it is open to the court to draw an inference based on [the child's] refusal to provide a sample.'

[94] [2006] EWHC 3545 (Fam), [2007] 2 FLR 26.

and understanding'.[95] In that case a child, T, was placed shortly after his birth with a woman who was assumed to be his paternal grandmother and brought up by her. Her son had been identified by T's teenage mother as his father and he had acknowledged his paternity. On T's 10th birthday, he was visited by a man (the applicant in the case) who had had a relationship with T's mother around the time of his conception. The applicant was accompanied by a friend, who tactlessly introduced the applicant to T as his real father. Shortly thereafter the applicant made applications for residence, contact, and parental responsibility in respect of T, in which the issue of T's paternity was raised. T had had a difficult childhood, experiencing educational and behavioural problems, and was described as 'a troubled and angry person'. T was adamant that he wanted nothing to do with the applicant and was 'deeply resistant to scientific testing'. Hedley J saw consent as integral to the workings of Part III of the 1969 Act and focused on whether a sample should be taken from T in his best interests pursuant to section 21(3) of the Family Law Reform Act 1969.

Hedley J found that T's opposition was his own view expressed at a 'highly emotive stage of his life', and was satisfied that while it was in T's best interests to know the truth sooner rather than later, it was not in T's interests to press the issue at this turbulent point his life. His Lordship thus gave a direction that the applicant be tested, but stayed without limit of time a similar direction in relation to T, in the hope that T would be encouraged to think about the issue and if he eventually agreed to be tested the results could be made known to the applicant.

It should be noted therefore that the child's interests can be considered at two distinct stages, first under section 20, and if a direction is given then possibly again under section 21. There are different approaches to welfare at each stage and judges must take care not to confuse the two tests.[96]

2.4.2 Failure to comply with a direction

Key legislation

Section 23(1) of the Family Law Reform Act 1969 provides that:

Where a court gives a direction under section 20 of this Act and any person fails to take any step required of him for the purpose of giving effect to the direction, the court may draw such inferences, if any, from that fact as appear proper in the circumstances.

Where paternity proceedings arise in relation to a child who is born to a married woman, and where consent to scientific testing is refused by one of the adults concerned, the legal position is made more complicated by the presumption of legitimacy. Section 23(2) separates the presumption of legitimacy from claiming relief in reliance on the presumption. In a case in which a party who is relying on the presumption refuses to be tested, or to allow the child to be tested, the court may dismiss the claim for relief even though there may be an absence of evidence to rebut the presumption. An example might be where a married woman alleges that a man other than her husband is the father of her child for child support purposes. Where the man denies paternity, but refuses to be tested, it seems that it would be possible for a court to order that the man should be liable to make child support payments, even though there is an absence of evidence to rebut the presumption of legitimacy. However, where a husband relies on the presumption of legitimacy and refuses to be tested, the inference will be drawn that he is not the father of the child.

---

[95] Ibid, [24].   [96] See eg *Re L (A Child)* [2009] EWCA Civ 1239, [2010] 2 FLR 188.

2.4.3 Inferences to be drawn from a failure to comply with a direction

What inferences may a court properly draw from the refusal of a person to be tested in the face of the court's direction? This question arose in *Re A (A Minor) (Paternity: Refusal of Blood Test)*.[97] In that case a mother was having a sexual relationship with three different men around the time of her child's conception. In the circumstances each could equally have been the child's father but the mother claimed child support maintenance against only one, Mr G, a 'prosperous businessman' who 'lived a luxurious life'.[98] A direction for testing to ascertain paternity was made in the proceedings but Mr G failed to cooperate. His argument was that he should not be put at risk of a finding of paternity when two other men were also 'in the frame' yet not similarly at risk. The judge dismissed the application, finding that he could not conclude on the balance of probabilities that Mr G was the father, and could not draw an inference from the failure to be tested that Mr G knew that he was the father. The Court of Appeal overturned the judge's decision, remitting the case for hearing of the level of maintenance that Mr G should pay. Waite LJ (Sir Ralph Gibson agreeing) held that the judge had fallen into error in so limiting his powers of inference under section 23(1) of the Family Law Reform Act 1969. The court explained that those powers are 'wholly at large and unconfined' and 'amply wide enough to extend to an inference drawn as to the very fact which is in issue in the proceedings, namely the child's actual paternity'.[99] In determining what inference should be drawn in the case, Waite LJ explained that genetic testing can now achieve certainty, and commented:

> Any man who is unsure of his own paternity and harbours the least doubt as to whether the child he is alleged to have fathered may be that of another man now has it within his power to set all doubt at rest by submitting to a test. It has ceased, therefore, to be possible for any man in such circumstances to be forced against his will to accept paternity of a child whom he does not believe to be his.
>
> Against that background of law and scientific advance, it seems to me to follow, both in justice and common sense, that if a mother makes a claim against one of the possible fathers, and he chooses to exercise his right not to submit to be tested, the inference that he is the father of the child should be virtually inescapable. He would certainly have to advance very clear and cogent reasons for this refusal to be tested—reasons which it would be just and fair and reasonable for him to be allowed to maintain.[100]

The court found the father's reason for refusal irrelevant. It held that the issue was one of evidence, not equity, and that the court 'should find proven forensically what G, by his refusal has prevented from being established scientifically'.[101]

Subsequently, courts have adopted a robust approach where one of the parties has refused to be tested and have taken full advantage of their entitlement to draw such inferences as appear proper.

In *Re G (Parentage: Blood Sample)*[102] Thorpe LJ added:

> The court must be astute to discern what are the real motivations behind the refusal. It should look critically at proffered explanation or justification. It should only uphold an explanation that is objectively valid, demonstrating rationality, logicality, and consistency. Anything less will usually lead to an adverse inference.[103]

In that case the applicant sought a contact order in respect of a child whom he believed he had conceived with his former wife. Several directions for testing were made in the

[97] [1994] 2 FLR 463, CA.   [98] Ibid, 470.   [99] Ibid, 472.
[100] Ibid, 472–473.   [101] Ibid, 473.   [102] *Re G (Parentage: Blood Sample)* [1997] 1 FLR 360, CA.
[103] Ibid, 367.

proceedings after the mother put the applicant's paternity in issue by suggesting that she had had sexual intercourse with another man around the time of the child's conception. Despite the directions, the applicant refused to be tested. The applicant declared that he was 99.9 per cent certain that he was the child's father but was unwilling to undergo testing. This was because the child would be upset if she were to be told that he was not the father, and the mother would use that finding to thwart his contact. In the absence of scientific evidence the judge declared that the applicant was the child's father on the bases, *inter alia*, that he could not be satisfied that sexual intercourse had not taken place between the parties at the relevant time; that the applicant had been registered as the father on the child's birth certificate; and that the mother had only put the child's paternity in issue two and a half years after the child's birth. The Court of Appeal held that the judge had misdirected himself in not drawing an adverse inference against the father for his failure to undergo testing. The court noted the illogicality of the father's stance, and that his assessment of the probabilities was wrong: on the evidence he could have no better than a 50 per cent chance of being the father. While acknowledging that counsel was correct that the absence of scientific testing did not alter those probabilities, the court pointed out that the proper inference permitted by section 23 of the Family Law Reform Act 1969 was held in *Re A (A Minor) (Paternity: Refusal of Blood Test)*[104] to be a 'forensic inference', and commented:

> The forensic process is advanced by presenting the truth to the court. He who obstructs the truth will have the inference drawn against him. The inexorable advance of science cannot be ignored.[105]

In summary, therefore, except in respect of a child the courts cannot compel the availability of necessary scientific evidence to ascertain paternity. They can merely direct such evidence be made available in the hope that the direction will be complied with. Where it is not, a proper inference (presumably that the refusal to comply is made to hide the truth) may be drawn. Indeed, it has been said that an inference could be drawn even where no direction has been given if there has been a failure to provide the best evidence, 'even if the inference is not as strong as when the court's direction is flouted'.[106]

2.5 DISCLOSURE OF PARENTAGE TO CHILDREN

As we have seen, the courts have increasingly taken the view that normally the truth about a child's parentage should emerge, and that attempts to obstruct this process should be met by the drawing of adverse inferences. In *Re D (Paternity)* Hedley J observed that this approach has obvious merits: 'truth...is easier to handle than fiction and also it is designed to avoid information coming to a young person's attention in a haphazard, unorganized and indeed sometimes malicious context'.[107]

However, concern has been expressed that the shift in the case law may be going too far too quickly in one direction.[108] There is a risk that the focus on ascertaining the truth is applied in practice almost as a blanket rule. Family dynamics vary from one household to another, particularly over an issue as sensitive as contested paternity. Directions for scientific tests may force disclosure at a time which may not fit in with the child's pace and

---

[104] [1994] 2 FLR 463, CA.   [105] Ibid, 466–467.
[106] *Re H (A Minor) (Blood Tests: Parental Rights)* [1997] Fam 89 at 103.
[107] [2006] EWHC 3545 (Fam), [2007] 2 FLR 26 (Hedley J).
[108] J. Fortin, 'Children's Right to Know Their Origins–Too Far, Too Fast?' [2009] Child and Family Law Quarterly 336–355.

sense of security, or may deliver a body blow to a recovering marriage which is still fragile with regard to the previous relationship which led to the child's birth. If forcing scientific testing on an unwilling married couple has a destructive effect on their personal relationship, or on the husband's relationship with the child, this may be more harmful to the child than giving him knowledge of the true facts during childhood. While some men may have no difficulty in treating another man's child as their own even where there is doubt about the child's paternity, other men may find it emotionally impossible to continue to respond to the child as their own where the fact of their non-paternity is established by incontrovertible evidence. Cultural factors may sometimes play a significant role in these responses.[109]

There is an argument, therefore, that while the courts should be aware of the benefits of truth and the child's interests in knowing his or her origins, they should also be able to respond flexibly to parentage disputes in a manner which is able to acknowledge the complexity of adult relationships, and which is perceptive of the family life of the particular child concerned.

Even where scientific testing has established that a man is the father of a child, it does not follow that the child will necessarily come to know of that paternity. In *J v C*[110] a child believed that his mother's long-term partner was his father, although in proceedings for contact by a man, J, DNA testing confirmed that J was the father. The proceedings were adjourned to determine whether the child's conception was forced, as the mother claimed, or consensual as J claimed. By the time of the hearing, the whereabouts of the father were unknown and the application was not pursued. The question arose, however, whether the court could, and should, of its own motion direct that the child be informed about his true father. Presuming that he had the necessary jurisdiction, Sumner J concluded that he should not do so in this case because of the mother's vulnerability to mental illness, explaining that the advantage of the child learning the truth was 'outweighed by the impact it would be likely to have on his mother and family upon whom he is so dependent'.[111] However, his Lordship urged the family to take advice, commenting that for the boy to know sooner rather than later might be to his advantage, rather than waiting until 16 when the impact might be greater given the turmoil of puberty.[112]

3 LEGAL PARENTHOOD

3.1 MOTHERHOOD

Lord Simon of Glaisdale in the *Ampthill Peerage Case* stated that motherhood, although 'a legal relationship, is based on a fact, being proved demonstrably by parturition'.[113] These words do not equate giving birth with motherhood; they speak of proving motherhood. It could be argued therefore that, as a matter of the *common law*, the underlying basis for motherhood might be the genetic connection, as *evidenced by* parturition. Usually of course there is no issue because the woman carrying the child will also be the genetic mother. However, a woman can now give birth to a child to whom she is not genetically related, for example where an embryo is implanted in her which has been created with the egg of another woman. Is the woman who gave birth the mother of the child or is the woman who

---

[109] See eg in the context of contact: *Re B (Contact: Stepfather's Opposition)* [1997] 2 FLR 579.
[110] [2006] EWHC 2837 (Fam), [2007] 1 FCR 365 (Sumner J).   [111] Ibid, [12].   [112] Ibid, [14].
[113] [1977] AC 547 at 577.

donated her egg the mother? Later in this chapter we shall explore the competing arguments in this situation. The law in statute, however, answers this question unequivocally.

Key legislation

Section 33 of the Human Fertilisation and Embryology Act (HFEA) 2008 provides:

> The woman who is carrying or has carried a child as a result of the placing in her of an embryo or of sperm and eggs,[114] and no other woman, is to be treated as the mother of the child.[115]

An identical provision is to be found in section 27 of the HFEA 1990, which applies prior to implementation of the 2008 Act. Whichever provision applies, however, the law is clear that the woman who gives birth to a child is the child's mother whether or not the child is genetically related to her.

Talking point

As Baroness Hale commented in *Re G (Children) (Residence: Same-Sex Partner)*:[116]

> While this may be partly for reasons of certainty and convenience, it also recognises a deeper truth: that the process of carrying a child and giving him birth (which may well be followed by breast-feeding for some months) brings with it, in the vast majority of cases, a very special relationship between mother and child, a relationship which is different from any other.[117]

3.2 FATHERHOOD

3.2.1 The general rule

The general rule in English law, subject to provisions of the Human Fertilisation and Embryology Acts (discussed in the following sections), is that a child's father is the man whose sperm resulted in the child's conception. Unless a statutory provision applies to the contrary, the child's father will be his or her genetic father.[118] In most cases, therefore, the issue of who, in law, is the father of a child will simply be a question of the child's *parentage*.

3.2.2 Assisted conception and fatherhood

The fatherhood of a child conceived through assisted conception may be determined by one of three different statutes, depending upon the date of the child's conception: the Family Law Reform Act 1987, the HFEA 1990, or the HFEA 2008.

Key legislation

Section 27 of the Family Law Reform Act 1987 was the first provision to regulate fatherhood in cases of assisted conception, and to recognise legal parenthood in a case where there was

---

[114] Whether this happened in the UK or elsewhere: see s 33(3).

[115] The provision does not apply to the extent that the child is treated by virtue of adoption as not being the woman's child: see s 33(2).

[116] [2006] 4 All ER 241.   [117] Ibid, [34].

[118] Illustrated by the *Leeds* case discussed in Section 3.7.

no blood relationship between the adult and child concerned.[119] It allowed fatherhood to be conferred on the mother's husband in a case of her artificial insemination by another man. It came into force on 4 April 1988 and provided:

(1) Where after the coming into force of this section a child is born in England and Wales as the result of the artificial insemination of a woman who—

(a) was at the time of the insemination a party to a marriage (being a marriage which had not at that time been dissolved or annulled); and

(b) was artificially inseminated with the semen of some person other than the other party to that marriage,

then, unless it is proved to the satisfaction of any court by which the matter has to be determined that the other party to that marriage did not consent to the insemination, the child shall be treated in law as the child of the parties to that marriage and shall not be treated as the child of any person other than the parties to that marriage.

The HFEA 1990, which was brought into force on 1 August 1991, introduced, in sections 27–29, new provisions regulating parenthood in light of scientific advances in assisted reproduction techniques.[120] As we have seen, the Act clarified who was to be the mother of a child in cases of egg donation. Section 28(2) of the 1990 Act adopted the same formula as section 27 of the Family Law Reform Act 1987 with respect to a woman's husband acquiring legal fatherhood, with some necessary re-wording to extend its substance beyond artificial insemination to other forms of assisted conception. Section 27 of the 1987 Act therefore became otiose for the future, and the 1990 Act provided[121] that it was not to have effect in relation to children carried as a result of artificial insemination after the commencement of relevant provisions of the 1990 Act. Section 27 of the Family Law Reform Act 1987 still remains applicable, however, to determining parenthood in the case of some children conceived through artificial insemination prior to implementation of sections 27–29 of the 1990 Act. Indeed, as we shall see later, the Court of Appeal had occasion to interpret and apply it as recently as 2006 in *J v C and Another*.[122]

The 1990 Act was groundbreaking in introducing (in s 28(3)) a provision which allowed the male partner of a woman, to whom she was not married, to become the legal father of a child to whom he was not genetically related, provided the couple were having treatment services together at a licensed clinic.

Part II of the HFEA 2008 sets out, in sections 33–48, a new scheme for determining parenthood in cases of assisted reproduction. Those provisions will apply only to children carried by women as a result of the placing in them of embryos or of sperm and eggs, or their artificial insemination (as the case may be) after their commencement,[123] and sections 27–29 of the 1990 Act do not have effect after that time.[124] The 2008 Act's provisions on parenthood were implemented on 6 April 2009, except for section 54 (parental orders) which was implemented on 6 April 2010. The new Act is the product of a

---

[119] Following a recommendation of the Law Commission in its *Report on Illegitimacy* (Law Com No 118, 1982), paras 12.1–12.27.

[120] The Act was preceded by the *Report of the Committee of Inquiry into Human Fertilisation and Embryology* (the Warnock Committee) (Cmnd 9314, 1984) and a White Paper, *Human Fertilisation and Embryology: A Framework for Legislation* (Cm 259, 1987).   [121] In s 49(4).

[122] [2006] EWCA Civ 551, [2007] Fam 1.   [123] HFEA 2008, s 57(1).   [124] Ibid, s 57(2).

public consultation[125] and pre-legislative scrutiny of a draft Bill.[126] In substance many of the relevant sections of the new Act are re-enactments of provisions in the 1990 Act, sometimes with amendments to take account of problems which were highlighted by case law. The principal change to the law on parenthood effected by the 2008 Act is to extend to female civil partners provisions which formerly only applied to married couples, and to extend to female partners who are not civil partners those provisions which formerly applied only to heterosexual unmarried couples.

While it is the new Act which applies to children who are born now, the 1990 Act and its case law will remain important to determine the parenthood of children born before implementation of the 2008 Act. A knowledge of the 1990 Act and its case law is also likely to prove helpful in understanding the genesis of some of the 2008 provisions, and how the re-enacted provisions are likely to be interpreted. In what follows, we set out and explain relevant provisions of the 1990 Act and their case law, and then examine the changes effected by the 2008 Act.

3.3 THE HUMAN FERTILISATION AND EMBRYOLOGY ACT 1990

The provision of assisted conception by clinics is regulated by the Human Fertilisation and Embryology Authority under the HFEA 1990 and a Code of Practice.[127] The Act sets out in section 13 conditions of licences for treatment, which include, in section 13(5), the requirement that: 'A woman shall not be provided with treatment services unless account has been taken of the welfare of any child who may be born as a result of the treatment (including the need of that child for supportive parenting), and of any other child who may be affected by the birth.' Section 13(5) was amended by the HFEA 2008 to remove what used to be a reference to the child's need for a father.[128] There are also restrictions on certain forms of treatment unless suitable counselling has been given.[129] The storage[130] and use of a person's genetic material are closely controlled by the requirement of written consent within Schedule 3 to the 1990 Act,[131] and a suitable opportunity for counselling must be given before consent is given.[132] Schedule 3, paragraph 5, makes clear that a person's gametes must not be used for the purposes of treatment services unless there is an effective Schedule 3 consent,[133] although this is not required where the gametes are being used for the person and another receiving treatment services together.[134]

---

[125] Department of Health, *Review of the Human Fertilisation and Embryology Act—A Public Consultation* (London: Department of Health, 2005).

[126] Human Tissue and Embryos (Draft) Bill (Cm 7087), which was based on a White Paper, *Review of the Human Fertilisation and Embryology Act: Proposals for Revised Legislation (including establishment of the Regulatory Authority for Tissue and Embryos)* (Cm 6989, December 2006). The Bill was scrutinised by the Joint Committee on the Human Tissue and Embryos (Draft) Bill Session 2006–07: see *Human Tissue and Embryos (Draft) Bill Volume 1: Report* HL Paper 169-I, HC Paper 630-I, published 1 August 2007.

[127] See HFEA 1990, s 25 and Code of Practice.

[128] For the arguments on this issue, see L. Smith, 'Clashing Symbols? Reconciling Support for Fathers and Fatherless Families After the Human Fertilisation and Embryology Act 2008' [2010] Child and Family Law Quarterly 46–70. See also G. Douglas, 'Assisted Reproduction and the Welfare of the Child' (1993) 46(2) Current Legal Problems 53–74; E. Blyth, 'The United Kingdom's Human Fertilisation and Embryology Act 1990 and the Welfare of the Child: A Critique' (1995) 3 International Journal of Children's Rights 417–438; E. Jackson, 'Conception and the Irrelevance of the Welfare Principle' (2002) 65 Modern Law Review 176–203.

[129] HFEA 1990, s 13(6) and Sch 3ZA, Pt 1.   [130] See Sch 3, para 8.

[131] Schedule 3, para 1. See eg *R v Human Fertilisation and Embryology Authority, ex p Blood* [1997] 2 All ER 687, CA (collection of husband's sperm while unconscious using electro-ejaculation was unlawful). See also *L v Human Fertilisation and Embryology Authority and Secretary of State* [2008] EWHC 2149 (Fam).

[132] Schedule 3, para 3.   [133] Ibid, para 5(1).   [134] Ibid, para 5(3).

These provisions protect individual autonomy in the use of genetic material and consequently a person's wish whether to have a child. However, their application in some situations has led to 'hard cases'.

In *Evans v UK*[135] Natalie Evans was diagnosed with pre-cancerous ovaries and told that her ovaries would need to be removed. She was advised to harvest some of her eggs to secure the possibility of future IVF treatment, and also that there were higher prospects of successfully having a child if, instead of freezing her eggs, embryos created with her partner, J, were frozen. The couple were told that it was possible for either to withdraw his or her consent at any time before the embryos were implanted. But J reassured Ms Evans that they would not split up and that she did not need to consider the freezing of her eggs. They entered into the necessary consents by signing relevant forms. However, the relationship subsequently broke down, and J wrote to the clinic stating that the embryos should be destroyed.

Evans sought an injunction requiring J to restore his consent, and a declaration that J could not vary his earlier consent. She claimed that her rights under Articles 8, 12, and 14 of the ECHR were breached, and the embryos were entitled to protection under Article 2. These claims were denied by the Court of Appeal, and permission to appeal to the Lords was refused, so Evans took her case to the European Court of Human Rights and the case ultimately came before the Court's Grand Chamber. Unanimously the Court held that Article 2 was not violated. A majority held that Article 8 of the ECHR was engaged but that the Article 8 rights of J and Natalie Evans were each engaged and entirely irreconcilable. Either Evans would be denied parenthood or J would be forced into it. The Court also held that the case did not simply involve 'a conflict between individuals; the legislation in question also served a number of wider, public interests, in upholding the principle of the primacy of consent and promoting legal clarity and certainty.'[136] In addition, as there was no uniform approach in Europe the state had to be afforded a wide margin of appreciation,[137] and the absolute nature of the consent requirement was held not inconsistent with Article 8.[138] Similarly, there was no breach of Article 8 together with Article 14. The dissenting judges held that the bright-line consent rule precluded any balancing of the competing interests in the case and its application on the facts was disproportionate to the impact on the applicant in the circumstances and gave no weight to J's reassurances. Craig Lind, in a commentary on the case,[139] has argued that there should be less sympathy for J because 'people who have sexual relations (and even those who approach clinics for procreative help) take a risk of children emerging that they were not planning to have, however carefully they set out to protect themselves against that eventuality'.[140] He argues that the desire for genetic parenthood embedded (socially) within us 'should give rise to a more nuanced…public policy position than the one accepted in the legislation and by the courts in this case'.[141] Lind also makes the point that there may have been indirect discrimination, in the sense that it is much easier to store sperm than it is to store eggs, so Ms Evans was in a position that no man would ever be in. Lind thus argues for a more nuanced approach in such cases, allowing 'personalised justice, appropriately tailored to the human tragedies that can beset anyone's life'.[142]

---

[135] [2007] 2 FCR 5 (Grand Chamber, ECtHR).
[136] Ibid, para 74.   [137] At para 81.   [138] At para 89.
[139] C. Lind, '*Evans v United Kingdom*—Judgments of Solomon: Power, Gender and Procreation' [2006] Child and Family Law Quarterly 576.   [140] Ibid, 583.
[141] Ibid, 587.   [142] Ibid, 592.

3.4 SECTION 28: THE LEGAL BUT NOT BIOLOGICAL FATHER

Section 28(2) and (3) of the HFEA 1990 allow a man who is not genetically related to a child to become the child's legal father. Section 28(5) clarifies that those provisions do not apply 'to any child who, by virtue of the rules of common law, is treated as the legitimate child of the parties to a marriage.' So, in the case of a child born to a married woman, section 28 does not apply to make a man other than the woman's husband the child's father, or to make a child fatherless, unless and until the presumption of legitimacy is rebutted.

3.4.1 The mother's husband and assisted conception

Key legislation

Section 28(2) of the HFEA 1990 provides:

If—

(a) at the time of the placing in her of the embryo or the sperm and eggs or of her insemination, the woman was a party to a marriage, and

(b) the creation of the embryo carried by her was not brought about with the sperm of the other party to the marriage,

then, subject to subsection (5) below, the other party to the marriage shall be treated as the father of the child unless it is shown that he did not consent to the placing in her of the embryo or the sperm and eggs or to her insemination (as the case may be).

Section 28(2) applies whether or not the conception was assisted through a so-called self-help method of artificial insemination or with professional help. It also applies whether the assisted conception took place in the UK or elsewhere.[143] The word 'marriage' in section 28 means a marriage subsisting at the time, unless a judicial separation was then in force, and includes a void marriage if at the relevant time either or both of the parties reasonably believed that the marriage was valid.[144]

The subsection treats the mother's husband as the child's father 'unless it is shown that he did not consent'. The meaning of this phrase was considered *obiter* by McFarlane J in *Re G (Surrogacy: Foreign Domicile)*.[145] In that case a surrogate mother, Mrs J, who was artificially inseminated with the sperm of Mr G, remained married to her estranged husband, raising the possibility that her husband could be the father of the surrogate child who was now living with the commissioning parents, Mr G and his wife. It was contended that the absence of Mrs J's husband's consent to the procedure demonstrated that he did not consent. McFarlane J disagreed, observing that the words 'it is shown' require the court to be *satisfied* that the husband did not consent, and the absence of clear evidence of consent does not mean that it is shown that a person has not consented.[146] Mrs J's evidence, however, was that her husband was aware of her general intention to act as a surrogate mother and had no objection to her doing so, but was not aware of the particular surrogacy procedure which led to the child's conception. He was therefore not in a

---

[143] HFEA 1990, s 28(8).

[144] Ibid, s 28(7). 'Void' in this context probably does not include a marriage which is void because the parties are not respectively male and female: see the discussion in Section 3.9 of *J v C and Another* [2006] EWCA Civ 551, [2007] Fam 1, a case on the similarly worded s 27 of the Family Law Reform Act 1987.

[145] [2007] EWHC 2814 (Fam), [2008] 1 FLR 1047 at [30]–[39].   [146] Ibid, [39].

position either to consent or not consent to the particular arrangement. The husband failed to respond to correspondence requesting clarification. In the absence of further evidence from the husband and on the evidence presented, McFarlane J declared that it was shown that the husband did not consent to his wife's insemination.[147] It was also proved that the child was conceived as a result of the artificial insemination and, the presumption of legitimacy having been rebutted, therefore Mr G was in law the child's father.

3.4.2 Assisted conception and unmarried couples

Key legislation

Section 28(3) of the HFEA 1990 provides:

(3) If no man is treated, by virtue of subsection (2) above, as the father of the child but—

    (a) the embryo or the sperm and eggs were placed in the woman, or she was artificially inseminated, in the course of treatment services provided for her and a man together by a person to whom a licence applies, and

    (b) the creation of the embryo carried by her was not brought about with the sperm of that man,

then, subject to subsection (5) below, that man shall be treated as the father of the child.

It has been said that subsections (2) and (3) of section 28 are mutually exclusive.[148] Section 28(3) allows a man who is neither married to the child's mother nor genetically related to the child to become the child's legal parent.

3.4.3 Licensed treatment

Unlike section 28(2), this provision applies only to treatment services[149] by a person to whom a licence applies, that is clinics which are licensed by the Human Fertilisation and Embryology Authority. Section 28(3) does not, therefore, apply to treatment provided abroad. For this reason, in *U v W (Attorney General Intervening)*[150] Wilson J held that twins born to a couple who received treatment by artificial insemination of the mother by donor sperm at a clinic in Rome were fatherless. Consequently, the mother's partner, from whom she was now estranged, had no duty to support the children under the Child Support Act 1991.[151]

3.4.4 In the course of treatment services provided for a woman and a man together

The requirement that treatment services are provided for the woman and man together does not require that there is any physical treatment of the man. In *U v V (Attorney General Intervening)*[152] Wilson J held that in the provision of treatment services with donor sperm what has to be demonstrated is that 'the doctor was responding to a request for that form of treatment made by the woman and the man as a couple'. In other words, there must be a

---

[147] Ibid, [37].

[148] *Leeds Teaching Hospital NHS Trust v A and others* [2003] 1 FCR 599, [2003] EWHC 259 (QB).

[149] Defined in the HFEA 1990, s 2(1).

[150] [1998] Fam 29.

[151] It was held that the restriction of provision of services in another state of the EU did not breach Art 59 of the Treaty of Rome. The restriction could be justified on policy grounds.

[152] [1998] Fam 29.

'joint enterprise', in the sense that the *services* are provided *for the man too*. It is clear that there can be no joint enterprise where a man's sperm is to be used after his death.[153]

However, having treatment services together involves more than the man simply being present with the woman at the medical practitioner's premises and paying for the treatment. In *Re Q (Parental Order)*[154] Johnson J held in such circumstances that an unmarried woman who was acting as a surrogate mother to a married couple was not having treatment services with the husband. It seems, therefore, that the section envisages that the joint enterprise is one in which the couple treated are seeking to be parents of the resulting child together.[155]

In *Re R (IVF: Paternity of Child)*[156] the question was whether section 28(3) applied where a man had participated during much of the treatment provided, but had separated from the woman by the time the embryo which led to the child's birth was placed within her. The child's mother's partner, B, became infertile following treatment for testicular cancer and the couple sought treatment at a licensed clinic. The mother signed a consent form to IVF with donor sperm (matched to the physical characteristics of the mother and B), and B countersigned acknowledging that he and the mother were being treated together and he would be recognised as the legal father of any resulting child. Two embryos were placed in the mother, and the remaining embryos were frozen for future use. The mother and B then separated and the mother formed a new relationship with another man. The mother did not tell the clinic of the separation but continued to have treatment with some of the remaining embryos, which resulted in the birth of a baby girl. B knew nothing of this later treatment until he found out that the mother was pregnant. B applied for a parental responsibility order in respect of the child and the issue of whether he was the child's father arose in the proceedings. At first instance Hedley J found that B was the father. Laying emphasis on clarity, simplicity, and certainty, his Lordship held that the parties should be regarded as still in a joint enterprise until it was expressly ended by being brought to the attention of the clinic.[157] The Court of Appeal allowed the mother's appeal. Hale LJ (delivering the judgment of the court) said that conferring parenthood was a 'serious matter' and section 28(3) should 'only apply to those cases which clearly fall within the footprint of the statutory language'.[158] The Court of Appeal's analysis of the structure of section 28(2) and (3) revealed that both subsections saw the critical time for determining legal parenthood as the point at which the embryo or the sperm and eggs are placed in the woman. The court concluded:

> There must be a point in time when the question has to be judged. The simple answer is that the embryo must be placed in the mother at a time when treatment services are being provided for the woman and the man together.

Applying this approach to the facts, the couple had separated at the relevant time and thus B could not be the father pursuant to section 28(3). The child therefore had no legal father.

B's appeal to the House of Lords was dismissed.[159] Lord Walker of Gestingthorpe, with whom the rest of the Appellate Committee agreed, was content to adopt the Court of

---

[153] *R v Human Fertilisation and Embryology Authority, ex p Blood* [1997] 2 All ER 687, CA.

[154] [1996] 1 FLR 369.

[155] Although not a case on s 28(3), *Re B (Parentage)* [1996] 2 FLR 15 appears to suggest that the man and the woman need not necessarily be intimate partners, provided they are embarked upon a joint enterprise of producing a child for whom the man will be the parent.

[156] [2003] Fam 129, CA (Morritt V-C, Hale and Dyson LJJ).

[157] [2002] 2 FLR 843 at [10].　　　　　[158] Ibid, [20].

[159] *Re R (A Child) (IVF: Paternity)* [2005] UKHL 33, [2005] 2 AC 621.

Appeal's reasoning as to the interpretation of section 28(3),[160] adding the observation that:

> important though certainty is, it is even more important that the very significant legal relationship of parenthood should not be based on a fiction (especially if the fiction involves a measure of deception by the mother).[161]

His Lordship clarified, however, that this 'does not imply the view that no weight should be given to the perspective (or perception) of medical staff at the clinic'.[162] He explained:

> The clinic's perception is one element to be taken into account in answering the factual question which the Court of Appeal posed, following the language of section 28(3). The idea of providing treatment services to two people 'together' does involve a 'mental element'...and the perceptions of the medical staff at the clinic are part of that. But they cannot be the decisive element if they are based partly on deception, and if the rest of the evidence shows that at the material time there is no longer any 'joint enterprise' between the woman and her ex-partner.[163]

Where a person is treated as the father by virtue of section 28, no other person is to be treated as the father of the child,[164] and in general that person is treated as the father for all purposes.[165] The legal fatherhood conferred by section 28 is the same as that conferred on a biological father. In *Re CH (Contact: Parentage)*[166] a husband was the legal father of a child born to his wife by artificial insemination by donor sperm. The marriage broke down after an episode of drunken violence by the husband and the mother sought to deny the husband contact with the child. She argued that he should not be treated in the same way as a child's biological father. It was held that the same general approach to contact applied to all men who were regarded in law as the father of a child, irrespective of biological connection.

3.5 THE HUMAN FERTILISATION AND EMBRYOLOGY ACT 2008

Section 28(2) and (3) of the HFEA 1990 is replicated, in its basic substance, by sections 35–38 of the HFEA 2008.[167] Section 35 adopts wording similar to section 28(2). The substance of section 28(3) of the 1990 Act appears in sections 36 and 37 of the new Act, but the wording of the new Act seeks to set out more precisely the circumstances in which the man and the woman will be receiving treatment services together, in order to deal with the difficulties

---

[160] Ibid, [41].   [161] Ibid, [42].

[162] Ibid, [43]. As the House acknowledged, this point had been made by Craig Lind in a commentary on the Court of Appeal's decision: see C. Lind, '*In re R (Paternity of IVF Baby)*—Unmarried Paternity under the Human Fertilisation and Embryology Act 1990' [2003] Child and Family Law Quarterly 327 at 332–333.

[163] Lord Hope of Craighead had earlier observed that the Court of Appeal's 'simple approach' left open what he saw as the issue in the appeal, namely how it is to be determined whether the services were being provided for the woman and the man together (at [14] and [16]). In his Lordship's view the question should be determined in the light of all of the evidence, including the perspectives of client and clinic, neither of which has priority (at [19]).

[164] Section 28(4). Section 28(2) and (3) do not apply, however, to any child to the extent that the child is treated by virtue of adoption as not being the man's child: s 28(5).

[165] HFEA 1990, s 29(1). There is an exception where the child is conceived when the father is deceased. In such a case, which is discussed in Section 3.8.3, the father is only permitted to become the father for the purpose of registration on the child's birth certificate.

[166] [1996] 1 FLR 569.

[167] See J. McCandless and S. Sheldon, 'The Human Fertilisation and Embryology Act (2008) and the Tenacity of the Sexual Family Form' (2010) 72(2) Modern Law Review 175–207 for discussion of the 2008 Act's focus on the sexual family model and its resistance to the possibility that a child can have two 'mothers' or indeed two 'fathers'.

that were presented in *Re R (A Child) (IVF: Paternity)*.[168] This is achieved by requiring that 'agreed fatherhood conditions', set out in section 37, are satisfied. The provisions are complex, and it is convenient to set them out in full.

Key legislation

Section 36 provides:

If no man is treated by virtue of section 35 as the father of the child and no woman is treated by virtue of section 42 as a parent of the child but—

(a) the embryo or the sperm and eggs were placed in W, or W was artificially inseminated, in the course of treatment services provided in the United Kingdom by a person to whom a licence applies,

(b) at the time when the embryo or the sperm and eggs were placed in W, or W was artificially inseminated, the agreed fatherhood conditions (as set out in section 37) were satisfied in relation to a man, in relation to treatment provided to W under the licence,

(c) the man remained alive at that time, and

(d) the creation of the embryo carried by W was not brought about with the man's sperm,

then, subject to section 38(2) to (4), the man is to be treated as the father of the child.

The 'agreed fatherhood conditions', are met in relation to a man (M) in relation to treatment provided to a woman (W) under licence if, but only if:

(a) M has given the person responsible a notice stating that he consents to being treated as the father of any child resulting from treatment provided to W under the licence,

(b) W has given the person responsible a notice stating that she consents to M being so treated,

(c) neither M nor W has, since giving notice under paragraph (a) or (b), given the person responsible notice of the withdrawal of M's or W's consent to M being so treated,

(d) W has not, since the giving of the notice under paragraph (b), given the person responsible—

(i) a further notice under that paragraph stating that she consents to another man being treated as the father of any resulting child, or

(ii) a notice under section 44(1)(b) stating that she consents to a woman being treated as a parent of any resulting child, and

(e) W and M are not within prohibited degrees of relationship in relation to each other.

---

[168] [2005] UKHL 33, [2005] 2 AC 621.

3.6 LESBIAN COUPLES, ASSISTED CONCEPTION, AND PARENTHOOD

Sections 42–44 of the HFEA 2008 extend the substance of sections 35–37 of the 2008 Act to female same-sex couples. Section 42(1) applies in the case of a woman who is in a civil partnership at the time of treatment, and provides:

> If at the time of the placing in her of the embryo or the sperm and eggs or of her artificial insemination, W was a party to a civil partnership, then subject to section 45(2) to (4), the other party to the civil partnership is to be treated as a parent of the child unless it is shown that she did not consent to the placing in W of the embryo or the sperm and eggs or to her artificial insemination (as the case may be).

Sections 43 and 44 apply to a female couple who are not in a civil partnership but who are undergoing treatment services together. Section 43 is in similar terms to section 36, with necessary modifications to accommodate the fact that in this case the treatment is being provided to two women. Section 44 then sets out a series of 'female parenthood conditions' which must be fulfilled if the partner of the child's mother is to acquire legal parenthood. Again, the conditions are similar to those in section 37, with necessary modifications to accommodate the same-sex circumstances. The mother's partner who fulfils the conditions of sections 43 and 44 becomes the child's other legal parent.

3.7 BIOLOGY: THE DEFAULT POSITION

Where a child is conceived by assisted conception but for some reason the requirements of the legislation are not fulfilled, then the child's father will be determined by biological connection, as illustrated in *Leeds Teaching Hospitals NHS Trust v A*.[169] In that case Mr and Mrs A, a white couple, consented to treatment under the HFEA 1990 whereby Mrs A was to be inseminated with her husband's sperm. Mr and Mrs B, a black couple, were also undergoing treatment at the same clinic and Mr B's sperm was erroneously injected into Mrs A's egg. The error became clear when twins of mixed heritage were born to Mrs A. It was agreed that Mr and Mrs A would raise the twins, but the question arose as to who was the legal father. It was clear that Mr A had not consented to his wife's treatment with Mr B's sperm, so section 28(2) could not apply to make Mr A the father. In addition, the clinic's error vitiated the concept of 'treatment together' in section 28(3).

In the absence of any person being the father within section 28, the fall-back position was the genetic connection between Mr B and the children, and Mr B was therefore the father. Mr and Mrs A's right to respect for family life was engaged, but any interference with it by declaring Mr B the father was justified and proportionate, since it preserved the truth about the personal identity of the twins, and there were mechanisms, for example adoption, by which Mr A could acquire security in respect of his relationship with the children.

3.8 PERSONS NOT REGARDED IN LAW AS A PARENT

There are situations in which the law expressly states that a person will not be regarded in law as a child's parent.

---

[169] *Leeds Teaching Hospital NHS Trust v A and others* [2003] EWHC 259 (QB), [2003] 1 FCR 599.

3.8.1 Anonymous sperm donors

Section 28(6)(a) of the HFEA 1990 provides that where sperm is used in accordance with consent required by Schedule 3, paragraph 5, then the sperm donor is not treated as the father. There is a similar provision in section 41(1) of the 2008 Act.

3.8.2 Access to information about donors

The Human Fertilisation and Embryology Authority (Disclosure of Donor Information) Regulations 2004 make provision regulating the disclosure of donor information.[170] The Human Fertilisation and Embryology Authority is required to keep a register of donor information, and under section 31ZA of the HFEA 1990 a person who has attained the age of 16 may make a request of the Authority for information about any donor to whom he or she may be genetically related,[171] and request whether there are other donor-conceived children of the donor (ie, genetic siblings of the applicant). The available information the Authority is required to supply about the donor is contained in the regulations. A range of information which is not capable of identifying the donor can be obtained at age 16: general physical characteristics such as sex, ethnic group, eye and skin colour; year of birth; medical history; religion, occupation, interests, and skills and why the donor provided sperm, eggs, or embryos; marital status, and whether the donor has children.[172] Under section 31ZA the Authority must supply information about the number of, sex, and birth year of genetic siblings. Upon reaching the age of 18, an applicant is also entitled to identifying information supplied by donors after 31 March 2005. The information includes the donor's name, date and place of birth, appearance, and last postal address.[173] At age 18, identifying information about donor-conceived genetic siblings can also be obtained, provided the siblings have consented to its release.[174] Identifying information is only provided in adulthood and there is no duty upon parents to disclose the fact that a child has been conceived as a result of donor insemination. It may be questioned therefore whether the law adequately protects the child's interests in obtaining information about biological origins during minority. As Andrew Bainham has observed, the current position may place a child born as a result of donor sperm to a mother and her heterosexual partner at a disadvantage compared with a similar child born to a mother and her lesbian partner since in the latter case the existence of the donor will eventually be obvious to the child.[175]

3.8.3 Use of deceased man's sperm

Section 28(6)(b) of the 1990 Act provides that where sperm, or an embryo created with a man's sperm, is used after a man's death, then the man is not to be treated for any purposes as the resulting child's father. A similar provision is found in section 41(2) of the 2008 Act.

---

[170] For discussion of this issue, see eg E. Blyth and A. Farrand, 'Anonymity in Donor-Assisted Conception and the UN Convention on the Rights of the Child' (2004) 12 International Journal of Children's Rights 89–104; C. Jones, 'The Identification of "Parents" and "Siblings": New Possibilities Under the Reformed Human Fertilisation and Embryology Act' in J. Herring, J. Wallbank, and S. Choudhry (eds), Rights, Gender and Family Law (Abingdon: Routledge-Cavendish, 2009), pp 219–238.

[171] Under s 31ZC, the Authority may notify the donor that a request under s 31ZA(2)(a) has been made.

[172] Regulation 2(2).

[173] Regulation 2(3). The Authority may also keep a voluntary contact register of persons who wish to have contact: HFEA 1990, s 31ZF.   [174] HFEA 1990, s 31ZE.

[175] A. Bainham, 'Arguments about Parentage' (2008) 67(2) Cambridge Law Journal 322–351 at 336.

However, the general rule is subject to an exception.[176] Where sperm is used, or an embryo placed in woman, after a man's death, in circumstances where, but for the death, he would have been the child's father, then the man can be the father for the purpose of enabling the man's particulars to be entered as those of the child's father in a register of live births but the man is to be treated in law as *not* being the father of the child for any other purpose.[177] In order for the provisions to apply, the man must have consented in writing to use after his death, and the child's mother must elect within 42 days of the birth to have the man registered on the birth certificate.

3.8.4 Use of embryo after mother's partner's death

A similar rule is now applied in the case of legal parenthood of a mother's same-sex partner.[178] If an embryo resulting in the mother's child is created when the mother is in a civil partnership, or in the course of licensed treatment with the mother's same-sex partner, and the partner dies before the embryo is implanted, then the partner can be the legal parent for the purpose of birth registration. The conditions of the partner's consent and the mother's election are the same as those discussed earlier in relation to fathers.

3.9 TRANSSEXUAL PERSONS AND PARENTHOOD

As discussed in more detail in Chapter 1, the Gender Recognition Act 2004[179] now permits a transsexual person to acquire a new gender as a matter of law. An application must be made to a Gender Recognition Panel to obtain a Gender Recognition Certificate. The Act does not require the transsexual person to have had gender reassignment surgery but to provide evidence of gender dysphoria and make various statutory declarations. Unless a person's gender has been changed by this process, English law holds that a person's sex is determined by reference to biological criteria at birth.[180] Once the certificate is obtained, the newly acquired gender becomes that person's gender for all purposes, subject to certain provisions of the Gender Recognition Act 2004. A Gender Recognition Certificate does not have retrospective effect. Section 9(2) of the 2004 Act provides that the certificate does not affect things done or events occurring before the certificate; and section 12 specifically provides that the fact that a person's gender has become the acquired gender under the 2004 Act does not affect the status of the person as the father or mother of a child. So, for example, if a person gives birth to a child and then acquires a Gender Recognition Certificate changing her gender to male, the person will now be a man but will also remain the child's mother. It is also possible for a female-to-male transsexual person to become a father of a child through sections 35 and 36 of the HFEA 2008. A female-to-male transsexual person with a Gender Recognition Certificate can now validly marry a woman, and so it is possible that section 35 could apply to confer fatherhood on the transsexual person. As the woman's husband, he will be the father of any child conceived by assisted conception unless it is shown that he did not consent to the treatment. If not married, he could acquire fatherhood by undergoing treatment services together with a woman at a licensed clinic. Even if a female-to-male transsexual person does not have a Gender Recognition Certificate, 'he' (she as a matter of law) could still become a parent of the child using sections 43 and 44 of the HFEA 2008 which confer parenthood on the female partner of the child's mother. 'He' would then be a parent, but not a father.

---

[176] See HFEA 1990, s 28(5A)–(5I) and HFEA 2008, s 39.
[177] HFEA 1990, s 29(3B) and HFEA 2008, s 39.   [178] See HFEA 2008, s 46.
[179] For an outline of the Act's provisions, see S. Gilmore, 'The Gender Recognition Act 2004' [2004] Family Law 741.   [180] *Corbett v Corbett (Otherwise Ashley)* [1971] P 83.

It is now possible as a matter of law for someone to be the mother of one child and the father of another. Furthermore, someone who is regarded in law as a man, but who has not undergone gender reassignment surgery and therefore still has female reproductive organs, could give birth to a child. To complicate matters further, that person may have been fertilised by a male-to-female transsexual person who similarly has not had surgery. Whether, in this situation, the person giving birth would be regarded as the mother or the father of the child has yet to arise for decision. These scenarios raise the possibility of male mothers and female fathers. It may not be long, however, before the courts are confronted with difficult cases like these.

In *J v C and Another*[181] Mr J and Mrs C went through a ceremony of marriage. Mr J was 30 and had been suffering from gender dysphoria. Although born as a female, Mr J had lived as a man since aged 17. The couple lived together for a number of years with the wife in ignorance of the true facts. In the process of a divorce she became aware from Mr J's birth certificate that 'he' was a woman and then sought a decree of nullity of marriage.

Two children had been conceived to the couple by artificial insemination by donor, one of whom, E, was still under 18. E was conceived prior to 1 August 1991 when the 1990 Act came into force, so the relevant statute which applied was section 27 of the Family Law Reform Act 1987. Mr J sought orders under section 8 of the Children Act 1989 in respect of E. By the time the case came to court, Mr J had obtained a Gender Recognition Certificate recognising his acquired male gender. The question arose as to whether he was the child's father so as not to require leave to make those applications (ie, did he fall within section 10(4) of the Children Act 1989?). It was contended for Mr J that the word 'marriage' in section 27 includes a void marriage[182] and therefore the provision applied to him.[183] The Court of Appeal observed, however, that section 27 talks of 'a party to a marriage' and 'the other party to the marriage' and concluded that this wording suggested that the parties referred to in section 27 must be respectively male and female. Presumably the same reasoning would be applied to relevant provisions of the Human Fertilisation and Embryology Acts.[184] Furthermore, Mr J's Gender Recognition Certificate did not affect that interpretation since the Gender Recognition Act 2004 makes clear, in section 9(2), that the certificate does not have retrospective effect. Accordingly the court concluded that Mr J is not and never was E's parent.

Prior to enactment of the Gender Recognition Act 2004, the European Court of Human Rights in *X, Y and Z v UK*[185] afforded the UK a wide margin of appreciation on the issue of legal recognition of transsexual parenthood. It found no violation of Article 8 of the ECHR where English law refused to register a female-to-male transsexual person as the father of a child born to 'his' female partner as a result of artificial insemination by donor. Since that time there has undoubtedly been increased legal recognition of transsexualism within states, and perhaps such a wide margin of appreciation could no longer be assumed. However, it seems unlikely that English law would be found to be in breach of the Convention in similar circumstances today following enactment of the Gender Recognition Act 2004.

---

[181] [2006] EWCA Civ 551.   [182] See s 27(2).

[183] Matrimonial Causes Act 1973, s 11(c), provides that a marriage is void if the parties are not respectively male and female.

[184] HFEA 2008, s 49, defines a marriage in s 35 to include a void marriage, provided either or both of the parties reasonably believed at the time that the marriage was valid. The definition of marriage in the HFEA 1990, s 28(2), is in the same terms.

[185] *X, Y and Z v UK* [1997] 2 FLR 892. See C. Lind, 'Perceptions of Sex in the Legal Determination of Fatherhood—*X, Y and Z v UK*' [1997] Child and Family Law Quarterly 401.

3.10 SURROGACY AND PARENTAL ORDERS

Occasionally a woman may be willing to act as a surrogate mother[186] for a couple who are unable to have children. The Surrogacy Arrangements Act 1985 provides that no surrogacy arrangement[187] is enforceable by or against any of the persons making it.[188] Furthermore, negotiating a surrogacy arrangement on a commercial basis and advertising surrogacy are both illegal activities.[189] Otherwise, however, a surrogacy arrangement is not unlawful. If the commissioning couple are to become the child's parents they will need to adopt the child or apply for a parental order, 'an order providing for a child to be treated in law as the child of the applicants'.[190] The law on adoption is dealt with in detail in Chapter 11. Here we concentrate on the possibility of obtaining a parental order. The requirements for the making of a parental order were formerly contained in section 30 of the HFEA 1990. The HFEA 2008 repealed section 30 and the law on parental orders is now regulated by section 54 of the 2008 Act.[191] Of course, any orders made under section 30 of the 1990 Act prior to the change in the law remain in force and are unaffected. The main difference that the new legislation brings is a broadening of the categories of possible applicants. Under section 30 of the 1990 Act it was possible to make an order only in favour of a married couple. Under the new legislation applicants may be either a husband and wife, civil partners of each other, or 'two persons who are living as partners in an enduring family relationship and are not within prohibited degrees of relationship in relation to each other.'[192] The conditions for making an order remain, in substance, similar to those under the 1990 Act, and the case law relating to section 30 is likely to remain useful in interpreting the new provision.

In deciding whether to make a parental order, the court must apply the child's welfare as the paramount consideration.[193] In order for an order to be made the child must have been carried by a woman who is not one of the applicants, as a result of the placing in her of an embryo or sperm and eggs or her artificial insemination[194] and the gametes of at least one of the applicants must have been used to bring about the creation of the embryo. In other words, at least one of the applicants must be genetically related to the child.[195] In addition, the court must be satisfied of various conditions in section 54(3)–(8).

---

[186] For a useful collection of essays on this topic, see R. Cook, S. Day Sclater, and F. Kaganas, *Surrogate Motherhood International Perspectives* (Oxford: Hart, 2003). For an account of the development of the law, see Hale LJ's judgment in *Briody v St Helen's and Knowsley Area Health Authority* [2001] EWCA Civ 1010, [2001] 2 FLR 1094. For criticism of the law, see K. Horsey and S. Sheldon, 'Still Hazy After All These Years: The Law Regulating Surrogacy' (2012) 20(1) Medical Law Review 67–89; and K. Horsey, 'Challenging Presumptions: Legal Parenthood and Surrogacy Arrangements' [2010] Child and Family Law Quarterly 449 (law should reflect pre-conception intentions, supporting the use of enforceable agreements).

[187] Defined in the Surrogacy Arrangements Act 1985, s 1.   [188] Ibid, s 1A.

[189] Ibid, ss 2 and 3. Indeed, giving legal recognition to any commercial element in surrogacy is viewed as contrary to public policy: see *Briody v St Helen's and Knowsley Area Health Authority* [2001] EWCA Civ 1010, [2001] 2 FLR 1094 (woman unable to claim cost of commercial surrogacy arrangement in California as part of damages against Health Authority for negligently causing her infertility).

[190] See HFEA 2008, s 54(1).   [191] Together with s 55, which makes supplementary provision.

[192] Ibid, s 54(2). For discussion of prohibited degrees of relationship, see Chapter 1.

[193] Adoption and Children Act 2002, s 1 (see Chapter 11), applies to applications under the HFEA 2008, s 54 with necessary modifications: see the Human Fertilisation and Embryology (Parental Orders) Regulations 2010 (SI 2010/985), reg 2, Sch 1.

[194] This applies whether the woman was in the UK or elsewhere at the relevant time: see s 54(10).

[195] The court is not precluded from disposing of an application by a couple where the genetically related parent dies prior to the application being determined by the court: *A v P (Surrogacy: Parental Order: Death of Application)* [2011] EWHC 1738 (Fam), [2011] Fam Law 1080.

(i) The application for the order must be made within six months of the child's birth.[196]

(ii) At the time of the application and the making of the order the child's home must be with the applicants and either or both of the applicants must be domiciled in the UK, Channel Islands, or Isle of Man. In *Re G (Surrogacy: Foreign Domicile)*[197] McFarlane J pointed out, in relation to the same requirement in section 30(7) of the 1990 Act, that this provision is mandatory, and accordingly it is impossible for commissioning parents who are both not so domiciled to obtain a parental order.[198] His Lordship suggested that such arrangements were to be discouraged because of the likely legal complications. The case concerned a Turkish couple, Mr and Mrs G, who, with the help of a British surrogacy agency, Childlessness Overcome Through Surrogacy (COTS), engaged the services of Mrs J, a surrogate mother in England. Mrs J's egg was fertilised with Mr G's sperm and a child was born. Mr and Mrs G then applied for a parental order, during which proceedings it became apparent that Mr and Mrs G did not fulfil the domicile requirements. The resulting 'mess' required seven High Court hearings at a cost of £35,000 to the taxpayer, eventually resulting in an order under section 84(2) of the Adoption and Children Act 2002. This provision allows the court to grant parental responsibility to persons who the court is satisfied intend to adopt the child outside the British Islands.[199] McFarlane J was sufficiently concerned by the surrogacy agency's lack of awareness of the legal requirements 'to question whether some form of inspection or authorization should be required in order to improve the quality of advice' given, and sent a copy of his judgment to the relevant Minister of State for consideration.[200]

(iii) At the time of the making of the order both applicants must have attained the age of 18.[201]

(iv) The court must be satisfied that the woman who carried the child and any other parent of the child (who is not one of the applicants) 'have freely, and with full understanding of what is involved, agreed unconditionally to the making of the order'.[202] This does not require the agreement of someone who cannot be found or who is incapable of giving agreement.[203] The agreement of the woman who carried the child is ineffective if it is given by her less than six weeks after the child's birth.[204]

(v) The court must be satisfied that:

no money or other benefit (other than for expenses reasonably incurred) has been given or received by either of the applicants for or in consideration of—

(a) the making of the order,

(b) any agreement required by subsection (6),

(c) the handing over of the child to the applicants, or

(d) the making of arrangements with a view to the making of the order,

unless authorised by the court.[205]

---

[196] HFEA 2008, s 54(3). Within the period of six months beginning with the day on which the section comes into force, couples who were not eligible to apply under the 1990 Act may apply for an order in respect of a child born before implementation of s 54: see s 54(11).

[197] [2007] EWHC 2814 (Fam), [2008] 1 FLR 1047.   [198] Ibid, [15].

[199] See ibid, [46]–[50].

[200] Ibid, [29]. See D. Howe, 'International Surrogacy—A Cautionary Tale' [2008] Family Law 60. See for some of the problems, *Re X (children) (Parental Order: Foreign Surrogacy)* [2008] EWHC 3030 (Fam), [2009] Fam 71; L. Theis QC, 'A Trek Through the Thorn Forest' [2009] Family Law 239; and *Re K (Minors: Foreign Surrogacy)* [2010] EWHC 1180, and *Re IJ (A Child) (Overseas Surrogacy: Parental Order)* [2011] EWHC 921 (Fam), [2011] 2 FLR 646.   [201] Section 54(5).

[202] Section 54(6).   [203] Section 54(7).   [204] Ibid.   [205] Section 54(8).

The courts have held, in relation to a similar provision in the 1990 Act, that authorisation may be given retrospectively.[206] In *X (Children) (Parental Order: Foreign Surrogacy)*[207] Hedley J drew from the authorities that in terms of the policy considerations the court should 'pose itself three questions: (1) was the sum paid disproportionate to reasonable expenses? (2) Were the applicants acting in good faith and without "moral taint" in their dealings with the surrogate mother? (3) Were the applicants party to any attempt to defraud the authorities?'[208] In *Re S (Parental Order)*[209] his Lordship added that the court should be astute not to be involved in anything resembling payment for children, should ensure that commercial surrogacy is not used to circumvent childcare laws and to place children in unsuitable arrangements, and that money is not used to overbear the will of a surrogate.[210] However, the law now requires the child's welfare be not merely the first consideration (as it was in relation to s 30 of the 1990 Act) but the paramount consideration on an application under section 54,[211] and in *Re L (A Child) (Parental Order: Foreign Surrogacy)*[212] Hedley J commented that the effect of the change in the law must be to weigh the balance between public policy considerations and welfare decisively in favour of welfare and that 'it will only be in the clearest case of the abuse of public policy that the court will be able to withhold an order if otherwise welfare considerations support its making.'[213] So 'if it is desired to control commercial surrogacy arrangements, those controls need to operate before the court process is initiated i.e. at the border or even before'.[214] His Lordship emphasised, however, that 'notwithstanding the paramountcy of welfare, the court should continue carefully to scrutinise applications for authorisation under section 54(8) with a view to policing the public policy matters'.[215]

An example of the conflict with which the courts are presented in this context is provided by *In the Matter of C (A Child)*.[216] In that case a couple, Mr and Mrs X, agreed to pay a surrogate mother, SM, expenses of £12,000 some of which was said to relate to loss of earnings. This was higher than the level of reasonable expenses recommended by COTS which had assisted in bringing the parties together. SM duly gave birth to a child, C, who lived with Mr and Mrs X from birth, and Mr and Mrs X applied for a parental order. It transpired, however, that SM had been on income support which she continued to claim, and thus some of the expenses claimed did not relate to loss of earnings. The issue for Wall J was whether in these circumstances he should authorise the payment retrospectively. In exercising his discretion, applying the degree of taint approach, Wall J weighed the following points:[217] (i) the sum paid was not disproportionate; (ii) Mr and Mrs X had not known that SM was on income support until after the pregnancy; (iii) Mr and Mrs X entered into the memorandum 'in good faith and without corrupt intent';[218] (iv) the responsibility for allegedly defrauding the Department of Social Security was SM's alone; and (v) it was manifestly in C's best interests to be brought up by Mr and Mrs X.

Once an order is made under section 54 the child becomes the child of the applicants, and the woman who gave birth is no longer recognised as the mother. However, it should be noted that proceedings under section 54 are family proceedings for the purposes of the

---

[206] See *Re Q (A Minor) (Parental Order)* [1996] 1 FLR 369, Johnson J, and *In the Matter of C (A Child)* [2002] EWHC 157 (Fam).   [207] [2008] EWHC 3030 (Fam), [2009] Fam 71.

[208] Ibid, [21], drawing on *Re Adoption Application (Payments for Adoption)* [1987] Fam 81 and *In the Matter of C (A Child)* [2002] EWHC 157 (Fam).   [209] [2009] EWHC 2977, [2010] 1 FLR 1156.

[210] Ibid, [7].

[211] Human Fertilisation and Embryology (Parental Orders) Regulations 2010 (SI 2010/985), reg 2, Sch 1.

[212] [2010] EWHC 3146, [2011] Fam 106.   [213] Ibid, [10].   [214] Ibid.

[215] See also Sir Nicholas Wall P in *Re X and Y (Children: Foreign Surrogacy)* [2011] EWHC 3147 (Fam), endorsing Hedley J's approach.   [216] [2002] EWHC 157 (Fam).

[217] Ibid, [34].   [218] Ibid, [20].

Children Act 1989, so a court could make an order under section 8 of that Act instead of or in addition to the section 54 order. However, it seems most unlikely that an order under section 8 would be made unless either an issue arose over contact with the child, or one or other of the child's legal parents changed his or her mind about agreeing to the section 54 order during the course of the proceedings or, as in *Re P (Residence: Appeal)* a parent has been deceived by a surrogate mother.[219] In that case, in a desperate bid to have further children of her own, a woman deceived couples by holding herself out as a surrogate mother then telling them that she had miscarried. The father of one of the children found out about the deception and sought a residence order in respect of his child who was 18 months old. Coleridge J transferred residence to the biological father and his wife.

4 MAKING SENSE OF THE LAW ON PARENTHOOD

4.1 RATIONALES FOR ATTRIBUTING PARENTHOOD

4.1.1 Biology

As we have seen, English law's default position on parenthood is to appeal to biological connection.[220] In favour of that approach is the fact that, at least in name, all children will have parents,[221] whereas a move away from that approach raises the possibility of increasing numbers of children who may only have a mother.[222] Legal recognition of gestational mothers not only acknowledges that in most cases there will also be a genetic connection between mother and child, but recognises the mother's physical involvement in producing the child, the importance of maternal bonding during gestation, and that relinquishing the child may have an adverse effect on the mother's psychological health. In addition, there are arguments that not to recognise the gestational mother risks her exploitation or commodification in surrogacy arrangements. Furthermore, as Rebecca Probert has observed, an appeal to gestation provides greater certainty, particularly in cases of surrogacy involving more than one commissioning couple (perhaps unbeknown to each other).[223]

4.1.2 Intent-based parenthood

Another approach is intent-based parenthood.[224] There are several examples of this approach in English law. It might be argued that the law in section 28(6) of the HFEA 1990 and section 41 of the HFEA 2008, reflects a sperm donor's intention *not* to become a parent; and in cases of surrogacy arrangements or adoption, the commissioning couple or adoptive parents might be said to intend to become parents of the child. As Gillian Douglas points out, however, this basis of attributing parenthood is not unproblematic. It 'implies a preparedness to recognise the free alienability of parental responsibility', that

---

[219] *Re P (Residence: Appeal)* [2007] EWCA Civ 1053, [2008] 1 FLR 198.

[220] There are several components: genetic and gestational roles, biological features of the act of coitus, and biological factors (eg hormonal changes) affecting post-natal behaviour. M. Johnson, 'A Biomedical Perspective on Parenthood' in A. Bainham et al., *What is a Parent?* (Oxford: Hart, 1999), ch 3.

[221] J. Shapiro, 'Changing Ways, New Technologies and the Devaluation of the Genetic Connection to Children' in M. Maclean (ed), *Family Law and Family Values* (Oxford: Hart, 2005), p 93.

[222] Ibid.

[223] R. Probert, 'Families, Assisted Reproduction and the Law by Rebecca Probert' [2004] Child and Family Law Quarterly 273.

[224] See eg the role of intention to address the competing claims of genetic and gestational parents in the Californian Supreme Court decision of *Johnson v Calvert* 5 Cal 4th 84, 851 P2d 776 (1993).

is, the child as a form of property that can be transferred to others. She quite rightly asks: 'should lack of intention be a means of avoiding parenthood?'[225]

Arguing in favour of intent-based parenthood in the context of surrogacy arrangements, Hill[226] observes that the context in which the child is being conceived (eg through donation of sperm or egg) cannot be ignored and that in such contexts the arguments in favour of gestational mothers may not be so powerful. Expectations may affect feelings, both in respect of the impact of relinquishing the child and the bonding process. Hill also reminds us of bonding processes between a child and his or her adoptive parents, and that arguments about the psychological effects of relinquishing a child might also apply in favour of a commissioning couple in a surrogacy arrangement. A further argument in support of an intent-based approach is that it avoids any gender stereotyping.[227]

4.1.3 Welfare

An appeal to the child's welfare is also sometimes evident in attributing parenthood. While adopters or those seeking a parental order may intend to be parents, the making of an adoption order or parental order is ultimately the decision of a court, applying the child's welfare as its paramount consideration. The view that children's welfare should be more widely the underlying basis for attributing parenthood has been advocated by Professor James Dwyer.[228] Focusing on children's relationship rights, Dwyer interrogates philosophically the approach in many jurisdictions whereby children are allocated to their natural parents without scrutiny of the parents' suitability. He argues, therefore, that in each case the child's welfare should be considered before allocating child and parent to each other. Apart from the obvious practical difficulties of implementing this approach, it risks imposing a state view about appropriate lifestyles and parenting.[229]

4.1.4 Responsibility/causation

As Rebecca Probert[230] points out, intent-based parenthood does not fit well with English law's treatment of a child conceived as a consequence of a 'one night stand', where the child is not necessarily intended. Probert suggests, therefore, that 'responsibility' in terms of causation may be a more appropriate underlying basis for attribution of parenthood in such cases.

4.1.5 Function

Another way of deciding whether someone is a parent is to look at parents' functions and examine who is performing those functions. Such an approach, as Shapiro points out, 'ensures a high degree of correspondence between those who are social parents and those

---

[225] G. Douglas, 'The Intention to be a Parent and the Making of Mothers' (1994) 57(4) Modern Law Review 636 at 640.

[226] J. Hill, 'What Does it Mean to be a "Parent"? The Claims of Biology as the Basis for Parental Rights' (1991) 66 New York University Law Review 353.

[227] M. Shultz, 'Reproductive Technology and Intent-Based Parenthood: An Opportunity for Gender Neutrality' (1990) Wisconsin Law Review 297.

[228] J. G. Dwyer, 'The Relationship Rights of Children' (New York, Cambridge University Press, 2006). For reviews, see S. Gilmore, 'The Relationship Rights of Children' (2008) 22(2) International Journal of Law, Policy and the Family 273; and C. Sawyer, 'Review Article: A Brave New World Order' [2007] Child and Family Law Quarterly 518.

[229] For criticism, see the review by S. Gilmore, 'The Relationship Rights of Children' (2008) 22(2) International Journal of Law, Policy and the Family 273 at 281; see also C. Sawyer, 'Review Article: A Brave New World Order' [2007] Child and Family Law Quarterly 518.

[230] R. Probert, 'Families, Assisted Reproduction and the Law' [2004] Child and Family Law Quarterly 273.

who will gain legal recognition', but the analysis may be 'intrusive, time-consuming and expensive', and there is 'little consensus about what it means to act like a parent'.[231]

5 CRITICISM OF THE LAW

Emily Jackson is critical of the law's assumption that a child can only have two parents.[232] She argues that the law has been 'stymied by the principle of parental exclusivity', leading to law which is 'spectacularly confused and confusing',[233] and 'unable adequately to accommodate increasingly complex reproductive arrangements'.[234] Jackson contends that '[t]ransparency and descriptive accuracy' require 'a model of parenthood that is capable of accommodating its social and technical fragmentation'.[235] This, as she points out, would not necessarily mean an increase in the number of persons having parental responsibilities, for there could be in some cases an extension of 'symbolic recognition of parenthood' without necessarily conferring rights or duties upon such persons.[236] On Jackson's view, therefore, the current law need not necessarily deny legal recognition (as it does) to the genetic role of the egg donor or the gestational function of the surrogate mother who has given up her child to a commissioning couple.[237]

Andrew Bainham has argued that there appears to be a form of 'status anxiety' among those caring for children. He identifies a pervasive concern 'that their status be improved and a strong desire to gain the full status associated with parenthood'.[238] He argues that 'caution is required in assuming too readily that what looks like a parent must be a parent'.[239]

Bainham is thus critical of the HFEA 2008 insofar as it extends the status of legal parenthood to a wider range of individuals who do not have any biological connection with the child. He argues that:

> while it may be appropriate to give to the lesbian partner and other social parents parental responsibility (depending on the extent to which the individual actually performs parenting functions), it is inappropriate to make that person the legal parent because this is to distort and misrepresent kinship.[240]

Illustrating the point, he observes that the lesbian parent's parents become grandparents, yet the sperm donor and his family drop entirely out of the 'parenthood' picture.[241] As Bainham observes, these developments contrast with the focus on ascertaining biological truth in the case law on establishing paternity.

---

[231] J. Shapiro, 'Changing Ways, New Technologies and the Devaluation of the Genetic Connection to Children' in M. Maclean (ed), *Family Law and Family Values* (Oxford: Hart, 2005), p 92.

[232] E. Jackson, 'What is a Parent?' in A. Diduck and K. O'Donovan (eds), *Feminist Perspectives on Family Law* (Abingdon: Routledge-Cavendish, 2006), p 60.   [233] Ibid.

[234] Ibid, p 66.   [235] Ibid, p 74.   [236] Ibid, p 70.

[237] See also J. Wallbank, 'Too Many Mothers? Surrrogacy, Kinship and the Welfare of the Child' [2002] Medical Law Review 271, arguing for focus on child's rights to a link with biological mother.

[238] A. Bainham, 'Status Anxiety? The Rush for Family Recognition' in F. Ebtehaj, B. Lindley, and M. Richards (eds), *Kinship Matters* (Oxford: Hart, 2006), p 58.

[239] Ibid, p 61; and see A. Bainham, 'Birthrights? The Rights and Obligations Associated with the Birth of a Child' in J. Spencer and A. Pedain (eds), *Freedom and Responsibility in Reproductive Choice* (Oxford: Hart, 2006).

[240] A. Bainham, 'Arguments about Parentage' (2008) 67(2) Cambridge Law Journal 321–355 at 341. See also T. Callus, 'First 'Designer Babies, now À La Carte Parents' [2008] Family Law 143.

[241] Bainham, ibid.

6 ALLOCATION OF PARENTAL RESPONSIBILITY

Legal parenthood of itself carries with it certain important legal incidents, such as the duty to maintain a child.[242] However, in the Children Act 1989 there is a further concept, 'parental responsibility', defined for the purpose of the Act in section 3(1) as 'all the rights, duties, powers, responsibilities and authority which by law a parent of a child has in relation to the child and his property'.[243] If a person, including a parent, is to have these additional legal relations, he or she must have parental responsibility. The Children Act 1989 sets out who has parental responsibility and the means by which those who do not have it may acquire it.

English law distinguishes in the allocation of parental responsibility between married and unmarried parents.

Key legislation

Section 2(1) of the Children Act 1989 provides:

Where a child's father and mother were married to each other at the time of his birth, they shall each have parental responsibility for the child.

In the case of unmarried parents, section 2(2) provides:

Where a child's mother and father were not married to each other at the time of his birth—

(a) the mother shall have parental responsibility for the child;

(b) the father shall not have parental responsibility for the child, unless he acquires it in accordance with the provisions of this Act.

The words 'being married to each other at the time of the child's birth' in section 2(1) are extended[244] to include some relationships in which the parties clearly were not, as a matter of fact, married to each other at the time of the child's birth. Parents who are parties to a void marriage fall within section 2(1) provided that at the time of the child's conception, or the time of the marriage if later, either or both of them reasonably believed that the marriage was valid.[245] This reasonable belief is presumed unless the contrary is shown.[246] This means that both parents enjoy parental responsibility if, for example, one of the parents was aged under 16 at the date of the marriage, provided either or both of them did not realise this. It means that a man who is already married to someone else, and who knowingly enters into a bigamous marriage, has parental responsibility for any child of that marriage if his 'wife' reasonably believed that their marriage was valid at one of the relevant times.

The phrase 'married to each other at the time of the child's birth' also applies to parents who marry after the child's birth.[247] The father acquires parental responsibility from the date of the marriage.

---

[242] Child Support Act 1991, s 1.   [243] See Children Act 1989, s 3(2) and (3).

[244] Section 2(3) stipulates that subs (1) must be read with s 1 of the Family Law Reform Act 1987, which in turn refers to s 1 of the Legitimacy Act 1976.   [245] Legitimacy Act 1976, s 1(1).

[246] Ibid, s 1(4).

[247] Family Law Reform Act 1987, s 1(3)(b), ie, a legitimated person within the meaning of the Legitimacy Act 1976, s 10.

Section 2(1) now also applies in the case of the child's mother and a female parent who acquires legal parenthood pursuant to section 42 or 43 of the HFEA 2008.

In addition, the parents of adopted children are included within the definition of parents married to each other at the time of the child's birth.[248]

Finally, parents of any person who is otherwise treated in law as legitimate also fall within section 2(1).[249] This provision draws in those cases, usually where there is a foreign element, where a child is treated by law as a child of parents who are married at the time of the child's birth even though this is not factually the case.

All other parents are treated as parents who were not married to each other at the time of the child's birth. The combined effect of section 2(1) and (2) of the Children Act 1989 is that mothers always have parental responsibility, as do fathers who are married to the child's mother. By contrast, a father who is not married to the child's mother does not automatically obtain parental responsibility: he is thus treated differently in two ways—less favourably than the unmarried mother and less favourably than a father who is married to the mother. To understand this position, which on its face may seem unjustifiably discriminatory, it is necessary briefly to explain how the law has developed.

Historically, parental responsibility in respect of a child born out of wedlock vested solely in the mother.[250] The current law emerged from the Law Commission's examination of the status of illegitimacy in the late 1970s. Initially the Commission favoured complete abolition of the status of illegitimacy,[251] including any difference between fathers based on marital status. However, following consultation the Commission changed its view,[252] explaining that its initial proposal had provoked 'serious anxiety' in a 'significant body of well-informed and experienced commentators',[253] many of whom suggested that parental rights should vest automatically 'only in a class of fathers defined so as to exclude the "unmeritorious"'.[254] The Commission concluded that it would be wrong to ignore the reported concerns where they could not be shown to be without foundation[255] and, being unable to define a class of unmeritorious fathers,[256] recommended that the unmarried father should not acquire parental rights automatically but should be entitled to seek a court order conferring parental rights and duties.[257]

Section 4 of the Family Law Reform Act 1987 was enacted, which enabled an unmarried father to obtain a status similar to a married father. The essence of that provision was re-enacted in section 4 of the Children Act 1989, with some changes to take account of the shift in terminology in that Act from parental rights and duties to 'parental responsibility', and the order is now known as a 'parental responsibility order'.[258] Section 4 of the Children Act 1989 further strengthened the unmarried father's position with another mechanism

---

[248] Family Law Reform Act 1987, s 1(3)(c).   [249] Ibid, s 1(3)(d).

[250] *Barnardo v McHugh* [1891] AC 388.

[251] Law Commision, *Illegitimacy* (Law Com WP No 74, 1979). See A. Bainham, 'The Illegitimacy Saga' in R. Probert and C. Barton (eds), *Fifty Years in Family Law Essays for Stephen Cretney* (Cambridge: Intersentia, 2012) and S. Cretney, *Family Law in the Twentieth Century A History* (Oxford: Oxford University Press, 2003), ch 15.   [252] Law Commission, *Illegitimacy* (Law Com No 118, 1982).

[253] Ibid, para 4.46.

[254] Ibid, para 4.27. For criticism of the Working Paper's conclusions see M. Hayes (1980) 43 MLR 299, and see the concerns of the National Council for One-parent Families, cited in Law Com No 118, fn 91.

[255] Ibid, para 4.49. It might equally have been said that the onus should be on those asserting.

[256] Ibid, paras 4.28–4.43.

[257] Ibid, para 4.50. See also Law Commission, *Illegitimacy (Second Report)* (Law Com No 157, 1986), para 1.1. Law Commission, *Illegitimacy* (Law Com No 118, 1982), para 7.26. Compare the views of the Scottish Law Commission (Law Com No 135, 1992), paras 2.36–2.50 concluding that 'both parents of the child should have parental responsibilities and rights whether or not they are or have been married to each other'. See A. Bainham, 'Reforming Scottish Children Law—Sense from North of the Border' (1993) 5(1) Journal of Child Law 3 at 5–7.   [258] Now in Children Act 1989, s 4(1)(c).

for acquiring parental responsibility, namely a formal agreement between the mother and the father, known as a 'parental responsibility agreement'.[259]

In the late 1990s there was a further public consultation on the law on parental responsibility, issued by the Lord Chancellor's Department.[260] Its tone was sympathetic to unmarried fathers, explaining that discrimination against unmarried fathers is 'increasingly seen as unacceptable, in view of the large numbers of children who are born to unmarried parents, many of whom are likely to be in stable relationships.'[261] The Consultation Paper commented that it was 'clearly impossible to assume that most unmarried fathers are irresponsible or uninterested in their children, and do not deserve a legal role as parents'.[262] However, as Sheldon notes, 'it is equally unconvincing to assert that all unmarried fathers *are* assuming such a useful and positive role'.[263]

Following consultation,[264] a new provision was inserted[265] into section 4 of the Children Act 1989 conferring parental responsibility on a father through joint registration of the father's name on the child's birth certificate.[266] While welcomed by some, the amendment has been criticised by others for diluting the degree of commitment needed for fathers to acquire parental responsibility, for placing the onus on women to apply to revoke parental responsibility where problems arise, and for doing 'little to enhance and promote the relationships between children and their fathers in any practical way'.[267]

6.1 ACQUISITION OF PARENTAL RESPONSIBILITY BY AN UNMARRIED FATHER

There are thus now three methods within section 4 of the Children Act 1989 by which an 'unmarried father' may acquire parental responsibility.

Key legislation

Section 4, as amended, provides:

(1) Where a child's father and mother were not married to each other at the time of his birth, the father shall acquire parental responsibility for the child if—

    (a) he becomes registered as the child's father…;

    (b) he and the child's mother make an agreement (a 'parental responsibility agreement') providing for him to have parental responsibility for the child; or

    (c) the court, on his application, orders that he shall have parental responsibility for the child.

---

[259] Now in ibid, s 4(1)(b).

[260] Lord Chancellor's Department, *1. Court Procedures for the Determination of Paternity, 2. The Law on Parental Responsibility for Unmarried Fathers* (March 1998). The Consultation Paper set out several options for reform.

[261] Law Com No 118, para 51. In 2000 almost 40 per cent of live births occurred outside marriage, 80 per cent of which were jointly registered, 75 per cent of which were to parents living at the same address: see (2002) 32 Social Trends at 47.   [262] Law Com No 118, para 51.

[263] S. Sheldon, 'Unmarried Fathers And Parental Responsibility: A Case For Reform?' (2001) 9 Feminist Legal Studies 93 at 112.

[264] For an account of some of the responses to the consultation, see S. Sheldon, 'Unmarried Fathers And Parental Responsibility: A Case For Reform?' (2001) 9 Feminist Legal Studies 93.

[265] By the Adoption and Children Act 2002, s 111.

[266] Children Act 1989, s 4(1)(a). See D. Sharp, 'Parental Responsibility—Where Next?' [2001] Family Law 606 and J. Masson, 'The Impact of the Adoption and Children Act 2002 Part I—Parental Responsibility' [2003] Family Law 581. For criticism of the provision, see J. Wallbank, 'Clause 106 of the Adoption and Children Bill: Legislation for the "Good" Father?' (2002) 22(2) Legal Studies 276.

[267] Wallbank, ibid, 278.

6.1.1 Section 4(1)(a): registration of father on child's birth certificate

Section 4(1)(a) of the Children Act 1989 provides that the father of a child will have parental responsibility if he is registered as the father on the child's birth certificate.

Its effect is not as extensive as might at first appear. First, the provision is not retrospective. Section 4(1)(a) was implemented on 1 December 2003 so acquisition of parental responsibility in this way only applies in respect of registrations on or after that date. Thus the father of a newly born child who is registered as the father now, is in a better position vis-à-vis parental responsibility than the man who was registered prior to 1 December 2003 and has cared for the child for many years. In addition, currently the registration of an unmarried father can only be effected with the mother's agreement' (ie, jointly), or where the father has a court order which already recognises his legal parenthood.[268] In *AAA v ASH, Registrar General for England and Wales and the Secretary for Justice*[269] a father who had contracted an Islamic marriage with his child's mother which was not valid in English law attended alone to register his child's birth. Sir Christopher Sumner held that the father (being an unmarried father) had not registered in compliance with the relevant provisions and the 'registration' had not conferred parental responsibility. Schedule 6 to the Welfare Reform Act 2009[270] (which at the time of writing has yet to be implemented) inserts new sections 2A and 2B into the Births and Deaths Registration Act 1953 imposing a duty upon a mother to disclose information about a child's father, the scope of which will be prescribed by regulations. The mother is not required to provide the information if she declares that the child has no father,[271] the father has died, she does not know his identity or whereabouts, or the father lacks capacity within the meaning of the Mental Capacity Act 2005.[272] The mother also does not have to provide the information if she has reason to fear for her safety or that of the child if the father is contacted in relation to the registration of the birth.[273] Schedule 6 further introduces provisions whereby the alleged father can be contacted to acknowledge parentage,[274] or his parentage ascertained by scientific testing with consent,[275] and the fact that he is the father then registered. The effect of these provisions will be to reduce a mother's control over birth registration and thus over acquisition of parental responsibility.

However, currently section 4(1)(a) does little to improve the position of unmarried fathers where the mother is resistant to his involvement in decisions concerning the child's upbringing. The general effect of section 4(1)(a), however, is likely to be a gradual decrease in the proportion of unmarried fathers who do not have parental responsibility, resulting eventually in only a small proportion of fathers who will not have it.

6.1.2 Section 4(1)(b): parental responsibility agreement

Section 4(1)(b) of the Children Act 1989 enables the unmarried father to acquire parental responsibility by agreement with the mother. The agreement must be made in accordance

---

[268] Registered means registered under any of paras (a), (b), and (c) of s 10(1) or under s 10A(1) of the Births and Deaths Registration Act 1953.

[269] [2009] EWHC 636 (Fam), [2010] 1 FLR 1.

[270] For the policy behind this provision, see Department for Work and Pensions, *Joint Birth Registration: Recording Responsibility* (Cm 7293, June 2008), and the preceding Green Paper *Joint Birth Registration: Promoting Parental Responsibility* (Cm 7160, 2007). For discussion, see S. Sheldon, 'From "Absent Objects of Blame" to "Fathers Who Want to Take Responsibility": Reforming Birth Registration Law' (2009) 31(4) Journal of Social Welfare and Family Law 373–389 (reflecting a genetic understanding of parent as actively engaged) and A. Bainham, 'What is the Point of Birth Registration?' [2008] Child and Family Law Quarterly 449.

[271] By virtue of the HFEA 2008, s 41.

[272] Births and Deaths Registration Act 1953, s 2B(3) and (4).   [273] Ibid.

[274] Ibid, s 2C. The father can also declare his parentage: see s 2D.   [275] Ibid, s 2E.

with regulations:[276] on the relevant set form;[277] signed and witnessed; and registered in the Principal Registry of the Family Division in London. The signatures must be witnessed by a lay justice or an officer of the court. It is important for parents to understand that, once made, the agreement cannot be revoked by the parties; it can only be ended by a court.

The making of a parental responsibility agreement is not itself an exercise of parental responsibility. In *Re X (Minors) (Care Proceedings: Parental Responsibility)*[278] a mother wished to share parental responsibility with the child's father. The child was in the care of the local authority and the local authority wanted, if possible, to prevent the father gaining parental responsibility. Wilson J held that a local authority's power under section 33(3)(b) of the Children Act 1989 to control the extent to which the parents of a child in its care may meet their parental responsibility, could not be exercised to prevent the child's mother from entering a parental responsibility agreement. Since the father was signing the agreement necessarily without parental responsibility, it would be paradoxical to conclude that in doing the same the mother was exercising her parental responsibility.[279] Furthermore, the local authority would not have been able to prevent the acquisition of parental responsibility through marriage, and a good reason ought to be shown for adopting a different result in the case of parental responsibility acquired by way of a parental responsibility agreement.[280]

There has been a low (some might say disappointing) uptake in the use of parental responsibility agreements.[281] The low uptake probably reflects at least two factors. There is evidence that many unmarried parents are unaware that the unmarried father lacks parental responsibility, especially when he is cohabiting with the mother, and also unaware of the possibility of making an agreement.[282] In addition, research by Pickford[283] identified the father's reluctance to broach with the mother the subject of making an agreement for fear that it may disrupt their relationship.

6.1.3 Section 4(1)(c): application for a parental responsibility order

If a father who desires parental responsibility has been unable to secure it in the ways discussed earlier (ie, with the mother's agreement), he will need to seek parental responsibility from a court. Usually he would do so by applying for a parental responsibility order (PRO) under section 4(1)(c) of the Children Act 1989.[284] The applicant for a PRO under section 4 of the Act must be the child's legal father,[285] and jurisdiction should not be founded upon a concession that the applicant is the child's father.[286] An application for

---

[276] Parental Responsibility Agreement Regulations 1991 (SI 1991/1478), as amended by the Parental Responsibility Agreement (Amendment) Regulations 2005 (SI 2005/2808) and the Parental Responsibility Agreement (Amendment) Regulations 2009 (SI 2009/2026) (in force 1 September 2009).

[277] Form C(PRA1).   [278] [2000] Fam 156.   [279] Ibid, 161.   [280] Ibid.

[281] Especially as no fee is imposed when the agreement is registered at the Principal Registry of the Family Division.

[282] R. Pickford, 'Unmarried Fathers and the Law' in A. Bainham, S. Day Sclater, and M. Richards (eds), *What is a Parent? A Socio-Legal Analysis* (Oxford: Hart, 1999); and see S. McRae, *Cohabiting Mothers, Changing Marriage and Motherhood* (London: Policy Studies Institute, 1993), pp 70–71.

[283] Pickford, ibid.

[284] The child need not be living within the jurisdiction: see *Re S (Parental Responsibility: Jurisdiction)* [1998] 2 FLR 921.

[285] *R v Secretary of State for Social Security, ex p W* [1999] 2 FLR 604, FD, Johnson J, at 607D: 'there is no jurisdiction to make an order in favour of anyone who is not the father'. *Re S (Parental Responsibility: Jurisdiction)* [1998] 2 FLR 921.

[286] *Re D (A Child) (IVF Treatment)* [2001] 1 FLR 972, CA (Butler-Sloss P, Hale and Arden LJJ) *per* Arden LJ at [42]. See also Hale LJ at [36] and [37] and Butler-Sloss P at [10].

a PRO is a discrete application which must be determined separately from other matters, such as contact between the parent and child.[287]

6.1.3.1 The courts' general guidance

How do the courts decide such applications? The Court of Appeal has taken the view that there is no doubt that a father's acquisition of parental responsibility for a child is a matter with respect to the child's upbringing,[288] and that section 1(1) of the Children Act 1989 applies to the making of a PRO[289] and a court must treat the child's welfare as its paramount consideration. Because the court is considering whether to make an order under the Children Act 1989, section 1(5) also applies: the court shall not make the order unless it is better for the child than making no order at all. Use of the checklist of matters bearing on a child's welfare in section 1(3), however, is not mandatory,[290] although factors within it, for example the child's ascertainable wishes and feelings,[291] may well be relevant. Within the confines of the relevant statutory criteria, the PRO is 'the subject of a discretion cast in the widest terms',[292] and the Court of Appeal has explained that:

> In every case it is a matter of weighing in the balance the various factors in favour and against granting parental responsibility and deciding, on the facts of the individual case, whether an order for parental responsibility is in the interests of the child.[293]

The courts have provided guidance on how to approach a PRO application, but it is important not to lose sight of the court's wide discretion and its basic task as set out earlier. Guidance stems both from cases decided under section 4 of the Family Law Reform Act 1987 and from those decided under section 4 of the Children Act 1989 which replaced it. In *Re CB (A Minor) (Parental Responsibility Order)*[294] Waite J said that, in his view, Parliament intended to carry forward the case law decided under the 1987 Act.

The Court of Appeal has approached applications for a PRO from the perspective that prima facie it must be 'for the child's benefit or welfare that it has an absent parent sufficiently concerned and interested to want to have a parental responsibility order'.[295] The court has seen the order as potentially impacting positively on the child's welfare in two senses. First, it may promote a degree of father involvement which allows the father

---

[287] *Re H (A Child: Parental Responsibility)* [2002] EWCA Civ 542 (15 April 2002) at [14], applying *Re C and V (Contact and Parental Responsibility)* [1998] 1 FLR 392, CA (contact and parental responsibility distinct questions to be addressed from different perspectives). See also *Re CB (A Minor) (Parental Responsibility Order)* [1993] 1 FLR 920, FD (Waite J).

[288] *In the Matter of Z (Children)* [2008] EWCA Civ 1556 at [13]. In fact, the courts have asserted this rather than reaching a reasoned conclusion on the matter, and the point is not beyond doubt. See for arguments to the contrary, S. Gilmore, 'Parental Responsibility and the Unmarried Father—A New Dimension to the Debate' [2003] Child and Family Law Quarterly 21, esp at 31–34.

[289] See eg *Re H (Parental Responsibility)* [1998] 1 FLR 855, CA.

[290] Children Act 1989, s 1(4), and *Re H and A (Minors)*, 19 January 1993, CA (Balcombe and Waite LJJ), Lexis-Nexis Professional.

[291] See eg *In the Matter of TB; A Community and Hospitals Trust*, Transcript GILF3498, 25 September 2001, Gillen J (High Court of Northern Ireland).

[292] *Re CB (A Minor) (Parental Responsibility Order)* [1993] 1 FLR 920, FD, Waite J at 922G.

[293] *Re P (Parental Responsibility)* [1998] 2 FLR 96 at 107F–G. See also Lord Woolf MR in *Re P (Parental Responsibility)* [1997] 2 FLR 722 at 728H: 'the judge had to weigh in the balance the various factors in favour and against granting parental responsibility.' And *Re H (Parental Responsibility)* [1998] 1 FLR 855, CA at 859H–860A *per* Butler-Sloss LJ: 'the duty in each case to take into account all the relevant circumstances and to decide whether the order proposed is in the best interests of the child.'

[294] [1993] 1 FLR 920, FD. Although the case law post-dates enactment of the Children Act 1989.

[295] *Re G (A Minor) (Parental Responsibility Order)* [1994] 1 FLR 504, CA at 508C.

to contribute practically to the promotion of the child's welfare[296] and, secondly, the order itself may impact upon the child's self-esteem.

Talking point

Ward LJ explained in *Re S (Parental Responsibility)*,[297] that a child's self esteem is aided by a positive favourable image of an absent father. Therefore it is important to:

> ensure that the law confers upon a committed father that stamp of approval, lest the child grow up with some belief that he is in some way disqualified from fulfilling his role and that the reason for the disqualification is something inherent which will be inherited by the child, making her struggle to find her own identity all the more fraught.[298]

The Court of Appeal has sought to provide guidance on the factors which are likely to indicate that the father's involvement will promote the child's welfare. In *Re H (Minors) (Local Authority: Parental Rights) (No 3)*,[299] Balcombe LJ, delivering the Court of Appeal's judgment, said:

> In considering whether to make an order...the court will have to take into account a number of factors of which the following will undoubtedly be material (although there may well be others, as the list is not intended to be exhaustive):
>
> (1) the degree of commitment which the father has shown towards the child; (2) the degree of attachment which exists between the father and the child;[300] and (3) the reasons of the father for applying for the order.[301]

In *Re G (A Minor) (Parental Responsibility Order)*[302] his Lordship explained that where the *Re H* criteria are fulfilled, 'prima facie it would be for the welfare of the child that such an order should be made';[303] and in *Re Et (Parental Responsibility: Blood Tests)*[304] added that in such a case he 'would require to be convinced by cogent evidence that the child's welfare would be adversely affected by the making of such an order.'[305]

Later decisions have cautioned against the *Re H* criteria being elevated to the status of a statutory definition and have emphasised that they are 'subordinate to the welfare principle and therefore must not divert attention from other considerations which bear upon the child's welfare.'[306] As Ward LJ explained in *Re C and V (Contact and Parental Responsibility)*, they represent:

> some, though not all, of the factors which might be material in answering a much more general question as to whether [a] particular father shows genuine concern for the child

---

[296] See *Re G (A Minor) (Parental Responsibility Order)* [1994] 1 FLR 504, CA.

[297] [1995] 2 FLR 648, CA.

[298] Ibid, 657H. Said in *Re P (Parental Responsibility)* [1998] 2 FLR 96 at 107B, to reflect 'current psychiatric and sociological thinking'. The self-esteem argument will not always be relevant, eg in the case of a severely disabled child: see eg *Re M (Contact) (Parental Responsibility)* [2001] 2 FLR 342, FD (Black J).

[299] [1991] Fam 151.

[300] This appears to be a two-way process: see *Re B (A Minor)*, 17 October 1995, CA (Hale J and Russell LJ).

[301] Ibid, 158D, building on Ward J's judgment in *D v Hereford and Worcester County Council* [1991] Fam 14, [1991] 1 FLR 205, in which, as his Lordship later explained in *Re P (Parental Responsibility)* [1997] 2 FLR 722, CA at 724, he had 'ventured to put a test in the most general terms of whether or not the father had behaved, or would behave, with parental responsibility for the child'.

[302] [1994] 1 FLR 504, CA.   [303] Ibid, 508D. See also *Re P* [1998] 2 FLR 96, CA at 106B.

[304] [1995] 1 FLR 392, Saville and Mann LJJ agreeing.   [305] Ibid, 398G.

[306] *M v M (Parental Responsibility)* [1999] 2 FLR 737, FD, Wilson J at 743B–C.

and a genuine wish to assume the mantle of responsibility in law which nature has already thrust upon him.[307]

However, Balcombe LJ's judgments have established the *Re H* criteria as highly significant factors in each case, and they are regarded as the 'starting point'[308] for considering an application.[309] In each case, therefore, the court considers the father's commitment to the child, the attachment between father and child (and vice versa), and the reasons for the application.

6.1.3.2 Commitment

A father's commitment can be demonstrated in various ways. Commitment (and attachment) might be demonstrated through contact with the child. In *Re J (Parental Responsibility)*,[310] for example, Stuart-White J focused on a father's contact with his 11-year-old child, albeit concluding that contact five or six times in her lifetime did not demonstrate sufficient commitment to warrant the making of a PRO.

Commitment might also be shown through payment of maintenance.[311] While a failure to pay maintenance may evidence some lack of commitment, a deliberate failure to pay maintenance will not necessarily result in denial of a PRO. In *Re H (Parental Responsibility: Maintenance)*[312] the father had never missed contact with his children and had pursued applications to the court when contact had been denied by the mother. His application for parental responsibility was genuinely motivated and there was existing attachment between the father and his children. However, while the father had provided some clothing for the children, he obstinately refused to pay maintenance, claiming that it would be wrongly used by the mother to buy alcohol and cigarettes. Unimpressed by this attitude, the trial judge had adjourned the application for parental responsibility to enable the father to demonstrate his commitment to the children by assisting in their financial upkeep. The Court of Appeal held that, while the judge was rightly critical of the father for not providing financially for his children, he ought not to have used 'the weapon of withholding a parental responsibility order for the purpose of exacting from the father what may be regarded as his financial dues'. In doing so the judge had placed undue emphasis on the father's financial shortcomings at the expense of paying proper regard to the father's other merits, and had also been unmindful of the need to avoid delay. The decision is, of course, not uncontroversial. For some, the idea that a father should enjoy the rights associated with parental responsibility in circumstances where he has shown himself determined not to pay towards his child's support will be seen as divesting the notion of parental responsibility of any significant moral content and as giving an undesirable message to fathers about what having responsibility for a child entails.

6.1.3.3 Attachment

The second factor which the courts will look closely at is the degree of attachment between father and child (and vice versa). They have tended to apply this criterion quite rigidly. Where, however, the mother has unjustifiably prevented the father from establishing contact with the child, a rigid focus on attachment is arguably unduly harsh to the father.[313]

---

[307] *Re C and V (Contact and Parental Responsibility)* [1998] 1 FLR 392 at 397G–H *per* Ward LJ.

[308] *Re H (Parental Responsibility)* [1998] 1 FLR 855, CA at 859H *per* Butler-Sloss LJ.

[309] They have been described as the 'most material considerations': see *Re S (A Minor) (Stay of Proceedings)* [1993] 2 FLR 912, CA at 917E. [310] [1999] 1 FLR 784, FD (Stuart-White J).

[311] Ibid. [312] [1996] 1 FLR 867, CA.

[313] See S. Gilmore, 'Parental Responsibility and the Unmarried Father—A New Dimension to the Debate' [2003] Child and Family Law Quarterly 21.

It is suggested that in such cases the lack of attachment should be viewed in all the circumstances and given very little, if any, weight if the father is genuine and committed. A lack of attachment will not, however, necessarily result in dismissal of the father's application; the court sometimes adjourns the application to allow time to establish it.

6.1.3.4 Reasons for applying

The third of the *Re H* criteria looks to whether the father has genuine, bona fide, reasons for applying. It does not require the father to have specific reasons for applying for parental responsibility; the purpose is to identify the father whose motives for wanting parental responsibility are improper. In *M v M (Parental Responsibility)*[314] Wilson J held that this criterion, and indeed the definition of parental responsibility in section 3 of the Children Act 1989, presupposes that a father is capable of reason. In declining to grant parental responsibility to a father who had a very low IQ (partly caused by a motorcycle accident) his Lordship held that it was not appropriate to grant parental responsibility to a father who did not have the mental ability to exercise it appropriately.

Apart from the exceptional case where a father is mentally incapable of exercising parental responsibility, 'an order is not precluded merely because parental rights may not in practice be exercisable'.[315] The inability to exercise some or all parental responsibilities might occur, for example, because the father is ill or in prison or the child is in the care of a local authority. In *Re C (Minors) (Parental Rights)*[316] Waite J (sitting in the Court of Appeal) explained that circumstances might arise when a father (perhaps through mental illness) had to 'step out of his children's lives altogether', but his parental responsibility does not become 'a dead letter or a mere paper title'. It has 'real and tangible value, not only as something he can cherish for the sake of his own peace of mind, but also as a status carrying with it rights in waiting'.[317] In that case, the unmarried parents of two children had parted and there was medical evidence to the effect that the mother's mental stability would be at risk if the father was allowed contact with the children. The court therefore determined that contact should be denied for the time being. However, in relation to the parental rights and duties order Waite J concluded that while the prospective enforceability of parental rights is a relevant consideration, there is nothing within the legislation to suggest that it should be an overriding consideration, and it could never be right to refuse a parental rights and duties order on the automatic ground that it would be vitiated by an inability to enforce it.[318]

6.1.3.5 The parental responsibility order generally characterised as designed to confer a status

The courts have viewed the PRO as 'designed not to do more than confer on the natural father the status of fatherhood which a father would have when married to the mother'.[319]

---

[314] [1999] 2 FLR 737.

[315] *W v Ealing London Borough Council* [1993] 2 FLR 788, CA (Stephen Brown P, Simon Brown and Peter Gibson LJJ) at 796C–D, drawing on *Re C (Minors) (Parental Rights)* [1992] 1 FLR 1, where the Court of Appeal held that whilst prospective enforceability of an order is a relevant factor, it is not an overriding one, and an order cannot be vitiated automatically because the powers conferred are not immediately exercisable.

[316] [1992] 1 FLR 1, CA.

[317] Ibid, 3G–4B. See also, *Re S (A Minor) (Stay of Proceedings)* [1993] 2 FLR 912, CA at 918A *per* Lloyd LJ: 'a matter to which the father may well attach importance for its own sake'.

[318] For another example, see *Re H (Minors) (Local Authority: Parental Rights) (No 3)* [1991] Fam 151, sub nom *Re H (Illegitimate Children: Father: Parental Rights) (No 2)* [1991] 1 FLR 214.

[319] *Re C and V (Contact and Parental Responsibility)* [1998] 1 FLR 392 at 397. For discussion of parental responsibility as a status, see J. Eekelaar, 'Parental Responsibility—A New Legal Status?' (1996) 112 LQR 233.

Furthermore it has been said that 'on any view an order for parental responsibility gives the father no power to override the decision of the mother, who already has such responsibility: in the event of disagreement between them on a specific issue relating to the child, the court will have to resolve it'.[320]

6.1.3.6 Court should not focus unduly on how parental responsibility may be exercised

In *Re S (Parental Responsibility)*,[321] the Court of Appeal, emphasising that the purpose of a PRO is to confer status, held that when deciding whether to grant parental responsibility it is 'wrong to place undue and therefore false emphasis on the rights and duties and the powers comprised in "parental responsibility"'.[322] It explained that the 'wide exercise of s 8 orders can control the abuse, if any, of the exercise of parental responsibility which is adverse to the welfare of the child'.[323] As Ward LJ put it in *Re C and V (Contact and Parental Responsibility)*:[324]

> It is perfectly proper to inquire what reasons impelled the application, but, unless those reasons are demonstrably improper and wrong, the court should not on this application regulate how parental responsibility will in fact be exercised.[325]

The application of these principles is strikingly illustrated by the facts of *Re S (Parental Responsibility)*.[326] In that case the father was acknowledged on the child's birth certificate and had cohabited with the mother in a committed relationship for four years. The parents' relationship broke down when the child was about one year old. The father continued to have regular contact with his daughter, from which the child benefited, and he contributed to the child's housing costs, maintenance, and nursery school fees, apart from a period of three months when he was out of work. About a year later the father was arrested and subsequently pleaded guilty to possession of obscene photographs of children that the authorities had intercepted in his post. The mother reacted by severing the contact, but the child became deeply distressed and her behaviour at school deteriorated. Consequently the mother allowed contact to be resumed, initially supervised, but over time the supervision was relaxed and eventually the child had staying contact with the father. Upon the father's application for a PRO, the judge, concerned by the father's conviction and his potential to interfere in the mother's care of the child, refused the application. The Court of Appeal allowed the father's appeal. Ward LJ, delivering the leading judgment, held that the judge 'rightly had regard to the fact of his conviction' but 'however disreputable the conviction, it was not one which demonstrably and directly affected the child in her day-to-day life' given the existing contact arrangements. The judge had failed to appreciate that the scope for the father to interfere was not material,[327] and had 'failed to appreciate the emphasis that Balcombe LJ placed upon children growing up in the knowledge that their father is committed enough to wish to have parental responsibility conferred upon him'. In Ward LJ's view, the father's commitment and the uncontroverted attachment and affection between father and child abundantly satisfied the requirements for the making of a PRO, and there had been no cogent reason, indeed little reason at all, for refusing the order. The decision is clearly a controversial one. For some, the idea that

---

[320] *Re P (A Minor) (Parental Responsibility Order)* [1994] 1 FLR 578 at 584G–585D (the mother in that case had a residence order which meant that the father could not exercise parental responsibility inconsistently with that order: see the Children Act 1989, s 2(8)).

[321] *Re S (Parental Responsibility)* [1995] 2 FLR 648, CA.   [322] Ibid, 657F.   [323] Ibid.

[324] [1998] 1 FLR 392.   [325] Ibid, 397.   [326] [1995] 2 FLR 648, CA.

[327] Especially as there was a paucity of evidence to justify that finding.

a father with this sort of conviction should be granted parental responsibility will be perceived as distasteful and wrong.[328]

The approach in *Re S* was also adopted by the Court of Appeal in *Re C and V (Contact and Parental Responsibility)*.[329] In that case the child suffered with a medical problem which required the mother's experienced management of a tracheotomy tube in order to maintain the child's health. Upon the breakdown of the parents' relationship the mother resisted the father's wish to maintain contact with his son and to acquire parental responsibility. The judge refused the father's application for a contact order. He was influenced by the court welfare officer's reluctant conclusion that attempts to enforce contact would be strongly resisted and prove highly stressful to the mother, which anxiety could have a detrimental impact on her capacity to care for the child. For similar reasons, the judge dismissed the father's application for a PRO. The Court of Appeal (Ward LJ again delivering the leading judgment) held that, while the judge had not been plainly wrong to deny contact, he had misdirected himself in applying the same reasoning to the PRO application. The judge had failed to make specific findings about the father's commitment.[330] The parents had had a four year relationship, the father had been present at the child's birth, during the relationship he had assisted in looking after the boy (including on occasions performing the suction necessary to clear his tube), and the court welfare officer reported that the father's concern for the child was genuine.[331] On those facts, the Court of Appeal had no difficulty finding that the father fulfilled the necessary tests to acquire parental responsibility, and the father's potential use of parental responsibility in the circumstances of this case was not a material factor.

In *Re P (Parental Responsibility)*[332] the Court of Appeal clarified further that while an order 'will not usually be refused simply because, through hostility to the child's mother or an excess of zeal, he may seek to exercise parental responsibility inappropriately', where:

> the father intends to use a parental responsibility order for improper or inappropriate ends to try to interfere with and possibly undermine the mother's care of the child, then clearly the court retains the discretion to refuse a parental responsibility order even if part of the father's likely abuse of the order can be contained by prohibited steps orders under s 8 of the Children Act 1989.[333]

6.1.3.7 Hedging the order and conditional orders

As we have seen, a distinction is made between a parent with improper motives and one who may simply be overzealous in his desire to exercise parental responsibility. Hostility between the parties and/or lack of mutual respect, while clearly relevant insofar as it impacts upon the child's welfare, is not per se sufficient to deny a father parental responsibility.[334] Where there is a risk that the father may be overzealous, or where it is not felt to be appropriate for the father to exercise parental responsibility in a particular area of the child's life, these concerns might be addressed by way of undertakings from

---

[328] F. Kaganas, 'Responsible or Feckless Fathers?—*Re S (Parental Responsibility)*' [1996] Child and Family Law Quarterly 165.   [329] [1998] 1 FLR 392, CA.

[330] Ibid, 397.   [331] Ibid, 398.   [332] *Re P (Parental Responsibility)* [1998] 2 FLR 96.

[333] Ibid, 107–108.

[334] *Re D (A Minor)* [1995] 3 FCR 783, FD (Sir Stephen Brown P). See also *Re S (A Minor) (Parental Responsibility)* [1995] 3 FCR 564, FD (Sir Stephen Brown P) at 568B, criticising the welfare officer's 'undue reliance upon the difficult relationship between the parties as being a relevant factor to take into account'. See eg *Re M (Contact: Family Assistance: McKenzie Friend)* [1999] 1 FLR 75, CA (Ward and Roch LJJ) at 80E–F: commenting of the father that there was 'no evidence whatever to suggest that he has behaved irresponsibly towards the children, however irresponsible he may have been to [the mother] as her partner.'

the father, by hedging the order with conditions, or indeed making the order conditional on the imposition of certain conditions.[335]

In *Re D (Contact and Parental Responsibility: Lesbian Mothers and Known Father)*[336] a lesbian couple, A and C, advertised for a man who would father a child. Mr B responded, and with A he fathered a girl, D. The lesbian couple's view was that Mr B would be acknowledged as D's father, but that he would play a minimal role in her life (eg contact once every three weeks or so). However, once the child was born, it became clear that Mr B envisaged a greater role in D's life. He sought parental responsibility, which the couple opposed.

They were concerned about Mr B's potential to interfere in their upbringing of the child. The concern was based upon Mr B's past behaviour. For example, D suffered from arthritis and the father wrote a letter to D's medical consultant which embarrassingly suggested that A and C had concerns about the treatment D was receiving. On another occasion, D was to attend a school open day on her 4th birthday, but B wanted to see her that day. Mr B had said that he would locate the school, and the mothers had been worried that he would turn up on the day and cause difficulties which might prejudice D's chance of getting a place at the school.

Black J was not convinced that it was appropriate simply to apply the existing principles to the novel facts of this case, and expert evidence was provided to the court by Dr Claire Sturge, Consultant Child and Adolescent Psychiatrist.[337] She advised that a third parent would be confusing for the child and her sense of security would be strongest if responsibility for her lay within the nuclear family. She suggested that the solution would be for the father to be officially recognised in some way, but not to be involved in the nitty-gritty of her daily life. Black J was concerned about Mr B's potential to interfere but in the end these concerns were eased by Mr B agreeing to be bound by undertakings not to interfere in matters of D's schooling and medical treatment. Black J granted a PRO, making clear that the order was made in reliance upon those restrictions.[338] Thus, by 'means of this more than usually detailed parental responsibility order' her Ladyship hoped that the respective statuses of the parties could properly be recognised.[339]

The courts' willingness to grant parental responsibility with one hand and then substantially control its exercise with the other, and the consequent characterisation of parental responsibility as a mere status, has led Helen Reece to comment that, at least in some cases, English law has seen a degrading of the concept of parental responsibility in recent years from the notion of 'parental authority' to 'nothing more than official approval'.[340]

6.1.3.8 Cases where the child particularly needs a father with parental responsibility

There may be features of a case which particularly suggest that the child needs another parent with parental responsibility and which therefore may make the granting of a PRO

---

[335] It is not possible, however, to suspend a PRO. In *Re G (Parental Responsibility Order)* [2006] 2 FLR 1092, CA, the court overturned a judge's decision to grant a PRO suspended provided the mother supply information about the child's education and health. Hedley J observed that while this could be achieved by a raft of specific issue orders, to do so would be most unusual. Instead, the Court of Appeal adjourned the PRO application with liberty to restore, upon the mother's undertakings to provide information to the father about the child's education and health.

[336] [2006] 1 FCR 556, FD (Black J).   [337] Ibid, [24]–[28].   [338] Ibid, [91].

[339] Ibid, [93].

[340] H. Reece, 'The Degradation of Parental Responsibility' in R. Probert, S. Gilmore, and J. Herring (eds), *Responsible Parents and Parental Responsibility* (Oxford: Hart, 2009), p 102.

more likely.[341] An example is where the mother herself has acted irresponsibly. As Thorpe J commented in *S v R*, a case in which the whereabouts of the children were unknown as the mother had relocated without the father's knowledge in breach of a contact order:[342] 'if the mother is going to behave irresponsibly in relation to her obligations there is all the more need for [the child] to be supported by another adult with parental responsibility.' Another reason might be where a mother is very ill[343] and it is helpful to confer parental responsibility to secure another parent with parental responsibility in the event of her likely death.[344]

6.1.3.9 When will a parental responsibility order be denied?

Most applications for parental responsibility orders are successful and it is relatively rare for parental responsibility to be completely denied. The Court of Appeal has explained that in such cases it is 'irresponsibility in the father's behaviour, or his abuse or likely abuse of parental responsibility which may disqualify him'.[345] A number of case law examples of such behaviours are discussed in the following sections.

6.1.3.9.1 Inappropriate use cases

One category of case in which parental responsibility is sometimes denied is where the father's motive for possessing parental responsibility appears to be improper; what has been termed[346] the 'inappropriate use' cases. *W v Ealing London Borough Council*[347] provides an example. The children were in the care of the local authority, and leave had been given to the authority to terminate contact between the children and their parents prior to placing the children with long-term foster parents with a view to their adoption. The children had been prepared for separation from their parents, and two possible adoptive families had been found, neither of whom wanted contact between the children and their mother and father to continue. In these circumstances Connell J dismissed the father's application for parental responsibility as introductions to the prospective adopters were imminent and to change the situation would have left the children in limbo or confused them. A further ground was that the father would not have been in any position to play any significant role in the future. Dismissing the father's appeal, the Court of Appeal found that the father's only reason for applying for a PRO was 'the hope that he might thereby thwart the making of an adoption order'[348] and held that in those circumstances Connell J had been entitled to refuse the order and thus eliminate that risk. The Court of Appeal pointed out that that approach is not inconsistent with earlier expressed principles, commenting:

> the principle that an order is not precluded merely because parental rights may not in practice be exercisable is no authority for the converse proposition that an order must be made in such circumstances.[349]

---

[341] *Re E (Parental Responsibility: Blood Tests)* [1995] 1 FLR 392 at 398H; *Re A (A Minor)* [1996] 1 FCR 5, FD (Thorpe J).   [342] *S v R* [1993] 1 FCR 331, FD (Thorpe J).

[343] See eg *Re S (A Minor)*, 5 October 1994, CA (Neill LJ, Wilson J) (mother seriously ill with neuro-degenerative disorder).

[344] *Re W (A Minor)*, 16 March 1994, CA (Balcombe and Hobhouse LJJ); *Re D (Minors)*, 20 March 1995, CA (Butler-Sloss, Morritt, and Hutchison LJJ).

[345] Ibid, 108C–D.   [346] *Re M (Contact) (Parental Responsibility)* [2001] 2 FLR 342 (Black J).

[347] [1993] 2 FLR 788, CA.   [348] At 796C.

[349] At 796C–D. Indeed, it has been held that, where the father's use of parental responsibility is likely to be inappropriate, the existence of a care order is 'insufficient protection to merit the granting of a parental responsibility order without more': see *In the Matter of TB; A Community Hospitals Trust*, Transcript GILF3498, 29 September 2001, High Court of Northern Ireland (Gillen J).

Parental responsibility has also been denied where the father will seek to use parental responsibility to unsettle the mother and undermine her day-to-day care of the child. An example is provided by *Re M (Contact) (Parental Responsibility)*.[350] The case concerned a 17-year-old girl, KM, who suffered from cerebral palsy, functioned at the level of a six-month-old, and was totally dependent for all her needs. She was living with the mother and the mother's partner. Since the parents' separation, the father and his family had frequently complained to the authorities about the mother's care of KM. In addition, the family alleged that the mother's partner represented a risk of sexual abuse to her based on his previous trial (albeit acquittal) for the sexual assault of a 13-year-old girl. As a result of these tensions, there had been a series of angry confrontations between the families. Upon the father's application for a PRO, Black J found that to a significant extent the father's motivation was concern for KM and therefore she 'should start well-disposed to the father's application'. However, her Ladyship was concerned that the father would 'seek to misuse such an order as a "make weight" in future dealings with those in authority such as the police, social services, the school and doctors, about KM'. She was concerned that the father and the wider family misunderstood the nature of a PRO and saw it as providing some sort of right to intervene. She concluded therefore that there was a very real problem of potential misuse which in the extreme circumstances of the case could not be prevented by hedging the order with safeguards in the form of restrictions on the exercise of parental responsibility. Accordingly her Ladyship held that it was not in KM's interests to grant parental responsibility where the father 'would be highly likely to misuse it to lend weight to future interference in her care, thus continuing the stress on the mother and potentially undermining her ability to care properly for KM'. KM required a settled existence free from stress, particularly in light of her special needs.

A further example of concern about a father's likely interference is provided by the case of *Re P (Parental Responsibility)*.[351] In that case there was a very substantial disparity in the parties' ages: the mother was 26 and the father 78. The judge found that they had met and began having sexual intercourse when the mother was just 15 years old, the father having convinced her that if she had sexual intercourse with him she would be saved from the devil. They subsequently cohabited and had a daughter together. They separated when the child was four years old and the father continued to have extensive contact. The contact ceased, however, and only resumed as supervised contact at a contact centre, when the mother became aware that the father was in possession of a number of photographs of pre-pubescent children in obscene or suggestive poses, some of whom were his grandchildren. A psychological report on the father disclosed that he had difficulties with sexual boundaries. In addition, the father was very critical of the mother's care of the child, on many occasions reporting to social services his concerns, which were found to be without foundation. He made a groundless allegation that the mother's new cohabitant was sexually abusing the child and he had taken a video of the child supposedly disclosing the same. The father indicated in evidence that he would use parental responsibility to monitor the child's health and schooling and to approve, or disapprove, of babysitters to ensure that they were not paedophiles. The judge's decision to deny parental responsibility because it would be used to undermine the mother's care of the children was upheld by the Court of Appeal. The judge did not base the denial of parental responsibility upon any potential risk of sexual abuse which the father might pose to the child. However, the Court of Appeal considered the matter *obiter*. The court commented that the issues of contact and parental responsibility are not wholly irrelevant to each other and if the judge had relied upon the fact that the father posed a sufficient risk to the child in the future to

---

[350] [2001] 2 FLR 342.   [351] [1998] 2 FLR 96, CA.

necessitate the indefinite supervision of his contact, she would have been entitled to deny parental responsibility on that basis too. The court indicated that the judge would have had to ask herself: 'whether a man who had no understanding of sexual boundaries and who posed a risk to his daughter such that his contact to her had to be supervised for the indefinite future, was fit to have parental responsibility to his child.'

A final, and more recent, example is provided by *Re B (Role of Biological Father)*,[352] which might be contrasted with *Re D (Contact and Parental Responsibility: Lesbian Mothers and Known Father)*,[353] discussed in Section 6.1.3.7. In *Re B* lesbian civil partners, CV and S, had a child conceived through insemination of CV with the sperm of S's brother, TJ. Three months into the pregnancy the lesbian partners became estranged from the donor father. The father asserted that it was intended that he have a real, albeit limited, role. The lesbian partners had envisaged a more distant relationship. TJ applied for parental responsibility and contact which the lesbian partners resisted.

Hedley J made no order with respect to the PRO application. His Lordship was concerned that TJ would seek to exercise parental responsibility forcefully to assert his views which would undermine the lesbian parents' status. In these circumstances, in contrast to the decision in *Re D (Contact and Parental Responsibility: Lesbian Mothers and Known Father)*,[354] Hedley J could see no benefit of a restricted grant of parental responsibility. His Lordship granted contact four times a year (on one occasion at a family gathering), the purpose of which was not to allow the development of status or a relationship which would threaten the autonomy of CV and S. Hedley J explained that the contact order was made merely:

> so that without artificiality [the child] can picture TJ as someone significant but not ordinarily important in his life yet someone with whom (in time and if he so wishes) he can explore the implications of the kind man who enabled him to be and he can ask questions to satisfy his own natural curiosity.[355]

Thus in this case parental responsibility was denied to preserve the lesbian couple's autonomy in light of the risk of the father's interference, although a contact order was used to preserve some link and the child's knowledge of his father. In a subsequent case,[356] Hedley J used the concepts of principal and secondary parenting to describe the intended respective roles of the child's mother and her female partner, and the child's father and his male partner. However, in *A v B and another (Contact: Alternative Families)*[357] the Court of Appeal cautioned against the use of such concepts,[358] and also expressed concerns about the practice of referring to the child's father as a donor, since it may misleadingly give the impression that the father is giving his child away.[359] The Court of Appeal eschewed giving further general guidance on how to address parenting disputes in cases involving 'alternative families', emphasising that each case is fact-specific.[360]

---

[352] [2007] EWHC 1952 (Fam) [2008] 1 FLR 1015[2008] 1 FLR 1015. See also *R v E and F (Female Parents: Known Father)* [2010] EWHC 417 (Fam), [2010] 2 FLR 383 and S. Blain and A. Worwood, 'Alternative Families and Changing Perceptions of Parenthood' [2011] Family Law 289.

[353] [2006] 1 FCR 556, FD (Black J)   [354] Ibid.

[355] *Re B (Role of Biological Father)* [2007] EWHC 1952 (Fam), [2008] 1 FLR 1015[2008] 1 FLR 1015 at [29].

[356] *ML v RW* [2011] EWHC 2455 (Fam) at [16].   [357] [2012] EWCA Civ 285, [2012] 1 FCR 510.

[358] Ibid, [30].   [359] Ibid, [48] and [49].

[360] Ibid, [23] and [39]. For research on lesbian mothers' perspectives, see L. Smith, 'Is Three a Crowd? Lesbian Mothers' Perspectives on Parental Status in Law' [2006] Child and Family Law Quarterly 231–252.

6.1.3.9.2 The father's previous behaviour

The second broad category of case when parental responsibility may be denied is where the father's previous behaviour demonstrates the inappropriateness of his being granted parental responsibility.

In some cases the father may have physically harmed the mother or child. In *Re T (A Minor) (Parental Responsibility: Contact)*[361] the mother was violently assaulted by the father when she was six months pregnant, requiring hospital attendance, which brought the relationship to an end. The father assaulted the mother again when he visited her at work and, following a dispute, headbutted the mother when she had the 7-month-old child in her arms. In addition, the father refused to return the child following contact sessions, including on one occasion for a period of nine days. The Court of Appeal dismissed the father's appeal against Ewbank J's decision to deny him parental responsibility, expressing the view that it was 'clearly the right decision'[362] in a case of 'cruel and callous behaviour in respect of a young child, with no thought for her welfare'.[363]

In *Re H (Parental Responsibility)*[364] the parents' relationship had broken down and the child spent Friday nights with his father. On return from one such visit, the child was considerably distressed and had a severe bruise and a scratch on his face. Subsequent medical examination disclosed that the child had several disturbing bruises on other parts of his body, including on his chest and trunk, inner and outer part of the ear, along the shaft of his penis, and on his scrotum. The father denied that he had caused the injuries and he subsequently applied for contact and parental responsibility. The father could demonstrate commitment to the child, the child was attached to him, and he had genuine reasons for fostering the relationship, and since the child's injuries had been discovered the child had continued to enjoy excellent supervised contact with the father. The judge, however, concluded that contact should continue to be supervised, and held that on all the facts the father was not suitable to hold parental responsibility. He concluded that, contrary to the father's denial, the father had injured the child[365] and also found, with the support of expert evidence, that some of the child's injuries were characteristic of not just over chastisement or a moment of frustration or anger but connoted something more sinister, in the nature of deliberate cruelty and possibly sadistic abuse. The father's appeal to the Court of Appeal was dismissed. The court commented that 'the judge was fully justified in deciding that a man who behaved like that to his son and made no attempt to come to terms with what he had done, was not fit to have parental responsibility for the child' and explained that:

> the appropriateness of the order has to be considered on the particular facts of each individual case. If, reviewing all the circumstances, the judge considers that there are factors adverse to the father sufficient to tip the balance against the order proposed, it would not be right to make the order, even though the three [*Re H* criteria] can be shown by the father.[366]

A father might demonstrate irresponsibility in other ways. In *Re P (Parental Responsibility)*[367] the two children had been born when their father was serving a term

---

[361] [1993] 2 FLR 450, CA.   [362] Ibid, 457.   [363] Ibid, 456.   [364] [1998] 1 FLR 855, CA.

[365] In reaching this conclusion, the judge had evidence that the father had previously been cautioned by the police for striking another two-year-old child heavily in the face.

[366] [1998] 1 FLR 855, CA at 860.

[367] [1997] 2 FLR 722, CA. See also the obiter comments of Ward LJ at 726E–F, providing further examples of factors which could be weighed against a father as demonstrating that he had devalued his responsibility: a father who for selfish or misguided reasons chose to abandon his family to work abroad or broke up the family through reckless acts of drunkenness.

of 15 years' imprisonment for robbery. The father played little or no part in the children's lives, apart from having contact with them during the time that he had been in prison. Having returned to the family on a home visit, he spent his time committing another robbery for which he was sentenced to a further term of 15 years' imprisonment. The judge declined to make a PRO. Refusing the father's appeal, the Court of Appeal held that the judge's decision could not be said to be plainly wrong. The court explained that a prisoner does not lose his personal rights when sentenced to imprisonment except insofar as his imprisonment makes this necessary, and is entitled to apply for parental responsibility. However, as Lord Woolf MR explained:

> If a parent behaves in a manner which he should appreciate can, and is likely to, result in his being sentenced for a long period of imprisonment, he should be taken to realise that this has a damaging effect on his children. It is an act of irresponsibility on his part towards his children. When, as here, you have a pattern of criminal conduct, the court is entitled to take into account as a relevant factor, not a conclusive factor, that conduct in deciding whether or not it is appropriate to grant that parent parental responsibility.[368]

A mother's reaction to the father's previous behaviour can also be a reason for denying parental responsibility. In *Re L (Contact: Genuine Fear)*[369] the mother had an intense fear of the father, who when much younger had been a 'Hell's Angel' with a violent past. The mother's fear arose principally from her knowledge that previously the father had been convicted of stabbing his wife and her solicitor in the Royal Courts of Justice, and stabbing his wife's boyfriend on another occasion. At the time of the hearing, however, the father had not been convicted of any offence for 15 years. Because of the mother's phobia of the father (as the judge described it), the father only had indirect contact with the child. There was no contact at all with the mother and the father did not know where the child lived or went to school. In these circumstances, Bruce Blair QC, sitting as a Deputy High Court Judge, concluded[370] that, while parental responsibility can be regarded as 'a status carrying with it rights in waiting',[371] the chance of the father having any meaningful say in the child's life was 'wholly imaginary rather than real'. It would 'barely, in practice, confer a status' and would cause additional distress to the mother which could be communicated to the child. Accordingly, the judge made no order as to parental responsibility.

6.2 SHOULD UNMARRIED FATHERS BE AFFORDED EQUAL TREATMENT?

Should the law give parental responsibility automatically to all fathers irrespective of marital status? The debate surrounding this issue is a complex one, with several different strands.

6.2.1 Human rights arguments

In *Re Z (Children)*[372] the Court of Appeal held that it was inapt that a father's argument that the current law is discriminatory should be developed, 'the most obvious reason [being] that it has already been considered and rejected in the European Court of Human Rights in the case of *B v United Kingdom*'.[373] In *B v UK*[374] the unmarried parents of a child separated and the mother, who was Italian, relocated to Italy taking the child with her. The English courts held that the removal of the child from the jurisdiction was not

---

[368] Ibid, 728.   [369] [2002] 1 FLR 621, FD.   [370] Ibid, [49]–[53].
[371] See *Re C (Minors) (Parental Rights)* [1992] 1 FLR 1, CA.   [372] [2008] EWCA Civ 1556.
[373] Ibid, [15].   [374] [2000] 1 FLR 1.

unlawful as the mother had sole parental responsibility, and therefore the father's consent to removal was not required. Furthermore, his application to have the child returned was dismissed. The father complained of a breach of Articles 8 and 14 of the ECHR in that his right to respect for family life was not protected in the same way as a married father. The complaint was declared inadmissible on the basis of 'an objective and reasonable justification for the difference of treatment', namely the range of possible relationships between children and unmarried fathers which vary 'from ignorance and indifference to a close stable relationship indistinguishable from the conventional family-based unit'.[375]

However, the court's reasoning in *B v UK* was scant and several arguments can be mounted against it. First, there is no obvious link between marriage and the range of different unmarried fathers and thus it is very difficult to see the latter as an objective and reasonable justification for the use of the former to discriminate. The connection between parental responsibility and marriage might be defended on the basis of seeking to encourage parents to marry and thus to bring up children in a relationship which is regarded as generally more stable than cohabitation. However, marriage is not necessarily an indicator of the quality of a parent/child relationship. Furthermore, there is a difficulty for the man who wishes to marry but his partner does not. The Scottish Law Commission did not accept the link with marriage in this context, noting a situation, which it doubted was in line with current social thinking, whereby:

> a man who abandoned his wife when she was pregnant, and never saw his child, would have full parental responsibilities and rights, whereas a man who was cohabiting with the mother of his child and playing a full paternal role would have none.[376]

Furthermore, in *Marckx v Belgium*[377] the European Court of Human Rights held that Belgian law breached an unmarried mother's right to respect for family life in its requirement that she undergo a process of formal recognition as the child's mother and thus its failure to recognise a legal relationship between the mother and child from the moment of birth. It is difficult to see why the same reasoning should not apply in the case of a man whose paternity has been established, for example through DNA testing.[378] Moreover, the *Marckx* case made clear that its ruling was not dependent on a wish to take care of the child, as the Court commented that 'it may happen that also a married mother might not wish to bring up her child, and yet, as far as she is concerned, the birth alone will have created the bond of affiliation'.[379] In *Marckx* the Court also found that the child's Article 14 right to enjoy the rights under the Convention free from discrimination had been breached when taken in conjunction with Article 8. This presumably would afford a child of an unmarried father scope to argue that his or her human rights are breached by being treated differently from a similar child whose parents are married. As Andrew Bainham has pointed out, the European Court of Human Rights in *Johnston v Republic of Ireland*[380] appears to have recognised that 'parents and

---

[375] For a similar conclusion on the law in Scotland, see *McMichael v UK* (1995) 20 EHRR 205, and the excellent analysis by G. Branchflower, 'Parental Responsibility and Human Rights' [1999] Family Law 34.

[376] Scottish Law Commission, *Report on Family Law* (Scot Law Com No 135, 1992), para 2.36.

[377] (1979–80) 2 EHRR 14. For detailed discussion of this case and its impact, see W. Pintens and J. M. Scherpe, 'The *Marckx* Case: A "Whole Code of Family Law"?' in S. Gilmore, J. Herring, and R. Probert (eds), *Landmark Cases in Family Law* (Oxford: Hart, 2011), p 155.

[378] G. Branchflower, 'Parental Responsibility and Human Rights' [1999] Family Law 34; A. Bainham, 'When is a Parent Not a Parent? Reflections on the Unmarried Father and His Child in English Law' (1989) 3 International Journal of Law, Policy and the Family 208–239 at 212.

[379] *Marckx* at para 39, a point made by Branchflower, ibid.   [380] (1986) 9 EHRR 203.

children have *mutual* rights to respect for their family life'.[381] He argues, therefore, that it follows that discrimination against the child represents discrimination against the father, and vice versa.[382]

6.2.2 Unmeritorious fathers and potentially negative exercise of parental responsibility

As the Strasbourg case law shows, the arguments against giving all fathers parental responsibility automatically have tended to focus on the fact that unmarried fathers inhabit a spectrum, and on the potentially negative exercise of parental responsibility[383] by some unmarried fathers.[384] However, this argument has been rendered very weak now by case law which indicates that parental responsibility does not give a father power to interfere in the resident parent's day-to-day care of the child, and which characterises parental responsibility as a status, and as one which can be hedged with conditions that can degrade it to almost nothing.[385] Furthermore, as Wilson J pointed out in *Re P (A Minor) (Parental Responsibility Order)*[386] one does not need parental responsibility to cause disturbance if minded to do so.[387]

The Law Commission cited the dramatic example of a rapist automatically gaining parental responsibility[388] which, while likely to elicit an emotive response, is a dubious example on which to draw to inform a general policy. As Barton has observed, drawing on Painter's research on the incidence of rape within marriage,[389] 'the vast majority of rapine children are legitimate'.[390] Furthermore, the rapist might be dealt with by way of an exception,[391] although the practical and emotional difficulties for the mother of proving such an exception should not be underestimated.

It might also be said that if the fact that a man is unmeritorious is a valid basis for denying a father rights in relation to his child, should that basis not apply to all fathers

---

[381] A. Bainham, 'When is a Parent Not a Parent? Reflections on the Unmarried Father and His Child in English Law' (1989) 3 International Journal of Law, Policy and the Family 208–239 at 215.

[382] Compare S. Sheldon, 'Unmarried Fathers and Parental Responsibility: A Case for Reform?' (2001) 9 Feminist Legal Studies 93 at 106–107.

[383] Whether parental responsibility can be exercised negatively is debatable since at least in the view of the House of Lords in *Gillick*, parental rights exist for the benefit of the child and are exercisable only insofar as they are necessary for the child's protection.

[384] Commentators have observed the English Law Commission's 'apparent willingness to equate the psychological needs of unmarried mothers with the best interests of their children': see A. Bainham, 'When is a Parent Not a Parent? Reflections on the Unmarried Father and His Child in English Law' (1989) 3 International Journal of Law, Policy and the Family 208–239 at 231. P. Townsend and A. Baker, 'Unmarried Fathers—Are We Ending Discrimination at Last?' (1998) 162(13) Justice of the Peace 236. See also Scottish Law Commission No 135, at para 2.40.

[385] See H. Reece, 'The Degradation of Parental Responsibility' in R. Probert, S. Gilmore, and J. Herring (eds), *Responsible Parents and Parental Responsibility* (Oxford: Hart, 2009). Of course, the point cuts both ways: it might be said that if possession of parental responsibility makes little difference in practice, the unmarried father does not really need it.   [386] [1994] 1 FLR 578, FD (Wilson J).

[387] And as Eekelaar has pointed out, the father might equally be vulnerable to harassment on the part of the mother: J. Eekelaar, 'Second Thoughts on Illegitimacy Reform' [1985] Family Law 261.

[388] Described as an 'extreme and no doubt unrealistic example' (Law Com WP No 74, 1979, para 3.9).

[389] K. Painter, *Wife Rape, Marriage and the Law—Survey Report: Key Findings and Recommendations* (Manchester: Faculty of Economic and Social Studies, University of Manchester, 1991).

[390] C. Barton, 'Equal Responsibility for all Fathers?' (1998) 142(17) Solicitors Journal 401.

[391] Although the Law Commission concluded that, given the availability of abortion, such a man was likely to be 'statistically insignificant' so as not to merit special provision to exclude him as an unmeritorious father (para 4.30).

irrespective of marital status?[392] It could be argued that all parents should initially have parental responsibility which should be revocable where it is inappropriate for the holder to have it.[393] The debate has centred, however, on the unmeritorious unmarried father, with little discussion of the potential also for unmeritorious mothers or unmeritorious married fathers. This prompts the question whether there is anything per se about motherhood or married fatherhood which would justify different treatment of unmarried fathers.

6.2.3 Are unmarried fathers less worthy than mothers?

There are strong arguments in favour of according parental responsibility automatically to all mothers: the physical nurture of the child during pregnancy, and (usually) ensuing attachment, together with the fact that nature delivers the child into the mother's care. Moreover, as Sheldon points out, it is 'somewhat easier to generalise about unmarried mothers' in that 'most unmarried mothers *are* assuming an active parenting role'.[394] However, fathers can be heavily committed at the pre-natal stage and it is not only fathers' parenting abilities and commitments to their children that vary. Consider, for example, the case of a mother who abuses drugs and/or alcohol, damaging her foetus, and who is unable to care appropriately for her child.[395] She will still obtain parental responsibility automatically and cannot have it removed except by way of her child's adoption. Furthermore, as the child grows older, arguments about the mother's role in pregnancy must surely decline in significance, yet the discrimination against the unmarried father extends beyond the child's infancy, throughout the child's life.[396]

The debate about similarities or differences between mothers and fathers has been made more complex by the Gender Recognition Act 2004, which allows a person to change his or her gender. It is now possible for a person to be the mother of one child and the father of another. In such a case, the same unmarried person would have automatic parental responsibility *qua* mother in relation to one child, but *qua* father would have to acquire it in accordance with the provisions of the Children Act 1989. While, of course, this is simply the consequence of applying section 2 of the Children Act 1989 to an admittedly unusual case, there is perhaps something rather revealing about the fact that the law here treats the same person differently according to his or her gender.[397]

6.2.4 Should the law reflect social change and attitudes?

An argument in favour of according parental responsibility automatically to all fathers is based on social change as evidenced by statistics which show an increasing proportion of births outside marriage to parents in cohabiting relationships.[398] In England and Wales in

---

[392] See generally J. M. Scherpe, 'Establishing and Ending Parental Responsibility: A Comparative View' in R. Probert, S. Gilmore, and J. Herring (eds), *Responsible Parents and Parental Responsibility* (Oxford: Hart, 2009).

[393] See ibid for comparative discussion. See also H. Conway, 'Parental Responsibility and the Unmarried Father' (1996) 146 New Law Journal 782.

[394] S. Sheldon, 'Unmarried Fathers and Parental Responsibility: A Case For Reform?' (2001) 9 Feminist Legal Studies 93 at 112.

[395] It might also be said that except in the limited period and circumstances in which a lawful abortion is permitted, the mother's connection with the child during pregnancy is the imposed consequence of conception, rather than evidence of commitment to her child based on choice.

[396] An observation made in a different context by the Constitutional Court of South Africa in *Fraser v Children's Court Pretoria North and Others* (CCT31/96) [1997] ZACC 1, 1996 (8) BCLR 1085, 1997 (2) SA 218.   [397] S. Gilmore, 'The Gender Recognition Act 2004' [2004] Family Law 741 at 744.

[398] The English Law Commission arguably attached excessive weight to parents' formal legal relationships when the tide was moving (and has been since) towards greater recognition of *de facto* relationships:

2007 there were 690,013 live births, of which 305,550 were outside marriage.[399] A further argument is based on the perceptions of such parents. Research by Ros Pickford[400] found that three-quarters of a random sample of unmarried fathers were unaware that there is a difference in legal status between unmarried and married fathers. Almost all 'expressed great surprise, and many were very annoyed or angry'[401] when informed that they did not have parental responsibility. The fathers' views of the law were based upon their assumption 'that marriage is not a relevant criterion for distinguishing fathers in terms of the legal rights' which 'derived from cultural beliefs such as in the existence of "common-law" marriage, or from their experience of other areas of law such as child support',[402] in which every father is liable to maintain his child.

Indeed it has been argued that if all fathers have financial support responsibilities to their children they should also be accorded other responsibilities.[403] By contrast, however, concerns have been expressed that linking child support and parental responsibility may commodify children.[404] In addition, it might be argued that mere biological connection should not found a duty of child support.[405]

6.2.5 Does the current law encourage irresponsibility?

It may also be argued that the perception of unmarried fathers as prima facie not worthy of parental responsibility does little to encourage them to play an active and responsible role in their children's lives.[406] Indeed, the real discrimination may lie in the fact that all mothers are required to accept their parental responsibility yet all fathers are not. As Bainham has pointed out, if the unmarried father represents a problem, it may be one of '*indifference* rather than interference'.[407] However, Sheldon has observed that the idea that granting parental responsibility will encourage more men to take responsibility for their children lacks empirical support, and comments that:

> On balance, it seems rather improbable that a status of which the vast majority of the population has remained demonstrably in ignorance, which accords limited advantages

---

see R. Ingleby, 'Law Commission No 118: Illegitimacy' (1984) Journal of Social Welfare Law 170–174. This may be attributable to the Commission's goal of not debasing the institution of marriage (para 4.39).

[399] *Review of the National Statistician on Births and Patterns of Family Building in England and Wales, 2007* (ONS, 2008).

[400] R. Pickford, *Fathers, Marriage and the Law* (London: Family Policy Studies Centre for the Joseph Rowntree Foundation, 1999); and for a discussion, see R. Pickford, 'Unmarried Fathers and the Law' in A. Bainham, S. Day Sclater, and M. Richards, *What is a Parent? A Socio-Legal Analysis* (Oxford: Hart, 1999), pp 143–159. See also I. Dey and F. Wasoff, 'Mixed Messages: Parental Responsibilities, Public Opinion and the Reforms of Family Law' (2006) 20 International Journal of Law, Policy and the Family 225, who report figures from the Scottish Social Attitudes Survey showing that in 2004 34 per cent of respondents said unmarried fathers had the same rights as married fathers (with 13 per cent 'don't knows').

[401] Pickford, in Bainham et al ibid, p 149.   [402] Ibid, p 146.

[403] See, eg H. Conway, 'Parental Responsibility and the Unmarried Father' (1996) 146 New Law Journal 782.

[404] See S. Sheldon, 'Unmarried Fathers and Parental Responsibility: A Case for Reform?' (2001) 9 Feminist Legal Studies 93 at 107.

[405] Whether such a view is in children's general interests or would be politically acceptable is debatable.

[406] The Scottish Law Commission commented that the law 'may be seen as encouraging irresponsibility in some men' (at para 2.37). '[T]hat is no reason for the law to encourage and reinforce an irresponsible attitude' (at para 2.39).

[407] A. Bainham, 'When is a Parent Not a Parent? Reflections on the Unmarried Father and His Child in English Law' (1989) 3 International Journal of Law, Policy and the Family 208–239 at 231.

and which gives no right to contact with children is likely to have much influence on men's commitment towards parenting.[408]

6.2.6 Should parental responsibility follow active parenting?

Ruth Deech has argued that a father's claim to parental rights lies in his active involvement in the child's life,[409] making a distinction between the absent father (even one who cares *about* his child) and the father who cares *for* his child. She argues that only 'the father who offers the child a home to the best of his ability should have any authority over the child' and suggests that the question should be not be 'does the absent unmarried father have too few rights, but does he have too few responsibilities'.

Talking point

Deech argues that:

Fatherhood that does not encompass a fair share of [the day-to-day practical parenting tasks] is an empty egotistical concept and has the consequences that the man does not know the child sufficiently well to be able sensibly to take decisions about education, religion, discipline, medical treatment, change of abode, adoption, marriage and property. Therefore the absent unmarried father, as contrasted with the cohabiting father, should not automatically be entitled to these rights.[410]

She concedes, however, that criticism of absent fathers is 'to recognise, not to decry, the importance of a father's involvement',[411] and admits that her argument concerning parental involvement could apply equally to the absent married father and the absent unmarried mother.[412] In contrast to Deech's position, however, it may be argued that cohabitation is not necessarily an indicator of commitment to a child. Indeed, in some situations the most committed thing a father might do is to withdraw from the family home. Furthermore, a father's absence from the home does not necessarily preclude his taking decisions if apprised of relevant facts/information. Undoubtedly, a caring parent's close involvement with the child could arguably obscure clear judgement whereas absence might produce a more detached (objective) decision.

---

[408] S. Sheldon, 'Unmarried Fathers and Parental Responsibility: A Case for Reform?' (2001) 9 Feminist Legal Studies 93 at 108.

[409] R. Deech, 'The Unmarried Father and Human Rights' (1992) 4 Journal of Child Law 3. See also S. Sheldon, 'Unmarried Fathers and Parental Responsibility: A Case for Reform?' (2001) 9 Feminist Legal Studies 93 at 114–115; chapters by C. Smart and M. L. Fineman in C. Smart and S. Sevenhuijsen (eds), *Child Custody and the Politics of Gender* (London: Routledge, 1989); J. Wallbank, 'Clause 106 of the Adoption and Children Bill' (2002) Legal Studies 276 at 295.

[410] R. Deech, 'The Unmarried Father and Human Rights' (1992) 4 Journal of Child Law 3 at 8.

[411] Ibid, at 8.

[412] Deech (ibid) goes on to maintain that as long as marriage remains as a status, 'then a logical distinction has to remain between the unmarried father and the married father'. At this point her argument becomes difficult to defend, for it contends that a distinction should be maintained between parents based on marital status, but ultimately argues for a position which eschews such status as the criterion for attributing parental responsibility; and, while arguing for a non-discriminatory approach, it endorses the distinction between married and unmarried fathers, which discriminates in its general assumption that marital fathers *are*, and non-marital fathers *are not*, caring parents.

6.2.7 The child's right to dual parenting?

Linked to this is an argument that focuses on the child's right to have the input of both parents. It might be argued, however, that providing another adult with decision-making powers in relation to the child does not necessarily promote the child's rights.[413]

6.2.8 The case law on parental responsibility orders

A further argument in favour of according parental responsibility automatically to all fathers relates to the case law on applications for a PRO. First, most applications are successful,[414] begging the question whether it would be more cost-effective to require mothers in the rare remaining cases to apply to divest a father of his parental responsibility. It might be argued, however, that such an approach ignores the issue of the delay which will occur while legal proceedings are taken, fails to give weight to the potential for disruption of the child's upbringing, and is also open to the more profound objection that it makes too many assumptions about the efficacy of legal proceedings in dealing with family conflict.

Secondly, Gilmore, in a critical analysis of the case law,[415] has identified a number of anomalies and inconsistencies in the case law, and on occasions a rigid application of the *Re H* criteria, working to the injustice of some fathers (eg requiring proof of attachment in circumstances where the mother's behaviour has prevented attachment). In addition he has pointed out that the courts' requirement that the father demonstrate positive criteria such as commitment and attachment is out of line with the policy debate which informed the PRO, where the concern was not that fathers should have to show that they are meritorious, but with excluding the unmeritorious father. Gilmore argues that this judicial failure to articulate clear, consistent, and just principles which reflect the relevant policy background may add further impetus to the call for allocation of parental responsibility to all fathers irrespective of marital status.

6.2.9 Certainty

Perhaps the strongest argument in favour of retaining the current position is certainty. Currently, there is documentary evidence that a holder of parental responsibility has parental responsibility: a marriage certificate, a birth certificate, or some court record of agreement or order. If all fathers had parental responsibility by reason of legal parenthood, in the case of an unmarried father the only way of knowing whether he has parental responsibility would be to ascertain paternity.[416]

6.2.10 The need for ongoing evaluation of the arguments

One final criticism that can be made of the law in this area relates to the manner of its incremental development. When the Lord Chancellor's Department consulted in 1998 the current legal position was taken as the starting point. While account was taken of social change, there was no attempt to re-evaluate the soundness or otherwise of the Law Commission's *arguments* in light of the subsequent views of the Scottish Law Commission, academic commentary, social change, or the developing case law on PROs. For example, the Law Commission's argument that automatic parental responsibility would discourage

---

[413] Ibid.

[414] In 2010 there were 5,520 orders made in 5,980 disposals: see *Judicial and Court Statistics 2010*, Table 2.4.

[415] S. Gilmore, 'Parental Responsibility and the Unmarried Father—A New Dimension to the Debate' [2003] Child and Family Law Quarterly 21.

[416] R. Pickford, 'Unmarried Fathers and the Law' in A. Bainham, S. Day Sclater, and M. Richards, *What is a Parent? A Socio-Legal Analysis* (Oxford: Hart, 1999), p 154.

mothers from identifying the child's father is now dated, since the law now connects acquisition of parental responsibility to birth registration, and the law's new policy is that joint birth registration should be the norm.[417]

The increased methods by which the unmarried father can acquire parental responsibility and the declining proportion of fathers, who consequently will not have it, may have a dampening effect on any appetite for further change. In such a climate it is easy to lose sight of the fact that recent changes do not fully eradicate discrimination against unmarried fathers. The arguments are well known to commentators who have followed the law's development, and it is easy to portray this debate as a series of well-worn arguments both for and against the current position which are fairly evenly balanced.[418] It is possible, however, that what has been missing from recent policy debate is ongoing *evaluation* of the arguments.

6.3 ACQUISITION OF PARENTAL RESPONSIBILITY BY A FEMALE PARENT

Section 4ZA of the Children Act 1989 provides that a parent (other than the child's mother) who acquires legal parenthood under section 43 of the HFEA 2008 may acquire parental responsibility in similar ways to the unmarried father, as discussed earlier: through birth registration,[419] a formal parental responsibility agreement, or a PRO. Whether the courts will adopt similar principles to those established in relation to unmarried fathers remains to be seen, although it is possible that a more liberal approach may be adopted, given that the female parent will necessarily have embarked upon a formal process to acquire legal parenthood.

6.4 ACQUISITION OF PARENTAL RESPONSIBILITY BY A STEP-PARENT

Section 4A of the Children Act 1989 provides a method by which a step-parent (defined as the spouse or civil partner[420] of the child's parent) can acquire parental responsibility. For the provision to apply the child's parent (who is the step-parent's partner) must have parental responsibility for the child. The parent and step-parent couple can agree that the step-parent shall have parental responsibility although if the child's other parent also has parental responsibility the agreement of both parents is required.[421] Such an agreement is a parental responsibility agreement in the same way as an agreement under section 4(1)(b), discussed in Section 6.1.2, and the same formalities apply in order to give effect to it. In addition, a court may, on the application of the step-parent, provide for the step-parent to have parental responsibility for the child.[422] In *Re R (Parental Responsibility)*[423] a child had been brought up by his mother and her husband for nearly three years, the husband believing the child to be his. However, it transpired that the child had been fathered by another man, and the husband and the mother were now divorcing. The husband sought parental responsibility under section 4A(1)(b). Peter Jackson J declined the application holding that

---

[417] Welfare Reform Act 2009, sch 6; Department for Work and Pensions, *Joint Birth Registration: Recording Responsibility* (Cm 7293, June 2008), and the preceding Green Paper *Joint Birth Registration: Promoting Parental Responsibility* (Cm 7160).

[418] See eg, J. Herring, *Family Law*, 4th edn (London: Pearson, 2009).

[419] There were 22 registrations in 2009 and 335 in 2010: 'Live births in England and Wales by characteristics of mother 2010' (ONS, 2011).

[420] As amended by the Civil Partnership Act 2004, s 75(2).   [421] Children Act 1989, s 4A(1)(a).

[422] Ibid, s 4A(1)(b).   [423] [2011] EWHC 1535 (Fam), [2011] 2 FLR 1132.

'in normal circumstances the beneficiary of such an order will be a person who might be described as an incoming step-parent who wishes to bring up a child together with the parent with parental responsibility and will be centrally participating in the upbringing of the child in future', and that 'the other situations in which an order might be made are likely to be limited'. His Lordship noted that it was only by chance that the power in section 4A existed at all, as it would not do so if the couple were already divorced.

6.5 FURTHER METHODS OF ACQUIRING PARENTAL RESPONSIBILITY

So far we have been exploring the methods of acquiring parental responsibility which are reserved to a child's parent or step-parent. There are several other ways of acquiring parental responsibility which are open to a wider range of persons and which, in some cases, also provide additional methods by which a parent can acquire parental responsibility.

6.5.1 Parental responsibility conferred by a residence order

A residence order is an order in section 8 of the Children Act 1989, which allows the court to settle the arrangements as to the person or persons with whom a child lives. It makes sense that the person who is caring for the child should have all the rights, duties, powers, and authority which are seen as necessary to provide for a child's upbringing.

In the case of a successful application by the child's father, section 12(1) provides that the residence order be accompanied by a PRO in the father's favour. Similarly section 12(1A) provides that where a court makes a residence order in favour of a woman who is a parent of the child by virtue of section 43 of the HFEA 2008, the court must also make an order under section 4ZA of the Children Act 1989 giving her parental responsibility. In each case the PRO cannot be revoked during the currency of the residence order[424] and even if the residence order is subsequently brought to an end the parent retains his or her PRO.

In the case of any other (ie, non-parent) applicant, section 12(2) provides that the residence order confers parental responsibility during the currency of the order. Parental responsibility follows the order and if the order is subsequently revoked parental responsibility is lost. Section 12(3) provides that the parental responsibility conferred by section 12(2) does not confer the right to agree, or refuse to agree, to the making of an adoption order or an order under section 84 of the Adoption and Children Act 2002, nor the right to appoint a guardian for the child.

The law relating to the application for, and making of, residence orders and shared residence orders (including for reasons of conferring parental responsibility) is dealt with in detail in Chapter 9.

6.5.2 Parental responsibility conferred in child protection proceedings

Sometimes the parental care provided for a child may fall below that which can reasonably be expected, and the state may need to intervene to care and protect the child. Some of the court orders which can be obtained in that context confer parental responsibility upon the applicant, usually the local authority (eg an emergency protection order or a care order).[425] These orders and their effects are discussed in detail in Chapter 10.

---

[424] Children Act 1989, s 12(4).   [425] See ibid, ss 44(5) and 33.

6.5.3 Adoption

When an adoption order is made under the Adoption and Children Act 2002, the legal parenthood and parental responsibility of the child's (previous) parents is extinguished and acquired by the adoptive parent or parents.[426] The law on adoption is discussed in more detail in Chapter 11.

6.5.4 Special guardianship

A means of providing some security in the relationship between a child and his or her substitute carer, without the full family transplant effect of adoption, is by way of a special guardianship order (SGO).[427] This order, which can be made in private law or public law proceedings, provides the successful applicant with parental responsibility which may be exercised exclusively by the special guardian(s). The parental responsibility of others, while not extinguished, cannot be exercised while the SGO is in force, and some restrictions are placed on the ability of parents to apply to court in respect of the child. The law on special guardianship, including case law guidance on how the courts decide between the making of a SGO or an adoption order, is discussed in detail in Chapter 11.

6.5.5 Appointment of a guardian

In contrast to special guardianship, guardianship under section 5 of the Children Act 1989 is concerned with providing the child with a person with parental responsibility[428] in the event of the death of a person or persons who had parental responsibility for the child. A guardian may only be appointed in accordance with the provisions of section 5,[429] which provides that the appointment may be made by a court or by certain individuals.

A court may, by order, appoint a guardian for the child, either of its own motion in family proceedings or upon application by an individual.[430] The court can make the guardianship order if the child has no parent with parental responsibility for him or her, if the child's only or last surviving special guardian has died, or if the child's parent, guardian, or special guardian in whose favour a residence order has been made, has died while the residence order was in force.[431] Such an appointment may have an advantage over a residence order in a case where a child has been orphaned, because a guardian obtains greater powers. The guardian can in turn appoint a guardian for the child, and the guardian's agreement to the child's adoption is required.

The individuals[432] who may appoint a guardian are a parent who has parental responsibility for the child, a child's guardian, or a child's special guardian. The appointment can be achieved in a relatively informal manner: although it can be made by deed or will, it is also sufficient if it is simply 'made in writing, is dated and is signed by the person[433] making the appointment'.[434]

---

[426] Adoption and Children Act 2002, ss 46 and 67.   [427] Children Act 1989, ss 14A–14F.

[428] By s 5(6), a person appointed as a guardian has parental responsibility for the child.

[429] Children Act 1989, s 5(13).

[430] Ibid, s 5(1) and (2). As noted earlier, a local authority cannot appoint a guardian.

[431] Ibid, s 5(1). Provided that any surviving parent did not also have that residence order made in his or her favour: see ibid, s 5(9).

[432] Who may act alone or jointly: see ibid, s 5(10).

[433] Or signed at the direction of such person in the presence of two witnesses who each attest the signature.

[434] Children Act 1989, s 5(5). The appointment is not effective unless these requirements are fulfilled.

6.5.5.1 When does the individual's appointment of a guardian take effect?

A guardian's appointment does not take effect unless both parents with parental responsibility have died,[435] or unless immediately before the death of the person making the appointment a residence order in favour of the deceased was still in force[436] and the residence order was not also made in favour of a surviving parent,[437] or unless the person making the appointment was the child's only (or last surviving) special guardian.

The general policy, therefore, is that where the parents are living with the child together in harmony appointment of a guardian should only take effect when both parents die. The effect is to preclude any sharing of parental responsibility with the guardian appointed by the deceased parent. It is an approach which might not necessarily be welcomed by all parents, given that the benefits and burdens of bringing up children are often easier to manage when the task is shared. The Law Commission, however, when recommending that the law be changed from the common law position under which the testamentary guardianship took effect from death, was influenced (perhaps unduly so) by the notion that the deceased spouse was seeking to rule the other from the grave.[438]

Where the parents are estranged each may be less content with the notion that the surviving parent will have sole responsibility for the child's upbringing, and they may wish to appoint a guardian to have parental responsibility in conjunction with the survivor. This may be particularly likely where a parent anticipates his or her premature death and wants a relative to have care of his or her children; or where a parent has remarried and wants the new spouse to be the child's guardian. In such a case, the appointment will only take immediate effect if the deceased spouse had a sole residence order prior to his or her death. In some cases the child may no longer be living with his parents, being cared for by a special guardian. In such a case, the law permits an only or last surviving special guardian to make an appointment which takes immediate effect upon his or her death. In such cases, parental responsibility is shared by the guardian with any surviving person who has parental responsibility.

Appointment of a guardian revokes any earlier appointment unless the intention is to appoint an additional guardian.[439] An appointment can also be revoked expressly in writing[440] or by deliberate destruction of the instrument which created it.[441] An appointment in favour of a spouse or civil partner is revoked by subsequent divorce/dissolution or annulment of that relationship unless the appointment shows a contrary intention.[442]

7 DURATION OF PARENTAL RESPONSIBILITY

Parental responsibility within the Children Act 1989 is defined *in relation to the child*. As 'child' is defined for the purpose of the Act as a person under the age of 18,[443] 'parental responsibility' within the meaning of the Children Act 1989 ends when a child attains 18. In the case of parental responsibility allocated automatically by operation of law, parental responsibility continues until the child's majority and cannot be removed except by way of adoption or a parental order. Parental responsibility conferred by an emergency protection order, SGO, care order, or on a non-parent by way of a residence order, exists only during the currency of the order and will come to an end if, for example, the order is discharged or expires. Parental responsibility conferred by birth registration, parental

---

[435] Ibid, s 5(7)(a).   [436] Ibid, s 5(7)(b).   [437] Ibid, s 5(9).
[438] Law Com No 172, para 2.27.   [439] Children Act 1989, s 6(1).   [440] Ibid, s 6(2).
[441] Ibid, s 6(3).   [442] Ibid, s 6(3A) and (3B).   [443] Ibid, s 105.

responsibility agreement, or PRO only ceases if a court so orders[444] upon the application of any person who has parental responsibility for the child or, with leave of the court, of the child himself or herself.[445]

8 REMOVAL OF PARENTAL RESPONSIBILITY

Cases involving applications for the removal of parental responsibility are rare. In *Re P (Terminating Parental Responsibility)*[446] Singer J provided some guidance on their disposal which has been approved by the Court of Appeal. In that case the child had been admitted to hospital aged 9 weeks with a skull fracture which had left her permanently physically and mentally disabled. Evidence showed that she had also suffered rib and leg fractures at other times, suggesting systematic abuse over time. The child, who was two and a half at the time of the hearing, had been taken into care and was thriving with long-term foster parents. The father subsequently pleaded guilty to offences relating to the commission of the child's injuries and was in prison. At an earlier stage, however, when the father and mother maintained common cause that neither had caused the injuries, the mother entered into a parental responsibility agreement with the father. The mother later maintained that had she known that the father was the perpetrator she would not have done so.

Upon the mother's application to revoke the parental responsibility agreement, Singer J held that section 1(1) of the Children Act 1989 should apply to its determination in the same way that it applied to an application to grant parental responsibility. He considered it pertinent to consider what would have been the court's response had the father been applying for a PRO. His Lordship explained, however, that he started 'from the proposition that parental responsibility—both wanting to have it and its exercise—is a laudable desire which is to be encouraged rather than rebuffed' and postulated as a first principle 'that parental responsibility once obtained should not be terminated in the case of a non-marital father on less than solid grounds, with a presumption for continuance rather than for termination'.[447]

Revoking the parental responsibility agreement, Singer J could see no element of parental responsibility which the father could in the present or foreseeable circumstances exercise in a way which would benefit the child. In addition, its continuance had considerable potential ramifications for future adversity to the child: it would give a message to others that the father had not forfeited parental responsibility; it might undermine the mother's confidence in the stability of the child's placement; it could be unsettling to the foster parents; and it imposed an unrealistic demand on the local authority in requiring them to consider the father's potential exercise of parental responsibility when exercising their powers under the care order.

In *Re M (Minors)*[448] the Court of Appeal endorsed the principles enunciated by Singer J as 'exactly the appropriate way in which a judge should approach an application of this

---

[444] Ibid, ss 4(2A), 4ZA(5), and 4A(3).

[445] Ibid, ss 4(3) and (4), 4ZA(6) and (7), and 4A(3) and (4). Leave may only be granted if the court is satisfied that the child has sufficient understanding to make the proposed application.

[446] [1995] 1 FLR 1048, FD.

[447] At 1052. His Lordship added that it

> should not be allowed to become a weapon in the hands of the dissatisfied mother of the non-marital child: it should be used by the court as an appropriate step in the regulation of the child's life where the circumstances really do warrant it and not otherwise.

[448] Court of Appeal, 11 October 1995 (unreported) (Hale J and Pill LJ).

nature'. However, Hale J explained that rather than asking whether a PRO would have been made, the court's task might more relevantly be put as evaluating 'how he has gone about meeting that responsibility since the order was made and what benefit the children have derived from it or may be expected to derive from it in the future'. The case concerned a father's appeal against discharge of a PRO which had been made by consent. The Court of Appeal dismissed the appeal, holding that there had been strong evidence to discharge the order. The father had done everything he could to undermine the mother and make her life a misery and the children had not benefited from parental responsibility in the past, nor were they likely to in future.

8.1 THE POSITION OF PERSONS WITHOUT PARENTAL RESPONSIBILITY

A person might have the care of a child while neither being a parent nor having parental responsibility within the meaning of section 3 of the Children Act 1989. What is the legal position of such a person? First, as Munby J pointed out in *R (G) v Nottingham City Council*[449] any person may intervene to prevent an actual or threatened criminal assault taking place, and a 'threat of immediate significant violence is enough, particularly if it involves a young child'.[450]

Key legislation

Secondly, in some circumstances reliance might be placed on section 3(5) of the Children Act 1989, which provides:

A person who—

(a) does not have parental responsibility for a particular child; but

(b) has care of the child,

may (subject to the provisions of this Act) do what is reasonable in all the circumstances of the case for the purpose of safeguarding or promoting the child's welfare.

The scope of this broad provision turns on what view is taken of what it is reasonable to do in all the circumstances of a case. It is possible, for example, that reliance could be placed on section 3(5) by medical personnel to obtain consent to medical treatment from a child's carer where persons with parental responsibility cannot be contacted, at least in respect of orthodox forms of treatment. The reasonableness might turn on the seriousness of the medical condition, the complexity of the decision to consent and its impact, and whether treatment could be delayed to allow a parent to be contacted. It might be entirely reasonable to use section 3(5) to consent to a child's broken arm being set, where the child's parent is on an overnight flight and cannot be contacted by telephone. It might not be viewed as reasonable to consent in the same way to a limb amputation which could be delayed to the following day. In *R (G) v Nottingham City Council*[451] Munby J explained that there might also be 'circumstances in which a hospital could rely upon s 3(5) as justifying action taken in relation to a child in its medical care, despite the absence of parental consent and the absence of any court order' where medical intervention is 'required in order to preserve the child's life or to protect a child from irreversible harm in circumstances of such urgency that there is not even time to make an urgent telephone application to a

---

[449] [2008] EWHC 152 (Admin), [2008] 1 FLR 1660, QBD.   [450] Ibid, [21].   [451] Ibid.

judge'.[452] In such a situation the doctor could even act despite a parental refusal of consent if the parent is acting unreasonably or contrary to the child's best interests.[453]

Another context in which this question may arise is where the person with care forms the view that it would be against the interests of the child to return him to the care of a parent. For example, if parents returned home drunk and a babysitter formed the opinion that it would be unsafe to leave the child in the house with them, could she lawfully remove the child from the premises and take the child to her own home? It would seem desirable that the law should authorise such a properly motivated action, and section 3(5) would almost certainly cover this situation.

More difficult is the position when a child is being accommodated by a local authority under section 20 of the Children Act 1989, and a parent wishes immediately to remove his or her child from that accommodation. A local authority does not have parental responsibility for an accommodated child, and section 20(8) specifically states that any person who has parental responsibility may at any time remove the child from accommodation provided by the local authority under that section. Whether section 3(5) would allow a foster parent, or a person in charge of a children's home, to refuse to hand the child over in express disregard of section 20(8) has yet to be determined. It would seem desirable that section 3(5) should provide such persons with protection for a very short period, during which time, for example, steps are being taken to invoke police protection.

9 THE NATURE AND SCOPE OF PARENTAL RESPONSIBILITY[454]

9.1 THE COMPLEXITY OF PARENTAL RESPONSIBILITIES

Section 3(4) of the Children Act 1989 makes clear that the fact that a person has, or does not have, parental responsibility for a child shall not affect any obligation which the parent may have in relation to the child (such as a statutory duty to maintain the child) or any rights which, in the event of the child's death, the parent (or any other person) may have in relation to the child's property. In this way English law is able to maintain a distinction between a parent and a parent who additionally has parental responsibility within the meaning of the Children Act 1989.[455] The suggestion in the definition of parental responsibility in section 3 of the Children Act 1989 that a person with parental responsibility has *all* the rights, duties, powers, responsibilities, and authority which by law a parent has in relation to a child is slightly misleading, however, as acquisition of parental responsibility does not confer all of the duties that parents owe to their children. First, as we have seen there may be some limitations on the content of parental responsibility depending on how it has been acquired. Secondly, the duty to make child support payments pursuant to the Child Support Act 1991 can only be imposed upon a child's parent.[456] Thirdly, the definition

---

[452] Ibid, [24].   [453] Ibid, [25].

[454] There is burgeoning literature on the nature of responsibility within family law. Here we are concerned with parental responsibility in the sense of responsibilities to or for the child.

[455] For the view that the difference is rather limited, see J. Eekelaar, 'Rethinking Parental Responsibility' [2001] Family Law 426. For criticism of Eekelaar's arguments, see S. Gilmore, J. Herring, and R. Probert, 'Parental Responsibility—Law, Issues and Themes' in R. Probert, S. Gilmore, and J. Herring, *Responsible Parents and Parental Responsibility* (Oxford: Hart, 2009), ch 1.

[456] The duty to maintain in the Child Support Act 1991, s 1, is owed in respect of a 'qualifying child', which definition requires the existence of a non-resident *parent*. While the courts see conferring parental responsibility as a matter with respect to the child's upbringing, to which Children Act 1989, s 1(1) applies, s 105(1) defines a child's upbringing as excluding his or her maintenance. See further N. Wikeley, 'Financial Support for Children

in section 3 of the Act refers to parental responsibility in relation to a child, who for the purpose of the Act is a person who has not attained 18 years.[457] Parental responsibility under the Children Act 1989 does not therefore include any duties which a parent might owe to an adult child.[458] A parent's responsibilities and the concept of parental responsibility are not, therefore, the same, and only a parent who has parental responsibility has the full complement of parental 'rights' and responsibilities.

The law is complicated further by the fact that, as John Eekelaar has observed,[459] there are rules relating to when parenthood and parental responsibility respectively are a necessary and/or sufficient condition of imposing a duty on a person, or for that person acting in matters relating to the child. Sometimes only a parent will have a duty: for example the duty to make child support payments pursuant to the Child Support Act 1991. Sometimes simply having parental responsibility will suffice—for example in the case of consenting to the child's marriage.[460] On occasions, however, it is necessary to be both a parent *and* to have parental responsibility, for example in order to consent to the child's adoption.[461] In yet other cases either being a parent *or* having parental responsibility will suffice. For example, under section 10(4) of the Children Act 1989 either a parent or a person with parental responsibility can apply for any order under section 8 of the Act without leave of the court. In some cases, however, the exercise of parental rights (eg the right to appoint a guardian or to object to a child's adoption) requires that the parent has parental responsibility for the child within the meaning of the Children Act 1989.

9.2 STATUTORY GUIDANCE ON THE NATURE AND EXERCISE OF PARENTAL RESPONSIBILITY IN SECTION 2 OF THE CHILDREN ACT 1989

Section 2 of the Children Act 1989 provides some general statutory guidance on the nature and exercise of parental responsibility.

9.2.1 Parental responsibility may be shared

First, as will already be apparent, section 2(5) provides that more than one person (whether a parent or not) may have parental responsibility at the same time. Furthermore, section 2(6) makes clear that a person who has parental responsibility 'shall not cease to have that responsibility solely because some other person subsequently acquires parental responsibility for the child'.

9.2.2 Each holder of parental responsibility may act alone in meeting his or her parental responsibility

Section 2(7) of the Children Act 1989 provides that each holder of parental responsibility may act alone in meeting his parental responsibility. Section 2(7) clarifies, however, that

---

after Parental Separation: Parental Responsibility and Responsible Parenting' in R. Probert, S. Gilmore, and J. Herring (eds), *Responsible Parents and Parental Responsibilty* (Oxford: Hart, 2009).

[457] Children Act 1989, s 105(1).

[458] Eg the duty to maintain a child within the Child Support Act 1991 extends to adult children under 19 years who are receiving full-time education which is not advanced: s 55(1)(b). See also s 55(7) and (8) and the Child Support (Maintenance Calculation Procedure) Regulations 2000 (SI 2001/157) Sch 1, para 5(1) in relation to short-term provision to persons under 19 who have just left full-time education.

[459] J. Eekelaar, 'Rethinking Parental Responsibility' [2001] Family Law 426.

[460] See R. Probert, 'Parental Responsibility and Children's Partnership Choices' in R. Probert, S. Gilmore, and J. Herring, *Responsible Parents and Parental Responsibility* (Oxford: Hart, 2009).

[461] Adoption and Children Act 2002, ss 47 and 52(6).

this does affect the operation of any enactment which requires the consent of more than one person with parental responsibility. An example of such an enactment is section 13, which provides that where a residence order is in force with respect to a child, the child's surname cannot be changed nor can the child be taken out of the jurisdiction for more than a month without the consent of all persons with parental responsibility. Section 2(8) further clarifies that the fact that a person has parental responsibility does not entitle him or her to act in any way which would be incompatible with an order made under the Act. So, for example, if a mother has a residence order, it would not be possible for the father to exercise his parental responsibility to suggest that the child attend a school so far away from the mother's home that that decision would be incompatible with the residence order.

The courts have interpreted section 2(7), apparently contrary to its clear wording and the background to the provision, to mean that there is still a 'right to be consulted on schooling, serious medical problems and other important occurrences in the child's life'.[462] As John Eekelaar has observed,[463] this interpretation of section 2(7) places a difficulty in the way of according parental responsibility to all fathers, since it would sometimes place a very onerous duty upon the mother to trace, or even to identify, the father, causing delays in decision making about the child.

9.2.3 Parental responsibility cannot be surrendered or transferred

No doubt there is many a parent who has been tempted to say: 'Give me a break; have my parental responsibility for the day.' The law does not permit this; parental responsibility cannot be surrendered or transferred except by court order.[464] However, the law does permit a holder of parental responsibility to 'arrange for some or all of it to be met by one or more persons acting on his behalf'[465] as, for example, where a parent delegates the exercise of parental responsibility to a childminder.[466]

9.3 THE CONTENT AND SCOPE OF PARENTAL RESPONSIBILITY

There is no definitive list of the 'rights, duties, powers, responsibility and authority' which constitute parental responsibility and, unlike some jurisdictions,[467] English law has not sought to define in statute the particular legal incidents attaching to parental responsibility. These must be found therefore in the common law and in particular statutory provisions.

The precise nature and content of parental responsibilities is likely to vary according to the particular aspect of parental responsibility concerned.[468] At a general level, however, the

---

[462] *Re H (Parental Responsibility)* [1998] 1 FLR 855 at 859A *per* Butler-Sloss LJ. For specific examples of exceptions to s 2(7), see *Re G (Parental Responsibility: Education)* [1994] 2 FLR 964; *Re PC (Change of Surname)* [1997] 2 FLR 730; *Re J (Specific Issue Orders: Child's Religious Upbringing and Circumcision)* [2000] 1 FLR 571. For criticism, see J. Eekelaar, 'Do Parents have a Duty to Consult?' (1998) 114 LQR 337; J. Eekelaar, 'Rethinking Parental Responsibility' [2001] Family Law 426; and S. Maidment, 'Parental Responsibility—Is there a Duty to Consult?' [2001] Family Law 518.

[463] J. Eekelaar, 'Rethinking Parental Responsibility' [2001] Family Law 426–430.

[464] Children Act 1989, s 2(9).   [465] Ibid.

[466] The making of the arrangement does not affect any liability of the person making it which may arise from any failure to meet any part of his parental responsibility: see s 2(11).

[467] Eg in Scotland see the Children (Scotland) Act 1995, ss 1 and 2.

[468] For an attempt to provide detailed accounts of the nature and content of some major areas of parental responsibility, see R. Probert, S. Gilmore, and J. Herring (eds), *Responsible Parents and Parental Responsibility* (Oxford: Hart, 2009).

scope of parental responsibility is perhaps best understood as a sphere of liberty[469] within which those with parental responsibility are granted the primary responsibility for the child's upbringing free from outside interference.[470] Although section 3 refers to the holder having 'rights', it will rarely be the case that a parental right will be a claim-right in the sense that someone else has a correlative duty. For example, a mother might say 'I have a right to dress my child as I wish in expensive clothing', but it is clear that she does not have a right to do so in the sense that someone else has a corresponding duty to provide such clothing. She has a liberty to dress her child as she wishes, and others do not have a right to meddle in her decision. It can be seen that the word 'right' can be used rather loosely in different senses and it is important in this context to be clear about the sense in which it is used.

Talking point

Where do the bounds of that sphere of liberty lie?[471] In *Gillick v West Norfolk and Wisbech Area Health Authority and Department of Health and Social Security*[472] (hereafter *Gillick*), Lord Fraser of Tullybelton said:

> parental rights to control a child do not exist for the benefit of the parent. They exist for the benefit of the child and they are justified only in so far as they enable the parent to perform his duties towards the child, and towards other children in the family.[473]

In that important decision (which is discussed in detail in Chapter 8) the House of Lords held that a doctor could prescribe contraceptive treatment for a girl under 16 years old without her parents' knowledge and consent provided the doctor was satisfied, *inter alia*, that it was in the child's best interests to do so without parental knowledge.

Lord Fraser's dictum, taken together with the overall ruling in the case, may suggest that parental discretion must be exercised in a child's best interests. This might suggest that parental rights are characterised as entirely 'child-centred'. However, as Andrew Bainham points out, welfare is 'so inherently vague a standard of behaviour'[474] that in day-to-day dealings with children this may translate (in the words of Bernard Dickens) to 'a parental discretion to employ control over children for purposes not violating children's interests, but equally not advancing their welfare or best interests'.[475] This allows recognition of what, it is submitted, is the better view of the nature of parental rights, namely that there are some aspects of parental discretion which are parent-centred.[476] Examples

---

[469] Or Hohfeldian privileges see W. N. Hohfeld, *Fundamental Legal Conceptions As Applied in Judicial Reasoning* (New Haven, CT: Yale University Press, 1919); and see *per* Lord Oliver of Aylmerton in *Re KD (A Minor) (Access: Principles)* [1988] 2 FLR 139 at 153.

[470] *Parental* responsibility rather than *state* responsibility: see J. Eekelaar, 'Parental Responsibility: State of Nature or Nature of the State' [1991] Journal of Social Welfare and Family Law 37.

[471] See generally B. M. Dickens, 'The Modern Function and Limits of Parental Rights' (1981) 97 LQR 462, and the discussion in A. Bainham, *Children, Parents and the State* (London: Sweet & Maxwell, 1988), p 48, and generally ch 3; and S. Gilmore, 'The Limits of Parental Responsibility' in R. Probert, S. Gilmore, and J. Herring, *Responsible Parents and Parental Responsibility* (Oxford: Hart, 2009).

[472] [1986] 1 AC 112.

[473] Ibid, 170 D–E. See also *per* Lord Scarman: 'Parental rights are derived from parental duty and exist only so long as they are needed for the protection of the person and property of the child' (at 22).

[474] A. Bainham, *Children, Parents and the State* (London: Sweet & Maxwell, 1988), p 59.

[475] B. M. Dickens, 'The Modern Function and Limits of Parental Rights' (1981) 97 LQR 462 at 464, cited in A. Bainham, *Children, Parents and the State* (London: Sweet & Maxwell, 1988), p 58.

[476] See A. McCall Smith, 'Is Anything Left of Parental Rights?' in E. Sutherland and A. McCall Smith (eds), *Family Rights: Family Law and Medical Advance* (Edinburgh: Edinburgh University Press, 1990) and A. Bainham,

include a parent's choice over a child's religious upbringing (which may be protected to a greater degree than some other aspects of parental responsibility since it may be regarded as an aspect of a parent's rights to religious freedom)[477] or the choice of the child's home.[478] It may also be argued that there are parental interests which derive from the parent's investment of time and energy in parenting, that is, aspects of the parent's family life which should be respected independently.

9.3.1 Potential legal restrictions on the exercise of parental responsibility

In practice, therefore, the law permits parents discretion in matters of parental responsibility provided the discretion does not conflict with any parental legal duties, nor violate the child's interests in such a way that the law has declared unacceptable. *Legal* control of parental responsibility does not, therefore, preclude all parental harm to children. Several sources of potential legal restriction on the exercise of parental responsibility can be identified.[479] First, there are restrictions imposed by the criminal law. In particular, the extent to which a parent may use corporal punishment to discipline a child is limited by offences against the person,[480] although parents (and those acting *in loco parentis*) still have a defence of reasonable punishment to a charge of common assault.[481] Secondly, there are specific legal provisions in Parts IV and V of the Children Act 1989 which permit the state to intervene to protect and/or care for a child when the child is suffering or is at risk of suffering significant harm attributable to lack of reasonable parental care. Thirdly, it is possible for an individual to challenge aspects of the exercise of parental responsibility in private law proceedings. In deciding an issue with respect to the child's upbringing a court is required to treat the child's welfare as its paramount consideration. Thus, it is possible that an exercise of parental responsibility could be overridden by the court on that basis although a court may be reluctant to intervene on matters in respect of which there is room for reasonable disagreement.[482] A fourth potential restriction on the exercise of parental responsibility is the child's right to make his or her own decisions. The extent to which (if at all) English law recognises the child's autonomy interest as a restraint on parental responsibility is a complex issue[483] which is discussed in detail in Chapter 8. Fifthly, it is possible that parents' powers are automatically qualified by a requirement of reasonableness, in the sense that a parent must not act unreasonably. The point has been made by Andrew Bainham,[484] by reference to some decisions in which courts have made *ex post facto* adjudications that a parent exceeded his lawful authority:[485] in *R v D*[486] the House of Lords upheld a father's

---

'Is Anything Now Left of Parental Rights?' in R. Probert, S. Gilmore, and J. Herring (eds), *Responsible Parents and Parental Responsibility* (Oxford: Hart, 2009) (discussing the difference between parent-centred and child-centred parental rights—what Bainham terms the independence and priority theses).

[477] See R. Taylor, 'Parental Responsibility and Religion' in R. Probert, S. Gilmore, and J. Herring (eds), *Responsible Parents and Parental Responsibility* (Oxford: Hart, 2009).

[478] *Re E (Residence: Imposition of Conditions)* [1997] 2 FLR 638.

[479] See S. Gilmore, J. Herring, and R. Probert, 'Parental Responsibility: Law, Issues and Themes' in R. Probert, S. Gilmore, and J. Herring, *Responsible Parents and Parental Responsibility* (Oxford: Hart, 2009), esp pp 13–15.

[480] Under the Offences Against the Person Act 1861.

[481] Children and Young Persons Act 1933, s 1(7) and Children Act 2004, s 58. For a full account of the law, see S. Choudhry, 'Parental Responsibility and Corporal Punishment' in R. Probert, S. Gilmore, and J. Herring (eds), *Responsible Parents and Parental Responsibility* (Oxford: Hart, 2009), pp 165–183.

[482] See eg *Re W (Residence Order)* [1999] 1 FLR 869, CA where the issue was nudity in the home.

[483] See the discussion in S. Gilmore, 'The Limits of Parental Responsibility' in R. Probert, S. Gilmore, and J. Herring (eds), *Responsible Parents and Parental Responsibility* (Oxford: Hart, 2009).

[484] A. Bainham, *Children, Parents and the State* (London: Sweet & Maxwell, 1988), pp 54–57.

[485] Ibid, p 56.   [486] [1984] AC 778.

conviction for kidnap of his 5-year-old son) and in *R v Rahman*[487] the Court of Appeal upheld a father's conviction for false imprisonment of his teenage daughter. In the former case, the unlawfulness of the father's act turned upon a presumed lack of consent on the part of the child, which may be equated with the reasonableness of the act. In the latter, the detention was in such circumstances 'as to take it out of the realm of reasonable discipline'[488] The analysis suggests that in dealings with a child a third party may need to have regard to the reasonableness of a parent's view.[489] However, other than in cases requiring confidentiality, cases of necessity, or requiring the child's very short-term protection, a third party would be wise to be cautious in overriding the perceived unreasonable views of a parent who has parental responsibility, without seeking court approval.[490]

9.4 THE LINK WITH CHAPTERS THAT FOLLOW

We have now examined all the concepts associated with 'being a parent' in English law: parentage, parenthood, and parental responsibility. In the chapters that follow, we explore the various ways (discussed earlier) in which parental rights and responsibilities may be restricted. In Chapter 8 we explore the concept of children's rights, including the important debate concerning the scope of children's autonomy; in Chapter 9 we look at how the courts decide issues or disputes surrounding the exercise of parental responsibility in private law disputes; and in Chapter 10 we examine the role of the state in childcare and protection.

DISCUSSION QUESTIONS

1. Do children have a right to know of their biological origins? Critically assess the courts' approach to establishing legal parentage; have they gone too far too fast?

2. To what extent are (a) biological connection, (b) intention, and (c) a child's welfare important in attributing legal parenthood in English law? To what extent do you think these factors should be important? Is the law on parenthood coherent? Should it be?

3. A father who has not married his child's mother does not automatically gain parental responsibility for the child. Discuss the policy behind this position, and assess the case for reform of the law on parental responsibility for 'unmarried fathers'.

4. Assess the case law on parental responsibility orders. Should the courts adopt different principles in the case of so-called 'alternative families'?

FURTHER READING

BAINHAM, A., 'Arguments about Parentage' (2008) 67(2) Cambridge Law Journal 321

BAINHAM, A., 'What is the Point of Birth Registration?' [2008] Child and Family Law Quarterly 449

BAINHAM, A., DAY SCLATER, S., and RICHARDS, M. (eds), *What is a Parent? A Socio-Legal Analysis* (Oxford: Hart, 1999)

---

[487] (1985) 81 Cr App R 349.
[488] A. Bainham, *Children, Parents and the State* (London: Sweet & Maxwell, 1988), pp 54–57.
[489] Ibid, p 57.   [490] See *Glass v UK* (App no 61827/00) [2004] 1 FLR 1019.

CALLUS, T., 'First Designer Babies, now À La Carte Parents' [2008] Family Law 143

EEKELAAR, J., 'Rethinking Parental Responsibility' [2001] Family Law 426

FORTIN, J, 'Children's Right to Know Their Origins—Too Far, Too Fast?' [2009] Child and Family Law Quarterly 336

GILMORE, S., 'Parental Responsibility and the Unmarried Father—A New Dimension to the Debate' [2003] Child and Family Law Quarterly 21

HILL, J., 'What Does it Mean to be a "Parent"? The Claims of Biology as the Basis for Parental Rights' (1991) 66 New York University Law Review 353

HORSEY, K. and SHELDON, S., 'Still Hazy After All These Years: The Law Regulating Surrogacy' (2012) 20(1) Medical Law Review 67

JACKSON, E., 'What is a Parent?' in A. Diduck and K. O'Donovan (eds), *Feminist Perspectives on Family Law* (Abingdon: Routledge-Cavendish, 2006)

LOWE, N., 'The Meaning and Allocation of Parental Responsibility: A Common Lawyer's Perspective' (1997) 11(2) International Journal of Law, Policy and the Family 192

MCCANDLESS, J. and SHELDON, S., 'The Human Fertilisation and Embryology Act (2008) and the Tenacity of the Sexual Family Form' (2010) 72(2) Modern Law Review 175

PROBERT, R., 'Families, Assisted Reproduction and the Law' [2004] Child and Family Law Quarterly 273

PROBERT, R., GILMORE, S., and HERRING, J. (eds), *Responsible Parents and Parental Responsibility* (Oxford: Hart, 2009)

SHELDON, S., 'From "Absent Objects of Blame" to "Fathers Who Want to Take Responsibility": Reforming Birth Registration Law' (2009) 31(4) Journal of Social Welfare and Family Law 373

SMITH, L., 'Is Three a Crowd? Lesbian Mothers' Perspectives on Parental Status in Law' [2006] Child and Family Law Quarterly 231

SMITH, L., 'Clashing Symbols? Reconciling Support for Fathers and Fatherless Families After the Human Fertilisation and Embryology Act 2008' [2010] Child and Family Law Quarterly 46

8

CHILDREN'S RIGHTS

INTRODUCTION

This chapter introduces some theoretical discussions concerning children's rights and examines some 'core' legal provisions and case law in which the issue of the legal protection of children's interests has been explored. Much of the chapter explores what is perhaps the most challenging question raised by children's rights in practice: the extent to which the law allows, and should allow, children to make their own decisions. Indeed, this chapter follows on directly from the last on parental responsibility because such rights are potentially one constraint on the exercise of parental responsibility.

1 FUNDAMENTAL DEBATES SURROUNDING CHILDREN'S RIGHTS[1]

Any discussion of children's rights is immediately complicated by the fact that each of the words in the phrase 'children's rights' raises debate.

1.1 CONCEPTIONS OF A RIGHT: WILL THEORY V INTEREST THEORY

The first difficulty is that theorists do not agree on the concept of a right.[2] There are two main theories of rights. The Interest Theory holds that rights derive from persons' interests. On this view, a person will have a right simply if that person's interest is sufficient

---

[1] The following are good starting points into the literature: J. Fortin, *Children's Rights and the Developing Law*, 3rd edn (Cambridge: Cambridge University Press, 2009); D. Archard, *Children Rights and Childhood* (London: Routledge, 2004) and the works cited in his bibliographical essay at pp 231–242; M. D. A. Freeman, *The Moral Status of Children: Essays on the Rights of the Child* (The Hague: Martinus Nijhoff, 1997); P. Alston, S. Parker, and J. Seymour (eds), *Children, Rights and the Law* (Oxford: Clarendon Press, 1992); M. D. A. Freeman, *The Rights and the Wrongs of Children* (London: Frances Pinter, 1983); B. Franklin (ed), *The New Handbook of Children's Rights Comparative Policy and Practice* (London: Routledge, 2002); P. Alderson, *Young Children's Rights*, 2nd edn (London: Jessica Kingsley, 2008). For a detailed practitioner work, see A MacDonald, *The Rights of the Child Law and Practice* (Bristol: Family Law, 2011).

[2] See eg, J. Waldron (ed), *Theories of Rights* (Oxford: Oxford University Press, 1984); M. H. Kramer, N.E. Simmonds, and H. Steiner, *A Debate Over Rights: Philosophical Enquiries* (Oxford: Oxford University Press, 1998).

ground for holding another to be subject to a duty. By contrast, the Will Theory holds that one can only talk meaningfully about a person having a right if the person can waive, or exercise, enforcement of the right. In other words, while the Interest Theory protects a person's interests independently of his or her choices, the Will Theory draws a necessary connection between the idea of a person having a right and the exercise of the person's will with respect to the right. Of course, babies and very young children will not have the necessary knowledge or understanding to exercise their will in this way, so the will theory conceptually denies some children the very possibility of having rights. This point was made by the late Professor Neil MacCormick, who used the case of children's rights to test the appropriateness of general theories of rights.[3] MacCormick argued that the will theory should be rejected as a general theory because of its inability to accommodate fully the case of children's rights. In the case of children at least, the interest theory is more apposite. As Michael Freeman has put it: 'Children have interests to protect before they develop wills to assert, and others can complain on behalf of younger children when those interests are trampled on.'[4]

1.2 SHOULD CHILDREN HAVE RIGHTS?

If it is accepted that children are capable of possessing rights, a further question arises as to whether children should be accorded (legal) rights. Several philosophical justifications for children's rights have been put forward. Michael Freeman has sought out a moral justification for children's rights based on the notion of autonomy. He argues that rights protect the integrity of a person in leading his or her life, based on a belief in equality and respect for autonomy. For Freeman, to 'believe in autonomy is to believe that anyone's autonomy is as morally significant as anyone else's'.[5] We should therefore respect a child's autonomy, treating the child as a person and as a right-holder[6] (although Freeman also acknowledges that children's autonomy must be seen in the context of their sometimes lesser abilities/capacities). By contrast, Katherine Federle is concerned that the justification for children's rights should not be tied to children's capacities or incapacities.[7] She argues that while the interest theory 'does not automatically exclude children from the class of rights-holders, it does define children's interests in terms of their incapacities'[8] and there is a tendency to empower adults to intervene in children's lives rather than empowering children.[9] The kinds of rights that Federle envisions are thus not premised upon capacity but upon power or more precisely, powerlessness. In other words, rights exist to remedy powerlessness and should flow downhill to the least powerful. Paternalistic justifications thus become unacceptable.

---

[3] N. MacCormick, 'Children's Rights: A Test Case for Theories of Rights' in N. MacCormick, *Legal Right and Social Democracy* (Oxford: Clarendon Press, 1982). For analysis and criticism of the will theory, see also J. G. Dwyer, 'The Conceptual Possibility of Children Having Rights', appendix in *The Relationship Rights of Children* (Cambridge: Cambridge University Press, 2006).

[4] M. D. A. Freeman, 'Taking Children's Rights More Seriously' in P. Alston, S. Parker, and J. Seymour (eds), *Children, Rights and the Law* (Oxford: Clarendon Press, 1992), 52, at 58.

[5] Freeman, ibid, p 64.   [6] Ibid, p 65.

[7] K. H. Federle, 'On the Road to Reconceiving Rights for Children: A Post-Feminist Analysis of the Capacity Principle' (1993) De Paul Law Review 983; K. H. Federle, 'Rights Flow Downhill' (1994) 2 International Journal of Children's Rights 343; K. H. Federle, 'Looking Ahead: An Empowerment Perspective on the Rights of Children' (1995) 68(4) Temple Law Review 1585. Federle's treatment of power may require further refinement: see H. Lim and J. Roche, 'Feminism and Children's Rights' in J. Bridgeman and D. Monk (eds), *Feminist Perspectives on Child Law* (London: Cavendish, 2000), pp 238–241.

[8] K. H. Federle, 'Rights Flow Downhill' (1994) 2 International Journal of Children's Rights 343 at 354.

[9] Ibid, 365.

Another argument in favour of rights has been advanced by Martha Minow, who highlights the ability which rights may have to forge connection with others, by providing a procedural basis for communication.[10] The importance of rights in this sense may have particular resonance for children, providing them with an appropriate status for communication with adults.

By contrast, some argue that rights are not the most appropriate basis for regulating close personal relationships. As David Archard explains, there is a standpoint in this context 'that rights talk is morally impoverished and neglects an alternative ethical view of the world, in which the affectionate, caring interdependence which ideally characterises the parent–child relationship assumes an exemplary significance'.[11] Similarly, Onora O'Neill has argued[12] that if we care about children's lives we may have good reasons to focus on adults' obligations to children rather than appealing to children's fundamental rights.[13] O'Neill's preference for a focus on obligations is founded on her observation that there are some obligations, such as being kind and helping to develop others' capacities, which are imperfect obligations because the precise obligations and to whom they are owed are not specified. Consequently, such obligations have no allocated right-holders and therefore no counterpart set of rights. The analysis provides useful insights: that a shift to the idiom of rights risks excluding and neglecting some things that may matter to children[14] because such things drop out of the picture if, approaching from a right's perspective, no right-holder can be identified; and that 'rights-based approaches are incomplete in that they tell us nothing about what should be done when nobody has a right to its being done'.[15] Supporting her argument, O'Neill contends that children are unlike other oppressed groups claiming rights. Children are 'more fundamentally but less permanently powerless; their main remedy is to grow up'.[16]

Against these views, however, Michael Freeman has argued that criticism of rights as impoverished idealises adult–child relations and presents a myth of childhood as a golden age,[17] yet the realities of many children's lives are different. A child who is being abused within a family may well see greater value in having a 'public' right to claim protection. Freeman also doubts that children's dependency is quite as different from other oppressed groups as O'Neill suggests, in that childhood can be artificially prolonged and is determined by those in authority.[18] This brings us neatly to another difficulty encountered in the phrase 'children's rights', namely the meaning of 'child' and of 'childhood'.

1.3 CHILDREN AND CHILDHOODS

Who is to be regarded as a child, and consequently the boundary between childhood and adulthood, is socially constructed by the laws of a particular society.[19]

---

[10] M. Minow, 'Interpreting Rights: An Essay for Robert Cover' (1987) Yale Law Journal 1860.

[11] D. Archard, *Children Rights and Childhood* (London: Routledge, 2004), p 112, and for criticism of the point, see pp 118–123.

[12] O. O'Neill, 'Children's Rights and Children's Lives' (1988) 98 Ethics 445–463, also published in P. Alston, S. Parker, and J. Seymour (eds), *Children, Rights and the Law* (Oxford: Clarendon Press, 1992).

[13] Alston et al, ibid, p 39.   [14] Ibid, pp 35–36.   [15] Ibid, p 39.

[16] Ibid. For criticism of O'Neill's arguments, see eg T. D. Campbell, 'The Rights of the Minor: As Person, As Child, As Juvenile, As Future Adult' in Alston et al, ibid, pp 12–16; M. D. A. Freeman, 'Taking Children's Rights More Seriously' in Alston et al, ibid, pp 56–61.   [17] Freeman, ibid, pp 55–56.

[18] Ibid, p 56.   [19] See in England and Wales, Family Law Reform Act 1969, s 1.

1.3.1 Debating the adult/child boundary

The fact that childhood and adulthood are socially constructed raises profound questions as to whether such a distinction can be justified and, if so, as to the setting and 'policing' of the boundary. The boundary was challenged by child liberationist ideology in the 1960s and 1970s which, placing great emphasis on individual autonomy, proposed an extension of adult's rights to children (such as the right to live independently, the right to drive, to take drugs, and to have sex).[20] Although politically naïve, child liberationist ideology was important in highlighting the issue of children's rights.[21] More moderate versions of this perspective might now argue that children should not be discriminated against simply on the basis of their age.

An argument for having a boundary between adulthood and childhood derives from the fact that in the early stages of a person's life paternalism is essential for survival. If we accept this fundamental need, then removal of the adult/child distinction would be purchased at the, arguably unacceptable, price of opening the door generally to paternalism beyond childhood.[22] It might also be objected that the setting of any boundary is arbitrary but that objection, if pursued to its logical limit, is capable of supporting the conclusion that either everyone or no one stands in need of paternalistic protection.[23]

1.3.2 Policing the adult/child boundary

If we accept that a boundary is necessary and inevitably arbitrary, how is the boundary to be decided and policed? There will be some adults with lesser abilities than children and some children with greater abilities than some adults. But societies are also concerned with efficiency and may need to take account of factors such as administrative convenience. Choosing a particular age as the starting point for adulthood (or for deciding whether a child is prima facie competent to do certain things, such as drive a car or have sexual intercourse) is more convenient than having to assess in each individual case whether a person is so competent. The drawing of such lines, however, can render some results which, at first blush, may seem surprising. A striking example is provided by Jonathan Herring, who observes that a child aged 16 may lawfully have sexual intercourse with his or her MP, but cannot vote for him or her.[24] However, those two activities are clearly different (unless you have attended some rather unusual polling stations!). It is as well also to recall that the setting of any boundary is not simply a matter of empirical finding, but also of judgement. If children were enfranchised, arguably our view of the vote would change rather our view of children.[25] Furthermore, once set, the boundary introduces a quantitative distinction between adults and children, which

---

[20] Eg R. Farson, *Birthrights* (London: Collier Macmillan, 1974) and J. Holt, *Escape from Childhood* (Harmondsworth: Penguin, 1975). For a cross-section of the diverse origins of this ideology, see P. Adams et al, *Children's Rights* (London: Longman, 1972) and for an overview, see D. Archard, *Children Rights and Childhood* (London: Routledge, 2004), ch 5 and L. Fox Harding, *Perspectives in Child Care Policy* (London, Longman, 1997) ch 5.

[21] M. D. A. Freeman, *The Rights and Wrongs of Children* (London: Frances Pinter, 1983).

[22] F. Schrag, 'The Child in the Moral Order' (1977) 52 Philosophy 167 at 176.

[23] R. Lindley, 'Teenagers and Other Children' in G. Scarre (ed), *Children, Parents and Politics* (New York: Cambridge University Press, 1989), p 78.

[24] J. Herring, *Family Law*, 5th edn (London: Longman, 2011), p 435.

[25] J. Hughes, 'Thinking about Children' in G. Scarre (ed), *Children, Parents and Politics* (New York: Cambridge University Press, 1989), p 48.

treats (or has treated) everyone equally, namely the amount of time allocated to acquire experience before adulthood.[26]

1.4 DIFFERENT CHILDHOODS

Talking point

It is not just the law that socially constructs, nor only the boundaries of childhood that are socially constructed. The nature of childhood is contingent on matters such as the particular time, society, and culture in which the child lives.[27] Children may experience very different childhoods at different times[28] in different parts of the world.

For example, child labour has a very different meaning for a child in England (perhaps doing a paper round for pocket money) compared with a child living in a country where daily child labour is required for family survival. For the drafters of international conventions seeking to set out children's rights, there are evident tensions between striving for universal rights and recognising cultural pluralism.[29] We may need to exercise caution when talking in general terms about 'children's rights'.

1.4.1 Society's perceptions of children

The social construction of childhood has clear implications for how children are perceived within society. Given its juxtaposition with adulthood it would not be surprising that perhaps the dominant vision of childhood is as a vulnerable and dependent period, children as beings who need to be nurtured into adulthood. This dominant perception may render less visible children's potential to exercise autonomy,[30] or indeed the role of children as actors in society (eg as carers[31]).

A further, interesting, point made by Carole Smith[32] is that the childhood/adulthood distinction may offer some explanation for resistance to granting children the right to make their own decisions, particularly where those decisions might lead to irreparable harm or death. As Smith observes:

> we are not prepared to withdraw our protection or to abandon the legal distinction between children and adults. To do so would strike at the very heart of the adult-child

---

[26] G. Scarre, 'Children and Paternalism' (1980) 55 Philosophy 117.

[27] See A. James, C. Jenks, and A. Prout, *Theorizing Childhood* (Cambridge: Polity Press, 1998); C. Jenks, *Childhood* (London: Routledge, 1996); A. James and A. Prout (eds), *Constructing* and *Reconstructing Childhood* (London: Falmer Press, 1997); P Ariès, *Centuries of Childhood: A Social History of Family Life* (London: Jonathan Cape, 1962).

[28] See eg A. Wade, 'Being Responsible: "Good" Parents and Children's Autonomy' in J. Bridgeman, H. Keating, and C. Lind (eds), *Responsibility, Law and the Family* (Aldershot: Ashgate, 2008), p 211, comparing across generations parents' attitudes to children's freedom.

[29] On which, see M. D. A. Freeman, 'Children's Rights and Cultural Pluralism' in *The Moral Status of Children* (The Hague: Martinus Nijhoff, 1997).

[30] See the discussion in C. Smith, 'Children's Rights: Judicial Ambivalence and Social Resistance' (1997) 11 International Journal of Law, Policy and the Family 103, esp at 106–110.

[31] See eg V. Morrow, 'Responsible Children and Children's Responsibilities? Sibling Caretaking and Babysitting by School-age Children' in J. Bridgeman, H. Keating, and C. Lind (eds), *Responsibility, Law and the Family* (Aldershot: Ashgate, 2008), p 105, and generally Part 2 of this book.

[32] C. Smith, 'Children's Rights: Judicial Ambivalence and Social Resistance' (1997) 11 International Journal of Law, Policy and the Family 103.

relationship which enables adults to locate themselves emotionally, as being affectionate, caring, protective, and socially, as being responsible for moulding the next generation of citizens.[33]

2 CATEGORISING CHILDREN'S RIGHTS: THE INTERESTS CHILDREN MIGHT PLAUSIBLY CLAIM

If the category of 'child' and the possibility of children being right-holders are accepted, it remains to consider the various interests that children might plausibly claim. The word 'plausibly' here is carefully chosen. As John Eekelaar has pointed out, there is a difference between 'welfarism' (ie, actions motivated solely by the purpose of promoting another's welfare) and the idea of a person having a right, which is related to the perception that people make claims.[34] Eekelaar's purpose in making this point is not to suggest that very young (incompetent) children should be denied rights, but to emphasise that even in such cases it 'could never be enough to assert simply that an action will be in the child's welfare'. He argues that if we are to talk of a child's right in the context of such actions, we 'need to think how the action could be one which the child might plausibly want'.[35] In a seminal article on children's rights,[36] Eekelaar identified three general categories of interests that children might plausibly claim: basic, developmental, and autonomy interests. By these, he means the following:

- **Basic interest**

Children's general physical, emotional, and intellectual care within the social of immediate caregivers (as a minimal expectation).[37]

- **Developmental interest**

Children's 'equal opportunity to maximise the resources available to them during their childhood (including their own inherent abilities) so as to minimize the degree to which they enter adult life affected by avoidable prejudices incurred during childhood. In short their capacities are to be developed to their best advantage.'[38]

- **Autonomy interest**

Children's freedom to choose their own lifestyle and to enter social relations according to their own inclinations uncontrolled by the authority of the adult world, whether parents or institutions.[39]

The value of such categorisation is that it draws attention to the potential interaction of the various interests. The child's developmental interest is likely to be promoted by

---

[33] Ibid, 135.

[34] J. Eekelaar, 'The Importance of Thinking That Children Have Rights' in P. Alston, S. Parker, and J. Seymour (eds), *Children, Rights and the Law* (Oxford: Clarendon Press, 1992), p 221. Eekelaar adds that 'a claim simply that people should act to further my welfare as they define it is in reality to make no claim at all'. See also his discussion of isolating interests pertaining to the child, in 'The Emergence of Children's Rights' (1986) 6 Oxford Journal of Legal Studies 161 at 169.

[35] J. Eekelaar, 'The Importance of Thinking That Children Have Rights' in P. Alston et al, ibid, p 230 (ie, via an hypothetical *process*). See also J. Eekelaar, 'The Interests of the Child and the Child's Wishes: The Role of Dynamic Self-Determinism' (1994) 8 International Journal of Law and the Family 42.

[36] J. Eekelaar 'The Emergence of Children's Rights' (1986) 6 Oxford Journal of Legal Studies 161.

[37] Ibid, 170.   [38] Ibid, 170.   [39] Ibid, 171.

exercises of autonomy, perhaps especially if those exercises of autonomy are accompanied by mistakes from which a child learns. There is also, as Freeman points out, a false dichotomy between protecting children and protecting their other interests. As he explains, '[c]hildren who are not protected, whose welfare is not advanced, will not be able to exercise self-determination: on the other hand, a failure to recognise the personality of children is likely to result in an undermining of their protection with children reduced to objects of intervention'.[40] However, there are also occasions when the various interests can conflict.[41] An example, which will be picked up in discussion of case law later in this chapter, is the competent adolescent who wishes to refuse medical treatment where the refusal will lead to irreparable harm or death. The autonomy and basic interests are in stark conflict in such cases. Theorists have reflected on ways of addressing these types of conflict.

2.1 EEKELAAR'S FUTURE-ORIENTED CONSENT AND FREEMAN'S LIBERAL PATERNALISM

Eekelaar suggested that in seeking to reconcile a conflict between children's basic interests and their decisions, 'some kind of imaginative leap may be required' to 'guess what a child might retrospectively have wanted once it reaches a position of maturity'.[42] Eekelaar acknowledges that the values of the adult world may intrude but that is to be openly accepted, encouraging debate about them.[43] Eekelaar suggests that while some adults might not approve of the fact that their autonomy was thwarted in childhood so as not to leave them at a disadvantage as against other children in realising their life-chances in adulthood, it seems improbable that this would be a common view. Hence, he concludes that the autonomy interests may be ranked 'subordinate to the basic and developmental interests' but that 'where they may be exercised without threatening these two interests, the claim for their satisfaction must be high'.[44]

Michael Freeman, drawing on John Rawls's theory of justice,[45] reaches a similar view, his version of 'liberal paternalism'.[46] Put simply, Rawls posited general principles of justice, using as a starting point the idea that people would be ignorant of their own position within a society. Freeman observes that if the persons participating in this hypothetical social contract did not know whether or not they were children, it is probable that most would wish to mature to an independent adulthood. The participants would know of children's limited capacities and how the actions of those with limited capacities could limit the exercise of autonomy in the future as an adult. Thus, there would be acceptance of interventions which would preclude action or conduct which would frustrate the achievement of the goal of reaching an autonomous adulthood. Freeman would thus defend a version of paternalism to avoid such irrationality.

---

[40] M. D. A. Freeman, 'Laws Conventions and Rights' (1993) 7(1) Children and Society 37 at 42.

[41] Eg, if we allow a young child to exercise his or her autonomy interest by walking in the middle of a motorway, the child's basic interest is likely soon to be compromised.

[42] J. Eekelaar 'The Emergence of Children's Rights' (1986) 6 Oxford Journal of Legal Studies 161 at 170.

[43] Ibid.

[44] Ibid. See also J. Eekelaar, 'The Importance of Thinking That Children Have Rights' in P. Alston, S. Parker, and J. Seymour (eds), Children, Rights and the Law (Oxford: Clarendon Press, 1992), pp 230–231.

[45] J. Rawls, A Theory of Justice (Oxford: Oxford University Press, 1973).

[46] See M. D. A. Freeman, The Rights and Wrongs of Children (London: Frances Pinter, 1983) and M. D. A. Freeman, 'Taking Children's Rights More Seriously' in P. Alston, S. Parker, and J. Seymour (eds), Children, Rights and the Law (Oxford: Clarendon Press, 1992), pp 66–69.

While these are useful methods of seeking to reconcile some of children's conflicting interests, one must perhaps be careful not to see children merely in terms of future adults. The point has been made by Tom Campbell, who classifies minors' interests in such a way as to highlight some interests which are distinctively children's. Campbell suggests thinking about the rights of the minor as person, as child, as juvenile, and as future adult. This recognises the interests that children may have in the here and now at different stages of their development, such as the right to play as a child for its own sake.[47]

3 LEGAL PROTECTION OF CHILDREN'S INTERESTS

To what extent, if at all, are the various categories of interests identified by Eekelaar protected by English law? Children's basic interests in survival and avoidance of harm are protected by various child protection measures in Parts IV and V of the Children Act 1989, which are explored in detail in Chapter 10. Indirectly, children are also protected by the criminal law, both general offences and specific offences against children, such as sexual offences or child neglect. There is also a raft of legal provisions which seek to secure children's developmental interests through their education.[48] The extent to which the law recognises a child's autonomy interest is a matter of considerable debate, however, and will now be explored in some detail. In English law the issue of children's autonomy has been explored principally in the context of children's medical treatment.

3.1 RECOGNITION OF CHILDREN'S AUTONOMY INTEREST?

3.1.1 *Gillick v West Norfolk and Wisbech Area Health Authority*

Key case

The leading case is the House of Lords' decision in *Gillick v West Norfolk and Wisbech Area Health Authority and Department of Health and Social Security*.[49] The case arose out

---

[47] See T. D. Campbell, 'The Rights of the Minor: As Person, As Child, As Juvenile, As Future Adult' in P. Alston et al, ibid, pp 21–22.

[48] Discussion of education law is beyond the scope of this book, but see A. Bainham, *Children The Modern Law*, 3rd edn (Bristol: Family Law, 2005), ch 16.

[49] [1986] 1 AC 112. For an assessment of the case's impact on children's rights, see J. Fortin, 'The *Gillick* Decision—Not Just A High-Water Mark' in S. Gilmore, J. Herring, and R. Probert, *Landmark Cases in Family Law* (Oxford: Hart, 2011). The case has attracted a lot of commentary: see G. Austin, 'Righting a Child's Right to Refuse Medical Treatment, Section 11 of the New Zealand Bill of Rights Act and the *Gillick* Competent Child' (1992) 7(4) Otago Law Review 578; A. Bainham, 'The Balance of Power in Family Decisions' (1986) 45(2) Cambridge Law Journal 262; A. Bainham, *Children, Parents and the State* (London: Sweet & Maxwell, 1988), ch 3; S. de Cruz, 'Parents, Doctors and Children: The *Gillick* Case and Beyond' [1987] Journal of Social Welfare and Family Law 93; J. Devereux, 'The Capacity of a Child in Australia to Consent to Medical Treatment—*Gillick* Revisited?' (1991) 11(2) Oxford Journal of Legal Studies 283 at 289–294; J. Eekelaar, 'The Eclipse of Parental Rights' (1986) 102 LQR 4 and 'The Emergence of Children's Rights' (1986) 6 Oxford Journal of Legal Studies 161; M. Jones, 'Consent to Medical Treatment by Minors after *Gillick*' (1986) 2 Professional Negligence 41; I. Kennedy, 'The Doctor, the Pill and the 15-Year-Old Girl' in I. Kennedy, *Treat Me Right: Essays in Medical Law and Ethics* (Oxford: Oxford University Press, 1988) ch 5; S. Lee, 'Towards a Jurisprudence of Consent' in J. Eekelaar and S. Ball (eds), *Oxford Essays in Jurisprudence* (Oxford: Oxford University Press, 1987), ch 9; J. Montgomery, 'Children as Property?' (1988) 51 Modern Law Review 323; P. Parkinson, 'The *Gillick* Case—Just What has it Decided?' [1986] Family Law 11; G. L. Peiris, 'The *Gillick* Case: Parental Authority, Teenage Independence and Public Policy'

of Mrs Victoria Gillick's objection to a DHSS Memorandum of Guidance[50] which advised that in exceptional circumstances a doctor could prescribe contraception to a girl under 16 without her parents' knowledge or consent. Having failed to receive an assurance from the West Norfolk and Wisbech Area Health Authority that her own children would not be so treated without her knowledge, Mrs Gillick sought a declaration in the High Court that the Memorandum gave advice which was unlawful. She was unsuccessful before Woolf J at first instance,[51] won a unanimous victory in the Court of Appeal,[52] but was ultimately defeated in the House of Lords by a majority of 3 to 2.[53]

Mrs Gillick's 'crusade',[54] which provoked considerable public debate,[55] was translated into three strands of legal argument. It was contended that a doctor could not lawfully prescribe contraceptives to a girl under 16 without parental consent because: (i) the girl could not consent to medical treatment;[56] (ii) to do so would infringe parental rights; and (iii) it would constitute the criminal offence of aiding unlawful sexual intercourse.[57] The narrow criminal law point found favour only in Lord Brandon's dissent and will not be examined further. The other two arguments have an important bearing on the legal relationship between parents and children and were considered in detail by the majority. Lord Fraser and Lord Scarman each delivered opinions on the substantive issues. Lord Scarman agreed with Lord Fraser, and Lord Bridge agreed with both opinions. It is proposed to examine the opinions in turn since, as we shall see, identifying what the case represents as a precedent is a complex issue.

3.1.2 Lord Fraser

Lord Fraser began his opinion by examining Mrs Gillick's contention that a child under 16 could not consent to medical treatment. Mrs Gillick had relied on several statutory provisions, in particular section 8 of the Family Law Reform Act 1969, which gave children who had attained the age of 16 years a statutory right to consent to medical treatment. Lord Fraser concluded that no statutory provision cited by counsel compelled that conclusion, and that section 8 of the 1969 Act had been enacted merely for the avoidance of doubt. In Lord Fraser's opinion, a girl under 16 could lawfully consent to contraceptive advice, examination, and treatment, provided 'she has sufficient understanding and intelligence to know what they involve'.[58]

[1987] Current Legal Problems 93; G. Williams, 'The *Gillick* Saga' [1985] New Law Journal 1156–1158 and 1179–1182.

[50] HN(80)46, Section G (as revised). See [1986] 1 AC 112 at 179–180.   [51] [1984] QB 581.

[52] [1986] 1 AC 112, CA (Eveleigh, Fox, and Parker LJJ).

[53] Lord Fraser of Tullybelton, Lord Scarman, and Lord Bridge of Harwich; Lord Brandon of Oakbrook and Lord Templeman dissenting. It has been observed that their Lordships' disagreement was 'largely, perhaps entirely, brought about by divergent views on policy': G. Williams, 'The *Gillick* Saga' [1985] New Law Journal 1156 at 1157 (eg Lord Brandon viewed the lawfulness of the activities countenanced by the Memorandum of Guidance as itself a matter of public policy, [1986] 1 AC 112 at 195 F–G).

[54] As Lord Templeman referred to it: see [1986] 1 AC 112 at 206 G–H.

[55] For an analysis of the public portrayal of the debate, drawing on newspaper coverage at the time, see S. Gilmore, 'The Limits of Parental Responsibility' in R. Probert, S. Gilmore, and J. Herring, *Responsible Parents and Parental Responsibility* (Oxford: Hart, 2009).

[56] The position prior to *Gillick* was obscure. See P. D. G. Skegg, 'Consent to Medical Procedures on Minors' (1973) 36 Modern Law Review 370 and A. Samuels, 'Can a Minor (Under 16) Consent to a Medical Operation?' [1984] Family Law 30.   [57] Contrary to the Sexual Offences Act 1956, ss 5, 6, and 28(1).

[58] [1986] 1 AC 112 at 170A.

Lord Fraser then examined Mrs Gillick's argument, supported by nineteenth-century authorities such as *In Re Agar-Ellis*,[59] that she had in law complete authority over her children and thus control over their medical treatment. Lord Fraser declared that the nineteenth-century authorities were an historical curiosity and no longer authoritative, and held as a matter of general principle that:

> parental rights to control a child do not exist for the benefit of the parent. They exist for the benefit of the child and they are justified only in so far as they enable the parent to perform his duties towards the child, and towards other children in the family.[60]

Rejecting also the view that the child's intellectual ability was irrelevant, he approved Lord Denning's opinion in *Hewer v Bryant*[61] that:

> the legal right of a parent to the custody of a child ends at the 18th birthday: and even up till then, it is a dwindling right which the courts will hesitate to enforce against the wishes of the child, and the more so the older he is. It starts with a right of control and ends with little more than advice.[62]

Lord Fraser explained that '[s]ocial customs change, and the law ought to, and does in fact, have regard to such changes when they are of major importance'.[63] Explaining perceptions of the parent/child relationship in the late twentieth century, he said:

> It is, in my view, contrary to the ordinary experience of mankind, at least in Western Europe...to say that a child or a young person remains in fact under the complete control of his parents until he attains the definite age of majority, now 18 in the United Kingdom, and that on attaining that age he suddenly acquires independence. In practice most wise parents relax their control gradually as the child develops and encourage him or her to become increasingly independent. Moreover the degree of parental control actually exercised over a particular child does in practice vary considerably according to his understanding and intelligence and it would, in my opinion, be unrealistic for the courts not to recognise these facts.[64]

It is less clear, however, whether Lord Fraser translated this description of good practice in relation to children's evolving independence into legal principle. In Lord Fraser's opinion, once absolute parental rights were abandoned the solution in the appeal had to be found in the idea of the child's best interests. For Lord Fraser the 'only practicable course [was] to entrust the doctor with a discretion to act in accordance with his view of what is best in the interests of the girl who is his patient.'[65] He identified five conditions of which the doctor would need to be satisfied if he were to be justified in proceeding without a parent's consent or knowledge:

> (1) that the girl (although under 16 years of age) will understand his advice; (2) that he cannot persuade her to inform her parents or to allow him to inform the parents that she is seeking contraceptive advice; (3) that she is very likely to begin or to continue having sexual intercourse with or without contraceptive treatment; (4) that unless she receives contraceptive advice or treatment her physical or mental health or both are likely to suffer; (5) that her best interests require him to give her contraceptive advice, treatment or both without the parental consent.[66]

---

[59] (1883) 24 ChD 317.

[60] [1986] 1 AC 112 at 170D–E, supporting this view, if necessary, by reference to *Blackstone's Commentaries*, 17th edn (1830), vol 1, p 452.

[61] [1970] 1 QB 357.   [62] Ibid, 369.   [63] [1986] 1 AC 112 at 171F.   [64] Ibid, 171D–F.

[65] Ibid, 174B–C.   [66] Ibid, 174D–E.

It should be noted that the condition in (5) is not simply that treatment be in the child's best interests, but that it be in the child's interests to have such treatment *without parental consent*.[67] Arguably, the guidelines show, in the context of medical practice with its special feature of patient confidentiality, how the doctor must negotiate parents' interests with children's interests in decision making: the doctor must ensure, in what is an extension[68] of his clinical judgement, that the parents' duty of protection can be safely abandoned.[69]

3.1.3 Lord Scarman

Lord Scarman agreed with Lord Fraser's opinion but felt that the importance of the case also necessitated his expressing his views in his own words. Drawing on similar authorities, he concluded that the underlying principle of the law, as exposed by Blackstone and acknowledged in the case law, is that 'parental right yields to the child's right to make his own decisions when he reaches a sufficient understanding and intelligence to be capable of making up his own mind on the matter requiring decision'.[70] Lord Scarman suggested that earlier 'age of discretion' cases, and specifically *R v Howes*,[71] may afford 'a clue to the true principle of the law'.[72] These cases were ones in which a father issued a writ of habeas corpus to secure the return of his child who had left home without consent. The courts would refuse an order if the child had attained an age of discretion. By analogy with the Abduction Acts, the first of which appeared in the sixteenth century, the age of discretion was set at 14 for boys and 16 for girls. In *R v Howes* Cockburn CJ rejected the argument that a girl could be emancipated from her father before the age of 16, pointing out that legal recognition of her precocity might risk her harm. Drawing on *R v Howes*, Lord Scarman explained that the principle underlying the habeas corpus cases was that 'an order would be refused if the child had *sufficient intelligence and understanding to make up his own mind*'.[73] and continued:

> While it is unrealistic to treat a 16th century Act as a safe guide in the matter of a girl's discretion,...we can agree with Cockburn CJ as to the principle of the law—the attainment by a child of an age of sufficient discretion to exercise a *wise choice in his or her interests*.[74]

Applying these principles to the medical context of the case, Lord Scarman explained that:

> as a matter of law the parental right to determine whether or not their minor child below the age of 16 will have medical treatment terminates if and when the child achieves a sufficient understanding and intelligence to enable him or her to understand fully what

---

[67] Cf G. Williams, 'The *Gillick* Saga' [1985] New Law Journal 1179–1182 at 1179, who in setting out what he terms Lord Fraser's five ethical precepts leaves out the words which refer to parental consent in ethical precept number five. Williams's omission is hardly surprising, however, since he views the parental rights issue in *Gillick* as a misdirection of judicial effort (at 1182).

[68] For detailed arguments supporting the view that Lord Fraser extends the doctor's role see I. Kennedy, 'The Doctor, the Pill and the 15-Year-Old Girl' in I. Kennedy, *Treat me Right: Essays in Medical Law and Ethics* (Oxford: Oxford University Press, 1988), pp 94–95.

[69] Cf Kennedy, ibid, p 94, who suggests that Lord Fraser takes this view as a matter of public policy.

[70] [1986] 1 AC 112 at 186D.   [71] (1860) 3 E & E 332.   [72] [1986] 1 AC 112 at 183F.

[73] Ibid, 187D.

[74] Ibid, 187H–188A (emphasis added). Fortin argues that Lord Scarman's statement that the age of discretion was the attainment of 'sufficient discretion to enable him or her to exercise a *wise* choice' was merely a factual description of how the ages of discretion were chosen and did not suggest that he himself confined the notion of *Gillick* competence to those with a capacity for wisdom: see J. Fortin, 'The *Gillick* Decision— Not Just a High-Water Mark' in S. Gilmore, J. Herring, and R. Probert (eds), *Landmark Cases in Family Law* (Oxford: Hart, 2011), pp 206–207.

is proposed. It will be a question of fact whether a child seeking advice has sufficient understanding of what is involved to give a consent valid in law.[75]

He went on to impose a stringent test for the child's capacity, going beyond mere understanding of the nature of the advice given. Lord Scarman explained that in the context of providing a girl with contraceptive advice and treatment:

> There are moral and family questions, especially her relationship with her parents; long-term problems associated with the emotional impact of pregnancy and its termination; and there are the risks to health of sexual intercourse at her age, risks which contraception may diminish but cannot eliminate. It follows that a doctor will have to satisfy himself that she is able to appraise these factors before he can safely proceed upon the basis that she has at law capacity to consent to contraceptive treatment.[76]

3.1.4 Lord Bridge of Harwich

Lord Bridge addressed a procedural point raised by the case, but otherwise simply agreed with both Lord Fraser and Lord Scarman on the substantive issue. Lord Bridge's failure to expand might be seen as rather unhelpful given the different emphases in the other two majority judgments. As we have seen, Lord Fraser took a welfare approach, whereas in Lord Scarman's opinion there is a much stronger focus on the child's capacities. These different approaches have led to the suggestion that the case may have no clear *ratio decidendi*.[77] The fact that Lord Bridge felt able to agree with both opinions, however, may suggest that he did not see the two other majority opinions as representing wholly inconsistent positions.[78]

3.2 INTERPRETING *GILLICK*

Given the differences in the majority opinions, it is perhaps not surprising that academics have been divided in their assessment of the decision.[79] Undoubtedly *Gillick* is a 'landmark decision for children's rights'[80] emancipating children from nineteenth-century views of absolute parental authority, but whether it is a case about children's autonomy rights which accorded to children general rights to make their own decisions, as some have claimed,[81] is debatable. Within academic work, perhaps the most prominent and

---

[75] [1986] 1 AC 112 at 188–189.   [76] Ibid, 189D.

[77] P. Parkinson, 'The *Gillick* Case—Just What has it Decided?' [1986] Family Law 11.

[78] The position is made even more interesting by Lord Templeman's dissenting opinion, which appeared to accept that a child might make his or her own decisions, but that having contraception under 16 was not one of them.

[79] J. Eekelaar, 'The Eclipse of Parental Rights' (1986) 102 LQR 4 and 'The Emergency of Children's Rights' (1986) 6 Oxford Journal of Legal Studies 161. Compare A. Bainham, 'The Balance of Power in Family Decisions' (1986) 45(2) Cambridge Law Journal 262 and S. Gilmore, 'The Limits of Parental Responsibility' in R. Probert, S. Gilmore, and J. Herring (eds), *Responsible Parents and Parental Responsibility* (Oxford: Hart, 2009). And for a defence of the children's rights interpretation of *Gillick*, see J. Fortin, 'The *Gillick* Decision—Not Just a High-Water Mark' in S. Gilmore, J. Herring, and R. Probert (eds), *Landmark Cases in Family Law* (Oxford: Hart, 2011).

[80] As the Children's Legal Centre described it at the time: see (1985) 22 Childright 11; and see Fortin, ibid.

[81] This was the Children's Legal Centre's perception of its landmark status: 'the first legal judgment which unequivocally recognises the right of young people to make decisions about their lives and their bodies if they are old enough to have a mature appreciation of the issues and to make up their own minds' (ibid, 16). And this approach was said to apply to 'every area of children's lives other than those regulated by statute'. Many suggestions for its future application soon emerged in the pages of *Childright*. For a summary, see 'Wider Implications of *Gillick*' (1986) 26 Childright 17. For a general discussion of the 'potentially far-reaching implications' of what

influential proponent of this view is John Eekelaar. Eekelaar focused on passages in Lord Scarman's opinion in which Lord Scarman referred to parental rights yielding[82] or terminating,[83] and observed that:

> The significance of Lord Scarman's opinion with respect to children's autonomy interests cannot be over-rated. It follows from his reasoning that, where a child has reached capacity, there is no room for a parent to impose a contrary view, *even if this is more in accord with the child's best interests.* For its legal superiority to the child's decision can rest only on its status as a parental right. But this is extinguished when the child reaches full capacity.[84]

Eekelaar maintained that Lord Fraser should not be taken to have expressed a different view, pointing out that the part of Lord Fraser's opinion dealing with parental rights 'is placed firmly within the context of medical treatment, whereas Lord Scarman discusses parental rights on a general level'.[85]

Thus, in Eekelaar's view, *Gillick* involved a reconciliation of the autonomy interest with the basic and developmental interests 'through the empirical application of the concept of the acquisition of full capacity',[86] namely intellectual understanding supplemented by emotional maturity. It accorded to children a decision-making power which, once granted, could be exercised without adult restraint. He declared, therefore, that *Gillick* had conferred on children 'in wider measure than ever before, that most dangerous but most precious of rights: the right to make their own mistakes'.[87]

By contrast, another leading child law scholar, Andrew Bainham, suggests that *Gillick* 'represents a small but significant shift towards the thinking of the child liberationist school'[88] but that we should not 'equate this with a policy of legal autonomy or independence for children'.[89] For Bainham, the majority speeches in *Gillick* 'support a participatory model of decision making, ... according to parents *and* children qualified or relative autonomy'.[90]

One of the authors of this book, Stephen Gilmore, has questioned more directly whether Eekelaar's interpretation of *Gillick* is the most plausible.[91] He has argued that

---

was clearly perceived as a 'fundamental shift in legal doctrine', see S. M. Cretney, '*Gillick* and the Concept of Legal Capacity' (1989) 105 LQR 356.

[82] [1986] 1 AC 112 at 186D.   [83] Ibid, 188H.

[84] (1986) 6 Oxford Journal of Legal Studies 161 at 181. The case would thus apparently require a reorientation of the court's approach to wardship and custody disputes on divorce (see J. Eekelaar, '*Gillick* in the Divorce Court' (1986) 136 New Law Journal 184), where welfare would now have to defer to the competent child's wishes.

[85] (1986) LQR at 6. Eekelaar also argued ((1986) LQR 7) that Lord Fraser's conditions (2) to (5) are matters for professional discipline only and have no reference to legal liability (see also J. Montgomery, 'Children as Property?' (1988) 51 Modern Law Review 323 at 339 ('they are obiter, and if they have force it is as the content of the doctor's duty of care in negligence'); A. Grubb, 'Contraceptive Advice and Medical Treatment for Children' [1986] Cambridge Law Journal 3 at 5. However, Silber J has since held that Lord Fraser's guidelines are legal conditions. Even if they were not legal conditions the fact that they have no reference to legal liability does not mean that they can be entirely ignored.

[86] (1986) Oxford Journal of Legal Studies 161 at 181.

[87] Ibid, 182. It is a view that he thought may not ultimately find favour with the judiciary: J. Eekelaar, '*Gillick*: Further Limits on Parents' Rights to Punish' (1986) 28 Childright 9.

[88] A. Bainham, 'The Balance of Power in Family Decisions' (1986) 45(2) Cambridge Law Journal 262 at 275.

[89] Ibid.   [90] A. Bainham, *Children, Parents and the State* (London: Sweet & Maxwell, 1988), p 72.

[91] S. Gilmore, 'The Limits of Parental Responsibility' in R. Probert, S. Gilmore, and J. Herring, *Responsible Parents and Parental Responsibility* (Oxford: Hart, 2009); but compare J. Fortin, 'The *Gillick* Decision—Not Just a High-Water Mark' in S. Gilmore, J. Herring, and R. Probert (eds), *Landmark Cases in Family Law* (Oxford: Hart, 2011), p 199, who argues that many of the attempts to dilute the impact of Lord Scarman's views can be answered (see pp 206–208).

Gillick is essentially a case about children's *welfare* not their autonomy interests.[92] This is demonstrated in the public debate surrounding the litigation, counsel's arguments, and their Lordships' characterisation of the issues, all of which focused on resolving the potentially conflicting claims of doctors and parents to know what was in a child's best interests.[93] Indeed their Lordships had rejected an application by the Children's Legal Centre to make submissions or instruct counsel as *amicus curiae* on behalf of children in general.[94] These are reasons for some caution regarding a children's autonomy rights reading of *Gillick*.

Remember that Eekelaar focused heavily on parts of Lord Scarman's opinion, and then argued that Lord Fraser's focus on child welfare in the case should be seen as confined to the medical aspects of the case and not detract from Lord Scarman's general approach. By contrast, Gilmore points out that Lord Scarman agreed with Lord Fraser's opinion, and therefore Lord Scarman's opinion should be read in light of that agreement. Defending a children's autonomy rights reading of Lord Scarman's opinion, Jane Fortin[95] has countered that Lord Scarman's 'words of agreement with Lord Fraser's opinion were unsurprising, given their joint view that Mrs Gillick's application was unfounded' and that 'he clearly agreed with much of Lord Fraser's assessment of the preceding case law'.[96] However, it should be recalled that Lord Scarman agreed with Lord Fraser's *speech* not just the outcome and he did not qualify his agreement[97] so he should on the face of it be taken to have agreed with all of it.

Gilmore questions why Lord Fraser's welfare approach in the medical context should not be seen as *reflecting* their Lordships' earlier general conclusions as to the point at which parental right yields. He also points out that the fact that Lord Scarman drew on case law on the ages of discretion, the aim of which was to protect children, makes it difficult to conclude that Lord Scarman envisaged the law allowing children to make decisions that would lead to their irreparable harm. These arguments should be borne in mind when thinking about the difficult question of what was meant in *Gillick* by the point at which parental right yields to the child's right.

So what did *Gillick* establish as a matter of law? It would certainly be difficult to see *Gillick* as a binding precedent for the view that children have the right to make their own mistakes.[98] The most *Gillick* could represent as a binding precedent would be the child's power to consent to medical treatment offered without parental knowledge or consent because it is considered in the child's best interests to do so. At its most abstract, it endorses a child's power to accept someone else's bona fide, yet possibly mistaken, view of what is in a child's interests. Put simply, the 'reasoning of Lords Fraser and Scarman was built upon

[92] S. Gilmore, 'The Limits of Parental Responsibility' in R. Probert, S. Gilmore, and J. Herring, *Responsible Parents and Parental Responsibility* (Oxford: Hart, 2009).

[93] See also Eekelaar's own comment: '[t]he public debate which surrounded the litigation tended to revolve around the competing claims of parents and doctors to determine children's interests' (1986) 6 Oxford Journal of Legal Studies 161 at 178.

[94] (1985) *Legal Action* 3. The DHSS consented but Mrs Gillick did not. No reasons were given by their Lordships.

[95] J. Fortin, 'The *Gillick* Decision—Not Just a High-Water Mark' in S. Gilmore, J. Herring, and R. Probert (eds), *Landmark Cases in Family Law* (Oxford: Hart, 2011) pp 199, 205–207.   [96] Ibid, p 206.

[97] Except by saying that the issues were so important that he wished to express his opinion in his own words.

[98] S. Gilmore, 'The Limits of Parental Responsibility' in R. Probert, S. Gilmore, and J. Herring, *Responsible Parents and Parental Responsibility* (Oxford: Hart, 2009).

a consideration of the best interests of the sexually active minor, not upon the right of the minor to be sexually active',[99] or indeed to demand contraceptive treatment.

That is not to say that the general principles articulated by Lord Scarman were not groundbreaking. As Fortin contends, in terms of *Gillick*'s landmark status 'it does not matter what the precise effects of the majority decision were'.[100] *Gillick* 'undeniably placed the idea of children's autonomy rights in the legal consciousness in a way which had not previously existed'.[101] It also undoubtedly had an influence on the Children Act 1989.[102] However, it is maintained that it is still important to distinguish between what it achieved as a matter of law and what it promised. Essentially what *Gillick* achieved was to create a climate of expectation that a child will be consulted, and his or her wishes and feelings will be taken into account, when any important decision is made in respect of his or her upbringing. What *Gillick* did *not* achieve was to create a rule that the wishes and feelings of a child will always prevail over the wishes and feelings of the persons with parental responsibility, even though the child has sufficient competence to understand the full implications of the decision to be made. The opportunity to suggest the incorporation of such a rule in legislation was afforded during the massive review of child law which took place before the Children Act 1989 was enacted, but no suggestion for such a rule was made.

3.3 *AXON*: A HUMAN RIGHTS CHALLENGE TO *GILLICK*

Key case

Over 20 years after *Gillick* was decided, and following implementation of the Human Rights Act 1998, a human rights challenge was mounted to the approach in *Gillick* by Ms Sue Axon, in the context of abortion advice and treatment and an updated version of the relevant Guidance.[103] Ms Axon had had an abortion when she was younger, which had caused her personal difficulties, and she did not want her daughters to be offered such advice or treatment without her knowledge; she wanted the opportunity to give her daughters the benefit of her own experience. In judicial review proceedings[104] she sought a declaration that medical

---

[99] S. Gilmore, J. Herring, and R. Probert, 'Introduction: Parental Responsibility—Law, Issues and Themes' in R. Probert, S. Gilmore, and J. Herring, *Responsible Parents and Parental Responsibility* (Oxford: Hart, 2009), p 4.

[100] J. Fortin, 'The *Gillick* Decision—Not Just a High-Water Mark' in S. Gilmore, J. Herring, and R. Probert (eds), *Landmark Cases in Family Law* (Oxford: Hart, 2011) p 199, at p 222.

[101] S. Gilmore, J. Herring, and R. Probert, 'Introduction: Parental Responsibility—Law, Issues and Themes' in R. Probert, S. Gilmore, and J. Herring, *Responsible Parents and Parental Responsibility* (Oxford: Hart, 2009), p 6. See H. Teff, *Reasonable Care, Legal Perspectives on the Doctor/Patient Relationship* (Oxford: Clarendon Press, 1994), p 152: undeniable that *Gillick* 'came to be seen as a symbolic milestone in the enfranchisement of children'.

[102] See eg children's rights to refuse assessment in ss 38(6), 43(8), and 44(7). However, see *South Glamorgan County Council v W and B* [1993] 1 FLR 574 in which the inherent jurisdiction was used to override the child's refusal, discussed in more detail in Chapter 10. See C. Lyon 'What's Happened to the Child's "Right" to Refuse?—*South Glamorgan County Council v. W and B*' (1994) 6(2) Journal of Child Law 84.

[103] Guidance for Doctors and other Health Professionals on the Provision of Advice and Treatment to Young People under 16 on Contraception, Sexual and Reproductive Heath (29 July 2004), gateway reference No 3382. Relevant parts of the Guidance are set out at [2006] EWHC 37 (Admin), [2006] QB 539 at [22]–[24].

[104] *R (Axon) v Secretary of State for Health* [2006] EWHC 37 (Admin). For comment, see J. Bridgeman, 'Case Comment: Young People and Sexual Health: Whose Rights? Whose Responsibilities?' [2006] Medical Law Review 418; R. Taylor, 'Reversing the Retreat from *Gillick*? *R (Axon) v Secretary of State for Health*' [2007] Child and Family Law Quarterly 81.

professionals are under no obligation to maintain confidentiality in relation to abortion advice and treatment unless disclosure might prejudice the child's physical or mental health. She also argued (and sought declarations to the effect) that the Guidance misrepresented *Gillick*, and failed to discharge the state's positive obligation to give practical and effective protection to her rights under Article 8(1) of the European Convention on Human Rights (ECHR). Silber J rejected her claims, holding that there was no such misrepresentation, and that the approach in *Gillick* 'was and is of general application to *all* forms of medical advice and treatment', including therefore abortion advice and treatment. Silber J clarified that Lord Fraser's guidelines are legal pre-conditions[105] and to be strictly observed. He also indicated that Lord Fraser's first condition, that the child understands the advice, was to be read in light of Lord Scarman's stringent test for capacity, and explained that 'all relevant matters' were included within the meaning of 'understanding'.[106]

Addressing Ms Axon's argument based on Article 8(1) of the ECHR, Silber J held that 'any right to family life on the part of a parent dwindles as their child gets older and is able to understand the consequence of different choices and then to make decisions relating to them'[107] and that 'this autonomy must undermine any article 8 rights of a parent to family life'.[108] Accordingly:

> parents do not have article 8 rights to be notified of any advice of a medical professional after the young person is able to look after himself or herself and make his or her own decisions.[109]

In reaching this conclusion, Silber J commented that 'the right of young people to make decisions about their own lives by themselves at the expense of the views of their parents has now become an increasingly important and accepted feature of family life'.[110] He saw this 'change in the landscape of family matters, in which rights of children are becoming increasingly important' as a reason for not retreating from the approach in *Gillick*.[111] He concluded that there was nothing in the Guidance which interferes with a parent's Article 8 rights since the medical professional must act in the child's best interests.[112] Alternatively, any infringement could be justified under Article 8(2). He held that the legislative objective (of reducing unwanted pregnancies and addressing sexually transmitted diseases) is sufficiently important to justify limiting parents' Article 8 rights; and Lord Fraser's guidelines were rationally connected to that objective and impaired freedom no more than necessary to achieve it.[113]

4 CHILDREN'S RIGHTS IN CASES OF REFUSAL OF MEDICAL TREATMENT

Gillick v West Norfolk and Wisbech Area Health Authority was concerned with whether a competent child could *consent* to medical treatment, and whether such consent could be countermanded by a person with parental responsibility. In two subsequent decisions

---

[105] *Axon* ibid at [110] and [111].
[106] Ibid, [154]. See also the passage from Lord Scarman's opinion set out at n 76.   [107] Ibid, [129].
[108] Ibid, [130].   [109] Ibid, [132].
[110] Citing as illustrations Arts 16(1) and 12(1) of the United Nations Convention on the Rights of the Child and the judgment of Thorpe LJ in *Mabon v Mabon* [2005] EWCA Civ 634, [2005] Fam 366.
[111] *Axon* at [80].   [112] Ibid, [134].   [113] Ibid, [150]–[152].

of the Court of Appeal, *Re R (A Minor) (Wardship: Consent to Treatment)*[114] and *Re W (A Minor) (Medical Treatment: Court's Jurisdiction)*,[115] and in a series of High Court judgments,[116] the tension between child autonomy and child protection has acquired a sharper practical focus, as the issue has switched to the validity of a child's *refusal* of consent in circumstances where a failure to undergo treatment might result in irreparable harm or death.

4.1 *RE R (A MINOR) (WARDSHIP: CONSENT TO TREATMENT)*

In *Re R* a local authority initiated wardship proceedings in respect of a girl, R, aged 15 years 10 months, who had a history of family problems and psychiatric illness, characterised by violent and suicidal behaviour. R, who was the subject of an interim care order,[117] had been placed with the consent of the local authority, in an adolescent psychiatric unit, where the treatment regime included, when necessary, compulsory administration of anti-psychotic medication. The local authority initially consented to the administration of anti-psychotic medication. In one of her lucid periods, R refused her medication. A social worker, who had experience with cases involving persons who are mentally ill, then had a three-hour telephone conversation with R after which he decided that R sounded lucid and rational and he did not regard her as 'sectionable'.[118] The local authority therefore took the view that they could not give permission for R to have drugs administered against her will. The adolescent unit refused to care for R without a free hand in the administration of her medication, and the wardship application therefore sought leave for administration of the medication without R's consent.

The application came before Waite J who heard evidence from a consultant child psychiatrist, Dr R.[119] In a written report, Dr R concluded that when he had seen R five days before the hearing she had been 'of sufficient maturity and understanding to comprehend the treatment being recommended and was rational'. He cautioned, however, that should she not continue with treatment her more florid psychotic behaviour was likely to return and she might become a serious suicidal risk. In his oral evidence, Dr R explained that he was familiar with the decision in *Gillick* which, in his view, required in R's case a consideration of 'whether, having regard to her development and

---

[114] [1992] Fam 11 (Lord Donaldson MR, Staughton and Farquharson LJJ), hereafter *Re R*. See A. Bainham, 'The Judge and the Competent Minor' (1992) 108 LQR 194; G. Douglas, 'The Retreat from *Gillick*' (1992) 55 Modern Law Review 569; P. Fennell, 'Informal Compulsion: The Psychiatric Treatment of Juveniles under Common Law' [1992] Journal of Social Welfare and Family Law 311; J. Masson, 'Adolescent Crisis and Parental Power' [1991] Family Law 528; J. Montgomery, 'Parents and Children in Dispute: Who Has the Final Word?' (1992) 4 Journal of Child Law 85; J. Murphy, 'Circumscribing the Autonomy of "*Gillick* Competent" Children' (1992) 43(1) Northern Ireland Legal Quarterly 60; S. Parker and J. Dewar [1992] Journal of Social Welfare and Family Law 143 (case commentary on *Re R*); R. Thornton, 'Multiple Keyholders—Wardship and Consent to Medical Treatment' [1992] Cambridge Law Journal 34; J. Urwin, '*Re R*: The Resurrection of Parental Powers?' (1992) 8 Professional Negligence 69.

[115] [1993] Fam 64 (Lord Donaldson MR, Balcombe and Nolan LJJ), hereafter *Re W*. See J. Eekelaar, 'White Coats or Flak Jackets? Doctors, Children and the Courts—Again' (1993) 109 LQR 182; H. Houghton-James, 'The Child's Right to Die' [1992] Family Law 550; N. Lowe and S. Juss, 'Medical Treatment—Pragmatism and the Search for Principle' (1993) 56 Modern Law Review 865; J. Masson, '*Re W*: Appealing from the Golden Cage' (1993) 5(1) Journal of Child Law 37; M. Mulholland, '*Re W (A Minor)*: Autonomy, Consent and the Anorexic Teenager' (1993) 9(1) Professional Negligence 21; R. Thornton, 'Minors and Medical Treatment—Who Decides?' [1993] Cambridge Law Journal 34.   [116] Discussed at Section 4.3.

[117] The case was decided pre-Children Act 1989, so the restrictions on the use of wardship in s 100 of that Act did not apply.

[118] That is, liable to be made the subject of an application under ss 2 and 3 of the Mental Health Act 1983.

[119] The summary of this evidence below is taken from *Re R* [1992] Fam 11 at 19–21.

maturity, she understands the nature of the implications of the treatment proposed', and concluded that when he had seen her, R was 'mature enough to understand the nature of the proposal'. Waite J, stating *obiter* that a judge in wardship could not override the refusal of a competent child, granted the local authority's application on the ground that R's mental condition precluded her from achieving such competence.

On appeal, James Munby QC for the Official Solicitor, acting as R's guardian ad litem, contended that Waite J was wrong as to R's competence, but was correct as to the powers of the judge in wardship. Relying on Lord Scarman's judgment in *Gillick*, he argued that parental rights to consent are terminated when a child achieves capacity to consent, and since the court in wardship steps into the parents' shoes the court is equally precluded from exercising its powers against the child's wishes.

The Court of Appeal rejected these arguments. It was by no means satisfied that R understood the implications of the treatment being withheld, as distinct from understanding what was proposed to be done by way of treatment. The evidence had established that R's mental state fluctuated, so that even if, on a good day, she was capable of reaching the standard of competence required to meet the *Gillick* criteria, on other days she was not only *Gillick* incompetent, she was actually sectionable. Lord Donaldson MR ruled that 'no child in that situation can be regarded as "*Gillick* competent"... "*Gillick* competence" is a developmental concept and will not be lost or acquired on a day-to-day or week-to-week basis. In the case of mental disability, that disability must also be taken into account, particularly where it is fluctuating in effect.'[120] Farquharson LJ observed that: 'The *Gillick* test is not apt to a situation where the understanding and capacity of the child varies from day to day according to the effect of her illness.'[121]

This sufficed to dispose of the case, but in response to a request from counsel for their Lordships to clarify the legal position, the court went further. It held that in wardship the child's wishes could be overridden irrespective of competence, the court's powers being wider than those of parents. Lord Donaldson alone made further *obiter* comments concerning the relationship between parents' and children's powers of consent, in a passage which bears extended citation:

What Mr. Munby's argument overlooks is that Lord Scarman was discussing the parents' right '*to determine* whether or not their minor child below the age of 16 will have medical treatment' (my emphasis) and this is the 'parental right' to which he was referring at p. 186D. A right of determination is wider than a right to consent. The parents can only have a right of determination if *either* the child has no right to consent, that is, is not a keyholder, *or* the parents hold a master key which could nullify the child's consent. I do not understand Lord Scarman to be saying that, if a child was '*Gillick* competent', to adopt the convenient phrase used in argument, the parents ceased to have an independent right of consent as contrasted with ceasing to have a right of determination, that is, a veto. In a case in which the '*Gillick* competent' child refuses treatment, but the parents consent, that consent *enables* treatment to be undertaken lawfully, but in no way determines that the child shall be so treated. In a case in which the positions are reversed, it is the child's consent which is the enabling factor and again the parents' refusal of consent is not determinative. If Lord Scarman intended to go further than this and to say that in the case of a

---

[120] [1992] Fam 11 at 25–26 *per* Lord Donaldson MR. The concept of 'competence' was subsequently developed in *Re C (Refusal of Medical Treatment)* [1994] 1 FLR 31 where Thorpe J ruled that the decision-making process should be approached in three stages: (i) comprehending and retaining treatment information; (ii) believing it; and (iii) weighing it in the balance to arrive at a choice. This test was applied in *A Metropolitan Borough Council v DB* [1997] 1 FLR 767 where the court ruled that a 17-year-old pregnant girl who was addicted to drugs, living in squalid conditions, and had a phobia against needles failed to satisfy each stage of the test. Compulsory medical treatment of the girl was therefore authorised.   [121] Ibid, 32.

'*Gillick* competent' child, a parent has no right either to consent or to refuse consent, his remarks were obiter, because the only question in issue was Mrs Gillick's alleged right of veto. Furthermore, I consider that they would have been wrong.[122]

Lord Donaldson's analysis, distinguishing between determination and consent, has been criticised by some commentators. Andrew Bainham has argued that if a doctor is faced with a conflict between parent and child and 'proceeds on the basis of the parent's view, he is in reality giving effect to a parental veto over the child's view, and thus the distinction between determination and consent falls apart'.[123] In similar vein, Gillian Douglas[124] views consent as part of the right to determine, not an alternative to it, illustrating her point by way of two examples: first, if I have the right to determine that my 1-year-old child is inoculated, then I have power to consent to the giving of an injection; secondly, if I do not have power to determine the length of a 15-year-old's hair, then I cannot have power to consent to its being cut against the child's wishes.

It seems, however, that Lord Donaldson was interpreting the word 'determine' differently, in the sense of an *exclusive* power to decide. Lord Donaldson would respond to Douglas's first example by pointing out that it is only because the child cannot consent that parental consent is determinative. To the second, presumably Lord Donaldson would say: 'Though the parent can consent to haircuts, she cannot be said to have a right to determine the issue of haircuts if she cannot prevent the child consenting to a particular haircut.' So the arguments here reduce to arguments over which of different possible meanings of the word 'determine' Lord Scarman used in *Gillick* and it was of course Lord Donaldson's job to interpret that word.

Lord Donaldson offered two principal arguments in support of his view that there can be concurrent consents in parent and child. First, he could not agree that, to avoid being sued in trespass, the law required a doctor 'to determine as a matter of law in whom the right of consent resided at the particular time in relation to the particular treatment'.[125] This, he felt, would place doctors in 'an intolerable dilemma' when, for example, there was a dispute between parents and a child nearing the age of 16.[126] This appeal to legal certainty seems out of step with the flexible approach of the Lords in *Gillick*.[127] Neither *Gillick* nor section 8 of the Family Law Reform Act 1969 seem directed at protecting doctors from litigation,[128] and it may be that 'it is no more difficult to determine the child's competence when the child is refusing'.[129] As Parker and Dewar have argued, consequentialist justifications appear to point the other way[130] since to place the doctor

---

[122] [1992] Fam 11 at 23E–H.

[123] A. Bainham, 'The Judge and the Competent Minor' (1992) 108 LQR 194 at 198.

[124] G. Douglas, 'The Retreat from *Gillick*' (1992) 55 Modern Law Review 569 at 575.

[125] [1992] Fam 11 at 24A–C.

[126] Ibid. Although also acknowledged by at least one commentator as a 'significant theoretical problem', see; J. Montgomery, 'Parents and Children in Dispute: Who Has the Final Word?' (1992) 4 Journal of Child Law 85 at 87.

[127] G. Austin, 'Righting a Child's Right to Refuse Medical Treatment, Section 11 of the New Zealand Bill of Rights Act and the *Gillick* Competent Child' (1992) 7(4) Otago Law Review 578 at 585. As Murphy observes, whilst the House of Lords held that parental rights exist for the benefit of the child, 'it is difficult to see why in *Re R* the Master of the Rolls held them to exist also for the benefit of the doctor': J. Murphy, 'Circumscribing the Autonomy of "*Gillick* Competent" Children' (1992) 43(1) Northern Ireland Legal Quarterly 60 at 62.

[128] R. Thornton, 'Multiple Keyholders—Wardship and Consent to Medical Treatment' [1992] Cambridge Law Journal 34 at 36.

[129] A. Grubb, 'Treatment Decisions: Keeping it in the Family' in A. Grubb (ed), *Choices and Decisions in Health Care* (Chichester: Wiley, 1993), p 63.

[130] S. Parker and J. Dewar, [1992] Journal of Social Welfare and Family Law 143 143 (case commentary on *Re R*) at 146–147.

at some risk might operate as a presumption in favour of competence and of complying with the child's wishes.[131]

Lord Donaldson's second argument suggested that section 8 of the Family Law Reform Act 1969 was inconsistent with counsel's interpretation of Lord Scarman's speech.[132] So far as material, section 8 provides:

> (1) The consent of a minor who has attained the age of 16 years to any…medical treatment, which in the absence of consent would constitute a trespass to the person, shall be as effective as it would be if her were of full age; and where a minor has by virtue of this section given an effective consent to any treatment it shall not be necessary to obtain any consent for it from his parent or guardian;…
>
> (3) Nothing in this section shall be construed as making ineffective any consent which would have been effective if this section had not been enacted.

Lord Donaldson indicated that if parental power to consent was extinguished upon a child's acquisition of capacity to consent, then not only would it not be necessary to obtain a parent's consent as section 8(1) provides, it would be legally impossible. He further argued that section 8(3) 'would create problems since, if the section had not been enacted, a parent's consent would undoubtedly have been effective *as a consent*'.[133] These arguments are not without merit. Furthermore, as Gilmore and Herring have argued in a detailed analysis of the background to section 8,[134] its parliamentary history and the approach of the Latey Committee Report[135] which recommended the provision does not suggest that the intention was that parental powers of consent would be extinguished upon the child achieving capacity. While, as Eekelaar has observed, section 8(3) 'cannot be construed as imposing a restraint in perpetuity on the later development of the common law'[136] there does not seem to be any reason why the statute should not provide some indication, or confirmation, of the appropriate interpretation of the common law.[137]

To summarise, then, Lord Donaldson was clearly of the opinion that in a case where a '*Gillick* competent' child refuses treatment, but someone with parental responsibility consents, that treatment can lawfully be given to the child. He acknowledged that the child's refusal of consent will be a very important factor in the doctor's decision whether or not to treat, but held that it does not stop treatment going ahead if consent is obtained from another person with parental responsibility.

4.2 *RE W (A MINOR) (MEDICAL TREATMENT: COURT'S JURISDICTION)*

Lord Donaldson's approach in *Re R* attracted considerable criticism and an opportunity to reconsider his approach was presented by the case of *Re W (A Minor) (Medical Treatment:*

---

[131] Ibid, 146.   [132] [1992] Fam 11 at 24F–G.

[133] Ibid, 24G–H. In *Re W* [1993] Fam 64 at 77, Lord Donaldson reiterated these arguments, where additionally he described s 8(3) as 'preserving the common law immediately before the Act, which undoubtedly gave parents a power to consent for all children up to the age of 21'.

[134] S. Gilmore and J. Herring, '"No" is the Hardest Word: Consent and Children's Autonomy' [2011] Child and Family Law Quarterly 3, esp at 17–19.

[135] *Report of the Committee on the Age of Majority* (Cmnd 3342, 1967).

[136] J. Eekelaar, 'The Emergence of Children's Rights' (1986) 6 Oxford Journal of Legal Studies 161 at 184.

[137] S. Gilmore and J. Herring, '"No" is the Hardest Word: Consent and Children's Autonomy' [2011] Child and Family Law Quarterly 3, esp at 19.

Court's Jurisdiction).[138] A 16-year-old child, W, who was in the care of a local authority, developed anorexia nervosa and was admitted to an adolescent residential unit for treatment. Following a deterioration in W's condition, the local authority obtained leave to invoke the inherent jurisdiction of the High Court. By the time the case came to court the girl's weight had dropped to such a low level that, should she continue to lose weight for more than a few days, her capacity to have children in later life would be put seriously at risk, and a little later her life itself might be in danger. Contrary to W's wishes and the advice of her consultant, the local authority sought the court's permission to transfer W from her adolescent unit where she was consenting to treatment, to a unit specialising in eating disorders and to treat her there, if necessary without her consent. Thorpe J held[139] that W had sufficient understanding to make an informed decision but nevertheless that he had jurisdiction to authorise treatment and should do so in W's best interests.

W's case differed materially from *Re R* in two respects: she had attained the age of 16, and by section 8 of the Family Law Reform Act 1969 had a statutory power to consent to medical treatment; and had been adjudged competent. On appeal to the Court of Appeal, W contended that section 8 had provided her with an absolute right to determine whether or not she received medical treatment, and accordingly under the principle in *A v Liverpool City Council*[140] the court was precluded from accepting jurisdiction. The Court of Appeal rejected this interpretation of section 8,[141] and held that a judge exercising the inherent jurisdiction had power to override the wishes of a competent 16- or 17-year-old.

Lord Donaldson again ventured 'to doubt whether Lord Scarman meant more than that the *exclusive* right of the parents to consent to treatment terminated',[142] a doubt now shared by Balcombe LJ,[143] although Lord Donaldson now acknowledged that he 'may well be wrong'.[144] Despite this concession, however, he reiterated his view that there could be concurrent consents, although he now preferred the analogy of the legal flak-jacket (providing the doctor with a shield against a claim in battery) to his earlier keyholder analogy since keys are capable of both locking and unlocking.[145] Balcombe LJ agreed. Nolan LJ appeared to have some reservations about this point.

Lord Donaldson MR emphasised, however, that the wishes of a competent child were of the greatest clinical importance. In response to the 'hair-raising' possibility, which had been canvassed before him in argument, of abortions being carried out by doctors with the consent of parents on unwilling 16- and 17-year-olds, he was content to place reliance on medical ethics to act as a restraining influence in such cases. Balcombe LJ was also of the opinion that a doctor would not terminate the pregnancy of a mentally competent 16-year-old merely upon the consent of the child's parents. He added that it would seem inevitable that the matter would have to come before the court in such highly unlikely circumstances. Nolan LJ offered the child the strongest safeguard when he said:

> We are not directly concerned with cases in which the jurisdiction of the court has not been invoked, and in which accordingly the decision on treatment may depend upon the consent of the child or of the parent. I for my part would think it axiomatic, however, in order to avoid the risk of grave breaches of the law that in any case where time permitted, where major surgical or other procedures (such as an abortion) were proposed, and whereby the parents or those in loco parentis were prepared to give consent but the child

---

[138] [1993] Fam 64. See criticism of *Re R* at 75.
[139] *Re J (a Minor)*, The Times, 14 May 1992.   [140] [1982] AC 363.
[141] [1993] Fam 64 at 77B–C *per* Lord Donaldson MR, at 87H *per* Balcombe LJ, at 92E–H *per* Nolan LJ.
[142] Ibid, 76C.   [143] Ibid, 87E–F.   [144] Ibid.   [145] Ibid, 78D–E.

(having sufficient understanding to make an informed decision) was not, the jurisdiction of the court should always be invoked.[146]

The court was united, however, in its view that a court has the power to override a minor's consent to medical treatment. With regard to the court's approach, Lord Donaldson indicated that 'good parenting involves giving minors as much rope as they can handle without an unacceptable risk that they will hang themselves' and that it was self-evident that the well-being, welfare, or interests of the minor:

> involves giving them the maximum degree of decision-making which is prudent. Prudence does not involve avoiding all risk, but it does involve avoiding taking risks which, if they eventuate, may have irreparable consequences or which are disproportionate to the benefits which could accrue from taking them.[147]

Balcombe LJ stressed that 'the judge should approach the exercise of the discretion with a predeliction to give effect to the child's wishes on the basis that prima facie that will be in his or her best interests'.[148] He added that W's wishes should have been respected 'unless there were very strong reasons for rejecting them'. Nolan LJ was certain that a court had not only the power, but also the inescapable responsibility, of deciding what should be done in W's case, guided by the welfare principle in section 1(1) of the Children Act 1989, and the checklist of matters in section 1(3) to which a court is required to have regard. However, he commented:

> I am very far from asserting any general rule that the court should prefer its own view of what is in the best interests of the child to those of the child itself. In considering the welfare of the child, the court must not only recognise but if necessary defend the right of the child, having sufficient understanding to make an informed decision, to make his or her own choice.[149]

4.3 AUTHORISING THE USE OF REASONABLE FORCE[150]

In cases subsequent to *Re W* judges have not hesitated, where necessary, to authorise the use of reasonable force in order to ensure a child's treatment. In *Re C (Detention: Medical Treatment)*[151] a cautious and conscientious approach was taken by Wall J to ordering the detention of a minor (aged 16) against her will for the purpose of giving her medical treatment for anorexia nervosa. He held that in the exercise of the inherent jurisdiction of the court he had power to direct that the girl reside at a clinic, and to authorise the use of reasonable force (if necessary)[152] to detain her in the clinic. He also found that while he must have regard to the child's wishes and feelings, he could override these if they were not in her best interests, but that where the child had capacity to give or refuse consent, then the weight which the court should give to her wishes and feelings would increase. However, Wall J acknowledged that an order for the detention of a minor aged 16 against her will was a draconian remedy. In the instant case, because the girl's civil liberties were involved, he held that the order should be time-limited and have built into it stringent

---

[146] [1993] Fam 64 at 94.   [147] Ibid, 81.   [148] Ibid, 644.   [149] [1992] 4 All ER 627 at 648.

[150] See generally, J. Fortin, 'Children's Rights and the Use of Physical Force' [2001] Child and Family Law Quarterly 243.

[151] [1997] 2 FLR 180. See P. de Cruz, 'Adolescent Autonomy, Detention for Medical Treatment and *Re C*' (1999) 62 Modern Law Review 595.

[152] See also *A Metropolitan Borough Council v DB* [1997] 1 FLR 767.

safeguards to protect the girl's interests, ensuring that she suffered the least distress and retained the greatest dignity.[153]

Despite their concern for the welfare of the children concerned, this and other rulings are nonetheless open to criticism. By exercising the inherent jurisdiction of the High Court in those cases where the child is suffering from a mental illness or serious mental disturbance, judges are by-passing the protective measures which are built into the Mental Health Act 1983,[154] and they may as a result be exposing children to medical and behavioural regimes and treatment processes to which far more stringent safeguards apply where adults are involved.

4.3.1 Is there a need to seek the authorisation of a court?

In *Re K, W and H (Minors) (Medical Treatment)*.[155] Thorpe J said that applications for orders authorising medical treatment, made by a hospital in respect of three highly disturbed 15-year-old girls who might not wish to consent in the future to the emergency use of medication, had been misconceived and unnecessary. He ruled that the girls were not '*Gillick* competent' to make decisions about their own medical treatment but that, even if they were, it was clear that the law allowed treatment to be given provided that someone with parental responsibility had given consent. An alarming feature of this case was that the judge took the view that the law was 'perfectly clear in this field', and that 'where more than one person has the power to consent, only a refusal by all having that power will create a veto'.[156] He rejected the hospital's appraisal of the situation as being highly complex and confusing. Thorpe J's approach stands in some contrast to that of Nolan LJ set out earlier. It is suggested that Thorpe J's certain approach in *Re K, W and H (Minors)* coupled in that case with a finding that the girls did not have sufficient competence to instruct their own lawyers, despite the beliefs of their lawyers to the contrary, bodes ill for competent and incompetent children who are in conflict with persons with parental responsibility in relation to medical decisions.[157] It illustrates the dangers of translating reasoned judgments, in which various reservations are expressed, into a simplified rule of law. It is important, therefore, that some of the thinking of the judges in *Re W (A Minor) (Wardship: Medical Treatment)* about the weight to be given to the competent child's wishes in medical cases is not lost.

---

[153] Interestingly, Wall J took the view that the girl's 'best safeguard is legal representation and access to the court though her lawyers' and that any order should give her liberty to apply at short notice. In this way, Wall J gave open endorsement to the view that children, like adults, should be entitled to turn to the courts when their liberties are at stake.

[154] See J. Masson, '*Re W*: Appealing from the Golden Cage' (1993) 5(1) Journal of Child Law 37.

[155] [1993] 1 FLR 854. Even though at the time of his judgment the only ruling on parental consent and *Gillick* competence had been in *Re R (A Minor) (Wardship: Medical Treatment)*, on which only Lord Donaldson MR had expressed a concluded view. For commentary, see P. Bates, 'Children in Secure Psychiatric Units: *Re K, W and H*—"Out of Sight, Out of Mind"?' (1994) 6(3) Journal of Child Law 131.

[156] [1993] 1 FLR 854.

[157] See also *South Glamorgan County Council v W and B* [1993] 1 FLR 574 which is discussed in Chapter 10. C. Bridge, 'Adolescents and Mental Disorder: Who Consents to Treatment?' (1997) 3 Medical Law International 51, suggests that differentiation should be made between three different categories of adolescent disturbance: the competent young person who refuses treatment that an adult may refuse; the rebellious teenager, whose refusal is triggered by simple teenage angst; and the mentally ill teenager, whose refusal is triggered by illness. She submits that adolescent autonomy needs to be more fully understood and the Mental Health Act 1983 more readily used in treating young people.

4.4 CRITICISM OF *RE R* AND *RE W*:[158] THE DISTINCTION BETWEEN CONSENT AND REFUSAL

Nigel Lowe and Satvinder Juss support the approach in *Re W* as one which consistently seeks to protect children by facilitating medical treatment easily when it is in a child's best interests, whilst at the same time protecting children from their own, and their parents, 'wrong-headed decisions'.[159] This reflects the view that:

> The consequences of withholding consent to treatment are usually much more significant and potentially dangerous than simply giving consent—unless one believes that most treatments are either unnecessary or are likely to be more dangerous than the condition for which they were prescribed.[160]

However, as Gillian Douglas has pointed out, the position is not as straightforward as this suggests, since there may be more than one recognised medical view and thus a choice between treatments. Douglas also argues that a refusal of consent should be given greater weight because overriding it involves both 'intellectual and bodily' interference with a person's autonomy.[161]

Attention has also been drawn to alleged anomalies that *Re W* creates. Jo Bridgeman points to the 'strange position' of a 17-year-old mother, who has far more control over her child's medical treatment than her own, for whereas she can both consent and refuse consent to her child's medical treatment, the mother's refusal of consent can be overridden by her own parents.[162] Furthermore, Margaret Brazier makes the powerful point that:

> In practical terms legal principles which result in a mother having no say as to whether her teenage daughter agrees to an abortion, no right even to know of the operation, but being able to require that same daughter to undergo abortion against her will, are odd in the extreme.[163]

In contrast to Lowe and Juss's viewpoint, therefore, many academic commentators have criticised *Re W* as entrenching in English law an illogical distinction between consent to and refusal of treatment.[164] It is a criticism supported by the admission of Balcombe LJ

---

[158] In addition to the commentaries on these individual cases, several commentaries have addressed both *Re R* and *Re W*: J. Bridgeman, 'Old Enough to Know Best?' (1993) 13 Legal Studies 69; L. Edwards, 'The Right to Consent and the Right to Refuse; More Problems with Minors and Medical Consent' [1993] Juridical Review 52; A. Grubb, 'Treatment Decisions: Keeping it in the Family' in A. Grubb (ed), *Choices and Decisions in Health Care* (Chichester: Wiley, 1993), p 37; J. K. Mason, 'Master of the Balancers; Non-Voluntary Therapy under the Mantle of Lord Donaldson' [1993] Juridical Review 115; J. Murphy, 'W(h)ither Adolescent Autonomy?' [1992] Journal of Social Welfare and Family Law 529.

[159] N. Lowe and S. Juss, 'Medical Treatment—Pragmatism and the Search for Principle' (1993) 56 Modern Law Review 865 at 871–872.

[160] J. Pearce, 'Consent to Treatment During Childhood, The Assessment of Competence and Avoidance of Conflict' (1994) 165 British Journal of Psychiatry 713 at 713. See also Mason and McCall Smith, who observe that 'while consent involves acceptance of an experienced view, refusal rejects that experience–and does so from a position of limited understanding': J. K. Mason and R. A. McCall Smith, *Law and Medical Ethics* (London, 1999), at p 160.

[161] G. Douglas, 'The Retreat from *Gillick*' (1992) 55 Modern Law Review 569 at 576.

[162] J. Bridgeman, 'Old Enough to Know Best?' (1993) 13 Legal Studies 69 at 80. It is possible to argue, however, that the 'strange position' encountered by the child mother in Bridgeman's example is not a consequence of legal inconsistency, but of the fact that unusually a 'child mother' falls into both categories of 'child' and 'mother'. The law consistently requires of a parent, whether adult or child, that powers of consent are exercised in the child's best interests. In any event, the alleged anomaly is more apparent than real since it seems inevitable that by the time the child is capable of exercising a choice to refuse medical treatment, the child's mother will be an adult.

[163] M. Brazier, *Medicine, Patients and the Law* (London: Penguin, 1992), p 346.

[164] J. Bridgeman, 'Old Enough to Know Best?' (1993) 13 Legal Studies 69 at 80.

himself in *Re W* that '[i]n logic there can be no difference between an ability to consent to treatment and an ability to refuse treatment'.[165] Many commentators have found difficulty understanding how a child could be competent to consent yet lack capacity to refuse.[166] In a recent article, however, Stephen Gilmore and Jonathan Herring have sought to explain how in certain circumstances this is possible, and to offer a partial defence of Lord Donaldson's concurrent consents approach.[167] They argue that it is important to distinguish the following two ways of saying no to treatment:

> (1) A 'rejection of proposed treatment'. Here the child is offered the option of consenting to a particular treatment. The child considers the proposed treatment and indicates that he or she does not consent to it; or, in other words, declines to provide consent to that particular treatment.
>
> (2) A 'refusal of treatment'. Here the child has decided not to have any treatment whatsoever. It is not merely the patient's wish to decline particular treatment, but a decision to refuse all treatment, a conscious decision to incur the consequences of a total failure to treat.[168]

Gilmore and Herring maintain that these definitions carry at least two significant distinctions: first as to the capacity required of the child in each case; and, secondly, that they involve asking two different questions. Rejection of proposed treatment involves asking, 'do I assent or not to the treatment proposed?'; a refusal of treatment involves the question 'do I refuse all treatment, understanding all the consequences which ensue from that decision?' They draw from this analysis that:

> it does not necessarily follow from the fact that a child has capacity to consent (and/ or capacity to decline consent) to certain specific treatment, X, that he or she will have capacity to refuse all treatment...the child considering whether or not to consent will not necessarily have addressed the 'refusal of treatment' question (not least because he or she may only have been told by the doctor about the proposed treatment). In a case in which the child has capacity to consent to X but does not fully understand the consequences of a total failure to treat, parental responsibility to consent is not fully extinguished by the child's capacity and it is necessary for a parent to have the power to consent to treatment, including, if necessary, treatment X.[169]

4.5 THE SO-CALLED 'RETREAT FROM *GILLICK*'

A popular, if not dominant, characterisation of the case law amongst academic lawyers, arising from the radical children's autonomy rights interpretation of *Gillick* and harsh

---

[165] [1993] Fam 64 at 88B–C.

[166] See discussion in S. Gilmore and J. Herring, '"No" is the Hardest Word: Consent and Children's Autonomy' [2011] Child and Family Law Quarterly 3.

[167] Ibid; and see also S. Gilmore and J. Herring, 'Children's Refusal of Medical Treatment: Could *Re W* be Distinguished?' [2011] Family Law 715.

[168] S. Gilmore and J. Herring, 'Children's Refusal of Medical Treatment: Could *Re W* be Distinguished?' [2011] Family Law 715. For criticism of these arguments see E. Cave and J. Wallbank, 'Minors' Capacity to Refuse Treatment: A Reply to Gilmore and Herring' [2012] Medical Law Review, arguing *inter alia* that the distinctions made by Gilmore and Herring are not workable in clinical practice since from 'a clinician's point of view, competence cannot always be judged in relation to specific treatment, but instead must relate to the decision'. For a response, see S. Gilmore and J. Herring, 'Children's Refusal of Treatment: The Debate Continues' [2012] Fam Law 973.

[169] Ibid, 716. They go on to argue that *Re W* might be distinguished in a future case of a fully competent child on the basis that the girl in *Re W* was only shown to have capacity to consent and not to refuse all treatment.

criticism of the post-*Gillick* cases, *Re R* and *Re W*, is that the *Gillick* case represented a high-water mark for children's autonomy rights, from which there has since been a recession.[170] However, as should be apparent from the foregoing account of the case law, whether or not there has been a retreat from *Gillick* rather depends upon one's interpretation of that case. The existence of a retreat from *Gillick* is complicated by two further factors. First, Lord Donaldson indicates explicitly on at least two occasions that his reasoning in *Re W* on the conflict between parent and minor is *obiter*.[171] Secondly, since *Gillick* only dealt with the issue of consent to medical treatment, it was perfectly permissible to distinguish *Gillick* on its facts and formulate a different rule in relation to refusal of consent. It is pertinent to recall the words of Lord Scarman himself in *Gillick* that the case was 'the beginning, not the conclusion, of a legal development in a field glimpsed by one or two judges in recent times ... but not yet fully explored'.[172] It should not be overlooked that the decision in *Gillick* in part *acquires* its meaning from its application in *Re R* and *Re W*. Thus, as Hamilton has commented, it may be:

> incorrect to view *Re W* as a great step backwards in children's rights or as an emasculation of the *Gillick* principle; rather it constitutes a recognition that the autonomy granted in *Gillick* only applies to cases where a decision does not cause irreversible damage to health.[173]

These arguments reveal a rather complex picture concerning the existence, nature, and extent of any so-called retreat from *Gillick*.

4.6 WILL A CHILD EVER BE CONSIDERED SUFFICIENTLY COMPETENT TO REFUSE LIFE-SAVING TREATMENT?

In *Re E (A Minor) (Wardship: Medical Treatment)*[174] a boy, A, who was a few months short of his 16th birthday, was being treated in hospital for leukaemia. He and his parents were Jehovah's Witnesses and for religious reasons they refused consent to the use of any blood transfusions. The replacement blood products were needed to replenish A's blood cells which were diminishing as a result of the drugs that were being administered to him. If the hospital continued to treat without transfusions A's prospects of remission were much

---

[170] Found perhaps most explicitly in Douglas's oft-cited commentary on *Re R*, proclaiming in its title 'the retreat from *Gillick*', (G. Douglas, 'The Retreat from *Gillick*' (1992) 55 Modern Law Review 569) but see also J. Bridgeman, 'Old Enough to Know Best?' (1993) 13 Legal Studies 69 at 80 ('leaps and bounds away from the approach in *Gillick*'); S. Cretney and J. Masson, *Principles of Family Law* (London: Sweet & Maxwell, 1997), pp 593–595; M. Freeman, *The Moral Status of Children: Essays on the Rights of the Child* (The Hague: Martinus Nijhoff, 1997), p 345 ('a false dawn'); C. Lyon and P. de Cruz, *Child Abuse*, 2nd edn (Bristol: Family Law, 1993), p 379 ('the already very marked retreat from the principles of the *Gillick* decision'); J. Roche, 'Children's Rights: In the Name of the Child' [1995] Journal of Social Welfare and Family Law 281 at 282. It is a view which has spread unquestioned to other disciplines: see eg V. Bell, 'Governing Childhood: Neo-Liberalism and the Law' (1993) 22(3) Economy and Society 390 (sociology); C. Smith, 'Children's Rights: Judicial Ambivalence and Social Resistance' (1997) 11 International Journal of Law, Policy and the Family 103 at 110–120 (social work); D. Dickenson and D. Jones, 'True Wishes: The Philosophy and Developmental Psychology of Children's Informed Consent' (1995) 2(4) Philosophy, Psychiatry and Psychology 287 at 291 (psychology): 'it seems *clear* that the English courts, through case-law, are swinging towards care and protection' (emphasis added), although there is little if any analysis of *Gillick* in the paper; J. Pearce, 'Consent to Treatment During Childhood, The Assessment of Competence and Avoidance of Conflict' (1994) 165 British Journal of Psychiatry 713 at 714 (child psychiatry); J. Pilcher, 'Contrary to *Gillick*: British Children and Sexual Rights since 1985' (1997) 5 International Journal of Children's Rights 299 (sociology).

[171] [1993] Fam 64 at 79E: 'that is not this case'; and at 76D–E: 'but even that is not the issue before this court. That is whether *the court* has such a power'.   [172] [1986] 1 AC 112 at 176C.

[173] C. Hamilton, 'Editorial' (1993) 5(1) Journal of Child Law 1.   [174] [1993] 1 FLR 386.

diminished[175] and the state of his blood cells meant that there would be a risk within a day or so of a stroke or heart attack caused by internal bleeding. The hospital issued a summons in wardship seeking leave to treat A as appropriate, including with the transfusions. The application was granted by Ward J, who found that A was not of sufficient intelligence, understanding, and maturity to refuse. He commented:

> I find that A is a boy of sufficient intelligence to be able to take decisions about his own well-being, but I also find that there is a range of decisions of which some are outside his ability fully to grasp their implications. Impressed though I was by his obvious intelligence, by his calm discussion of the implications, by his assertion even that he would refuse well knowing that he may die as a result, in my judgment A does not have a full understanding of the whole implication of what the refusal of that treatment involves...
>
> I am quite satisfied that A does not have any sufficient comprehension of the pain he has yet to suffer, of the fear that he will be undergoing, of the distress not only occasioned by that fear but also—and importantly—the distress he will inevitably suffer as he, a loving son, helplessly watches his parents' and his family's distress. They are a close family, and they are a brave family, but I find that he has no realization of the full implications which lie before him as to the process of dying. He may have some concept of the fact that he will die, but as to the manner of his death and to the extent of his and his family's suffering I find he has not the ability to turn his mind to it nor the will to do so.[176]

Ward J added, however, that the child's competence to refuse is not the issue in wardship where the welfare of the child dominates the decision, and a judgement has to be taken objectively. He agreed that the court, 'exercising its prerogative of protection, should be very slow to allow an infant to martyr himself'. Ward J emphasised, however, that the child's wishes and feelings are an important factor in ascertaining the child's welfare and, having regard to the closeness of A's attaining 16, A's wishes and feelings were a very important matter, weighing very heavily in the scales.[177] But Ward J was also far from satisfied that at the age of 15 A's will was fully free,[178] and concluded that when balanced against the need for the chance to live a precious life, the decision to refuse transfusions was inimical to A's well-being.[179] However, despite the court's ruling, once A reached the age of 18, he exercised his right as an adult to refuse treatment and died.[180]

A similar case arose after the decisions in *Re R* and *Re W* in *Re S (A Minor) (Consent to Medical Treatment)*.[181] A 15½-year-old girl, S, had suffered since birth from the most serious form of thalassaemia.[182] Her treatment required monthly hospitalisation for blood transfusion and daily injections to her abdomen. Unlike *Re E*, therefore, this involved ongoing, long-term treatment rather than a one-off response to the development of an illness. When S was 10 years old, her mother began attending Jehovah's Witness meetings, although S's treatment continued with the consent of her father. When S was

---

[175] Forty per cent to 50 per cent rather than possibly a 70 per cent chance if transfusions were administered.   [176] [1993] 1 FLR 386 at 391.

[177] Ward J had rejected an argument based on s 8 of the Family Law Reform Act 1969 because A had not attained the age of 16. But the emphasis on the age of 16 here suggests that Ward J might have viewed s 8 as giving children aged 16 both the right to consent and refuse. As noted earlier in this chapter, however, that is a view not shared by the Court of Appeal in *Re W*.

[178] In that his volition had been 'conditioned by the very powerful expressions of faith to which all members of the creed adhere': see [1993] 1 FLR 386 at 393.   [179] [1993] 1 FLR 386 at 393.

[180] As reported by counsel, Mr Daniel, to Johnson J in a subsequent case *Re S (A Minor) (Consent to Medical Treatment)* [1994] 2 FLR 1065 at 1075.

[181] [1994] 2 FLR 1065.

[182] A condition in which the body cannot produce red blood cells which carry oxygen around the body, so transfusion is necessary for survival. There are also problems with extraction of iron from the body.

15, however, she failed to attend one of her monthly appointments, indicating that she now refused blood as an adherent to the Jehovah's Witness faith. The social services department became concerned for S's welfare and sought use of the inherent jurisdiction[183] to permit the treatment. By the time the application came before the court, S had missed two monthly appointments and there was a risk that she could die within weeks. Johnson J granted the application. He noted the strong emphasis that had to be given to S's wishes and feelings, as required by *Re W*, but found on the facts that S was not competent. She was confused as to the facts surrounding her illness; fed up with her treatment and thus susceptible to influence from her mother[184] and other Jehovah's Witnesses; and she did not fully understand the implications of her decision. In similar vein to Ward J in *Re E*, Johnson J commented:

> It seems to me that an understanding that she will die is not enough. For her decision to carry weight she should have a greater understanding of the manner of death and pain and the distress.[185]

In *Re L (Medical Treatment: Gillick Competence)*[186] a 14-year-old girl sustained severe scalds to over half of her body when she fell into a hot bath, possibly because she had had an epileptic fit. In order to survive, she required surgery, which had an 80 per cent chance of success. The operations would require blood transfusions but the girl, who was described as mature for her age, expressed a strong and sincere wish as a Jehovah's Witness not to have blood products. If she did not have the treatment, however, she would suffer a particularly horrible death: gangrene would supervene, followed by a very distressing time. The surgeon concerned did not feel that it was appropriate to explore in detail with her[187] the manner of her death. Sir Stephen Brown P found that the girl had led a sheltered life[187] and held that she was not *Gillick* competent in the context of all the necessary details which it would be appropriate for her to be able to form a view about. His Lordship had no hesitation in holding that it was in the girl's best interests to permit the operation and that that would have been the appropriate order even if she had been *Gillick* competent. Caroline Bridge is critical of the court's approach, commenting:

> The fact that she had not been told, by either her doctor or her family, of the distressing nature of her predicted death meant that L lacked vital information. Without it she could not properly understand her predicament and could not make a valid decision. She was, effectively, denied the ability to give informed consent. She was certainly denied an informed refusal. She was simply not informed about the risks (of gangrene, for example) yet an understanding of risk is integral to making a valid decision.[188]

---

[183] It is not clear from the decision how this was possible and why leave to apply for a specific issue order was not pursued. There is no indication that the child was in care: see the Children Act 1989, ss 9 and 100.

[184] Johnson J had cited *Re T (An Adult) (Consent to Medical Treatment)* [1993] Fam 95, where the Court of Appeal drew attention to two important outside influences on patient decision making: the strength of will of the patient and the relationship of the persuader to the patient (eg the influence of parents on their children).   [185] [1994] 2 FLR 1065 at 1076.

[186] [1998] 2 FLR 810. See C. Bridge, 'Religious Beliefs and Teenage Refusal of Medical Treatment' (1999) 62 Modern Law Review 585–594.

[187] Ibid, 813, although, as Bridge points out (ibid, 590), 'quite how a more robust and worldly upbringing could equip a 14 year old to make life and death decisions more soundly is difficult to imagine'. See also ibid, 589, where Bridge comments:

> the High Court is suggesting that the concept of *belief* is one which can only be properly arrived at with the passage of time, that it is akin to the development of cognitive functioning and the demands of maturity, rationality, intelligence and understanding. It is suggested here that belief is alien to these attributes. Its existence or otherwise should not form part of the assessment of adolescent competence.

[188] Ibid, 591.

In *Re M (Medical Treatment: Consent)*[189] a 15-year-old girl, M, suffered heart failure and was close to death unless she had a heart transplant. A few weeks earlier she had been a healthy active girl. While her mother consented, M refused to consent to the transplant. The hospital concerned sought authorisation to carry out the operation. Johnson J took great pains to ensure that the girl was represented at short notice. The Official Solicitor reported (following an interview with M) that she did not want someone else's heart as she would feel different, nor to take medication for the rest of her life. At the same time, however, she did not want to die. On this evidence the Official Solicitor submitted that while M was intelligent and her wishes should carry considerable weight, events had 'overtaken her so swiftly that she had not been able to come to terms with her situation'.[190] In those circumstances Johnson J held that making the order sought was in M's best interests.

In *Re P (Medical Treatment: Best Interests)*[191] a boy, John, aged 16 years 10 months, suffered from hypermobility syndrome, a condition in which blood vessels are fragile and susceptible to bleeding. He had been admitted to hospital with a suspected rupture of his aorta. He and his parents objected to any blood transfusion because of their religious beliefs as Jehovah's Witnesses. That crisis had passed and the hospital had not at that time sought to treat John with blood products because operating was felt to be too dangerous. However, the hospital sought leave to administer blood should John's situation should become immediately life-threatening in future, and if in the professional opinion of those treating John such treatment were needed. Johnson J made the order sought, with the additional proviso that blood would only be administered if no other treatment was possible. In passing Johnson J commented that:

> there may be cases as a child approaches the age of 18 when his refusal would be determinative. A court will have to consider whether to override the wishes of a child approaching the age of majority when the likelihood is that all that will have been achieved will have been deferment of an inevitable death and for a matter only of months.[192]

In addition, he acknowledged that in the case of a young man of nearly 17 with established convictions, there were weighty reasons why the order should not be made.[193] However, he concluded that John's best interests would be met by making the order, 'looking at the interests of John in the widest possible sense—medical, religious, social, whatever they be'.[194]

4.6.1 Comment

In none of the decisions discussed earlier was the child concerned permitted to refuse medical treatment. While many may agree with the outcomes in the cases, some of the reasoning by which the decisions were reached is susceptible to criticism. The courts have set the level of children's competence to refuse at a very high level. Arguably the standard is one that many adults would not fulfil if required to demonstrate it, and it has been suggested such a test is unfair to children.[195] Secondly, in some cases[196] children have been prevented in their own best interests from having all the necessary information to make an informed decision. This has allowed the court to sidestep the crucial issue of reconciling the child's welfare and autonomy interests. Thirdly, as Bridge has

---

[189] [1999] 2 FLR 1097. See R. Huxtable, '*Re M (Medical Treatment: Consent)* Time to Remove the "Flak Jacket"' [2000] Child and Family Law Quarterly 83.
[190] [1999] 2 FLR 1097 at 1100.   [191] [2003] EWHC 2327, [2004] 2 FLR 1117.
[192] Ibid, [9].   [193] Ibid, [11].   [194] Ibid, [12].
[195] D. Archard and M. Skivenes, 'Balancing a Child's Best Interests and a Child's Views' (2009) 17 International Journal of Children's Rights 1 at 10.   [196] *Re E* and *Re L*.

pointed out, the case law involving children's religious beliefs seems to suggest that 'the concept of *belief* is one which can only be properly arrived at with the passage of time, that it is akin to the development of cognitive functioning and the demands of maturity, rationality, intelligence and understanding'. Yet, as she points out, 'belief is alien to these attributes. Its existence or otherwise should not form part of the assessment of adolescent competence.'[197] A fourth criticism is that the courts examine the child's *Gillick* competence, yet then go on to declare that irrespective of that assessment the outcome is dictated by the child's best interests. Why adopt a functional test of capacity unless it is to be used? Or, perhaps there is some force in Bridge's point:

> that judges should not go through the pretence of applying a functional test of capacity when the outcome of the young person's decision is not one that they, or probably society, would countenance. The law should openly declare that welfare reigns when grave decisions with momentous outcomes are considered and recognise that adolescent autonomy is, inevitably, circumscribed.[198]

Finally, it is notable that in none of the cases are children's rights under the ECHR articulated, including those which were decided after 'incorporation' of Convention rights into English law by the Human Rights Act (HRA) 1998.

This brings us neatly to the final section of this chapter which examines the extent to which children's rights have been articulated and protected by the ECHR and the HRA 1998.[199]

5 CHILDREN AND THE EUROPEAN CONVENTION ON HUMAN RIGHTS

The ECHR protects all persons irrespective of age, so when Convention rights were directly protected in English law by the HRA 1998, clearly 'the notion of children being rights holders could no longer be treated by the courts merely as an abstract proposition'.[200] Section 6 of the HRA 1998 provides that it is unlawful for a court to act in a way which is incompatible with Convention rights. However, the ECHR was not designed to deal with some of the subtler human rights issues which emerge within family law and takes no account of the differences between adults and children. It lacks any guidance on reconciling children's and parents' interests; and it has a narrow focus on civil and political rights, omitting social and economic rights.[201] Jane Fortin also highlighted a danger that the Act might effect a change of legal principles in ways which might endanger rather than promote children's rights, for example through greater focus on adults' rights. Thus children's advisers would need to display ingenuity in interpreting the Convention to children's benefit.[202]

---

[197] C. Bridge 'Religious Beliefs and Teenage Refusal of Medical Treatment' (1999) 62 Modern Law Review 585 at 589.

[198] Ibid, 594. See also M. Brazier and C. Bridge, 'Coercion or Caring: Analyzing Adolescent Autonomy' (1996) 16(1) Legal Studies 84–109.

[199] See generally S. Choudhry and J. Herring, *European Human Rights and Family Law* (Oxford: Hart, 2010), esp ch 6; U. Kilkelly, *The Child and the European Convention on Human Rights* (Ashgate: Dartmouth, 1999).

[200] J. Fortin, 'The HRA's Impact on Litigation Involving Children and their Families' (1999) 11 Child and Family Law Quarterly 237 at 255.

[201] Ibid.

[202] J. Fortin, 'The HRA's Impact on Litigation Involving Children and their Families' (1999) 11 Child and Family Law Quarterly 237 at 241.

The Articles of the Convention perhaps most likely to be employed in family disputes are Article 2 (right to life), Article 3 (prohibition on inhuman or degrading treatment), Article 5 (right to liberty and security of person), Article 6 (right to a fair trial), and Article 8 (the right to respect for private and family life).[203] Their impact on the domestic law is discussed at appropriate points throughout this book.

In several academic articles since implementation of the HRA, Professor Fortin has examined the developing impact the Act has had on legal recognition of children's rights.[204] Her conclusion, like that of others too,[205] is that there has been a rather patchy recognition of children's Convention rights. In some areas, such as children's claims within the education system or in cases of young offenders' engagement with the youth justice system, there is a ready use of Convention rights. There have also been some notable uses of the Convention in cases in which children's freedoms are a focus for the court, or are obviously apparent from the issues. An example is provided by *Re Roddy (A Child) (Identification: Restrictions on Publication)*.[206] In that case a local authority had sought care proceedings in respect of a girl, Angela Roddy, who had become pregnant at the age of 12 by a boy, X, of a similar age. Her case came to public attention amidst controversy that the Catholic Church had allegedly paid her not to have an abortion. Angela's baby was also taken into care. The local authority obtained injunctions protecting from publication the identities of Angela and X. When she was aged 16 (and described as a mature and articulate young person), Angela applied to the court to have the injunction lifted to the extent that it would enable her to tell to the press her experiences of the care system. Munby J recognised that a child is as much entitled to the protection of the European Convention as anyone else[207] and that Angela had a right to freedom of expression within Article 10 of the ECHR and also that the right to respect for private life within Article 8 protected 'the right to share what would otherwise be private with others'.[208] Munby J concluded that Angela was 'of an age, and has sufficient understanding and maturity, to decide for herself whether that which is private, personal and intimate should remain private or whether it should be shared with the whole world'.[209] Referring to the judgments in *Re W*, Munby J commented:

> In my judgment (and I wish to emphasise this) it is the responsibility—it is the duty—of the court not merely to recognise but, as Nolan LJ said, to defend what, if I may respectfully say so, he correctly described as the right of the child who has sufficient understanding to make an informed decision, to make his or her own choice. This is not mere pragmatism, although as Nolan LJ pointed out, any other approach is likely to be both futile and counter-productive.

[203] These Articles are highlighted by Fortin, ibid, who discusses some of the issues in which they have arisen.

[204] J. Fortin, 'Children's Rights: Are the Courts Now Taking Them More Seriously?' (2004) 15 Kings College Law Journal 253; J. Fortin, 'Accommodating Children's Rights in a Post Human Rights Act Era' (2006) 69 Modern Law Review 299; J. Fortin, 'A Decade of the HRA and its Impact on Children's Rights' [2011] Family Law 176.

[205] See eg D. Bonner, H. Fenwick, and S. Harris-Short, 'Judicial Approaches to the Human Rights Act' (2003) 52(3) International Comparative Law Quarterly 549: 'In many cases "judicial reasoning under the Human Rights Act" is most conspicuous by its absence. The attitude of many members of the family bench and the higher appeal Courts when called upon to apply the Convention rights to family law matters has been cautious and defensive—even openly hostile'; and S. Harris-Short, 'Family Law and the Human Rights Act 1998: Judicial Restraint or Revolution' (2005) 17(3) Child and Family Law Quarterly 329.

[206] [2003] EWHC 2927 (Fam), [2004] 2 FLR 949. See also *Mabon v Mabon* [2005] 3 WLR 460 and see J. Fortin, 'Children's Representation Through the Looking Glass' [2007] Family Law 500.

[207] [2003] EWHC 2927 (Fam), [2004] 2 FLR 949 at [37].   [208] Ibid, [35] and [36].

[209] Ibid, [56].

It is also, as he said, a matter of principle. For, as Balcombe LJ recognised, the court must recognise the child's integrity as a human being. And we do not recognise Angela's dignity and integrity as a human being—we do not respect her rights under Arts 8 and 10—unless we acknowledge that it is for her to make her own choice, and not for her parents or a judge or any other public authority to seek to make the choice on her behalf.[210]

Another example is *R (Axon) v Secretary of State for Health*[211] discussed earlier in this chapter.

In the main, however, there has been rather limited engagement with the implications of the HRA 1998 in private law cases involving children. Section 1 of the Children Act 1989 provides that whenever a court determines a matter with respect to a child's upbringing, the child's welfare shall be the court's paramount (currently interpreted to mean the sole) consideration. As discussed in detail elsewhere in this book[212] there has been a failure to acknowledge the difference between the paramountcy principle (in which the child's welfare is the sole focus) and the requirements of the Convention (in which it is not, and the interests of others must also be considered). A notable exception to this blindness to the Convention in private law cases is the issue of a child's paternity, where the courts have been much more ready to articulate the various interests involved within Article 8.[213]

Children's rights under the Convention are seldom articulated in public law child protection cases too, where the focus has rather been on protection of parents' Article 8 rights against inappropriate state intervention in family life.[214]

Fortin suggests, convincingly, that the different approaches may in part be explained by procedural factors, and the judicial response may reflect the nature of the application.[215] In many children cases the issues are handled before the courts as disputes between parents, which risks ignoring or sidelining children's rights.[216] A striking example is *R (On the application of Williamson) v Secretary of State for Education and Employment*[217] in which parents who believed in the availability of corporal punishment in schools argued that the statutory ban on corporal punishment in schools[218] infringed their rights to religious freedom under Article 9 of the Convention. The argument was unsuccessful but, as Baroness Hale observed,[219] the case was clearly about children's rights yet there was a failure to put any case from the children's perspective.

6 CONCLUSION

The issue of children's rights raises many theoretical and practical debates. Particularly challenging issues are the extent to which English law does, and should, recognise a child's autonomy interest. As we have seen, the case law on these issues is not easy to navigate. The issues have been addressed by the courts in the context of children's medical treatment.

---

[210] Ibid, [57].   [211] [2006] EWHC 37 (Admin), [2006] 2 FLR 206.   [212] See Chapter 9.
[213] A point made by J. Fortin, 'Children's Rights: Are the Courts Now Taking Them More Seriously?' (2004) 15 King's College Law Journal 253 at 270. See Bodey J's decision in *Re T (Paternity: Ordering Blood Tests)* [2001] 2 FLR 1190, discussed in Chapter 7.
[214] See J. Masson, 'Protecting Children or Protecting Human Rights' (2010 unpublished paper presented at Staffordshire University), cited in J. Fortin, 'A Decade of the HRA and its Impact on Children's Rights' [2011] Family Law 176 at 179.   [215] See Fortin, ibid, 180.
[216] J. Fortin, 'Children's Rights: Are the Courts Now Taking Them More Seriously?' (2004) 15 Kings College Law Journal 253.   [217] [2005] UKHL 15, [2005] AC 246.
[218] Under the Education Act 1996, s 548.   [219] [2005] UKHL 15, [2005] AC 246 at [71].

Controversially, the courts have held that while a child can consent validly to medical treatment, his or her refusal of treatment might be overridden by parental consent.

This raises an important practical question: what might a '*Gillick* competent' child do when medical or psychiatric treatment is authorised by persons with parental responsibility, but without the child's consent? It is suggested that he or she would be best advised to seek leave to apply either for a specific issue order, or for a prohibited steps order, under section 8 of the Children Act 1989, or that he or she should seek leave to make an application for the exercise by the High Court of its inherent jurisdiction. Similarly, where the child concerned is younger and unable to initiate proceedings, a relative or other interested third party anxious about the child's predicament could seek leave to invoke the jurisdiction of the courts. Court involvement would act as a safeguard to detect whether those exercising parental responsibility for the child were abusing their powers and whether any decisions made were giving paramountcy to the interests of the child. The availability and use of section 8 orders in a wide range of matters concerning the care and upbringing of children, and the inherent jurisdiction of the High Court, are each discussed in the next chapter.

DISCUSSION QUESTIONS

1. To what extent has English law recognised a child's right to make his or her own decisions?

2. Has there been a retreat from *Gillick*?

3. Do you agree with Lord Donaldson's judgments in *Re R* and *Re W*? Should the law allow a competent child to refuse life-saving medical treatment? Why or why not?

FURTHER READING

ALDERSON, P., *Young Children's Rights*, 2nd edn (London: Jessica Kingsley, 2008)

ALSTON, P., PARKER, S., and SEYMOUR, J. (eds), *Children, Rights and the Law* (Oxford: Clarendon Press, 1992)

ARCHARD, D., *Children Rights and childhood* (London: Routledge, 2004)

BAINHAM, A., 'The Balance of Power in Family Decisions' (1986) 45(2) Cambridge Law Journal 262

BAINHAM, A., 'The Judge and the Competent Minor' (1992) 108 Law Quarterly Review 194

BRIDGEMAN, J., 'Old Enough to Know Best?' (1993) 13 Legal Studies 69

CAVE, E. and WALLBANK, J., 'Minors' Capacity to Refuse Treatment: A Reply to Gilmore and Herring' [2012] Medical Law Review

DOUGLAS, G., 'The Retreat from *Gillick*' (1992) 55 Modern Law Review 569

EEKELAAR, J., 'The Emergence of Children's Rights' (1986) 6 Oxford Journal of Legal Studies 161

EEKELAAR, J., 'White Coats or Flak Jackets? Doctors, Children and the Courts—Again' (1993) 109 LQR 182

FORTIN, J., *Children's Rights and the Developing Law*, 3rd edn (Cambridge: Cambridge University Press, 2009)

FORTIN, J., 'The *Gillick* Decision—Not Just A High-Water Mark' in S. Gilmore, J. Herring, and R. Probert (eds), *Landmark Cases in Family Law* (Oxford: Hart, 2011)

FRANKLIN, B. (ed), *The New Handbook of Children's Rights Comparative Policy and Practice* (London: Routledge, 2002)

FREEMAN, M. D. A., *The Rights and the Wrongs of Children* (London: Francis Pinter, 1983)

FREEMAN, M. D. A., *The Moral Status of Children: Essays on the Rights of the Child* (The Hague: Martinhus Nijhoff, 1997)

GILMORE, S., 'The Limits of Parental Responsibility' in R. Probert, S. Gilmore, and J. Herring, *Responsible Parents and Parental Responsibility* (Oxford: Hart, 2009)

GILMORE, S. and HERRING, J., '"No" is the Hardest Word: Consent and Children's Autonomy' [2011] Child and Family Law Quarterly 3

GILMORE, S. and HERRING, J., 'Children's Refusal of Treatment: The Debate Continues' [2012] Fam Law 973

LOWE, N. and JUSS, S., 'Medical Treatment—Pragmatism and the Search for Principle' (1993) 56 Modern Law Review 865

ROCHE, J., 'Children's Rights: In the Name of the Child' [1995] Journal of Social Welfare and Family Law 281

9

PRIVATE LAW DISPUTES AND ISSUES IN CHILDREN CASES

INTRODUCTION

As explained in Chapter 7, there may be several different persons with parental responsibility for a child and scope, therefore, on occasions for disagreement on matters concerning a child's upbringing. Disputes are perhaps most likely to occur on relationship breakdown, when heightened emotion and bitterness surrounding the break-up may make agreement difficult. The courts may then ultimately be charged with resolving the matter. They may be asked to decide, for example, with whom a child shall live, whether a parent and child should have contact, or some other specific issue, such as which school a child is to attend. In this chapter, we examine how the courts resolve such private disputes. Before examining the various orders at the courts' disposal and the courts' decisions in specific areas, it is convenient first to set out some general principles for deciding children cases which are contained in section 1 of the Children Act 1989.

1 THE COURTS' FOCUS ON CHILD WELFARE: BACKGROUND

In deciding matters with respect to a child's upbringing the courts look to the welfare of the child concerned. The Court of Chancery introduced the child's interests as a justification for awarding care of a child to the child's mother in cases of dispute with the father.[1] A similar approach emerged in statute[2] and eventually, by section 1 of the Guardianship of Infants Act 1925, the child's welfare became the 'first and paramount' consideration in such cases. That provision, which meant that the parents' 'legal claims were to be ignored and the child's welfare was to prevail',[3] remained the law for many decades, being later

---

[1] See eg *De Manneville v De Manneville* (1804) 10 Ves 54 and *Wellesley v Duke of Beaufort* (1827) 2 Russ Rep 1. By the early 1890s, the child's welfare had become the 'dominant matter' in such determinations. See *R v Gyngall* [1893] 2 QB 232 and *Re McGrath* [1893] 1 Ch 143. For a general review of the emergence of the welfare principle see J. C. Hall, 'The Waning of Parental Rights' (1972) 31 Cambridge Law 248–265.

[2] The Guardianship of Infants Act 1886 provided that the child's welfare was to be a consideration for the court in custody disputes between parents.

[3] [2006] 2 FLR 629 at 638, at [27] *per* Baroness Hale of Richmond.

consolidated with minor changes of terminology in section 1 of the Guardianship of Minors Act 1971. The ascendancy of child welfare in court decision making thus emerged as a by-product of a struggle to equalise the legal position of mothers and fathers. To this day, however, the paramountcy of the child's welfare remains the golden thread that runs through court decision making in children cases. It is now found in section 1 of the Children Act 1989.

1.1 DECISION-MAKING PRINCIPLES IN SECTION 1 OF THE CHILDREN ACT 1989

1.1.1 The paramountcy principle

Key legislation

Section 1(1) of the Children Act 1989 provides:

When a court determines any question with respect to

(a) the upbringing of a child; or

(b) the administration of the child's property or the application of any income arising from it,

the child's welfare shall be the court's paramount consideration.

The general approach in section 1(1) is supplemented by further provisions in subsections (2)–(5). Before examining how the courts have interpreted and applied the paramountcy principle, it is convenient first to set out the scope of application of the paramountcy principle and the supplementary principles in section 1.

1.1.2 When does the paramountcy principle apply?

1.1.2.1 Any proceedings

Section 1(1) applies to *any* relevant court determinations,[4] in all proceedings where the requirements of the subsection are fulfilled, for example the exercise of the High Court's inherent jurisdiction in matters with respect to a child's upbringing.

1.1.2.2 Upbringing or administration of child's property

However, it is necessary in each case to ask whether the question is with respect to the administration of the child's property or to the child's upbringing.[5] Upbringing is defined in section 105 of the Children Act 1989 to include 'the care of the child but not his maintenance', but is otherwise left to the courts to interpret. In *Re Z (A Minor) (Freedom of Publication)*[6] Ward LJ acknowledged that it 'is not always easy to decide when a question of upbringing is being determined',[7] but explained that it is 'one which relates to how the child is being reared'.[8] In *Re X (A Child) (Injunctions Restraining Publication)*[9] Bracewell J added that:

The words 'reared' and 'upbringing' carry a meaning of the bringing up, care for, treatment, education, and instruction of the child by its parents or by those who are substitute

---

[4] Compare s 1(5) of the Children Act 1989, discussed in Section 1.4.

[5] The courts have not always done so explicitly: an example is the issue of a child's name, which has been assumed to be a matter with respect to the child's upbringing.   [6] [1997] Fam 1.

[7] See [1997] Fam 1 at 28.   [8] Ibid, 29.   [9] [2001] 1 FCR 541.

parents. It involves a process where the parent is the subject and the child is the object, so that s 1(1) of the 1989 Act applies only to those actions of which the child is the object and not to those in which the child is the subject.[10]

1.1.2.3 Child's welfare must be directly in issue

The child's welfare is paramount only if the child's upbringing falls to be 'decided as a matter directly in issue'.[11] As Ward LJ explained in Re Z (in the previous section), the child's upbringing must be the 'central issue'. For example, as explained in Chapter 7, it has been held that the paramountcy principle does not apply to the question whether scientific tests should be directed to determine paternity, since the interests of justice as well as the child's welfare are engaged on such applications.[12] Similarly, a child's welfare is not directly in issue where the question is whether the child's allegedly violent parent should be 'ousted' from the family home.[13]

1.1.2.4 Paramountcy must not be impliedly or expressly excluded by other provisions

The last example illustrates that the paramountcy principle also does not apply where another statutory provision expressly or impliedly excludes its operation. The aim of Part IV of the Family Law Act 1996 is to provide a comprehensive scheme for regulating occupation of the family home in cases of domestic violence, and the statute sets out specific criteria that must be applied in such cases. The implication is that Parliament intended those specific criteria to apply rather than the paramountcy principle. Similarly, it has been held that the paramountcy principle does not apply to Part III of the Children Act 1989, and in particular to a local authority's application to place a child in secure accommodation pursuant section 25 of the Act.[14] One of the grounds upon which a child can be so accommodated is that he is likely to injure other persons if he is kept in any other description of accommodation.[15] This requirement to consider danger to others is clearly incompatible with treating the child's welfare as paramount.[16]

Sometimes statutory provisions are explicit that the paramountcy principle does not apply (eg where the court is making orders for a child's maintenance),[17] or a statute may explicitly adopt a different emphasis on child welfare: for example, when making financial provision and property adjustment ancillary to divorce, a court must give *first* (not paramount) consideration to the welfare whilst a minor of any child of the family.[18]

---

[10] Ibid, 546, respectfully agreeing with what she described as the careful analysis by Munby J in *Kelly v BBC* [2001] 1 All ER 323 at 348 et seq.

[11] *Richards v Richards* [1984] AC 174 at 203, [1983] 2 All ER 807 at 815 (Lord Hailsham of St Marylebone LC).

[12] *S v S; W v Official Solicitor* [1970] 3 All ER 107.

[13] *Richards v Richards* [1984] AC 174, a decision under previous legislation, the Matrimonial Homes Act 1983. The relevant legislation is now in the Family Law Act 1996, Pt IV. See Chapter 3.

[14] *Re M (A Minor) (Secure Accommodation Order)* [1995] Fam 108.

[15] Children Act 1989, s 25(1)(b).

[16] *Re M (A Minor) (Secure Accommodation Order)* [1995] Fam 108, *per* Butler-Sloss LJ, Hoffmann LJ agreeing. Hoffmann LJ added a further reason: s 25 was derived from the Child Care Act 1980 which did not have a provision equivalent to s 1(1) of the Children Act 1989. The court also held that application of s 1(5) of the Children Act 1989 is incompatible with the duty in s 25 to make an order if the criteria are fulfilled. See Section 1.4 for discussion of s 1(5).

[17] The definition of upbringing in s 1 does not include the child's maintenance: see the Children Act 1989, s 105(1).   [18] Matrimonial Causes Act 1973, s 25(1).

1.1.2.5 Cases involving the welfare of more than one child

In a case involving more than one child the court will need to consider, as a matter of statutory construction, which child's upbringing is the one with respect to which the court is determining a question.[19] In *Birmingham City Council v H (A Minor)*[20] a 14-year-old girl, M, gave birth to a little boy, R. M, who had a history of absconding and volatile behaviour and was considered to be beyond parental control, was in secure accommodation. There was evidence that M's care of R had been inadequate and that she had on occasions treated him roughly. Connell J granted the local authority care orders in respect of both M and R. Within the care proceedings, M applied under section 34(3) of the Children Act 1989 for contact with her baby, and the local authority applied under section 34(4) for permission to refuse M contact with R. The evidence suggested that M might harm herself if she were prevented from having contact with her baby. However, there was also some evidence that contact might present a risk of physical harm to R, and if contact were to take place in secure accommodation, as proposed, it could prove distressing to both the child and mother. Connell J held that R's welfare (and not M's) was paramount on these applications and granted the council permission to refuse contact. On M's appeal, the Court of Appeal set aside Connell J's order.[21] The Court of Appeal explained that the approach to contact is a matter of substantive law and should not depend upon the fact that procedurally M's application was made under section 34(3) in R's care proceedings rather than under section 34(2) in M's care proceedings. As it was impossible to treat the upbringing of both children as paramount, the issue of contact required a weighing in the balance of the respective interests of M and R.[22] Applying that approach the court concluded that contact would be positively beneficial to M and, provided it was adequately monitored, should not be detrimental to R.[23]

On the local authority's appeal, the House of Lords unanimously held that the Court of Appeal had erred in law and restored Connell J's order. Lord Slynn, delivering the leading opinion, found the solution in the appeal through an analysis of the structure of section 34. His Lordship held that in the applications under section 34(3) and (4) R's welfare was paramount, and when the court had decided that it was appropriate to authorise the local authority to refuse contact, there could be no value in making an order under subsection (2) allowing contact between M (as a child, and whose welfare would be paramount) and a named person, her son R.[24] As Douglas points out, however, this is unconvincing since 'one could equally put things the other way round. If the mother had applied, as a child in care under section 34(2), and it had been decided that she should be allowed to have contact with her son, there would have been no point in making a refusal order under section 34(4).'[25] As Thornton observes, 'to point out that only one of

---

[19] In the draft Bill suggested by the Law Commission in its Report No 172 (1988), prior to the enactment of the 1989 Act, it was provided that, when determining any question under the Act, the welfare of 'any child likely to be affected' should be the court's only concern. That provision was not adopted by Parliament.

[20] [1994] 2 AC 212.   [21] [1993] 1 FLR 883, CA.

[22] The courts have subsequently acknowledged that in some exceptional cases, such as a decision to separate conjoined twins to preserve the life of one, there may be no alternative but to weigh the children's respective interests: see *Re A (Children) (Conjoined Twins: Surgical Separation)* [2001] Fam 147.

[23] [1993] 1 FLR 883, 894.

[24] A rather puzzling aspect of Lord Slynn's reasoning is the suggestion that such an order could be made in the family proceedings in question. The family proceedings in which the applications under s 34(3) and (4) were made were the proceedings under Pt IV of the Children Act 1989 in respect of R. In those family proceedings, where the child concerned is R, it is submitted that the word 'child' in s 34(2) would refer to R, not M.

[25] G. Douglas, 'In Whose Best Interests?' (1994) LQR 379 at 381.

two contradictory orders should be made does not answer the question of the basis upon which the court is to choose between them'.[26] It is submitted that overall this decision was a disappointing response to the problems raised in the appeal. The House failed to seize the opportunity to deliver a judgment of principle on how the courts should deal with cases involving children's conflicting interests.[27] However, the *Birmingham* case has been interpreted as putting in place a general approach to construction where the welfare of two children is implicated in a case.[28]

1.2 SECTION 1(2): 'DELAY LIKELY TO PREJUDICE THE CHILD'S WELFARE'

Key legislation

Section 1(2) of the Children Act 1989 recognises the harm that delay in deciding a child's case can potentially cause to the child. It provides:

In any proceedings in which any question with respect to the upbringing of a child arises, the court shall have regard to the general principle that any delay in determining the question is likely to prejudice the welfare of the child.

The courts recognise, however, that a planned and purposeful delay may be warranted if it will ultimately achieve an outcome in the child's welfare. For example, more time may be required for an investigation to be completed[29] or to produce a report for the court[30] so that the court can take a fully informed decision.

1.3 SECTION 1(3): THE WELFARE CHECKLIST

Within the confines of section 1(1), the court is given a very wide discretion when deciding children's cases. The Children Act 1989 provides, in section 1(3)(a)–(g), a checklist of factors, most of which were derived from earlier case law and are widely accepted to be relevant to the promotion of a child's welfare, in order to exercise some control and structure over decision making, designed to achieve balanced decisions after the court has consciously weighed all the factors which it ought to take into account. As Baroness Hale explained in *Re G (Children) (Residence: Same-Sex Partner)*, 'in any difficult or finely balanced case...it is a great help to address each of the factors in the list, along with any others which may be relevant, so as to ensure that no particular feature of the case is given more weight than it should properly bear'.[31]

---

[26] R. Thornton, 'Children and Children's Children: Whose Welfare is Paramount?' [1994] Cambridge Law Journal 41 at 43.

[27] G. Douglas, 'In Whose Best Interests?' (1994) LQR 379 at 382.

[28] See in relation to siblings *Re S (Contact: Application by Sibling)* [1998] 2 FLR 897, FD (Charles J), *Re F (Contact: Child in Care)* [1995] 1 FLR 510, FD (Wilson J), and *Re T and E (Proceedings: Conflicting Interests)* [1995] 1 FLR 581, FD (Wall J); and see *F v Leeds City Council* [1994] 2 FLR 60 at 63 (applied to the Children Act 1989, s 31).

[29] *C v Solihull MBC* [1993] 1 FLR 290 and see also *Hounslow LBC v A* [1993] 1 FLR 702 (delay required to complete local authority investigations).   [30] See *Re W (Welfare Reports)* [1995] 2 FLR 142, CA.

[31] [2006] UKHL 43, [2006] 4 All ER 241 at [40].

Key legislation

Section 1(3) provides:

In the circumstances mentioned in subsection (4), a court shall have regard in particular to—

(a) the ascertainable wishes and feelings of the child concerned (considered in the light of his age and understanding);

(b) his physical, emotional and educational needs;

(c) the likely effect on him of any change in his circumstances;

(d) his age, sex, background and any characteristics of his which the court considers relevant;

(e) any harm which he has suffered or is at risk of suffering;

(f) how capable each of his parents, and any other person in relation to whom the court considers the question to be relevant, is of meeting his needs;

(g) the range of powers available to the court under this Act in the proceedings in question.

Section 1(4) indicates that the checklist *must* be considered where a court is considering whether to make, vary, or discharge an order under section 8 of the Children Act 1989, and the making, variation, or discharge is opposed by any party to the proceedings. It must also be applied where the court is considering whether to make, vary, or discharge a special guardianship order[32] or an order under Part IV of the Act (ie, a care order or supervision order).[33]

Where all, or most, of the factors in the checklist point in one direction, the decision on what will best promote the child's welfare may be relatively straightforward, and indeed a court ruling is unlikely to be necessary. However, the complexity of children cases often means that the matters listed in the checklist pull in different directions. For example, the child's age may point to an order being made that she should live with her mother rather than an older relative but there may be evidence to suggest that the mother might cause the child to suffer harm. The court must then determine whether the factor specified in paragraph (d) should be given greater weight than the factor specified in paragraph (e) and in this it must be guided by the factors in the other paragraphs, which again are likely to conflict and to point to different outcomes. Thus, opinion evidence may have been given that the child is likely to be badly affected by a change in her circumstances, which raises the considerations in paragraphs (b) and (c), but that if she were to remain with the mother it is unlikely that the mother could meet some of her needs, which raises paragraph (f).

1.4 NO ORDER UNLESS BETTER FOR THE CHILD

Key legislation

Section 1(5) of the Children Act 1989 provides:

Where a court is considering whether or not to make one or more orders under this Act with respect to a child, it shall not make the order or any of the orders unless it considers that doing so would be better for the child than making no order at all.

---

[32] See Chapter 11.   [33] See Chapter 10.

Unlike the paramountcy principle, section 1(5) applies only when the court is making an order under the Children Act 1989. In *K v H (Child Maintenance)*[34] Sir Stephen Brown P held that section 1(1) sets the scene for the rest of section 1, and that section 1(5) is principally directed to orders relating to the upbringing of a child, the administration of a child's property, or the application of any income arising from it. His Lordship held therefore that section 1(5) does not apply to applications for financial provision for children under Schedule 1 to the Children Act 1989, since section 1(1) does not apply to such applications.

Section 1(5) derives from a recommendation of the Law Commission in its Report *Guardianship and Custody*.[35] The Commission was concerned about the practice prior to the Children Act 1989 whereby court orders were used in almost all divorce cases involving children.[36] The relationship between parents and children was formalised and characterised in legal language without much thought as to whether this was either desirable in the interests of children or wanted by their parents.[37] The courts' approach could be perceived by some as unnecessarily intrusive when parents were able to agree. Section 1(5) thus encapsulates the idea that court orders are designed to achieve a purpose and should not be granted automatically and without thought as to their consequences, but only where the court is satisfied that the order will improve matters for the child.

As the section puts it, the law's concern is to identify those cases where the proposed order will be better for the child than making no order. Sometimes section 1(5) has loosely been termed the 'no order principle', which risks associating the principle unduly with the idea of 'non-intervention'. As Andrew Bainham has observed, and as acknowledged in case law, the principle is more accurately paraphrased as the 'no *unnecessary* order principle'.[38] Munby J commented in *Re X and Y*[39] that section 1(5) at least 'requires that the court ought not to make unnecessary orders', for example 'if the parties can reach agreement between themselves'.[40] Many parents are able to make arrangements about their children, sometimes without assistance. Professional help may be useful in those cases where the parents initially cannot agree. Even where acceptable arrangements prove difficult to negotiate, a court order may not be necessary, although it may be advisable for the lawyers to incorporate the arrangements in a written agreement.

However, it does not follow that in every case in which a negotiated agreement is achieved an order will be unnecessary. To defer automatically to agreements would mean that the welfare principle had been 'hi-jacked by non-interventionism'[41] and, of course, some agreements may not promote a child's welfare.[42] As the Law Commission commented: 'in many, possibly most, uncontested cases an order is needed in the children's own interests, so as to confirm and give stability to the existing arrangements, to clarify the respective roles of the parents, to reassure the parent with whom the children will be living, and even to reassure the public authorities responsible for housing and income support that such arrangements

---

[34] [1993] 2 FLR 61.   [35] Law Com No 172 (1988).

[36] See further J. Priest and J. Whybrow, *Custody Law in Practice in the Divorce and Domestic Courts*, supplement to Law Com WP No 96 (1986).

[37] In court the following dialogue would be typical: 'The children are living with you Mrs Smith?' 'Yes.' 'They see their father regularly?' 'Yes.' 'You have no objection to Mr Smith having reasonable access to them?' 'No.' 'The court orders custody, care and control to Mrs Smith and reasonable access to Mr Smith.'

[38] A. Bainham, 'Changing Families and Changing Concepts' (1998) Child and Family Law Quarterly 1.

[39] [2001] 2 FCR 398.

[40] Ibid, 417, citing by way of example the decision of Millett LJ in *Re T (Adoption: Contact)* [1995] 2 FLR 251 at 257–258.

[41] A. Bainham, 'The Privatisation of the Public Interest in Children' (1990) 53 Modern Law Review 206.

[42] See J. Craig, 'Everybody's Business: Applications for Contact Orders by Consent' [2007] Family Law 26.

have been made'.[43] In *Re G (Children)*[44] after protracted and difficult negotiations an agreement was struck whereby the father would receive his parental responsibility by consent in return for his agreeing that the mother should have the security of a residence order made in her favour in respect of the children. The District Judge, however, refused counsel's invitation to make the orders by consent. The judge took the view that section 1(5) dictated that there was a presumption against making an order and, as there was no longer any dispute about the matter, there was no good reason to upset that presumption. Allowing the mother's appeal, the Court of Appeal commented that the subsection:

> is perfectly clear. It does not…create a presumption one way or another. All it demands is that before the court makes any order it must ask the question: will it be better for the child to make the order than make no order at all? The section itself gives the test to be applied and the question to be asked. If judges in each case do just that then they cannot go wrong, it being axiomatic that every case is different, and each case will depend upon its own peculiar facts.[45]

The court identified three reasons why in this case the order should have been made: (i) in providing peace of mind to the mother it was an important factor producing stability in the children's lives; (ii) it was advantageous to the children in dissipating bitterness and mistrust between the parents; and (iii) in a case where an agreement has been carefully negotiated a court should not be astute to go behind it; the court should have paid respect to the parents' views that an order would be beneficial to the management of the children's lives.

Section 1(5) has also been treated, particularly in the context of public law proceedings, as establishing the principle that the court should proceed from a 'non-interventionist' or 'least interventionist' approach.[46] In such cases section 1(5) may also have the desirable effect of promoting considered forward planning for children, in that persons seeking an order must normally explain to the court why an order is needed and what they will do with the order if it is granted. It will be seen in the following that courts may not make certain orders once a child has been placed in the care of a local authority. Hence, there may be all the more reason for a court to be satisfied, at the outset, that an order which vests major decision-making powers in a local authority will be better for the child than making no order at all.

2 THE MEANING OF 'PARAMOUNTCY'

Key case

The leading case on the meaning of the paramountcy principle is *J and Another v C and Others*.[47] The issue was whether a boy should be returned to the care of his natural parents in Spain or whether he should remain with his English foster parents with whom he had spent

---

[43] Law Com No 172 (1988), para 3.2. See eg *B v B (A Minor) (Residence Order)* [1992] 2 FLR 327 (appropriate to make a residence order in favour of a grandmother so that, amongst other matters, she had authority to consent to her grandchild going on school trips).   [44] [2005] EWCA Civ 1283, [2006] 1 FLR 771.

[45] Ibid, 774.

[46] See Law Com No 172 (1988), para 3.4. See also *B v B (A Minor) (Residence Order)* [1992] 2 FLR 327 at 328B 'state shall not intervene in the life of children and their families unless it is necessary to do so'; *Re DH (A Minor) (Child Abuse)* [1994] 1 FLR 679 at 707F *per* Wall J: courts where possible should 'seek to withdraw the shadow of litigation from parties' lives'; *Re O (Care or Supervision Order)* [1996] 2 FLR 755 at 760A *per* Hale J; see also *Oxfordshire County Council v L (Care or Supervision Order)* [1998] 1 FLR 70 at 74E: 'the less Draconian order was likely to be better for the child than the more Draconian or interventionist one.'

[47] [1970] AC 668. See N. Lowe, '*J v C*: Placing The Child's Welfare Centre Stage' in S. Gilmore, J. Herring, and R. Probert (eds), *Landmark Cases in Family Law* (Oxford: Hart, 2011), ch 3.

most of his childhood. The Spanish parents had come to England to improve their financial position. The families met when shortly after the child's birth the mother was found to be suffering from tuberculosis, and the foster parents looked after the child until the mother's discharge from hospital. The parents then returned with the child to Spain. However, they were living on low wages 'in what were virtually slum conditions'[48] and in the summer heat of Madrid the child's health rapidly deteriorated. At the parents' request, therefore, the child returned to England to stay with the foster parents. The parents were happy for this arrangement to continue while they sought to improve their financial position. They became concerned, however, when they received a tactless letter from the foster mother. This described how the boy (then 5 years old) had integrated with the foster family, had grown up as an English boy, and how it would be most disturbing for him to have to return to Madrid. The parents requested the child's return and Surrey County Council, in whose official care the child was, applied to have him made a ward of court. Ungoed-Thomas J, applying the child's welfare as the first and paramount consideration under section 1 of the Guardianship of Infants Act 1925, confirmed the wardship and committed the child's care to the foster parents. An appeal to the Court of Appeal was dismissed and the parents appealed to the House of Lords. There were considerable delays at each stage of the proceedings and by the time the case came before the House of Lords the child was 10½ years old. He had not seen his parents since he was 3 years old and had spent all but 27 months of his life with the foster parents. The parents were now living in suitable modern accommodation and their financial position was much improved.

Dismissing the parents' appeal, the House clarified that the paramountcy principle was not confined to custody disputes as between parents,[49] and applied equally to a dispute between unimpeachable parents and a third party.[50]

Lord MacDermott (with whom Lord Pearson expressly agreed) explained that the words 'shall regard the welfare of the infant as the first and paramount consideration':

> mean more than that the child's welfare is to be treated as the top item in a list of items relevant to the matter in question. I think they connote a process whereby, when all the relevant facts, relationships, claims and wishes of parents, risks, choices and other circumstances are taken into account and weighed, the course to be followed will be that which is most in the interests of the child's welfare as that term has now to be understood. That is the first consideration because it is of first importance and the paramount consideration because it rules upon or determines the course to be followed.[51]

As the facts of *J v C*[52] illustrate, the principle that the child's welfare must be the court's paramount consideration sometimes exists uneasily alongside the idea that it is parents (usually) who enjoy parental responsibility and the right to bring up their own children. That social norm and the welfare principle may sometimes pull in different directions.

---

[48] [1970] AC 668 at 690.

[49] As suggested by the second limb of the section and by the preamble to the Act, which referred to equality between the sexes:

> Whereas Parliament by the Sex Disqualification (Removal) Act, 1919, and various other enactments, has sought to establish equality in law between the sexes, and it is expedient that this principle should obtain with respect to the guardianship of infants and the rights and responsibilities conferred thereby.

Disapproving *Re Carroll* [1931] 1 KB 317.

[50] [1970] AC 668, at 692 *per* Lord Guest and at 702 *per* Lord MacDermott.   [51] Ibid, 710–711.

[52] [1970] AC 668.

In *J v C* the House of Lords rejected the proposition that there was any presumption in favour of the natural parents of the child. Lord MacDermott put their position in this way:

In applying section 1, the rights and wishes of parents, whether unimpeachable or otherwise, must be assessed and weighed in their bearing on the welfare of the child in conjunction with all other factors relevant to that issue.

While there is now no rule of law that the rights and wishes of unimpeachable parents must prevail over other considerations, such rights and wishes, recognised as they are by nature and society, can be capable of ministering to the total welfare of the child in a special way, and must therefore preponderate in many cases...[53]

In *Re KD (A Minor) (Ward: Termination of Access)*[54] the House of Lords was invited to reconsider Lord MacDermott's approach in light of the European Court of Human Rights' recognition that contact between a child and parent is a fundamental element of family life protected by Article 8 of the European Convention on Human Rights (ECHR).[55] A local authority had applied to terminate contact between a mother and her son so that they could place him for adoption. The boy had been separated from his mother since he was nine months old, and at the date of the decision giving rise to the appeal he had been with foster parents for two and a half years. There was 'only the most shadowy possibility' of re-establishing the child with the mother.[56] The child had displayed signs of distress on access visits, and there was a risk that continued access would disturb the stability of his developing relationship with the foster parents. Granting the local authority's application, the judge concluded that contact provided no benefit to the boy and that he might suffer harm if it continued. On the mother's appeal, it was contended that the judge's exercise of discretion was flawed by an error in principle. Counsel submitted (based in part upon Article 8 of the ECHR) that a natural parent has a legal right to have contact with his or her child which must prevail where there is no positive evidence that contact will be damaging. It was said on the mother's behalf that the judge had merely concluded that the child *might* suffer harm, not that contact would be damaging. The House held that although the judge, in her use of the term 'might', had couched her findings in mild terms, her judgment effectively 'amounted to a finding that there was a present risk of harm from continued access'.[57] Since there had been a finding that continued contact was harmful, it was strictly unnecessary to express an opinion on counsel's primary contention regarding a parent's legal right of access. However, as the point had been fully argued, the House went on to consider, *obiter*, whether the welfare principle, as understood in *J v C*, applied to the termination of contact between a child and his parent or whether such an approach was inconsistent with Article 8 of the ECHR.

Lord Oliver, delivering an opinion with which the House unanimously agreed, could not discern any conflict between pronouncements of the European Court of Human Rights[58] and the principles laid down in *J v C*,[59] stating that:

Such conflict as exists is, I think, semantic only and lies in differing ways of giving expression to the single common concept that the natural bond and relationship between parent and child gives rise to universally recognised norms which ought not to be

---

[53] Ibid, 715. Lord MacDermott also quoted FitzGibbon LJ in the Irish case of *Re O'Hara* [1900] 2 IR 232 at 240:

In exercising the jurisdiction to control or to ignore the parental right the court must act cautiously, not as if it were a private person acting with regard to his own child, and acting in opposition to the parent only when judicially satisfied that the welfare of the child requires that the parental right should be suspended or superseded.

See also Lord Oliver of Aylmerton in *Re KD (A Minor) (Ward: Termination of Access)* [1988] AC 806 at 828.

[54] [1988] AC 806.

[55] Counsel cited in support *R v UK* (Case 6/1986/104/152), The Times, 9 July 1987.

[56] [1988] AC 806 at 829.   [57] Ibid, 820.

[58] In *R v UK* (Case 6/1986/104/152), The Times, 9 July 1987.   [59] [1970] AC 668.

gratuitously interfered with and which, if interfered with at all, ought to be so only if the welfare of the child dictates.

Lord Oliver could see nothing in the jurisprudence of the European Court which contradicted or cast doubt on that decision or calls for reappraisal of it. His Lordship considered the debate to be 'one without content',[60] explaining:

> If the child's welfare dictates that there be access, it adds nothing to say that the parent has also a right to have it subject to considerations of the child's welfare. If the child's welfare dictates that there should be no access, then it is equally fruitless to ask whether that is because there is no right to access or because the right is overborne by considerations of the child's welfare.[61]

That the court's focus is solely on the child's welfare in matters concerning a child's upbringing was emphasised by the House of Lords in *Re B (A Minor) (Wardship: Sterilisation)*.[62] There the House was called upon to decide whether a 17-year-old girl with 'very limited intellectual development'[63] should be sterilised. The girl, who had the mental capacity of a 6-year-old child,[64] was showing signs of sexual awareness and drive. However, she did not understand the relationship between sexual intercourse and pregnancy. Because her menstrual cycle was irregular there was a risk that any pregnancy would only be discovered after an abortion would be possible. It was likely that any pregnancy would require a Caesarean section delivery and subsequently it would be difficult to prevent her from opening up the wound, preventing healing of the post-operative scar. The girl displayed no maternal feelings and there was no prospect of her caring for a child. The only feasible alternative to sterilisation to prevent pregnancy was use of the progesterone pill, although its effectiveness was speculative.[65] The case had attracted media attention, with suggestions that it raised issues of eugenics and of sterilisation for social purposes. On behalf of the ward, counsel cited the decision of the Supreme Court of Canada in *In re Eve*[66] which had distinguished between sterilisation for 'therapeutic'[67] and 'non-therapeutic' purposes respectively, and had held that sterilisation should never be authorised for 'non-therapeutic' purposes. The House of Lords regarded this distinction as 'quite irrelevant to the correct application of the welfare principle'[68] which was the 'only consideration involved'.[69] As Lord Oliver of Aylmerton[70] explained:

> The primary and paramount consideration is only whether [measures taken] are for the welfare and benefit of this particular young woman situate as she is situate in this case.[71]

He went on to emphasise what the case was *not* about:

> this case is not about sterilization for social purposes; it is not about eugenics; it is not about the convenience of those whose task it is to care for the ward or the anxieties of her family; and it involves no general principle of public policy.[72]

---

[60] [1988] AC 806 at 827.   [61] Ibid, and see also *per* Lord Templeman to similar effect at 812.
[62] [1988] 1 AC 199.   [63] Ibid, 207.
[64] Ibid. Her ability to express herself was at the level of a 2-year-old.
[65] There were concerns about the ability to administer the pill every day, and its reaction with anticonvulsant drugs that she would also be taking.   [66] 31 DLR (4th) 1.
[67] In the sense of treatment of some malfunction or disease. See [1988] 1 AC 199 at 211.
[68] Ibid, at 204 *per* Lord Hailsham of St Marylebone LC, with whom Lord Bridge of Harwich, Lord Templeman, and Lord Brandon of Oakbrook agreed. Lord Oliver of Aylmerton described it as 'entirely immaterial': see [1988] 1 AC 199 at 211. See also Lord Bridge expressly at 205.
[69] Ibid, at 202 *per* Lord Hailsham LC.
[70] With whom Lord Bridge of Harwich, Lord Templeman, and Lord Brandon of Oakbrook expressly agreed.   [71] Ibid, 211.
[72] Ibid, 212.

Following the House of Lords' guidance in *J v C* and *Re KD*, there were several Court of Appeal cases which gave expression to the position of parents in the application of the paramountcy principle in different ways, some making reference to a 'parental right'[73] and others not.[74] As Waite LJ commented in *Re W (A Minor) (Residence Order)*,[75] those authorities illustrated:

> the difficulty of finding, within the infinite variety of circumstances in which the welfare of a child may fall to be applied as the paramount consideration, some principle which does precise justice to the element in every child's welfare represented by the advantage of maintaining the ties of nature with its own parent.

In *Re W* the Court of Appeal suggested that the law was 'best and most succinctly expressed' by Lord Donaldson of Lymington in *Re H (A Minor) (Custody: Interim Care and Control)*[76] when he indicated that by use of the term 'parental right', all that was meant was that the welfare principle was to be applied with 'a strong supposition that, other things being equal, it is in the interests of the child that it shall remain with its natural parents. But that has to give way to particular needs in particular situations.'[77]

An opportunity for the House of Lords to clarify the position arose in *Re G (Children) (Residence: Same-Sex Partner)*.[78] The parties, CG and CW, had lived together in a lesbian relationship for seven years. With a view to the couple having a family, CG had given birth to two girls conceived using sperm from an anonymous donor. The couple's relationship broke down, however, and there was a dispute concerning CW's contact with the girls. CW eventually obtained a shared residence order, although the order provided that the children's time was to be spent primarily in the mother's household. The mother had given evidence that she wished to relocate from her home in Leicester to Cornwall and, because of concern that the proposed move was in part designed to frustrate CW's contact, a condition of the mother's residence order was that she live in the Leicester area.[79] The mother defied this condition, relocating without telling CW, who had to issue applications under the Family Law Act 1986 to find the girls. Contact had been maintained since the children had been found. However, in light of this episode, CW applied for the residential arrangements to be changed so that the children's primary home would be with her. Bracewell J granted the application, reversing the times allocated to each home, because her Ladyship had no confidence that if CG remained the primary carer she would promote the children's close relationship with CW. The Court of Appeal dismissed the mother's appeal. However, a further appeal to the House of Lords was allowed. The case again raised the issue of principle of what weight is to be attached to the fact that one party, CG, was the natural and legal parent of the child and the other, CW, was not.

Baroness Hale delivered an opinion with which the rest of the Appellate Committee agreed. Her Ladyship set out the law in *J v C* and made brief reference to the principal Court of Appeal authorities, quoting in particular Lord Donaldson's formulation of the law in *Re H (A Minor) (Custody: Interim Care and Control)*.[80] Baroness Hale then said that the statutory position is plain, as expressed by Lord MacDermott in *J v C*: the welfare of the child 'rules upon or determines the course to be followed'; and she explained that there 'is no question of a parental right'.[81] She cited with approval the Law Commission's view in its

[73] Eg *Re K (A Minor) (Custody)* [1990] 2 FLR 64, CA.
[74] Eg *Re W (A Minor) (Residence Order)* [1993] 2 FCR 589, CA.   [75] [1993] 2 FLR 625 at 639.
[76] [1991] 2 FLR 109, CA.   [77] Ibid, 113.   [78] [2006] UKHL 43, [2006] 4 All ER 241.
[79] Such conditions are unusual. For further discussion, see Section 5.8.7.
[80] [1991] 2 FLR 109, CA.   [81] [2006] UKHL 43, [31].

Working Paper No 96,[82] which preceded the Children Act 1989, that: 'The welfare test itself is well able to encompass any special contribution which natural parents can make to the emotional needs of their child.'

Baroness Hale went on to say that none of this means that the fact of parentage is irrelevant.[83] She explained that the position in English law is akin to that in Australian law as explained by Lindenmayer J in *Hodak v Newman*:[84]

> the fact of parenthood is to be regarded as an important and significant factor in considering which proposals better advance the welfare of the child. Such fact does not, however, establish a presumption in favour of the natural parent, nor generate a preferential position in favour of the natural parent from which the court commences its decision making process.[85]

The House held that the Court of Appeal had allowed the unusual context of the case to distract them from these principles of universal application, and had failed to explore the important and significant factor that CG is the natural mother of the children in every sense of that term: genetic, gestational, and psychological.[86]

Lord Scott commented that 'mothers are special' and was unable to accept that the circumstances came even close to justifying the change of primary home from the mother to the partner.[87]

Lord Nicholls, in a speech with which Lord Rodger agreed, added that:

> In reaching its decision the court should always have in mind that in the ordinary way the rearing of a child by his or her biological parent can be expected to be in the child's best interests... I decry any tendency to diminish this factor. A child should not be removed from the primary care of his or her biological parents without compelling reason. Where such a reason exists the judge should spell this out explicitly.[88]

One might have thought that Baroness Hale's opinion in *Re G* would represent the last word on the meaning of the paramountcy principle. However, only three years later the Supreme Court was required to clarify the position in *Re B (A Child) (Residence)*,[89] in which Lord Nicholls' dictum appeared to have caused some confusion. The case concerned a boy, Harry, who was nearly 4 years old, who had lived with his maternal grandmother since birth because his parents had been incapable of caring for him in his early years. The father applied for a residence order in respect of Harry so that he could join the father's new family. In granting the grandmother a residence order with staying contact to both parents, the justices indicated that '*Re G*... stated that a child should not be removed from primary care of biological parents'. The Court of Appeal agreed with a judge's conclusion that the justices' decision was plainly wrong. However, the grandmother's appeal to the Supreme Court was allowed in a judgment of the whole court delivered by Lord Kerr. While the justices had misapprehended the real import of *Re G* they had nevertheless applied the child's welfare as paramount, carefully evaluating the evidence and weighing competing factors. The Supreme Court noted that the justices' misreading of *Re G* appeared to be an erroneous reliance upon Lord Nicholls's opinion and took the opportunity to clarify the opinions in *Re G*.

The Supreme Court indicated that the principal message from *Re G* was to give the final quietus to the notion that parental rights have any part to play in the assessment of where

---

[82] *Review of Child Law: Custody* (Law Com WP No 96, 1986), para 6.22.

[83] [2006] UKHL 43, [2006] 4 All ER 241 at [31].

[84] (1993) 16 Fam LR 1, approved by the Full Court of the Family Court of Australia in *Rice v Miller* (1993) 16 Fam LR 970 and *Re Evelyn* [1998] FamCA 55.   [85] [2006] UKHL 43, [2006] 4 All ER 241 at [27].

[86] Ibid, [44].   [87] Ibid, [3].   [88] Ibid, [2].   [89] [2009] UKSC 5.

the best interests of a child lay. If, and insofar as that required reaffirmation, the Supreme Court underscored the point again, stating:

> All consideration of the importance of parenthood in private law disputes about residence must be firmly rooted in an examination of what is in the child's best interests. This is the paramount consideration. It is only as a contributor to the child's welfare that parenthood assumes any significance. In common with all other factors bearing on what is in the best interests of the child, it must be examined for its potential to fulfil that aim.[90]

The child's welfare 'must be the dominant and overriding factor that ultimately determines disputes about residence and contact and there can be no dilution of its importance by reference to extraneous matters'.[91]

The court pointed out that Lord Nicholls had been careful to qualify his statement that 'the rearing of a child by his or her biological parent can be expected to be in the child's best interests' with the words 'in the ordinary way'. He did not propound any general rule to the effect that a child should not be removed from the primary care of biological parents.[92] His opinion was set firmly in the context of his acknowledgement that the child's welfare is paramount. Lord Nicholls 'was doing no more than reflecting common experience that, in general, children tend to thrive when brought up by parents to whom they have been born'. The Supreme Court added, however, that 'many disputes about residence and contact do not follow the ordinary way' and therefore 'although one should keep in mind the common experience to which Lord Nicholls was referring, one must not be slow to recognise those cases where that common experience does not provide a reliable guide'.[93]

So where does this leave the law? The decisions in *Re G* and *Re B* have confirmed that in applying section 1(1) of the Children Act 1989 the child's welfare is the court's sole consideration and that any whittling down of the protection that principle affords to children should not be entertained. A clear message has been given that attempts to emphasise a parent's position should avoid references to a 'parental right'. It is striking, however, that this view has been reached without any reference to the Human Rights Act (HRA) 1998 and consideration of parents' (and others') rights to respect for family life in Article 8 of the ECHR. As discussed later in this chapter, this is one in a line of cases interpreting and applying the paramountcy principle which do not really engage with the question whether treating the child's welfare as the sole consideration can survive the enactment of the HRA 1998.

It is a pity that Baroness Hale in *Re G* did not engage more fully with the Court of Appeal's case law. It will be recalled that her Ladyship neither expressly approved nor disapproved any of the Court of Appeal tests. This leaves rather unclear the status of the earlier Court of Appeal authorities and their consistency or otherwise with pronouncements in the House of Lords/Supreme Court. For example, it is rather unclear whether Lord Donaldson's view that there is a 'strong supposition that, other things being equal, it is in the interests of the child that it shall remain with its natural parents' survives *Re G*. This depends on whether it can be reconciled with Lindenmayer J's view in *Hodak v Newman* (cited with approval by Baroness Hale as reflecting English law) that the fact of parenthood does not 'generate a preferential position in favour of the natural parent from which the court commences its decision making process'. It is clear that Lindenmayer J saw a 'preferential position' as

---

[90] Ibid, [37].   [91] Ibid, [34].   [92] See ibid, [34].   [93] Ibid, [35].

distinct from, and additional to, a presumption. To what extent (if at all) is that very widely expressed restriction consistent with Lord Donaldson's approach and, indeed, Lord Nicholls's view that the court 'should always have in mind that in the ordinary way the rearing of a child by his or her biological parent can be expected to be in the child's best interests'?[94] The courts must now recognise the special way in which parenthood can minister to the child's welfare, yet not generate a preferential position in favour of the natural parent.

While the courts have explained that there is no parental right nor preferential position for parents, the emphasis which the courts will place on the position of parents has probably not altered in substance. The focus of recent decisions has been on how expression is properly given to that emphasis: the courts have clarified that it is encompassed within the application of the welfare principle, in the view that parenthood is an 'important and significant factor' bearing on the question of which proposals better advance the child's welfare. Lord Nicholls's speech in Re G was not intended to detract from the paramountcy principle. His statements must be seen in the context of the application of section 1 of the Children Act 1989, as guidance seeking to ensure that the child's welfare is treated as paramount.

Each case will turn upon its own facts. However, it seems likely that the approach in earlier case law[95] that parents should not be prevented from caring for their child simply on the basis of a balancing exercise which concludes that substitute parents could offer the child a more advantageous style of upbringing will not alter.[96]

An illustration of how the parents' position is not easily displaced is provided by Re M (Child's Upbringing)[97] which raised cross-cultural issues similar to those which arose in J v C. Great weight was given by the trial judge and the Court of Appeal to the notion that a 10–year-old South African boy's development 'must be, in the last resort and profoundly, Zulu development and not Afrikaans or English development'.[98] The boy had been living in England with a South African woman and her family for about four years during which time he had only intermittent contact with his natural family. Expert evidence was given that abrupt separation from his 'psychological' family would cause him severe trauma. Nonetheless, the court ordered that he be returned to South Africa. Neill LJ justified this conclusion by asserting that the boy had a right to be reunited with his Zulu parents. Similarly, Ward LJ asserted that the child's roots were in South Africa and that he therefore ought to return to his family there.[99]

The court's characterisation of the child's right as the 'right to be brought up by the parents who gave birth to him' is interesting. The child certainly may not regard it as his 'right' to be brought up by his parents who, to him, may be strangers compared with his substitute parents whom he regards as his family. There appears to have been some recognition of this point in Re H (A Child: Residence)[100] in which the Court of Appeal commented that 'the biological parent may not always be the natural parent in the eyes of the child' and in cases where the child has been for long in the settled care of a non-parent, the court must arrive at its choice applying the statute.

---

[94] [2006] UKHL 43 at [2].   [95] See the 2nd edition of this book.
[96] See eg Re D (A Child) (Residence: Natural Parent) [2000] 1 FCR 97, FD (Johnson J) and Re K (A Minor) (Wardship: Adoption) [1991] 1 FLR 57 (danger of social engineering recognised).
[97] [1996] 2 FCR 473. Contrast Re H (A Minor: Custody) [1990] 1 FLR 51.
[98] [1996] 2 FCR 473, 485.   [99] Ibid, 495.   [100] [2002] 3 FCR 277.

3 IS SECTION 1(1) OF THE CHILDREN ACT 1989 COMPATIBLE WITH THE REQUIREMENTS OF THE HUMAN RIGHTS ACT 1998?

The Supreme Court has confirmed the strong interpretation given to the word 'paramountcy' in section 1(1) of the Children Act 1989 in *J v C* and other House of Lords' decisions. Indeed the position has arguably been strengthened, with the added message that our Supreme Court justices should not contemplate any change 'which might have the effect of weakening the protection given to children under the present law'.[101] In reaching those decisions, however, there was no engagement at all with the question whether the paramountcy principle so interpreted is compatible with the requirements of the HRA 1998. This failure is not a new phenomenon. Several commentators have high-lighted previous judicial failures (some might say instances of unwillingness) to engage fully with the issue, as evidenced by rather dubious reasoning in several cases in which the judiciary has asserted that the balancing of interests required under section 1(1) and 1(3) of the Children Act 1989 is the same as that required by Article 8 of the ECHR.[102] It has been suggested that any difference between the requirements of Article 8 of the ECHR and section 1 of the Children Act 1989 is merely semantic,[103] or that the paramountcy principle is recognised in the jurisprudence of the European Court of Human Rights.

In *Payne v Payne*[104] Thorpe LJ commented that 'the jurisprudence of the European Court of Human Rights inevitably recognises the paramountcy principle, albeit not expressed in the language of our domestic statute'[105] citing in support a statement in *Johansen v Norway*[106] that: 'the court will attach particular importance to the best interests of the child, which...may override those of the parent.'[107] A similar view was taken in *Re S (Contact: Promoting Relationship with Absent Parent)*[108] citing in support the view of the European Court in *Yousef v The Netherlands*:

> that in judicial decisions where the rights under art 8 of parents and those of a child are at stake, the child's rights must be the paramount consideration. If any balancing of interests is necessary, the interests of the child must prevail (see *Elsholz v Germany* [2001] ECHR 25735/94 at para 52 and *TP and KM v UK* [2001] ECHR 28945/95 at para 72).[109]

However, as several commentators have cogently argued,[110] Article 8 of the ECHR and section 1 of the Children Act 1989 do not merely express the same thing in a different way

---

[101] See *per* Baroness Hale of Richmond in *Re G (Children) (Residence: Same-Sex Partner)* [2006] UKHL 43 at [30].

[102] *Payne v Payne* [2001] EWCA Civ 166, [2001] Fam 473; *Re H (Contact Order) (No 2)* [2002] 1 FLR 23; *Re B (Adoption: Natural Parent)* [2001] UKHL 70, [2002] 1 FLR 196; *Re KD (A Minor) (Ward: Terminating Access)* [1988] AC 806 at 825.

[103] *Re KD (A Minor) (Ward: Terminating Access)* [1988] AC 806 at 825. See also *Re B (Adoption: Natural Parent)* [2001] UKHL 70, [2002] 1 FLR 196, discussed further in Chapter 11.

[104] [2001] EWCA Civ 166, [2001] Fam 473, confirmed on several occasions: see Sections 5.14.1 et seq.

[105] Ibid, [38].   [106] (1996) 23 EHRR 33 at 72, para 78.

[107] [2001] EWCA Civ 166, [2001] Fam 473 at [39].

[108] [2004] EWCA Civ 18, [2004] 1 FLR 1279 at [15].

[109] (App no 33711/96) (2003) 36 EHRR 20, at para 73.

[110] J. Herring, 'The Human Rights Act and the Welfare Principle in Family Law: Conflicting or Complementary?' (1999) 11 Child and Family Law Quarterly 223; S. Harris-Short, 'Case Commentary: Putting the Child at the Heart of Adoption?—*Re B (Adoption: Natural Parent)*' (2002) 14(3) Child and Family Law Quarterly 325; D. Bonner, H. Fenwick, and S. Harris-Short, 'Judicial Approaches to the Human Rights Act' (2003) 52(3) International and Comparative Law Quarterly 549.

and, even if they do, their different processes are not without significance. As Jonathan Herring observes, the Convention requires the court to take into account the interests of parents which do not directly bear upon the child's welfare. There is also a qualitative difference between applying the welfare principle and Article 8: the former is a determination of *fact*, the latter a matter of *judgement*.[111] The ECHR requires a weighing of respective interests: an outcome (ie, respect for family life) is prescribed unless overridden by considerations specified in Article 8(2), and interference with a parent's right must be proportionate. The words represented by ellipsis and omitted from Thorpe LJ's quotation from *Johansen v Norway* in *Payne* are '*depending on their nature and seriousness*'. The quotation in full actually reads: 'the court will attach particular importance to the best interests of the child, which depending on their nature and seriousness may override those of the parent.'[112]

Thus, while the interests of the child may justify interference with the parent's right, they cannot do so automatically.[113] Reliance on *Yousef v The Netherlands* is also problematic since it is clear from the cases footnoted by the court that the word 'paramount' was not being used in the same sense as the domestic authorities.[114]

The better view, therefore, may be that some reformulation of the paramountcy principle is required in light of human rights jurisprudence. Choudhry and Fenwick have argued that the correct approach now requires what has been termed a 'parallel analysis'. In this process, the participants in any dispute start presumptively equal and interference with the Article 8(1) rights of each must be considered in accordance with the requirements of Article 8(2). The participants' rights are then weighed against each other in an ultimate balancing exercise, in which the child's welfare is privileged but not automatically decisive.[115] In the majority of cases the outcome will probably be the same whether one adopts the paramountcy principle or a parallel analysis. However, the process by which a decision is reached, in the sense of whether it accords respect to individuals' independent interests, is arguably important too. This point appears to be overlooked in the domestic case law.

There is thus considerable debate (and doubt) surrounding the correct interpretation of section 1(1) in light of the HRA 1998, and academic criticisms of the paramountcy principle have assumed a more pressing and practical significance. It is useful, perhaps, to think of the academic criticism as having two strands: the first examines welfare decision making per se; the second focuses on the elevation of the child welfare to the sole consideration.

4 CRITICISM OF THE WELFARE PRINCIPLE

4.1 'WELFARE' AS A DECISION-MAKING CRITERION

In defence of the welfare principle, Herring has pointed to several of its virtues:[116]

---

[111] Herring, ibid.

[112] *Payne v Payne* [2001] EWCA Civ 166, [2001] Fam 473 at [39].

[113] See D. Bonner, H. Fenwick, and S. Harris-Short, 'Judicial Approaches to the Human Rights Act' (2003) 52(3) International and Comparative Law Quarterly 549.

[114] Ibid, fn 154.

[115] S. Choudhry and H. Fenwick, 'Taking the Rights of Parents and Children Seriously: Confronting the Welfare Principle under the Human Rights Act' (2005) 25(3) Oxford Journal of Legal Studies 453.

[116] J. Herring, 'Farewell Welfare?' (2005) 27(2) Journal of Social Welfare and Family Law 159–171.

[it] focuses the court's attention on the person whose voice may be the quietest both literally and metaphorically and who has the least control over whether the issue arrives before the court or in the way it does. The child may also be the person with whom the court is least able to empathise.[117]

In addition, it is 'probably one of the most accurately understood legal principles among the general public'[118] and, since child welfare is something about which parents are likely to agree at least in principle, it is a useful basis for achieving negotiated settlements.[119]

Two further important attractions of the 'welfare principle' are its flexibility and adaptability. Because it does not specify a particular outcome but merely guides in a very general way, it is flexible in its particular application to the facts of individual cases. Moreover, it can accommodate to changes over time in 'accepted' notions of child welfare, following social change and new insights from research evidence. Of course, this feature of the principle means that court decisions in earlier times must be read cautiously.

Yet, these last-mentioned advantages are also viewed as a source of criticism of the principle. In 1975, Robert Mnookin drew attention to the indeterminacy of welfare decision making.[120] He illustrated the point with the example of a dispute concerning custody of a child. Should the child live with dad or with mum? Mnookin pointed out that, in order to answer this question in a rational way, it would be necessary to specify the possible outcomes for the child and then ascertain their probability. Thus, the decision-maker requires considerable information and must contend with various competing theories and bodies of knowledge about human behaviour. Therefore, it can be argued that the welfare principle makes predicting the outcome of a case (and consequently the ability to achieve a negotiated settlement) more difficult than if a clearer rule were applied. Furthermore, the flexible application of the welfare principle to children's individual circumstances may cause delay and be expensive.[121] These decision costs could be cut down by introducing a rule-based approach, such as a rule (or presumption) in a custody case in favour of the person who was the child's primary caretaker before breakdown of the parents' relationship, although the concomitant disadvantage of a rule is that it may lack sufficient flexibility in interpretation and application and lead to different cases being treated alike.[122]

A further criticism of the welfare principle is its potential lack of transparency. It may be unclear what factors have weighed heavily with the judge in reaching his or her decision and it is possible that, under the guise of the child's welfare, other values can be smuggled in. An example given by Helen Reece[123] is the attitude displayed in older case law in the 1980s, which stated that all things being equal it was better for children to be brought up with a father and a mother rather than by same-sex parents. Reece makes a powerful point that it is not just the child before the court who may be affected by such a ruling; it

---

[117] J. Herring, 'The Human Rights Act and the Welfare Principle in Family Law: Conflicting or Complementary?' (1999) 11(3) Child and Family Law Quarterly 223.

[118] J. Herring, 'Farewell Welfare?' (2005) 27(2) Journal of Social Welfare and Family Law 159 at 168.

[119] Ibid, 163.

[120] R. H. Mnookin, 'Child-Custody Adjudication: Judicial Functions in the Face of Indeterminacy' (1975) 39(3) Law and Contemporary Problems 226–293. See also S. Parker, 'The Best Interests of the Child—Principles and Problems' in P. Alston (ed), The Best Interests of the Child: Reconciling Culture and Human Rights (Oxford, Clarendon Press, 1994).

[121] As Herring points out this may be compounded by evidential difficulties of ascertaining what happened in private and at times of heightened emotion: 'Farewell Welfare?' (2005) 27(2) Journal of Social Welfare and Family Law 159 at 160.

[122] See C. Schneider, 'Discretion and Rules: A Lawyer's View' in K. Hawkins (ed), The Uses of Discretion (Oxford, Clarendon Press, 1992), on the relative benefits of discretion and rules.

[123] H. Reece, 'The Paramountcy Principle: Consensus or Construct?' (1996) 49 Current Legal Problems 267–304.

stigmatises as living in inferior environments all children who are living perfectly happily with same-sex parents.[124]

While the criticisms mentioned have force, they need also to be kept in some perspective. The problem of indeterminacy can sometimes be solved by drawing on a consensus, particularly as to what does not promote children's welfare.[125] If one parent has harmed the child and the other has not, it may be patently clear in whose favour a dispute about the child's sole residence should be decided. Furthermore, as Herring observes, judges appear to be striving not to let their personal views influence their decisions, at least not overtly.[126] Case law indicates that the judicial focus is on the practical consequences for the child of parental behaviour and that the courts avoid making value judgements about parents' lifestyles, for example on matters such as religion and sexuality.

4.2 CRITICISMS OF THE PARAMOUNTCY OF THE CHILD'S WELFARE

The second strand of criticism of section 1(1) of the Children Act 1989 relates to English law's elevation of child welfare to the paramount consideration.

Helen Reece[127] has pointed out that while the paramountcy principle commands a strong consensus of support its foundations are not strong on rational argument. First, Reece makes the strong point that general arguments that children's welfare should be treated as paramount are somewhat undermined by the narrow scope of the application of the paramountcy principle, in that it only applies in court decision making.[128] If it is an appropriate approach to ordering the lives of children and parents, why does it not apply in all decisions or actions concerning children?[129] Reece also shows that are a number of questionable assertions which are commonly advanced to justify treating children's welfare as paramount, for example that children are vulnerable and need protection. As Reece observes, it is a fallacy that protection requires priority: it does not follow that in order to protect a child adequately his or her welfare must be the sole consideration. She illustrates the point with the example of a parent seeking to take three children of different ages safely across a road, during which the parent's attentions will not be directed solely to one child, nor solely to the children, in ensuring that the whole family crosses safely. As Reece and other commentators have argued, the paramountcy principle is unjust in its focus solely on the child, and falls foul of the Kantian ethic that persons are ends in themselves and not merely to be viewed as means to the promotion of others' welfare.[130]

---

[124] See ibid and H. Reece, 'Subverting the Stigmatization Argument' (1996) 23(4) Journal of Law and Society 484–505.

[125] Although any consensus as to how welfare is promoted is itself contingent on a vast array of historical and political decisions relating to how we are governed, see S. Parker, 'The Best Interests of the Child—Principles and Problems' in P. Alston (ed), *The Best Interests of the Child: Reconciling Culture and Human Rights* (Oxford, Clarendon Press, 1994).

[126] J. Herring, 'Farewell Welfare?' (2005) 27(2) Journal of Social Welfare and Family Law 159 at 162.

[127] H. Reece, 'The Paramountcy Principle: Consensus or Construct? (1996) 49 Current Legal Problems 267–304.

[128] See for discussion, J. Herring, 'The Human Rights Act and the Welfare Principle in Family Law: Conflicting or Complementary?' (1999) 11(3) Child and Family Law Quarterly 223.

[129] The United Nations Convention on the Rights of the Child, Art 3 does not make the child's welfare paramount; it is merely the primary consideration.

[130] See eg J. Elster, 'Solomonic Judgments: Against the Best Interest of the Child' (1987) 54(1) University of Chicago Law Review 1–45. Elster argues that the child's welfare should be privileged whilst avoiding excessive harm to others. For a similar approach, see J. Eekelaar, 'Beyond the Welfare Principle' [2002] Child and Family Law Quarterly 237.

5 SECTION 8 ORDERS

Key legislation

Section 8 of the Children Act 1989 contains four orders (referred to as 'section 8 orders')[131] whose purpose is to deal flexibly with practical issues concerning a child's upbringing.[132] They are defined in section 8 as follows:

'a contact order' means an order requiring the person with whom a child lives, or is to live, to allow the child to visit or stay with the person named in the order, or for that person and the child otherwise to have contact with each other;

'a prohibited steps order' means an order that no step which could be taken by a parent in meeting his parental responsibility for a child, and which is of a kind specified in the order, shall be taken by any person without the consent of the court;

'a residence order' means an order settling the arrangements to be made as to the person with whom a child is to live; and

'a specific issue order' means an order giving directions for the purpose of determining a specific question which has arisen, or which may arise, in connection with any aspect of parental responsibility for a child.

A specific issue order could be made in most of the situations which are covered by the meanings given to the other three section 8 orders. However, section 9(5) of the Children Act 1989 provides that:

No court shall exercise its powers to make a specific issue or prohibited steps order—

(a) with a view to achieving a result which could be achieved by making a residence or contact order.

This ensures that residence and contact orders are defined consistently, and prevents residence or contact orders being substituted by specific issue or prohibited steps orders, particularly in uncontested cases, 'to achieve much the same practical results but without the same legal effects'.[133] As we shall see, in particular in the case of a residence order significant legal consequences flow from the order.

5.1 GIVING DIRECTIONS AND IMPOSING CONDITIONS ON SECTION 8 ORDERS

Key legislation

The flexibility of section 8 orders is enhanced by section 11(7), which provides:

(7) A section 8 order may—

(a) contain directions about how it is to be carried into effect;

---

[131] The term 'section 8 order' is used in s 8 itself to describe the orders.

[132] See Ward LJ in *Re G (Residence: Restriction on Further Applications)* [2008] EWCA Civ 1468, [2009] 1 FLR 894, CA at [18], commenting in discussion of a residence order that it 'simply regulates a factual state of affairs'.

[133] *Review of Child Law: Guardianship and Custody* (Law Com No 172, 1988), para 4.19.

> (b) impose conditions which must be complied with by any person—
>
> > (i) in whose favour the order is made;
> >
> > (ii) who is a parent of the child concerned;
> >
> > (iii) who is not a parent of his but who has parental responsibility for him; or
> >
> > (iv) with whom the child is living,[134]
> >
> > and to whom the conditions are expressed to apply;
>
> (c) be made to have effect for a specified period, or contain provisions which are to have effect for a specified period;
>
> (d) make such incidental, supplemental or consequential provision as the court thinks fit.

This provision 'confers a wide and comprehensive power to make orders which will be effective'.[135] However, section 11(7) supplements a section 8 order and it does not entitle the court to give directions and impose conditions which fall outside the scope of the main order. In *D v N (Contact Order: Conditions)*[136] a judge attached conditions to a defined contact order which included, *inter alia*, orders relating to the father obtaining a passport for the child, entering or telephoning the mother's place of work, entering premises owned by relatives of the mother and molesting these relatives, and removing the child from the mother. Sir Stephen Brown P held that these conditions were outside the powers of the court when adding conditions to a contact order. He stated that very great care should be exercised before what were in effect injunctive orders were brought under the umbrella of section 11(7) powers. The case law on section 11(7) is explored at various points later in this chapter in discussion of its use with particular section 8 orders.

5.2 THE FAMILY ASSISTANCE ORDER[137]

Section 16 of the Children Act 1989 provides a court with power to make a family assistance order in any family proceedings in which the court could make an order under Part II of the Act. The order, which is usually made of the court's own motion, is 'intended to provide focused short-term help to a family to overcome the problems and conflicts associated with their parents' separation'.[138] The order may require a local authority to make an officer of the authority available,[139] 'to advise, assist and (where appropriate) befriend any person named in the order' or require a Children and Family Court Advisory and Support Service (Cafcass) officer (or Welsh family proceedings officer) to do the same. The persons who may be named in the order are: any parent, guardian, or special guardian of the child; any person with whom the child is living or in whose favour a contact order is in force with respect to the child; or the child concerned.[140] The order may direct such person(s) to 'take such steps as may be so specified with a view to enabling the officer concerned to be kept informed of the address of any person named in the order and to be allowed to visit any such person'. The order may be made on its own or (more usually) alongside the making of a section 8 order. In the latter case, the order 'may direct the officer concerned to report to the court on such matters relating to the section 8 order

---

[134] There is no power to impose a condition on any other person: see *Re M (Judge's Discretion)* [2001] EWCA Civ 1428, [2002] 1 FLR 730.

[135] *Re O (Contact: Imposition of Conditions)* [1995] 2 FLR 124, CA at 128. [136] [1997] 2 FLR 797.

[137] See R. Little, 'In Practice: Family Assistance Orders: Rising to the Challenge' [2009] Fam Law 435.

[138] Children Act 1989 Guidance and Regulations (2008), vol 1, para 2.67. [139] Section 16(1).

[140] Section 16(2).

as the court may require (including the question whether the section 8 order ought to be varied or discharged).'[141]

There are some constraints on the making of the order. It can only be made with the consent of every person named in the order (other than the child).[142] In the case of a direction to a local authority, the local authority must agree to the making of the order, or the child concerned must be, or will be, living in local authority's area.[143] The order can have effect for a maximum period of 12 months[144] although it can be renewed.[145]

The making of a family assistance order clearly has resource implications for any local authority which is subject to the order. This is illustrated by the case of *Re C (Family Assistance Order)*.[146] Johnson J had made a family assistance order with a view to a local authority assisting in re-establishing a boy's relationship with his mother. The boy had earlier applied for and been granted a residence order so that he could live with his aunt and uncle. The application had attracted considerable, and hurtful, press publicity, being an early case under the Children Act 1989 in which, as the press put it, a child had sought to 'divorce his parents'. Counsel for the local authority came back to court to tell Johnson J that the local authority simply did not have the resources to carry out the order. Johnson J saw no reason to question the local authority's opinion and was of the view that there was no remedy which would be appropriate or sensible. While an order directed to the director of social services, endorsed with a penal notice, could be made so that enforcement proceedings could ensue, that would be totally contrary to the best interests of the boy and the childcare system as a whole.[147]

Re C can be contrasted with *Re E (Family Assistance Order)*.[148] A mother was convicted of the manslaughter of her child's father and was detained in a psychiatric unit. The child, aged 6, was living with a paternal aunt. A local authority had been assisting in facilitating contact between the child and the mother (arranging and paying for some transport). The child moved from that local authority's area and the new local authority in whose area the child was living was reluctant to take on any role with respect to maintenance of contact because of its cost and resource implications. Bennett J explained that because the child was living in the local authority's area an order could be made against the new local authority even though it did not agree to the order. If such an order were made, the local authority would have to consider whether or not facilitating contact was to be part of the assistance they gave the child. However, his Lordship observed that 'under such an order it would be their duty to advise, assist and befriend' the child and the judge could not 'see that they could reasonably exclude providing facilities for [the child] to have supervised contact with her mother'. The question for the court, however, was whether it should exercise its discretion to make the order in the case of a reluctant authority. It was argued on behalf of the authority that a family assistance order should not be used to make long-term provision for a child in the way proposed. Making the order, Bennett J said that although generally speaking section 16 of the Children Act 1989 is aimed at the short term and the court will lean against simply making one family assistance order after another for a substantial period of time, there was nothing else in this case

---

[141] Section 16(6).   [142] Section 16(3).   [143] Section 16(7).

[144] Section 16(5). The period was extended from six months by the Children and Adoption Act 2006, s 6(1), (4).

[145] See *Re E (Family Assistance Order)* [1999] 2 FLR 512, FD (Bennett J) discussed later in this section.

[146] [1996] 1 FLR 424, FD.

[147] See also *S v P (Contact Application: Family Assistance Order)* [1997] 2 FLR 277, FD (HHJ Callman) rejecting a suggestion that a local authority undertake duties to escort a child to visit his father in prison under the guise of a family assistance order (see esp at 279).   [148] [1999] 2 FLR 512, FD (Bennett J).

that the court could do under the Children Act to ensure that the child's contact with the mother continued, which everyone agreed was in the child's best interests.

5.3 THE COURTS' POWERS TO MAKE A SECTION 8 ORDER

Section 10 of the Children Act 1989 sets out several situations in which the courts have power to make a section 8 order. The Act designates certain proceedings as 'family proceedings', and empowers a court to make a section 8 order 'in any family proceedings in which a question arises with respect to the welfare of any child'. The power can be exercised either upon an application[149] or of the court's 'own motion'.[150] Thus, where the court takes the view that a section 8 order would be in the child's best interests, it can make such an order even though no application for an order has been made.[151]

'Family proceedings', for the purpose of the Children Act 1989, means any proceedings 'under the inherent jurisdiction of the High Court in relation to children'[152] or under any of the enactments listed under section 8(4). These enactments are:

- Parts I, II, and IV of the Children Act 1989;
- the Matrimonial Causes Act 1973;
- Schedule 5 to the Civil Partnership Act 2004;
- the Adoption and Children Act 2002;
- the Domestic Proceedings and Magistrates' Courts Act 1978;
- Schedule 6 to the Civil Partnership Act 2004;
- Part III of the Matrimonial and Family Proceedings Act 1984;
- the Family Law Act 1996;
- sections 11 and 12 of the Crime and Disorder Act 1998.

The availability of section 8 orders in family proceedings recognises that often an issue about a child arises in the context of other proceedings, and it would be wasteful of time and resources, and more stressful for the parties, if different proceedings had to be commenced to resolve inter-related family matters. The jurisdiction in family proceedings also allows a court to choose how best to respond to an application, since it is not limited to making the order which has been sought. For example, a court might decide that there is sufficient evidence to enable it to make a care order under section 31, but that the child's interests would better be served by making a residence order in favour of a concerned relative. Perhaps the most obvious example is divorce proceedings in which issues about the child's future residence and contact with a non-resident parent will invariably arise. Indeed, in any proceedings for a decree of divorce or nullity of marriage, or a decree of judicial separation, section 41 of the Matrimonial Causes Act 1973 enjoins the court to consider, in relation to any children of the family, 'whether (in the light of the arrangements which have been, or are proposed to be, made for their upbringing and welfare) it should exercise any of its powers under the Children Act 1989 with respect to any of them'.[153]

---

[149] Children Act 1989, s 10(1)(a).   [150] Ibid, s 10(1)(b).

[151] The order could be made even in favour of a person who would be ineligible to apply for an order: see *Gloucestershire County Council v P* [1999] 2 FLR 61; see also Children Act 1989 Guidance and Regulations (2008), vol 1, para 2.45.   [152] Children Act 1989, s 8(3).

[153] Exceptionally, the need to make appropriate arrangements for the children may delay the making of a decree absolute: see s 41(2).

A section 8 order may also be made upon a free-standing application under section 10(2) of the Act. For example, in the case of the separation of parents who are not married, there would be no divorce proceedings in which a section 8 order might be made. A parent could, however, make a free-standing application to the court for an order should a dispute arise about a child's upbringing. An application for a section 8 order is itself 'family proceedings' since it is made under Part II of the Children Act 1989, which is one of the enactments listed in section 8(4) of the Act (as listed earlier).

5.4 WHO MAY APPLY FOR A SECTION 8 ORDER?

The law is mindful that section 8 orders can have a major impact on the life of a child and on those who have parental responsibility. Some applications might be wholly without merit, could waste valuable court time, and could divert attention and resources from those genuine cases in need of resolution. A balance is achieved by designating certain persons as entitled to apply for section 8 orders, and by allowing all other persons to apply only if the court is first prepared to give them leave. In addition, there are special rules which apply to children, local authorities, and local authority foster parents.

5.4.1 Persons entitled to apply for any section 8 order

Section 10(4) of the Children Act 1989 provides:

> (4) The following persons are entitled to apply to the court for any section 8 order with respect to a child—
>
> > (a) any parent, guardian or special guardian of the child;
> >
> > (aa) any person who by virtue of section 4A has parental responsibility for the child;
> >
> > (b) any person in whose favour a residence order is in force with respect to the child.

The entitlement of all parents to apply for any section 8 order recognises their prime position. It is also a provision which comes to the assistance of the unmarried father since entitlement to apply does not depend on possession of parental responsibility. Since parental responsibility may be shared, it is essential for holders of parental responsibility to have access to a court to resolve a dispute or issue by means of a section 8 order.

5.4.2 Persons entitled to apply for a residence order or contact order

Section 10(5) identifies a privileged group of persons who are entitled to apply for a residence or contact order.

> (a) any party to a marriage (whether or not subsisting) in relation to whom the child is a child of the family;
>
> (aa) any civil partner in a civil partnership (whether or not subsisting) in relation to whom the child is a child of the family;
>
> (b) any person with whom the child has lived for a period of at least three years;
>
> (c) any person—
>
> > (i) in any case where a residence order is in force with respect to the child, has the consent of each of the persons in whose favour the order was made;
> >
> > (ii) in any case where the child is in the care of a local authority, has the consent of that authority; or
> >
> > (iii) in any other case, has the consent of each of those (if any) who have parental responsibility for the child.

The uniting characteristic which accords these persons special treatment is that to require them to seek the court's leave to apply would amount to a meaningless formality because it would almost invariably be granted.[154] Given the close relationships listed in section 10(5), it is curious that there is no entitlement to apply for a specific issue or prohibited steps order.

5.4.2.1 Any party to a marriage or civil partnership in relation to whom a child is a child of the family

A person who is or has been a child's parent's spouse or civil partner (ie, a step-parent or former step-parent) is entitled to apply for a residence or contact order provided that he or she has treated the child as a child of their family.[155] Sometimes a husband may falsely believe that he is the father of his wife's child and not discover the true facts until after the marriage has broken down. In a case of this kind the child will nonetheless be a child of the family because he will have been treated as such, albeit on a mistaken basis.[156] Consequently, although not the father of the child, the husband will be entitled to apply for a contact or residence order.

5.4.2.2 Any person with whom the child has lived for a period of at least three years

Any person with whom the child has lived for a period of at least three years is entitled to apply for a residence or contact order.[157] Section 10(10) provides that the period of three years need not be continuous but must not have begun more than five years before, or ended more than three months before, the making of the application. This three-year provision recognises that it is in the interests of children that persons who have provided a child with a home over a considerable period of time are able to apply for an order, either to secure that position or to ensure that contact with the child is maintained. Furthermore, no one is able to pre-empt an application simply by removing the child, as there is the three-month period of grace within which proceedings can be commenced. Three years is an arbitrary period which may bear no relationship either to a child's sense of time or to the strength of his personal attachments. These will vary considerably according to the child's particular circumstances, and will be influenced by the child's age, personality, and stage of development. However, the chosen period seeks to strike a balance between recognising the importance of a child's attachments to persons other than parents, and not exposing parents to the threat of legal proceedings, and the fear of losing their children to substitute carers, without the preliminary safeguard of an application for leave.

5.4.2.3 Any person who has the necessary consents

Where a person is not entitled to apply under any of the provisions already discussed, he or she may still be entitled provided necessary consents have been obtained as detailed in section 10(5)(c). Where there are persons in whose favour a residence order was made, the consent of each is required in order to confer entitlement on an applicant. In such circumstances, others who share parental responsibility for the child have no power to give or withhold consent.

In a case where the child is in the care of a local authority it is the consent of the authority which confers entitlement to apply.[158] In any other case, that is to say when there is no residence order in force and the child is not in local authority care, a person is entitled to

---

[154] See Law Com No 172 (1988), para 4.45.   [155] As defined in s 105(1).

[156] *W (RJ) v W (SJ)* [1971] 3 All ER 303.   [157] Section 10(5)(b).

[158] Section 9(1) prohibits a court from making any section 8 order other than a residence order with respect to a child in care, so in fact an application for a residence order is the only one which can be made in relation to a child in care. See discussion at Section 5.6.1.

apply who has the consent of each of those (if any) who have parental responsibility for the child. Where there is no one with parental responsibility to provide consent, then a potential applicant clearly cannot obtain consent and, unless otherwise entitled to apply, would require the leave of the court.

5.4.3 Relatives and foster parents: entitlement to apply for a residence order

A local authority foster parent or a relative[159] of the child is entitled to apply for a residence order with respect to a child if the child has lived with the foster parent or relative for a period of at least one year immediately preceding the application.[160] If such persons have had the care of the child for less than one year, it would be necessary to examine whether the person could apply by reason of falling within section 10(5) of the Act. In the case of a local authority foster parent, where the child is being looked after by the local authority under a care order, he or she would need the consent of the local authority under section 10(5)(c)(ii) in order to be entitled to make an application for a residence order. But where the child is an accommodated child (ie, looked after by the authority but not compulsorily in its care by way of a care order) then before the foster parent can be entitled to apply, he or she would either have to obtain the consent of each person with a residence order under section 10(5)(c)(i); or in any other case, the consent of each of those (if any) who have parental responsibility for the child under section10(5)(c)(iii). Where the relationship between the foster parent(s) and the natural parent(s) is good, the provisions relating to the consent of persons with parental responsibility could be important if, shortly after placement of the child, a dispute arose between the child's parents and the local authority as to the most appropriate foster placement for the child. In a case of this kind the parents might be willing to consent to the foster parents making an application for a residence order despite objections from the local authority.

5.5 LEAVE TO APPLY FOR A SECTION 8 ORDER

We have examined the limited class of persons who are entitled to apply for section 8 orders. However, the door of the court is not necessarily closed to non-entitled persons. Subject to some special rules which apply to applications by local authorities and local authority foster parents, which will be discussed later, any person may seek the leave of the court to apply for any section 8 order either in family proceedings or on a free-standing application.[161] When deciding whether to grant leave the court must have regard to criteria in section 10(9) of the Children Act 1989, which are discussed in detail in the following section. The court must give reasons for its decision.[162]

Whether leave is granted to a non-entitled person is usually of crucial importance to that person. Often an applicant for leave has been excluded from the child's life by the persons who have parental responsibility or by plans for the child's future. Several such cases

---

[159] 'Relative', in relation to a child, means a grandparent, brother, sister, uncle, or aunt (whether of the full blood or half blood or by marriage or civil partnership) or step-parent: see Children Act 1989, s 105.

[160] Section 10(5A) and (5B).

[161] An alternative route to a hearing for a non-entitled person is to apply to be joined as a party to existing family proceedings. A party has the opportunity to adduce evidence and to make submissions with a view to persuading a court to exercise its own motion powers to make a section 8 order in his or her favour. In *G v Kirklees Metropolitan Borough Council* [1993] 1 FLR 805 Booth J stated that the criteria which apply to an application for leave are equally applicable to an application to be joined as a party.

[162] *T v W (Contact: Reasons For Refusing Leave)* [1996] 2 FLR 473, FD (Connell J).

involve grandparents[163] and there have been calls in some quarters for grandparents to be included in the category of persons who can apply automatically for a section 8 order.[164] As Gillian Douglas has commented, striking a balance between 'enabling a grandparent to seek the court's help in securing his relationship with the grandchild, and on the other, preventing "interfering" grandparents or others from challenging parents' control over their children, is not an easy one'.[165] Examining the growing research evidence,[166] Douglas comments that the 'very wide range of grand-parenting styles and patterns of family behaviour that develop across the three generations suggests that, for the moment, it is wise to be cautious about the reasons for grandparents' applications to seek orders, and to probe carefully the nature and quality of their relationship with the parents and grandchildren. This is precisely what section 10(9) allows the court to do.'[167]

5.5.1 The criteria on an application for leave

Key legislation

Section 10(9) of the Children Act 1989 provides:

Where the person applying for leave to make an application for a section 8 order is not the child concerned, the court shall, in deciding whether or not to grant leave, have particular regard to—

(a) the nature of the proposed application for the section 8 order;

(b) the applicant's connection with the child;

(c) any risk there might be of that proposed application disrupting the child's life to such an extent that he would be harmed by it; and

(d) where the child is being looked after by a local authority—

(i) the authority's plans for the child's future; and

(ii) the wishes and feelings of the child's parents.

---

[163] For consideration of the position before the Children Act 1989, see G. Douglas and N. V. Lowe, 'Grandparents and the Legal Process' (1990) Journal of Social Welfare Law 89.

[164] For discussions of this debate, see C. Barton, '*Troxel et vir v Granville*—Grandparent Visitation Rights in the United States Supreme Court' [2001] Child and Family Law Quarterly 101; F. Kaganas and C. Piper, 'Grandparents and Contact: "*Rights v Welfare*" Revisited' (2001) 15 International Journal of Law, Policy and the Family 250.

[165] G. Douglas, 'Case Commentary—*Re J (Leave To Issue Application For Residence Order)*—Recognising Grandparents' Concern or Controlling Their Interference?' [2003] Child and Family Law Quarterly 103. See for an example within case law of these tensions: *Re F and R (Section 8 Order: Grandparent's Application)* [1995] 1 FLR 524, FD (Cazalet J) in which the grandmother stated that she had a close relationship with her grandchildren, yet the parents maintained that she interfered and was not interested in seeing the children.

[166] G. Dench and J. Ogg, *Grandparenting in Britain: A Baseline Study* (London: Institute of Community Studies, 2002) (found more likely to be maternal grandparents involved); G. Douglas and N. Ferguson, 'The Role of Grandparents in Divorced Families' (2003) 17 International Journal of Law, Policy and the Family 41 (showed variety in roles grandparents play); A. Richards, *Second Time Around—A Survey of Grandparents Raising their Grandchildren* (London: Family Rights Group, 2001) (may be cultural differences).

[167] G. Douglas, 'Case Commentary—*Re J (Leave To Issue Application For Residence Order)*—Recognising Grandparents' Concern or Controlling Their Interference?' [2003] Child and Family Law Quarterly 103.

Notice first that this provision is concerned with applications for leave by persons other than the child concerned in the application. Applications by the child concerned are governed by section 10(8) of the Act which is discussed in Section 5.5.2.1.

In *Re A and others (Minors) (Residence Orders: Leave to Apply)*[168] the Court of Appeal ruled that the paramountcy principle in section 1(1) of the Children Act 1989 does not apply to an application for leave under section 10(9) since the court is not determining a question with respect to the upbringing of the child concerned[169] and some of the criteria in section 10(9) would be otiose if the whole matter were subject to the overriding provision of section 1(1).

For several years, the leading decision dictating the courts' approach to a leave application under section 10(9) was *Re M (Care: Contact: Grandmother's Application for Leave)*,[170] a case which was not directly concerned with section 10(9), but instead with section 34(3) of the Children Act 1989, which concerns applications for leave to apply for contact with a child who is in the care of the local authority. The leading decision now is *Re J (Leave to Issue Application for Residence Order)*,[171] which directly considered section 10(9). However, in order to understand fully the position following *Re J*, it is necessary briefly to refer to *Re M*.

The Court of Appeal recognised that section 10(9) did not directly govern applications for contact with a child in care,[172] but held that it would be anomalous if the court, in exercising its discretion under section 34, did not have in mind the criteria contained in section 10(9). The Court of Appeal thus imported into the task of exercising discretion under section 34(3) the four statutory criteria that Parliament had applied in section 10(9). In addition Ward LJ (with whom Butler-Sloss and Simon Brown LJJ agreed) added a threefold test to be applied in exercise of the court's discretion, as follows:

(1) If the application is frivolous or vexatious or otherwise an abuse of the process of the court, of course it will fail.

(2) If the application for leave fails to disclose that there is any eventual real prospect of success, if those prospects of success are remote so that the application is obviously unsustainable, then it must also be dismissed...[173]

(3) The applicant must satisfy the court that there is a serious issue to try and must present a good arguable case[174]... —is there a real issue which the applicant may reasonably ask the court to try and has he a case which is better than merely arguable yet not necessarily one which is shown to have a better-than-even chance, a fair chance, of success?[175]

---

[168] [1992] Fam 182, [1992] 3 All ER 872.

[169] Citing *F v S (Adoption: Ward)* [1973] Fam 203, [1973] 1 All ER 722 in support.

[170] [1995] 2 FLR 86, CA.

[171] [2003] 1 FLR 114, CA. For a commentary on this decision and a stimulating discussion of the role of grandparents in children's lives, see G. Douglas, 'Case Commentary—*Re J (Leave To Issue Application For Residence Order)*—Recognising Grandparents' Concern or Controlling Their Interference?' [2003] Child and Family Law Quarterly 103.

[172] Because no court can make a section 8 order, other than a residence order, in respect of a child in the care of a local authority: see Children Act 1989, s 9(1).

[173] Citing *W v Ealing London Borough Council* [1993] 2 FLR 788, approving *Cheshire County Council v M* [1993] 1 FLR 463.

[174] The door of the court appears to have been opened even wider by Butler-Sloss LJ's statement (*obiter*) in *Re G (Child Case: Parental Involvement)* that the test for an application for leave was whether there was 'an arguable case'.

[175] [1995] 2 FLR 86 at 98.

In *Re J (Leave to Issue Application for Residence Order)*[176] a mother's history of psychiatric illness meant that she was unable to care for her child. The local authority considered placing the 18-month-old child with the maternal grandmother, Mrs J, who was aged 59, but concluded that bringing up the child would be too great a burden at that age. Mrs J therefore sought leave to apply for a residence order. The judge refused to grant leave and the grandmother appealed. Thorpe LJ (with whom Ferris J agreed) commented[177] that the statutory checklist in section 10(9) needs to be given its proper recognition and weight. He further observed that 'The statutory language is transparent. Nowhere does it import any obligation on the judge to carry out independently a review of future prospects.'[178] Thorpe LJ added[179] that, while the threefold test formulated by Ward LJ in *Re M* 'has the laudable purpose of excluding from the litigation exercise applications which are plainly hopeless', that guidance was given not directly in relation to the discharge of the judicial task under section 10(9). Thorpe LJ was 'anxious at the development of a practice that seems to substitute the test, "has the applicant satisfied the court that he or she has a good arguable case" for the test that Parliament applied in s 10(9)', an anxiety heightened by enactment of the HRA 1998 and rights under Articles 6 and 8 of the ECHR thereby protected in English law. The Court of Appeal concluded that:

> Whilst the decision in *Re M (Care: Contact: Grandmother's Application for Leave)* no doubt served a valuable purpose in its day and in relation to s 34(3) applications, it is important that trial judges should recognise the greater appreciation that has developed of the value of what grandparents have to offer, particularly to children of disabled parents. Judges should be careful not to dismiss such opportunities without full inquiry. That seems…to be the minimum essential protection of Arts 6 and 8 rights that Mrs J enjoys, given the very sad circumstances of the family.[180]

In *Re R (Adoption: Contact)*[181] Wall LJ said that he understood Thorpe LJ in *Re J* in essence to be disapproving the test devised by Ward LJ in *Re M*.[182] However, his Lordship went on usefully to clarify that *Re J* does not prohibit 'a broad assessment of the merits of a particular application'.[183] What it prohibits 'is the determination of the application on the "no reasonable prospects of success" criterion'.[184]

In *Re H (Children)*[185] Thorpe LJ explained that:

> The whole purpose of the decision in *Re J* was to draw the attention of trial judges to the need to adopt a careful review of the s 10(9) criteria and not to replace those tests simply with a broad evaluation of the applicant's future prospects of success.

It is unclear whether or not Ward LJ's test is completely erased from applications under section 10(9) or whether that approach in *Re M* survives to be applied together with a careful focus on the statutory criteria. However, *Re J* has usefully drawn attention to the need to ensure that any assessment of the merits of a case does not usurp careful attention to the criteria in section 10(9), to which we now turn.

---

[176] [2002] EWCA Civ 1364, [2003] 1 FLR 114, CA.   [177] Ibid, [17].   [178] Ibid, [14].
[179] Ibid, [18].   [180] Ibid, [19].   [181] [2005] EWCA Civ 1128, [2006] 1 FLR 373.
[182] Ibid, [41]. However, Thorpe LJ did not say so in terms; he merely observed that the guidance in *Re M* was not made directly in relation to s 10(9).
[183] Ibid, [46]. There are several dicta in the Court of Appeal which acknowledge that the merits are relevant on a leave application. See eg Wall LJ in *Re H (Leave to Apply for Residence Order)* [2008] 2 FLR 848 at [14] and Wilson LJ at [33].   [184] [2005] EWCA Civ 1128, [2006] 1 FLR 373 at [46].
[185] [2003] EWCA Civ 369, [2003] All ER (D) 290 (Feb).

5.5.1.1 The nature of the proposed application

The first factor, in paragraph (a) of the checklist in section 10(9), is the nature of the proposed application. In *Re R (Adoption: Contact)*,[186] a case in which a 17-year-old girl was applying for post-adoption contact with her younger half-sibling, Wall LJ observed that examining the nature of the proposed application may involve 'a consideration of the jurisprudence surrounding the circumstances in which such orders may or may not be made'.[187] In refusing leave in that case, the Court of Appeal commented that the judge was 'bound to have regard to the fact that, under the jurisprudence which has developed, contact orders in adoption proceedings are of themselves unusual'.[188] In *Re C (A Minor) (Adopted Child: Contact)*[189] the court was concerned to shield the adoptive parents from unnecessary anxiety, and it took the view that an application for leave could safely be refused without adoptive parents' involvement. It therefore ruled that the Official Solicitor should be brought in as respondent in a case of this kind, his function being to represent the child's interests. Only if, having heard from the applicant and from the Official Solicitor and/or the local authority, the court was satisfied that the natural parent had made out a prima facie case for leave should notice be given to the adoptive parents. In this way the court would ensure that no application for leave was granted without the adoptive parents having first been given an opportunity to oppose it. The court refused the natural parent leave to apply for either a specific issue order, which would result in her learning the identity of the adoptive parents, or a contact order. It held that adoption orders are intended to be permanent and final, and that a fundamental question such as contact should not be subsequently reopened unless there is some fundamental change in circumstances.[190]

5.5.1.2 The applicant's connection with the child

Under section 10(9)(b) the court must consider the applicant's connection with the child. This criterion is often closely linked to the nature of the proposed application and is directed to ascertaining whether the applicant can demonstrate a genuine relationship with, and a legitimate concern about, some matter relating to the child's upbringing. The word 'connection' is a broad one, embracing not merely any legal relationship between the child and the applicant but also *de facto* connections. For example, in *G v F (Shared Residence: Parental Responsibility)*[191] the applicant who had lived in a lesbian relationship with the child's mother had behaved towards the child as a joint parent. After the couple separated the applicant continued to play a substantial part in the little boy's upbringing until he was 3, when staying contact with the applicant ceased. When granting the leave requested, Bracewell J observed that the applicant's close connection with the child made this a clear case where leave should be granted.

A judge's exercise of discretion may be vitiated by a failure to give sufficient emphasis to the applicant's connection with the child. In *Re H (Leave to Apply for Residence Order)*[192] three half-siblings had been taken into care because of their mother's drug addiction. The second child, aged 9, had been adopted by a couple who wished to adopt the third child, aged 4, who had been freed for adoption and was living with foster carers. The second child's adoptive parents, Mr and Mrs A, wanted to adopt the third child. Because of some concerns about their age, however, the local authority/adoption agency preferred a third, considerably younger, couple. Mr and Mrs A therefore applied to the court for leave to

---

[186] [2005] EWCA Civ 1128, [2006] 1 FLR 373.   [187] Ibid, [50].   [188] Ibid, [45].
[189] [1993] 2 FLR 431.
[190] Ibid. See also *Re T (Adopted Children: Contact)* [1995] 2 FLR 792 and *X and Y v A Local Authority (Adoption: Procedure)* [2009] EWHC 47 (Fam) (McFarlane J), [2009] 2 FLR 984.
[191] [1998] 2 FLR 799.   [192] [2008] 2 FLR 848.

make an application for a residence order. The judge refused leave, having described Mr and Mrs A's connection with the third child as only indirect. The Court of Appeal allowed Mr and Mrs A's appeal, holding that the judge had erred in giving insufficient weight to (i) the fact that Mr and Mrs A are the legal parents of the third child's half-sibling; (ii) the principle that half-siblings should be brought up together wherever that is possible;[193] and (iii) the evidence that Mr and Mrs A were wholly capable of caring for the children.[194]

The fact that the applicant has close family ties with a child is of course not determinative, and it may not outweigh different considerations in the other paragraphs of section 10(9). In *Re A (A Minor) (Residence Order: Leave to Apply)*[195] a request was made by an aunt for leave to apply for a residence order in the course of care proceedings which were already underway. The trial court took the view, which was confirmed on appeal, that sufficient persons were already involved in the case, and that to join another would not be in the interests of the child because it would lead to delays and be disruptive.[196]

5.5.1.3 Any risk of disruption causing harm

The court is required under section 10(9)(c) to have particular regard to 'any risk there might be of the proposed application disrupting the child's life to such an extent that he would be harmed by it'. Indeed, it is regarded as a 'factor of crucial significance'.[197] 'Harm' for these purposes means ill-treatment or the impairment of health and development as defined by section 31(9) and (10) and section 105(1) of the Children Act 1989.[198] As the Court of Appeal in *Re M (Care: Contact: Grandmother's Application for Leave)*[199] recognised, it follows from these definitions that a 'child's upset, unhappiness, confusion or anxiety, needs to be sufficiently severe before it can amount to an impairment of emotional, social or behavioural development'.[200]

Secondly, as Wall LJ pointed out in *Re R (Adoption: Contact)*,[201] section 10(9)(c) 'refers to the risk of disruption posed by the application, not by the outcome of the application'.[202] This point was also stressed by Thorpe LJ in *Re H (Children)*,[203] explaining that it is 'a risk of what the trial of the proposed application might do to disrupt the life of the child, not what the grant of that application might do to disrupt the life of the child'.[204] So the question is not whether the applicant if granted the application would prove to be a potentially disruptive factor in the child's life, it is whether the applicant's litigation (during that process) would prove to be a disruptive factor.[205] As Ward LJ commented in *Re M (Care: Contact: Grandmother's Application for Leave)*:[206]

> The very knowledge that litigation is pending can be sufficiently unsettling to be harmful; if leave is given, the process of investigating the merits of the application can be sufficiently disruptive if it involves the children in more interviews, psychiatric investigations and so

---

[193] See discussion in Section 5.7.2.   [194] [2008] 2 FLR 848 at [25].

[195] [1993] 1 FLR 425.

[196] See also *C v W (A Minor) (Contact: Leave to Apply)* [1998] 1 FCR 618 (father repeatedly failed to attend hearings; not in child's best interests to allow him to continue litigating).

[197] *Re M (Care: Contact: Grandmother's Application for Leave)* [1995] 2 FLR 86 at 95. *A fortiori* where the child is in care.

[198] See *Re A and others (Minors) (Residence Orders: Leave to Apply)* [1992] Fam 182, [1992] 3 All ER 872.

[199] [1995] 2 FLR 86.   [200] Ibid, 96.   [201] [2005] EWCA Civ 1128, [2006] 1 FLR 373.

[202] Ibid, [55].   [203] [2003] EWCA Civ 369, [2003] All ER (D) 290 (Feb).   [204] Ibid, [26].

[205] Ibid. Contrast *Re A (A Minor) (Residence Order: Leave to Apply)* [1993] 1 FLR 425 in which Hollings J was 'satisfied that the right approach is to consider not just the effect of the application being made, which the child may not even know of, but also what effect there might be of disrupting the child's life if the application succeeded' (at 428).   [206] [1995] 2 FLR 86.

forth. The stressfulness of litigation may impair the ability of those who have care of the child properly to discharge their responsibility to the child's detriment.[207]

5.5.1.4 The local authority's plans for the child

Under section 10(9)(d)(i), in a case where a child is being looked after by a local authority a court is required to have particular regard to the authority's plans for the child's future. In *Re A and others (Minors) (Residence Orders: Leave to Apply)*[208] the Court of Appeal explained how a court should approach a case where a local authority has plans for the child's future which are inconsistent with the application for leave. It reasoned as follows: a local authority has a duty under section 22(3) to safeguard and promote the welfare of any child in its care and:

> Accordingly, the court should approach the application for leave on the basis that the authority's plans for the child's future are designed to safeguard and promote the child's welfare and that any departure from those plans might well 'disrupt the child's life to such an extent that he would be harmed by it'.[209]

This ruling highlights the dilemma faced by courts when a challenge is made to the way in which a local authority is choosing to exercise its statutory powers, namely when it is proper for a court to substitute its own judgement for the judgement of the authority about what decision will best promote the welfare of the child. *Re A and others (Minors) (Residence Orders: Leave to Apply)*[210] makes clear that the decision whether or not to grant leave is one for a court, and the fact that a child is in care does not detract from the court's decision-making function. However, the Court of Appeal ruled that a court must take as its starting point the notion that the local authority is under a statutory duty to promote the child's welfare, and *a fortiori* the authority's plans are therefore designed to advance the welfare of the child. Thus, the court created what appears to amount to an assumption in favour of not disrupting the authority's plans for the child, thus in practice requiring the applicant to provide arguments/evidence why the local authority's plans should be disrupted.

The phrase 'being looked after' by a local authority embraces both a child being provided with accommodation by the authority (ie, voluntarily) and one in care under a care order.[211] In relation to an accommodated child the authority does not have parental responsibility, and it could be somewhat anomalous to give significant weight to the local authority's plans for a child's future in circumstances when it does not have the power to implement these plans. It might therefore be maintained that less weight ought to be given to the authority's plans for an accommodated child than when the child is in care.

5.5.1.5 The wishes and feelings of the child's parents

In any case in which the local authority is looking after a child, section 10(9)(d)(ii) requires that the wishes and feelings of the child's parents be taken into account. It will be recalled that in *Re A and others (Minors) (Residence Orders: Leave to Apply)*[212] the Court of Appeal held that the judge had erred in applying the paramountcy principle to a leave application. The reason was that it would mean that the judge could not consider independently the mother's wishes and feelings. In that case, the mother was not even notified of the foster mother's application in respect of her four children in the care of a local authority. The Court of Appeal stated that by failing to give the mother notice the

---

[207] Ibid, 96.   [208] [1992] Fam 182.   [209] Ibid, 193.   [210] [1992] Fam 182.
[211] Children Act 1989, s 23.   [212] [1992] Fam 182, [1992] 3 All ER 872.

judge had deprived himself of information which was necessary for the proper exercise of his discretion.

5.5.2 Without notice applications for leave

A request for leave to apply for a section 8 order can be made without notice before a single magistrate or judge. However, the courts have been cautious regarding the hearing of without notice applications. The leave decision is important and while there may well be cases of urgency, or other circumstances, which make it right to grant leave without notice to the other side, in the ordinary case the interests of justice require that notice be given to parties who are likely to be affected if leave is granted, so that they can adduce evidence and make submissions.[213] In *Re W (Contact Application: Procedure)*[214] Wilson J stated that in almost all cases applications should be on notice, but gave an example from his experience of an exceptional type of case in which a without notice application might be made: where a mature teenage child has left home and seeks leave to apply for a residence order to secure his or her position in the home of another family member. In such a case the application might be granted and a short interim residence order put in place. In *Re SC (A Minor) (Leave to Seek Residence Order)*,[215] however, the court held that where the applicant for leave is a child, it is desirable that everyone with parental responsibility should be given notice of the application even though an application for leave can be made without notice. In *Nottinghamshire County Council v P*[216] the Court of Appeal stated that it was wholly inappropriate for a local authority to apply without notice before a single justice for leave to issue an application for a prohibited steps order. The court added that, in future, any such application should be transferred to the county court and that it should not be dealt with without notice.

5.5.3 The child concerned and leave

The Children Act 1989 recognises that in some instances children should be given the opportunity to initiate proceedings for a section 8 order on their own behalf. Children (as a category) do not fall within the categories of persons who are entitled to apply for a section 8 order,[217] although a child is entitled to make a leave application. Applications by children for leave fall into two categories.

First there are cases in which the child applicant is also the child with respect to whom the court may make the section 8 order (ie, the child concerned). Such applications are subject to section 10(8) of the Children Act 1989, which provides:

> where the person applying for leave to make a section 8 application is the child concerned, the court may only grant leave if it is satisfied that he has sufficient understanding to make the proposed application for the section 8 order.[218]

A Practice Direction[219] provides that applications under section 10(8) of the Children Act 1989 must be heard in the High Court, and there have therefore been several reported first instance decisions concerning such applications. In *Re SC (A Minor) (Leave to Seek*

---

[213] *Re M (Prohibited Steps Order: Application for Leave)* [1993] 1 FLR 275 at 278F–G *per* Johnson J.

[214] [2000] 1 FLR 263.   [215] [1994] 1 FLR 96.   [216] [1993] 3 All ER 815.

[217] Except in cases of variation of an order in which the child is named in the order (see s 10(6) and *Re W (Application for Leave: Whether Necessary)* [1996] 3 FCR 337).

[218] Much of the case law examining the level of understanding required of the child to pursue proceedings on his or her own has arisen in the context of the question of whether a child should be permitted to dispense with the services of a guardian ad litem during existing proceedings and be separately represented.

[219] Practice Direction Children Act 1989—Applications By Children [1993] 1 FLR 668.

Residence Order)[220] Booth J pointed out that a court has a discretion whether to grant leave even if it has been established under section 10(8) that the child has sufficient understanding to make the application and that it is right for the court to have regard to the likelihood of success of the proposed application, and to be satisfied that the child is not embarking on proceedings which are doomed to failure. Her Ladyship also clarified that, as the initial application for leave does not raise any question about the child's upbringing, the child's welfare is not the court's paramount consideration, a view which has been endorsed in subsequent decisions.[221] It has been said, however, that, although not paramount, the child's interests are 'very much at the centre of the court's thinking' on a leave application.[222]

In *Re SC (A Minor) (Leave to Seek Residence Order)*[223] a girl aged 14 years 8 months who had been in care for eight years and had had several failed foster placements, applied for leave to apply for a residence order to live with a friend, Mrs B. The local authority had earlier assessed Mrs B as a foster parent but had found her not to be suitable. The court recognised that in such a case, where the person with whom the child wishes to live may be unlikely to succeed on her own leave application, the child's application, to which the criteria in section 10(9) do not apply,[224] may provide a way of circumventing the more stringent criteria in section 10(9). However, the court did not think that that should prevent the child from being able to apply. On the facts Booth J granted leave.

In *Re C (A Minor) (Leave to Seek Section 8 Orders)*[225] a 15-year-old girl was seeking leave to apply for a residence order to live at the home of a friend and her family, and for a specific issue order to go on holiday with them to Bulgaria. In relation to the residence order, Johnson J took the view that there was no identifiable advantage in making a residence order at that time. He therefore adjourned the child's application for leave. In relation to the application for leave to apply for a specific issue order, he took the view that this was not the kind of issue which Parliament had envisaged as being litigated in a court when it allowed children to make applications for leave. Johnson J said that 'this jurisdiction is one which should be reserved for the resolution of matters of importance' and he did not consider that the question whether the child should go on a two-week holiday to Bulgaria was such a matter. He therefore refused the child's leave application.

In *Re C (Residence: Child's Application for Leave)*[226] an articulate 14-year-old girl, who was not content for her views to be put forward by a welfare officer, was seeking the leave of the court to apply for an order which, if granted, would enable her to live with her mother rather than her father. Granting the application, Stuart White J carefully applied the guidance in the earlier cases, finding that the child was of sufficient understanding to make the application, that it was impossible to say that the application could not succeed, and that the application concerned a 'matter of very considerable importance.'[227] A similar case, albeit with a contrasting outcome, is *Re H (Residence Order: Child's Application for Leave)*.[228] A very bright 12-year-old, whose intelligence was put on the 99th percentile for age and whose comprehension, social awareness, and abilities with respect to interpersonal

---

[220] [1994] 1 FLR 96.

[221] *Re C (Residence: Child's Application for Leave)* [1995] 1 FLR 927, FD (Stuart-White J). There had earlier been a conflict in the authorities, but in *Re H (Residence Order: Child's Application for Leave)* [2000] 1 FLR 780 Johnson J agreed with Booth J's approach, resiling from the view he earlier expressed in *Re C (A Minor) (Leave to Seek Section 8 Orders)* [1994] 1 FLR 26.

[222] *Re C (Residence: Child's Application for Leave)* [1995] 1 FLR 927 at 929 *per* Stuart White J.

[223] [1994] 1 FLR 96.

[224] *Re C (A Minor) (Leave to Seek Section 8 Orders)* per Johnson J. See also Charles J in *Re S (A Minor) (Adopted Child: Contact)* [1999] Fam 283 at 291.   [225] [1994] 1 FLR 26.

[226] [1995] 1 FLR 927.   [227] Ibid.   [228] [2000] 1 FLR 780 (Johnson J).

relationships were 'very superior', applied for leave to apply for a residence order to live with his father upon his parents' divorce. The child's wish to live with the father was supported by the father. Johnson J concluded that the child had 'sufficient understanding' for the purpose of section 10(8) of the Children Act 1989. However, his Lordship refused the application on the basis that there was no argument or any cross-examination which could be addressed to the court on behalf of the child which would not in any event be addressed to the court on behalf of the father. There were disadvantages, such as the child seeing all the evidence in a case pending between parents and 'the spectre (a word [chosen] deliberately) of a mother being faced across a courtroom by solicitor or counsel acting on behalf of the child she bore'.[229]

In some cases a leave application may create a difficult practical problem, namely where is the child to live in the period between the application for leave and the hearing? The child may be living with a parent or other person, such as a step-parent, in circumstances of considerable animosity. An interim order temporarily to settle the arrangements as to the person with whom the child is to live would seem helpful, but it is doubtful whether one can be made at the leave to apply stage. The difficulty is that that step would interfere in a parent's parental responsibility on the basis of incomplete information and could be influential against the parent at trial. Therefore, where the child should live pending the hearing for leave raises some awkward questions of principle as well as the practical question of what should be done.

5.5.4 Where the child seeking leave is not the 'child concerned'

Where the child seeking leave is not 'the child concerned', the applicant child must satisfy the criteria in section 10(9) in the same way as any other applicant for leave. Moreover, in *Re S (Contact Application by Sibling)*[230] it was held that the court was not required to have exclusive regard to the criteria in section 10(9) where the case concerned an applicant child. The child's understanding remained a relevant consideration, as did the application's chances of success.

5.5.5 Restriction on leave applications by local authority foster parents

There is a restriction on leave applications by local authority foster parents. Section 9(3) of the Children Act 1989 provides:

A person who is, or was at any time within the last six months, a local authority foster parent of a child may not apply for leave to apply for a section 8 order with respect to the child unless—

(a) he has the consent of the authority;

(b) he is a relative of the child; or

(c) the child has lived with him for at least one year preceding the application.

Why are local authority foster parents who require the court's leave singled out for special treatment? One of the many aims of the Children Act 1989 is to instil confidence in parents in state provision of social services for children in need and in care. Parents are encouraged to work in partnership with local authorities for the benefit of their children. Foster parents may often have more material possessions than a parent, and the opportunities afforded in the foster home to develop and enhance a child's physical, emotional, and educational progress may be superior to those that a parent is able to provide. These are all matters which are relevant to the application of the welfare

---

[229] Ibid, 783.   [230] [1998] 2 FLR 897.

principle which governs the determination of applications for section 8 orders. If a foster parent could apply like any other person for leave to apply for a residence order, a parent might be fearful of making temporary arrangements for his or her child with a local authority. This could rebound to the general disadvantage of children in need and in care, because parents might be tempted to make private arrangements for their children which are less appropriate to their child's needs, or they might become hostile to a foster placement simply because it appeared to be particularly well suited to their child's circumstances.

Unless a foster parent is a relative, or has looked after the child for at least one year, he or she must obtain the consent of the local authority to apply to the court for leave to apply for a section 8 order. Unless that consent is forthcoming, the foster parent is precluded from seeking a section 8 order. The consent provision is also there to reassure local authorities that they can develop their fostering services without losing control over the children.

In *Re P (A Minor) (Leave to Apply: Foster Parents)*[231] the question arose whether the local authority had the entitlement to give consent under section 9(3)(a) to a foster parent's application for leave to apply for a residence order, where the child was an accommodated child, and where the local authority therefore did not have parental responsibility for the child. It was argued that if a local authority were able to give consent under section 9(3), this would, in effect, allow the authority to circumvent the clear prohibition in section 9(2) that no application may be made by a local authority for a residence order or a contact order. Hale J dismissed this argument. She said that it was absolutely plain from the wording that the consent of the local authority accommodating the child was the consent which was needed. While this ruling was unremarkable on the point of law which it settled, the argument raised by counsel that this was a back-door way of allowing a local authority to apply for a residence order was uncomfortably close to the mark. However, it does expose an uncomfortable tension between the various policies which underpin different provisions in the Act. The ruling makes it clear that a local authority, where it takes the view that the welfare of the child requires that he should remain in the care of his foster parents, but where it also takes the view that it does not have sufficient grounds to satisfy the test for making a care order, can encourage the foster parents to make their own application for leave to apply for a residence order.[232] If a foster parent were to obtain a residence order, and if the local authority were to continue to make contributions towards the foster parents' costs of accommodating the child, and perhaps to continue to supervise the child on a voluntary basis too, the distinction between state intervention and private law applications would arguably become blurred, to an unacceptable degree.

Section 9(3)(c) allows a local authority foster parent with whom the child has lived for at least one year to apply to a court for leave to apply for a section 8 order without first obtaining the consent of the local authority. The difference between that provision and section 10(5A) which entitles a local authority foster parent to apply for a residence order is that the entitlement in section 10(5A) arises where the child has been living with the foster parent for a period of at least one year *immediately preceding the application*. If the foster parent had had the child living with him or her for at least one year but had since ceased to

---

[231] [1994] 2 FCR 1093.

[232] Which indeed was close to what happened in *Re P (A Minor) (Leave to Apply: Foster Parents)*. The local authority was also acting as an adoption agency in respect of the child. The parents, who were Orthodox Jews, objected to the foster parents as adoptive parents because they were not Orthodox Jews. The court granted the foster parents leave to apply for a residence order.

look after the child, the foster parent would not be entitled to apply under section 10(5A). The foster parent would require leave (unless otherwise entitled) but would not be subject to the requirement of the local authority's consent since the child had lived with the foster parent for at least one year.

Once six months have elapsed since the foster parent last looked after the child, the foster parent is free to apply to the court for leave. Of course, the difficulty in overcoming the hurdle of the criteria in section 10(9) would almost certainly be accentuated by the lapse of time. However, a foster parent who was determined to apply for leave once the six months had elapsed might persuade the local authority to consent to her making a leave application at once. This would resolve the matter at an early stage and allow the child's future to be planned without the threat of future litigation.

5.6 RESTRICTIONS ON APPLICATIONS FOR, AND THE USE OF, SECTION 8 ORDERS

Section 10(3) of the Children Act 1989 provides that section 10 is subject to the restrictions imposed by section 9.

5.6.1 In respect of a child in care

Section 9(1) provides that:

> No court shall make any section 8 order, other than a residence order, with respect to a child who is in the care of a local authority.

This provision reflects an underlying policy within the Children Act 1989, that while the making of a care order is a decision for a court, once a local authority is entrusted via the care order with parental responsibility for the child, the courts should not supervise a local authority's day-to-day decision making with respect to the child. Thus, it is the local authority which can determine matters relating to the child's upbringing.[233] If courts were permitted to entertain applications for specific issue and prohibited steps orders in respect of a child in care this would give individuals the opportunity to challenge a local authority's exercise of parental responsibility. It would also give the courts power to dictate to local authorities how they should carry out their statutory powers and duties. That would conflict with the principle that the courts should not supervise, other than by judicial review, an area of discretion conferred on the local authority by Parliament.[234]

Why may a residence order be made with respect to a child in care but none of the other section 8 orders? A residence order not only settles the arrangements as to the person with whom the child is to live, it discharges a care order and brings to an end a local authority's parental responsibility for the child. Thus, a residence order goes to the source of the local authority's powers and not to the manner in which they are being exercised.

5.6.2 A local authority may not apply for a residence order or contact order

Section 9(2) provides that:

> No application may be made by a local authority for a residence order or contact order and no court shall make such an order in favour of a local authority.

---

[233] Except issues relating to contact (see Children Act 1989, s 34).
[234] *A v Liverpool City Council* [1981] 2 All ER 385.

Why is a local authority prohibited from seeking leave to apply for either a residence or contact order, yet permitted to apply for leave to apply for a specific issue or prohibited steps order? Section 9(2) is directed at those cases where a local authority does not have a care order. Its aim is to prevent a local authority from obtaining parental responsibility for a child otherwise than through making an application in care proceedings. A local authority may not apply for a contact order for similar reasons. Such an order could enable the authority to have enforceable contact with a child other than through obtaining a supervision order in an application brought in care proceedings.[235]

5.7 RESIDENCE ORDERS

An application for a residence order commonly arises when the child's parents' relationship breaks down and the parents no longer live together. Each parent may wish to provide a home for the child. If the parents are unable to agree about the child's future living arrangements, it may ultimately fall to the court to decide the issue upon a contested application (or cross-applications) for a residence order. Other persons, such as relatives or foster parents, may also be caught up in this type of dispute. In some cases it may be appropriate for more than one person to have a residence order, for example where two grandparents are looking after their grandchild. In such a case, where the persons concerned will live together in the same household, the order is known as a joint residence order. It is also possible for a residence order to be made in favour of two or more persons who do not live together in the same household. In that case the order is referred to as a shared residence order.

A residence order is 'an order settling the arrangements to be made as to the person with whom a child is to live'. It is thus not directly concerned with *where* the child shall live in the sense of the location of the child's home; rather, it defines *the person(s) with whom the child shall live*. However, that is not to say that the issue of where the child will live is not relevant to the question of with whom the child shall live. As Butler-Sloss LJ explained in *Re E (Residence: Imposition of Conditions)*:[236]

> The correct approach is to look at the issue of where the children will live as one of the relevant factors...If the case is finely balanced between the respective advantages and disadvantages of the parents, the proposals put forward by each parent will assume considerable importance.

Every case is different and must be decided upon its own unique facts.[237] The court will apply section 1(1) of the Children Act 1989, considering in particular the factors in the checklist in section 1(3) and weighing each in a balancing exercise aimed at ascertaining where the child's welfare lies and ultimately whether the application(s) should be granted or not. For example, the court is required to consider under paragraph (f) of the checklist how capable each of the child's parents is of caring for the child and, under paragraph (g), any harm the child has suffered or is at risk of suffering. The fact that one parent is for some reason incapable of caring for the child appropriately may prove highly significant to the outcome. Under these headings the court might also consider the extent to which a resident parent will facilitate contact with a non-resident parent. In *Re A (A Minor) (Custody)*[238] Butler-Sloss LJ said that the approach of a parent to contact is highly relevant

---

[235] *F v Cambridgeshire County Council* [1995] 1 FLR 516 (wrong for a local authority to be made a party to contact proceedings, and it is not open to a local authority to invite a court to refuse to make a contact order).   [236] [1997] 2 FLR 638, CA.

[237] *Re H (Shared Residence: Parental Responsibility)* [1995] 2 FLR 883: 'each case will depend upon its own facts'; *Re T* [2009] EWCA Civ 388: 'every case is fact sensitive' (at [6]).   [238] [1991] 2 FLR 394.

to the determination of whether the child should live with him or her.[239] As we shall see later in this chapter, the courts are increasingly willing to use a change of residence (or at least the threat thereof) as a means of enforcing contact.

In many cases, however, each parent will be able to provide a reasonable standard of care for the child, and the decision about which parent will better provide for the child's welfare often turns on considerations in the checklist such as those relating to the child's physical, emotional, and educational needs (para (b)), and the child's age, sex, background, and any characteristics of his which the court considers relevant (para (d)). The court must also consider the ascertainable wishes and feelings of the child in light of his or her age and understanding (under para (a)). This too can be a powerful factor influencing the court's decision in a particular case, whether the wishes and feelings are evidenced by the statements of an articulate teenager or, for example, through a toddler's clinginess to a particular parent.

Of particular importance in residence disputes is paragraph (c), which directs a court to consider the likely effect on the child of any change in his circumstances. Of course, when parents part there is inevitably a change of circumstances for the children, though if one parent remains in the former family home with the children, he or she has a clear advantage under that head. Continuity is generally regarded as desirable for a child because it assists in giving a sense of security at a time when the child may feel vulnerable and threatened by the parents' separation. Bonds are likely to exist not only between the child and the parent with whom he is living, but also between the child and other members of the household, neighbours, friends, and companions at school. Thus, the parent who keeps the children in the immediacy of relationship breakdown is most likely, all other things being equal, to obtain a residence order. Parents seeking legal advice should be made fully aware of this bias towards the status quo. Even where a parent leaves the family home with the children, delays in litigation may mean that the new arrangements will have assumed some importance by the time of a court hearing. *Re B (Residence Order: Status Quo)*[240] illustrates the force of the status quo. The trial judge transferred residence from the father to the mother, taking the view that the child could only enjoy such contact if she was under the control of the mother. Allowing the father's appeal, the Court of Appeal agreed with counsel's submission that the judge was wrong to put speculative improvements in contact over continuity of care. The contact difficulties needed to be tackled but not by the drastic measure of upsetting the status quo, which in this case was of overwhelming importance for securing the child's future.

In addition to the statutory checklist structuring the court's exercise of discretion, the appellate courts have also developed guideline general principles to assist judges.

5.7.1 The relevance of the child's age and sex

In *Re W (A Minor) (Residence Order)*,[241] Lord Donaldson MR expressed the view that there is a rebuttable presumption of fact that the best interests of a baby are served by being with its mother.[242] In saying this his Lordship laid stress on the word 'baby' and indicated that different considerations apply in the case of a child. In *Re W* the mother initially agreed that her baby would be looked after by the father, who duly collected the baby from the hospital shortly after the child's birth and was caring for the child. Shortly thereafter the mother changed her mind and sought the return of the child. A judge had ordered that the status quo be maintained pending the preparation of reports. Allowing the mother's appeal, the Court of Appeal substituted an interim residence order in her favour, Balcombe LJ commenting that 'it hardly requires saying that a baby of under four

---

[239] Ibid, 400.   [240] [1998] 1 FLR 368.   [241] [1992] 2 FLR 332, CA.   [242] Ibid, 336.

weeks old would normally be with his or her natural mother'. Agreeing with Balcombe LJ, Lord Donaldson added that it had not really been possible for a status quo to be established in the very short period of three weeks that the father had cared for the child.

Apart from this presumption of fact in the case of a baby, there is no presumption that one parent should be preferred to another parent at a particular age of the child or because of the child's sex. In *Re S (A Minor) (Custody)*[243] Butler-Sloss LJ explained that 'it is natural for young children to be with their mothers' but where there is a dispute 'it is a consideration but not a presumption'.[244] In *Re A (A Minor) (Custody)*[245] her Ladyship added that:

> In cases where the child has remained throughout with the mother and is young, particularly when a baby or a toddler, the unbroken relationship of the mother and child is one which it would be very difficult to displace, unless the mother was unsuitable to care for the child.[246]

In *Re A (A Minor) (Custody)*[247] a mother left the matrimonial home with her 12-year-old daughter, leaving four of her children with the father, including a 6-year-old girl, K. Upon the mother's custody application the judge, apparently starting from the proposition that girls naturally go with their mothers, awarded custody of K to the mother. At the time of the mother's application, the father had been caring for the girl (with the assistance of a full-time housekeeper and a girlfriend) for nearly 12 months. Allowing his appeal, the Court of Appeal held that the judge had applied the wrong test and also failed to take sufficient account of the status quo. Butler-Sloss LJ distinguished the situation where there has been a continuum of care by the mother (as described earlier) from one as here where the mother and child have been separated and she seeks the return of the child.

The approach in *Re S (A Minor) (Custody)* and *Re A (A Minor) (Custody)* was reflected in the House of Lords decision in *Brixey v Lynas*,[248] an appeal from Scotland in which the English case law was cited. In that case the parents, who were disputing the custody of a young child, were from very different backgrounds. As the House of Lords put it, the father was 'comfortably middle class, while the mother had had none of the educational and social advantages which he had had'. The child had been living with the mother when the Glasgow Sheriff Court granted custody to the father, taking the view that 'as a member of the father's family the child would have all the advantages of comfort, education and a strong and stable moral framework which they can offer'.[249] Allowing the mother's appeal, the Court of Session, First Division, found[250] that the sheriff had failed to take account of the important factor that during infancy the child's need for her mother is stronger than the need for a father. The Court of Session explained that this principle did not create any presumption in favour of the mother, nor rule of law, but reflected a generally recognised belief that a mother is ordinarily better able, for whatever reason, to minister to a very young child's needs than is a father. The father appealed to the House of Lords, contending *inter alia* that that approach amounted to a maternal preference and thus sexual prejudice. Dismissing the father's appeal, Lord Jauncey, in an opinion which had the full agreement of the House, commented that 'to ignore the fact that in normal circumstances, and I stress the word normal, a mother is better able than a father to fulfil

---

[243] [1991] 2 FLR 388, CA.

[244] Ibid, 390. See also *Re A (A Minor) Custody)* [1991] 2 FLR 394 at 400: 'There is no presumption which requires the mother, as mother, to be considered as the primary caretaker in preference to the father.'

[245] [1991] 2 FLR 394.   [246] Ibid, 400.   [247] Ibid.   [248] [1996] 2 FLR 499, HL (Sc).

[249] Ibid, 500.

[250] See *Brixey v Lynas*, 1994 SLT 847, and for comment see E. Sutherland, 'Mother Knows Best', 1994 SLT (News) 375.

the needs of a very young child is to ignore what is generally accepted to be reality'. He rejected the father's argument about sexual prejudice with the following words:

> To suggest that any recognition of the normal mother's natural ability to look after a very young child amounts to sexual discrimination is absurd. Nature has endowed men and women with very different attributes and it so happens that mothers are generally better fitted than fathers to provide for the needs of very young children. This is no more discriminatory than the fact that only women can give birth.[251] Every case must be considered on its own facts.[252]

Summarising the legal position, which can probably be taken also to reflect the House of Lords' view of the law of England and Wales, Lord Jauncey explained:

> the advantage to a very young child of being with its mother is a consideration which must be taken into account in deciding where lie its best interests in custody proceedings in which the mother is involved. It is neither a presumption nor a principle but rather recognition of a widely held belief based on practical experience and the workings of nature. Its importance will vary according to the age of the child and to the other circumstances of each individual case such as whether the child has been living with or apart from the mother and whether she is or is not capable of providing proper care. Circumstances may be such that it has no importance at all. Furthermore it will always yield to other competing advantages which more effectively promote the welfare of the child. However, where a very young child has been with its mother since birth and there is no criticism of her ability to care for the child only the strongest competing advantages are likely to prevail.[253]

5.7.2 Young siblings should normally be brought up together

In *C v C (Minors: Custody)*[254] the Court of Appeal held that young siblings should, wherever possible, be brought up together in the same household, so that they may be an emotional support to each other following the family breakdown as they grow up. The children's mother moved out of the family home with the 7-year-old daughter, leaving their 4-year-old son with the father. She then obtained her own accommodation and applied for residence of both children. Noting that there was satisfactory contact between the boy and the mother, the judge made a split custody order confirming the existing arrangements. The Court of Appeal held that the judge had erred, and that a split order should not be made unless there were strong factors to warrant it.

In *B v B (Minors) (Custody, Care and Control)*[255] the High Court clarified that although it is desirable that siblings are brought up together, this factor is not of such importance always to override other factors in the balancing exercise, and particularly so where there is a large age gap between children. Upon the breakdown of the parents' relationship the older two children (aged 10 and 9) lived with the father and the youngest (aged 2) with the mother. The older children wished to stay with their father and the youngest child was bonded with the mother. In those circumstances the status quo was confirmed by the court.

In a case in which there is a baby and a young child, the presumption of fact that the baby's best interests are best served by being with the mother, combined with the desirability of siblings being brought up together, will often lead to the conclusion that both children should be with the mother.

---

[251] Of course, now following the Gender Recognition Act 2004 that is not wholly true.
[252] [1996] 2 FLR 499 at 504.   [253] Ibid, 505.   [254] [1988] 2 FLR 291, CA.
[255] See also *B v B (Residence Order: Restricting Applications)* [1991] 1 FLR 402, FD.

5.7.3 A parent's sexual orientation

There have been several cases in which the relevance of a parent's sexual orientation has been raised. The European Court of Human Rights in *Salgueiro da Silva Mouta v Portugal*[256] has held that, in the case of any relationship between a child and parent which constitutes family life within Article 8 of the ECHR, a decision regarding a child's residence in which a person's sexual orientation is of itself a decisive factor would constitute a breach of Articles 8 and 14 taken together. In *Salgueiro da Silva Mouta* a child's parents had divorced and the father was cohabiting in a homosexual relationship. The child's residence was initially with the mother. However, the mother failed to allow the father contact with the child,[257] and for that reason a court subsequently reversed the child's residence in favour of the father. The Lisbon Court of Appeal, however, allowed the mother's appeal against that decision, the majority commenting in the course of judgment that homosexuality 'is an abnormality and children should not grow up in the shadow of abnormal situations'.[258] The European Court of Human Rights unanimously found that the Lisbon court had made a distinction based on the father's sexuality which was not acceptable under the ECHR.

In light of this ruling, the leading domestic authority on this issue, the Court of Appeal decision in *C v C (A Minor) (Custody: Appeal)*[259] must be viewed with considerable caution, although it has never been overruled. In that case the court had to choose between parents of a 6-year-old girl who both clearly loved the child and could give her good physical care. The father had remarried and was living with his new wife; the mother was living with a lesbian partner. The trial judge gave the care of the child to the mother, holding that her lesbian relationship was not a matter to put into the balancing exercise since its impact on the child would be much the same whether she visited her mother from time to time or lived with her permanently. Allowing the father's appeal and remitting the case for a fresh hearing, the Court of Appeal ruled that the judge had been plainly wrong to engage in the balancing operation as if there were no lesbian relationship.

Glidewell LJ expressed the view that 'despite the vast changes over the past 30 years or so in the attitudes of our society generally to the institution of marriage, to sexual morality, and to homosexual relationships... a lesbian relationship between two adult women is an unusual background in which to bring up a child'. Balcombe LJ added that:

> It is still the norm that children are brought up in a home with a father, mother and siblings (if any) and, other things being equal, such an upbringing is most likely to be conducive to their welfare. If, because the parents are divorced, such an upbringing is no longer possible, then a very material factor in considering where the child's welfare lies is which of the competing parents can offer the nearest approach to the norm.[260]

It is submitted that, in light of *Salgueiro da Silva Mouta* and the requirements of the HRA 1998, a domestic court would be highly unlikely to view this norm as a lawful justification for deciding a residence application in favour of a heterosexual parent rather than a homosexual parent. It should be noted that the assertions in *C v C* were made over 20 years ago[261] and must be viewed in light of increased social and legal recognition of same-sex relationships and parenting. By contrast with *C v C*, in *G v F (Shared Residence:*

---

[256] *Salgueiro da Silva Mouta v Portugal* (App no 33290/96) [1999] ECHR, [2001] 1 FCR 653, ECtHR.

[257] Faciliation of contact was not aided by the fact that the maternal grandparents were Jehovah's Witnesses and had strong religious objections to the father's homosexuality.

[258] [2001] 1 FCR 653 at 664 (para 14 of the judgment).   [259] [1991] 1 FLR 223.

[260] Ibid, 231.   [261] It was decided on 24 August 1990.

Parental Responsibility)²⁶² Bracewell J granted leave to apply for a shared residence order to the applicant who had formerly been in a lesbian relationship with the respondent, holding that sexual orientation is merely a background circumstance and that it would be 'entirely wrong…and unsustainable to seek, in any way, to reflect against the applicant by reason of the nature of her relationship with the respondent'.²⁶³ It is submitted that the correct approach is as follows. As *C v C* makes clear that the parent's relationship (whether homosexual or heterosexual) cannot simply be ignored; it is one of the circumstances of the case. However, a parent's sexuality cannot be relevant per se, for to choose on that basis would be discriminatory; the nature of the parent's relationship is relevant only insofar as it impacts on the child's welfare.

5.7.4 Religious beliefs and practices

Sometimes a parent may object to the other parent's religious beliefs and/or practices, and fear the impact on the child of those beliefs.

In *Hoffmann v Austria*²⁶⁴ the European Court of Human Rights held that to draw a distinction between parents in a custody dispute simply on the basis of one parent's religion is a violation of that parent's rights under Articles 8 and 14 of the ECHR taken together. In that case the parents of two children had been married as Roman Catholics, and Austrian legislation provided that during the marriage, in the absence of an agreement, 'neither parent may decide without the consent of the other that the child is to be brought up in a faith different from that shared by both parents at the time of their marriage'.²⁶⁵ The mother had subsequently converted to the Jehovah's Witness faith and the parents divorced. In a dispute over custody of the children, the Austrian Supreme Court awarded custody of the children to the father. The court took account of the practical consequences of the religious convictions of the Jehovah's Witnesses, including their rejection of holidays such as Christmas and Easter which are customarily celebrated by the majority of the Austrian population, their opposition to the administration of blood transfusions, and in general their position as a social minority living by its own distinctive rules.²⁶⁶ The European Court of Human Rights commented that, depending on the circumstances of the case, those factors may be capable of tipping the scales in favour of one parent or the other. However, the Austrian court had also drawn on the said legislation in reaching its decision, noting that the mother was seeking to bring up the children in a religion other than that of the marriage. The European Court of Human Rights found that the Austrian Supreme Court had regarded the legislation as a decisive factor and had thus discriminated unlawfully simply on the basis of religion.²⁶⁷

The case can be compared with *Ismailova v Russia*²⁶⁸ in which the parents married as Muslims and the mother converted to the Jehovah's Witness faith. Upon the parents' divorce the father sought and obtained custody of the couple's children, aged 7 and 4. In the course of granting residence to the father, the Russian courts noted that the mother and the children had been living in cramped conditions in a three-room flat with the maternal grandparents and the mother's three brothers. Jehovah's Witness meetings were held a few times a week at the flat and the children had been frightened by some of the things they had heard. For example, they had become frightened of rain and wind, being worried that a worldwide flood and earthquake would take place. The mother claimed a violation of Articles 8 and 14 of the ECHR in that she had been unlawfully discriminated

---

²⁶² [1998] 2 FLR 799. ²⁶³ Ibid, 805.
²⁶⁴ *Hoffmann v Austria* (App no 12875/87) [1993] ECHR 25, (1994) 17 EHRR 293, [1994] 1 FCR 193, ECtHR.
²⁶⁵ Federal Act on the Religious Education of Children, art 2(2).
²⁶⁶ *Hoffmann v Austria*, para 32. ²⁶⁷ Ibid, para 33. ²⁶⁸ [2008] 1 FLR 533.

against in the custody proceedings on the basis of her religion. The European Court of Human Rights found no violation, explaining that the domestic courts' decisions had not been based upon the mother's membership of the Jehovah's Witnesses but upon the impact of her religious practices upon the children's interests. Furthermore, this was only one aspect of the decision, which was also based on the children's financial, housing, and general living conditions.[269]

The English authorities have similarly drawn a distinction between religion and the effect of religious practices. They have seen as material such factors as indoctrination or isolation arising from religious practices.[270] In *Re T (Minors) (Custody: Religious Upbringing)*[271] the Court of Appeal made clear that it is not for the court to pass any judgement on the beliefs of the parents where they are socially acceptable and consistent with a decent and respectable life. The case concerned the custody of three children in wardship proceedings: two 15-year-old twin girls and their 8-year-old sister. The parents' marriage broke down as a result of the mother's interest in, and commitment to, the Jehovah's Witness faith. Evidence was given that Jehovah's Witnesses do not celebrate Christmas or birthdays and the life of that community became more important than the wider community. The judge regarded it of critical importance that if the mother were given custody the children would be withdrawn from ordinary family life, and was apprehensive of the children's possible alienation from the father.

A welfare report showed that the mother was bringing up the children as well adjusted, and the girls wanted to be with their mother. The judge awarded custody to the father. Allowing the mother's appeal, Scarman LJ commented that there was no reason why the mother should not espouse the beliefs and practices of the Jehovah's Witnesses for there was nothing immoral or socially obnoxious about them. The judge had given too much weight to the father's only complaint against the mother, namely her religious beliefs, and too little weight to the success of the mother in bringing up the children.

In *M v H (Education: Welfare)*[272] the child's residence was shared between the parents. The child lived for most of the time in Germany with the mother, who was a Jehovah's Witness, but spent considerable time also with the father in England, who was a Catholic. The question arose as to where the child should be educated, with consequent impact on the child's residence arrangements. Charles J decided that the child should be educated in England, supporting his decision with the view that thereby the likely social effects on the child of the mother's beliefs and practices as a Jehovah's Witness would have far less weight.[273]

Sometimes a parent's fears about the other parent's religious beliefs may have an impact upon the welfare of the child and this may need to be reflected in the court's order. An example, albeit in the context of a contact dispute, is *Wright v Wright*[274] where the mother's fear that the father would indoctrinate the child justified denial of the father's contact because the mother's emotional reaction if contact took place would be damaging to the child.

5.7.5 The child's background

A child's religious heritage is of course a relevant consideration on any application, being part of the child's background within section 1(3)(d) of the Children Act 1989, and an important factor where the child's religion is a powerful aspect of the family's way of life.[275] The weight

---

[269] Ibid, [62].

[270] See eg *Re R (Residence: Religion)* [1993] 2 FLR 163 (father withdrawn from religious sect and thus affecting ability to have contact with child).   [271] (1981) 2 FLR 239. The case was decided in 1975.

[272] [2008] EWHC 324 (Fam), [2008] 1 FLR 1400.

[273] Ibid, [107]–[110]. The child would likely have a wider circle of friends and be able to celebrate birthdays and Christmas.   [274] (1981) 2 FLR 276.

[275] *Re P (Section 91(14) Guidelines) (Residence and Religious Heritage)* [1999] 2 FLR 573, CA.

given to the child's religion will vary according to the facts of each case.[276] Even where religious practices are not a source of concern, the child's religion may in some cases need to defer to other welfare considerations. In *Re P (Section 91(14) Guidelines) (Residence and Religious Heritage)*[277] a girl with Down's Syndrome was born to Orthodox Jewish parents (the father was a Rabbi) who were initially unable to care for her. From the age of 17 months the child was placed with experienced foster parents who were non-practising Catholics. When the child was 8 years old the parents sought the return of their daughter. The judge concluded that the child should not be moved given her attachment to the foster parents. Upholding that decision, the Court of Appeal held that the 'undoubted importance for an Orthodox Jew of his religion which provides in itself a way of life which permeates all activities, is a factor to be put in the balancing exercise' but also noted that religious and cultural heritage could not be the overwhelming factor, nor displace the weighty welfare factors.[278]

5.8 SHARED RESIDENCE[279]

Section 11(4) of the Children Act 1989 provides:

> Where a residence order is made in favour of two or more persons who do not themselves all live together, the order may specify the periods during which the child is to live in the different households concerned.[280]

This provision followed a recommendation of the Law Commission which saw 'no reason why such orders should be actively discouraged given evidence from the USA that, where practicable, such arrangements could work well'.[281] It was never the expectation or intention that they would be a common form of order.[282] However, section 11(4) could 'be taken to be an encouragement to make more use of shared residence orders than hitherto'.[283]

5.8.1 On what bases can the court make a shared residence order?

In *Re A (Joint Residence: Parental Responsibility)*[284] Sir Mark Potter P explained that there are three possible bases for making a shared residence order:

(i) where it provides legal confirmation of the factual reality of a child's life;[285]

(ii) where it is the means by which to confer parental responsibility on an individual who would otherwise not be able to apply for a free-standing parental responsibility order;[286]

---

[276] Ibid, 585.   [277] [1999] 2 FLR 573, CA.   [278] Ibid, 586.

[279] See generally, S. Gilmore, 'Court Decision-Making in Shared Residence Order Cases—A Critical Examination' [2006] Child and Family Law Quarterly 478; S. Gilmore, 'Shared Residence: A Summary of the Courts' Guidance' [2010] Family Law 285; R. George and P. Harris, 'Parental Responsibility and Shared Residence Orders: Parliamentary Intentions and Judicial Interpretations' (2010) 22 Child and Family Law Quarterly 151; S. Harris-Short, 'Resisting the March Towards 50/50 Shared Residence. Rights, Welfare and Equality in Post-Separation Families' (2010) 22 Journal of Social Welfare and Family Law 257–274.

[280] The subsection is 'permissive and its purpose is to direct the court's attention to the need, if it arises, to allocate the periods during which the child is "to live in the different households concerned"': *Re H (A Child)* [2002] EWCA Civ 2005 at [33]. It is thus possible to make a shared residence order where persons in whose favour the order is made are living together in the same property (eg a house or flat), but not sharing households.

[281] Law Com No 172 (1988), para 4.12.

[282] '[P]artly because most children will still need the stability of a single home, and partly because in the cases where shared care is appropriate there is less likely to be a need for the court to make any order at all': see Children Act 1989 Guidance and Regulations (HMSO, 1991), vol 1: Court Orders, para 2.28 at p 10.

[283] *Re W (A Minor)*, CA (6 December 1993).

[284] [2008] EWCA Civ 867, [2008] 2 FLR 1593, CA.   [285] Ibid, [66].   [286] Ibid, [70].

(iii) 'where, in a case where one party has the primary care of a child, it may be psychologically beneficial to the parents in emphasising the equality of their position and responsibilities'.[287]

5.8.1.1 Reflecting the underlying reality of where the children live their lives

A shared residence order is usually made where it 'provides legal confirmation of the factual reality of a child's life',[288] and it has been said that it 'is not intended to deal with issues of parental status';[289] the latter is recognised in 'parental responsibility' which gives an 'equal say in how the children are to be brought up'.[290] A shared residence order will commonly reflect an arrangement whereby the child moves back and forth between the parents' respective households spending several days in each. However:

> The fact that the parents' homes are separated by a considerable distance does not preclude the possibility that the children's year will be divided between the homes of the two separated parents in such a way as to validate the making of a shared residence order.[291]

Furthermore, the children need not spend their time evenly, or more or less evenly, in the households concerned.[292] In *Re K (Shared Residence Order)*[293] the parents shared the child's time 40/60[294] in favour of the mother, and the father applied to increase this to 50/50 shared care reflected in a shared residence order. The judge, having concluded that the time should not be increased, refused to make a shared residence order. The Court of Appeal allowed the appeal with regard to the judge's refusal to reflect the arrangements in a shared residence order. Wilson LJ explained:

> a ruling in favour of an equal division of time and for a shared residence order, do not stand or fall together...the convenient course is...to rule first upon the optimum division of the child's time in his interests and then, in the light of that ruling, to proceed to consider whether the favoured division should be expressed as terms of a shared residence order or of a contact order.[295]

The material question, therefore, is whether the time spent with each parent can properly be characterised as shared residence. In *Re H (Children)*[296] Ward LJ explained that his:

> practical test is to postulate the question, ask the children, where do you live? If the answer is 'I live with my mummy but I go and stay with my daddy regularly', then you have the answer to your problem. That answer means a residence order with mummy and contact with daddy, but if the situation truly is such that the children say, 'Oh, we live with

---

[287] Ibid, [66].

[288] *Re A (Joint Residence: Parental Responsibility)* [2008] EWCA Civ 867, [2008] 2 FLR 1593, CA at [66] *per* Sir Mark Potter P.

[289] *Re H (Children)* [2009] EWCA Civ 902. See also *Re F (Children)* [2003] EWCA Civ 592 at [21].

[290] [2009] EWCA Civ 902 at [11]. Note, however, that a residence order has an impact upon existing parental responsibility and a holder of a residence order will have greater rights than someone with parental responsibility who does not have a residence order: see discussion in Section 5.9.2.

[291] *Re F (Children) (Shared Residence Order)* [2003] EWCA Civ 592, [2003] 2 FLR 397 at [21].

[292] This was recognised in the Law Commission Report which preceded the Children Act 1989 (Law Commission, *Family Law: Review of Child Law* (Law Com No 172, 1988), para 4.12) and has been stated in several decisions: see *A v A (Shared Residence)* [2004] EWC 142 (Fam), [2004] 1 FLR 1195 at [115] *per* Wall J; *Re F (Shared Residence Order)* [2003] EWCA Civ 592, [2003] 2 FLR 347 at [10] and [34]; *Re W (Shared Residence Order)* [2009] EWCA Civ 370, [2009] 2 FLR 436, CA at [17].   [293] [2008] 2 FLR 380, CA.

[294] While common to express the shared time as a percentage, such statistics are 'usually only of limited value'. See *Re F (Shared Residence Order)* [2003] EWCA Civ 592, [2003] 2 FLR 397 at [30], and *Re W (Shared Residence Order)* [2009] EWCA Civ 370, [2009] 2 FLR 436, CA at [17] *per* Wilson LJ.   [295] Ibid, [6].

[296] [2009] EWCA Civ 902, Moore-Bick LJ concurring.

mummy for part of the time and with daddy for the other part of the time', then you have the justification for making a shared residence order.[297]

In other words: from the child's perspective, are the existing, or proposed, arrangements appropriately characterised as shared residence? At some point the child–parent contact will be such that it is better expressed in a contact order. In *Re W (Children) (Residence Order)*,[298] for example, Thorpe LJ held that it is:

> not open to a judge to make a shared residence order in circumstances such as this where the children sleep perhaps 320 days of the year with their mother and visit their father on a pattern of contact which, although regular and frequent, is at the lower end of what is conventionally ordered.[299]

5.8.1.2 Conferring parental responsibility where not otherwise possible

Re A (Joint Residence: Parental Responsibility) confirmed that a second basis for the making of a shared residence order is as a means of conferring parental responsibility 'on an individual who would otherwise not be able to apply for a free-standing parental responsibility order'.[300] A child had been brought up for two years on the erroneous assumption that the mother's cohabitant, A, was the child's father. Upon the breakdown of the adults' relationship the child continued to enjoy good contact with A, who represented his only father figure. The Court of Appeal upheld a shared residence order which envisaged that the mother would remain the primary carer and was made principally to confer (by s 12(2) of the Children Act 1989) parental responsibility on A (who could not otherwise acquire it). The occasions on which a shared residence order will be needed to confer parental responsibility, however, have been reduced by the increased free-standing methods by which parental responsibility can be acquired.[301]

5.8.1.3 Can an order be made for the psychological benefit of a parent?

In *Re A (Joint Residence: Parental Responsibility)*[302] Sir Mark Potter P appeared to introduce a further distinct category of case in which the making of a shared residence order would be justified: 'where, in a case where one party has the primary care of a child, it may be psychologically beneficial to the *parents* in emphasising the equality of their position and responsibilities.'[303] However, it is submitted that this view is not consistent with the parliamentary intention behind residence orders,[304] finds no support in earlier authorities, nor is it consistent with the child focus required by section 1(1) of the Children Act

---

[297] Ibid, [11].   [298] [2003] EWCA Civ 116.

[299] Ibid, [9], Chadwick LJ agreeing. Cf *Re W (Shared Residence Order)* [2009] EWCA Civ 370, [2009] 2 FLR 436, CA (shared residence made when father seeing child 25 per cent of the time).

[300] *Re A (Joint Residence: Parental Responsibility)* [2008] EWCA Civ 867, [2008] 2 FLR 1593 at [70], drawing on *Re H (Shared Residence: Parental Responsibility)* [1995] 2 FLR 883.

[301] Eg Children Act 1989, ss 4ZA and 4A.   [302] [2008] 2 FLR 1593.

[303] Ibid, [66], Sir Robin Auld and Scott Baker LJ agreeing (emphasis added). His Lordship appeared to draw on a passage of Ward LJ's judgment in *Re H (Shared Residence: Parental Responsibility)* [1995] 2 FLR 883 at 889, which drew attention to the different psychological impact which residence and contact respectively may have. For criticism, see S. Gilmore, 'Shared Residence: A Summary of the Courts' Guidance' [2010] Family Law 285 (arguing this was a misreading of *Re H*, where the making of a shared residence order was firmly rooted in the psychological benefit to the *child* not the parent).

[304] See P. G. Harris and R. H. George, 'Parental Responsibility and Shared Residence Orders: Parliamentary Intentions and Judicial Interpretations' [2010] Child and Family Law Quarterly 151. See also A. Grand, 'In Practice: Disputes between Parents: Time for a New Order?' [2011] Family Law 74, suggesting that residence orders have become the new custody orders and that it is time for a newly worded order: a 'parental time order' which would deal only with time and avoid any references to parental status.

1989 as emphasised by the House of Lords in *Holmes-Moorhouse v Richmond-Upon-Thames LBC* (discussed in the next section).[305] Sir Mark Potter P's statement appears to be a misreading of some earlier authority which suggests that, in addition to reflecting the reality, a shared residence order may incidentally carry with it additional benefits. As Wall LJ commented in *Re P (Shared Residence Order)*:[306]

> Such an order emphasises the fact that both parents are equal in the eyes of the law and that they have equal duties and responsibilities as parents. The order can have the additional advantage of conveying the court's message that neither parent is in control and that the court expects parents to co-operate with each other for the benefit of their children.[307]

In *T v T (Shared Residence)*[308] a shared residence order had been made in favour of the child's mother and father, who respectively were living in same-sex relationships. The mother's partner, L, was not a party to the shared residence order although the judge had granted her parental responsibility. The mother and her partner argued that the shared residence order should not have been made and contended instead for a joint residence order in favour of the mother and her partner. The Court of Appeal held that the judge's exercise of discretion could not be criticised. However, it was submitted that, if the mother died, there would then be nothing to stop the father from asserting that the children should immediately go to live full time with him as the last surviving holder of a residence order. In light of that submission and the father's agreement to L being included in a shared residence order, the Court of Appeal made a shared residence order in favour of the mother, father, and L. Black LJ observed, however, that 'it cannot be anticipated that considerations relating to what may happen in the aftermath of an untimely death will regularly tip the balance in favour of a joint residence order in circumstances such as the present ones. In many cases, there will be a profusion of much more pressing factors that dictate another outcome.'[309]

5.8.2 Deciding whether it is appropriate to make a shared residence order: general guidance

The starting point for considering the courts' approach to a shared residence order is the House of Lords' decision in *Holmes-Moorhouse v Richmond-Upon-Thames LBC*.[310] Unusually, this case did not concern a dispute between parents, but rather the impact of a shared residence order upon a housing authority's duties under the Housing Act 1996. Accordingly, the House was not provided with an opportunity fully to engage with earlier Court of Appeal authorities on shared residence. However, it made some important statements on the nature of shared residence and how shared residence applications should be approached.

A judge had ordered the father of four children to leave the rented family home and made a shared residence order that the children live with the father on alternate weeks and half of the school holidays. The court's order rendered the father homeless and a question arose for the housing authority as to whether, as the father claimed, he was a priority housing need within section 189(1) of the Housing Act 1996, being 'a person with whom dependent children... might reasonably be expected to reside'. The father argued that the shared residence order put him into this category. The relevant housing authority disagreed and ultimately appealed the matter to the House.

---

[305] [2009] UKHL 7, [2009] 1 FLR 904 See further, S. Gilmore, 'Shared Residence: A Summary of the Courts' Guidance' [2010] Family Law 285.

[306] [2005] EWCA Civ 1639, [2006] 2 FLR 347 at [22].

[307] Ibid, [22], repeated in *Re K (Shared Residence Order)* [2008] 2 FLR 380, CA, Buxton LJ agreeing.

[308] [2010] EWCA Civ 1366.   [309] Ibid, [47].   [310] [2009] UKHL 7, [2009] 1 FLR 904.

Lord Hoffmann delivered the leading opinion. He acknowledged that 'shared residence orders are not nowadays unusual'[311] but cautioned that a court 'should not make a shared residence order unless it appears reasonably likely that both parties will have accommodation in which the children can reside'.[312] The court's decision 'must be taken in the light of circumstances as they are or may reasonably expected to be'.[313]

Lord Hoffmann noted that the housing authority's decision imported wider considerations than those of a court making a shared residence order, and the fact that a court had made an order did not necessarily require the authority to provide the necessary accommodation. Indeed, in practice it would only be in exceptional circumstances that it would be reasonable to expect the authority to so conclude given that a substantial part of the property would remain empty half of the time.[314]

Baroness Hale of Richmond (with whom Lord Walker and Lord Neuberger expressly agreed) delivered a concurring opinion from a family lawyer's perspective, which Lord Hoffmann described as 'required reading by family judges dealing with residence orders'.[315] Her Ladyship emphasised that the court's focus in shared residence applications is the children, commenting that the application of the paramountcy principle in section 1(1) of the Children Act 1989 'means that it must choose from the available options the future which will be best for the children, not the future which will be best for the adults'.[316] In addition, her Ladyship emphasised the importance of considering the children's wishes and feelings, explaining that:

> these ought to be particularly important in shared residence cases, because it is the children who will have to divide their time between two homes and it is all too easy for the parents' wishes and feelings to predominate.[317]

Echoing Lord Hoffmann's opinion, Baroness Hale underlined the fact that:

> Family court orders are meant to provide practical solutions to the practical problems faced by separating families. They are not meant to be aspirational statements of what would be for the best in some ideal world which has little prospect of realisation. Ideally there may be many cases where it would be best for the children to have a home with each of their parents. But this is not always or even usually practicable.[318]

The Court of Appeal decisions on shared residence orders, still influenced by the pre-Children Act approach in *Riley v Riley*,[319] initially adopted a cautious approach, holding that they were only to be made in exceptional[320] or unusual[321] circumstances. However, a shift came in *D v D (Shared Residence Order)*.[322] In that case an arrangement had been settled for some time whereby the children spent 38 per cent of their time with their father. The children were doing well. There was a high level of animosity between the parents, however, and the judge was convinced that the mother was using her sole residence order as a weapon in her 'war' with the father. The judge therefore made a shared residence order with a view to diminishing the parental conflict. The mother appealed,

---

[311] Ibid, [7]; and see the similar statement by Sir Mark Potter P in *Re A Joint Residence: Parental Responsibility)* [2008] EWCA Civ 867, [2008] 2 FLR 1593, CA at [66].

[312] [2009] UKHL 7, [2009] 1 FLR 904 at [8].   [313] Ibid.

[314] Ibid, [21].   [315] Ibid, [26].   [316] Ibid, [30].

[317] Ibid, [36]. See also *Re R (Residence: Shared Care: Children's Views)* [2005] EWCA Civ 542, [2006] 1 FLR 491.   [318] Ibid, [38].

[319] [1986] 2 FLR 429.

[320] *Re H (A Minor) (Shared Residence)* [1994] 1 FLR 717: 'it must be an order which would rarely be made and would depend upon exceptional circumstances.'

[321] *A v A (Minors) (Shared Residence Order)* [1994] 1 FLR 669, CA.   [322] [2001] 1 FLR 495, CA.

contending, in light of the earlier authorities, that the making of a shared residence order required exceptional circumstances, or at least demonstration of a positive benefit to the children, none of which, it was alleged, existed so as to justify the judge's order.

Hale LJ considered that there was a positive benefit to the children in making a shared residence order, and the judge's exercise of discretion was not open to challenge. Her Ladyship said that if 'it is either planned or has turned out that the children are spending substantial amounts of their time with each of their parents then...it may be an entirely appropriate order to make'. She added that she would not place 'any gloss on the legislative provisions, which are always subject to the paramount consideration of what is best for the children concerned'.[323] Dame Elizabeth Butler-Sloss P agreed that the earlier case law 'was unduly restrictive' and that the Court of Appeal 'should not impose restrictions upon the wording of the statute not actually found within the words of the section'.[324] In Re W (Shared Residence Order)[325] Wilson LJ helpfully confirmed that D v D now represents the better view.[326]

Building on D v D (Shared Residence Order)[327] the Court of Appeal has held that in such cases some justification for not making a shared residence order is required. In Re A (Children) (Shared Residence),[328] for example, the Court of Appeal overturned a judge's refusal to make a shared residence order in favour of a mother who had a child staying with her four nights per week and half of the school holidays. The court held that the judge 'should have given the greatest weight to ensuring that the order duly reflected the realities, unless there were some counterbalancing welfare consideration that prevented that sensible outcome'.[329] In Re P (Children) (Shared Residence Order)[330] Wall LJ explained that the making of a shared residence order 'involves the exercise of a judicial discretion and does not automatically follow because children divide their time between their parents in proportions approaching equality', adding, however, that 'where that does happen...a shared residence order is most apt to describe what is actually happening on the ground; and...good reasons are required if a shared residence order is not to be made'.[331]

Lord Hoffmann's comment in Holmes-Moorhouse that 'shared residence orders are not nowadays unusual'[332] could be seen as offering some support at House of Lords level to this shift in the case law. However, it should also be recalled that Baroness Hale explained that shared residence orders are not usually practicable. Thus, while shared residence orders are not to be regarded as unusual orders, neither are they to be regarded as routinely of benefit to children. There is no reason to adopt a negative approach to shared residence, but its appropriateness in the individual case must be carefully considered applying the child's welfare as the paramount consideration.

Somewhat surprisingly, in light of the authorities, in Re AR (A Child: Relocation)[333] Mostyn J said that a shared residence order 'is nowadays the rule rather than the exception'. In one sense this is right; such orders are no longer exceptional. However, care must

---

[323] Ibid, [32].

[324] Ibid, [39]. See S. Gilmore, 'Court Decision-Making in Shared Residence Order Cases: A Critical Examination' (2006) 18(4) Child and Family Law Quarterly 478–498 for difficulties with some of the reasoning in D v D.   [325] [2009] EWCA Civ 370, [2009] 2 FLR 436.

[326] Ibid, [13], citing [31]–[32] of Hale LJ's judgment in D v D (Shared Residence Order) [2001] 1 FLR 495. See also Re C (A Child) [2006] EWCA Civ 235 at [19]: 'the whole tenor of authority is against the identification of restricted circumstances in which shared residence orders may be made'.   [327] [2001] 1 FLR 495.

[328] [2002] EWCA Civ 1343, [2003] 3 FCR 656.   [329] Ibid, [10].

[330] [2005] EWCA Civ 1639, [2006] 1 FCR 309.   [331] Ibid, [22].

[332] [2009] UKHL 7, [2009] 1 FLR 904 at [7].   [333] [2010] EWHC 1346 (Fam), [2010] 2 FLR 1577.

be taken in saying that they are the rule. In *T v T (Shared Residence)*[334] the Court of Appeal was clear that Mostyn J's statement 'is to go too far. Whether or not a joint or shared residence order is granted depends upon a determination of what is in the best interests of the child in the light of all the factors in the individual case.'[335] Furthermore, Sir Nicholas Wall P has stated extra-judicially that: 'if shared parenting orders as a concept are to become the norm, the initiative, in my view, must come from Parliament'.[336]

Alongside the courts' general approach, the courts have provided some guidance on the circumstances in which shared residence might be appropriate.

5.8.3 Proposed arrangements must be clear and not likely to cause the child confusion

In *A v A (Minors) (Shared Residence Order)*[337] the Court of Appeal held that it would be unlikely that a shared residence order would be made where there were:

> concrete issues still arising between the parties which had not been resolved, such as the amount of contact, whether it should be staying or visiting contact or another issue such as education, which were muddying the waters and which were creating difficulties between the parties which reflected the way in which the children were moving from one parent to the other in the contact period.[338]

5.8.4 Where parents are not capable of working in harmony

Parents' 'inability to work in harmony is not a reason for declining to make an order for shared residence'.[339] Nor is it, by itself, a reason for making a shared residence order.[340] However, there may be cases of deliberate and sustained marginalisation of one parent by the other, where the inability to work in harmony may sometimes provide a reason for making the order[341] in order to try to prevent such marginalisation by granting each party the same type of order.[342] There are also some cases in which parents, although granted contact:

> are nevertheless rightly refused shared residence on the basis that their motivation seems to be to strike at the other parent's role in the management of the child's life. In any application for an order for shared residence, the court should … be alert to discern such malign motivation.[343]

5.8.5 Should there be a presumption of shared residence?

How the law should respond to post-separation parenting disputes is controversial. Some argue on behalf of non-resident parents[344] that the usual award of residence to one parent

---

[334] [2010] EWCA Civ 1366, CA.   [335] Ibid, [26].

[336] In an address to Families Need Fathers in September 2010, reported in Elizabeth Walsh, 'Newsline Extra: The Shape of Things to Come' [2010] Family Law 1232.

[337] [1994] 1 FLR 669.

[338] Ibid, 678. Compare *Re C (A Child)* [2006] EWCA Civ 235 at [21] (classic case for shared residence where child's school was close to both homes and child was happy, confident, and had a sense of belonging in each home).

[339] *Re W (Shared Residence Order)* [2009] EWCA Civ 370, [2009] 2 FLR 436.

[340] Ibid, [15], explaining Wall J's decision in *A v A (Shared Residence)* [2004] EWHC 142 (Fam), [2004] 1 FLR 1195 at [124].

[341] See eg *Re G (Residence: Same-Sex Partner)* [2006] UKHL 43, [2006] 2 FLR 629, HL.

[342] *Re W (Shared Residence Order)* [2009] EWCA Civ 370, [2009] 2 FLR 436.

[343] *Re K (Shared Residence Order)* [2008] 2 FLR 380, CA at [21] *per* Wilson LJ. *Re M (Children) (Residence Order)* [2004] EWCA Civ 1413 (order made unworkable by the father's domestic violence, rigidity, and failure to cooperate over arrangements for the children, and manipulation of the children by involving them in inappropriate discussions).

[344] Since most non-resident parents are fathers, the arguments have been publicised by fathers' rights organisations: see R. Collier, 'Fathers 4 Justice, Law and the New Politics of Fatherhood' (2005) 17 Child and

and contact to the other should be supplanted with a norm of shared residence, or even automatic *equal* division of parenting time.[345] Should there be a presumption of shared residence in all cases? [346]

Research has not demonstrated any 'clear linear relationship between shared time and improving children's outcomes';[347] child well-being is most strongly connected to the quality of the post-separation parenting arrangement, although the amount of time a parent spends with the child is not irrelevant to quality. Shared residence can thus facilitate the opportunity for good quality parenting[348] from both parents in the normal setting of the parents' households. Furthermore, there are some studies that have reported positive outcomes for children in shared residence, and some studies comparing shared residence with other arrangements show modest comparative benefits of shared residence in some areas of child adjustment.[349] The evidence does not, therefore, suggest that a negative stance should be taken to shared residence.

However, reviews of research on the well-being of children in such arrangements would also caution against the introduction of a general presumption of shared residence.[350] If the parents of four children are to put in place a shared residence arrangement in which the children have their own permanent spaces in the parents' respective homes, the parents each require a home with sufficient accommodation for four children. Not surprisingly, research shows that parents who self-select such arrangements tend to be well educated and well resourced, perhaps with flexible work arrangements, and involvement in childcare when the relationship was intact.[351]

Successful arrangements also tend to involve cooperative, child-focused parents. These are not features typically exemplified by parents who are fighting over shared residence in the courts, and the research suggests that, in cases of high parental conflict,

Family Law Quarterly 511 and R. Collier and S. Sheldon (eds), *Fathers' Rights Activism and Law Reform in Comparative Perspective* (Oxford: Hart, 2006).

[345] H. Rhoades 'The Rise and Rise of Shared Parenting Laws: A Critical Reflection' (2002) 19 Canadian Journal of Family Law 75; H. Rhoades and S. B. Boyd, 'Reforming Custody Laws: A Comparative Study' (2004) 18(2) International Journal of Law, Policy and the Family 119.

[346] For debate, see S. Johnson, 'Shared Residence Orders: For and Against' [2009] Family Law 131 (arguing in favour of shared residence, and drawing attention to s 1(3)(g) of the Children Act which directs the court to consider, 'the range of powers available to the court in determining questions about children').

[347] B. Fehlberg, B. Smyth, M. Maclean, and C. Roberts, 'Legislating for Shared Time Parenting After Separation: A Research Review' (2011) 25(3) International Journal of Law, Policy and the Family 318 at 321.

[348] Children benefit from authoritative parenting: see P. R. Amato and J. G. Gilbreth, 'Nonresident Fathers and Children's Well- Being: A Meta-Analysis' (1999) 61 Journal of Marriage and the Family 557.

[349] S. Gilmore, 'Contact/Shared Residence and Child Well-Being—Research Evidence and its Implications for Legal Decision Making' (2006) 20 International Journal of Law, Policy and the Family 344–365.

[350] For reviews and discussion of the research, see B. Fehlberg, B. Smyth, M. Maclean, and C. Roberts, 'Legislating for Shared Time Parenting After Separation: A Research Review' (2011) 25(3) International Journal of Law, Policy and the Family 318 at 321; L. Trinder, 'Shared Residence: A Review of Recent Research Evidence' [2010] Child and Family Law Quarterly 475; S. Gilmore, 'Shared Parenting: The Law and the Evidence (Part 2)' (2010) 20 Seen and Heard 21–35; S. Harris-Short, 'Resisting the March Towards 50/50 Shared Residence: Rights, Welfare and Equality in Post-Separation Families' (2010) 32(3) Journal of Social Welfare and Family Law 257–274, esp at 263 et seq; S. Gilmore, 'Contact/Shared Residence and Child Well-Being—Research Evidence and its Implications for Legal Decision Making' (2006) 20 International Journal of Law, Policy and the Family 344–365.

[351] See B. Fehlberg, B. Smyth, M. Maclean, and C. Roberts, 'Legislating for Shared Time Parenting After Separation: A Research Review' (2011) 25(3) International Journal of Law, Policy and the Family 318 at 322, and references cited therein.

the courts should be particularly cautious about making a shared residence order.[352] In such situations, when the child is spending lengthy periods in each household, a child can become particularly caught between the parents' conflict, with consequent harmful effects on the child's well-being.

There is also some evidence from Australia that overnight 'shared care of children under four years of age had an independent and deleterious impact',[353] the repeated disruption of the child's care arguably causing stress and consequent developmental and behavioural problems.

In addition, some children can find shared residence burdensome,[354] for example having to carry their belongings to and fro between different homes and accommodating different rules/practices in each home. As the House of Lords acknowledged in *Holmes-Moorhouse*, it is very important to listen to the views of the children concerned since they are the ones who will have to live with the arrangement. Research from Norway by Skørten and Barlindhaug suggests that there is a danger that shared residence arrangements can be put in place by parents without consulting the children concerned.[355] Their analysis showed that particularly where the child had a highly educated father there was a danger of the child not being consulted. Very plausibly, Skørten and Barlindhaug argue that such well-educated fathers, who may be engaged in childcare as well as being breadwinners, may see their shared physical care of the child in terms of their right, which can undermine the child's say.[356]

As Sonia Harris-Short has pointed out,[357] in the UK such appeals to fairness, justice, and equality based on fathers' increasingly hands-on role in children's upbringing are not unproblematic, since empirical evidence on father involvement 'points very clearly to the wide gulf that exists between the rhetoric and the reality of parenting practices within the UK'.[358] She argues that the child's future interests should be firmly grounded in the realities of family life, since the pre-separation pattern of care is likely to be an important factor in the child's ability to adjust successfully within a post-separation shared care arrangement.[359] As Harris-Short notes, the debates are 'notably quiet as to whether

---

[352] See J. McIntosh, B. Smyth, M. Kelaher, Y. Wells, and C. Long, *Post-Separation Parenting Arrangements and Developmental Outcomes for Infants and Children* (Victoria: Family Transitions for the Australian Government Attorney-General's Department, 2010). For discussion see J. McIntosh and R. Chisholm, 'Cautionary Notes on the Shared Care of Children in Conflicted Parental Separation' (2008) 14(1) Journal of Family Studies 37–52; J. McIntosh and R. Chisholm, 'Shared Care and Children's Best Interests in Conflicted Separation—A Cautionary Tale from Current Research' (2008) 20(1) Australian Family Lawyer 1; C. M. Buchanan, E. E. Maccoby, and S. M. Dornbusch, 'Caught Between Parents: Adolescents' Experience in Divorced Homes' (1991) 62(5) Child Development 1008; C. M. Buchanan, E. E. Maccoby, and S. M. Dornbusch, *Adolescents After Divorce* (Cambridge, MA: Harvard University Press, 1996).

[353] McIntosh et al, ibid, 9.

[354] See eg the interviews with children reported in C. Smart, 'From Children's Shoes to Children's Voices' (2002) 40(3) Family Court Review 307–319, and the research in C. Smart, B. Neale, and A. Wade, *The Changing Experience of Childhood: Families and Divorce* (Cambridge: Polity Press, 2001).

[355] K. Skørten and R. Barlindhaug 'The Involvement of Children in Decisions about Shared Residence' (2007) 21 International Journal of Law, Policy and the Family 373–385.

[356] Ibid, 382.

[357] S. Harris-Short, 'Resisting the March Towards 50/50 Shared Residence: Rights, Welfare and Equality in Post-Separation Families' (2010) 32(3) Journal of Social Welfare and Family Law 257–274 at 266.

[358] Ibid, 268. See the analysis of the research at 267–268.   [359] Ibid, 270–271.

the child's welfare similarly demands that he or she spends a substantial and significant amount of time with both parents when living within the intact family'.[360]

The recent experience of legislating to encourage shared-time parenting in Australia also suggests caution. The law there was changed in 2006 so that judges were to consider whether it would be in the best interests of a child and reasonably practicable to order equal time or substantial and significant time with both parents. The reforms led to a marked increase in court-ordered shared residence (paradoxically, the types of cases in which shared residence may be most risky[361]). The provisions were misunderstood as introducing a starting point of equal time, and discouraged mothers from disclosing family violence because they believed that this starting point meant there was no point in doing so.[362]

Having examined the evidence and the experience in Australia, the Family Justice Review[363] recommended no change to the law. However, the Government has recently indicated that, contrary to that advice, it intends to legislate with a form of words which will give emphasis to the idea that both parents should have a meaningful relationship with a child upon parental relationship breakdown.

5.9 ATTACHING CONDITIONS TO A RESIDENCE ORDER

To what extent is it appropriate to attach a condition to a residence order? The most common issue which arises in this context is whether the court can impose a condition limiting residence to a particular geographical location. In *Re E (Residence: Imposition of Conditions)*[364] the Court of Appeal held that while the wording of section 11(7) of the Children Act 1989 is wide enough to give the court power to restrict a parent's right of residence to a specified area of the UK, such a restriction would sit uneasily with what is meant by a residence order.

Butler-Sloss LJ explained:

A general imposition of conditions on residence orders was clearly not contemplated by Parliament and where the parent is entirely suitable and the court intends to make a residence order in favour of that parent, a condition of residence is in my view an unwarranted imposition upon the right of the parent to choose where he/she will live within the UK or with whom. There may be exceptional cases, for instance, where the court, in the private law context, has concerns about the ability of the parent to be granted a residence order to be a satisfactory carer but there is no better solution than to place the child with that parent. The court might consider it necessary to keep some control over the parent by way of conditions which include a condition of residence.[365]

In *Re S (A Child) (Residence Order: Condition) (No 2)*[366] Butler-Sloss LJ clarified that the examples given earlier were just that and were not intended to limit the use of section 11(7)

---

[360] S. Harris-Short, 'Building a House Upon Sand: Post-Separation Parenting, Shared Residence and Equality—Lessons from Sweden' [2011] Child and Family Law Quarterly 344 at 369, drawing on the experience in Sweden, on which see also A. Newnham, 'Shared Residence: Lessons from Sweden' [2011] Child and Family Law Quarterly 251.

[361] L. Trinder, 'Shared Residence: A Review of Recent Research Evidence' [2010] Child and Family Law Quarterly 475.   [362] See Fehlberg et al, 236–330.

[363] *Family Justice Review Final Report* (Ministry of Justice, November 2011), and see Ministry of Justice and Department for Education, *The Government Response to the Family Justice Review: A System with Children and Families at its Heart* (Cm 8273, February 2012), paras 59–64.

[364] [1997] 2 FLR 638, CA.

[365] Ibid, 642. See on the issue of with whom the parent will live, *Re D (Minors) (Residence: Imposition of Conditions)* [1996] 2 FLR 281, CA.   [366] [2002] EWCA Civ 1795, [2002] 1 FCR 138.

to particular exceptional categories.[367] Her Ladyship observed that section 11(7) provides 'a safety net to allow for the exercise of discretion under the provisions of s 1 where the paramountcy of the welfare of the child exceptionally requires the court to impose restrictions upon the primary carer which otherwise would be unacceptable',[368] adding that an 'exceptional case means truly exceptional and there will be few of them'.[369] Earlier, in *Re S (A Child) (Residence Order: Condition)*[370] Clarke LJ had commented that 'no case will be an exceptional case unless the absence of such a condition would be incompatible with the welfare of the child'.[371] As Lowe et al comment, for the court to impose conditions save in exceptional circumstances 'would be an unsustainable restriction on adult liberties and would be likely to have an adverse effect on the welfare of the child by denying the primary carer reasonable freedom of choice'.[372]

In *Re E*, upon the breakdown of the parents' relationship the mother, who was from Blackpool, proposed to relocate there with the children. The father, a Nigerian, wanted the children to remain in London close to his family, a view supported by the court welfare officer who felt strongly that the children fitted more easily into the multiracial and multicultural lifestyle of London. The Court of Appeal held that these circumstances were not exceptional and the judge had not been justified in adding a condition that the mother should reside in London in the former matrimonial home.

By contrast, in *Re H (Children: Residence Order: Condition)*[373] the circumstances were found to fall into the category of exceptional.[374] The mother had a problem with alcohol abuse which she was seeking to address, but had not yet achieved abstinence. The judge made a residence order to the father, but also prohibited the children's relocation with the father to Northern Ireland. The evidence showed that the proposed removal and the mother's consequent loss of contact with the children would be perceived by her as akin to a bereavement, the effect of which would be devastating, not only defeating her search for abstinence but capable of plunging her into accelerated alcoholic decline.[375] The Court of Appeal dismissed the father's appeal against the prohibited steps order, commenting that this was 'rightly classified as a highly exceptional case'.[376]

The circumstances were also exceptional in *Re S (A Child) (Residence Order: Condition) (No 2)*.[377] The mother wished to relocate with the child from London to Cornwall to live with her new partner. The child suffered from Down's Syndrome with associated medical problems. She was attached to the father and would find change in her routine difficult to manage. As Laws LJ succinctly summed up in upholding the judge's order preventing relocation:

> The combination of this little girl's disability and medical problems, the limits of her understanding, her foreshortened life expectancy, and the practicalities of travel between South London and Cornwall amply suffice to produce that result.[378]

---

[367] Ibid, [17]. See also *Re S (A Child) (Residence Order: Condition)* [2001] EWCA Civ 847, [2001] 3 FCR 154 at [34] *per* Clarke LJ.

[368] [2002] EWCA Civ 1795, [2002] 1 FCR 138 at [17].

[369] Ibid, [23]. See also in *Re S (A Child) (Residence Order: Condition)* [2001] EWCA Civ 847, [2001] 3 FCR 154 at [35] *per* Clarke LJ: 'should only be imposed in genuinely exceptional cases'.

[370] [2001] EWCA Civ 847, [2001] 3 FCR 154.   [371] Ibid, [37].

[372] N. Lowe et al, *International Movement of Children* (Bristol: Jordan Publishing, 2004), p 90.

[373] [2001] EWCA Civ 1338, [2001] 2 FLR 1277.

[374] In *Re B (Prohibited Steps Order)* [2007] EWCA Civ 1055, [2008] 1 FLR 613, CA Thorpe LJ acknowledged that he had not perhaps sufficiently clearly stated in *Re H* that the circumstances of the case clearly took the case into the exceptional category (at [7] and [8]).

[375] [2001] EWCA Civ 1338, [2001] 2 FLR 1277, [28].

[376] Ibid, [30].   [377] [2002] EWCA Civ 1795, [2002] 1 FCR 138.   [378] Ibid, [38].

B v B (Residence: Condition Limiting Geographic Area)[379] illustrates that the motive for relocation and the preparedness of the parent to facilitate contact following the move, may also be significant. In that case the mother was hostile to the father and his contact with their 6-year-old child. She had made applications to relocate with the child to Australia to get away from the father and now wished to move from the South of England to Newcastle. The father wished the child to remain at school in the South of England. The High Court found that the mother could not be relied on to facilitate contact and that it was not in the child's interests to move in circumstances where the child's contact with the father would depend upon the mother ensuring that the child boarded an aeroplane for London. Viewing the circumstances of the case as exceptional, the court attached a condition to the mother's residence order providing that she was to live in an area bounded by the A4 to the north, the M25 to the west, and the A3 to the south and east until further order.

In *Re L (Shared Residence Order)*[380] the Court of Appeal held that the principles concerning imposition of conditions on a residence order apply in the same way to cases in which there are shared residence orders. Wall LJ explained[381] that a shared residence order must not be seen as an automatic bar to relocation or a trump card against relocation. There may be cases in which it is determinative of welfare, yet there will be others where it will plainly be in the best interests of the child to relocate, notwithstanding the existence of a shared residence order.

Another issue which has arisen is whether the courts can exercise control over the persons living with the child who is subject to a residence order. The courts have been clear that there is no jurisdiction under the Children Act 1989 to oust a person from his or her home by way of a section 8 order,[382] and section 11(7) does not permit the court to attach conditions which have the effect of interfering with a clear right of occupation of property.[383] Nor does section 11(7) permit a court to make a residence order to a parent containing either a condition that the children are not brought into contact with a partner, or a condition ordering her not to allow her partner to reside at her address.[384] It may in any event be unrealistic to put faith in the efficacy of such a protective measure to safeguard the children from harm. Only the residential parent would be under a duty to ensure that the condition was obeyed and no one would have a duty to inform the court where the condition was broken. Therefore, such a condition could be broken with impunity, possibly placing the child at risk, yet the inclusion of the condition might generate a false sense of security that the child was being properly protected. It is suggested, therefore, that the courts' cautious approach to conditions in section 8 orders is sensible. It strikes a proper balance between recognising that courts have extensive powers to make orders for the benefit of children and acknowledging that parents have a right to conduct their lives in the manner they choose.

5.10 THE LEGAL CONSEQUENCES OF A RESIDENCE ORDER

The legal consequences of a residence order are broadly: (i) that it confers parental responsibility on persons who would not otherwise have it; (ii) it diminishes the existing parental responsibility of the non-residential parent; and (iii) it discharges a care order.

---

[379] [2004] 2 FLR 979.

[380] [2009] EWCA Civ 20, [2009] 1 FLR 1157. See R. George, 'Re L (Internal Relocation: Shared Residence Order) [2009] EWCA Civ 20, [2009] 1 FLR 1157' [2010] Journal of Social Welfare and Family Law 71.

[381] [2009] EWCA Civ 20, [2009] 1 FLR 1157 at [52].

[382] *Re D (Prohibited Steps Order)* [1996] 2 FLR 273 at 278.   [383] Ibid, 279.

[384] *Re D (Residence: Imposition of Conditions)* [1996] 2 FLR 281.

5.10.1 A residence order confers responsibilities and rights

The person who provides the child with a home will normally make most, or all, of the day-to-day decisions about the child's upbringing. Section 12(2) of the Children Act 1989 recognises this by providing that the holder of a residence order shall have parental responsibility for the child concerned while the residence order is in force.[385]

There is a further reason why a person who is caring for a child may wish to have a residence order. If the child is subsequently taken into local authority care, even though the residence order is discharged by the making of the care order, the status of having previously had a residence order could still prove important. Section 34 of the Children Act 1989 provides that a local authority shall allow the child reasonable contact with 'a person in whose favour a residence order was in force immediately before the care order was made'. It also entitles such a person to apply for a contact order under section 34 when there is a dispute with the local authority about what arrangements are reasonable. More generally, when a child is being looked after by a local authority it must involve any person with parental responsibility in decision making about the child.

5.10.2 A residence order diminishes the parental responsibility of the non-residential parent

Section 8 orders are practical mechanisms for resolving issues or disputes; they are not supposed fundamentally to alter any existing parental responsibility. However, a residence order undoubtedly does give some additional 'rights' to the residential parent, and does diminish the parental responsibility of the non-residential parent in various ways:

(i) Parental responsibility cannot be exercised in a way which is incompatible with the residence order.[386]

(ii) It is normally the case that a person who takes, or sends, a child out of the UK without the consent of a parent with parental responsibility commits an offence.[387] However, such a person does not commit an offence where he has a residence order, and where he takes or sends the child from the UK for less than one month.[388] The aim of the one-month provision is to allow holidays abroad to be taken without prior consent or the court's approval.

(iii) Appointment of a guardian does not take effect when there is a surviving parent with parental responsibility unless the deceased parent had a residence order.[389] It is only in the latter situation that the guardian shares parental responsibility with the surviving parent. This could expose the non-residential parent to forms of interference in the child's upbringing which he would not experience where no residence order had been made, and to that extent it may diminish his or her parental responsibility.

(iv) The normal rule that the consent of each parent with parental responsibility to the marriage of their child aged under 18 is abrogated when a residence order is in force: only the consent of the person who has a residence order which is needed.[390]

(v) A residence order also affects who may confer entitlement to apply for a residence or contact order on a third party.[391]

---

[385] While a residence order must usually reflect the child's living arrangements, the courts have recognised that, exceptionally, a residence order may be used to confer parental responsibility on an individual where no other mechanism exists to achieve that result: see eg *Re H (Shared Residence: Parental Responsibility)* [1995] 2 FLR 883.

[386] Children Act 1989, s 2(8).   [387] Child Abduction Act 1984, s 1.

[388] Children Act 1989, s 13.   [389] Ibid, s 5(7).   [390] Marriage Act 1949, s 3.

[391] Children Act 1989, s 10(5)(c).

(vi) As discussed in Chapter 10, a local authority may not provide accommodation for a child if any person with parental responsibility is willing and able to provide, or to arrange for accommodation to be provided, for the child.[392] Furthermore, any person with parental responsibility may remove the child at any time from local authority accommodation.[393] This rule does not apply when a residence order is in force.[394] Thus, for example, if parents divorce and no residence order is made, the parent who does not have the day-to-day care of the child can prevent the child going into local authority accommodation, and can remove the child who is being accommodated at any time. But where there is a residence order and the residential parent wants the child to be accommodated, the local authority has a discretion as to whether to accommodate the child against the wishes of the non-residential parent. When the authority is insistent on accommodating the child, the remedy for the aggrieved parent is to apply for a residence order.

5.10.3 A residence order discharges a care order

When a child is the subject of a care order only a very limited class of persons are entitled to apply for the order to be discharged.[395] Fathers without parental responsibility, relatives, and other interested persons fall outside this class. However, section 91(1) of the Children Act 1989 provides that a residence order discharges a care order. Thus, it may be possible for a relative, or other interested person, to take steps to bring a care order to an end by obtaining a residence order. This is a vitally important provision where a relative wishes to look after a child but where a local authority refuses to place the child in the care of that relative.

5.11 CONTACT ORDERS

Most commonly when parents part, any child(ren) will be living with one parent and the so-called 'non-resident parent' will normally wish to continue to see them regularly. If post-separation contact is contested in principle, or if there is a dispute as to its nature and/or frequency, a court may need to consider the matter, and if necessary make a contact order.

Key legislation

A contact order is defined in section 8(1) of the Children Act 1989 as:

an order requiring the person with whom a child lives, or is to live, to allow the child to visit or stay with the person named in the order, or for that person and the child otherwise to have contact with each other.

As can be seen, the order may provide for face-to-face contact between a person and the child, usually termed 'direct contact', and which could include overnight stays at the non-resident parent's home (known as 'staying contact'). Notice from the definition of a contact order that an order for direct contact places an obligation upon the resident parent to allow contact;[396] the order is 'not directed at the child to submit to, still less to be forced into,

---

[392] Ibid, s 20(7).   [393] Ibid, s 20(8).   [394] Ibid, s 20(9).

[395] Ibid, s 39(1): persons with parental responsibility, the child, or the local authority.

[396] It follows that, in the case of direct contact, one 'cannot have a contact order without having first determined who the person is with whom a child lives': see *Re B (A Child: Contact)* [2001] EWCA Civ 1968 at [9]. See also *In the matter of S (A Child)* [2010] EWCA Civ 705: court only has power to make an order in the terms of the definition of a contact order.

visits or staying with the absent parent',[397] nor is any duty placed upon the person named in the order. In *Re LW (Children) (Enforcement and Committal: Contact); CPL v CH-W and others*[398] the Court of Appeal considered what was meant by the word 'allow' within the definition of a contact order in the context of an application to commit a father for breach of an order. The order stated that the father was to 'allow' contact and to make the child available. He had presented the child for the mother on the doorstep of his home but did no more, and contact did not take place because the child refused to go. Munby LJ said that 'to "allow" is to concede or to permit; to "make available" is to put at one's disposal or within one's reach. That was the father's obligation; no more and no less.'[399] The judge, however, had erroneously seen the father's obligation as to take steps within the exercise of his parental responsibility to ensure that contact took place. Munby LJ commented:

> The father may have been under a parental or moral obligation to do these things, but on the wording of these orders he was not, in my judgment, under any legal obligation such as to render him in breach of the orders for failing to do them, let alone for failing to achieve—to 'ensure'—that contact actually took place. Nor...was the father under a legally enforceable obligation to take such steps in the exercise of his parental discipline, guidance and encouragement as were reasonable in all the circumstances to ensure that contact took place.[400]

The definition of a contact order in section 8 of the Children Act 1989 also recognises that contact can be maintained with a child in a variety of ways other than (or in addition to) direct contact. In some situations, it may not be possible, or it may not be appropriate, for direct contact to take place. In these circumstances a court may order indirect contact, for example in a traditional way by means of letters, cards, presents for birthdays and Christmas, and telephone calls. The court can be creative in embracing opportunities for indirect contact, and with advances in technology the options for maintaining indirect contact have increased through such mechanisms as texting, emailing, Skype, or Facetime video-calls over the internet, and social networking sites. In *Re B (Section 91(14) Order: Duration)*,[401] for example, the court sought to introduce contact between a child and father by the father, with the assistance of the local authority, making a video recording about his life.

In *Re O (Contact: Imposition of Conditions)*[402] the mother of a boy aged 2 was implacably opposed to the father's direct contact with him. The father therefore sought and was granted only indirect contact. The order provided that the mother was to: send to the father photographs of the child every three months; send the father copies of all reports pertaining to the child's progress at nursery or play group; inform the father and supply to him medical reports in the event of the child suffering a significant illness; and accept delivery of all cards and presents for the child via the postal system and read and show such deliveries to the child. The mother challenged the court's jurisdiction to impose these conditions upon her, citing in support the decision of Wall J in *Re M (A Minor) (Contact: Conditions)*.[403] In that case magistrates had directed a mother to write a letter every three months to the child's father, who was in prison, telling him about the progress of his child. They also ordered the mother to read letters from the father to the child. Wall J held that the magistrates had acted beyond their powers. He said that the effect of their order would have been to require the parents to have contact with each other, and that the

[397] *Re M (Minors)*, CA (26 January 2000).
[398] [2010] EWCA Civ 1253, [2011] 1 FCR 78.   [399] Ibid, [76].   [400] Ibid.
[401] [2003] EWCA Civ 1966, [2004] 1 FLR 871.   [402] [1995] 2 FLR 124, CA.
[403] [1994] 1 FLR 272.

court had no power to make such an order. Moreover, he was 'profoundly unhappy' about orders which required a parent to be proactive in facilitating contact such as reading communications to the child, and said that although the court may have had jurisdiction to give such a direction, nonetheless it should not have done so unless satisfied that the other parent consented, and was willing to undertake the task. He added that in the case of written communications any such order must also be subjected to the right of the resident parent to censor what is written if it is unsuitable for the child. He ruled that the direction was wrong in principle, and unwise on the facts, and therefore that it could not stand. The Court of Appeal in *Re O* rejected the mother's contentions, held that the judge's approach could not be faulted, and rejected Wall J's approach. Sir Thomas Bingham MR disagreed with the notion that an order should not be made otherwise than with the resident parent's consent because this was 'tantamount to saying that a mother's withholding of consent and expression of unwillingness to do something is enough to defeat the court's power to order that it should be done'.[404] Furthermore, his Lordship dissented from the view that the mother should be encouraged to think that she could only read what, in her judgement, should be read. He explained:

> if an absent parent abuses the right of contact by writing inappropriate, offensive, insulting or obscene material, then there is a remedy to be exercised by curtailing such an order, and of course the [resident parent] need not read such material. But that is something quite different from saying that she enjoys any general right of deciding what should be read and what should not.[405]

The Master of the Rolls observed that the court 'has ample power to compel the mother to send photographs, medical reports and school reports in order to promote meaningful contact'.[406] Commenting robustly on the mutual obligations of parents to facilitate contact, he said:

> If the caring parent puts difficulties in the way of indirect contact by withholding presents or letters or failing to read letters to a child who cannot read, then such parents must understand that the court can compel compliance with its orders; it has sanctions available and no residence order is to be regarded as irrevocable. It is entirely reasonable that the parent with the care of the child should be obliged to report on the progress of the child to the absent parent.[407]

Agreeing, Swinton Thomas LJ was clear that the court 'can impose conditions which require positive steps to be taken by one parent or the other in order to facilitate the contact' and he gave examples: a condition that the father must provide transport for the child or the mother is to be responsible for the expenses incurred in travel.

This robust defence of the efficacy of contact orders in the context of indirect contact stands in contrast to the outcome in the case of the direct contact order in *Re LW (Children) (Enforcement and Committal: Contact); CPL v CH-W and others*. That decision suggests that a direct contact order expressed baldly by reference to the order's definition in section 8 does not require positive steps to be taken beyond simply allowing the child to have contact. It may be, therefore, that practitioners will in future wish to use section 11(7) to impose conditions on direct contact orders so as to augment the resident parent's duties in respect of facilitating contact.

The case law leaves open the question of whether, and in what circumstances, a parent or other person can be ordered to take active steps to facilitate direct contact. In *Re M (A Minor) (Contact: Conditions)* the court was clear that there was power under section 11(7)

---

[404] [1995] 2 FLR 124 at 131.   [405] Ibid, 132.   [406] Ibid, 132.   [407] Ibid, 130.

to direct the residential parent to keep the other parent informed of the child's whereabouts as a necessary condition of contact taking place. In *Re O (Contact: Imposition of Conditions)* the Court of Appeal were certain that a mother must comply with an order to send photographs at regular intervals.[408] But these orders were a long way away from requiring the residential parent to take the child to visit the non-residential parent. Perhaps the solution lies in making this kind of cooperation a condition of making the residence order to that parent, thus squarely placing the burden of facilitating direct contact on the residential parent. However, the problem of enforcing the order[409] if the residential parent refused to cooperate would remain.

Occasionally it may be thought that contact should be informally supervised by a relative, or by the staff of an organisation which provides a setting for facilitating contact, usually known as a contact centre. These centres provide a particularly useful service where contact poses some risk to the child and must therefore be carefully observed, or where there is so much distrust and animosity between the parents that contact will only be possible if it takes place in a neutral setting.[410]

5.11.1 Contact a fundamental element of respect for family life

The existing relationship between a parent and child clearly attracts some legal protection. Article 9(3) of the United Nations Convention on the Rights of the Child[411] provides that:

> States Parties shall respect the right of the child who is separated from one or both parents to maintain personal relations and direct contact with both parents on a regular basis, except if it is contrary to the child's best interests.[412]

And the European Court of Human Rights has held on several occasions that:

> the mutual enjoyment by parent and child of each other's company constitutes a fundamental element of family life, even if the relationship between the parents has broken down, and domestic measures hindering such enjoyment amount to an interference with the right protected by Art 8 of the Convention.[413]

As Article 8(2) makes clear, any interference must be 'in accordance with the law' and pursue legitimate aims within the meaning of Article 8(2), principally in this context the protection of the 'health or morals' and the 'rights and freedoms' of others, notably the child. Interference must also be 'necessary in a democratic society'. In determining whether a measure is so necessary, the court 'will consider whether, in the light of the case as a whole, the reasons adduced to justify this measure were relevant and sufficient for the purposes of Art 8, para 2'.[414] The review requires a fair balance to be struck between the interests of the

---

[408] Ibid, 133.   [409] Enforcement is discussed in detail below at Section 5.12.

[410] On which see A. Perry and B. Rainey, 'Supervised, Supported and Indirect Contact Orders: Research Findings' (2007) 21 International Journal of Law, Policy and the Family 21; on the dangers of supervised contact, see C. Humphreys and C. Harrison, 'Squaring the Circle: Contact and Domestic Violence' [2003] Family Law 419.

[411] Adopted 20 November 1989, entered into force 2 September 1990, 1577 UNTS 3.

[412] See also United Nations Convention on the Rights of the Child, Arts 7, 8, and 18(1), which are usefully identified and discussed in A. Bainham, 'Contact as a Right and Obligation' in A. Bainham, B. Lindley, M. Richards, and L. Trinder (eds), *Children and Their Families: Contact, Rights and Welfare* (Oxford: Hart, 2003), p 62.

[413] *Johansen v Norway* (App no 17383/90) (1997) 23 EHRR 33 at para 52; *Bronda v Italy* (App no 22430/93) (2001) 33 EHRR 4 at para 51; *Elsholz v Germany* (App no 25735/94) (2002) 34 EHRR 58 at para 43; *Kosmopoulou v Greece* (App no 60457/00) [2004] 1 FLR 800 at [47].

[414] *Elsholz*, ibid, para 48.

child and parent.[415] It has been said, however, that 'consideration of what lies in the best interest of the child is of crucial importance in every case of this kind'[416] and that:

> particular importance must be attached to the best interests of the child which, depending on their nature and seriousness, may override those of the parent. In particular, the parent cannot be entitled under Art 8 of the Convention to have such measures taken as would harm the child's health and development.[417]

5.11.1.1 Is there a right of contact?

Andrew Bainham has suggested that these international conventions recognise a right of contact as between parent and child.[418] He recognises that the protection afforded is not absolute, and therefore describes the right as a fundamental presumption 'which may be rebutted—but only for good reason'.[419] However, Stephen Gilmore has questioned whether it is helpful to talk of a right if the term 'presumption' is needed to describe it. As he points out, a right and a presumption are different things.[420] Gilmore argues that the right protected in Article 8 is a right to respect for family life, and only one (albeit fundamental) element of that right is respect for contact. There are other aspects of family life which may require respect, such as remaining free from a risk of domestic violence.[421]

5.11.2 The courts' general approach to contact between a child and parent

In the case of a minor child[422] and parent the domestic courts' general policy is that contact 'should be maintained wherever this is practical'.[423] There is, however, no automatic expectation that contact will be maintained or established in the case of persons other than parents. It has been said, for example, that contact between a child and step-parent is not presumed.[424] In the case of persons other than parents with whom the child may have a psychological link, the burden lies on the person who wishes to have contact to establish a case for making an order. The most usual situation in which a contact dispute arises, however, is between parents upon the breakdown of

---

[415] *Olsson v Sweden (No 2)* (App no 13441/87) (1994) 17 EHRR 134 at para 90; *Elsholz v Germany* (App no 25735/94) (2002) 34 EHRR 58 at para 50.

[416] *Elsholz*, ibid, para 48; *Hoppe v Germany* (App no 28422/95) [2003] 1 FLR 384.

[417] *Johansen v Norway* (App no 17383/90) (1997) 23 EHRR 33 at para 78; *Elsholz* ibid, para 50; *Ignaccolo-Zenide v Romania* (App no 31679/96) (2001) 31 EHRR 7 at para 94; *Nuutinen v Finland* (App no 32842/96) (2002) 34 EHRR 15 at para 128; *Sahin v Germany* (App no 30943/96) [2003] 2 FLR 671 at [42]. For a summary of the Strasbourg jurisprudence, see *Re C (A Child) (Direct Contact: Suspension)* [2011] EWCA Civ 521 at [37]–[42], commenting at [43] that the 'domestic jurisprudence, if somewhat differently expressed, is to the same effect' (see at [44]–[47] for a partial anthology of the domestic authorities).

[418] A. Bainham, 'Contact as a Right and Obligation' in A. Bainham, B. Lindley, M. Richards, and L. Trinder (eds), *Children and Their Families: Contact, Rights and Welfare* (Oxford: Hart, 2003).

[419] Ibid, p 75.

[420] S. Gilmore, 'Disputing Contact: Challenging some Assumptions' [2008] Child and Family Law Quarterly 285.

[421] As discussed later, the domestic case law rejects the use of the term 'right' in this context.

[422] There is no assumption of contact between a parent and an adult child, even one under a disability: see *Re D-R (Adult: Contact)* [1999] 1 FLR 1161, CA.

[423] *Re B (A Minor) (Contact: Stepfather's Opposition)* [1997] 2 FLR 579. For an interesting recent analysis of the case law, arguing that the courts 'aim to change attitudes as well as conduct by attempting to manage the emotions that are thought to feed conflict', see F. Kaganas, 'Regulating Emotion: Judging Contact Disputes' [2011] Child and Family Law Quarterly 63.

[424] *Re H (A Minor) (Contact)* [1994] 2 FLR 776, CA.

their relationship and it is on the guidance given by the courts in that context that we focus here.

In *Re O (Contact: Imposition of Conditions)*,[425] Sir Thomas Bingham MR provided a summary of the principles that apply in contact cases involving a parent, which has been described by a senior judge[426] as 'the definitive exposition' of the law.[427]

First of all Sir Thomas Bingham MR observed that overriding all else as provided in section 1(1) of the 1989 Act, the welfare of the child is the paramount consideration.[428] Of course, in a disputed application the checklist of factors in section 1(3) of the Children Act 1989 must be applied. Indeed in *Re M (Contact: Welfare Test)*,[429] Wilson J (sitting in the Court of Appeal) said that he found it helpful to cast the issues in a contact case into the framework of the checklist of considerations set out in section 1(3) of the Children Act 1989 and to ask:

> whether the fundamental emotional need of every child to have an enduring relationship with both his parents (s 1(3)(b)) is outweighed by the depth of harm which, in the light, inter alia, of his wishes and feelings (s 1(3)(a)), this child would be at risk of suffering (s 1(3)(e)) by virtue of a contact order.[430]

In *Re H (Contact Order (No 2))*[431] the Court of Appeal commented that:

> a proper application of the checklist in s 1(3) of the Children Act 1989 is equivalent to the balancing exercise required in the application of Art 8, which is then a useful cross-check to ensure that the order proposed is in accordance with the law, necessary for the protection of the rights and freedoms of others and proportionate.

Secondly, in *Re O* the Master of the Rolls explained that:

> Where parents of a child are separated and the child is in the day-to-day care of one of them, it is almost always in the interests of the child that he or she should have contact with the other parent. The reason for this scarcely needs spelling out. It is, of course, that the separation of parents involves a loss to the child, and it is desirable that that loss should so far as possible be made good by contact with the non-custodial parent, that is the parent in whose day-to-day care the child is not.[432]

His Lordship drew on *Re H (Minors) (Access)*,[433] in which it was stated that the question was whether there are any cogent reasons why a parent should be denied contact with his children, and that it is necessary to balance the risk of possible temporary upset against the long-term benefits which will accrue from maintaining contact.[434]

---

[425] [1995] 2 FLR 124 at 128–130. For comment, see S. Jolly, 'Implacable Hostility, Contact, and the Limits of Law' (1995) 7 Child and Family Law Quarterly 228.

[426] Wall J as he then was, currently the President of the Family Division.

[427] In *Re P (Contact: Supervision)* [1996] 2 FLR 314 at 328.

[428] His Lordship added that: 'It cannot be emphasised too strongly that the court is concerned with the interests of the mother and the father only insofar as they bear on the welfare of the child.'

[429] [1995] 1 FLR 274, CA.   [430] Ibid.   [431] [2002] 1 FLR 22.

[432] *Re O* [1995] 2 FLR 124, CA at 128, drawing upon Balcombe LJ's judgment in *Re H (Minors) (Access)* [1992] 1 FLR 148, CA at 152 and Latey J's judgment in *M v M (Child: Access)* [1973] 2 All ER 81, DC.

[433] [1992] 1 FLR 148, CA at 152.

[434] Ibid 153, a view described in *Re J (A Minor) (Contact)* [1994] 1 FLR 729 as well established, and followed in many cases.

The third principle identified by Sir Thomas Bingham MR was that 'the court has power to enforce orders for contact, which it should not hesitate to exercise where it judges that it will overall promote the welfare of the child to do so'.

Fourthly, the Master of the Rolls acknowledged that cases unhappily and infrequently, but occasionally, arise in which a court is compelled to conclude that in existing circumstances an order for immediate direct contact should not be ordered. It is convenient to explain this in Section 5.10.6 on implacable hostility.

Fifthly, his Lordship observed that 'in cases in which, for whatever reason, direct contact cannot for the time being be ordered, it is ordinarily highly desirable that there should be indirect contact'.

In *In re L (A Child) (Contact: Domestic Violence) In re V (A Child) In re M (A Child) In re H (Children)*[435] (hereafter *Re LVMH*) Dame Elizabeth Butler-Sloss P respectfully agreed with Sir Thomas Bingham's review of the leading authorities on contact and his restatement of the main principles.[436] Her Ladyship emphasised again the court's duty to apply section 1(1) of the Children Act 1989 having regard to all the circumstances. Thorpe LJ in agreeing with Butler-Sloss P's judgment, similarly endorsed that approach and the law as set out in *Re O*. Thorpe LJ went on, however, in a judgment with which Waller LJ agreed, to make further comments about the courts' general approach to contact. Thorpe LJ observed that the language of the judges in explaining the basis of decision making in relation to contact has shifted over the years,[437] in judgments sometimes reflective of social attitudes and assumptions of their time.[438] He noted that contact had been described as a parental right,[439] the child's right,[440] and that judicial statements about how applications for contact should be determined have also used the term 'presumption'[441] or 'principle'.

Thorpe LJ saw difficulty with the language of rights in this context, recognising that the word 'right' is a confusing word, particularly if used loosely.[442] The word is often used by lawyers in a strong sense of a claim-right, with a correlative duty imposed upon another which ensures that the claim is fulfilled. Because the issue of court-ordered contact is always subject to the child's welfare it is not possible always to say that there is a duty to uphold contact and thus that there is a claim right to contact.

Thorpe LJ was also wary of the use of presumptions in the context of deciding contact applications, highlighting that a presumption alters the burden of proof and the consequent danger 'that the identification of a presumption will inhibit or distort the rigorous search for the welfare solution' or 'be used as an aid to determination when the individual advocate or judge feels either undecided or overwhelmed'.[443] While acknowledging that the distinction may be fine, Thorpe LJ preferred the term 'assumption', commenting that:

> it perhaps more accurately reflects the base of knowledge and experience from which the court embarks upon its application of the welfare principle in each disputed contact application.[444]

---

[435] [2001] Fam 260, CA.   [436] Ibid, 274.   [437] Ibid, 291.   [438] Ibid, 294.

[439] See eg *S v S* [1962] 1 WLR 445 at 448 *per* Willmer LJ.

[440] See eg *M v M (Child: Access)* [1973] 2 All ER 81 at 85, *per* Wrangham J; *A v L (Contact)* [1998] 1 FLR 361 at 365, Holman J describing contact as 'a fundamental right of a child'.

[441] See S. Gilmore, 'Disputing Contact: Challenging Some Assumptions' [2008] Child and Family Law Quarterly 285 for an account of judicial use of the term 'presumption' in the context of contact applications.

[442] See the observation of Ormrod LJ in *A v C* [1985] FLR 445 at 455, and of Lord Oliver of Aylmerton in *Re KD (A Minor) (Ward: Termination of Access)* [1988] AC 806, both cited by Thorpe LJ.

[443] *Re LVMH* [2001] Fam 260, CA at 295.   [444] Ibid, 295.

His Lordship doubted 'that sufficient distinction had been made in the authorities between cases in which contact is sought in order to maintain an existing relationship, to revive a dormant relationship or to create a non-existent relationship', and commented:

> The judicial assumption that to order contact would be to promote welfare should surely wane across that spectrum. I would not assume the benefit with unquestioning confidence where a child has developed over its early years without any knowledge of its father, particularly if over those crucially formative years a psychological attachment to an alternative father has been achieved.[445]

5.11.2.1 Should there be an assumption in favour of contact?

In reaching the conclusion that the benefits of contact should be assumed, Thorpe LJ relied on the Sturge/Glaser psychiatric report which he saw as fully identifying 'the benefits which children derive from continuing contact with the absent parent'.[446] However, the Sturge/Glaser report emphasises that cases are fact-sensitive and identifies a range of benefits and detriments of contact which may or may not apply depending on the facts. As Dr Sturge has explained, the true position is that the report fully identifies the benefits which children derive from continuing contact with the absent parent *when certain conditions are met.*[447]

Reviews of the research evidence on the connection between contact arrangements and child well-being show that it is not contact per se but the quality of contact that is important to children's well-being.[448] There is a range of factors potentially impacting on the relationship between child well-being and post-separation parenting arrangements, such as the quality of the parents' relationship and the personalities of those involved.[449] As Stephen Gilmore has argued, the complexity revealed by the research 'does not advocate a form of legal decision-making which relies on generalisations'.[450] Furthermore, given the deleterious effects of conflict on child well-being,[451] the adoption of a presumption (or indeed an assumption) in favour of contact seems particularly contraindicated in disputed contact cases, with their profile of high conflict demonstrated in recent research.[452]

---

[445] Ibid, 294–295.   [446] Ibid, 365.

[447] Correspondence with S. Gilmore, as discussed in S. Gilmore, 'Disputing Contact: Challenging Some Assumptions' [2008] Child and Family Law Quarterly 285.

[448] S. Gilmore, 'Contact/Shared Residence and Child Well-Being: Research Evidence and its Implications for Legal Decision-Making' (2006) 20 International Journal of Law, Policy and the Family 344 at 358.

[449] See eg J. Dunn, 'Annotation: Children's Relationships with their Nonresident Fathers' (2004) 45(4) Journal of Child Psychology and Psychiatry 659; S. Gilmore, 'Contact/Shared Residence and Child Well-Being: Research Evidence and its Implications for Legal Decision-Making' (2006) 20 International Journal of Law, Policy and the Family 344; J. Hunt, *Researching Contact* (London: National Council for One Parent Families, 2003).

[450] S. Gilmore, 'Contact/Shared Residence and Child Well-Being: Research Evidence and its Implications for Legal Decision-Making' (2006) 20 International Journal of Law, Policy and the Family 344 at 358–359. See also J. Hunt with C. Roberts, *Child Contact with Non-Resident Parents*, Family Policy Briefing 3 (Oxford: University of Oxford, 2004).

[451] See G. T. Harold and M. Murch, 'Inter-Parental Conflict and Children's Adaptation to Separation and Divorce: Theory, Research and Implications for Family Law, Practice and Policy' [2005] Child and Family Law Quarterly 185.

[452] S. Gilmore, 'Contact/Shared Residence and Child Well-Being: Research Evidence and its Implications for Legal Decision-Making' (2006) 20 International Journal of Law, Policy and the Family 344 at 359. See eg A. Buchanan, J. Hunt, H. Bretherton, and V. Bream, *Families in Conflict: Perspectives of Children and Parents on the Family Court Welfare Service* (Bristol: Policy Press, 2001); L. Trinder, J. Connolly, J. Kellett, and C. Notley,

Given the courts' approach to contact set out earlier, it is not surprising that denial of contact is rare. What are the circumstances in which contact might be denied?

5.11.3 Contact in cases of child abuse

Since each case must be decided upon its facts, the courts have been reluctant to subscribe to general principles that there should be no contact in specified circumstances. There is thus no principle that direct contact will be denied even where the applicant has abused a child,[453] however serious the abuse.[454] Abuse is, however, in every case 'an extremely important factor to be taken into account',[455] and on the facts of a particular case can constitute a justification for denying contact.[456] In *L v L (Child Abuse: Access)*,[457] however, contact was ordered despite the father's sexual abuse of his daughter. The evidence disclosed a close bond between father and child; the child had benefited from contact and was socially well adjusted, showing no signs of disturbance from the abuse. The child's welfare could be safeguarded by supervision of contact and undertakings not to question the child about the abuse. However, the Court of Appeal has also pointed out[458] that limited contact under supervised conditions has the disadvantage that it may take place infrequently and in artificial surroundings. Furthermore, at some stage a child is likely to enquire why contact is taking place under these conditions and, if given the true answer, this could lead to difficulties.

The magnitude of the distress suffered by the non-abusing parent when sexual or other abuse is discovered or alleged, and the impact any contact order will have will be relevant to the court's decision. An anxious and distressed residential parent, who is fearful for her child's safety, may be unable to give an abused child the balanced and calm care which such a child needs.

5.11.4 Contact in the context of domestic violence[459]

The Children Act 1989 defines harm so as to include impairment of health or development 'suffered from seeing or hearing the ill-treatment of another'.[460] The dangers of domestic

---

A Profile of Applicants and Respondents in Contact Cases in Essex, DCA Research Series 1/05 (2004); A. Perry and B. Rainey, 'Supervised, Supported and Indirect Contact Orders: Research Findings' (2007) 21 International Journal of Law, Policy and the Family 21 at 29.

[453] The abused child may not necessarily be the child who is the subject of the application: see for an example *P v B* [2003] EWHC 327 (Fam).

[454] *H v H (Child Abuse: Access)* [1989] 1 FLR 212, CA; *L v L (Child Abuse: Access)* [1989] 2 FLR 16, CA; *Re E-L (A Child) (Contact)* [2003] EWCA Civ 1947 at [8]: 'There is simply no principle or practice that would justify an inevitable conclusion for the termination of direct contact from the bare finding of past inappropriate sexual conduct.'

[455] *H v H* [1989] 1 FLR 212, CA at 219.

[456] Eg *Re R (A Minor) (Child Abuse: Access)* [1988] 1 FLR 206, CA. Allegations 'should be speedily investigated and resolved, not left to fester unresolved and a continuing source of friction and dispute' and once findings have been made 'everybody must thereafter approach the case on the basis of the facts as judicially found': *Re D (Intractable Contact Dispute: Publicity)* [2004] 1 FLR 1226 at [54]. Where contact is denied with one child in a household because of abuse, then according to Fox LJ in *S v S (Child Abuse: Access)* [1988] 1 FLR 213, CA, contact should be denied to all the children since an order which distinguished between the children would be destructive of family cohesion and likely to cause tensions in the household. Where a court has not made any finding about alleged sexual abuse, it should be careful not to impugn a parent's character by what it says: see *Sanchez Cardenas v Norway* (App no 12148/03) [2007] ECHR 763.

[457] [1989] 2 FLR 16, CA.

[458] *R (A Minor) (Child Abuse: Access)* [1988] 1 FLR 206, CA and *S v S (Child Abuse: Access)* [1988] 1 FLR 213, CA.

[459] See The Rt Hon Lord Justice Wall, 'Domestic Violence and Access: The Impact on Families and Enforcement Problems' [2009] International Family Law 22.

[460] Children Act 1989, s 31 as amended by s 120 of the Adoption and Children Act 2002.

violence for children are well documented.[461] Some research demonstrates a correlation between domestic violence and child abuse,[462] and shows that some children witnessing domestic violence may experience psychological harm.[463] There is a risk that contact can be used as an opportunity for ongoing abuse and control of a former partner and may be associated with a risk of emotional manipulation of the child within contact.[464] In light of this evidence, some commentators have called for a presumption against contact where domestic violence is proved,[465] as in New Zealand, where such an approach is contained within legislation.[466]

The issue attracted considerable policy debate in the 1990s. There emerged a concern that the courts' general approach to ordering contact was obscuring a proper consideration of the dangers of doing so in cases involving domestic violence.[467] In a study of county court practice in 1996 and 1997, Bailey-Harris et al[468] found that there was in practice a strong rebuttable presumption in favour of ordering contact,[469] the effect of which was to downplay the genuine and rationally based concerns of resident parents, and erroneously to characterise such parents as unjustifiably hostile to contact.[470] The research concluded that 'the presumption in favour of contact has achieved such force that it virtually amounts to a rule yielding to a different outcome only in very exceptional circumstances',[471] and that research on domestic violence 'appears to have had little impact in practice on attitudes of judges and legal practitioners'.[472]

In 1999 the Lord Chancellor's Department issued on behalf of the Children Act Sub-Committee of the Lord Chancellor's Advisory Board on Family Law (CASC) a consultation paper on contact and domestic violence, the responses to which confirmed a widespread

---

[461] For an overview of the effects of domestic violence, see O. Mills, 'Effects of Domestic Violence on Children' [2008] Family Law 165; M. Hester and L. Radford *Domestic Violence and Child Contact Arrangements in England and Denmark* (Bristol: Policy Press, 1996); C. Humphreys and R. K. Thiara 'Neither Justice Nor Protection: Women's Experiences of Post-separation Violence' (2003) 25(3) Journal of Social Welfare and Family Law 195.

[462] M. Hester 'One Step Forward and Three Steps Back? Children, Abuse and Parental Contact in Denmark' (2002) Child and Family Law Quarterly 267; L. Bowker, M. Arbitell, and J. McFerron, 'On the Relationship Between Wife Beating and Child Abuse' in K. Yllo and M. Bograd (eds), *Feminist Perspectives on Wife Abuse* (London: Sage, 1989).

[463] M. Hester, C. Pearson, and N. Harwin *Making an Impact: Children and Domestic Violence* (London: Jessica Kingsley, 2000). Children's reactions vary: see C. McGee, *Childhood Experiences of Domestic Violence* (London: Jessica Kingsley, 2000).

[464] J. Pryor and B. Rodgers, *Children in Changing Families: Life After Parental* Separation (Oxford: Blackwell, 2001), p 207.

[465] M. Kaye, 'Domestic Violence, Residence and Contact' (1996) 8 Child and Family Law Quarterly 285; M. Fineman, 'Domestic Violence, Custody and Visitation' (2002) 36 Family Law Quarterly 211.

[466] Domestic Violence Act 1995 (New Zealand).

[467] R. Bailey-Harris, J. Barron, and J. Pearce, 'From Utility to Rights? The Presumption of Contact in Practice' (1999) 13 International Journal of Law, Policy and the Family 111 at 129.

[468] R. Bailey-Harris, J. Barron, J. Pearce, and G. Davis, *Monitoring Private Law Applications Under the Children Act 1989* (London: Nuffield Foundation, 1998).

[469] R. Bailey-Harris, J. Barron, and J. Pearce, 'From Utility to Rights? The Presumption of Contact in Practice' (1999) 13 International Journal of Law, Policy and the Family 111.

[470] J. Wallbank, 'Castigating Mothers: The Judicial Response to "Wilful" Women in Disputes Over Paternal Contact in English Law' (1998) 20(4) Journal of Social Welfare and Family Law 357; C. Smart and B. Neale, 'Arguments Against Virtue—Must Contact Be Enforced?' (1997) 27 Family Law 332.

[471] Bailey-Harris et al above, 126.   [472] Ibid, 129.

problem.[473] CASC's subsequent Report[474] recommended 'Good Practice Guidelines', in the form of a Practice Direction, heightening judicial awareness of the impact of domestic violence and the need for fact-finding in such cases.[475]

Shortly before the Report was published, the issue of contact and domestic violence came before the Court of Appeal in four consolidated appeals, *Re LVMH*.[476] The Court of Appeal was given advance sight of the CASC Report and took the opportunity to incorporate a summary of the CASC guidelines into its judgments. The court also had the benefit of an expert psychiatric report on the subject of contact and domestic violence (known as the Sturge/Glaser report).[477] This report identified various advantages and disadvantages of contact depending on the circumstances, emphasised that the focus must be on the particular child and circumstances, and suggested that there should be an assumption against contact in cases of proven domestic violence. The Court of Appeal was thus provided with a perfect opportunity to offer general guidance on the approach to contact in cases of domestic violence.

Dame Elizabeth Butler-Sloss P acknowledged that the courts' general approach to contact may 'sometimes have discouraged sufficient attention being paid to the adverse effects on children living in the household where violence has occurred' and advised[478] that family judges and magistrates 'need to have a heightened awareness of the existence of and consequences (some long-term) on children of exposure to domestic violence'. The court gave guidance on how allegations of domestic violence should be addressed:

Where allegations of violence material to the outcome of a case are made 'those allegations must be adjudicated upon and found proved or not proved.'

The court 'should consider the conduct of both parties towards each other and towards the children, the effect on the children and on the residential parent, and the motivation of the parent seeking contact. Is it a desire to promote the best interests of the child or a means to continue violence and/or intimidation or harassment of the other parent?'

'In cases of serious[479] domestic violence, the ability of the offending parent to recognise his or her past conduct, to be aware of the need for change and to make genuine efforts to do so, will be likely to be an important consideration'; assertions, 'without evidence to back it up, may well not be sufficient.'[480]

---

[473] Although there had been some signs of a changing judicial attitude within case law: see R. Bailey-Harris, 'Contact—Challenging Conventional Wisdom?' (2001) 13(4) Child and Family Law Quarterly 361; F. Kaganas and S. Day Sclater, 'Contact and Domestic Violence—The Winds of Change' [2000] Family Law 630.

[474] Advisory Board on Family Law Children Act Sub-Committee, *A Report to the Lord Chancellor on the Question of Parental Contact in Cases Where There Is Domestic Violence* (Lord Chancellor's Department, 2000).

[475] Ibid, para 1.5, appendix 2 and para 3.6.4. The Sub-Committee was not persuaded of the 'need to move immediately to legislation', ibid, para 1.8. Opinion was divided on this point: see para 3.5. In the view of the Sub-Committee, the law, properly understood, contained all the necessary mechanisms for dealing with domestic violence in this context, ibid, para 1.5, appendix 2 and para 3.6.4.

[476] [2001] Fam 260, CA. For comment see F. Kaganas, '*Re L (Contact: Domestic Violence); Re V (Contact: Domestic Violence); Re M (Contact: Domestic Violence); Re H (Contact: Domestic Violence)*: Contact and Domestic Violence' (2000) 12 Child and Family Law Quarterly 311.

[477] C. Sturge and D. Glaser, 'Contact and Domestic Violence—The Experts' Court Report' (2000) 30 Family Law 615.

[478] [2001] Fam 260, CA at 272–273.

[479] This reference to serious violence appears in Butler-Sloss P's summary; earlier she referred to cases of *proved* domestic violence.

[480] Here Butler-Sloss P explained that Wall J in *Re M (Contact: Violent Parent)* [1999] 2 FLR 321 at 333 suggested that 'often in cases where domestic violence had been found, too little weight had been given to

However, noting that domestic violence comes in many forms, and contrary to the advice given in the Sturge/Glaser report, the Court of Appeal confirmed the view expressed in earlier case law,[481] that 'as a matter of principle, domestic violence of itself cannot constitute a bar to contact'[482] and there is 'no presumption that, on proof of domestic violence, the offending parent has to surmount a prima facie barrier of no contact'.[483] Thorpe LJ, agreeing with Dame Elizabeth Butler-Sloss P's judgment, said that this would risk creating 'an excessive concentration on past history and an over-reflection of physical abuse within the determination of individual cases'.[484] He agreed with Waller LJ's succinct summary that:

Talking point

domestic violence is not to be elevated to some special category; it is one highly material factor amongst many which may offset the assumption in favour of contact when the difficult balancing exercise is carried out by the judge applying the welfare principle and the welfare checklist, s 1(1) and (3) of the Children Act 1989.[485]

It can be argued that the court's considering only a presumption in which the basic facts include any type of domestic violence meant that the conclusion against use of a presumption became almost inevitable. The approach fails to distinguish between, for example, levels of seriousness of the domestic violence or whether the violence is likely to be repeated or not.[486]

The filtering down of the guidance in *Re LVMH* to trial courts appears to have been patchy,[487] and in *Re H (Contact: Domestic Violence)*[488] the Court of Appeal made clear that the guidelines in this seminal decision must be followed and that it was wholly unacceptable for the judge in that case to have made only a passing 'incomplete and highly selective' reference to it.[489]

In *Re C (Domestic Violence: Fact-Finding Hearing)*[490] Thorpe LJ commented that the judgments in *Re LVMH* 'had a wide impact and perhaps the members of this court gave insufficient attention to the burden that they were placing on judges'.[491] Accordingly there is now a Practice Direction which makes clear that it is a matter of discretion for the judge to order a fact-finding preliminary hearing and a judge does not have to provided he gives

---

the need for the father to change' and 'that the father should demonstrate that he was a fit person to exercise contact and should show a track record of proper behaviour.'

[481] Eg *Re H (Leave to Apply for Residence Order)* [2008] 2 FLR 848.

[482] *Re H (Contact: Domestic Violence)* [1998] 2 FLR 42, CA; *Re LVMH* [2001] Fam 260, CA.

[483] *Re LVMH*, ibid, 273.   [484] Ibid, 300.   [485] Ibid, 301.

[486] J. Herring, 'Connecting Contact: Contact in a Private Law Context' in A. Bainham, B. Lindley, M. Richards, and L. Trinder (eds), *Children and Their Families: Contact, Rights and Welfare* (Oxford: Hart, 2003), p 105.

[487] As acknowledged by the Government: see HM Government, *Parental Separation: Children's Needs and Parents' Responsibilities* (Cm 6273, 2004), para 48.

[488] [2005] EWCA Civ 1404, [2006] 1 FLR 943.

[489] Ibid, [76]. See also *Re K and S (Children) (Contact: Domestic Violence)* [2005] EWCA Civ 1660, [2006] 1 FCR 316 in which the Court of Appeal found difficulty understanding how over four years since its pronouncements its guidance could be overlooked, and found this a 'most serious deficiency in the trial process' (at [27]). See, however, *Re F (A Child) (Contact Order)* [2001] 1 FCR 422, CA (requiring the father to demonstrate that he was fit to have contact was not justified).

[490] [2009] EWCA Civ 994, [2010] 1 FLR 1728.

[491] Ibid, [14]. See Hedley J's comments in *S v S (Interim Contact)* [2009] EWHC 1575 (Fam), [2009] 2 FLR 1586 at 1587 to 1588 as to the pressures increases in requests for fact-finding hearings were placing on the judiciary.

reasons for declining so to do.[492] The Practice Direction, *Residence and Contact Orders: Domestic Violence and Harm*,[493] provides detailed practice guidance on dealing with any case in which a question arises about residence or contact and in which it is alleged, or there is otherwise reason to suppose, that the child or a party has experienced domestic violence perpetrated by another party or that there is a risk of such violence. This provides for initial screening of cases by Cafcass and if there is a domestic violence issue then the court may give directions about the conduct of the hearing and for written evidence to be filed by the parties before the hearing.[494] Where a fact-finding hearing is necessary,[495] the hearings should be conducted by the same judge or, in the magistrates' court, by at least the same chairperson of the justices.[496]

Where there are findings of domestic violence, the court 'should only make an order for contact if it can be satisfied that the physical and emotional safety of the child and the parent with whom the child is living can, as far as possible, be secured before during and after contact'.[497] If the court nevertheless considers that direct contact is in the child's best interests it should in particular consider[498] whether or not contact should be supervised, whether to impose a condition such as that the party in whose favour the order is made should seek treatment,[499] whether the contact should be for a specified period, and whether the order should be reviewed. If so, the court should set a date for review. The court should 'always make clear how its findings on the issue of domestic violence have influenced its decision'.[500]

5.11.5 Children's wishes and feelings[501]

Sometimes a child may find existing contact unsatisfying or otherwise problematic, or the idea of proposed contact may be distressing for the child. In such circumstances, where appropriate, the child's wishes and feelings concerning the contact may constitute a powerful reason for denying or discontinuing contact. In *Re C (Contact: No Order for*

---

[492] See eg *Re C (Domestic Violence: Fact-Finding Hearing)* [2009] EWCA Civ 994, [2010] 1 FLR 1728 (judge correctly declined fact-finding hearing given that the issues had already been determined in criminal proceedings).

[493] [2009] 2 FLR 1400, reissuing in revised form Practice Direction: Residence and Contact Orders: Domestic Violence and Harm [2008] 2 FLR 103 to reflect the decision of the House of Lords in *Re B (Care Proceedings: Standard of Proof)* [2008] UKHL 35, [2009] 1 AC 11.

[494] [2009] 2 FLR 1400 at [8]. Where there is a need for special arrangements to secure the safety of any party or child attending any hearing, the court shall ensure that appropriate arrangements are made for the hearing and for all subsequent hearings (at [9]).

[495] See also President's Guidance in Relation to Split Hearings [2010] 2 FLR 1897. In an appropriate case, costs of the hearing might be recovered: see *Re J (Costs of Fact-Finding Hearing)* [2009] EWCA Civ 1350, [2010] 1 FLR 1893 (mother entitled to costs where allegations proved and none alleged shown to be untrue).

[496] [2009] 2 FLR 1400 at [15]. Compare *M v A (Contact: Domestic Violence)* [2002] 2 FLR 921: where magistrates hold fact-finding hearing, the final hearing should be heard by the same bench (at [19] and [20]). A fact-finding hearing should not be abandoned before hearing all the evidence: *Re Z (Unsupervised Contact: Allegations of Domestic Violence)* [2009] EWCA Civ 430, [2009] 2 FLR 877 (judge abandoned fact-finding hearing after incident in which mother attacked father's partner in the court precinct). See also *Re FH (Dispensing with Fact-Finding Hearing)* [2008] EWCA Civ 1249, [2009] 1 FLR 349, CA (in context of care proceedings). Furthermore, a submission of no case to answer is inappropriate on a fact-finding hearing in Children Act proceedings as the judge sits in a quasi-inquisitorial role: *Re R (Family Proceedings: No Case to Answer)* [2009] EWCA Civ 1619, [2009] 2 FLR 83.

[497] [2009] 2 FLR 1400 at [26]. The Practice Direction sets out at [27] particular matters which the court should consider.   [498] Ibid, [28].

[499] Subject to necessary consents.   [500] [2009] 2 FLR 1400, [30].

[501] For the view that within post-separation parenting debates there is an emerging image of the autonomous responsible child and increasing account taken of children's wishes, see F. Kaganas and A. Diduck, 'Incomplete Citizens: Changing Images of Post-Separation Children' (2004) 67 Modern Law Review 959.

Contact)[502] Connell J upheld the decision of justices to cease all contact between a father and an 8-year-old boy. Initially there had been direct contact between the boy and his father but this ceased following the boy's allegation of sexual abuse by the father's new stepson. The boy told his school that he would kill himself because of unhappiness about contact and, when indirect contact was attempted by letters and cards, he had destroyed the father's communications. Connell J acknowledged that ordinarily an order for indirect contact should be made, but the circumstances in this case were not ordinary and the justices' decision was open to them on the facts.

The child may have concerns about the parent's behaviour during contact, but where the behaviour stems from the parent's personality/characteristics, account must be taken of the child's need to know and accept the parent as he or she is. It has been said that children:

> have to know the parents that they have. It is generally not considered to be in the best interests of children to wish that they had different parents from those that they have. The more that they know the parents, the healthier their approach is likely to be.[503]

In *Re B (Minors: Access)*,[504] for example, a father was described as genuinely fond of his two children (aged 12 and 11) but socially awkward and prone to exhibit eccentric and even bizarre behaviour which was capable of baffling and distressing them. For example, the children had complained that while they were in a field the father got out his cigarette lighter and tried to set fire to some of the grass where they were sitting. There was another occurrence when one of the children had been embarrassed by being given a children's bible by the father, which was wrapped up in a piece of newspaper with a photograph of a nude woman on it. The children also found visits to their father lacking stimulus, and had no desire to see him. The Court of Appeal held, however, that the children's interests required 'that they should have the opportunity of gradually understanding those attributes in their father'.[505] The court thus ordered limited contact which, whilst avoiding 'the distress involved in over-frequent contact', would 'prevent the father from becoming an unknown quantity in the children's minds, elevated, perhaps through absence, to a status inviting fear or fantasy in crucial teenage years'.[506]

In *Re F (Minors) (Denial of Contact)*,[507] however, a judge held that two boys aged 12 and 9 should not have the reality of their father's transsexualism 'forced on them at all costs'.[508] The children had difficulty making a connection between the father they had in the past and their father in his new gender and were 'steadfast in their present wish not to see their father'. A psychiatrist gave evidence that contact was 'preferable but without the boys having to be forced', and the judge was not prepared to coerce the boys into having contact. The Court of Appeal upheld the judge's decision, declaring that he 'quite rightly gave the views of the boys very considerable weight'.[509]

Although the courts may be able to uphold a child's wishes not to have contact, and indeed thwart a child's wish to have contact,[510] they recognise that, at least in the case of teenage children, it may be impossible and counterproductive to force the child to have contact where he or she does not want it.[511] In *Re S (Contact: Children's Views)* it was recognised that children aged 16, 14, and 12 are 'entitled to have their views on contact

---

[502] [2000] 2 FLR 723 (Fam).   [503] *Re L (Minors)*, CA (10 June 1998).
[504] [1992] 1 FLR 140, CA.   [505] Ibid, 146.   [506] Ibid.
[507] [1993] 2 FLR 677, CA. See also *Re J (Minors)*, CA (2 October 1997) and cf *Re L (Contact: Transsexual Applicant)* [1995] 2 FLR 438 (Fam).   [508] [1993] 2 FLR 677, CA at 683.
[509] Ibid, 684.
[510] *Re H (Minors)*, CA (3 December 1999) (child's wishes overridden by expert opinion).
[511] Ibid; *Re R (A Minor)*, CA (12 March 1998).

respected' and that an alternative to ordering contact was to listen to the children, to try persuasion, and to try to provide opportunities for negotiation.[512]

5.11.5.1 Parental alienation

However, where a child's 'attitudes are or may be shaped by the influences of others, the child's wishes and the child's understanding are to be considered in that light'.[513] There are several reported decisions involving a parent who has imbued the children with a negative attitude to the other parent,[514] in some cases to the extent of falsely persuading a child that the other parent has abused the child,[515] or coaching the child to make such allegations.[516] A judge must sufficiently address the origins of a child's alienation from a parent and must make sufficient findings on that issue.[517] Some commentators have suggested that there is a particular syndrome associated with this type of behaviour which has been termed 'parental alienation syndrome'. However, this characterisation of the problem as a syndrome has been cogently criticised in academic commentary[518] and is not recognised in English law.[519] It has been said that the behaviour is better characterised as an aspect of a parent's implacable hostility to contact.[520]

5.11.6 Parent's implacable hostility

Where contact is accompanied by negative feelings about the arrangements (eg tension, anger, or tears on the part of the resident parent), there is likely to be a conflict for the child in that the child may wish to avoid precipitating those emotions. The courts recognise that in such circumstances ordering contact may sometimes do more harm than good.

In *Re B (A Minor) (Access)*[521] it was accepted that 'implacable hostility' to contact could constitute an exception to the courts' general principle that a child should grow up in the knowledge of both his parents. The exception applied where 'to enforce, impose or seek to enforce or seek to impose access is going to have adverse effects on the child and injure it'.[522] Therefore, it may be that in some cases 'the welfare of the child requires the court to inflict injustice upon a parent with whom the child is not resident'.[523]

---

[512] [2002] EWHC 540 (Fam), [2002] 1 FLR 1156 at 1170.

[513] *Re M (Minors)*, CA (26 January 2000). By contrast, a child's wish to have contact, expressed in the face of parental loyalty, may be given considerable weight: see *P v B* [2003] EWHC 327 (Fam) at [43].

[514] See eg *P v P* [2003] EWHC 151 (Fam), and cf *Re O (Contact: Withdrawal of Application)* [2003] EWHC 3031 (Fam), [2004] 1 FLR 1258 at [93] (allegation made but not upheld).

[515] *Re M (Intractable Contact Dispute: Interim Care Order)* [2003] EWHC 1024 (Fam), [2003] 2 FLR 636.

[516] *V v V (Children) (Contact: Implacable Hostility)* [2004] EWHC 1215 (Fam), [2004] 2 FLR 851.

[517] *Re T (A Child: Contact)* [2002] EWCA Civ 1736, [2003] 1 FLR 531 (cause of child's sudden and adamant refusal to stay with the father not adequately investigated).

[518] C. S. Bruch, 'Parental Alienation Syndrome And Alienated Children—Getting It Wrong In Child Custody Cases' (2002) 14(4) Child and Family Law Quarterly 381.

[519] *Re O (Contact: Withdrawal of Application)* [1995] 2 FLR 124, CA at [92].

[520] C. Sturge and D. Glaser, 'Contact and Domestic Violence—The Experts' Court Report' (2000) 30 Family Law 615 at 622:

> The essential and important difference is that the Parental Alienation Syndrome assumes a cause (seen as misguided or malign on the part of the resident parent) which leads to a prescribed intervention whereas the concept (which no one claims to be a 'syndrome') is simply a statement aimed at the understanding of particular situations but for which a range of explanations is possible and for which there is no single and prescribed solution, this depending on the nature and individuality of each case.

[521] [1984] FLR 648, CA.

[522] Ibid, 649. See also *Re BC (A Minor) (Access)* [1985] FLR 639, CA.

[523] *Re J (A Minor) (Contact)* [1994] 1 FLR 729, CA at 736.

In *Re D (A Minor) (Contact: Mother's Hostility)*,[524] Waite LJ described this point as now 'well settled'.[525] In that case the mother left the father when she was six months pregnant, alleging that he treated her with violence, drank excessively, and had brought into the household another woman. Following the break-up the father appeared at the mother's home at night on occasions causing a disturbance and delivered her clothes back to her in a slashed condition. There followed injunction proceedings at which the father appeared with 12 associates and caused such intimidation to the mother's family that they had to leave the court by a private exit. A year after the child's birth, the father sought contact, claiming to be a reformed character. The judge dismissed the contact application on the basis that, while the father might be reformed, the indelible impression his behaviour had left on the mother meant that it would be injurious to the child to force the mother to allow contact. The father's appeal was dismissed. Waite LJ saw:

> no reason to think that the judge fell into any error of principle in deciding, as he clearly did on the plain interpretation of his judgment, that the mother's present attitude towards contact puts D at serious risk of major emotional harm if she were to be compelled to accept a degree of contact to the natural father against her will.[526]

In *Re O (Contact: Imposition of Conditions)* Sir Thomas Bingham MR drew attention to this use of the words 'serious risk of major emotional harm' and added that:

> The court should not at all readily accept that the child's welfare will be injured by direct contact. Judging that question the court should take a medium-term and long-term view of the child's development and not accord excessive weight to what appear likely to be short-term or transient problems.[527]

In *Re D (Contact: Reasons for Refusal)*,[528] Hale J, giving judgment in the Court of Appeal, reviewed the authorities and concluded that in a case of implacable hostility:

> the court will be very slow indeed to reach the conclusion that contact will be harmful to the child. It may eventually have to reach that conclusion but it will want to be satisfied that there is indeed a serious risk of major emotional harm before doing so.[529]

Waite LJ's reference in *Re D (A Minor) (Contact: Mother's Hostility)*[530] to 'a serious risk of major emotional harm' was descriptive of the judge's findings in that case. Interestingly, however, Hale J's summary of the law appears to elevate the absence of error of principle on the facts of *Re D (A Minor) (Contact: Mother's Hostility)* to the status of a principle based on the facts of that case. The criterion adopted by the Court of Appeal in *Re O (Contact: Imposition of Conditions)* when discussing *Re D (A Minor) (Contact: Mother's Hostility)*,[531] in line with earlier case law, is simply injury to the child's welfare.[532]

In each case the impact on the child of the resident parent's implacable hostility will need to be weighed against the medium or long-term benefits to the child of contact. The

---

[524] [1993] 2 FLR 1, CA.   [525] Ibid, 7.   [526] Ibid.   [527] [1995] 2 FLR 124, CA.
[528] [1997] 2 FLR 48, CA.   [529] Ibid, 53. See also *Re P (Contact: Discretion)* [1998] 2 FLR 696 (Fam).
[530] [1993] 2 FLR 1, CA.   [531] Ibid.
[532] Eg there does not seem to be any reason why implacable hostility should not be a reason for denying contact where the mother's reaction to contact produces anxieties which would impact upon her ability to manage her child's medical treatment with consequent impact upon the child's physical well-being. The relevance of a child's physical illness and of the impact of proposed contact upon a parent's ability to care for a child has been acknowledged in other cases: see *Re H (A Child: Parental Responsibility)* [2002] EWCA Civ 542 and *Re C and V (Contact and Parental Responsibility)* 1998] 1 FLR 392.

conclusion may not always be that the child's overall welfare will not be promoted by contact,[533] but in some cases the impact of the hostility may be determinative.[534]

However, parental hostility to contact is viewed as 'a very unattractive argument to place before a court'[535] and should never of itself be a reason for not ordering contact.[536] The Court of Appeal is anxious that there should not be 'a selfish parents' charter'.[537]

5.11.7 Genuine fear

In *Re D (Contact: Reasons for Refusal)*,[538] the Court of Appeal was anxious to ensure that the phrase 'implacable hostility' is not wrongly used. Hale J indicated that the term 'implacable hostility' is properly applied in cases where there is hostility and also no good reason can be discerned either for the hostility or for the opposition to contact. Hale J observed that it is 'rather different in the cases where the judge or the court finds that the mother's fears, not only for herself but also for the child, are genuine and rationally held'.

In *Re K (Contact: Mother's Anxiety)*,[539] for example, the father of a 5-year-old boy had been violent to the mother on several occasions and on one occasion had ransacked the mother's home leaving it 'virtually devoid of furnishing and any kind of domestic equipment'.[540] In addition, when the child was not yet two years old he had been kidnapped in brutal circumstances by his father and the paternal grandfather, who had entered the mother's home at 3.30 a.m. and had torn the child away from her.[541] After the father was released from prison, having served a sentence of imprisonment for the kidnapping, he sought and was awarded supervised contact three times a year. After two contact sessions, which had gone well and which the child had enjoyed, the mother applied to vary the contact order to indirect contact in light of the stress the contact caused her. As a result of her experiences with the father, the mother experienced a real and uncontrollable stress and anxiety about the child's direct contact with the father, which became palpable and was conveyed to the child. In the circumstances, Wall J ordered indirect contact only, finding that direct contact would expose the child, via the mother's reaction, to insupportable stress, placing the child in a fraught emotional state in which his loyalties would be torn, ultimately resulting in severe emotional harm.[542]

Provided the resident parent's fears are genuine, they need not necessarily be rationally held.[543] In *Re L (Contact: Genuine Fear)*[544] the father of a 7-year-old boy had treated the mother with violence during the relationship. During his early adult life he had been a 'Hell's Angel' and professional 'biker' with strong right-wing tendencies. In the 1980s he was sentenced to five years' imprisonment for causing grievous bodily harm with intent when he stabbed both his former wife and her solicitor in the precincts of the Royal Courts of Justice and then subsequently stabbed the mother's boyfriend in a separate incident. He had also been convicted on another occasion of possession of a shotgun without a certificate. This, his last criminal conviction, had occurred some 15 years prior to the hearing. The parents had split up when the child was 4 and the mother was living at an

---

[533] See eg *Re E (A Minor: Access)* [1987] 1 FLR 368.
[534] See eg *Re J (A Minor) (Contact)* [1994] 1 FLR 729 (10-year-old child's experience of contact arrangements associated with acrimony, recrimination, and family upset, telling court welfare officer that he did not wish to see his father again).   [535] *Re H (A Minor) (Contact)* [1994] 2 FLR 776, CA at 783.
[536] See *Re W (A Minor) (Contact)* [1994] 2 FLR 441 (abdication of judicial responsibility to decline to make contact order simply on the basis that the mother would not obey it).
[537] *Re H (A Minor) (Contact)* [1994] 2 FLR 776 at 782.   [538] [1997] 2 FLR 48, CA.
[539] [1999] 2 FLR 703.   [540] Ibid, 709.   [541] Ibid, 708–709.   [542] Ibid, 715.
[543] See *Re M (Contact: Family Assistance: McKenzie Friend)* [1999] 1 FLR 75, CA and *Re P (Contact: Discretion)* [1998] 2 FLR 696 (Fam).   [544] [2002] 1 FLR 621.

address unknown to the father, for fear that he would seek revenge upon her for leaving him. In denying the father direct contact, the judge found that the mother had a phobia of the father. Although not based on rational thinking,[545] it was genuine and intense such that the child would suffer marked emotional harm if an order for direct contact were made and the child were exposed to its emotional effect upon the mother, which would be profound and possibly destabilising.[546]

As *Re H (Contact Order) (No 2)*[547] illustrates, the effect of contact upon the primary carer's health may be the most important factor bearing upon the child's welfare, even where contact might take place safely. In that case the father of two children, aged 9 and 5, suffered from Huntington's disease, a progressive neurodegenerative disorder, which had adverse effects on his mood and personality. On one occasion during staying contact with the children, the father took the children out in his car. Concealed from the children, he had with him petrol and sleeping pills. He telephoned the mother and members of his own family, announcing that he intended to take his own life and the children's lives too. Fortunately, a member of the public became alarmed at the father's behaviour, called the police, and the children were saved. As a result of this incident the mother opposed direct contact, although she was content to facilitate indirect contact. Wall J found that contact which was properly supervised, and preceded by a careful assessment of the father's mood, could take place without the children coming to harm. However, nothing could reassure the mother (who was suffering from acute post-traumatic stress disorder) about the children's safety when in the presence of their father; she was aware that the father had been trained in the Special Air Service (SAS) and that he had the knowledge and strength to kill the children should his mood change suddenly. For example, she was concerned that if the children were sitting on the father's lap he could break their necks in an instant. Wall J found that there was 'a real risk—indeed a likelihood—of the mother suffering a nervous breakdown if an order for face-to-face contact between the children and their father [was] imposed on her'.[548] He concluded that the most important factor in an assessment of the children's welfare in this case was 'the need to protect and promote the mental and physical health of the children's primary carer'. It was especially important that the mother was healthy because of the degeneration in the father's health and his reduced life expectancy. Wall J thus made no order on the application for contact, holding that it was for the mother to decide on appropriate contact.[549]

The cases disclose a tension between the principle that risk of harm must be based upon facts proved on the balance of probabilities and a person's erroneously held view, which as a fact itself may impact on the child's welfare.

5.11.8 Step-parent opposition and the risk of destabilising the child's present family unit

Where a parent has formed a secure family unit with another partner, and particularly when the partner has acted as the child's parent in circumstances in which the child is unaware of his or her natural parent, there can sometimes be a risk that an application for contact by the child's other parent will destabilise the mother's new family unit. This may sometimes arise because the new partner is hostile to any proposed contact.

[545] In light of the facts set out earlier, this conclusion of the judge is perhaps one with which not everyone might agree.   [546] [2002] 1 FLR 621, [42].
[547] [2002] 1 FLR 22, FD (Wall J).   [548] Ibid, [45].
[549] See also *Re A (A Child) (Contact: Sexual Abuse)* [2002] EWCA Civ 1595 at [24] (recognising the need to address a mother's fears, even where findings of fact did not support the mother's viewpoint. In that case the court ordered supervised contact to allay a mother's fears that the father had sexually abused the children, despite a judge's conclusion that sexual abuse had not taken place).

The courts recognise that in such situations the child's welfare may sometimes dictate that contact must be denied. In *Re B (Contact: Stepfather's Opposition)*[550] the parents of a child split up shortly after the child's birth. The mother remarried and the only father figure the child had known was the stepfather. When the child was 9 years old the father sought contact. The stepfather, who was a Sikh, was implacably opposed to contact and was threatening to reject the mother as well as the child. As a matter of the stepfather's cultural background it was simply not acceptable to him that there could be two father figures involved in the child's life. Recognising the genuineness with which those feelings were held, the court took the view that the serious harm that the break-up of the family would cause the child outweighed the real injustice to the father and therefore ruled that the interests of the child must prevail. However, the court hoped that the stepfather might in the future come to a different view.[551] The outcome chimes with the statement of Thorpe LJ in *Re LVMH* that he would not assume the benefit of contact with unquestioning confidence 'where a child has developed over its early years without any knowledge of its father, particularly if over those crucially formative years a psychological attachment to an alternative father has been achieved'.[552]

5.12 FACILITATION AND ENFORCEMENT OF CONTACT

Parental obduracy may continue despite the fact that a contact order has been made. Cases of this kind are extremely difficult for practitioners to handle and for courts to manage. How the courts have dealt with such situations in the past has attracted criticism and policy debate. In March 2001, CASC issued another consultation paper, on the subject of facilitation and enforcement of contact.[553] It was followed by a report to the Lord Chancellor entitled *Making Contact Work*.[554] The consultation and report were prompted in part by parents' concerns that orders were easily flouted, and that the courts seemed reluctant or powerless to enforce them. The report identified a court process which was too slow,[555] unpredictable,[556] and adversarial,[557] with sometimes a lack of judicial continuity in case management.[558] Improved court procedures were recommended, and the President of the Family Division subsequently published a Private Law Programme to improve the management of private family law cases[559] (which has since been revised to take account of subsequent developments).[560] CASC also concluded that the current

---

[550] [1997] 2 FLR 579, CA.

[551] See also *Re H (A Minor) (Parental Responsibility)* [1993] 1 FLR 484, CA (stepfather of a 2-year-old boy wrote to the natural father saying that his marriage to the mother would be put at risk if the father continued to have contact with the child. The court therefore refused contact on the ground that the child's welfare would not be served if he lost his present home and security because his mother's marriage broke down).

[552] [2000] Fam 260 at 294–295.

[553] *Making Contact Work: A Consultation Paper from the Children Act Sub-Committee of the Lord Chancellor's Advisory Board on Family Law (CASC) on the Facilitation and Enforcement of Contact* (Lord Chancellor's Department, 2001).

[554] *Making Contact Work: A Report to the Lord Chancellor on the Facilitation of Arrangements for Contact Between Children and their Non-Residential Parents and the Enforcement of Court Orders for Contact* (Lord Chancellor's Department, 2002).

[555] Ibid, para 10.37 (eg delay caused by obtaining reports, see para 10.40).

[556] Ibid, para 10.38.

[557] Ibid, para 10.39. See also paras 10.14 and 10.11 for a list of specific problems identified.

[558] Ibid, para 10.38. Similar concerns about the inadequacy of the system were subsequently expressed by the judiciary: see eg *V v V (Children) (Contact: Implacable Hostility)* [2004] EWHC 1215 (Fam), [2004] 2 FLR 851 at [7]–[12]; *Re D (Intractable Contact Dispute: Publicity)* [2004] EWHC 727, [2004] 1 FLR 1226.

[559] See www.dca.gov.uk/family/plpguide.pdf.

[560] Practice Direction: Revised Private Law Programme [2010] 2 FLR 717.

powers of enforcement of contact orders were 'seriously deficient' and that legislation was required to provide a more flexible range of options.[561] Most of CASC's recommendations were carried forward by the Government,[562] which introduced new measures to facilitate contact and enforce contact orders,[563] enacted in the Children and Adoption Act 2006. A survey conducted by the Office of National Statistics (ONS)[564] showed that most parents managed to reach their own agreements on post-separation contact, and that only about 10 per cent of children did not have any contact with a non-resident parent. So the Government's aim was to encourage more parents to agree contact arrangements,[565] whilst also providing more sophisticated mechanisms for facilitation and enforcement of contact for the more difficult cases.[566] As a whole, a changing role for Cafcass was envisaged, reducing resources spent on report writing to enable greater focus on provision of conciliation and support services.

5.12.1 Facilitating contact

Section 16(4A) of the Children Act 1989 was one of several provisions inserted into that Act by the Children and Adoption Act 2006[567] to increase the courts' powers to facilitate contact. It provides that if the court makes a family assistance order with respect to a child and the order is to be in force at the same time as a contact order made with respect to the child, the family assistance order may direct the officer concerned to give advice and assistance as regards establishing, improving, and maintaining contact to such of the persons named in the order as may be specified in the order.

Part 1 of the Children and Adoption Act 2006 also inserted into the Children Act 1989 sections 11A–11P, which supplement existing measures for facilitating and enforcing contact.

5.12.1.1 Contact activity directions and conditions

Section 11A of the Act allows a court to make a contact activity direction whenever a court is considering whether to make provision about contact with a child by way

---

[561] See *Making Contact Work*, para 14.55 for the detail. For criticism, see J. Eekelaar, 'Contact—Over the Limit' (2002) 32 Family Law 271.

[562] *Government's Response to the Report of the Children Act Sub-Committee of the Lord Chancellor's Advisory Board on Family Law 'Making Contact Work'* (2002); Department for Constitutional Affairs and Department for Education and Skills, *The Government's Response to the Children Act Sub-Committee (CASC) Report: 'Making Contact Work'* (2004); HM Government, *Parental Separation: Children's Needs and Parents' Responsibilities* (Cm 6273, 2004).

[563] Children and Adoption Bill 2005, 2005–06 HL-96 54/1, which was preceded by the Draft Children (Contact) and Adoption Bill (Cm 6462, 2005). For comment, see J. Masson and C. Humphreys, 'Facilitating and Enforcing Contact: the Bill and the Ten Per Cent' (2005) 35 Family Law 548. See House of Commons and House of Lords Joint Committee on the Draft Children (Contact) and Adoption Bill 'Draft Children (Contact) and Adoption Bill Volume 1: Report' (2004–05) HC 400-I, HL 100-I.

[564] A. Blackwell and F. Dawe, 'Non-Resident Parent Contact' (London: Department for Constitutional Affairs, 2003).

[565] HM Government, *Parental Separation: Children's Needs and Parents' Responsibilities* (Cm 6273, 2004), para 10.

[566] Research revealed the complexity of contact disputes, and that the courts' approach to decision making did not correlate with some of the factors parents regarded as important (such as blame for the breakdown of a relationship, or non-payment of child support): C. Smart, V. May, A. Wade, and C Furniss, *Residence and Contact Disputes in Court Volume 1*, Research Series 6/03 (London: Department for Constitutional Affairs, 2003), esp ch 6. The Government also had regard to existing research: see HM Government, *Children's Needs, Parents' Responsibilities: Supporting Evidence for Consultation Paper.*

[567] Inserted by the Children and Adoption Act 2006, s 6(1), (3).

of a contact order.[568] The direction can only be made when there is a dispute about contact.[569] A contact activity direction is 'a direction requiring an individual who is a party to the proceedings to take part in an activity that promotes contact with the child concerned.'[570] Note, therefore, that a contact activity direction may only be imposed on a very limited category of person, a party to the proceedings, and is made at the stage when the court is considering whether to make, vary, or discharge a contact order. A contact activity direction cannot be made when the court is finally disposing of the proceedings as it relates to contact.[571] The direction specifies the activity and the person providing the activity.[572] Section 11A(5) explains that the activities include, in particular:

(a) programmes, classes and counselling or guidance sessions of a kind that—

    (i) may assist a person as regards establishing, maintaining or improving contact with a child;

    (ii) may, by addressing a person's violent behaviour, enable or facilitate contact with a child;

(b) sessions in which information or advice is given as regards making or operating arrangements for contact with a child, including making arrangements by means of mediation.[573]

In considering whether to make a contact activity direction, the welfare of the child concerned is the court's paramount consideration.[574]

A contact activity direction is to be contrasted with a contact activity *condition* under section 11C of the Act,[575] which may be imposed when the court actually makes (or varies) a contact order. This can require an individual 'to take part in an activity that promotes contact with the child concerned'.[576] It can be imposed on a wider range of individuals than just the parties. Section 11C(3) provides that the condition can be imposed on a person if he or she is:

(a) for the purposes of the contact order so made or varied, the person with whom the child concerned lives or is to live;

(b) the person whose contact with the child concerned is provided for in that order; or

(c) a person upon whom that order imposes a condition under section 11(7)(b).

There are some limitations on what may be ordered by way of a contact activity direction or condition. No individual may be required to undergo medical or psychiatric examination, assessment, or treatment or to take part in mediation.[577] In addition, no direction or condition can be made in respect of a child, unless the child is the parent of the child concerned in the proceedings.[578] Contact activity directions and conditions can only be imposed on persons who are habitually resident in England and Wales.[579]

---

[568] Children Act 1989, s 11A(1). This includes varying or discharging a contact order. Contact activity directions do not apply to contact orders in adoption proceedings. Such contact orders are excepted orders under the Act: see s 11B(4) and (5).   [569] Ibid, s 11B(1).

[570] Ibid, s 11A(3).   [571] Ibid, s 11A(7).   [572] Ibid, s 11A(4).

[573] Section 11F(1) provides that the 'Secretary of State may by regulations make provision authorising him to make payments to assist individuals who are subject to contact activity directions or conditions in paying relevant charges or fees'.   [574] Children Act 1989, s 11A(9).

[575] Again specifying the activity and the person providing it: see ibid s 11C(4).   [576] Ibid, s 11C(2).

[577] Ibid, s 11A(6).   [578] Ibid, s 11B(2) and s 11D(1).   [579] Ibid, s 11B(7) and s 11D(3).

Before making a contact activity direction or condition, the court must satisfy itself of the following matters in section 11E(2)–(4):

(2) The first matter is that the activity proposed to be specified is appropriate in the circumstances of the case.

(3) The second matter is that the person proposed to be specified as the provider of the activity is suitable to provide the activity.

(4) The third matter is that the activity proposed to be specified is provided in a place to which the individual who would be subject to the direction (or the condition) can reasonably be expected to travel.

The court must obtain and consider information about the individual who would be subject to the direction or the condition and the likely effect of the direction or the condition on him.[580] This may in particular include information as to 'any conflict with the individual's religious beliefs' and 'any interference with the times (if any) at which he normally works or attends an educational establishment'.[581]

5.12.1.2 Monitoring contact and contact activities

Section 11G of the Children Act 1989 provides that upon making a contact activity direction or condition, the court may request a Cafcass officer or Welsh family proceedings officer to 'monitor, or arrange for the monitoring of, the individual's compliance with the direction (or the condition); and to report to the court on any failure by the individual to comply with the direction (or the condition). It is the officer's duty to comply with the request.'[582] Section 11H provides for similar monitoring of, and reporting on, an individual's compliance with a contact order.[583] The monitoring cannot exceed a period of 12 months.[584] The request for monitoring can be made at any time during the course of the proceedings as they relate to contact with the child concerned.[585] The section applies to an individual if the contact order:

(a) requires the individual to allow contact with the child concerned;

(b) names the individual as having contact with the child concerned; or

(c) imposes a condition under section 11(7)(b) on the individual.[586]

Paragraph (b) is a curious provision. It allows the monitoring of compliance with contact of a person who is not a resident parent, yet no legal duty of compliance is imposed on such a person.

5.12.1.3 Warning notices

Section 11I provides that where the court makes (or varies) a contact order, it is to attach to the contact order (or the order varying the contact order) a notice warning of the consequences of failing to comply with the contact order.[587] The warning notice is important, not only in bringing attention to the consequences of breach, but also because, as we shall

---

[580] Ibid, s 11E(5).   [581] Ibid, s 11E(6).   [582] Ibid, s 11G(3).

[583] Again, the contact order is defined to exclude an excepted order s 11H(10) 'within the meaning given by section 11B(4)'.   [584] Section 11H(6).

[585] Section 11H(5).

[586] Section 11H(3). The court may order any individual falling within subs (3) to take such steps as may be specified in the order with a view to enabling the Cafcass officer or Welsh family proceedings officer to comply with the court's request for monitoring: see s 11H(8).

[587] See S. Evans, 'To Warn or Not To Warn: Contact Enforcement' [2009] Fam Law 530.

see, it is a pre-condition to the making of an enforcement order under section 11J of the Children Act 1989.

5.12.2 Enforcement of contact

In *Glaser v UK*[588] the European Court of Human Rights made clear that there is an obligation on states to take measures to reunite parents and children but it is not an absolute obligation. While national authorities must do their utmost, any obligation to apply coercion must be limited since the interests/rights of all concerned must be taken into account, and more particularly the best interests of the child. The key consideration is whether authorities have taken all necessary steps as can be reasonably demanded in the special circumstances of each case. In that case a mother did not comply with a contact order made in 1993. She relocated to Scotland without the father's knowledge. He eventually located the children with the assistance of the English court and he brought successful proceedings in Scotland for enforcement of the English contact order. Contact was finally re-established in 2000. The father claimed a breach of Articles 8 and 6 of the ECHR. Finding no violation, the Court observed that the applicant's difficulties flowed from the unilateral actions of the mother and the authorities could not have reasonably undertaken any more coercive step at any point.

The reason the duty to reunite is not absolute is that in some circumstances enforcing contact may be more harmful than the loss of contact to the child. As Butler-Sloss P commented in *Re S (Contact: Promoting Relationship with Absent Parent)*:[589]

Talking point

there is a limit beyond which the court should not strive to promote contact and the court has the overriding obligation to put the welfare of the child at the forefront and above the rights of either parent.

Re O (Contact: Withdrawal of Application)[590] provides an illustration of a case in which it was felt that the issue of contact should not be pushed further. The father wrongly believed that the mother was alienating his 12-year-old son. In fact the boy found frequent weekend staying contact with his father disruptive of his social life and the father's telephone calls on other occasions excessive. The father was described as rigid in his attitude and was relentlessly pursuing contact. Because of the difficulties with contact, the father applied to withdraw his application for contact. Wall J made clear that the court will go to great lengths before terminating contact[591] and that if there had been any prospect of repairing the relationship between the father and the child he would not have allowed the father to withdraw his application.[592] However, his Lordship was clear that there was no prospect of change in the father's attitude and no reasonable prospect of meaningful contact and he allowed the father to withdraw the application.

However, care must be taken to ensure that the conclusion that contact cannot be made to work is not reached prematurely. The court will need to consider the child's long-term best interests. In *Re S (Contact: Promoting Relationship with Absent Parent)*[593] the parents

---

[588] [2001] 1 FLR 153.   [589] [2004] EWCA Civ 18, [2004] 1 FLR 1279 at [28].
[590] [2003] EWHC 3031 (Fam), [2004] 1 FLR 1258.
[591] Ibid, [89].   [592] Ibid, [88].
[593] [2004] EWCA Civ 18, [2004] 1 FLR 1279.

were initially on good terms upon the breakdown of their relationship and the father had contact with their child. There was then an allegation of domestic violence and the parents' relationship deteriorated. The Recorder found that the mother was primarily responsible for the failure of contact and that she had no intention of making it work. In light of this conclusion, the Recorder made an order for indirect contact only. The Court of Appeal allowed the father's appeal, ordering a child psychiatric report, and commenting that it is:

> most important that the attempt to promote contact should not be abandoned until it was clear that the child would not benefit from continuing the attempt.[594]

In the case like this, of a child under 7 and a genuinely motivated father, the decision to abandon the hope of direct contact was premature; the problems should have been explored.

Similarly, in *Re M (Contact: Long-Term Best Interests)*[595] the Court of Appeal concluded that there was a need to continue to pursue the possibility of contact to prevent long-term harm to the children. In that case the non-resident parent was the mother of two children aged 15 and 13. The mother suffered from a psychiatric illness and when the younger child was just 2 years old she had picked him up by the side of his head. The social services department was involved and the parents' marriage broke down. The mother had contact until an incident when the mother was refused contact and attempted physically to take the child. The father and his wife referred to this incident as an 'abduction' and since that time (some eight years previously) the mother had not had contact. The children subsequently refused to have contact with the mother out of fear of the mother. The judge ordered a two-year moratorium on direct contact, during which time it was hoped that the mother might re-establish a relationship through indirect contact. However, during that time the father did not encourage the children with regard to contact and they remained unaware of the mother's communications. The children expressed the view that they did not want contact with their mother. In these circumstances the judge made a more limited order for indirect contact by way of progress reports and photographs to the mother. The mother's appeal was allowed. The judge had been plainly wrong. While the wishes of teenage children ordinarily carry great weight, the children's understanding had been corrupted by the malignancy of the views they had been force-fed by the father. The case was to be transferred to the High Court to consider whether the children should be separately represented and an expert's opinion was required. Scott Baker LJ commented:

> Where, as in this case, the court has the picture that a parent is seeking, without good reason, to eliminate the other parent from the child's, or children's lives, the court should not stand by and take no positive action. Justice to the children and the deprived parent... require the court to leave no stone unturned that might resolve the situation and prevent long-term harm to the children.

If a court concludes that there is a case for enforcing contact, further welfare considerations may arise concerning the impact of the enforcement measures upon the child. There are various measures which can be adopted.

5.12.2.1 Committal

One option for enforcing contact is for the non-resident parent to make an application to commit an obdurate parent to prison for contempt in failing to obey the court's order. This presents a court with an extremely difficult dilemma: on the one hand, there is a

---

[594] Ibid.   [595] [2006] 1 FLR 627, CA.

legitimate view that a parent cannot be permitted to continue to flout the court's orders with impunity; on the other hand, in many cases an order committing the resident parent to prison is likely to cause harm to the child. In *Churchard v Churchard* Ormrod LJ, in a judgment with which Brandon LJ agreed, was firmly of the view that such applications were futile and damaging, and should not be made, observing that 'The court is only concerned with the welfare of the children and ought not to trouble itself too much about its own dignity.'[596]

This approach was doubted by Ward LJ, with whom Beldam LJ agreed, in *A v N (Committal: Refusal of Contact).*[597] Whilst the court accepted that the child's welfare was a material consideration on an application to commit, it rejected the submission that the child's welfare was the paramount consideration.[598] In *Re F (Contact: Enforcement)*[599] Hale J, acknowledging the correctness of this approach, observed, however, that 'if a court is to put enforcement above the risk of harm to the child, it must be very clear indeed about the correctness of the orders it is seeking to enforce'.

In *A v N* the mother had 'flagrantly set herself upon a course of collision with the court's order' and had been given 'endless opportunities to comply' and the judge had 'bent over backwards to accommodate her'. Eventually the judge's patience ran out and he put into effect a suspended order committing the mother to prison for 42 days. Dismissing the mother's appeal, Ward LJ said:

> In my judgment, it is time that it is realised that against the wisdom of the observations of Ormrod LJ is to be balanced the consideration that orders of the court are made to be obeyed. They are not made for any other reason...it is perhaps appropriate that the message goes out in loud and clear terms that there does come a limit to the tolerance of the court to see its orders flouted by mothers even if they have to care for their young children. If she goes to prison it is her fault, not the fault of the judge...The Children Act 1989 makes it [the judge's] duty...to determine what is in the child's best interests. He, not this mother, has to decide whether contact will promote this child's welfare...He did not commit this mother to preserve his own dignity. He was concerned to preserve the due administration of justice which depends on orders of the court being obeyed.[600]

Subsequent case law has echoed these sentiments,[601] and the shift in the case law was summed up in *B v S*[602] by Wilson LJ, with whom Ward LJ agreed, when he said:

> The days are long gone when mothers can assume that their role as carers of children protects them from being sentenced to immediate terms of imprisonment for clear, repeated and deliberate breaches of contact orders.[603]

However, the courts have still accepted that this sanction should be used sparingly in children cases. As the Court of Appeal acknowledged in *Re S (Minors: Access):*[604]

> it is a rare case—although I would not go so far as to say it can never happen—that the welfare of the child requires that the custodial parent be sent to prison for refusing to give the other parent access.[605]

---

[596] [1984] FLR 635 at 638.   [597] [1997] 1 FLR 533.   [598] Ibid, 540.
[599] [1998] 1 FLR 691.   [600] [1997] 1 FLR 533, 541–542. See also Beldam LJ to like effect at 542.
[601] See eg *Re S (Contact Dispute: Committal)* [2004] EWCA Civ 1790, [2005] 1 FLR 812 at [14].
[602] [2009] EWCA Civ 548.
[603] Ibid, [16]. See also *Re LW (Children) (Enforcement and Committal: Contact); CPL v CH-W and others* [2010] EWCA Civ 1253 at [96]: 'Committal is—has to be—an essential weapon in the court's armoury'.
[604] [1990] 2 FLR 166.   [605] Ibid, 170.

In *Re LW (Children) (Enforcement and Committal: Contact); CPL v CH-W and others*[606] Munby LJ agreed with the common trope that committal is or ought to be a last resort. However, his Lordship went on to caution that that handy aphorism should not be misunderstood, explaining:

> Committal should not be used unless it is a proportionate response to the problem nor if some less drastic remedy will provide an adequate solution. But this does not mean that one has to wait unduly before having resort to committal, let alone waiting so long that the moment has passed and the situation has become irretrievable.... on occasions, the understandable reluctance to resort to such a drastic remedy as committal means that when recourse to it is first proposed it is too late for committal, whereas a willingness to grasp the nettle by making a committal order at an earlier stage might have ended up making all the difference... The threat, or if need be the actual implementation, of a very short period of imprisonment—just a day or two—may at an earlier stage of the proceedings achieve more than the threat of a longer sentence at a much later stage in the process. I do not suggest this as a panacea—this is an area in which there is no panacea—but it is something which, I suggest, is worth keeping in mind.[607]

Proceedings for committal are a criminal charge for the purposes of Article 6 of the ECHR.[608] It follows the burden of proving guilt, to the criminal standard of proof, lies on the person seeking committal; the defendant is entitled to be represented;[609] and the defendant has a right against self-incrimination[610] and is not obliged to give evidence. A Practice Direction[611] seeks to ensure that committal proceedings in family proceedings safeguard the defendant's rights. Procedural irregularities which fail to protect the defendant's rights will lead to a committal order being overturned.[612]

Contempt of court 'involves a contumelious, that is to say a deliberate, disobedience to the order'.[613] It is necessary, therefore, that the order is clear on its face as to what those affected by the order are required to do or abstain from doing.[614]

---

[606] [2010] EWCA Civ 1253, [2011] 1 FLR 1095.

[607] Ibid, [108]. For earlier views on the potential usefulness of short prison sentences, see *Re M (Intractable Contact Dispute: Interim Care Orders)* [2003] EWHC 1024 (Fam), [2003] 2 FLR 636 at [117] and *Re D (Intractable Contact Dispute: Publicity)* [2004] EWHC 727 (Fam), [2004] 1 FLR 1226 at [57].

[608] The implications of Art 6 are usefully highlighted in *Hammerton v Hammerton* [2007] EWCA Civ 248, [2007] 2 FLR 1133, esp at [9].

[609] See ECHR, Art 6(3)(c), and *Re K (Contact: Committal Order)* [2002] EWCA Civ 1559, [2003] 1 FLR 277 at [21] and [23]; *Benham v UK* (1996) 22 EHRR 293 at 324; and *Re G (Contempt: Committal)* [2003] EWCA Civ 489, [2003] 1 WLR 2051, [2003] 2 FLR 58 at [22]. The obligation to afford a defendant representation imposed by virtue of ECHR, Art 6(3)(c) is not, however, unlimited (see *Re K* at [34] *per* Mance LJ (as he then was)).

[610] See *Re G (Contempt: Committal)* [2003] EWCA Civ 489, [2003] 1 WLR 2051, [2003] 2 FLR 58 at [22] and, eg, *Saunders v UK* (1996) 23 EHRR 313 and *R v Mushtaq* [2005] UKHL 25, [2005] 1 WLR 1513 at [53].

[611] Practice Direction (Family Proceedings: Committal) [2001] 1 WLR 1253, sub nom President's Direction: (Committal Applications and Proceedings in which a Committal Order may be made) [2001] 1 FLR 949.

[612] As Wall LJ explained in *Hammerton v Hammerton* [2007] EWCA Civ 248, [2007] 2 FLR 1133 at [35]: 'Provided the contemnor has had a fair trial and the order has been made on valid grounds, the existence of a defect in the committal application or in the order served will not result in it being set aside except insofar as the interests of justice require that to be done.' See *M v P (Contempt: Committal); Butler v Butler* [1993] Fam 167, [1993] 1 FLR 773 and *Rayden & Jackson on Divorce and Family Matters*, 18th rev edn (London: LexisNexis UK, 2005), vol 1(1), para 30.23.

[613] *Re A (Abduction: Contempt)* [2008] EWCA Civ 1138, [2009] 1 WLR 1482, [2009] 1 FLR 1 at [6].

[614] *Re S-C (Contempt)* [2010] EWCA Civ 21, [2010] 1 FLR 1478 at [17]. See *Re LW (Children) (Enforcement and Committal: Contact); CPL v CH-W and others* [2010] EWCA Civ 1253 as to what must be proved.

5.12.2.2 The use of residence orders to enforce contact

As Sir Thomas Bingham MR pointed out in *Re O (Contact: Imposition of Conditions)*[615] 'no residence order is to be regarded as irrevocable'[616] although 'orders transferring children from one parent to another are very rare and usually only taken as a matter of last resort'.[617] More recently the Court of Appeal has endorsed the propriety in an appropriate case of making a suspended residence order, providing for a future transfer of residence upon a further failure to comply with any conditions imposed. In *Re A (Suspended Residence Order)*[618] the judge found that the father had sexually abused the mother's daughter from a previous relationship, although he had not abused his own two sons. Contact had been ordered between the father and the boys but the mother, who believed that the father had also abused them, resisted contact and the father had not seen his sons (who were by then 8 and 11) for two years. The paternal grandparents made an application for a residence order with a view to effecting a reintroduction of the boys to their father. Coleridge J took the view that a transfer of residence would not be as harmful, in the long term, as the boys being 'continually and unrelentingly exposed to their mother's false beliefs combined with her unremitting hostility to the paternal family undiluted by contact'. He therefore made the requested residence order but suspended it provided the mother complied with a defined contact order. The mother's appeal against this order was dismissed by the Court of Appeal.[619] The mother subsequently failed to comply with the order and Coleridge J was forced to implement his threat. The mother's further appeal to the Court of Appeal against the transfer of residence to the grand-parents was dismissed.[620] Although the suspended order was not, of itself, effective in this case, it seems likely that this type of order will prove an attractive, and probably an effective, option in other cases.

In an appropriate case, however, an order may be made for an immediate transfer of residence to address failure of contact.[621] In *Re S (Transfer of Residence)*[622] an immediate transfer of residence was made despite the child's objections. A boy aged 11 had been the subject of contact proceedings between his parents since he was one year old and had not seen his father for the last three years. The mother was implacably opposed to contact, and the child's expressed view that he did not wish to see his father, was said to be the product of parental alienation. Despite the boy's wishes to the contrary, therefore, the judge made an order for transfer of residence, having greater confidence in the father's ability to meet the child's overall needs.[623] In *Re A (Residence Order)*[624] the Court of Appeal indicated that if such an order is made there should be a narrow opportunity for the current resident parent to approach the Court of Appeal for relief, for example by stay of the order to the next working day.

5.12.2.3 The use of a section 37 direction

In some intractable contact disputes the children concerned may be suffering significant harm as a result of a parent's behaviour. Such cases will probably be relatively rare but, where the circumstances warrant it, the judge has the option of giving a direction to a local authority pursuant to section 37 of the Children Act 1989 to investigate the child's

---

[615] [1995] 2 FLR 124, CA.   [616] Ibid, 130.

[617] *Re R (A Child)* [2009] EWCA Civ 1316 at [4] *per* Wall LJ.

[618] [2009] EWHC 1576 (Fam), [2010] 1 FLR 1679.   [619] *Re D (Children)* [2009] EWCA Civ 1551.

[620] *Re D (Children)* [2010] EWCA Civ 496.

[621] See *per* Munby LJ in *Re LW (Children) (Enforcement and Committal: Contact); CPL v CH-W and others*, CA (4 November 2010).   [622] [2010] EWHC 192 (Fam), [2010] 1 FLR 1785.

[623] See also *Re C (Residence Order)* [2007] EWCA Civ 866, [2008] 1 FLR 211 (transfer ordered where mother had new baby and committal to prison not appropriate).   [624] [2007] EWCA Civ 899.

circumstances. In *Re M (Intractable Contact Dispute: Interim Care Orders)*[625] the mother had succeeded in alienating two children from their father and paternal grandparents, by doing her best to instil in the children the false belief that they had been sexually abused by their father, and that one of the children had been physically maltreated and sexually abused by the grandparents. The court found that the allegations were false, and that actually the children were suffering significant emotional harm as a result of the behaviour of the mother who lacked all insight into the damage she was causing the children. In the circumstances Wall J gave a section 37 direction.[626] The local authority, having investigated, sought and obtained an interim care order and the children were removed from the mother to foster parents where they could begin a process of reintroduction to the father and his family, free from the mother's control. The case was finally disposed of by making a residence order in favour of the father combined with a supervision order in favour of the local authority for two years, with contact between the children and the mother to be in the discretion of the local authority. Wall J made clear, however, that section 37 is 'a well-focused tool, to be used only when the case fits its criteria'.[627] There must therefore be reasonable grounds for believing that the child concerned is suffering or is likely to suffer significant harm. The action contemplated by the direction must be in the child's best interests, and thought through; there must be 'a coherent care plan of which temporary or permanent removal of the child from the resident parent is an integral part'.[628] The reasons for the direction should be clearly spelled out. The children should be separately represented[629] and preferably the section 37 report should be supported by professional or expert advice.[630]

5.12.2.4 Enforcement orders

Section 11J of the Children Act 1989 provides a new mechanism for enforcing a contact order, known as an enforcement order. Section 11J(2) provides:

> If the court is satisfied beyond reasonable doubt that a person has failed to comply with the contact order, it may make an order (an 'enforcement order') imposing on the person an unpaid work requirement.[631]

The order cannot be made unless the court is satisfied that the person concerned was given a warning notice under section 11I or was informed of the terms of such notice prior to the failure.[632]

---

[625] [2003] EWHC 1024 (Fam), [2003] 2 FLR 636.

[626] Note that when a court gives a section 37 direction, it also has power to make an interim care order under s 38(1)(b) of the Children Act 1989, but immediate making of such an order was not felt to be necessary.   [627] [2003] EWHC 1024 (Fam), [2003] 2 FLR 636 at [8].

[628] Ibid, [11].

[629] The definition of 'specified proceedings' (s 41(6)(b)) includes private law proceedings for contact or residence orders in which the court has given a direction under s 37(1) and has made or is considering whether to make an interim care order. In these circumstances a children's guardian must be appointed under s 41(1) unless the court is satisfied that it is not necessary to do so in order to safeguard the children's interests (see ibid, at [9] and see [15]–[16]).   [630] Ibid, [17].

[631] Subject to the restrictions in ss 11K and 11L: see s 11J(8). Section 11K(4) provides that a 'court may not make an enforcement order against a person unless the person is habitually resident in England and Wales; and an enforcement order ceases to have effect if the person subject to the order ceases to be habitually resident in England and Wales'. Section 11K(2) provides that a court 'may not make an enforcement order against a person in respect of any failure to comply with a contact order occurring before the person attained the age of 18'. More than one enforcement order in relation to the same person on the same occasion can be made: see s 11J(10).

[632] Section 11K(1).

There is a defence in section 11J(3) of 'reasonable excuse'. This provides that the court 'may not make an enforcement order if it is satisfied that the person had a reasonable excuse for failing to comply with the contact order', the proof of which lies on the person claiming to have had a reasonable excuse, and the standard of proof is the balance of probabilities.[633] It is necessary to keep the question of reasonable excuse entirely separate and distinct from the logically prior question of breach.[634] There will be no breach where it is beyond the defendant's power to comply, for example 'when contact is prevented or delayed by unforeseen and insuperable transport or weather problems'.[635] However, reasonable excuse arises where, although it was within the power of the defendant to comply, he has a reasonable excuse for not doing so, for example where it is necessary to take the child to a doctor rather than going to contact.

An enforcement order can only be made upon an application; the court cannot under this provision enforce the order of its own motion. Those who can apply are (i) the person with whom the child concerned lives or is to live; (ii) the person whose contact with the child concerned is provided for in the contact order; (iii) any individual subject to a condition under section 11(7)(b) or a contact activity condition imposed by the contact order; or (iv) the child concerned.[636] In the case of a child applicant the child must obtain the leave of the court before making such an application,[637] which may be granted only if the court is satisfied that he or she has sufficient understanding to make the proposed application.[638]

Before making the order, which may be a suspended order,[639] the court must be satisfied that:

(a) making the enforcement order proposed is necessary to secure the person's compliance with the contact order or any contact order that has effect in its place;

(b) the likely effect on the person of the enforcement order proposed to be made is proportionate to the seriousness of the breach of the contact order.[640]

The court must also be satisfied that 'provision for the person to work under an unpaid work requirement imposed by an enforcement order can be made in the local justice area in which the person in breach resides or will reside'.[641] The court must obtain and consider information about the person and the likely effect of the enforcement order on him,[642] including any conflict with the person's religious beliefs; and any interference with the times (if any) at which he normally works or attends an educational establishment.[643]

The court must also 'take into account the welfare of the child who is the subject of the contact order'.[644]

Where the court makes an enforcement order, it is to attach to the order a notice warning of the consequences of failing to comply with the order,[645] and the court is to ask a Cafcass officer or Welsh family proceedings officer to monitor and report on compliance with the order.[646]

---

[633] Section 11J(4).

[634] Re LW (Children) (Enforcement and Committal: Contact); CPL v CH-W and others [2010] EWCA Civ 1253, [2011] 1 FLR 1095.

[635] Ibid, [40] per Munby LJ, adding 'one thinks of the sudden and unexpected grounding of the nation's airlines by volcanic ash'.   [636] Children Act 1989, s 11J(5).

[637] Ibid, s 11J(6).   [638] Ibid, s 11J(7).   [639] Ibid, s 11J(9).   [640] Ibid, s 11L(1).

[641] Ibid, s 11L(2).   [642] Ibid, s 11L(3).   [643] Ibid, s 11L(4).   [644] Ibid, s 11L(7).

[645] Ibid, s 11N.

[646] Ibid, s 11M. Schedule A1, Pt 1 makes provision as regards an unpaid work requirement, and Pt 2 makes provision in relation to the revocation and amendment of enforcement orders and failure to comply with such orders.

5.12.2.5 Compensation for financial loss

Section 11O(2) of the Children Act 1989 provides that if the court is satisfied that an individual has failed to comply with a contact order and another person (as defined by the section) has suffered financial loss by reason of the breach, it may make an order requiring the individual in breach to pay the person compensation in respect of his financial loss.[647] Unlike in the case of an enforcement order, the breach need only be proved to the civil standard (balance of probabilities).[648] The order can only be made on an application by the person who claims to have suffered financial loss. Those who may claim compensation are the person with whom the child concerned lives or is to live; the person whose contact with the child concerned is provided for in the contact order; an individual subject to a condition under section 11(7)(b) or a contact activity condition imposed by the contact order; or the child concerned.[649]

An order can only be made if prior to the breach the individual was given a copy of, or was otherwise informed of the terms of, a notice under section 11I relating to the order.[650] There is also a defence that the court is satisfied that the individual in breach had a reasonable excuse for failing to comply with the contact order,[651] the burden of proof as to which lies on the individual claiming to have had a reasonable excuse.[652] The amount of compensation is to be determined by the court, but may not exceed the amount of the applicant's financial loss.[653] In determining the amount of compensation payable by the individual in breach, the court must take into account the individual's financial circumstances[654] and the welfare of the child concerned.[655] An amount ordered to be paid as compensation may be recovered by the applicant as a civil debt.[656]

5.13 PROHIBITED STEPS ORDER

A prohibited steps order means:

> an order that no step which could be taken by a parent in meeting his parental responsibility for a child, and which is of the kind specified in the order, shall be taken by any person without the consent of the court.

This order is limited to controlling areas of parental responsibility which a parent could exercise. In *Croydon London Borough Council v A*[657] it was held that the trial court had been plainly wrong to make an order that the parents could not have contact with each other, as contact between parents has nothing to do with the exercise of parental responsibility. Similarly, a prohibited steps order cannot be used as a means to oust a parent from the home.[658] Nor may such an order be made where its purpose is to prevent a father from staying overnight at the matrimonial home at the conclusion of contact with his children.[659]

---

[647] A court may not require an individual to pay compensation in respect of a failure by him to comply with a contact order where the failure occurred before the individual attained the age of 18: see s 11P.

[648] See *Re LW (Children) (Enforcement and Committal: Contact); CPL v CH-W and others* [2010] EWCA Civ 1253, [2011] 1 FLR 1095 at [38].

[649] As in the case of the child's application for an enforcement order, where the person proposing to apply for an order is the child concerned, the child must obtain the leave of the court, which may grant leave to the child concerned only if it is satisfied that he or she has sufficient understanding to make the proposed application (see s 11O(7) and (8)). [650] Children Act 1989, s 11P.

[651] Ibid, s 11O(3).   [652] Ibid, s 11O(4).   [653] Ibid, s 11O(9).   [654] Ibid, s 11O(10).

[655] Ibid, s 11O(14).   [656] Ibid, s 11O(11).   [657] [1992] Fam 169, CA.

[658] *Nottinghamshire County Council v P* [1993] 2 FLR 134.

[659] *Re D (Prohibited Steps Order)* [1996] 2 FLR 273.

Such use of a prohibited steps order would amount to the importation by the back door of an occupation order, which is governed by Part IV of the Family Law Act 1996.[660]

While the order is limited to aspects of parental responsibility, it can be used to control the behaviour of 'any person' towards a child, including therefore persons who do not have parental responsibility. Thus in *Re M (A Child) (Prohibited Steps Order: Appeal)*[661] a father sought a prohibited steps order preventing the child's stepfather from looking after a baby alone. The father's concern was that the stepfather was over 70 years old, suffered from angina, and might have a heart attack while caring for the child.

5.13.1 Can a prohibited steps order be used to prevent contact?

It will be recalled that section 9(5)(a) of the Children Act 1989 provides that a prohibited steps order cannot be made with a view to achieving a result which could be achieved by making a residence or contact order. If it is also recalled that in *Nottinghamshire County Council v P*[662] it was held that the term 'contact order' includes an order for no contact, the result of section 9(5)(a) is that a prohibited steps order cannot be made where it would be a disguised form of a 'no contact' order.

In *Re H (Prohibited Steps Order)*[663] the trial judge made a prohibited steps order against the mother (with whom the children were residing) to prevent the children from having contact with the abuser of one child. He declined to make a prohibited steps order against the abuser on the ground that he had no jurisdiction as the abuser was not a party to the proceedings. The Court of Appeal held that the judge was in error in making a prohibited steps order against the mother because this directly contravened section 9(5); a prohibited steps order against the mother would achieve the same result as a contact order requiring the mother not to allow contact with the abuser, and could be enforced in the same way. However, a prohibited steps order which required the abuser not to seek contact with the children did not contravene section 9(5) and such an order could and should be made.[664]

5.13.2 Preventing removal

Removal of children from the UK without the consent of all those with parental responsibility is a criminal offence,[665] but parents and others may either not be aware of this or they may be prepared to break the criminal law. In addition, section 13 of the Children Act 1989 provides that a person with a residence order can take or send the child out of the UK for a period of less than one month without either the consent of all those with parental responsibility or the court's leave.[666] In some situations any removal from the jurisdiction could expose the child to the risk of being taken permanently abroad and a prohibited steps order may therefore be necessary to obviate this risk. Certainly it is advisable that such an order is sought by a person with parental responsibility where there is a perceived risk of the child being taken overseas without consent, for once a child has been taken from the country there may be difficulties securing the child's return. A person without parental responsibility, such as an unmarried father or other close relative, may be particularly well advised to apply for a prohibited steps order preventing removal from the jurisdiction, for such persons have no right to prevent a child being taken abroad. Where they enjoy a close

---

[660] See Chapter 3.   [661] [2002] All ER (D) 401 (Nov).   [662] [1993] 2 FLR 134.
[663] [1995] 1 FLR 638.
[664] The court confirmed that it had this power despite the fact that the abuser was not a party to the proceedings. See ibid at 642, for discussion of the procedural difficulties which might arise in such without notice proceedings, and the court's suggested solution to them. See also M. Roberts, 'Ousting Abusers—Children Act 1989 or Inherent Jurisdiction? *Re H (Prohibited Steps Orders)*' (1995) 7 Child and Family Law Quarterly 243.
[665] Child Abduction Act 1984, s 1.   [666] See also ibid, s 1(4).

relationship with the child, a court could well be persuaded to prohibit the child's removal unless those with parental responsibility first gained the permission of the court.[667]

A prohibited steps order might also be used to prohibit a child's relocation within the UK[668] although, as we have seen, an order restricting a resident parent's movements within the UK will only be made exceptionally.

5.14 SPECIFIC ISSUE ORDER[669]

A specific issue order means:

> an order giving directions for the purpose of determining a specific question which has arisen, or which may arise, in connection with any aspect of parental responsibility for a child.

The order will normally resolve a dispute about an aspect of parental responsibility. However, there need not necessarily be an issue between the parties. In *Re HG (Specific Issue Order: Sterilisation)*[670] a girl aged nearly 18 had severe epilepsy and a form of chromosomal deficiency which meant that she was an infant in terms of abilities. She lived in a school which meant she was likely at some time to be at risk of sexual relationships leading to pregnancy. The contraceptive pill was not suitable because of her epilepsy. It was accepted by all that it would be disastrous for the girl if she were to become pregnant because she would not be capable of understanding what was happening to her. Her parents wished to raise the question whether their daughter could be sterilised by making an application as the child's next friend[671] for a specific issue order. The case thus raised the question whether a specific issue order could be made when there was no issue (or dispute) between the persons having parental responsibility. It was held that the fact that a 'question has to be answered is what gives rise to the issue, not that there are protagonists on either side of the debate'.[672]

The issue which the order addresses must be one 'in connection with any aspect of parental responsibility for a child'. In *Re HG* the court had been confronted with an argument that, since the non-therapeutic sterilisation of a child required court approval,[673] the question of whether a child should be sterilised could not be one in connection with an aspect of parental responsibility. Thus, as the argument went, a specific issue order could not be made to sanction the operation. Peter Singer QC (sitting as Deputy High Court Judge) opined that it would be contrary to the philosophy of the Children Act 1989 if the definition of a specific issue order and of parental responsibility in section 3 of the

---

[667] See *Re WB (Residence Orders)* [1995] 2 FLR 1023.

[668] See *Re B (Prohibited Steps Order)* [2007] EWCA Civ 1055, [2008] 1 FLR 613 in which, however, the order was not granted.

[669] See S. Gilmore, 'The Nature, Scope and Use of the Specific Issue Order' [2004] Child and Family Law Quarterly 367.

[670] [1993] 1 FLR 587, FD.

[671] The Children Act 1989, s 10(7) entitles any person who falls within a category of persons prescribed by rules of court to apply for a section 8 order, and rules of court provide that a person under a disability may begin and prosecute proceedings by her next friend, in this case the parents. The parents could, of course, have made their own application for a specific issue order; however they were not entitled to legal aid to make an application themselves and legal proceedings in the High Court are very expensive. On the other hand, they could obtain legal aid to bring proceedings on behalf of their child. The court found this approach to be acceptable.

[672] *Re HG (Specific Issue Order: Sterilisation)* [1993] 1 FLR 587 (Peter Singer QC, sitting as a deputy High Court judge) at 595D–E.

[673] See *Re B (A Minor) (Wardship: Sterilisation)* [1988] AC 199.

Children Act 1989 were approached too restrictively. He held that the fact that a High Court judge must rule on sterilisation did not take from the parents their responsibility to form their own conclusion and to take the necessary steps to implement that conclusion. Indeed, the court suggested that it may be one of the responsibilities of parenthood to bring the issue of sterilisation before a judge.

Clearly, however, there will be some issues which affect a child but which are outside the scope of the order, as illustrated by *Re J (Specific Issue Order: Leave to Apply)*.[674] In that case a child claimed to be a 'child in need' for the purposes of section 17 of the Children Act 1989. He sought leave to apply for a specific issue order which would deem him to be such a child. Wall J ruled that, as a matter of statutory construction, it was clear that it was the intention of Parliament that the exercise of a local authority's powers and duties under Part III of the Act should not be subject to judicial scrutiny or control except by means of judicial review. Accordingly, a specific issue order was inapposite to determine the question whether or not the applicant was a child in need. Moreover, the decision whether a child was a child in need was not a specific question which arose 'in connection with any aspect of parental responsibility'. Such a question must relate to the application of the exercise of parental responsibility to particular facts.[675]

A specific issue order may be of particular value to a parent in a situation where the child has his home elsewhere. The parent in charge of the day-to-day care of the child will make most decisions about the child's upbringing, but the other parent still retains an interest in these decisions and, where they are in dispute, the issue can be placed before a court and the court asked to decide. The order may also be of value to a third party who wishes to challenge a decision of a person with parental responsibility. In *Re F (Specific Issue: Child Interview)*[676] a father was accused of assaulting the mother of two children and had been committed for trial. His solicitor wished to interview the children because they may have witnessed the alleged assault. The mother, who had sole parental responsibility for the children, refused to consent to the interview taking place. Dismissing the mother's appeal against the granting of a specific issue order permitting the solicitor to interview the children, the Court of Appeal held that the interview would be an ordeal which the boys would want to be spared if possible, but that that consideration had to be weighed against the advantages of securing a fair trial.

The specific issue order has been used across a range of issues[677] such as medical treatment/surgical intervention,[678] disputes surrounding children's education,[679] and disclosure of information.[680] Two particularly prominent issues, upon which we now focus, are relocation from the jurisdiction and disputes concerning a child's name.

[674] [1995] 1 FLR 669.
[675] *Re HG* and *Re J* are not easy to reconcile: see S. Gilmore, 'The Nature, Scope and Use of the Specific Issue Order' [2004] Child and Family Law Quarterly 367.
[676] [1995] 1 FLR 819.
[677] See S. Gilmore, 'The Nature, Scope and Use of the Specific Issue Order' [2004] Child and Family Law Quarterly 367.
[678] *Re C (Welfare of Child: Immunisation)* [2003] EWHC 1376 (Fam), [2003] 2 FLR 1054, affirmed by the Court of Appeal in *Re B (A Child) (Immunisation)* [2003] EWCA Civ 1148, [2003] 2 FLR 1095; *Re C (HIV Test)* [1999] 2 FLR 1004, upholding Wilson J's decision in *Re C (A Child) (HIV Testing)* [2000] Fam 48; *Re R (A Minor) (Blood Transfusion)* [1993] 2 FLR 757 (Booth J); *Re J (Specific Issue Order: Child's Religious Upbringing and Circumcision)* [2000] 1 FLR 571.
[679] *Re A (Specific Issue Order: Parental Dispute)* [2001] 1 FLR 121; *Re Z (A Child) (Specific Issue Order: Religious Education)* [2002] EWCA Civ 501.
[680] Eg *Re K (Specific Issue Order)* [1999] 2 FLR 280 and *Re F (Specific Issue: Child Interview)* [1995] 1 FLR 819, discussed earlier in this section.

5.14.1 Authorising the child's removal from the jurisdiction

The question of a child's removal from the jurisdiction is an issue which arises relatively frequently before the courts[681] and has attracted a large body of case law.[682] Relocation disputes may be a growing phenomenon, arising from increases in family breakdown, greater international mobility, and changes in dating patterns (eg couples meeting over the internet).[683] The fact that cases tend to come before the courts is prompted by at least two factors. First, in many cases this is likely to be a contentious issue: if a child is taken out of the jurisdiction it is almost inevitable that the child will be unable to enjoy regular contact with the other parent, especially where the child is young. Secondly, the Child Abduction Act 1984 provides that it is a criminal offence for a person to take or send a child out of the UK without 'the appropriate consent'.[684] This safeguard means that before such removal is lawful, either all persons with parental responsibility for the child must have consented to the child's removal or the leave of the court must first have been obtained. Section 13(1)(b) of the Children Act 1989 reinforces this safeguard by providing that:

> Where a residence order is in force with respect to a child, no person may—
>
> (b) remove [the child] from the United Kingdom;
>
> without either the written consent of every person who has parental responsibility for the child or the leave of the court.

Of course families commonly travel abroad for holidays, and the stringent nature of this provision could prove very disruptive and inconvenient for the parent with whom the child is living. Section 13(2) therefore contains some amelioration by providing that a person with a residence order may take the child out of the jurisdiction for a period of up to one month without first obtaining such consents or the court's leave.[685]

In the event that a parent is resisting the other's long-term (permanent) relocation with the child, the court's authorisation will need to be sought. This can be achieved by seeking a specific issue order or, if there is a residence order in force, by seeking leave pursuant to section 13 of the Children Act 1989.[686]

5.14.1.1 Payne v Payne: *general guidance*

The leading decision is *Payne v Payne*,[687] in which the Court of Appeal held that the implementation of the HRA 1998 did 'not necessitate a revision of the fundamental approach

---

[681] See Thorpe LJ's comment in *Re G (Leave to Remove)* [2007] EWCA Civ 1497, [2008] 1 FLR 1587 at [18] that the volume of such applications for permission to appeal and hearings is not inconsiderable.

[682] For useful accounts of the case law see M. Hayes, 'Relocation Cases: Is the Court of Appeal Applying the Correct Principles?' [2006] Child and Family Law Quarterly 351 and R. George, 'The Shifting Law: Relocation Disputes in New Zealand and England' (2009) 12 Otago Law Review 107.

[683] P. Parkinson, J. Cashmore, and J. Single, 'The Need for Reality Testing in Relocation Cases' (2010) 44(1) Family Law Quarterly 1–34 at 2–3.

[684] Defined in s 1(3).

[685] Children Act 1989, s 13(3). Also, when making the residence order the court may grant the leave required by s 13(1)(b), either generally or for specified purposes.

[686] There is some rather sterile debate in the case law as to whether a specific issue order can be sought where a residence order is in force or whether in such a case the appropriate route is to apply for leave under s 13. See S. Gilmore, 'The Nature, Scope and Use of the Specific Issue Order' [2004] Child and Family Law Quarterly 367 and R. George, 'Changing Names, Changing Places: Reconsidering Section 13 of the Children Act 1989' [2008] Family Law 1121.

[687] [2001] Fam 473. For commentary, see A. Perry, 'Case Commentary: Leave to Remove Children from the Jurisdiction: *Payne v Payne*' [2001] Child and Family Law Quarterly 455; A. Bainham, 'Taking Children Abroad: Human Rights, Welfare and the Courts' [2001] Cambridge Law Journal 489.

to relocation applications' in decisions over the preceding 30 years deriving from *Poel v Poel*.[688] Reviewing those decisions, the court concluded that:

> relocation cases have been consistently decided upon the application of the following two propositions: (a) the welfare of the child is the paramount consideration; and (b) refusing the primary carer's reasonable proposals for the relocation of her family life is likely to impact detrimentally on the welfare of her dependent children. Therefore her application to relocate will be granted unless the court concludes that it is incompatible with the welfare of the children.[689]

The court emphasised that 'in most relocation cases the most crucial assessment and finding for the judge is likely to be the effect of the refusal of the application on the mother's future psychological and emotional stability';[690] and in 'any evaluation of the welfare of the child as the paramount consideration great weight must be given to this factor'.[691] The court explained, however, that there is no presumption that the reasonable proposals of the custodial parent should receive endorsement,[692] since this would be to risk breaching the respondent's rights under Articles 8 and 6 of the ECHR.[693] In order to 'guard against the risk of too perfunctory an investigation resulting from too ready an assumption that the mother's proposals are necessarily compatible with the child's welfare', however, the court suggested, at paragraph [40], the following approach:

> (a) Pose the question: is the mother's application genuine in the sense that it is not motivated by some selfish desire to exclude the father from the child's life? Then ask is the mother's application realistic, by which I mean founded on practical proposals both well researched and investigated? If the application fails either of these tests refusal will inevitably follow.
> (b) If however the application passes these tests then there must be a careful appraisal of the father's opposition: is it motivated by genuine concern for the future of the child's welfare or is it driven by some ulterior motive? What would be the extent of the detriment to him and his future relationship with the child were the application granted? To what extent would that be offset by extension of the child's relationships with the maternal family and homeland? (c) What would be the impact on the mother, either as the single parent or as a new wife, of a refusal of her realistic proposal? (d) The outcome of the second and third appraisals must then be brought into an overriding review of the child's welfare as the paramount consideration, directed by the statutory checklist insofar as appropriate.

At paragraph [41], Thorpe LJ added:

> In suggesting such a discipline I would not wish to be thought to have diminished the importance that this court has consistently attached to the emotional and psychological wellbeing of the primary carer. In any evaluation of the welfare of the child as the paramount consideration great weight must be given to this factor.

In *Re B (Leave to Remove: Impact of Refusal)*[694] the court emphasised the importance of paragraph [41] and that it is as much a part of the discipline set out as if it had been expressed in paragraph [40](c). The approach in paragraphs [40] and [41] are commonly referred to as the *Payne* discipline.

---

[688] [1970] 1 WLR 1469. For a detailed assessment of this case, see R. Taylor, '*Poels* Apart: Fixed Principles and Shifting Values in Relocation Law' in S. Gilmore, J. Herring, and R. Probert, *Landmark Cases in Family Law* (Oxford: Hart, 2011). The court's reasoning in *Poel* was followed and developed in a line of pre-Children Act 1989 case law: see eg *Nash v Nash* [1973] 2 All ER 704; *Chamberlain v De La Mare* (1982) 4 FLR 434; *Lonslow v Hennig* [1986] 2 FLR 378; *Belton v Belton* [1987] 2 FLR 343; *Re F (A Ward) (Leave to Remove Ward Out of the Jurisdiction)* [1988] 2 FLR 116.   [689] [2001] Fam 473 at [26].
[690] Ibid, [26].   [691] Ibid, [41].   [692] Ibid, [40].   [693] Ibid.
[694] [2004] EWCA Civ 956, [2005] 2 FLR 239 at [14].

Butler-Sloss P in *Payne* agreed with Thorpe LJ. She went on to emphasise that all relevant factors need to be considered, including the following matters which, although not exclusive of other important matters which arise in an individual case, should be kept at the forefront of the judge's mind:[695]

(a) The welfare of the child is always paramount.

(b) There is no presumption created by section 13(1)(b) in favour of the applicant parent.

(c) The reasonable proposals of the parent with a residence order wishing to live abroad carry great weight.

(d) Consequently the proposals have to be scrutinised with care and the court needs to be satisfied that there is a genuine motivation for the move and not the intention to bring contact between the child and the other parent to an end.

(e) The effect upon the applicant parent and the new family of the child of a refusal of leave is very important.

(f) The effect upon the child of the denial of contact with the other parent and in some cases his family is very important.

(g) The opportunity for continuing contact between the child and the parent left behind may be very significant.[696]

In *Re B (Children) (Removal from Jurisdiction); Re S (A Child) (Removal from Jurisdiction)*[697] the Court of Appeal offered the following extension to subparagraph (c) of paragraph [40] of the judgment in *Payne* (see the earlier quotation): 'Where the mother cares for the child or proposes to care for the child within a new family, the impact of refusal on the new family and the stepfather or prospective stepfather must also be carefully evaluated.' In those cases two mothers successfully appealed against refusal of leave to relocate.[698] In *Re B* the mother of two children, aged 10 and 6 years, who had divorced the children's father, wished to relocate to South Africa to be with her new partner, an affluent South African businessman who needed to live in South Africa to run his business interests there. In *Re S* the facts were similar. The mother of a 6-year-old child had formed a relationship with a man from the Philippines who had a right to live in Western Australia. They were soon to marry and she wished to relocate to Perth to live with him. He had a good salary there in a rather specialised job as a facial surgeon's clinical assistant. Overturning the judges' respective decisions, the Court of Appeal held that in each case insufficient weight had been given to the welfare as a whole of the new family. Thorpe LJ explained that the Court of Appeal had previously indicated that inter-ference with reasonable decisions, particularly of step-parents, is something the court should undertake with considerable hesitation if the children are to continue to live with that step-parent.[699] His Lordship added:

The mother's attachment and commitment to a man whose employment requires him to live in another jurisdiction may be a decisive factor in the determination of a relocation

---

[695] *Payne v Payne* [2001] Fam 473 at [85].

[696] In *Re D (Leave to Remove: Appeal)* [2010] EWCA Civ 50, [2010] 2 FLR 1605 Wall LJ observed (at [18]) that 'the best summary of the approach which judges are required to take to these difficult decisions is contained in the judgment of the President, Dame Elizabeth Butler-Sloss in *Payne v Payne* at paras [85] to [88]'.

[697] [2003] EWCA Civ 1149, [2003] 2 FLR 1043. See also on the significance of re-marriage, *Re H (Application to Remove from the Jurisdiction)* [1998] 1 FLR 848.

[698] The cases were heard consecutively but the Court of Appeal gave judgment on them together.

[699] *Chamberlain v De la Mare* (1983) 4 FLR 434 at 443H *per* Ormrod LJ and see also Griffiths LJ at 445, as endorsed by Butler-Sloss P in *Payne v Payne* at [73].

application. That does not entail putting the needs and interests of an adult before the welfare of the children. Rather the welfare of the children cannot be achieved unless the new family has the ordinary opportunity to pursue its goals and to make its choices without unreasonable restriction…

That consideration applies with greater force in the case where the child's stepfather is a foreign national. There, as well as work, all his history, his family ties and his loyalties pull in the same direction. If the court frustrates that natural emigration it jeopardises the prospects of the new family's survival or blights its potential for fulfilment and happiness. That is manifestly contrary to the welfare of any child of that family. That is a reality which the court determining an application for relocation simply has to recognise.[700]

5.14.1.2 *The scope of* Payne

In *Re B (Leave to Remove: Impact of Refusal)*[701] Thorpe LJ explained that the principles set out in *Payne* apply generally to all applications by a primary carer. The court rejected counsel's submission that different principles might apply in a case in which, unlike in *Payne*, the relocation could be regarded as a 'lifestyle choice'.[702] There may, however, be some rare cases the facts of which are so unusual that it may not be apt to apply the discipline in *Payne* or aspects of it. In *Re J (Leave to Remove: Urgent Case)*[703] there were cross-applications for residence orders by the parents of two children aged 14 and 11. The children were living with their Bulgarian father and had expressed strong views that they did not wish to see their mother. The father went bankrupt and his home had burnt to the ground. He wished urgently to return to Bulgaria where he had been offered a job. The paternal grandparents had been supporting the father financially and had been paying the children's school fees but they too were proposing to relocate, selling their home to buy a property in Bulgaria. The judge allowed the relocation and the mother appealed contending that the father had not established that practical arrangements for the children's home and school had been made. The Court of Appeal held that the judge had been correct in the unusual circumstances to recognise 'the extraordinary and driving consideration that a sound future for the family could only be achieved by the father recovering an earning capacity in some other economy'.[704] Thorpe LJ commented:

The judge ultimately had to decide between a mother's proposal for a residence order to be implemented in this jurisdiction and a father's residence order application to be implemented in another state. In those circumstances the discipline suggested in paras [40] and [41] of my judgment in *Payne v Payne* hardly applies.[705]

5.14.1.3 *Does* Payne *apply in shared residence cases?*

In *Re Y (Leave to Remove From Jurisdiction)*[706] Hedley J expressed the view that in a shared residence case the guidance in *Payne* should not be applied and that the court should simply apply section 1(1) and (3) of the Children Act 1989.[707] This approach was endorsed by

---

[700] *Re B (Children) (Removal from Jurisdiction); Re S (A Child) (Removal from Jurisdiction)* [2003] EWCA Civ 1149, [2003] 2 FLR 1043 at [8] and [12].   [701] [2004] EWCA Civ 956, [2005] 2 FLR 239 at [14].

[702] See also Charles J's deprecation of the development of sub-classes of case in *Re C (Permission to Remove from Jurisdiction)* [2003] EWHC 596 (Fam), [2003] 1 FLR 1066 at [24](2) which was cited by Thorpe LJ.

[703] [2006] EWCA Civ 1897, [2007] 1 FLR 2033, CA.   [704] Ibid, [28].   [705] Ibid, [27].

[706] [2004] 2 FLR 330.   [707] Ibid, [14]–[16].

Thorpe LJ in *K v K (Relocation: Shared Care Arrangement).*[708] Thorpe LJ emphasised that what is significant is not simply the label of shared residence but the substance of:

> the practical arrangements for sharing the burden of care between two equally committed carers. Where each is providing a more or less equal proportion and one seeks to relocate externally then…the approach…in paragraph 40 in *Payne v. Payne* should not be utilised. The judge should rather exercise his discretion to grant or refuse by applying the statutory checklist in section 1(3) of the Children Act 1989.[709]

However, Black LJ indicated that she 'would not put *Payne* so completely to one side' in cases of shared care. She did not see '*Re Y* as representative of a different line of authority from *Payne*', but rather 'as a decision within the framework of which *Payne* is part', exemplifying 'how the weight attached to the relevant factors alters depending upon the facts of the case'.[710] Her Ladyship was concerned that cases should not get bogged down with preliminary skirmishes over the label to be applied to a child's arrangements or with arguments about whether a case is 'a *Payne* case' or a '*Re Y* case'. Moore-Bick LJ merely agreed with Thorpe LJ that the judge had failed to give sufficient consideration to authority subsequent to *Payne*.[711] This leaves the position rather unclear and is made even more complicated by the fact that some 12 years earlier Thorpe LJ had delivered the Court of Appeal's judgment in *Re C and M (Children)*[712] holding that the approach in *Poel v Poel* (as endorsed in *Payne*) does not apply where there is a shared residence arrangement in place. That case was not cited so arguably *K v K* is decided *per incuriam*.[713] It remains to be seen, however, whether the court will follow its earlier decision or whether Black LJ's approach will prevail.

5.14.2 Applying the *Payne* discipline

5.14.2.1 Are the applicant's proposals genuine and realistic?

The court must be satisfied that the relocating parent's proposals are genuine and realistic. However, in *Re F and H (Children: Relocation)*[714] the Court of Appeal explained that:

> the bar as to practicalities that must be jumped by the relocation applicant is set at a wide variety of heights depending on the facts and circumstances of the case.[715]

In that case a Texan mother of two girls aged 11 and 5 wished to relocate with her children back to Texas after six years in England. Although the mother failed to provide any clear information about the school that the little girls would attend in Texas and as to the mother's employment or earning capacity,[716] the judge permitted the relocation, commenting that the mother was resourceful and would ensure that the children were appropriately cared for and educated. The Court of Appeal held that the judge had not erred, holding that the 'bar is set particularly low where the primary carer is returning to the completely familiar home life after such a brief absence'.[717]

---

[708] [2011] EWCA Civ 793, [2011] 2 FLR at [35]. For commentary, see R. George, 'Reviewing Relocation? *Re W (Relocation: Removal Outside Jurisdiction)* [2011] EWCA Civ 345 and *K v K (Relocation: Shared Care Arrangement)* [2011] EWCA Civ 793' [2012] Child and Family Law Quarterly 110.

[709] Ibid, [57].   [710] Ibid, [144].   [711] Ibid, [87].   [712] [1999] EWCA Civ 2039.

[713] R. George, 'Reviewing Relocation? *Re W (Relocation: Removal Outside Jurisdiction)* [2011] EWCA Civ 345 and *K v K (Relocation: Shared Care Arrangement)* [2011] EWCA Civ 793' [2012] Child and Family Law Quarterly 110.   [714] [2007] EWCA Civ 692, [2008] 2 FLR 1667.

[715] Ibid, [9].

[716] Especially since the contact regime that had been put in place required the mother to be absent from work for eight weeks a year.   [717] [2007] EWCA Civ 692, [2008] 2 FLR 1667 at [9].

Provided they are realistic, the applicant's proposals need not necessarily be supported by detailed evidence. In *Re G (Removal from Jurisdiction)*[718] a mother who had obtained an international diploma in anatomy, physiology, and massage, intended to relocate with her 5-year-old twins from Yorkshire to Argentina, to work as a complementary therapist. The judge was suspicious of the potential of her qualifications, and of such a practice. The Court of Appeal doubted the validity of the judge's conclusion that the mother had fallen short by producing no evidence of business conditions or of demand for her services or of her ability to provide them on a commercial basis.[719] However, leave may be refused where the applicant's proposals are ill thought out. In *K v K (A Minor) (Removal from Jurisdiction)*[720] a mother, who was born in the USA, applied to take the child of the marriage, who was nearly 4, to the USA where the mother proposed to pursue postgraduate education. Refusing leave, Thorpe J found that she had paid insufficient attention to the practicalities of pursuing postgraduate studies in the USA. He also found that the mother had an underlying resilience which would enable her to cope with refusal and that the continuation of the relationship between the child and her father was of very great importance.[721]

5.14.2.2 *Detriment to the non-relocating parent*

As part of the discipline in *Payne*, the court must ask: what would be the extent of the detriment to the parent who opposes relocation and his or her future relationship with the child were the application granted? In some cases the child's relationship with the respondent parent has proved material to the outcome. However, it seems to be rare in the more recent reported decisions for this factor to be material to the outcome.[722] As Mostyn J commented in *Re AR (Relocation)*, the Court of Appeal's approach in *Payne* has a tendency to bring about 'the almost invariable success of the application, save in those cases where it is demonstrably irrational, absurd or malevolent'.[723] *Re B (Leave to Remove)*[724] is a relatively rare example in recent years of a reported decision in which leave has been denied. The Court of Appeal upheld a judge's decision to refuse a mother's application for relocation, despite the fact that the mother had had a reactive depression to the family break-up which would be exacerbated by a refusal, because the effect of relocation would be to alienate the children from their father. *Re AR* itself is another example where a child's contact with the father proved an important factor bearing on the child's overall welfare, albeit in the more unusual situation of a shared care arrangement. The father was English and the mother French. The mother and child had previously lived in France but she had returned to London for postgraduate study, during which time the father, who had care of the child 40 per cent of the time, had established a close relationship with the child. The mother sought leave to remove the child to France again upon the completion

---

[718] [2005] EWCA Civ 170, [2005] 2 FLR 166.

[719] See also *Re M-K (A Child) (Relocation Outside the Jurisdiction)* [2006] EWCA Civ 1013, [2007] 1 FLR 432 (mother wishing to relocate to Brazil merely had a law degree but claimed to be an advocate, although she had an offer to work in her uncle's law firm—the judge focused unduly on the mother's description of her qualifications as affecting her credibility, with which she was given no fair opportunity to deal).

[720] [1992] 2 FLR 98.

[721] See also *M v A (Wardship: Removal from Jurisdiction)* [1993] 2 FLR 715 (mother's plans to relocate to Canada were ill thought out and failed to accommodate the needs and wishes of children aged 12 and 9) and *M v M (Minors) (Jurisdiction)* [1993] Fam Law 396 (Israeli mother refused leave to take her children permanently to Israel because they did not want to be uprooted from their father, schools, and the UK).

[722] For an earlier example, see *Tyler v Tyler* [1989] 2 FLR 158.   [723] Ibid, [7].

[724] [2008] EWCA Civ 1034, [2008] 2 FLR 2059.

of her course. Mostyn J refused leave and made a shared residence order, albeit with the mother as the principal carer.

In *J v S (Leave to Remove)*[725] Eleanor King J also highlighted the significance of the child's existing attachments, commenting:

> It is important that no court dealing with these cases shrinks from examining what the children involved will lose if the application is granted. For my part, I do not subscribe to the view that email and Skype are tolerable substitutes for [informal direct contact]...Often, even on the most restrictive application of the *Payne* discipline, the loss of frequent informal contact between father and child will be considered to be too high a price to pay to satisfying a primary carer's desire to relocate. In such circumstances even the knowledge that the mother will be bitterly disappointed and resentful will not drive a court to the conclusion that the children's interests lie in allowing relocation.[726]

However, on the facts her Ladyship concluded that a Japanese mother should be allowed to relocate back to Japan. The mother suffered with a long-term gastrointestinal illness associated with stress and depression and she would suffer long-term ill health and distress in the event that she was not able to return to Japan. This would be harmful to the welfare of the children, who were aware of the mother's fragile emotional state. In addition, the court was satisfied that the mother would not seek to minimise the strength of and the importance of the relationship between the father and the children.

In reaching her conclusion, Eleanor King J observed[727] that in conducting the balancing exercise she was bound by the discipline of *Payne*, not limited to the questions set out by Thorpe LJ, but also with the judgment of Butler-Sloss P at the forefront of her mind. *Payne* is thus considered only under the umbrella of the paramountcy rule and using the welfare checklist as a tool to assist, whilst always bearing in mind the Article 8 rights of the children. Her Ladyship, while recognising that Thorpe LJ's judgment[728] in *Payne* still resonated strongly and was highly material to the case before her, unhesitatingly agreed with counsel's submission that the court:

> must be careful not to allow itself to become confined in a strait-jacket, with the series of questions presenting the only test...Care must be taken to ensure that the question of the impact of refusal of the mother is but one component of an assessment of the best interests of the boys and not the only feature.[729]

5.14.2.3 *Impact of refusal on the applicant in its effect on child welfare*

As noted, the impact of refusal on the applicant is a powerful factor. However, it is not essential for the relocating parent to demonstrate a negative emotional impact of refusal in order to be successful. In *Re W (A Child) (Removal from Jurisdiction)*[730] the mother suffered with mental health problems, as a result of which she was permitted only indirect contact with her child who lived with the father. The father wished to relocate with his new wife to Australia where his brother lived, a desire which he had had for several years and which he made known to the mother during their relationship some five years earlier. The judge regarded the only impediment to the relocation as the possibility of reviving direct contact with the mother. In the context of the mother's illness, the judge regarded this as an unrealistic prospect and did not regard the disbenefit to the child of relocating as high. Even though the father had not given evidence of the impact of a refusal upon

---

[725] [2010] EWHC 2098 (Fam), [2011] 1 FLR 1694.   [726] Ibid, [99].   [727] Ibid, [82].
[728] Especially *Payne* [2001] EWCA Civ 166, [2001] Fam 473 at [31].
[729] [2010] EWHC 2098 (Fam) at [81].   [730] [2005] EWCA Civ 1614, [2006] 1 FCR 346.

him, the Court of Appeal held that the judge's decision was a balanced exercise of discretion and could not be said to be flawed.

5.14.2.4 Impact of removal on the child's welfare

The court is concerned with the impact of the removal on the welfare of the child primarily as a minor, not as an adult. This point was made in *Re A (Leave to Remove: Cultural and Religious Considerations)*[731] in which the child's father raised cultural and religious considerations as arguments against the removal. Resisting the relocation to Holland (the mother's husband's homeland), the father argued that it would deny the boy the benefit of his father's guidance on the Muslim faith and he would have no prospect of succeeding to the mantle of head of the family in adulthood, which brought status and benefits within the family. McFarlane J observed that this was a matter relating to the child's life as an adult and, although not irrelevant, the court's 'primary task is to give paramount consideration to Y's upbringing as a child'.[732] He concluded that the balance was strongly in favour of the relocation. The father's religious guidance of the child could be achieved through contact.

5.14.3 Criticism of *Payne*

Payne v Payne has attracted considerable criticism by judges, practitioners, and academics.[733] It may be argued that the heavy emphasis on the emotional reaction of the primary carer represents an illegitimate gloss on the purity of the paramountcy principle,[734] or indeed on the process of fairly weighing the interests in the case. Through an analysis of case law applying *Payne*, Mary Hayes has argued that the approach in *Payne* fetters the complex balancing approach required by the welfare checklist and contends that following *Payne* there has emerged an increasingly rigid body of precedent which disempowers trial judges and undermines and devalues the emphasis that might otherwise be placed upon the unique features of each case.[735] As Hayes points out, the effect of *Payne* is that the judge does not start his or her investigation with an open mind and the series of questions set out by Thorpe LJ is not balanced. While the judge must give emphasis to

---

[731] [2006] EWHC 421 (Fam), [2006] 2 FLR 572.   [732] Ibid, [40].

[733] See eg M. Hayes, 'Relocation Cases: Is the Court of Appeal Applying the Correct Principles?' [2006] Child and Family Law Quarterly 351; J. Herring and R. Taylor, 'Relocating Relocation' [2006] Child and Family Law Quarterly 517; P. Pressdee, 'Relocation, Relocation, Relocation: Rigorous Scrutiny Revisited' [2008] Family Law 220; C. Geekie, 'Relocation and Shared Residence: One Route or Two?' [2008] Family Law 446; R. George, 'The Shifting Law: Relocation Disputes in New Zealand and England' (2009) 12 Otago Law Review 107; M. Freeman, *Relocation: The Reunite Research* (London: Reunite, 2009); F. Judd and R. George, 'International Relocation: Do We Stand Alone?' [2010] Family Law 63.

[734] See *Re AR (A Child: Relocation)* [2010] EWHC 1346 (Fam), [2010] 2 FLR 1577 at [8] *per* Mostyn J.

[735] M. Hayes, 'Relocation Cases: Is the Court of Appeal Applying the Correct Principles?' [2006] Child and Family Law Quarterly 351. R. H. George, 'Reassessing Relocation: A Comparative Analysis of Legal Approaches to Disputes Over Family Migration After Parental Separation in England and New Zealand', DPhil Thesis, University of Oxford (2010), p 100 observes that of 23 international relocation judgments from the Court of Appeal since 1999, only four ended with relocation being refused; by contrast, 13 of the 23 cases were refused by the trial judges. As Judd and George have commented, in the current relocation climate it is hard to envisage a case in which granted relocation will be overturned on appeal (citing pre-*Payne* examples of *M v M (Removal from Jurisdiction)* [1993] 1 FCR 5 and *M v M (Minors) (Removal from Jurisdiction)* [1992] 2 FLR 303 (re-trial)): 'International Relocation: Do We Stand Alone?' [2010] Family Law 63. See also Chadwick LJ's criticism in *Re C (Leave to Remove from Jurisdiction)* of the degree of critical analysis to which Thorpe LJ subjected a trial judgment; and generally on this point in the context of international child abduction: *Re J (Child Returned Abroad: Convention Rights)* [2005] UKHL 40, [2005] 2 FLR 802. See, however, the recent case *Re S (Relocation: Interests of Siblings)* [2011] EWCA Civ 454 ,[2011] 2 FLR 678, where the Court of Appeal overturned a judge's decision to grant leave to relocate, albeit on unusual facts.

the primary carer's reactions, the judge is not instructed to have any preconceptions when carrying out an assessment of the detriment to the other parent. Furthermore, there is no reference to the impact on the latter's family.[736]

In *Re H (Leave to Remove)*,[737] Wilson LJ rightly cautioned that 'one must beware of endorsing a parody' of *Payne*, stressing that:

Both Thorpe LJ, at para 26(a), and Dame Elizabeth Butler-Sloss P, at para 85(a), stressed that, in the determination of applications for permission to relocate, the welfare of the child was the paramount consideration. It is only against the subsidiary guidance to be collected from *Payne* that criticisms can perhaps more easily be levelled.[738]

As we have seen in the case law discussed earlier, however, the *Payne* discipline is regularly applied in practice in deciding cases.

There is some evidence that the concerns are shared by some practitioners. Robert George's interviews with 22 practitioners[739] revealed *Payne* as a 'coherent and well-understood approach to relocation disputes, but one which divides practitioners and causes significant discomfort for many who work with it'.[740] In *Re D (Leave to Remove: Appeal)*,[741] Wall LJ acknowledged the considerable criticism of *Payne* and that 'there is a perfectly respectable argument for the proposition that it places too great an emphasis on the wishes and feelings of the relocating parent, and ignores or relegates the harm done of children by a permanent breach of the relationship which children have with the left behind parent'.[742] His Lordship considered that that would in the right case constitute a 'compelling reason' for an appeal to be heard by the Supreme Court.[743] In *Re AR (A Child: Relocation)*[744] Mostyn J called for an urgent review of the ideology of *Poel/Payne* by the Supreme Court, commenting that the impact on the primary carer 'deserves its own berth and as such deserves its due weight, no more, no less'.[745] 'The problem with the attribution of great weight to this particular factor is that, paradoxically, it appears to penalise selflessness and virtue, while rewarding selfishness and uncontrolled emotion.'[746] His Lordship pointed out that 'the one word that is missing from *Payne* is, in fact, *sacrifice*'.[747] Mostyn J added[748] that the very obvious and critically important right of a child to have the meaningful participation of both of his parents in his upbringing (as protected by Art 8 of the ECHR) is sometimes 'lost in the relocation cases'. Jonathan Herring and Rachel

---

[736] Hayes also notes that the discipline contains no indication that the wishes and feelings of the children are important.   [737] [2010] EWCA Civ 915, [2010] 2 FLR 1875.

[738] Ibid, [21].   [739] Seven judges, seven barristers, five solicitors, and three court welfare officers.

[740] R. H. George, 'Reassessing Relocation: A Comparative Analysis of Legal Approaches to Disputes Over Family Migration After Parental Separation in England and New Zealand', DPhil Thesis, University of Oxford (2010), p 201. Some attractive features of *Payne* were also highlighted: it ensures that the court looks to medium/long-term welfare of the child, provides some certainty as to the process by which the court decides, and some clarity as to the information the court would require in evidence. There may be a gender split (at p 221) with women preferring *Payne*.   [741] [2010] EWCA Civ 50, [2010] 2 FLR 1605.

[742] Ibid, [33]. In *Re H (Leave to Remove)* [2010] EWCA Civ 915, [2010] 2 FLR 1875 (discussed in note 752) Wilson LJ (at [23]) questioned the use of the word 'ignores' in this quotation, but agreed that contact with the non-resident parent is relegated.   [743] Ibid, [34].

[744] [2010] EWHC 1346 (Fam), [2010] 2 FLR 1577.

[745] Reiterating some points he had made as counsel in *Re G (Leave to Remove)* [2007] EWCA Civ 1497, [2008] 1 FLR 1587.

[746] Ibid, [12]. See the endorsement of this paradox by Eleanor King J in *J v S* [2010] EWHC 2098 (Fam) at [96].

[747] *Re AR (A Child: Relocation)* [2010] EWHC 1346 (Fam), [2010] 2 FLR 1577 at [8]. However, compare Robert George who observes that this is an adult-centred analysis and that the issue is not about whether the parent is 'stoical' or 'uncontrolled', but about what effect her state of mind may have on the child: see R. George, 'The International Relocation Debate' [2012] Journal of Social Welfare and Family Law 141.

[748] [2010] EWHC 1346 (Fam), [2010] 2 FLR 1577 at [53].

Taylor have also called attention to the fact that there is a failure in relocation disputes to analyse the various interests of the child and the parties as arguably required by Article 8 of the ECHR.[749]

The point made by Mostyn J about 'sacrifice' is a powerful one. Against a focus on personal autonomy in this context, it could be said that parental responsibility requires parents and step-parents to negate their own wishes and feelings. A man who marries a woman who already has children knows that she has responsibilities to those children, and that they may have a father with whom they have a relationship which ought to be maintained. To feel bitter, frustrated, and resentful about an inability to relocate may be a natural response, but these are arguably also self-indulgent emotions and ones which should not be placed at the forefront of the court's approach. It could be said that restrictions on mobility should simply be regarded as one of the burdens of bringing up children, and recognition that the parental responsibility of the natural parents is shared throughout the children's minority. Childhood passes rapidly, and when the children are old enough to express an informed opinion they can be asked whether the benefits of visiting a loved parent outweigh the opportunities offered by moving to a new country.

Despite the criticism, in *Re W (Relocation: Removal Outside Jurisdiction)*[750] Wall P indicated[751] that undue prominence has been accorded to his statements in *Re D (Leave to Remove: Appeal)*[752] and described *Payne* as 'not only the latest leading case on "relocation" in the English jurisprudence, but also a reserved decision of this court and binding on us'.[753] Reviewing that decision, he concluded that:

> the decision falls to be taken on what the court perceives to be in the best interests of the children concerned. Their welfare is our paramount consideration. The court must also apply the criteria and guidance set out in *Payne v Payne*.[754]

Lloyd LJ was slightly more circumspect in endorsing *Payne* as binding, noting only that trial judges had regarded it as so.[755] Elias LJ added (at para [156]): '*Payne* is binding, to the extent at least that guiding principles can be said to bind a court.' In *K v K (Relocation: Shared Care Arrangement)*[756] Moore-Bick LJ, having referred to *Re W*, accepted that *Payne* is binding but added that 'it is binding in the true sense only for its ratio decidendi'.[757] He observed that 'the only principle of law enunciated in *Payne v Payne* is that the welfare of the child is paramount; all the rest is guidance'.[758] And added that:

> where this court gives guidance on the proper approach to take in resolving any particular kind of dispute, judges at all levels must pay heed to that guidance and depart from it only

---

[749] J. Herring and R. Taylor, 'Relocating Relocation' [2006] Child and Family Law Quarterly 517.

[750] [2011] EWCA Civ 345, [2011] 2 FLR 409.

[751] *Re W* [2011] EWCA Civ 345, [2011] 2 FLR 409 at [128].

[752] [2010] EWCA Civ 50, [2010] 2 FLR 1605.

[753] [2011] EWCA Civ 345, [2011] 2 FLR 409 at [13]. Interestingly, however, in March 2010 Thorpe LJ, as the Head of International Family Justice in England and Wales, at an International Judicial Conference on Cross-Border Family Relocation in Washington DC signed the Washington Declaration on International Family Relocation, with a view to harmonising the approach to relocation across states (see [2010] 2 International Family Law 211). The Declaration, which has no force of law, sets out a number of factors relevant to decisions on international relocation but, significantly, does not place emphasis on the emotional impact of refusal. Indeed as Wilson LJ observed in *Re H (Leave to Remove)* [2010] EWCA Civ 915, [2010] 2 FLR 1875 at [27], it may place insufficient weight on that factor. For discussion of the Washington Declaration and subsequent international developments, see R. George, 'The International Relocation Debate' [2012] Journal of Social Welfare and Family Law 141.

[754] *Re W*, [23].   [755] Ibid, [148].   [756] [2011] EWCA Civ 793.

[757] Ibid, [86]. See S. Gilmore, 'The *Payne* Saga: Precedent and Family Law Cases' [2011] Fam Law 970.

[758] Ibid, and see also at [141] *per* Black LJ.

after careful deliberation and when it is clear that the particular circumstances of the case require them to do so in order to give effect to fundamental principles.[759]

As Black LJ put it, the guidance:

> must be heeded for all the reasons that Moore-Bick LJ gives but as guidance not as rigid principle or so as to dictate a particular outcome in a sphere of law where the facts of individual cases are so infinitely variable.[760]

5.14.4 Relocation debate and research

The issue of relocation is hotly debated[761] in the academic literature, with two broad factions, one emphasising the importance of supporting the primary caretaker relationship, and the other focusing on the importance to the child of maintaining a relationship with both parents.[762] There is, however, a paucity of empirical evidence concerning the impact of relocation on parents and children.[763]

There is only one published empirical study in England of individuals involved in relocation cases, work undertaken for the child abduction charity Reunite[764] by Marilyn Freeman.[765] Freeman carried out a series of semi-structured interviews with 36 parents who were involved in 34 relocation cases between 1999 and 2009. The interviewees were 25 fathers, 23 of whom resisted relocation, and 11 mothers all of whom sought relocation. In 22 of the 34 cases (nearly 65 per cent) relocation was granted. The interviews revealed several themes. Post-relocation contact was difficult to maintain, both practically and because of the cost of staying in touch, and could be easily thwarted from a distance. There were also concerns that outcomes after relocation were not monitored. Many interviewees were concerned that Cafcass officers' objectivity seemed compromised by the prevailing approach of the courts. A majority of interviewees urged a more child-centric approach, with appointment of a guardian to protect the child's interests and a more

---

[759] Ibid, [86].   [760] Ibid, [142].

[761] See for a cross-section of perspectives: C. Bruch and J. Bowermaster, 'The Relocation of Children and Custodial Parents: Public Policy, Past and Present' (1995) 30 Family Law Quarterly 245; J. Kelly and M. Lamb, 'Developmental Issues in Relocation Cases Involving Young Children: When, Whether, and How?' (2003) 17 Journal of Family Psychology 193; C. Bruch, 'Sound Research or Wishful Thinking in Child Custody Case? Lessons from Relocation Law' (2006) 40 Family Law Quarterly 281; P. Stahl and L. Drozd (eds), *Relocation Issues in Child Custody Cases* (Binghamton, NY: Haworth Press, 2006); W. Austin, 'Relocation, Research, and Forensic Evaluation, Part I: Effects of Residential Mobility on Children of Divorce' (2008) 46 Family Court Review 137; see also articles in (2011) 23(2) Child and Family Law Quarterly.

[762] See the discussion in J. Herring and R. Taylor, 'Relocating Relocation' [2006] Child and Family Law Quarterly 517 at 519–522, who conclude:

> With so little agreement between researchers, the evidence to date is not capable of founding a general theory of harm to the child in relocation cases nor of providing conclusive support for a presumption either for or against relocation. At best the research evidence tells us that we should be aware of the potential harm to the child both due to any diminution in the quality of parenting of the resident parent and loss of contact with the non-resident parent.

[763] See N. Taylor, M. Gollop, and M. Henaghan, *Relocation Following Parental Separation: The Welfare and Best Interests of Children Research Report* (Centre for Research on Children and Families and Faculty of Law, University of Otago, Dunedin, June 2010) for an excellent account of the existing empirical research on relocation following parental separation (at ch 3), and an extensive bibliography of relevant literature; see also the review of research by N. Taylor and M. Freeman, 'International Research Evidence on Relocation: Past, Present and Future' (2010) 44(3) Family Law Quarterly 317–339 and B. Horsfall and R. Kaspiew, 'Relocation in Separated and Non-Separated Families: Equivocal Evidence from the Social Science Literature' (2010) 24 Australian Journal of Family Law 34. See C. Bruch, 'Sound Research or Wishful Thinking in Child Custody Case? Lessons from Relocation Law' (2006) 40 Family Law Quarterly 281 for a critical account of some of the literature.   [764] See www.reunite.org.

[765] M. Freeman, 'Relocation: The Reunite Research Project' [2010] International Family Law 161.

scientific approach to the impact of relocation on the child. The left-behind parents, who comprised the majority within this study, spoke of the devastation the relocation had brought to their lives, although there was also some evidence of such emotional difficulties caused to parents who were thwarted in their wish to relocate. The research provides an important insight into the very real impact of relocation, particularly for left-behind parents. However, as Judd and George observe,[766] it would be difficult to draw broad conclusions from it as to how relocation law should be developed.

There have also been recent studies in other jurisdictions, for example in Australia and New Zealand. A prospective longitudinal study of relocation disputes is being carried out by Professor Parkinson and colleagues at the University of Sydney.[767] In a reported phase of the study, 80 parents,[768] 40 men (all opposing relocation) and 40 women (all but one relocating) in 71 cases[769] were interviewed at two points 18 months apart. The study cautions that the fact that contact is ordered does not mean that it will occur or do so with anticipated frequency. The study suggested that 'distant relocations may impose financial burdens on parents which may make the planned levels of contact unsustainable in the long-term'.[770] There was also evidence in some cases of difficulties arising over contact which, particularly in overseas relocations, was difficult to enforce and of concerns about the burden of travel on young children. Parkinson et al suggest that judges should 'reality test' any proposed contact and may need to ask whether the relocation would still be in the child's best interests if the proposed contact did not take place.[771] A similar study has been carried out in New Zealand by Taylor, Gollop, and Henaghan[772] interviewing 114 parents and 44 children in 100 families. The study has highlighted the diversity and complexity of relocation disputes,[773] revealing many different relocation sequences. Another study by Behrens, Smyth, and Kaspiew[774] carried out in-depth interviews with 38 separated parents (27 fathers and 11 mothers) involved in contested relocation proceedings in Australia[775] and found that the largest group of cases involved families in which the relocation dispute was only one source of conflict. For most of such cases, poor or abusive inter-parental relationships continued after relocation. This suggests that a court's consideration of the likely outcomes following the relocation dispute may need to take account of these wider issues. The difficulty of comparing international research should be noted, however, because different countries take quite different approaches to relocation disputes.[776]

---

[766] F. Judd and R. George, 'International Relocation: Do We Stand Alone?' [2010] Family Law 63 at 66, referencing C. O'Flinn, 'Back in the Fold' (2009) 159 New Law Journal 1416.

[767] Reported in P. Parkinson, J. Cashmore, and J. Single, 'The Need for Reality Testing in Relocation Cases' (2010) 44(1) Family Law Quarterly 1–34. The Hon Richard Chisholm is also one of the researchers.

[768] And 19 children.   [769] Ten of these involved relocations to other countries.   [770] At 33.

[771] Ibid, 34.

[772] N. Taylor, M. Gollop, and M. Henaghan, *Relocation Following Parental Separation: The Welfare and Best Interests of Children Research Report* (Centre for Research on Children and Families and Faculty of Law, University of Otago, Dunedin, June 2010). See also M. Henaghan, 'Relocation Cases—The Rhetoric and the Reality of a Child's Best Interests—A View from the Bottom of the World' [2011] Child and Family Law Quarterly 226.

[773] See N. Taylor, M. Gollop, and M. Henaghan, 'Relocation Following Parental Separation in New Zealand: Complexity and Diversity' [2010] International Family Law 97.

[774] R. Kaspiew, J. Behrens, and B. Smyth, *Relocation Disputes in Separated Families Prior to the 2006 Reforms: An Empirical Study* (2011) 86 Family Matters 70 (Australian Institute of Family Studies journal).

[775] In 2002 to 2005.

[776] See R. George, 'Practitioners' Views on Children's Welfare in Relocation Disputes: Comparing Approaches in England and New Zealand' [2011] Child and Family Law Quarterly 178 on how the differences might play out in practice, and R. George, 'The International Relocation Debate' [2012] Journal

5.14.5 Change of a child's surname[777]

Another issue which has attracted a considerable amount of case law[778] is what surname a child should bear. The leading authority is the House of Lords' decision in *Dawson v Wearmouth*.[779] The relationship between the unmarried parents of a baby boy called Alexander broke down within three weeks of the child's birth. Shortly thereafter, the mother, without consulting the father, registered Alexander with the surname Wearmouth. This was the name of her former husband, by whom she had two children bearing that surname, and whose name she had retained. Alexander's father, Mr Dawson, sought a specific issue order to change the child's surname to his. The trial judge, who approached the matter as if it had come before him before the child's birth was registered, directed that Alexander be known by the surname Dawson. On the mother's appeal, the Court of Appeal held that the judge had erred in principle. The court explained that the surname which appears on a child's birth certificate cannot be altered and consequently 'as a matter of principle registration is a profound matter'. The court held that registration is thus a 'major factor to be taken into account in the exercise of the court's discretion'.[780] Exercising its discretion afresh, the court held that the connection the mother and Alexander's half-siblings had to the name Wearmouth meant that that was a 'perfectly natural and logical choice for her to make' and could not be justly criticised as alien merely because it was also the name of the mother's ex-husband. The court went on to say that those factors, 'coupled with the all-important fact already stressed that this was the child's duly registered name' were 'very powerful factors in the mother's favour' which could 'only be displaced by strong countervailing considerations'.[781]

Mr Dawson appealed to the House of Lords contending, *inter alia*, that the Court of Appeal gave too much emphasis to registration. The appeal was dismissed. Lord Mackay, delivering the House's opinion, observed that the facts of this case could be distinguished from one in which there had been substantial usage of a father's name. He held that the correct approach is to apply section 1(1)[782] and (5) of the Children Act 1989, 'and not make an order for the change of name unless there is some evidence that this would lead to an improvement from the point of view of the welfare of the child'.[783] Lord Mackay held that on a fair reading, the Court of Appeal was not suggesting that the registration was conclusive of the issue, but that circumstances justifying the change would be required and that there were no such circumstances of sufficient strength to do so in this case.

Lord Jauncey, while not formally dissenting, commented on two matters. First, he did not accept that registration is necessarily a major factor in every case, the weight given to

of Social Welfare and Family Law 141 for an overview of the different approaches and discussion of the possibility of harmonisation.

[777] See J. Herring, 'The Shaming of Naming: Parental Rights and Responsibilities in the Naming of Children' in R. Probert, S. Gilmore, and J. Herring (eds), *Responsible Parents and Parental Responsibility* (Oxford: Hart, 2009). In the context of a child in care, see the Children Act 1989, s 33(7) and *Re S (Change of Surname)* [1999] 1 FLR 672; in the context of special guardianship, see *Re L (Special Guardianship: Surname)* [2007] EWCA Civ 196, [2007] 2 FLR 50.

[778] For useful accounts of the case law, see A. R. Bond, 'Reconstructing Families—Changing Children's Surnames' [1998] Child and Family Law Quarterly 17; M. Hayes, '*Dawson v Wearmouth*: What's in a Name? A Child by Any Other Name is Surely Just as Sweet?' [1999] Child and Family Law Quarterly 423; and N. Gosden, 'Children's Surnames—How Satisfactory is the Current Law?' [2003] Family Law 186.

[779] [1999] 2 AC 308. See M. Hayes, ibid.   [780] [1998] Fam 75 at 82.   [781] Ibid, 83.

[782] See also Ward LJ in *Re C (Change of Surname)* 1998] 2 FLR 656 at 660 to the effect that change of a child's surname is a matter with respect to a child's upbringing.

[783] [1999] 2 AC 308 at 320–321. Lord Hobhouse of Woodborough said that the applicant 'has to make out a positive case in accordance with section 1 of the Act that it is in the interests of the child that the order should be made. If he fails to make out that *positive* case, his application will fail' (at 326).

which must always depend upon the surrounding circumstances as they affect the welfare of the child. Secondly, his Lordship observed that a child's surname at birth is 'not simply a name plucked out of the air'; rather, normally the child is given the father's surname as a biological label, demonstrating the child's connection with the father and telling 'the world at large that the blood of the name flows in its veins'. Lord Jauncey considered that in a case such as this the court should have regard to the importance of maintaining a paternal link; the very real possibility that the mother might remarry and take a new husband's surname; and the fact that the child may wonder why he or she bears a name which is that of neither of the parents but rather that of a man with whom the child has no connection and whom it may never have seen. Lord Jauncey was left in doubt as to whether the Court of Appeal gave proper weight to these important matters in exercising their discretion.

Lord Hobhouse commented that the child's registered name represents the status quo and provides an important part of the background against which the court has to assess what will be in the interests of the child's welfare. He added that it is 'not without importance', 'has practical implications', and, 'other things being equal, it is in the long-term interests of the child that the name by which he is known should also be the name which appears on his birth certificate'. Lord Hobhouse expressed disapproval of how the Court of Appeal had expressed itself. He made clear that registration is a relevant and, maybe, important factor in assessing where the balance of advantage for the child's welfare lies but should not be treated as an 'all-important' factor which requires to be 'displaced by strong countervailing considerations', adding:

> Each case depends upon its own facts.... the registered surname is a relevant factor which must be taken into account and may, in certain cases, like any other relevant factor make the difference between whether an order is made or not.[784]

Dawson v Wearmouth was applied in *Re A (Change of Name)*[785] on similar facts and the same outcome was reached, although the process by which the Court of Appeal reached its decision raises some interesting issues. The parents of a child were Somalis. Within three months of her divorce, the mother conceived the child by a new partner (the father). The mother registered the child in the name of her former husband. The father was successful before the judge at first instance in obtaining a change of the name to that which the father claimed was required by the Somali custom of patrilineal naming. On the mother's appeal, the Court of Appeal received expert evidence on Somali cultural practices with regard to the naming of children and relevant Muslim law. Fatal to the father's case was that the evidence showed that the name for which the father was contending would not be the name in accordance with Somali custom for patrilineal naming. Instead, it showed that where, as here, the mother conceived in such proximity to her divorce, Muslim law provided that the child was regarded as the legitimate child of the mother's former husband and registered accordingly. In light of these findings the Court of Appeal held that there was no justification for changing the name and the judge had been wrong. Chadwick LJ commented that it would not be right 'without very good reason, to deny the child the benefit of a fiction which is conferred by custom and practice within a community for whom...illegitimacy is regarded as a much more serious stigma than divorce'.[786] This comment is interesting, as the court appears to recognise as a basis for its decision a cultural practice which adopts a view which Parliament has sought to eradicate from the laws of England and Wales. English law no longer regards illegitimacy as a stigma. The fact that the court sought out, and placed emphasis upon, the evidence of cultural practices

---

[784] Ibid, 328–329.   [785] [2003] EWCA Civ 56, [2003] 2 FLR 1.   [786] Ibid, [20].

in this case is also interesting, particularly when compared with *Dawson v Wearmouth*, in which the father's argument concerning the custom of patrilineal naming appeared only to strike a chord with Lord Jauncey. As Hale LJ observed in *Re R (Surname: Using Both Parents')*,[787] Lord Jauncey's view in *Dawson v Wearmouth* was a minority view. Her Ladyship added respectfully 'that the majority view was more consistent with the modern law'[788] and that it was:

a matter of great sadness...that it is so often assumed, and even sometimes argued, that fathers need that outward and visible link in order to retain their relationship with, and commitment to, their child. That should not be the case. It is a poor sort of parent whose interest in and commitment to his child depends upon that child bearing his name. After all, that is a privilege which is not enjoyed by many mothers, even if they are not living with the child. They have to depend upon other more substantial things.[789]

The Court of Appeal's approach in *Re A* does not sit easily alongside *Dawson*. One wonders what the Court of Appeal's ruling in *Re A* would have been had all the expert evidence supported the father's case. Would that cultural context have justified an outcome different from Mr Dawson's case? The case law raises some obvious but important questions: can it be right that cultural considerations are given emphasis in one case and not the other, in relation to one culture and not another?

As *Dawson v Wearmouth* makes clear, the status quo is clearly a factor for the court to consider. The court will wish to consider not only the registered surname but also the current legal and *de facto* position regarding the child's use of surname. Any changes of circumstances of the child since the original registration may be relevant. There may have been changes of name since registration, and the history regarding the child's surname is likely to be relevant. The reasons for any previous or proposed change will also be considered.

Reasons 'based on the fact that the child's name is or is not the same as the parent making the application do not generally carry much weight'.[790] One must be careful, however, how this is understood. Insofar as this is seen as a problem for the parent it is of little account.[791] So reasons such as the convenience of medical or school records are likely to be of little weight.[792] However, it has been said that the case law is not to be read as meaning 'that considerations of confusion, anxiety and embarrassment for the child were of little account'.[793] As we saw in the cases discussed earlier, the impact a name has may depend upon the facts and circumstances of the particular case. However, the courts have taken the view that, given the number of births outside marriage, generally there is no reason to suppose that a child will be 'embarrassed or particularly unusual in being registered at...school in a different name from the current surname of her mother'.[794] As Wilson J observed in *Re B (Change of Surname)*:[795]

In these days of such frequent divorce and remarriage, of such frequent cohabitation outside marriage, and indeed increasingly of preservation of different surnames even

---

[787] [2001] EWCA Civ 1344, [2001] 2 FLR 1358, CA.   [788] Ibid, [13].   [789] Ibid, [18].

[790] *Re W (A Child) (Illegitimate Child: Change of Surname); Re A (A Child); Re B (Children)* [2001] Fam 1, CA at [9].

[791] *Re R (Surname: Using Both Parents')* [2001] EWCA Civ 1344, [2001] 2 FLR 1358 at [16].

[792] *Re T (Change of Surname)* [1998] 2 FLR 620 at 624A.

[793] *Re R (Surname: Using Both Parents')* [2001] EWCA Civ 1344, [2001] 2 FLR 1358 at [16].

[794] *Note: Re F (Child: Surname)* [1993] 2 FLR 837 at 838E *per* Ralph Gibson LJ.

[795] [1996] 1 FLR 791.

within marriage, there is, in my view, no opprobrium nowadays upon a child who carries a surname different from that of the adults in his home.[796]

The lawfulness of any change of name may need to be considered in light of the Court of Appeal's view in *Dawson v Wearmouth* that a dispute about a child's surname 'must be referred to the court for determination whether or not there is a residence order in force and whoever has or has not parental responsibility'.[797]

Re C (Change of Surname)[798] held that where a surname has been lawfully changed[799] and is subsequently challenged, the correct approach is to look at whether the change has been in the child's interests.

The security of the foundation of a parent's name may be a relevant factor. In *Re R (Surname: Using Both Parents')*[800] the mother, who was intending to relocate to Spain, unilaterally had begun calling her child by the name of her own stepfather, which the mother had adopted since the child's birth. The judge ordered the change of name on the basis that it was in the child's interests to be brought up within a family with one name. On the father's appeal, Thorpe LJ commented that the relatively insecure foundation of the proposed name militated against change to that name.[801] This was a name which the maternal grandmother used informally but not for all formal purposes. Thorpe LJ pointed out that whether it was a name that the mother would bear in the long term was 'obviously an open question'.[802] Applying *Dawson v Wearmouth*, the Court of Appeal held that the judge had been wrong to order a change of surname, there being no evidence that a change would be in the child's interests. The court drew attention to the fact that it is customary in Spain for children to take two surnames, one from the paternal family and one from the maternal family. Hale LJ commented that 'parents and courts should be much more prepared to contemplate the use of both surnames in an appropriate case, because that is to recognise the importance of both parents'. The court thus urged the parents 'to consider the good sense of imitating Spanish custom'.[803]

A parent's change of name may be relevant. In *Re C (Change of Surname)*[804] the children, aged 8 and 7, had originally been known by their mother's maiden name. When the parents parted the father obtained a residence order and he subsequently caused the children to be known by his surname (not realising that he was prohibited from making this change). Proceedings were issued and the father was granted leave to cause the children to be known by his surname. The mother sought leave to appeal. She did not seek to prevent the daily use by the children of their father's name, but she did want them to retain her name for official purposes. Refusing the mother's application, the Court of Appeal noted that the mother had since married, had taken her husband's surname, and no longer used her maiden name. Therefore, although the stamp of parenthood reflected by a surname should not lightly be erased, retention of the mother's maiden name would not significantly assist in preserving the link between her and her children.

The child's wishes and feelings may prove important to the outcome in a particular case. In *Re PC (Change of Surname)*[805] Holman J said of children aged 12½ and 10 that 'it would be wrong of me even to contemplate trying to effect any reversal of the position which has now been reached without knowing their wishes and feelings and degree of

---

[796] Ibid, 795.

[797] [1998] 2 FLR 656 at 662–663. See Ward LJ at 664 endorsing the view that an order should be sought if there is a dispute.   [798] Ibid.

[799] On the facts of the case that conclusion might be doubted given that *Dawson v Wearmouth* was merely clarifying the existing legal position.   [800] [2001] EWCA Civ 1344, [2001] 2 FLR 1358, CA.

[801] Ibid, [8].   [802] Ibid.   [803] Ibid, [12] *per* Thorpe LJ, echoed by Hale LJ at [20].

[804] [1998] 1 FLR 549.   [805] [1997] 2 FLR 730, FD.

understanding'. However, in *Re B (Change of Surname)*[806] the Court of Appeal confirmed the trial judge's refusal to permit a mother's application for the names of three teenage children to be changed to that of their stepfather despite the fact that they strongly wished this. The children were extremely hostile towards their father and to seeing him,[807] and contact had not taken place for five years. Since their mother's remarriage the children had been known informally by their stepfather's surname, although formal records (such as school reports) bore their father's surname. The children reported that this situation was a source of embarrassment. Wilson J remarked that 'orders nowadays which run flatly counter to the wishes of normal children aged 16, 14 and 12 are virtually unknown to family law'.[808] However, his Lordship went on to draw a distinction between an application by the children's mother to lift an existing prohibition on change of name and imposing an order on the children in the teeth of their opposition.[809] He pointed out that the order did not oblige the children to do anything which they were refusing to do and that they could not be prevented from informally using their stepfather's name. However, he asserted that only the father's name should be recorded on formal documents and that the order prevented the mother from causing the children to be known by a new surname. He concluded that the grant of leave:

> would have sent out a wholly inappropriate message to the children, namely that the court agreed with them that their father was of the past, not of the present. Save following adoption, a father, while he lives, is always of the present.[810]

Despite this reasoning, which emanated from the basic principle that it is of fundamental importance for every child to have an enduring relationship with both parents, the decision sits uneasily with Lord Scarman's opinion in *Gillick v West Norfolk and Wisbech Area Health Authority*.[811] In light of that decision, was it right that the court should take the view that it had an unfettered right to impose its own view of welfare on competent adolescent children in order to prevent them from choosing the name by which they wished to be known formally? Adolescent children are usually very certain that they know their own minds, know what is good for them, and know what will cause them harm. It may be that the children's decision in *Re B (Change of Surname)* was mistaken, and that they would come to regret it. But their choice was relatively harmless (in the sense that it would not lead them positively to suffer harm in the same way that, say, refusal of medical treatment might). If there was ever a situation, therefore, to which the principles in *Gillick* ought to apply, this was it. Having said that, this was undoubtedly a difficult case and Wilson J's anxiety that to agree to the change of name would be interpreted by the child as an endorsement of the children's negative opinion of the father is understandable. However, that might have been handled by carefully giving reasons for the court's decision. Against the court's approach is the danger that, when the determined adolescent's wishes are thwarted, resulting resentment may be counterproductive to fostering good interpersonal relationships with the father. However, on the facts of the case, perhaps the relationships could not have got any worse.

---

[806] [1996] 1 FLR 791, CA.

[807] As demonstrated by their practice of destroying birthday and Christmas cards the father had sent, their refusal to travel on local buses in case the father, who was a bus driver, was driving, and their habit of referring to the father as 'him at Blyth'.   [808] [1996] 1 FLR 791, 794.

[809] Ibid, 794–795. The prohibition had been automatically imposed upon the making of a custody order to the mother at divorce.   [810] Ibid, 795–796.

[811] [1986] AC 112.

The parents' marital status is also a factor. In *Re W (A Child) (Illegitimate Child: Change of Surname); Re A (A Child); Re B (Children)*[812] Butler-Sloss LJ, having provided a useful summary of the House of Lords decision in *Dawson v Wearmouth*, added:

> In the case of a child whose parents were married to each other, the fact of the marriage is important[813] and I would suggest that there would have to be strong reasons to change the name from the father's surname if the child was so registered...Where the child's parents were not married to each other, the mother has control over registration. Consequently on an application to change the surname of the child, the degree of commitment of the father to the child, the quality of contact, if it occurs, between father and child, the existence or absence of parental responsibility are all relevant factors to take into account.[814]

Re A (A Child) and *Re B (Children)*[815] illustrate some circumstances in which a change from the father's registered name may be warranted. In *Re A (A Child)* a boy, aged 10, had exactly the same name as his father, who was described as 'a notorious criminal'. The father had been sentenced to 21 years' imprisonment for offences of violence and the earliest he would be released from prison would be when the boy was 17. The parents had divorced and the mother sought a specific issue order to change the boy's name to her maiden name. The district judge made the order, having found that the mother had a genuine, deep-seated fear that, because of the father's notoriety, the boy was at real risk of harm from being taunted, victimised, or the subject of attack if his identity became known within the locality to which she had recently moved. The district judge's order was over-turned by a circuit judge and the mother appealed to the Court of Appeal, which restored the district judge's decision.[816] In *Re B (Children)* the father of two young girls had been convicted of two offences of indecent assault of a 17-year-old girl and had pleaded guilty to indecent assault of his 11-year-old niece. The mother applied to change the children's surnames to her own name. The judge made the requested order in light of the peripheral part the father was likely to play in the future life of the two girls, which was upheld by the Court of Appeal.

Another case in which it was held to be necessary to permit a change of name is *Re S (Change of Names: Cultural Factors)*.[817] The mother was a Muslim who, at the age of 17 had eloped with a 22-year-old Sikh man to marry at Gretna Green. The couple subsequently had a child, who was 3 years old at the hearing. There were considerable tensions between the parents' respective religions and cultures and the mother's actions had been attended by great shame and anger on the part of her family, which had disowned her. The parents' relationship broke down and the mother became reconciled with her family and wished to move back to her original community. The mother wished to make a fresh

---

[812] [2001] Fam 1, CA.

[813] Compare *Re C (Change of Surname)* [1998] 2 FLR 656 at 660C–D: 'The judge's reference to finding more merit in the father's case had he not declined to marry the mother is an irrelevant consideration'.

[814] [2001] Fam 1, CA at 7G. See eg *Re P (Parental Responsibility)* [1997] 2 FLR 722, CA, discussed in Chapter 7. The children's father had been denied a parental responsibility order because of his irresponsibility in committing an offence of robbery while on home leave from prison. As part of a fresh start in a new town, the children were using the mother's maiden name, by which the children were now known at school. Ward LJ agreed with counsel that the fact that the father had failed in his application for parental responsibility much reduced his prospects of success on his application for change of name.

[815] [2001] Fam 1, CA.

[816] See also in a public law context, *Re M, T, P, K and B (Care: Change of Name)* [2000] 2 FLR 645 (where the children were frightened their family would locate them).

[817] [2001] 2 FLR 1005 (Wilson J). See S. Jivraj and D. Herman, 'It is Difficult for a White Judge to Understand: Orientalism, Racialisation, and Christianity in English Child Welfare Cases' [2009] Child and Family Law Quarterly 283.

start, eliminating the father from her life. The child had recognisably Sikh names and the mother applied to change the child's names so that he was not stamped within the Muslim community as a Sikh and she was not stamped as the 'slag' who had a relationship with a Sikh.[818] There was expert evidence to the effect that in order for the mother and child to be able to integrate into the community the child would need to be known by Muslim names. Wilson J therefore ordered that the child should have Muslim names for use on a day-to-day basis, but that the child should retain his Sikh names formally (eg for the purpose of obtaining a passport) in order to maintain his connection with that part of his family and cultural background.

5.15 RESTRICTING APPLICATIONS FOR SECTION 8 ORDERS UNDER SECTION 91(14)

The court has power to prevent applications without the prior leave of the court. This may be achieved by exercising the inherent jurisdiction of the High Court[819] or a statutory power within section 91(14) of the Children Act 1989. This provides:

> On disposing of any application for an order under this Act, the court may (whether or not it makes any other order in response to the application) order that no application for an order under this Act of any specified kind may be made with respect to the child concerned by any person named in the order without leave of the court.

As Waite LJ observed in *B v B (Residence Order: Restricting Applications)*,[820] section 91(14), tucked away amongst 17 subsections which are largely administrative in character:

> represents a substantial interference with the fundamental principle of public policy enshrined in our unwritten constitution that all citizens enjoy a right of unrestricted access to the Queen's courts.

In *Re P (A Minor) (Residence Order: Child's Welfare)*,[821] however, Butler-Sloss LJ explained that it is only 'a partial restriction', which does not breach Article 6 of the ECHR, in that it merely prohibits an immediate inter partes hearing. The purpose of the bar is to prevent issues relating to a child's upbringing being the subject of constant disruptive, unnecessary, and often highly contentious litigation.[822] It thereby protects the other parties and the child from being drawn into the proposed proceedings unless or until a court has ruled that the application should be allowed to proceed.[823] An order made under section 91(14) should do nothing to prevent a meritorious application.

Notice that section 91(14) requires that the court specify the order(s) to which it is to apply[824] and that it only applies to orders under the Children Act 1989.[825] An absolute prohibition on making any application to the court 'would have to be made under the

---

[818] [2001] 2 FLR 1005 at 1008.

[819] See eg *Re H (Child Orders: Restricting Applications)* [1991] FCR 896.

[820] [1997] 1 FLR 139 at 146.

[821] [2000] Fam 15, sub nom *Re P (Section 91(14) Guidelines) (Residence and Religious Heritage)* [1999] 2 FLR 573.   [822] See eg *Re N (Section 91(14) Order)* [1996] 1 FLR 356.

[823] [2000] Fam 15 at 38.

[824] Thus it is wrong to make an order at large without specifying the orders to which it applied.

[825] *Re M (Education: Section 91(14) Order)* [2007] EWCA Civ 1550, [2008] 2 FLR 404.

inherent jurisdiction of the court'.[826] In *Stringer v Stringer*[827] the Court of Appeal held that it is not permissible to attach any conditions to a section 91(14) order except those allowed by the section itself, that is relating to the type of relief to which it is to apply and its duration. The court was concerned that attaching conditions could have the effect, in a case in which the condition might not be achievable, of imposing an absolute bar on applying to the court which was not the purpose of section 91(14).[828] The court over-turned a judge's order to the extent that it required a psychological or psychiatric report indicating that the father had engaged in treatment before the father was allowed to apply for leave. While no such condition can be attached to a section 91(14) order, the Court of Appeal observed that it is plainly permissible for a judge to tell a litigant that unless he or she addresses a particularly issue and can show that he or she has addressed it, any appli-cation for permission to apply is unlikely to succeed.[829] Thus a non-binding incentive for change can be given.

An application for a section 91(14) order should usually be issued in advance on notice and be supported by evidence.[830] There may, however, be cases which require an exception to that approach. For example, the need for an order may only become apparent during the hearing,[831] whether upon a party's application or arising on the court's own initiative. In *Re C (Litigant in Person: Section 91(14) Order)*[832] Wall LJ said that it is of the utmost impor-tance that parties or those affected by the order, particularly if they are litigants in person, should '(a) understand that such an application is being made, or that consideration is being given to making a s 91(14) order; (b) understand the meaning and effect of such an order; and (c) have a proper opportunity to make submissions to the court in answer to the application or to the suggestion that a s 91(14) order be made.'[833] A proper opportunity for a litigant in person to understand the effect of the order and to respond to it may require an adjournment for the application to be made on notice in writing.[834]

In *Re P (A Minor) (Residence Order: Child's Welfare)*[835] Butler-Sloss LJ, reviewing ear-lier authorities, provided useful guidance, in the context of section 91(14) orders, on the power to restrict access to the court.[836] In order to illustrate her Ladyship's guidance by reference to other case law and to deal with subsequent case law developments, it is convenient to deal with the guidance under two subheadings: (i) when section 91(14) orders may be made and (ii) the duration of orders.

---

[826] Butler-Sloss LJ in *Re P (A Minor) (Residence Order: Child's Welfare)*, citing *Re R (Residence: Contact: Restricting Applications)* [1998] 1 FLR 749 at 760 *per* Wilson J.

[827] [2006] EWCA Civ 1617, [2007] 1 FLR 1532.

[828] The court's reasoning on this point was provided in its judgment on the application for permission to appeal which preceded the appeal: see *Re S (Permission to Seek Relief)* [2006] EWCA Civ 1190, [2007] 1 FLR 482 at [73]–[75].

[829] *Stringer v Stringer* [2006] EWCA Civ 1617, [2007] 1 FLR 1532 at [10].

[830] See *Re C-J (Section 91(14) Order* [2006] EWHC 1491 (Fam), [2006] 2 FLR 1213 at [19]; *Re S (Permission to Seek Relief)* [2006] EWCA Civ 1190, [2007] 1 FLR 482 at [91]; *Re C (Litigant in Person: Section 91(14) Order)* [2009] EWCA Civ 674, [2009] 2 FLR 1461 at [13].

[831] *Re S (Permission to Seek Relief)* [2006] EWCA Civ 1190, [2007] 1 FLR 482 at [91].

[832] [2009] EWCA Civ 674, [2009] 2 FLR 1461.

[833] Ibid, [13]. For an example of an order made in breach of the guidance in *Re C (Litigant in Person: Section 91(14) Order)* [2009] EWCA Civ 674, [2009] 2 FLR 1461, see *Re A (Contact: Section 91(14))* [2009] EWCA Civ 1548, [2010] 2 FLR 151, in which Wilson LJ commented at [17], that 'this court spends a surprising and unfortunate amount of its time in reversing orders under s 91(14) made on the inappropriately summary basis here exemplified.'

[834] *Re C (Litigant in Person: Section 91(14) Order)* [2009] EWCA Civ 674, [2009] 2 FLR 1461 at [13].

[835] [2000] Fam 15.

[836] The guidelines apply also to restrictions made under the inherent jurisdiction: see *Harris v Harris; Attorney-General v Harris* [2001] 2 FLR 895, FD.

5.15.1 When may section 91(14) orders be made?

In *Re P (A Minor) (Residence Order: Child's Welfare)*[837] Butler-Sloss LJ explained that the power to restrict applications involves an exercise of discretion in which the court must weigh all the relevant circumstances, treating the child's welfare as the paramount consideration.[838] An 'important consideration is that to impose a restriction is a statutory intrusion into the right of a party to bring proceedings before the court and to be heard in matters affecting his/her child.' Accordingly:

> The power is therefore to be used with great care and sparingly, the exception and not the rule...It is generally to be seen as a useful weapon of last resort in cases of repeated and unreasonable applications.

Re R (Residence: Contact: Restricting Applications)[839] graphically illustrates the frequency with which some parents may seek to bring proceedings under section 8 of the Children Act 1989. Between 1993 and 1996 a father had made no fewer than 18 applications for orders—15 to review contact arrangements with his child and three for residence. When hearing the father's latest application, the judge refused to make a residence order and made an order under section 91(14) restricting his right to bring further applications before the court. Dismissing the father's appeal against this restriction, the Court of Appeal held that when exercising its discretion to make an order under section 91(14), the best interests of the child must be weighed against the applicant's fundamental freedom of access to the courts without going through an initial screening process. The court found that this particular father was committed to his child and had steadily built up a relationship with him. It acknowledged that a section 91(14) order was a substantial interference with the applicant's fundamental right to raise issues affecting his child's welfare before a court, but it ruled that such a right had to be exercised consistently with the welfare of the child. In this regard, a court had to take account of the emotional effect on the residential parent of frequent applications to change a child's residence. As Wilson J said, 'nothing can raise the temperature of a family dispute more than an ill-considered, unfounded application for a residence order...Even worse can be the effect of a residence application when the applicant expresses himself or herself in intemperate and bilious terms.'[840]

Where the child's welfare dictates, the court can also make an order under section 91(14) where there is no past history of making unreasonable applications.[841] In such cases 'the court will need to be satisfied first that the facts go beyond the commonly encountered need for a time to settle to a regime ordered by the court and the all too common situation where there is animosity between the adults in dispute or between the local authority and the family and, secondly, that there is a serious risk that, without the imposition of the restriction, the child or the primary carers will be subject to unacceptable strain'.[842] For example, in *Re F (Restrictions on Applications)*[843] the mother had obtained an injunction under Part IV of the Family Law Act 1996 restraining the father from violence, threats of violence, from harassment, from communication except via solicitors, and from approaching within 100 metres of the mother's home. In light of the Cafcass officer's recommendation that face-to-face contact would 'alarm and unsettle the children', the father withdrew his application for contact. The judge added a direction that the father

---

[837] [2000] Fam 15.   [838] That is, s 91(14) is to be read together with s 1(1) of the Children Act 1989.

[839] [1998] 1 FLR 749.   [840] Ibid, 759.

[841] *Re F (Children) (Restriction on Applications)* [2005] EWCA Civ 499, [2005] 2 FLR 950.

[842] *Re P (A Minor) (Residence Order: Child's Welfare)* [2000] Fam 15. See also *B v B (Residence Order: Restricting Applications)* [1997] 1 FLR 139 at 145, citing *Re H (Child Orders: Restricting Applications)* [1991] FCR 896 at 899.   [843] [2005] EWCA Civ 499, [2005] 2 FLR 950.

should not be permitted to apply without leave for a period of two and a half years. Drawing attention to the guidance in *Re P*, the Court of Appeal held that the absence of repeated applications did not make the order wrong in principle; the judge had been entitled to take into account the history of the case from its inception and to protect the children's welfare in the way he had.[844]

However, it is not appropriate to make a section 91(14) order simply to achieve 'breathing space'.[845] In *Re G (Residence: Restriction on Further Applications)*[846] the Court of Appeal overturned an order made on that basis. The father sought shared residence but was awarded instead generous contact. The judge, taking the view that the father was entrenched in his wish for 50/50 shared care, imposed a section 91(14) restriction. The Court of Appeal pointed out that the father's applications had been reasonable, there was no evidence of harm to the child, nor had the mother reached 'saturation point' so that she was suffering in a way which impacted adversely on the child's welfare. The court said that the breathing space should be achieved simply by giving the order time to work itself out.[847]

5.15.2 Duration of a section 91(14) order

In *Re P (A Minor) (Residence Order: Child's Welfare)*[848] Butler-Sloss LJ explained that a restriction may be imposed with or without limitation of time. Unless revoked, the latter type of order will run until it ceases upon the child attaining 18 years of age.[849] In *Re S (Permission to Seek Relief)*[850] the Court of Appeal added that such an order (or indeed orders expressed to last until a child is 16) should be 'the exception rather than the rule' and 'the reasons for making them should be fully and carefully set out'.[851] Of course, all section 91(14) orders are exceptional, so as Wilson LJ pointed out in *Re J (A Child) (Restriction on Applications)*,[852] this means only that along the spectrum of exceptional cases 'orders of such duration should be made only in respect of cases at the egregious end, which merit the strongest degree of forensic protection for the child from further ill-founded conflict'.[853] This is because in the majority of cases the use of section 91(14) is still part of the court's 'over-arching strategy, which is to preserve and foster relationships wherever possible'.[854] Although there may be a minority of cases in which the court has reached the end of the road, in most cases therefore the court will need carefully to consider whether the duration of the order is compatible with its objective to restore the parent/child relationship.[855]

As Butler-Sloss P explained in *Re P*:

> The degree of restriction should be proportionate to the harm it is intended to avoid. Therefore the court imposing the restriction should carefully consider the extent of the restriction to be imposed and specify, where appropriate, the type of application to be restrained and the duration of the order.[856]

---

[844] See also *Re J (A Child) (Restriction on Applications)* [2007] EWCA Civ 906, [2008] 1 FLR 369.

[845] *Re G (Residence: Restriction on Further Applications)* [2008] EWCA Civ 1468, [2009] 1 FLR 894. See also *Re C-J (Section 91(14) Order)* [2006] EWHC 1491 (Fam), [2006] 2 FLR 1213, FD (Coleridge J) and *B v B (Residence Order: Restricting Applications)* [1997] 1 FLR 139, CA—not to be used because the judge feels that 'the dust should be allowed to settle and a quietus be imposed on the family differences' (at 146 *per* Waite LJ).   [846] [2008] EWCA Civ 1468, [2009] 1 FLR 894.

[847] *Re G (Residence: Restriction on Further Applications)* [2008] EWCA Civ 1468, [2009] 1 FLR 894 at [14].

[848] [2000] Fam 15.

[849] See s 93(13) and *Re J (A Child) Restriction on Applications* [2008] 1 FLR 369 at [16].

[850] [2006] EWCA Civ 1190, [2007] 1 FLR 482.   [851] Ibid, [85].

[852] [2007] EWCA Civ 906, [2008] 1 FLR 369.   [853] Ibid, [17].

[854] [2006] EWCA Civ 1190, [2007] 1 FLR 482 at [90].

[855] *Re B (Section 91(14) Order: Duration)* [2004] 1 FLR 871 at [16].   [856] [2000] Fam 15 at 38.

As Wilson J observed in the Court of Appeal in *Re R (Residence: Contact: Restricting Applications)*[857] the setting of a term to the order is not without its potential difficulties. For example, apart from the difficulty in forecasting what would be the appropriate length of time before the applicant's rights revived, an order of fixed duration almost invites a fresh application at the expiry of the specified term.

In *Re B (Section 91(14) Order: Duration)*[858] a father applied for direct contact with his 9-year-old daughter, with whom he had not had contact for three years, and then only for four periods of supervised contact. The judge made an order for indirect contact, which included the local authority's assistance in preparing a video about him and his life to show the daughter. The judge then added a direction under section 91(14) that there should be no further applications for the remainder of the child's minority because of the risk of emotional damage to the child. Allowing an appeal against that order, the Court of Appeal held that the objective of the court to restore the relationship was 'best achieved by limiting the s 91(14) prohibition to any application for direct contact and by setting the moratorium at a 2-year duration to enable the bespoke solution of video contact to be given a fair chance to shift attitudes and inhibitions'.[859] Similarly, in *Re D (A Child)*[860] it was held to be wrong in principle to impose a section 91(14) order for a period of five years where the consequence of doing so would make it very difficult for the father to seek contact once that period had expired. The order would be replaced by an order for a period of two years, permitting the father to maintain indirect contact during that period.

The circumstances of a particular case may, however, warrant an order which is imposed to last until the child's majority. In *Re J (A Child) (Restriction on Applications)*[861] the parents of a 12½-year-old severely autistic boy had been involved in a forensic struggle over him on and off for his whole life, initially in private law proceedings and latterly in care proceedings. A care order had been made because the mother's volatility and distress in dealing with the child's special difficulties made it inappropriate for him to be in her home. The local authority placed the child with the father. The mother sought to discharge the care order and during the hearing made several statements that she would never accept the care order. In those circumstances, Munby J made an order under section 91(14), to run for five and a half years until the child reached his majority, that the mother should not be permitted to apply to discharge the care order. This was upheld by the Court of Appeal.

5.15.3 Leave applications where a section 91(14) restriction exists

When a court is determining whether to grant an application for leave to apply for the section 91(14) restriction to be lifted, or for leave to proceed notwithstanding the bar, what factors should influence the court's discretion? In *Re A (Application for Leave)*[862] the Court of Appeal held that a Recorder had been wrong to apply the criteria in section 10(9) of the Children Act 1989 to such an application. One reason given by the court was that very often the person who has been barred by section 91(14) will be an applicant who would otherwise be entitled to apply for a section 8 order under section 10(4) or (5) of the Children Act 1989. In such cases it would not seem right to apply the section 10(9) leave criteria, which include the applicant's connection with the child. Thorpe LJ held therefore that permission for leave to apply in the context of a section 91(14) bar is a distinct application and his Lordship favoured 'the simplest of tests': 'Does this application demonstrate that there is any

---

[857] [1998] 1 FLR 749.   [858] [2004] 1 FLR 871.
[859] Ibid, [16]. See also *Radovanovic v Austria* (App no 42703/98) (2005) 41 EHRR 6, EtCHR.
[860] [2010] EWCA Civ 470.   [861] [2007] EWCA Civ 906, [2008] 1 FLR 369.
[862] [1998] 1 FLR 1.

need for renewed judicial investigation? If yes, then leave should be granted.'[863] In *Re P (A Minor) (Residence Order: Child's Welfare)*[864] Butler-Sloss LJ expressed the approach slightly differently: 'the applicant must persuade the judge that he has an arguable case with some chance of success'.[865] In *Re S (Permission to Seek Relief)*,[866] however, the Court of Appeal saw no inconsistency in those respective approaches, which were seen as complementing each other: a judge will not 'see a need for renewed judicial investigation into an application which he does not think sets out an arguable case'.[867] The court went on to say that where a section 91(14) order has been imposed because of particular conduct, that conduct must have been addressed if the application for permission to apply is to warrant a renewed judicial investigation or to present an arguable case.[868]

There are statements in *Re N (Section 91(14) Order)*[869] and in *Re A (Application for Leave)*[870] that an application for permission to apply should be determined inter partes. However, in *Re S (Permission to Seek Relief)*[871] the Court of Appeal said that it is open to a judge in certain sensitive circumstances[872] to direct that in the first instance an application is not to be served on the other party and be considered by the judge on the papers,[873] although an applicant for permission to appeal should not be denied an oral hearing if he or she seeks one.[874]

5.16 LOCAL AUTHORITY APPLICATIONS FOR SECTION 8 ORDERS

A local authority may seek a court's leave to apply for a specific issue or prohibited steps order.[875] This affords local authorities the opportunity to seek a court's assistance to make a ruling on one aspect of the exercise of parental responsibility, without otherwise interfering in the day-to-day control exercised by parents, and others, over a child's upbringing. This raises questions about which proceedings are the most appropriate when a local authority is the applicant; should it apply under the public law provisions in Parts IV and V of the Children Act 1989 or for a specific issue order?[876]

In *Nottinghamshire County Council v P*[877] the Court of Appeal held that a local authority which believed a child to be at risk of suffering significant harm should proceed by way of an application for a care or supervision order and not use the private law provisions. This ruling means that where a local authority takes the view that it is safe to leave a child with one parent, but that the other parent presents a serious risk to the child, the local authority must seek to persuade the caring parent to apply for orders which will be effective to protect the child. This is likely to mean orders under section 8 and under legislation which permits a court to restrict a parent's access to the home.[878] Where the caring parent refuses, or is too frightened, to take such action, the local authority then has no

---

[863] Ibid, 4.   [864] [2000] Fam 15.

[865] Ibid, 38. See also *Re G (Child Case: Parental Involvement)* [1996] 1 FLR 857, CA.

[866] [2006] EWCA Civ 1190, [2007] 1 FLR 482.   [867] Ibid, [78].   [868] Ibid, [79].

[869] [1996] 1 FLR 356.   [870] [1998] 1 FLR 1 at 3E–F.

[871] [2006] EWCA Civ 1190, [2007] 1 FLR 482.

[872] Eg in the case of a fragile resident parent who may be adversely affected by the application which may be unmeritorious or unlikely to succeed.   [873] [2006] EWCA Civ 1190, [2007] 1 FLR 482 at [94].

[874] Ibid, [95].

[875] Except when it already has a care order, and the Children Act 1989, s 9(1) therefore applies.

[876] Or, indeed, for leave to apply to invoke the inherent jurisdiction of the High Court, discussed in Section 5.17.   [877] [1993] 2 FLR 134.

[878] See Family Law Act 1996, Pt IV, discussed in Chapter 3.

alternative but to apply for an order in care proceedings.[879] Where a local authority will not take such steps, it appears that a court is powerless to direct it to do so.

The choice of which proceedings are appropriate will depend on the nature of the local authority's concerns about the child. It has been said that where a child's parents are 'caring, committed and capable and where only one issue arises for decision, albeit one of the gravest significance' to the child's welfare it is wholly inappropriate for a court to make even an interim care order.[880] Such single issues have tended to arise in cases in which all persons with parental responsibility are refusing to agree to a child receiving medical treatment because the treatment runs counter to the parents' most profound and sincerely held beliefs. Usually it will be the local authority which will initiate legal proceedings on behalf of the child because it is under a statutory duty to intervene when a child is at risk of significant harm. In *Re R (A Minor) (Blood Transfusion)*[881] the issue to be resolved was whether a child should have a blood transfusion. Booth J ruled that a local authority should make an application for leave to apply for a specific issue order where such an application is possible[882] and where there is no need for any other public law order to safeguard the child's welfare. It was held that such cases should be determined, wherever possible, by a High Court judge.

Where a child is already the subject of a care order or interim care order, the local authority already has parental responsibility for the child and could exercise parental responsibility to consent to treatment.[883] However, the courts have taken the view that where such a decision is to be made against the strongly held beliefs of the child's parents, it should be made by a High Court judge.[884] If the child is in the care of a local authority a court is prevented by section 9(1) of the Children Act 1989 from making any section 8 order other than a residence order. Consequently, a specific issue order cannot be made in relation to a child in care. This was the position confronting the High Court in *Re O (A Minor) (Medical Treatment)*.[885] The parents who were Jehovah's Witnesses were refusing to authorise blood transfusions for their gravely ill child. A family proceedings court made an emergency protection order in ex parte proceedings followed by an interim care order, and the case was then transferred for hearing to the High Court. Johnson J was asked to express a view about the most appropriate legal framework in which such decisions should be made. He agreed with counsel, who had been unanimous in rejecting all proceedings governed by the Children Act 1989, and ruled that the inherent jurisdiction of the High Court was the only appropriate route in the circumstances.[886] In such a case a local authority should make an application under section 100(3) of the Children Act 1989 for leave to invoke the exercise of the court's inherent jurisdiction. We explain this jurisdiction, and restrictions on its use, in the next section.

---

[879] An exclusion requirement could be attached to an emergency protection order or interim care order, thus preserving the child's residence with the parent who is not a risk to the child: see further Chapter 10.

[880] *Re O (A Minor) (Medical Treatment)* [1993] 2 FLR 149.

[881] [1993] 2 FLR 757.

[882] Sometimes, for example when a child is in care, it will not be possible to obtain a specific issue order: see Children Act 1989, s 9 and the discussion in Section 5.17.

[883] An emergency protection order made under the Children Act 1989, s 44, also confers limited parental responsibility on the local authority, and this can be exercised insofar as necessary to safeguard the child's welfare.

[884] Eg *Re R (A Minor) (Blood Transfusion)* [1993] 2 FLR 757 and *Re O (A Minor) (Medical Treatment)* [1993] 2 FLR 149.

[885] [1993] 2 FLR 149.

[886] Recall that the proceedings are family proceedings, and the High Court is entitled to make any section 8 order when exercising its inherent jurisdiction.

5.17 THE INHERENT JURISDICTION OF THE HIGH COURT

The inherent jurisdiction of the High Court in children cases dates back to feudal times. Its origins lie in the duty of the sovereign, as *parens patriae*, to take care of vulnerable subjects.[887] One way of seeking the High Court's use of its inherent jurisdiction is by making a child a ward of court.[888] A child becomes a ward as soon as an application in wardship is made, that is to say the jurisdiction takes effect even before any order is made, and no important step in the child's life can be taken without the court's leave.[889] At the hearing, if the wardship is not discharged, the High Court takes control over the child's upbringing but will then delegate powers to make decisions to the persons who are responsible for looking after the child. The difference between asking the High Court to exercise its inherent jurisdiction and warding a child is that the court, when exercising its inherent jurisdiction, simply adjudicates on a particular aspect of the child's welfare; it does not place the child under the long-term control of the court.

There are rules in section 100 of the Children Act 1989 restricting a local authority's use of wardship and the inherent jurisdiction,[890] which are discussed in the next section. However, nothing in the 1989 Act prevents others who have a genuine interest in the upbringing of a child from warding the child, or from otherwise asking the High Court to exercise its inherent jurisdiction to deal with a specific issue which has arisen. However, to use the jurisdiction when other remedies under the Children Act 1989 are denied, or have been used and exhausted, would turn the inherent jurisdiction into an alternative code for resolving disputes about children, with its own body of case law separate and distinct from cases decided under the Act. This would seriously undermine the Act and its associated procedures.

The inherent jurisdiction is therefore usually used to fill any gaps where otherwise there may be no jurisdiction to intervene. An example is provided by *Re X (A Minor) (Adoption Details: Disclosure)*.[891] Under the Adoption Act then in force,[892] the Registrar-General had a mandatory duty to keep a register of adopted children and had to allow any person to search the index and to have a certified copy of any entry. The fear in this case was that the birth mother, who was an aggressive and violent woman, of whom the child was terrified, would discover the child's whereabouts if she had access to this information. The Court of Appeal ruled that the High Court could order that the Registrar-General should not reveal details of the adoption recorded on the register to any person without the leave of the court. Another need for the use of wardship arose where a contract for surrogate parenthood was involved, and where there appeared to be a need to throw a ring of care around the child, but where care proceedings were inappropriate.[893]

5.17.1 The inherent jurisdiction and local authorities

Historically, local authorities could invite the High Court to exercise its inherent jurisdiction in wardship to make up for apparent deficiencies in the statutory child protection framework. Wardship was used to safeguard children when other procedures and remedies were unavailable or had failed. In return, the local authority relinquished some of its control over a child to

---

[887] See J. Seymour, 'Parens Patriae and Wardship Powers: Their Nature and Origins' (1994) 14 Oxford Journal of Legal Studies 159.

[888] See generally, and for its use especially prior to the Children Act 1989, N. Lowe and R. White, *Wards of Court*, 2nd edn (London: Barry Rose, 1986).

[889] See *Re S (Infants)* [1967] 1 All ER 202 at 209 *per* Cross J.

[890] See M. Parry, 'The Children Act 1989: Local Authorities, Wardship and the Revival of the Inherent Jurisdiction' [1992] Journal of Social Welfare and Family Law 212.

[891] [1994] 2 FLR 45.

[892] Adoption Act 1976, now superseded by the Adoption and Children Act 2002: see Chapter 11.

[893] *Re C (A Minor) (Wardship: Surrogacy)* [1985] FLR 846. See for another example *D v N (Contact Order: Conditions)* [1997] 2 FLR 797.

the court, and before it took any important step in the child's life which related to his upbringing it was required to refer the matter back to the court. Section 100 of the Children Act 1989 makes plain that it is no longer open to local authorities to ask the High Court to exercise the inherent jurisdiction as an alternative to taking proceedings under the Act. Section 100(2) provides that no court shall exercise the inherent jurisdiction to put a child in care, under local authority supervision, or into local authority accommodation. Nor may the jurisdiction be used for the purpose of conferring on any local authority the power to determine any question which has arisen, or which may arise, in connection with any aspect of parental responsibility for the child.[894] In *Devon County Council v S*,[895] Thorpe J drew a distinction between a local authority seeking to have protective powers conferred upon it through resort to the inherent jurisdiction, which is prohibited by section 100(2)(d), and a local authority inviting the court to exercise its inherent powers to make an order which does not give any powers to the local authority. The local authority could invite the court to exercise its own powers under the inherent jurisdiction where the purpose of the order was to prevent an abuser from having contact with children living at home with their mother.

The High Court may only grant a local authority leave to apply for the exercise of the court's inherent jurisdiction if it is satisfied both that the desired result cannot be achieved by any other order for which the local authority is entitled to apply and that there is reasonable cause to believe that if the court's inherent jurisdiction is not exercised the child is likely to suffer significant harm.[896]

The reason for this restriction on the High Court's powers is that if a local authority could invoke the inherent jurisdiction, or make a child a ward of court, whenever it wished to do so, this could enable the authority to obtain parental responsibility for a child other than by satisfying the threshold test for care proceedings.[897] The threshold test lays down a minimum standard which, if established, allows a court to authorise a child's placement in the care of a local authority. It is a universal standard applicable in all cases to all local authorities and the structure of the Children Act 1989 makes it absolutely clear that the test cannot be circumvented.

However, when a child is in the care of a local authority, sometimes a specific question may arise in connection with an aspect of the authority's parental responsibility where it takes the view that a court should be the decision-maker rather than itself. Examples might be where a child in care is seeking an abortion against her parents' wishes;[898] where sterilisation is believed to be in a child's best interests;[899] where a '*Gillick* competent' child is refusing consent to medical treatment;[900] or where a child and his parents are refusing to consent to medical treatment on religious or other grounds.[901] The strict legal position is that because the local authority has parental responsibility it has the right to give the requisite consents to the medical treatment which is in issue. But these questions raise sensitive and controversial moral dilemmas, and it may be thought that a court, rather than the local authority, ought to be the final decision-maker. Because a local authority with care of a child cannot apply for a specific issue order in relation to that child, the local authority may properly turn to the High Court's inherent jurisdiction for assistance.

What is the position where a parent or a third party wishes to invoke the inherent jurisdiction in order to challenge a decision made by a local authority in the exercise of

---

[894] Children Act 1989, s 100(2).   [895] [1994] 1 FLR 355.

[896] Children Act 1989, s 100(4) and (5).   [897] In ibid, s 31(2).

[898] Eg *Re B (Wardship: Abortion)* [1991] 2 FLR 426.

[899] The sterilisation of a minor in virtually all cases requires the prior sanction of a High Court judge: Practice Note [1990] 2 FLR 530; *Re B (A Minor) (Wardship: Sterilisation)* [1987] 2 FLR 314.

[900] Eg *Re W (A Minor)(Medical Treatment)* [1992] 4 All ER 627. See Chapter 8.

[901] Eg *Re B (A Minor) (Wardship: Medical Treatment)* (1982) 3 FLR 717, FD.

their parental responsibility? By placing a prohibition on specific issue orders being made in respect of children in care, section 9(1) of the Children Act 1989 makes it plain that Parliament did not intend that parents, or others, should be able to bring proceedings under the Act to challenge any of the many day-to-day decisions made by local authorities with respect to the children for whom they are responsible. Similarly it was recognised by the House of Lords in *A v Liverpool City Council*[902] as a fundamental principle of law that the High Court will not exercise its inherent jurisdiction where this would interfere with the discretionary powers which Parliament has clearly given to local authorities.

Where, by contrast, the issue to be resolved does not involve an exercise of parental responsibility by the local authority the High Court may be able to intervene. In *Re M (Care: Leave to Interview Child)*[903] a solicitor acting for a father in criminal proceedings wished to interview the father's two sons for the purpose of preparing his defence. The boys were the subject of interim care orders, and while the local authority did not object to them being interviewed, there was disagreement about the conditions under which the interview should be carried out. The issue for the court was whether it could intervene under its inherent jurisdiction, or whether the decision was one for the local authority alone. Hale J held that local authorities have the same powers as parents when exercising their parental responsibility. These powers are not unlimited, and they may not be exercised in ways which infringe the rights of others. Here justice required that the father, who faced very serious charges, should be permitted properly to prepare his defence. The court had powers under its inherent jurisdiction to determine how the solicitor should interview the children and it would exercise these powers whether or not the local authority agreed.

How local authorities, which have special responsibilities towards children in need and children suffering, or likely to suffer, significant harm, have responded to the child care and protection framework, and how courts have approached child care and protection cases, are both considered in the next chapter.

DISCUSSION QUESTIONS

1. Should the paramountcy principle in section 1(1) of the Children Act 1989 be abandoned? If so, what, if anything, could replace it?

2. Is shared residence the norm upon parental separation? Should it be?

3. Is there a right of contact between a non-resident parent and child in English law?

4. Should the courts assume that contact between a non-resident parent and a child is beneficial?

5. In cases of dispute, the relocation of a parent to a different country requires a difficult decision for a court between a parent wishing to start a new life and the parent left behind. Critically evaluate the English courts' approach.

FURTHER READING

BAINHAM, A., 'Contact as a Right and Obligation' in A. Bainham, B. Lindley, M. Richards, and L. Trinder (eds), *Children and Their Families: Contact, Rights and Welfare* (Oxford: Hart, 2003), p 62

---

[902] [1981] 2 All ER 385.   [903] [1995] 1 FLR 825.

CHOUDHRY, S. and FENWICK, H., 'Taking the Rights of Parents and Children Seriously: Confronting the Welfare Principle under the Human Rights Act' (2005) 25(3) Oxford Journal of Legal Studies 453

COLLIER, R. and SHELDON, S. (eds), *Fathers' Rights Activism and Law Reform in Comparative Perspective* (Oxford: Hart, 2006)

EEKELAAR, J., 'Beyond the Welfare Principle' [2002] Child and Family Law Quarterly 237

FEHLBERG, B., SMYTH, B., MACLEAN, M., and ROBERTS, C., 'Legislating for Shared Time Parenting After Separation: A Research Review' (2011) 25(3) International Journal of Law, Policy and the Family 318

GEORGE, R., 'The International Relocation Debate' [2012] Journal of Social Welfare and Family Law 141

GEORGE, R. and HARRIS, P., 'Parental Responsibility and Shared Residence Orders: Parliamentary Intentions and Judicial Interpretations' [2010] Child and Family Law Quarterly 151

GILMORE, S., 'The Nature, Scope and Use of the Specific Issue Order' [2004] Child and Family Law Quarterly 367

GILMORE, S., 'Contact/Shared Residence and Child Well-Being—Research Evidence and its Implications for Legal Decision Making' (2006) 20 International Journal of Law, Policy and the Family 344

GILMORE, S., 'Court Decision-Making in Shared Residence Order Cases—A Critical Examination' [2006] Child and Family Law Quarterly 478

GILMORE, S., 'Disputing Contact: Challenging Some Assumptions' [2008] Child and Family Law Quarterly 285

GILMORE, S., 'Shared Residence: A Summary of the Courts' Guidance' [2010] Family Law 285

HARRIS, P. G. and GEORGE, R. H., 'Parental Responsibility and Shared Residence Orders: Parliamentary Intentions and Judicial Interpretations' [2010] Child and Family Law Quarterly 151

HARRIS-SHORT, S., 'Resisting the March Towards 50/50 Shared Residence. Rights, Welfare and Equality in Post-Separation Families' (2010) 32 Journal of Social Welfare and Family Law 257–274

HERRING, J., 'The Human Rights Act and the Welfare Principle in Family Law: Conflicting or Complementary?' (1999) 11 Child and Family Law Quarterly 223

HERRING, J., 'Farewell Welfare?' (2005) 27(2) Journal of Social Welfare and Family Law 159

KAGANAS, F., 'Regulating Emotion: Judging Contact Disputes' [2011] Child and Family Law Quarterly 63

LOWE, N., '*J v C*: Placing The Child's Welfare Centre Stage' in S. Gilmore, J. Herring, and R. Probert (eds), *Landmark Cases in Family Law* (Oxford: Hart, 2011)

PERRY, A. and RAINEY, B., 'Supervised, Supported and Indirect Contact Orders: Research Findings' (2007) 21 International Journal of Law, Policy and the Family 21

REECE, H., 'The Paramountcy Principle: Consensus or Construct?' (1996) 49 Current Legal Problems 267

STURGE, C. and GLASER, D., 'Contact and Domestic Violence—The Experts' Court Report' (2000) 30 Family Law 615

TRINDER, L., 'Shared Residence: A Review of Recent Research Evidence' [2010] Child and Family Law Quarterly 475

10

CHILDREN NEEDING SERVICES, CARE, AND PROTECTION

INTRODUCTION: A LIBERAL STANDARD

The care and protection of children is in most cases a natural parental instinct and will be perceived by parents as their moral duty.[1] However, if analysed philosophically, the moral duty arguably falls on a society as a whole.[2] How the care and protection of children are achieved in a particular society is a matter of political choice. The state could, for example, adopt a form of licensed parenthood,[3] checking on parenting abilities prior to allocating parents to children, although this would, in many cases, present obvious diffi-culties in predicting future parenting abilities. An even more extreme method would be to adopt a collectivist approach to children's care and upbringing, with the state directly concerned in all children's upbringing. Recognising the danger in this approach of indoc-trination and social engineering, however, the law places value on the upbringing of children within families. As Baroness Hale explained in *Re B (Care Proceedings: Standard of Proof):*[4]

Families in all their subversive variety are the breeding ground of diversity and individuality. In a free and democratic society we value diversity and individuality. Hence the family is given special protection in all the modern human rights instruments including the European Convention on Human Rights (Article 8), the International Covenant on Civil and Political Rights (Article 23) and throughout the United Nations Convention on the Rights of the Child. As McReynolds J famously said in *Pierce v Society of Sisters* (1925) 268 US 510, 535, 'The child is not the mere creature of the State'.[5]

---

[1] See C. Barton and G. Douglas, *Law and Parenthood* (London: Butterworths, 1995), ch 2.

[2] Based on a general moral duty to promote human flourishing: see J. Eekelaar, 'Are Parents Morally Obliged to Care for Their Children?' (1991) 11(3) Oxford Journal of Legal Studies 340.

[3] See eg H. LaFollette, 'Licensing Parents' (1980) 9 Philosophy and Public Affairs 182; C. P. Mangel, 'Licensing Parents: How Feasible?' (1988) 22 Family Law Quarterly 17; J. C. Westman, *Licensing Parents: Can We Prevent Child Abuse and Neglect?* (Cambridge, MA: Perseus Books, 1994); M. Freeman, 'The Right to Responsible Parents' in J. Bridgeman, H. Keating, and C. Lind (eds), *Responsibility, Law and the Family* (Aldershot: Ashgate, 2008); J. G. Dwyer, *The Relationship Rights of Children* (New York: Cambridge University Press, 2006). [4] [2008] UKHL 35, [2009] 1 AC 11.

[5] Ibid, [20].

Of course, with this view in mind a society could simply defer to parental care within individual families.[6] But experience shows that sometimes individuals with parental responsibility for a child may be unable properly to fulfil their parental responsibilities without some assistance from the state, or there may be a need for the state to intervene in family life[7] to protect a child or to provide alternative care for the child. Recognising the benefits of family life, but also the need to safeguard and promote the welfare of children, English law thus takes a middle ground, adopting a so-called 'liberal standard'.[8] This presumes that the upbringing of children within families is desirable and that the state does not intrude unless there is consent or stated conditions for state intervention are fulfilled. As we shall see, this approach requires the law to identify the point at, and basis upon, which the state is entitled to intervene.[9] In this chapter we seek to explain how English law expresses this liberal standard of state intervention in family life.

The relevant law is principally set out in the Children Act 1989, which repealed earlier legislation and radically altered the law on child care and child protection.[10] In order to understand the current law, it is helpful briefly to consider some of the deficiencies in the previous law and the various factors which influenced the change.

---

[6] For a view approaching this, see J. Goldstein, A. Freud and A. Solnit, *Before the Best Interests of the Child* (New York, Free Press, 1979), p 9:

> The child's need for safety within the confines of the family must be met by law through its recognition of family privacy as the barrier to state intrusion upon parental autonomy in childrearing.

[7] On one view, the notion that there is a private sphere of family life into which the state intervenes is a myth: see F. E. Olsen, 'The Myth of State Intervention in the Family' (1984–85) 18 University of Michigan Journal of Law Reform 835–864 at 837: 'Because the state is deeply implicated in the formation and functioning of families, it is nonsense to talk about whether the state does or does not intervene in the family', criticised by L. D. Houlgate, 'What is Legal Intervention in the Family? Family Law and Family Privacy' (1998) 17 Law and Philosophy 141–158 (because nothing can count as non-intervention the conclusion that there is no such thing as non-intervention is logically empty).

[8] D. Archard, *Children: Rights and Childhood*, 2nd edn (London: Routledge, 2004).

[9] In thinking about state intervention in terms of explicit interventions to protect and care for children, sight should not be lost of the more subtle ways in which the state's policies exercise 'governance' over families through, eg, the education system and health advice/monitoring. As Archard explains, a 'therapeutic medical model stipulates a norm of familial "health" which, by means of professionals, insinuates into the "private" life of families.' (D. Archard, ibid, 155). See J. Donzelot, *The Policing of Families: Welfare versus the State* (London: Hutchinson, 1980), drawing on the work/methodology of Michel Foucault.

[10] For excellent detailed accounts of the law and policy in this area see eg L. Hoyano and C. Keenan, *Child Abuse Law and Policy Across Boundaries* (Oxford: Oxford University Press, 2007); C. Lyon, *Child Abuse* (Bristol: Family Law, 2006 reprint). For critique of child protection systems, see B. Lonne, N. Parton, J. Thomson, and M. Harries, *Reforming Child Protection* (Abingdon: Routledge, 2009).

1 BACKGROUND[11]

1.1 THE INADEQUACIES OF THE PREVIOUS LAW

The law on child care and protection prior to the Children Act 1989 had developed piecemeal along three main strands[12] and was unsatisfactory in several respects.[13] One strand was the law relating to the care of children who were orphaned or whose parents were otherwise unable to care for them, which manifested itself perhaps most memorably in the nineteenth-century workhouses, as depicted in Charles Dickens' novel, *Oliver Twist*.[14] The modern version of this provision, prior to the Children Act 1989, emerged in the Children Act 1948,[15] later consolidated in the Child Care Act 1980. Under those provisions a local authority could assume parental rights and duties in respect of a child in its care administratively, simply by passing a council resolution.[16]

A second strand of law allowed an application to be made to a court for a care order committing a child into the care of a local authority. Section 1 of the Children and Young Persons Act 1969 provided that a child who was in need of care and control could be taken into care on various grounds, for example a child who was ill-treated or neglected or one who had committed an offence. The merging within the grounds of children who were victims of neglect and delinquent children who were viewed as a threat to society arose out of increasing concerns in the 1960s about childhood delinquency and a policy decision to deal with such children where possible by providing alternative care rather than through the penal system.[17] Importantly, this meant that the grounds for making a care order made no explicit reference to a lack of reasonable parental care because that criterion was not relevant in the case of the juvenile offender where the focus was on commission of an offence. Consequently, prior to the Children Act 1989, parents were not parties in care proceedings. There were also problems with shorter term child protection measures. A local authority could obtain a 'place of safety order'[18] to remove a child immediately to its care for 28 days. Parents had no right to challenge the order or the local authority's decisions regarding access to the child.

The third strand was the use of the inherent jurisdiction of the High Court to place a child in care. Instead of applying for a care order local authorities would issue a summons in wardship and then ask the judge to commit the child into the care of the local

---

[11] See S. Cretney, *Family Law in the Twentieth Century—A History* (Oxford: Oxford University Press, 2003), ch 20; J. Masson, 'From Curtis to Waterhouse: State Care and Child Protection in the UK 1945–2000' in S. Katz, J. Eekelaar, and M. Maclean (eds), *Cross-Currents: Family Law Policy in the US and England* (Oxford: Oxford University Press, 2000), ch 26 (p 565); B. Hale et al, *The Family, Law and Society: Cases and Materials*, 5th edn (Oxford: Oxford University Press, 2005), ch 11, esp p 530 et seq; N. Parton, *The Politics of Child Abuse* (Basingstoke: Macmillan, 1985) N. Parton, *Governing the Family* (Basingstoke: Macmillan, 1991).

[12] For an account, see R. Dingwall, J. Eekelaar, and T. Murray, *The Protection of Children: State Intervention and Family Life* (Oxford: Basil Blackwell, 1983), ch 1.

[13] See M. Hayes, 'Removing Children from their Families—Law and Policy Before the Children Act 1989' in G. Douglas and N. Lowe (eds), *The Continuing Evolution of Family Law* (Bristol: Jordan Publishing, 2009).

[14] The tone for the law was set as early as the Poor Relief Act of 1601, 43 Eliz c 2.

[15] Preceded by the Monckton Report (Cmd 6636, 1945) the *Report of the Care of Children Committee* (Cmd 6922, 1946) (The Curtis Committee); S. Cretney, 'The State as a Parent: The Children Act 1948 in Retrospect' in *Law, Law Reform and the Family* (Oxford: Clarendon Press, 1998), ch 9; S. Cretney, 'The Children Act 1948—Lessons For Today?' [1997] Child and Family Law Quarterly 359; and S. Cretney, 'The State as a Parent: The Children Act 1948 in Retrospect' (1998) 114 LQR 419–459.

[16] Child Care Act 1980, s 3.

[17] J. Eekelaar, R. Dingwall, and T. Murray, 'Victims or Threats? Children in Care Proceedings' (1982) 4(2) Journal of Social Welfare and Family Law 68–82.   [18] Children and Young Persons Act 1969, s 28.

authority. Thus, the statutory grounds in the Children and Young Persons Act 1969 could be bypassed, and a child could be placed in care simply by applying the child's welfare as the first and paramount consideration. There was in this process no threshold barrier to state intervention and, in theory at least, a child could be placed in care simply on the basis that the child would fare better with substitute carers than with his or her parents.[19]

The law was clearly complex, lacking overall coherence, and in need of rationalisation. The need for change was recognised in 1984 by a House of Commons Committee,[20] and consequently an Interdepartmental Working Group was set up to review the law. Its report entitled the *Review of Child Care Law*[21] formed the core of the new philosophy and framework for state intervention in family life within the public law provisions of the Children Act 1989. The ensuing legislation sought to retain positive features of earlier legislation, such as the philosophy of providing support for children and families within the Children Act 1948. At the same time, however, it sought to deal with the various criticisms which have been highlighted by distinguishing more clearly between voluntary and compulsory intervention in family life, ensuring that there was only one route into local authority care when a threshold for state intervention had been passed; and to ensure that the interests of parents (and children) were appropriately protected.[22]

The relevant legislation is in Parts III, IV, and V of the Children Act 1989 and associated Schedules. Part III contains various provisions which facilitate local authorities' working in partnership with parents to safeguard and promote the welfare of children in their area; Part IV provides the legal framework for compulsory intervention by way of care or supervision of children; and Part V addresses investigation and emergency protection. The Act is supplemented, of course, by a lot of subordinate legislation and also by Guidance.[23]

The changes were also influenced by research,[24] which showed that, in general, there was precipitate intervention and overuse of emergency intervention, a picture graphically illustrated by the Cleveland Child Abuse Inquiry.[25] Over 200 children in the north-east of England were taken from their parents by social workers based on disputed allegations of sexual abuse founded on medical diagnoses by two paediatricians. The inquiry found that social workers had deferred unduly to the medical diagnosis, rather than considering it against the full family context. Magistrates had then effectively 'rubber-stamped' the applications for emergency orders. The inquiry highlighted the need for greater protection of parents' and children's rights. Seeking to address those concerns, the law now gives competent children the right to refuse medical assessments, has reduced the time children can be kept away from home following emergency intervention, and ensures

---

[19] M. Hayes, 'Removing Children from their Families—Law and Policy Before the Children Act 1989' in G. Douglas and N. Lowe (eds), *The Continuing Evolution of Family Law* (Bristol: Jordan Publishing, 2009), pp 99–101.   [20] Short Report, Social Services Committee (London: HMSO, 1984) (HC 360).

[21] DHSS, *Review of Child Care Law: Report to Ministers of an Inter-Departmental Working Party* (London: HMS0, 1985).

[22] Neatly summarised in the White Paper that preceded the Act: see Secretary of State for Social Services *The Law on Child Care and Family Services* (Cm 62, 1987). Not surprisingly, the Act discloses a number of different perspectives: see L. Fox-Harding, 'The Children Act in Context: Four Perspectives on Child Care Law and Policy' (1991) 13 Journal of Social Welfare and Family Law 179.

[23] See the various updated volumes of *The Children Act 1989 Guidance and Regulations*, available from the Department for Children Schools and Families, at www.education.gov.uk.

[24] J. Packman, *Who Needs Care? Social Work Decisions About Children* (Oxford: Blackwell, 1986).

[25] Secretary of State for Social Services, *Report of the Inquiry into Child Abuse in Cleveland* (Cmnd 412, 1988). See N. Parton, 'Sexual Abuse, the Cleveland Affair and the Private Family' in N. Parton, *Governing the Family* (Basingstoke: Macmillan, 1991).

contact between parent and child during this period.[26] In contrast to the picture painted by research and by the Cleveland affair, other inquiry reports into the deaths of children highlighted failures to intervene and deficiencies in practice.[27] Of particular influence on the law was the inquiry into the death of Kimberley Carlile.[28] Kimberley, aged 4, was killed by her stepfather, Nigel Hall, after a visiting social worker was refused access to the family home. This highlighted the need for clearer legal provisions on gaining access to children in cases of suspected abuse.

1.2 ONGOING PRACTICE CONCERNS: THE CLIMBIÉ REPORT AND THE CHILDREN ACT 2004

Following implementation of the Children Act 1989, further concerns were expressed about the workings of the child protection system in practice, most notably with regard to inter-agency communication. Lord Laming's inquiry into the death of Victoria Climbié[29] found that she suffered appalling abuse at the hands of her great aunt and the great aunt's partner, and remained unprotected despite the fact that she was known to 'four social services departments, two child protection teams of the Metropolitan Police Service (MPS), a specialist centre managed by the NSPCC, and she was admitted to two different hospitals because of suspected deliberate harm.'[30] The report recommended structural changes to the child protection system, which led to the Children Act 2004.

1.3 THE CHILDREN ACT 2004

The Children Act 2004 was enacted with a view to ensuring that all organisations that work with children 'share a commitment to safeguard and promote their welfare' that is under-pinned by statutory duties,[31] and that there are in place appropriate strategies to achieve the same. The relevant provisions of the 2004 Act are found in Part 2, which is concerned with children's services. First, the law seeks to give out the clear message that everyone who is professionally involved with children and young people shares responsibility for safeguarding and promoting their welfare. Local authorities that are children's services authorities,[32] headed by a Director of Children's Services, have specific statutory duties aimed at safeguarding and promoting children's welfare.[33] Section 11 of the Children Act 2004 requires various other bodies to ensure that their services and functions are discharged with regard to the need to safeguard and promote the welfare of children: for example, National Health

---

[26] A Government-commissioned programme of research into child protection was initiated following the Cleveland Inquiry Report. A summary of the findings of 20 studies from that research programme was published in 1995: Department of Health, *Child Protection: Messages from Research* (London: HMSO, 1995), for a critique see C. Wattam, 'The Social Construction of Child Abuse for Practical Policy Purposes—A Review of Child Protection: Messages from Research' (1996) 8 Child and Family Law Quarterly 189. See also D. Gough, *Child Abuse Interventions: A Review of the Research Literature* (London: HMSO, 1993).

[27] N. Parton and N. Martin, 'Public Inquiries, Legalism and Child Care in England and Wales' (1989) 3 International Journal of Law and the Family 21–39.

[28] London Borough of Greenwich, *A Child in Mind: Protection of Children in a Responsible Society: Report of the Commission of Inquiry into the Circumstances Surrounding the Death of Kimberley Carlile* (1987).

[29] Lord Laming, *The Victoria Climbié Inquiry: Report of an Inquiry by Lord Laming* (Cm 5730, January 2003). See H. Conway, 'The Laming Inquiry—Victoria Climbié's Legacy' [2002] Family Law 755.

[30] Ibid, Summary Peport, p 3.   [31] Appendix 1.

[32] A metropolitan district council; district councils where there is no county council, a London Borough Council, the Common Council of the City of London, the Council of the Isles of Scilly.

[33] Children Act 2004, s 18.

Services,[34] the police, probation, and prison services, youth offending teams, and secure training centres.[35] Other statutes respectively place similar duties on those carrying out education functions,[36] on the Children and Family Court Advisory and Support Service (Cafcass),[37] and on the UK Border Agency.[38]

While each of these agencies has its own duties, the law also seeks to bring together relevant agencies to cooperate on the strategy for safeguarding and promoting children's welfare. Section 10 of the Children Act 2004 requires each local authority in England to make arrangements to promote cooperation between the authority and its relevant partners (as defined in s 10(4))[39] and such other persons or bodies as the authority considers appropriate.[40] The arrangements are to be made with a view to improving the well-being of children in the authority's area so far as relating to: physical and mental health and emotional, social, and economic well-being; protection from harm and neglect; and education, training, and recreation.[41] The relevant partners have a duty to cooperate with the local authority in making the arrangements.[42] So section 10 is the legal foundation for what are called Children's Trusts (ie, the bringing together of the local authority and its relevant partners with a view to cooperating regarding children's well-being in the area). By section 9A of the Children Act 2004 the Secretary of State can now set targets for safeguarding and promoting the welfare of children in a local authority's area.

Section 13 of the 2004 Act requires each children's services authority to establish a Local Safeguarding Children Board,[43] the objective of which is to coordinate and ensure the effectiveness of what is done by the organisations on the Board for the purposes of safeguarding and promoting the welfare of children in the relevant local authority's area.[44]

The legislation is supplemented by guidance on inter-agency cooperation, *Working Together to Safeguard Children*,[45] and on how social work assessments are to be carried out.[46]

2 PART III OF THE CHILDREN ACT 1989

Part III of the Children Act 1989 is concerned with the duty of every local authority to provide support for children and their families. It recognises that families sometimes

[34] Primary care trusts, NHS trusts, NHS foundation trusts, strategic health authorities, designated special health authorities.

[35] See Children Act 2004, s 11(1) for the full list of persons/bodies to whom the section applies.

[36] See Education Act 2002, ss 175 and 157 and regulations; Children Act 1989, s 87 (accommodation at independent schools); Child Care Act 2006, s 40 (duty in respect of Early Years Foundation Stage).

[37] Criminal Justice and Court Services Act 2000.

[38] Borders, Citizenship and Immigration Act 2009, s 55.

[39] These include health, education, police, and probation services amongst others. The full list of relevant partners is set out in s 10(4).

[40] Being persons or bodies of any nature who exercise functions or are engaged in activities in relation to children in the authority's area.

[41] Section 10(3) provides that: 'In making arrangements under this section a [local authority] in England must have regard to the importance of parents and other persons caring for children in improving the well-being of children.'   [42] Children Act 2004, s 10(5).

[43] See Children Act 2004, ss 13–16 and the Local Safeguarding Children Boards Regulations 2006 (SI 2006/90) (made under s 13(2)); Local Safeguarding Children Boards (Amendment) Regulations 2010 (SI 2010/622) (made under s 13(4)).   [44] See Children Act 2004, s 14.

[45] See HM Government, *Working Together to Safeguard Children: A Guide to Inter-Agency Working to Safeguard and Promote the Welfare of Children* (London: TSO, March 2010), issued pursuant to the Local Authority Social Services Act 1970, s 7, and with which local authorities must therefore comply in carrying out their social services functions.

[46] Department of Health, *Framework for the Assessment of Children in Need and Their Families* (London: HMSO, 2000).

require help in bringing up children. A large body of regulations and guidance has been issued which provides further detail on how this Part (and other Parts) of the Act should be implemented.[47]

In carrying out its functions under Part III, the local authority can call on the support of other agencies, any local authority, local housing authority, health authorities,[48] or any other authorised person.[49] Under section 27 an authority whose help is so requested 'shall' comply with the request 'if it is compatible with their own statutory or other duties and obligations and does not unduly prejudice the discharge of any of their functions'.[50]

In *R v Northavon District Council, ex p Smith*,[51] a housing authority decided that the applicant and his wife were homeless and in priority need because they had five children, but that they had become homeless intentionally within section 60(1) of the Housing Act 1985. The housing authority therefore declined to provide accommodation in response to a request made under section 27 by the social services department. The House of Lords ruled that section 27 did not enable a local authority to require a housing authority to exercise its powers to provide housing. Instead it imposed a duty of cooperation between social services and housing authorities, both of which had together to do the best they could to carry out their respective responsibilities for children and housing.

Fundamental to the thinking in Part III of the Children Act 1989 is the principle that it is normally in the best interests of children to be brought up by their own families, and the expectation is that a local authority will, where possible, work in partnership with parents.[52] Part III seeks to facilitate this process by setting out the duty of every local authority to provide services for children in need and powers to provide services for other children.

Key legislation

Section 17, the opening provision, states that:

(1) It shall be the general duty of every local authority…

    (a) to safeguard and promote the welfare of children within their area who are in need; and

    (b) so far as is consistent with that duty, to promote the upbringing of such children by their families,

by providing a range and level of services appropriate to those children's needs.

For the purpose of facilitating the discharge of the general duty in section 17, further provisions are set out in Part I of Schedule 2 to the Act. These are discussed in more detail later. For the moment, however, we need to examine the scope of section 17.

---

[47] Some details concerning the provision of services under Pt III, the regulation of child-minding, private foster care, community homes, and voluntary homes are beyond the scope of this book. For greater detail, see updated volumes of *The Children Act 1989 Guidance and Regulations*, available from the Department for Children Schools and Families at www.education.gov.uk. See too, M. D. A. Freeman, *Children, Their Families and the Law* (Basingstoke: Macmillan, 1992).

[48] Any local health board, special health authority, primary care trust, NHS trust, or NHS foundation trust.   [49] Children Act 1989, s 27(1).

[50] Ibid, s 27(2).   [51] [1994] 2 FLR 671, HL.

[52] See particularly Department of Health, *The Challenge of Partnership in Child Protection: Practice Guide* (London: HMSO, 1995); F. Kaganas, M. King, and C. Piper (eds), *Legislating for Harmony—Partnerships under the Children Act 1989* (London: Jessica Kingsley, 1996).

2.1 WHO ARE 'CHILDREN IN NEED'?

Section 17(10) provides that a child shall be taken to be in need if:

   (a) he is unlikely to achieve or maintain, or to have the opportunity of achieving or maintaining, a reasonable standard of health or development without the provision for him of services by a local authority under this Part;

   (b) his health or development is likely to be significantly impaired, or further impaired, without the provision for him of such services; or

   (c) he is disabled,

and 'family', in relation to such a child, includes any person who has parental responsibility for the child and any other person with whom he has been living.[53]

Section 17(11) explains what is meant by 'disabled', 'development', and 'health'. It provides:

For the purposes of this Part, a child is disabled if he is blind, deaf or dumb or suffers from mental disorder of any kind or is substantially and permanently handicapped by illness, injury or congenital deformity or such other disability as may be prescribed; and in this Part—
   'development' means physical, intellectual, emotional, social or behavioural development; and
   'health' means physical or mental health.

Thus it can be seen that the definition of a child in need focuses both on a child who is disabled and on a child who is at risk of impaired health or development unless preventive steps are taken. These steps may include not only the provision of services for the child himself but also their provision for any member of his family, if they are provided with a view to safeguarding or promoting the child's welfare.[54] Before determining what (if any) services to provide for a particular child in need, a local authority shall, so far as is reasonably practicable and consistent with the child's welfare:

   (a) ascertain the child's wishes and feelings regarding the provision of those services; and

   (b) give due consideration (having regard to his age and understanding) to such wishes and feelings of the child as they have been able to ascertain.[55]

There is power within section 17(6) to give assistance in kind or in cash. Under section 17A and regulations there is power to make direct payments[56] to assist a person with parental responsibility for a disabled child, a disabled person with parental responsibility for a child, or a disabled child aged 16 or 17.

Where a local authority fails to provide a service for a child in need which it 'shall' provide, it will be in breach of its statutory duty. However, evaluative judgement or discretion is also built into many of the duties within Part III and Schedule 2; often the provision made must either be 'reasonable' or 'as is appropriate'. Because local authority social services departments are under a duty not only to provide services for children in need in their area but also for other needy members of the community, and because they

---

[53] Schedule 2, para 1 provides that a local authority must 'take reasonable steps to identify the extent to which there are children in need within their area' and para 2 provides that the local authority must keep a register of disabled children.   [54] Section 17(3).

  [55] Section 17(4A).

  [56] See Community Care, Services for Carers and Children's Services (Direct Payments) (Wales) Regulations 2004 (SI 2004/1748); Community Care, Services for Carers and Children's Services (Direct Payments) (England) Regulations 2009 (SI 2009/1887).

are operating with limited budgets, standards of reasonableness and appropriateness may sometimes be low.[57]

The nature of the duty in section 17(1) was explored by the House of Lords in three conjoined appeals, *R (G) v Barnet London Borough Council; R (W) v Lambeth London Borough Council; R (A) v Lambeth London Borough Council*.[58] In each case the claimants were single parent mothers. In the *Barnet* case, G, a Dutch national of Somali origin, came to England with her son to look for the child's father. She claimed that she left the Netherlands because she was ostracised by the Somali community on account of her son's illegitimacy. G did not qualify for income support or housing provision in England. The relevant local authority, Barnet LBC, said that if the mother refused to return to the Netherlands, it would place the child with foster parents but would not provide the mother with accommodation. In the second case, W was intentionally homeless. The local authority took the view that, should the need arise, accommodation could be arranged for her two children alone.[59] The third case concerned A, two of whose three children were autistic. She claimed that the accommodation the local authority had provided was not suitable for her children's needs. The children had severe learning difficulties and required constant supervision. The family had been housed in a ground-floor two-bedroom flat, with no enclosed garden or play area, very close to a road which presented a danger to the children should they run out of the front door or climb out of a ground-floor window. In each case the children were 'in need' (because of disability or the parents' homelessness). In each case, it was argued that the effect of section 17(1) of the Children Act 1989 was that the respondent local authorities owed a duty to each individual child in need to provide that child with residential accommodation to enable the child to live with his or her mother if an assessment showed that that was required to meet the children's needs. However, the House of Lords, by a majority of 3 to 2,[60] held that section 17(1) is a general 'framework' duty 'owed to the local population and did not result in a mandatory duty to meet the assessed needs of every individual child regardless of resources'.[61] This interpretation was supported by the wording of section 17, for example its reference to a 'general duty',[62] particularly when contrasted with the more specific duties set out in Schedule 2 to the Act.[63] To read the section as imposing the duty contended for, would have had the effect of 'turning the social services department of the local authority into another kind of housing department'.[64]

2.2 PROVISION OF SERVICES: SCHEDULE 2 TO THE CHILDREN ACT 1989

2.2.1 Services for children in need living with their families

Schedule 2 supplements section 17, providing that local authorities 'shall make such provision as they consider appropriate' for the following services: advice, guidance and

---

[57] Hence the frequent complaint that the principles in Pt III are excellent but that the resources to implement them have not been provided. See eg *R v Royal Borough of Kingston upon Thames, ex p T* [1994] 1 FLR 798, where the local authority were unable to accommodate two Vietnamese sisters together, partly because of resource constraints.   [58] [2003] UKHL 57, [2004] 2 AC 208.

[59] Under the Children Act 1989, s 20, which is discussed in detail in Section 2.3.

[60] Lord Hope of Craighead, Lord Scott of Foscote, and Lord Millett; Lord Nicholls of Birkenhead and Lord Steyn dissenting.

[61] See paras [85] and [91] *per* Lord Hope of Craighead; the quoted description of the effect of the decision is that of Baroness Hale of Richmond in *R (G) v Southwark London Borough Council* [2009] UKHL 26, [2009] 2 FLR 380 at [23].

[62] At [107]–[109] *per* Lord Millett.   [63] See eg at [119] *per* Lord Scott of Foscote.

[64] At [93] *per* Lord Hope of Craighead.

counselling; occupational, social, cultural, or recreational activities; home help; assistance with travelling; or to enable the child concerned and his family to have a holiday.[65] Local authorities are also required to provide family centres within their area[66] where the child, his parents, any person with parental responsibility, and any other person who is looking after him may attend for occupational, social, cultural, or recreational activities; advice, guidance, and counselling; and where such a person may be provided with accommodation while he is receiving such advice, guidance, or counselling.[67] In relation to disabled children, paragraph 6 of Schedule 2 provides that every local authority shall provide services designed to minimise the effect on disabled children within its area of their disabilities; and to give such children the opportunity to lead lives which are as normal as possible; and to assist individuals who provide care for such children to continue to do so, or to do so more effectively, by giving them breaks from caring. Under section 18, a local authority 'shall' provide day care for pre-school children in need as is appropriate; it 'may' provide such care for other children.

2.2.2 Avoiding the need for compulsory intervention

Several provisions within Schedule 2 to the Act are concerned with providing services to avoid the need for compulsory intervention in the family. Schedule 2, paragraph 4(1) provides that every local authority 'shall take reasonable steps, through the provision of services under Part III of this Act, to prevent children within their area suffering ill-treatment or neglect'. More specifically, paragraph 5 provides that where it appears that a child is suffering, or is likely to suffer, ill-treatment at the hands of another person who is living on the same premises the local authority 'may' assist that person to obtain alternative accommodation, and such assistance may include the provision of cash. Even where there may be serious concerns about a child, paragraph 7 provides that a local authority shall take reasonable steps designed to reduce the need to bring proceedings for a care or supervision order or other legal proceedings with respect to children.

2.2.3 Keeping families together

As we have seen, the guiding principle behind the duty to provide services to children in need is to promote the upbringing of children by their families. With that principle in mind, paragraph 10 of Schedule 2 provides that where any child who is in need and whom the relevant local authority are not looking after is living apart from his family, they shall take such steps as are reasonably practicable to enable him to live with his family or to promote contact between him and his family. The duty applies if, in the local authority's opinion, it is necessary to do so in order to safeguard or promote the child's welfare. This provision envisages a situation such as where the family home has burnt down or been flooded and parents and children are respectively being accommodated by different relatives in separate homes. In such a situation the local authority may become under a duty so far as reasonably practicable to keep the family together.

Sometimes it may not be possible to keep children and their families together and a child may need instead to live away from home. In certain circumstances a local authority may have a duty under section 20 of the Children Act 1989 to provide accommodation for children.[68]

---

[65] Schedule 2, para 8.   [66] Not merely children in need.
[67] Schedule 2, para 9; qualified by 'as they consider appropriate'.
[68] In such a case there is a duty under para 8A of Sch 2 to promote contact between each accommodated child and that child's family.

2.3 PROVISION OF ACCOMMODATION FOR CHILDREN

Local authorities have a general duty to take steps, so far as reasonably practicable, to secure sufficient appropriate accommodation for the children whom the local authority may need to look after.[69] Like section 17, this is a duty to children in need in general.

Key legislation

In addition, section 20(1) of the Children Act 1989 provides:

Every local authority shall provide accommodation for any child in need within their area who appears to them to require accommodation as a result of—

(a) there being no person who has parental responsibility for him;

(b) his being lost or having been abandoned; or

(c) the person who has been caring for him being prevented (whether or not permanently, and for whatever reason) from providing him with suitable accommodation or care.

Section 20(6) of the Children Act 1989 specifically provides that:

Before providing accommodation under this section, a local authority shall, so far as is reasonably practicable and consistent with the child's welfare—

(a) ascertain the child's wishes and feelings regarding the provision of accommodation; and

(b) give due consideration (having regard to his age and understanding) to such wishes and feelings of the child as they have been able to ascertain.

Unlike the duty in section 17 of the Children Act 1989, this duty is owed to individual children. In *R (G) v Southwark London Borough Council*[70] (the facts of which are discussed later in this chapter), the House of Lords indicated that applying section 20(1) 'involves an evaluative judgment on some matters but not a discretion'.[71] Baroness Hale of Richmond, who delivered the leading opinion, set out the following series of questions which must be considered when deciding whether section 20 applies.[72]

(1) Is the applicant a child?

The first question is whether the local authority is dealing with a child. In most cases it will be clear from a person's birth certificate or other formal documentation that a person is under 18 and therefore a child for the purpose of the Children Act 1989, as defined in section 105(1) of the Act. However, with increasing numbers of young persons seeking asylum in England and Wales and arriving without such documentation, and requiring accommodation, sometimes an issue can arise as to whether a person is a child for the purpose of section 20. Such questions arose in *R (On the application of A) v Croydon London Borough Council; R (On the application of M) v Lambeth London Borough Council*.[73] The Supreme Court held that the term 'child' within the Children Act 1989 is 'defined in wholly objective terms'[74] and is not simply a matter of a local authority's opinion

---

[69] Children Act 1989, s 22G.   [70] [2009] UKHL 26, [2009] 2 FLR 380.   [71] Ibid, [31].

[72] Ibid, [28]. Her Ladyship acknowledged that the series of questions was adopted from Ward LJ's judgment in *R (A) v Croydon London Borough Council; R (M) v Lambeth London Borough Council* [2008] EWCA Civ 1445, [2009] 1 FLR 1324 at [75].

[73] [2009] UKSC 8, [2009] 3 FCR 607.   [74] Ibid, [32].

as to whether a person is a child.[75] In other words, it is a jurisdictional fact going to the operation of the Children Act 1989. If there is a dispute, therefore, ultimately it will be a court which will be responsible for deciding that question of fact.

(2) Is the applicant a child 'in need'?

By contrast, whether a child is 'in need' within the meaning of the Act is a question of judgement to be left to the relevant local authority. The local authority's judgement can only be interfered with on the principle set out in *Associated Provincial Picture Houses Ltd v Wednesbury Corp*[76] (ie, if no local authority could rationally have reached that conclusion). In most cases in which a child is without a home, he or she is likely to be 'in need'.[77] However, as Baroness Hale pointed out in *R (G) v Southwark London Borough Council*[78] there may be rare instances where such a child is not in need: for example, a child whose home has been temporarily damaged by fire or flood who can afford hotel accommodation.

(3) Is the child within the local authority's area?

(4) Does he or she appear to the local authority to require accommodation?

(5) Is the need the result of the various factors set out in section 20(1)(a)–(c)?

The child's situation must fall within one of the paragraphs within section 20(1). An example of the use of section 20(1) might be where a single parent mother is taken ill and admitted to hospital and thus prevented from looking after her child. However, section 20(1) would not apply, for example, where a child has been living independently for some time and may lose his or her accommodation.[79] The words 'being prevented from providing him with suitable accommodation or care' in section 20(1)(c) have been given a wide construction, so that children do not suffer from the shortcomings of their parents or carers.[80] As Lord Hope of Craighead commented in *R (G) v Barnet London Borough Council; R (W) v Lambeth London Borough Council; R (A) v Lambeth London Borough Council*[81] the words 'for whatever reason' indicate that the widest possible scope must be given to this provision. So this paragraph would embrace a child who has been excluded from home by a parent or a situation where a parent is intentionally homeless.[82]

(6) What are the child's wishes and feelings regarding the provision of accommodation?

(7) And the linked question: having regard to the child's age and understanding, what due consideration is to be given to those wishes and feelings?

In *R (G) v Southwark London Borough Council*[83] Baroness Hale of Richmond made clear that 'there is nothing in s 20 which allows the local authority to force their services upon

---

[75] This view was supported by ss 25 and 46 of the Children Act 1989, which permit the keeping of a child in secure accommodation and police protection respectively. These provisions would not apply to an adult whatever the relevant authorities believed to be a person's age. See [2009] UKSC 8, [2009] 3 FCR 607 at [17]–[19].   [76] [1948] 1 KB 223, CA.

[77] See *R v Northavon District Council, ex p Smith* [1994] 2 AC 402, [1994] 2 FLR 671 at 406 and 672 respectively *per* Lord Templeman; and see *per* Lord Nicholls of Birkenhead in *R (G) v Barnet London Borough Council; R (W) v Lambeth London Borough Council; R (A) v Lambeth London Borough Council* [2003] UKHL 57, [2004] 1 FLR 454 at [19]: 'A child without accommodation is a child in need.'

[78] [2009] UKHL 26, [2009] 2 FLR 380 at [28](2).

[79] The example was given by Baroness Hale at [2009] UKHL 26, [2009] 2 FLR 380 at [28](5).

[80] Ibid, [28](5).

[81] [2003] UKHL 57, [2004] 2 AC 208, [2003] 3 WLR 1194, [2004] 1 FLR 454 at [100].

[82] *R (G) v Barnet London Borough Council; R (W) v Lambeth London Borough Council; R (A) v Lambeth London Borough Council* [2003] UKHL 57, [2004] 1 FLR 454 at [24]; see also *Attorney-General ex rel Tilley v Wandsworth London Borough Council* [1981] 1 WLR 854, *sub nom Attorney-General ex rel Tilley v London Borough of Wandsworth* (1981) 1 FLR 377.   [83] [2009] UKHL 26, [2009] 2 FLR 380 at [28](6).

older and competent children who do not want them.'[84] Her Ladyship had commented in the earlier case *R(M) v Hammersmith and Fulham London Borough Council*[85] that:

> there may well be cases in which there is a choice between s 17 and s 20, where the wishes of the child, at least of an older child who is fully informed of the consequences of the choices before her, may determine the matter. It is most unlikely that s 20 was intended to operate compulsorily against a child who is competent to decide for herself. The whole object of the 1989 Act was to draw a clear distinction between voluntary and compulsory powers and to require that compulsion could only be used after due process of law.[86]

2.4 WAYS IN WHICH THE CHILD CAN BE ACCOMMODATED

The ways in which a child may be accommodated are set out in section 22C of the Children Act 1989. This provides that unless it would not be consistent with the child's welfare or would not be reasonably practicable,[87] the child should be placed with a parent or someone who has parental responsibility.[88] Otherwise the child's placement can be with a relative or friend, a local authority foster parent, or in a children's home.[89] The local authority must give preference to placing the child with a relative or friend.[90] So far as reasonably practicable it must place the child within its area[91] and ensure the placement allows the child to live near home, does not disrupt the child's education or training, allows the child to live with any siblings, and that if the child is disabled the accommodation is suitable to the child's needs.[92] It will be recalled that in the cases *R (G) v Barnet London Borough Council; R (W) v Lambeth London Borough Council; R (A) v Lambeth London Borough Council*[93] which were discussed earlier in relation to section 17 of the Children Act 1989, the mothers of the children concerned were arguing that they should be provided with accommodation together with their children. It was argued on the appellants' behalf that the duty to accommodate children if possible with a parent meant that the local authority had a duty also to provide accommodation for the mothers concerned. The House of Lords rejected this view indicating that such provisions are concerned with placement, not housing, and assume that a parent of the child already has accommodation which the child might share.[94]

2.5 THE STATUS OF A 'LOOKED AFTER' CHILD

For children who are in need in the circumstances of section 20(1), the provision of accommodation is of obvious practical benefit to the child. However, being a child accommodated by the local authority can bring with it a status which is of wider benefit. Section 22 of the Children Act 1989 defines a category of children referred to as 'looked after by the local authority' and to whom certain duties are owed. The category includes both a child who is in the care of the local authority[95] (under a care order) and for whom the local authority therefore has parental responsibility, *and* a child who has been provided with accommodation by a local authority exercising its social services functions (in particular

---

[84] As supported by s 20(11) discussed later.   [85] [2008] UKHL 14, [2008] 1 FLR 1384.

[86] Ibid, [43].   [87] Section 22C(4).

[88] Including in the case of a child in care, a person who had parental responsibility for the child under a residence order prior to the care order being made: s 22B(3).

[89] Registered under the Care Standards Act 2000, Pt 2.   [90] Children Act 1989, s 22C(7).

[91] Ibid, s 22C(9).   [92] Ibid, s 22C(8).

[93] [2003] UKHL 57, [2004] 2 AC 208, [2003] 3 WLR 1194, [2004] 1 FLR 454.

[94] Ibid, [38].

[95] The local authority has a duty to provide accommodation for a child in its care: see s 22A.

those under the Children Act 1989)[96] provided that the local authority has done so for a continuous period of more than 24 hours.[97] Section 22 excludes from this definition accommodation provided under section 17 of the Children Act 1989, so accommodation provided under that section does not give rise to the status of being looked after.[98]

A local authority has several duties in relation to 'looked after' children. There is a duty to safeguard and promote the child's welfare,[99] including in particular a duty to promote the child's educational achievement;[100] and to make such use of services available for children cared for by their own parents as appears to the authority reasonable in his case.[101] In addition, there is a duty to maintain the child 'in other respects apart from the provision of accommodation'.[102] These duties mean that, 'although the local authority do not have "parental responsibility" for a child who is accommodated under s 20, they are nevertheless replacing to some extent the role played by a parent in the child's life, and are expected to look after the child in all the ways that a good parent would'.[103] Before making any decision with respect to a child whom it is looking after, or proposing to look after, a local authority shall, so far as is reasonably practicable, ascertain the wishes and feelings of the child, the child's parents, any person who has parental responsibility for the child, and any other person whose wishes and feelings the authority considers to be relevant, regarding the matter to be decided.[104] In the case of the child, in making any decision the local authority must give due consideration to the wishes and feelings ascertained, having regard to his or her age and understanding. In addition the local authority must give due consideration to the child's religious persuasion, racial origin, and cultural and linguistic background.[105]

Schedule 2, paragraph 19A provides that it is 'the duty of the local authority looking after a child to advise, assist and befriend him with a view to promoting his welfare when they have ceased to look after him'. The fact that a child is, or has been, accommodated by the local authority can in some circumstances bring into effect further duties which are owed when the child has ceased to be looked after. There are different categories of children to whom additional duties are owed.

2.5.1 An 'eligible child'

The first category is known as an 'eligible child' as defined in Schedule 2, paragraph 19B. An eligible child is aged 16 or 17 who has been looked after by a local authority for 13 weeks, or periods amounting in all to 13 weeks, which began after he reached the age of 14 and ended after he reached the age of 16.[106] In such a case the local authority must arrange for the child to have a personal adviser,[107] and prepare what is called a pathway plan[108] and keep it under regular review.[109]

---

[96]   Children Act 1989, s 22(1).   [97]   Ibid, s 22(2).

[98]   Ibid, 22(1)(b). Similarly, provision of accommodation under s 23B and s 24B.

[99]   Section 22(1)(a).   [100]   Section 22(3A).

[101]   The emphasis on keeping families together whilst at the same time safeguarding and promoting the child's welfare can again be seen in this provision.   [102]   Section 22B.

[103]   Per Baroness Hale of Richmond in *R (M) v Hammersmith and Fulham London Borough Council* [2008] UKHL 14, [2008] 1 FLR 1384 at [20].   [104]   Section 22(4).

[105]   Section 22(5).

[106]   Children Act 1989, Sch 2, para 19B(2)(b) and Care Planning, Placement and Case Review (England) Regulations 2010 (SI 2010/959), reg 40. The rules are modified in the case of a series of short-term placements, see reg 48.   [107]   Schedule 2, para 19C.

[108]   Ibid, para 19B(4).   [109]   Ibid, para 19B(5).

2.5.2 A 'relevant child'

A second category of child is a 'relevant child', as defined in section 23A of the Children Act 1989. A relevant child is a child who is aged 16 or 17 and who is not being looked after by any local authority and who, before last ceasing to be looked after, was an eligible child (as defined in the previous section). In such a case, the authority which last looked after the child (known as the responsible authority) has certain functions in relation to the child which are set out in section 23B. It must take reasonable steps to keep in touch with a 'relevant child', appoint a personal adviser and carry out an assessment, and prepare a pathway plan if one has not already been prepared. The authority has a duty to safeguard and promote the child's welfare and, unless they are satisfied that his welfare does not require it, to support the child by maintaining him and providing suitable accommodation and support,[110] which may be in cash.[111]

2.5.3 'Former relevant children'

Once a person reaches the age of 18 he or she is no longer a child and, of course, also no longer falls within the definitions of an eligible or relevant child. However, in defined circumstances some persons who were formerly looked after by a local authority will be owed duties by the authority into their early adult life. There is a further category of children known as 'former relevant children' to whom such duties are owed. They are any person who was being looked after by a local authority when the child attained the age of 18 and who immediately before ceasing to be looked after was an eligible child; or any person who has been a relevant child for the purposes of section 23A (and would be one if he were under 18). The local authority has a duty to take reasonable steps to keep in touch with a former relevant child,[112] to continue the appointment of his or her personal adviser, and to keep the pathway plan under review. There is also a duty to give assistance as set out in section 24B(1) and (2), or other assistance, as the child's welfare and educational or training needs require it. These duties always subsist until the former relevant child reaches the age of 21.[113] However, if the former relevant child's pathway plan sets out a programme of education or training which extends beyond his 21st birthday, then the assistance of the kind referred to in section 24B(2), to the extent that his welfare and his educational or training needs require it, continues for as long as the former relevant child is pursuing the programme.[114] The local authority has a duty to pay an amount of money to such a person who is pursuing higher education.[115] Even in a case where these duties have ceased, duties in respect of the former relevant child's education may be resurrected provided he or she is under 25 and informs the authority that he or she is pursuing or wishes to pursue a programme of education.[116] Again, the local authority has duties to appoint a personal adviser and to prepare a pathway plan. In addition, there is a duty to assist by contributing to living expenses incurred in connection with the programme and by making a grant to meet educational expenses.[117]

As can be seen, a local authority's decision to accommodate a child pursuant to section 20 of the Children Act 1989 can have significant long-term resource implications for the local authority, which may be required to provide assistance to a person into his or her mid-twenties. There is a big difference between those duties and the duty which a local housing authority owes to a young homeless person, even if in priority need. It would not be surprising, therefore, if some local authorities took steps to avoid incurring duties

---

[110] Section 23B(8).   [111] Section 23B(9).   [112] Section 23C(2).   [113] Section 23C(6).
[114] Section 23C(7).   [115] Section 23C(5A).
[116] Section 23CA(1), inserted by Children and Young Persons Act 2008, s 22(2).
[117] Section 23CA(5).

under section 20.[118] In *R (M) v Hammersmith and Fulham London Borough Council*[119] the House of Lords made clear that a deliberate policy to avoid responsibilities under the 1989 Act by shifting them onto a housing department, while understandable, would be unlawful.[120] *R (M) v Hammersmith and Fulham London Borough Council*[121] concerned a teenager, M, with troubling behaviour who had been excluded from school at 14 and had never returned to school. She had become involved with the criminal justice system, with court cases pending. M presented to the local authority housing department with a letter written by her mother, who had an inoperable stomach tumour, saying that M, who was then 16, could no longer stay in her home because she had broken every rule that had been laid down. The local housing authority acted to provide M with accommodation pursuant to its interim duty under section 188(1) of the Housing Act 1996. That duty applies if the local housing authority 'have reason to believe that an applicant may be homeless, eligible for assistance and have a priority need.' The relevant provision in M's case dealing with priority need was article 3 of the Homelessness (Priority Need for Accommodation) (England) Order 2002 which defines persons aged 16 or 17 as in priority need. However, the Order specifically excepts relevant children under section 23A of the Children Act 1989 or children to whom a local authority owe a duty to provide accommodation under section 20 of the Children Act 1989. 'Thus, in the longer term, the Children Act duties supersede the Housing Act duties.'[122] Although there was official Guidance[123] which recommended a joint assessment of children aged 16 or 17 and advised that in cases of uncertainty about whether section 20 applied a housing authority should contact the relevant social services authority, at no stage did the local housing authority refer the matter to the local authority children's services department.

M was housed in a succession of temporary placements in bed and breakfast hotel accommodation and in a hostel, from which she was evicted. Thereafter she lived with her sister, who had a baby, in one-bedroom accommodation not suitable for three people. Subsequently, M was sentenced for various offences, which sentences included a four-month detention and training order. While in custody M found out that she was pregnant and reached the age of 18. Proceedings for judicial review were issued on M's behalf while she was in custody, in order to try to secure accommodation for her upon her release. If M had been accommodated by the local authority under section 20 prior to her custody, she would of course be a recipient of the various duties discussed earlier. M's case ultimately reached the House of Lords on her appeal, where her argument was that the local authority had in fact been acting under section 20 of the Children Act 1989 when they thought they were acting under section 188 of the 1996 Act. The House of Lords dismissed the appeal, holding that no duty under section 20 had arisen since M's situation had never been drawn to the attention of the local social services authority. This outcome has been criticised by Jenny Driscoll and Kathryn Hollingsworth,[124] who observe that it could be argued that the housing department acted ultra vires by failing to have regard to the Code of Guidance, given that that was mandated by statute,[125] and referral to the social

---

[118] See the comment of Baroness Hale of Richmond in *R (M) v Hammersmith and Fulham London Borough Council* [2008] UKHL 14, [2008] 1 FLR 1384 at [24].

[119] [2008] UKHL 14, [2008] 1 FLR 1384.   [120] Ibid, [33].   [121] Ibid.   [122] Ibid, [15].

[123] *Homelessness Code of Guidance for Local Authorities* (Office of the Deputy Prime Minister, 2002), para 8.37.

[124] J. Driscoll and K. Hollingsworth, 'Accommodating Children in Need: *R (M) v Hammersmith and Fulham London Borough Council* [2008] Child and Family Law Quarterly 522.

[125] The guidance was issued pursuant to s 182 of the Housing Act 1996, which provides that local authorities 'shall have regard to such guidance'.

services authority was crucial to securing M's rights under the Children Act. Driscoll and Hollingsworth argue that there should be a legal duty to consider referral.

The reverse situation occurred in *R (G) v Southwark London Borough Council*.[126] A mother had excluded her 17-year-old son, A, from her home and he was 'sofa surfing' (sleeping on friends' sofas or in cars). He consulted solicitors and was advised to present at the children's services department of the local authority asking for urgent assessment of his needs under section 17 of the Children Act 1989 and for accommodation under section 20(1). A detailed assessment was carried out, identifying his housing and educational needs and revealing that he may be involved in gang activity. The local authority took the view that section 20 was 'not appropriate' and that his needs could be provided merely through provision of housing and other support. Judicial review proceedings were commenced challenging the local authority's decision which ultimately reached the House of Lords on A's appeal. The House of Lords unanimously allowed the appeal. A's circumstances fell within section 20(1), that duty had arisen, and the local authority 'were not entitled to "side-step" it by giving the accommodation a different label'.[127] The result was that A was accommodated by the local authority, became an eligible child within the meaning of paragraph 19B(2) of Schedule 2 to the Act, and, upon reaching 18, a 'former relevant child' within the meaning of section 23C(1), with all the attendant responsibilities attaching to the local authority.

2.6 REPRESENTATIONS AND COMPLAINTS RELATING TO PART III

Under section 26(3) of the Children Act 1989, local authorities are required to establish procedures for considering representations, including complaints, about how they are discharging their functions under Part III of the Children Act 1989.[128] Those entitled to use the procedures are any child being looked after by the local authority, a child in need, the child's parent, any other person who has parental responsibility for the child, any local authority foster parent, and 'such other person as the authority considers has a sufficient interest in the child's welfare to warrant his representations being considered by them'.[129] The duty under section 26(3) also applies in respect of persons using the local authority's adoption and special guardianship services.[130] Section 26A provides that every local authority shall make arrangements for the provision of assistance to children who make or intend to make representations under section 26,[131] including assistance by way of representation.[132]

---

[126] [2009] UKHL 26, [2009] 2 FLR 380.

[127] Ibid, [28]. For earlier case law in which there were similar labelling issues, giving a similar message: see *H, Barhanu and B v Wandsworth Hackney and Islington LBC* [2007] EWHC 1082 (Admin), [2007] 2 FLR 822; *R (L) v Nottinghamshire County Council* [2007] EWHC 2364 (Admin), [2007] All ER (D) 158 (Sept); *London Borough of Southwark v D sub nom R (On the Application of D) v A Local Authority* [2007] EWCA Civ 182, [2007] 1 FLR 2181, [2007] Family Law 701; *R (S) v Sutton London Borough Council* [2007] EWCA Civ 790, (2007) 10 CCLR 625.

[128] These include complaints about day care, services to support children within the family home, accommodation of a child, after care, and decisions relating to the placement of a child or the handling of a child's case. Section 24D of the Children Act 1989 also requires establishment of a similar procedure for the purpose of considering representations by a relevant child for the purposes of s 23A or a young person falling within s 23C, a person qualifying for advice and assistance, or a person falling within s 24B(2), about the discharge of functions in relation to him.

[129] Section 26(3).   [130] Section 26(3B) and (3C).   [131] Children Act 1989, s 26A(1).

[132] Ibid, s 26A(2).

The procedures established under section 26 must be publicised.[133] Regulations set out the way in which they should operate and each authority must use the regulations as the basis for the creation of their own procedure.[134]

A complainant must usually make his representations about a matter no later than one year after the grounds to make the representations arose.[135] The procedure has three stages. The first stage is local resolution of the complaint under regulation 14.[136] The local authority must consider and try to resolve the representations as soon as is reasonably practicable, usually within ten working days.[137] Where, however, the matter is not resolved, the complainant or, where one has been appointed, his advocate may request orally or in writing that the representations be investigated by the local authority together with an independent person, under regulation 17.[138] The response must be notified within 25 working days. If there is dissatisfaction with this outcome, the complainant can request that the matter be considered by a review panel[139] in accordance with regulation 19, which must meet within 30 days of the request. The panel consists of three independent persons,[140] one of whom will chair the panel. Within five days of meeting the panel must produce recommendations. Within 15 working days of receiving the panel's recommendations the local authority must, together with the independent person appointed under regulation 17, consider the recommendations and determine (i) how the authority will respond to them; and (ii) what they propose to do in the light of them, and send to the complainant its response and proposals, along with information about making a complaint to a Local Commissioner.[141]

This procedure goes some way towards mitigating the limited role of the courts in supervising how local authorities carry out their statutory duties to children in need, children being accommodated, and children in care. The courts have no involvement with children in need and accommodated children, and later in this chapter it will be seen that once a care order is made, the court's role comes to an end and it has no jurisdiction to intervene in how the local authority is looking after a child. It is therefore crucial that a person with a grievance about a child's treatment by the local authority should have somewhere to turn and that there should be at least some independent element in the conduct of an inquiry into that grievance. It should also be stressed that one purpose behind the establishment of this procedure was to give children being looked after by local authorities an avenue for making complaints about the care they are receiving. Tragically, some children, particularly those in residential care, are victims of abuse from the very people with whom they have been placed to protect them from harm. Although the procedures set up by section 26 are not designed to investigate allegations of child abuse, it is one method open to children to bring what is happening to them to the attention of others in the local authority. Where the

---

[133] Section 26(8). For interesting research about the variable nature of this publicity, see C. Williams and H. Jordan, *Factors Relating to Publicity Surrounding the Complaints Procedure under the Children Act 1989* (1996) 8 Child and Family Law Quarterly 337.

[134] Children Act 1989 Representations Procedure (England) Regulations 2006 (SI 2006/1738). For Wales the procedure is set out in SI 2005/3365. References hereafter are to the English regulations.

[135] Ibid, reg 9(1). The local authority may still consider the representation if it would not be reasonable to expect the complainant to have made the representations within the time limit; and it is still possible to consider the representations effectively and fairly.

[136] Unless the complainant and the local authority agree that the representations should not be so considered, see reg 14(1). [137] The period can be extended in the case of a complex representation.

[138] Reg 15(2). [139] Reg 18.

[140] The independent person appointed in accordance with regulation 17 may not be a member of the panel, reg 19(3).

[141] Reg 20.

complaints procedure is fully pursued and where the panel make recommendations then normally the local authority must abide by those recommendations unless it has substantial reasons for not doing so, and its failure to do so may be actionable in judicial review.[142]

The complaints procedure must first be exhausted before any proceedings for judicial review can be pursued. Another remedy might be to pursue a claim for breach of a Convention right under the Human Rights Act 1998.

2.7 THE VOLUNTARY NATURE OF 'ACCOMMODATION'

The philosophy of Part III of the Children Act 1989 is to encourage local authorities to work in partnership with parents and persons with parental responsibility, and to promote mutual confidence and trust. The thinking is that parents and others should be able to turn to local authorities for positive help and support in bringing up their children, and that they should not have cause to fear that they may lose their children into state care if they take advantage of the services provided. Such fear may be very real in a case where a person with parental responsibility is encouraged to agree to his child being accommodated under section 20, because he or she thereby as a matter of fact loses a measure of control over the child's upbringing. Reassurance is provided by subsections (7) and (8), which together make clear that accommodation under section 20 may only be provided, or continue to be provided, if the persons with parental responsibility for the child do not object.

Key legislation

Section 20(7) provides that:

A local authority may not provide accommodation under this section for any child if any person who—

(a) has parental responsibility for him; and

(b) is willing and able to—

    (i) provide accommodation for him; or

    (ii) arrange for accommodation to be provided for him,

objects.

It can be seen that section 20(7) does not require a local authority to obtain the consent of persons with parental responsibility before a child is received into accommodation. Such a provision would prove unworkable for the practical reason that it may not always be possible to contact such persons. However, where there is a positive objection from a person with parental responsibility, the local authority may not accommodate the child where the objecting person can make his or her own arrangements for the child.

The voluntary nature of accommodation is further underlined by section 20(8) which provides that in a case in which a child has been accommodated: 'Any person who has parental responsibility for a child may at any time remove the child from accommodation provided by or on behalf of the local authority under this section.' The voluntary nature of accommodation was made clear in *R v Tameside Metropolitan Borough Council*,

---

[142] *R v Avon County Council, ex p M* [1994] 2 FLR 1006.

ex parte J.[143] In that case a 13-year-old girl with multiple severe disabilities, autistic tendencies, and challenging behaviour had lived with her parents until she was 9 when the
parents could no longer cope. The girl was thereafter accommodated by the local authority under section 20 and placed at a residential home for disabled children which was
near the parents' home and also near the school that she attended. The local authority
subsequently suggested that she be moved to live with foster parents, a move to which
the parents objected. Despite the parents' objections the local authority began to initiate
contact between the child and the proposed foster parents with a view to the move. The
child, acting by her mother as litigation friend, sought permission to apply for judicial
review of the local authority's decision. Granting permission, Scott Baker J explained that
the 'unspoken word in Pt III of the 1989 Act is co-operation—co-operation between the
parents and the local authority to work together in the best interests of the child'.[144] A
local authority accommodating a child is 'able to exercise mundane day-to-day powers of
management' but a 'mere power of management cannot override the wishes of the parent
with parental responsibility'.[145] His Lordship held that the general duty of a local authority to safeguard and promote the welfare of children within its area who are in need[146]
does not entitle a local authority to accommodate a child in a (foster) placement against
the wishes of those with parental responsibility.[147] Equally, his Lordship made clear that
the parents cannot dictate where the local authority must accommodate the child. If there
is an impasse, the local authority must ask whether there is a risk of significant harm to
the child if its view does not prevail and if so it may be necessary for the local authority
to invoke its compulsory powers of intervention. If the parents unreasonably refuse all
the local authority has to offer then the local authority can argue that it has discharged its
duty. Scott Baker J was of the view that in such a situation if the parents were unable to
accommodate the child, 'then the significant harm threshold is likely to be crossed and
the ultimate answer may be a care order'.[148] As we shall see later in this chapter, even when
a care order is made, those with parental responsibility retain it and any overriding of
parental responsibility will need to have regard to the right to respect for private and family life within Article 8 of the European Convention on Human Rights (ECHR).

2.7.1 The position of the father who does not have parental responsibility

Section 20(7) refers to persons with parental responsibility. A father who is not married to
his child's mother is in a vulnerable position if he has not acquired parental responsibility.
He has no enforceable right to object to his child being accommodated and he is not entitled
to remove his child from accommodation at any time. However, his position is not entirely
bleak. The general duty of a local authority is to promote the upbringing of children by their
families[149] and a local authority is not required to receive the child into accommodation
when a family member is offering to look after the child. In a case where the child is already
being accommodated, the local authority can bring the accommodation arrangement to
an end, or where it continues to accommodate the child, the local authority 'shall' make
arrangements to enable an accommodated child to live with a parent unless that would not
be reasonably practicable or consistent with his welfare. Thus, an unmarried father who
does not have parental responsibility should only find himself in conflict with the local
authority when placement with him appears to the authority to be against the interests

---

[143] [2000] 1 FCR 173.   [144] Ibid, 180.

[145] Ibid, recognising that the 'distinction between management decisions and decisions which ultimately
require the consent of those with parental responsibility may not always be an easy one to define' (at 181).

[146] Under Children Act 1989, s 17.   [147] [2000] 1 FCR 173 at 183.   [148] Ibid, 181.

[149] Children Act 1989, s 17(1), discussed in Section 2.1.

of the child. Where the father objects to the authority's approach his remedy would be to apply for a residence order. In determining the merits of his application, the court would give paramount consideration to the welfare of the child, but presumably in a case in which the parent could offer appropriate care the court would give considerable weight to the fact that a parent was offering to provide a home for a child in a case where the alternative offered was foster care or accommodation in a residential home.

2.8 SOME QUALIFICATIONS TO THE VOLUNTARY NATURE OF 'ACCOMMODATION'

Section 20(7) and (8) do not apply where a residence order is in place nor when the High Court's inherent jurisdiction has settled the child's carer; nor when the child concerned is 16 or over.

2.8.1 Where there is a residence order or a person has the child's care by virtue of the High Court's inherent jurisdiction

A parent with parental responsibility is placed in a similar position to the unmarried father discussed earlier, where there is a residence, or other, order settling the arrangements as to the person with whom the child is to live in favour of another person. Section 20(9) provides that:

Subsections (7) and (8) do not apply while any person—

(a) in whose favour a residence order is in force with respect to the child; or

(b) who has care of the child by virtue of an order made in the exercise of the High Court's inherent jurisdiction with respect to children,

agrees to the child being looked after in accommodation provided by or on behalf of the local authority.

Where more than one person has the benefit of a residence order, all such persons must agree to the child being accommodated.[150]

The thinking lying behind subsection (9) is that it is the voice of the person who has had the benefit of the residence order which should prevail in dealings with the local authority. Where there has been an estrangement between parents, between parents and others, or where some other reason has led to a residence order being made, a court must have decided that it is better for the child to make a residence order than not to make an order.[151] The thinking is that it is normally in the interests of the child that the person with the residence order should be able to make arrangements about where the child will live, including placing him with a local authority, in spite of the objections of a parent or other person with parental responsibility.[152]

2.8.2 Where the child is 16

Another exception to the voluntary principle is where a child who has reached the age of 16 agrees to being accommodated. Section 20(11) provides that in these circumstances subsections (7) and (8) do not apply. Subsection (11) is an important example of how the law has moved towards allowing a child to determine his own upbringing

---

[150] Section 20(10).

[151] Section 1(5): see Chapter 9; or the High Court has intervened in the exercise of its inherent jurisdiction.

[152] For criticism, see A. Bainham *Children the New Law* (Bristol: Family Law, 1990), para 4.26.

in the face of objections from a parent or other person with parental responsibility. It assumes that a child of 16 is old enough, and has reached a sufficient level of understanding, to make an informed choice about where he wishes to live. In many cases this will be correct. The thinking is that a child of 16 is approaching full adulthood so that he or she should be entitled to leave home and to seek assistance from a local authority in obtaining properly regulated accommodation.[153] Where already accommodated, the child should be entitled to remain with the persons with whom he or she has been living in the face of parental objection. Subsection (11) also assists the local authority, because it need not consider instituting care proceedings to assist the mature child in a case where the persons with parental responsibility refuse to agree to the child being accommodated.

The disadvantage of subsection (11) is that it may sometimes place parents and others with parental responsibility in an intolerable position in a case where they do not wish the child to be accommodated. The fact that a child chooses to put himself into, or to remain in, local authority accommodation may be a matter of very great concern to them. Children being looked after by a local authority come from a variety of backgrounds, some of which are very disturbed. An accommodated child who comes from a 'good home' may live on premises where he or she associates with children who have been involved in prostitution, drug abuse, and various types of crime. The child's desire to remain in accommodation may be because these alternative forms of lifestyle seem attractive at an age which is notoriously associated with rebellion against parental norms. While those charged with the duty of looking after older accommodated children make every effort to ensure that such children are not involved in unhealthy, dangerous, and criminal forms of activity, there may be little they can do to prevent a determined child from becoming so involved. Local authorities do not have the power to restrict the liberty of delinquent children whom they are looking after, for more than 72 hours in any period of 28 consecutive days,[154] unless given specific authority to do so by a court.[155]

It would seem that the obvious solution would be for the persons with parental responsibility to apply for a residence order as this would have the effect of overriding the child's decision to be accommodated. However, such persons are normally powerless to obtain a residence order once a child is 16. Section 9(7) provides that a court shall not make any section 8 order with respect to a child who has reached the age of 16 unless it is satisfied that the circumstances of the case are exceptional. It is suggested that a person with parental responsibility should either seek to persuade a court to treat the case as exceptional or should seek the leave of the High Court to invoke the exercise of the inherent jurisdiction. Once decision-making power had been taken from the child and placed in the court, the court's decision would be determined by the view it took of the child's best interests, in relation to which the child's wishes and feelings would be but one element.

---

[153] The local authority must accommodate a child aged 16 who is in need and whose welfare 'is likely to be seriously prejudiced if they do not provide him with accommodation' (s 20(3)). It may accommodate any child aged between 16 and 21 where to do so would 'safeguard or promote his welfare' (s 20(5)) and see *Re T (Accommodation by Local Authority)* [1995] 1 FLR 15 where a local authority's decision to refuse formally to accommodate a 17-year-old child was quashed in proceedings for judicial review.

[154] Children (Secure Accommodation) Regulations 1991 (SI 1991/1505), reg 10(1).

[155] The Children Act 1989, s 25, enables a court to make a secure accommodation order on specified grounds for a maximum period of three months.

2.8.3 Accommodated children who need care or protection

Accommodation may be used by a local authority as an alternative to bringing care proceedings in a case where there are concerns and fears about the manner in which a child is being looked after.[156] While the voluntary nature of accommodation arrangements made under section 20 is in keeping with the partnership philosophy of the Act, in some cases subsections (7) and (8) may be difficult to reconcile with a local authority's child protection duties.

Some of the tensions in such cases can be addressed by careful forward planning between the local authority and the persons with parental responsibility. This type of planning enables the local authority and persons with parental responsibility to agree in advance about any problems which might arise through the strict enforcement of rights under section 20(8). For example, a parent might be prepared to agree that the best interests of a child are not normally served by a precipitate and unplanned removal from accommodation, and that at least a brief period of notice is normally better for the child.

The advantage of this type of formal planning between a local authority and persons with parental responsibility is that it reinforces the philosophy that local authorities, parents, and others should work together in partnership and that each should trust the other. In this regard, warning parents and others in a written agreement that precipitate removal might lead to an application for an emergency protection order is honestly to reflect the reality. It tells them in no uncertain terms that a 'voluntary' arrangement might be transformed into a compulsory arrangement if their cooperation is withdrawn. Injecting this note of realism into accommodation arrangements may better promote the child's sense of security with his current carers, and the child can be reassured that his wishes and feelings will be taken into account before there is any sudden change of plan.

The disadvantage of agreements of this kind is that terms which require persons with parental responsibility to give a period of notice before removing a child from accommodation undermine the principle that the arrangement is voluntary. Parliament was insistent that no notice period should be included in section 20(8) in the face of very great pressure to include at least a brief period.[157] Local authorities are in a much stronger position than parents when suggesting what terms should be included, and they are likely to tell parents what the arrangements will be, however much this is couched in the language of mutual agreement. There is a risk that written accommodation agreements will take on a spurious authority in the eyes of those who are party to them, so that local authorities may feel that they can 'contract out' of the law's provisions, and parents and others may feel 'bound' by the terms and not be aware of their rights under section 20(8).

Research by Judith Masson indicates that in practice the boundary between voluntariness and coercion may be blurred.[158] Reflecting an obvious tension between risk assessment and working in partnership, Masson found that agreements between parents and the local authority were not always freely negotiated:

> Rather, they were conditions imposed on parents, which allowed the social services department to conclude that the issue of the children's care could remain a matter determined by the department and need not be brought before a court.[159]

---

[156] The care provided is regulated by the Care Planning, Placement and Case Review (England) Regulations 2010 (SI 2010/959).

[157] House of Commons Debate, Standing Committee B, 18 May 1989, cols 137–154; House of Lords, Official Report, 20 December 1988, col 1335.

[158] J. Masson, 'Police Protection—Protecting Whom?' (2002) Journal of Social Welfare and Family Law 157; J. Masson, 'Emergency Intervention to Protect Children: Using and Avoiding Legal Controls' [2005] Child and Family Law Quarterly 75.

[159] Masson, 'Emergency Intervention to Protect Children', ibid, 82.

This *de facto* compulsion does not carry with it the safeguards of formal compulsory intervention. Furthermore, the failure to comply with an agreement was then sometimes seen as a reason, and further ground, for compulsory intervention.

2.8.4 No compulsory removal without court sanction

Except in the case of police protection, a court order is required if a child is to be compulsorily removed from parental care. Astonishingly, the need to make this rather obvious point judicially arose in *R (G) Nottingham City Council*.[160] An 18-year-old woman who had been in local authority care and had a troubled history, including alcohol/drug abuse and self harm, was about to deliver her child in hospital. Following a child protection meeting, the local authority intended to apply for an interim care order in respect of the baby immediately upon birth. Details of the plan were sent to all hospitals in the region. A 'birth plan' was prepared for the hospital medical staff by the Nottingham City NHS Primary Care Trust, which referred to the child protection meeting and indicated that the child was to be removed at birth. The plan made no reference, however, to the need first for a court order authorising removal. Two hours after the birth, the hospital staff, in accordance with the birth plan and express instructions from a social worker,[161] removed the baby from his mother to a different room in the hospital. In judicial review proceedings before Munby J[162] counsel for the mother applied for an immediate order that the mother and her son be reunited since the removal was done without legal authority and in breach of the rights of the mother and the baby under Article 8 of the ECHR. Munby J ordered that, provided there was no lawful authority to remove the child, the NHS Hospital Trust was to take steps forthwith to reunite the mother and baby. They were reunited within minutes of the order being made.

It had been submitted on behalf of the local authority that the birth plan was a plan to accommodate K within the meaning of section 20 of the Children Act 1989.[163] The argument was founded on nothing more than the assertion that the mother knew and understood the details of the birth plan and that she did not raise objection to it nor to the removal of her newborn baby.[164] Munby J stated that these submissions were 'as divorced from legal substance' as they were remote from the emotional and hormonal realities of the woman's condition.[165] He continued:

> I am not suggesting that consent to the accommodation of a child in accordance with s 20 is required by law to be in writing—though, that said, a prudent local authority would surely always wish to ensure that an alleged parental consent in such a case is properly recorded in writing and evidenced by the parent's signature. Nor am I disputing that there may be cases where a child has in fact, and without parental objection, been accommodated by a local authority for such a period as might entitle a court to infer that the parent had in fact consented.[166]

However:

> To equate helpless acquiescence with consent when a parent is confronted in circumstances such as this with the misuse (or perhaps on another occasion the misrepresentation) of

---

[160] [2008] EWHC 152 (Admin), [2008] 1 FLR 1660.

[161] This latter fact emerged in subsequent proceedings: see *R (G) v Nottingham City Council and Nottingham University Hospital* [2008] EWHC 400, [2008] 1 FLR 1668, QBD at [44].

[162] There were already judicial review proceedings before the court in respect of the woman, challenging a pathway plan for her under the leaving care legislation (discussed in Section 2.5). *R (G) v Nottingham City Council and Nottingham University Hospital* [2008] EWHC 400, [2008] 1 FLR 1668, QBD.

[163] Ibid, [48].   [164] Ibid, [51].   [165] Ibid, [52].   [166] Ibid, [53].

non-existent authority by an agent of the State is, in my judgment, both unprincipled and, indeed, fraught with potential danger.[167]

Munby J made clear what he considered ought to be obvious, namely that 'social workers have no power to remove children from their parents unless they have first obtained judicial sanction for what they are proposing to do'[168] and also emphasised that 'the powers conferred on the police by s 46 are *not* given to either local authorities or social workers'.[169] He added that 'the same goes, of course, for a hospital and its medical staff'[170] and that 'no baby, no child, can be removed simply as the result of a decision taken by officials in some room'.[171]

2.8.5 Qualifications

His Lordship clarified, however, that this is subject to two qualifications. First, a person is entitled to intervene 'in order to prevent an actual or threatened criminal assault taking place'.[172] Secondly, section 3(5) of the Children Act 1989 provides that 'a person who has care of a child may (subject to the provisions of the Children Act 1989) do what is reasonable in all the circumstances of the case for the purpose of safeguarding or promoting the child's welfare.'[173] This, or the doctrine of necessity, would for example allow medical care in order to protect a child from irreversible harm or death in circumstances of such urgency that other lawful authorisation could not be invoked.[174] In such situations, as Munby J explained, 'Law, medical ethics and common sense march hand in hand.'[175] In the *Nottingham* case, neither of the qualifications applied.

However, they might be relied on if a parent sought to remove a child from local authority accommodation in circumstances where the child would be at risk. A local authority might also be protected for a brief period by its general duty to safeguard and promote the welfare of a looked after child. There are overwhelming policy reasons why the local authority should not be compelled to hand the child over immediately, for the child might suffer the feared significant harm which will form the basis of an application for the emergency protection order. This reasoning is assisted by the Court of Appeal's ruling in *F v Wirral Metropolitan Borough Council*[176] that there is no separate tort of interference with parental rights. If a local authority were to be sued for retaining a child in breach of section 20(8), the plaintiff would have the burden of establishing that a tort had been committed against the *child*, and not against the person with parental responsibility. A separate possibility for speedy intervention might be, as Munby J also notes, to involve the police.

3 SIGNIFICANT HARM: THE THRESHOLD FOR COMPULSORY INTERVENTION

With the intention of drawing a clear distinction between voluntary and compulsory interventions in family life, the Children Act 1989 establishes a threshold for compulsory

---

[167] Ibid, [55].

[168] [2008] 1 FLR 1660, [17]. The sanction could be 'either an emergency protection order in accordance with s 44 of the Children Act 1989 or an interim care order in accordance with s 38 of the Act or perhaps, in an exceptional case (and subject to s 100 of the Act), a wardship order made by a judge of the Family Division of the High Court.'   [169] Ibid, [15].

[170] Ibid, [17].   [171] Ibid, [18].

[172] Ibid, [21], adding that: 'Any threat of immediate significant violence is enough, particularly if it involves a young child.'   [173] Ibid, [23].

[174] Ibid, [25].   [175] Ibid, [26].

[176] [1991] 2 All ER 648; for a useful comment see A. Bainham (1990) 3 Journal of Child Law 3.

intervention in family life based on the concept of 'significant harm'. As we shall see, the standard of proof with regard to this threshold criterion[177] varies according to the nature of the intervention.

Key legislation

'Harm' is defined in section 31(9) to mean:

ill-treatment or the impairment of health or development including, for example, impairment suffered from seeing or hearing the ill-treatment of another;
    'development' means physical, intellectual, emotional, social or behavioural development;
    'health' means physical or mental health; and
    'ill-treatment' includes sexual abuse and forms of ill-treatment which are not physical.

The definition of harm is thus very wide and covers all types of conceivable harm to the child.[178] It specifically recognises the deleterious effects on child well-being of exposure to (domestic) violence.

For the state to be entitled to intervene compulsorily, however, the harm must be 'significant'. This requirement means that not all falling off in standards of parenting causing harm to the child will permit state intervention.

In *Humberside County Council v B*[179] Booth J accepted,[180] indeed found 'very apt and helpful', counsel's submission that significant should be defined 'in accordance with dictionary definitions, first as being harm that the court should consider was either considerable or noteworthy or important' and 'as harm which the court should take into account in considering a child's future'.[181] In *Re L (Care: Threshold Criteria)*[182] Hedley J cautioned that it 'would be unwise to a degree to attempt an all embracing definition of significant harm … Significant harm is fact specific and must retain the breadth of meaning that human fallibility may require of it.' Whether or not a child is suffering significant harm must therefore be seen in the context of all the circumstances of the case and in relation to the particular child with whom the court is concerned. A child may be exceptionally vulnerable in one way or another. In *Humberside County Council v B*[183] Booth J cited an example given in argument by counsel of a child who suffers from brittle bones, in whose case 'a push or a slap might be of great significance, whereas in the case of a child who does not so suffer it may be a minimal incident'.[184] But of course this cuts both ways: it is possible on this view that the impact of ill-treatment or other types of unacceptable parenting on a resilient child who is able to withstand the treatment or behaviour, may fall outside the scope of the meaning of 'significant harm' where the harm is not considerable, noteworthy, or important. However, where the standards of parenting of those who are looking after the child show no sign of being capable of change, so that the child will sustain the effects of poor parenting continued over a considerable period of time, it is suggested that such a child might be one whom a local authority should take steps to protect on the basis that he

---

[177] As it has come to be known: see [1993] 1 FLR 257 at 261 *per* Booth J.

[178] The definition now includes seeing or hearing domestic violence. See Social Services Inspectorate and Department of Health, *Domestic Violence and Social Care* (London: HMSO, 1995); P. Parkinson and C. Humphries, 'Children who Witness Domestic Violence: The Implications for Child Protection' (1998) 10 Child and Family Law Quarterly 147.   [179] [1993] 1 FLR 257.

[180] Ibid, 265.   [181] Ibid, 263.   [182] [2007] 1 FLR 2050 at [51].

[183] [1993] 1 FLR 257.   [184] Ibid, 263.

is 'likely' to suffer significant harm, because the harm he is presently suffering is likely to become 'considerable, noteworthy, or important'.

The inclusion of likely harm as a basis for taking child protection action allows for intervention before any actual harm is suffered.[185] Where a child is not presently suffering significant harm, it may be even more difficult for the local authority to determine when it is appropriate to intervene on the basis that a child is 'likely' to suffer significant harm. Professionals who engage in child protection work are aware that some parents and other carers may have little appreciation of the vulnerability of babies and small children to suffering significant harm. In the case of babies a shaking which is relatively mild by adult standards may lead to disastrous consequences such as brain damage, impairment of sight, or even death.[186] A parent with learning difficulties may not be able to be trusted always to test that water in which a child is bathed is of the correct temperature, yet for a child to be scalded may be fatal or it may have permanent serious consequences for the child's appearance, health, and development. When setting standards, and evaluating the risk of harm occurring to a child, the question to be resolved is: when should the parents and others be allowed the opportunity to demonstrate whether it is safe for the child to remain in their care, and when is it proper to intervene to prevent predicted harm from occurring?

3.1 HEALTH OR DEVELOPMENT: COMPARISON WITH SIMILAR CHILD

Key legislation

Some assistance on the meaning of significant harm is provided by section 31(10), which provides:

Where the question of whether harm suffered by a child is significant turns on the child's health or development, his health or development shall be compared with that which could reasonably be expected of a similar child.[187]

In *Re O (A Minor) (Care Order: Education: Procedure)*[188] the meaning of 'significant harm', in the context of a child's intellectual, emotional, social, and behavioural development was considered, and parallels were drawn with a similar child. *Re O* concerned a 15-year-old girl who had been truanting from school for three years. Considerable efforts had been made by the local education authority to secure the girl's attendance at school, but to no avail. The main thrust of the local authority's application for a care order, which was supported by the guardian ad litem, was that if the girl's absenteeism was not arrested, it would have a profound effect on her ability to cope in adult life. Although there was anxiety about

---

[185] Eg *F v Leeds City Council* [1994] 2 FLR 60 where the court found that the mother's dangerously egocentric behaviour posed an unacceptable risk to her child. See also *Re A (A Minor) (Care Proceedings)* [1993] 1 FCR 824 where three children had already been removed from their mother. When a fourth child was born, the local authority immediately obtained an emergency protection order and commenced care proceedings on the basis of likely significant harm.

[186] For discussion of such cases and difficulties with expert opinion evidence in that context, see J. Bettle and J. Herring, 'Shaken Babies and Care Proceedings' [2011] Family Law 1370.

[187] For criticism of the similar child concept, see M. D. A. Freeman, 'Care After 1991' in D. Freestone (ed), *Children and the Law* (Hull: Hull University Press, 1990). Cf A. Bainham, 'Care after 1991—A Reply' (1993) 3 Journal of Child Law 99.   [188] [1992] 2 FLR 7.

her intellectual and educational development,[189] the real concern related to her emotional and social development. It was said that her refusal to go to school 'will have a major impact on her self-esteem, her self-confidence and her perception of herself... it will also seriously impair her ability to relate to peers and adults in a more formal way. This will inhibit [the girl's] development because school is, of course, not only about intellectual learning, it also provides young people with necessary social and relationship skills.'[190]

On appeal from magistrates who made a care order, Ewbank J ruled that it had been entirely open to the magistrates to come to the view that the girl's intellectual and social development was suffering, and was likely to suffer, significant harm. He said 'if a child does not go to school and is missing her education, it is not difficult to draw the conclusion that, if she had gone to school and had not truanted, she would have improved her intellectual and social development'. With regard to the comparison to be made with a similar child he said 'in the context of this type of case, "similar child" means a child of equivalent intellectual and social development, who has gone to school, and not merely an average child who may or may not be at school'.[191] Ewbank J therefore confirmed the care order, and the care plan that the girl should go to a children's home and should be taken to school from there until a pattern of attendance had been achieved, when consideration would be given to sending her home.[192]

Presumably the meaning of 'similar' in this context needs to take account of environmental, social, and cultural characteristics of the child. It seems that a similar child is a child with similar attributes, that is, a child of the same age, sex, and ethnic origin. Where a child has learning difficulties he should be compared with a child with similar learning difficulties. Where the child was born prematurely the child's achievement of developmental milestones should be compared with those achieved by other premature babies. Where the child has a spurt in growth in weight and height if put into hospital or foster care, and comparison is made with a similar child, the question to be asked is would a similar child demonstrate such a growth spurt under these conditions. Where such a child would not, the question then arises whether the first child has been malnourished or otherwise treated in an abusive manner which has led to his or her failing to grow and put on weight, or whether there is some organic cause for the condition.

More contentious is the question of how far a disadvantaged child should be compared to a similar disadvantaged child, or how far he should be compared with a child who has benefited from greater material, social, and intellectual advantages. An example might be of children living in deprived circumstances in an inner city area. It might be expected that some such children will be poorly clothed, have few toys or books, be fed on a diet which is not very healthy, and not receive much intellectual stimulus from those who are caring for them. It is suggested that it could probably be maintained that a child who is looked after in this way is being treated in no worse a manner than many other children living in deprived circumstances, and that the standard of care he is receiving amounts to good enough parenting in the light of his background. However, it is suggested that deprivation and relative poverty do not provide a reasonable excuse for a child being dressed in filthy clothing, for complete lack of attention to personal hygiene, for not seeking medical attention when the child is ill, and for no interest being taken in his

---

[189] The evidence was that the girl had in fact acquired educational skills so that, in comparative terms, she was of about average ability. [190] [1992] 2 FLR 7 at 11–12.

[191] Ibid, 12.

[192] See J. Fortin, 'Significant Harm Revisited' (1993) 5 Journal of Child Law 151, who argues that the facts did not justify removing a child from her parents, that it was wrong to use removal into state care to deal with a child's lack of self-esteem and self-confidence, and that an application for an education supervision order would have been the appropriate response. See too R. White (1992) 142 New Law Journal 396.

intellectual and emotional development. Decision-makers must, of course, take account of poverty, but where one or more of these conditions applies to a child, then it seems proper to conclude that the level of care has fallen below the minimum standard which is acceptable.

In *Re L (Care: Threshold Criteria)*[193] Hedley J explained that for harm to be significant 'it is clear that it must be something unusual; at least something more than the commonplace human failure or inadequacy'. Hedley J observed that as a matter of policy it is 'recognised in law, that children are best brought up within natural families'[194] and that it follows inexorably:

Talking point

that society must be willing to tolerate very diverse standards of parenting, including the eccentric, the barely adequate and the inconsistent. It follows too that children will inevitably have both very different experiences of parenting and very unequal consequences flowing from it. It means that some children will experience disadvantage and harm, while others flourish in atmospheres of loving security and emotional stability. These are the consequences of our fallible humanity and it is not the provenance of the state to spare children all the consequences of defective parenting. In any event, it simply could not be done.[195]

Similarly, in *Re K; A Local Authority v N and Others*[196] Munby J commented[197] that:

the court must always be sensitive to the cultural, social and religious circumstances of the particular child and family. And the court should, I think, be slow to find that parents only recently or comparatively recently arrived from a foreign country—particularly a country where standards and expectations may be more or less different, sometimes very different indeed, from those with which they are familiar—have fallen short of an acceptable standard of parenting if in truth they have done nothing wrong by the standards of their own community.[198]

The passages from the judgments of Hedley J and Munby J were endorsed by Ward LJ in *Re MA (Care Threshold)*,[199] who observed that, given the underlying philosophy of the Act, 'the harm must...be significant enough to justify the intervention of the State and disturb the autonomy of the parents to bring up their children by themselves in the way they choose'.[200] The citation and endorsement of the passages in *Re L* and *Re K* (set out in the preceding paragraphs) in the context of the decision in *Re MA*, however, has been a

---

[193] [2007] 1 FLR 2050 at [51].

[194] Citing in support Lord Templeman in *Re KD (A Minor: Ward) (Termination of Access)* [1988] AC 806 at 812:

> The best person to bring up a child is the natural parent. It matters not whether the parent is wise or foolish, rich or poor, educated or illiterate, provided the child's moral and physical health are not in danger. Public authorities cannot improve on nature.

[195] [2007] 1 FLR 2050 at [50].

[196] [2005] EWHC 2956 (Fam), [2007] 1 FLR 399.

[197] In the context of considering the threshold for making a care order pursuant to s 31 of the Children Act 1989.

[198] [2005] EWHC 2956 (Fam), [2007] 1 FLR 399 at [26].

[199] [2009] EWCA Civ 853, [2010] 1 FLR 431 at [51]. For commentary on this case, see H. Keating, 'Re MA: The Significance of Harm' [2011] Child and Family Law Quarterly 115 and J. Hayes, M. Hayes, and J. Williams, '"Shocking" Abuse Followed by a 'Staggering Ruling': Re MA (Care Threshold)' [2010] Family Law 166.   [200] [2009] EWCA Civ 853, [2010] 1 FLR 431 at [54].

matter of concern for some commentators. That was a case in which there was no suggestion that the parents were claiming any cultural justification for the alleged ill-treatment of their children. As Hayes et al comment:

> any reference to the value placed by society on 'diversity and individuality' cannot be used to justify child cruelty or exposing young children to the risk of significant harm. Our developed laws of child protection are rooted in the protection of the rights and freedoms of all children within our society.[201]

4 INVESTIGATION

4.1 INVESTIGATING WHETHER A CHILD IS SUFFERING, OR IS LIKELY TO SUFFER, SIGNIFICANT HARM

A local authority have a duty in section 47 of the Children Act 1989 to investigate cases in which it is suspected that a child may be suffering or likely to suffer significant harm.[202]

Key legislation

Section 47(1) provides:

Where a local authority—

(a) are informed that a child who lives, or is found, in their area—

    (i) is the subject of an emergency protection order; or

    (ii) is in police protection;…

(b) have reasonable cause to suspect that a child who lives, or is found, in their area is suffering, or is likely to suffer, significant harm,

the authority shall make, or cause to be made, such enquiries as they consider necessary to enable them to decide whether they should take any action to safeguard or promote the child's welfare.

There is an identical duty where the local authority itself has obtained an emergency protection order with respect to a child.[203] The duty in section 47(1)(b) is triggered when

---

[201] J. Hayes, M. Hayes, and J. Williams, '"Shocking" Abuse Followed by a 'Staggering Ruling: *Re MA (Care Threshold)*' [2010] Family Law 166. However, research does not suggest that a change to the threshold is required: see J. Brophy et al, *Significant Harm: Child Protection Litigation in a Multi-Cultural Setting* (London: Department for Constitutional Affairs, 2003) (examining cultural context in care proceedings and not recommending any change to the threshold criteria); J. Brophy, J. Jhutti-Johal, and C. Owen, 'Assessing and Documenting Child Ill-Treatment in Ethnic Minority Households' [2003] Family Law 756:

> no 'single issue' cases where allegations of significant harm to a child rested unequivocally on behaviours/ attitudes defended as culturally acceptable by a parent but that professionals argued were unacceptable within western European assessments of ill-treatment.

[202] In *D v D (County Court Jurisdiction: Injunctions)* [1993] 2 FLR 802, the Court of Appeal ruled that the trial judge did not have jurisdiction to issue a direction which had the effect of inhibiting a local authority from carrying out its investigative function in response to a suspicion of child abuse in proceedings brought by parents for residence orders. Whether a High Court judge has such power was doubted, but left open: ibid, 811.

[203] Section 47(2).

the local authority has *reasonable cause to suspect* that a child is suffering, or is likely to suffer, significant harm. In *R (S) v Swindon Borough Council and another*[204] Scott Baker J commented that:

> the threshold is quite low. This is hardly surprising as [the local authority's] obligation is to investigate ie make enquiries with a view to deciding whether to take any action to safeguard or promote the child's welfare.[205]

In that case, the claimant was a widower with three children, who had begun a relationship with a woman who had a daughter, K, then aged 9. The claimant was found not guilty on seven charges of the indecent assault of K over an 18-month period. He had subsequently formed a relationship with a Mrs X, who had two daughters aged 11 and 7. The claimant and Mrs X wished to set up home together with their respective children and the claimant therefore wrote to Swindon Borough Council asking what social services intended to do. Mr X (the father of Mrs X's children) approached his local social services department expressing concern about his children's contact with the claimant. The local authorities concerned (the defendants in the case) took the view that K's allegations were to be believed and that the claimant could pose a risk to children, particularly children other than his own living in the same household, and therefore some consideration would need to be given to a plan to protect the children. The claimant applied for judicial review of those decisions, contending that the defendants had to be satisfied of the likelihood of significant harm before intervening. Scott Baker J dismissed the claim and, having drawn attention to the precise wording of section 47, observed that there was nothing at the criminal trial which ought to have led the defendants to the conclusion that what K had said was so unlikely to be true that they no longer had any reasonable cause to suspect the likelihood of significant harm. His Lordship explained that, although a local authority would 'no doubt look carefully at the result of a criminal trial and any matters of significance that emerged in the course of it', the fact of an acquittal does 'not prevent a local authority from forming a view which is adverse to the acquitted person',[206] and 'the various statutory duties under the 1989 Act must, if they are in play, be discharged'.[207]

Enquiries under section 47 are in particular directed towards establishing three things: whether the authority should make any application to the court, or exercise any of their other powers under the Children Act 1989 with respect to the child; whether it would be in the best interests of a child who is the subject of emergency protection to be in local authority accommodation; and whether, in the case of a child who has been taken into police protection, it would be in the child's best interests for the local authority to ask for an application to be made for an emergency protection order under section 46(7).[208]

Once the duty to make enquiries is in place, several other duties follow, or may follow depending on the circumstances. By section 47(4) the local authority is under a duty to take such steps as are reasonably practicable to obtain access to the child 'unless they are satisfied that they already have sufficient information with respect to him'. Section 47(6) follows up this provision by providing that where, in the course of the section 47 enquiries, any officer of the local authority concerned[209] is refused access to the child concerned or is denied information as to his whereabouts, 'the authority shall apply for an emergency protection order, a child assessment order, a care order or a supervision order with respect

---

[204] [2001] EWHC (Admin) 334, [2001] 3 FCR 702. See also *Gogay v Hertfordshire County Council* [2001] 1 FLR 280, CA at [49]: 'a s 47 investigtion does not generally infringe the legal rights of anyone involved. It merely imposes on the local authority a duty to carry the investigation far enough to reach a conclusion' (employee should not be suspended simply because there is a s 47 investigation).

[205] [2001] 3 FCR 702, [36].   [206] Ibid, [37].   [207] Ibid, [37].   [208] Section 47(3).

[209] Or any person authorised by the authority to act on its behalf in connection with those enquiries.

to the child unless they are satisfied that his welfare can be satisfactorily safeguarded without their doing so'.

Section 47(9) emphasises the importance of inter-agency cooperation by placing a duty on specified persons (listed in s 47(11))[210] to assist the local authority in conducting its enquiries unless it would be unreasonable in all the circumstances of the case.[211] Of course, the value of different agencies working together in the early detection and prevention of child abuse is emphasised in the guidance issued under the Act. The conduct of an investigation under section 47 requires not only the cooperation of other agencies, but also the cooperation of persons with parental responsibility for the child. Section 47 does not give a local authority any coercive powers; nothing in section 47 empowers a local authority to enter premises, despite the fact that one of its duties when conducting its investigation is to take such steps as are reasonably practicable to obtain access to the child.[212] Rather, the local authority is reliant on the person who has care of the child allowing them to see the child. However, cooperation from such a person may be forthcoming when the local authority's duty under section 47(6) is explained to him or her. It is suggested that only rarely should a local authority be satisfied that a child's welfare can be satisfactorily safeguarded without applying for a court order when the local authority has not actually seen, and (where appropriate) talked to, the child. It is a dangerously optimistic reaction to a suspicion of abuse which has not been properly investigated. Tragically, several children who have died at the hands of those looking after them are those children to whom social workers and others have not insisted on having proper access.[213]

If, at the conclusion of their enquiries, the local authority decides not to apply for a court order in respect of the child, it must decide whether it is appropriate to review the case at a later date and, if so, set a date for the review.[214] If a local authority concludes that it should take action to safeguard or promote the child's welfare it shall take that action (so far as it is both within its power and reasonably practicable for it to do so).[215] However, there may be no need for legal intervention even where significant harm is discovered. Where parents and other persons caring for the child are willing to work with social workers and other professionals in addressing the concerns which have arisen, it may be decided that the child can be adequately protected if he or she remains at home while work with the family is attempted.

4.2 CHILD ASSESSMENT ORDERS

Where access to a child is denied, or where information is denied as to the child's whereabouts, the local authority must apply for a court order unless it is satisfied that the child's welfare can otherwise be satisfactorily safeguarded. Normally the most appropriate response in such cases is to apply for an emergency protection order (discussed in

---

[210] The persons specified are any local authority, any local housing authority, health authorities, and any other person authorised by the Secretary of State. Surprisingly, and arguably wrongly, the police are omitted from this list. See further E. Birchall and C. Hallett, *Working Together in Child Protection* (London: HMSO, 1995); C. Hallett, *Inter-Agency Coordination in Child Protection* (London: HMSO, 1995).

[211] Section 47(10).   [212] Section 47(4).

[213] For a classic and horrific recent example, see *Birmingham City Council v AG and A* [2009] EWHC 3720 (Fam), [2010] 2 FLR 580 (child starved to death after social worker failed to gain access to child's household). See also *A Child in Mind: The Report on the Death of Kimberley Carlile* (Greenwich London Borough Council, 1987). See too *A Child in Trust: Report on the Death of Jasmine Beckford* (London Borough of Brent, 1988); *Whose Child: Report on the Death of Tyra Henry* (London Borough of Greenwich, 1987); see Department of Health and Social Security, *Child Abuse: A Study of Inquiry Reports 1973–1981* (London: HMSO, 1982), Department of Health, *Child Abuse: A Study of Inquiry Reports 1980–89* (London: HMS0, 1991).

[214] Section 47(7).   [215] Section 47(8).

Section 5). Sometimes, however, even when access to a child is obtained, persons with parental responsibility or those caring for a child may prevent a proper assessment from taking place by refusing to allow the child to be medically, or otherwise, examined. Where an assessment of the child is being frustrated in this way, the most appropriate response might be for a local authority or the NSPCC to apply for a child assessment order[216] under section 43 of the Children Act 1989. The effect of this order is to place any person who is in a position to produce the child under a duty to produce him to the persons named in the order, and to comply with the court's directions.[217] Only a local authority or an authorised person[218] can apply for a child assessment order.

Key legislation

Section 43(1) provides that a child assessment order may be made if, but only if, the court is satisfied that:

(a) the applicant has reasonable cause to suspect that the child is suffering, or is likely to suffer, significant harm;

(b) an assessment of the child's health or development, or the way in which he has been treated, is required to enable the applicant to determine whether or not the child is suffering, or is likely to suffer, significant harm; and

(c) it is unlikely that such an assessment will be made, or be satisfactory, in the absence of an order under this section.

The standard of proof which must be satisfied is thus one of reasonable cause for suspicion only, and accordingly the type of intervention allowed is strictly limited. The order must specify the date on which the assessment is to begin and gives the local authority a time-limited period as specified in the order, up to a maximum of seven days from that date, in which to discover whether there is any real foundation to its suspicion.[219] The court takes control over the type of assessment which should take place, and may give such directions as it thinks fit. The order authorises any person carrying out an assessment to do so in accordance with the terms of the order.[220] Those carrying out the assessment are limited as to where the assessment is carried out: a child may only be kept away from home where this is in accordance with directions specified in the order; where it is necessary for the purposes of the assessment; and where it is for such period, or periods, as may be specified in the order.[221] Where a child is to be kept away from home, the court must give directions about contact arrangements.[222] The voice of the child may also be determinative in a case of this kind. A child who has sufficient understanding to make an informed decision may refuse to submit to a medical, psychiatric, or other assessment.[223]

It is up to the court to determine how far a child assessment order can be used as a 'fishing expedition' to discover whether the suspicion that the child is suffering, or is likely to suffer, significant harm is soundly based. It is not clear to what extent it would be

---

[216] That is the title given to an order under s 43 of the Children Act 1989: see s 43(2). For a general evaluation of the child assessment order see R. Lavery, 'The Child Assessment Order—A Reassessment' (1996) 8 Child and Family Law Quarterly 41. See also G. Mitchell, 'The Child Assessment Order—A Breach of Principle?' [1991] XIII(I) Liverpool Law Review 53.

[217] Section 43(6); this person may not, of course, be a person with parental responsibility.

[218] Ie, a person authorised for the purpose of s 31 of the Children Act 1989 (currently only the NSPCC), see s 43(13).   [219] Section 43(5).

[220] Section 43(6) and (7).   [221] Section 43(9).   [222] Section 43(10).   [223] Section 43(8).

appropriate for the court to be very specific in the type of assessment it authorises, and to what extent it can leave this to the discretion of the local authority. Very little use has been made of the child assessment order and there does not appear to be any reported case law directly in relation to this order.[224] It seems that the court is expected to be cautious about authorising removal of the child from the home. A fine balance must be struck between taking the steps which are needed to discover whether or not the local authority's decisions can be verified and causing unnecessary distress and anxiety to a child and his or her parents in a case where there is nothing untoward happening. The caution surrounding the structure of child assessment orders can be partly explained by the crisis which occurred in Cleveland in the period immediately preceding the passing of the Children Act 1989.[225]

It is important to appreciate that a child assessment order is not the appropriate order in a case in which a child requires emergency protection. Section 43(4) provides that no court shall make a child assessment order if it is satisfied that there are grounds for making an emergency protection order and that it ought to make such an order rather than a child assessment order. This provision is designed to obviate the risk of children being left in a position of immediate danger because the wrong proceedings have been commenced. For the same reason, a court may treat an application for a child assessment order as an application for an emergency protection order.[226]

4.3 THE POWER OF A COURT TO DIRECT A SECTION 37 INVESTIGATION IN FAMILY PROCEEDINGS

One of the times when the welfare of a child may come under scrutiny is when an application is made to a court in family proceedings. Sometimes the evidence may give rise to concern, or even alarm, and the court may take the view that the position of a child should be further investigated. One response is to request a welfare report under section 7. Where there is serious concern about the upbringing of a child, such that the court takes the view that it may be appropriate to make a care or supervision order with respect to him, section 37 provides that the court may direct a local authority to undertake an investigation of the child's circumstances. In responding to this direction, and when undertaking its investigation, the local authority must consider whether it should apply for a care or supervision order, provide services or assistance for the child or his family, or take any other action with respect to the child. Because it is the court which is instigating the inquiry, it may wish to specify particular matters which it would like the local authority to look into.[227]

Where a local authority undertakes an investigation under a direction given under section 37 and decides not to apply for a care or supervision order, it must give the court its reasons. It must also inform the court of any service or assistance which it has provided, or intends to provide, for the child and his family, and of any other action which it has taken, or proposes to take, in relation to the child. However, it was held in *Nottinghamshire*

---

[224] There is information which suggests that social workers are unhappy about the alienating effect of such an order, and consider that there is no need for an order where parents can be persuaded to cooperate, see J. Dickens, 'Assessment and the Control of Social Work: Analysis of Reasons for the Non-Use of the Child Assessment Order' [1993] Journal of Social Welfare and Family Law 88.

[225] *Report of the Inquiry into Child Abuse in Cleveland 1987* (Cm 412, 1988). For an account of the effect of the Cleveland Inquiry on the work of those involved with child sexual abuse see A. Bentovim, *Cleveland 10 Years On—A Mental Health Perspective* [1998] Family Law 153–157, 202–207, and 267–269.

[226] Section 43(3).

[227] See eg *Re H (A Minor) (Section 37 Direction)* [1993] 2 FLR 541.

County Council v P[228] that a court has no power to direct the local authority to initiate care proceedings where it is not satisfied with the authority's reasons for failing to do so. *Nottinghamshire County Council v P* is an example of a case where who had the final decision-making power was crucial to its outcome. On the one hand, the trial judge and the Court of Appeal were in no doubt that a care order was necessary to prevent the children from suffering further significant harm; on the other hand, the local authority was obdurate in its refusal to pursue an application for a care order. The decision-making power lay with the local authority and, as Sir Stephen Brown P said, 'if a local authority doggedly resists taking the steps which are appropriate to the case of children at risk of suffering significant harm it appears that the court is powerless.'[229] Where, during the course of its section 37 investigation, the local authority uncovers matters which lead it to believe that a child is being abused, it can, of course, take steps to protect the child by making an application in care proceedings.

4.4 LOCAL AUTHORITY RESPONSES TO SIGNIFICANT HARM

Determining which is the most effective response to a discovery that a child is suffering, or is likely to suffer, significant harm is not easy for local authorities. Detailed guidance on the procedures to be adopted by the local authority children's social care department and other relevant agencies in fulfilment of the local authority's duties to safeguard children is set out in *Working Together to Safeguard Children: A Guide to Inter-Agency Working to Safeguard and Promote the Welfare of Children.*[230] In outline, the procedures are as follows. Following referral by a member of the public or professional, the local authority will carry out an initial assessment. The initial assessment may reveal that no further action is required, or perhaps that the child is in need and merely requires the provision of services. However, the initial assessment may suggest actual or likely significant harm. In such a case, following a strategy discussion, a section 47 investigation will be initiated. If there are concerns about a child's immediate safety there will be an immediate strategy discussion with police and other agencies as appropriate, legal advice will be obtained, and appropriate emergency action taken. If a section 47 investigation is warranted, a core assessment is led by a social worker, with contributions from other relevant professionals, and if concerns are substantiated a child protection conference is convened within 15 days of the strategy discussion. The initial child protection conference brings together family members, the child concerned (where appropriate), and those professionals most involved with the child and family. The purpose is to analyse and consider, in an inter-agency setting, the evidence obtained and to decide what future action is required in order to safeguard and promote the welfare of the child. If the conclusion is that the child is likely to suffer significant harm in the future, the decision will be to provide inter-agency help and intervention through a formal child protection plan. The chair of the conference determines which category of abuse or neglect the child has suffered or is likely to suffer (physical, emotional, sexual abuse or neglect) for recording on the child's social care record.[231] The conference will formulate in as much detail as possible an outline child protection plan. The local authority or the NSPCC will carry statutory responsibility for the child's welfare, with a social worker given lead responsibility for the case. There will be ongoing assessment by a core group of

---

[228] [1993] 2 FLR 134.   [229] Ibid, 148.

[230] London: TSO, March 2010, published by HM Government.

[231] In 2011, there were 42,700 children with such records in England (18,700 for neglect, 12,100 for emotional abuse, 4,500 physical abuse, 2,300 sexual abuse, and 5,000 multiple categories) (figures from the NSPCC).

professionals, refining the child protection plan. A child protection review conference[232] is held within three months of the initial child protection conference and further reviews at intervals of not more than six months for as long as the child remains the subject of the child protection plan. At these various stages the local authority will be considering whether concerns about significant harm remain and what if any measures, including legal measures, need to be implemented.

During these processes, the priority must be to ensure that the child is adequately protected. In compliance with Article 3 of the ECHR a local authority has a duty to prevent inhuman and degrading treatment of which it has knowledge or ought to have knowledge. In *Z and Others v UK*[233] a violation was found where a local authority took little action for several years in respect of children about whom there were serious concerns. The children had suffered psychological damage and neglect which should have been prevented.

5 PROTECTING CHILDREN IN AN EMERGENCY[234]

Sometimes there will be concern about the child's situation of such urgency that immediate steps to protect the child may be justified. In these circumstances an application can, and indeed should, be made under section 44 of the Children Act 1989 for an emergency protection order (EPO).

5.1 WHAT IS AN EMERGENCY PROTECTION ORDER?

An EPO operates as a direction to any person who is in the position to do so to comply with a request to produce the child. In addition, it authorises either the child's removal to accommodation provided by the applicant or the prevention of his removal from any hospital or other place in which he is currently being accommodated.[235] It is an offence intentionally to obstruct a person exercising these powers.[236] An EPO also gives the applicant parental responsibility for the child.[237] Clearly an order which authorises, for example, the sudden removal of a child from his home, sometimes without any prior warning, and gives parental responsibility to a third party is a powerful order with potential for traumatic effects on a child, his parents, and wider family, who may all become shocked, angry, or distressed when an EPO is obtained. The law therefore imposes tight control over when an EPO may be granted. The government guidance issued prior to the introduction of the Children Act 1989 states that the purpose of an EPO 'is to enable the child in a genuine emergency to be removed from where he is or be kept where he is, if and only if this is what is necessary to provide immediate short-term protection'.[238] In *Re X (Emergency Protection Orders)*[239] McFarlane J stressed the words 'genuine emergency' and 'only what is necessary to provide immediate short-term protection'.[240]

There is further tight control over the duration of the order and the powers which may be exercised in relation to the child while an order is in force. The order can be made

---

[232] For some of the difficulties surrounding case conferences see D. Savas, 'Parental Participation in Case Conferences' (1996) 8 Child and Family Law Quarterly 57; J. Thoburn, A. Lewis, and D. Shemmings, *Paternalism or Partnership? Family Involvement in the Child Protection Process* (London: HMSO, 1995).

[233] [2000] 2 FLR 603.

[234] See J. Masson et al, *Protecting Powers: Emergency Intervention for Children's Protection* (Chichester: Wiley, 2007).   [235] Section 44(4).

[236] Section 44(15).   [237] Section 44(4)(c).

[238] *Children Act 1989—Guidance and Regulations* (London: HMSO, 1991), vol 1, p 51.

[239] [2006] EWHC 510 (Fam), [2006] 2 FLR 701.   [240] Ibid, [63].

initially for up to eight days, and then renewed once for up to a further seven days[241] but only where the court has reasonable cause to believe that the child is likely to suffer significant harm if the order is not extended. The fact that the order can initially be made for eight days does not mean that it should automatically be made for eight days. The court should consider the appropriate duration of the order in the circumstances of the case.

Section 44(5)(a) provides that the powers to remove the child or prevent the child's removal shall only be exercised 'in order to safeguard the welfare of the child'. Furthermore, if those powers are exercised, section 44(10) provides that if it appears that it is safe for the child to be returned, or allowed to be removed from the place in question, the applicant for the EPO shall return the child[242] or (as the case may be) allow him to be removed. Section 44(12) provides, however, that the applicant 'may again exercise his powers with respect to the child (at any time while the emergency protection order remains in force) if it appears to him that a change in the circumstances of the case makes it necessary for him to do so'.

Section 44(5)(b) provides that the person in whose favour the order is made 'shall take, and shall only take, such action in meeting his parental responsibility for the child as is reasonably required to safeguard or promote the welfare of the child (having regard in particular to the duration of the order)'. Thus, the parental responsibility conferred by an EPO is a very limited form. It is submitted, for example, that the parental responsibility conferred would not give the applicant power to authorise any major medical or psychiatric treatment without the agreement of a parent or other person with parental responsibility, unless the child is in urgent need of such treatment.

It is submitted, however, that the applicant would have parental responsibility to permit the child to be examined, or otherwise assessed, provided it is exercised to promote the child's welfare. An assessment or examination may be viewed as promoting the child's welfare as without the assessment/examination it may not be possible to establish whether the child is indeed suffering, or likely to suffer, significant harm, and to what that harm is attributable. However, the applicant's powers in this regard are subject to section 44(6)(b) which provides that when the court makes an EPO (or at any time during its currency)[243] it may give various directions as it considers appropriate with respect to the medical or psychiatric examination or other assessment of the child including a direction to the effect that there should be no such examination or assessment of the child, or no such examination or assessment unless the court directs otherwise.[244] The child may, if he is of sufficient understanding to make an informed decision, refuse to submit to the examination or other assessment.[245] Again, these provisions address concerns which were identified in the Cleveland inquiry[246] in 1988.

The court may also give directions with respect to the contact which is, or is not, to be allowed between the child and any named person.[247] Subject to such directions, the applicant must allow the child reasonable contact[248] with his parents or any person

---

[241] Children Act 1989, s 45(1), (5), and (6).

[242] Section 44(11) provides that this should be to the person from whose care he was removed; or if that is not reasonably practicable, a parent of his, any person who is not a parent of his but who has parental responsibility for him; or such other person as the applicant (with the agreement of the court) considers appropriate.   [243] Section 44(9).

[244] Section 44(8).

[245] Section 44(7).   [246] *Report of the Inquiry into Child Abuse in Cleveland 1987* (Cm 412, 1988).

[247] Section 44(6)(a).   [248] Section 44(13).

who has parental responsibility for him and various other persons closely connected to the child, as listed in section 44(13).[249] This provision reflects the assumption which permeates the Act that maintaining contact between a child and his parents, and others who have parental responsibility for him, is normally in the best interests of the child and must, therefore, be permitted unless a court authorises otherwise. Such contact may not, in the applicant's opinion, be in the interests of the child, and it is important that the applicant draws this to the attention of the court where he believes this to be the case.

5.2 THE GROUNDS FOR MAKING AN EMERGENCY PROTECTION ORDER

Unlike a child assessment order, an EPO can be made without notice. Indeed, in some cases it is essential to do so, for if the person caring for the child were to be alerted in advance to the fact that an application for an order was being made, this could expose the child to an even greater risk of suffering significant harm.[250]

Key legislation

The grounds for making an EPO are set out in section 44(1), which provides:

Where any person ('the applicant') applies to the court for an order to be made under this section with respect to a child, the court may make the order if, but only if, it is satisfied that—

(a) there is reasonable cause to believe that the child is likely to suffer significant harm if—

(i) he is not removed to accommodation provided by or on behalf of the applicant; or

(ii) he does not remain in the place in which he is then being accommodated;

(b) in the case of an application made by a local authority—

(i) enquiries are being made with respect to the child under section 47(1)(b); and

(ii) those enquiries are being frustrated by access to the child being unreasonably refused to a person authorised to seek access and that the applicant has reasonable cause to believe that access to the child is required as a matter of urgency;[251]

---

[249] The other categories are: any person with whom he was living immediately before the making of the order; any person in whose favour a contact order is in force with respect to him; any person who is allowed to have contact with the child by virtue of an order under s 34; any person acting on behalf of any of those persons.

[250] Judith Masson's study of the use of EPOs found variations in the use of 'without notice' applications within different areas. In some areas there were quite high proportions (eg in one area just under 50 per cent of applications), and in areas where the courts were more reluctant to hear applications without notice, 'on notice' applications were much more likely to be preceded by police protection (in one area, in 53 per cent of cases): see J. Masson, 'Emergency Intervention to Protect Children: Using and Avoiding Legal Controls' [2005] Child and Family Law Quarterly 75.

[251] Paragraph (c) makes similar, but not identical, provisions in the case of enquiries made by an authorised person, presently only the NSPCC.

Unlike the child assessment order, *any person* can apply for an emergency protection order via section 44(1)(a), although the 'frustrated access' grounds in section 44(1)(b) and (c) are open only to a local authority and the NSPCC respectively. Paragraph (a) requires that the court has reasonable cause to believe that the child is likely to suffer significant harm unless an EPO is made. In seeking to establish this ground the applicant can put any information before the court, and the court can take it into account regardless of any enactment or rule of law which would otherwise prevent it from doing so, provided that, in the opinion of the court, it is relevant to the application.[252] The applicant must further persuade the court that there is a causative link between the harm being likely to occur and the child being removed from, or remaining in, his present accommodation. Thus, for example, if the child is reasonably believed to have suffered a serious non-accidental injury, but if the person who is suspected of having injured the child has been remanded in custody pending a criminal trial, and the person presently caring for him is not impli-cated in the abuse in any way, it is suggested that it is most unlikely there are grounds for making an EPO. On the other hand, where the alleged abuser has moved out of the home, but where there is uncertainty about where he is living, or whether he will stay away from the child, there may be grounds for an order being made. Where the alleged abuser is still in the home, or intends to discharge the child from hospital, there are likely to be very clear grounds for making the order.

Paragraph (b) is aimed at those cases where a local authority is making section 47 enquiries about the child in order to decide what action they should take to safeguard or promote his welfare.[253] In conducting such enquiries, the local authority must normally obtain access to the child.[254] This provision reflects the findings made in various enquiries which have been conducted into cases where child protection procedures have failed to protect children from being killed as a result of ill-treatment and neglect. These enquiries have emphasised that it is usually imperative that access is obtained to a child where there is a suspicion that he or she is suffering, or is likely to suffer, significant harm.[255] Unless the child is seen, and in the case of a young child physically examined for signs of injuries, ill-treatment, or neglect, and where appropriate (for example in the case of an older child) spoken to in private as well, it may be very easy for a parent to conceal significant harm to the child from a concerned professional. It should be noted that when an application is made under section 44(1)(b) a court is empowered to make an EPO on the basis that the applicant has reasonable cause to *suspect* that the child is suffering, or is likely to suffer, significant harm[256] and has reasonable cause to believe that access to the child is urgently required. This is a lesser standard than the requirement that the court should have rea-sonable cause to *believe* that such harm is likely to occur, which must be proved in rela-tion to applications made under section 44(1)(a). Clearly, where access is being refused, it may be impossible for the applicant to obtain the evidence to substantiate a belief, and therefore a reasonable suspicion provides an adequate basis for an order being made when taken together with access being unreasonably refused.[257]

---

[252] Section 45(7).

[253] On s 47 generally, see Section 4.1.

[254] Section 47(4).

[255] See particularly *A Child in Mind: The Report on the Death of Kimberley Carlile* (Greenwich London Borough Council, 1987).

[256] As this is the wording of s 47(1)(b) under which the enquiry was initiated.

[257] Section 44 (3) provides that any person seeking access to a child in connection with enquiries shall, on being asked to do so, produce some duly authenticated document as evidence that he is such a person.

Key case

In *X Council v B (Emergency Protection Order)*[258] Munby J gave guidance on the use of the EPO jurisdiction. In that case a family had endured significant levels of stress as a result of their children's illnesses. The local authority became concerned at the mother's histrionic reaction to the situation, her alleged mismanagement of the children's medication, and failure to engage appropriately with medical services and offered therapies. When the mother was unwilling to discuss the matter at a strategy meeting, the local authority obtained without notice EPOs, each lasting for eight days, and the three younger children were taken into foster care. The local authority subsequently obtained interim care orders but the issues were satisfactorily resolved through negotiation. Accordingly, the case came before Munby J on the local authority's application to withdraw its application for care orders. Leave was granted. However, Munby J was concerned by some aspects of the way in which the children had entered care via the EPO. While his Lordship considered that the without notice application could be justified because of the possibility that the mother might administer medication and thus thwart the local authority's investigation, he was concerned that the order had been made to last for more than 24 or 48 hours, the time necessary to carry out tests, and that the children had been removed to foster care. His Lordship therefore took an opportunity to explain the human rights context in which the EPO jurisdiction operates. He acknowledged that 'there are cases where the need for such highly intrusive emergency intervention is imperatively demanded'[259] and that in principle the European Court of Human Rights has recognised that emergency removal of children is entirely compatible with the ECHR, including in cases of without notice applications.[260] He observed, however, that an EPO is 'a terrible and drastic remedy'[261] that the European Court had stressed in the context of the removal of a newborn baby that such an order is a 'draconian' and 'extremely harsh' measure, requiring 'exceptional justification' and 'extraordinary compelling reasons'.[262] In his Lordship's view these principles should equally apply to cases of the removal of older children, who, unlike the newborn, will be conscious of what is happening to them in circumstances which may be frightening and/or distressing to the children.[263]

Munby J said that it is important that both the local authority and justices approach every application for an EPO 'with an anxious awareness of the extreme gravity of the relief being sought and a scrupulous regard for the European Convention rights of both the child and the parents'.[264] The Strasbourg jurisprudence, as recognised by the Court of Appeal, repeatedly emphasised that intervention 'must be proportionate to the legitimate aim of protecting the welfare and interests of the child'.[265] Munby J observed that this proportionality was all the more necessary in the context of interim care orders or EPOs 'when there have as yet been no adverse findings against the parent(s)'.[266] Citing *Haase v Germany* at paragraphs [90]–[95], his Lordship drew particular attention to the fact that the test is one of 'necessity' and there is

---

[258] [2004] EWHC 2015 (Fam), [2005] 1 FLR 341 (Munby J).

[259] Ibid, [35], citing from his judgment in *Re M (Care Proceedings: Judicial Review)* [2003] EWHC 850 (Admin), [2003] 2 FLR 171 at [40].

[260] *K and T v Finland* (2000) 31 EHRR 484, [2000] 2 FLR 79; [2001] 2 FLR 707, *P, C and S v UK* (2002) 35 EHRR 31, [2002] 2 FLR 631; *Venema v Netherlands* [2003] 1 FLR 552; *Covezzi and Morselli v Italy* (2003) 38 EHRR 28; and *Haase v Germany* [2004] 2 FLR 39.

[261] [2004] EWHC 2015 (Fam), [2005] 1 FLR 341 at [34].   [262] Ibid.   [263] Ibid.

[264] Ibid, [41].

[265] See *Re O (Supervision Order)* [2001] EWCA Civ 16, [2001] 1 FLR 923 at [28]; *Re B (Care: Interference with Family Life)* [2003] 2 FLR 813 at [34]; *Re O (Care or Supervision Order)* at 760; *Oxfordshire County Council v L (Care or Supervision Order)* [1998] 1 FLR 70 at 74.

[266] *X Council v B* [2004] EWHC 2015 (Fam), [2005] 1 FLR 341 at [44].

a requirement that there be 'imminent danger'.[267] At paragraph [57] of his judgment, Munby J provided a useful summary of the important points. The essential points (adapting Munby J's words) were:

(1)   An EPO should not be made unless the Family Proceedings Court (FPC) is satisfied that it is both necessary and proportionate and that no other less radical form of order will achieve the essential end of promoting the welfare of the child. Separation is only to be contemplated if immediate separation is essential to secure the child's safety: 'imminent danger' must be 'actually established'.

(2)   Any order must provide for the least interventionist solution consistent with the preservation of the child's immediate safety.

(3)   No EPO should be made for any longer than is absolutely necessary to protect the child.

(4)   The evidence in support of the application for an EPO must be full, detailed, precise, and compelling.[268] Unparticularised generalities will not suffice. The sources of hearsay evidence must be identified. Expressions of opinion must be supported by detailed evidence and properly articulated reasoning.

(5)   Save in wholly exceptional cases, parents must be given adequate prior notice of the date, time, and place of any application by a local authority for an EPO. They must also be given proper notice of the evidence the local authority is relying upon.

(6)   There must be compelling reasons for a without notice application which will normally be appropriate only if the case is genuinely one of emergency or other great urgency or if there are compelling reasons to believe that the child's welfare will be compromised if the parents are alerted in advance to what is going on. In such a case there is a duty to make the fullest and most candid and frank disclosure of all the relevant factual and legal matters known to them.

(7)   The FPC must 'keep a note of the substance of the oral evidence' and must also record in writing not merely its reasons but also any findings of fact.

(8)   Parents against whom an EPO is made without notice are entitled to be given, if they ask, proper information as to what happened at the hearing and to be told, if they ask: (i) exactly what documents, bundles, or other evidential materials were lodged with the FPC either before or during the course of the hearing; and (ii) what legal authorities were cited to the FPC.

(9)   The local authority, even after it has obtained an EPO, is under an obligation to consider less drastic alternatives to emergency removal (see s 44(5)).

(10) Section 44(10)(a) and (11)(a) impose on the local authority a continuing duty to exercise exceptional diligence in keeping the case under review day by day so as to ensure that parent and child are separated for no longer than is necessary to secure the child's safety.

(11) Arrangements for contact must be driven by the needs of the family, not stunted by lack of resources.

In *Re X (Emergency Protection Orders)*[269] McFarlane J agreed with each and every one of the observations in paragraph [57] of Munby J's judgment, indicating that they should

---

[267]   See ibid, [46].

[268]   For criticism, see J. Masson, 'Emergency Protection Good Practice and Human Rights' [2004] Family Law 882.

[269]   [2006] EWHC 510 (Fam), [2006] 2 FLR 701.

be required reading for every magistrate and justices' clerk involved in an EPO application.[270] His Lordship advised that the key points made by Munby J in *X Council v B* should be copied and made available to the justices hearing an EPO on each occasion such an application is made and it is the duty of the applicant for an EPO to ensure that the *X Council v B* guidance is brought to the court's attention.

McFarlane J added that the hearing ought to be tape-recorded or a verbatim note taken, and that 'unless there is a very good reason to the contrary, the parents should always be given a full account of the material submitted to the court, the evidence given at the hearing, the submissions made to support the application and the justices' reasons whether the parents ask for this information or not'.[271] In *Re X* a child was on the Child Protection Register in the category of 'emotional harm' and social workers had concerns about the mother's personality. Within two hours of a case conference which had concluded that low-level intervention by way of a psychiatric assessment of the child's mother and a psychological assessment of the child should proceed, the local authority without notice obtained an EPO. The application was prompted by the fact that the mother had presented with the child at a local hospital for a check up as the child was complaining of abdominal pain. A nurse had contacted the social services department reporting that the mother was insisting on the child seeing a doctor despite the fact that a triage nurse had assessed the child and considered that there was no problem. Several elements of the social work team manager's evidence in support of the EPO application were misleading, incomplete, or wrong, presenting a seriously distorted picture to the bench. For example, the nurse's account became inflated to the fact that the mother was demanding further investigations and *treatment*, and the court was also told that the mother was suffering from fabricated or induced illness syndrome[272] despite the fact that this had never been professionally diagnosed. McFarlane J made clear that this 'is not a diagnosis that can be made by social workers acting alone, it is a matter that requires skilled medical appraisal'[273] and must be approached with care and caution in accordance with guidance. His Lordship considered that the processes by which the EPO was obtained were badly flawed.[274] The central errors were that there was no emergency, no imminent danger of harm that justified X's removal, the local authority testimony was partial, inaccurate, and misleading, and the application was made against legal advice. McFarlane J indicated that a local authority lawyer in such circumstances must consider him/herself under a duty to present the case and to ensure that it is presented fairly and that the bench is fully aware of the legal context.[275] Evidence given to the justices should come from the best available source. Where there has been a case conference with respect to the child, the most recent case conference minutes should be produced to the court.[276]

The manner in which the case had been heard was also found wanting. The magistrates had fitted the case round a busy list rather than making separate appropriate time for it and had not separately considered the issue of whether a without notice application could be justified. They had also failed to give full reasons for their decision. McFarlane J gave the following additional guidance on types of cases which will rarely warrant an EPO:[277]

> mere lack of information or a need for assessment can never of themselves establish the existence of a genuine emergency sufficient to justify an EPO. The proper course in such a

---

[270] Ibid, [65].   [271] Ibid, [66].

[272] Fabricating or inducing illness in her child. See for a full discussion of the child protection implication of this problem: Department for Education and Skills, *Safeguarding Children in Whom Illness is Fabricated or Induced* (London: TSO, 2008).   [273] [2006] EWHC 510 (Fam), [2006] 2 FLR 701 at [67].

[274] *Re X* [2006] EWHC 510 (Fam), [2006] 2 FLR 701 at [71].

[275] Ibid, [88].   [276] Ibid, [101].   [277] Ibid, [101].

case is to consider application for a child assessment order or issuing s 31 proceedings and seeking the court's directions under s 38(6) for assessment;...

cases of emotional abuse will rarely, if ever, warrant an EPO, let alone an application without notice;...

cases of sexual abuse where the allegations are inchoate and non-specific, and where there is no evidence of immediate risk of harm to the child, will rarely warrant an EPO;...

cases of fabricated or induced illness, where there is no medical evidence of immediate risk of direct physical harm to the child, will rarely warrant an EPO;...

justices faced with an EPO application in a case of emotional abuse, non-specific allegations of sexual abuse and/or fabricated or induced illness, should actively consider refusing the EPO application on the basis that the local authority should then issue an application for an interim care order.

5.3 INCLUDING AN EXCLUSION REQUIREMENT IN AN EMERGENCY PROTECTION ORDER

Sometimes a preferable response to removal of the child is for action to be taken against the person who is alleged to be endangering him or her. Section 44A(1)[278] provides that the court may include an exclusion requirement in an EPO provided that the conditions in section 44A(2) are satisfied. An exclusion requirement can require the person concerned to leave a dwelling-house in which he is living with the child, prohibit the person entering it, and exclude the person from a defined area in which the relevant dwelling-house is situated.[279]

In essence the conditions require the court to be satisfied that if a person is excluded from the house where the child lives there is reasonable cause to believe that in the case of an order made under section 44(1)(a) the child will not be likely to suffer significant harm even though not removed, or in the case of an order made on the grounds mentioned in paragraph (b) or (c) of section 44(1), that the enquiries referred to in those paragraphs will cease to be frustrated.[280] The court must also ensure that another person living in the same house consents to the exclusion order and is able and willing to give to the child the care which it would be reasonable to expect a parent to give him. The reason why an exclusion requirement is in addition to, rather than an alternative to, an EPO is to give the local authority the power immediately to remove the child where the cooperation of the person caring for the child is withdrawn or the exclusion requirement is otherwise broken.

The attraction of using an exclusion requirement is much stronger where the applicant can be confident that it will be backed up by strong enforcement powers. This is recognised in the legislation. A power of arrest may be attached to an exclusion requirement.[281] This permits a police officer to arrest without warrant any person whom he has reasonable cause to believe to be in breach of the requirement.[282] Consequently, any breach of the order should lead to the arrest of the person excluded and this should avoid the necessity to remove the child, except in those cases where the person caring for the child has colluded in the breach. If the applicant removes the child from the house to other accommodation for more than 24 hours the exclusion requirement ceases to have effect.[283]

Under section 44B a court may accept an undertaking from the relevant person in any case where it has power to include an exclusion requirement in the EPO, but a power of

---

[278] Inserted, together with s 44B by the Family Law Act 1996, s 52, Sch 6, para 3.
[279] Section 44A(3).   [280] Including, where appropriate, a defined area around the house (s 44A(3)).
[281] Section 44A(5).   [282] Section 44A(8).   [283] Section 44A(10).

arrest may not be added to an undertaking.[284] The undertaking is enforceable as if it were an order of the court.[285]

5.4 EXECUTING THE EMERGENCY PROTECTION ORDER: THE ASSISTANCE OF THE POLICE AND HEALTH CARE PROFESSIONALS

When making an EPO the court may direct that the applicant, on exercising any powers conferred by the order, be accompanied by a medical practitioner, nurse, or midwife, if he so chooses.[286] This provision may assist in preventing removal of a child from the home in a case where fears about his health and safety prove to be unfounded. Section 44(5)(a) provides that the applicant shall only exercise the power to remove, or to prevent the removal of, the child in order to safeguard the welfare of the child. In a case where a doctor is willing to accompany the applicant (who will normally be a social worker) to the child's home, a medical examination of the child in the home might sometimes reveal that there is nothing to give rise to concern that the child is suffering, or is likely to suffer, significant harm. In such a case the child should be left where he is. In a case where the child has been removed or retained under an EPO, and where it appears to the applicant that it is safe to return the child, or to allow him to be removed, the child must be returned or his removal must be allowed.[287]

Sometimes an applicant for an EPO may be unsure of the child's whereabouts or be denied entry to premises where he suspects the child to be. Sometimes he may have reasonable cause to believe that there is another child on the premises with respect to whom an EPO ought to be made. In cases of this kind the applicant should apply for orders under section 48(3) and (4) which authorise him to enter premises and search for the children concerned. However, such orders do not authorise the applicant to break into premises by force; where force is needed the police must be involved and a warrant obtained under section 48(9).[288] In difficult cases, particularly where it is anticipated that those looking after the child will respond to being served with an EPO with violence, police involvement is likely to be an added feature of the implementation of the order.

5.5 APPLYING TO DISCHARGE AN EMERGENCY PROTECTION ORDER

The child, a parent, anyone with parental responsibility for the child, or any person with whom the child was living immediately before the making of the order may apply for the EPO to be discharged.[289] However, this provision does not apply in a case where such a person was given at least one day's clear notice of the hearing at which the order was made, and was present at that hearing.[290] Allowing the order to be challenged gives some measure of safeguard to the interests of those persons affected by a without notice application; whereas those persons who had the opportunity to attend the hearing, and did attend, are not further entitled to challenge the order.

---

[284] Section 44B. Undertakings are permitted despite a firm recommendation to the contrary by the Law Commission, see *Domestic Violence and Occupation of the Family Home* (Law Com No 207, 1992), para 6.15.

[285] Section 44B(3)(a).   [286] Section 45(12).   [287] Section 44(10).

[288] See too the Police and Criminal Evidence Act 1984, s 17(1)(e), which authorises the police to enter premises without a warrant where there is an immediate risk to life or limb.   [289] Section 45(8).

[290] Section 45(11); also, an application to discharge cannot be made where the order has been extended under s 45(5).

5.6 CHALLENGING THE MAKING OF, OR REFUSAL TO MAKE, AN EMERGENCY PROTECTION ORDER

Section 45(10) provides that no appeal may be made against the making of, or refusal to make, an EPO or against any direction given by the court in connection with such an order. In *Essex County Council v F*,[291] Douglas Brown J held that section 45(10) allows no scope for the use of the appellate process, and he ruled that if magistrates act unreasonably in refusing to make an order the only possible remedy is in proceedings brought in judicial review. But, of course, judicial review proceedings are totally impracticable in an emergency situation; they are not designed to provide speedy relief.[292] Douglas Brown J arrived at his ruling in *Essex County Council v F* with considerable regret because the facts 'cried out for the intervention of the court'; however, he took the view that the words of the statute gave him no alternative.[293]

It is suggested that the combined effect of section 45(10) and the ruling in *Essex County Council v F* is particularly alarming when it is recalled that applications for an EPO are often heard by a single magistrate. It cannot be acceptable that nothing further can be done to protect a child in a case where, as in the *Essex* case, the court's decision is plainly wrong. In that case, the mother promised the local authority that she would not remove the child from her foster parents until the hearing of the application in care proceedings, which would come before the court a few days later. However, other mothers might not be so compliant, and the fact that the child was secure in the *Essex* case may have lulled the judge into a false sense of security. It is the precedent force of *Essex County Council v F* in relation to other cases which makes the decision so disturbing. A child could be put in grave danger by the wrongful refusal of a court to make an EPO. He might even be badly injured or killed. It cannot be acceptable that the courts are apparently powerless to protect a child in circumstances of this kind.

It is therefore necessary to search for possible solutions and to consider what might be done if a case of this kind arose again. One possibility might be for the local authority to make a fresh application for an EPO to a judge, probably a High Court judge. Where a child's safety is gravely at risk, a judge might find that he has the power to make the order requested. There is no actual precedent which prevents the judge from making such an order, and he would be likely to be very aware of his own personal responsibility for any possible tragic outcome of his refusal to do so.

Another possibility might be to make an application for leave to invoke the inherent jurisdiction of the High Court. Section 100(4) allows use of the court's inherent jurisdiction where the court is satisfied that the result which the authority wishes to achieve could not be achieved through the making of any order other than in the exercise of the court's inherent jurisdiction. The local authority might thus rely on section 100(4) and ask the court to make an order placing the child in the care of an individual (but not, of course, an order which placed the child in the care of the local authority, or in local authority accommodation, as this is prohibited by section 100(2)). The court might, for example, order that the child be kept in hospital or live with a relative or friend of the family or possibly even with the local authority foster parents with whom he has been living, but only in their personal capacity and not as agents of the local authority.

---

[291] [1993] 1 FLR 847.

[292] On the possibility of the use of judicial review, see Munby J in *X Council v B* [2004] EWHC 2015 (Fam) at [40].

[293] See also the concerns of Johnson J in *Re P (Emergency Protection Order)* [1996] 1 FLR 482.

6   POLICE PROTECTION: CHILDREN ACT 1989, SECTION 46

The police have their own separate powers to remove children to suitable accommodation and to keep them there, or to prevent the child's removal from hospital or any other place. A police constable may exercise these powers where he has reasonable cause to believe that the child would otherwise be likely to suffer significant harm.[294] Section 46, together with Home Office Circular 017/2008, provides a code of guidance on how the police should exercise their powers, and how they should inform the parents and liaise with the local authority once they have taken the child into police protection. No child may be kept in police protection for more than 72 hours.[295] However, while a child is being kept in police protection, a designated officer may apply on behalf of the appropriate authority for an EPO to be made under section 44 with respect to the child.[296]

In *Langley v Liverpool City Council*[297] the Court of Appeal considered the relationship between an EPO and the use of police protection. All of the Langley family were profoundly deaf, apart from one of their four children, Callum, aged 4. The father also had Usher's Syndrome, which meant that he had tunnel vision and night blindness. He was registered blind. Despite this disability the father persisted in driving his car with the children, which was a matter of great concern to the local authority. The local authority became aware that Mr Langley had driven with Callum and the two older children from Liverpool to Derby where the older children were to be assessed for several days at the Royal School for the Deaf. The local authority obtained an EPO in respect of these three children and foster parents were alerted. By the time the EPO had been obtained, the parents and Callum had returned by car to Liverpool, although the local authority could not locate the whereabouts of the family who were not at home. Later the same evening the social worker asked the police to assist in finding the family and they were finally located at home. On locating the family the police officer concerned spoke to a member of the social work emergency duty team, who indicated that they wanted Callum to be taken into care. The police officer decided to remove Callum to foster care. The following day the social workers executed the EPO in respect of the other two children by removing them from the school. In claims by the parents a judge found against the police and the council that the children's removals were unlawful, and the police and the council appealed to the Court of Appeal. The judge had held that, if an EPO is in force, the police cannot invoke section 46, and the only part that the police can play is by assisting, authorised by a warrant under section 48(9). The Court of Appeal disagreed with this analysis, holding that there 'is nothing in the language of the Act which compels the conclusion that s 46 cannot be invoked where an EPO is in force'.[298] However, the court held that 'discretionary statutory powers must be exercised to promote the policy and objects of the statute'[299] and that 'the statutory scheme clearly accords primacy to s 44'.[300] The court

---

[294] Section 46(1).   [295] Section 46(6).   [296] Section 46(7).

[297] [2005] EWCA Civ 1173, [2006] 1 FLR 342.   [298] Ibid, [30].

[299] Ibid, [33], citing *Padfield and Others v Minister of Agriculture, Fisheries and Food and Others* [1968] AC 997 at 1030C.

[300] *Langley* [2005] EWCA Civ 1173, [2006] 1 FLR 342 at [38]. At [37] the court pointed to a number of important differences between the s 44 and s 46 regimes. They include the following. First, the court can give directions with respect to contact, examinations and assessments. This is a valuable power not available to the police. Secondly, an EPO gives the applicant parental responsibility, whereas while a child is being kept in police protection under s 46 neither the constable nor the designated officer has parental responsibility. Thirdly, no child can be kept in police protection for more than 72 hours, whereas an EPO may have effect for a period not exceeding 8 days (s 45(1)), and this period may be extended by up to 7 days (s 45(5)).

therefore held that 'where a police officer knows that an EPO is in force, he should not exercise the power of removing a child under s 46, unless there are compelling reasons to do so'.[301] The court explained that: '(i) removal of children should usually be effected pursuant to an EPO; and (ii) s 46 should be invoked only where it is not practicable to execute an EPO. In deciding whether it is practicable to execute an EPO, the police must always have regard to the paramount need to protect children from significant harm.'[302] The court held on the facts that there had been no compelling reason to use section 46; the police officer should have requested the emergency duty team to execute the EPO. Accordingly the police were liable for the unlawful removal of Callum, and the council had also acted unlawfully in 'ordering' Callum's removal.

Langley was applied in *A v East Sussex County Council and Chief Constable of Sussex Police*.[303] A baby was admitted to hospital after the mother alerted the emergency services to the fact that the child had stopped breathing. Two days later the medical staff thought the child fit for discharge. However, the mother, who had suffered post-natal depression and who was described as an anxious mother, had reported two further incidents of the child stopping breathing, although no one else had witnessed these events and no explanation could be found. The consultant doctor was concerned that this might be a case of factitious illness and that it was not safe for the child to go home without professional supervision. The mother was uncooperative, indicating that she wished to take the child home with only family supervision, and on one occasion 'kicked off' threatening to take the child home. The child was removed into foster care using the power of police protection in section 46. The mother subsequently agreed to go with the child to a mother and baby unit and following a positive assessment the mother and baby were allowed to go home. Proceedings were discontinued. The mother then brought a claim under section 7 of the Human Rights Act 1998 against the police and East Sussex County Council, the issue being whether the actions of the respondents were lawful and proportionate. The judge dismissed the claim and the mother's appeal to the Court of Appeal was dismissed. The Court of Appeal held that in the circumstances the judge had been entitled to reach the view that the respondents' actions were lawful. Applying *Langley v Liverpool City Council*,[304] the court held that on the facts as honestly and reasonably believed by the respondents at the time it had not been practicable to execute an EPO. Given the consultant's opinion regarding the child's safety, the fact that there was no agreement that the mother would not exercise her otherwise lawful right to remove the child, and the fact that the social services and police would not necessarily be able to keep track of her once she left, section 46 was required urgently to avert potential danger to the child. Hedley J (with whom Jackson and Carnwath LJJ agreed) commented:

> Sadly the experiences of the appellant simply illustrate the truth that viable child protection procedures in any society will sometimes inflict what turns out to have been unnecessary distress on families. That does not make them or the exercise of them thereby unlawful.[305]

In *Re D (Unborn Baby)*[306] the question arose as to whether it was lawful for the local authority to conceal from a pregnant mother and her partner its plan to remove the child immediately upon birth by way of police protection under section 46 of the Children Act 1989. The mother was in prison as a result of an assault against her own child. On an occasion of supervised contact she had blindfolded and gagged the child before threatening

[301] Ibid, [36].   [302] Ibid, [40].   [303] [2010] EWCA Civ 743, [2010] 2 FLR 1596.
[304] [2005] EWCA Civ 1173, [2006] 1 FLR 342.   [305] [2010] EWCA Civ 743, [21].
[306] [2009] EWHC 446 (Fam), [2009] 2 FLR 313.

her with a knife over a period of 15 minutes. Since arriving in prison the mother had attempted suicide and had made worrying statements that her children would be better off dead than in the care of the local authority. She had been described by a psychologist as 'an emotionally desperate woman' who 'remains likely to engage in impulsive acts when frustrated and angry'. In these circumstances, the local authority had real concerns that she might lash out at her child if she were aware that the child was to be removed shortly after birth. As the child was not yet born, the court did not have any powers under the Children Act 1989 nor could the court exercise its inherent jurisdiction.[307] The local authority therefore sought declaratory relief,[308] declaring that its proposed future course of conduct would be lawful. Munby J held that the same principles that apply regarding the necessity and proportionality of state intervention in family life applied to the question before him.[309] The test is therefore: 'Is the step which the local authority is proposing to take, that is, the step of not involving the parents in its planning and not communicating to the parents its plan for immediate removal at birth, something which is justified by "the overriding necessity of the interests of the child" or something which is "essential to secure [the child's] safety"?'[310]

Munby J had no hesitation in concluding that in the circumstances 'the very stringent test' for the local authority lawfully to take this 'very drastic and highly unusual step' was 'more than adequately met'.[311] His Lordship emphasised, however, that it will only be in very unusual and exceptional cases that a local authority will be so justified.[312]

Judith Masson's study of police protection[313] found that one of the main categories of use was in response to requests by social workers out of hours, for example in the case of emergency duty teams lacking court work experience. The prior existence of police protection then tended to reinforce the local authority's case on a subsequent application for an EPO. In light of her findings, Masson rightly questions whether these practices surrounding emergency intervention adequately secure accountability and protect parents' rights.[314]

7 INTERIM CARE AND SUPERVISION ORDERS

Where the local authority concludes that the only way to provide the child with the protection needed is for it either to share parental responsibility with his or her parents or to have the power formally to supervise the child's upbringing, it must bring an application for a care order or supervision order. Research shows that care proceedings are not brought without good reason.[315] Most cases contain multiple allegations of parenting

---

[307] See *Re F (In Utero) (Wardship)* [1988] Fam 122, [1988] 2 FLR 307.

[308] On which see *Re F (Mental Patient: Sterilisation)* [1990] 2 AC 1, [1989] 2 FLR 376.

[309] [2009] EWHC 446 (Fam), [2009] 2 FLR 313 at [11].   [310] Ibid.   [311] Ibid, [15] and [23].

[312] His Lordship was of the view that the factual situation was rather different from that in *P, C and S v UK* (App no 56547/00) (2002) 35 EHRR 31, [2002] 2 FLR 631, ECtHR in which a risk of poisoning to the child could be more easily controlled on the birth of the child. See [26].

[313] J. Masson, 'Police Protection—Protecting Whom?' (2002) Journal of Social Welfare and Family Law 157.

[314] J. Masson, 'Emergency Intervention to Protect Children: Using and Avoiding Legal Controls' [2005] Child and Family Law Quarterly 75 at 94–96. Dame Margaret Booth, *Delay in Public Law Children Act Cases—Second Report* (1996) found that in some areas police protection powers, rather than EPOs, were used when the crisis arose out of hours: at para 8.15.

[315] J. Masson, J. Pearce, and K. Bader with O. Joyner, J. Marsden, and D. Westlake, *Care Profiling Study* (Ministry of Justice, March 2008).

failures, in respect of parents who have multiple vulnerability factors (eg alcohol/drug abuse, mental health problems, chaotic lifestyles).[316]

Key legislation

Section 31(2) of the Children Act 1989 provides:

A court may only make a care order or supervision order if it is satisfied—

(a) that the child concerned is suffering, or is likely to suffer, significant harm; and

(b) that the harm, or likelihood of harm, is attributable to—

(i) the care given to the child, or likely to be given to him if the order were not made, not being what it would be reasonable to expect a parent to give to him; or

(ii) the child's being beyond parental control.

When an application is first made in care proceedings it would be most unusual for either the local authority, or the other parties to the proceedings, to be in a position fully to present their case. Moreover, the court will wish to have an independent investigation of the child's circumstances. Meanwhile arrangements must be made about where the child will live and with whom he may have contact. Sometimes the local authority will be satisfied that the child can be protected from harm if he remains living at home pending the final hearing of their application. It may, for example, be able to persuade the person whom it alleges is causing significant harm to the child to move away from the premises.[317] Sometimes a relative or friend of the child will offer to look after him and this may give the child the protection needed. In a case of this kind it may be appropriate to make a residence order to the person offering to care for the child, in which case section 38(3) provides that the court must make an interim supervision order unless satisfied that the child's welfare will be satisfactorily safeguarded without such an order being made. Sometimes the local authority will offer to accommodate the child under section 20, and his parents, and any others with parental responsibility, may be willing to comply with this arrangement. It is where voluntary arrangements of this nature cannot be agreed, or where the local authority takes the view that it will not give the child sufficient protection, or where the local authority takes the view that it needs to have parental responsibility for the child during the period preceding the final hearing, that it is likely to make an application for an interim order.

Section 38(1) provides that where in any proceedings for a care order or supervision order[318] the proceedings are adjourned, the court may make an interim care order or an interim supervision order. There is also power to make an interim order where the court gives a direction under section 37(1) that the local authority should investigate the child's circumstances.

---

[316] J. Brophy, *Research Review: Child care proceedings under the Children Act 1989*, DCA Research Series 5/06 (May 2006).

[317] It may assist that person to obtain alternative accommodation under Sch 2, para 5. It may also assist a parent to bring proceedings under Pt IV of the Family Law Act 1996 for an occupation order excluding a spouse, partner, or other 'associated person' from the home; see Chapter 3. See also the possibility of an exclusion requirement in s 38A, discussed in Section 7.6.

[318] But not in an application to extend a supervision order: see *Re A (Supervision Order: Extension)* [1995] 1 FLR 335.

7.1 DURATION OF INTERIM ORDERS AND RENEWAL

Section 38(4) makes provision for various time limits to be imposed when an interim order is made; in essence these provide that the maximum period for the initial interim order is eight weeks and that subsequent orders may be made to last for a maximum of four weeks.[319] The temporary nature of an interim order allows the court to maintain a degree of control over the steps taken by the local authority in the interim period. Issues can be raised about how the local authority is exercising its parental responsibility under the order each time an application is made for the renewal of the order. Where the court is dissatisfied with action taken by the local authority it can refuse to make a further interim order.[320] In *Re G (Minors) (Interim Care Order)*,[321] Waite LJ commented that:

> the clear intention to be inferred from s 38 of the Act [is] that Parliament intended the regime of an interim care order to operate as a tightly run procedure closely monitored by the court and affording to all parties an opportunity of frequent review as events unfold during the currency of the order. That purpose would be frustrated if a practice were to be allowed to grow up under which renewals of interim care orders were sought routinely by local authorities without any attempt to keep the court up to date with progress, or granted by the court perfunctorily without any of the inquiries necessary to eliminate the risk of essential disclosure being lost through administrative lethargy.

In *Re B (Interim Care Orders: Renewal)*[322] Black J held that the court has a discretion to control its procedure and evidence on an application for renewal of an interim care order. In that case a local authority had obtained an interim care order in respect of a boy, aged 9. The boy was home schooled and the local authority had concerns that, although bright and intellectually ahead of many of his peer group, he was emotionally and socially immature and would benefit from mixing with peers at school. The mother was strongly opposed to the local authority's intervention and the case came before a District Judge on the fourth contested application for renewal of the interim care order in six months. On this fourth occasion the District Judge refused to have a fully contested hearing and limited counsel for the mother's submissions to any change of circumstances. On appeal the mother contended that her rights under Article 6 of the ECHR and her procedural rights under Article 8 had been breached by the District Judge's approach. Black J dismissed the appeal, holding that while there is clearly no rule to the effect that no renewal application can be fully contested unless a change of circumstances is shown, a judge's discretion can be exercised in an appropriate case (such as this) to concentrate upon changes of circumstance.[323]

7.2 INTERIM CARE AND SUPERVISION ORDERS: THE THRESHOLD

An application for an interim care or supervision order 'must be approached in two stages'.[324] The first stage is the threshold contained in section 38(2) of the Children Act 1989, which provides that a court shall not make an interim care order or an interim supervision order unless it is satisfied that there are *reasonable grounds for believing* that

---

[319] The position is slightly more complicated than as described; however, there is nothing in s 38 which prevents a number of consecutive interim orders from being made. See s 38(4), (5), and (10).

[320] See *Re G (Minors) (Interim Care Order)* [1993] 2 FLR 839, CA.   [321] Ibid.

[322] [2001] 2 FLR 1217, FD.

[323] Ibid, 1223–1224. See at 1224 where the factors that are likely to be important are highlighted.

[324] *Re GR (Care Order)* [2010] EWCA Civ 871, [2011] 1 FLR 669 at [33].

the circumstances with respect to the child are as mentioned in section 31(2). This means that the court does not have to be satisfied in fact that the grounds exist but simply that there are reasonable grounds for believing that they do.[325] Thus, evidence which might not be sufficient to satisfy the court at a final hearing may be acceptable to discharge the lower standard for an interim care order. An interim care order can be made despite the fact that a parent, relative, or other person who has not caused the child to suffer, and is not likely to cause the child to suffer, significant harm is offering to look after the child pending the final hearing.[326]

7.3 DECIDING WHETHER OR NOT TO GRANT THE ORDER

If the threshold is passed, the court must then go on to consider as a discrete issue whether or not to grant the order. This is a question to which section 1 of the Children Act 1989 applies, which must be applied having regard to the purpose of an interim order which is to 'establish a holding position pending a full hearing'.[327] As the Court of Appeal put it in *Re G (Minors) (Interim Care Order)*,[328] the 'making of an interim care order is an essentially impartial step, favouring neither one side nor the other, and affording no one, least of all the local authority in whose favour it is made, an opportunity for tactical or adventitious advantage'.[329] Thorpe LJ explained in *Re LA (Care: Chronic Neglect)*[330] that 'the decision taken by the court on an interim care order application must necessarily be limited to issues that cannot await the fixture and must not extend to issues that are being prepared for determination at that fixture'.[331] An application for an interim order is not a trial run for the final hearing, and the courts have ruled that evidence, and the cross-examination of witnesses, should be restricted to the issues which are essential at the interim stage.[332]

A local authority may wish, by way of an interim care order, to remove a child from home and place a child with another parent,[333] a relative, or a foster carer, or continue an existing removal which began under an EPO. The courts have provided guidance on how to approach applications for interim care orders in such cases. In *Re LA (Care: Chronic Neglect)*[334] Thorpe LJ extracted from earlier Court of Appeal authorities[335] the proposition

---

[325] *Re B (A Minor) (Care Order: Criteria)* [1993] 1 FLR 815 (Douglas Brown J).

[326] *Re M (A Minor) (Care Order: Threshold Conditions)* discussed in Section 8.2 in detail.

[327] *Re GR (Care Order)* [2010] EWCA Civ 871, [2011] 1 FLR 669 at [35].   [328] [1993] 2 FLR 839, CA.

[329] Ibid, 845. It was common ground in *Re G* that the threshold criteria in s 31 were fulfilled, and the court pointed out that in such a case the making of an interim care order is a neutral method of preserving the status quo. See the apparent endorsement of this decision in *Re B (Care Proceedings: Interim Care Order)* [2009] EWCA Civ 1254, [2010] 1 FLR 1211 at [52] and [53]. See also *per* Baroness Hale of Richmond in *Re G (Interim Care Order: Residential Assessment)* [2006] 1 AC 576 at [57]: 'This does not pre-judge the eventual outcome of the case'.   [330] [2009] EWCA Civ 822, [2010] 1 FLR 80.

[331] Ibid, [7], drawing on *Re H (A Child) (Interim Order)* [2002] EWCA Civ 1932, [2003] 1 FCR 350 at [38] and [39].

[332] *Hampshire County Council v S* [1993] 1 FLR 559; *Re W (A Minor) (Interim Care Order)* [1994] 2 FLR 892.

[333] The placement could be outside the jurisdiction with permission granted under Sch 2, para 19 of the Children Act 1989. See *Islington London Borough Council v EV* [2010] EWHC 3240 (Fam), [2011] 1 FLR 1681 (assessment of 4-year-old boy's placement with Turkish father in Turkey following mother's mental illness).

[334] [2009] EWCA Civ 822, [2010] 1 FLR 80.

[335] *Re H (A Child) (Interim Order)* [2002] EWCA Civ 1932, [2003] 1 FCR 350 at [39] and *Re K and H* [2006] EWCA Civ 1898, [2007] 1 FLR 2043 at [16].

that 'separation is only to be ordered if the child's safety demands immediate separation'. [336] Thus, for example, in *Re K and H*[337] the Court of Appeal had so held in setting aside orders which removed children from their father's care because of concerns that he was facing serious criminal charges for drug offences. The facts did not disclose a need for immediate separation.

Thorpe LJ's analysis of the authorities was endorsed by Wall LJ in *Re B (Care Proceedings: Interim Care Order)*.[338] The case concerned a boy aged 6 and a girl aged 2. The boy was found on a visit to his home to be living in such alarming conditions that he was immediately removed under police protection and the parents were arrested on suspicion of child cruelty or wilful neglect. The boy was being kept in a filthy, poorly furnished bedroom, possibly in darkness, with no toys. These conditions were in marked contrast to the conditions in which the younger sister lived. She had 'a nicely decorated, furnished bedroom replete with appropriate toys'.[339] Subsequently, interim care orders were sought in respect of both children. The judge refused to make an order in respect of the girl. On appeal, the Court of Appeal found that the judge had directed himself immaculately by asking the following question: 'whether the continued removal of [the girl] from the care of her parents is proportionate to the risk of harm to which she will be exposed if she is allowed to return to her parents' care?' However, the judge's conclusion had seriously understated the treatment of the boy and was plainly wrong. Wall LJ found that there was abundant material from which to conclude that the child's safety, 'using that word in a broad sense to include her psychological welfare', did require interim protection.[340] In *Re GR (Care Order)*[341] the Court of Appeal invited particular attention to Wall LJ's definition of 'safety', commenting that the concept of safety is not confined to physical safety and includes the child's emotional safety or psychological welfare.[342] In *Re B (Interim Care Order)*[343] the Court of Appeal said that the test enunciated by the trial judge, which was approved in *Re B (Care Proceedings: Interim Care Order)*,[344] 'is one which can be universally applied'.[345]

Re B (Interim Care Order) provides an example of a case in which the test in *Re LA* was plainly met.[346] In that case there was a long history of domestic violence between the parents and the local authority sought interim care orders to remove two children, aged 9 and 11, to foster care pending the local authority's assessment of the mother's ability to disengage from the father and to parent the children appropriately on her own. The Court of Appeal held that the judge had been correct to make the orders, there being an abundance of evidence that the exercise could only safely be attempted if the children were not living with the mother.[347]

By contrast, in *Re F (Care Proceedings: Interim Care Order)*[348] the test in *Re LA* was not satisfied. In that case a mother gave birth to twins. Her four older children had been taken into care, one within the previous year. It was common ground that the parents were competent to deliver good enough standards of care to the children in the interim.

---

[336] In *Re L (Care Proceedings: Removal of Child)* [2008] 1 FLR 575, Ryder J sought to articulate the test by reference to the following words: 'an imminent risk of really serious harm ie whether the risk to [the child's] safety demands immediate separation'. However, the words 'imminent risk of really serious harm' had apparently caused some confusion and Thorpe LJ in *Re LA (Care: Chronic Neglect)* took the opportunity to reassert the test as traditionally understood.   [337] [2006] EWCA Civ 1898, [2007] 1 FLR 2043.

[338] [2009] EWCA Civ 1254, [2010] 1 FLR 1211.

[339] The judge's description, cited at [22] of the Court of Appeal's judgment.

[340] [2009] EWCA Civ 1254, [2010] 1 FLR 1211 at [56].

[341] [2010] EWCA Civ 871, [2011] 1 FLR 669.   [342] Ibid, [42].

[343] [2010] EWCA Civ 324, [2010] 2 FLR 283.   [344] [2009] EWCA Civ 1254, [2010] 1 FLR 1211.

[345] [2010] EWCA Civ 324, [2010] 2 FLR 283 at [21].   [346] Ibid, [19].

[347] Ibid, [13].   [348] [2010] EWCA Civ 826, [2010] 2 FLR 1455.

However, the judge, placing emphasis on the history, made interim care orders removing the children from the parents on the basis that the children were at risk of emotional harm. Thorpe LJ held that the orders should be set aside: the judge had wrongly strayed into matters which fell to be addressed at the final hearing and her conclusion on the facts did 'not begin to meet the high threshold set by the authorities'.[349] Hedley J agreed, adding that while the child's welfare is the paramount consideration, fairness to parents is a matter that should be in the mind of the court at every stage of the proceedings. His Lordship observed that it 'can hardly be in the welfare of a child for the parents not to be given a fair opportunity for that child to be able to be brought up by them rather than by strangers'.[350] Sir Nicholas Wall P agreed with both judgments, observing that the same conclusion would have been reached had the trial judge correctly applied the test in *Re B*: in his Lordship's view, it 'would not have been a proportionate exercise of discretion to remove a child in the circumstances of this case'.[351] That is not to say that emotional harm can never justify an interim care order.[352]

In *Re M (Interim Care Order: Removal)*[353] the Court of Appeal made clear that a judge must consider the risk to the child from removal as well as the risks alleged by the local authority. In that case, R, the youngest of four children, aged 2, was removed under an interim care order to foster care, although the local authority had been unable to implement interim care orders in respect of the three older children, who absconded home and were living with the parents. The local authority's concerns related to domestic violence. The court saw the short-term risk to the child from the domestic violence over a four-month period awaiting trial as a relatively insignificant one of being caught in some physical cross-fire given that there was no evidence of anything of that sort happening in the past. It also saw the continuation of the order as difficult to defend given that the judge had allowed the older children, who were at greater risk from the domestic violence, to remain at home.[354] The court also found that the judge had failed to put in the balance risk of harm to R of short-term emotional harm of deprivation of her parents, siblings, and home.[355] The court concluded that 'the very high standard that must be established to justify the continuing removal of a child from home' had not been made good and set aside the order.

There have been concerns that the test for making an interim care order is in some cases too high. Darren Howe[356] expresses concern that chronic situations (such as the domestic violence situation in *Re M (Interim Care Order: Removal)*[357] discussed earlier) and long-term neglect cases sit uncomfortably with the current test for interim removal and children in such situations are unlikely to be protected. He comments that 'we should not be leaving children in neglectful situations for months on end' pending final hearings. Andrew Bainham has highlighted the opposite problem; that in some circumstances in practice the bar may be set too low and interim care orders are being made too readily by lower courts.[358] Bainham's concern is with a prevalent practice whereby parents neither consent to nor oppose the making of the first interim care order. Of particular concern is the fact that in many cases the parents' position is unlikely to represent a true lack of opposition because of various pressures (eg the perception of the need to cooperate to achieve reunification with the child, and a wish to avoid an interim court ruling on the

---

[349] Ibid, [23].   [350] Ibid, [29].   [351] Ibid, [32].

[352] See eg *Re A (Children) (Interim Care Order)* [2001] 3 FCR 402 (emotional abuse from failure to protect children from local community's influence over children giving evidence against their father in criminal proceedings).   [353] [2005] EWCA Civ 1594, [2006] 1 FLR 1043.

[354] Ibid, [25].   [355] Ibid, [23] and [24].

[356] D. Howe, 'Removal of Children at Interim Hearings: Is the Test Now Set Too High?' [2009] Family Law 320.   [357] [2005] EWCA Civ 1594, [2006] 1 FLR 1043.

[358] A. Bainham, 'Interim Care Orders: Is the Bar Set Too Low?' [2011] Family Law 374.

threshold criteria). The reason for the local authority's application will usually be that it will want parental responsibility and to have a more secure basis to promote the child's welfare during the care proceedings. However, Bainham points out that, in contrast to the Court of Appeal's characterisation of interim care orders as 'neutral' holding orders, this is not a credible view from the perspective of parents. Bainham argues that to achieve the local authority's aims without the juggernaut of care starting to roll by way of an interim care order, a solution might be to extend availability of the parental responsibility orders and agreements to local authorities, provided they have already instituted care proceedings. Alternatively, he argues, it might be possible to introduce a new, intermediate order, with new nomenclature which avoids at the interim stage the pejorative connotations which entering care has for many parents.

7.4 INTERIM CARE ORDERS AND ASSESSMENT

In the period between first making an application in care proceedings and the final hearing a local authority will normally wish to carry out a careful assessment of the child, his parents, his siblings, and others, such as relatives, who are important persons in his or her life. The purpose of this assessment is to give the local authority a clearer idea about the nature of the harm which the child is suffering, or is likely to suffer, and to whom it can be attributed. The local authority also needs to give close attention to whether a care or supervision order is the most appropriate response to the child's circumstances, and to decide on the arrangements it wishes to make for the future care of the child should it obtain a care order. Where the local authority has been granted an interim care order it will have parental responsibility for the child and thus will have the necessary powers in relation to the child to enable it to carry out a proper assessment. Indeed, as we have seen, this may well be one of the reasons why the local authority has sought an interim care order. The general principle is that where a court makes a care order, be it an interim order or a final order, it loses its powers over the child's upbringing and gives control to the local authority.[359] A care order is a 'care order' whether the order made is interim or final[360] and a court cannot normally attach conditions or give directions about where the child shall live once a care order has been made.[361] However, one exception to this principle is to be found in section 38(6) and (7) of the Children Act 1989, which empower the courts to exercise a large measure of control over the assessment process despite the fact that an interim care order is in force.

Section 38(6) provides:

> Where the court makes an interim care order, or interim supervision order, it may give such directions (if any) as it considers appropriate with regard to the medical or psychiatric examination or other assessment of the child;[362] but if the child is of sufficient

---

[359] This principle stems from the pre-Children Act 1989 ruling of the House of Lords in *A v Liverpool City Council* [1982] AC 363; and see M. Hayes, 'The Proper Role of Courts in Child Care Cases' (1996) 8 Child and Family Law Quarterly 201. For a different view see J. Dewar, 'The Courts and Local Authority Autonomy' (1995) 7 Child and Family Law Quarterly 15.   [360] Section 31(11).

[361] *Re T (A Minor) (Care Order: Conditions)* [1994] 2 FLR 243; *Re L (Interim Care Order: Power of Court)* [1996] 2 FLR 742.

[362] In *Re W (Assessment of Child)* 1998] 2 FLR 130 the Court of Appeal held that the power in s 38(6) is wide enough to direct that an assessment be undertaken by a named individual although the court recognised that its jurisdiction is limited by the fact that it cannot compel an individual who is either unable or unwilling to carry out the assessment. The court commented that it should not encourage applications naming individuals and that if it is intended to name an individual the court should ascertain in advance that the individual is willing to act. The court suggested that a better practice might be to direct that the assessment

understanding to make an informed decision he may refuse to submit to the examination or other assessment.

Section 38(7) provides:

A direction under subsection (6) may be to the effect that there is to be—

(a) no such examination or assessment; or

(b) no such examination or assessment unless the court directs otherwise.

These directions may be given when the interim order is made, or at any time when it is in force, and an application may be made at any time for a direction to be varied.[363] Subsection (6) reflects the need of the court to obtain information and guidance from doctors, social workers, and others about the child and his circumstances in order to assist it to determine whether the threshold test has been crossed, and to decide what order, if any, to make.

A local authority must comply with a direction under section 38(6) or (7).[364]

The scope of the court's powers under section 38(6) and their inter-relationship with the powers of the local authority at the interim stages of a child protection case were considered by the House of Lords in *Re C (Interim Care Order: Residential Assessment)*.[365] C had suffered very serious and unexplained injuries while being looked after by his parents. An interim care order was made and C was placed with foster parents. C's parents, who were immature, lacked family support, and had a difficult relationship with each other, nonetheless had extensive contact with C and showed progress in caring for him. A clinical psychologist and the guardian ad litem, were firmly of the view that a proper evaluation of the parents' ability to care for C should be carried out before a final order was made, and that such an evaluation could only be carried out by means of an in-depth assessment at a residential unit. Hogg J ordered that the residential assessment take place, rejecting the local authority's submission that the court had no jurisdiction under section 38(6) to make such an order. The Court of Appeal reluctantly allowed the authority's appeal and gave leave to appeal to the House of Lords.

The point of construction for the House of Lords was whether the Court of Appeal had been correct to take a narrow view of the words 'other assessment of the child' in section 38(6) and to rule that they had to be construed as *ejusdem generis* with the words 'medical or psychiatric examination'. Their Lordships held that this narrow construction was wrong, that the words were wide enough to embrace a joint assessment of the child and his parents together. Accordingly, they ruled that Hogg J did have jurisdiction to order a residential assessment.[366] Lord Browne-Wilkinson, who delivered the sole

be carried out by a 'suitably qualified individual' as in *Berkshire County Council v C and Others* [1993] Fam 203, [1993] 1 FLR 569, [1993] 2 WLR 475, FD

[363] Section 38(8).

[364] *Re O (Minors) (Medical Examination)* [1993] 1 FLR 860. The local authority were unsuccessful in their appeal against a direction from justices that the children concerned should be tested to discover whether they were HIV positive.

[365] [1997] 1 FLR 1. For further discussion, see C. Smith, 'Judicial Power and Local Authority Discretion— The Contested Frontier' (1997) 9 Child and Family Law Quarterly 243.

[366] Their Lordships accepted that orders under s 38(6) have significant cost implications but held that this was not a reason for refusing to make an order, rather it was a matter the court should take into account when exercising its discretion. In *Re W (Assessment of Child)* [1998] 2 FLR 130, the Court of Appeal commented that local authority resources, both human and financial, and legal aid funds should all be borne in mind. Consequently, such applications should not be encouraged. See too, *Berkshire County Council v C* [1993] 1 FLR 569; *Re M (Residential Assessment Directions)* [1998] 2 FLR 371.

speech, pointed out that the interaction between a child and his parents and others looking after him is an essential element in making any assessment of the child.[367] He stated
that section 38(6) should be construed purposively so as to give effect to the underlying
intentions of Parliament, namely to enable the court to obtain the information necessary
for its own decision.[368]

The House of Lords had another occasion to consider section 38(6) in *Re G (A Minor)*
(Interim Care Order: Residential Assessment).[369] In that case the mother's second child had
died from a non-accidental injury in circumstances in which a judge was unable to decide
which of the parents had caused the injuries. The mother's first child, by another man, was
protected by being placed with his father. The mother then formed a more promising relationship with another man and they had a girl, Ellie. After a period of assessment of the
mother's ability to address the issues surrounding the death of her second child, Johnson J
held that he had no power under section 38(6) to direct at the local authority's expense a
further period of psychotherapy for the mother because it fell on the side of therapy rather
than assessment. The Court of Appeal allowed an appeal, holding that the essential question was not one of distinguishing between therapy and assessment but whether what is
sought can broadly be classified as assessment to enable the court to obtain the information necessary for its decision. On appeal to the House of Lords, the issue was whether
on the true construction of section 38(6) the Court of Appeal had correctly identified the
essential question for the court. The House of Lords allowed the appeal. Baroness Hale of
Richmond delivered the leading opinion, with which there was unanimous agreement.
Examining the legislative history of section 38(6) and (7) she concluded that the purpose of the provisions is 'not only to enable the court to obtain the information it needs,
but also to enable the court to control the information-gathering activities of others'.[370]
The emphasis is always on 'information obtaining' and there is nothing in the Act which
permits a court to order the provision of services to anyone[371] and it 'cannot be a proper
use of the court's powers under section 38(6) to seek to bring about change'.[372] The House
concluded that what is directed under section 38(6) must be:

> an examination or assessment of the child, including where appropriate her relationship
> with her parents, the risk that her parents may present to her, and the ways in which those
> risks may be avoided or managed, all with a view to enabling the court to make the deci-
> sions which it has to make under the Act with the minimum of delay. Any services which
> are provided for the child and his family must be ancillary to that end. They must not be
> an end in themselves.[373]

Baroness Hale preferred to express no concluded view on the issue of whether or not the
court has power to direct the local authority or any of the parties to fund the assessment.[374]
But on the assumption that it does, her Ladyship said that the cost of any proposed
assessment must be relevant to the court's decision.[375]

---

[367] The court has no power to order the parents to take part in any assessment against their wishes.

[368] '[T]he court is to have such powers to override the views of the local authority as are necessary to
enable the court to discharge properly its function of deciding whether or not to accede to the local authority's application to take the child away from its parents by obtaining a care order' [1997] 1 FLR 1 at 7. Their
Lordships acknowledged that assessments had financial implications and that account of these should be
taken by the court.   [369] [2006] 1 AC 576.

[370] Ibid, [64].   [371] Ibid, [65].   [372] Ibid, [67].   [373] Ibid, [69].

[374] See, however, Lord Scott of Foscote's account of the position of the Legal Services Commission, at
[20]–[23].

[375] On which see Holman J [1998] 2 FLR 371 at 382: the assessment should not be contrary to the best
interests of the child, should be 'necessary' to enable the court to reach a proper decision and should not

While Baroness Hale noted in the course of her opinion that the issue of the distinction between assessment and treatment had arisen in cases after *Re C*, her Ladyship did not directly address that issue. However, Lord Scott of Foscote (with whom Lord Mance agreed) examined those authorities.

Lord Scott agreed with Holman J's analysis in *Re M (Residential Assessment Directions)*.[376] In that case Holman J directed that a residential assessment take place, but limited the assessment period to the first eight weeks of the proposed programme because thereafter it shifted to treatment rather than assessment.[377] After referring to Lord Browne-Wilkinson's conclusions in *Re C*, Holman J concluded that the courts' powers:

> are limited to a process that can properly be characterized as 'assessment' rather than 'treatment', although no doubt all treatment is accompanied by a continuing process of assessment. And they are limited to a process which bona fide involves the participation of the child as an integral part of what is being assessed.[378]

Lord Scott also agreed with the analysis of Thorpe and Simon Brown LJJ in *Re D (Jurisdiction: Programme of Assessment or Therapy)*.[379] There it was held that a 'programme for assessment can encompass within it an element of therapy or treatment' but if 'the programme is essentially one for treatment rather than one for assessment it... must be held to be outside the court's powers to order'.[380] A judge had ordered a six-month residential assessment of a mother who was drug dependent. This involved the treatment of her underlying emotional and psychological disorder by a psychotherapist independent of the residential unit and the treatment of her drug addiction by that unit. The mother's capacity to relate to her baby was not substantially in question, although her care of the baby would be closely supervised and assessed during her stay. The Court of Appeal allowed the local authority's appeal, finding that the proposed programme clearly fell outside the limits of any programme which as a matter of fact and degree could properly be characterised as one primarily designed for the purpose of assessment rather than treatment. The programme's 'therapeutic component was altogether too prominent, its length altogether too long'.[381]

Lord Scott disagreed, however, with the conclusion of the Court of Appeal in *Re B (Interim Care Order: Directions)*.[382] There the court gave a direction that a mother and child be assessed at a mother and baby unit where the focus was on improving parents' childcare skills. Lord Scott was of the view that 'an assessment of the success of the programme in improving the parenting skills of the parents could not... be described as "an examination or assessment of the child"'. An assessment of mother/child attachment can be regarded as an assessment of the child, whereas assessment of the mother's ability to respond to professional concerns cannot.

Having reviewed the authorities, Lord Scott concluded that in *Re G* 'the main purpose of the proposed programme was therapy for the mother in order to give her the opportunity of change so as to become a safe and acceptable carer for Ellie'.[383] In his Lordship's

---

make unreasonable demands of a local authority. Contrast Hobhouse LJ in *Re B (Psychiatric Therapy for Parents)* [1999] 1 FLR 701 (paramountcy of child's welfare and cost relevant).

[376] [1998] 2 FLR 371.

[377] His Lordship commented that the words in s 38(6) are 'limited to a process that can properly be characterised as "assessment" rather than "treatment"' and 'to a process which bona fide involves the participation of the child as an integral part of what is being assessed'.

[378] See also *Re B (Psychiatric Therapy for Parents)* [1999] 1 FLR 701.

[379] [1999] 2 FLR 632, reiterating the approach in *Re B*, ibid.

[380] [1999] 2 FLR 632 at 641 *per* Simon Brown LJ and at 637–639 *per* Thorpe LJ.

[381] At 641 *per* Simon Brown LJ.   [382] [2002] 1 FLR 545.   [383] [2006] 1 AC 576 at [14].

view this purpose did not fall within section 38(6) 'notwithstanding that the results of the programme would be valuable and influential in enabling the court to decide whether a care order in respect of Ellie should be made and that if the purpose were to be achieved it would very greatly benefit Ellie'.[384]

Lord Clyde also recognised the distinction as a matter of language between assessment and treatment but commented that:

> without engaging in the terminological distinction it should be enough to recognise that the jurisdiction of the court is confined to obtaining information about the current state of affairs, including perhaps a forecast of what future progress might be possible, and does not extend to a continuing survey of the effects of treatment.[385]

In cases in which there are professional recommendations both of assessment and therapy, there will need to be careful consideration therefore of the precise nature of that which is being ordered under section 38(6) as distinct from interventions otherwise taking place. In *Re L and H (Residential Assessment)*[386] a mother had a history of struggling to care for her children. Her first child was cared for by the maternal grandmother, the second and third had been adopted outside the family, and the fourth child was in foster care following emergency protection. A comprehensive report of a consultant clinical psychologist prepared in the course of care proceedings relating to the fourth child recommended a residential parenting assessment to assess the mother's parenting ability and the ability of the parents' relationship to withstand the stresses of parenting. The psychologist also recommended that the mother and her partner would benefit from concurrent therapeutic interventions (in the form of cognitive behavioural therapy and couple therapy). Before the hearing the mother's fifth child, M, was born and was joined to the care proceedings. The mother's application for a section 38(6) assessment in line with the psychologist's recommendation was rejected by the judge on the grounds that it involved a therapeutic element and was concerned with the parents' relationship not with the child. The Court of Appeal allowed the mother's appeal and ordered assessment. The judge had misinterpreted the nature of the recommended assessment which did not contain therapeutic interventions. The therapeutic interventions were to take place concurrently, organised by others.[387] The proposed assessment in this case was on all fours with that in *Re C*.[388] The Court of Appeal was left with the feeling that the denial of an assessment to the parents was unfair and stressed that 'the hearing of the proceedings should be fair (or, to put the matter in the language of the European Convention, Art 6 compliant) and that the court should have before it all the relevant evidence necessary for the decision'.[389] The court acknowledged that there would be some cases in which professional advice might be unanimous that an assessment would serve no useful purpose (eg a parent who had been found to have grievously harmed a child but was still in denial about it or a parent who refused to acknowledge that a convicted paedophile was a danger to her children). However, where as in this case there was powerful, well-reasoned, objective, and balanced professional evidence that an assessment was worthwhile, that was a 'a powerful pointer to the propriety of such an order'.[390]

---

[384] Ibid.   [385] Ibid, [31].   [386] [2007] EWCA Civ 213, [2007] 1 FLR 1370.   [387] See at [32].
[388] Ibid, [76].
[389] Ibid, [85]. See for another example *Re K (Care Order)* [2007] EWCA Civ 697, [2007] 2 FLR 1066 (two-day assessment ordered to avoid jeopardising 'the essential requirement of fairness to the mother in seeking to resist the care order'—see at [7]).
[390] Ibid, [88] and [91]. There is, of course, no question of a parent having a right to a further assessment. The court must ask whether a further assessment will assist the judge in reaching the right conclusion: see *Re J (Residential Assessment: Rights of Audience)* [2009] EWCA Civ 1210, [2010] 1 FLR 1290 at [10].

As these cases illustrate, section 38(6) assessments tend to be thought of in terms of residential assessments in institutional settings. However, in *Re A (Residential Assessment)*[391] Munby J made clear that it 'applies to any "examination" (medical or psychiatric) or any "assessment", whether short or long, and in whatever setting'.[392] His Lordship held, contrary to a local authority's contention, that justices had not erred in directing an assessment of a child whilst living at the home of her paternal aunt and great-grandmother. The aunt had a conviction which in the local authority's opinion would disqualify her under the relevant fostering regulations,[393] and contended therefore that the effect of the direction was to put in place an unregulated placement. Munby J pointed out that the House of Lords in *Re C* made clear that a direction which specified the venue at which a residential assessment was to take place did not wrongly interfere with the local authority's power under the Children Act 1989 to determine a child's place of residence under a care order, including an interim care order. In their Lordships' opinion, the power is concerned with a child's placement not his assessment. Munby J held that to accept the local authority's argument would be to read into section 38(6) restrictions which are not there.[394] Any concern that it was a placement unregulated by statute could be met by the fact that it was a placement regulated by the court, in that the court was satisfied that it was a safe and suitable placement. Against such an approach, however, is the fact that in some cases the court's order requires a local authority on which it is conferring parental responsibility to act against its better judgement and to take risks with which it disagrees. In such circumstances there may be an argument that the court should take its own steps to secure the safety of the child during the assessment period, for example by making an interim residence order (which could contain conditions and directions) coupled with an interim supervision order.[395]

7.5 THE CHILD'S RIGHT TO REFUSE TO BE ASSESSED

Section 38(7) was included in the Act partly in response to matters raised in the Cleveland inquiry.[396] The report revealed that children who were suspected of having been sexually abused were subjected to repeated medical examinations and prolonged interviews which caused them a considerable degree of distress. Additional safeguards for the child appear in the final words of section 38(6) which provide that where a child is of sufficient understanding to make an informed decision he may refuse to submit to a medical or psychiatric examination or other assessment. However, the scope of this safeguard for the child has been limited by the ruling in *South Glamorgan County Council v W and B*[397] that the inherent jurisdiction can be used to override it. A girl refused to comply with the court's direction and the court found that she was competent to make an informed decision. The court then gave leave to the local authority to bring proceedings to invoke the exercise of the court's inherent jurisdiction to authorise that the child be assessed and treated without her consent. Leave was granted because the court was satisfied that the result which the local authority wished to achieve could not be achieved through the making of any order made otherwise than in the exercise of the court's inherent jurisdiction, and for which

---

[391] [2009] EWHC 865 (Fam), [2009] 2 FLR 443 (Munby J).

[392] Ibid, [59]. The point became an academic one in the case but Munby J agreed to deliver a judgment on this matter of pubic interest since he had heard full argument.

[393] Fostering Services (Wales) Regulations 2003 (SI 2003/237), reg 38(2).

[394] [2009] EWHC 865 (Fam), [2009] 2 FLR 443 at [63].

[395] In *Re T (A Minor) (Care Order: Conditions)* [1994] 2 FLR 423 at 435 it was acknowledged by Nourse LJ that a placement at home could be achieved in this fashion.

[396] *Report of the Inquiry into Child Abuse in Cleveland 1987* (Cm 412, 1988).

[397] [1993] 1 FLR 574.

the local authority were entitled to apply. It therefore fulfilled the requirements of section 100(5) of the Children Act 1989. It was put to the court that the court's power under the inherent jurisdiction to override in a proper case the wishes of a child, and to give consent for medical treatment, had been abrogated by section 100. This view was rejected by the court on the grounds that the court had always been able to override the wishes of a competent child, and that it would require very clear words in a statute to take that right away.

There were compelling reasons why the child in *South Glamorgan County Council v W and B* should receive psychiatric assessment and treatment, and it is easy to appreciate why the court was determined to override her refusal. However, the difficulty with the ruling is that Parliament had specifically legislated, in section 38(6), that a child with sufficient competence could refuse to comply with a direction from a court that she undergo such an assessment. Thus Parliament appeared deliberately to have circumscribed the powers of a court in the face of a refusal from the child. The ruling in *South Glamorgan County Council v W and B* allowed the inherent jurisdiction to be used to give powers to the court which were denied it by statute.

7.6 INTERIM CARE ORDERS AND EXCLUDING THE ALLEGED ABUSER FROM THE HOME

In the same way that an exclusion requirement can be added to an EPO (see the discussions of sections 44A and 44B in Section 5.3), section 38A provides that an exclusion requirement can be attached to[398] an interim care order[399] provided that the conditions in section 38A(2) are satisfied. These conditions are:

Key legislation

(a) that there is reasonable cause to believe that, if a person ('the relevant person') is excluded from a dwelling house in which the child lives, the child will cease to suffer, or cease to be likely to suffer, significant harm, and

(b) that another person living in the house (whether a parent of the child or some other person)—

    (i) is able and willing to give the child the care which it would be reasonable to expect a parent to give to him, and

    (ii) consents to the inclusion of the exclusion requirement.

The court may attach a power of arrest to an exclusion requirement[400] and a police constable may arrest without warrant any person whom he has reasonable cause to believe to be in breach of the requirement.[401] Section 38B allows for exclusion from the home to be regulated by undertakings rather than a court order.

7.7 THE ROLE OF THE CHILDREN'S GUARDIAN

Unless there is someone who has the duty to be the voice of the child, and who has a duty to safeguard the child's interests before the court, there is a risk that the child's

---

[398] An exclusion requirement can only be made as an addition to, and not as an alternative to, an interim care order.

[399] Sections 38A and 38B were inserted by the Family Law Act 1996, s 52, Sch 6, para 1. For further discussion, see *Domestic Violence and Occupation of the Family Home* (Law Com No 207, 1992), paras 6.15–6.22.

[400] Section 38A(5).   [401] Section 38A(8).

perspective will be inadequately represented. Because care proceedings can often involve babies and young children who lack the capacity properly to instruct a lawyer, the normal safeguards afforded by separate legal representation do not assist the child to any great extent. A lawyer has only limited opportunities to make a close and independent investigation into the circumstances surrounding a child client's case, and he or she is likely therefore to feel obliged to support the local authority's perception of the case unless instructions are received from someone who has the authority to make enquiries and to represent the child's position. A children's guardian is such a person.[402] The need for children's guardians (formerly referred to as guardians ad litem) and the dangers inherent in an unopposed application being allowed to proceed without any separate investigation being conducted on behalf of the child, were graphically illustrated by the tragic circumstances of the death of Maria Colwell[403] following the discharge of her care order and her return to her mother and stepfather. At that time no one had the duty to give an account of Maria's wishes and feelings to the court, and no one had the duty to make an assessment, independent of the one made by the local authority, of whether Maria's mother and stepfather might ill-treat her, or otherwise cause her harm, were she to be returned to their care. Following the Colwell case, guardians were introduced, initially in respect of unopposed applications to discharge a care order, but gradually their use has been extended to other proceedings. Section 41 of the Children Act 1989 now provides a list of specified proceedings in which a court must appoint a children's guardian unless satisfied that it is not necessary to do so in order to safeguard the child's interests.[404] A failure to appoint a guardian where the case for the child's interests being separately represented is clear may leave a court open to successful judicial review.[405]

A children's guardian appointed in specified proceedings will be a Cafcass officer or Welsh family proceedings officer.[406] They are trained and experienced in social work. Section 41(2) of the Children Act 1989 provides that they shall be appointed in accordance with rules of court;[407] and be under a duty to safeguard the interests of the child in the manner prescribed by such rules.[408] The relevant rules are set out in Part 16 of the Family Procedure Rules 2010, supplemented by Practice Direction 16A—Representation of Children, and rule 16.20(5) provides that the children's guardian's duties must be exercised in accordance with the Practice Direction. The children's guardian must 'act on behalf of the child upon the hearing of any application in proceedings with the duty of safeguarding the interests of the child',[409] and 'must also provide the court with such other assistance as it may require'.[410] In doing so the guardian must have regard to the

---

[402] See www.nagalro.com for further information on the role of children's guardians.

[403] *Report of the Committee of Inquiry into the Care and Supervision provided in relation to Maria Colwell* (London: HMSO, 1974) (Chairman: T. G. Field-Fisher QC).

[404] Section 41(1) and (6): on an application to make or discharge a care order including when the court is considering making a residence order with respect to a child who is the subject of a care order; on an application to make, vary, or discharge a supervision order; when a direction has been made in family proceedings and the court has made, or is thinking of making, an interim care order; when an application is made with respect to contact with a child in care; in respect of any proceedings brought under Pt V; on an appeal in relation to any of the above proceedings, and an appeal in relation to s 34 of the Children Act 1989 (contact with a child in care). The list of specified proceedings does not include an application for an education supervision order under s 36 of the Act. See *Essex County Council v B* [1993] 1 FLR 866.

[405] *R v Pontlottyn Juvenile Court, ex p R* [1990] FCR 900.

[406] As set out in Children Act 1989, s 41 and Family Procedure Rules, r 16.17. See the functions of the services set out in Criminal Justice and Court Services Act 2000, s 12 and Children Act 2004, s 35.

[407] Section 41(2)(a). See Family Procedure Rules, rr 16.3 and 12.6 on the appointment of a children's guardian in specified proceedings.   [408] Section 41(2)(b)

[409] Family Procedure Rules, r 16.20(1).   [410] Ibid, r 16.20(2).

principle in section 1(2) (that delay will normally be prejudicial to the child's welfare) and the matters in section 1(3) of the Children Act 1989 (the so-called welfare checklist). The children's guardian's duties are set out in Part 3 of Practice Direction 16A.

The guardian must appoint and instruct a solicitor to represent the child,[411] attend all directions, appointments, and hearings unless excused from so doing, and advise the court on various specified matters, such as the child's wishes and the child's level of understanding.[412] The guardian is responsible for serving and accepting service of documents on behalf of the child. Occasionally the child may wish to give instructions to a solicitor which conflict with those of the guardian. This is most likely to arise where the guardian forms the view that it would be in the interests of the child if a care order were made and the child does not want to go into care. In such a case, provided that the solicitor is satisfied that the child is able, having regard to his understanding, to give instructions on his own behalf, the rules provide that the solicitor must conduct the case in accordance with the instructions received from the child.[413] The guardian will nonetheless continue to investigate the case on behalf of the child, and must perform all his or her duties set out in the rules and Practice Direction other than his or her duty to appoint a solicitor for the child.[414] These provisions are an example of how the law seeks to balance giving due weight to the child's right to be respected as an individual, and to have access to the type of legal safeguards which are given to adults, and the concern of the law to ensure that the welfare of children is afforded proper protection in proceedings designed to secure their safety and well-being.

The Practice Direction states that the guardian must carry out such investigations as may be necessary to carry out his or her duties, and in particular must contact or seek to interview such persons as he or she thinks appropriate or as the court directs.[415] The guardian must also obtain such professional assistance, such as a report from an expert, which he or she thinks appropriate, or which the court directs the guardian to obtain.[416] The guardian has a right to inspect and take copies of any local authority records[417] and adoption agency records,[418] and where he or she thinks that they may assist in the determination of the case, they must be brought to the attention of the court.[419] Following investigations, the children's guardian must, unless the court directs otherwise, file a written report advising on the interests of the child for the final hearing.[420] The parents and other parties must have the opportunity to read the report in advance of the hearing. This is particularly important where the guardian is supporting the local authority's application for a care order, for the persons affected are entitled to know details of the case which is being made against them, so that they can prepare their own case properly. Once the court has made its decision, the guardian has the responsibility (where appropriate) to convey the court's decision in a manner appropriate to the child's age and understanding.

---

[411] Ibid, r 6.2, unless a solicitor has already been appointed or the children's guardian is authorised to and intends to have conduct of the proceedings on behalf of the child (r 6.3). The court has power to appoint a solicitor for the child (see Children Act 1989, s 41(3)). For guidance to solicitors on acting in the absence of a guardian, see the Law Society Practice Note: Acting in the Absence of a Children's Guardian [2010] 1 FLR 1632.   [412] Practice Direction 16A, 6.6.

[413] See *Re H (A Minor) (Care Proceedings: Child's Wishes)* [1993] 1 FLR 440; *Re P (Representation)* [1996] 1 FLR 486.

[414] See *Re M (Minors) (Care Proceedings: Child's Wishes)* [1994] 1 FLR 749 where Wall J laid down guidelines to be followed where the views of the guardian ad litem conflict with those of the child.

[415] Practice Direction 16A, 6.1(a).

[416] Ibid, 6.1(b).   [417] Children Act 1989, s 42.   [418] Adoption and Children Act 2002, s 103.

[419] Practice Direction 16A, 6.10. Where the local authority's care plan is adoption, the guardian has the right to see the case record in relation to the prospective adopters even though this is normally confidential: *Re T (A Minor) (Guardian ad Litem: Case Record)* [1994] 1 FLR 632.

[420] Practice Direction 16A, 6.8(a).

8 THE FINAL HEARING IN CARE PROCEEDINGS

8.1 THE THRESHOLD TEST

At the final hearing the court must be satisfied, on the balance of probabilities, that the threshold test in section 31(2) has been made out before it has jurisdiction to make either a care order or a supervision order. It is convenient to set this out again:

A court may only make a care order or a supervision order if it is satisfied—

(a) that the child is suffering, or is likely to suffer, significant harm; and

(b) that the harm, or likelihood of harm, is attributable to—

    (i) the care given to the child, or likely to be given to him if the order were not made, not being what it would be reasonable to expect a parent to give to him; or

    (ii) the child's being beyond parental control.

In *Newham London Borough v AG*,[421] Sir Stephen Brown P issued a warning against courts taking a too legalistic approach to the analysis of the language of section 31(2). He said 'of course, the words of the statute must be considered, but I do not believe that Parliament meant them to be unduly restrictive when the evidence clearly indicates that a certain course should be taken in order to protect the child'.[422] As we shall see, however, the wording of section 31(2) has generated much case law, including several House of Lords/Supreme Court decisions.

The threshold test has several elements. It will be satisfied where it is shown that the child 'is suffering' significant harm or where it is shown that he or she is 'likely to suffer' such harm. In either case it must be shown that the significant harm is attributable either to a lack of reasonable parental care or to the child's being beyond parental control. Each part of the test will now be analysed.

8.2 'IS SUFFERING SIGNIFICANT HARM'

The words of the threshold test relating to the child suffering significant harm are expressed in the present tense. It must be shown that the child 'is suffering' significant harm.

Before a final application is made in care proceedings there is always some considerable lapse of time between the commencement of the case and the final hearing while enquiries are made on behalf of the child by the child's guardian. By the time of the final hearing, when full evidence is given to substantiate the allegation that the child is suffering, or is likely to suffer, significant harm, protective steps will already have been taken. Indeed the child may be positively thriving in his new environment and clearly not so suffering in a literal sense. Difficult questions about the proper interpretation of section 31(2) have consequently arisen in cases where a relative, or other person, is offering to care for the child, and where there is no evidence to suggest that the child would positively come to harm if cared for by that person. Such cases not only give rise to awkward questions about the proper meaning of the language of section 31(2), they also raise fundamental issues of social policy, and go to the root of child protection practices and procedures. Essentially they pose the question 'when is it right for the state to be allowed to impose its own view

---

[421] [1993] 1 FLR 281.   [422] Ibid, 289.

on what would be best for the child when this view is at variance with the sincerely held wishes of members of the child's family?'[423]

Key case

Re M (A Minor) (Care Order: Threshold Conditions)[424] concerned a 2-year-old child. His parents were married and he had three half-siblings. In October 1991, when M was four months old, his father murdered his mother[425] in a very brutal manner in the presence of all the children. The police immediately obtained a place of safety order in respect of all the children.[426] After a week the three half-siblings went to live with Mrs W, the mother's maternal cousin, and in August 1992 she obtained a residence order which gave her parental responsibility for them.[427] However Mrs W, who was a lady in her mid-fifties, felt unable to care for M because he was so young and because of the special needs of the older children. M was therefore accommodated by the local authority and placed with a short-term foster mother. In May 1992 the local authority applied for a care order in respect of M. Members of the father's family and Mrs W separately applied for residence orders, but before the final hearing the paternal relatives had discontinued their application. The final hearing was not until February 1993. Mrs W, who had managed to care for the older children, now felt able to care for M. The local authority were of the opinion that Mrs W could now also care for M. They therefore supported her application and were no longer pursuing their application for a care order. However, M's guardian ad litem recommended that a care order be made with a view to M being adopted outside the family.[428] The question therefore arose whether the grounds for making a care order had been made out and, if they had, whether such an order should be made in light of the suggestion that the child should be adopted.[429]

Bracewell J found that the threshold conditions for making a care order had been established and that the child's interests would be best served by a care order being made with a view to his adoption. Mrs W appealed, supported by the local authority.[430] The Court of Appeal disapproved Bracewell J's interpretation of the wording of the statute, holding that the words 'is suffering or is likely to suffer' in the present tense were not fulfilled at the date of disposal (ie, at the final hearing); it also disagreed with her judgment for reasons of social policy. Balcombe LJ, who gave the judgment of the court, said that the facts of *Re M* were analogous with a case where a child's parents have both been killed in a motor accident, but where relatives offer to

---

[423] This is a dilemma to which social workers and other professionals are constantly exposed when discussing a child's future at a child protection case conference.

[424] [1994] 3 All ER 298.

[425] For guidance on dealing with cases where one parent has unlawfully killed the other, see *Re A and B (One Parent Killed by the Other)* [2011] 1 FLR 783. The perpetrator's family should not necessarily be discounted as future carers of the child. The view at [1] of the guidance that the threshold will always be met where one parent has killed the other is probably too broadly expressed.

[426] Under the Children and Young Persons Act 1969, s 28, now repealed.

[427] Children Act 1989, ss 8 and 12(2), and see Chapter 9.

[428] The father, who had by now been sentenced to life imprisonment for murder, supported the guardian ad litem's recommendation.

[429] A difficult feature in analysing this case is that the local authority were not seeking a care order, and although the court could make a care order on the recommendation of the guardian ad litem, she could not impose her view on the local authority on what should happen to the child if the care order was made.

[430] One of the many curious features of this case is that once a care order is made it is up to the local authority, and not the court, to decide about the child's future upbringing. Therefore the local authority could have chosen to disregard the judge's opinion that the child should be placed for adoption and have placed the child in the care of Mrs W, thus obviating the necessity for an appeal. However, for reasons which are not explained, the local authority appears to have conceded its decision-making powers to the court, and to have treated Bracewell J's view that adoption would best promote the welfare of the child as a ruling which was binding upon it.

care for the child, and said that for it to be open to a court to say that the second threshold condition was satisfied on facts of this kind would amount to a form of 'social engineering'.[431]

The House of Lords reversed the decision of the Court of Appeal and restored the care order which had been made by Bracewell J.[432] The House condemned the Court of Appeal's apparent pre-occupation with whether the present tense drafting of the statute was satisfied at the date of the final hearing. Rather, Lord Mackay LC ruled that:

> Where, at the time the application is to be disposed of, there are in place arrangements for the protection of the child by the local authority on an interim basis which protection has been continuously in place for some time, the relevant date with respect to which the court must be satisfied is the date at which the local authority initiated the procedure for protection under the Act from which these arrangements followed. If after a local authority had initiated protective arrangements the need for these had terminated, because the child's welfare had been satisfactorily provided for otherwise, in any subsequent proceedings it would not be possible to found jurisdiction on the situation at the time of the initiation of these arrangements. It is permissible only to look back from the date of disposal to the date of initiation of protection as a result of which local authority arrangements had been continuously in place thereafter to the date of disposal.[433]

Thus, where there has been a continuum of protective measures between the first initiation of proceedings and the final hearing, the fact that the child is being currently well cared for does not preclude the making of a care order. Lord Mackay endorsed the view that the point of time at which the court has to consider whether a continuing situation exists is at the moment in time immediately before the process of protection is first put into motion.[434]

It was accepted by most commentators that the House of Lords' ruling on this point was in accordance with the purpose of the legislation, and that it struck the correct balance between giving respect to the rights of families to make provision for children who are suffering, or at risk of suffering, significant harm, and allowing local authority and court involvement with such children.[435]

Re L (Care: Threshold Criteria)[436] illustrates how the temporal dimension of the threshold criteria, as explained in *Re M*, applies. Care proceedings were brought in respect of two children, aged 11 and 7, whose parents had learning disabilities. The family first came to the local authority's attention when the elder child was sexually assaulted by a man whom the father knew to be a sex offender and allowed to stay in the family home. The offender was imprisoned and, after working with the family on preventing such risks in the future, the local authority closed its file. Two years later the local authority became involved again because of concerns about domestic violence and an allegation that one of the children had been beaten with a belt. The case was remitted by the Court of Appeal for

---

[431] [1994] 1 All ER 424 at 432.

[432] Somewhat curiously, the appeal to the House of Lords was pursued not by the child's guardian ad litem but by the father. It is suggested that it was wrong for anyone other than the child to have been allowed to pursue the appeal. It is suggested that the fact that the father took the same view of the child's interests as the guardian ad litem should have been treated as irrelevant. It was a classic situation where the court should have assumed that there might at some stage be a conflict of interest between parent and child.

[433] [1994] 3 All ER 298, 305.

[434] This approach applies to both limbs of s 31(2)(a) of the Children Act 1989 (ie, also to 'is likely to suffer significant harm'): see *Southwark London Borough Council v B* [1999] 1 FCR 550, FD (Charles J).

[435] M. Hayes (1995) 58 Modern Law Review 878; A. Bainham (1994) 53 Cambridge Law Journal 458; J. Whybrow (1994) 6 Journal of Child Law 177. For a contrary view, see J. Masson (1994) 6 Journal of Child Law 170.

[436] [2007] 1 FLR 2050 (Hedley J). The case had been remitted by the Court of Appeal for rehearing: see *Re L (Children) (Care Proceedings: Significant Harm)* [2006] EWCA Civ 1282, [2007] 1 FLR 1068.

rehearing (ultimately by Hedley J). Both the Court of Appeal[437] and Hedley J[438] held that it would be impermissible to rely on the historic matter of the sexual assault to address the question in the present whether the children are suffering significant harm. However, it would be going too far to say that it could not figure in an assessment of whether the children were then likely to suffer significant harm. As Hedley J put it, the court 'cannot, as a matter of law, close its mind to matters that have happened in the past... What it can do is take account of the extent to which anybody else regarded those matters as potentially of significant harm in considering whether or not to take it into account itself.'[439] Here it was clear that the local authority had closed its case on the sexual offender issue and did not consider it of any future significance.

The House of Lords' interpretation of the relevant date for proving the threshold criteria raises the question of whether evidence which emerges between the relevant date and the date of the hearing can be used. In *Re G (Children) (Care Order: Evidence)*[440] the Court of Appeal clarified that information acquired after the relevant date as to the state of affairs at the relevant date can be taken into account. Hale LJ offered the following obvious examples: 'further medical evidence about the injuries which promoted removal, new complaints by the child about other forms of abuse within the home or admissions made by the parents'.[441] However, later events cannot be relied upon unless they are capable of showing what the position was at the relevant time. For example, the inability of the parents to care for the child as a result of a complete collapse or mental illness brought on by the stress of the proceedings could not be relied on in the existing proceedings.[442]

Once the jurisdiction point had been resolved in *Re M (A Minor) (Care Order: Threshold Conditions)*[443] the House of Lords had to consider whether to confirm the residence order to Mrs W, or restore the care order made by Bracewell J. By the time the appeal reached the House of Lords the child had been living for several months with Mrs W and, because he was thriving in her care, all parties were agreed that there was no question of the child being taken from her at that time and placed for adoption. Somewhat astonishingly, however, their Lordships restored the care order. Lord Mackay gave as his reason for so doing that there was a possibility in the longer term of difficulties and the care order would enable the local authority to monitor the progress of the child. Also, a care order would give them the power to determine the extent to which the father should be allowed to meet his parental responsibility for the child.[444] Lord Templeman said that a care order would have the advantage for Mrs W that it would enable her to turn to the local authority for advice and help if necessary. He also expressed the view that it would have the advantage for the child that the local authority would be able to monitor his progress and intervene with speed if anything went wrong.

It is regrettable that there was virtually no discussion in the House of Lords of the important and controversial social policy issues raised by the case. No attempt was made to deal with Balcombe LJ's telling analogy with a case where a child's parents have been killed in a motor accident. No comparison was made between the results which would be produced by the competing interpretations of section 31(2).[445] At no stage did their Lordships address the question of fundamental difficulty posed by Bracewell J's ruling, namely when is it a proper

---

[437] *Re L (Children) (Care Proceedings: Significant Harm)* [2006] EWCA Civ 1282, [2007] 1 FLR 1068 at [13] *per* Wilson LJ.   [438] [2007] 1 FLR 2050 at [34] and [35].

[439] Ibid, [35].   [440] [2001] EWCA Civ 968, [2001] 2 FCR 757.   [441] Ibid, [13] and [22].

[442] An example given by Hale LJ, ibid, [14].   [443] [1994] 3 All ER 298.

[444] Under s 33(3)(b).

[445] Eg where significant harm is caused by one parent at a time when the other parent is absent from the home, and where the local authority take steps to protect the child during that parent's absence, on his return the absent parent would not be able to claim that the court has no jurisdiction to make a care order. The local authority would be able to overcome the threshold test and the absent parent would be in the same position as Mrs W.

application of the welfare principle to make an order which will result in a child being adopted when a relative is offering to care for him. It is suggested that the ruling was unsatisfactory with respect to their Lordships' approach to the choice of orders available. The justification given by Lords Mackay and Templeman for making a care order was an untenable application of the welfare principle. The statement that a care order would enable Mrs W to turn to the local authority for help and advice was undoubtedly correct. But such help and advice would almost certainly have been forthcoming in any event and, even if it were not, surely its desirability cannot justify permitting the state to take over parental responsibility? In relation to the court's continuing concerns about the child, these could adequately have been alleviated by making a residence order to Mrs W, possibly with conditions attached, and coupling it with a supervision order. The supervisor would have been charged with the duty to advise, assist, and befriend the child,[446] which would inevitably have involved giving help and advice to the child's carer. Moreover it was Mrs W, not the local authority, who would have responsibility for making the day-to-day decisions about the child's upbringing, but the House of Lords was expecting her to carry out this function without the benefit of a residence order and without the parental responsibility which such an order confers. The statement that a care order would enable the local authority to determine the extent to which the father should meet his parental responsibility for the child does not bear close examination. He was serving a life sentence for murder and had been recommended for deportation on his release. Thus, he would have no part to play in the child's life in the foreseeable future, if at all. Also, the child's siblings similarly needed protection from the father exercising parental responsibility at some time in the future, but it would have been inconceivable that anyone could have successfully pleaded that this would justify making a care order in respect of them too. Any problems could clearly have been dealt with by orders under section 8.[447]

8.3 'OR IS LIKELY TO SUFFER SIGNIFICANT HARM'

The inclusion of 'likely' significant harm within the threshold test allows for an order to be made where the court finds that the child is at risk of such harm even where no significant harm to the child has yet occured. In *Re H (A Minor) (Section 37 Direction)*,[448] Scott Baker J ventured the opinion that when looking at the likelihood of significant harm, the court is not limited to looking at the present and the immediate future. He said 'if a court concludes that a parent, or a carer, is likely to be unable to meet the emotional needs of a child in the future—even if years hence—my view is that the condition in section 31(2) would probably be met'.[449]

8.4 PROVING ACTUAL OR LIKELY SIGNIFICANT HARM

Key case

The leading decision on what is required in order to prove the threshold criteria is *Re H and Others (Minors) Sexual Abuse: Standard of Proof)*.[450] Four girls aged 15, 13, 8, and 2

---

[446] Section 35(1).

[447] For further commentary, see M. Hayes, 'Care by the Family or Care by the State?' (1995) 58 Modern Law Review 878.   [448] [1993] 2 FLR 541.

[449] He did not need to resolve the question because no application had been made for a care or supervision order. The case concerned an application by a lesbian couple for a residence order in respect of a baby girl. Scott Baker J ordered the local authority to undertake an investigation under s 37(1).

[450] [1996] AC 563. For further comment, see M. Hayes, 'Reconciling Protection for Children with Justice for Parents' (1997) 17 Legal Studies 1; I. Hemingway and C. Williams, '*Re M and R: Re H and R*' [1997] Family Law 740; C. Keenan, 'Finding that a Child is at Risk from Sexual Abuse: *Re H (Minors) (Sexual*

were living with their mother and Mr R, who was the father of the younger two children and stepfather of the older two. The eldest girl, D, alleged that Mr R had sexually abused her from the age of 7 or 8. Mr R was charged with having raped D, although acquitted on all counts. Relying on the different standard of proof in civil proceedings, the local authority nevertheless instituted care proceedings in respect of the three younger daughters on the ground that they were likely to suffer significant harm.[451] The local authority's case was based solely on the alleged sexual abuse of D. The trial judge concluded that he could not be sure 'to the requisite high standard of proof' that D's allegations were true. He therefore found that the threshold criteria were not made out in respect of the younger children. However, he added: 'This is far from saying that I am satisfied the child's complaints are untrue...If it were relevant, I would be prepared to hold that there is a real possibility that her statement and her evidence are true.' The local authority's appeal (ultimately to the House of Lords) against the judge's finding that the threshold was not crossed, was dismissed by a majority of 3 to 2. Lord Nicholls of Birkenhead gave the speech for the majority with which Lords Goff and Mustill agreed; Lords Lloyd and Browne-Wilkinson dissented.

8.4.1 Meaning of 'likely'

Their Lordships were unanimous that 'likely' in the context of the threshold test did not mean more likely than not.[452] They ruled that for the purposes of section 31(2)(a) 'likely' is being used 'in the sense of a real possibility, a possibility that cannot sensibly be ignored having regard to the nature and gravity of the feared harm in the particular case'.[453] As Lord Nicholls of Birkenhead explained, if the word 'likely' were given the meaning 'more likely than not' it would have the effect of preventing courts from making care and supervision orders in cases in which it was as likely as not that the child would suffer significant harm, as well as in cases in which the court was satisfied that there was a real possibility of significant harm to the child in the future.[454]

8.4.2 Evidence establishing significant harm or likely significant harm

There must be facts, proved to the court's satisfaction if disputed, on which the court can properly conclude that the child is suffering harm. An alleged but non-proven fact is not a fact for this purpose. Similarly with the second limb: there must be facts from which the court can properly conclude there is a real possibility that the child will suffer harm in the future.[455] Lord Nicholls offered three reasons: the word 'satisfied' in section 31(2) is the 'language of proof, not suspicion';[456] otherwise the effect would be to reverse the burden of proof; and it would be odd if unproven facts which could not show that the child is suffering harm could nonetheless be used to infer future harm. In an important passage, however, Lord Nicholls went on to place this conclusion in context 'by noting,

---

Abuse: Standard of Proof (1997) 60 Modern Law Review 857; H. Keating, 'Shifting Standards in the House of Lords—*Re H and Others (Minors) (Sexual Abuse: Standard of Proof)*' (1996) 8 Child and Family Law Quarterly 157.

[451] The eldest daughter was being accommodated by the local authority with the agreement of her parents.

[452] See Lord Browne-Wilkinson [1996] AC 563 at 572 and at 576 *per* Lord Lloyd of Berwick.

[453] [1996] AC 563 at 565 *per* Lord Nicholls, approving *Newham London Borough Council v AG* [1993] 1 FLR 281. Lord Nicholls said that by parity of reasoning the word likely also bore the same meaning in ss 43, 44, 46, and 31(2)(b) ('care given to the child or "likely" to be given him').

[454] For an example of a Recorder getting the test wrong, see *Re R (Care Order: Threshold Criteria)* [2009] EWCA Civ 942, [2010] 1 FLR 673.

[455] [1996] AC 563, at 590.   [456] Ibid.

and emphasising, the width of the range of facts which may be relevant when the court is considering the threshold conditions.' He said:

> The range of facts which may properly be taken into account is infinite. Facts include the history of members of the family, the state of relationships within a family, proposed changes within the membership of a family, parental attitudes, and omissions which might not reasonably have been expected, just as much as actual physical assaults. They include threats, and abnormal behaviour by a child, and unsatisfactory parental responses to complaints or allegations. And facts, which are minor or even trivial if considered in isolation, when taken together may suffice to satisfy the court of the likelihood of future harm. The court will attach to all the relevant facts the appropriate weight when coming to an overall conclusion on the crucial issue.[457]

Lord Nicholls also stressed that that it is 'open to a court to conclude there is a real possibility that the child will suffer harm in the future although harm in the past has not been established'. He observed that there will be cases where, although alleged maltreatment itself is not proved, the evidence establishes a combination of profoundly worrying features affecting the care of the child, on the basis of which facts it would be open to a court to find a likelihood of significant harm. He concluded, however, that in this case there was only one relevant fact in issue, namely whether Mr R had sexually abused D.[458] Lord Nicholls (for the majority) held, therefore, that once the trial judge had been unable to find on the balance of probabilities that D had been abused there was no evidence upon which he could infer that the younger girls were likely to suffer significant harm. The judge's suspicions or lingering doubts could not form a proper basis for concluding that likely significant harm had been established.

The dissenting Law Lords took a different view as to what was open to the judge. Lord Lloyd expressed the opinion that evidence which is insufficient to establish the truth of an allegation to a required standard of proof nevertheless remains evidence in the case. It need not be disregarded. The trial judge's conclusion that there was a real possibility that the evidence of D was true was a finding based on her evidence coupled with a number of other 'micro' facts which supported her account. It was not a mere suspicion that Mr R was an abuser, it was a finding of risk based on facts. Therefore, it was open to the judge to find that the younger daughters were likely to suffer significant harm.[459] Lord Browne-Wilkinson, agreeing with Lord Lloyd's reasoning, illustrated the point by way of a striking example:[460]

> Say that in 1940 those responsible for giving air-raid warnings had received five unconfirmed sightings of approaching aircraft which might be enemy bombers. They could not, on balance of probabilities, have reached a conclusion that any one of those sightings was of an enemy aircraft: nor could they logically have put together five non-proven sightings so as to be satisfied that enemy aircraft were in fact approaching. But their task was not simply to decide whether enemy aircraft were approaching but whether there was a risk of an air-raid. The facts relevant to the assessment of such risk were the reports that unconfirmed sightings had been made, not the truth of such reports. They could well, on the

---

[457] [1996] AC 563 at 591.

[458] Such cases will be relatively rare, but see *Re P (A Minor) (Care: Evidence)* [1994] 2 FLR 751 and *Re P (Sexual Abuse: Standard of Proof)* [1996] 2 FLR 333. For an example of where a local authority failed to prove that the children had been sexually abused but where there was substantial other evidence of significant harm to the children, see *Re G and R (Child Sexual Abuse: Standard of Proof)* [1995] 2 FLR 867.

[459] For further analysis of difficulties of proof in child protection cases, see M. Hayes, 'Reconciling Protection of Children With Justice for Parents' [1997] 17 Legal Studies 1.

[460] [1996] AC 563 at 572–573.

basis of those unconfirmed reports, have been satisfied that there was a real possibility of an air-raid and given warning accordingly.

Lord Browne-Wilkinson also identified a number of what he called micro facts which fell short of proving that D had been abused, but which were nevertheless established as facts and from which it might be inferred that there was a real possibility of harm to the younger children.[461]

There seems to be nothing in these dissenting opinions with which Lord Nicholls would disagree as a matter of general principle.[462] Where the majority and minority part company is in their respective views of the relevance of the so-called micro facts in the unusual circumstances of this case which had been fought solely on the basis that the eldest girl, D, had been sexually abused. While the minority would have held that the micro facts were still relevant, the majority took the view that those facts 'lead nowhere relevant in this case if they do not lead to the conclusion that [D] was abused'.[463]

In *Re B (Children) (Care Proceedings: Standard of Proof) (Cafcass Intervening)*[464] the House of Lords re-visited its decision in *Re H*. The facts were similar to *Re H* in that among the matters in dispute was whether Mr B, the father of a 9-year-old girl and a 6-year-old boy, had sexually abused their 16-year-old stepsister, R. Charles J was unable to decide whether the sexual abuse had occurred and reasoned as follows: 'I am unable to conclude that there is no real possibility that Mr B sexually abused R as she asserts or substantially as she asserts and I have therefore concluded that there is a real possibility that he did.'[465] The House of Lords pointed out that the law operates a binary system in which facts in issue are either proved or not[466] and that it was not open to a judge to sit on the fence as Charles J had done. However, Charles J's reasoning squarely raised once again the principle of whether a likelihood of significant harm could be inferred from a real possibility that facts existed (in other words from suspicions). The children's guardian[467] invited the House to depart from its reasoning in *Re H* and to uphold Charles J's conclusion. The House unhesitatingly declined that invitation, stating that Lord Nicholls's reasons 'remain thoroughly convincing'.[468] Baroness Hale explained that:

Talking point

The threshold is there to protect both the children and their parents from unjustified intervention in their lives. It would provide no protection at all if it could be established on the basis of unsubstantiated suspicions: that is, where a judge cannot say that there is no real possibility that abuse took place, so concludes that there is a real possibility that it did. In other words, the alleged perpetrator would have to prove that it did not.

---

[461] Eg that D had been consistent in her story from the time of her first complaint; that her statement was full and detailed; that there were opportunities for such abuse by Mr R and that he had been lying in denying that he had ever been alone either with D or with any of the other children; that one of the younger children had made statements which indicated that she had witnessed 'inappropriate' behaviour between Mr R and D; that the mother suspected that something had been going on between Mr R and D.

[462] Assuming that the evidence to which Lord Lloyd refers and the sightings (as opposed to what exactly was being sighted) in Lord Browne-Wilkinson's example are facts established on the balance of probabilities.

[463] [1996] AC 563 at 592.

[464] [2008] UKHL 35, [2009] AC 11. For commentary, see J. Hayes, 'Farewell to the Cogent Evidence Test: *Re B*' [2008] Family Law 859; H. Keating, 'Suspicions, Sitting on the Fence and Standards of Proof' [2009] Child and Family Law Quarterly 230.   [465] Cited at [2008] UKHL 35, [2009] AC 11 at [30].

[466] See [2008] UKHL 35, [2009] AC 11 at [20] *per* Lord Hoffmann and at [31] and [32] *per* Baroness Hale of Richmond.   [467] With the support of the local authority and the child's mother.

[468] [2008] UKHL 35, [2009] AC 11 at [54].

The House pointed out that it is difficult to see how reasons for interference with a child's right to respect for family life could be 'relevant and sufficient' as required by the European Court of Human Rights[469] if unproven allegations are the only basis for inferring that the child is at risk of harm.

8.4.3 The use of expert evidence

In many cases the judge will be assisted by medical expert evidence in deciding whether the threshold criteria are fulfilled.[470] In *Re U (Serious Injury: Standard of Proof); Re B*[471] the Court of Appeal made clear that a local authority should not refrain from proceedings or discontinue proceedings simply because there is substantial disagreement between experts. That is because in care proceedings the judge 'invariably surveys a wide canvas, including detailed history of the parents' lives, their relationship and their interaction with professionals. There will be many contributions to this context, family members, neighbours, health records, as well as observation of professionals such as social workers, health visitors and children's guardian.' A case must be decided on the totality of the evidence and each piece of information needs 'to be weighed and assessed in the context of all the other pieces of information'.[472] However, where there is undisputed expert opinion evidence, 'the judge ought not to reject it without sound and articulated reason'.[473] Similarly, if a judge prefers the evidence of one expert over another, he or she must have a sound basis, and provide a reasoned explanation, for doing so.[474]

Cases in which there is a series of unexplained episodes of harm to a child which are not capable of medical explanation, or where there is disagreement between medical experts as to the possible causes, can be particularly difficult for the courts. Some such cases have been the subject of criminal prosecutions of parents. For example, in *R v Cannings*,[475] three of the defendant's four children died in early infancy and she was convicted of the murder of two of them. The conviction was quashed because there was no evidence other than the children's breathing having stopped and a serious disagreement among experts as to the cause. Fresh evidence of hereditary factors indicating a possible genetic cause was admitted. The court concluded that a natural cause could not be excluded as a reasonably possible explanation. The court took the opportunity to give guidance on inferences to be drawn from the evidence in such cases. In *Re U (Serious Injury: Standard of Proof); Re B*[476]

---

[469] Citing for example *K and T v Finland* (2000) 31 EHRR 484; *Scozzari and Giunta v Italy* (2000) 35 EHRR 243; and *Kutzner v Germany* (2002) 35 EHRR 653.

[470] It is possible for the expert evidence to be provided by a clinician who is treating, or has treated, the child provided the therapeutic relationship is not wholly incompatible with an issue before the court: see *O-M, GM (and KM) v The Local Authority, LO and EM* [2009] EWCA Civ 1405, [2010] 2 FLR 58. Eg a clinician who is treating a child for sexual abuse on the basis that the abuse happened, would not be capable of giving expert opinion on whether it did occur.   [471] [2004] EWCA Civ 567, [2004] 2 FLR 263.

[472] *Leeds City Council v YX and ZX (Assessment of Sexual Abuse)* [2008] EWHC 802 (Fam) at [106] *per* Holman J (medical evidence apparently diagnostic of sexual abuse had to be assessed in context of child's express denial that abuse occurred: care order application dismissed). See also *Lancashire County Council v D and E* [2008] EWHC 832 (Fam) (Charles J) (a judge is entitled to reject a plausible account, even where backed by medical documentation, and such an approach does not result in a reversal of the burden of proof): see *Re M (Fact-Finding Hearing: Burden of Proof)* [2008] EWCA Civ 1261, [2009] 1 FLR 1177 (mother's well-documented unstable knees rejected as reason for fall and consequent injury to baby).

[473] *Re D (Care Order: Evidence)* [2010] EWCA Civ 1000, [2011] 1 FLR 447 at [24].

[474] See *Re M-W (Care Proceedings: Expert Evidence)* [2010] EWCA Civ 12, [2010] 2 FLR 46 at [39] and [43].

[475] [2004] EWCA Crim 1, [2004] 1 All ER 725 (judge entitled to prefer factual evidence of witnesses over expert's psychological profile.)   [476] [2004] EWCA Civ 567, [2004] 2 FLR 263.

the Court of Appeal held that the following considerations emphasised in *R v Cannings* are of direct application in care proceedings.[477]

(i)   The cause of an injury or an episode that cannot be explained scientifically remains equivocal.

(ii)   Recurrence is not in itself probative.

(iii) Particular caution is necessary in any case where the medical experts disagree, one opinion declining to exclude a reasonable possibility of natural cause.

(iv)   The court must always be on guard against the over-dogmatic expert, the expert whose reputation or *amour propre* is at stake, or the expert who has developed a scientific prejudice.

(v)   The judge in care proceedings must never forget that today's medical certainty may be discarded by the next generation of experts or that scientific research will throw light into corners that are at present dark.[478]

The application of some of these principles is neatly illustrated by one of the cases heard in *Re U (Serious Injury: Standard of Proof); Re B*.[479] In *Re B* the mother of a disabled child was a paediatric nurse. The child was being treated on the hospital wards where the mother worked. The child suffered 11 episodes of potentially life-threatening rigor in six days, at times when the mother was nearby. All six experts agreed that infection was the most likely cause of the child's rigors, but only two opined that deliberate introduction of infection via a cannula attached to the child was the most likely cause. The latter view rested partly on the foundation that science had no other explanation. Bracewell J[480] concluded that the threshold criteria were made out having regard to the frequency and severity of the rigors without medical explanation, together with other circumstantial evidence.[481] The mother had a history of self-harm and depression and had admitted feeling panicky and physically ill in the presence of the child. She was present at the relevant times and had the relevant knowledge to interfere with the cannula. The Court of Appeal held that the judge's conclusions from the expert evidence and her treatment of the frequency of rigors as in some way probative were wrong, although ultimately Bracewell J's decision was upheld as the Court of Appeal concluded that the circumstantial evidence alone entitled her to so find.

As *Re B* illustrates, a parent's personality may be an important factor in the judge's assessment. However, the Court of Appeal has cautioned against undue reliance on personality (or psychometric) testing in assessing the credibility of a party or witness, and has stated that such testing does not ordinarily have any place in care cases. It is the task of the judge, not the expert, to assess credibility.[482]

Where a non-accidental injury to a child has been proved and there is more than one child in the same household it will be highly unusual for that finding of harm not to justify the inference that protection of the other child(ren) is required. If the court is not to find the threshold met in respect of an uninjured child, the judge must give a full and

---

[477]   Ibid, [23].

[478]   Ibid. See also comments of Ryder J in *Lancashire County Council v R* [2008] EWHC 2959 (Fam), [2010] 1 FLR 387 at [52]–[55].   [479]   [2004] EWCA Civ 567, [2004] 2 FLR 263.

[480]   [2002] EWHC 20 (Fam), [2004] 2 FLR 200.

[481]   See also *Re B (Non-Accidental Injury)* [2002] EWCA Civ 752, [2002] 2 FLR 1133 at [25] (a judge would fail in his primary protective function if he acceded to a submission that just because a doctor could not give a confident diagnosis, therefore there was no risk of harm).

[482]   *Re S (Care: Parenting Skills: Personality Tests)* [2004] EWCA Civ 1029, [2005] 2 FLR 658 at [57] *per* Ward LJ, at [66] *per* Arden LJ, and at [71] *per* Scott Baker LJ. See also the concerns expressed in *Re L (Children) (Care Proceedings: Significant Harm)* [2006] EWCA Civ 1282, [2007] 1 FLR 1068.

reasoned explanation of why that view has been reached. The Court of Appeal so held in *Re K (Care: Threshold Criteria)*[483] where the judge had found that one or other of the parents of two children aged 6 and 1 had suffocated the 1-year-old, yet the judge had not found the threshold fulfilled in respect of the 6-year-old. The Court of Appeal held that it was inadequate for the judge simply to say that the discrete episode of violence to the baby could be compartmentalised as not affecting the older child.[484]

8.5 THE BURDEN AND STANDARD OF PROOF IN CARE PROCEEDINGS

In addition to examining the legal issues already mentioned, the House of Lords in *Re H and Others (Minors) (Sexual Abuse: Standard of Proof)*,[485] took the opportunity to explain the burden and standard of proof in care proceedings. Lord Nicholls of Birkenhead explained that the burden of establishing the threshold criteria lies on the applicant. The criteria 'must be affirmatively established to the satisfaction of the court'.[486] All their Lordships agreed that the standard of proof which applies to the threshold test is the ordinary civil standard of balance of probability.[487] As Lord Nicholls explained, the balance of probability standard means that 'a court is satisfied an event occurred if the court considers that, on the evidence, the occurrence of the event was more likely than not'. However, their Lordships differed on whether any further gloss should be placed on this test. The majority took the view that a generous degree of flexibility is built into the preponderance of probability standard and sought to explain this. Lord Nicholls therefore added that when assessing the probabilities 'the court will have in mind as a factor, to whatever extent is appropriate in the particular case, that the more serious the allegation the less likely it is that the event occurred and, hence, the stronger should be the evidence before the court concludes that the allegation is established on the balance of probability'.[488] He emphasised that this does not mean that the standard of proof is higher than the balance of probabilities;[489] rather 'it means only that the inherent probability or improbability of an event is itself a matter to be taken into account when weighing the probabilities and deciding whether, on balance, the event occurred. The more improbable the event, the stronger must be the evidence that it did occur before, on the balance of probability, its occurrence will be established'.[490] His Lordship said that this had been expressed neatly by Ungoed-Thomas J in *Re Dellow's Will Trusts*[491] in the following words: 'The more serious the allegation the more cogent is the evidence required to overcome the unlikelihood of what is alleged and thus to prove it'.[492] Lord Nicholls added that this approach provided a method of dealing with the instinctive feeling that even in civil proceedings a court should be more sure before finding serious allegations proved than when deciding less serious or trivial matters.

---

[483] [2005] EWCA Civ 1226, [2006] 2 FLR 868.   [484] Ibid, [40] and [42].

[485] [1996] AC 563. For further comment, see M. Hayes, 'Reconciling Protection for Children with Justice for Parents' (1997) 17 Legal Studies 1; I. Hemingway and C. Williams, '*Re M and R: Re H and R*' [1997] Family Law 740; C. Keenan, 'Finding that a Child is at Risk from Sexual Abuse: *Re H (Minors) (Sexual Abuse: Standard of Proof)*' (1997) 60 Modern Law Review 857; H. Keating, 'Shifting Standards in the House of Lords—*Re H and Others (Minors) (Sexual Abuse: Standard of Proof)*' [1996] Child and Family Law Quarterly 157.

[486] [1996] AC 563 at 586.   [487] Ibid, 586 and 587.   [488] Ibid, 586.

[489] Indeed, he expressly rejected a so-called third standard of proof, somewhere between the criminal standard and simple balance of probabilities: see [1996] AC 563 at 587.   [490] Ibid, 586.

[491] [1964] 1 WLR 451 at 455.

[492] Adding that this substantially accords with the approach adopted by Morris LJ in *Hornal v Neuberger Products Ltd* [1957] 1 QB 247 at 266. On this test, see J. R. Spencer, 'Evidence in Child Abuse Cases: Too High a Price for Too High a Standard?' (1994) 6 Journal of Child Law 160.

Lord Lloyd, in his dissenting speech, expressed the opinion that the standard of proof under section 31(2)[493] ought to be the simple balance of probability however serious the allegations involved. In reaching this conclusion his Lordship was influenced by the fact that section 31(2) merely represents a threshold and by no means dictates that a care order will be made. However, Lord Lloyd was concerned that unless the threshold criteria are met the local authority can do nothing to protect the child however grave the anticipated injury to the child, or however serious the apprehended consequences, adding:

> This seems to me to be a strong argument in favour of making the threshold test lower rather than higher. It would be a bizarre result if the more serious the anticipated injury, whether physical or sexual, the more difficult it became for the local authority to satisfy the initial burden of proof, and thereby ultimately, if the welfare test is satisfied, secure protection for the child.[494]

Furthermore, Lord Lloyd did not find helpful the majority's gloss about the cogency of the evidence needed to tip the balance of probabilities, and was concerned that 'there is a danger that the repeated use of the words will harden into a formula, which, like other formulas (especially those based on a metaphor) may lead to misunderstanding'.[495]

Baroness Hale of Richmond later observed in *Re B (Children) (Care Proceedings: Standard of Proof) (Cafcass Intervening)*[496] that 'Lord Lloyd's prediction proved only too correct'.[497] Despite the care with which Lord Nicholls sought to explain that the standard of proof is the balance of probabilities, his 'nuanced explanation left room for the nostrum, "the more serious the allegation, the more cogent the evidence needed to prove it", to take hold'. In addition, more confusion was created when in *R (McCann) v Crown Court at Manchester*[498] Lord Steyn cited Lord Nicholls's approach in *Re H (Minors) (Sexual Abuse: Standard of Proof)*[499] in support of there being in some cases a 'heightened civil standard' of proof.[500]

In *Re B (Children) (Care Proceedings: Standard of Proof) (Cafcass Intervening)*,[501] there-fore, the House of Lords agreed that, in light of the difficulties that misinterpretation of Lord Nicholls's gloss had seemingly caused, it was time to 'loosen its grip and give it its quietus'.[502] Indeed, the House went further and announced 'loud and clear' that the standard of proof in care proceedings 'is the simple balance of probabilities, neither more nor less'.[503] Baroness Hale explained that the consequences of care proceedings are serious either way and:

> Neither the seriousness of the allegation nor the seriousness of the consequences should make any difference to the standard of proof to be applied in determining the facts. The inherent probabilities are simply something to be taken into account, where relevant, in deciding where the truth lies.[504]

---

[493] His Lordship confined his comments to s 31(2). In the absence of argument he was not prepared to endorse the wider view, expressed by Millett LJ in the Court of Appeal, that the standard in all civil cases should be the simple balance of probabilities.   [494] [1996] AC 563 at 577.

[495] Ibid, 578.   [496] [2008] UKHL 35, [2009] AC 11   [497] Ibid, [64].   [498] [2003] 1 AC 787.

[499] [1996] AC 563 at 586D–H.

[500] *R (McCann) v Crown Court at Manchester* [2003] 1 AC 787 at [37]. As Baroness Hale observed in *Re B* Lord Nicholls's suggestion that the court should be 'more sure' in relation to serious allegations could be read as suggesting a higher standard than the simple preponderance of probabilities (see [2008] UKHL 35, [2009] AC 11 at [62]). See also the ambiguity in Lord Bingham of Cornhill's opinion in *B v Chief Constable of the Avon and Somerset Constabulary* [2001] 1 WLR 340. The dicta in *McCann* and *B v Chief Constable* were applied in care proceedings by Bodey J in *Re ET (Serious Injuries: Standard of Proof) (Note)* [2003] 2 FLR 1205, until the Court of Appeal corrected the position in *Re U (A Child) (Department for Education and Skills intervening)* [2005] Fam 134 at [13]. The developments in the case law on standard of proof are explored by Lord Hoffmann at [2008] UKHL 35, [2009] AC 11 at [5]–[12].

[501] [2008] UKHL 35, [2009] AC 11.   [502] Ibid, [64].   [503] Ibid, [70].

[504] Ibid. Lord Hoffmann stated that having regard to the inherent probabilities was a matter required by common sense not law (see at [15]).

As to the seriousness of any allegation, her Ladyship pointed out that:

> there is no logical or necessary connection between seriousness and probability. Some seriously harmful behaviour, such as murder, is sufficiently rare to be inherently improbable in most circumstances. Even then there are circumstances, such as a body with its throat cut and no weapon to hand, where it is not at all improbable. Other seriously harmful behaviour, such as alcohol or drug abuse, is regrettably all too common and not at all improbable.[505]

Baroness Hale also emphasised that the context in which allegations are made is important, commenting:

> Nor are serious allegations made in a vacuum. Consider the famous example of the animal seen in Regent's Park. If it is seen outside the zoo on a stretch of greensward regularly used for walking dogs, then of course it is more likely to be a dog than a lion. If it is seen in the zoo next to the lions' enclosure when the door is open, then it may well be more likely to be a lion than a dog.[506]

What do these dicta mean when translated to the child abuse context of the cases? The fact that an allegation of child abuse is a serious allegation does not affect the standard of proof. It is necessary in all cases simply to show that the allegation is more probably true than not. As to the inherent probabilities, the fact that, looking to the general population, it is unlikely that a stepfather is sexually abusing his stepdaughter is simply something to be taken into account, where relevant, in deciding where the truth lies. The difficulty may be in knowing when the inherent (general) probabilities are to be regarded as relevant or, even if relevant, how they are to be taken into account. For example, to what extent, if at all, is the general improbability of a stepfather having sexually abused his stepdaughter to be regarded as relevant in a particular case? There is an argument that once an allegation of sexual abuse has been made the relevant sample has shifted from the general population to stepdaughters who have made an allegation of serious abuse against a stepfather. While the position in the general population has a bearing on the likelihood (in general) of a parent being wrongly accused, once an allegation is made, arguably the more pertinent probability relates to the likelihood of a child making a false allegation.[507] It is submitted that the courts will need to think carefully in individual cases about the relevance of general inherent probabilities. In some cases the issue of relevance will be more clear-cut than in others: for example, if there is evidence that a baby has suffered a non-accidental injury in unknown circumstances, the fact that such non-accidental injuries are relatively rare in the general population is clearly neither here nor there.

8.6 HARM ATTRIBUTABLE TO CARE NOT BEING WHAT IT WOULD BE REASONABLE TO EXPECT A PARENT TO GIVE

Key legislation

The second limb of section 31(2), in (b), requires proof that:

… the harm, or likelihood of harm, is attributable to—

(i) the care given to the child, or likely to be given to him if the order were not made, not being what it would be reasonable to expect a parent to give to him.

---

[505] Ibid, [72].   [506] Ibid.
[507] H. Keating, 'Shifting Standards in the House of Lords—*Re H and Others (Minors) (Sexual Abuse: Standard of Proof)*' [1996] Child and Family Law Quarterly 157.

The phrase 'attributable to' connotes a causal connection between the harm or likelihood of harm and the care given or likely to be given, but the connection 'need not be that of a sole or dominant or direct cause and effect: a contributory causal connection suffices'.[508] So, for example, if a parent entrusts a child to the care of another without checking that person's suitability and the third party injures the child, the harm may be regarded as attributable to the inadequate care of the parent as well as to the actions of the third party.[509] By contrast, section 31(2)(b) would not be fulfilled where a child is harmed in the circumstances of a 'one-off temporary entrustment of the child to a person reasonably believed by the parents to be suitable'.[510] However, if the parent is unsuitable to care for the child, the threshold may be fulfilled even though the parent has entrusted the child's care to others who are looking after the child appropriately. In *H v Trafford Borough Council*[511] the mother, who engaged in prostitution and was addicted to drugs, asked neighbours to babysit for her baby and then disappeared for six weeks. Although the mother reappeared briefly she disappeared again and the following year she indicated that she did not now wish to resume care of her child. The local authority decided to commence care proceedings even though the child was being properly looked after by the neighbours. Wall J held that there should not be a narrow construction of section 31 which would prevent intervention to protect such a child. The magistrates were entitled to find that the child would be likely to suffer significant harm as the mother could have reclaimed the child at any time, thus exposing the child to the dangers of her lifestyle.

It has been said that where a child has suffered injuries, it is not open to a local authority simply to use the fact of those injuries as a basis for submitting that the threshold criteria are reached and that the parents are responsible. In *CL v East Riding Yorkshire Council, MB and BL (A Child)*[512] a father tripped and fell while carrying a seven-week-old baby and the baby struck his head on the floor suffering a skull fracture and brain injury. The judge found the threshold fulfilled on the basis that the child had suffered this serious injury while in the care of the parents.[513] The Court of Appeal held that the judge had been wrong to do so. The court commented that 'a child may receive serious accidental injuries whilst in the care of his or her parents, even where those parents are both conscientious and competent' and such injuries do not fall within section 31(2) of the Children Act 1989. The court held that that provision, 'translated into everyday language and experience' means that a local authority 'must prove that an injury is non-accidental'.[514] The occurrence of the injuries, by itself, was not sufficient to satisfy the threshold. This decision suggests that a child might not be protected from a very accident-prone parent. Yet, it may legitimately be asked whether a child who has suffered significant harm attributable

---

[508] *Lancashire County Council v B* [2002] 2 AC 147 at 162, echoing Donaldson J in *Walsh v Rother District Council* [1978] ICR 1216 at 1220.

[509] The example was given by Lord Nicholls of Birkenhead in *Lancashire County Council v B* [2002] 2 AC 147 at 162.

[510] Ibid, 165.   [511] [1997] 3 FCR 113.   [512] [2006] EWCA Civ 49, [2006] 2 FLR 24.

[513] A further feature of the case was that the parents did not immediately summon an ambulance, and the judge found that the parents had failed to protect the child after the injury. This was not criticised on appeal. On failure to protect, see also *Re W (Care: Threshold Criteria)* [2007] EWCA Civ 102, [2007] 2 FLR 98 (mother could not be said to have failed to protect her child where there was no finding that the child's father, a sex offender, had sexually abused the child. A risk of future harm could also not be established on the basis of her former relationship with the father, as there was no evidence that she was likely to forge another relationship with child abuser).

[514] [2006] EWCA Civ 49, [52]. See also *Re J (Care Proceedings: Injuries)* [2009] 2 FLR 99, FD (Hogg J).

to several accidental injuries at the hands of his or her parents is receiving care which it would be reasonable to expect a parent to give.[515]

8.6.1 Care must fall below an objectively acceptable level

The care given or likely to be given 'must fall below an objectively acceptable level'.[516] The focus is not on the care it would be reasonable to expect the actual child's parent or carer to give, but on what it would be reasonable to expect 'a parent' to give to the child. Furthermore, 'an absence of a reasonable standard of parental care need not imply that the parents are at fault'.[517] As Hughes LJ observed in *Re D (Care Order: Evidence)*[518] if it were otherwise, 'the protection afforded to children would be very limited indeed, if not entirely illusory. It would in effect then be limited to protection against the parent who was fully able to provide proper care but either chose not to do so or neglected through fault to do so. That is not the meaning of s 31(2). It is abundantly clear that a parent may unhappily fail to provide reasonable care even though he is doing his incompetent best.'[519] If the threshold did not adopt an objective test, it would mean that a child could not be protected from persons with serious physical incapacities, serious or unpredictable mental illness, or (severe) learning disabilities.[520]

8.6.1.1 Parents with learning disabilities

The Court of Appeal has made clear that, in cases involving parents with learning disabilities, a care order is never made simply on the basis of the parent's learning disability.[521] To do so would be impermissible social engineering.[522] Equally, however, the court has observed that there is no issue of discrimination in this context in judging a learning disabled parent by the standards expected of a non-disabled parent.[523]

Although the objective nature of the test is easily stated and defended, cases involving learning disabled parents raise difficult questions in practice concerning the human rights of such individuals[524] and the extent to which they should be supported in parenting tasks.[525] In *Kutzner v Germany*[526] the German authorities removed parental responsibility from the learning disabled parents of two children. The European Court of Human Rights found in the circumstances a breach of parents' rights to respect for family life as guaranteed by Article 8

---

[515] Cf the similar approach of HHJ Bryant at first instance in *Re B (Fact-Finding Hearing: Evidence)* [2008] EWCA Civ 1547, [2009] 2 FLR 14, described by the Court of Appeal (at [6]) as 'singular to himself'. HHJ Bryant declined to approach the issue on what the Court of Appeal said was 'a commonplace basis: were these injuries accidental or non-accidental?'

[516] *Lancashire County Council v B* [2002] 2 AC 147 at 162.

[517] Ibid.   [518] [2010] EWCA Civ 1000, [2011] 1 FLR 447.

[519] Ibid, [35], and see also *Lancashire County Council v B* [2002] 2 AC 147 at 162; and for an example, see *Re G and A (Care Order: Freeing Order: Parents with a Learning Disability)* [2006] NI Fam 8 (parents' lack of insight would require 24-hour support which was impractical).

[520] See A. Bond, *Care Proceedings and Learning Disabled Parents: A Handbook for Family Lawyers* (Bristol: Jordan Publishing, 2011) for definitions, a useful overview of research evidence on parents with learning disabilities, and discussion of the relevant law, policy, and guidance.

[521] *Re L (Children) (Care Proceedings: Significant Harm)* [2006] EWCA Civ 1282, [2007] 1 FLR 1068 at [52].   [522] Ibid, [49].

[523] *Re D (A Child) (Care Order: Evidence)* [2010] EWCA Civ 1000, [2011] 1 FLR 447. Note, however, Munby J's suggestion in *Re G (Care: Challenge To Local Authority's Decision)* [2003] EWHC 551 (Fam), [2003] 2 FLR 42 at [59] that a local authority may have to work harder to fulfil its duty to ensure such parents understand the local authority's concerns.

[524] See eg United Nations Convention on the Rights of Persons with Disabilities, particularly in this context Art 23(2).

[525] See Department of Health and Department for Education and Skills, *Good Practice Guidance on Working with Parents with a Learning Disability* (London: TSO, 2007).

[526] (App no 46544/99) [2003] 1 FCR 249.

of the ECHR. The Court commented that it was 'questionable whether the domestic administrative and judicial authorities [had] given sufficient consideration to additional measures of support as an alternative to what is by far the most extreme measure, namely separating the children from their parents'.[527] Clearly this raises an issue for any court about whether a care order is a proportionate response in the context of available support which could be provided to the child's parent(s). But it also potentially raises an issue with respect to the threshold criteria. Is the question whether the significant harm is attributable to 'the care given to the child not being what it would be reasonable to expect a parent to give' to be viewed in light of the provision of available support to a parent? Hedley J thought so in *LBH (A Local Authority) v KJ and IH*[528] in the slightly different context of a parent's care of a severely disabled child. His Lordship commented that parents do not expose themselves to compulsory state intervention in family life simply on the ground that the child's needs are beyond their capacities however assiduously they devote themselves to the care of the child (except where a child is beyond parental control).[529] He was also of the view that neither can it:

be the case that a local authority can fail to put in the support properly required to enable a child to be cared for at home (absent expert evidence that a child could never be cared for at home because of disability whatever reasonable support was provided) and then use that failure as grounds for compulsory intervention under Part IV of the Act...each would involve a violation of Article 8(1) (as all such interventions on the face of it necessarily must) and that such violation in those circumstances would not be justifiable under Article 8(2).[530]

He added:

a parent cannot be said to be responsible for a falling below the standard of 'reasonable care' if the public authorities cannot or do not provide what would be reasonably necessary to support that parent.

It has been suggested that the same reasoning could be applied to the support which might reasonably be provided to enable a learning disabled parent to parent his or her child appropriately.[531] However, the analogy with *LBH (A Local Authority) v KJ and IH*[532] is an uneasy one. Hedley J's concern in *LBH* is that parenting should not be found wanting in circumstances where 'a parent' (ie, parents generally) would not cope without support. By contrast, if the same approach is extended to learning disabled parents the emphasis is not on what could be expected of a 'a parent' generally; instead the focus is on what could reasonably be expected of the particular learning disabled parent with available support.

8.6.1.2 Unknown perpetrator cases

Key case

A particular difficulty in interpreting section 31(2)(b) arises where a child suffers a non-accidental injury but it is not possible to identify the perpetrator, for example when a child is being looked after by more than one person, sometimes in more than one household, and it is unclear when, and by whom, the child has suffered the injury. The issue came before the House of Lords in *Lancashire County Council v B*.[533] A paid childminder, who had a child of her own (child B) looked after a baby girl, child A, while A's parents were at

---

[527] Ibid, [75].   [528] [2007] EWHC 2798 (sitting in the Barnet County Court).
[529] Ibid, [20].   [530] Ibid, [21].
[531] See A. Bond, *Care Proceedings and Learning Disabled Parents: A Handbook for Family Lawyers* (Bristol: Jordan Publishing, 2011), pp 61–62.
[532] [2007] EWHC 2798 (sitting in the Barnet County Court).   [533] [2002] 2 AC 147.

work. Otherwise, A's parents looked after her. After this arrangement had been in place for two months, A, who was then seven months old, was found to have sustained serious non-accidental head injuries. The local authority applied for care orders in respect of A and B (who was only a month older than A), relying exclusively on the injury sustained to A. The judge found that the injuries to A had been inflicted by a member of household A or household B[534] but not both, but was unable to say which of A's mother, A's father, or B's mother was the perpetrator. The judge was of the view that, having so found, the threshold criteria could not be fulfilled and he dismissed the care applications.[535] On the local authority's appeal, the Court of Appeal dismissed the appeal in respect of B, applying the approach to the standard of proof required by *Re H*. The court explained that since it had not been established as a matter of fact that B's mother had harmed A, there was no factual basis (as opposed to suspicion) from which the inference could be drawn that B was at risk in his household.[536] There was no appeal in respect of B. However, the Court of Appeal allowed the appeal in respect of A, and A's case subsequently came before the House of Lords on A's parents' appeal. The House of Lords dismissed the appeal, holding that the threshold was fulfilled. The House could not believe that Parliament intended the threshold criteria to operate so as to preclude protection of a child injured in the circumstances of A's case.[537] Lord Nicholls of Birkenhead, delivering an opinion with which there was unanimous agreement, held that the phrase 'care given to the child' normally refers primarily to the care given to the child by a parent or parents or other primary carers. However, the matter stands differently in a case in which the child's care is shared between primary carers and other carers and the court is unable to distinguish between the care given by those respective carers. Lord Nicholls said that in such a case 'the phrase "care given to the child" is apt to embrace not merely the care given by the parents or other primary carers; it is apt to embrace the care given by any of the carers'.[538] The House recognised that this interpretation meant that parents who were wholly innocent will face the possibility of losing their child but the factor outweighing all others is 'the prospect that an unidentified, and unidentifiable, carer may inflict further injury on a child he or she has already severely damaged'.[539]

This reasoning would similarly apply in a case in which a child has been injured in the care of both parents and it is not possible to establish which parent has caused the first child to suffer significant harm. Indeed in *Re CB and JB (Care Proceedings: Guidelines)*[540] Wall J ruled on such facts that the threshold was fulfilled. In that case the child who had been harmed had a sibling and Wall J went further to hold that a finding that the first child's injuries must have been caused by either the mother or the father gave rise to a real possibility, a possibility which could not sensibly be ignored, that the unharmed sibling would also suffer significant harm were he to be left in the care of both or either of his parents.[541] This aspect of the decision was distinguished by the judge at first instance in *Lancashire County Council v B* and the Court of Appeal held that the judge had been correct in the conclusion that he reached in respect of child B in that case. However, the

---

[534] The judge excluded B's father as a possible perpetrator.

[535] The judge applied a dictum of Wall J in *Re G (A Minor) (Care Order: Threshold Conditions)* [1995] Fam 16 at 20, which suggested that the lack of care must be shown to be attributable to the parents.

[536] For criticism of the Court of Appeal's approach, see J. Hayes, 'The Threshold Test and the Unknown Perpetrator' [2000] Family Law 260.   [537] [2002] 2 AC 147 at 165.

[538] [2002] 2 AC 147, 166.   [539] Ibid, 167.   [540] [1998] 2 FLR 211.

[541] As Wall J said (at 220): 'the argument to the contrary…strikes at the whole philosophy of child protection embodied in the Children Act 1989'.

Court of Appeal in the *Lancashire* case did not comment further on the correctness or otherwise of Wall J's reasoning in *Re CB and JB*. It is not easy to reconcile the two decisions. This has been illustrated by John Hayes,[542] who points to the difficulty the *Lancashire* case creates on facts somewhere between the two cases. Imagine, he says, a case in which child A in the *Lancashire* case had a twin, child C, living in the same household, but who had suffered no harm. On the Court of Appeal's reasoning in the *Lancashire* case, A (who has been harmed) can be protected on the basis of suspicion that the parents were responsible for the harm, but the twin cannot. Hayes argues that the Court of Appeal's tortuous reasoning could be avoided if the court focused on the question whether, even without identifying a perpetrator, there was a 'real possibility' of harm.

Wall J's reasoning in *Re CB and JB* is now also difficult to reconcile with a dictum of the Supreme Court's decision in *Re S-B (Children) (Care Proceedings: Standard of Proof)*,[543] which applied the same approach as the Court of Appeal in the *Lancashire* case, this time to siblings. In *Re S-B* a child, Jason, suffered non-accidental bruising when aged 4 weeks. The parents separated and the mother subsequently gave birth to another child, William. Care proceedings were brought in respect of William because of what had happened to Jason. The trial judge was unable to decide which of Jason's parents was responsible for the injuries, but found the threshold crossed in respect of William on the basis that there was a real possibility that the mother had injured Jason. Baroness Hale stated[544] that the judge's approach was not permissible since *Re H* made clear that the finding of a real possibility of future harm had to be based upon findings of fact made on the balance of probabilities.

Re CB and JB and *Re S-B* can be distinguished, however, in at least one arguably material respect. In *Re CB and JB* the parents were still living together at the relevant time for establishing the threshold criteria (although the father was subsequently removed from the scene because he was imprisoned for offences not related to harm of the child). Thus at the relevant time the risk of future harm to the sibling could be inferred from the established fact that the child had been harmed by someone in the household to which the child would be returned. By contrast, in *Re S-B* by the relevant time for establishing the threshold in respect of William, the parents had separated. This is, however, a very fine point of distinction in unknown perpetrator cases, for, as Wall J pointed out in *Re CB and JB*, the absence of a finding that it was one parent rather than the other who has harmed a child does not eliminate the risk if one of the parents leaves or is removed and a child is left with the other parent.

The reasoning in *Re S-B* was cited by the Court of Appeal in *Re F (Interim Care Order)*.[545] In that case a man had two children of different mothers. The first child, J, had been the subject of care proceedings in which there had been a finding of non-accidental injury perpetrated by one of the parents. The father set up home with another woman and had another child, C. In care proceedings alleging a risk of harm to C from his father, the trial judge held that the threshold criteria could not be fulfilled. In refusing leave to appeal to the Supreme Court, the Court of Appeal endorsed the judge's approach and commented that: 'No doubt there are hard and worrying cases. But the requirement of proven factual foundation is a bulwark against the state's removal of a child from his family, which I consider very precious.'[546] Mary Hayes has commented, however, that this 'was an inadequate and detached response to the creation by

---

[542] J. Hayes, 'The Threshold Test and the Unknown Perpetrator' [2000] Family Law 260.

[543] [2009] UKSC 178, [2010] 1 AC 678. See Ian Goldrein QC, 'There is Only So Much Juice in an Orange: *Re SB*' [2010] Family Law 196; J. Hayes, 'Ensuring Equal Protection for Siblings' [2010] Family Law 505. *Re CB and JB* was cited to the Supreme Court but was not referred to in the judgment.

[544] [2009] UKSC 178, [2010] 1 AC 678 at [49].

[545] [2011] EWCA Civ 258, [2011] 2 FLR 856. For comment, see M. Hayes, 'Why Didn't the Courts Protect this Child? *Re SB and Re F*' [2012] Family Law 169.   [546] Ibid, [15].

law of a very dangerous situation for children.[547] She argues that the approach in *Re F*, relying on paragraph [49] of *Re S-B*, conflates the tests in section 31(2)(a) and (b) respectively. As Mary Hayes points out, *Re H* did not 'make any observations or rulings on whether the threshold test can be crossed where a court finds it impossible to determine who in a pool of possible perpetrators has caused the proven harm.'[548] It does not, therefore, provide a reason for not applying to a case like this the more liberal approach to section 31(2)(b) in cases of unknown perpetrators as set out by the House of Lords in the *Lancashire* case. There is no reason to conflate the two sub-paragraphs of section 31(2).[549] Unlike in *Re H*, in *Re F* there was no doubt that harm to J had been perpetrated, and the harm was attributable to either the mother or the father. In the absence of knowledge of who the perpetrator actually was, the conclusion must surely be that there is a real possibility that C is at risk. This is consistent with the view that a possible perpetrator remains just that at the welfare stage of proceedings when assessing future risks. The inappropriateness of the approach at paragraph [49] of *Re S-B* can be illustrated by an example: imagine that either parent (but not both) is found to be a possible perpetrator of significant harm to a child who is taken into care. The parents then separate and each has a child with a new partner. One of the children is at risk, but neither can be protected. A further difficulty with the approach adopted in *Re S-B* is that, as John Hayes has pointed out,[550] it is extremely difficult to reconcile with an earlier House of Lords decision in *Re O and another (Minors) (Care: Preliminary Hearing)*[551] in which on facts essentially indistinguishable from those in *Re S-B* the House of Lords accepted that the threshold criteria were fulfilled. In *Re J (Children)*[552] the Court of Appeal held that it would be wholly inappropriate for it to do other than follow *Re S-B*. However, McFarlane LJ concluded that there was a pressing need for the issue to be determined by the Supreme Court. His Lordship's analysis suggested that *Re S-B* may not be compatible with Lord Nicholls's opinions in earlier decisions, which indicated a different approach 'between cases where absolutely no past harm has been proved, and those where past harm is established but the identity of the actual perpetrator cannot be proved.'[553]

8.6.1.3 Orphans and abandoned children

Difficult questions as to whether a child can be said to be suffering significant harm attributable to lack of reasonable parental care and whether a care order can be made have arisen in cases in which children are orphaned or abandoned. In *Birmingham City Council v D; Birmingham City Council v M*[554] these questions arose with respect to children from two different families who were orphans, accommodated by the local authority, with no family members available to be appointed as their guardians. The local authority argued that the absence of parental responsibility in any person imperilled the children because they would not be fully empowered to deal with crises and emergencies, and that therefore the children were at risk of suffering significant harm. The application was resisted by the children's guardians ad litem, who said that the needs of orphans were addressed by the accommodation provisions in the Act.[555] Thorpe J rejected the local authority's application for the following reason:

> section 31 is plainly designed to protect families from invasive care orders unless there is a manifest need evidenced by a perceptible risk of significant harm ... in these cases the local authority does not seek to invade, but to protect and compensate children who have been

---

[547] M. Hayes, 'Why Didn't the Courts Protect this Child? *Re SB and Re F*' [2012] Family Law 169.
[548] Ibid.
[549] Ibid.   [550] J. Hayes, 'Ensuring Equal Protection for Siblings' [2010] Family Law 505.
[551] The case involved conjoined appeals and is cited in full as *Re O and another (Minors) (Care: Preliminary Hearing); Re B (A Minor)* [2003] UKHL 18, [2004] 1 AC 523. The argument here relates to *Re O*.
[552] [2012] EWCA Civ 380.   [553] Ibid, at paras [128] and [131].
[554] [1994] 2 FLR 502 (Thorpe J).   [555] Sections 20, 22, and 23.

bereft of parental support. I have every sympathy with the local authority's motives and their aims, but I must construe section 31 sensibly and realistically. If there is some shortcoming in the statutory framework it is not for me to remedy the deficiency by a strained construction of section 31, particularly in the light of the opposition of the guardians ad litem.[556]

This illustrates that even where the proposals made by a local authority are entirely well meaning, and arguably in the child's best interests, they cannot be authorised by a court unless the grounds for an order are first established. Here Thorpe J took the view that the language of the relevant provision prevented the court from intervening, even had it wished to do so.

In *Re SH (Care Order: Orphan)*[557] the court was faced with a similar situation: an 11-year-old boy was being accommodated by the local authority; he was an orphan and no member of his extended family was prepared to care for him. However, the facts differed in one vital respect. The boy was accommodated by the local authority following allegations of sexual abuse by his father, in which the mother and a half-sister were also implicated. While the child was accommodated, his mother and father died in quick succession. The local authority continued to look after the boy, and two months after he became an orphan the local authority sought a care order. Hollis J held that the threshold criteria could be fulfilled applying *Re M (A Minor) (Care Order: Threshold Conditions)*.[558] There was evidence that the child was suffering significant harm when the local authority first took steps to rescue him and on that basis counsel conceded that the threshold could be fulfilled at the date of the hearing. It may be doubted whether that concession was correctly made. Lord Mackay in *Re M* made clear that jurisdiction can only be founded at an earlier date where protective measures are continuously in place to the date of disposal, and cannot be so founded where the need for protection has terminated prior to that date. It is submitted that the House of Lords did not just mean that, following intervention, there must be continuous accommodation of the child to the date of disposal. For the House of Lords' approach to make sense, surely the protective measures referred to must be those that were put in place to avoid the harm which is relied upon at the hearing to fulfil the threshold. Once the parents were dead, the need to protect the children from sexual abuse ceased. From that point, the boy, although continuing to be accommodated, was accommodated for a different reason, because he was orphaned.

However, having accepted that the threshold was crossed, Hollis J went on to consider whether a care order should be made. At this stage, the fact that no one had parental responsibility for the child was influential on Hollis J. When giving his reasons for concluding that a care order was in the child's best interests, he said that although the local authority had extensive powers under Part III of the Children Act 1989 it did not have the powers it might need when caring for the boy. Moreover, the guardianship provisions in section 5 were not apt to cover the situation because they were designed to confer guardianship upon an individual, not on an artificial individual such as the director of social services.

In the case of an orphaned child, whether the threshold test can be established appears, therefore, to turn on the court's view of the child's total situation. Being an orphan is not enough to overcome the threshold test, but where the fact of being an orphan is linked to other facts together they may provide sufficient evidence to establish that the child is suffering, or is likely to suffer, significant harm.[559]

---

[556] [1994] 2 FLR 502 at 504–505.   [557] [1995] 1 FLR 746.

[558] [1994] 2 AC 424, which approved *Northamptonshire County Council v S* [1993] Fam 136, [1992] 3 WLR 1010.

[559] The Children Act Advisory Committee recommended that the position of children for whom no one has parental responsibility is in urgent need of review, CAAC Report 1994/5, p 32.

Cazalet J applied similar reasoning to an abandoned child in *Re M (Care Order: Parental Responsibility)*.[560] He held that the threshold test was established in the case of a baby who had been abandoned when only a few days old on the steps of a health centre. While there was a good chance, therefore, that the child would be found, Cazalet J reasoned that the fact of abandonment, with all the risks it entailed, meant the child was suffering significant harm immediately before he was found. Furthermore, and importantly, he held it was likely that the child would suffer significant harm in view of the fact that he would grow up having no knowledge of his background. Such lack of knowledge would probably cause him to have distressing fantasies about his origins and he would be deprived of a sense of belonging. Upon medical examination the child had been found to be developmentally delayed and to have some bone abnormalities. Cazalet J concluded that the child's future required firm and positive decisions which may have to be taken by the local authority at short notice and that it should therefore have parental responsibility with a view to implementing its care plan, which was to place the child for adoption.

8.7 THE HARM IS ATTRIBUTABLE TO THE CHILD'S BEING BEYOND PARENTAL CONTROL

Occasionally a child may be suffering, or be likely to suffer, significant harm not because of a failure of reasonable parental care, but because he is beyond parental control.[561] Examples might be where a child has become addicted to drugs or is sexually promiscuous, but no doubt there are many other situations in which parents become powerless to influence the child's behaviour. An example arose in *M v Birmingham City Council*[562] where Stuart-White J held that the words 'beyond parental control' are 'a substantial expression capable of describing a state of affairs in the past, in the present or in the future according to the context in which it falls to be applied' and assumed, without deciding the point, that parental control refers to 'the parent of the child in question and not to parents, or reasonable parents, in general'.[563]

It is suggested that those initiating care proceedings, and courts when determining an application brought in care proceedings, should be wary of improper reliance being placed on the beyond control provision. Where parents, or others, have truly tried their best to make reasonable arrangements for the child's upbringing it is right that they should not be stigmatised as causing the child to suffer, or to be likely to suffer, significant harm because the care they have given the child, or are likely to give the child, is not what it would be reasonable to expect a parent to give to him. However, it is equally stigmatising for the child to be found to be beyond parental control in a case where the fault lies with those who have brought him up. Such a finding is likely to influence the arrangements which are made about how the child will be looked after if a care order is made, or the types of activities in which the child will be required to take part if a supervision order is made. Justice to a child requires that he should only be labelled as beyond control where there is cogent evidence to support this allegation. Where a child is badly behaved, or otherwise apparently out of control, it may be comparatively easy to prove that the child is bringing harm upon himself. It may be far harder to prove wrongdoing or other failure by a parent which has led to the child coming to harm, or to be likely to come to harm. It seems likely that there is a risk that the attribution to the child of the cause of harm to the child, rather than the parent, might sometimes be selected as the basis for bringing proceedings, or making an order, because it is easier to

---

[560] [1996] 2 FLR 84.   [561] Section 31(2)(b)(ii).

[562] [1994] 2 FLR 141. The child, aged 13, was very seriously disturbed and behaving in an uncontrollable fashion, such that she was posing a serious risk to herself and those around her.   [563] Ibid, 147.

prove. However, just as it is wrong to label a parent as having caused his child to come to harm unless there is evidence to substantiate this, so too it is wrong to label a child as being beyond parental control if the true cause of his coming to harm is because his parents, or others, have failed to give him reasonable parental care.

8.8 THE WELFARE QUESTION IN CARE PROCEEDINGS[564]

Once established, the threshold criteria allow the court to make a care order or a supervision order. But proof of the grounds is permissive only. It by no means follows that those orders will always be in the child's best interests. Whether an order is made and, if so which, must be considered applying the child's welfare as the paramount consideration (section 1 of the Children Act 1989). The checklist in section 1(3) must also be applied,[565] and the court must be satisfied that the making of an order is better for the child than making no order at all.[566]

8.9 ISSUES SURROUNDING APPLICATION OF THE CHECKLIST IN CARE PROCEEDINGS

8.9.1 Proof of harm in section 1(3)(e)

Paragraph (e) of the welfare checklist directs the court to have regard to 'any harm which [the child] has suffered or is at risk of suffering'. Thus, harm must be considered both at the threshold and welfare stages. Several issues have arisen for the courts on this provision.

8.9.1.1 Unknown perpetrators at the disposal stage

In *Re O and another (Minors) (Care: Preliminary Hearing); Re B (A Minor)*[567] the House of Lords considered how the welfare stage of proceedings should be approached in unknown perpetrator cases following its earlier ruling in the *Lancashire County Council* cases (discussed in Section 8.6.1.2). The appeals in *Re O* and *Re B* arose from the different approach which the Court of Appeal had adopted in each case. In *Re B* a 1-year-old child had been killed in the care of his parents in circumstances in which neither could be exonerated as the perpetrator. The parents subsequently split up. In care proceedings in respect of the child's 6-year-old elder sibling the Court of Appeal held that a judge cannot in these circumstances disregard the risk that the mother presents as a primary carer for the child. In *Re O* a six-month-old child suffered a skull fracture and neither parent could be exculpated. The parents parted when the child was admitted to hospital, the father was subsequently imprisoned, and the mother thereafter gave birth to the couple's second child. The local authority sought care orders in respect of both children. By contrast with *Re B* the Court of Appeal held that a judge should proceed on the basis that the first child was not injured by her mother and the mother presented no risk to the children. Lord Nicholls of Birkenhead, delivering the House of Lords' decision, concluded that the approach in *Re B*:

> would be a self-defeating interpretation of the legislation. It would mean that, in 'uncertain perpetrator' cases, the court decides that the threshold criteria are satisfied but then lacks

---

[564] Sometimes this is referred to as the welfare *stage*. However, the House of Lords has commented that there are not two stages in care proceedings: see *Re B (Children) (Sexual Abuse: Standard of Proof)* [2008] UKHL 35 at [74].   [565] It is mandatory in applications under Pt IV of the Children Act 1989: see s 1(4).   [566] Section 1(5).   [567] [2003] UKHL 18, [2004] 1 AC 523.

the ability to proceed in a sensible way in the best interests of the child. The preferable interpretation of the legislation is that in such cases the court is able to proceed at the welfare stage on the footing that each of the possible perpetrators is, indeed, just that: a possible perpetrator.[568]

However, his Lordship added that the 'importance to be attached to that possibility, as to every feature of the case, necessarily depends on the circumstances.'[569]

8.9.1.2 Other cases of unproved allegations

Another question the courts have had to address is how section 1(3)(e) is to be applied in a case in which the threshold criteria are proved on one ground such as neglect, but not on another. To what extent (if at all) can the court take into account at the welfare stage the possibility that the non-proven allegation may be true? The Court of Appeal considered the issue in *Re M and R (Child Abuse: Evidence)*[570] in light of the House of Lords' decision in *Re H (Minors) (Sexual Abuse: Standard of Proof).*[571] In *Re M and R* the threshold test had been passed because the children had been emotionally abused. However, the trial judge declined to make a final care order because although there was a real possibility that sexual abuse had occurred, the judge ruled that the evidence of sexual abuse was not sufficient to prove the allegations to the requisite standard.[572] The local authority appealed, supported by the guardian ad litem. The question of law was whether the judge's conclusion that there was a real possibility that sexual abuse had occurred could be taken into consideration when the court was considering what order (if any) to make, and it was asserted on behalf of the child that there was sufficient evidence of sexual abuse for the purposes of section 1(3)(e). The Court of Appeal held that where there is a dispute at the welfare stage of the proceedings over whether the child has suffered, or is at risk of suffering, significant harm the court must apply the same reasoning as in *Re H*. It must reach a conclusion based on facts, not on suspicion or doubts.[573] In *Re P (Sexual Abuse: Standard of Proof)*[574] the Court of Appeal adopted the same approach to section 1(3)(e) in private law proceedings. These points did not call for decision in the House of Lords in *Re O and another (Minors) (Care: Preliminary Hearing); Re B (A Minor)*.[575] However, Lord Nicholls reviewed the authorities and found attractive the conclusions of the Court of Appeal in both cases.[576]

8.9.2 The range of orders at the court's disposal: section 1(3)(g)

Within the checklist, section 1(3)(g) specifically requires the court to have regard to the range of possible orders at its disposal. The court may conclude that a care order should be made or it may decide that a supervision order will afford the child sufficient protection against suffering further significant harm. The courts' approach to choosing between these orders is discussed later in the text once the legal effects of each of the orders has been considered. In some cases, however, neither order may be deemed appropriate. In some cases the court may determine that no useful purpose will be served by the local authority continuing to have involvement with the child, and that it is better for the child if no order at all is made. Sometimes a different order, for example a residence order, may be thought to be the most appropriate response, particularly where a relative is offering

---

[568] Ibid, [28].   [569] Ibid, [31].   [570] [1996] 2 FLR 195.   [571] [1996] AC 563.

[572] Despite the unanimous opinion evidence of three consultant psychiatrists that two children of the family had probably been abused.

[573] [1996] 2 FLR 195, see Butler-Sloss LJ at 203. For a critique, see I. Hemingway and C. Williams, 'Re M and R: Re H and R' [1997] Family Law 740; contra see D. Bedingfield, *The Child in Need* (Bristol: Family Law, 1998), p 343.   [574] [1996] 2 FLR 333, CA.

[575] [2003] UKHL 18, [2004] 1 AC 523   [576] Ibid, [45].

to look after the child. A residence order can be made subject to conditions or it could be coupled with a supervision order where this seems necessary for the purpose of protecting the child.[577] A family assistance order may be a helpful adjunct to a residence order, particularly where there may be difficulties about contact arrangements with the child.[578] A prohibited steps order might suffice, for example where the child may be protected by prohibiting a specified person from having any contact with the child.

Even when parties to the proceedings agree about which order is most suitable, the decision is nonetheless one for the court to make. The parties might, for example, all agree that the threshold for care is established but that the child can be adequately protected by a supervision order. The court, on the other hand, might be unhappy with this arrangement, and take the view that a care order is the only order which will properly safeguard the child from suffering further significant harm. In these circumstances it should make a care order. However, there must in general be cogent and strong reasons to force a more draconian order upon the local authority than that for which it has asked, and it is wrong to make a care order simply to encourage or oblige a local authority to fulfil its statutory duties towards children in need.[579] Similarly, the court can, of course, refuse to make a care order even though the local authority's application is supported by the children's guardian. However, where a court departs from a recommendation made by the guardian it must give particularly full and clear reasons for reaching a different decision.[580]

9 THE LOCAL AUTHORITY'S CARE PLAN AND RESPECTIVE ROLES OF THE LOCAL AUTHORITY AND COURT

The local authority is required by section 31A of the Children Act 1989 to prepare a care plan setting out the local authority's plan for the child's future care, keep the plan under review, and revise it if necessary.[581]

The adequacy and appropriateness of the care plan will be important factors in the court's decision whether to make a care order. That crucial decision, with its long-term implications, is the responsibility of the court. With the exception of the issue of contact between the child and individuals which is regulated by section 34 of the Children Act 1989,[582] the court cannot monitor implementation of the care plan once a care order is made.[583] The court cannot attach any conditions to a care order, or ask the guardian to report back on how the order is working, for this would amount to an attempt to regulate the manner in which a local authority exercise its powers under the order.[584] The court

---

[577] See *Re DH (A Minor) (Child Abuse)* [1994] 1 FLR 679; *Re FS (Child Abuse: Evidence)* [1996] 2 FLR 158.

[578] See *Leeds City Council v C* [1993] 1 FLR 269.

[579] *Oxfordshire City Council v L (Care or Supervision Order)* [1998] 1 FLR 70.

[580] *S v Oxfordshire County Council* [1993] 1 FLR 452; *Leicestershire County Council v G* [1994] 2 FLR 329.

[581] See Care Planning, Placement and Case Review (England) Regulations 2010 (SI 2010/959) and the Fostering Services (England) Regulations 2011 (SI 2011/581) for the prescribed information and the manner in which it is to be presented. *Re J (Care: Care Plan)* [1994] 1 FLR 253; *Re K (Care Proceedings: Care Plan)* [2007] EWHC 393 (Fam).

[582] Discussed further in Section 14.

[583] See *Re S (Minors) (Care Order: Implementation of Care Plan)*; *Re W (Minors) (Care Order: Adequacy of Care Plan)* [2002] 2 AC 291.

[584] *Kent County Council v C* [1993] 1 FLR 308; *Re B (A Minor) (Care Order: Review)* [1993] 1 FLR 421; *Re T (A Minor) (Care Order: Conditions)* [1994] 2 FLR 423.

will only become involved in further litigation about the child where an application is made which would have the effect of discharging the care order[585] or where an application is made for a contact order under section 34. Thus, once the order is made, parental responsibility lies with the local authority and effectively all decision-making powers about the child are henceforth vested in the local authority and taken from the court.[586] The court, therefore, needs to have a clear idea of the nature of the local authority's plans for the child before it transfers decision-making powers to the authority.[587]

In *Re J (Minors) (Care: Care Plan)*[588] Wall J said that, wherever possible, evidence to support the care plan should be provided, though he acknowledged that the extent and nature of the evidence will vary from case to case, and that the local authority may have been inhibited from formulating long-term plans until sure of obtaining a care order.[589]

The court 'cannot dictate to the local authority what the care plan is to say'[590] and 'if it seeks to alter the local authority's care plan, must achieve its objective by persuasion rather than by compulsion'.[591] The point at which the court passes responsibility to the local authority is a matter of discretion,[592] and 'one for fine judgment, reflecting sensitivity, realism and an appropriate degree of judicial understanding of what can and cannot sensibly be expected of the local authority'.[593] One possibility where the court disagrees with the care plan is to make an interim care order to afford the local authority time to reconsider. However, an interim order 'is to be used for its intended purpose and not to be extended to providing a continuing control over the actions of the local authority',[594] although in an appropriate case the court can properly require the local authority to reconsider its care plan more than once.[595]

Ultimately, however, the court's role is limited to deciding whether an order should be made or not. As Nourse LJ explained in *Re T (A Minor) (Care Order: Conditions)*:[596]

> it is the duty of any court hearing an application for a care order carefully to scrutinise the local authority's care plan. If it does not agree with the care plan, it can refuse to make a care order...The cases in which it is appropriate to take such a course will no doubt be rare.[597]

---

[585] As when a direct application is made to discharge the care order under s 39; or where an application is made for a residence order which, if made, would have the effect of discharging the care order (s 91(1)).

[586] Once a care order is made it lasts until the child reaches 18 unless it is brought to an end earlier by order of a court (s 91(12)).

[587] This sometimes gives rise to the question whether the court is in a position to make a final order or whether it should make an interim order: see Section 7.

[588] *Re J (Minors) (Care: Care Plan)* [1994] 1 FLR 253.

[589] Eg they are unlikely to arrange a potential adoption placement until certain that they will obtain a care order, but they could give the court some idea of how easy such an arrangement would be to make.

[590] *Re L (Care Proceedings: Human Rights Claims)* [2003] EWHC 665 (Fam), [2003] 2 FLR 160 at [11].

[591] *Re K (Care Proceedings: Care Plan)* [2008] 1 FLR 6 at [15].

[592] See eg Butler-Sloss LJ in *Re L (Sexual Abuse: Standard of Proof)* [1996] 1 FLR 116 at 124 and *Re R (Care Proceedings: Adjournment)* [1998] 2 FLR 390 at 399.

[593] *Re K (Care Proceedings: Care Plan)* [2008] 1 FLR 6 at [16].

[594] *Re L (Sexual Abuse: Standard of Proof)* [1996] 1 FLR 116 at 125. See also *per* Hale LJ in *Re W and B; Re W (Care Plan)* [2001] EWCA Civ 757, [2001] 2 FLR 582 at [67].

[595] *Re K (Care Proceedings: Care Plan)* [2008] 1 FLR 6 at [18]. See eg *Re X; Barnet London Borough Council v Y and X* [2006] 2 FLR 998.

[596] [1994] 2 FLR 423.

[597] Ibid, 429, drawing on Wall J's judgment in *Re J (Minors) (Care: Care Plan)* [1994] 1 FLR 253 at 257–262. See also *per* Butler-Sloss LJ in *Re L (Sexual Abuse: Standard of Proof)* [1996] 1 FLR 116 at 126.

In such cases, however, the court may ultimately be faced with the dilemma that, while it does not agree with the care plan, failure to make a care order will mean that unsuitable parents retain unfettered parental responsibility for a child. This was illustrated in stark form in *Re S and D (Children: Powers of Court)*[598] where the judge was in the unenviable position of disagreeing with the local authority's plan to place the children at home because he was convinced that it would place the children at grave risk of suffering further significant harm.[599] He therefore purported to protect the children through coupling a supervision order with private law orders designed to prevent the children's removal from their foster parents, but in this regard he acted outside his powers.[600] Balcombe LJ, when asked to provide guidance to other courts faced with a similar dilemma, gave the unequivocal response that, regrettably, the judge has no alternative but to choose between the lesser of two evils:

> He may make a care order knowing that the local authority will then act in a way which he considers to be undesirable; or he may make no care order, which will often, as here, leave an unsuitable parent with parental responsibility for the children.[601]

9.1 REVIEWING IMPLEMENTATION OF THE CARE PLAN

The House of Lords in *Re S (Minors) (Care Order: Implementation of Care Plan); Re W (Minors) (Care Order: Adequacy of Care Plan)*[602] recognised that in the case of a young child who is the subject of a care order who would not have the capacity to initiate further proceedings before the court, the absence of a mechanism for reviewing the implementation of a care plan might breach the child's human rights. For that reason, an amendment was made to section 26 of the Children Act 1989, together with regulations, to ensure that care plans are kept under review. Independent reviewing officers are employed to monitor the process and are able to refer appropriate cases to Cafcass. Cafcass officers are then able to initiate proceedings on the child's behalf under section 7 of the Human Rights Act 1998 or by way of judicial review.

10 THE LEGAL EFFECT OF A CARE ORDER[603]

When a care order is made, the local authority gains parental responsibility for the child, which is shared with persons who already have parental responsibility.[604] However, there are some statutory limits imposed on the parental responsibility conferred on the local authority. Section 33(6)(a) provides that an authority is not permitted to 'cause the child to be brought up in any religious persuasion other than that in which

---

[598] [1995] 2 FLR 456. For another example, see *R (Care Proceedings: Adjournment)* [1998] 2 FLR 390.

[599] There was overwhelming evidence that the mother could not provide an adequate standard of parenting and a suggestion that she was suffering from Munchausen's syndrome by proxy.

[600] The Court of Appeal held that the orders were in breach of ss 9(5) and 100(2)(b).

[601] [1995] 2 FLR 456 at 463. For a similar example of local authority obduracy, see *Nottinghamshire County Council v P* [1993] 3 All ER 815.

[602] [2002] 2 AC 291.

[603] A useful analysis of the Children Act 1989 s 33 is provided by Baker J in *Re A and D (Local Authority: Religious Upbringing)* [2010] EWHC 2503 (Fam), [2011] 1 FLR 615 at [70] et seq.

[604] Unless the care order has discharged the order which originally conferred parental responsibility. A residence order is discharged when a care order is made so any parental responsibility which is conferred only while the residence order is in force would be ended. Parental responsibility is not lost solely because some other person subsequently acquires it (s 2(6)).

he would have been brought up if the order had not been made.'[605] In *Re A and D (Local Authority: Religious Upbringing)*[606] a Muslim father of a child who had been placed under a care order with maternal grandparents who were Catholics, contended that this provision means that a local authority must ensure that the child is brought up in the religion to which he 'belonged' at the time of the making of the care order. Rejecting this contention, Baker J drew attention to the fact that the nature of a child's religious persuasion, and parental control over it, evolves as the child matures.[607] He also pointed out that either or both parents might change religion after a care order is made. Indeed, in this case the child's mother, who had been a convert to Islam, had reconverted to Catholicism. In light of these observations, his Lordship held that 'the subtle and careful language used in s 33(6)(a) requires an equally subtle and careful interpretation, rather than the inflexible, and...unworkable, interpretation for which the father contends'.[608] He held that the local authority's duty under section 33(6)(a), like all its statutory duties under the Children Act 1989, is subject to its overriding duty under section 17(1) and section 22(3) to safeguard and promote the child's welfare.[609] The local authority must have regard to any parent's change of religion and, as the child develops and makes his own choices, must respect the child's personal autonomy and freedom of conscience, provided again that by doing so it is safeguarding his welfare. The court rejected the father's claims that section 33(6)(a) and his rights under Articles 8 and 9 of the ECHR had been infringed. The local authority was entitled, and correct, to adopt its policy of trying to ensure that the child was bought up with an understanding of his mixed and varied heritage, and given the opportunity to develop his own thinking, and was demonstrating a proportionate empathy with the different belief systems in the family.

A local authority also do not have the right to agree or refuse to agree to the making of an adoption order, or an order under section 84 of the Adoption and Children Act 2002, with respect to the child[610] or the right to appoint a guardian for the child.[611] While a care order is in force, no person may cause the child to be known by a new surname; remove him or her from the UK, without either the written consent of every person who has parental responsibility for the child or the leave of the court.[612]

Section 33(3)(b) goes on to state that the local authority has the power to determine the extent to which a parent, guardian, special guardian, or a person who has parental responsibility for the child by way of section 4A of the Children Act 1989, may meet his or her parental responsibility for the child. Thus, it can be seen that the local authority and others with parental responsibility are not equal holders of parental responsibility; decision making has been firmly vested by statute in the local authority. However, the local authority's power of control is not an unfettered one. It cannot be exercised unless the local authority is satisfied that it is necessary to safeguard or promote the child's welfare. It is also subject to any right, power, duty, or authority which persons mentioned in section 33(3)(b) have in relation to the child and his or her property by virtue of any other enactment. Furthermore, a parent who has care of the child subject to the care order remains entitled to do whatever is reasonable in the circumstances to safeguard or promote the child's welfare.[613]

---

[605] Section 33(6)(a).   [606] [2010] EWHC 2503 (Fam), [2011] 1 FLR 615.
[607] Ibid, [73].   [608] Ibid, [74].   [609] Ibid, [75].   [610] Section 33(6)(b)(ii).
[611] Section 33(6)(b) (iii).
[612] Section 33(7). See *Re S (A Minor) (Change of Surname)* [1999] 1 FCR 304 (court granting leave to a 15-year-old *Gillick* competent girl to change her surname to that of her maternal aunt and uncle, with whom she was living under a care order).   [613] Section 33(5).

It will be recalled that a child who is subject to a care order is a 'looked after' child under Part III of the Children Act 1989, so the duties in sections 22 to 22G (discussed earlier) in relation to placement, and consultation about the placement, apply. It is possible for a child to be placed at home with his parents despite being in the care of the local authority. Clearly, where it was the parents who caused, or failed to protect, the child from suffering, or being likely to suffer, significant harm, safeguards are needed to ensure the safety of the child when this arrangement is made. There are special regulations about such placements which require the local authority to be sure that the placement of the child is the most suitable way of performing its duty to safeguard and promote the child's welfare, to make regular visits and to review the placement as necessary.[614]

While, as we have seen, the court does not retain any supervisory jurisdiction over a care plan when exercising its jurisdiction under the Children Act 1989 or in wardship, the court's power to intervene in judicial review proceedings or when exercising its jurisdiction under the Human Rights Act 1998 remains. A local authority must therefore continue to be mindful of its human rights obligations when exercising powers under a care order.

In *Re G (Care: Challenge to Local Authority's Decision)*[615] a care order had been made, approving a care plan to rehabilitate children with their parents. Two years later, at a meeting to which the parents were not invited, the local authority decided to alter the plan and to remove the children because of increasing concerns. The local authority eventually reverted to its original plan of rehabilitation, and the case came before Munby J on an application for leave to withdraw the proceedings. In the course of granting leave, however, his Lordship took the opportunity to emphasise that Article 8 of the ECHR provides not only substantive protection but also significant procedural safeguards[616] and 'guarantees fairness in the decision-making process at *all* stages of child protection'[617] including when the local authority is implementing its care plan. Munby J stated that:

> The fact that a local authority has parental responsibility for children pursuant to s 33(3) (a) of the Children Act 1989 does not entitle it to take decisions about those children without reference to, or over the heads of, the children's parents. A local authority, even if clothed with the authority of a care order, is not entitled to make significant changes in the care plan, or to change the arrangements under which the children are living, let alone to remove the children from home if they are living with their parents, without properly involving the parents in the decision-making process and without giving the parents a proper opportunity to make their case before a decision is made.[618]

11 SUPERVISION ORDERS

A supervision order places a child under the supervision of a designated local authority,[619] initially for a period of one year.[620] The order ceases after that period unless extended for

---

[614] Care Planning, Placement and Case Review (England) Regulations 2010 (SI 2010/959).

[615] [2003] EWHC 551 (Fam), [2003] 2 FLR 42.

[616] Ibid, [30].

[617] Ibid, [35], citing *Re L (Care: Assessment: Fair Trial)* [2002] EWHC 1379 (Fam), [2002] 2 FLR 730 at [88].

[618] [2003] EWHC 551 (Fam), [2003] 2 FLR 42 at [43]. See also *Re M (Care: Challenging Decisions by Local Authority)* [2001] 2 FLR 1300, FD.

[619] As defined in s 31(8). The order can be imposed upon any local authority in whose area the child is, or will, live but in other cases requires the local authority's agreement: see Sch 3, para 9(1).

[620] Schedule 3, para 6(1). The making of the order brings to an end any earlier supervision order or care order: see Sch 3, para 10.

such period(s) as the court may specify,[621] although it may not be extended to run beyond the end of the period of three years beginning with the date on which it was made.[622] The general duties of the supervisor are set out in section 35 of the Children Act 1989, and further detailed provisions are found in Parts I and II of Schedule 3.

Section 35 provides that it is the duty of the supervisor to advise, assist, and befriend the supervised child and to take such steps as are reasonably necessary to give effect to the order.[623] Furthermore, where the order is not wholly complied with, or where it appears no longer to be necessary, the supervisor must consider whether an application should be made to vary or discharge the order.[624] So compliance with the order cannot be directly enforced but clearly if the supervisor becomes anxious that supervision is not enough to protect the child from suffering significant harm, he or she should approach the court again for its reconsideration of the appropriate form of protection for the child. In an emergency, steps should be taken to obtain an emergency protection order.

The provisions within Schedule 3 enable a highly structured supervision order to be made which may afford the child adequate protection. A supervision order can be supplemented and strengthened by giving the supervisor additional powers. The order may require the supervised child to comply with directions given from time to time by the supervisor which require the child to do all or any of the following: live at a particular place; present to a person or persons at specified places and times; and participate in specified activities.[625] There is no power to give directions in respect of medical or psychiatric treatment or examination.[626] The directions can be given to the child without the child's consent, although in the case of an older child, the child's willingness to comply with such directions may be a relevant practical consideration as to whether the order is appropriate.[627] The order may also require the child to submit to medical or psychiatric examination and treatment.[628] In addition, the order can require the child to keep the supervisor informed of his or her address and allow the supervisor to visit.[629] Similarly, a 'responsible person', meaning any person who has parental responsibility for the child and any other person with whom the child is living,[630] can be required to inform as to the child's address (if known) and, if living with the child, required to allow the supervisor reasonable contact with the child.[631]

In many cases the child will be too young to control his own upbringing in any way and to express a view on the directions and requirements imposed. Directions are likely to include such matters as that the child should go to a day nursery, attend a clinic, and go to a family centre on specified days. In such cases, cooperation from the persons looking after the child is normally essential if the supervision order is to work. Consequently, there is power, with the consent of a responsible person, to impose further obligations on that person,[632] to ensure that the supervised child complies with the directions imposed and any examination or treatment ordered. The order may also include a requirement that the responsible person complies with any directions given by the supervisor that he attends at certain places for the purpose of taking part in specified activities.

---

[621] Schedule 3, para 6(3).

[622] Schedule 3, para 6(4). It is not possible to substitute a care order on an application to extend a supervision order: see *Re A (Supervision Order: Extension)* [1995] 1 FLR 335, CA.

[623] Section 35(1)(a) and (b).   [624] Section 35(1)(c).   [625] Schedule 3, para 2(1).

[626] Schedule 3, para 2(3).

[627] This may be particularly relevant where the significant harm is attributable to the child's being beyond parental control.

[628] The usual proviso about the competent child agreeing to such examination or treatment applies: Sch 3, paras 4(4) and 5(5).   [629] Schedule 3, para 8(1).

[630] Schedule 3, para 1.   [631] Schedule 3, para 8(2).   [632] Schedule 3, para 3.

But even where the responsible person consents, the supervisor has no powers to secure direct compliance with the obligations. The supervisor's only 'sanction' in the case of non-cooperation is to consider seeking variation or discharge of the order.[633] It is, therefore, entirely inappropriate for a supervision order to be made where it is the court's intention that the local authority should be able to control the situation.[634]

In *Re H (Supervision Order)*,[635] the children concerned were living with their mother and having contact with their father. He had served a sentence of imprisonment for sexual assaults on his stepchild. He was anxious to receive treatment for his behaviour and therefore readily agreed to attend at a specialist clinic. It was agreed by all parties, and by the court, that a supervision order was appropriate. But the mother, father, and guardian ad litem sought an order under Schedule 3 that the local authority should direct the father to attend a particular course of treatment at the clinic. The local authority contended that the court had no power to make such a direction. Bracewell J upheld the local authority's contention. She drew a contrast between the power of the court to direct that the child submit to a medical or psychiatric examination or treatment, and its powers to make orders in respect of a responsible person. She held that requirements as to treatment of the child are wholly the responsibility of the court, and must be specified in the order itself. However, she held that the imposition of obligations on a responsible person fell into a wholly different category, namely that such directions are solely a matter for the supervisor, and that it is not open to the court to order the local authority to give any such directions. Clearly, if a court were entitled to impose such an obligation on a local authority, this would amount to a form of court control over local authority expenditure. Services provided by clinics of this kind are an expensive resource, and therefore it is for the local authority, rather than the court, to decide whether use should be made of such services as part of the authority's child protection strategy.

In *Re M (A Minor) (No 2) (Appeal)*[636] Ward J justified declining to make a supervision order on the ground that confidence between the parents and the local authority had been 'irredeemably destroyed'. He reached this conclusion despite having found that the mother, by failing to obtain medical attention for the child, had caused the child to suffer, and to be likely to suffer, significant harm, and that the child was dangerously ill by the time she was taken to hospital. Against these findings, the issue of confidence between the parents and the local authority seems slight. Unless the local authority is authorised to make regular checks on a child's progress, there are real dangers that the child may slip through the net of child protection procedures. There is clear authority for the proposition that it is appropriate for a court to make a care order even though parties, the guardian, and the court itself all agree that the child should not be removed from his parents; and even where the local authority only wishes and proposes that there should be a supervision order.[637]

12   DECIDING BETWEEN A CARE ORDER OR SUPERVISION ORDER

In most cases in which it is acknowledged that longer term protection of a child is required, the court will be deciding whether that protection is more appropriately afforded by

---

[633] Section 35.   [634] *Re R and G (Minors) (Interim Care or Supervision Orders)* [1994] 1 FLR 793.
[635] [1994] 2 FLR 979.
[636] [1994] 1 FLR 59. For critical commentary, see J. R. Spencer, 'Evidence in Child Abuse Cases: Too High a Price for Too High a Standard?' (1994) 6 Journal of Child Law 160, and the editorial by M. Hayes in the same issue.   [637] *Re B (Care or Supervision Order)* [1996] 2 FLR 693.

way of a care order or a supervision order.[638] In *Re S (J) (A Minor) (Care or Supervision Order)*[639] HHJ Coningsby QC, sitting as a Family Division judge, pointed out that there is a tendency to look at those orders under the same umbrella because the statutory criteria for making them are the same. Where the local authority's plan is to place the child in the day-to-day care of a parent, the difference between the orders, at least superficially, is likely to be least visible.[640] However, HHJ Coningsby QC engaged in a careful analysis of the essential features of each order in that context,[641] and cautioned that supervision 'should not in any sense be seen as a sort of watered-down version of care'.[642] He observed that the concept of parental responsibility is at the heart of the difference. If granted a care order, the local authority has parental responsibility and 'the whip hand as far as control is concerned'.[643] In addition, a duty is imposed on the local authority to safeguard and promote the child's welfare.[644] If the child is placed at home with parents,[645] the placement is subject to the Care Planning, Placement and Case Review (England) Regulations 2010[646] which impose duties on the local authority to monitor the welfare of the child in the placement by way of regular visits,[647] and to review the placement if the visit reveals that the placement may not be safeguarding the child's interests.[648] By contrast, parental responsibility and the obligation to safeguard the child's welfare do not pass to the local authority under a supervision order; they remain with the parent(s). Unlike a care order, a supervision order is also time limited (up to three years where extended). Finally, and importantly, the supervision order 'has less teeth than the care order' since, apart from the supervisor's access to the child (which can be enforced by a warrant under s 102), its provisions cannot be directly enforced, and breaches can only be evidence in further proceedings.[649]

So how is the court to choose between these different orders? First, the chosen order must be a proportionate response. A care order rather than a supervision order should be made only if the stronger order is necessary for the proper protection of the child.[650] In *Re O (Care or Supervision Order)*[651] Hale J stated that it was accepted by all parties that the court should begin with a preference for the less interventionist rather than the more interventionist approach and that this should be considered to be in the better interests of the child unless there are cogent reasons to the contrary;[652] and her Ladyship acknowledged that 'one must always beware an over-authoritarian or Draconian approach which has not been demonstrated to be necessary in the best interests of the children in the particular case yet'.[653] In that case there were long-standing concerns about the health and development

---

[638] See G. Brasse, 'Supervision or Care Orders?' [1997] Family Law 351.   [639] [1993] 2 FLR 919, FD.

[640] It has been argued that there is a need for a third, intermediate, order in such situations (a protected parental placement order), a supervision order with conditions attached and power to remove the child for 72 hours where a condition is breached: see A. A. Gillespie, 'Establishing a Third Order in Care Proceedings' [2000] Child and Family Law Quarterly 239.   [641] See especially 947–951.

[642] *Re S(J) (A Minor) (Care or Supervision Order)* [1993] 2 FLR 919 at 950 *per* Judge Coningsby QC; see too *Leicestershire County Council v G* [1994] 2 FLR 329.

[643] *Re S(J) (A Minor) (Care or Supervision Order)* [1993] 2 FLR 919 at 948.

[644] Children Act 1989, s 22.

[645] It is not wrong in law to make a care order where it is proposed to leave a child in the day-to-day care of parents: see *Re T (A Minor) (Care or Supervision Order)* [1994] 1 FLR 103 at 105–106, citing *M v Westminster City Council* [1985] FLR 325.   [646] SI 2010/959.

[647] Ibid, reg 28.   [648] Ibid, reg 30.

[649] See *Croydon London Borough Council v A (No 3)* [1992] 2 FLR 350. See also *per* Bracewell J in *Re T (A Minor) (Care or Supervision Order)* [1994] 1 FLR 103 at 106.

[650] *Re W (A Minor) (Interim Care Order)* [1994] 2 FLR 892; *Oxfordshire County Council v L (Care or Supervision Order)* [1998] 1 FLR 70.   [651] [1996] 2 FLR 755.

[652] Ibid, 760.   [653] Ibid, 763.

of six children, who for the foreseeable future were to remain living with their parents. The parents had demonstrated some improvement and the local authority had intensified its involvement with the family. The sole issue was whether the children's welfare would be better served by a supervision order, sought by the local authority, or a care order, as argued by the children's guardian. The justices made a care order. Substituting a supervision order as more appropriate on the facts of the case, Hale J found that, as well as erring in the process of balancing relevant evidence, the justices had gone straight to the more draconian order without fully considering the effect of a supervision order. They had also failed to consider the case in the context of all of the local authority's duties under Part III of the Children Act 1989. The choice of order is linked to these duties to provide services to prevent children in their area suffering ill-treatment or neglect and to reduce the need to take proceedings for care or supervision orders, and Hale J emphasised that Parliament intended that these services should be offered.[654]

It has been said that an appropriate general approach is for the court to consider 'whether, in the light of gravity of the case as a whole, the local authority ought to have imposed upon it the extra duties'[655] which a care order brings. The need to put in place an appropriate level of protection is likely to be the decisive factor in any case. In *Re D (A Minor) (Care or Supervision Order)*[656] a father had been convicted of cruelty to a two-month-old baby who had died from a fractured skull and other injuries.[657] A decade later he set up home with another woman and had another child. The local authority sought a supervision order in respect of the child, taking the view that the child was thriving and a care order would undermine working cooperatively with the parents. Ewbank J held that the child's protection was the decisive factor and the local authority's views were not an appropriate reason to make a supervision order where it would not afford the child sufficient protection.[658]

In some cases, the extent to which the order allows a quick response may be a major factor influencing the court. In *S (J) (A Minor) (Care or Supervision Order)*,[659] for example, the judge concluded that 'this is a case where things could occur so rapidly and so dangerously that the care order procedure is needed'.[660] While the local authority may, of course, apply for an EPO, it may be in the interests of the child that the authority should not have first to take this step before intervening. A care order may also act as an incentive to parents to comply with the care plan because they know that non-compliance may lead to their child being taken from them.[661] Such strong pressure cannot be exerted where a supervision order is in place.

In weighing the relative merits of a care order or a supervision order, a judge must properly advert to the difference between the two orders.[662] In *Re V (Care or Supervision*

---

[654] For a similar case substituting a supervision order, see *Oxfordshire County Council v L (Care or Supervision Order)* [1998] 1 FLR 70.

[655] *Re S(J) (A Minor) (Care or Supervision Order)* [1993] 2 FLR 919 at 957.   [656] [1993] 2 FLR 423.

[657] The father was acquitted of the baby's murder. A 4-year-old child had also suffered injury in the household.   [658] See esp at 429.

[659] [1993] 2 FLR 919, FD.

[660] *Re S(J) (A Minor) (Care or Supervision Order)* [1993] 2 FLR 919 at 953. See also *Re R and G (Minors) (Interim Care or Supervision Orders)* [1994] 1 FLR 793, in which the justices apparently misunderstood the nature of a supervision order in thinking that the local authority could thereby force children to attend a family centre against their parents' wishes.

[661] See eg Bracewell J's comment in *Re T (A Minor) (Care or Supervision Order)* [1994] 1 FLR 103, CA at 107, that the judge 'was justified in reaching the conclusion that the existence of a care order would concentrate the minds of the parents on their responsibilities'.

[662] *Re S (Care or Supervision Order)* [1996] 1 FLR 753 at 759 *per* Beldam LJ.

Order)[663] the judge had misunderstood the nature of a supervision order. A 16-year-old boy, S, who suffered with spastic quadriplegia and learning disabilities, was withdrawn from a special school by his mother. The father took a different view, agreeing with professional opinion that S's attendance at the school was beneficial. The local authority became concerned that S was regressing and sought a care order. The judge declined to make a care order for fear that it would put great strain on the parents' marriage. Instead, he made a supervision order subject to a condition that S continue to attend the school. The Court of Appeal held that the judge had erred, in that the 'concept of a supervision order subject to conditions cannot be fitted into the framework of the Children Act legislation'.[664] While the judge had been correct to give weight to the impact of the order on the parents' relationship, the impact of loss of school attendance on the child's welfare (which prevailed) was more significant, and a care order was required to ensure the child's attendance. It was particularly important on the facts that a care order be made because the boy was only three weeks off his 17th birthday, by which time neither order could be made.[665]

A care order can be made where the local authority is merely seeking a supervision order,[666] although Hale J commented in *Re O (Care or Supervision Order)*[667] that 'if the court is to impose upon the authority an order other than that for which it asks, there should be very cogent reasons indeed to do so'.[668] In *Re C (Care or Supervision Order)*,[669] for example, Sir Stephen Brown P upheld the decision of justices to make a care order (in respect of a 6-month-old baby whose seven siblings had all been taken into care), where the local authority was merely seeking a supervision order.[670]

By contrast with these cases in which care orders were made, two cases provide further illustrations of circumstances in which a supervision order might be appropriate. In *Re B (Care or Supervision Order)*[671] the father of six children had absconded when due to stand trial for indecent assault of one of his daughters, and the children were living with the mother under a residence order which prohibited the children's contact with the father. Holman J found that the children's pressing needs were to be closely monitored and to undertake work with child protection professionals. His Lordship took into account as relevant, although not decisive, the social worker's view that the mother and children would react unfavourably to a care order, thus undermining the relationship of trust established with the social worker. Similarly in *Re C (Care or Supervision Order)*[672] a child was injured when the mother left him in the care of his father, whom the mother knew to be violent. The father was imprisoned and the child was living with the mother. Sumner J found that in the circumstances the risk to the child from the mother (eg setting up home with another violent man) was very low, and a supervision order represented a proportionate response.[673]

---

[663] *Re V (Care or Supervision Order)* [1996] 1 FLR 776, CA.

[664] Ibid, 785. See also *Re S (Care or Supervision Order)* [1996] 1 FLR 753 where a judge erroneously attached conditions to a supervision order to try to protect a child from sexual abuse.

[665] Children Act 1989, s 31(3).   [666] Ibid, s 31(5).   [667] [1996] 2 FLR 755.   [668] Ibid, 759.

[669] [1999] 2 FLR 621.

[670] It is possible, however, that Sir Stephen Brown P questioned the emphasis in Hale J's judgment in *Re O*, following up her words quoted earlier with a comment that 'in point of fact' the case before him came down to the question of discretion: ibid, 624.   [671] [1996] 2 FLR 693.

[672] [2001] 2 FLR 466.

[673] Ibid, [52]. See also *Re O (Care Order: Discharge of Care Order)* [1999] 2 FLR 119 (discharging care order and making supervision order).

13 DISCHARGE OF CARE ORDERS

Care orders may be discharged on the application of any person who has parental responsibility for the child, the child himself or the local authority.[674] There is no obligation on the applicant to satisfy the court that the threshold requirements no longer apply. The court has a discretionary jurisdiction from the outset and the welfare principle and welfare checklist apply.[675] Where, after hearing from the applicant, the court feels that the application stands no realistic prospect of success it is entitled to exercise its discretion and stop the case without hearing all the evidence.[676]

The requirement in section 1(3)(e) that the court shall have regard to any harm which the child has suffered or is at risk of suffering therefore normally takes on a particular significance in discharge cases. The relevant time at which the risk must be considered is the risk current at the date of the discharge hearing.[677] In *Re S (Discharge of Care Order)*,[678] the Court of Appeal acknowledged that there are rare instances where justice to both children and adults requires the court which is hearing the discharge application to question not merely the relevance but also the soundness of the findings of fact made in the original proceedings. Although this amounts to a relaxation of the ordinary rules of issue estoppel, the court explained that such willingness 'does not originate from laxity or benevolence but from recognition that where children are concerned there is liable to be an infinite variety of circumstances whose proper consideration in the best interests of the child is not to be trammelled by the arbitrary imposition of procedural rules'.[679]

A judge is entitled to take into account the continuing effect, or lack of effect, of the care order.[680] In *Re C (Care: Discharge of Care Order)*[681] the Court of Appeal upheld a judge's decision to discharge a care order where the local authority could not give proper effect to it because a 15-year-old boy repeatedly absconded to his mother's home, and thus the effect of the care order was to set up conflict.[682] However, it will be recalled that the point at which a child leaves care is relevant to the local authority's duties to provide ongoing support under the leaving care provisions, and the Court of Appeal added that the order's lack of effect 'needed to be balanced against the potential advantages under the leaving care provisions of preserving an empty husk of a care order'.[683]

---

[674] Section 39(1). The child does not first require the leave of the court to make an application (unlike the position in private proceedings under s 10): *Re A (Care: Discharge Application by Child)* [1995] 1 FLR 599.

[675] See *Re S (Discharge of Care Order)* [1995] 2 FLR 639 at 643 *per* Waite LJ.

[676] *Re S and P (Discharge of Care Order)* [1995] 2 FLR 782.

[677] *Re S (Discharge of Care Order)* [1995] 2 FLR 639.   [678] [1995] 2 FLR 639.   [679] Ibid, 646.

[680] *Re C (Care: Discharge of Care Order)* [2009] EWCA Civ 955, [2010] 1 FLR 774.   [681] Ibid.

[682] Discharge applications can cause particular problems where it is clear that the local authority's care plan is not working, yet it cannot be said that the parents have improved sufficiently for it to be safe to return the child to their care, see G. Posner, 'Applications to Discharge Care Orders' [1998] Family Law 623.

[683] *Re C (Care: Discharge of Care Order)* [2009] EWCA Civ 955, [2010] 1 FLR 774 at [22]. On the facts of the case the leaving care provisions did not apply because the child had been living with his mother: see Children (Leaving Care) (England) Regulations 2001, reg 4(5). However, the court indicated that for a local authority to seek discharge in order to avoid the effect of the leaving care provisions would be an improper ground: see *Re C* at [31].

14   CONTACT WITH A CHILD IN CARE[684]

Key legislation

Paragraph 15(1) of Schedule 2 positively promotes the maintenance of contact by providing that:

Where a child is being looked after by a local authority, the authority shall, unless it is not reasonably practicable or consistent with his welfare, endeavour to promote contact between the child and—

(a) his parents;

(b) any person who is not a parent of his but who has parental responsibility for him; and

(c) any relative, friend or other person connected with him.

Other provisions in the Children Act 1989 reinforce this general principle: local authorities are required to make efforts to secure that a child is accommodated near his home; parents and persons with parental responsibility should be told where the child is living;[685] and it is recognised that parents, relatives, and friends of a child in care may be too poor to afford the travelling costs involved in visiting the child, and the local authority has a discretion to make payments towards defraying these and other expenses.[686]

At the time when an application is made for a final care order, the local authority's attitude towards contact between the child and his parents will normally form part of its care plan for the child. Section 34(11) provides that before making a care order the court must consider the contact arrangements which the local authority has made, or proposes to make, and must invite the parties to the proceedings to comment on those arrangements. The court is empowered at this stage[687] to make any order it thinks appropriate in relation to contact, either on application[688] or in the exercise its own motion powers.[689] However, in many cases an order will not be necessary.[690] This is because the law takes as its starting point the rule that a child must be allowed to have reasonable contact with his parents and other important persons in his life even though he has been removed from their care.[691] Contact is normally therefore a matter to be arranged by agreement between the local authority, the child, the parents, and other interested persons.

---

[684] See Department of Health and Social Services Inspectorate, *Contact Orders Study: A Study of Local Authority Decision Making around Contact Applications under Section 34* (London: HMSO, 1994).

[685] Unless, in the case of a child in care, this would prejudice the child's welfare: Sch 2, para 15(2), (3), and (4).   [686] Schedule 2, para 16.

[687] Section 34(10).   [688] Eg under s 34(2) or (3).

[689] Section 34(5). In *Re S (A Minor) (Care: Contact Order)* [1994] 2 FLR 222 at 226 Sir Francis Purchas commented that 'it must be extremely rare that a judge would wish to do so'.

[690] See *Re L (Minors) (Care Proceedings: Contact)* [1998] 3 FCR 339 at 347 *per* Wilson J.

[691] Section 34(1). By contrast, where, unusually, parents of a child in care are refusing to have anything to do with him they cannot be compelled to have contact with him. Where parents are preventing a child in care from having contact with siblings, the child may seek the leave of the court to apply for a contact order under s 8. See *Re F (Contact: Child in Care)* [1995] 1 FLR 510.

Key legislation

Section 34(1) provides:

Where a child is in the care of a local authority, the authority shall (subject to the provisions of this section) allow the child reasonable contact with—

(a)   his parents;

(b)   any guardian or special guardian of his;

(ba) any person who by virtue of section 4A has parental responsibility for him;

(c)   where there was a residence order in force with respect to the child immediately before the care order was made, the person in whose favour the order was made; and

(d)   where, immediately before the care order was made a person had care of the child by virtue of an order made in the exercise of the High Court's inherent jurisdiction with respect to children, that person.

In this context, therefore, contact at the discretion of the local authority means 'reasonable contact'.[692] In *Re P (Minors) (Contact with Children in Care)*,[693] Ewbank J stated that 'reasonable' implies contact which has been agreed between the local authority and the parents or, if there is no such agreement, contact which is objectively reasonable. Clearly, what is reasonable will vary according to the particular circumstances,[694] and in some cases the evidence may justify quite restricted contact as reasonable.[695]

14.1 REGULATING CONTACT WITH A CHILD IN CARE IN CASES OF DISAGREEMENT

Where the local authority and the parents, or other specified persons, cannot agree over contact arrangements, an application can be made under section 34 for the court to determine the matter, and a section 34 order is enforceable by committal proceedings should, for example, a foster parent be hostile to a parent's contact with a child.[696] Under section 34(2) the local authority or the child may apply to the court to make such order as it considers appropriate with respect to the contact which is allowed between the child and any named person. However, the effect of section 34(8) and the Care Planning, Placement and Case Review (England) Regulations 2010[697] is that the local authority can depart from the order with the agreement of the person in whose favour the order is made, provided that any child, being of sufficient age and understanding, also agrees.[698]

---

[692] Cf *L v London Borough of Bromley* [1998] 1 FLR 709: order that contact should be at the discretion of the local authority made in relation to a person who falls within s 34(1) means that the local authority must allow and arrange reasonable contact between the child and that person, and it is not inapt for the court to indicate the frequency which it has in mind.   [693] [1993] 2 FLR 156.

[694] On the facts of *Re P* two and a half hours unsupervised contact per month was said to be reasonable, unless the children requested more contact.

[695] See eg *Re C (Care: Contact)* [2009] EWCA Civ 959, [2010] 1 FLR 895, where the Court of Appeal upheld a care plan which restricted contact between a mother, who had been the sole carer of two children aged 9 and 7, to four times per year, which was justified by reference to expert evidence (see at [56]).

[696] See *Re P-B (Contact: Committal)* [2009] 2 FLR 66, CA. Exceptionally a penal order might be attached.   [697] SI 2010/959.

[698] See ibid, reg 8(4).

Under section 34(3) any person mentioned in section 34(1)(a)–(d) is similarly entitled to apply for a contact order.[699] Any other person who is aggrieved about the amount of contact may apply for a contact order provided that the court first gives leave.[700]

The Children Act 1989 does not contain specific criteria for determining whether an application for leave under section 34 should be granted. Detailed guidance on how this vacuum should be filled was given in *Re M (Care: Contact: Grandmother's Application for Leave)*.[701] Ward LJ stated that while it is clear that section 10(9) which deals with leave to apply for section 8 orders does not govern contact with a child in care, it is equally clear that it could be anomalous were the court not to take account of the factors specified in section 10(9) when exercising its discretion to grant leave.[702]

14.2 AUTHORISING THE LOCAL AUTHORITY TO DENY CONTACT

In *Re B (Minors) (Care: Contact: Local Authority's Plans)*[703] Butler-Sloss LJ said that it is clear that the discretion to refuse to allow contact, or otherwise to determine what contact is reasonable, is firmly vested in the courts and not in the local authority.[704] She said that the proposals of the local authority, based on their appreciation of the best interests of the child, must command the greatest respect and consideration from the court, but that the duty to decide is in the court. Consequently, 'the court may have the task of requiring the local authority to justify their long-term plans to the extent only that those plans exclude contact between parent and child'. It is for the court to determine whether such a plan is in the best interests of the child.[705]

Section 34(6) empowers the local authority to refuse to allow the contact that would otherwise be required by virtue of section 34(1) if satisfied that: it is necessary to do so in order to safeguard or promote the child's welfare; the refusal is decided upon as a matter of urgency; and it does not last for more than seven days. Section 34(4) provides that upon the application of the local authority or the child the court may make an order authorising the authority to refuse to allow contact between the child and a named person within section 34(1). Although section 34 does not actually say so in terms, the implication of section 34(4) and (6) when read together is that, outside the exception in subsection (6), court authorisation for denial

---

[699] Section 34(3)(a). Where a court in earlier proceedings has made an order authorising that there should be no contact between a child and his parent, if an application is later made under s 34 a court is entitled to act robustly and to dismiss the application without hearing oral evidence: *Cheshire County Council v M* [1993] 1 FLR 463.

[700] Section 34(3)(b). As such persons are not entitled to contact within s 34(1), an order that their contact should be at the discretion of the local authority means only that the authority should endeavour to promote it unless it is not practicable or consistent with the welfare of the child (Sch 2, para 15(1)(c)); see *L v London Borough of Bromley* [1998] 1 FLR 709.

[701] [1995] 2 FLR 86. See discussion in Chapter 9, Section 5.5.

[702] Eg a court might be faced with an application by a grandparent for leave to apply for a residence order in relation to a child in care, or alternatively a contact order. For the first application, she would need leave of the court under s 10(9); for the second under s 34(3).

[703] [1993] 1 FLR 543.

[704] Butler-Sloss LJ said that her own earlier judgment in *Re S (A Minor) (Access Application)* [1991] 1 FLR 161 should be read 'with considerable caution'.

[705] Where the nature and extent of contact is an integral part of the local authority's care plan it is not permissible for a judge to adjourn proceedings for future consideration of what is reasonable contact since the judge would be 'straying into the forbidden territory of supervising the administration of the local authority's arrangements for rehabilitation': *Re S (A Minor) (Care: Contact Order)* [1994] 2 FLR 222 at 226 *per* Simon Brown LJ.

of contact is required.[706] Where the court authorises refusal, the local authority is in control over when contact is actually brought to an end. The authority may determine whether, for example, contact should be gradually phased out, whether there should be a final 'goodbye' visit, or whether contact should terminate forthwith.

Authorising the termination of contact is a draconian decision and one which courts will not make lightly.[707] In *Re E (A Minor) (Care Order: Contact)*[708] Simon Brown LJ recognised that 'although the value of contact may be limited by the parent's inadequacy, it may still be of fundamental importance to the long-term welfare of the child, unless of course it can be seen that in a given case it will inevitably disturb the child's care'.[709] He set out four reasons why contact may still be of importance:

> first, in giving the child the security of knowing that his parents love him and are intere-
> sted in his welfare; secondly, by avoiding any damaging sense of loss to the child in seeing
> himself abandoned by his parents; thirdly, by enabling the child to commit himself to the
> substitute family with the seal of approval of the natural parents; and, fourthly, by giving
> the child the necessary sense of family and personal identity.[710]

In some cases, however, a local authority may decide to abandon any attempt to rehabilitate the child with his or her family because of the danger a parent presents to the child, and adoption may be their long-term plan for the child. In such a case a court might also conclude that no further contact would be appropriate, for example because the parent could play no appropriate future role or would perhaps undermine the child's placement.[711] In a less clear-cut case the question of denial of contact may arise in the context of deciding whether the rehabilitation of the child with his family should be attempted when balancing the prospects of success against the fact that delay in determining a question about the child's upbringing is likely to prejudice the welfare of the child.[712]

Even where it is believed that the child needs the security of a settled placement away from the parents, the difficulty is to know how much time and effort should be given to exploring arrangements with potential for the parents continued contact with a child before an order authorising termination of contact.[713] In *Re E (A Minor) (Care Order: Contact)*[714] a local authority sought permission to refuse contact between children and parents in light of its plan to place the child for closed adoption. Expert evidence had been given that the children would benefit from contact and that the parents would not undermine an alternative open placement. The local authority had not yet investigated the possibility of finding suitable prospective adopters who would accept a degree of face-to-face contact with the parents. The judge granted the local authority's application, being of the view that he should not make an order incompatible with the local authority's plans unless the children's welfare dictated otherwise. The Court of Appeal held that the judge had failed to apply the correct

---

[706] See *per* Butler-Sloss LJ in *Re B (Minors) (Care: Contact: Local Authority's Plans)* [1993] 1 FLR 543 at 547: 'a presumption of continuing reasonable contact... unless or until a court order under s 34(4)'.

[707] See Thorpe LJ in *Re H (Termination of Contact)* [2005] 2 FLR 408 at [11]: 'The function of the judge in upholding the Parliamentary intention of s 34 and in granting s 34(4) orders restrictively and stringently is an important one.' [708] [1994] 1 FLR 146.

[709] *Re E (A Minor) (Care Order: Contact)* [1994] 1 FLR 146, CA at 154 *per* Simon Brown LJ.

[710] Ibid, 154–155.

[711] See eg *Birmingham City Council v H* in which Connell J authorised the local authority to terminate contact, having concluded that it was very unlikely that the 15-year-old mother, whose behaviour towards her child which had caused anxiety, would make significant progress in her ability to care for the child.

[712] Section 1(2).

[713] See *L v London Borough of Bromley* [1998] 1 FLR 709 allowing an appeal from justices who had failed to take account of the unlikelihood of finding adopters who could tolerate a high level of contact.

[714] [1994] 1 FLR 146.

test, as set out in *Re B*, and that had the judge done so he must inevitably have recognised that it was premature to authorise termination of contact in the circumstances.[715]

Denial of contact will be authorised where the child's safety demands it. In *Re K (Contact)*[716] a fight broke out between parents at a supervised contact session and the mother threw her baby 18 inches to the supervisor. Munby J authorised refusal of contact until a case management conference when more stringent conditions for supervised contact might be put in place.

The courts also recognise that contact must not be allowed to destabilise or endanger the local authority's plans for a child. As Thorpe J said in *Re N (Minors) (Care Orders: Termination of Parental Contact)*[717] 'it is always tempting to keep doors open against possible developments in an uncertain future, but the future must be surveyed in terms of probabilities and not low possibilities'. The three children concerned had suffered very severe significant harm at the hands of their parents, and as a consequence had special needs and would be difficult to place with long-term foster or adoptive parents. Thorpe J found that the search for a permanent new family would be made more difficult if the children continued to have a relationship with their parents in the interim. He therefore concluded that the need for an order authorising the refusal of contact had been plainly established.[718]

However, an order under section 34(4) must not be made merely in anticipation of its future use. In *Re L (Sexual Abuse: Standard of Proof)*[719] a judge made a care order, taking the view that there was still a possibility of rehabilitation of the mother with the children. He nevertheless terminated contact,[720] his motive being to save the local authority the necessity of making a further application to the court should the authority wish to bring contact to an end. The Court of Appeal held that the judge had been wrong to hand over prematurely to the local authority the residual responsibility for contact arrangements which should still have vested in the court.

An order authorising a local authority to terminate contact is not a final order, and an application may be made under section 34(9) for the order to be discharged.[721] On such an application the child's welfare is paramount. The burden is on the applicant to show that there has been some material change in circumstances and that the application is not a disguised form of appeal.[722]

In *Re W (A Child) (Parental Contact: Prohibition)*[723] the Court of Appeal held that section 34 'does not create a prohibitory jurisdiction',[724] so the court cannot prohibit contact which the local authority consider advantageous to the child's welfare.[725]

---

[715] See also *Re S (Care: Parental Contact)* [2004] EWCA civ 1397, [2005] 1 FLR 469 (order inappropriate where also a finding that contact will be beneficial). [716] [2008] 2 FLR 581.

[717] [1994] 2 FCR 1101 at 1107.

[718] See also *Re SW (A Minor) (Care Proceedings)* [1993] 2 FLR 609 in which Booth J held that the justices were correct to exercise their own motion powers to order no contact between a child and his mother in circumstances where there was no realistic chance that the child would return to live with her, where the local authority's plan was to find a permanent substitute family for the child, and where the children's guardian supported this plan. [719] [1996] 1 FLR 116.

[720] The local authority had not sought a section 34(4) order; it was made at the request of the guardian ad litem.

[721] Section 34(9). The only express statutory restriction on making any kind of section 34 order is that provided by s 91(17). [722] *Re T (Termination of Contact: Discharge of Order)* [1997] 1 FLR 517.

[723] [2000] Fam 130. [724] Ibid, 138.

[725] Cf the Court of Appeal's view in *Re D and H (Care: Termination of Contact)* [1997] 1 FLR 841 that s 34(2) should not be used to phase out contact against the local authority's view. Even if such a jurisdiction existed, as Ewbank J held in *Kent County Council v C* [1993] 1 FLR 308, it would be foolish to exercise it because the effect of Children Act 1989, s 34(8) and the Contact with Children Regulations 1991 (SI 1991/891), reg 3, is that an order can be departed from by agreement.

To summarise, a court has the power to authorise a local authority to terminate contact with the persons specified in section 34(1), either on an application made by the local authority or in the exercise of its own motion powers. However, the court cannot compel the authority to do so. Similarly, where the court makes an order under section 34(2) regulating contact arrangements between the child and a specified person, these can only be altered by the local authority where the person affected by the contact order agrees, and an order of the court can be overridden where such an agreement is made.

In the next chapter, we examine the law on adoption, which may be one of the local authority's options for long-term substitute care of a child who requires protection.

DISCUSSION QUESTIONS

1. To what extent, if at all, should the notion of 'significant harm' take account of cultural factors?

2. Explain the approach to proof of the threshold criteria in section 31(2) of the Children Act 1989 following *Re H* [1996] AC 563 and *Re B (Children)* [2009] AC 11. Do you think the approach to proof of likely harm adequately protects children? How does the approach of the dissenting judges in *Re H* differ?

3. Is paragraph [49] of *Re S-B* [2010] 1 AC 678 compatible with Lord Nicholls's trilogy of opinions in *Re H* [1996] AC 563, *Lancashire County Council v B* [2002] AC 147, and *Re O and another; Re B* [2004] 1 AC 523? (See *Re J (Children)* [2012] EWCA Civ 380.)

4. Does the law on child protection strike an appropriate balance between the role of the courts and that of local authorities?

FURTHER READING

BAINHAM, A., 'Interim Care Orders: Is the Bar Set Too Low?' [2011] Family Law 374

BETTLE, J. and HERRING, J., 'Shaken Babies and Care Proceedings' [2011] Family Law 1370

CONWAY, H., 'The Laming Inquiry—Victoria Climbie's Legacy' [2002] Family Law 755

CRETNEY, S., *Family Law in the Twentieth Century—A History* (Oxford: Oxford University Press, 2003), ch 20

EEKELAAR, J., 'Are Parents Morally Obliged to Care for Their Children?' (1991) 11(3) Oxford Journal of Legal Studies 340

FREEMAN, M., 'The Right to Responsible Parents' in J. Bridgeman, H. Keating, and C. Lind, *Responsibility, Law and the Family* (Aldershot: Ashgate, 2008)

GILLESPIE, A. A., 'Establishing a Third Order in Care Proceedings' [2000] Child and Family Law Quarterly 239

HALE, B. et al., *The Family, Law and Society: Cases and Materials*, 5th edn (Oxford: Oxford University Press, 2005)

HAYES, M., 'Removing Children from their Families—Law and Policy Before the Children Act 1989' in G. Douglas and N. Lowe (eds), *The Continuing Evolution of Family Law* (Bristol: Jordan Publishing, 2009)

HAYES, J., 'Ensuring Equal Protection for Siblings' [2010] Family Law 505

HAYES, M., 'Why Didn't the Courts Protect this Child? *Re SB and Re F*' [2012] Family Law 169

HAYES, J., HAYES, M., and WILLIAMS, J., ' "Shocking" Abuse Followed by a 'Staggering Ruling': *Re MA (Care Threshold)*' [2010] Family Law 166

HOWE, D., 'Removal of Children at Interim Hearings: Is the Test Now Set Too High?' [2009] Family Law 320

KEATING, H., 'Suspicions, Sitting on the Fence and Standards of Proof' [2009] Child and Family Law Quarterly 230

KEATING, H., '*Re MA*: The Significance of Harm' [2011] Child and Family Law Quarterly 115

LONNE, B., PARTON, N., THOMSON, J., and HARRIES, M., *Reforming Child Protection* (Abindgon: Routledge, 2009)

LORD LAMING, *The Victoria Climbié Inquiry: Report of an Inquiry by Lord Laming* (Cm 5730, January 2003)

MASSON, J., 'From Curtis to Waterhouse: State Care and Child Protection in the UK 1945–2000' in S. Katz, J. Eekelaar, and M. Maclean (eds), *Cross-Currents: Family Law Policy in the US and England* (Oxford: Oxford University Press, 2000)

MASSON, J., 'Police Protection—Protecting Whom?' (2002) Journal of Social Welfare and Family Law 157

MASSON, J., 'Emergency Intervention to Protect Children: Using and Avoiding Legal Controls' [2005] Child and Family Law Quarterly 75

PARTON, N., *The Politics of Child Abuse* (Basingstoke: Macmillan, 1985)

PARTON, N., *Governing the Family* (Basingstoke: Macmillan, 1991)

11

ADOPTION AND SPECIAL GUARDIANSHIP

INTRODUCTION

This chapter explores two methods by which a child who is unable to live with his or her parents may be provided with a suitable long-term secure alternative family placement: adoption and special guardianship.

1 ADOPTION

Adoption in English law[1] is effected by the making of an adoption order under the Adoption and Children Act (ACA) 2002. It achieves an 'almost "total legal transplant" of a child from one family to another'.[2] The child is treated as if born to the adoptive parent(s) and the parental responsibility of the birth parents is extinguished.[3] The practice of adoption has a long history, although the legal regulation of adoption is relatively recent, the first English statute regulating adoption being the Adoption Act 1926. The early legislation and the idea of adoption as a total legal transplant were developed in relation to a traditional model of adoption of 'a young unmarried mother giving up her healthy new born baby, reluctantly but voluntarily, to a married couple who are unable to have children of their own'.[4] In the inter-war period adoption was seen as a method of dealing discreetly with births of illegitimate children and, in the decades following the Second World War, as largely a service for infertile couples.[5] However, baby adoptions peaked in 1968, followed by a rapid decline reflecting increased availability of contraception and abortion, and a decline in the stigmas accompanying lone motherhood and illegitimacy.[6] The law has since been developed in several statutes,[7] as the law has sought

---

[1] For international perspectives, see K. O'Halloran, *The Politics of Adoption: International Perspectives on Law, Policy and Practice*, 2nd edn (Vienna: Springer, 2009).

[2] *Re P (Adoption: Unmarried Couple)* [2008] UKHL 38.

[3] See ACA 2002, ss 46 and 67, discussed in detail in Sections 7.6.1 and 7.8.2.

[4] *Re P (Adoption: Unmarried Couple)* [2008] UKHL 38 at [89].

[5] See J. Lewis, 'Adoption: The Nature of Policy Shifts in England and Wales, 1972–2002' (2004) 18(2) International Journal of Law, Policy and the Family 235 at 238.

[6] Ibid. Lewis cites figures showing that in 1975, 4,548 babies under one year old (21 per cent) were adopted, which figures had by 1999 declined to merely 196 (5 per cent).

[7] For the history see S. Cretney, *Family Law in the Twentieth Century—A History* (Oxford: Oxford University Press, 2003), ch 17; N. V. Lowe, 'English Adoption Law: Past, Present and Future' in S. Katz, J. Eekelaar, and M. Maclean (eds), *Cross-Currents: Family Law and Policy in the US and England* (Oxford: Oxford University Press, 2000), ch 14; and I. Dey, 'Adapting Adoption: A Case of Closet Politics?' (2005) 19(3) International Journal of Law, Policy and the Family 289.

to respond to social change and various policy shifts with regard to adoption.[8] As well as its use in relation to babies, adoption has also been used to cement the relationship between a child and step-parent 'when an unmarried, widowed or divorced mother married'[9] and step-parent adoption increased following reform of divorce law and the ensuing rise in the divorce rate. As explained in Chapter 7, parents can now share parental responsibility with a step-parent, under section 4A of the Children Act 1989, without displacing the parents' role and, while circumstances still exist in which step-parent adoptions may be appropriate, their number has also declined.

By contrast, a third category of adoptions, namely of children who are looked after by the state and are in need of a new family, is increasing.[10] In the 1970s, following enact-ment of the Children Act 1975, adoption was aligned with local authority childcare pro-fessional services and increasingly seen as part of the state childcare system.[11] Given the shortcomings for children of life spent in local authority care, adoption came to be seen as a favourable method of achieving permanency for children who could not be rehabili-tated with their parents. In contrast to the traditional model of adoption, which provided a family with a child, this form of adoption was concerned with providing a family for the child. These types of adoptions require adoptive parents who can meet the additional challenges which such adoptions present. As Baroness Hale has commented:

> Apart from the particular parenting problems these children might present, there might also be the stress of a contested adoption if the birth parents did not agree and a need for continued contact of some sort between the child and her birth family.[12]

Unsurprisingly, the rate of disruption of placement in the case of older children adopted out of care is greater than for children placed as babies.[13] As Nigel Lowe[14] has pointed out, the adoption of children from state care does not fit well with the model of the child as a one-off gift/donation to a family, characteristic of the traditional form of adoption. Lowe argues that a contract/services model better fits adoptions of children from state care: the adopters are providing a service to the local authority and the birth parents in bringing up the adoptive children and, given the on-going challenges as noted earlier, there should be adequate on-going provision of post-adoption support to adopters in this role.

It was against this changing face of adoption that the current law of adoption, in the ACA 2002,[15] was enacted; indeed, as we shall see, it was arguably seen as the solution to

---

[8] See J. Lewis, 'Adoption: The Nature of Policy Shifts in England and Wales, 1972–2002' (2004) 18(2) International Journal of Law, Policy and the Family 235; C. Bridge, 'Adoption Law: A Balance of Interests' in J. Herring (ed), *Family Law: Issues, Debates, Policy* (Cullompton: Willan, 2001).

[9] *Re P* [2008] UKHL 38 at [90].

[10] In 2000, prior to enactment of the current legislation, there were 2,700 adoptions of looked after children, accounting for more than half of adoptions that year: see I. Dey, 'Adapting Adoption: A Case of Closet Politics?' (2005) 19(3) International Journal of Law, Policy and the Family 289.

[11] Following recommendations of the Houghton Committee, *Report of the Departmental Committee on the Adoption of Children* (Cmnd 5107, 1972).   [12] *Re P* [2008] UKHL 38 at [91].

[13] See eg C. Dance and A. Rushton, 'Predictors of Outcome for Unrelated Adoptive Placements made During Middle Childhood' (2005) 10 Child and Family Social Work 269. Disruptions for adolescents are even higher: see eg D. Howe, D. Shemmings, and J. Feast, 'Age at Placement and Adult Adopted People's Experience of Being Adopted' (2001) 6 Child and Family Social Work 337. Success in baby adoptions is quite usual: see J. Castle, C. Beckett, and C. Groothues, 'Infant Adoption in England: A Longitudinal Account of Social and Cognitive Progress' (2000) 24 Adoption and Fostering 26.

[14] N. Lowe, 'The Changing Face of Adoption—The Gift/Donation Model versus the Contract/Services Model' [1997] Child and Family Law Quarterly 371.

[15] On which, see generally in detail, C. Bridge and H. Swindells QC, *Adoption: The Modern Law* (Bristol: Family Law, 2003). For a brief overview, see D. Cullen, 'The Adoption and Children Act 2002' [2003] Family Law 235 and S. Mahmood, 'Adoption and Children Act 2002: Where Are We So Far?' [2004] Family Law 449.

some of the problems of the childcare system.[16] The Act is the product of two reviews of the law, one which began in the early 1990s and one in 2000. The law on adoption was not examined in the various reviews of child law in the run-up to enactment of the Children Act 1989. However, a similar process reviewing adoption law began shortly thereafter, in 1992, with a consultation document[17] produced by an interdepartmental working group.[18] A White Paper followed[19] and a Draft Bill[20] was published in 1996. However, the Bill was shelved following a change of government. Adoption reform gained further impetus some four years later when the Waterhouse Inquiry into the abuse of children in care homes in North Wales identified the drift of children in care as an issue.[21] The then Prime Minister, Tony Blair, led a review[22] of childcare policy and practice to see whether local authorities might be encouraged to make more use of adoption to achieve permanent new families for children. The review identified a problem with the low number of children adopted out of care each year (only 4 per cent of looked after children) and with the length of time children remained in care before a suitable adoptive home was found. In 1999 the average length of time a child had spent in care before an adoption order was made was two years and 10 months.[23] As Sonia Harris-Short neatly summarised the message emerging from the review: 'too many children are in care for too long; these children need a family who can meet their needs on a permanent basis; adoption can provide such a family; adoption law, therefore, needs to be reformed to achieve "more adoptions more quickly".'[24] A subsequent White Paper[25] recommended changes in practice, including setting time limits and targets for social workers. It also promised a change in the law. The government's fast-track adoption approach was not universally admired. Harris-Short described the proposals as misconceived and not radical enough in their failure to target appropriate adopters for children in care, commenting:

> Imposing time-limits and target figures on battle weary social workers is not going to have the dramatic effect the Government is hoping for. The fundamental problem … is that the majority of potential adoptive parents still seem to expect 'trouble-free babies' and not older children with 'challenging backgrounds and complex needs'. There are, therefore, not enough babies to satisfy the demands of adopters and not enough adopters to satisfy the demands of children in need. It is unrealistic to expect that by simply telling child care

---

[16] J. Lewis, 'Adoption: The Nature of Policy Shifts in England and Wales, 1972–2002' (2004) 18(2) International Journal of Law, Policy and the Family 235. For background to the Act, see C. Bridge, 'Adoption Law: A Balance of Interests' in J. Herring (ed), *Family Law: Issues, Debates, Policy* (Cullompton: Willan, 2001).

[17] Department of Health and Welsh Office, Report to Ministers of the Interdepartmental Working Group, *Review of Adoption Law* (London: HMSO, 1992).

[18] Comprising the family law team of the Law Commission and members of relevant government departments.

[19] Department of Health and Welsh Office, Home Office, Lord Chancellor's Department, *Adoption: The Future* (Cm 2288, 1993).

[20] Department of Health and Welsh Office, *Adoption: A Service for Children, Draft Bill* (1996).

[21] Sir Ronald Waterhouse (Waterhouse Inquiry), *Lost in Care—Report of the Tribunal of Inquiry into the Abuse of Children in the Former County Council Areas of Gwynedd and Clwyd since 1974* (London: TSO, 2000).

[22] HM Government, Performance and Innovation Unit, *Prime Minister's Review: Adoption: Issued for Consultation* (London: TSO, July 2000). See C. Barton, 'Adoption: The Prime Minister's Review' [2000] Family Law 731.

[23] HM Government, Performance and Innovation Unit, *Prime Minister's Review of Adoption* (London: TSO, 2000), p 13.

[24] S. Harris-Short, 'The Adoption and Children Bill—A Fast Track to Failure?' [2001] Child and Family Law Quarterly 405. Harris-Short also indicated that it was probably fair to add 'as cheaply as possible'.

[25] Department of Health, *Adoption: A New Approach: A White Paper* (Cm 5017, 2000). On the extent to which the 2002 Act met the aims of the Paper, see D. Cullen, 'Adoption—A (Fairly) New Approach' [2005] Child and Family Law Quarterly 475.

professionals to do 'more of the same, more quickly', this fundamental difficulty is going to disappear.[26]

Nevertheless, a Bill which resembled in structure the 1996 Draft Bill was introduced into Parliament,[27] and eventually became the ACA 2002. As the Bill passed through Parliament, a particularly hotly debated issue related to who is eligible to adopt.[28] At that time, only a joint adoption by a married couple or adoption by a single person was permitted. Neither the Bill as originally presented, nor the various preceding reviews,[29] advocated any broadening of the eligibility criteria.

Talking point

Amendments made in the House of Commons to allow unmarried couples, including same-sex couples, to adopt were initially resisted by the House of Lords. The issue of allowing same-sex couples to adopt was particularly hard fought but eventually the amendments were passed.[30] The Government sought to diffuse opposition by emphasising that extension of the eligibility criteria constituted a pragmatic reform to avoid delay in adoptions and serve the welfare of children who needed to be adopted, although no doubt the 'real' issue was the law's compliance with human rights requirements; the Houses' Joint Committee on Human Rights expressed the view that 'a blanket ban on unmarried couples becoming eligible to adopt children would amount to unjustifiable discrimination on the ground of marital status, violating article 14 combined with article 8'.[31] As Ian Dey has argued, the Government's approach was arguably a case of 'closet politics', which denied a full airing of the issue of same-sex adoption in principle. Dey argues that this 'strategy failed to challenge popular prejudices; indeed, by implying that only the interests of children matter, it tacitly legitimated them'.[32]

The strategy was successful, however, in achieving a desired outcome which was consistent with the overall policy focus of ensuring that more children are adopted more speedily from care and provided with permanent homes at less cost to the state than if they remained in state care.

---

[26] S. Harris-Short 'The Adoption and Children Bill—A Fast Track to Failure?' [2001] Child and Family Law Quarterly 405.

[27] An Adoption and Children Bill went through most of its stages in the House of Commons in 2001 but was lost when the 2001 General Election was called. The same Bill was introduced in the 2001–02 session. See C. Barton, 'Adoption and Children Bill—Don't Let Them Out of Your Sight' [2001] Family Law 431 and S. Harris-Short, 'The Adoption and Children Bill—A Fast Track to Failure?' [2001] Child and Family Law Quarterly 405.

[28] See the useful account of the debates by Baroness Hale in *Re P* [2008] UKHL 38 at [93]–[98].

[29] See Department of Health and Welsh Office, Report to Ministers of the Interdepartmental Working Group, *Review of Adoption Law* (London: HMSO, 1992), paras 26.10–26.14.; Department of Health and Welsh Office, Home Office, Lord Chancellor's Department, *Adoption: The Future* (Cm 2288, 1993), para 4.40, endorsing the 'the general preference of authorities, adoption agencies and their staffs for adoption by married couples'; the 2000 Review and White Paper contained no discussion of the issue.

[30] For an account of the debate, see I. Dey, 'Adapting Adoption: A Case of Closet Politics?' (2005) 19(3) International Journal of Law, Policy and the Family 289.

[31] 24th Report of the Session 2001–02, *Adoption and Children Bill: as amended by the House of Lords on Report*, HL Paper 177 (28 October 2002), para 25.

[32] I. Dey, 'Adapting Adoption: A Case of Closet Politics?' (2005) 19(3) International Journal of Law, Policy and the Family 289 at 307; see also A. Marshall, 'Comedy of Adoption—When is a Parent not a Parent?' [2003] Family Law 840.

With a view to addressing the overarching policy aim, the 2002 Act had four main objectives. As explained by Wall LJ in *Re F (Placement Order)*:[33] 'The first was to simplify the process. The second was to enable a crucial element of the decision making process to be undertaken at an earlier stage. The third was to shift the emphasis to a concentration on the welfare of the child; and the fourth was to avoid delay.'[34] To these ends, the Act provides the legal framework for adoption services maintained by local authorities, and places the responsibility for placement of children for adoption in the hands of adoption agencies. The adoption process has two main stages. In the first, the child is placed for adoption, either by consent of the parents or by a 'placement order' after certain conditions are fulfilled and a court has decided that parental consent may be dispensed with. The Act introduces the paramountcy of the child's welfare as the criterion for all decisions relating to adoption and, as we shall see later in this chapter, that approach is particularly controversial as a criterion for dispensing with parental consent. The second stage of the adoption process involves an application to the court by prospective adopters for an adoption order. Certain conditions must be fulfilled before an application may be made, for example that the child has had his or her home with the adopter(s) for a certain period of time (which depends on the type of adoption). Further conditions must be complied with before an adoption order may be made. In many cases consent to the child's adoption will have been obtained much earlier in the adoption process at the placement stage, thus ensuring that the child's adoption is not thwarted at the last minute, although in limited circumstances the adoption application may be opposed. Before making an order, the court is required to consider post-adoption contact between the child and his or her birth parent(s) or other relatives. In what follows, we explain the central features of the Act and how they have been interpreted in case law.

2 THE ADOPTION SERVICE

The Act places a duty upon each local authority to maintain services which collectively are referred to as 'the Adoption Service'.[35] The Service is to be designed to meet the needs, in relation to adoption, of:

(a) children who may be adopted, their parents and guardians,

(b) persons wishing to adopt a child, and

(c) adopted persons, their parents, natural parents and former guardians.

The local authority must provide facilities for arranging the adoption of children and providing adoption support services.[36] At the request of the persons listed, a local authority is under a duty to carry out an assessment of that person's needs for adoption support services.[37]

The Act provides that certain functions relating to adoption are to be carried out by adoption agencies. An adoption agency can either be a local authority or a registered adoption society,[38] that is, an adoption society registered under Part 2 of the Care Standards Act 2000.[39] The Act and secondary legislation provide for the regulation of adoption

---

[33] [2008] EWCA Civ 439, [2008] 2 FLR 550.   [34] Ibid, [72].   [35] ACA 2002, s 2(1).

[36] Ibid, s 3(2).

[37] Ibid, s 4; and see Adoption Support Services Regulations 2005 (SI 2005/691). See also ACA 2002, s 8 for the meaning of an adoption support agency.

[38] ACA 2002, s 2(1).   [39] Ibid, s 2(2).

agencies' functions in relation to adoption,[40] and how and by whom they are managed.[41] Provision is also made for independent review of the decisions of adoption agencies.[42]

3 DECISION MAKING IN RELATION TO ADOPTION

Section 1 of the ACA 2002 sets out some considerations which apply 'whenever a court or adoption agency is coming to a decision relating to the adoption of a child'.[43] Section 1 is similar to, but not exactly the same as, section 1 of the Children Act 1989. By section 1(2) of the ACA 2002 the paramount consideration of the court *or adoption agency* must be the child's welfare *throughout his life*. Therefore, unlike section 1 of the Children Act 1989, section 1(2) of the ACA 2002 is not confined to court decision making. By section 1(3) the court or adoption agency 'must at all times bear in mind that, in general, any delay in coming to the decision is likely to prejudice the child's welfare'.

Key legislation

There follows in section 1(4) a checklist of matters to which (among others) the court or adoption agency must have regard:

(a) the child's ascertainable wishes and feelings regarding the decision (considered in the light of the child's age and understanding),

(b) the child's particular needs,

(c) the likely effect on the child (throughout his life) of having ceased to be a member of the original family and become an adopted person,

(d) the child's age, sex, background and any of the child's characteristics which the court or agency considers relevant,

(e) any harm (within the meaning of the Children Act 1989 (c 41)) which the child has suffered or is at risk of suffering,

(f) the relationship[44] which the child has with relatives,[45] and with any other person in relation to whom the court or agency considers the relationship to be relevant, including—

   (i) the likelihood of any such relationship continuing and the value to the child of its doing so,

   (ii) the ability and willingness of any of the child's relatives, or of any such person, to provide the child with a secure environment in which the child can develop, and otherwise to meet the child's needs,

   (iii) the wishes and feelings of any of the child's relatives, or of any such person, regarding the child.

By section 1(5) an adoption agency, in placing a child for adoption, 'must give due consideration to the child's religious persuasion, racial origin and cultural and linguistic

---

[40] Ibid, s 9, and see Adoption Agencies Regulations 2005 (SI 2005/389).   [41] ACA 2002, s 10.

[42] Ibid, s 12, and see Independent Review of Determinations (Adoption and Fostering) Regulations 2009 (SI 2009/395).

[43] ACA 2002, s 1(1). See s 1(7) for assistance on the meaning of 'coming to a decision relating to the adoption of a child'.   [44] The term 'relationship' here is not confined to legal relationships: see s 1(8).

[45] The term 'relative' includes the child's mother or father: see s 1(8).

background'. The court or adoption agency must also always consider the whole range of powers available to it in the child's case;[46] and the court must not make any order unless it would be better for the child than not doing so.[47]

4 ADOPTION AGENCIES' ROLE IN ASSESSING SUITABLE ADOPTIONS

The role of an adoption agency, with regard to particular children and potential adopters, is to decide whether a child is suitable for adoption, whether prospective adopters are in general suitable, and whether a proposed placement of a particular child with prospective adopters should be approved. The Adoption Agencies Regulations 2005 provide that an adoption agency must have one or more adoption panels[48] whose job it is to advise the agency in relation to adoption decisions. Each panel must comprise an independent Chair of the Panel and a minimum of three other persons, at least one of whom must be a registered social worker with at least three years' relevant post-qualification experience.[49]

Where an agency is considering adoption for a child, the agency is under a duty to open a case file relating to a child's adoption, in which is recorded relevant information/documents, such as records of proceedings, decisions, relevant consent, court orders etc.[50] The agency must, so far as reasonably practicable, provide counselling for, and ascertain the wishes and feelings of, the child[51] and parents.[52] The agency is required to obtain information on the child as specified in Schedule 1 to the Regulations, and must arrange for the child to be medically examined and a report obtained,[53] including so far as is reasonably practicable information about the child's family and the health of parents and siblings.[54] A report, known as the child's permanence report, containing the information which has been compiled, is then passed, with other relevant reports, to the adoption panel for its consideration.[55] The panel then considers whether the child should be placed for adoption and makes a recommendation to the agency.[56] The agency must then come to a decision, taking into account the recommendation of the panel.

The agency is under a duty to carry out a similar process with regard to considering a prospective adopter's suitability to adopt a child, compiling a range of information for a case file.[57] The agency must arrange for police checks to be carried out, and a person cannot be considered as suitable to adopt if convicted or cautioned for specified offences.[58] As noted earlier, the law now permits adoption by an unmarried couple, including same-sex adopters. However, this fact may not of itself ensure that unmarried couples, and perhaps particularly same-sex adopters, will be on a level playing field with married couples in the adoption process. Indeed, work by Emma Hitchings and Tracey Sagar[59] reporting on interviews with a small sample of social workers working in the field of adoption, suggested that same-sex adopters might be more likely to be offered very damaged children, children who had proved difficult to place with others. There may also still be an

---

[46] ACA 2002, s 1(6).   [47] Ibid.   [48] Adoption Agencies Regulations 2005, reg 4.
[49] Ibid, regs 3 and 6.   [50] Ibid, reg 12.   [51] Ibid, reg 13.   [52] Ibid, reg 14.
[53] Ibid, reg 15.   [54] Ibid, reg 16.
[55] Ibid, reg 17. The adoption agency must obtain, so far as is reasonably practicable, any other relevant information which may be requested by the adoption panel and send that information to the panel (reg 17(3)).   [56] Ibid, reg 18.
[57] Ibid, reg 22.   [58] Ibid, reg 23.
[59] E. Hitchings and T. Sagar, 'The Adoption and Children Act 2002: A Level Playing Field for Same-Sex Adopters?' [2002] Child and Family Law Quarterly 60.

expectation that same-sex couples should adopt distinct role differentiation as in many heterosexual relationships so as apparently not to confuse the adopted child. The law is clear, however, that it would be unlawful to discriminate against prospective adopters solely on the basis of marital status[60] or sexuality.[61]

The agency is under a duty to provide prospective adopters with preparation for adoption.[62] A prospective adopter's report is compiled by the agency[63] and sent to the adoption panel, which makes recommendations as to the prospective adopters' suitability.[64] The adoption agency is charged with the duty of making the decision as to the suitability of an adopter, taking account of the recommendation of the panel. The Suitability of Adopters Regulations 2005 set out the range of information which the agency must consider in reaching a decision about the suitability of adopters.[65] In determining the suitability of a couple to adopt a child, the agency must have proper regard to the need for stability and permanence in their relationship. If the adopter is deemed unsuitable, the decision must be given in writing, with reasons. If the prospective adopter is dissatisfied with the decision, he or she can apply to have it reviewed by an independent review panel.[66]

The next stage is matching of the child with prospective adopters. Again, the agency is under duties to compile information regarding proposed placement (a placement report) which together with other relevant reports is put before the panel for recommendation.[67] The adoption panel makes a recommendation[68] which the agency is under a duty to consider when making its decision.[69] If the placement is approved and the prospective adopters wish to proceed, before the child is placed the agency must send the prospective adopters a placement plan and notify the prospective adopters' general medical practitioner and the local authority of the placement.[70]

4.1 CAN INFORMATION ABOUT ADOPTION BE WITHHELD FROM THE CHILD'S FATHER AND OTHER RELATIVES?

As noted earlier, the adoption agency is under a duty to compile considerable information about the child as set out in Schedule 1 to the Adoption Agencies Regulations 2005, including information, as required by regulation 16, about the child's parents and relatives in Schedule 1, paragraph 3. However, cases sometimes arise in which the mother of a child wishes to give up her child for adoption without the father's knowledge or without informing her own family. The mother may even refuse to disclose who is the father. To what extent should the mother's wish for confidentiality be respected in such cases? Is the agency still required to collect the information specified in the regulations? In *Re L (Adoption: Contacting Natural Father)*[71] the mother of a girl had concealed her pregnancy from her family, left hospital two hours after the birth without seeing her baby, and requested that the baby be adopted. The mother maintained that she was unable (or as professionals suspected, unwilling) to disclose the father's identity. She was also adamant that her own family should not be informed of the child's birth. The local authority, with whom the child was accommodated, sought leave to invoke the inherent jurisdiction

---

[60] *Re P* [2008] UKHL 38.

[61] *EB v France* (App no 43546/02) [2008] 1 FLR 850, ECtHR. For comment on this case, see I. Curry-Sumner, '*EB v France*: A Missed Opportunity?' [2009] Child and Family Law Quarterly 356. Note also the Equality Act 2010, ss 12 and 29.   [62] Adoption Agencies Regulations 2005, reg 24.

[63] Ibid, reg 25.   [64] Ibid, reg 26.   [65] SI 2005/1712, and see ACA 2002, s 45.

[66] ACA 2002, s 12, and see Independent Review of Determinations (Adoption and Fostering) Regulations 2009 (SI 2009/395).   [67] Adoption Agencies Regulations 2005, reg 31.

[68] Ibid, reg 32.   [69] Ibid, reg 33.   [70] Ibid, reg 35.

[71] [2007] EWHC 1771 (Fam), [2008] 1 FLR 1079.

of the High Court for orders that it need not take further steps to identify the child's father nor inform or consult members of the maternal family concerning the intended adoption. Munby J, held that respecting the mother's wishes was lawful[72] and made the orders sought. However, he took the view that a further attempt should be made to obtain information from the mother about the father, and directed that the mother disclose details about the father. The mother subsequently told the judge from the well of the court (ie, not in the witness box under oath) that she was unable to provide further information and Munby J concluded that no further steps could sensibly be undertaken. While his Lordship was of the view that the court had the necessary power under the inherent jurisdiction to order the mother to disclose the father's identity, he found deeply unattractive,[73] and smacking too much of the Inquisition to be tolerable,[74] the idea that the mother should be cross-examined in order to compel her to reveal the father's name. It would, in his Lordship's view, be wrong to coerce the mother in this way.[75]

Where the identity of the child's father is known, a question may still arise as to whether he should be told of the child's existence and any plans for adoption. If a father does not have parental responsibility, his consent to adoption is not required. Under the rules of court a local authority is able to ask the High Court for directions on the need to give a father who does not have parental responsibility notice of the intention to place a child for adoption. The court has power to direct that a father be joined as a party to adoption proceedings. Equally, however, the child can be placed for adoption and an adoption order made without notice to a father who does not have parental responsibility. The authorities on whether a father should be told of proceedings with respect to his child have arisen similarly in the context of care proceedings and adoption proceedings.

In *Re A (Father: Knowledge of Child's Birth)*[76] the Court of Appeal dismissed a mother's appeal against Mostyn J's refusal of a declaration that the mother's husband (the child's father) not be told of the child's birth. The parents, who were in their forties with grown-up children, had been granted asylum from Afghanistan where the father and his family had suffered terribly at the hands of the Taliban.[77] As a result of his experiences, the father suffered mental health problems and was prone to unpredictable, frightening behaviour, including domestic violence. The mother's pregnancy was identified after it was possible for her to have an abortion, and she concealed the pregnancy and birth from the father and her son, although her daughters were aware of it. The mother feared the father's reaction to knowledge of the baby. However, the expert evidence did not support the mother's case that knowledge of the child would be adverse to the father's equilibrium.[78]

Black LJ (with whom Longmore LJ agreed) reviewed earlier authorities and concluded that the thrust of the case law[79] was that 'the court will not be persuaded to sanction the withholding of information about the existence of a child from that child's parent or to dispense with service on him of proceedings relating to the child in anything other than exceptional circumstances where there are ... strong countervailing factors'.[80]

---

[72] At [11], drawing on Holman J's judgment in *Z County Council v R* [2001] 1 FLR 365 at 367.

[73] Ibid, [38].   [74] Ibid, [40].   [75] Ibid, [41].   [76] [2011] EWCA Civ 273, [2011] 2 FLR 123.

[77] Relatives had been murdered and the father himself had been kidnapped and beaten up.

[78] [2011] EWCA Civ 273, [2011] 2 FLR 123 at [16].

[79] For a review of some of the case law, see A. Bainham, 'Can We Protect Children and Protect Their Rights?' [2002] Family Law 279.

[80] [2011] EWCA Civ 273, [2011] 2 FLR 123 at [37]. See also *Re H and G (Adoption: Consultation of Unmarried Fathers)* [2001] 1 FLR 745 at [48]; *Re C (Adoption: Disclosure to Father)* [2005] EWHC 3385 (Fam), [2006] 2 FLR 589 at [17] ('very compelling reasons'); *Birmingham City Council v S, R and A* [2006] EWHC 3065 (Fam), [2007] 1 FLR 1223 at [73] ('cogent and compelling grounds').

Accordingly, Mostyn J had been correct to conclude that the evidence was 'so deficient as to be incapable of satisfying any test of exceptionality'[81] and the father should not be denied knowledge of the child's existence.

As Munby J indicated in *Re L (Adoption: Contacting Natural Father)*,[82] however, 'every case is different and has to be decided having regard to its own unique circumstances'.[83] In *Re X (Care: Notice of Proceedings)*[84] the father was the brother-in-law of the mother, a 17-year-old Bangladeshi girl. The issue was whether the father, who did not know of the child's birth, should be served with notice of care proceedings. If the relationship between the mother and father became known in their community the overall effect would be a catastrophic destruction of the family. Stuart-White J decided that the father should not be given notice. In *Re H; Re G (Adoption: Consultation of Unmarried Fathers)*[85] Butler-Sloss P gave further examples of countervailing circumstances, such as rape or other serious domestic violence that placed the mother at serious physical risk.[86] However, in *Re A (Father: Knowledge of Child's Birth)*[87] the Court of Appeal made clear that the authorities 'do not impose a requirement of significant physical risk'.[88]

Key case

In *Re C (A Child) (Adoption: Duty of Local Authority)*[89] the court approached the matter 'from a slightly different angle'.[90] There an unmarried mother concealed her pregnancy from her family and placed her baby for adoption at birth. The child had been conceived as a result of a 'one-night stand'. The mother was opposed to the local authority making enquiries to see if any of the child's birth family would be suitable carers. The mother did not think that either of her divorced parents could care for the child, nor was there evidence that her siblings could do so. The judge held that the local authority was under a duty to inform itself of as much of the child's background as it was able and gave directions accordingly. On appeal, the Court of Appeal held that the judge had been wrong in principle and set aside his exercise of discretion. Arden LJ delivered the leading judgment, with which Thorpe LJ expressly agreed. Lawrence Collins LJ delivered a separate short judgment concurring in the result.

Arden LJ approached the case as a matter of statutory construction, holding that section 1 of the 2002 Act applied. Her Ladyship held, therefore, that there is no duty to make enquiries which are not in the interests of the child to make, and enquiries 'are not in the interests of the child simply because they will provide more information about the child's background'.[91] The question for the court in this case was who would look after the child on a long-term basis applying the child's welfare as paramount, and the fact that the judge considered that the child would benefit from knowledge of her father in adult life was not sufficient to animate the exercise of discretion.[92]

---

[81] Ibid, [17].   [82] [2007] EWHC 1771 (Fam), [2008] 1 FLR 1079.   [83] Ibid, [25].

[84] [1996] 1 FLR 186.   [85] [2001] 1 FLR 745 at [48].

[86] See also *Z County Council v R* [2001] 1 FLR 365 (relatives suffering illness which made it impossible for them to care for the child).   [87] [2011] EWCA Civ 273, [2011] 2 FLR 123.

[88] Ibid, [45]. Insofar as there may have been statements inconsistent with that view in Mostyn J's judgment (about which there was doubt), those statements were overruled.

[89] [2007] EWCA Civ 1206, [2008] Fam 54. For comment, see B. Sloan, '*Re C (A Child) (Adoption: Duty of Local Authority)*—Welfare and the Rights of the Birth Family in "Fast Track" Adoption Cases' [2009] Child and Family Law Quarterly 87.

[90] As Black LJ put it in *Re A (Father: Knowledge of Child's Birth)* [2011] EWCA Civ 273, [2011] 2 FLR 123.

[91] [2007] EWCA Civ 1206, [2008] Fam 54 at [3].   [92] Ibid, [21].

> Arden LJ commented:
>
> I do not consider that this court should require a preference to be given as a matter of policy to the natural family of a child. Section 1 [of the 2002 Act] does not impose any such policy. Rather, it requires the interests of the child to be considered. That must mean the child as an individual. In some cases, the birth tie will be very important, especially where the child is of an age to understand what is happening or where there are ethnic or cultural or religious reasons for keeping the child in the birth family. Where a child has never lived with her birth family, and is too young to understand what is going on, that argument must be weaker. In my judgment, in a case such as this, it is (absent any application by any member of the family, which succeeds) overtaken by the need to find the child a permanent home as soon as that can be done.

In this case the child was four months old and making attachments to the foster parents. In those circumstances, exercising the discretion afresh, the Court of Appeal found that the overriding need was to find the child a permanent home before the bond with the foster parents developed further.[93] The court's approach has been criticised for adopting a narrow interpretation of welfare which unduly emphasises permanence and the avoidance of delay criterion in the statute over other welfare factors, particularly as the requirement to examine the child's welfare throughout his or her life suggests a careful and broad assessment of welfare considerations.[94] In *Re A (Father: Knowledge of Child's Birth)*[95] the court commented that there is no reason to suppose that the court in *Re C* was contemplating a radical departure from the earlier authorities (discussed earlier), observing that Arden LJ in *Re C* clearly recognised that the circumstances in which a father would remain in ignorance about the child would be exceptional.[96]

The court in *Re C* also examined the human rights context under the European Convention on Human Rights (ECHR) to the situation presented. The right to respect for family life in Article 8 presupposes the existence of family life.[97] In the case of a father and a child born out of wedlock, whether family life exists within the meaning of Article 8 will depend on the circumstances, including the nature of the relationship between the natural parents and the demonstrable interest in and commitment by the natural father to the child both before and after the birth.[98] It can be established, therefore, where there are sufficiently close *de facto* family ties, for example arising through cohabitation.[99] However, family life may be established in the case of a potential relationship, although

---

[93] Ibid, [56] *per* Lawrence Collins LJ.

[94] B. Sloan, '*Re C (A Child) (Adoption: Duty of Local Authority)*—Welfare and the Rights of the Birth Family in "Fast Track" Adoption Cases' [2009] Child and Family Law Quarterly 87.

[95] [2011] EWCA Civ 273, [2011] 2 FLR 123 (Black LJ at [40], Longmore LJ agreeing).

[96] See *Re C* [2007] EWCA Civ 1206, [2008] Fam 54 at [24].

[97] See eg *Marckx v Belgium* (1979) 2 EHRR 330 at para 31; *Johnson v UK* (1999) 27 EHRR 296 at para 62. Arden LJ also held that near relatives, particularly grandparents automatically have an Art 8 right to respect for family life (citing *Marckx v Belgium* (1979) 2 EHRR 330 at para 45); see *Re C* at [31] *per* Arden LJ and at [53] *per* Lawrence Collins LJ. This is a doubtful statement since, as several commentators have pointed out, *Marckx* suggests that family life could include ties between grandparents and grandchildren, but this does not mean that it arises simply by reason of formal kinship links. See B. Sloan, '*Re C (A Child) (Adoption: Duty of Local Authority)*—Welfare and the Rights of the Birth Family in "Fast Track" Adoption Cases' [2009] Child and Family Law Quarterly 87, citing A. Bainham and F. Kaganas.

[98] See *Rozanski v Poland* (App no 55339/00) [2006] 2 FLR 1163.

[99] It need not involve cohabitation: see *Söderbäck v Sweden*: family life where only small amount of contact between father and daughter.

the father must have had some relationship with the mother and expressed his commitment to the child in some way, even if there was no cohabitation.[100] Moreover, in *Pini v Romania*[101] the Strasbourg Court stated that intended family life may, in some circumstances, be enough to establish a right to respect for one's family life. Arden LJ concluded that in the circumstances of the case before her, the father had no Article 8 right which could be violated by adoption of the child without his knowledge. Lawrence Collins LJ observed that even if Article 8 were engaged, it would be difficult to envisage a situation in which there could be an interference with the exercise of that right where the father does not know (or care) about the existence of the child. Furthermore, his Lordship was of the view that the protection of the rights of the mother and child would plainly justify the interference with any such right.[102]

5 RULES RELATING TO PARENTAL CONSENT IN ADOPTION CASES

Parental consent (and where necessary dispensing with it) plays an important role at various stages of the adoption process. It is convenient at the outset of our discussion of the legal framework for adoption, to set out some rules of interpretation which apply when there is a reference in the Act to any parent or guardian of a child giving or withdrawing consent to the placement of a child for adoption, or consent to the making of an adoption order (including a future adoption order).[103] The rules are set out in section 52.

Section 52(3) provides that consent given by the mother to the making of an adoption order is ineffective if it is given less than six weeks after the child's birth. Where consent can be validly given, section 52(5) makes clear that what is meant is 'consent given unconditionally and with full understanding of what is involved; but a person may consent to adoption without knowing the identity of the persons in whose favour the order will be made'.

Section 52 also clarifies whose consent is required. By section 52(6) 'parent' means a parent with parental responsibility. Furthermore, section 52(9) and (10) provide that if the child has been placed under section 19 with the consent of one parent, and at a later time the other parent of the child acquires parental responsibility for the child, the other parent is to be treated as having given consent at the earlier time in the same terms as the parent who consented. In such circumstances, even though an unmarried father may have acquired parental responsibility and may refuse consent to the making of an adoption order, his refusal would be ineffective to prevent the adoption.

6 PLACEMENT FOR ADOPTION

The first stage in the legal process of adoption is placement of the child. Section 18 of the ACA 2002 authorises an adoption agency to place a child for adoption provided the agency is satisfied that the child ought to be placed for adoption.[104] A child under six

---

[100] *Nylund v Finland* (App no 27110/95) (unreported) 29 June 1999; cf *G v Netherlands* (App no 16944/90) (1993) 16 EHRR CD 38; see *Re C* at [31]. See also *Görgülü v Germany* (family life where significant relationship ending before father aware of pregnancy).

[101] (2005) 40 EHRR 132, [2005] 2 FLR 596 at para 143: although holding that there was no family life in the case of persons who had obtained adoption orders but had not had care of the children concerned, the Court indicated that the requirement for *de facto* ties 'does not mean that all intended family life falls entirely outside the ambit of Art. 8'.   [102] *Re C* at [55].

[103] See s 52(2).   [104] Section 18(2).

weeks old may be lawfully placed with a prospective adopter provided the agency has obtained the written consent of the parents.[105] In the case of a child who is aged six weeks or over, the agency may only place the child with parental consent given under section 19 of the Act, or pursuant to a court order known as a placement order, under section 21.

6.1 MEANING OF 'PLACING A CHILD FOR ADOPTION'

Placing a child for adoption is defined in section 18(5) of the Act as placing a child for adoption with prospective adopters and includes, where the child is already living with persons, leaving the child with them as prospective adopters.[106] In *Coventry City Council v O (Adoption)*[107] the Court of Appeal[108] held that 'a child is not "placed" for adoption until he begins to live with the proposed adopters or, if he is already living with them in their capacity as foster carers, when the adoption agency formally allows him to continue to live with them in their fresh capacity as prospective adopters'.[109] This the court saw as the natural construction of the verb 'place'.[110] The court thus overruled Coulson J's ruling in *R (W) v Brent London Borough Council*[111] that placement had occurred when a local authority resolved to place a child with identified adopters (ie, the date of ratification of the placement). It should also be noted that section 18(5) refers to placement with 'prospective adopters', not merely 'potential adopters'.[112] It is important to be clear precisely when a child is or is not placed for adoption because various legal incidents flow from being placed.

6.2 PLACEMENT BY AGENCY WITH PARENTAL CONSENT (S 19)

Key legislation

Section 19(1) provides:

Where an adoption agency is satisfied that each parent or guardian of a child has consented to the child—

(a) being placed for adoption with prospective adopters identified in the consent, or

(b) being placed for adoption with any prospective adopters who may be chosen by the agency,

and has not withdrawn the consent, the agency is authorised to place the child for adoption accordingly.

---

[105] Adoption Agencies Regulations 2005, reg 35.

[106] However, see s 44(8):

Where—

(a) a local authority have placed a child with any persons otherwise than as prospective adopters, and

(b) the persons give notice of intention to adopt,

the authority are not to be treated as leaving the child with them as prospective adopters for the purposes of section 18(1)(b).

[107] [2011] EWCA Civ 729, [2011] 2 FLR 936.

[108] Lord Wilson of Culworth, Lord Neuberger of Abbotsbury, and Dame Janet Smith DBE.

[109] [2011] EWCA Civ 729, [2011] 2 FLR 936 at [44].

[110] See also the Adoption Agencies Regulations 2005, reg 35(2), cited by the court, which requires an adoption agency to send to a prospective adopter with whom it has decided to place a child an 'adoption placement plan' which, by para 3 of Sch 5, must identify the '[d]ate on which it is proposed to place the child for adoption with the prospective adopter'.   [111] [2010] EWHC 175 (Admin), [2010] 1 FLR 1914.

[112] For the distinction, see *Re S (Placement Order: Revocation)* [2008] EWCA Civ 1333, [2009] 1 FLR 503, which is discussed further in Section 6.7.

Under section 20(1), a parent or guardian who consents to the child being placed for adoption may at the same or any subsequent time consent to the making of a future adoption order. Notice can also be given to the adoption agency that the person consenting does not wish to be informed of an application for an adoption order.[113]

Consent given under sections 19 and 20 has momentous consequences for the future of child and parent,[114] and there can come a point when the consent cannot be withdrawn. Section 52(4) provides that withdrawal of any consent to the placement of a child for adoption, or of any consent given under section 20, is ineffective if it is given after an application for an adoption order is made. At that stage the adoption process is too far down the line to permit withdrawal of consent. Given these effects of sections 19 and 20, section 52 also specifies that consent under those provisions must be given in a form prescribed by rules,[115] and must be withdrawn in a form prescribed by rules, or alternatively in the case of withdrawal simply by giving notice to the agency.[116]

In *A Local Authority v GC and others*[117] the parents signed forms when a child was only four weeks old consenting to placement for adoption with prospective adopters under section 19, and purportedly giving advance consent to adoption under section 20. On a subsequent application to adopt the child, the justices' clerk noticed that the consent to adoption had been obtained before the child attained six weeks of age. The case came before Eleanor King J on the issue of whether the consent to placement was effective despite the fact that the child was under six weeks at the time. Her Ladyship noted that under section 18 placement of a child when aged under six weeks is an exception to the rule that placement can only take place pursuant to section 19 or 21 of the 2002 Act. (Regulation 35 of the Adoption Agencies Regulations 2005 provides that a child may be placed when still under six weeks provided there is a written agreement with the child's parent.) It was not necessary therefore for Eleanor King J to decide whether on the facts of the case there had been an effective section 19 placement, since, as her Ladyship found, the written consent meant that the child had been placed pursuant to a written agreement as required by the regulations and accordingly was an authorised placement. However, she stated that good practice and common sense suggest that section 19 consents should be obtained after the child attains the age of six weeks. Her Ladyship went on to hold that consent to placement when a child is under six weeks old cannot be relied on as a basis for making an adoption order,[118] since the law positively requires that the mother's consent to adoption is valid only once the child has attained the age of six weeks.[119] Therefore, as the child's parents were now no longer consenting to the child's adoption, the court needed to be satisfied that parental consent should be dispensed with.[120]

6.3 PLACEMENT ORDERS

A child can also be placed with prospective adopters pursuant to a 'placement order' under section 21 of the Act. This is a court order authorising a local authority to place a child for adoption with prospective adopters chosen by the authority.[121]

---

[113] Section 20(4).
[114] The effects of consent to placement are explored in more detail in Section 6.6. For a summary, see Eleanor King J in *A Local Authority v GC and Others* [2008] EWHC 2555 (Fam) at [21].
[115] Section 52(7).   [116] Section 52(8).   [117] [2008] EWHC 2555 (Fam), [2009] 1 FLR 299.
[118] Ibid, [34].
[119] See s 52, in accordance with the European Convention on the Adoption of Children 1967.
[120] See s 47(4).   [121] Section 21(1).

Key legislation

Under section 22(1) a local authority is under a duty to apply for a placement order if:

(a) the child is placed for adoption by them or is being provided with accommodation by them,

(b) no adoption agency is authorised to place the child for adoption,

(c) the child has no parent or guardian or the authority consider that the conditions in section 31(2) of the 1989 Act are met, and

(d) the authority are satisfied that the child ought to be placed for adoption.

Note that the wording is 'ought to be placed' rather than 'will be placed', and it has been held that a local authority can be satisfied that the child ought to be placed for adoption within the meaning of section 22(1)(d) 'even though it recognises the reality that a search for adoptive parents may be unsuccessful and that, if it is, the alternative plan will have to be for long-term fostering'.[122] In other words, there is 'no objection in principle to dual planning in appropriate cases'.[123]

6.3.1 Placement order must be preceded by the correct procedure

An application for a placement order must be preceded by compliance with the regulations which set out the procedure by which the agency must reach its decision whether the child should be placed for adoption. The framework laid down by Parliament cannot be bypassed or short-circuited.[124] If a judge becomes aware of a material irregularity in that procedure, the proceedings should be adjourned to allow the adoption agency to consider the matter in accordance with the regulations. The hearing before the judge cannot rectify those procedural difficulties.[125] In *Re B (Placement Order)*[126] there was a failure on the part of the local authority to provide the adoption agency panel with relevant expert reports in breach of the 2002 Act and the Adoption Agencies (Wales) Regulations 2005.[127] The Court of Appeal set out guidance,[128] the essence of which was that 'panel members should be made fully and properly aware of all the available material relevant to their decision'.[129]

6.3.2 Conditions for making a placement order

The court may not make a placement order in respect of a child unless the child is subject to a care order, or the court is satisfied that the conditions for making a care order are satisfied, or the child has no parent or guardian. In other words, the state may only intervene to place the child for adoption if there has at some stage been a finding that the child is suffering or likely to suffer significant harm attributable to a want of reasonable parental care or the child is orphaned. In addition, in any case in which a parent or guardian is still living, the court must be satisfied that each parent or guardian has consented

---

[122] *Re P (Placement Orders: Parental Consent)* [2008] EWCA Civ 535, [2008] 2 FLR 625 at [137].

[123] Ibid.

[124] *Re B (Placement Order)* [2008] EWCA Civ 835, [2008] 2 FLR 1404 at [70]; and see also at [99]: 'the Regulations are there to be honoured and obeyed in their entirety'.

[125] Contrast *Re P-B* [2006] EWCA Civ 1016, where the agency's failure to fulfil its statutory duty was undiscovered until after the making of the placement order.

[126] [2008] EWCA Civ 835, [2008] 2 FLR 1404.   [127] SI 2005/1313.

[128] [2008] EWCA Civ 835, [2008] 2 FLR 1404 at [81].   [129] Ibid, [84].

to the child being placed for adoption with any prospective adopters who may be chosen by the local authority and has not withdrawn consent,[130] or that the parent's or guardian's consent should be dispensed with.

6.3.3 Dispensing with consent

Key legislation

Section 52(1) provides that:

The court cannot dispense with the consent of any parent or guardian of a child to the child being placed for adoption or to the making of an adoption order in respect of the child unless the court is satisfied that—

(a) the parent or guardian cannot be found or lacks capacity (within the meaning of the Mental Capacity Act 2005) to give consent, or

(b) the welfare of the child requires the consent to be dispensed with.[131]

In *Re P (Placement Orders: Parental Consent)*[132] the Court of Appeal commented that the best guidance it could give to judges approaching the question of dispensation under section 52(1)(b) is 'to apply the statutory language with care to the facts of the particular case'.[133] The court held that deciding whether or not to dispense with parental consent to a placement order is a decision relating to the adoption of a child, and accordingly section 1(2) of the 2002 Act requires the court to treat 'the child's welfare throughout his life' as its 'paramount consideration'.[134] The court went on to give 'paramount' in this context the same meaning as in Lord MacDermott's famous dictum in *J v C*,[135] namely that the child's welfare 'rules upon and determines the course to be followed'. However, the court added that welfare in the context of adoption means welfare determined having regard to the matters set out in section 1(4) of the 2002 Act, which provides a far wider checklist of factors than that provided in section 1(3) of the Children Act 1989.[136] The court highlighted that the focus on the child's welfare 'throughout his life' emphasises that adoption has lifelong implications, and therefore a judge exercising his powers under section 52(1)(b) 'has to be satisfied that the child's welfare now, throughout the rest of his childhood, into adulthood and indeed throughout his life, requires that he or she be adopted'.[137] This is reinforced by section 1(4)(c), which specifically directs attention to the consequences for the child 'throughout his life'—and by section 1(4)(f). Thus, a judge must address the question in section 52(1)(b) whether 'the welfare of the child requires the consent to be dispensed with', and answer it by reference to section 1 of the 2002 Act, and in particular by a careful consideration of all the matters identified in section 1(4).[138] There is therefore no so-called 'enhanced welfare test' in adoption cases as compared with other situations in which

---

[130] Section 21(3)(a).
[131] On the previous law, see s 16(2)(b) of the Adoption Act 1976, *Re W (An Infant)* [1971] 2 All ER 49, [1971] AC 682, and Lord Wilberforce's parent '(hypothetically) endowed with mind and temperament capable of making reasonable decisions'—see *Re D (Adoption: Parent's Consent)* [1977] 1 All ER 145 at 130, [1977] AC 602 at 625.   [132] [2008] EWCA Civ 535, [2008] 2 FLR 625.
[133] Ibid, [117].   [134] Ibid, [114].   [135] [1969] 1 All ER 788 at 821, [1970] AC 668 at 711.
[136] [2008] EWCA Civ 535, [2008] 2 FLR 625 at [115].
[137] Ibid, [128]. For an example, see *Re Q (Adoption)* [2011] EWCA Civ 1610.   [138] *Re P* ibid, [116].

children's welfare is paramount. The vital difference is simply between the wording of section 1 of the 1989 Act and section 1 of the 2002 Act.[139]

The court commented that 'the word "requires" in s 52(1)(b) is a perfectly ordinary English word',[140] adding, however, that the word takes its colour from the statutory context in which it is used. Here the context is that of determining whether the child's welfare requires *adoption* rather than something short of adoption.[141] The court emphasised that the judge must 'be aware of the importance to the child of the decision being taken' adding that there 'is, perhaps, no more important or far-reaching decision for a child than to be adopted by strangers'.[142] It held that the Strasbourg jurisprudence also provides the context in which the word 'requires' is used, and the word was chosen as best conveying the essence of the Strasbourg jurisprudence.[143] Reviewing the main principles on state interference with the rights of children and parents under Article 8 of the ECHR (which will usually be engaged in this context),[144] the court explained that any interference must be in accordance with the law, pursue a legitimate aim, and be necessary in a democratic society (implying the existence of a 'pressing social need').[145] Intervention must represent a proportionate response to achieving the legitimate aim (in this context, protection of the child's welfare). The court stated that in assessing what is proportionate the judge must always bear in mind that adoption without parental consent is the most extreme interference with family life, and therefore cogent justification must exist.[146] Thus, the court held that, viewed from the perspective of the Strasbourg jurisprudence, the word 'requires' has 'the connotation of the imperative, what is demanded rather than what is merely optional or reasonable or desirable'.[147] The court emphasised the 'need for care, sensitivity and intellectual rigour on the part of judges hearing applications for placement orders'.[148] The judge must not apply section 1(4) simply as a mantra, nor act as a rubber stamp; the 'underlying facts, properly analysed, must support the judicial conclusion'.[149]

The court's approach here is a valiant attempt, within the constraints of the paramountcy principle as interpreted by the House of Lords/Supreme Court, to place emphasis on the child's interest in the birth family not being disintegrated by adoption. However, as discussed in detail in Chapter 9, there are strong arguments that the paramountcy principle, as interpreted in *J v C*, is not consistent with the requirements of the ECHR and Strasbourg jurisprudence which requires separate articulation of the Article 8 interests of the child and parents concerned.[150] The divergence between the paramountcy principle and Article 8 'encompasses both the reasoning process each requires and the substantive outcomes likely to be produced'.[151] Despite acknowledgement during the review of adoption law in the early 1990s that 'the permanent legal severance of the relationship between child and birth parents should be justified by clear and significant advantage to the child compared with less permanent options',[152] the paramountcy principle was introduced into adoption law with little justification other than seeking consistency with

---

[139] Ibid, [127].   [140] Ibid.   [141] Ibid, [126].   [142] Ibid, [116].   [143] Ibid, [125].
[144] Ibid, [119].

[145] See the discussion at [119]–[124], citing *Re C and B (Children) (Care Order: Future Harm)* [2000] 2 FCR 614 at [33]; *Haase v Germany* [2005] 3 FCR 666 at [93]; *Re O (A Child) (Supervision Order: Future Harm)* [2001] EWCA Civ 16, [2001] 1 FCR 289 at [28]; *Re B (Children) (Care: Interference with Family Life)* [2003] EWCA Civ 786, [2004] 1 FCR 463 at [34]; *Re O (Minors) (Care or Supervision Order)* [1997] 2 FCR 17 at 22: *Johansen v Norway* (1996) 23 EHRR 33 at para 78.

[146] See [2008] EWCA Civ 535, [2008] 2 FLR 625 at [124].   [147] Ibid, [125].   [148] Ibid, [132].
[149] Ibid, [131].

[150] See in the context of adoption reform, S. Choudhry, 'The Adoption and Children Act 2002, the Welfare Principle and the Human Rights Act 1998—A Missed Opportunity?' [2003] Child and Family Law Quarterly 119.   [151] Ibid.

[152] *Adoption the Future* (Cm 2288, 1993), p 263.

the approach in the Children Act 1989.[153] This change troubled commentators even prior to enactment of the Act.[154] It has been suggested that if the same welfare test is used for whether an order should be made as well as for dispensing with consent, then the latter becomes a foregone conclusion and there is also a risk of social engineering,[155] although it has also been observed that there may be cases in which it is in the child's interests to be adopted, but not in the child's interests to be adopted without parental consent.[156]

6.3.4 Child must be suitable for placement

For an order to be made, it must be possible to say at the time of making the order that the order is in a child's best interests. In *Re T (Placement Order)*[157] a judge made care orders and placement orders in respect of boys aged 7 and 5, who had suffered neglect and inappropriate parenting by their parents, both of whom had significant learning disabilities. The boys were described by two experienced independent social workers as the most damaged and needy they had ever encountered in their work. The local authority's long-term plan was for the children to be adopted. However, it was proposed first to place the children with specialist therapeutic foster parents for six months and possibly a year, so as to help the children to learn how to form secure attachments. The children's father challenged the placement orders. Allowing his appeal and setting aside the placement orders, the Court of Appeal explained that, while mere uncertainty as to whether adoption will actually follow is not a reason for not making a placement order,[158] in this unusual case it was not simply a matter of potential difficulty of placement; rather the boys were not yet suitable for placement for adoption.[159] It had, therefore, not yet been possible to say that adoption was actually in the boys' best interests and the placement order was premature.[160]

6.4 CONSEQUENCES OF A PLACEMENT ORDER

The effect of a placement order is that certain orders under the Children Act 1989 cease to have effect, and certain orders under that Act can no longer be made, or in some cases applications are restricted by a leave requirement. On the making of a placement order, any order mentioned in section 8(1) of the Children Act 1989 and any supervision order ceases to have effect,[161] and no court can make a prohibited steps order, specific issue order, supervision order, or child assessment order in respect of the child.[162] No residence order or special guardianship order may be made unless leave of the court has been obtained under section 29(4) and (5) respectively, or the applicant has obtained leave under section 47 to oppose an adoption order. An existing care order does not cease to exist, but does not have effect at any time when the placement order is in force.[163] These effects of a placement order are intended to ensure that (with limited exceptions) the adoption agency and prospective adopter are in control of the child's future day-to-day welfare pending a court decision concerning adoption, without the risk of interference from others via court orders. An exception is made where the applicant has been granted

[153] *Adoption: A New Approach* (Cm 5017, 2000), paras 2.11. and 4.14.

[154] E. Cooke, 'Dispensing with Parental Consent to Adoption—A Choice of Welfare Tests' [1997] Child and Family Law Quarterly 259.

[155] S. Harris-Short, 'The Adoption and Children Bill—A Fast Track to Failure?' [2001] Child and Family Law Quarterly 405.

[156] E. Cooke, 'Dispensing with Parental Consent to Adoption—A Choice of Welfare Tests' [1997] Child and Family Law Quarterly 259.   [157] [2008] EWCA Civ 248, [2008] 1 FLR 1721.

[158] Ibid, [17].   [159] Ibid, [18].   [160] Ibid.

[161] ACA 2002, s 29(2).   [162] Ibid, s 29(3).   [163] Ibid, s 29(1).

leave under relevant provisions to apply for a residence order or special guardianship order. Another exception is that an application for a contact order under section 8 of the Children Act 1989 is still permitted, as contact is ultimately under court control, and it may be that in future such an application will be heard alongside an application for an adoption order. Apart from such a case,[164] where a placement order is in force, applications relating to contact with the child concerned are regulated by sections 26 and 27 of the ACA 2002 not the Children Act 1989.

6.5 PLACEMENT AND CONTACT

On an adoption agency being authorised to place a child for adoption, or placing a child for adoption who is less than six weeks old, any provision for contact under section 8 or 34 of the Children Act 1989 ceases to have effect,[165] and no application can be made for contact under the 1989 Act. Instead, contact becomes regulated by sections 26 and 27 of the 2002 Act. Section 27(4) provides that before making a placement order the court must consider the arrangements which the adoption agency has made, or proposes to make, for allowing any person contact with the child, and invite the parties to the proceedings to comment on those arrangements. Section 26(2) provides for the making of a contact order 'requiring the person with whom the child lives, or is to live, to allow the child to visit or stay with the person named in the order, or for the person named in the order and the child otherwise to have contact with each other' (thus defined in the same way as in s 8 of the Children Act 1989). The court can make a contact order of its own initiative when making a placement order,[166] or an application for an order under this section may be made by:

(a) the child or the agency,

(b) any parent, guardian or relative,

(c) any person in whose favour there was provision for contact under the 1989 Act which ceased to have effect by virtue of subsection (1),

(d) if a residence order was in force immediately before the adoption agency was authorised to place the child for adoption or (as the case may be) placed the child for adoption at a time when he was less than six weeks old, the person in whose favour the order was made,

(e) if a person had care of the child immediately before that time by virtue of an order made in the exercise of the High Court's inherent jurisdiction with respect to children, that person,

(f) any person who has obtained the court's leave to make the application.

An order under section 26 may provide for contact on any conditions the court considers appropriate.[167] The courts' approach to on-going contact in adoption cases is discussed further later in this chapter.

6.6 EFFECT OF PLACEMENT OR AUTHORISATION TO PLACE

Where a child is placed for adoption or an agency is authorised to place a child under section 19, or a placement order is in force in respect of a child, the agency concerned

---

[164] See ibid, s 26(5).

[165] Ibid, s 26(1) and (6). Any contact activity direction (see Children Act 1989, s 11A) relating to contact with the child is also discharged.   [166] ACA 2002, s 26(4).

[167] Ibid, s 27(5).

has parental responsibility for the child and, while the child is placed with prospective adopters, they too have parental responsibility.[168] However, in such circumstances a person may not cause the child to be known by a new surname or remove the child from the UK (except for a period of less than one month by a person who provides the child's home[169]), unless the court gives leave or each parent or guardian of the child gives written consent.[170] Where a child is placed for adoption under section 19 or an adoption agency is authorised to place a child for adoption under that section, a parent or guardian of the child may not apply for a residence order, and a guardian may not apply for a special guardianship order, unless an application for an adoption order has been made and the parent or guardian has obtained the court's leave to oppose the adoption order.[171]

Where a child is placed for adoption, there is authorisation to place, or a local authority is seeking a placement order, the stability of the child's current home placement (whether placed with prospective adopters or accommodated by the local authority) is protected to some extent by prohibitions on the child's removal. Where a child is placed for adoption by an adoption agency, or accommodated by an agency which is authorised to place the child, no person other than the agency is allowed to remove the child from the placement or accommodation.[172] Similarly, where a child is accommodated by a local authority and the authority has applied for a placement order which has not yet been disposed of, the child may only be removed from accommodation by the local authority or by a person who has the leave of the court.[173]

These general prohibitions on removal of a child are subject to sections 31–33 which provide for the child to be returned following a period of notice. If a parent or guardian informs the agency that he or she wishes the child to be returned and the child is accommodated but not placed for adoption, the agency must return the child within seven days beginning with the request. If the child is placed otherwise than under section 19 (eg as a baby under six weeks old), then the agency must give notice of the parents' request to the prospective adopters, who similarly must return the child within seven days, whereupon the agency must return the child to the parents.[174] In the case of a child who is placed pursuant to section 19 and consent to placement has been withdrawn, the same procedure applies except that the time frame for return of the child is 14 days, not seven.[175] None of these requirements to return the child applies, however, if an application for a placement order is, or has been, made and has not been disposed of.[176] If a child is placed for adoption and an application for a placement order fails, prospective adopters must return the child to the local authority on a date determined by the court.[177] In each of the cases mentioned, a failure on the part of prospective adopters to return the child as required constitutes a criminal offence.

6.7 DURATION, AND REVOCATION, OF A PLACEMENT ORDER

Once made, the placement order remains in force until an adoption order is made in respect of the child, or the child reaches the age of 18, marries, or forms a civil partnership, or the placement order is revoked under section 24 of the Act. The court may revoke a placement order if, on an application for an adoption order, it determines not to make the adoption order.[178] In addition, it may revoke the placement order on the application of any person. An important effect of making an application for revocation is to be found in section 24(5) of the Act. It provides that where such an application has been made and not

---

[168] Ibid, s 25.   [169] Ibid, s 28(4).   [170] Ibid, s 28(2) and (3).   [171] Ibid, s 28(1).
[172] Ibid, s 30(1) and (3).   [173] Ibid, s 30(2).   [174] Ibid, s 31.   [175] Ibid, s 32.
[176] Ibid, s 31(2) and (3).   [177] Ibid, s 33.   [178] Ibid, s 24(4).

disposed of and the child has not yet been placed for adoption by the authority, the child may not without the court's leave be placed for adoption under the placement order.

While any person may apply for revocation, section 24(2) places some restrictions on applications. It provides that:

> an application may not be made by a person other than the child or the local authority authorised by the order to place the child for adoption unless—
>
> (a) the court has given leave to apply, and
>
> (b) the child is not placed for adoption by the authority.

As paragraph (b) makes clear, an application for leave to revoke a placement order can only be made at a time when the child is not already placed for adoption. As provided in section 18(5), this means placed with prospective adopters. In *Re S (Placement Order: Revocation)*[179] a mother applied for leave to revoke a placement order, contending that her change of circumstances meant she could now safely care for her child. The local authority's plan for the child was adoption, and the child was placed with a foster carer who, while not making a specific commitment to adopt, had not precluded the possibility of her family adopting the child. In these circumstances the judge held that the child was placed with potential adopters and the leave application was precluded by section 24(2)(b). The Court of Appeal allowed the mother's appeal and remitted the case to the judge for rehearing. The court held that the statute required placement with prospective adopters, not merely potential adopters. The court pointed out that the word 'prospective' is defined 'as an adjective attributive of a person expected or expecting to be something particular in the future; alternatively, as something likely to happen at a future date. "Potential", by contrast, is defined as an adjective having or showing the capacity to become or develop into something in the future.'[180] The court made clear that placement for adoption only takes place once the child in question is matched to prospective adopters. Here only the first stage in the adoption process had been completed, namely whether adoption was in the child's best interests. The foster carer had not been approved in principle, let alone matched, as a prospective adopter for the child.[181] The foster carer had no more than the potential to emerge at a later stage as a prospective adopter.[182]

Section 24(2)(b) proved crucial in *Re F (Placement Order)*.[183] In that case, a girl, who was just under two years old at the date of the Court of Appeal's judgment, had been conceived following a casual relationship between her parents. The father, who had initially been unaware that he was the father, was served with care proceedings in respect of the child in which the local authority's plan was for the child's adoption. However, the father was hospitalised with a heart attack and took no part in the proceedings. The local authority was granted a placement order. Some months thereafter, after consulting solicitors, the father applied for leave to revoke the placement order under section 24(2). The solicitors sent the local authority a fax informing them of the father's application and asking the authority to confirm by return fax that the child had not yet been placed. There was no response to the fax. The authority convened an informal strategy meeting and, on the day before the hearing of the father's application, the local authority placed the child with prospective adopters. At the hearing, the local authority then simply relied on section 24(2)(b) and the judge reluctantly agreed that in the circumstances no application to revoke could be made and therefore leave could not be granted. The father appealed, arguing that respect for his human rights required that words should be read into section 24(5) pursuant to section 3 of the Human Rights Act 1998 so that

---

[179] [2008] EWCA Civ 1333, [2009] 1 FLR 503.

[180] Ibid, [7].   [181] Ibid, [8].   [182] Ibid, [9].   [183] [2008] EWCA Civ 439, [2008] 2 FLR 550.

the prohibition in that subsection on placing a child when an application to revoke a placement order has been made should also apply when an application for leave to apply to revoke
a placement order has been made. In this way, the local authority would have been prevented
from placing the child once the father made his application for leave.

The Court of Appeal, by a majority,[184] dismissed the father's appeal, holding that it
was impossible to read section 24(5) as contended for by the father. Indeed, section 24(5),
read as part of the whole scheme for adoption under the 2002 Act, was 'human rights
compliant'.[185] The majority reached this conclusion with regret, not because of any doubts
about the law but because of the conduct of the local authority adoption agency in this
case.[186] Wall LJ commented that the 'disgraceful conduct of the agency in this case is an
example of the worst kind of sharp practice',[187] which demonstrated 'a profound if not
total misunderstanding of its functions under the 2002 Act'.[188] It was 'an abuse of power,
and wholly unacceptable'.[189] Wall LJ suggested[190] that were such behaviour to be repeated
it could be the subject of an application for judicial review, and his Lordship could see no
reason why the Administrative Court should not declare unlawful such a decision. The
decision to place the child for adoption could be quashed. Directions could be given for
hearing the application for leave to revoke, and in the meantime an injunction could be
put in place restraining the local authority from placing the child for adoption. Wall LJ
went on to indicate what should have happened in this case as a matter of good practice.[191]
Either the father's solicitors should have sought an undertaking from the local authority
that the child would not be placed pending the hearing of the father's application or, in
the absence of such an undertaking, should have sought an injunction in similar terms.
Alternatively, the local authority should have replied, explained that its plans to place the
child were at an advanced stage, and then sought leave of the court to place the child.

Section 24(3) provides that the court 'cannot give leave under subsection (2)(a) unless
satisfied that there has been a change in circumstances since the order was made'. In *M v
Warwickshire County Council*[192] two children were taken into care because their mother
abused alcohol and crack cocaine, rendering her incapable of looking after them appropriately. Care orders and placement orders had been made in respect of the children. However,
the mother had since achieved significant improvements in her life and was applying for
leave to revoke the placement orders. She had abstained from drugs, was no longer abusing
alcohol, kept the home in a fit state, and had managed to hold down a part-time job. The
judge found that there was a change of circumstances and that once he had so found he
was obliged to grant leave. On appeal by the local authority, the Court of Appeal held that
the judge had been right on these facts to find a change of circumstances, but had erred in
granting leave automatically, since the grant of leave involves an exercise of discretion.[193]
The court went on to provide guidance on what should be a court's general approach to
exercising discretion under section 24(3). The court explained that section 1(7) of the 2002
Act makes clear that section 1 of that Act does not apply to an application for leave to
revoke a placement order under section 24(2).[194] Thus the child's welfare is not the paramount consideration on an application for leave to revoke a placement order, although the
court made clear that it is still, of course, a factor in the exercise of discretion. The court was

---

[184] Wall and Wilson LJJ; Thorpe LJ dissenting.
[185] [2008] EWCA Civ 439, [2008] 2 FLR 550 at [63] *per* Wall LJ, Wilson LJ agreeing.
[186] [2008] EWCA Civ 439, [2008] 2 FLR 550 at [1].
[187] Ibid, [93]. Indeed, the worst his Lordship had ever encountered in a career spanning nearly 40 years
(see at [78]).   [188] Ibid, [39].
[189] Ibid, [44].   [190] Ibid, [94].
[191] See [97] et seq.   [192] [2007] EWCA Civ 1084, [2008] 1 FLR 1093.   [193] Ibid, [30].
[194] Ibid, [22].

of the view that, as in the case of many other leave applications in areas of family law, the court should ask whether the applicant would have a real prospect of success.[195] However, the court made clear that the prospect of success can only be a relevant factor to the exercise of discretion; 'it cannot be written in stone that the prospect of success has to be real'.[196] In other words, the court was merely commending those words as 'a reasonable working assumption, likely to be apt to the vast majority of applications'.[197] The Court of Appeal, in the words of Wilson LJ, went on to explain the overall correct approach, highlighting the relationship between child welfare and prospect of success:

> on establishment of a change in circumstances, a discretion arises in which the welfare of the child and the prospect of success should both be weighed.... the requisite analysis of the prospect of success will almost always include the requisite analysis of the welfare of the child. For, were there to be a real prospect that an applicant would persuade the court that a child's welfare would best be served by revocation of the placement order, it would surely almost always serve the child's welfare for the applicant to be given leave to seek to do so. Conversely, were there not to be any such real prospect, it is hard to conceive that it would serve the welfare of the child for the application for leave to be granted. But I hesitate to suggest that analysis of welfare will always be satisfactorily subsumed within an analysis of prospect.[198]

In *M v Warwickshire County Council*, by the time the mother made her application for leave to revoke, the children had been in long-term foster care for three years, over half of their lives. In difficult circumstances the children had eventually been well matched to proposed adopters.[199] The Court of Appeal noted that the only realistic aspiration that the mother would have at a revocation hearing would be an adjournment pending a full professional assessment of her parenting capacity, and the present adopters might not be relied on to tolerate the ensuing delay. In all the circumstances, the Court of Appeal held that the mother's application for leave must be refused.

6.7.1 Revocation even when child will not be returned to parents

As *NS-H v Kingston Upon Hull City Council and MC*[200] demonstrates, occasionally it will be proper for a court to grant parental leave to revoke a placement order notwithstanding the absence of any real prospect that a court would find it to be in the interest of the child to return to live with the parent.[201] In that case a young boy who had very low weight for his age was taken into care and a placement order was also made. However, he continued to fail to thrive when living with foster parents and the local authority changed its care plan. The authority now intended to move him to new foster parents, and accepted that an adoptive home could only be found once he began to thrive. The child's mother sought leave to apply to revoke the placement order. There was no question in this case of the boy returning to live with his mother as it had been found that his initial failure to thrive was the result of the mother's defective attachment to the boy and her own past eating disorder, which had led to her mishandling of his feeding. The Court of Appeal overturned the judge's refusal to grant leave, holding that, applying the correct test (in the *Warwickshire* case, as set out earlier) the judge could only have concluded that leave should be granted.[202]

---

[195] Ibid, [27].   [196] Ibid.   [197] Ibid.   [198] Ibid, [29].

[199] Finding adopters had not proved easy apparently because of the children's ethnicity, the fact that one of them had cerebral palsy, and the father of the other child had been diagnosed with paranoid schizophrenia.   [200] [2008] EWCA Civ 493, [2008] 2 FLR 918, CA.

[201] Ibid, [1].

[202] See at [27]. The court added, at [31], that in exercising discretion the court should guard against an opportunistic attempt to use an application for improper, collateral purposes.

7 APPLICATIONS TO ADOPT

Following placement, the next step in the adoption process is for the prospective adopter(s) to make an application to adopt the child. The effect of making the application is that the child may not be placed with any other prospective adopter until the application is disposed of.[203] The Act defines who may adopt and be adopted, and thus the nature of an adoption application, and also sets out certain preliminaries which must be complied with before the application may be made.

7.1 WHO MAY ADOPT?

An application for an adoption order may be made by a couple or by one person.[204] Each adopter must have been habitually resident in a part of the British Islands for a period of not less than one year ending with the date of the application.[205] In addition, the individual applicant, or at least one member of a couple, must be domiciled in a part of the British Islands.[206]

7.1.1 Adoption by a couple

An adoption order may be made on the application of a couple under section 50 of the 2002 Act. With one exception, both of the couple must have attained the age of 21 years. Where one of the couple is the mother or the father of the person to be adopted the age requirement is less stringent. An application can be made provided the parent has attained the age of 18 years and the other person of the couple has attained the age of 21 years.[207]

7.1.1.1 Meaning of couple

For the purpose of the 2002 Act, section 144(4) defines a couple as:

(a)   a married couple, or

(aa) two people who are civil partners of each other, or

(b)   two people (whether of different sexes or the same sex) living as partners in an enduring family relationship.

Section 145(5) provides that the definition in section 144(4)(b) does not include two people one of whom is the other's parent, grandparent, sister, brother, aunt, or uncle, in each case whether of the full blood or half blood. The list of excluded relationships in section 144(5) includes such relationships as would exist but for adoption, and also a child's relationship with his or her adoptive, or former adoptive, parents, but no other adoptive relationships.[208]

The definition is silent as to whether the couple must live at the same address. This issue arose in *Re T and M (Adoption)*.[209] In that case, two women who were a couple each separately adopted a child while living in Nicaragua. The separate adoptions were necessary because Nicaragua did not permit adoption by a same-sex couple. One of the women was Nicaraguan and adopted a child, C, who was a member of her extended family, while the other woman, who was from the USA, adopted a child, J, from an orphanage. The women

---

[203]   ACA 2002, s 18(4).   [204]   Ibid, s 49.   [205]   Ibid, s 49(3).   [206]   Ibid, s 49(2).
[207]   Ibid, s 50(1).   [208]   Ibid, s 144(6).
[209]   [2010] EWHC 964 (Fam), [2011] 1 FLR 1487 (Hedley J).

and the children came to live in the UK. However, J's previous experiences of abandonment by her parents led to difficulties in her relationship with the Nicaraguan woman (J's adoptive mother's partner). This led the women to set up two separate households close to each other, although they remained a couple and saw each other daily. J lived in one household with her adoptive mother, and C moved between the households in a shared residence arrangement. The couple then applied to adopt C as a couple and Hedley J (having first recognised at common law the validity of the Nicaraguan adoption order in respect of C) was required to consider whether the women were a couple, notwithstanding the fact that they were living in separate properties. Hedley J held that the words 'living as partners in an enduring family relationship' were 'no doubt chosen so as not to require the residence of both in the same property', which he did not see as unusual given that many a parent has had to work abroad leaving the rest of the family at home. He held that what is required is 'first, an unambiguous intention to create and maintain family life, and secondly, a factual matrix consistent with that intention,'[210] adding that that 'is clearly a question of fact and degree in each case.'[211] Applying that approach, his Lordship found on the facts that the parties were within the ambit of section 144(4)(b) and thus entitled to make a joint application to adopt, since they lived in a committed and exclusive relationship and spent significant time as a unit of four, consistent with the background to the case and the shared-care arrangement.[212]

In *Re WM (Adoption: Non-Patrial)*,[213] a case under the former legislation (the Adoption Act 1976), Johnson J was required to consider whether an adoption order could be made in favour of a married couple who had separated. His Lordship made the order, noting that there was no specific provision in the legislation which prevented an order being made in favour of a separated couple. The 1976 Act provided (as does the 2002 Act—see discussion at Section 7.3.1.2) that an adoption order could not be made unless there had been sufficient opportunities to view the couple with the child in the home environment. However, in this case the social worker concerned had had sufficient opportunity to do so prior to the separation. Johnson J suggested, however, that had that not been the case it would seem that that provision would have proved a bar to making the order. The same reasoning would presumably apply to the similar provision under the 2002 Act.

7.1.2 Adoption by one person

An application to adopt can be made by one person under section 51 of the 2002 Act. In such a case, the applicant must have attained the age of 21 years and must fall into one of the following categories:

(1) The person is not married or a civil partner.[214]

(2) The court is satisfied that the person is the partner of a parent of the person to be adopted.[215] For the purposes of the 2002 Act, a person is the partner of a child's parent if the person and the parent are a couple but the person is not the child's parent.[216]

(3) The person is married or a civil partner, but the court is satisfied that:

  (a) 'the person's spouse or civil partner (as the case may be) cannot be found,

  (b) the spouses or civil partners have separated and are living apart, and the separation is likely to be permanent, or

---

[210] Ibid, [16].   [211] Ibid.   [212] Ibid, [17].   [213] [1997] 1 FLR 132, FD.
[214] ACA 2002, s 51(1).   [215] Ibid, s 51(2).   [216] Ibid, s 50(7).

(c) the person's spouse or civil partner is by reason of ill-health, whether physical or mental, incapable of making an application for an adoption order.'[217]

7.1.3 Adoption by the child's mother or father

Special considerations apply on an application by the mother or father of the person to be adopted. Such an application may not be made unless the court is satisfied that:

(a) the other natural parent is dead or cannot be found,

(b) ...there is no other parent,[218] or

(c) there is some other reason justifying the child's being adopted by the applicant alone.[219]

Where the court makes an adoption order on such an application, the court must record that it is satisfied as to the fact mentioned in paragraph (a) or (b) or, in the case of paragraph (c), record the reason.[220]

In *Re B (A Minor) (Natural Parent)*[221] the House of Lords considered a provision in section 15(3) of the Adoption Act 1976 which was in similar terms. In that case an adoption order was sought in respect of a 3-year-old girl by one of her natural parents (the father), with the consent of the child's mother. The mother had had a brief relationship with the father and initially he was unaware of the mother's pregnancy and the birth of his daughter. The mother gave up the child for adoption at birth. Purely by chance the local authority became aware of the father's whereabouts, and when contacted by them he expressed his desire to look after the child.[222] The child had been placed with the father and he had since looked after her successfully. There was no issue as to whether the father should continue to care for his daughter; the issue was whether he should become her sole adoptive parent, the legal effect of which would be to remove the mother's legal parenthood and parental responsibility so that the child would have no maternal relations. The father was anxious that the mother might marry and wish to take over the care of the child in the future. His case was that the mother's continuing status as a parent with parental responsibility would perpetuate insecurity for him and that this would potentially affect the child's stability. Bracewell J made the adoption order.[223] However, the Court of Appeal reversed her decision,[224] holding that section 15(3) was to be interpreted to require that 'that there be some reason, comparable to the death, disappearance or anonymous sperm donation of the other natural parent, "justifying" his or her exclusion, not only from parental responsibility for but also from the whole life and lineage of the

---

[217] See ibid, s 51(3) in relation to a married person, and s 51(3A) for the corresponding provision in relation to a civil partner.

[218] By virtue of assisted conception provisions under the Human Fertilisation and Embryology Acts as specified in subs (5). The provisions are—(a) section 28 of the Human Fertilisation and Embryology Act 1990 (disregarding subsections (5A) to (5I) of that section), or (b) sections 34 to 47 of the Human Fertilisation and Embryology Act 2008 (disregarding sections 39, 40 and 46 of that Act).   [219] ACA 2002, s 51(4).

[220] Ibid.

[221] [2001] UKHL 70, [2002] 1 FLR 196. See S. Harris-Short, '*Re B (Adoption: Natural Parent)* Putting the Child at the Heart of Adoption?' [2002] Child and Family Law Quarterly 325; A. Bainham, 'Unintentional Parenthood: The Case of the Reluctant Mother' [2002] Cambridge Law Journal 288.

[222] Upon the father being located, the mother had registered the father on the child's birth certificate and had entered into a parental responsibility agreement with him.

[223] *B v P (Adoption by Unmarried Father)* [2000] 2 FLR 717.

[224] *Re B (Adoption by One Natural Parent to Exclusion of Other)* [2001] 1 FLR 589 (Dame Elizabeth Butler-Sloss P and Potter and Hale LJJ).

child'.[225] On the father's appeal, the House of Lords restored Bracewell J's order, holding that the Court of Appeal's interpretation had been unduly restrictive.[226] The House could see no reason to place this unexpressed limitation on the section[227] since there may be other situations when the welfare of the child justifies the exclusion of a natural parent, such as abandonment or persistent neglect or ill-treatment of the child.[228] The House recognised that 'permanent exclusion of the child's mother from the life of the child is a drastic and detrimental consequence of adoption so far as the child is concerned' and that the circumstances in which such an order will be justified are likely to be exceptional,[229] but added that how 'serious this loss is likely to be depends on the circumstances of the case'.[230] The House was of the view that 'all that is required, is that the reason, whatever it be, must be sufficient to justify the exclusion of the other parent'.[231] The court explained that the reason must be sufficient to outweigh the adverse consequences such an order may have by reason of the exclusion of one parent from the child's life. Consent of the excluded parent is not of itself a sufficient reason, but it is a factor to be taken into account. Its weight will depend on the circumstances. Whether any particular reason satisfies this test depends on the circumstances.[232]

The House held that it could not be said that Bracewell J had been plainly wrong to conclude that the child's best interests required the adoption order even though this would have the consequence of excluding the mother. According to the House, the judge's approach identified the pressing social need for adoption (the need to safeguard and promote the child's welfare) and represented the court's considered view on proportionality so as to fulfil the requirements of Article 8 of the ECHR.

7.2 WHO MAY BE ADOPTED?

An adoption order may not be made in relation to a person who has attained the age of 19 years[233] nor in relation to a person who is or has been married[234] or a civil partner.[235] Furthermore, an application for an adoption order may only be made if the person to be adopted has not attained the age of 18 years on the date of the application.[236] So an adoption order can be made in respect of a person at any time before his or her 19th birthday, provided the application was made while that person was still a minor. An adoption order may be made even if the child to be adopted is already an adopted child.[237]

7.3 PRELIMINARIES TO ADOPTION

There are certain preliminaries which must be complied with before an adoption application may be made.

7.3.1 Child must live with the adopter(s)

First, an application may not be made unless the child has lived with the adopter(s) for a specified period of time. The precise period depends on the type of adoption. The rules are set out in section 42.

(i) If the child was placed for adoption by an adoption agency or in pursuance of an order of the High Court, or the applicant is a parent of the child, 'the child must have had

---

[225] Ibid, [34].   [226] [2001] UKHL 70, [2002] 1 FLR 196 at [24].   [227] Ibid.   [228] Ibid, [23].
[229] Ibid, [27].   [230] Ibid, [22].   [231] Ibid, [24].   [232] Ibid, [24].
[233] ACA 2002, s 47(9).   [234] Ibid, s 47(8).   [235] Ibid, s 47(8A).   [236] Ibid, s 49(4).
[237] Ibid, s 46(5).

his home with the applicant or, in the case of an application by a couple, with one or both of them at all times during the period of *ten weeks* preceding the application'.[238]

(ii) If the applicant or one of the applicants is the partner of a parent of the child, 'the child must have had his home with the applicant or, as the case may be, applicants at all times during the period of *six months* preceding the application'.[239]

(iii) If the applicants are local authority foster parents, then 'the child must have had his home with the applicants at all times during the period of *one year* preceding the application'.[240]

(iv) In any other case, 'the child must have had his home with the applicant or, in the case of an application by a couple, with one or both of them for not less than *three years* (whether continuous or not) during the period of five years preceding the application'.[241]

7.3.1.1 Leave to make the adoption application where conditions in section 42(4) and (5) not fulfilled

In the last two cases mentioned (points (iii) and (iv) above), the conditions do not prevent an application being made if the court gives leave to make it under section 42(6). In *ASB and KBS v MQS (Secretary of State for the Home Department Intervening)*[242] a 15-year-old boy was brought from Pakistan to England by his mother on a six-month visitor's visa, which could not be extended. The mother returned to Pakistan, leaving the child with his uncle and aunt. The child had remained after expiry of the visa and had spent over two years with the aunt and uncle who now wanted to adopt the boy. There was a genuine relationship of parent and child between the applicants and the boy, he had settled at school, and had a network of friends. As the boy had not had his home with the couple for not less than three years during the five years preceding the application, leave to apply was required, pursuant to section 42(6).

In *Re A; Coventry County Council v CC and A*[243] the Court of Appeal had applied to section 42(6) the approach to a leave application as set out in *M v Warwickshire County Council*[244] in respect of an application under section 24(2), that is, the child's welfare and whether the application had a real prospect of success were both relevant considerations. Applying that approach,[245] Bennett J granted leave, finding that the immigration matters were not sufficient to persuade him to refuse leave.[246] However, Bennett J accepted that Lord Hoffmann's statement in *Re B (Adoption Order: Nationality)*[247] (a case on the Adoption Act 1976) that the court will not make an adoption order when adopters merely wish to assist the child to acquire a right of abode, applied also to applications under the 2002 Act.[248] Bennett J cautioned that it remained the court's obligation to be on its guard against misuse of adoption proceedings in that way.[249] His Lordship commented that:

> such action is most unlikely to (indeed I would go so far as to say, cannot) be in the child's best interests. For the proposed adopters would have proved to have been irresponsible, indeed thoroughly devious if not dishonest and thus not acting in the child's best interests in a fundamental respect. Thus such behaviour ought to preclude the child being committed, indeed committed irrevocably, by adoption to the care of such applicants.[250]

---

[238] Ibid, s 42(2), emphasis added. The requirement under s 42(2)(a) can be fulfilled in a placement abroad: see *Re A (Adoption: Removal)* [2009] EWCA Civ 41, [2010] Fam 9; *ECC (The Local Authority) v SM* [2010] EWHC 1694 (Fam), [2011] 1 FLR 234 at [13] *per* Hedley J.

[239] ACA 2002, s 42(3), emphasis added.   [240] Ibid, s 42(4), emphasis added.

[241] Ibid, s 42(5), emphasis added.   [242] [2009] EWHC 2491 (Fam) (Bennett J).

[243] [2007] EWCA Civ 1383, [2008] 1 FLR 959.   [244] [2007] EWCA Civ 1084, [2008] 1 FLR 1093.

[245] Ibid, [45] and [46].   [246] Ibid, [43] and [46].   [247] [1999] 2 AC 136 at 141.

[248] [2007] EWCA Civ 1084, [2008] 1 FLR 1093 at [38].   [249] Ibid, [35].   [250] Ibid, [38].

7.3.2 Sufficient opportunities to see the child in the home environment

Under section 42(7), an adoption order may not be made unless the court is satisfied that sufficient opportunities to see the child with the applicant or, in the case of an application by a couple, both of them together in the home environment have been given to the adoption agency concerned or, in any other case, to the local authority within whose area the home is. In *Re A (Adoption: Removal)*[251] the Court of Appeal held that the word 'home' is not geographically defined[252] and that in the case of a foreign adoption the more comfortable meaning for home environment is the adopters' home abroad.[253]

7.3.3 Adoption agency must submit report

Where an application for an adoption order relates to a child placed for adoption by an adoption agency, the agency must submit to the court a report on the suitability of the applicants and on any other matters relevant to the operation of section 1, and assist the court in any manner the court directs.[254]

7.3.4 Child not placed by adoption agency: notice of intention to adopt and report

Where proposed adopters wish to adopt a child who is not placed for adoption with them by an adoption agency an adoption order may not be made unless the proposed adopters have given notice to the appropriate local authority of their intention to apply for the adoption order.[255] The notice must be given not more than two years, or less than three months, before the date on which the application for the adoption order is made.[256] Where leave to make an application to adopt would be required, notice may not be given until leave has been obtained.[257] On receipt of the notice of intention to adopt, the local authority 'must arrange for the investigation of the matter and submit to the court a report of the investigation', which in particular must 'so far as practicable, include the suitability of the proposed adopters and any other matters relevant to the operation of section 1 in relation to the application'.[258]

7.4 CONDITIONS FOR MAKING AN ADOPTION ORDER

Where a child has a parent or guardian an adoption order may not be made unless one of certain conditions set out in section 47 is fulfilled. The first condition, set out in section 47(2), is that, in the case of each parent or guardian of the child, the court is satisfied:

(a) that the parent or guardian consents to the making of the adoption order,

(b) that the parent or guardian has consented under section 20 (and has not withdrawn the consent) and does not oppose the making of the adoption order, or

(c) that the parent's or guardian's consent should be dispensed with.[259]

The second condition, set out in section 47(4), is that:

(a) the child has been placed for adoption by an adoption agency with the prospective adopters in whose favour the order is proposed to be made,

(b) either—

   (i) the child was placed for adoption with the consent of each parent or guardian and the consent of the mother was given when the child was at least six weeks old, or

   (ii) the child was placed for adoption under a placement order, and

(c) no parent or guardian opposes the making of the adoption order.

---

[251] [2009] EWCA Civ 41, [2010] Fam 9. [252] Ibid, [60]. [253] Ibid, [65].
[254] ACA 2002, s 43. [255] Ibid, s 44(1) and (2). [256] Ibid, s 44(3). [257] Ibid, s 44(4).
[258] Ibid, s 44(5) and (6). [259] Ibid, s 47(2).

7.5 COURT'S LEAVE REQUIRED TO OPPOSE MAKING OF ADOPTION ORDER

Section 47(3) and (5) provide with regard to the first and second conditions respectively that a parent or guardian may not oppose the making of an adoption order without the court's leave. Section 47(7) provides that the court 'cannot give leave under subsection (3) or (5) unless satisfied that there has been a change in circumstances since the consent of the parent or guardian was given or, as the case may be, the placement order was made'.

In *Re W (Adoption Order: Set Aside and Leave to Oppose)*[260] the Court of Appeal said that it cannot be too strongly emphasised that an application for permission to oppose an adoption application 'is an absolute last ditch opportunity and it will only be in exceptionally rare circumstances that permission will be granted after the making of the care order, the making of the placement order, the placement of the child, and the issue of the adoption order application'.[261] The applicant who wishes successfully to oppose an adoption application has three fences to jump:

> The first is to establish the necessary change of circumstances. The second is then to satisfy the court that, in the exercise of discretion, it would be right to grant permission. The third and final stage would of course be to persuade the court at the opposed hearing to refuse the adoption order and to reverse the direction in which the child's life has travelled since the inception of the original public law care proceedings.[262]

7.5.1 Change of circumstances

In *Re M (Adoption: Leave to Oppose)*[263] a child had been made the subject of a care order after a finding that she had sustained ten fractures non-accidentally. The parents subsequently obtained a report from an expert in the USA which suggested that the child suffered from a metabolic bone disorder which made her susceptible to fractures. In subsequent adoption proceedings the parents of the child sought leave to oppose the making of an adoption order on the basis of new evidence contained in the report. Her Honour Judge Newton, sitting as a judge of the High Court, held that this new evidence, even taken at its highest, was not capable of being a change of circumstances within the meaning of section 47(7).[264] Even if the fresh evidence were accepted it could not amount to a change of circumstances since the findings in the care proceedings had not been overturned. The fresh evidence was a matter for the Court of Appeal on an appeal against the care order, not a matter for the adoption court.[265]

7.5.2 Exercising discretion on the application for leave

In *Re P (A Child) (Adoption: Leave Provisions)*[266] Ward LJ explained that:

> the question of leave falls to be decided by the application of s 1 of the 2002 Act to the facts of the case. The paramount consideration of the court must be the child's welfare throughout his or her life.[267]

Section 47 is thus a rare case where the paramountcy of the child's welfare applies to a leave application. In *Re W (Adoption Order: Set Aside and Leave to Oppose)*[268] the Court of

---

[260] [2010] EWCA Civ 1535, [2011] 1 FLR 2153.   [261] Ibid, [17].
[262] Ibid, [18] *per* Thorpe LJ.
[263] [2010] 1 FLR 238 (HHJ Newton sitting as judge of the High Court).   [264] Ibid, [25].
[265] Ibid, [32].   [266] [2007] EWCA Civ 616, [2007] 2 FLR 1069.   [267] Ibid, [55].
[268] [2010] EWCA Civ 1535, [2011] 1 FLR 2153.

Appeal gave guidance on exercising its broad discretion whether or not to grant permission under section 47(5).[269] Thorpe LJ, while acknowledging that each case must depend upon its particular facts, said that the 'judge must have great regard to impact of the grant of permission on the child within the context of the adoptive family'.[270] His Lordship suggested that if the facts are such that opposition to the adoption order would have a profoundly upsetting effect on the adopters and the child, such a consequence should not be contemplated unless the applicant 'demonstrates prospects of success that are not just fanciful and not just measureable'; in Thorpe LJ's opinion, with which other members of the court agreed, the prospects of success 'should have substance' or 'solidity'.[271] In *Re W* a boy, aged 5 years 10 months at the date of the appeal, had been removed from his mother's care when he was 2 years old because of her drug addiction and consequent inability to care for him. He was subsequently placed for adoption under a placement order when he was 4. An adoption order was subsequently made without the mother being informed of the proceedings. The mother, who had liberated herself from her drug dependency, sought to set aside the adoption order and permission to oppose the adoption application. Holman J set aside the order and allowed the mother permission to oppose. The Court of Appeal, applying the approach set out, allowed the adopters' appeal, finding that the judge had under-weighed the very powerful current imperatives in favour of adoption and overvalued the much more speculative aspects of the future.[272] The mother's recovery had simply come too late.

7.6 EFFECT OF AN ADOPTION ORDER

An adoption order is an order made by the court on an application under section 50 or 51.[273] The order gives parental responsibility for the child to the adopters or adopter.[274] It also operates to extinguish 'the parental responsibility which any person other than the adopters or adopter has for the adopted child immediately before the making of the order',[275] although it 'does not affect parental responsibility so far as it relates to any period before the making of the order'.[276] The adoption order also extinguishes 'any duty arising by virtue of an agreement[277] or an order of a court to make payments, so far as the payments are in respect of the adopted child's maintenance or upbringing for any period after the making of the adoption order'.[278]

7.6.1 Status conferred by adoption

As from the date of the adoption[279] an adopted person is to be treated in law as if born as the child of the adopters or adopter,[280] is the legitimate child of the adopters or adopter and, if adopted by a couple or one of a couple under section 51(2), is to be treated as the child of the relationship of the couple in question.[281] The adopted person is to be treated in law as not being the child of any person other than the adopters or adopter.[282]

---

[269] Ibid, [20].   [270] Ibid.   [271] Ibid.   [272] Ibid, [25].   [273] ACA 2002, s 46(1).
[274] Ibid.   [275] Ibid, s 46(2).   [276] Ibid, s 46(3)(a).
[277] Subject to subs (4) which provides that subs (2)(d) does not apply to a duty arising by virtue of an agreement:
     (a) which constitutes a trust, or
     (b) which expressly provides that the duty is not to be extinguished by the making of an adoption order.
[278] Ibid, s 46(2)(d).   [279] Ibid, s 67(5).   [280] Ibid, s 67(1).
[281] Ibid, s 67(2).
[282] Ibid, s 67(3). This is subject to subs (4) which provides:
    In the case of a person adopted by one of the person's natural parents as sole adoptive parent, subsection (3)(b) has no effect as respects entitlement to property depending on relationship to that parent, or as respects anything else depending on that relationship.

The rules are adapted differently to the case of an order made on an application under section 51(2) by the partner of a parent of the adopted child. In such a case the order does not affect the parental responsibility of that parent or any duties with respect to child maintenance.[283] The adopted child is treated in law as not being the child of any person other than the adopter and the other one of the couple.[284]

The status conferred by adoption 'applies for the interpretation of enactments or instruments passed or made before as well as after the adoption, and so applies subject to any contrary indication…and has effect as respects things done, or events occurring, on or after the adoption'.[285] However, the status conferred by adoption does not apply for the purpose of the prohibited degrees of relationship for marriage or civil partnership,[286] nor for the purpose of sexual offences in sections 64 and 65 of the Sexual Offences Act 2003 (sex with an adult relative).[287] It also does not apply for the purpose of the British Nationality Act 1981, the Immigration Act 1971, or any other provision of law which determines British citizenship or the status of a British National (Overseas).[288]

The Act indicates that the relationship established by the adoption order may be described as an adoptive relationship and the adopter(s) as the child's adoptive mother/father/parent as the case may be.[289]

7.7 SETTING ASIDE AN ADOPTION ORDER

As the outlined provisions show, adoption is the process whereby a child becomes a permanent and full member of a new family, and is treated as if born to the adopters.[290] Adoption orders are perceived 'as final, and as putting the adoptive parents fully in control'.[291] Thus, the imposition of conditions on adoption orders will be very rare.[292] In *Re S (A Minor) (Adoption: Blood Transfusion)*,[293] for example, the prospective adopters were Jehovah's Witnesses and they indicated that they could not consent to the child having a blood transfusion should one become necessary. The Court of Appeal held that it had been wrong for the judge to impose a condition of the adoption that the adoptive parents give an undertaking obliging them to involve the High Court if the contingency arose. The courts recognise the impact that not respecting that peculiar finality of adoption orders might have on the integrity of the adoption system and on prospective adopters coming forward to adopt. It will be very rare that an adoption order will be set aside.

The courts have set aside adoption orders in some cases where there has been a procedural irregularity involving a denial of natural justice,[294] such as when a parent has not been informed of an application for an adoption order. In *Re B (Adoption: Jurisdiction to Set Aside)*[295] Sir Thomas Bingham MR added that he would have 'little hesitation in holding that the court could set aside an adoption order which was shown to have been obtained by fraud'.[296] Otherwise, however, the courts have been very strict in their refusal to allow adoption orders to be challenged, except by way of appeal, even where there has been a very clear and fundamental error which causes (sometimes extreme) hardship. A powerful

---

[283] Ie, the duties as mentioned in s 46(2)(d).   [284] ACA 2002, s 67(3).   [285] Ibid, s 67(6).
[286] Ibid, s 74(1)(a).   [287] Ibid, s 74(1)(b).   [288] Ibid, s 74(2).   [289] See ibid, s 68.
[290] Ibid, s 67, and see *per* Wall LJ in *Webster v Norfolk County Council and the Children (By their Children's Guardian)* [2009] EWCA Civ 59, [2009] 1 FLR 1378 at [145].   [291] *Webster*, ibid, [146].
[292] *Re S (A Minor) (Adoption: Blood Transfusion)* [1995] 2 FCR 177, CA.   [293] Ibid.
[294] See this characterisation of the case law in *Re B (Adoption: Jurisdiction to Set Aside)* [1995] Fam 239 at 245H and 252F. See for examples *Re F(R) (An Infant)* [1970] 1 QB 385; *Re RA (Minors)* (1974) 4 Fam Law 182; and *Re F (Infants) (Adoption Order: Validity)* [1977] Fam 165.   [295] [1995] Fam 239.
[296] Ibid, 252G.

example is provided by the Scottish Court of Session case of *J v J and C's Tutor*.[297] In that case a couple adopted a child whom they believed to be healthy but later found out that the child had a severe brain injury. The Scottish Court of Session unanimously held that it was no ground for revocation of the adoption order. That case was cited with apparent approval by Sir Thomas Bingham MR in *Re B (Adoption: Jurisdiction to Set Aside)*,[298] who commented that any discrepancy in English and Scottish authority on the issue of setting aside an adoption order was undesirable. In *Re B* the appellant, a man in his mid-thirties, had been adopted when he was three months old by an orthodox Jewish couple and brought up a Jew, but he later found out that his natural father was a Muslim Arab from Kuwait. As Simon Brown LJ put it, it 'is difficult to imagine a more ill-starred adoption placement'.[299] The appellant had wished to settle in Israel but had been suspected of being an Arab spy and had been asked to leave, and he also was not accepted in Kuwait. His adoptive parents were deceased and he now sought to set aside the adoption order. The Court of Appeal, albeit with sympathy for the appellant, unanimously dismissed the appeal, holding that the circumstances of the case provided no basis for setting aside the order. In so holding, the Court of Appeal recognised the strong policy considerations against doing so. Simon Brown LJ commented:

> Exceptional though this case undoubtedly is and strong though [the appellant's] grievance, more important still is the integrity of the adoption system; its inviolability must be the ultimate imperative.[300]

These public policy considerations mean that an adoption order will not necessarily be set aside even where natural parents have suffered a serious injustice in losing their children to adoption.[301] In *Webster v Norfolk County Council and the Children (By Their Children's Guardian)*[302] three of Mr and Mrs Webster's children were taken into care and adopted by strangers, following findings in care proceedings that their 2-year-old child had suffered non-accidental injuries resulting in six fractures. The child had a feeding problem and on the advice of their doctor the parents had been feeding the child soya milk only. The child's diet was rejected by the experts in the case as a cause of the fractures. Care proceedings were subsequently brought in respect of a fourth child born to the couple. Those proceedings were withdrawn, however, when fresh expert evidence showed that the older child's fractures had not been caused through abuse, but by a rare case of scurvy as a result of the diet. Nearly three years after the older children had been adopted, Mr and Mrs Webster sought leave to appeal out of time, to adduce the fresh evidence, and ultimately to have the adoptions set aside. The Court of Appeal unanimously dismissed the application, holding that it was far too late to seek to disturb the orders, having regard to the social importance of not undermining the irrevocability of adoption orders, and to the interests of the children, who by then had been settled with the adoptive parents for four years.

A case which was viewed by the Court of Appeal as wholly exceptional, and in which leave to appeal out of time was granted and an appeal against an adoption order was successful, is *Re M (Minors) (Adoption)*.[303] In that case, a father who was leaving the country to live in the USA agreed to his two daughters' adoption by their mother and stepfather, with whom the girls were then living. However, the mother had terminal cancer and died three months later. The father's consent to adoption was given in ignorance of

---

[297] 1948 SC 636.   [298] [1995] Fam 239.   [299] Ibid, 249E.   [300] Ibid, 251E.
[301] *Webster v Norfolk County Council and the Children (By Their Children's Guardian)* [2009] EWCA Civ 59, [2009] 1 FLR 1378 at [148].   [302] [2009] EWCA Civ 59, [2009] 1 FLR 1378.
[303] [1991] 1 FLR 458.

the mother's illness. He had since remarried and the children wished to live with him and his new wife, and the stepfather also agreed that that was the best course for the children. The Court of Appeal set aside the adoption order, holding that ignorance of the mother's illness vitiated his consent. The court made clear that it was in no way setting a precedent for any related set of facts in some other case. Moreover, in *Re B (Adoption: Jurisdiction to Set Aside)*[304] the Court of Appeal held that there were some important points of distinction between *Re M* and the case before it: the mistake in *Re B* as to religion or ethnicity could not vitiate consent; *Re M* was a case of permission to appeal out of time following a very short period of time rather than an application to set aside; it was a case involving minor children (rather than an adult) and the outcome was demanded by their best interests; and no injustice would result to any party as all were agreed as to the correctness of the eventual outcome.[305]

7.8 OPENNESS IN ADOPTION AND ON-GOING CONTACT[306]

Over time, probably reflecting the changing landscape of those adopted, there has been a movement towards greater openness in adoptions. As Lindley points out the term 'open adoption' 'encompasses a very broad range of circumstances and arrangements'.[307] It ranges from the idea of adoptive parents being open with their children by telling them about their adoption,[308] through so-called letterbox contact with the child's natural family by way of letters, cards, presents, photographs etc, to face-to-face contact with the child's natural parents and/or other relatives. One aspect of increasing openness surrounding adoption is the facility which adopted persons now have in adulthood to obtain information about their birth families.

7.8.1 Access to information

The 2002 Act makes provision for an adoption contact register to allow adoptees and relatives the opportunity to indicate that they would like contact.[309] The Act also makes provision for the disclosure of information to adopted persons. The disclosure is in most cases in the hands of the adoption agency concerned. The Act and regulations prescribe the information that must be kept relating to a person's adoption.[310] The information must be kept secure and for at least 100 years.[311] Certain information is regarded as 'protected information' as defined in section 57 of the Act. This is information which identifies or enables a person to be identified, information which would enable the adopted person to obtain a certified copy of the record of his birth, or information about an entry

---

[304] [1995] Fam 239.   [305] Ibid, 247.

[306] See J. Eekelaar, 'Contact and the Adoption Reform' in A. Bainham, B. Lindley, M. Richards, and L. Trinder (eds), *Children and Their Families: Contact, Rights and Welfare* (Oxford: Hart, 2003); C. Bridge, 'Adoption and Contact: The Value of Openness' [1994] Journal of Child Law 147; D. Casey and A. Gibberd, 'Adoption and Contact' [2000] Family Law 39; and C. Smith and J. Logan, 'Adoptive Parenthood as a "Legal Fiction"—Its Consequences for Direct Post-Adoption Contact' [2002] Child and Family Law Quarterly 281.

[307] B. Lindley, 'Open Adoption—Is the Door Ajar?' [1997] Child and Family Law Quarterly 115.

[308] Referred to by some as communicative openness as opposed to structural openness: see eg E. Neil, 'Post-Adoption Contact and Openness in Adoptive Parents' Minds: Consequences for Children's Development' (2009) 39 British Journal of Social Work 303.

[309] ACA 2002, s 80, and see J. Haskey and E. Errington, 'Adoptees and Relatives Who Wish to Contact One Another: The Adoption Contact Register' (2001) 104 Population Trends 18.

[310] ACA 2002, s 56, and Disclosure of Adoption Information (Post-Commencement Adoptions) Regulations 2005 (SI 2005/888): see reg 4.

[311] Disclosure of Adoption Information (Post-Commencement Adoptions) Regulations 2005, regs 5 and 6.

relating to the adopted person in the Adoption Contact Register.[312] Section 57 provides that such information may only be disclosed to a person by the agency in pursuance of the group of sections 56–65 of the Act. It is an offence to disclose such information in contravention of this provision.[313] An adopted person who has attained the age of 18 years has the right, at his request, to receive from the appropriate adoption agency any information which would enable him to obtain a certified copy of the record of his birth, unless the High Court orders otherwise.[314] The High Court may make such an order, on an application by the appropriate adoption agency, if satisfied that the circumstances are exceptional. An example of an exceptional case is provided by the case of *R v Registrar General, ex p Smith*.[315] In that case the appellant was a patient in a secure mental hospital following conviction for murder of a stranger and manslaughter of his prison cell-mate while under the psychotic belief that the cell-mate was his adoptive mother. The court held that the Registrar-General had not acted unlawfully in denying the appellant access to a copy of his birth certificate for the reason that his natural mother might thereby be endangered.

The adult adopted person is also entitled to receive any prescribed information which the agency was required to disclose to the adopters.[316] Section 61 of the Act provides that if a person applies for disclosure of protected information and none of the information is about a person who is a child at the time of the application, then the agency is not required to proceed with the application unless it considers it appropriate to do so. If it does proceed, it must take all reasonable steps to obtain the views of any person the information is about as to the disclosure of the information about him. The agency may then disclose the information if it considers it appropriate to do so. In deciding those matters the agency must consider the welfare of the adopted person, any views obtained, and all the circumstances of the case. Where any of the information sought is about a person who is a child at the time of the application, then section 62 applies. The same approach as described for section 61 is taken, except that the agency must take all reasonable steps to obtain the views of any parent or guardian of the child, and the views of the child, if the agency considers it appropriate to do so having regard to his age and understanding and to all the other circumstances of the case. If the information relates to an adopted child, the child's welfare must be the paramount consideration, or in the case of any other child, the agency must have particular regard to the child's welfare.

An adoption agency must provide written information about the availability of counselling to any person who is seeking information under section 60, 61, or 62 of the Act,[317] and there is a duty to secure counselling for those who wish it.

7.8.2 Post-adoption contact

The most extensive aspect of openness is, of course, post-adoption direct contact with the child's natural family.[318] The value of such contact is a matter which has been hotly debated amongst commentators, as have the inferences which can validly be drawn from research

---

[312] Adoption agencies are permitted to disclose other information: ACA 2002, s 58.

[313] ACA 2002, s 59, and Disclosure of Adoption Information (Post-Commencement Adoptions) Regulations 2005, reg 21.   [314] ACA 2002, s 60.

[315] [1991] 1 FLR 255, CA.   [316] ACA 2002, s 60.

[317] Ibid, s 63 and Disclosure of Adoption Information (Post-Commencement Adoptions) Regulations 2005, reg 16.

[318] See J. Masson, 'Thinking about Contact—A Social or a Legal Problem?' [2000] Child and Family Law Quarterly 15. Masson argues that it is preferable to think of contact in terms of social rather than legal problem, noting that even though the courts have been wary of post-adoption contact in the face of adopters' opposition, a social work practice surrounding openness and adoption has emerged.

evidence.[319] Several arguments can be put in favour of open adoption.[320] Ryburn[321] has suggested that while each case must be looked at individually, the starting point should be recognition that post-adoption contact may have benefits for all concerned. Ryburn argues that contact may help birth parents to resolve the grief of their loss of the child; it can serve the information needs of the child and in some cases this may mean that facts can helpfully replace the child's possibly negative speculation or fantasy about the birth parent(s) (eg about the nature of a parent's mental illness). Contact may also provide adopters with a source of up-to-date information with which to deal with the child's questions, together with a sense of security and permanence in the parenting role. Smith and Logan,[322] in a review of research, have observed that there is certainly evidence from several studies that 'children, adoptive parents and birth family members value contact and can *experience* it as beneficial',[323] and conclude from their survey:

> First, there appears to be increasing professional support for post-adoption contact and many adoptive parents are willing to facilitate this. Secondly, it is possible to maintain helpful contact with birth parents, notwithstanding their opposition to adoption. Thirdly, many adopters experience contact as beneficial for their children and for themselves and express satisfaction with contact arrangements. Fourthly, adopted children may value contact and want it to continue. Fifthly, contact does not seem to interfere with adoptive parents' sense of security or their perceived status as parents.[324]

Smith and Logan's own research, interviewing adoptive parents in 61 families, also shows, however, that for some adoptive parents the practical and emotional burdens of contact are not insignificant (eg having to take days off work to facilitate it and having to encounter parents with very different social backgrounds and parenting expectations to their own).[325]

---

[319] See the debate surrounding the evidence in the following: D. Quinton, A. Rushton, C. Dance, and D. Mayes, 'Contact Between Children Placed Away from Home and Their Birth Parents: Research Issues and Evidence' (1997) 2(3) Clinical Child Psychology and Psychiatry 393; M. Ryburn, 'In Whose Best Interests?—Post-Adoption Contact with the Birth Family' [1998] Child and Family Law Quarterly 53; D. Quinton, J. Selwyn, A. Rushton, and C. Dance, 'Contact with Birth Parents in Adoption—A Response to Ryburn' [1998] Child and Family Law Quarterly 349.

[320] For arguments on the benefits of openness, see eg A. Mullender (ed), *Open Adoption: The Philosophy and Practice* (London: BAAF, 1991); M. Adcock, J. Kaniuk, and R. White (eds), *Exploring Openness in Adoption* (Significant Publications, 1993); J. Fratter, *Adoption with Contact* (London: BAAF, 1996), ch 1; J. Triseliotis, J. Shireman, and M. Hundleby, *Adoption; Theory, Policy and Practice* (London: Cassell, 1997), ch 4.

[321] M. Ryburn, 'In Whose Best Interests?—Post-Adoption Contact with the Birth Family' [1998] Child and Family Law Quarterly 53.

[322] C. Smith and J. Logan, 'Adoptive Parenthood as a "Legal Fiction"—Its Consequences for Direct Post-Adoption Contact' [2002] Child and Family Law Quarterly 281.

[323] Citing H. D. Grotevant and R. G. McRoy, *Openness in Adoption: Exploring Family Connections* (Thousand Oaks, CA: Sage, 1998) (adoptive parents less fearful); J. Logan and C. Smith, 'Adoption and Direct Post-Adoption Contact' (1999) 23(4) Adoption and Fostering 58 (adoptive parents in 61 families interviewed; advantages identified for 92 per cent of the children concerned); R. P. Barth and M. Berry, *Adoption and Disruption: Rates, Risks and Responses* (New York: Aldine DeGruyter, 1988), p 120 (79 per cent contact, 31 per cent found helpful); M. Ryburn, 'A Study of Post-Adoption Contact in Compulsory Adoptions' (1996) 26(5) British Journal of Social Work 627 (adopters indicated advantages); J. Fratter, *Adoption with Contact: Implications for Policy and Practice* (London: BAAF, 1996) (perceived as contributing to child's welfare).

[324] 'Adoptive Parenthood as a "Legal Fiction"—Its Consequences for Direct Post-Adoption Contact' [2002] Child and Family Law Quarterly 281 at 285.

[325] J. Logan and C. Smith, 'Adoption and Direct Post-Adoption Contact' (1999) 23(4) Adoption and Fostering 58.

While there is some evidence about how contact is *experienced*, there is little evidence of the impact (if any) that post-adoption contact has on long-term *outcomes* for children. Grotevant and Roy studied 171 children[326] aged between 4 and 12 who were adopted as babies and compared child outcomes according to the openness of the placement (including completely closed adoption, those with indirect contact, and those with fully open face-to-face contact with birth parents[327]). The research found no significant differences 'for self-esteem, curiosity, satisfaction and socio-emotional adjustment by openness level'.[328] The authors commented that these results 'are not compatible with assertions raised by critics of openness stating that such arrangements will damage children's self-esteem and cause confusion. But neither do these findings support the hypothesis that more openness enhances these outcomes.'[329] This research is useful. However, one should be cautious about generalising its findings in relation to 'baby adoptions' to other adoptions, such as the many adoptions which now take place through the system of state care when children are older. As Quinton and Selwyn observe:

> We know little about the consequences of contact for adult adjustment, especially for children with the experiences and profiles of those currently being placed. Moreover, the extent of difficulties many of the children face may militate against finding substantial differences in outcome related to contact, since many improvements in emotional and behavioural adjustment may be hard won, whatever the circumstances.[330]

The debates surrounding post-adoption contact have not gone unnoticed by the judiciary. Lord Carswell commented in *Down Lisburn Health and Social Services Trust v H*:[331]

> There have been some differences of opinion in the published literature about the desirability of contact, which is propounded by some as universally beneficial, while others are more cautious and urge a degree of flexibility of approach and avoidance of doctrinaire policies. They point out that in the wrong case contact can lead to disturbance of the children and impose a significant burden on the adopting parents. There is, however, general agreement that in appropriate cases contact can contribute to reassurance and security and a feeling of identity for adopted children and help to dispel feelings of rejection...[332]

His Lordship therefore went on to caution that when 'considering post-adoption contact courts must exercise care in assessing the effect which contact is likely to have on the particular child in the particular circumstances of the case, bearing in mind the paramountcy of the welfare of the child'.[333] As a matter of the courts' general approach, however, post-adoption contact between children and their birth parents has historically been perceived as highly exceptional, and the effect the 2002 Act has had on this approach

---

[326] Sourced from 190 adoptive families from 35 agencies across the USA.

[327] Note that a study by Neil compared letterbox contact with direct contact but did not find any significant differences in terms of child outcome: see E. Neil, 'Post-Adoption Contact and Openness in Adoptive Parents' Minds: Consequences for Children's Development' (2009) 39 British Journal of Social Work 303.

[328] H. D. Grotevant and R. G. McRoy, *Openness in Adoption: Exploring Family Connections* (Thousand Oaks, CA: Sage, 1998), p 103.

[329] Ibid.

[330] D. Quinton and J. Selwyn, 'Adoption: Research, Policy and Practice' [2006] Child and Family Law Quarterly 459.

[331] [2006] UKHL 36, [2007] 1 FLR 121 [2007] 1 FLR 121, a case on appeal from Northern Ireland.

[332] Ibid, [44]. See Department of Health, *Adoption Now: Messages from Research* (Chichester: Wiley, 1999) for an overview of research findings in this context.

[333] [2006] UKHL 36,[2007] 1 FLR 121 [2007] 1 FLR 121 at [44].

is rather unclear. In the pre-Children Act 1989 case, *Re C (A Minor) (Adoption Order: Conditions)*,[334] Lord Ackner commented that:

> The cases rightly stress that in normal circumstances it is desirable that there should be a complete break, but that each case has to be considered on its own particular facts. No doubt the court will not, except in the most exceptional case, impose terms or conditions as to access to members of the child's natural family to which the adopting parents do not agree. To do so would be to create a potentially frictional situation which would be hardly likely to safeguard or promote the welfare of the child. Where no agreement is forthcoming the court will, with very rare exceptions, have to choose between making an adoption order without terms or conditions as to access, or to refuse to make such an order and seek to safeguard access through some other machinery, such as wardship. To do otherwise would be merely inviting future and almost immediate litigation.[335]

Indeed, in early case law the Court of Appeal went so far as to suggest that on-going contact between a child and his or her birth parent(s) was repugnant to the purpose of adoption to effect a transplant of legal parenthood and parental responsibility; in other words, if contact were appropriate, it could be doubted whether the severance of the legal ties which adoption effects is the necessary intervention.[336] After implementation of the Children Act 1989, even against a background of post-adoption contact becoming more common in practice, and of increasing judicial recognition of the value of post-adoption contact,[337] court-imposed post-adoption contact was still perceived to be highly unusual.[338] As the Court of Appeal put it in *Re R (A Child) (Adoption: Contact)*,[339] 'the imposition on prospective adopters of orders for contact with which they are not in agreement is extremely, and remains extremely unusual'.

However, section 46(6) of the 2002 Act now provides that before making an adoption order, 'the court must consider whether there should be arrangements for allowing any person contact with the child; and for that purpose the court must consider any existing or proposed arrangements and obtain any views of the parties to the proceedings'. Furthermore, section 26(5) specifically envisages an application for contact being made at the same time as an adoption order is applied for. In *Re P (Placement Orders: Parental Consent)*,[340] the Court of Appeal indicated that the 2002 Act thus 'envisages the court exercising its powers to make contact orders post adoption, where such orders are in the interests of the child concerned'.[341] In *Re P* there was universal recognition that the relationship between siblings needed to be preserved and in such circumstances it was the court's responsibility to make orders for contact.[342] Indeed, the court went as far as to say that it was highly likely that a plan to place the children with adopters who were unwilling to facilitate sibling contact would provide a basis for granting leave to apply to revoke the placement order concerned.[343] The court was unclear, however, whether its 'views on contact on the facts of this particular case presage a more general sea change in post adoption contact overall'.

---

[334] [1989] 1 AC 1.   [335] [1989] 1 AC 1 at 18.

[336] See *per* Oliver LJ in *Re V (A Minor) (Adoption: Dispensing with Agreement)* [1987] 2 FLR 89 at 98.

[337] *Re G (Children: Contact)* [2002] EWCA Civ 761, [2002] 3 FCR 377 and in the dissenting speech of Baroness Hale of Richmond in the Northern Ireland case of *Down Lisburn Health and Social Services Trust v H* [2006] UKHL 36, [2007] 1 FLR 121.

[338] See eg *Re T (A Minor) (Contact after Adoption)* [1995] 2 FCR 537.

[339] [2005] EWCA Civ 1128, [2007] 1 FCR 149 at [49].

[340] [2008] EWCA Civ 535, [2008] 2 FLR 625.   [341] Ibid, [154].   [342] Ibid, [151].

[343] Ibid, [150].

In *Oxfordshire County Council v X, Y and J*[344] the Court of Appeal did not see the discussion of the implications of sections 26, 27, and 46(6) of the 2002 Act in *Re P* as affecting the approach to contact where an adoption order has already been made. The court held that in such a case the judge must apply the checklist in section 1(3) of the Children Act 1989, together with the approach set out in *Re R* (ie, that contact against the wishes of the child's adoptive parent(s) would be extremely unusual). In that case the child's natural parents sought an order that the adoptive parents provide to them an annual photograph of the child. The adoptive parents did not object to the parents viewing a photograph annually, but objected to the parents retaining the photograph, fearing that the parents might use it to trace the child, perhaps by placing a copy on the internet. The judge at first instance, assessing the risk of disruption to the placement as very small, granted the application, but the Court of Appeal overturned it. The judge had failed to apply the correct approach as set out in *Re R*. The 'essential question was whether the adoptive parents' fear of such a risk was unreasonable in the sense that it had no reasonable basis'[345] since the court's focus had to be on the child's welfare and in the court's view there was a clear link between the fears of the adoptive parents, and their sense of security, and the welfare of their daughter. The court commented:

> It is beyond argument that the welfare of so young a child in the early stages of her adoption depended upon the stability and security of her new parents, the adoptive parents. To undermine that stability by fuelling or failing to heed their fears that their daughter's natural parents might seek to trace her is to damage her welfare.[346]

The court observed that given the effect of an adoption order 'it is very far from obvious, to say the least, that the natural parents can thereafter have any Art 8 rights at all vis-à-vis a child who is no longer their child'.[347] Since, however, the point had not been fully argued before the court, the court said no more about it, except to make clear that even if the natural parents had Article 8 rights capable of being engaged in the application (and the court did not assume, let alone decide, that they did), those rights would not have sufficed to tip the balance in their favour.[348] Kirsty Hughes and Brian Sloan are critical of this aspect of the decision, arguing that there was scope for the court to have required full argument on this important issue, and also to engage more fully with all the Article 8 interests that were involved, for example the child's right to respect for private life, in the sense of the child's interest in her image and its retention by others.[349]

8 SPECIAL GUARDIANSHIP

The ACA 2002 introduced another option for permanency planning for children who are unable to live with their birth parents, namely a special guardianship order (SGO).[350]

---

[344] [2010] EWCA Civ 581, [2011] 1 FLR 272. For comment, see K. Hughes and B. Sloan, 'Post-Adoption Photographs: Welfare, Rights and Judicial Reasoning' [2011] Child and Family Law Quarterly 393.

[345] Ibid, [28].   [346] Ibid, [29].

[347] Ibid, [43]. The position in the Strasbourg jurisprudence is rather unclear; see for discussion K. Hughes and B. Sloan, 'Post-Adoption Photographs: Welfare, Rights and Judicial Reasoning' [2011] Child and Family Law Quarterly 393.

[348] [2010] EWCA Civ 581, [43].

[349] K. Hughes and B. Sloan, 'Post-Adoption Photographs: Welfare, Rights and Judicial Reasoning' [2011] Child and Family Law Quarterly 393.

[350] A similar concept, custodianship, had been introduced by the Children Act 1975, following a recommendation of the Houghton Committee's Report (Cmnd 5107, 1972), aimed at providing long-term security for care of a child without the need for adoption. For the history, see S. Cretney, *Family Law in the Twentieth*

Section 115 of the 2002 Act inserted sections 14A–14F of the Children Act 1989, making provision for such orders.[351] Their purpose was to provide an option for meeting the needs of some children for a permanent family placement without the complete transplant of legal parenthood involved in adoption.[352] The aim was to meet the needs of children 'where adoption is not appropriate, and to modernise the law so as to reflect the religious and cultural diversity of our country today'.[353] As the White Paper that preceded the 2002 Act commented:

> Adoption is not always appropriate for children who cannot return to their birth parents. Some older children do not wish to be legally separated from their birth families. Adoption may not be best for some children being cared for on a permanent basis by members of their wider birth family. Some minority ethnic communities have religious and cultural difficulties with adoption as it is set out in law. Unaccompanied asylum-seeking children may also need secure, permanent homes, but have strong attachments to their families abroad. All these children deserve the same chance as any other to enjoy the benefits of a legally secure, stable permanent placement that promotes a supportive, lifelong relationship with their carers, where the court decides that is in their best interests.[354]

Section 14A of the Children Act provides that a 'special guardianship order' is an order appointing one or more individuals to be a child's 'special guardian' (or special guardians).[355] A special guardian must be aged 18 or over and must not be a parent of the child.[356]

Key legislation

Those who are entitled to apply for a SGO are:

(a) any guardian of the child;

(b) any individual in whose favour a residence order is in force with respect to the child;

(c) any individual listed in subsection (5)(b) or (c) of section 10 (as read with subsection (10) of that section);

(d) a local authority foster parent with whom the child has lived for a period of at least one year immediately preceding the application;

(e) a relative with whom the child has lived for a period of at least one year immediately preceding the application.[357]

Century—A History (Oxford: Oxford University Press, 2003), chs 17 and 20. The provisions were elaborate and little used and were not implemented until 1988, by which time the adoption provisions of the 1975 Act had been consolidated in the Adoption Act 1976: see *Re S (Adoption Order or Special Guardianship Order)* [2007] EWCA Civ 54, [2007] 1 FLR 819 at [5]–[9].

[351] Implemented on 30 December 2005. The provisions are supplemented by the Special Guardianship Regulations 2005 (SI 2005/1109), and with guidance: see Department for Children, Schools and Families, *The Children Act 1989 Guidance and Regulations Volume 1: Court Orders* (London: TSO, 2008), paras 2.59–2.66.

[352] See generally L. Jordan and B. Lindley (eds), *Special Guardianship: What Does it Offer Children Who Cannot Live with Their Parents?* (London: Family Rights Group, 2006).

[353] White Paper, *Adoption: A New Approach* (Cm 5017, 2000), para 5.9.   [354] Ibid, para 5.8.

[355] Children Act 1989, s 14A(1).   [356] Ibid, s 14A(2).

[357] Ibid, s 14A(5). Section 9(3) applies in relation to an application for leave to apply for a SGO as it applies in relation to an application for leave to apply for a section 8 order (see s 14A(4)).

The order can also be made in family proceedings, either on application or of the court's own motion.[358] Three months' notice of the application must be given to the relevant local authority (either the local authority for the area in which the potential applicant lives or a local authority which is looking after the child concerned).[359] The local authority then has to investigate and prepare a report. Section 14A(11) makes clear that the 'court may not make a special guardianship order unless it has received such a report'. A court cannot therefore make an order of its own motion unless a report has already been prepared, although it will suffice merely to provide any information which may be missing from existing reports before the court, rather than producing an entirely new report.[360]

Key legislation

The effect of a SGO is that while the order remains in force:[361]

(a) a special guardian appointed by the order has parental responsibility for the child in respect of whom it is made; and

(b) subject to any other order in force with respect to the child under this Act, a special guardian is entitled to exercise parental responsibility to the exclusion of any other person with parental responsibility for the child (apart from another special guardian).

However, this does not affect the operation of any enactment or rule of law which requires the consent of more than one person with parental responsibility in a matter affecting the child; or any rights which a parent of the child has in relation to the child's adoption or placement for adoption.[362]

While a SGO is in force with respect to a child, no person may cause the child to be known by a new surname or remove him from the UK, without either the written consent of every person who has parental responsibility for the child or the leave of the court.[363] However, on making a SGO the court may give leave for these purposes.[364]

An application can be made to discharge a SGO,[365] including an application by the child concerned, although in such a case the court may only grant leave if it is satisfied that he has sufficient understanding to make the proposed application.[366] A step-parent who has parental responsibility, or any person who immediately before the making of the SGO had parental responsibility, also requires the leave of the court to apply to discharge the order. The court may not grant leave to such persons unless it is satisfied that there has been a significant change in circumstances since the making of the SGO.[367] In *Re G (Special Guardianship Order)*[368] it was held that there was no relevant difference

---

[358] Ibid, s 14A(6).

[359] Ibid, s 14A(7). On provisions relating to notice and leave within s 14A, see *Birmingham City Council v R* [2006] EWCA Civ 1748, [2007] 1 FLR 563 (and see tables on who can apply as of right and who needs leave).

[360] *Re S (Adoption Order or Special Guardianship Order) (No 2)* [2007] EWCA Civ 90, [2007] 1 FLR 855 at [14] and [15].

[361] Unless discharged earlier, the order comes to an end upon the child's reaching age 18: Children Act 1989, s 91(13).

[362] Section 14C(2).

[363] Section 14C(3). This does not prevent the removal of a child, for a period of less than three months, by a special guardian of his (s 14C(4)).

[364] Section 14B(2). See for a case in which grandparents' application for change of surname was rejected, *Re L (Special Guardianship: Surname)* [2007] EWCA Civ 196, [2007] 2 FLR 50.

[365] Section 14D. The persons who can apply are listed in subs (1).

[366] Section 14D(4).   [367] Section 14D(5).   [368] [2010] EWCA Civ 300, [2010] 2 FLR 696.

between the 'significant change in circumstances' test in section 14D(5) and the change in circumstances' test in section 24(3) of the ACA 2002. Therefore the same approach as adopted in relation to section 24(3) should be taken, as set out in *M v Warwickshire County Council*.[369] So the welfare of the child and the prospects of success of the application must be weighed.

A SGO discharges a care order and an order under section 34 of the Children Act 1989.[370] A SGO also discharges a residence order.[371]

In *Re S (Adoption Order or Special Guardianship Order)*[372] the Court of Appeal provided some general guidance on the nature and use of SGOs,[373] and particularly on how the court should approach a choice between adoption and special guardianship.

The court emphasised the importance of the issues raised by special guardianship, explaining that:

> special guardianship is an issue of very great importance to everyone concerned with it, not least, of course, the child who is its subject. It is plainly not something to be embarked upon lightly or capriciously, not least because the status it gives the special guardian effectively prevents the exercise of parental responsibility on the part of the child's natural parents, and terminates the parental authority given to a local authority under a care order (whether interim or final).[374]

The court explained that the examples given in the White Paper 'are only illustrations' and that there can be 'no routine solutions'[375] and that:

> There is nothing in the statutory provisions themselves which limits the making of a special guardianship order or an adoption order to any given set of circumstances. The statute itself is silent on the circumstances in which a special guardianship order is likely to be appropriate, and there is no presumption contained within the statute that a special guardianship order is preferable to an adoption order in any particular category of case. Each case must be decided on its particular facts; and each case will involve the careful application of a judicial discretion to those facts.[376]

The court drew attention to the distinctions between the status of children who are adopted and those who are subject to a SGO,[377] and also to the equally fundamental differences between the status and powers of adopters and special guardians.[378] The court recognised that 'it is a material feature of the special guardianship regime that it is "less

---

[369] [2007] EWCA Civ 1084, [2008] 1 FLR 1093.   [370] See Children Act 1989, s 91(5A).

[371] *Re S (Adoption Order or Special Guardianship Order)* [2007] EWCA Civ 54, [2007] 1 FLR 819 at [30].

[372] [2007] EWCA Civ 54, [2007] 1 FLR 819.

[373] The guidance was endorsed by the then President of the Family Division, Potter P, and also incorporated in, and endorsed by the judges in, two other cases: *Re M-J (Adoption Order or Special Guardianship Order)* [2007] EWCA Civ 56, [2007] 1 FLR 691 and *Re AJ (Adoption Order or Special Guardianship Order)* [2007] EWCA Civ 55, [2007] 1 FLR 507. For discussion of the case law, see A. Hall, 'Special Guardianship—Themes Emerging from Case-Law' [2008] Family Law 244.

[374] Repeating what the court had said at [78] in *Birmingham City Council v R* [2006] EWCA Civ 1748, [2007] 1 FLR 563.

[375] *Re S (Adoption Order or Special Guardianship Order)* [2007] EWCA Civ 54, [2007] 1 FLR 819 at [43].

[376] Ibid, [47]. See, however, the findings in A. Hall, 'Special Guardianship and Permanency Planning: Unforeseen Consequences and Missed Opportunities' [2008] Child and Family Law Quarterly 359 and 'Special Guardianship: A Missed Opportunity—Findings from Research' [2008] Family Law 148 that aspirations for reducing the number of looked after children may not have been met.

[377] *Re S (Adoption Order or Special Guardianship Order)* [2007] EWCA Civ 54, [2007] 1 FLR 819 at [44].

[378] Ibid, [46]. For a full account of the differences, see the table set out in *Re AJ (Adoption Order or Special Guardianship Order)* [2007] EWCA Civ 55, [2007] 1 FLR 507 at 524–525.

intrusive" than adoption'.[379] It also observed that when a child is adopted by a member of his own family 'the "skewing" or "distorting" effect of adoption' is 'a factor which the court must take into account'. However, the court noted that, as the cases illustrate, different weight will be placed on that factor in different circumstances.[380] The court observed that where a SGO is made a parent still has a right to apply for any section 8 order other than a residence order, and therefore 'it must be accepted that special guardianship does not always provide the same permanency of protection as adoption'.[381] This 'is a factor, which, in a finely balanced case, could well tip the scales in favour of adoption'.[382] Finally, the court indicated that it has jurisdiction to impose a SGO on an unwilling party,[383] but whether or not it should do so will depend on the facts, the nature of the refuser's case, and the welfare of the child. The court was clear, however, that if the court concludes that a SGO would best serve the child's welfare then the court should make it.[384]

In *Re S (Adoption Order or Special Guardianship Order)*[385] the Court of Appeal upheld a judge's decision to make a SGO in favour of the child's foster mother rather than an adoption order because of the close relationship between the 6-year-old child and the natural mother. Applying its assessment set out above, that is, that each case must be assessed on its own facts, the court rejected the foster mother's argument that SGOs were intended to be used only in cases where family members would otherwise adopt, and not to replace adoption applications by non-family members. By contrast, in *Re M-J (Adoption Order or Special Guardianship Order)*[386] and *Re AJ (Adoption Order or Special Guardianship Order)*[387] the Court of Appeal upheld the judges' decisions to make adoption orders rather than SGOs in favour of relatives where the children had not been looked after by their respective parents since the age of six months, and where the adoption met the children's long-term needs for security and stability.

DISCUSSION QUESTIONS

1. When, if at all, should the law permit a child's adoption without a parent's knowledge? Is the courts' approach to this issue satisfactory?

2. Does English law adequately protect the interests of the birth parent in the adoption process? Should the law treat a child's welfare as paramount when considering whether to dispense with parental consent to adoption? Is the courts' approach to post-adoption contact satisfactory?

3. When, if at all, should it be possible to revoke an adoption order? Are policy considerations more important than justice in this context?

FURTHER READING

BRIDGE, C., 'Adoption and Contact: The Value of Openness' [1994] Journal of Child Law 147

BRIDGE, C., 'Adoption Law: A Balance of Interests' in J. Herring (ed), *Family law: Issues, Debates, Policy* (Cullompton: Willan, 2001)

---

[379] *Re S (Adoption Order or Special Guardianship Order)* [2007] EWCA Civ 54, [2007] 1 FLR 819 at [49].
[380] Ibid, [51].
[381] Note, however, that a restriction under Children Act 1989, s 91(14) could be imposed: see eg *Re K (Special Guardianship Order)* [2011] EWCA Civ 635. [382] Ibid, [68].
[383] Ibid, [74].   [384] Ibid, [77].   [385] [2007] EWCA Civ 54, [2007] 1 FLR 819.
[386] [2007] EWCA Civ 56, [2007] 1 FLR 691.   [387] [2007] EWCA Civ 55, [2007] 1 FLR 507.

BRIDGE, C. and SWINDELLS, H., *Adoption: The Modern Law* (Bristol: Family Law, 2003)

CASEY, D. and GIBBERD, A., 'Adoption and Contact' [2000] Family Law 39

CRETNEY, S. and LOWE, N. V., 'English Adoption Law: Past, Present and Future' in S. Katz, J. Eekelaar, and M. Maclean (eds), *Cross-Currents: Family Law and Policy in the US and England* (Oxford: Oxford University Press, 2000)

CURRY-SUMNER, I., '*EB v France*: A Missed Opportunity?' [2009] Child and Family Law Quarterly 356

DEY, I., 'Adapting Adoption: A Case of Closet Politics?' (2005) 19(3) International Journal of Law, Policy and the Family 289

EEKELAAR, J., 'Contact and the Adoption Reform' in A. Bainham, B. Lindley, M. Richards, and L. Trinder (eds), *Children and Their Families: Contact, Rights and Welfare* (Oxford: Hart, 2003)

HALL, A., 'Special Guardianship and Permanency Planning: Unforeseen Consequences and Missed Opportunities' [2008] Child and Family Law Quarterly 359

HALL, A., 'Special Guardianship—Themes Emerging from Case-Law' [2008] Family Law 244

HITCHINGS, E. and SAGAR, T., 'The Adoption and Children Act 2002: A Level Playing Field for Same-Sex Adopters?' [2002] Child and Family Law Quarterly 60

HUGHES, K. and SLOAN, B., 'Post-Adoption Photographs: Welfare, Rights and Judicial Reasoning' [2011] Child and Family Law Quarterly 393

JORDAN, L. and LINDLEY, B. (eds), *Special Guardianship: What Does it Offer Children Who Cannot Live with Their Parents?* (London: Family Rights Group, 2006)

LEWIS, J., 'Adoption: The Nature of Policy Shifts in England and Wales, 1972–2002' (2004) 18(2) International Journal of Law, Policy and the Family 235

SLOAN, B., '*Re C (A Child) (Adoption: Duty of Local Authority)*—Welfare and the Rights of the Birth Family in "Fast Track" Adoption Cases' [2009] Child and Family Law Quarterly 87.

SMITH, C. and LOGAN, J., 'Adoptive Parenthood as a "Legal Fiction"—Its Consequences for Direct Post-Adoption Contact' [2002] Child and Family Law Quarterly 281

BIBLIOGRAPHY

Introduction

BAINHAM, A., 'Men and Women Behaving Badly: Is Fault Dead in English Family Law?'(2001) 22(1) Oxford Journal of Legal Studies 219

BRIDGEMAN, J. and MONK, D., *Feminist Perspectives on Child Law* (London: Cavendish, 2000)

DEWAR, J., 'The Normal Chaos of Family Law' (1998) 61 Modern Law Review 467

DIDUCK, A., 'Family Law and Family Responsibility' in J. Bridgeman, H. Keating, and C. Lind (eds), *Responsibility, Law and the Family* (Aldershot: Ashgate, 2008)

DIDUCK, A. and KAGANAS, F., *Family Law, Gender and the State: Text, Cases and Materials* (Oxford: Hart, 2012)

DIDUCK, A. and O'DONOVAN, K. (eds), *Feminist Perspectives on Family Law* (Abingdon: Routledge-Cavendish, 2006)

EEKELAAR, J., *Family Law and Social Policy* (London: Weidenfeld & Nicholson, 1984)

EEKELAAR, J., *Family Law and Personal Life* (Oxford: Oxford University Press, 2006)

GILMORE, S., 'The *Payne* Saga: Precedent and Family Law Cases' [2011] Family Law 970

GLENNON, L., 'Obligations Between Adult Partners: Moving from Form to Function' (2008) 22 International Journal of Law, Policy and the Family 22

GLENNON, L., '*Fitzpatrick v Sterline Housing Association*: A Perfectly Pitched Stall' in S. Gilmore, J. Herring, and R. Probert (eds), *Landmark Cases in Family Law* (Oxford: Hart, 2011)

HUNTER, R., McGLYNN, C., and RACKLEY, E. (eds), *Feminist Judgments from Theory to Practice* (Oxford: Hart, 2010)

KING, M. and PIPER, C., *How the Law Thinks About Children*, 2nd edn (Aldershot: Ashgate, 1995)

MINISTRY OF JUSTICE, *Family Justice Review Final Report* (London: TSO, 2011)

MINISTRY OF JUSTICE AND DEPARTMENT FOR EDUCATION, *The Government Response to the Family Justice Review: A System with Children and Families at its Heart* (Cm 8273, February 2012)

O'DONOVAN, K., *Family Law Matters* (London: Pluto Press, 1993)

PARKER, S., 'Rights and Utility in Anglo-Australian Family Law' (1992) 55 Modern Law Review 311

PROBERT, R., 'Family Law—A Modern Concept?' [2004] Family Law 901

PROBERT, R. (ed), *Family Life and the Law Under one Roof* (Aldershot: Ashgate, 2007)

Chapter 1: The Formation of Adult Relationships

AUCHMUTY, R., 'What's So Special About Marriage? The Impact of *Wilkinson* v. *Kitzinger*' [2008] Child and Family Law Quarterly 475

AUCHMUTY, R., 'Beyond Couples' (2009) 17 Feminist Legal Studies 205

BAKER, H., 'Family Law Down Under: Can the Old World Learn from the New?' [2009] International Family Law 165

BAMFORTH, N., '"The Benefits of Marriage in All But Name"? Same-Sex Couples and the Civil Partnership Act 2004' [2007] Child and Family Law Quarterly 133

BARLOW, A., 'Legal Rationality and Family Property: What has Love Got to Do With It?' in J. Miles and R. Probert (eds), *Sharing Lives, Dividing Assets: An Interdisciplinary Study* (Oxford: Hart, 2009)

BARLOW A. and SMITHSON, J., 'Legal
Assumptions, Cohabitants' Talk and the
Rocky Road to Reform' [2010] Child and
Family Law Quarterly 328

BARLOW, A., BURGOYNE, C., and
SMITHSON, J., *The Living Together
Campaign: An Investigation of its Impact
on Legally Aware Cohabitants* (London:
Ministry of Justice, 2007)

BARLOW, A., BURGOYNE, C., CLERY, E., and
SMITHSON, J., 'Cohabitation and the Law:
Myths, Money and the Media' in A. Park,
J. Curtice, K. Thompson, M. Phillips, and
E. Clery (eds), *British Social Attitudes—The
24th Report* (London: Sage, 2008)

BARLOW, A., DUNCAN, S., JAMES, G., and
PARK, A., *Cohabitation, Marriage and the
Law: Social Change and Legal Reform in the
21st Century* (Oxford: Hart, 2005)

BESSANT, C., 'Transsexuals and Marriage
after *Goodwin v United Kingdom*' [2003]
Family Law 111

BORKOWSI, A., 'The Presumption of
Marriage' [2002] Child and Family Law
Quarterly 251

BRADNEY, A., 'Duress, Family Law and
Coherent Legal System' [1994] Modern
Law Review 963

BRADNEY, A., 'Developing Human Rights?
The Lords and Transsexual Marriages'
[2003] Family Law 585

BRIDGE, S., 'Financial Relief for Cohabitants:
Eligibility, Opt-Out and Provision on
Death' [2007] Family Law 1076

BRIDGE, S., 'Financial Relief for Cohabitants:
How the Law Commission's Scheme would
Work' [2007] Family Law 998

BURGOYNE, C. and SONNENBERG, S.,
'Financial Practices in Cohabiting
Heterosexual Couples: A Perspective from
Economic Psychology' in J. Miles and
R. Probert (eds), *Sharing Lives, Dividing
Assets, An Inter-Disciplinary Study* (Oxford:
Hart, 2009)

CHARLES, J. and BARLOW, A., '*W v W
(Nullity: Gender)* and *B v B (Validity
of Marriage: Transsexual)*—A New

Approach to Transsexualism and a Missed
Opportunity?' [2001] Child and Family
Law Quarterly

CHAU, P.-L. and HERRING, J., 'Defining,
Assigning and Designing Sex' (2002) 16
International Journal of Law, Policy and
the Family 327

CRETNEY, S., *Same Sex Relationships: From
'Odious Crime' to 'Gay Marriage'* (Oxford:
Oxford University Press, 2006)

DEECH, R., 'Civil Partnership' [2010] Family
Law 468

DEECH, R., 'Cohabitation' [2010] Family Law 39

DEECH, R., 'Cousin Marriage' [2010] Family
Law 619

DEECH, R., 'Sisters Sisters—And Other
Family Members' [2010] Family Law 375

DEPARTMENT OF TRADE AND INDUSTRY,
*Civil Partnership: A Framework for the
Legal Recognition of Same-Sex Couples*
(London: Women and Equality Unit, June
2003)

*Dicey, Morris and Collins on the Conflict of
Laws*, 14th edn (London: Sweet & Maxwell,
2010)

DNES, A., 'Rational Decision-Making and
Intimate Cohabitation' in J. Miles and
R. Probert (eds), *Sharing Lives, Dividing
Assets: An Interdisciplinary Study* (Oxford:
Hart, 2009)

DOUGLAS, G., PEARCE, J., and WOODWARD,
H., *A Failure of Trust: Resolving Property
Disputes on Cohabitation Breakdown*
(2007), available at www.law.cf.ac.uk/
researchpapers/papers/1.pdf

DOUGLAS, G., PEARCE, J., and WOODWARD,
H., 'The Law Commission's Cohabitation
Proposals: Applying them in Practice'
[2008] Family Law 1076

DUNCAN, S., BARLOW, A., and JAMES, G.,
'Why Don't They Marry? Cohabitation,
Commitment and DIY Marriage' [2005]
Child and Family Law Quarterly 383

EEKELAAR, J. and MACLEAN, M., 'Marriage
and the Moral Bases of Personal
Relationships' (2004) Journal of Law and
Society 244

FOREIGN & COMMONWEALTH OFFICE, *The Right to Choose: Multi-Agency Statutory Guidance for Dealing with Forced Marriage*, available at www.fco.gov.uk

GILMORE, S., '*Bellinger v Bellinger*—Not Quite Between the Ears and Between the Legs—Transsexualism and Marriage in the Lords' (2003) 15(3) Child and Family Law Quarterly 295

GILMORE, S., '*Corbett v Corbett*: Once a Man, Always a Man?' in S. Gilmore, J. Herring, and R. Probert, *Landmark Cases in Family Law* (Oxford: Hart, 2011)

GLENNON, L., 'Displacing the "Conjugal" Family in Legal Policy—A Progressive Move?' (2005) Child and Family Law Quarterly 17

GLENNON, L., 'The Limitations of Equality Discourses on the Contours of Intimate Obligations' in J. Wallbank, J. Herring, and S. Choudhry (eds), *Rights, Gender and Family Law* (Abingdon: Routledge, 2009)

GLENNON, L., '*Fitzpatrick v Sterling Housing Association*: A Perfectly Pitched Stall' in S. Gilmore, J. Herring, and R. Probert (eds), *Landmark Cases in Family Law* (Oxford: Hart, 2011)

GRANT BOWMAN, C., *Unmarried Couples, Law, and Public Policy* (Oxford: Oxford University Press, 2010)

HERRING, J., 'Relational Autonomy in Family Law' in J. Wallbank, J. Herring, and S. Choudhry (eds), *Rights, Gender and Family Law* (Abingdon: Routledge, 2009)

HERRING, J. and CHAU, P.-L., 'Assigning Sex and Intersexuals' [2001] Family Law 762

HOME OFFICE and FOREIGN & COMMONWEALTH OFFICE, *Forced Marriage: A Wrong Not a Right* (Consultation Paper, September 2005)

KIERNAN, K., 'Unmarried Cohabitation and Parenthood in Britain and Europe' (2004) 26(1) Journal of Law and Policy 33

LATEY COMMITTEE, Report of the Committee on the Age of Majority (1967)

LAW COMMISSION, *Report on Nullity of Marriage* (Law Com No 33, 1970)

LAW COMMISSION, *Sharing Homes: A Discussion Paper* (Law Com No 278, 2002)

LAW COMMISSION, *Cohabitation: The Financial Consequences of Relationship Breakdown* (Law Com CP No 179, 2006)

LAW COMMISSION, *Cohabitation: The Financial Consequences of Relationship Breakdown* (Law Com No 307, 2007)

LAW COMMISSION, *Intestacy and Family Provision Claims on Death* (Law Com CP No 191, 2009)

McNORRIE, K., 'Marriage is for Heterosexuals—May the Rest of Us Be Saved From It' [2000] Child and Family Law Quarterly 363

MINISTRY OF JUSTICE, *Judicial and Court Statistics 2009* (London: Ministry of Justice, 2010)

PROBERT, R., 'When are We Married? Void, Non-Existent and Presumed Marriages' [2000] 22 Legal Studies 398

PROBERT, R., 'The Right to Marry and the Impact of the Human Rights Act 1998' [2003] International Family Law 29

PROBERT, R., 'How Would *Corbett v Corbett* be Decided Today?' [2004] Family Law 382

PROBERT, R., '*Hyde v Hyde*: Defining or Defending Marriage?' [2007] Child and Family Law Quarterly 322

PROBERT, R., 'Common-Law Marriage: Myths and Misunderstandings' [2008] Child and Family Law Quarterly 1

PROBERT, R., 'Hanging on the Telephone: *City of Westminster v IC*' (2008) Child and Family Law Quarterly 395

PROBERT, R., 'The Cohabitation Bill' [2009] Family Law 150

SCHÄFER, L., 'Marrying an In-Law. The Future of Prohibited Degrees of Affinity and Consanguinity in English Law' [2008] Child and Family Law Quarterly 219

VALLANCE-WEBB, G., 'Forced Marriage: A Yielding of the Lips Not the Mind' [2008] Family Law 565

VOGLER, C., BROCKMANN, M., and WIGGINS, R., 'Intimate Relationships and

Changing Patterns of Money Management at the Beginning of the 21st Century' (2008) 37 British Journal of Sociology 455

WILLIAMS, C., POTTER, G., and DOUGLAS, G., 'Cohabitation and Intestacy: Public Opinion and Law Reform' [2008] Child and Family Law Quarterly 499

Chapter 2: The Dissolution of Adult Relationships

CRETNEY, S., 'The Divorce White Paper—Some Reflections' [1995] Family Law 302

CRETNEY, S., 'Marriage, Divorce and the Courts' [2002] Family Law 900

CRETNEY, S., Family Law in the Twentieth Century (Oxford: Oxford University Press, 2003

CRETNEY, S. and BIRD, R., Divorce: The New Law (Bristol: Family Law, 1996)

DAVIS, G. and MURCH, M., Grounds for Divorce (Oxford: Clarendon Press, 1988)

DEECH, R., 'Divorce—A Disaster?' [2009] Family Law 1048

EEKELAAR, J., 'Family Law—Keeping Us "On Message"' [1999] Child and Family Law Quarterly 387

FREEMAN, M. (ed), Divorce: Where Next? (Aldershot: Dartmouth, 1996)

FREEMAN, M., 'Divorce Gospel Style' [1997] Family Law 413

HASSON, E., 'Setting a Standard or Reflecting Reality? The "Role" of Divorce Law, and the Case of the Family Law Act 1996' [2003] International Journal of Law, Policy and the Family 338

HASSON, E., 'Wedded to "Fault": The Legal Regulation of Divorce and Relationship Breakdown' (2006) Legal Studies 267

HM GOVERNMENT, Royal Commission on Marriage and Divorce (Cmd 9678, 1956)

HM GOVERNMENT, Reform of the Grounds of Divorce: the Field of Choice (Cmd 3123, 1966)

HM GOVERNMENT, Report of the Matrimonial Causes Procedure Committee (HMSO, 1985)

HM GOVERNMENT, Consultation Paper: Looking to the Future (London: HMSO, 1993)

KAY, R., 'Whose Divorce is it Anyway?—The Human Rights Aspect' [2004] Family Law 892

LAW COMMISSION, Facing the Future: A Discussion Paper on the Ground for Divorce (Law Com No 170, 1988)

PROBERT, R., 'The Roos Case' in S Gilmore, J. Herring, and R. Probert (eds), Landmark Cases in Family Law (Oxford: Hart, 2011)

RESOLUTION, Family Law Protocol, 2nd edn (London: Resolution, 2006)

SHEPHERD, N., 'Ending the Blame Game: Getting No Fault Divorce Back on the Agenda' [2001] Family Law 122

STONE, L., Road to Divorce (Oxford: Oxford University Press, 1991)

Chapter 3: Protection from Domestic Violence and Occupation of the Family Home

AUSTRALIAN LAW REFORM COMMISSION, Domestic Violence (Report No 30, 1986)

BAILEY-HARRIS, R., BARRON, J., and PEARCE, J., 'From Utility to Rights? The Presumption of Contact in Practice' (1999) 13 International Journal of Law, Policy and the Family 111

BAINHAM, A., 'Changing Families and Changing Concepts—Reforming the Language of Family Law' (1998) 10 Child and Family Law Quarterly 1

BARRON, J., Not Worth the Paper...? The Effectiveness of Legal Protection for Women and Children Experiencing Domestic Violence (Bristol: Women's Aid Federation England, 1990)

BARRON, J., 'Five Years On: A Review of Legal Protection from Domestic Violence' (Bristol: Women's Aid, 2002)

BESSANT, C., 'Enforcing Non-Molestation Orders in the Civil and Criminal Courts' [2005] Family Law 640

BLACKSTONE, W., Commentaries on the Laws of England (1765)

BURTON, M., 'Criminalising Breaches of Civil Orders for Protection from Domestic Violence' [2003] Criminal Law Review 301

BURTON, M., 'Third Party Applications for Protections Orders in England and Wales: Service Provider's Views on Implementing Section 60 of the Family Law Act 1996 (2003) 25(2) Journal of Social Welfare and Family Law 137

BURTON, M., 'Case Commentary—*Lomas v Parle*—Coherent and Effective Remedies for Victims of Domestic Violence: Time for an Integrated Domestic Violence Court' [2004] Child and Family Law Quarterly 317

BURTON, M., *Legal Responses to Domestic Violence* (Abingdon: Routledge-Cavendish, 2008)

BURTON, M., 'Civil Law Remedies for Domestic Violence: Why are Applications for Non-Molestation Orders Declining?' (2009) 31(2) Journal of Social Welfare and Family Law 109

BURTON, M., *Legal Responses to Domestic Violence* (Abingdon: Routledge-Cavendish, 2008)

CHAPPELL, D. and STRANG, H., 'Domestic Violence—Findings and Recommendations of the National Committee on Violence' [1990] Australian Journal of Family Law 211

CHESNEY-LIND, M., 'Patriarchy, Crime and Justice: Feminist Criminology in an Era of Backlash' (2006) 1 Feminist Criminology 6

CHOUDRY, S. and HERRING, J., 'Righting Domestic Violence' (2006) 20 International Journal of Law, Policy and the Family 95

COOK, D. et al, *Evaluation of Specialist Domestic Violence Courts/Fast Track Systems* (London: Crown Prosecution Service/Department of Constitutional Affairs, 2004)

COPELON, R., 'Intimate Terror: Understanding Domestic Violence as Torture' in R. Cook (ed), *Human Rights of Women: National and International Perspectives* (Philadelphia, PA: University of Pennsylvania Press, 1994)

CRISIS, *Homeless Women, Still Being Failed Yet Striving to Survive* (London: Crisis, 2006)

DEPARTMENT FOR COMMUNITIES AND LOCAL GOVERNMENT, *Homelessness Code of Guidance for Local Authorities* (London: Department for Communities and Local Government, 2006)

DEPARTMENT FOR CONSTITUTIONAL AFFAIRS, DEPARTMENT FOR EDUCATION AND SKILLS, and DEPARTMENT OF TRADE, *Parental Separation: Children's Needs and Parents' Responsibilities* (Cm 6273, 2004)

DEPARTMENT OF HEALTH, *Secure Futures for Women: Making a Difference* (London: Department of Health, 2002)

DEPARTMENT OF HEALTH, *Into the Mainstream—Strategic Development of Mental Health Care for Women* (London: Department of Health, 2003)

DOBASH, R. and DOBASH, R., *Violence Against Wives: A Case Against the Patriarchy* (New York: Free Press, 1979)

DOBASH, R. and DOBASH, R., Violence Against Women in the Family' in S. Katz, J. Eekelaar, and M. Maclean, *Cross-Currents: Family Law Policy in the US and England* (Oxford: Oxford University Press, 2000)

DOBASH, R. and DOBASH, R., 'Women's Violence to Men in Intimate Relationships: Working on a Puzzle' (2004) British Journal of Criminology 324

DOBASH, R. et al, *Research Evaluation Programmes for Violent Men* (Edinburgh: The Scottish Office Central Research Unit, 1996)

EDWARDS, S., 'Police Attitudes and Dispositions in Domestic Disputes: The London Study' (1986) Police Journal (July)

EDWARDS, S., *Policing 'Domestic' Violence: Women, the Law and the State* (London: Sage, 1989)

FELSON, R. B. and MESSNER, S. F., 'The Control Motive in Intimate Partner Violence' (2000) 63 Social Psychology Quarterly 86

FRASER, A. S., 'Becoming Human: The Origin and Development of Women's

Human Rights Law' (1999) 21 Human Rights Quarterly 853

GELLES, R., 'Through a Sociological Lens: Social Structures and Family Violence' in R. Gelles and D. Loseke (eds), *Current Controversies on Family Violence* (Thousand Oaks, CA: Sage, 1993)

GELLES, R. and STRAUS, M., 'Determinants of Violence in the Family: Toward a Theoretical Integration' in R. Burr et al, (eds), *Contemporary Theories About the Family*, vol 1 (New York: Free Press, 1979)

GORE, S., 'In Practice: The Domestic Violence, Crime and Victims Act 2004 and Family Law Act 1996 Injunctions' [2007] Family Law 739

GRACE, S., *Policing Domestic Violence in the 1990s*, Home Office Research Study No 139 (London: Home Office, 1995)

HANMER, J. and SAUNDERS, S., *Well-Founded Fear* (London: Hutchinson, 1984)

HAYES, M., 'Non-Molestation Protection—Only Associated Persons Need Apply' [1996] Family Law 134

HAYES, M. and WILLIAMS, C., 'Domestic Violence and Occupation of the Family Home: Proposals for Reform' [1992] Family Law 497

HERRING, J. and CHOUDHRY, S., 'Domestic Violence and the Human Rights Act 1998: A New Means of Legal Intervention' (2006) Public Law 752

HESTER, M., 'Making It Through the Criminal Justice System: Attrition and Domestic Violence' (2005) 5(1)Social Policy and Society 79

HESTER, M., *Who Does What to Whom? Gender and Domestic Violence Perpetrators* (Bristol: University of Bristol in association with the Northern Rock Foundation, 2009)

HESTER, M. and WESTMARLAND, N., *Tackling Domestic Violence: Effective Interventions and Approaches*, Home Office Research Study 290 (London: Home Office, 2005)

HESTER, M., PEARSON, C., and HARWIN, N., *Making an Impact: Children and*

Domestic Violence—A Reader (London: Jessica Kingsley, 2007)

HESTER, M., WESTMARLAND, N., PEARCE, J., and WILLIAMSON, E., *Early Evaluation of the Domestic Violence, Crime and Victims Act 2004*, Ministry of Justice Research Series 14/08 (London: Ministry of Justice, 2008)

HESTER, M., et al, *Domestic Violence: Making it Through the Criminal Justice System* (University of Sunderland, Northern Rock Foundation and the International Centre for the Study of Violence and Abuse, 2003)

HILL, R. N., 'Protection from Harassment' [2005] Family Law 364

HM GOVERNMENT, *Safety and Justice: The Government's Proposals on Domestic Violence* (Cm 5847, 2003)

HM GOVERNMENT, Home Affairs Committee, 'Domestic Violence, Forced Marriage and "Honour"-Based Violence, Sixth Report of Session 2007–08, Vol I, HC 263-I

HM GOVERNMENT, *National Domestic Violence Delivery Plan: Annual Progress Report 2008-09* (London: HMSO, 2010)

HOME OFFICE, *Stalking—The Solutions: A Consultation Paper* (London: Home Office, 1996)

HOME OFFICE, *Domestic Violence Offenders: Characteristics and Offending-Related Needs* (London: Home Office, 2003)

HOME OFFICE, *Alcohol and Intimate Partner Violence* (London: Home Office, 2004)

HOME OFFICE, *Domestic Violence: A National Report* (London: Home Office, 2005)

HUMPHREYS, C. and THIARA, R. K., *Routes to Safety: Protection Issues Facing Abused Women and Children and the Role of Outreach Services* (Bristol: Women's Aid Federation England, 2002)

HUMPHREYS, C. and THIARA, R. K., 'Neither Justice nor Protection: Women's Experiences of Post-Separation Violence' (2003) 25 Journal of Social Welfare and Family Law 195

JAMES, B., 'Occupation Orders after Grubb', available at www.familylawweek.co.uk

JAMES, B., 'In Practice: Prosecuting Domestic Violence' [2008] Family Law 456

KAGANAS, F., 'Re L (Contact: Domestic Violence) ... Contact and Domestic Violence' (1999) 12 Child and Family Law Quarterly 311

KELLY, L., Surviving Sexual Violence (Cambridge: Polity Press, 1987)

LEES, S., 'Marital Rape and Marital Murder' in J. Hanmer and C. Itzin (eds), Home Truths about Domestic Violence: Feminist Influences on Policy and Practice: A Reader (Abingdon: Routledge, 2002)

LEONARD, K. E. and QUIGLEY, B. M., 'Drinking and Marital Aggression in Newlyweds: An Event-Based Analysis of Drinking and the Occurrence of Husband Marital Aggression' (1999) 60(4) Journal of Studies on Alcohol 537

LEWIS, R., 'Making Justice Work: Effective Legal Interventions for Domestic Violence' (2004) British Journal of Criminology 204

MACLEAN, M. and EEKELAAR, J., 'The Obligations and Expectations of Couples within Families' 26(2) Journal of Social Welfare and Family Law 117

MADDEN-DEMPSEY, M., 'What Counts as Domestic Violence: A Conceptual Analysis' [2006] 12 William and Mary Journal of Women and the Law 301

MARCUS, I., 'Reframing "Domestic Violence": Terrorism in the Home' in M. Fineman and R. Mykitiuk (eds), The Public Nature of Private Violence: The Discovery of Domestic Abuse (Abingdon: Routledge, 1994)

MARTIN, D., Battered Wives (New York: Pocket Books, 1976)

McQUIGG, R., 'The Responses of States to the Comments of the CEDAW Committee on Domestic Violence' (2007) 11(4) International Journal of Human Rights 461

MILES, J., 'Domestic Violence' in J. Herring (ed), Family Law: Issues, Debates, Policy (Cullompton: Willan, 2001)

MIRRLEES-BLACK, C., Domestic Violence: Findings from a New British Crime Survey Self-Completion Questionnaire, Home Office Research Study 191 (London: Home Office, 1999)

MULLENDER, A., Rethinking Domestic Violence (Abingdon: Routledge, 1996)

MULLENDER, A., Tackling Domestic Violence: Providing Support for Children who have Witnessed Domestic Violence (London: Home Office, 2005)

NOON, R., 'Compensation for Domestic Abuse after Singh v Bhaker', available at www.familylawweek.co.uk

PARMAR, A. and SAMPSON, A., 'Evaluating Domestic Violence Initiatives' (2007) British Journal of Criminology 671

PIZZEY, E., Scream Quietly or the Neighbours Will Hear (Harmondsworth: Penguin Books, 1974)

PLATT, J., 'The Domestic Violence, Crime and Victims Act 2004 Part 1: Is it Working?' [2008] Family Law 642

RADFORD, J. and STANKO, E., 'Violence Against Women and Children: The Contradictions of Crime Control under Patriarchy' in M. Hester, L. Kelly, and J. Radford (eds), Women, Violence and Male Power (Buckingham: Open University Press, 1996)

RADFORD, L., SAYERS, S., and AID FOR MOTHERS INVOLVED IN CONTACT ACTION (AMICA), Unreasonable Fears? Child Contact in the Context of Domestic Violence: A Survey of Mothers' Perception of Harm (Bristol: Women's Aid Federation England, 1999)

REECE, H., 'The End of Domestic Violence' (2006) Modern Law Review 770

REFUGE, Response to Domestic Violence, Crimes and Victims Bill (London: Refuge, 2004)

RICHARDS, L., Domestic Violence Murder Review Analysis of Findings (London: Metropolitan Police Service, 2003)

ROBINSON, A. and COOK, D., 'Understanding Victim Retraction in Cases of Domestic Violence: Specialist Courts, Government Policy, and Victim-Centred Justice' (2006) 9 Contemporary Justice Review 189

ROMITO, P., *A Deafening Silence: Hidden Violence against Women and Children* (Bristol: Policy Press, 2008)

ROSLEY, J., 'In Practice: Mother-in-Law Harassment: *Singh v Bhakar*' [2006] Family Law 968

RUBENS, T., 'Domestic Violence and Priority Need' (2008) Journal of Housing Law 28

SAUNDERS, H., *Twenty-Nine Child Homicides: Lessons Still to be Learnt on Domestic Violence and Child Protection* (Bristol: Women's Aid, 2004)

SCHNEIDER, E. M., *Battered Women and Feminist Lawmaking* (New Haven, CT: Yale University Press, 2000)

SENTENCING GUIDELINES COUNCIL, 'Overarching Principles: Domestic Violence' (2006)

SONI, B., 'Domestic Violence and Family Law: A New Era', available at www.family-lawweek.co.uk

STANKO, B., *Intimate Intrusions: Women's Experience of Male Violence* (London: Routledge, 1985)

STURGE, C. and GLASER, D., 'Contact and Domestic Violence—The Experts' Report' (2000) 30 Family Law 615

THOMAS, D. and BEASLEY, M., 'Domestic Violence as a Human Rights Issue' (1993) 15 Human Rights Quarterly 36

WALBY, S. and ALLEN, J., *Domestic Violence, Sexual Assault and Stalking: Findings from the British Crime Survey*, Home Office Research Study 276 (London: Home Office, 2004)

WALKLATE, S., 'What is to be Done About Violence Against Women? Gender, Violence, Cosmopolitanism and the Law' (2008) British Journal of Criminology 39

Chapter 4: Money and Property Distribution on Marriagte Breakdown

BAILEY-HARRIS, R., 'Comment on *GW v RW (Financial Provision: Departure from Equality)*' [2003] Family Law 388

BOELE-WOELKI, K., MILES, J., and SCHERPE, J. M. (eds), *The Future of Family Property in Europe* (Antwerp: Intersentia, 2011)

BRASSE, G., 'It's Payback Time! *Miller, McFarlane* and the Compensation Culture' [2006] Family Law 647

CLARK, B., 'Should Greater Prominence be Given to Pre-Nuptial Contracts in the Law of Ancillary Relief' [2004] Child and Family Law Quarterly 399

COOKE, E., 'Making the Clean Break Squeaky Clean' [1994] Family Law 268

COOKE, E., '*Miller/McFarlane*: Law in Search of Discrimination' [2007] Child and Family Law Quarterly 98

CRETNEY, S., 'The Family and the Law—Status or Contract? [2003] Child and Family Law Quarterly 403

DAVIS, G., CRETNEY, S., and COLLINS, J., *Simple Quarrels* (Oxford: Clarendon Press, 1994)

DAVIS, S., 'Equal Sharing: A Judicial Gloss Too Far?' [2008] Family Law 428

DOUGLAS, A., 'Comment on *Dixon v Marchant*' [2008] Family Law 306

DOUGLAS, G., 'Bringing an End to the Matrimonial Post Mortem: *Wachtel v Wachtel* and its Enduring Significance for Ancillary Relief' in S. Gilmore, J. Herring, and R. Probert (eds), *Landmark Cases in Family Law* (Oxford: Hart, 2011)

EDWARDS, J., 'Duration of Marriage: From "I Do", "I Promise" or "I May"?' [2004] Family Law 726

EEKELAAR, J., 'Some Principles of Financial and Property Adjustment on Divorce' (1979) LQR 253

EEKELAAR, J., 'Post-Divorce Financial Obligations' in S. Katz, J. Eekelaar, and M. Maclean (eds), *Cross-Currents: Family Law and Policy in the United States and England* (Oxford: Oxford University Press, 2000)

EEKELAAR, J., 'Uncovering Social Obligations: Family Law and the Responsible Citizen' in

M. Maclean (ed), *Making Law for Families* (Oxford: Hart, 2000)

EEKELAAR, J., 'Asset Distribution on Divorce—The Durational Element' (2001) 117 LQR 552

EEKELAAR, J., 'Back to Basics and Forward into the Unknown' [2001] Family Law 30

EEKELAAR, J., 'Shared Income After Divorce: A Step too Far' (2005) LQR 1

FISHER, L., 'The Unexpected Impact of *White*—Taking "Equality" Too Far' [2002] Family Law 108

GEORGE, R. H., HARRIS, P. G., and HERRING, J., 'Pre-Nuptial Agreements: For Better or For Worse?' [2009] Family Law 934

GERLIS, S., '*White*—The Unlearned Lesson' [2002] 32 Family Law 628

GILMORE, S., 'Duration of Marriage *and* Seamless Preceding Cohabitation?' [2004] Family Law 205

GLENDON, M. A., *The Transformation of Family Law; State, Law, and Family in the United States and Western Europe* (Chicago, IL: University of Chicago Press, 1989)

GLENNON, L., 'Obligations between Adult Partners: Moving from Form to Function?' (2008) 22(1) International Journal of Law, Policy and the Family 22

HAYES, M., 'Cohabitation Clauses in Financial Provision and Property Adjustment Orders: Law, Policy and Justice' (1994) 110 LQR 124

HERRING, J., 'Why Financial Orders on Divorce Should be Unfair' (2005) 19(2) International Journal of Law, Policy and the Family 218

HOME OFFICE, *Supporting Families: A Consultation Document* (London: Home Office, 1998)

HUGHES, S., 'Over the *Bard*erline' [2008] Family Law 670

JACKSON, E., WASOFF, F., MACLEAN, M., and DOBASH, R., 'Financial Support on Divorce: The Right Mixture of Rules and Discretion?' (1993) 7 International Journal of Law and the Family 230

LAW COMMISSION, *Report on Financial Provision in Matrimonial Proceedings* (Law Com No 25, 1969)

LAW COMMISSION, *Family Law: The Financial Consequences of Divorce: the Basic Policy: A Discussion Paper'* (Law Com No 103, 1980)

LAW COMMISSION, *Family Law: The Ground for Divorce* (Law Com No 192, 1990)

LAW COMMISSION, *Cohabitation: The Financial Consequences of Relationship Breakdown* (Law Com No 307, 2007)

LEWIS, J., 'Debates and Issues Regarding Marriage and Cohabitation in the British and American literature' (2001) 15(1) International Journal of Law, Policy and the Family 159

LORD SIMON OF GLAISDALE, *With All My Worldly Goods* (1964, Holdsworth Club)

MERRIGAN, D., 'Variation of Nominal Periodical Payment Orders' [2007] Family Law 1009

MILES, J., '*Charman v Charman (No 4)*—Making Sense of Need, Compensation and Equal Sharing after *Miller/McFarlane*' [2008] Child and Family Law Quarterly 378

MOOR, P., 'Key Developments in Ancillary Relief' [2008] Family Law 44

MORLEY, J., 'Enforceable Pre-Nuptial Agreements: Their Time Has Come' [2006] Family Law 772

O'DONOVAN, K., 'Flirting with Academic Categorizations—*McFarlane v McFarlane and Parlour v Parlour* [2005] Child and Family Law Quarterly 418

RESOLUTION, *A More Certain Future— Recognition of Pre-Marital Agreements in England and Wales* (London: Resolution, 2004)

SCHERPE, J. M., 'Fairness, Freedom and Foreign Elements—Marital Agreements in England and Wales After *Radmacher v Granatino*' [2011] Child and Family Law Quarterly 513

SCHERPE, J. M. (ed), *Marital Agreements and Private Autonomy in Comparative Perspective* (Oxford: Hart, 2012)

SMART, C., *The Ties That Bind* (Abingdon: Routledge, 1984)

ZUCKERMAN, A., 'Finality of Litigation—Setting Aside a Final Judgment' (2008) 27(2) Civil Justice Quarterly 151

Chapter 5: Property Disputes of Unmarried Cohabitants on Relationship Breakdown

ANDREWS, G., 'The Presumption of Advancement: Equity, Equality and Human Rights' (2007) Conveyancer and Property Lawyer 340

ARTHUR, S., LEWIS, J., MACLEAN, M., FINCH, S., and FITZGERALD, R., 'Settling Up: Making Financial Arrangements after Divorce or Separation' (National Centre for Social Research, 2002)

BAILEY-HARRIS, R. and WILSON, J., '*Jones v Kernott*—Another Helping of the Witches Brew?, available at www.familylawweek.co.uk

BARLOW, A., 'Cohabitation Law Reform—Messages from Research' (2006) 14 Feminist Legal Studies 167

BARLOW, A., BURGOYNE, C., and SMITHSON, J., *The Living Together Campaign—An Investigation of its Impact on Legally Aware Cohabitants* (London: Ministry of Justice, 2007)

BARLOW, A., BURGOYNE, C., CLERY, E., and SMITHSON, J., 'Cohabitation and the Law: Myths, Money and the Media' in A. Park et al (eds), *British Social Attitudes: The 24th Report* (London: Sage, 2008)

BARLOW, A., DUNCAN, S., JAMES, G., and PARK, A., 'Just a Piece of Paper? Marriage and Cohabitation in Britain' in A. Park, J. Curtice, K. Thomson, L. Jarvis, and C. Bromley (eds), *British Social Attitudes: The 18th Report* (London: Sage, 2001)

BARLOW, A., DUNCAN, S., JAMES, G., and PARK, A., *Cohabitation. Marriage and the Law: Social Change and Legal Reform in the 21st Century* (Oxford: Hart, 2005)

BATTERSBY, G., 'Ownership of the Family Home: *Stack v Dowden* in the House of Lords' [2008] Child and Family Law Quarterly 255

CHANDLER, A., 'Express Declarations of Trust, Rectification and Recissions: *Goodman v Gallant* Revisited' [2008] Family Law 1210

COOKE, E., 'Accounting Payments: Please Can We Get the Maths Right?' [2007] Family Law 1024

DEECH, R., 'The Case against the Legal Recognition of Cohabitation' (1980) 29 International and Comparative Law Quarterly 480

DIXON, M., 'The Never-Ending Story—Co-Ownership after *Stack v Dowden*' (2007) Conveyancer and Property Lawyer 456

DOBBS, C., 'Patterns of Pay: Results of the Annual Survey of Hours and Earnings 1997 to 2008' (2009) 3(3) Economic and Labour Market Review 24

DOUGLAS, G., PEARCE, J., and WOODWARD, H., Cardiff Law School Research Paper No. 1, 'A Failure of Trust: Resolving Property Disputes on Cohabitation Breakdown' (2007)

DOUGLAS, G., PEARCE, J., and WOODWARD, H., 'Cohabitants, Property and the Law: A Study of Injustice' (2009) 72(1) Modern Law Review 24

DUNCAN, S. and PHILLIPS, M., 'New Families? Tradition and Change in Modern Relationships' in A. Park et al (eds), *British Social Attitudes: The 24th Report* (London: Sage, 2008)

EEKELAAR, J. and MACLEAN, M., 'Marriage and the Moral Bases of Personal Relationships' (2004) 31(4) Journal of Law and Society 510

GARDNER, S., *An Introduction to Land Law* (Oxford: Hart, 2007)

GLENNON, L., 'Obligations between Adult Partners: Moving from Form to Function?'

(2008) 22(1) International Journal of Law, Policy and the Family 22

GLOVER, N. and TODD, P., 'The Myth of Common Intention' (1996) Legal Studies 325

GREER, S., 'Back to the Bad Old Days?' (2008) 158 New Law Journal 174

HARPUM, C., 'Cohabitation Consultation' [1995] 25 Family Law 657

HASKEY, J., 'Cohabiting Couples in Great Britain: Accommodation Sharing, Tenure and Property Ownership' (2001) 103 Population Trends 26

HESS, E., 'The Rights of Cohabitants: When and How Will the Law be Reformed' [2009] Family Law 405

KIERNAN, K., BARLOW, A., and MERLO, R., 'Cohabitation Law Reform and its Impact on Marriage: Evidence from Australia and Europe' (2007) 63 International Family Law 71

LAW COMMISSION, Sharing Homes: A Discussion Paper (Law Com No 278, 2002)

LAW COMMISSION, Cohabitation: The Financial Consequences of Relationship Breakdown (Law Com No 307, 2007)

LAW SOCIETY, Cohabitation: the Case for Clear Law. Proposals for Reform (London: Representation and Law Reform Directorate, 2002)

LORD NEUBERGER, 'The Conspirators, the Tax Man, the Bill of Rights and a Bit About the Lovers', Chancery Bar Association Annual Lecture, 10 March 2008, available at www.chba.org.uk/library/seminar_notes/news4

OFFICE FOR NATIONAL STATISTICS, Annual Survey of Hours and Earnings (2008)

OFFICE FOR NATIONAL STATISTICS, General Household Survey 2007 (2008)

PAWLOWSKI, M., 'Beneficial Entitlement—No Longer Doing Justice' (2007) Conveyancer and Property Lawyer 354

PISKA, N., 'A Common Intention or a Rare Bird? Proprietary Interests, Personal Claims and Services Rendered by Lovers Post-Acquisition: James v Thomas; Morris v Morris' [2009] Child and Family Law Quarterly 104

PISKA, N., 'Distinctions Without a Difference? Explaining Stack v Dowden' (2008) Conveyancer and Property Lawyer 451

PROBERT, R., 'Equality in the Family Home' (2007) Feminist Legal Studies 341

PROBERT, R., 'The Cohabitation Bill' [2009] Family Law 150

RALTON, A., 'Establishing a Beneficial Share: Rosset Revisited' [2008] Family Law 424

ROBERTSON, A., 'The Reliance Basis of Proprietary Estoppel Remedies' (2008) 72 Conveyancer and Property Lawyer 295

SMART, C. and STEVENS, P., Cohabitation Breakdown (London: FPSC/Rowntree, 2000)

SWADLING, W., 'The Common Intention Constructive Trust in the House of Lords: An Opportunity Missed' (2007) LQR 511

TENNANT, R., TAYLOR, J., and LEWIS, J., 'Separating from Cohabitation: Making Arrangements for Finances and Parenting', Department for Constitutional Affairs Research Report 7/2006 (London: DCA, 2006)

VOGLER, C., BROCKMANN, M., and WIGGINS, R., 'Intimate Relationships and Changing Patterns of Money Management at the Beginning of the Twenty-First Century' (2006) 57(3) British Journal of Sociology 455

WILSON, J., 'Tripping up on the TR1' [2006] Family Law 305

Chapter 6: Financial Support for Children

ABBOTT, D., 'The Child Support Act 1991: The Lives of Parents With Care Living in Liverpool' (1996) 18(1) Journal of Social Welfare and Family Law 21

BARTON, C., 'Third Time Lucky for Child Support?—The 1998 Green Paper' [1998] Family Law 668

BARTON, C., 'Child Support—Tony's Turn' [1999] Family Law 704

COLLIER, R., 'The Campaign Against the Child Support Act, Errant Fathers and Family Men' [1994] Family Law 384

COSTLEY-WHITE, T., 'Maintenance Liability for Students' [1999] Family Law 45

CRETNEY, S., Family Law in the Twentieth Century: A History (Oxford: Oxford University Press, 2003)

DAVIS, G., WIKELEY, N., YOUNG, R. et al, Child Support in Action (Oxford: Hart, 1998)

DEPARTMENT FOR WORK AND PENSIONS, A New System of Child Maintenance (Cm 6979, 2006)

DEPARTMENT FOR WORK AND PENSIONS, Strengthening Families, Promoting Parental Responsibility: The Future of Child Maintenance (Cm 7990, 2011)

DEPARTMENT FOR WORK AND PENSIONS, Government's Response to the Consultation on Strengthening Families, Promoting Parental Responsibility (Cm 8130, 2011)

DIDUCK, A., 'The Unmodified Family: The Child Support Act and the Construction of Legal Subjects' (1995) 22(4) Journal of Law and Society 527

DSS, Children Come First: The Government's Proposals on the Maintenance of Children (Cm 1263, 1990)

EEKELAAR, J., 'Families and Children: From Welfarism to Rights' in J. C. McCrudden and G. Chambers (eds), Individual Rights and the Law in Britain (Oxford, Oxford University Press, 1994)

FEHLBERG, B. and MACLEAN, M., 'Child Support Policy in Australia and the United Kingdom: Changing Priorities But A Similar Tough Deal for Children?' (2009) 23(1) International Journal of Law, Policy and the Family 1

GARNHAM, A. and KNIGHTS, E., Putting the Treasury First (London: Child Poverty Action Group, 1994)

GILLESPIE, G., 'Child Support—The Hand that Rocks the Cradle' [1996] Family Law 162

GILMORE, S., 'Re P (Child)(Financial Provision)—Shoeboxes and Comical Shopping Trips—Child Support From the Affluent to Fabulously Rich' (2004) 16(1) Child and Family Law Quarterly 103

GILMORE, S., 'Re B (Contact: Child Support)—Horses and Carts: Contact and Child Support' [2007] Child and Family Law Quarterly 357

GLENDINNING, C., CLARKE, K., and CRAIG, G., 'Implementing the Child Support Act' (1996) 18(3) Journal of Social Welfare and Family Law 273

HM GOVERNMENT, Improving Child Support (Cm 2745, 1995)

HM GOVERNMENT, Children First: A New Approach to Child Support (Cm 3992, 1998)

HM GOVERNMENT, A New Contract for Welfare: Children's Rights and Parents' Responsibilities (Cm 4349, 1999)

HM GOVERNMENT, Recovering Child Support: Routes to Responsibility (Cm 6894, July 2006)

HORTON, A., 'Improving Child Support—A Missed Opportunity' [1995] Child and Family Law Quarterly 26

MACLEAN, M., 'The Making of the Child Support Act: Policy Making at the Intersection of Law and Social Policy' (1994) 21(4) Journal of Law and Society 505

MACLEAN, M. and EEKELAAR, J., 'Child Support: The British Solution' (1993) 7 International Journal of Law and the Family 205

MACLEAN, M. with KURCZEWSKI, J., Making Family Law (Oxford: Hart, 2011)

MAHMOOD, S. and HALLAM, C., 'Schedule 1 and the CSA: Getting into the Top-up Zone' [2011] Family Law 266

MILLER, J., 'Children and Family Capital on Divorce' (1993) 5 Journal of Child Law 113

MILLER, G., 'Capital Provision for Children' (1997) 1 Private Client Business 51

MOSTYN, N., 'The Green Paper on Child Support' [1999] Family Law 95

PIRRIE, J., 'The Child Support, Pensions and Social Security Bill' [1999] Family Law 199

PRIEST, J. A., 'Child Support and the Non-Standard Earner—Pass the Heineken, Please! *Phillips v Peace*' [1997] Child and Family Law Quarterly 63

PRIEST, J. A., 'Capital Settlements and the Child Support Act' [1998] Family Law 115

THATCHER, M., *The Downing Street Years* (London: Harper Collins, 1995)

WALLBANK, J., 'The Campaign for Change of the Child Support Act 1991: Reconstructing the "Absent Father"'(1997) 6 Social and Legal Studies 191

WIKELEY, N., 'A Duty but Not a Right: Child Support after *R (Kehoe) v Secretary of State for Work and Pensions*' [2006] Child and Family Law Quarterly 287

WIKELEY, N., *Child Support Law and Policy* (Oxford: Hart, 2006)

WIKELEY, N., 'Child Support: Carrots and Sticks' [2008] Family Law 1102

WIKELEY, N., 'Child Support: The Brave New World' [2008] Family Law 1024

WORK AND PENSIONS SELECT COMMITTEE, *The Government's Proposed Child Maintenance Reforms* (London: TSO, 2011)

Chapter 7: A Child's Parents: Parentage, Parenthood, and Parental Responsibility

BAINHAM, A., *Children, Parents and the State* (London: Sweet & Maxwell, 1988)

BAINHAM, A., 'When is a Parent Not a Parent? Reflections on the Unmarried Father and His Child in English Law' (1989) 3 International Journal of Law, Policy and the Family 208

BAINHAM, A., 'Reforming Scottish Children Law—Sense from North of the Border' (1993) 5(1) Journal of Child Law 3

BAINHAM, A., 'Vasectomies, Lovers and Disputed Offspring: Honesty is the Best Policy (Sometimes)' (1996) 55 Cambridge Law Journal 444

BAINHAM, A., 'Parentage, Parenthood and Parental Responsibility: Subtle, Elusive Yet Important Distinctions' in A. Bainham et al, *What is a Parent? A Socio-Legal Analysis* (Hart, Oxford, 1999)

BAINHAM, A., 'Birthrights? The Rights and Obligations Associated with the Birth of a Child' in J. Spencer and A. Pedain (eds), *Freedom and Responsibility in Reproductive Choice* (Oxford: Hart, 2006)

BAINHAM, A., 'Status Anxiety? The Rush for Family Recognition' in F. Ebtehaj, B. Lindley, and M. Richards (eds), *Kinship Matters* (Oxford: Hart, 2006)

BAINHAM, A., 'Truth Will Out: Paternity in Europe' [2007] Cambridge Law Journal 278

BAINHAM, A., 'Arguments about Parentage' (2008) 67(2) Cambridge Law Journal 321

BAINHAM, A., 'What is the Point of Birth Registration?' [2008] Child and Family Law Quarterly 449

BAINHAM, A., 'Is Anything Now Left of Parental Rights?' in R. Probert, S. Gilmore, and J. Herring (eds), *Responsible Parents and Parental Responsibility* (Oxford: Hart, 2009)

BAINHAM, A., 'Welfare, Truth and Justice: The Children of Extra-Marital Liaisons' in S. Gilmore, J. Herring, and R. Probert (eds), *Landmark Cases in Family Law* (Oxford: Hart, 2011)

BAINHAM, A., 'The Illegitimacy Saga' in R. Probert and C. Barton (eds), *Fifty Years in Family Law Essays for Stephen Cretney* (Cambridge: Intersentia, 2012)

BAINHAM, A., DAY SCLATER, S., and RICHARDS, M. (eds), *What is a Parent? A Socio-Legal Analysis* (Oxford: Hart, 1999)

BARTON, C., 'Equal Responsibility for all Fathers?' (1998) 142(17) Solicitors Journal 401

BESSON, S., 'Enforcing the Child's Right to know her Origins: Contrasting Approaches under the Convention on the Rights of the Child and the European Convention on Human Rights' (2007) 21 (2) International Journal of Law, Policy and the Family 137

BLAIN, S. and WORWOOD, A., 'Alternative Families and Changing Perceptions of Parenthood' [2011] Family Law 289

BLYTH, E., 'The United Kingdom's Human Fertilisation and Embryology Act 1990 and the Welfare of the Child: A Critique' (1995) 3 International Journal of Children's Rights 417

BLYTH, E. and FARRAND, A., 'Anonymity in Donor-Assisted Conception and the UN Convention on the Rights of the Child' (2004) 12 International Journal of Children's Rights 89

BRANCHFLOWER, G., 'Parental Responsibility and Human Rights' [1999] Family Law 34

CALLUS, T., 'First 'Designer Babies, Now A La Carte Parents' [2008] Family Law 143

CHOUDHRY, S., 'Parental Responsibility and Corporal Punishment' in R. Probert, S. Gilmore, and J. Herring (eds), Responsible Parents and Parental Responsibility (Oxford: Hart, 2009)

CONWAY, H., 'Parental Responsibility and the Unmarried Father' (1996) 146 New Law Journal 782

COOK, R., DAY SCLATER, S., and KAGANAS, F., Surrogate Motherhood International Perspectives (Oxford: Hart, 2003)

CRETNEY, S., Family Law in the Twentieth Century A History (Oxford: Oxford University Press, 2003)

DEECH, R., 'The Unmarried Father and Human Rights' (1992) 4 Journal of Child Law 3

DEPARTMENT FOR WORK AND PENSIONS, Joint Birth Registration: Recording Responsibility (Cm 7293, June 2008)

DEPARTMENT OF HEALTH, Review of the Human Fertilisation and Embryology Act—A Public Consultation (London: Department of Health, 2005)

DEY, I. and WASOFF, F., 'Mixed Messages: Parental Responsibilities, Public Opinion and the Reforms of Family Law (2006) 20 International Journal of Law, Policy and the Family 225

DICKENS, B. M., 'The Modern Function and Limits of Parental Rights' (1981) 97 LQR 462

DOUGLAS, G., 'Assisted Reproduction and the Welfare of the Child' (1993) 46(2) Current Legal Problems 53

DOUGLAS, G., 'The Intention to be a Parent and the Making of Mothers' (1994) 57(4) Modern Law Review 636

DRAPER, H. and IVES, J., 'Paternity Testing: A Poor Test of Fatherhood' (2009) 31(4) Journal of Social Welfare and Family Law 407

DWYER, J. G., The Relationship Rights of Children (New York: Cambridge University Press, 2006)

EEKELAAR, J., 'Second Thoughts on Illegitimacy Reform' [1985] Family Law 261

EEKELAAR, J., 'Parental Responsibility: State of Nature or Nature of the State' [1991] Journal of Social Welfare and Family Law 37

EEKELAAR, J., 'Parenthood, Social Engineering and Rights' in D. Morgan and G. Douglas (eds), Constituting Families: A Study in Governance (Stuttgart: Steiner, 1994)

EEKELAAR, J., 'Parental Responsibility—A New Legal Status?' (1996) 112 LQR 233

EEKELAAR, J., 'Do Parents have a Duty to Consult?' (1998) 114 LQR 337

EEKELAAR, J., 'Rethinking Parental Responsibility' [2001] Family Law 426

FORTIN, J., 'Re F: "The Gooseberry Bush Approach"' (1994) 57 Modern Law Review 296

FORTIN, J., 'Children's Right to know Their Origins—Too Far, Too Fast?' [2009] Child and Family Law Quarterly 336

FREEMAN, T. and RICHARDS, M., 'DNA Testing and Kinship: Paternity, Genealogy and the Search for the "Truth" of our Genetic Origins' in F. Ebtehaj, B. Lindley, and M. Richards (eds), *Kinship Matters* (Oxford: Hart, 2006)

GILBERT, B., 'Paternity, Truth and the Interests of the Child—Some Problems of *Re H (Paternity: Blood Test)'* [1996] Child and Family Law Quarterly 361

GILMORE, S., 'Parental Responsibility and the Unmarried Father—A New Dimension to the Debate' [2003] Child and Family Law Quarterly 21

GILMORE, S., 'The Gender Recognition Act 2004' [2004] Family Law 741

GILMORE, S., 'The Relationship Rights of Children' (2008) 22(2) International Journal of Law, Policy and the Family 273

GILMORE, S., 'The Limits of Parental Responsibility' in R. Probert, S. Gilmore, and J. Herring (eds), *Responsible Parents and Parental Responsibility* (Oxford: Hart, 2009)

HERRING, J., *Family Law*, 4th edn (London: Pearson, 2009)

HILL, J., 'What Does it Mean to be a "Parent"? The Claims of Biology as the Basis for Parental Rights' (1991) 66 New York University Law Review 353

HM GOVERNMENT, *Report of the Committee of Inquiry into Human Fertilisation and Embryology* (Cmnd 9314, 1984)

HM GOVERNMENT, *Human Fertilisation and Embryology: A Framework for Legislation* (Cm 259, 1987)

HM GOVERNMENT, *Review of the Human Fertilisation and Embryology Act: Proposals for revised legislation (including establishment of the Regulatory Authority for Tissue and Embryos)* (Cm 6989, December 2006)

HM GOVERNMENT, *Joint Birth Registration: Promoting Parental Responsibility* (Cm 7160, 2007)

HM GOVERNMENT, *Joint Birth Registration: Promoting Parental Responsibility* (Cm 7160, 2008)

HOHFELD, W. N., *Fundamental Legal Conceptions As Applied in Judicial Reasoning* (New Haven, CT: Yale University Press, 1919)

HORSEY, K., 'Challenging Presumptions: Legal Parenthood and Surrogacy Arrangements' [2010] Child and Family Law Quarterly 449

HORSEY, K. and SHELDON, S., 'Still Hazy After All These Years: The Law Regulating Surrogacy' (2012) 20(1) Medical Law Review 67

HOWE, D., 'International Surrogacy—A Cautionary Tale' [2008] Family Law 60

INGLEBY, R., 'Law Commission No 118: Illegitimacy' (1984) Journal of Social Welfare Law 170

JACKSON, E., 'Conception and the Irrelevance of the Welfare Principle' (2002) 65 Modern Law Review 176

JACKSON, E., 'What is a Parent?' in A. Diduck and K. O'Donovan (eds), *Feminist Perspectives on Family Law* (Abingdon: Routledge Cavendish, 2006)

JOHNSON, M., 'A Biomedical Perspective on Parenthood' in A. Bainham et al, *What is a Parent?* (Oxford: Hart, 1999)

JONES, C., 'The Identification of "Parents" and "Siblings": New Possibilities Under the Reformed Human Fertilisation and Embryology Act' in J. Herring, J. Wallbank, and S. Choudhry (eds), *Rights, Gender and Family Law* (Abingdon: Routledge-Cavendish, 2009)

KAGANAS, F., 'Responsible or Feckless Fathers?—Re S (Parental Responsibility)' [1996] Child and Family Law Quarterly 165

LAW COMMISSION, *Illegitimacy* (Law Com WP No 74, 1979)

LAW COMMISSION, *Report on Illegitimacy* (Law Com No 118, 1982)

LAW COMMISSION, *Illegitimacy (Second Report)* (Law Com No 157, 1986)

LIND, C., 'Perceptions of Sex in the Legal Determination of Fatherhood—*X, Y and*

Z v UK' [1997] Child and Family Law Quarterly 401

LIND, C., '*In re R (Paternity of IVF Baby)—*Unmarried Paternity under the Human Fertilisation and Embryology Act 1990' [2003] Child and Family Law Quarterly 327

LORD CHANCELLOR'S DEPARTMENT, *1. Court Procedures for the Determination of Paternity, 2. The Law on Parental Responsibility for Unmarried Fathers* (March 1998)

MAIDMENT, S., 'Parental Responsibility—Is there a Duty to Consult?' [2001] Family Law 518

MASSON, J., 'The Impact of the Adoption and Children Act 2002 Part I—Parental Responsibility' [2003] Family Law 581

MASSON, J., 'Parenting by Being; Parenting by Doing—In Search of Principles for Founding Families' in J. R. Spencer and A. Du Bois-Pedain (eds), *Freedom and Responsibility in Reproductive Choice* (Oxford: Oxford University Press, 2006)

MCCALL SMITH, A., 'Is Anything Left of Parental Rights?' in E. Sutherland and A. McCall Smith (eds), *Family Rights: Family Law and Medical Advance* (Edinburgh: Edinburgh University Press, 1990)

MCCANDLESS, J. and SHELDON, S., 'The Human Fertilisation and Embryology Act (2008) and the Tenacity of the Sexual Family Form' (2010) 72(2) Modern Law Review 175

MCRAE, S., *Cohabiting Mothers, Changing Marriage and Motherhood* (London: Policy Studies Institute, 1993)

PAINTER, K., *Wife Rape, Marriage and the Law—Survey Report: Key Findings and Recommendations* (Manchester: Faculty of Economic and Social Studies, University of Manchester, 1991)

PICKFORD, R., *Fathers, Marriage and the Law* (London: Family Policy Studies Centre for the Joseph Rowntree Foundation, 1999)

PICKFORD, R., 'Unmarried Fathers and the Law' in A. Bainham, S. Day Sclater, and M. Richards (eds), *What is a Parent? A Socio-Legal Analysis* (Oxford: Hart, 1999)

PINTENS, W. and SCHERPE, J. M., 'The *Marckx* Case: A "Whole Code of Family Law"?' in S. Gilmore, J. Herring, and R. Probert (eds), *Landmark Cases in Family Law* (Oxford: Hart, 2011)

PROBERT, R., 'Families, Assisted Reproduction and the Law' [2004] Child and Family Law Quarterly 273

PROBERT, R., 'Parental Responsibility and Children's Partnership Choices' in R. Probert, S. Gilmore, and J. Herring (eds), *Responsible Parents and Parental Responsibility* (Oxford: Hart, 2009)

REECE, H., 'The Degradation of Parental Responsibility' in R. Probert, S. Gilmore, and J. Herring (eds), *Responsible Parents and Parental Responsibility* (Oxford: Hart, 2009)

ROTHSTEIN, M. A., MURRAY, T. H., KAEBNICK, G. E., and ANDERLIK MAJUNDER, M. (eds), *Genetic Ties and the Family. The Impact of Paternity Testing on Parents and Children* (Baltimore, MD: Johns Hopkins University Press, 2005)

SAWYER, C., 'Review Article: A Brave New World Order' [2007] Child and Family Law Quarterly 518

SCHERPE, J. M., 'Establishing and Ending Parental Responsibility: A Comparative View' in R. Probert, S. Gilmore, and J. Herring (eds), *Responsible Parents and Parental Responsibility* (Oxford: Hart, 2009)

SCOTTISH LAW COMMISSION, *Report on Family Law* (Scot Law Com No 135, 1992)

SHAPIRO, J., 'Changing Ways, New Technologies and the Devaluation of the Genetic Connection to Children' in M. Maclean (ed) *Family Law and Family Values* (Oxford: Hart, 2005)

SHARP, D., 'Parental Responsibility—Where Next?' [2001] Family Law 606

SHELDON, S., 'Unmarried Fathers and Parental Responsibility: A Case for Reform?' (2001) 9 Feminist Legal Studies 93

SHELDON, S., 'Fragmenting Fatherhood: The Regulation of Reproductive Technologies' (2005) 68(4) Modern Law Review 523

SHELDON, S., 'From "Absent Objects of Blame" to "Fathers Who Want to Take Responsibility": Reforming Birth Registration Law' (2009) 31(4) Journal of Social Welfare and Family Law 373

SHULTZ, M., 'Reproductive Technology and Intent-Based Parenthood: An Opportunity for Gender Neutrality' (1990) Wisconsin Law Review 297

SMART, C. and SEVENHUIJSEN, S. (eds), *Child Custody and the Politics of Gender* (London: Routledge, 1989)

SMITH, L., 'Is Three a Crowd? Lesbian Mothers' Perspectives on Parental Status in Law' [2006] Child and Family Law Quarterly 231

SMITH, L., 'Clashing Symbols? Reconciling Support for Fathers and Fatherless Families After the Human Fertilisation and Embryology Act 2008' [2010] Child and Family Law Quarterly 46

STEINER, E., 'Desperately Seeking Mother—Anonymous Births in the European Court of Human Rights' (2003) 15(4) *Child and Family Law Quarterly* 425

TAYLOR, R., 'Parental Responsibility and Religion' in R. Probert, S. Gilmore, and J. Herring (eds), *Responsible Parents and Parental Responsibility* (Oxford: Hart, 2009)

THEIS, L., 'A Trek Through the Thorn Forest' [2009] Family Law 239

TOWNSEND, P. and BAKER, A., 'Unmarried Fathers—Are We Ending Discrimination at Last?' (1998) 162(13) Justice of the Peace 236

WALLBANK, J., 'Clause 106 of the Adoption and Children Bill: Legislation for the "Good" Father?' (2002) 22(2) Legal Studies 276

WALLBANK, J., 'Too Many Mothers? Surrogacy, Kinship and the Welfare of the Child' [2002] Medical Law Review 271

WALLBANK, J., 'The Role of Rights and Utility in Instituting a Child's Right to Know her Genetic History' (2004) 13 Social and Legal Studies 245

WIKELEY, N., 'Financial Support for Children after Parental Separation: Parental Responsibility and Responsible Parenting' in R. Probert, S. Gilmore, and J. Herring (eds), *Responsible Parents and Parental Responsibilty* (Oxford: Hart, 2009)

Chapter 8: Children's Rights

ADAMS, P. et al, *Children's Rights* (London: Longman, 1972)

ALDERSON, P., *Young Children's Rights*, 2nd edn (London: Jessica Kingsley, 2008)

ALSTON, P., PARKER, S., and SEYMOUR, J. (eds), *Children, Rights and the Law* (Oxford: Clarendon Press, 1992)

ARCHARD, D., *Children Rights and Childhood* (London: Routledge, 2004)

ARCHARD, D. and SKIVENES, M., 'Balancing a Child's Best Interests and a Child's Views' (2009) 17 International Journal of Children's Rights 1

ARIÈS, P., *Centuries of Childhood: A Social History of Family Life* (London: Jonathan Cape, 1962)

AUSTIN, G., 'Righting a Child's Right to Refuse Medical Treatment, Section 11 of the New Zealand Bill of Rights Act and the *Gillick* Competent Child' (1992) 7(4) Otago Law Review 578

BAINHAM, A., 'The Judge and the Competent Minor' (1992) 108 LQR 194

BAINHAM, A., 'The Balance of Power in Family Decisions' (1986) 45(2) Cambridge Law Journal 262

BAINHAM, A., *Children, Parents and the State* (London: Sweet & Maxwell, 1988)

BAINHAM, A., *Children The Modern Law*, 3rd edn (Bristol: Family Law, 2005)

BATES, P., 'Children in Secure Psychiatric Units: Re K, W and H—"Out of Sight, Out of Mind"?' (1994) 6(3) Journal of Child Law 131

BELL, V., 'Governing Childhood: Neo-Liberalism and the Law' (1993) 22(3) Economy and Society 390

BRAZIER, M., *Medicine, Patients and the Law* (London: Penguin, 1992)

BRAZIER, M. and BRIDGE, C., 'Coercion or Caring: Analyzing Adolescent Autonomy' (1996) 16(1) Legal Studies 84

BRIDGE, C., 'Adolescents and Mental Disorder: Who Consents to Treatment?' (1997) 3 Medical Law International 51

BRIDGE, C., 'Religious Beliefs and Teenage Refusal of Medical Treatment' (1999) 62 Modern Law Review 585

BRIDGEMAN, J., 'Old Enough to Know Best?' (1993) 13 Legal Studies 69

BRIDGEMAN, J., 'Case Comment: Young People and Sexual Health: Whose Rights? Whose Responsibilities?' [2006] Medical Law Review 418

CAMPBELL, T. D, 'The Rights of the Minor: As Person, As Child, As Juvenile, As Future Adult' in P. Alston, S. Parker, and J. Seymour (eds), *Children, Rights and the Law* (Oxford, Clarendon Press, 1992)

CAVE, E. and WALLBANK, J., 'Minors' Capacity to Refuse Treatment: A Reply to Gilmore and Herring' [2012] Medical Law Review 1

CRETNEY, S. M., 'Gillick and the Concept of Legal Capacity' (1989) 105 LQR 356

CRETNEY, S. and MASSON, J., *Principles of Family Law* (London: Sweet & Maxwell, 1997)

CHOUDHRY, S. and HERRING, J., *European Human Rights and Family Law* (Oxford: Hart, 2010)

DE CRUZ, P., 'Adolescent Autonomy, Detention for Medical Treatment and *Re C*' (1999) 62 Modern Law Review 595

DE CRUZ, S., 'Parents, Doctors and Children: The *Gillick* Case and Beyond' [1987] Journal of Social Welfare and Family Law 93

DEVEREUX, J., 'The Capacity of a Child in Australia to Consent to Medical Treatment—*Gillick* Revisited?' (1991) 11(2) Oxford Journal of Legal Studies 283

DICKENSON, D. and JONES, D., 'True Wishes: The Philosophy and Developmental Psychology of Children's Informed Consent' (1995) 2(4) Philosophy, Psychiatry and Psychology 287

DOUGLAS, G., 'The Retreat from *Gillick*' (1992) 55 Modern Law Review 569

DWYER, J. G., 'The Conceptual Possibility of Children Having Rights', appendix in *The Relationship Rights of Children* (Cambridge: Cambridge University Press, 2006)

EDWARDS, L., 'The Right to Consent and the Right to Refuse; More Problems with Minors and Medical Consent' [1993] Juridical Review 52

EEKELAAR, J., '*Gillick*: Further Limits on Parents' Rights to Punish' (1986) 28 Childright 9

EEKELAAR, J., 'The Eclipse of Parental Rights' (1986) 102 LQR 4

EEKELAAR, J., 'The Emergence of Children's Rights' (1986) 6 Oxford Journal of Legal Studies 161

EEKELAAR, J., 'The Importance of Thinking That Children Have Rights' in P. Alston, S. Parker, and J. Seymour (eds), *Children, Rights and the Law* (Oxford: Clarendon Press, 1992)

EEKELAAR, J., 'White Coats or Flak Jackets? Doctors, Children and the Courts—Again' (1993) 109 LQR 182

EEKELAAR, J., 'The Interests of the Child and the Child's Wishes: The Role of Dynamic Self-Determinism' (1994) 8 International Journal of Law and the Family 42

FARSON, R., *Birthrights* (London: Collier Macmillan, 1974)

FEDERLE, K. H., 'On the Road to Reconceiving Rights for Children: A Post-Feminist Analysis of the Capacity Principle' (1993) De Paul Law Review 983

FEDERLE, K. H., 'Rights Flow Downhill' (1994) 2 International Journal of Children's Rights 343

FEDERLE, K. H., 'Looking Ahead: An Empowerment Perspective on the Rights of Children' (1995) 68(4) Temple Law Review 1585

FENNELL, P., 'Informal Compulsion: The Psychiatric Treatment of Juveniles under Common Law' [1992] Journal of Social Welfare and Family Law 311

FORTIN, J., 'The HRA's Impact on Litigation Involving Children and their Families' (1999) 11 Child and Family Law Quarterly 237

FORTIN, J., 'Children's Rights and the Use of Physical Force' [2001] Child and Family Law Quarterly 243

FORTIN, J., 'Children's Rights: Are the Courts Now Taking Them More Seriously?' (2004) 15 Kings College Law Journal 253

FORTIN, J., 'Accommodating Children's Rights in a Post Human Rights Act Era' (2006) 69 Modern Law Review 299

FORTIN, J., 'Children's Representation Through the Looking Glass' [2007] Family Law 500

FORTIN, J., *Children's Rights and the Developing* Law, 3rd edn (Cambridge: Cambridge University Press, 2009)

FORTIN, J., 'A Decade of the HRA and its Impact on Children's Rights' [2011] Family Law 176

FORTIN, J., 'The *Gillick* Decision—Not Just A High-Water Mark' in S. Gilmore, J. Herring, and R. Probert (eds), *Landmark Cases in Family Law* (Oxford: Hart, 2011)

FOX HARDING, L., *Perspectives in Child Care Policy* (London: Longman, 1997)

FRANKLIN, B. (ed), *The New Handbook of Children's Rights Comparative Policy and Practice* (Abingdon: Routledge, 2002)

FREEMAN, M. D. A., *The Rights and the Wrongs of Children* (London: Francis Pinter, 1983)

FREEMAN, M. D. A., 'Taking Children's Rights More Seriously' in P. Alston, S. Parker, and J. Seymour (eds), *Children, Rights and the Law* (Oxford: Clarendon Press, 1992)

FREEMAN, M. D. A., 'Laws Conventions and Rights' (1993) 7(1) Children and Society 37

FREEMAN, M. D. A., *The Moral Status of Children: Essays on the Rights of the Child* (The Hague: Martinus Nijhoff, 1997)

GILMORE, S., 'The Limits of Parental Responsibility' in R. Probert, S. Gilmore, and J. Herring (eds), *Responsible Parents and Parental Responsibility* (Oxford: Hart, 2009)

GILMORE, S. and HERRING, J., 'Children's Refusal of Medical Treatment: Could *Re W* be Distinguished?' [2011] Family Law 715

GILMORE, S. and HERRING, J., ' "No" is the Hardest Word: Consent and Children's Autonomy' [2011] Child and Family Law Quarterly 3

GILMORE, S. and HERRING, J., 'Children's Refusal of Treatment: The Debate Continues' [2012] Fam Law 973

GILMORE, S., HERRING, J., and PROBERT, R., 'Introduction: Parental Responsibility—Law, Issues and Themes' in R. Probert, S. Gilmore and J. Herring (eds), *Responsible Parents and Parental Responsibility* (Oxford: Hart, 2009)

GRUBB, A., 'Contraceptive Advice and Medical Treatment for Children' [1986] Cambridge Law Journal 3

GRUBB, A., 'Treatment Decisions: Keeping it in the Family' in A. Grubb (ed), *Choices and Decisions in Health Care* (Chichester: Wiley, 1993)

HAMILTON, C., 'Editorial' (1993) 5(1) Journal of Child Law 1

HARRIS-SHORT, S., 'Family Law and the Human Rights Act 1998: Judicial Restraint or Revolution' (2005) 17(3) Child and Family Law Quarterly 329

HERRING, J., *Family Law*, 5th edn (London: Longman, 2011)

HOLT, J., *Escape from Childhood* (Harmondsworth: Penguin, 1975)

HOUGHTON-JAMES, H., 'The Child's Right to Die' [1992] Family Law 550

HUGHES, J., 'Thinking about Children' in G. Scarre (ed), *Children, Parents and*

Politics (New York: Cambridge University Press, 1989)

JAMES, A. and PROUT, A. (eds), *Constructing and Reconstructing Childhood* (London: Falmer Press, 1997)

JAMES, A., JENKS, C., and PROUT, A., *Theorizing Childhood* (Cambridge: Polity Press, 1998)

JENKS, C., *Childhood* (London: Routledge, 1996)

JONES, M., 'Consent to Medical Treatment by Minors after *Gillick*' (1986) 2 Professional Negligence 41

KENNEDY, I., 'The Doctor, the Pill and the 15-Year-Old Girl' in I. Kennedy, *Treat me Right, Essays in Medical Law and Ethics* (Oxford: Oxford University Press, 1988)

KILKELLY, U., *The Child and the European Convention on Human Rights* (Dartmouth: Ashgate, 1999)

KRAMER, M. H., SIMMONDS, N. E., and STEINER, H., *A Debate Over Rights: Philosophical Enquiries* (Oxford: Oxford University Press, 1998)

LEE, S., 'Towards a Jurisprudence of Consent' in J. Eekelaar and S. Ball (eds), *Oxford Essays in Jurisprudence* (Oxford: Oxford University Press, 1987)

LIM, H. and ROCHE, J., 'Feminism and Children's Rights' in J. Bridgeman and D. Monk (eds), *Feminist Perspectives on child law* (London: Cavendish, 2000)

LINDLEY, R., 'Teenagers and Other Children' in G. Scarre (ed), *Children, Parents and Politics* (New York: Cambridge University Press, 1989)

LOWE, N. and JUSS, S., 'Medical Treatment—Pragmatism and the Search for Principle' (1993) 56 Modern Law Review 865

LYON, C., 'What's Happened to the Child's "Right" to Refuse?—*South Glamorgan County Council v. W and B*' (1994) 6(2) Journal of Child Law 84

LYON, C. and DE CRUZ, P., *Child Abuse*, 2nd edn (Bristol: Family Law, 1993)

MACCORMICK, N., 'Children's Rights: A Test Case for Theories of Rights' in N. MacCormick, *Legal Right and Social Democracy* (Oxford: Clarendon Press, 1982)

MACDONALD, A., *The Rights of the Child Law and Practice* (Bristol: Family Law, 2011)

MASON, J. K., 'Master of the Balancers; Non-Voluntary Therapy under the Mantle of Lord Donaldson' [1993] Juridical Review 115

MASSON, J., 'Adolescent Crisis and Parental Power' [1991] Family Law 528

MASSON, J., '*Re W*: Appealing from the Golden Cage' (1993) 5(1) Journal of Child Law 37

MASSON, J., 'Protecting Children or Protecting Human Rights' (2010 unpublished paper presented at Staffordshire University)

MINOW, M., 'Interpreting Rights: An Essay for Robert Cover' (1987) Yale Law Journal 1860

MONTGOMERY, J., 'Children as Property?' (1988) 51 Modern Law Review 323

MONTGOMERY, J., 'Parents and Children in Dispute: Who Has the Final Word?' (1992) 4 Journal of Child Law 85

MORROW, V., 'Responsible Children and Children's Responsibilities? Sibling Caretaking and Babysitting by School-Age Children' in J. Bridgeman, H. Keating, and C. Lind (eds), *Responsibility, Law and the Family* (Aldershot: Ashgate, 2008)

MULHOLLAND, M., '*Re W (A Minor)*: Autonomy, Consent and the Anorexic Teenager' (1993) 9(1) Professional Negligence 21

MURPHY, J., 'Circumscribing the Autonomy of "*Gillick* Competent" Children' (1992) 43(1) Northern Ireland Legal Quarterly 60

MURPHY, J., 'W(h)ither Adolescent Autonomy?' [1992] Journal of Social Welfare and Family Law 529

O'NEILL, O., 'Children's Rights and Children's Lives' (1988) 98 Ethics 445

PARKER, S. and DEWAR, J. 'Case Commentary on *Re R*' [1992] Journal of Social Welfare and Family Law 143

PARKINSON, P., 'The *Gillick* Case—Just What Has it Decided?' [1986] Family Law 11

PEARCE, J., 'Consent to Treatment During Childhood, the Assessment of Competence and Avoidance of Conflict' (1994) 165 British Journal of Psychiatry 713

PEIRIS, G. L., 'The *Gillick* Case: Parental Authority, Teenage Independence and Public Policy' [1987] Current Legal Problems 93

PILCHER, J., 'Contrary to *Gillick*: British Children and Sexual Rights since 1985' (1997) 5 International Journal of Children's Rights 299

RAWLS, J., *A Theory of Justice* (Oxford: Oxford University Press, 1973)

ROCHE, J., 'Children's Rights: In the Name of the Child' [1995] Journal of Social Welfare and Family Law 281

SAMUELS, A., 'Can a Minor (Under 16) Consent to a Medical Operation?' [1984] Family Law 30

SCARRE, G., 'Children and Paternalism' (1980) 55 Philosophy 117

SCHRAG, F., 'The Child in the Moral Order' (1977) 52 Philosophy 167

SKEGG, P. D. G., 'Consent to Medical Procedures on Minors' (1973) 36 Modern Law Review 370

SMITH, C., 'Children's Rights: Judicial Ambivalence and Social Resistance' (1997) 11 International Journal of Law, Policy and the Family 103

TAYLOR, R., 'Reversing the Retreat from *Gillick*? *R (Axon) v Secretary of State for Health*' [2007] Child and Family Law Quarterly 81

TEFF, H., *Reasonable Care, Legal Perspectives on the Doctor/Patient Relationship* (Oxford: Clarendon Press, 1994)

THORNTON, R., 'Multiple Keyholders—Wardship and Consent to Medical Treatment' [1992] Cambridge Law Journal 34

THORNTON, R., 'Minors and Medical Treatment—Who Decides?' [1993] Cambridge Law Journal 34

URWIN, J., '*Re R*: The Resurrection of Parental Powers?' (1992) 8 Professional Negligence 69

WADE, A., 'Being Responsible: "Good" Parents and Children's Autonomy' in J. Bridgeman, H. Keating, and C. Lind (eds), *Responsibility, Law and the Family* (Aldershot: Ashgate, 2008)

WALDRON, J. (ed), *Theories of Rights* (Oxford: Oxford University Press, 1984)

WILLIAMS, G., 'The *Gillick* Saga' [1985] New Law Journal 1156

Chapter 9: Private Law Disputes and Issues in Children's Cases

AMATO, P. R. and GILBRETH, J. G., 'Nonresident Fathers and Children's Well-Being: A Meta- Analysis' (1999) 61 Journal of Marriage and the Family 557

AUSTIN, W., 'Relocation, Research, and Forensic Evaluation, Part I: Effects of Residential Mobility on Children of Divorce' (2008) 46 Family Court Review 137

BAILEY-HARRIS, R., 'Contact—Challenging Conventional Wisdom?' (2001) 13(4) Child and Family Law Quarterly 361

BAILEY-HARRIS, R., BARRON, J., and PEARCE, J., 'From Utility to Rights? The Presumption of Contact in Practice' (1999) 13 International Journal of Law, Policy and the Family 111

BAILEY-HARRIS, R., BARRON, J., PEARCE, J., and DAVIS, G., *Monitoring Private Law Applications Under the Children Act 1989* (London: Nuffield Foundation, 1998)

BAINHAM, A., 'The Privatisation of the Public Interest in Children' (1990) 53 Modern Law Review 206

BAINHAM, A., 'Changing Families and
Changing Concepts' (1998) Child and
Family Law Quarterly 1

BAINHAM, A., 'Taking Children Abroad:
Human Rights, Welfare and the Courts'
[2001] Cambridge Law Journal 489

BAINHAM, A., 'Contact as a Right and
Obligation' in A. Bainham, B. Lindley,
M. Richards, and L. Trinder (eds), *Children
and Their Families: Contact, Rights and
Welfare* (Oxford: Hart, 2003)

BARTON, C., '*Troxel et vir v Granville*—
Grandparent Visitation Rights in the
United States Supreme Court' [2001] Child
and Family Law Quarterly 101

BLACKWELL, A. and DAWE, F., 'Non-
Resident Parent Contact' (London:
Department for Constitutional Affairs, 2003)

BOND, A. R., 'Reconstructing Families—
Changing Children's Surnames' [1998]
Child and Family Law Quarterly 17

BONNER, D., FENWICK, H., and
HARRIS-SHORT, S., 'Judicial Approaches
to the Human Rights Act' (2003)
52(3) International Comparative Law
Quarterly 549

BOWKER, L., ARBITELL, M., and
MCFERRON, J., 'On the Relationship
Between Wife Beating and Child Abuse'
in K. Yllo and M Bograd (eds), *Feminist
Perspectives on Wife Abuse* (London: Sage,
1989)

BRUCH, C., 'Parental Alienation Syndrome
and Alienated Children—Getting It Wrong
in Child Custody Cases' (2002) 14(4) Child
and Family Law Quarterly 381

BRUCH, C., 'Sound Research or Wishful
Thinking in Child Custody Case? Lessons
from Relocation Law' (2006) 40 Family
Law Quarterly 281

BRUCH, C. and BOWERMASTER, J., 'The
Relocation of Children and Custodial
Parents: Public Policy, Past and Present'
(1995) 30 Family Law Quarterly 245

BUCHANAN, C. M., MACCOBY, E. E., and
DORNBUSCH, S. M., 'Caught between
Parents: Adolescents' Experience in

Divorced Homes' (1991) 62(5) Child
Development 1008

BUCHANAN, C. M., MACCOBY, E. E., and
DORNBUSCH, S. M., *Adolescents After
Divorce* (Cambridge, MA: Harvard
University Press, 1996)

BUCHANAN, A., HUNT, J., BRETHERTON,
H., and BREAM, V., *Families in Conflict:
Perspectives of Children and Parents on
the Family Court Welfare Service* (Bristol:
Policy Press, 2001)

CHOUDHRY, S. and FENWICK, H., 'Taking
the Rights of Parents and Children
Seriously: Confronting the Welfare
Principle under the Human Rights Act'
(2005) 25(3) Oxford Journal of Legal
Studies 453

COLLIER, R., 'Fathers 4 Justice, Law and
the New Politics of Fatherhood' (2005) 17
Child and Family Law Quarterly 511

COLLIER, R. and SHELDON, S. (eds),
*Fathers' Rights Activism and Law Reform
in Comparative Perspective* (Oxford: Hart,
2006)

CRAIG, J., 'Everybody's Business:
Applications for Contact Orders by
Consent' [2007] Family Law 26

DENCH, G. and OGG, J., *Grandparenting in
Britain: A Baseline Study* (London: Institute
of Community Studies, 2002)

DOUGLAS, G., 'In Whose Best Interests?'
(1994) LQR 379

DOUGLAS, G., 'Case Commentary—*Re J
(Leave to Issue Application for Residence
Order)*—Recognising Grandparents'
Concern or Controlling Their
Interference?' [2003] Child and Family
Law Quarterly 103

DOUGLAS, G. and FERGUSON, N., 'The Role
of Grandparents in Divorced Families'
(2003) 17 International Journal of Law,
Policy and the Family 41

DOUGLAS, G. and LOWE, N. V.,
'Grandparents and the Legal Process'
(1990) Journal of Social Welfare Law 89

DUNN, J., 'Annotation: Children's
Relationships with their Nonresident

Fathers' (2004) 45(4) Journal of Child Psychology and Psychiatry 659

EEKELAAR, J., 'Beyond the Welfare Principle' [2002] Child and Family Law Quarterly 237

ELSTER, J., 'Solomonic Judgments: Against the Best Interest of the Child' (1987) 54(1) University of Chicago Law Review 1

FEHLBERG, B., SMYTH, B., MACLEAN, M., and ROBERTS, C., 'Legislating for Shared Time Parenting After Separation: A Research Review' (2011) 25(3) International Journal of Law, Policy and the Family 318

FINEMAN, M., 'Domestic Violence, Custody and Visitation' (2002) 36 Family Law Quarterly 211

FREEMAN, M., *Relocation: The Reunite Research* (London: Reunite, 2009)

GEEKIE, C., 'Relocation and Shared Residence: One Route or Two?' [2008] Family Law 446

GEORGE, R., 'The Shifting Law: Relocation Disputes in New Zealand and England' (2009) 12 Otago Law Review 107

GEORGE, R., 'Reassessing Relocation: A Comparative Analysis of Legal Approaches to Disputes Over Family Migration After Parental Separation in England and New Zealand', DPhil Thesis, University of Oxford (2010)

GEORGE, R., 'Practitioners' Views on Children's Welfare in Relocation Disputes: Comparing Approaches in England and New Zealand' [2011] Child and Family Law Quarterly 178

GEORGE, R., 'Reviewing Relocation? *Re W (Relocation: Removal Outside Jurisdiction)* [2011] EWCA Civ 345 and *K v K (Relocation: Shared Care Arrangement)* [2011] EWCA Civ 793' [2012] Child and Family Law Quarterly 110

GEORGE, R., 'The International Relocation Debate' [2012] Journal of Social Welfare and Family Law 141

GEORGE, R. and HARRIS, P., 'Parental Responsibility and Shared Residence Orders: Parliamentary Intentions and Judicial Interpretations' (2010) 22 Child and Family Law Quarterly 151

GILMORE, S., 'The Nature, Scope and Use of the Specific Issue Order' [2004] Child and Family Law Quarterly 367

GILMORE, S., 'Contact/Shared Residence and Child Well-Being—Research Evidence and its Implications for Legal Decision Making' (2006) 20 International Journal of Law, Policy and the Family 344

GILMORE, S., 'Court Decision-Making in Shared Residence Order Cases: A Critical Examination' (2006) 18(4) Child and Family Law Quarterly 478

GILMORE, S., 'Disputing Contact: Challenging Some Assumptions' [2008] Child and Family Law Quarterly 285

GILMORE, S., 'Shared Parenting: The Law and the Evidence (Part 2)' (2010) 20 Seen and Heard 21

GILMORE, S., 'Shared Residence: A Summary of the Courts' Guidance' [2010] Family Law 285

GILMORE, S., 'The *Payne* Saga: Precedent and Family Law Cases' [2011] Family Law 970

GOSDEN, N., 'Children's Surnames—How Satisfactory is the Current Law?' [2003] Family Law 186

GRAND, A., 'In Practice: Disputes between Parents: Time for a New Order?' [2011] Family Law 74

HALL, J. C., 'The Waning of Parental Rights' (1972) 31 Cambridge Law 248

HAROLD, G. T. and MURCH, M., 'Inter-Parental Conflict and Children's Adaptation to Separation and Divorce: Theory, Research and Implications for Family Law, Practice and Policy' [2005] Child and Family Law Quarterly 185

HARRIS-SHORT, S., 'Case Commentary: Putting the Child at the Heart of Adoption?—*Re B (Adoption: Natural Parent)*' (2002) 14 (3) Child and Family Law Quarterly 325

HARRIS-SHORT, S., 'Resisting the March Towards 50/50 Shared Residence. Rights,

Welfare and Equality in Post-Separation Families' (2010) 32 Journal of Social Welfare and Family Law 257

HARRIS-SHORT, S., 'Building a House Upon Sand: Post-Separation Parenting, Shared Residence and Equality—Lessons from Sweden' [2011] Child and Family Law Quarterly 344

HAYES, M., '*Dawson v Wearmouth*: What's in a Name? A Child by Any Other Name is Surely Just as Sweet?' [1999] Child and Family Law Quarterly 423

HAYES, M., 'Relocation Cases: Is the Court of Appeal Applying the Correct Principles?' [2006] Child and Family Law Quarterly 351

HENAGHAN, M., 'Relocation Cases—The Rhetoric and the Reality of a Child's Best Interests—A View from the Bottom of the World' [2011] Child and Family Law Quarterly 226

HERRING, J., 'The Human Rights Act and the Welfare Principle in Family Law: Conflicting or Complementary?' (1999) 11 Child and Family Law Quarterly 223

HERRING, J., 'Connecting Contact: Contact in a Private Law Context' in A. Bainham, B. Lindley, M. Richards, and L. Trinder (eds), *Children and Their Families: Contact, Rights and Welfare* (Oxford: Hart, 2003)

HERRING, J., 'Farewell Welfare?' (2005) 27(2) Journal of Social Welfare and Family Law 159

HERRING, J., 'The Shaming of Naming: Parental Rights and Responsibilities in the Naming of Children' in R. Probert, S. Gilmore, and J. Herring (eds), *Responsible Parents and Parental Responsibility* (Oxford: Hart, 2009)

HERRING, J. and TAYLOR, R., 'Relocating Relocation' [2006] Child and Family Law Quarterly 517

HESTER, M., 'One Step Forward and Three Steps Back? Children, Abuse and Parental Contact in Denmark' (2002) Child and Family Law Quarterly 267

HESTER, M. and RADFORD, L., *Domestic Violence and Child Contact Arrangements*

in England and Denmark (Bristol: Policy Press, 1996)

HESTER, M., PEARSON, C., and HARWIN, N., *Making an Impact: Children and Domestic Violence* (London: Jessica Kingsley, 2000)

HM GOVERNMENT, *Parental Separation: Children's Needs and Parents' Responsibilities* (Cm 6273, 2004)

HORSFALL, B. and KASPIEW, R., 'Relocation in Separated and Non-Separated Families: Equivocal Evidence from the Social Science Literature' (2010) 24 Australian Journal of Family Law 34

HUMPHREYS, C. and HARRISON, C., 'Squaring the Circle: Contact and Domestic Violence' [2003] Family Law 419

HUMPHREYS, C. and THIARA, R. K., 'Neither Justice Nor Protection: Women's Experiences of Post-Separation Violence' (2003) 25(3) Journal of Social Welfare and Family Law 195

HUNT, J., *Researching Contact* (London: National Council for One Parent Families, 2003)

HUNT, J. with ROBERTS, C., *Child Contact with Non-Resident Parents*, Family Policy Briefing 3 (Oxford: University of Oxford, 2004)

JIVRAJ, S. and HERMAN, D., 'It is Difficult for a White Judge to Understand: Orientalism, Racialisation, and Christianity in English Child Welfare Cases' [2009] Child and Family Law Quarterly 283

JOHNSON, S., 'Shared Residence Orders: For and Against' [2009] Family Law 131

JOLLY, S., 'Implacable Hostility, Contact, and the Limits of Law' (1995) 7 Child and Family Law Quarterly 228

JUDD, F. and GEORGE, R., 'International Relocation: Do We Stand Alone?' [2010] Family Law 63

KAGANAS, F., '*Re L (Contact: Domestic Violence); Re V (Contact: Domestic Violence); Re M (Contact: Domestic Violence); Re H (Contact: Domestic Violence)*: Contact and

Domestic Violence' (2000) 12 Child and Family Law Quarterly 311

KAGANAS, F., 'Regulating Emotion: Judging Contact Disputes' [2011] Child and Family Law Quarterly 63

KAGANAS, F. and DAY SCLATER, S., 'Contact and Domestic Violence—The Winds of Change' [2000] Family Law 630

KAGANAS, F. and DIDUCK, A., 'Incomplete Citizens: Changing Images of Post-Separation Children' (2004) 67 Modern Law Review 959

KAGANAS, F. and PIPER, C., 'Grandparents and Contact: "*Rights v Welfare*" Revisited' (2001) 15 International Journal of Law, Policy and the Family 250

KAYE, M., 'Domestic Violence, Residence and Contact' (1996) 8 Child and Family Law Quarterly 285

KELLY, J. and LAMB, M., 'Developmental Issues in Relocation Cases Involving Young Children: When, Whether, and How?' (2003) 17 Journal of Family Psychology 193

LAW COMMISSION, *Review of Child Law: Guardianship and Custody* (Law Com No 172, 1988)

LITTLE, R., 'In Practice: Family Assistance Orders: Rising to the Challenge' [2009] Family Law 435

LORD CHANCELLOR'S DEPARTMENT, *Making Contact Work: A Consultation Paper from the Children Act Sub-Committee of the Lord Chancellor's Advisory Board on Family Law (CASC) on the Facilitation and Enforcement of Contact* (2001)

LORD CHANCELLOR'S DEPARTMENT, Advisory Board on Family Law Children Act Sub-Committee, *A Report to the Lord Chancellor on the Question of Parental Contact in Cases Where There Is Domestic Violence* (2000)

LOWE, N., '*J v C*: Placing the Child's Welfare Centre Stage' in S. Gilmore, J. Herring, and R. Probert (eds), *Landmark Cases in Family Law* (Oxford: Hart, 2011)

LOWE, N. and White, R., *Wards of Court*, 2nd edn (London: Barry Rose, 1986)

LOWE, N. et al, *International Movement of Children* (Bristol: Jordan Publishing, 2004)

MASSON, J. and HUMPHREYS, C., 'Facilitating and Enforcing Contact: the Bill and the Ten Per Cent' (2005) 35 Family Law 548

McGEE, C., *Childhood Experiences of Domestic Violence* (London: Jessica Kingsley, 2000)

McINTOSH, J. and CHISHOLM, R., 'Cautionary Notes on the Shared Care of Children in Conflicted Parental Separation' (2008) 14(1) Journal of Family Studies 37

McINTOSH, J. and CHISHOLM, R., 'Shared Care and Children's Best Interests in Conflicted Separation—A Cautionary Tale from Current Research' (2008) 20(1) Australian Family Lawyer 1

McINTOSH, J., SMYTH, B., KELAHER, M., WELLS, Y., and LONG, C., *Post-Separation Parenting Arrangements and Developmental Outcomes for Infants and Children* (Victoria: Family Transitions for the Australian Government Attorney-General's Department, 2010)

MILLS, O., 'Effects of Domestic Violence on Children' [2008] Family Law 165

MINISTRY OF JUSTICE, *Family Justice Review Final Report* (November 2011)

MINISTRY OF JUSTICE and DEPARTMENT FOR EDUCATION, *The Government Response to the Family Justice Review: A System with Children and Families at its Heart* (Cm 8273, February 2012)

MNOOKIN, R. H., 'Child-Custody Adjudication: Judicial Functions in the Face of Indeterminacy' (1975) 39(3) Law and Contemporary Problems 226

NEWNHAM, A., 'Shared Residence: Lessons from Sweden' [2011] Child and Family Law Quarterly 251

PARKER, S., 'The Best Interests of the Child—Principles and Problems' in P. Alston, *The Best Interests of the Child: Reconciling Culture and Human Rights* (Oxford: Clarendon Press, 1994)

PARKINSON, P., CASHMORE, J., and SINGLE, J., 'The Need for Reality Testing in Relocation Cases' (2010) 44(1) Family Law Quarterly 1

PARRY, M., 'The Children Act 1989: Local Authorities, Wardship and the Revival of the Inherent Jurisdiction' [1992] Journal of Social Welfare and Family Law 212

PERRY, A., 'Case Commentary: Leave to Remove Children from the Jurisdiction: *Payne v Payne*' [2001] Child and Family Law Quarterly 455

PERRY, A. and RAINEY, B., 'Supervised, Supported and Indirect Contact Orders: Research Findings' (2007) 21 International Journal of Law, Policy and the Family 21

PRESSDEE, P., 'Relocation, Relocation, Relocation: Rigorous Scrutiny Revisited' [2008] Family Law 220

PRIEST, J. and WHYBROW, J., *Custody Law in Practice in the Divorce and Domestic Courts*, supplement to Law Com WP No 96 (1986)

PRYOR, J. and RODGERS, B., *Children in Changing Families: Life After Parental Separation* (Oxford: Blackwell, 2001)

REECE, H., 'Subverting the Stigmatization Argument' (1996) 23(4) Journal of Law and Society 484

REECE, H., 'The Paramountcy Principle: Consensus or Construct?' (1996) 49 Current Legal Problems 267

RHOADES, H., 'The Rise and Rise of Shared Parenting Laws: A Critical Reflection' (2002) 19 Canadian Journal of Family Law 75

RHOADES, H. and BOYD, S. B., 'Reforming Custody Laws: A Comparative Study' (2004) 18(2) International Journal of Law, Policy and the Family 119

RICHARDS, A., *Second Time Around—A Survey of Grandparents Raising their Grandchildren* (London: Family Rights Group, 2001)

ROBERTS, M., 'Ousting Abusers—Children Act 1989 or Inherent Jurisdiction? *Re H*

(Prohibited Steps Orders)' (1995) 7 Child and Family Law Quarterly 243

SCHNEIDER, C., 'Discretion and Rules: A Lawyer's View' in K. Hawkins (ed), *The Uses of Discretion* (Oxford, Clarendon Press, 1992)

SEYMOUR, J., 'Parens Patriae and Wardship Powers: Their Nature and Origins' (1994) 14 Oxford Journal of Legal Studies 159

SKØRTEN, K. and BARLINDHAUG. R., 'The Involvement of Children in Decisions About Shared Residence' (2007) 21 International Journal of Law, Policy and the Family 373

SMART, C., 'From Children's Shoes to Children's Voices' (2002) 40(3) Family Court Review 307

SMART, C. and NEALE, B., 'Arguments Against Virtue—Must Contact Be Enforced?' (1997) 27 Family Law 332

SMART, C., NEALE, B., and WADE, A., *The Changing Experience of Childhood: Families and Divorce* (Cambridge: Polity Press, 2001)

STAHL, P. and DROZD, L. (eds), *Relocation Issues in Child Custody Cases* (Binghamton, NY: Haworth Press, 2006)

STURGE, C. and GLASER, D., 'Contact and Domestic Violence—The Experts' Court Report' (2000) 30 Family Law 615

SUTHERLAND, E., 'Mother Knows Best', 1994 SLT (News) 375

TAYLOR, R., '*Poels* Apart: Fixed Principles and Shifting Values in Relocation Law' in S. Gilmore, J. Herring, and R. Probert (eds), *Landmark Cases in Family Law* (Oxford: Hart, 2011)

TAYLOR, N. and FREEMAN, M., 'International Research Evidence on Relocation: Past, Present and Future' (2010) 44(3) Family Law Quarterly 317

TAYLOR, N., GOLLOP, M., and HENAGHAN, M., *Relocation Following Parental Separation: The Welfare and Best Interests of Children Research Report* (Centre for Research on Children and Families and

Faculty of Law, University of Otago, Dunedin, June 2010)

THORNTON, R., 'Children and Children's Children: Whose Welfare is Paramount?' [1994] Cambridge Law Journal 41

TRINDER, L., 'Shared Residence: A Review of Recent Research Evidence' [2010] Child and Family Law Quarterly 475

TRINDER, L., CONNOLLY, J., KELLETT, J., and NOTLEY, C., *A Profile of Applicants and Respondents in Contact Cases in Essex*, DCA Research Series 1/05 (London: Department for Constitutional Affairs, 2004)

WALLBANK, J., 'Castigating Mothers: The Judicial Response to "Wilful" Women in Disputes Over Paternal Contact in English Law' (1998) 20(4) Journal of Social Welfare and Family Law 357

Chapter 10: Children Needing Services, Care, or Protection

ARCHARD, D., *Children: Rights and Childhood*, 2nd edn (Abingdon: Routledge, 2004)

BAINHAM, A., *Children the New Law* (Bristol: Family Law, 1990)

BAINHAM, A., 'Care after 1991—A Reply' (1993) 3 Journal of Child Law 99

BAINHAM, A., 'Interim Care Orders: Is the Bar set Too Low?' [2011] Family Law 374

BARTON, C. and DOUGLAS, G., *Law and Parenthood* (London: Butterworths, 1995)

BENTOVIM, A., *Cleveland 10 Years On—A Mental Health Perspective* [1998] Family Law 153

BETTLE, J. and HERRING, J., 'Shaken Babies and Care Proceedings' [2011] Family Law 1370

BIRCHALL, E. and HALLETT, C., *Working Together in Child Protection* (London: HMSO, 1995)

BOND, A., *Care Proceedings and Learning Disabled Parents A Handbook for Family Lawyers* (Bristol: Jordan Publishing, 2011)

BOOTH, Dame Margaret, *Delay in Public Law Children Act Cases—Second Report* (London: HMSO, 1996)

BRASSE, G., 'Supervision or Care Orders?' [1997] Family Law 351

BROPHY, J., *Research Review: Child Care Proceedings under the Children Act 1989*, DCA Research Series 5/06 (London: Department for Constitutional Affairs, May 2006)

BROPHY, J., JHUTTI-JOHAL, J., and OWEN, C., 'Assessing and Documenting Child Ill-Treatment in Ethnic Minority Households' [2003] Family Law 756

BROPHY, J. et al, *Significant Harm: Child Protection Litigation in a Multi-Cultural Setting* (London: Department of Constitutional Affairs, 2003)

CONWAY, H., 'The Laming Inquiry—Victoria Climbié's Legacy' [2002] Family Law 755

CRETNEY, S., 'The Children Act 1948—Lessons For Today?' [1997] Child and Family Law Quarterly 359

CRETNEY, S., 'The State as a Parent: The Children Act 1948 in Retrospect' in *Law, Law Reform and the Family* (Oxford: Clarendon Press, 1998)

CRETNEY, S., *Family Law in the Twentieth Century—A History* (Oxford: Oxford University Press, 2003)

DEPARTMENT FOR EDUCATION AND SKILLS, *Safeguarding Children in Whom Illness is Fabricated or Induced* (London: TSO, 2008)

DEPARTMENT OF HEALTH, *Child Abuse: A Study of Inquiry Reports 1980-89* (London: HMS0, 1991)

DEPARTMENT OF HEALTH, *Child Protection: Messages from Research* (London: HMSO, 1995)

DEPARTMENT OF HEALTH, *The Challenge of Partnership in Child Protection: Practice Guide* (London: HMSO, 1995)

DEPARTMENT OF HEALTH, *Framework for the Assessment of Children in Need and Their Families* (London: TSO, 2000)

DEPARTMENT OF HEALTH and DEPARTMENT FOR EDUCATION AND SKILLS, *Good Practice Guidance on Working with Parents with a Learning Disability* (London: TSO, 2007)

DEPARTMENT OF HEALTH and SOCIAL SERVICES INSPECTORATE, *Contact Orders Study: A Study of Local Authority Decision Making around Contact Applications under Section 34* (London: HMSO, 1994)

DEPARTMENT OF HEALTH AND SOCIAL SECURITY, *Child Abuse: A Study of Inquiry Reports 1973–1981* (London: HMSO, 1982)

DINGWALL, R., EEKELAAR, J., and MURRAY, T., *The Protection of Children: State Intervention and Family Life* (Oxford: Basil Blackwell, 1983)

DONZELOT, J., *The Policing of Families: Welfare versus the State* (London: Hutchinson, 1980)

DRISCOLL, J. and HOLLINGSWORTH, K., 'Accommodating Children in Need: *R (M) v Hammersmith and Fulham London Borough Council*' [2008] Child and Family Law Quarterly 522

DWYER, J. G., *The Relationship Rights of Children* (New York: Cambridge University Press, 2006)

EEKELAAR, J., 'Are Parents Morally Obliged to Care for Their Children?' (1991) 11(3) Oxford Journal of Legal Studies 340

EEKELAAR J., DINGWALL, R., and MURRAY, T., 'Victims or Threats? Children in Care Proceedings' (1982) 4(2) Journal of Social Welfare and Family Law 68

FORTIN, J., 'Significant Harm Revisited' (1993) 5 Journal of Child Law 151

FOX-HARDING, L., 'The Children Act in Context: Four Perspectives on Child Care Law and Policy' (1991) 13 Journal of Social Welfare and Family Law 179

FREEMAN, M. D. A., 'Care After 1991' in D. Freestone (ed), *Children and the Law* (Hull: Hull University Press, 1990)

FREEMAN, M. D. A., *Children, Their Families and the Law* (Basingstoke: Macmillan, 1992)

FREEMAN, M. D. A., 'The Right to Responsible Parents' in J. Bridgeman, H. Keating, and C. Lind (eds), *Responsibility, Law and the Family* (Aldershot: Ashgate, 2008)

GIBBONS, J., CONROY, S., and BELL, C., *Operating the Child Protection System: A Study of Child Protection Practices in English Local Authorities* (London: HMSO, 1995)

GILLESPIE, A. A., 'Establishing a Third Order in Care Proceedings' [2000] Child and Family Law Quarterly 239

GOLDSTEIN, J., FREUD, A., and SOLNIT, A., *Before the Best Interests of the Child* (New York, Free Press, 1979)

GOLDREIN, I., 'There is Only So Much Juice in an Orange: *Re SB*' [2010] Family Law 196

GOUGH, D., *Child Abuse Interventions: A Review of the Research Literature* (London: HMSO, 1993)

HALE, B. et al, *The Family, Law and Society: Cases and Materials*, 5th edn (Oxford: Oxford University Press, 2005)

HALLETT, C., *Inter-Agency Coordination in Child Protection* (London: HMSO, 1995)

HAYES, J., 'The Threshold Test and the Unknown Perpetrator' [2000] Family Law 260

HAYES, J., 'Farewell to the Cogent Evidence Test: *Re B*' [2008] Family Law 859

HAYES, J., 'Ensuring Equal Protection for Siblings' [2010] Family Law 505

HAYES, J., HAYES, M., and WILLIAMS, J., '"Shocking" Abuse Followed by a 'Staggering Ruling': *Re MA (Care Threshold)*' [2010] Family Law 166

HAYES, M., 'Care by the Family or Care by the State?' (1995) 58 Modern Law Review 878

HAYES, M., 'Reconciling Protection for Children with Justice for Parents' (1997) 17 Legal Studies 1

HAYES, M., 'Removing Children from their Families—Law and Policy Before the Children Act 1989' in G. Douglas and

N. Lowe (eds), *The Continuing Evolution of Family Law* (Bristol: Jordan Publishing, 2009)

HAYES, M., 'Why Didn't the Courts Protect this Child? *Re SB and Re F'* [2012] Family Law 169

HEMINGWAY, I. and WILLIAMS, C., '*Re M and R: Re H and R*' [1997] Family Law 740

HM GOVERNMENT, *Report of the Care of Children Committee* (Cmd 6922, 1946)

HM GOVERNMENT, *Report of the Committee of Inquiry into the Care and Supervision Provided in Relation to Maria Colwell* (London: HMSO, 1974)

HM GOVERNMENT, SECRETARY OF STATE FOR SOCIAL SERVICES, *The Law on Child Care and Family Services* (Cm 62, 1987)

HM GOVERNMENT, SECRETARY OF STATE FOR SOCIAL SERVICES, *Report of the Inquiry into Child Abuse in Cleveland* (Cmnd 412, 1988)

HM GOVERNMENT, *Working Together to Safeguard Children A guide to Inter-Agency Working to Safeguard and Promote the Welfare of Children* (London: TSO, March 2010)

HOULGATE, L. D., 'What is Legal Intervention in the Family? Family Law and Family Privacy' (1998) 17 Law and Philosophy 141

HOYANO, L. and KEENAN, C., *Child Abuse Law and Policy Across Boundaries* (Oxford: Oxford University Press, 2007)

KAGANAS, F., KING, M., and PIPER, C. (eds), *Legislating for Harmony—Partnerships under the Children Act 1989* (London: Jessica Kingsley, 1996)

KEATING, H., 'Shifting Standards in the House of Lords—*Re H and Others (Minors) (Sexual Abuse: Standard of Proof)*' (1996) 8 Child and Family Law Quarterly 157

KEATING, H., 'Suspicions, Sitting on the Fence and Standards of Proof' [2009] Child and Family Law Quarterly 230

KEATING, H., '*Re MA:* The Significance of Harm' [2011] Child and Family Law Quarterly 115

KEENAN, C., 'Finding that a Child is at Risk from Sexual Abuse: *Re H (Minors) (Sexual Abuse: Standard of Proof*' (1997) 60 Modern Law Review 857

LAFOLLETTE, H., 'Licensing Parents' (1980) 9 Philosophy and Public Affairs 182

LAVERY, R., 'The Child Assessment Order—A Reassessment' (1996) 8 Child and Family Law Quarterly 41

LAW COMMISSION, *Domestic Violence and Occupation of the Family Home* (Law Com No 207, 1992)

LONDON BOROUGH OF BRENT, *A Child in Trust: Report on the Death of Jasmine Beckford* (1988)

LONDON BOROUGH OF GREENWICH, *A Child in Mind: Protection of Children in a Responsible Society: Report of the Commission of Inquiry into the Circumstances Surrounding the Death of Kimberley Carlile* (1987)

LONDON BOROUGH OF GREENWICH, *Whose Child: Report on the Death of Tyra Henry* (1987)

LONNE, B., PARTON, N., THOMSON, J., and HARRIES, M., *Reforming Child Protection* (Abingdon: Routledge, 2009)

LORD LAMING, *The Victoria Climbié Inquiry: Report of an Inquiry by Lord Laming* (Cm 5730, January 2003)

LYON, C., *Child Abuse* (Bristol: Family Law, 2006 reprint)

MANGEL, C. P., 'Licensing Parents: How Feasible?' (1988) 22 Family Law Quarterly 17

MASSON, J., 'From Curtis to Waterhouse: State Care and Child Protection in the UK 1945–2000' in S. Katz, J. Eekelaar, and M. Maclean (eds), *Cross-Currents: Family Law Policy in the US and England* (Oxford: Oxford University Press, 2000)

MASSON, J., 'Police Protection—Protecting Whom?' (2002) Journal of Social Welfare and Family Law 157

MASSON, J., 'Emergency Intervention to Protect Children: Using and Avoiding

Legal Controls' [2005] Child and Family Law Quarterly 75

MASSON, J., PEARCE, J., and BADER K. with JOYNER, O., MARSDEN, J., and WESTLAKE, D., *Care Profiling Study* (London: Ministry of Justice, March 2008)

MASSON, J. et al, *Protecting Powers: Emergency Intervention for Children's Protection* (Chichester: Wiley, 2007)

MITCHELL, G., 'The Child Assessment Order—A Breach of Principle?' [1991] XIII(I) Liverpool Law Review 53

OLSEN, F. E., 'The Myth of State Intervention in the Family' (1984–85) 18 University of Michigan Journal of Law Reform 835

PACKMAN, J., *Who Needs Care? Social Work Decisions About Children* (Oxford: Blackwell, 1986)

PARKINSON, P. and HUMPHRIES, C., 'Children who Witness Domestic Violence: The Implications for Child Protection' (1998) 10 Child and Family Law Quarterly 147

PARTON, N., *The Politics of Child Abuse* (Basingstoke: Macmillan, 1985)

PARTON, N., *Governing the Family* (Basingstoke: Macmillan, 1991)

PARTON, N., 'Sexual Abuse, the Cleveland Affair and the Private Family' in N. Parton, *Governing the Family* (Basingstoke: Macmillan, 1991)

PARTON, N. and MARTIN, N., 'Public Inquiries, Legalism and Child Care in England and Wales' (1989) 3 International Journal of Law and the Family 21

POSNER, G., 'Applications to Discharge Care Orders' [1998] Family Law 623

SAVAS, D., 'Parental Participation in Case Conferences' (1996) 8 Child and Family Law Quarterly 57

SMITH, C., 'Judicial Power and Local Authority Discretion—The Contested Frontier' (1997) 9 Child and Family Law Quarterly 243

SOCIAL SERVICES INSPECTORATE and DEPARTMENT OF HEALTH, *Domestic Violence and Social Care* (London: HMSO, 1995)

SPENCER, J. R., 'Evidence in Child Abuse Cases: Too High a Price for Too High a Standard?' (1994) 6 Journal of Child Law 160

THOBURN, J., LEWIS, A., and SHEMMINGS, D., *Paternalism or Partnership? Family Involvement in the Child Protection Process* (London: HMSO, 1995)

WATTAM, C., *The Social Construction of Child Abuse for Practical Policy Purposes—A Review of Child Protection: Messages from Research* (1996) 8 Child and Family Law Quarterly 189

WESTMAN, J. C., *Licensing Parents: Can We Prevent Child Abuse and Neglect?* (Cambridge, MA: Perseus Books, 1994)

WILLIAMS, C. and JORDAN, H., 'Factors Relating to Publicity Surrounding the Complaints Procedure under the Children Act 1989' (1996) 8 Child and Family Law Quarterly 337

Chapter 11: Adoption and Special Guardianship

ADCOCK, M., KANIUK, J., and WHITE, R. (eds), *Exploring Openness in Adoption* (Significant Publications, 1993)

BAINHAM, A., 'Can We Protect Children and Protect Their Rights?' [2002] Family Law 279

BAINHAM, A., 'Unintentional Parenthood: The Case of the Reluctant Mother' [2002] Cambridge Law Journal 288

BARTH, R. P. and BERRY, M., *Adoption and Disruption: Rates, Risks and Responses* (New York: Aldine DeGruyter, 1988)

BARTON, C., 'Adoption: The Prime Minister's Review' [2000] Family Law 731

BARTON, C., 'Adoption and Children Bill—Don't Let Them Out of Your Sight' [2001] Family Law 431

BRIDGE, C., 'Adoption and Contact: The Value of Openness' [1994] Journal of Child Law 147

BRIDGE, C., 'Adoption Law: A Balance of Interests' in J. Herring (ed), *Family Law: Issues, Debates, Policy* (Cullompton: Willan, 2001)

BRIDGE, C. and SWINDELLS, H., *Adoption: The Modern Law* (Bristol: Family Law, 2003)

CASEY, D. and GIBBERD, A., 'Adoption and Contact' [2000] Family Law 39

CASTLE, J., BECKETT, C., and GROOTHUES, C., 'Infant Adoption in England: A Longitudinal Account of Social and Cognitive Progress' (2000) 24 Adoption and Fostering 26

CHOUDHRY, S., 'The Adoption and Children Act 2002, the Welfare Principle and the Human Rights Act 1998—A Missed Opportunity?' [2003] Child and Family Law Quarterly 119

COOKE, E., 'Dispensing with Parental Consent to Adoption—A Choice of Welfare Tests' [1997] Child and Family Law Quarterly 259

CRETNEY, S., *Family Law in the Twentieth Century—A History* (Oxford: Oxford University Press, 2003)

CULLEN, D., 'The Adoption and Children Act 2002' [2003] Family Law 235

CULLEN, D., 'Adoption—A (Fairly) New Approach' [2005] Child and Family Law Quarterly 475

CURRY-SUMNER, I., '*EB v France*: A Missed Opportunity?' [2009] Child and Family Law Quarterly 356

DANCE, C. and RUSHTON, A., 'Predictors of Outcome for Unrelated Adoptive Placements made During Middle Childhood' (2005) 10 Child and Family Social Work 269

DEPARTMENT FOR CHILDREN, SCHOOLS AND FAMILIES, *The Children Act 1989 Guidance and Regulations Volume 1: Court Orders* (London: TSO, 2008)

DEPARTMENT OF HEALTH, *Adoption Now: Messages from Research* (Chichester: Wiley, 1999)

DEPARTMENT OF HEALTH, *Adoption: A New Approach: A White Paper* (Cm 5017, 2000)

DEPARTMENT OF HEALTH and WELSH OFFICE, Report to Ministers of the Interdepartmental Working Group, *Review of Adoption Law* (1992)

DEPARTMENT OF HEALTH and WELSH OFFICE, *Adoption: A Service for Children, Draft Bill* (London: TSO, 1996)

DEPARTMENT OF HEALTH and WELSH OFFICE, Report to Ministers of the Interdepartmental Working Group, *Review of Adoption Law* (London: HMSO, 1992)

DEPARTMENT OF HEALTH and WELSH OFFICE, HOME OFFICE, LORD CHANCELLOR'S DEPARTMENT, *Adoption: The Future* (Cm 2288, 1993)

DEY, I., 'Adapting Adoption: A Case of Closet Politics?' (2005) 19(3) International Journal of Law, Policy and the Family 289

EEKELAAR, J., 'Contact and the Adoption Reform' in A. Bainham, B. Lindley, M. Richards, and L. Trinder (eds), *Children and Their Families: Contact, Rights and Welfare* (Oxford: Hart, 2003)

FRATTER, J., *Adoption with Contact: Implications for Policy and Practice* (London: BAAF, 1996)

GROTEVANT, H. D. and McRoy, R. G., *Openness in Adoption: Exploring Family Connections* (Thousand Oaks, CA: Sage, 1998)

HALL, A., 'Special Guardianship: A Missed Opportunity—Findings from Research' [2008] Family Law 148

HALL, A., 'Special Guardianship and Permanency Planning: Unforeseen Consequences and Missed Opportunities' [2008] Child and Family Law Quarterly 359

HALL, A., 'Special Guardianship—Themes Emerging from Case-Law' [2008] Family Law 244

HARRIS-SHORT, S., 'The Adoption and Children Bill—A Fast Track to Failure?' [2001] Child and Family Law Quarterly 405

HASKEY, J. and ERRINGTON, E., 'Adoptees and Relatives who Wish to Contact One Another: The Adoption Contact Register' (2001) 104 Population Trends 18

HITCHINGS, E. and SAGAR, T., 'The Adoption and Children Act 2002: A Level Playing Field for Same-Sex Adopters?' [2002] Child and Family Law Quarterly 60

HM GOVERNMENT, Performance and Innovation Unit, *Prime Minister's Review: Adoption: Issued for Consultation* (London: TSO, July 2000)

HOUGHTON COMMITTEE, *Report of the Departmental Committee on the Adoption of Children* (Cmnd 5107, 1972)

HOWE, D., SHEMMINGS, D., and FEAST, J., 'Age at Placement and Adult Adopted People's Experience of Being Adopted' (2001) 6 Child and Family Social Work 337

HUGHES, K. and SLOAN, B., 'Post-Adoption Photographs: Welfare, Rights and Judicial Reasoning' [2011] Child and Family Law Quarterly 393

JORDAN, L. and LINDLEY, B. (eds), *Special Guardianship: What Does it Offer Children Who Cannot Live with Their Parents?* (London: Family Rights Group, 2006)

LEWIS, J., 'Adoption: The Nature of Policy Shifts in England and Wales, 1972–2002' (2004) 18(2) International Journal of Law, Policy and the Family 235

LINDLEY, B., 'Open Adoption—Is the Door Ajar?' [1997] Child and Family Law Quarterly 115

LOGAN, J. and SMITH, C., 'Adoption and Direct Post-Adoption Contact' (1999) 23(4) Adoption and Fostering 58

LOWE, N., 'The Changing Face of Adoption—The Gift/Donation Model versus the Contract/Services Model' [1997] Child and Family Law Quarterly 371

LOWE, N. V., 'English Adoption Law: Past, Present and Future' in S. Katz, J. Eekelaar, and M. Maclean (eds), *Cross-Currents: Family Law and Policy in the US and England* (Oxford: Oxford University Press, 2000)

MAHMOOD, S., 'Adoption and Children Act 2002: Where Are We So Far?' [2004] Family Law 449

MARSHALL, A., 'Comedy of Adoption—When is a Parent not a Parent?' [2003] Family Law 840

MASSON, J., 'Thinking about Contact—A Social or a Legal Problem?' [2000] Child and Family Law Quarterly 15

MULLENDER, A. (ed), *Open Adoption: The Philosophy and Practice* (London: BAAF, 1991)

NEIL, E., 'Post-Adoption Contact and Openness in Adoptive Parents' Minds: Consequences for Children's Development' (2009) 39 British Journal of Social Work 303

O'HALLORAN, K., *The Politics of Adoption: International Perspectives on Law, Policy and Practice*, 2nd edn (Vienna: Springer, 2009)

QUINTON, D. and SELWYN, J., 'Adoption: Research, Policy and Practice' [2006] Child and Family Law Quarterly 459

QUINTON, D., RUSHTON, A., DANCE, C., and MAYES, D., 'Contact Between Children Placed Away from Home and Their Birth Parents: Research Issues and Evidence' (1997) 2(3) Clinical Child Psychology and Psychiatry 393

QUINTON, D., SELWYN, J., RUSHTON, A., and DANCE, C., 'Contact with Birth Parents in Adoption—A Response to Ryburn' [1998] Child and Family Law Quarterly 349

RYBURN, M., 'A Study of Post-Adoption Contact in Compulsory Adoptions' (1996) 26(5) British Journal of Social Work 627

RYBURN, M., 'In Whose Best Interests?—Post-Adoption Contact with the Birth Family' [1998] Child and Family Law Quarterly 53

SLOAN, B., 'Re C (A Child) (Adoption: Duty of Local Authority)—Welfare and the Rights of the Birth Family in "Fast Track" Adoption Cases' [2009] Child and Family Law Quarterly 87

SMITH, C. and LOGAN, J., 'Adoptive Parenthood as a "Legal Fiction"—Its Consequences for Direct Post-Adoption Contact' [2002] Child and Family Law Quarterly 281

TRISELIOTIS, J., SHIREMAN, J., and HUNDLEBY, M., Adoption; Theory, Policy and Practice (London: Cassell, 1997)

WATERHOUSE, SIR RONALD (Waterhouse Inquiry), Lost in Care—Report of the Tribunal of Inquiry into the Abuse of Children in the Former County Council Areas of Gwynedd and Clwyd since 1974 (London: TSO, 2000)

INDEX

abandoned children 648
abduction of children 537
abroad, taking children 503, 534, 537–49
abuse *see also* children needing services, care, and protection; domestic violence
  access to children 569–70
  allegations 390, 517–18, 531, 569, 583, 596, 608, 632–40, 647–50
  care, in 583–4
  children's guardian, role of 626
  Cleveland Child Abuse Inquiry 569, 624
  Climbié Report 570
  contact orders 512, 513, 517, 530–1, 534
  parental responsibility 404–5
  sexual abuse 633–5, 640
  significant harm threshold 633–5, 640
  Waterhouse Inquiry 671
  welfare checklist 650
accommodation *see* homelessness; local authority accommodation for children
adoption 669–707
  access to information 702–3
  address, adopters living at same 692–3
  adoption orders 476, 654, 669, 673, 680, 698–702
  Adoption Service 673–4
  age
    children 680–2, 696, 703
    parents 692, 693
  agencies 673–5
    assessing suitable adoptions, role in 674–6
    counselling 703
    decision-making 674–5
    information 702–3
    panels 675–6, 683
    placements 680–91
    regulation 673–4
    reviews 674
  appeals 689–90, 698–701
  applications 673, 692–707
  assessments 674–6, 686, 697
  authorisation to place, effect of 687–8

background of child 674–5, 701
best interests test 686, 695, 702
birth certificates, access to 702–3
birth parents
  adoption, by 692, 694–5
  on-going contact 702–7
  parental responsibility, extinguishment of 669
British citizenship 700
British Nationals (Overseas) 700
care orders 654, 690, 698
case files 675
change of circumstances 689–91, 698
child assessment orders 686
civil partners 46, 692, 700
cohabitants 51
conditions 673, 683–4, 696, 697–8
confidentiality 676
consent 680–2, 697
  age 680–2
  dispensing with consent 673, 684–6
  fathers 677, 680, 701–2
  rules 680
  withdrawal 682
consequences of placement orders 686–7
contact
  advantages and disadvantages 704–6
  letterbox 702, 707
  on-going 702–7
  orders 687
  post-adoption contact 703–7
  register 702–3
  siblings 706
couples 672, 675–6, 692–3
counselling 703
criminal offences 688, 703
decision-making 674–5
delay 673–4, 679, 691
discretion 690, 698–9
discrimination 676
dispensing with consent 673, 684–6
disruption of placement 670
divorce 670

domestic violence 678
domicile 692
duration of orders 688–9
effect of adoption orders 699–700
effect of placement or authorisation to place 687–8
eligibility 672, 675–6, 692–5
enhanced welfare test 684–5
fathers
  adoption by fathers 692, 694–5, 700
  consent 677, 680, 701–2
  identity 676–7
  parental responsibility 378, 677
  private and family life, right to respect for 679–80
  withholding information 676–80
final, orders as being 700
habitual residence 692
home environment, sufficient opportunities to see children in 697
Human Rights Act 1998 689–90
information 675, 676–80
  access 702–3
  criminal offences 703
  exceptional circumstances, withholding information in 677–8
  protected information, definition of 702–3
  withholding information from fathers and other relatives 676–80
inherent jurisdiction 562, 676–7
injunctions 690
judicial review 690
leave to make applications where conditions not fulfilled 696
leave to oppose adoption 698–9
letterbox contact 702, 707
live with adopters, children must 695–6
local authorities 669–74

adoption (*cont.*)
looked after children 670
maintenance, termination
of 699–700
married couples 42
medical examinations and
reports 675
mothers, adoption by 692,
694–5, 700
natural justice 700
notice of intention to adopt
and report 697
on-going contact 702–7
openness in adoption 702–7
opposition 686, 688, 698–9
panels 675–6, 683
paramountcy or welfare
principle 673–4, 678–9,
684–6, 690–1, 695–9, 703–6
parental responsibility 378,
402, 407, 654, 669–70, 677,
680, 699–700, 706
permanence reports 675
photographs 702, 707
placement 680–91
authorisation to place,
effect of 687–8
conditions for orders
683–4
consequences of
orders 686–7
definition 681
duration 688–9
effect of placement 687–8
orders 673, 682–8
plans 676
procedure 683
removal 688
reports 676
return of children,
revocation of orders
without 691
revocation 688–91, 701
police checks 675
policy 670, 673, 679, 701
post-adoption contact 703–7
potential adopters 681, 689
preliminaries 696–7
preparation 676
private and family life, right
to respect for 679–80, 685,
695, 707
procedural irregularity 700–1
procedure 683
prohibited degrees of
relationship 700
prohibited steps orders 686
proportionality 695
prospective adopters 681, 689

protected information,
definition of 702–3
reasons for decisions 676
register of contact
details 702–3
registered adoption
societies 673–4
relatives, withholding
information from 676–80
religion 674–5, 701–2
removal from placement 688
residence orders 686–7, 688
reports 676, 697–8
return of children 688, 691
reviews 674
revocation of orders 688–91,
701
same-sex couples 672, 675–6,
692
section 8 orders 476
separated couples 693
setting aside orders 700–2
sexual offences 700
siblings, contact with 706
single people 672, 693–5
social change 670
social workers 675, 686, 693
special guardianship orders
686–7, 688, 708, 710–11
specific issue orders 686
status conferred by
adoption 699–700
step-parents 670
suitable adoptions,
assessment of 674–6, 697
supervision orders 686
surrogacy 371
time limits and target
figures 670–1
unmarried couples 672,
675–6
welfare checklist 674, 684
who may adopt 672, 675–6,
692–5
who may be adopted 696
withholding information
from fathers and other
relatives 676–80
adultery 60, 67–8, 86
**advancement, presumption
of** 250
age
accommodation for
children 586–7
adoption 680–2, 692, 693,
696, 703
child support 317, 325, 327
children, rights of 416–17, 423
contact orders 558

divorce 62
looked after children 579–80
money and property
distribution on marriage
breakdown 184–7
parental responsibility of
fathers 377
residence orders 485–7, 558
section 8 orders 558–9
**alcohol and domestic
violence** 96, 112
ancillary relief *see* **money and
property distribution on
marriage breakdown**
ante-nuptial agreements 222–9
children 229
disclosure 224
enforcement 222–9
Europe 228
forum shopping 228
guidance 224–5
improper pressure 219
ousting the jurisdiction of
the court 227
post-nuptial
agreements 223–5
public policy 222–3, 229
safeguards 229
variation 223
**antisocial/narcissistic
personality and domestic
violence** 96
appeals and rehearings
adoption 689–90, 698–701
divorce 66–7
lump sums 232–4
matrimonial
home 231, 233
money and property
distribution on marriage
breakdown 230–42
periodical payments 232–4
separation agreements
231–2
**armed forces, overseas
marriages of** 38
arranged marriages 33
arrest
emergency protection
orders 608
exclusion requirement 625
forced marriages 37
harassment 147
interim care and supervision
orders 625
non-molestation orders
103–4, 108, 113–14
occupation orders 103–4,
140–4

assessments
adoption 674–6, 686, 697
child assessment orders
597–9, 686
Cleveland Inquiry 624
competency 625
directions 619–25
inherent jurisdiction 625
interim care and supervision
orders 619–25
looked after children 580, 582
medical or psychiatric
assessments 620–5
psychotherapy 621–3
refuse, child's right to 620,
624–5
residential assessments 620,
622–4
significant harm 600–1
treatment, distinguished
from 621–3
assisted fertilisation
agreed fatherhood
conditions 366
autonomy 361
biological connection 357–8,
367
civil partnerships 367, 369
Code of Practice 360
consent 360–1, 369
counselling 360
death, use of sperm
after 368–9
egg donations 357–8
embryos after mother's
partner's death, use of 369
embryos, father's consent to
destruction of 361
fathers and fatherhood 358–9,
361–9
Human Fertilisation
and Embryology Act
1990 360–5
Human Fertilisation and
Embryology Act 2008 360,
365–8
Human Fertilisation
and Embryology
Authority 360–1, 368
legal but not biological
fathers 362–5
legitimacy, presumption
of 362
lesbian couples 40, 46, 331, 367
licence conditions 360
licensed treatment 361, 366
life, right to 361
margin of appreciation 361
motherhood 357–8

mothers, husbands of 362–3
parenthood 367
private and family life, right
to respect for 361
same-sex couples 40, 46,
331, 367
sperm donors 365, 367–9
surrogacy 362–3
unmarried couples 363
woman and man together,
services provided
for 363–5
attachment to children 384–5,
476–7, 539–40, 543
autonomy
assisted fertilisation 361
children, rights of 414, 416,
417–28, 444–5
cohabitants 48, 53–4
medical treatment of children,
consent to 420–8
parental responsibility 410
religion 654

bankruptcy 293
banns 18
behaviour fact for divorce
68–71, 84, 86
best interests test *see also*
paramountcy or welfare
principle
accommodation for
children 588
adoption 686, 695, 702
child protection 572
children, rights of 422, 426–8
contact orders 526–7, 664
emergency protection
orders 603
medical treatment of children,
consent to 433–4, 436,
441–2
parentage 343–6, 353–4
residence orders 486–7, 497,
500
shared residence orders 497,
500
supervision orders 658–9
big money cases 63–4, 76, 170–6,
182, 187–9, 205–6
bigamy 21, 377
biological relationship
340–2, 350
adoption 692, 694–5, 702–7
assisted fertilisation 357–8, 367
egg donation 357–8
fathers and fatherhood 358
legal parenthood 367, 374, 376
motherhood 357–8

paramountcy or welfare
principle 456, 458–61
parental responsibility of
fathers 397
prohibited degrees of
relationship 16
recognition of interests
in knowing genetic
origins 346–56
surrogacy 371
birth certificates
adoption 702–3
fathers 379–80, 400
name, change of 549–50
parental responsibility 379–80,
400, 403
transsexuals 23–4, 29, 370
birth rate, decrease in 3
blood transfusions, refusal
of 438–42, 561
Booth Committee 61, 69, 78
breakdown of relationships
see **money and property**
distribution on marriage
breakdown; property
disputes of cohabitants on
relationship breakdown
Brussels II Revised 62, 64
burden of proof 638–40
businesses, contributions
to 275–7

Cafcass (Children and Family
Court Advisory and
Support Service) 7, 467,
571, 626, 653
capacity
children, rights of 414–15
consummation 26–7, 30
forced marriages 13–14
learning disabilities, persons
with 642–3
marriage 13–14, 25–7, 29,
30, 31, 38
mental disabilities/illness,
people with 13–14, 25, 29,
31, 112–13, 187
overseas marriages,
recognition of 38
parental responsibility of
fathers 380, 385
residence orders 484
care orders *see also* **care**
proceedings; interim care
and supervision orders
adoption 654, 690, 698
care plans 651–3
contact with children in
care 471–2, 483–4, 662–7

care orders (cont.)
  discharge of orders 502, 503, 504, 661, 710
  discretion 661
  emergency protection orders 659
  grounds 568
  issue estoppel 661
  legal effect 653–5
  looked after children 655
  monitoring 658
  paramountcy or welfare principle 569, 654–5, 661
  parental responsibility 653–5, 661
  religion 653–4
  residence orders 502, 503, 504
  significant harm threshold 614, 620, 628–38, 655
  special guardianship orders 710
  supervision orders 657–60
  welfare checklist 650–1, 661
care plans 651–3, 655
care proceedings 628–51
  actual significant harm 628–38
  allegations 650
  balance of probabilities 638–9
  burden of proof 638–40
  final hearings 628–51
  interim care and supervision orders 613–27
  likely harm 632–8
  parental control, where child is beyond 648–9
  proof 632–40
  reasonable parental care 640–8
  significant harm 628–48
  standard of proof 638–40
  threshold test of significant harm 628–48
  welfare checklist 649–51
carers as home-sharers 56–7
Carlile, Kimberley, inquiry into death of 570
change of circumstances 485, 615, 689–91, 698, 709
child assessment orders 686
child labour 417
child liberationist ideology 416
child protection see children needing services, care, and protection
child support 313–39
  adoption, termination on 699–700
  adult children, applications by 330

against whom orders can be made 331
age 317, 325, 327
another child, where non-resident partner is maintaining 319
applications 318, 329–31
apportionment 320
available orders 325–6, 330–1
basic rate 318–19
capital provision 324
capital transfers 321
care, orders against a person with 323–4
child, definition of 317
Child Maintenance and Enforcement Commission (C-MEC) 316, 318, 320–2
Child Maintenance and Other Payments Act 2008 316
child of the family, concept of 324–5, 331
Child Support Act 1991 313–22
Child Support Agency 314–16
Children Act 1989 329–38
civil partners 324
clean break 314–15
collection, applications for 318
county court, powers of 324
court's powers 324–38
court's residual role with respect to maintenance 321–4
criticism, response to 315
departure directions 315, 321
dependants, children as 327–9
disability, expenses attributable to a child's 323
discretion 326, 332–8
duration of orders 327, 331, 334
during marriage 243–4
educational expenses 322–3
enforcement 318, 321
expenses 321, 322–3
fair hearing, right to a 321
flat rate 319
flexibility 314–15
gross income scheme 316
habitual residence 317, 323
Henshaw Report 315–16
High Court, powers of 324, 331
legal parenthood 315
liability orders, applications for 321
lifestyle choices 321, 337–8

loss of confidence 315–16
lump sums 324, 326, 329, 330–1
magistrates' courts 321, 331
maintenance agreements 316, 318–19, 322, 338
maintenance calculation 314–16, 318–22
  applications 318
  apportionment 320
  basic rate 318–19
  existing maintenance agreements 322
  existing maintenance orders 322
  flat rate 319
  nil rate 319
  reduced rate 319
  shared care, reduction for 320
  topping up orders 322
  variations 320–1
maintenance orders 318–19, 322
marital status 324
Matrimonial Causes Act 1973 324–30, 333–4
nil rate 319
non-parents, maintenance by 326–7
paramountcy or welfare principle 332–4
parent, definition of 317
parental responsibility 314, 331, 392–3, 397, 406–7
paternity, lack of knowledge of 325
periodical payments 244, 324, 326, 327, 330–1, 334, 337–8
problems 314–15
property adjustment orders 330–1, 333
property transfers 321, 325, 330–1, 333
qualifying child, duty to maintain a 317–18
reduced rate 319
residence orders, applications by persons with 330
review of system 315–16
same-sex parents 331
Secretary of State 315
secured periodical payments 326, 327
shared care, reduction for 320
social parenthood 315, 331
special expenses 321
sperm donation 331

standard of living 326, 332–8
to whom Act applies 317
topping up orders 322
unborn children 325
unmarried parents 329–38
  against whom orders can
    be made 331
  applications on behalf of
    the child 329–30
  available orders 330–1
  Children Act 1989 329–38
  discretion 332–8
  duration of orders 331
  who can apply 329–30
variations 315, 320–2, 337
welfare benefits 313–14, 316
who can apply 329–30
children *see also* adoption; child
support; Children Act 1989;
children needing services,
care and protection; children,
rights of; consent to medical
treatment of children; local
authority accommodation
for children; paramountcy or
welfare principle; relocation
of children; wishes and
feelings of child
abduction 537
advancement, presumption
  of 250
ante-nuptial agreements 229
attachment to
  children 384–5, 476–7,
  539–40, 543
bankruptcy 293
behaviour allegations in
  divorce 69
child assessment
  orders 597–9, 686
civil partners 46, 324
clean break 196
cohabitants 48–51, 53–4, 294
  Child Maintenance
    and Enforcement
    Commission 50
  definition of
    cohabitation 54
  maintenance 50, 51
  rights and
    responsibilities 51
  section 8 orders 51
  vulnerability 48–9, 53
competency 353, 418–45,
  553, 625
definition 403, 406–7
disabilities, with 187, 323,
  573, 575
divorce 67, 69, 75–6, 81

domestic violence 94–5, 101,
  156–8
family, child of the 169–70,
  324–7, 331, 471
higher education or training,
  in 67
home rights 216
marriage 41, 43
matrimonial home 170,
  201–9, 211–16
Mesher orders 205–8, 211–14
money and property
  distribution on marriage
  breakdown 161, 169–70,
  183–4
name, change of 549–54
non-molestation
  orders 105–6, 108, 110–11
occupation orders 110,
  124–42
orphans 646–7
parental responsibility 216
property disputes of
  cohabitants 52, 250, 295–6,
  306, 307–8
remarriage 209, 212
sale of matrimonial
  home 203, 292–3
same-sex marriages 40
self-esteem 383
separation, dangers to
  children after 157–8
Statement of Arrangements
  for the Children 67
tenancies, transfers of 294
UN Convention on the Rights
  of the Child 246, 348,
  350–1, 507–8, 566
welfare reports 67
Children Act 1989 *see also*
  section 8 orders
accommodation for
  children 576–8, 582–4
child protection 567–90
child support 329–38
children, rights of 420, 427, 45
Climbié Report 570
complaints and
  representations 582–4
decision-making
  principles 448–54
family assistance orders 467–9
fathers, parental responsibility
  of 342, 377–93, 396
forced marriages 35
Human Rights Act 1998,
  compatibility with 462–3
local authorities, duties
  of 571–90

paramountcy or welfare
  principle 448–54, 462–3,
  465
parental responsibility 342,
  377–93, 396, 400–10
police protection 611–13
property disputes of
  cohabitants 295–6
significant harm
  threshold 35, 590–1
special guardianship
  orders 708
surrogacy 373–4
unmarried parents 329–38
**Children and Family Court
Advisory and Support
Service (Cafcass)** 7, 467, 571,
626, 653
**children cases, private law
disputes in** 447–565 *see also*
section 8 orders
**children needing services,
care, and protection**
566–668 *see also* **care orders;
supervision orders**
abandoned children 648
access to children in abuse
  cases 569–70
accommodation 576–8,
  582–90
background 568–71
best interests test 572
breach of statutory duty 573–4
Cafcass 7, 571
care plans 651–3, 655
care proceedings, final
  hearings in 628–51
Carlile, Kimberley, inquiry
  into death of 570
child assessment orders 597–9
Children Act 1989 567–90,
  611–13
Children Act 2004 570–1
children's guardian, role
  of 625–7
Children's Trust 571
Cleveland Child Abuse
  Inquiry 569
Climbié Report 570
complaints and
  representations 582–4
compulsory intervention 575,
  590–5
conferences 601
contact with children in
  care 662–7
cooperation between
  authorities 570–1
direct payments 573

**children needing services,
  care, and protection** (*cont.*)
disabilities, children
  with 573, 575
disciplines, interaction with
  other 7
diversity and
  individuality 566
emergency intervention
  569–70, 601–13
European Convention on
  Human Rights 566
experts 7
forced marriages 244
homelessness 572, 574
inadequacies of previous
  law 568–70
inherent jurisdiction to take
  child into care 568–9
interim care and supervision
  orders 613–27
International Covenant
  on Civil and Political
  Rights 566
investigations 595–601, 627
judicial review 584
keeping families
  together 572, 575
liberal standard 567–8
Local Safeguarding Children
  Board 571
looked after child, status
  of 578–82
need, children in 536, 573–5
ongoing practice
  concerns 570
paramountcy or welfare
  principle 569–73
parental responsibility 401,
  567, 573
place of safety orders 568
police protection 611–13
provision of services 574–5
reasonable parental care, lack
  of 640–8
representations and
  complaints 582–4
resources 574
respite care 575
Review of Child Care Law 569
review panels 583–4
section 37 investigations,
  court's power to
  order 599–600
significant harm
  threshold 590–7, 601
social workers 7, 569–70,
  589–90, 597, 600–1, 607,
  609, 611–13, 660

UK Border Agency 571
UN Convention on the Rights
  of the Child 566
wardship 568–9
wishes and feelings of
  child 573, 627
children, rights of 413–46
age 416–17, 423
adulthood, boundary
  with 415–18
autonomy 414, 416, 417–28,
  444–5
basic interests 418–19, 425
best interests test 422, 426–8
capacity 414–15
categorisation 418–19
child labour 417
child liberationist
  ideology 416
childhoods 415–18
Children Act 1989 420, 427,
  445
competency 418, 420–8, 444–5
conceptions of a right 413–14
consent to medical
  treatment 420–8
contraceptives 420–7
corporal punishment 444
criminal law 420–1
cultural pluralism 417
developmental
  interests 418–19, 425
different childhoods 417–18
discretion, age of 423, 426
discrimination 416
dual parenting 399
European Convention on
  Human Rights 428, 442–4
fair hearing, right to a 443
freedom of expression 443
fundamental debates 413–18
future-orientated
  consent 419–20
Gillick competency 353,
  420–45, 553
Human Rights Act
  1998 427–8, 442–4
inhuman or degrading
  treatment 443
interest theory 413–14
interests children can
  plausibly claim 418–20
legal protection of
  interests 420–8
liberal paternalism 419–20
life, right to 441
medical treatment 420–42,
  444–5
paramountcy principle 444–5

paternalism 414, 416, 419–20
private and family life, right
  to respect for 428, 443
Rawls's theory of justice 419
self-determination 419
should children have
  rights 414–15
social construction of
  childhood 416
society's perceptions of
  children 417–18
thought, conscience and
  religion, freedom of 444
treaties and conventions 417
voting 416–17
welfarism 418, 426
will theory 413–14
children's guardian 625–7
appointment 402–3
Cafcass officers 626
care plans 651–2
Colwell, Maria, death of 626
delay 627
duties 625–7
interim care and supervision
  orders 625–7
investigations 627
orphans 646–7
parental responsibility 402–3
Practice Direction 626–7
records 627
residence orders 503
solicitor, appointment of 627
welfare checklist 627, 651
Welsh family proceedings
  officers 626
wishes of the child 627
Children's Trust 571
civil partnerships 42–6
adoption 46, 692, 700
agreements 44
assisted fertilisation 367, 369
behaviour, dissolution due
  to 89
child support 324
children 46, 324
Civil Partnership Act 2004 5,
  38–40, 42–5, 88–9
contact orders 46
death, presumption of 89
definition 44
desertion 89
dissolution 45, 88–9
distinguished from
  marriage 38–9, 43, 45
domestic violence 43, 44, 46
financial provision 45, 89
formalities 44
heterosexual couples 55–6

home rights 46
irretrievable breakdown,
    dissolution due to 89
legal consequences 45–6
legal formation 44
legal recognition of families 5
lesbian couples 367
marriage 38–41
nullity 45
occupation orders 119–23,
    133–5, 138–9
overseas dissolution 89
overseas partnerships,
    recognition of 45, 89
parental responsibility
    agreements 46
property disputes of
    cohabitants 305
property orders 45, 89
registration 44
religion 43
residence orders 46
separation 44–5, 89
statistics 43–4, 89
surviving spouses 45–6
termination 44–5
clean break 194–8
children 196, 314–15
contributions 196
deferred clean breaks 162
duration of marriage 196
employment 195–6
extension of the term 197
hardship 195–6
just and reasonable test 194
Law Commission 161
lump sum 166
matrimonial home 202–3,
    206, 208
nominal orders 195
past contributions 196
periodical payments 164,
    195–8
physical and mental disabilities,
    persons with 187
policy 195
property adjustment
    orders 166–7
public interest 234–5
section 28(1A) directions 197
variation 237, 242
Cleveland Child Abuse
    Inquiry 569, 624
Climbié Report 570
cohabitants 46–55 see also
    property disputes of
    cohabitants on relationship
    breakdown
adoption 51

autonomy 48, 53–4
children 48–51, 53–4, 294
    Child Maintenance
        and Enforcement
        Commission 50
    definition of
        cohabitation 54
    maintenance 50, 51
    rights and
        responsibilities 51
    section 8 orders 51
    vulnerability 48–9, 53
civil partnerships for
    heterosexual couples 55
Cohabitation Bill 46, 48, 52,
    54–5, 57
commitment, level of 54,
    301–2
common law marriage 49, 55
death 50–1, 52
definition 47–8, 54
domestic violence 48–9, 50,
    51, 90
financial provision 48, 50
home rights 50, 90
home-sharers 56–7
ideological superiority
    of marriage,
    maintaining 307, 309–10
ideologues, romantics,
    pragmatists, and uneven
    couples 48
Inheritance (Provision for
    Family and Dependants)
    Act 1975 48, 51
increase 3, 46–7
intention of parties with
    regard to ownership of
    property 49, 90
intestacy 50–1, 90
Law Commission 46, 50–5
legal recognition of families 4
length of relationships 48, 55
Living Together
    campaign 49, 55
maintenance 49, 50, 51, 54
marriage
    commitment, level of 54,
        301–2
    comparison with
        cohabitation 54–5,
        294–5, 300–2, 305–10
    ideological superiority,
        maintaining 307,
        309–10
    policy 309–10
    reputation of marriage,
        with 20–1
    undermining 54, 302

matrimonial home,
    cohabitation precipitating
    sale or realisation of
    charge on 208–14
new partners, cohabitation
    after marriage breakdown
    with 165–6, 180–2, 208–14,
    233, 234–5, 242
non-molestation orders 51,
    90, 105–6, 108–9
occupation orders 50, 51, 90,
    123, 133–9
parental responsibility 51
pensions 54
periodical payments 54
policy 48, 53–4, 309–10
property rights 49, 50–4, 90
reform 52–5
relationship breakdown 49–50,
    52–5, 89–90
reputation of marriage,
    having 20–1
rights and obligations 50–1, 54
section 8 orders 51
social attitudes 46–7, 52
statistics 3, 47
tenancies, succession to 51
undermining marriage 54,
    302
vulnerability 48–51, 53,
    89–90
wills 51
Colwell, Marie, death of 626
commitment
    marriage, level of commitment
        in 54, 301–2
    parental responsibility of
        fathers 379, 384, 387, 392,
        396, 398
    property disputes of
        cohabitants 54, 301–2
    unmarried fathers 379
committal 527–9, 663
common law marriage 49, 55,
    301
compensation 102, 199, 533
    see also damages
competency
    assessments 625
    children, rights of 418, 420–8,
        444–5
    Gillick competency 353,
        420–44, 553
    medical treatment of children,
        consent to 419–42, 444–5
    name, change of 553
    parentage 353
complaints and
    representations 582–4

confidentiality 411, 676
connection with
  children 384–5, 476–7,
  539–40, 543
consent *see also* **consent to
  marriage; consent to medical
  treatment of children**
  adoption 673, 677, 680–2,
    684–6, 697, 701–2
  assisted fertilisation 360–1,
    369
  children, relocation of 537
  contact orders 471–2
  divorce 72–3, 85–7
  embryos, father's consent to
    destruction of 361
  family assistance orders 468
  fathers
    adoption 677, 680, 701–2
    embryos, consent to
      destruction of 361
  financial orders, variation
    of 236–7
  non-molestation
    orders 145
  occupation orders 145
  parentage 353–4
  parental responsibility 408
  residence orders 471–2
  section 8 orders 471–2, 482
  separation agreements 219–22,
    231–5
  special guardianship
    orders 709
consent to marriage 13, 25–33
  ceremony, mistake as to
    nature of 29
  conditional consent 31–2
  duress 27–8
  forced marriages 25–8, 33
  identity, mistake as to 28–9
  marriage 27–32
  mental disabilities, persons
    with 29
  mistake 28–9
  nullity 28–9
  overseas marriages,
    recognition of 38
  pregnancy by another
    man 31–2
  residence orders 503
**consent to medical treatment of
  children** 428–42
  authorisation of court,
    seeking 435
  autonomy 420–9, 437–8,
    441–2
  best interests test 433–4, 436,
    441–2

blood transfusions by
  Jehovah's Witnesses, refusal
  of 438–42, 561
children, rights of 420–8,
  444–5
competency 419–42, 444–5
consent and refusal, distinction
  between 436–7
Gillick competency 420–42,
  444–5
Human Rights Act 1998 442
life-saving treatment 438–42,
  561
paramountcy or welfare
  principle 441–2
parental responsibility 405–6,
  428–9
refusal of treatment 428–42
section 8 orders 561
use of reasonable force 434–5
wardship 429–32
constructive trusts 251, 266,
  268, 272–9, 282–4, 299–300
consummation of marriage 25,
  26–7, 30, 31
  forced marriage 26–7
  incapacity 26–7, 30
  religious marriage 26–7
  transsexuals 26
  voidable marriage 26–7
  wilful refusal 26–7
contact *see also* **contact orders;
  contact with child in care**
  adoption 702–7
  care, children in 471–2,
    483–4, 662–7
contact orders 504–33
  3 years, persons with whom
    child has lived for at
    least 471
  18, reaching age 558
  abuse 512, 513, 517, 530–1,
    534
  alienation of parent 518
  assumption in favour of
    contact 511–12
  behaviour of parent 517
  best interests test 526–7
  care, contract with child
    in 471–2, 483–4, 663–7
  child of the family 471
  Children Act Sub-Committee
    of the Lord Chancellor's
    Advisory Board on Family
    Law 522–3
  child's interest, contact almost
    always in 509
  civil partners 46
  committal 527–9

compensation for financial
  loss 533
conditions 505–7, 511,
  525–7, 530
consents 471–2
contact activity directions and
  conditions 525–7
contact centres 507
contempt of court 527–9
court's general
  approach 508–12
criminal convictions 520–1
definition 466, 504–5
destabilising present family
  unit, risk of 521–2
direct contact 504–6, 526–7
discretion 557
distress caused to residential
  parents 512, 514, 518–21
domestic violence 156–8,
  513–16, 520–1, 527
duration of orders 558–9
emergency protection
  orders 603
enforcement 510, 522–3,
  526–33
facilitation of contact 523–6
fair hearing, right to a 526, 529
family assistance orders 523
genuine fear 520–1, 527
guidelines 514–17
harm
  committal 528
  definition of 513
  enforcement 526
  risk 519
  section 37 directions 530–1
hostility of parent,
  implacable 518–21, 527,
  530–1
indirect contact 506, 510–12,
  517, 520–1, 527, 559
local authority care 471–2,
  483–4, 664–7
monitoring contact and
  contact activities 525
nature of proposed
  applications 476
opposition
  implacable hostility of
    parent 518–21, 527,
    530–1
  step-parents 521–2
paramountcy or welfare
  principle 509, 510, 512,
  518, 524, 527–8
parentage 351–6
parental alienation
  syndrome 518

parental responsibility 472,
483–4, 505
presumption 508–13
private and family life, right
to respect for 507–8, 526
prohibited steps orders 466,
534
religion 525
residence orders 503, 530
right of contact 508
section 37 directions 530–1
specific issue orders 466
step-parents 508, 521–2
supervised contact 507, 512,
516
suspended residence
orders 530
transsexuals 517
UN Convention on the Rights
of the Child 507–8
variations 524
warning notices 525–6
welfare checklist 509
when orders can be
made 557–8
who can apply 470–2
wishes and feelings of
child 516–18, 527
contact with child in care
agreements 662
best interests test 664
care orders 662
committal proceedings 663
consent 471–2
deny contact, courts
authorising local
authorities to 664–7
discretion 663–4
enforcement 663
expert evidence 665
leave to apply 664
paramountcy or welfare
principle 664– 6
parental responsibility
483–4
reasonable contact 663–4
regulation of contact in cases
of disagreement 663
section 8 orders 664
variation 667
wishes and feelings of
child 663
contempt of court 37, 113,
114–16, 140–2, 148, 527–9
contraceptives 420–7
contributions to family home
businesses, contributions
to 275–7
clean break 196

common intention 251,
254–84, 298–300
constructive trusts 251,
266, 268, 272–9, 282–3,
299–300
detrimental reliance 268,
271, 279–81
domestic contributions 271–4,
278, 281–2, 298–300, 304
economic disadvantage 306–7
financial contributions 205,
250–68, 270–84, 299–300
improvements 269–71, 279
indirect financial
contributions 261, 272–8,
282–3
indirect contributions 205,
251, 261, 267–8, 270–8,
282–3
joint names cases 248–9,
252–66, 271–4, 278, 281–3,
298–300
money and property
distribution on marriage
breakdown 187–90, 205
past contributions 196
proprietary estoppel 284–90
purchase price 251–2, 270,
274, 279–81, 309
qualifying contributions 306–7
reform 304, 306–7
resulting trusts 250–8, 265,
279, 282–3
sole name cases 252, 266–83
special contribution
argument 188–90
**control, children beyond
parental** 648–9
convenience, marriages of 33
co-ownership 205–8, 211–18
corporal punishment 410, 444
costs 183, 193, 201, 218
counselling 81–3, 86–7, 360, 703
criminal offences see also **arrest**
accommodation for
children 590
adoption 688, 703
bigamy 21, 377
children, rights of 420–1
contact orders 520–1
criminal injuries
compensation 102
divorce 69
domestic violence 99–103
emergency protection
orders 601
fathers, parental responsibility
of 386–7, 391–3, 395,
404–5, 411–12

forced marriages 34–5
fraud 221
harassment 146–8
marital rape 99
money and property
distribution on marriage
breakdown 192–3
non-molestation orders,
breach of 104, 108, 113–
17, 142
parental responsibility 386–7,
391–3, 395, 404–5, 411–12
removal of children 503,
534, 537
residence orders 503
separation agreements 221
sexual offences 99, 386–7,
390–1, 700
culture
children, rights of 417
name, change of 550–1,
554–5
paramountcy or welfare
principle 461
parentage 357
pluralism 417
relocation of children 544
scientific testing 357
significant harm
threshold 595

damages 35, 147–9, 177
see also **compensation**
de facto relationships 4–6
death
assisted fertilisation 368–9
cohabitants 50–1, 52
domestic violence, statistics
on deaths from 93, 158
home-sharers 56
presumption of death, decree
of 46, 88
property rights 42
separation agreements 231–2
sperm after death, use
of 368–9
definition of family law 2–3
delay
adoption 673–4, 679, 691
children's guardian, role
of 627
contact with child in care 665
divorce 66, 74–5, 82–3, 86
money and property
distribution 232
occupation orders 143–4
paramountcy or welfare
principle 451, 455, 464,
665, 673–4, 679, 691

delay (*cont.*)
   parental responsibility 399,
     408
   residence orders 477
desertion 71–2, 89
detrimental reliance 268, 271,
   279–81, 284–90
developmental interests 418–19,
   425
disabilities, persons with
   child support 323
   children 187, 323, 573, 575
   clean break 187
   expenses 323
   mental disabilities, persons
     with 13–14, 25, 29, 31,
     112–13, 187
   need, children in 573, 575
   parents 592, 642–3
   respite care 575
   significant harm
     threshold 592
   wishes and feelings of
     child 573
discipline of children
   410, 444
disciplines, interaction with
   other 7, 35
discretion
   adoption 690, 698–9
   care orders 661
   child support 326, 332–8
   children, rights of 423, 426
   contact orders 557, 663–4
   financial orders, variation
     of 237–8
   judges 6
   non-molestation orders 111,
     113
   occupation orders 122, 124–6,
     128–30, 136–9
   parentage 351
   parental responsibility 382,
     409–10
   pensions 200
   property disputes of
     cohabitants 307
   residence orders 485, 557
   rules 6–7
   sale of property 292
   section 8 orders 474, 557–8
discrimination
   adoption 676
   children, rights of 416
   Convention on the
     Elimination of All Forms
     of Discrimination against
     Women 154–6
   domestic violence 154–6

European Convention on
   Human Rights 16–17, 22,
   38–40, 56, 393–5
   fathers, against 378–9,
     393–400, 486–7
   home-sharers 56
   marriage 13, 22, 394–6
   marry, right to 13
   money and property
     distribution on marriage
     breakdown 170–6, 182, 188
   parental care, lack of
     reasonable 642
   parental responsibility of
     fathers 378–9, 393–400
   prohibited degrees of
     relationship 16–17
   religion 489–90
   residence orders 486–90
   same-sex couples 5, 39–40,
     488
   transsexuals and marriage 22
   unmarried fathers 378–9,
     393–400
disease, marriage to persons
   with venereal 25, 29, 30, 31
dissolution of adult
   relationships 59–90
   see also divorce
   civil partnerships 45, 88–9
   cohabitation 89–90
   death, decree of presumption
     of 88, 89
   judicial separation 87–8
distress, causing
   contact orders 512, 514,
     518–21
   parental responsibility of
     fathers 385, 387–8, 390, 393
   relocation of children 538–9,
     542–5, 548
divorce 59–88 *see also* money
   and property distribution on
   marriage breakdown
   1 year bar 66
   2 years desertion for 71–2
   2 years separation with
     consent 72–3, 87
   5 years separation 72–3, 74
   Acts of Parliament,
     through 59
   adoption 670
   adultery
     collusion 60, 67
     definition 68
     intolerability 67–8
     proof 68
     reconciliation, periods of 68
     waiting period 86

   age 62
   appeals 66–7
   attendance at court 67
   behaviour 68–71, 84, 86
   big money cases 63–4, 76
   Booth Committee 61, 69, 78
   Brussels II Revised 62, 64
   children
     16, under 67
     before divorce, making
       arrangements 81
     behaviour allegations 69
     Children Act 1989 67
     higher education or
       training, in 67
     legal effects of
       divorce 75–6
     parental responsibility,
       continuation of 76
     policy 67
     Statement of Arrangements
       for the Children 67
     welfare reports 67
   collusion 60, 67
   condonation 59–60
   consent 72–3, 85–7
   constructive desertion 72
   county courts 65
   criminal offences, conviction
     of 69
   criticism 78–81
   decrees absolute 66–7, 72,
     75–6
   decrees nisi 61, 66–7, 72
   defended divorces 67
   delay 66, 74–5, 82–3, 86
   desertion for 2 years 71–2
   developments in
     procedure 61
   domestic violence 75–6
   domicile 62, 76–7
   EU law 76
   Family Law Act 1996 81–4
   fault 79, 84–7
   five facts 64–75, 84
   forum shopping 63
   future of divorce law 84–6
   ground for divorce 64–5
   habitual residence 62
   hardship 73–5, 82
   Hemain injunctions 74
   higher education or training,
     children in 67
   history 59–61
   home rights 75–6
   illness, behaviour arising
     through 70–1
   information meetings,
     attendance at 81, 83, 86–7

Inheritance (Provision for
Family and Dependants)
Act 1975 75–6
intolerability 67–8
irretrievable breakdown 64–5,
68–9, 79–82, 85
jurisdiction to hear a
divorce 62–4, 76–8
Law Commission 32, 60, 73,
78–84
legal effects 75–6
living apart 73
living together
behaviour, after 71
desertion for 2 years 71–2
living apart 71–2, 73
same household, in the 73
Matrimonial Causes Act
1973 64–81
mediation and
counselling 81–3, 86–7
mixed system of fault and
no-fault divorce, proposal
for 79, 85
Morton Commission 60
nullity, distinguished
from 15, 32
obtaining a divorce 62–84
occupation orders 131–3
offences 59–60
oral evidence 61, 67
orders 82
overseas divorce, recognition
of 76–8
parental responsibility,
continuation of 76
petitions 65
policy 67–8, 85–6
preventing divorce, orders 82
procedure 65–6
promotion of institution of
marriage 86
Putting Asunder report 60
Queen's Proctor, intervention
by 66–7
reconciliation
adultery 68
certificates 66
condonation 59–60
encouraging 66–7, 71,
73, 79
reflection and
consideration, period
for 82, 83, 85
reflection and consideration,
period for 82, 83, 85
reform 61, 78–87
religious decrees 75
Scotland 87

separation
2 years with consent,
for 72–3, 87
5 years separation 72–3, 74
special preparation 73–5
special preparation 73–5
special procedure 61
state, interests of the 85
Statement of Arrangements
for the Children 67
statements of marital
breakdown 81–2
statistics 62
stay of proceedings in
England and Wales 64
stigma 31, 32
talaq (Islamic divorce) 77–8
timetable 66–7, 82, 86
trends 62
unilateral demand 85–6
waiting period 86
DNA testing 343–4, 349, 352, 357
domestic contributions 271–4,
278, 281–2, 298–300, 304
domestic violence 91–160 see
also non-molestation orders;
occupation orders
adoption 678
aggravating factors 99
alcohol 96, 112
antisocial/narcissistic
personality 96
asymmetry 93–4
attrition, high levels of 100–2
children
contact 156–8
effects on children 94–5,
101, 156–8
separation, dangers of
contact after 157–8
civil law remedies 103–18
civil partners 43, 44, 46
cohabitants 48–9, 50, 51, 90
contact orders 513–16,
520–1, 527
Convention on the
Elimination of All Forms
of Discrimination against
Women 154–6
criminal injuries
compensation 102
criminal law, role
of 99–103
deaths, statistics on 93, 158
definition 91–3, 150–1
dependency, relationships
of 96
divorce 75–6
drug abuse 96, 112

emotional and psychological
abuse 92–5, 104–5
evidence, reluctance to
give 101
explanations 96–8
failure to report abuse 93, 100
fair hearing, right to a 154
family violence, use of
term 92
feminist explanations 97–8
forced marriages 34, 36
gender-based violence 92–4,
97–8, 155–6
guidelines 514
harassment 146–9
harm, definition of 513
homelessness 149–53
home-sharers 55–6
human rights 153–6
inhuman or degrading
treatment 154
injunctions 146–9
interim care and supervision
orders 617–18
international human rights
law 154–6
Law Commission 145–6
leave relationships, reasons
for not 95–6
life, right to 154
local authority housing 149–53
marital rape 99
men, against 93–4, 102
multifaceted phenomenon
97–8
parental responsibility of
fathers 392
patriarchal social order 97–8
persons not protected 145–6
police, attitudes of 99–101
policy 513
positive obligations 154
prevalence 93–6
private and family life, right
to respect for 154
psychological explanations
96–7, 513
public interest 101
Sentencing Guidelines
Council 99
separation, violence after
95–6, 157–8
significant harm
threshold 591
social structural
explanations 96–8
Specialist Domestic Violence
Courts 100
statistics 93, 99–101, 158

domestic violence (*cont.*)
structural inequality 98
terminology 92
terrorism 92
threatening or intimidating
behaviour 91–2
treaties and conventions on
human rights 154–6
UN Declaration on
Elimination of Violence
against Women 92–3
under-reporting 93, 100
United Nations 92–3, 154–5
vulnerability 151–2
women's refuges 98
domicile 62, 372, 692
drug abuse and domestic
violence 96, 112
duress
forced marriages 27–8, 33, 35
marriage 25, 27–8, 32, 33
overborne will 27–8
Duxbury formula 166. 210–11

education 67, 322–3
egg donations 357–8
embryos, use of 361, 369
emergencies *see also* emergency
protection orders (EPOs)
child protection 569–70,
601–13
police protection under
Children Act 1989 611–13
significant harm threshold
600, 602–4, 608–9
emergency protection orders
(EPOs) 569–70, 601–10
access to child 604, 609
arrest 608
best interests test 603
care orders 659
causative link
requirement 604
challenging EPOs 610
contact, directions with
regard to 603
criminal offences 601
definition 601–3
discharge, applications for 609
duration of the order 601–2,
605
enforcement 608
enquiries 604
exclusion requirement 608–9
execution of orders 609
extension 602
frustrated access grounds 604
grounds 603–8
guidance 601

inherent jurisdiction of High
Court 610
interim care and supervision
orders 616
judicial review 610
medical examinations or
assessments 602, 607, 609
obstruction 601
parental responsibility 601–3
police 609, 611–12
proportionality 605–6, 612
removal for protection 601–2,
609
significant harm 602–4, 608–9
social workers 607, 609
supervision orders 659
suspicion 604
undertakings 607–8
without notice 603, 605, 609
emotional and psychological
abuse 92–5, 104–5
employment
child labour 417
clean break 195–6
EPOs *see* emergency protection
orders (EPOs)
estoppel *see* proprietary
estoppel emotional
European Convention on
Human Rights *see also* fair
hearing, right to a; life, right
to; private and family life,
right to respect for
child protection 566
children, rights of 428, 442–4
discrimination 16–17, 22,
38–40, 56, 393–5
freedom of expression 443
inhuman or degrading
treatment 154, 443, 601
liberty and security, right
to 144
life, right to 154, 361, 441
living instrument
doctrine 39–40
margin of appreciation 22,
361, 370
marry, right to 12–13, 22–4,
33, 39–40
same-sex marriages 38–9
thought, conscience, and
religion, freedom of 444,
654
exclusion requirements 123,
135, 292, 608–9, 625
experts
child protection 7
contact with children in
care 665

disagreement amongst
experts 636–8
disciplines, interaction with
other 7
section 37 directions 531
significant harm
threshold 636–8

fair hearing, right to a
child support 321
children, rights of 443
committal 529
contact orders 526, 529
domestic violence 154
interim care and supervision
orders 615
occupation orders 144, 154
parentage 347
relocation of children 538
section 8 orders 555
self-incrimination, privilege
against 529
false imprisonment 35
family, child of the 169–70,
324–7, 331, 471
family assistance orders 467–9,
523, 651
family home *see* matrimonial
home; property disputes of
cohabitants on relationship
breakdown
family life, right to respect for
see private and family life,
right to respect for
family proceedings, definition
of 469–70
fathers and fatherhood *see also*
parental responsibility of
fathers; parents
adoption
by fathers 692, 694–5, 700
consent 677, 680, 701–2
identity 676–7
parental responsibility 677
private and family
life, right to respect
for 679–80
withholding
information 676–80
agreed fatherhood
conditions 366
assisted reproduction 358–9,
361–9
biological connection 367
child support and lack
of knowledge of
paternity 325
consent
adoption 677, 680, 701–2

embryos, destruction
of 361
death, use of sperm
after 368–9
discrimination 378–9,
393–400, 486–7
embryos, father's consent to
destruction of 361
genetic connection 358
Human Fertilisation
and Embryology Act
1990 358–60
Human Fertilisation
and Embryology Act
2008 358–60
identity 676–7
information on fathers 380,
399–400, 676–80
knowledge of paternity, lack
of 325
legal parenthood 358–60, 376
legitimacy, presumption
of 342–6, 354, 362
lesbian couples 360, 368, 376,
388, 391, 488–9
paternity, child support and
lack of knowledge of 325
private and family life,
right to respect for 679–80
sperm donors 347–8, 351–2,
365, 367–9, 374–6
transsexuals and
marriage 369–70
withholding
information 676–80
features of family law 6–7
feelings of child see wishes and
feelings of child
feminist writers
definition of family law 2–3
domestic violence 97–8
fertility treatment see assisted
fertilisation
financial contributions 250–68,
270–84, 299–300
financial obligations of
marriage 14–15, 25, 41
financial provision see also
money and property
distribution on marriage
breakdown; property
disputes of cohabitants on
relationship breakdown
forced marriages 13–14, 15, 33–7
arranged marriages
distinguished 33
arrest, protection orders
with 37
capacity 13–14

Children Act 1989,
significant harm under 35
civil remedies 35
consent 27–8, 33, 35–6
consummation 26–7, 30
contempt of court 37
criminal offences 34–5
damages 35
definition 33, 36–7
domestic violence 34, 36
duress 27–8, 33, 35
false imprisonment 35
family law remedies 35
forced marriage protection
orders 36–7
Forced Marriage Unit 33–4
harassment 35
injunctions 35
multi-agency approach 35
nullity 33, 35–6
oral evidence 35
overseas, entered into 35–7
time limits 36
trespass to the person 35
undertakings 37
void marriages 33
voidable marriages 33
wardship and inherent
jurisdiction of High Court,
protection under 35–6
formation of adult
relationships 11–58
civil partnerships 42–6
cohabitation 46–55
home-sharers 55–7
marriage 11–42
non-formal
relationships 46–57
former relevant child 580–2
forum shopping 63, 228
foster parents 472, 481–4
fraud 221
freedom of expression 443

gender see also fathers and
fatherhood; mothers and
motherhood
Convention of the
Elimination of All Forms
of Discrimination against
Women 154–6
domestic violence 92–4,
97–8, 155–6
human rights 155–6
legal parenthood 375
marriage 21–5, 38–41
patriarchal social order 97–8
residence orders 485–7
stereotyping 375

UN Declaration on
Elimination of Violence
against Women 92–3
gender reassignment see
transsexuals and marriage
genetic relationships see
biological relationship
Gillick competency 353, 420–45,
553
grandparents 376, 473, 475,
484, 530–1
guardians see children's
guardian, role of; special
guardianship orders

habitual residence 62, 76–7, 692
harassment 146–9
arrest 147
civil remedies 146–7
contempt of court 148
course of conduct 147–8
criminal offences 146–8
damages 147–9
definition 147
domestic violence 146–9
fear of violence, putting
people in fear of 148
forced marriages 35
injunctions 146, 148–9
non-molestation orders 104–5,
109, 116, 147, 149
occupation orders 141–2
private nuisance 146
Protection from Harassment
Act 1997 109, 141–2,
146–9
restraining orders 148–9
sentencing 116
stalking 146
standard of proof 147–8
telephone calls 146
tort, creation of a 146–7
hardship
clean break 195–6
divorce 73–5, 82
financial orders, variation
of 237
judicial separation 87
matrimonial home 213–14
property disputes of
cohabitants 293–4, 303,
305, 309
tenancies, transfers of 294
harm see also significant harm
threshold
committal 528
contact orders 513, 519, 526,
528, 530–1
definition 513

harm (*cont.*)
    disruption causing
      harm 477–8
    domestic violence 92–5,
      104–5, 513
    emotional and psychological
      harm 92–5, 104–5
    residence orders 484
    section 8 orders 477–8
    section 37 directions 530–1
Hemain injunctions 74, 78
Henshaw Report 315–16
High Court *see* inherent
    jurisdiction of the High Court
holiday, taking children on 503,
    537, 575
home rights
    cohabitants 50, 90
    divorce 75–6
    marriage 42
    matrimonial home 216
    non-molestation orders 103
    occupation orders 119, 121,
      123, 124–5
    property disputes of
      cohabitants 246–7
homelessness
    children 152, 572, 574, 581–2
    Code of Guidance 150–1, 153
    definition of
      homelessness 149–50
    domestic violence 149–53
      associated persons 150
      Code of Guidance 150–1,
        153
      definition 150–1
    intentional homelessness
      150–3, 572, 574
    looked after children 581–2
    occupation orders 128
    priority need 151–2, 581
    vulnerable persons 151–2
home-sharers 56–7
homosexual couples *see* civil
    partnerships; same-sex
    couples; same-sex marriage
housing *see also* homelessness;
    local authority
    accommodation for children;
    matrimonial home
    domestic violence 149–53
    occupation orders 128
Human Fertilisation and
    Embryology Authority
    (HFEA) 360–1, 368
human rights *see also* European
    Convention on Human Rights;
    Human Rights Act 1998
    domestic violence 153–6

gender-based violence 155–6
International Covenant
    on Civil and Political
    Rights 566
treaties and
    conventions 154–6
Human Rights Act 1998
    adoption 689–90
    care plans 653, 655
    Children Act 1989,
      compatibility of 462–3
    children, rights of 427–8,
      442–4
    discrimination 5, 488
    domestic violence 154–5
    list of Convention rights 5–6
    medical treatment of children,
      consent to 442
    paramountcy or welfare
      principle 462–3
    positive obligations 154
    relocation of children 537–8
    residence orders 488
    same-sex couples 5
    transsexuals and
      marriage 23–4

identity rights 346–56
illegitimacy *see* legitimacy/
    illegitimacy
immigration 33
improvements 269–71, 279,
    288–9
information
    adoption 675, 676–80, 702–3
    confidentiality 411, 676
    criminal offences 703
    divorce 81, 83, 86–7
    exceptional circumstances,
      withholding information
      in 677–8
    fathers, on 380, 399–400,
      676–80
    meetings, attendance at 81,
      83, 86–7
    mothers, anonymity of 348
    protected information,
      definition of 702–3
    relatives, withholding
      information
      from 676–80
    separation agreements 221–2
    sperm donors 368
    withholding
      information 676–80
inherent jurisdiction of the
    High Court
    accommodation for
      children 586–7

adoption 562, 676–7
    assessments 625
    blood transfusions and
      Jehovah's Witnesses 561
    child protection 568–9
    emergency protection
      orders 610
    forced marriages 35–6
    interim care and supervision
      orders 625
    local authorities 562–4
    parental responsibility 563–4
    section 8 orders 555–6, 561–4
    wardship 35–6, 562–4, 568–9
inheritance *see* succession
Inheritance (Provision for
    Family and Dependants) Act
    1975 42, 48, 51, 75–6
inheritance tax 43, 56–7
inhuman or degrading
    treatment 154, 443, 601
injunctions
    adoption 690
    divorce 74
    domestic violence 146–9
    forced marriages 35
    harassment 146, 148–9
    Hemain injunctions 74, 78
in-law marriages 16–17
interim care and supervision
    orders 613–27
    arrest attached to exclusion
      requirement, power of 625
    assessments 619–25
    care plans 652
    change of circumstances 615
    children's guardian, role
      of 625–7
    Cleveland Inquiry 624
    decisions on whether to grant
      order 616–17
    directions 619–25
    domestic violence 617–18
    duration of orders 615–16
    emergency protection
      orders 616
    exclusion from home 625
    fair hearing, right to a 615
    guidance 616–17
    inherent jurisdiction 625
    medical or psychiatric
      assessments 620–5
    paramountcy or welfare
      principle 618–19
    parental responsibility 613,
      615, 619, 624
    parents, assessment of 619–21
    private and family life, right
      to respect for 615

proportionality 617
psychotherapy 621–3
reasonable grounds for
    belief 615–16
refuse assessments, child's
    right to 620, 624–5
renewal 615–16
residence orders 614
residential assessments 620,
    622–4
significant harm 614, 620
threshold 615–16
time limits 615
**International Covenant on Civil
    and Political Rights** 566
**internationalisation of family
    law** 6
intersexuals 25
intestacy 50–1, 88, 90
intolerability, divorce and 67–8
investigations
    child protection 597–601, 627
    children's guardian, role of 627
    section 37 investigations,
        court's power to
        order 599–600
    significant harm 595–7
irretrievable breakdown
    civil partners 89
    divorce 64–5, 68–9, 79–82, 85
    judicial separation 87

Jehovah's Witnesses
    blood transfusions, consent
        to 438–42, 561
    discrimination 489–90
    residence orders 489–90
**joint names, property
    in** 248–9, 252–66, 281–3,
    296–300
joint tenants 214–16
**judicial separation, decree
    of** 87–8

Law Commission
    clean break 161
    cohabitants 46, 50–5
    divorce 32, 60, 73, 78–84
    domestic violence 145–6
    fathers, parental responsibility
        of 399–400
    illegitimacy 378
    marriage formalities 31–3
    money and property
        distribution on marriage
        breakdown 161, 190–1
    non-molestation orders 103,
        105, 109–10, 145
    nullity of marriage 32

occupation orders 118, 126,
    128–9, 133, 139, 143, 145
paramountcy or welfare
    principle 453, 458–9
parental responsibility 395,
    399–400, 403
property disputes of
    cohabitants 247, 272–3,
    296, 298, 303, 304–8
shared residence orders 491
**learning disabilities, parents
    with** 642–3
legal aid 111, 117, 201, 217
legal parenthood 340–2, 357–76
    assisted fertilisation 362–5, 367
    biology 367, 374, 376
    causation 375
    child support 315
    criticism of the law 376
    definition 341
    fatherhood 341–2, 358–60,
        376
    gender stereotyping 375
    Human Fertilisation
        and Embryology Act
        1990 360–5, 374
    Human Fertilisation
        and Embryology Act
        2008 365–6, 374, 376
    Human Fertilisation and
        Embryology Authority 368
    intent-based
        parenthood 374–5
    lesbian couples 367, 376
    motherhood 357–8, 374, 400
    not regarded as parents,
        persons not 367–9
    paramountcy or welfare
        principle 375
    parentage 341–2
    parental responsibility 341–2,
        376
    rationales for attributing
        parenthood 374–6
    responsibility/causation 375
    social parents 375–6
    sperm donors 365, 368,
        374–5, 376
    surrogacy and parental
        orders 371–4, 375
    transsexuals 369–70
**legal recognition of
    families** 3–6
legitimacy/illegitimacy
    Law Commission 378
    name, change of 550–1
    parentage 342–6, 354
    parental responsibility of
        fathers 378

presumption of
    legitimacy 342–6, 354, 362
lesbian couples
    assisted fertilisation 40, 46,
        331, 367
    civil partnerships 367
    fathers and fatherhood 360,
        368, 376, 388, 391, 488–9
    legal parenthood 367, 376
    mothers 46, 331, 367, 376,
        378, 388, 391, 458–9
    parental responsibility 40, 46,
        331, 378, 388, 391
    residence orders 458–9,
        485–9
liberty and security, right to 144
life, right to 154, 361, 441
**life-saving treatment of children,
    refusal of** 438–42, 561
lifestyle choices 184, 238–40,
    329, 337–8, 540, 614, 641
**living together after
    divorce** 71–2, 73
local authorities *see also*
    **care orders; children
    needing services, care and
    protection; local authority
    accommodation for children;
    looked after children;
    supervision orders**
    adoption 669–74
    Children Act 1989 571–90
    domestic violence and
        housing 149–53
    family assistance orders 468
    fathers, parental responsibility
        of 381
    housing 149–53
    inherent jurisdiction 562–4
    medical treatment, consent
        to 561
    parental responsibility 381,
        401, 404, 406, 482–4, 560–1,
        564, 579, 652–5, 661
    prohibited steps orders 483–4,
        560–1
    resources 468
    section 8 orders 478–84,
        560–1
    specific issues orders 483,
        536, 560–1
    wishes and feelings of
        child 478–9
**local authority accommodation
    for children** 576–8
    16, where child is 586–7
    abuse in care 583–4
    agreements 588
    best interests test 588

local authority accommodation for children (*cont.*)
birth plans 589–90
care and protection, in need of 588–9
Children Act 1989 576–8, 582–4
coercion 588–9
complaints and representations 582–4
compulsory intervention 588–9
cooperation 585, 588
criminal assaults 590
homelessness 152, 572, 574, 581–2
inherent jurisdiction of High Court 586–7
looked after children 578–81
paramountcy or welfare principle 586, 590
parental responsibility 584–5, 587–90
planning 588
priority need 581
private and family life, right to respect for 585–6, 589
qualifications to voluntary nature 586–90
residence orders 471–2, 482–4, 504, 586
risk assessment 588–9
significant harm threshold 585
unmarried fathers without parental responsibility 585–6
voluntary nature 584–90
wishes and feelings of child 587
Local Safeguarding Children Board (LSCB) 571
lone parents *see* **single parents**
looked after children
accommodation 578–81
adoption 670
age 579–80
assessments 580, 582
background of children, consideration of 579
care orders 578, 655
Children Act 1989 578–82
educational achievement, duty to promote 579
eligible child, definition of 579, 580, 582
former relevant child 580–2
homelessness 581–2
local authorities 578–82

parental responsibility 579
pathway plans 579, 580
personal advisers 579, 580
relevant child
definition 580
former relevant child 580–2
safeguard and promote welfare, duty of local authorities to 579
status 578–82
wishes and feelings of child, parents and persons with parental responsibility 579
lump sums
appeals 232–4
child support 324, 326, 329, 330–1
clean break 166
during marriage 243–4
Duxbury formula 166
instalments 165, 236, 237–8
Matrimonial Causes Act 1973 161
matrimonial home 203
property disputes of cohabitants 304, 307–8
remarriage 165–6
variation 236, 237–8

maintenance *see also* **child support; money and property distribution on marriage breakdown**
agreements 316, 318–19, 322, 338
children 41, 43
cohabitants 49, 50, 51, 54
costs 163–4
definition of maintenance 163
periodical payments orders 164
remarriage 235
suit, pending 163–4, 235
variation 235
margin of appreciation 22, 361, 370
marital rape 99
marriage 11–42 *see also* **consent to marriage; forced marriage; money and property distribution on marriage breakdown; nullity of marriage**
adoption 42, 700
age 17
already married, where party is 21
approved premises, definition of 18–19

armed forces, overseas marriages of 38
arranged marriages 33
banns 18
bars to relief 30
bigamy, criminal offence of 21, 377
capacity to marry 13–14, 25–7, 29, 30, 31, 38
ceremonies 12, 18–20, 29
certificates 18
children 41, 43, 324
Christian concept 11–12, 18, 31–3
civil ceremonies 12, 18–20
civil partners
distinguished 38–9, 43, 45
cohabitants
commitment, level of 54, 301–2
comparison with marriage 54–5, 294–5, 300–2, 305–10
ideological superiority, maintaining 307, 309–10
policy 309–10
reputation of marriage, with 20–1
undermining 54, 302
commitment, level of 54, 301–2
consummation 25, 26–7, 30, 31
convenience, marriages of 33
cousins 16
death, presumption of 88
decline in marriage 300
definition 11–12
discrimination 13, 22, 394–6
duress 25, 27–8, 32, 33
fathers, parental responsibility of 377, 394–6
formalities
ceremonies 18–19
failure to comply 17–21
overseas marriages, recognition of 37–8
preliminary formalities 18
presumptions of marriage 20–1
home rights 42
identity, mistakes as to 28–9
ideological superiority, maintaining 307, 309–10
immigration 33
inheritance tax 43
in-laws 16–17
intersexuals 25

Law Commission 31–3
legal consequences 41–2
male and female, parties must be 21–5, 38–41
mental disabilities, persons with 13–14, 25, 29, 31
mistake 28–9
name, change of 554
non-marriages 14, 19–20
notice 18
overseas marriages, recognition of 37–8, 41
parental responsibility of fathers 377, 394–6
parents
  consent of 17
  parental responsibility 43
pensions 43
policy 309–10
polygamous marriages 12
pregnancy by another man 26, 29, 30, 31–2
presumptions of marriage 20–1
prohibited degrees of relationship 16–17, 700
rape within marriage 99
religion 11–12, 18–21, 26–7, 31–3, 38, 41
right to marry 12–13, 22–4, 33, 39–40
same-sex marriages 38–41
sham marriages 33
state's interest in marriage 13
statistics 12, 300
step-families 16
tax 43
transsexuals 21–5, 26, 29–30, 31
undermining marriage 54, 302
validity 13–41
venereal disease, persons with 25, 29, 30, 31
void marriages 14, 15–25, 33, 88, 377
voidable marriages 14, 25–33
voluntary union, as 11–12, 13
vulnerable adults, protection of 13–14
marry, right to
discrimination 13
European Convention on Human Rights 12–13, 22–4, 33, 39–40
living instrument doctrine 39–40
same-sex marriages 39–40
sham marriages 33

transsexuals 22–4
Martin **orders** 208–14
maternity *see* **mothers and motherhood**
matrimonial home 201–17
adulthood, postponement of realisation of share until children reach 205–8
age of parties 184–5
appeals 231, 233
big money cases 205–6
charges 205, 208–14, 216–17
children 201–9, 211–16
clean breaks 202–3, 206, 208
cohabitation precipitating sale or realisation of charge 208–14
contributions to welfare of family 187–90, 205
co-ownership 205–8, 211–18
costs 201
court, powers of 201–17
Duxbury principle 210–11
final orders, *Mesher* and *Martin* orders as 211–12
hardship 213–14
home rights 216
joint tenants 214–16
legal aid 201, 217
lump sums 203
Martin orders 208–14
Matrimonial Causes Act 1973 202–5
Mesher orders 205–8, 211–14
mortgages 216–17
moving house problem, overcoming 212–13
orders for sale 162, 167–8, 202–3, 307–8
paramountcy or welfare principle 170
pensions 199
periodical payments orders 203–4, 209–10, 213
policy 207
postponement of realisation of one party's share 205–8, 211–14
proceeds of sale 202–3, 212–15, 240–1
property adjustment orders 167, 205–14, 211
remarriage or cohabitation with new partner 165, 208–14, 233
retention of interest for each spouse 205
sale of property 167–8, 202–3, 208–14, 236

secured periodical payments orders 165
sole names, property transferred in 203–5
statutory charge 201, 217
tenancies, transfer of 217
triggering events 208–10
mediation on divorce 81–3, 86–7
medical examinations or assessments 602, 607, 609, 620–5, 656–7
medical treatment *see* **consent to medical treatment of children**
mental disabilities/illness, people with 13–14, 25, 29, 31, 112–13, 187 *see also* **capacity**
Mesher **orders** 205–8, 211–14
mistake, marriage and 28–9
money and property distribution on marriage breakdown 160–245 *see also* **child support; clean break; lump sums; matrimonial home; periodical payments orders; property adjustment orders**
age of parties 184–7
all the circumstances, having regard to 169, 185
ante-nuptial agreements 222–9
appeals and rehearings 230–42
background to current law 160–1
Barder test 230–5
before divorce, making arrangements 81
big money cases 63–4, 76, 170–6, 182, 187–9
capital 170–6, 178–9
children 161, 169–70, 183–4, 243–4
civil partners 45, 89
classification of property 182–3
conduct 189, 190–3
consent orders 236–7
costs penalties 183, 193
county court, applications to 243
courts' powers 163–8
criminal offences 192–3
damages 177
decrees nisi and decrees absolute, time between 66–7
deferred orders 162, 236

money and property
  distribution on marriage
  breakdown (*cont.*)
    dependants 183–4
    disclosure 183
    discretion 169–98
    discrimination 170–6, 182, 188
    divorce 61, 63, 66–7, 75–6, 81
    Domestic Proceedings and
      Magistrates' Courts Act
      1978 243
    duration of marriage 184–7
    during marriage, orders 243–4
    earning capacity 178–9, 187,
      240–2
    equality, yardstick of 63,
      170–6, 182, 188
    expectations of inheritance
      177
    Family Procedure Rules 2010
      161
    fault 190–3
    finality principle 230–5
    financial and property
      agreements 217–29
    financial needs, obligations
      and responsibilities 183–4
    financial order
      proceedings 161
    financial provision
      orders 161, 243–4
    financial resources of each
      spouse 177–83
    full and frank disclosure 183
    general directions 169–70
    guidance 170–6
    hardship 237
    High Court, applications
      to 243
    income 176, 178–9, 187
    inequitable to disregard,
      type of conduct which it
      is 191–3
    inheritance 177, 182–3
    judicial separation 88
    Law Commission 161, 190–1
    legal effects of divorce 75–6
    legislative framework 161–8
    lifestyle choices 184, 238–40,
      321, 337–8
    magistrates' courts,
      applications to 243–4
    maintenance pending
      suit 163–4, 235
    Matrimonial Causes Act
      1973 161–3
    matrimonial/non-matrimonial
      property, classification
      of 182–3

    mental disabilities 187
    minimal loss principle 161
    new partners 165–6, 180–2,
      208–14, 233, 234–5, 242
    nominal orders 243–4
    nullity of marriage 14–15,
      25, 41
    overseas divorces, recognition
      of 76–7
    paramountcy or welfare
      principle 169–70, 237
    pensions 162, 194, 198–201,
      236, 237–8
    personal injury, damages
      for 177
    physical disabilities 187
    policy 169–70
    power of sale 162, 167–8
    pre-marital cohabitation
      185–7
    price fluctuations 232–3
    public interest 230–5
    reasonable requirements
      ceiling 171–2, 188
    remarriage 180–2, 234–5
    resources provided by new
      spouse or partner 179–80
    secured periodical payments
      orders 161, 164–5, 236,
      237–8, 243–4
    separation agreements 217–22,
      231–5
    settlement orders 167, 308–9,
      329
    special contribution
      argument 188–90
    special protection in
      separation divorces 74–5
    standard of living before
      marriage breakdown 184
    statutory factors 177–94
    undertakings 168
    variation of financial
      provision orders 235–42
mortgages 123, 216–17
Morton Commission 60
mothers and motherhood
    see also **parents**
    alcohol and drugs, abuse
      of 396
    anonymity 348
    assisted fertilisation 362–3
    best interests of babies
      485–7
    egg donations 357–8
    fathers, unmarried mothers
      as less worthy than
      unmarried 396
    genetic connection 357–8

    Human Fertilisation and
      Embryology Act 1990 358
    legal parenthood 357–8,
      374, 400
    lesbian couples 46, 331, 367,
      376, 378, 388, 391, 458–9
    parental responsibility 377–8,
      396, 400
    residence orders 458–9,
      485–9
    surrogacy 362–3

name, change of child's
    birth certificates, names
      on 549–50
    culture 550–1, 554–5
    Gillick competency 553
    illegitimacy 550–1
    marital status of parents 554
    paramountcy or welfare
      principle 549
    parental responsibility 552
    religion 554–5
    residence orders 552
    specific issues orders 536,
      549–55
    wishes and feelings of
      child 552–3
need, children in 536, 573–5
**new partners, remarriage or
  cohabitation with** 165–6,
    180–2, 208–14, 233, 234–5, 242
no order principle 452–4
non-marriage 14, 19–20
non-molestation orders 103–17
    alcohol 112
    applications 105–10
    arrest, powers of 103–4, 108,
      113–14
    associated persons 103–4,
      105, 107–10
    breach
      arrest, powers of 103–4, 108
      criminal offence, as 104,
        108, 113–17, 142
      sentencing 114, 115–16
    children
      applicants, as 110
      occupation orders 110
      relevant child 105–6, 108,
        111
    civil partners 46
    cohabitants 51, 90, 105–6,
      108–9
    consent 145
    contempt of court 113,
      114–16
    criminal offence, breach as
      a 104, 108, 113–17, 142

criteria 110–11
definition 104–5
discretion 111, 113
drug abuse 112
emotional abuse 104–5
enforcement 113–17
harassment 104–5, 109, 116,
147, 149
home rights 103
Law Commission 103, 105,
109–10, 145
legal aid 111, 117
mental illness 112–13
occupation orders 110
police, applications by
the 145
relevant child 105–6, 108,
111
research 116–17
same-sex couples 108–9
sentencing 114, 115–16
standard of proof 111
third parties, applications
by 145
threats 104
undertakings 142
unintentional conduct 111–13
victims' right to enforce order
in civil courts 114–15
who can apply 105–10, 145
nuisance 146
nullity of marriage
civil partners 45
consent 28–9
decrees absolute 14–15
decrees nisi 14–15
divorce, distinguished
from 15, 32
financial and property
consequences 14–15,
25, 41
forced marriages 15, 28, 33,
35–6
gender recognition 29–30
intersexuals 25
Law Commission 32–3
mental disabilities, persons
with 28–9
mistake 28–9
non-marriages 19
pregnancy by another
man 29
religion 31–3
transsexuals 21, 30, 370
time limits 30, 36
voidable marriages 25, 30–1

occupation orders 118–45
applications 119–20

arrest, powers of 103–4, 140–4
associated persons 103–4,
120–1
balance of harm test 124–7,
134–9, 143–4
breach 103–4, 140–2
causation 126–7
checklist 124–5, 127–9, 130,
134–5, 139
children
balance of harm test 124–39
criteria 124–5
health, safety, and
well-being 128–9
non-molestation
orders 110
paramountcy
principle 126, 128
civil partners 46, 119–23,
129–32
cohabitants 50, 51, 90, 123,
129–35
conduct 126–9
consent 145
contempt of court 140–2
courts, approach of 122,
124–9, 136–40
criteria 124–5
declaratory occupation
orders 119, 121, 124–5
delay 143–4
discretion 122, 124–6, 128–30,
134–9
divorce 129–30
duration of orders 129, 134–5
enforcement 123–4, 140–4
entitled applicants 119–21,
129
ex parte orders 143–4, 154
exclusionary orders 123
existing right to occupy,
cohabitants or former
cohabitants with no 130–1
fair hearing, right to a 144, 154
fault 124
financial needs and
resources 128
former spouses, civil partners,
or cohabitants 129–32
granting occupation
rights 132–3
harassment 141–2
health, safety, and well-being
of parties or children 128–9
home rights 119, 121, 123,
124–5
homelessness 128
housing needs 128
interim orders 129

Law Commission 118, 126,
128–9, 133, 139, 143, 145
liberty and security, right
to 144
living areas, dividing up 122–3
neither party is entitled to
occupy, where 135
non-entitled occupants
119–20, 129–35
non-molestation orders 110
orders that can be made 121–4
ouster orders 124
police, applications by the 145
private and family life, right
to respect for 144
prohibited steps orders 533–4
regulatory occupation
orders 119, 137–9
relationship breakdown 130,
136
rent and mortgage payments,
responsibility for 123
repair and maintenance,
responsibility for 123
sentencing 141–2
spouses 119–23, 129–32
third parties, applications
by 145
undertakings 142–3
who can apply 119–21, 145
occupation, right of see **home
rights**
orders for sale 202–3, 307–8
orphans 646–7
ouster orders 124
**overseas dissolutions,
recognition of** 45, 89
**overseas divorce, recognition
of** 76–8
big money cases 76
domicile 76–7
EU law 76
financial orders 76–7
habitual residence 76–7
Hemain injunctions 78
refusal of recognition 77
talaq (Islamic divorce) 77–8
unconscientiously, oppressively,
or vexatiously, acting 78
overseas marriages
armed forces 38
forced marriages 35–7
recognition 37–9, 41
same-sex marriages 39, 41

**paramountcy or welfare
principle** 447–65 *see also* **best
interests test; welfare checklist**
accommodation for
children 586, 590

paramountcy or welfare principle (*cont.*)
  adoption 673–4, 678–9, 684–6, 690–1, 695–9, 703–6
  background 447–54
  biological parents 456, 458–61
  care orders 569, 618–19, 654–5, 661
  child protection 569–73
  child support 332–4
  Children Act 1989 448–54, 462–3, 465
  children, rights of 444–5
  contact orders 509–10, 512, 518, 524, 527–8, 664–6
  criticism 463–5
  cultural issues 461
  decision-making principles 448–54, 463–5
  definition 454–61
  delay 451, 455, 464, 665, 673–4, 679, 691
  directly in issue, welfare must be 449
  fathers, parental responsibility of 383–4, 386–7
  financial orders, variation of 237
  flexibility 464
  Human Rights Act 1998 462–3
  impliedly or expressly excluded by other provisions, must not be 449
  interim care and supervision orders 618–19
  Law Commission 453, 458–9
  legal parenthood 375
  looked after children 579
  matrimonial home 170
  medical treatment of children, consent to 441–2
  money and property distribution on marriage breakdown 169–70
  more than one child 450–1
  name, change of 549
  no order principle 452–4
  occupation orders 126, 128
  paramountcy principle 447–51, 453–63, 465
  parentage 345
  parental responsibility 383–4, 386–7, 409–10, 455
  police protection 612

  private and family life, right to respect for 456, 460, 462–3
  private law disputes 447–65
  religion 490–1
  relocation of children 538–9, 543–7
  residence orders 490–1, 496, 500–2
  same-sex parents 464–5
  section 8 orders 474, 478–82, 557–8
  shared residence orders 496, 500–2
  significant harm threshold 632, 649
  sterilisation 457
  supervision orders 618–19, 659
  surrogacy 371, 373
  transparency 464–5
  upbringing or administration of child's property 448–9
  when principle applies 448–51
parentage 341–57
  anonymity of mothers 348
  best interests of the child 343–6, 353–4
  consent 353–4
  contact orders 351–6
  cultural factors 357
  declarations of parentage 343–5
  definition 341
  disclosure to children 356–7
  discretion 351
  DNA testing 343–4, 349, 352, 357
  evidence 343–6, 351–7
  failure to comply with directions 354–6
  fair hearing, right to a 347
  genetic origins, recognition of interests in knowing 346–56
  Gillick competency 353
  identity rights 346–56
  inferences to be drawn from failure to comply directions 355–6
  legitimacy, presumption of 342–6, 354
  paramountcy principle 345
  parental responsibility 341–2, 350–4
  parenthood 341–2
  private and family life, right to respect for 346–9, 352

  proof of paternity 343–4
  scientific testing, directions for 343–6, 349, 351–7, 380
  sperm donation 347–8, 351–2
  UN Convention on the Rights of the Child 346, 348, 350–1
parental responsibility *see also* **parental responsibility of fathers**
  abuse, removal of responsibility due to 404–5
  accommodation for children 584–5, 587–90
  adoption 402, 407, 654
  agreements 46
  alcohol and drug abuse 396
  alone, each holder may act 407–8
  autonomy of child 410
  birth certificates 400, 403
  care orders 504, 653–5, 661
  care plans 652–3
  child, definition of 403, 406–7
  child protection 401, 567, 573
  child support 314, 441, 406–7
  Children Act 1989 400–10
  civil partners 46
  cohabitants 51
  complexity of responsibilities 406–7
  confidentiality 411
  consent, issues requiring 408
  consulted on various issues, right to be 408
  contact orders 472, 483–4, 505
  content and scope 408–11
  criminal offences 404–5
  delay 399, 408
  discipline 410
  discretion 409–10
  divorce 76
  duration 403–4
  emergency protection orders 601–3
  female parents 400
  guardians, appointment of 402–3
  guidance 407–8
  inherent jurisdiction 563–4
  interference, freedom from 409
  interim care and supervision orders 613, 615, 619, 624
  Law Commission 403

lesbian couples 40, 46, 331, 378, 388, 391
local authorities 381, 401, 404, 406, 482–4, 560–1, 564, 579, 652–5, 661
looked after children 579
marriage 43
medical treatment, consent to 405–6, 428–9
more than two people with parental responsibility 376
mothers 377–8, 396, 400
name, change of 554–5
nature and scope 406–11
non-resident parents, diminishing responsibility of 503–4
paramountcy or welfare principle 409–10, 455
parentage 350–4
parental responsibility agreements 400, 403–4
parental responsibility orders 351–4, 400, 404
position of persons without parental responsibility 405–6
prohibited steps orders 533–5
reasonableness 410–11
religion 410
relocation of children 537
removal 404–6
residence orders 401, 402, 403, 408, 472, 491, 493, 502–4
restrictions 410–11
section 8 orders 51, 472–3, 482–4, 560–1
shared residence orders 491, 493
shared responsibility 407
significant harm threshold 631–2
special guardianship orders 402, 709
specific issues orders 535–6
step-parents 400–1, 709
supervision orders 658
surrender 408
transfer 408
unmarried fathers 585–6
wishes and feelings 579
parental responsibility of fathers 377–411
acquisition by unmarried fathers 379–93
active parenting, parental responsibility following 398

adoption 378, 677
age 377
allocation 377–411
attachment 384–5
bigamy 377
biological connection 397
birth certificate, registration on 379–80, 400
capacity 380, 385
certainty 385
Children Act 1989 342, 377–93, 396
commitment, level of 379, 384, 387, 392, 396, 398
conditional orders 387–8
criminal convictions 386–7, 391–3, 395, 404–5, 411–12
definition 342, 377
denial, reasons for 389–93
disclosure of information on father 380, 399–400
discretion 382
discrimination and equal treatment 378–9, 385, 387–8, 393–400
domestic violence 392
dual parenting, child's right to 399
foreign element 378
how responsibility might be exercised, focus on 386–7
illegitimacy 378
inappropriate use cases 385, 389–91
interference from fathers 386, 390–1, 395, 409
irresponsibility, encouraging 397–8
joint enterprise, parental responsibility as a 364
Law Commission 395, 399–400
lesbian partners 378
local authorities 381
maintenance 384, 386, 397
marriage
adoption 378
date of marriage 377
discrimination 394–6
reasonable belief in validity 377
void marriages 377
mothers
fathers, as less worthy than 396
married couples 377–8
no power to override decisions 386, 390–1
non-legal parents 342

paramountcy or welfare principle 383–4, 386–7
parentage 341–2
parental responsibility agreements 379, 380–1
parental responsibility orders 364, 381–93, 395, 399, 404–5, 409, 411–12
applications 381–93
conditional orders 387–8
hedging the order 387–8
inappropriate use cases 385, 389–91
reasons for applying 385, 389–91
parenthood 341–2
policy 399
previous behaviour 392–3
private and family life, right to respect for 393–5
reasons for applying 385, 389–91
same-sex partners 378
scientific testing 380
self-esteem of child 383
sexual offences 386–7, 390–1
social change and attitudes, changes in 396–7, 399
status, as designed to confer a 385–6, 393, 395
time of birth, unmarried at 377–8
transsexuals 396
unmarried fathers 364, 377–93
acquisition, by 379–93
commitment, degree of 379
discrimination 378–9, 393–400
mothers, as less worthy than 396
parental responsibility orders 381–93
time of birth, unmarried at 377–8
unmeritorious fathers 378–9, 395–8
unmeritorious fathers 378–9, 395–8
void marriages 377
parents 340–412 *see also* **fathers and fatherhood; legal parenthood; mothers and motherhood; parentage; parental responsibility**
assessments 619–21
biological parents 340–2, 350, 456, 458–61
child support 317

parents (*cont.*)
control, where child is
beyond 648–9
definition 317
different senses of
parent 340–1
disabilities, with 592, 642–3
dual parenting, right to 399
interim care and supervision
orders 619–21
learning disabilities,
with 642–3
marriage, consent to 43
parental alienation
syndrome 518
single parents 3, 672, 693–5
social parents 315, 331,
340–1, 350
terminology 341–2
unmarried parents 329–38
wishes and feelings of
parents 478–9, 579
paternalism 414, 416, 419–20
paternity *see* fathers and
fatherhood
pathway plans 579, 580
patriarchal social order 97–8
pensions
cohabitants 54
compensation to off-set loss
of entitlements 199
discretion 200
duty to consider parties'
entitlements 199
earmarking orders 199–201
loss of entitlements 198–9
marriage 43
matrimonial home, transfer of
interest in 199
money and property
distribution on marriage
breakdown 162, 194,
198–201
pension-sharing orders 236,
237–8, 307–8
pension splitting 199, 200–1
periodical payments 199
property disputes of
cohabitants 307–8
variation 236, 237–8
periodical payments orders
appeals 232–4
capitalisation 233–4, 237–42
child support 244, 324, 326,
327, 330–1, 334, 337–8
clean break 164, 195–8
cohabitants 54, 209–10
consent orders 242
during marriage 243–4

extension 222, 238–40
maintenance 164
matrimonial home 203–4,
209–10, 213
money and property
distribution on marriage
breakdown 161, 164,
180–2, 232–3
new partners 180–2, 234, 242
pensions 199
price fluctuations 232–3
property disputes of
cohabitants 307–9
remarriage or cohabitation
with new partner 180–2,
209–10, 234
secured periodical payments
orders 161, 164–5, 235,
243–4, 326, 327
separation agreements 222
variation 235, 237–43
personal advisers 579, 580
personal injury, damages for 177
place of safety orders 568
plans
accommodation for
children 588
adoption 676
birth plans 589–90
care plans 651–3, 655
looked after children 579, 580
pathway plans 579, 580
significant harm
threshold 600
police
adoption and police
checks 675
domestic violence 99–101
emergency protection orders,
execution of 609
non-molestation orders,
applications for 145
occupation orders,
applications for 145
police protection under
Children Act
1989 611–13
polygamous marriages 12
post-nuptial agreements 223–5
poverty 593–4
pregnancy by another man,
marriage and 26, 29, 30,
31–2
pre-nuptial agreements *see*
ante-nuptial agreements
private and family life, right to
respect for
accommodation for
children 585–6, 589

adoption 679–80, 685, 695,
707
care plans 655
children, rights of 428, 443
contact orders 507–8, 526
de facto relationships 6
domestic violence 154
embryos, father's consent to
destruction of 361
fathers
adoption 679–80
embryos, consent to
destruction of 361
Gillick competency 428
identity rights 346–9
interim care and supervision
orders 615
occupation orders 144
paramountcy or welfare
principle 456, 460, 462–3
parentage 346–9, 352
parental care, lack of
reasonable 642–3
parental responsibility of
fathers 393–5
positive obligations 348
religion 654
relocation of children 538,
543, 545–6
residence orders 488–90
sale of property 293
same-sex couples 5, 488
significant harm
threshold 636
transsexuals and marriage 22,
24, 370
private law disputes in children
cases 447–565 *see also*
section 8 orders
private nuisance 146
prohibited degrees of
relationship
adoption 700
affinity 16
biological, moral, and social
reasons 16
consanguinity 16
cousins, genetic consequences
for children of marriage
between 16
discrimination 16–17
in-law marriages 16–17
step-parents and
step-children 16
prohibited steps orders
adoption 686
contact 466, 534
definition 466, 533
local authorities 483–4, 560–1

occupation orders 533–4
parental responsibility 533–5
relocation within UK 535
removal, preventing 534–5
residence orders 466
section 8 orders 533–5
welfare checklist 651
proof *see also* **standard of proof**
burden of proof 638–40
care proceedings, final
hearings in 632–40
paternity 343–4
significant harm
threshold 632–8
welfare checklist 649
property *see* **money and
property distribution on
marriage breakdown**
property adjustment orders
child support 330–1, 333
civil partners 45, 89
clean break 166–7
duration of marriage 186–7
during marriage 243–4
fairness and equality 63
history 61
judicial separation 88
legal effects of divorce 75–6
Martin orders 208–14
Matrimonial Causes Act 1973
162
matrimonial home 167,
205–14, 211
Mesher orders 205–8, 211–14
periodical payments
orders 165
property disputes of
cohabitants 246–7, 295,
304, 307–8
property transfer orders 166–7
settlement orders 167
variation 166, 236, 237–8
**property disputes of
cohabitants on relationship
breakdown** 48–55, 246–310
advancement, presumption
of 250
bankruptcy 293
beneficial ownership
establishing 248–50, 266–81
joint names cases 248–9,
252–66
quantification 252, 255–66,
274–7, 281–4, 296–7
sole name cases 252,
266–81
trusts of land 290–3
businesses, contributions
to 275–7

children
advancement, presumption
of 250
Children Act 1989
295–6
discretion 307
financial settlement orders,
proposal for 308
reform 52, 306, 307–8
tenancies, transfers
of 294
trusts of land 292–3
choosing to avoid relationship
regulation 48, 53, 300–1,
307
civil partnerships 305
Cohabitation Bill 46, 48,
52–4, 57, 308–10
commitment, level of 54,
301–2
common intention
ascertainment 256–8
constructive trusts 251,
266, 296, 299–300
contributions 251, 254–84,
298–300
detrimental reliance 268,
271, 279–81
evidence 279, 297–8
express common
intention 267–9
household finances,
organisation of 272,
297–8
inferred common
intention 269–81
joint names cases 256–66,
281–3, 296–9
purchase price
contributions 270, 274,
279–81
reform 296–8, 305, 310
resulting trusts 254–8
sole name cases 266–72
common law marriage
myth 49, 55, 301
constructive trusts 251,
266, 268, 272–9, 282–3,
299–300
contributions
businesses, contributions
to 275–7
common intention 251,
254–84, 298–300
constructive trusts 251,
266, 268, 272–9, 282–3,
299–300
detrimental reliance 268,
271, 279–81

domestic
contributions 271–4,
278, 281–2, 298–300, 304
economic
disadvantage 306–7
financial
contributions 250–68,
270–84, 299–300
improvements 269–71,
279, 288–9
indirect financial
contributions 261,
272–8, 282–3
indirect contributions 205,
251, 261, 267–8, 270–8,
282–3
joint names cases 248–9,
252–66, 281–3,
298–300
purchase price 251–2, 270,
274, 279–81, 309
purchase price resulting
trusts 251–2
qualifying
contributions 306–7
reform 304, 306–7
resulting trusts 250–8,
265, 279, 282–3
sole name cases 252,
266–83
criteria for determining
applications 291–2
declarations of trust 248, 252,
253–4, 262–3
deeds 247
detrimental reliance 268,
271, 279–81, 284–90
discretion 292, 307
domestic contributions 271–4,
278, 281–2, 298–300, 304
duration of relationship 47–8,
54, 260, 304, 306, 308
economic disadvantage 306–7
educating cohabitants about
legal position 301
equity, satisfying 289–90
evidence 279, 297–8
exclusion orders 292
express trusts 248–9, 253–4
financial contributions 250–68,
270–84, 299–300
Fowler v Barron 259–62
hardship 293–4, 303, 305, 309
home rights 246–7, 292
household finances,
organisation of 272, 297–8
ideologues, romantics,
pragmatists, and uneven
couples 48, 302

property disputes of cohabitants on relationship breakdown (*cont.*)
implied trusts 248, 249–51, 310
improvements 269–71, 279, 288–9
increase in cohabitation 3, 11, 46–7, 300
indirect financial contributions 261, 272–8, 282–3
indirect contributions 205, 251, 261, 267–8, 270–8, 282–3
inducement 287–8
joint names cases 248–9, 252–66, 281–3, 296–300
Jones v Kernott 262–4
Law Commission 247, 272–3, 296, 298, 303, 304–8
Law Society 304
legal ownership, establishing 247–8
Living Together campaign 55, 301
lump sum orders 304, 307–8
marriage
commitment, level of 54, 301–2
comparison with 54–5, 89–90, 294–5, 300–2, 305–10
decline in marriage 300
ideological superiority, maintaining 307, 309–10
policy 309–10
undermining 54, 302
non-couple situations 264–6, 304–6
opt-in/opt-out schemes 304, 308
orders for sale 307–8
pension-sharing orders 307–8
periodical payments orders 307–9
policy 48, 53, 309–10
principles 247–52
private and family life, right to respect for 293
property adjustment orders 246–7, 295, 304, 307–8
proprietary estoppel 275, 284–90
public opinion 46–7, 300
purchase price 251–2, 270, 274, 279–81, 309
quantification of beneficial interest 252, 255–66, 274–7, 281–4, 296–7

reasonable needs principle 308
reform 52, 296–310
resulting trusts 250–8, 265, 279, 282–3
sale
disputes 292–3
orders for sale 307–8
trusts of land 292–3
Scotland 308
separation agreements 307–8
settlement orders, proposal for 308
sole name cases 252, 266–83
Stack v Dowden 253–66, 273–83
statistics 47, 300–1
tenancies, transfers of 293–5
trusts of land 248–54, 290–3, 296, 305–6
Trusts of Land and Appointment of Trustees Act 1996 290–3
unconscionability 285
unequal shares, establishing that property is held in 254–6
unfair outcomes, property law principles producing 298–300
vulnerable parties, protection of 49–52, 302, 304, 306
writing 248
proportionality 290, 605–6, 612, 617, 695
proprietary estoppel
assurances or representation by owners, whether there were 285–6
beneficial interests 284
conduct found insufficient 288–9
constructive trusts 284
contributions 286–9
definition 284–5
detrimental reliance 284–90
equity, satisfying the 289–90
improvements 288–9
inducement 287–8
property disputes of cohabitants 275, 284–90
remedies 289–90
unconscionability 285
psychiatric examinations 620–5, 656–7
psychological factors *see also* **distress, causing**
antisocial/narcissistic personality and domestic violence 96

domestic violence 96–7, 513
relocation of children 538–9, 542–5, 548
shared residence orders 492, 493–4
psychotherapy 621–3
purchase price
contributions 251–2, 270, 274, 279–81, 309

Queen's Proctor, intervention by 66–7

rape 99
Rawls's theory of justice 419
reasonable parental care, lack of 640–8
abandoned children 648
causal connection 641
discrimination 642
learning disabilities, parents with 642–3
objectively acceptable level, care must fall below an 641–8
orphans 646–7
private and family life, right to respect for 642–3
standard of proof 644–5
third parties 641
unknown perpetrator cases 643–6
reasonableness
contact with children in care 663–4
interim care and supervision orders 615–16
money and property distribution on marriage breakdown 171–2, 188
parental care, lack of reasonable 640–8
parental responsibility 410–11
property disputes of cohabitants 308
relocation of children 539–40
reconciliation
adultery 68
certificates 66
condonation 59–60
divorce 59–60, 66–8, 71, 73, 79, 82, 83, 85
encouraging reconciliation 66–7, 71, 73, 79
reflection and consideration, period for 82, 83, 85
reform *see also* **Law Commission**
cohabitants 52–5

divorce 61, 78–87
property disputes of
cohabitants 296–310
relationship breakdown
see **money and property
distribution on marriage
breakdown; property
disputes of cohabitants on
relationship breakdown**
relatives
adoption 676–80
grandparents 376, 473, 475,
484, 530–1
residence orders 472
siblings 487, 706
significant harm
threshold 628–32
relevant child
definition 580
former relevant child 580–2
religion
adoption 674–5, 701–2
autonomy 654
blood transfusions and
Jehovah's Witnesses 438–42,
561
care orders 653–4
civil partners 43
consummation 26–7
contact orders 525
corporal punishment 444
discrimination 489–90
divorce 75, 77–8
marriage 11–12, 18–21, 26–7,
31–3, 38, 41
paramountcy or welfare
principle 490–1
parental responsibility 410
private and family life, right
to respect for 654
relocation of children 544
residence orders 489–91
talaq (Islamic divorce) 77–8
thought, conscience, and
religion, freedom of 444,
654
relocation of children
abduction 537
attachments, importance
of 539–40, 543
authorisation of the
court 537
consent 537
criminal offences 503, 534,
537
culture 544
debate and research 547–8
detriment to non-relocating
parent 539, 542–5, 548

evidence 542–4
fair hearing, right to a 538
genuine and realistic, whether
proposals are 541–2
holidays 537
Human Rights Act 1998 537–8
lifestyle choices 540
paramountcy or welfare
principle 538–9, 543–7
parental responsibility 537
Payne discipline 537–47
private and family life, right
to respect for 538, 543,
545–6
prohibited steps orders 534–5
psychological and emotional
stability of relocating
parent 538–9, 542–5, 548
reasonable decisions,
interference with 539–40
relevant factors 539
religion 544
removal from the
jurisdiction 503, 534,
537–49
residence orders 503, 534–5,
537, 539–41
return to previous home
country 541–3
shared residence 500–2, 540–3
specific issues orders 536,
537–49
step-parents 539–40
United Kingdom, within 535
**remarriage or cohabitation with
new partners** 165–6, 180–2,
208–14, 233, 234–5, 242
representations *see* **complaints
and representations**
reproduction *see* **assisted
fertilisation**
residence orders 484–504
3 years, persons with whom
child has lived for at
least 471
18, reaching age of 558
abroad, criminal offence
of taking or sending
child 503
accommodation for
children 586
adoption 686–7, 688
age, relevance of 485–7, 558
background of child 490–1
best interests test 486–7
capacity 484
care orders
discharging 502, 503, 504
interim 614

change of circumstances 485
change of residence 485
checklist 484–5
child of the family 471
child support 330
civil partners 46
conditions 651
connection with the
child 476–7
consents 471–2
contact orders 503, 530
continuity 485–6
criminal offence of taking or
sending child abroad 503
criteria 475
cultural heritage 491
definition 466, 484
delay 477
discharge 710
discretion 485, 557
discrimination
fathers, against 486–7
religion 489–90
sexual orientation 488
duration of orders 558–9
foster parents 472, 482
gender, relevance of 485–7
guardian, appointment of 503
harm 484
Human Rights Act 1998 488
interim orders 481, 485–6, 614
Jehovah's Witnesses 489–90
leave to apply 480–1
legal consequences 502–4
lesbian couples 458–9, 485–9
local authority care 471–2,
482–4, 504
location of home 484
marriage, consent to 503
mothers, best interests of
babies to be with 485–7
name, change of 552
paramountcy or welfare
principle 490–1
parental responsibility 401,
402, 403, 408, 472, 491,
493, 502–4
private and family life, right
to respect for 488–90
prohibited steps orders 466
relatives 472
religious practices and
beliefs 489–91
relocation 503, 534–5, 537,
539–41
removal from UK 534
residence orders 614
responsibilities and rights,
conferring 503

residence orders (*cont.*)
  sexual orientation of
    parents 488–9
  shared residence 484,
    491–502
  siblings to be kept
    together 487
  special guardianship
    orders 710
  specific issue orders 466
  status quo, bias towards
    the 485–7
  suspended residence
    orders 530
  welfare checklist 650–1
  when orders can be
    made 557–8
  who can apply 470–2
  wishes and feelings of
    child 485
respite care 575
restraining orders 148–9
resulting trusts 250–8, 265, 279,
  282–3
right to a fair hearing *see* **fair
  hearing, right to a**
**right to liberty and
  security** 144
right to life 154, 361, 441
**right to respect for private and
  family life** *see* **private and
  family life, right to respect for**

sale of property 208–15
  bankruptcy 203
  children 203, 292–3
  discretion 292
  exceptional
    circumstances 293
  orders for sale 162, 167–8,
    202–3, 307–8
  postponement 290–2
  private and family life, right
    to respect for 293
  proceeds of sale 202–3,
    212–15
  property disputes of
    cohabitants 307–8
  remarriage or cohabitation
    precipitating sale or
    realisation of charge 208–14
  trusts of land 292–3
  variation 236
same-sex couples *see also* **civil
  partnerships; lesbian couples**
  adoption 672, 675–6, 692
  child support 331
  discrimination 5, 39–40, 488
  Human Rights Act 1998 5, 488

legal recognition of
    families 4–5
  marriage 38–41
  non-molestation orders
    108–9
  paramountcy or welfare
    principle 464–5
  parental responsibility of
    fathers 378
  private and family life, right
    to respect for 5, 488
  residence orders 488–9
  tenancies, transfer of 4–5, 43,
    45–6, 217
same-sex marriage 38–41 *see
  also* **civil partnerships**
  children 40
  civil partnerships 38–41
  discrimination 39–40
  European Convention on
    Human Rights 38–9
  overseas marriages,
    recognition of 39, 41
  private and family life, right
    to respect for 39
  marry, right to 39–40
  transsexuals 41
scientific testing 343–6, 349,
  351–7, 380
section 8 orders 466–565 *see
  also* **contact orders; residence
  orders**
  18, reaching age 558–9
  adoption orders 476
  cohabitants 51
  conditions 466–7, 556
  connection with the
    child 476–7
  consent 471–2, 482
  contact with children in
    care 664
  court's powers 469–70
  criteria 473–9
  directions 466–7
  discretion 474, 557–8
  duration of orders 556, 558–9
  fair hearing, right to a 555
  family assistance orders
    467–9
  family proceedings, definition
    of 469–70
  foster parents 472, 481–4
  free-standing
    applications 470, 472
  grandparents 473
  harm 477–8, 560–1
  inherent jurisdiction of the
    High Court 555–6, 561–4
  interim orders 481

leave to apply 472–83
    child concerned 479–81
    not the child concerned,
      where child is 481
    restrictions 481–4,
      555–60
    without notice applications
      for leave 479–83
  local authorities
    foster parents, restrictions
      on leave applications
      by 481–4
    looked after children 478
    medical treatment, consent
      to 561
    parental responsibility
      482–4, 560–1
    plans for the child 478–9
    restrictions 483–4
    significant harm, risk
      of 560–1
    wishes and feelings of
      parents 478–9
  medical treatment, consent
    to 561
  nature of proposed
    applications 476
  no reasonable prospects of
    success criterion 475
  not the child concerned,
    where child is 481
  notice 556
  paramountcy or welfare
    principle 474, 478–82,
    557–8
  parental responsibility 51,
    472–3, 482–4, 560–1
  parents, wishes and feelings
    of 478–9
  prohibited steps orders 466,
    483–4, 533–5, 560–1, 651,
    686
  restrictions 481–4, 555–60
  specific issue orders 466, 476,
    483, 535–55, 560–1, 686
  unmarried parents 470
  when orders can be
    made 556–8
  who may apply 470–2
  wishes and feelings of
    parents 478–9
  without notice applications
    for leave 479–83
**secured periodical payments
  orders**
  child support 326, 327
  during marriage 243–4
  enforcement 164–5
  matrimonial home 165

money and property
distribution on marriage
breakdown 161, 164–5
variation 235
self-determination 419
**self-incrimination, privilege
against** 529
separation *see also* **divorce;
separation agreements**
children, dangers to 157–8
civil partners 44–5, 89
domestic violence after
separation 95–6, 157–8
judicial separation 87–8
separation agreements *see also*
ante-nuptial agreements
appeals 231–2
consent orders 219–22, 231–5
costs 218
death 231–2
enforcement 218, 221
fraud 221
full and frank
disclosure 221–2
improper pressure 219
legal advice 219
mistake 221
money and property
distribution on marriage
breakdown 217–22
ousting jurisdiction of the
court 218
periodical payments orders,
extension of 222
private agreements 217–18
property disputes of
cohabitants 307–8
settlement orders 167, 308–9,
329
sexual offences
abuse 633–5, 640, 650
adoption 700
marital rape 99
parental responsibility of
fathers 386–7, 390–1
sexual orientation *see* **civil
partnerships; lesbian
couples; same-sex couples;
same-sex marriage**
sham marriages 33
shared residence
orders 484, 491–502
50/50 care 492
bases 491–4
best interests test 497, 500
conditions 500–2
confusion, arrangements
must not cause 497
criteria 494–6

equality of positions and
responsibilities 492, 493–4
exceptional
circumstances 496–7, 500
good existing arrangements,
assumption of orders
reflecting 496–7
harmony, where parents are not
capable of working in 497
Law Commission 491
paramountcy or welfare
principle 496, 500–2
parental responsibility where
not otherwise possible,
conferring 491, 493
presumption, whether there
should be a 497–500
psychological benefit 492,
493–4
reality of how children live their
lives, reflecting the 491,
492–3, 496, 499–500
relocation 500–2
wishes and feelings of
child 495, 499
siblings
adoption and contact with
siblings 706
residence orders 487
**significant harm
threshold** 628–48
accommodation for
children 585
actual significant harm 628–38
allegations 633–6
assessments 600–1
burden of proof 638–40
care orders 614, 620, 628–38,
655
care proceedings, final
hearings in 628–48
child protection 590–7, 601
Children Act 1989 590–1
culture 595
definition of harm 591
disabilities, parents with 592
domestic violence 591
emergency action 600, 602–4,
608–9
evidence 628, 631–8
experts, disagreement
amongst 636–8
forced marriages 35
guidance 600
health or development
compared with similar
child 592–5
inhuman or degrading
treatment 601

interim care and supervision
orders 614, 620
investigations 595–7
keeping families together 594
likely harm 632–8
paramountcy or welfare
principle 632, 649
parental control, where child
is beyond 648–9
parental responsibility,
exercise of 631–2
plans 600
police protection 612
private and family life, right
to respect for 636
proof 632–8
reasonable parental care, lack
of 640–8
relative poverty 593–4
relatives 628–32
section 8 orders 560–1
sexual abuse 633–5, 640
social workers 600–1
standard of care 593–4
standard of proof 590–1,
633–5, 638–40
supervision orders 628–38
uninjured children,
protection of 637–8
single parents
adoption 672, 693–5
statistics 3
social changes 46–7, 52, 396–7,
399, 670
**social construction of
childhood** 416
social parenthood 315, 331,
340–1, 350, 375–6
social security 313–14, 316
social workers
adoption 675, 686, 693
child protection 7, 569–70,
589–90, 597, 600–1, 607,
609, 611–13, 660
emergency protection
orders 607, 609
interaction with other
disciplines 7, 35
police protection 611–13
significant harm
threshold 600–1
time limits and targets 671
sole name cases 252, 266–83
**solicitors, appointment
of** 627
**special guardianship
orders** 707–11
adoption 686–7, 688, 708,
710–11

special guardianship orders
(*cont.*)
   care orders, discharge of 710
   change of circumstances 709
   Children Act 1989 708
   consent 709
   notice 709
   parental responsibility 402,
      709
   residence orders, discharge
      of 710
   step-parents 709
specific issue orders 535–55
   adoption 686
   contact orders 466
   definition 466, 535
   local authorities 483, 536,
      560 1
   names, disputes as to
      children's 536, 549–55
   nature of proposed
      applications 476
   need, children in 536
   parental responsibility 535–6
   relocation 536, 537–49
   residence orders 466
   sterilisation 535
sperm donors
   anonymity 368
   child support 331
   death, use of sperm
      after 368–9
   fathers and fatherhood 347–8,
      351–2, 365, 367–9, 374–6
   identity rights 347–8
   information, access to 368
   intent-based
      parenthood 374–5
   legal parenthood 365, 368,
      374–5, 376
   parentage 347–8, 351–2
stalking 146
standard of living 184, 326,
   332–8
standard of proof
   balance of probabilities
      638–9
   care proceedings, final
      hearings in 638–9
   harassment 147–8
   non-molestation orders 111
   parental care, lack of
      reasonable 644–5
   significant harm
      threshold 590–1, 633–5,
      638–40
statistics
   civil partners 43–4, 89
   cohabitants 3, 47

domestic violence 93, 99–101,
   158
marriage 12, 300
property disputes of
   cohabitants 47, 300–1
single parents 3
statutory charge 201, 217
step-parents
   adoption 670
   contact orders 508, 521–2
   marriage with
      step-children 16
   parental responsibility 400–1,
      670, 709
   relocation of
      children 539–40
   special guardianship
      orders 709
sterilisation 457, 535
succession
   expectations of
      inheritance 177
   Inheritance (Provision for
      Family and Dependants)
      Act 1975 42, 48, 51, 75–6
   inheritance tax 43, 56–7
   intestacy 50–1, 88, 90
   money and property
      distribution on marriage
      breakdown 177, 182–3
   surviving spouses 42, 45–6, 51
   wills 51, 53, 260–1
supervision orders *see also* **care
   proceedings; interim care
   and supervision orders**
   additional powers 656
   adoption 686
   best interests test 658–9
   care orders 657–60
   child protection 655–7
   directions 656
   discharge 656–7
   duration 655–6
   emergency protection
      orders 659
   enforcement 656–7
   medical or psychiatric
      examination and
      treatment 656–7
   monitoring 658
   paramountcy or welfare
      principle 659
   parental responsibility 658
   reasonable contact of
      supervisor 656
   responsible person 656–7
   significant harm
      threshold 628–38
   specified activities 656

variation 656–7
welfare checklist 650–1
wishes and feelings of
   child 656
surrogacy and parental orders
   adoption 371
   Children Act
      proceedings 373–4
   commercial basis, on a 371,
      373
   conditions 372–3
   deception 374
   domicile 372
   enforcement 371
   expenses 373
   genetic relationship,
      requirement for 371
   Human Fertilisation
      and Embryology Act
      1990 371–3
   Human Fertilisation and
      Embryology Act 2008 371
   husbands of mothers 362–3
   illegality 371
   intent-based parenthood 375
   legal parenthood 371–4, 375
   paramountcy principle 371,
      373
   parental orders 371–4, 375
   policy 373
   who may apply 371–2

talaq (Islamic divorce) 77–8
tax 43, 56–7
**telephone calls, harassment
   by** 146
tenancies
   children 294
   cohabitants 51, 294–5
   compensation for
      transfer 294
   hardship 294
   legal recognition of
      families 3–5
   matrimonial home 217
   occupation orders 123
   property disputes of
      cohabitants 293–5
   relevant tenancy, definition
      of 217, 294–5
   rent, responsibility for 123
   same-sex couples 4–5, 43,
      45–6, 217
   succession 3–5, 51
   transfer 217, 293–5
terminology
   domestic violence 92
   family law 2
   parents 341–2

terrorism 92
thought, conscience, and
religion, freedom of 444, 654
transsexuals and marriage
birth certificates 23–4, 29, 370
chromosomal factors, gonadal
factors, genital factors, and
psychological factors
21–3, 25
consummation 26
contact orders 517
discrimination 22
fatherhood 369–70
Gender Recognition Act
2004 24, 29–30, 369–70
gender recognition
certificates 24, 26, 29–30,
369–70
Human Rights Act 1998 23–4
knowledge 30
legal parenthood 369–70
margin of appreciation 22, 370
marriage
consummation 26
marry, right to 22–4
nullity 21, 30, 370
same-sex marriages 41
nullity 21, 30, 370
parental responsibility of
fathers 396
private and family life, right
to respect for 22, 24, 370
retrospectivity 369–70
right to marry 22–4
same-sex marriages 41
voidable marriages 29–30, 31
treaties and conventions 6,
154–6, 417 see also particular
treaties and conventions
trespass of the person 35
trusts of land
bankruptcy 293
beneficial interests 290–3
constructive trusts 251,
266, 268, 272–9, 282–4,
299–300
criteria for determining
applications 291–2
exclusion orders 292
express trusts 248–9, 253–4
implied trusts 248, 249–51,
310
occupation of property,
disputes over 292
property disputes of
cohabitants 248–54, 290–3,
296, 305–6
resulting trusts 250–8, 265,
279, 282–3

sale of property,
disagreements over 292–3
sale of property,
postponement of 290–2
trusts for sale 292
Trusts of Land and
Appointment of Trustees
Act 1996 290–3
writing, declarations in 248

UK Border Agency
(UKBA) 571
UN Convention on the Rights
of the Child 246, 348, 350–1,
507–8, 566
unborn children, child support
for 325
unconscionability 285
United Nations (UN)
Convention on the
Elimination of All Forms
of Discrimination against
Women 154–6
Convention on the Rights of
the Child 246, 348, 350–1,
507–8, 566
Declaration on Elimination
of Violence against
Women 92–3
domestic violence 92–3,
154–5
unmarried cohabitants
see property disputes of
cohabitants on relationship
breakdown
unmarried couples see also
cohabitants; unmarried
fathers
accommodation for
children 585–6
adoption 672, 675–6
assisted fertilisation 363
child support 329–38
parental responsibility 377–93,
585–6
section 8 orders 470
time of birth, unmarried
at 377–8
unmarried fathers
commitment, degree of 379
discrimination 378–9,
393–400
mothers, unmarried fathers
as less worthy than
unmarried 396
parental responsibility 364,
378–400
time of birth, unmarried
at 377–8

unmeritorious fathers 378–9,
395–8
unreasonable behaviour fact for
divorce 68–71, 84, 86
utility and rights, tension
between 7

variation of financial provision
orders 235–42
capitalisation of periodical
payments orders 237–42
child support 315, 320–2, 337
clean break 237, 242
cohabitation with new
partners 242
consent orders 236–7
deferred orders 236
discretion 237–8
earning capacity 240–2
factors to be
considered 237–42
hardship 237
lifestyle choices 238–40
lump sums by
instalments 236, 237–8
maintenance pending
suit 235
matrimonial home 236,
240–1
paramountcy or welfare
principle 237
pension sharing orders 236,
235
periodical payments
orders 235, 237–43
property adjustment
orders 236, 237–8
sale of property orders 236
secured periodical payments
orders 235
timing of applications 236–7
venereal disease, marriage to
persons with 25, 29, 30, 31
views of child see wishes and
feelings of child
voting 416–17
vulnerability
children 48–9, 53
cohabitants 48–51, 53, 89–9
homelessness 151–2
home-sharers 56
marriage 13–14
property disputes of
cohabitants 49–52, 302,
304, 306

wardship
child protection 568–9
forced marriages 35–6

wardship (*cont.*)
  inherent jurisdiction 35–6,
    562–4, 568–9
  local authorities 562
  medical treatment of children,
    consent to 429–32
  surrogacy 562
Waterhouse Inquiry 671
welfare benefits 313–14, 316
welfare checklist
  adoption 674, 686
  allegations 650
  care orders 650–1, 661
  care proceedings 649–61
  Children Act 1989 451–2
  children's guardians 627,
    651
  family assistance orders 651

prohibited steps orders
  651
proof of harm 649
range of orders 650–1
residence orders 650–1
sexual abuse, unproven
  allegations of 650
supervision orders 650–1
unknown perpetrators at
  disposal stage 649–50
welfare principle *see*
  paramountcy or welfare
  principle
welfarism 418, 428
Welsh family proceedings
  officers 626
will theory 413–14
wills 51, 53, 260–1

wishes and feelings of child
  accommodation for
    children 587
  child protection 573, 627
  children's guardian, role of 627
  contact orders 516–18, 527,
    663
  disabled children 573
  looked after children 579
  name, change of 552–3
  parental alienation
    syndrome 518
  residence orders 485
  section 8 orders 478–9
  shared residence orders 495,
    499
  supervision orders 656
women's refuges 98